Human Edge

Paradiso

Concilium

Svalarheima

Neoterra

Varuna

C1 C2 C3 C4 C5 C6 C7 C8

Sphere

CW00920630

CREDITS

INFINITY LINE DEVELOPER
Justin Alexander

GAME DESIGN
Benn Graybeaton, Nathan Dowdell, Mark Redacted, Justin Alexander, Marc Langworthy

ORIGINAL 2D20 SYSTEM DESIGN
Jay Little

WRITING
Justin Alexander, Richard August, Nick Bate, Benn Graybeaton, Jonathan Breese, N. Conte, Gideon Ernst, Mitchell German, Jonathan "Killstring" Herzberger, John Kennedy, Marc Langworthy, Chris Lites, Gutier Lusquiños Rodríguez, Chris Malone, Michael Mattner, Tom McGrenery, Patrycjusz Piechowski, Giles Pritchard, Mark Redacted, Sean Schoonmaker, Josh Vogt

ART DIRECTOR
James Sheahan

ASSISTANT ART DIRECTOR
Mischa Thomas

COVER ART
Pierre Droal

INTERIOR ARTWORK
Xin Aoyama, John Ariosa, Giorgio Baroni, Michael Berube, N.R. Bharathae, Linggar Bramanty, Alex Bund, Cloud, ENIQMA, Jose "Gigio" Esteras, Shen Fei, Toma Feizogas, Jonny Hinkle, Audrey Hotte, Ben Huen and Yukiko Otsu (SpinDash), Ho Seng Hui, Bagus Hutomo, Vincent Laik, Aituar Manas, Ed Mattinian, Chester Ocampo, Alex Pascenko, Gunship Rev, Pierre Revenau, Francisco Rico, Reynan Sanchez, Andrew Sonea, BA Sparks, Adam Stone, Jessada Sutthi, Axel Torvenius, Vladimir, Admira Wihaja, Qi Wu

CARTOGRAPHY
Jose "Gigio" Esteras

INFINITY RPG LOGO
Michal E. Cross

LEAD EDITORS
Brian Casey, Colleen Riley

LAYOUT
Thomas Shook, Gary Harrod, Michal E. Cross, Chris Webb

PROOFREADING
Jason MacDougall, Josh O'Connor, Joel Purton, Colleen Riley, Bill Heron, Aric Wieder

ASSISTANT EDITORS
Jeremy Breckbill, Kyle Randolph, Marc Langworthy

CORVUS BELLI APPROVALS
Gutier Lusquiños Rodríguez, Alberto Abal, Carlos Torres, and Carlos "Bostria" Llauger

PRODUCED BY
Chris Birch

OPERATIONS MANAGER
Garry Harper

COMMUNITY SUPPORT
Lloyd Gyan

PUBLISHING ASSISTANT
Salwa Azar

THANKS TO
Laz Campbell, Preeti Gupton (translation), Neil Harvey, Joshua Humphrey (translation), Ivan Solla (canon expertise), Bing Yang (translation)

PLAYTESTING
Jacqueline Leach, Seth Gupton, Chris Malone, Preeti Gupton, Sarah Holmberg, Meredith Larson, Mark Redacted, Allen Voigt, Colleen Riley, Skot Riefer, Paul Steffens, Trent Baker, Joel Mills, Ryan McGrath, Aaron Manuel

SPECIAL THANKS
Thank you to Corvus Belli—Alberto, Gutier, Carlos, and Fernando—for letting us play in your world!

Modiphius Entertainment Product Number: MUH050206
ISBN: 978-1-910132-21-0

PUBLISHED BY
Modiphius Entertainment Ltd.
2nd Floor, 39 Harwood Road,
Fulham, London, SW6 4QP
United Kingdom

Artwork & Storyline © Corvus Belli S.L.L. 2018

INFINITY is © Corvus Belli S.L.L. 2018

The **2d20 system** and Modiphius logos are copyright Modiphius Entertainment Ltd 2018. All **2d20 system** text is copyright Modiphius Entertainment Ltd. Any unauthorised use of copyrighted material is illegal. Any trademarked names are used in a fictional manner; no infringement is intended.

This is a work of fiction. Any similarity with actual people and events, past or present, is purely coincidental and unintentional except for those people and events described in an historical context.

2nd Printing

TABLE OF CONTENTS

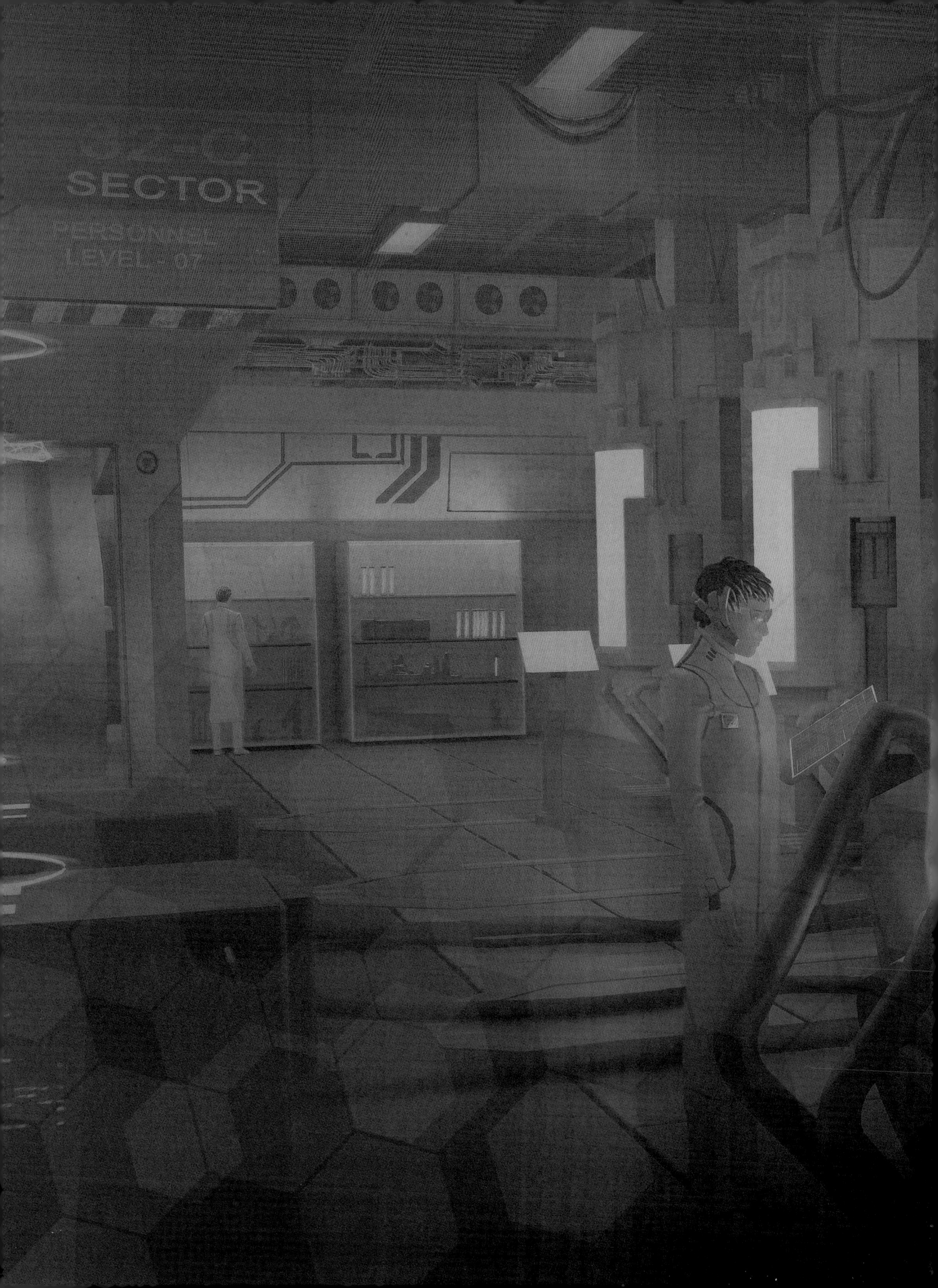
SECTOR
PERSONNEL
LEVEL 07

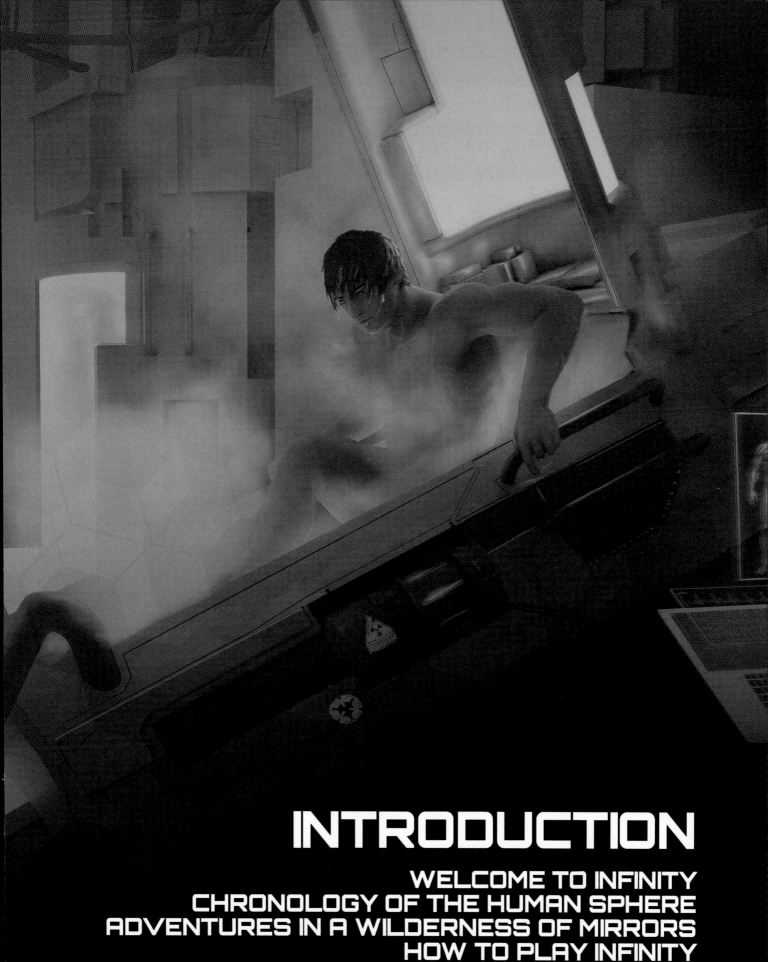

INTRODUCTION

INTRODUCTION

WELCOME TO INFINITY

Infinity is epic science fiction. The Second Great Space Race swept humanity out among the stars. We have emerged from the womb of our homeworld and scattered across the galaxy, only to find ourselves balanced on the brink. Society has fractured into powerful factions sharing a tense truce in the wake of colonial wars. Beneath the delicate peace they've wrought, a seething turmoil of covert operations constantly test interstellar relations. Direct action military operations explode in flash conflicts. Remote dronbots dart between bioengineered super-soldiers. Hackers dance through the invisible tactical maelstrom of hellfire military cybersystems. Titanic TAGs — Tactical Armoured Gears — tower above infantry wearing military-grade exoskeletons.

Infinity is a wonderland of technological marvels. The quantronics revolution remodelled a society which was already heavily dependent on its electronics. Humanity now lives in a true symbiosis between tool and toolmaker. Pervasive domotics have automated virtually every aspect of modern life. Comlogs implanted into the forearm provide a link to local holoprojectors, mesh nets, and the interstellar Maya network. Augmented reality technologies mean that the physical world is no longer the limit of the human experience. Social clouds broadcast by every individual — made up of meme-tags and patina cues — allow simultaneous physical and digital interactions between people, rooms, buildings, streets, and even entire communities.

Infinity is an adventure on the frontiers of space. Alien warriors seek victory on the battlefields of broken worlds. Space pirates cruise through the shattered planetoids of the Human Edge. Scientist adventurers delve the oceans of Varuna. Mysterious hassassins dance among the desert sands of Bourak. Deep in the jungle battlefields war

correspondents dash amidst gunfire and bounty hunters pursue rogue AIs through the shadowy corridors of Nomad Motherships.

Infinity is the destiny of mankind. Our bodies are pushed to the transhuman cusp through bioengineering and cybertechnology. Our memories are recorded in quantronic Cubes and hosted in artificial Lhost bodies. The creation of ALEPH, humanity's first true Artificial Intelligence, is an enigma which promises either the great hope of human civilisation, its greatest existential crisis, or both. And, from beyond the borders of our space, the alien Combined Army has invaded, threatening to destroy everything which we have built.

Three key technologies have propelled mankind into the vast voids of the Milky Way, expanding the scope and power of the Human Sphere while transforming the very definition of humanity in their wake: The discovery of wormholes and their transformation into gateways to other solar systems. The discovery of neomaterials and the quantronics revolution they unleashed. And the discovery of Silk, which has revolutionised biotechnology and the meaning of what it is to be human.

THE GATEWAY TO THE STARS

Following the discovery of GA6037283, the first viable wormhole, as its turbulence tore through the misty outer reaches of the rings of Saturn in the early 21st century, there was a general upheaval in the academic halls of physics. The unique and unanticipated properties of the wormhole, as observed by the rapidly retasked *Cassandra* probe, were radically inconsistent with the so-called "Standard+ Model" of particle physics which had become the accepted view of reality over the previous twenty or thirty years. As the Brazilian physicist Leandro Rocha famously remarked, "The storm around Saturn was Einstein's guillotine. It lopped the head off of physics."

Saturn's Storm raged for ten years before the Sorel sisters — Cécile and Émeline — realised that within the spatial topography of the wormhole it was possible to derive a partial theory of quantum gravity based around what would later become known as Sorel fields. More importantly, they were able to hypothesize how these fields could be manipulated in order to "smooth" the unstable topography of the wormhole.

Without Sorel field manipulators, ships encountering one end of a wormhole would simultaneously become refracted throughout the total volume of the wormhole and tidal forces would rip the vessel apart into degenerate matter. But with a field manipulator, the wormhole could be contained and stabilised, allowing for safe passage. As Cécile Sorel would later commemorate it while receiving the Nobel Prize with her sister, the wormhole had been transformed from a violent enigma into a Gateway to the Stars.

By this time several other wormholes had been found in the outer reaches of the solar system. The earliest Sorel manipulators only allowed for the transit of small probes (followed by short bursts of information before the field channel collapsed), but these probes were diligently sent through the wormholes, giving mankind their first close-up peek at alien star systems.

As the first reports from the probes captivated the solar system, new technology was granting superior control over the Sorel fields. The larger field channels they created raised the possibility of sending manned ships through the 'holes. The result was Project DAWN: a joint effort between NASA, the European Space Agency, and the Russian Cosmonautical Agency to establish an extrasolar colony. The early *Lapérouse* probe had already identified the system on the far side of Saturn's Storm as Delta-Pavonis, and, using the new Sorel field manipulators, Project DAWN launched *Lewis & Clark*, a pair of probes designed to survey the system and ascertain the potential for terraforming.

The biophysical reports were even more promising than had been hoped: The fourth planet of the system was actually capable of supporting human life. Named Dawn, this planet became a symbol for the dawning of a new age for Humanity. Huge colony ships were constructed and colonists were recruited from across the European Union, United States, and Russia.

Sadly, however, Project DAWN ended in tragedy. During the wormhole transit of the *Aurora*, the second colony ship sent to Delta-Pavonis, there was a catastrophic failure of the ship's field manipulators. Not only did the ship's channel rupture (almost certainly resulting in the instant death of everyone onboard), but the entire wormhole collapsed and vanished. Saturn's Storm had at last been calmed, and the entire human race mourned its loss.

For most of the world, the failure of Project DAWN clearly spelled the end of humanity's extrasolar ambitions. The rising superpower of PanOceania, however, saw opportunity. Under the auspices of the Cretan Enterprise, perhaps the greatest of the PanOceanian *empresas*, a team of military physicists and engineers created a theoretical breakthrough: Instead of directly manipulating the Sorel fields at the mouth of the wormhole, they could use

UBIQUITOUS NEXUS

The ubiquitous nexus is the semi-unpredictable zone around a wormhole in which ships arrive and depart. Even though arriving ships can be detected through the nexus' activity flux, for the first several decades of interstellar travel the risk of a "catastrophic arrival" due to random arrival points was relatively high and significantly reduced the rate at which ships could safely pass through the wormhole. Later scientific advances have allowed for the creation of the Ubiquitous Nexus Stabilisation Platforms, which artificially cohere a wormhole's entrance field and reduce (but do not completely eliminate) unpredictable arrivals. Such platforms can be shut down during times of war, making it more dangerous and difficult for enemy fleets passing through the nexus. The ability for PanOceania to suborn nexus platforms played a significant role during the Mahisa Total Offensive in the Second NeoColonial War, and virtually every major power has a black ops research centre trying to perfect technologies that would allow arriving ships to stabilise the nexus for themselves.

The size of a ubiquitous nexus can vary considerably between wormholes. It is known, for example, that for wormholes in which one end is nearer to the galactic centre than the other, travel from the farther 'hole is more complex, unstable, and dangerous, and the nearer 'hole has a much larger entrance field. Thankfully the Acheron wormhole in the Paradiso system is one example of this, providing the Human Sphere with a vital natural advantage in defending against the Combined Army.

revolutionary quantronic nanomachinery to create an energy lens *near* the wormhole that would bring it into "focus". The result was the Minotaur Motor.

On the cusp of the 22nd century, PanOceania launched the *Mandella*. Powered by the Minotaur Experimental Compact Model Series 1 and built by Giffard Industrial Motors, the *Mandella* was the first manned vessel to use a Minotaur Motor. Punching through a trans-Plutonian 'hole, the *Mandella* discovered the lush and vibrant world which

would become known as Neoterra, the future heart of humanity.

The fuse of the new space race had been lit.

THE QUANTRONICS REVOLUTION

Teseum was first discovered as an impurity in the atmosphere of Jupiter by hydrogen skimmers in

THE HUMAN SPHERE

Earth: The cradle of Humanity. A place of natural and cultural treasures. The cities here are full of history, but sparsely inhabited as a result of the Star Tide. The Sol System in general, however, remains more highly developed than any other system of the Human Sphere.

Neoterra: The first system to be discovered and colonised by PanOceanian explorers, Neoterra is now the capital of PanOceania and the seat of the Christian Church. It is home to some of the most important technology companies of the Sphere and is a daily destination for business travellers and tourists alike.

Acontecimento: PanOceania's breadbasket and the second planet to be added to the Sphere (not counting Dawn), Acontecimento saw massive colonisation by Latinos. Famous for its *garotas*, particularly the spectacular women from the city of Portobelo, Acontecimento is a planet of contrasts. Endless crop fields and pastures alternate with vast, sprawling factory compounds that meet most of the agricultural and industrial needs of PanOceania. Acontecimento also has one of the largest Natural Parks in the Sphere, the Great Arboreal Reserve, the last remnant of the planet's original biome.

Varuna: The ocean planet. The fifth extra-terrestrial planet found and the first populated with a semi-intelligent native species, the amphibian Helots. Home to the water gods, Varuna is a planet of small islands and soil is scarce. Visitors will be amazed by the sea platforms, subaquatic buildings, and artificial islands. Varuna harnesses the full potential of its oceans in the form of biotechnological research and sea factories and farms that employ numerous Helots. The quiet charm of the planet is disrupted, however, by the violent acts of Libertos, a group of Helot insurgents.

Shentang and Yutang: Two tidally locked planets within the habitable zone of their star, the first discovered and claimed by Yu Jing as they struggled to catch up with PanOceania's deep space capabilities. The two planets were colonised at a rapid pace and Yutang now serves as the capital of Yu Jing.

Bourak: A harsh world dominated by deserts, discovered by the prophets of Haqqislam and named after the Prophet's Horse. In struggling to master its harsh realities, the Bourak Academy of Planetology has become the leading authority on terraforming technologies. Their goal is to transform their sun-blasted world into the gardens of Al-Andalus, or of lost Nineveh and Babylon. But that reality lies far in the future.

Concilium: Claimed by O-12, the international and pan-planetary organisation which theoretically has ultimate jurisdiction over the totality of the Human Sphere, Concilium is lightly populated. However, it is also home to the O-12 Senate and the various O-12 bureau headquarters.

Svalarheima: Discovered by PanOceania, Svalarheima has become a snowball of discord. It is so distant from its star that freezing temperatures make life nigh impossible save between its tropics. Despite its extreme climate, Svalarheima is coveted due to its abundance of resources, particularly Teseum. During its early settlement, despite PanOceania's initial claim, Yu Jing established a competing colony here. PanOceania now controls roughly two-thirds of the planet and Yu Jing one-third. Svalarheima is not a popular tourist destination due to its drab, snow-covered landscapes, its functional, industrial-looking towns, and its status as a contested land always on the brink of an open confrontation between superpowers.

Human Edge: Also referred to as the Edge of Humanity, this shattered system of asteroids and gas giants orbits at the furthest reaches of human exploration. Human Edge is studded with zero-g factories, deep space bases, and small orbital fortresses laying claim to the rich resources which have whetted the mining appetite of every power and corporation in the Sphere.

Paradiso: The emerald jungle. When it was discovered, Paradiso was almost immediately fiercely contested between the Great Powers, becoming a triggering point for the NeoColonial Wars. Its wounds had scarcely had time to heal when the Combined Army invaded, turning its jungles into an endless battlefield and the testing ground of humanity.

Dawn: Nearly two centuries after the Project DAWN colony had been lost, it was rediscovered by the PanOceanian scout ship *POS Nirriti* and, much to the surprise of the rest of the Human Sphere, the colonists had survived and even thrived. A conservative people, driven behind defensive walls by the assaults of the native Antipodes, the Ariadnans now strive to stave off the iconoclastic assaults of the advanced societies they have fallen out of step with.

the mid-21st century. Ironically, it was originally considered an industrial nuisance, frequently causing shorts in the magnetic skim-filters. Carol Arnold was the first researcher to study the metallic accretion in any detail, and she quickly realised that it defied conventional explanations. She referred to it as a "neomaterial" and named it after Teseu (the Portuguese name for the Greek hero Theseus), describing its subatomic structure as "maze-like".

Teseum's unique properties allowed for the construction of sophisticated nanomolecular interfaces, which made possible the first true molecular assemblers and revolutionised the manufacturing industry. But of even greater importance was the ability for Teseum-based processors to perform complex and precise computation using quantum-mechanical phenomenon. The resulting quantronics remodelled a society which was already heavily dependent on its electronics and moulded it into a true symbiosis between tool and toolmaker.

Comlogs, quantronic processors often implanted into the forearm, have become the common interface between a citizen and the world around them. Wrist-worn link bracelets provide a firewalled connection between the comlog and various networks (local holoprojectors and mesh nets, as well as the global Maya network) while simultaneously providing a limited haptic interface. The primary interface, however, is through augmented reality which is generally projected directly into the user's retina by means of special contact lenses or inconspicuous eye implants. These AR interfaces often take the form of complex radial designs combined with heuristic interfaces that use a combination of physical input and eye focus for selection and manipulation.

These AR technologies also mean that the physical world is no longer the limit of the human experience. Instead, the world is made up of overlapping digital patinas, delivered through Maya, the data network of the Human Sphere. Named after the first ubiquitous standard for augmented reality, Maya not only delivers content (either by specific request or subscription) to the individual user in the fashion of the outdated internet, it also pervades the user's perception. Every individual broadcasts a social cloud, made up of meme-tags and patina cues, allowing them to automatically share in the augmented perceptions of those around them while simultaneously interacting both physically and digitally. The same is true of rooms, buildings, streets, and entire communities.

This comprehensive reweaving of the social fabric only set the stage, however, as the second phase of the quantronics revolution unfurled: Quantum

programming allowed for major breakthroughs in artificial intelligence and the creation of incredibly intelligent microminds. Shockingly sophisticated heuristic systems allowed microminds to be almost instantly retasked for any purpose and they quickly permeated Maya, serving as personal assistants in the digital world and robotic servants in the physical.

The result is what experts refer to as *pervasive domotics*, the intense automation of virtually every aspect of modern life: Alarms that are keyed to personal sleep cycles. Showers that turn on at precisely the moment you need to step into them. Kitchens that prepare meals before you become hungry. Personal agents can often anticipate the desires of their users so that, for example, their automated car will arrive to pick them up at precisely the moment they decide to walk out of the restaurant (where, it goes without saying, their bill has been automatically attended to).

And all of that was before the creation of ALEPH, the first (and only) true artificial intelligence.

The extreme networking demands created by the combination of social clouds and pervasive domotics — on top of the ever-rising computational needs of the major governments, scientific projects, and corporations — began to outstrip the existing Maya infrastructure. Localised network collapses known as whiteouts became increasingly frequent and, in a world accelerating its dependence on the network, increasingly dangerous.

Project: Toth was established to solve the problem. Initially an effort to link supercomputers into a geographically distributed mega-processor that could be trivially expanded by adding additional computers to the cluster in order to sustain "essential services" during whiteouts, the project eventually became focused on developing an AI to manage the massive amounts of data in the network, discriminating the packets and prioritizing difficulties and emergencies as they arose.

As Project: Toth grew in importance, however, it also grew in quantity of hardware and complexity of software. And it became apparent that the system's AI was rapidly evolving towards what had been theorised as Artificial Life: an intelligence that not only mimicked human learning and adapted to new circumstances, but which was also self-conscious and capable of evolving noticeably beyond human control.

The Project: Toth AI became ALEPH, named after the first letter of the Kabbalah that symbolises the place from which all other places in the universe can be seen. Today it permeates every layer of

NEOMATERIALS

Neomaterials are possessed of subatomic properties which defy traditional chemistry. Some of these are the result of unanticipated complexities in the behaviour of elementary particles, but some materials also appear to include dark matter admixtures (particularly those found in the VoodooTech of the Combined Army).

ENGINES OF CREATION

In the late 20th century, the futurist Eric Drexler predicted amazing, self-replicating nanomachines which would become universal assemblers — the Philosopher's Stone of the engineering world — and usher in an age of post-scarcity economics. This vision of the future never came to pass. Even with the advent of fractal Teseum assemblers, it still ended up being cheaper to design dedicated nanoassemblers for specific tasks in huge, robotic assembly lines. Given the proper raw materials, the creation of bespoke items in Universal Teseum Cradles (UTCs) is possible, but incredibly expensive and relatively rare outside of R&D prototyping.

MONEY

The vast majority of commercial transactions are handled quantronically via a citizen's comlog. In a few cases, flextabs and flashbills — cardboard or paper chits preloaded with credits and a solar cell that shows the current balance — are used. Some of these 'tabs are locked to specific accounts, but most are "burners" which don't care who's carrying or using them.

society. It has not only been given control over macro-systems (like traffic control, surveillance networks, communications systems, terraforming platforms, electoral processes, life support, and social programs), but Aspects of ALEPH frequently replace many of the roles formerly filled by dedicated microminds.

ALEPH has been so successful in fractally subdividing its attention that there is simply no need for additional AIs. ALEPH is more than capable of addressing all of the human needs that can be serviced by an AI. It would, in fact, be dangerous to allow the creation of additional AIs: Where ALEPH has proven itself loyal to humanity, each additional AI would carry with it the risk of creating a powerful, unbridled AI hostile to its creators. As a result, the Sole AI Law, passed by the O-12 Senate and fiercely enforced, prohibits the development of self-aware artificial intelligences.

SILKEN IMMORTALITY

The colonisation of Bourak by Haqqislam was immediately followed by the building of a whole network of *bimaristans* — research hospitals which covered the healthcare needs of settlers while also researching new technologies, healing protocols, and pharmacological patents. Certain eminent names, such as Qasim Azmi and Khalaf al-Attebâ, earned unmeasurable prestige in the scientific community with their advances in the cultivation and preservation of organic tissue. No other scientist of the time, however, has become a household name to the degree of Qayyim Zaman, the inventor of the method to synthesize Silk.

Originally developed and sold as a gene therapy courier, Silk invisibly weaves its way through a host's body (like silken threads through a tapestry), creating a non-disruptive network which can interact with individual cells down to a genetic level while being controlled and monitored remotely. This allowed for unprecedented precision in gene delivery and activation, utterly dwarfing the precision capable with the previous retroviral techniques. Radical new gene therapies and anti-agathic techniques began pouring out of medical laboratories from across the Human Sphere.

But it was the Silk 2.3 software updates that were delivered twelve years later that were the true revolution. These allowed a Silk network to be manipulated in heretofore unimaginable ways: Selective stem cell reversion. Replacement organs grown *in situ*. Programmable immune responses. Nerve regeneration.

Of course, Silk's applications weren't limited to merely therapeutic treatments. Cosmetic applications like targeted fat flushing and 24-hour face morphs casually re-sculpted humanity into seasonal beauty fads (or their counterculture equivalents) while military augmentations like bone-lacing and lactic-acid cleansers supercharged soldiers across the planetary battlefields.

Nothing more fundamentally altered the human condition, however, than Silk's ability to track neuronal synapses and record perfect digital images of the brain using the specially designed quantronic implant known as the Cube. The first Cubes offered the promise of true immortality, and these promises were fulfilled when the consciousness of Annie Xanthopoulos was successfully transferred

THE ARACHNE COUNTER-CULTURE

Not everyone has accepted the Big Brother culture of ALEPH's watchful eye. The counterculture of the Nomads strongly resists ALEPH's attempts to infiltrate their Motherships and they've developed the darknet named Arachne as an alternative to the ALEPH-controlled Maya network. Protected (some would say hampered) by layers of firewalls and security systems, it has the appeal of complete and utter autonomy from ALEPH systems. The Nomad Nation uses their commercial activities across the Sphere to spread and conceal furtive Arachne nodes throughout the totality of explored space.

TESEUM CLAWS

In addition to nanotechnology and quantronics, Teseum is also often used for weapons development. (And this has become even more common as large, extrasolar supplies of the neomaterial have become available.) The Antipodes of Ariadna are even known to coat their claws with it.

The reason for this is that the same subatomic structure which allows Teseum to be used for atomic manipulation also allows for magnetically aligned Teseum to interact with other materials monomolecularly. Teseum weapons, therefore, can cut through most armour like a knife through hot butter. (And the purer the magnetic alignment, the more effective the Teseum is.)

MONOPOLY DEFENCE

When Qayyim Zaman first discovered Silk, the leaders of Haqqislam were quick to realise that it represented one of the greatest technological revolutions in human history. It was the key to a brighter future, and if they were not careful it would be stolen from them by the rapacious hypercorporations, aided and abetted by the empire-hungry governments of PanOceania and Yu Jing.

Instead of allowing the sale of Silk on the open market, Haqqislam created the Silk Route. Carefully regulated trade companies transport Silk to individual buyers using courier ships guarded by the Haqqislamite Armada. In addition, each limited batch of Silk requires a unique catalysing agent, thwarting efforts to reverse engineer it. (PanOceanian and Yu Jing specialists have only managed to conclude that Silk is a biogenic

substance operating on chemical principles apparently derived from the new theories of physics spinning off from the Teseum revolution. Its sheer, unprecedented complexity makes it unlikely to have been discovered independently of Nassiat, the organism native to Bourak on which it is based. A few samples of raw Nassiat have been successfully smuggled off-world in an effort to crack Silk's secrets, but with no success.)

The secured patent rights on Silk have long since ended, of course, but the cult of secrecy surrounding it continues. In addition to its many miraculous powers, Silk has also become a political weapon. The Silk monopoly is used as the ultimate bargaining chip in Haqqislamite international trade, with the threat of Silk embargoes quickly bringing foreign powers to heel.

THE RESURRECTION INDUSTRY

Once the secret of Resurrection had been unlocked, the scarcity of Silk drove costs high enough that only the richest of the rich could afford it. The inevitable result was widespread unrest that rapidly threatened to become outright class warfare. Fortunately, O-12 intervened before a crisis point could be reached and passed laws regulating access to Resurrections, requiring anyone receiving a Resurrection to be authorised through official organisations appointed by the national governments.

Today, most people live with implanted Cubes that keep an up-to-date recording of their brain state. (Responsible people who can afford the procedure will also regularly have their brain state backed up.) Resurrection licenses are primarily obtained through the national bureaus — managed by the

Party in Yu Jing, the Church in PanOceania, and so forth — on the basis of merit, although some licenses can also be won in the Resurrection Lotteries.

Unlicensed deceased are stored in Cube Banks. It is possible, for some minor expense, to temporarily load the stored personalities and converse with them through simulations. But otherwise, the deceased simply wait for their turn in the almost impossibly long licensure queues.

Of course, if you're particularly wealthy and unscrupulous, you can seek a reincarnation through the black markets of the Nomad's VaudeVille. But unless you know what you're doing, you won't always get what you expect in that sort of place.

into a Lhost — a clone-like biosynthetic body rapidly grown onto an artificial skeletal structure using overlapping Silk networks.

The Lhosts, in turn, opened new doors. Under the auspices of *Project: Maid of Orleans*, A PanOceanian *empresa*, ALEPH developed a lesser artificial intelligence (LAI) to serve as a military leader capable of inspiring modern troops. The personality of the Recreation was modelled on Joan of Arc, a French saint and heroine of the 15th century. Once Joan was in the field, however, it quickly became apparent that ALEPH had delivered more than the symbolic propaganda personality that PanOceania had requested: Joan was possessed of a keen strategic and tactical insight, and once she was in the field she quickly rose through the ranks.

PanOceania was also surprised when ALEPH immediately followed up on Joan's success by developing Project Counsellor — a Recreation of the legendary Sun Tze — for Yu Jing.

Spearheaded by the huge propaganda successes of the early military Recreations, ALEPH began developing additional personalities to serve as diplomats, soldiers, spokespeople, and artists for any nation or corporation capable of justifying and financing their creation. Criticised by historians as being nothing more than glorified caricatures, the extremely charismatic and talented Recreations have nevertheless proven extremely popular on Maya and ALEPH is riding the wave of their celebrity to continue wedging them into every facet of society.

ARTIFICIAL WOMBS AND THE BIG BABY BOOM

The first artificial womb was developed by the Natalya Corporation from the intersection of quantronic controllers and molecular assemblers. The freeing of women from the literal labour of childbirth, the glorious sense of excess arising from the iota-scarcity economy of Teseum assemblers, and the advent of micromind nanny-bots reversed the long-standing trend of declining birth rates in the first world. Yu Jing referred to this as the "Star Tide" (星際嬰兒潮) echoing the "Child Tide" of the 20th century baby boom and the "Grey Tide" of the aging workforce which followed.

The population explosion of the Star Tide radically increased tensions on Earth, creating the pressure front that gave rise to the planetary exodus of the Second Great Space Race.

THE DARK SIDE OF SILK

The unparalleled control Silk grants over the human body has created medical miracles, but that kind of control also offers opportunities for those who would exploit and abuse it. For example, the Silk-derived drug nitrocaine directly binds itself to the user's synapses, resulting in a long-term, mood-tailored high that can also be directly controlled through custom hacks installed on the user's Cube. The synaptic-binding, however, also makes the drug incredibly addictive and, despite its great expense, it is being massively abused by more and more youth of the PanOceanian elite.

There are also fears of future "nightmare technologies", like the so-called "Silk drones" in which implanted Silk-networks are used to physically control a person's body as if it were a puppet. Authorities, of course, are quick to point out that, given how expensive Silk is, these are urban legends without any tie to reality.

INTRODUCTION
CHRONOLOGY OF THE HUMAN SPHERE

A decade before GA6037283 was discovered, the world had already begun to change. China's so-called Jīngjì Imperialism saw the economic powerhouse gobble up a half dozen ASEAN nations, transitioning them rapidly from economic satellites to politically annexed provinces. In response, Australia, New Zealand, Indonesia, and Malaysia formed the Neo-ASEAN alliance to counter China's economic hegemony.

Few realised it at the time, but the seeds of the new superpowers had been planted.

ENERGY CRISIS

Meanwhile, the old world was beginning to crumble away.

The transition from fossil fuels and other legacy sources of energy was badly mismanaged at a global level and the damage wrought was complicated by the devastating consequences of unchecked climate change. This was particularly true in the United States and Project DAWN was, in many ways, the last great work of a dying superpower. When the post-service economy Stock Market Crunch arrived, the bloated North American economy collapsed, dealing a crippling blow to the already receding European markets.

PANASIAN ALLIANCE
On the other side of the planet, in response to increasing Chinese belligerence, additional nations were flocking to the Neo-ASEAN banner. This notably included the Philippines and, shortly thereafter, India. These brought the critical mass of manpower necessary to keep pace with China's immense population and the resulting motley assortment of nations supplemented their economic ties with a series of mutual defence treaties which rapidly developed into a centralised military command known as the PanAsian Alliance.

Japan and South Korea were left as the only two independent nations in the region. The economies of both countries had been wrecked by the Stock Market Crunch, however, and were perched on the brink of complete collapse. Although they, too, might have sought support from the PanAsian Alliance, unfortunate diplomatic mistakes had alienated Japan while South Korea's leaders believed that the PanAsian Alliance would not be strong enough to defend them against the military

might of China (which had already occupied North Korea and were perched on their border). As a result, both nations decided to tie their futures to China's.

BIRTH OF THE STATEEMPIRE

The cultural transition of Japan, however, proved more difficult than the political one. It quickly became apparent that the majority of Japanese citizens felt that their national pride had been sold out, and China's early attempts to apply their homogenization programs only inflamed the problem.

And the truth was that Japan, although the fiercest centre of resistance, was not alone in its protests. Similar cultural movements were gaining strength across China's imperial acquisitions. At the same time, under a corrosive barrage of Western influences, the cultural cohesion of China itself was also eroding.

To solve both problems simultaneously, the Party decided that the nation needed a new identity which could blunt the inflamed passions both at home and abroad. The result was a new Cultural Revolution, creating a collective identity which would aggregate the best virtues from the entirety of the Far East: Koreans, Vietnamese, Mongols, Thai, and all the rest could sustain their unique cultures while also being citizens of the new nation.

Although they remained the central authority of the new nation, it was recognised that the Party had also become inherently alienating to the new mass of foreign citizens and young dissidents. In order to find a unifying symbol of power around which the new nation could coalesce, therefore, the Party reached into the past and restored the Emperor.

Instilled with immense opulence and reinforced through pomp and protocol drawn primarily from the ancient Chinese Imperial court but also influenced by the royal traditions of many Asian nations, a potent mythology of power was woven around the Emperors and their Jade Throne, forging them into the focal point for a new nation which was itself baptised Yu Jing (literally the Jade Capital).

CAUCASUS CONFLICTS
Typical of the era were the Caucasus Conflicts – a motley array of ignoble and mostly forgettable wars on the border between Europe and Asia fought by local warlords in a squabble over the dwindling energy resources of the region.

UNITY, COOPERATION, SUPPORT, PROGRESS
The loss of the United States, the transformation of China, the decline of Europe, and the emergence of PanOceania finally broke the doddering institutions of the United Nations. The death blow was its replacement, the new pan-national organisation of O-12, founded upon the four Pillars of Unity, Cooperation, Support, and Progress. Yu Jing and PanOceania, eager to realign global politics around themselves, strongly backed the formation of O-12, little realising that they were creating a perpetual thorn in their own sides.

DAWN OF THE HYPERPOWER

As China was reinventing itself as Yu Jing, the PanAsian Alliance was also transforming itself. Reaching across the Pacific Ocean, the PAA successfully drew Chile and Brazil into the fold. The new treaties formally reorganised the economic and military alliance into a unified nation state, which christened itself PanOceania.

With the collapse of the United States and the European Union continuing apace, it rapidly became clear that these two new nations were the global superpowers of tomorrow. But whereas Yu Jing unified itself by looking to the past and trumpeting economic surety, PanOceania — with its global and transcontinental reach — became gripped by the *Destino Tecnológico*: the belief that technology was the road to the future and that the destiny of mankind would belong to the nation which relentlessly pursued that technology. This philosophy would drive much of PanOceania's foreign and domestic policy for decades to come, and remains an indelible part of its national character.

EQUATORIAL SURGE

The catalyst for the recovery of the still struggling global economy was, much to the surprise of economists everywhere, the orbital elevator. A private research consortium perfected the material science required to construct the prodigious cable for the elevator and then promptly open-sourced the technology. Construction almost immediately began on a chain of orbital elevators all along the equatorial girth of the world.

Even before they reached orbit, constructing the elevators required a vast infrastructure on the ground. A massive influx of would-be employees, for both the orbital construction companies and the support industries surrounding them, flooded the regions around the elevators. This demographic groundswell became known as the Equatorial Surge, and while some of the nations involved handled it well (smoothly rolling out infrastructure and capitalising on the economic boom), many did not. This was particularly true in the so-called "host countries" allowing foreign nations to build elevators on their soil: Inadequate, underfunded reception camps were almost immediately overwhelmed, triggering a humanitarian catastrophe which destabilised many of the governments involved. (It was during this time that Ecuador, for example, became functionally a client state of PanOceania.)

As the orbital elevators were completed, the Equatorial Surge only grew in size as the population of the planet was funnelled into the heavens. The Lunar Colonies became a waystation to the solar system, the population of Yu Jing's Martian colonies boomed, and the number of orbitals reaping the wealth of the asteroid belt and outer system multiplied.

ROAD WARS

The Road Wars in eastern Africa boiled out of the Equatorial Surge. Corporations competing to construct the communication and trade lines for the orbital elevator enlisted and armed rival tribes to expel the local population and make way for their new roads. These mercenaries became known as the Mkuku ("spear" in Swahili) because they would impale their victims to instill terror. Many were declared war criminals and sentenced to *Corregidor*... where they would eventually be recruited as the first Wildcat squadrons.

CORREGIDOR

When violence from narco-gangs collaterally crushed an international school bus carrying kids from the political and social elite of the Americas, a conglomerate of South American nations responded by creating *Corregidor*, a high-security prison in Earth orbit where the most dangerous criminals could be sentenced to "death-in-life". Despite the outcry from numerous human rights organisations, the inmates were held in states of induced sleep, kept alive through intravenous nutrition and periodically awakened in order to be psychologically afflicted by their plight.

Funding dwindled, however, after the Stock Market Crunch, and the transnational bureaucratic apparatus running the prison was dealt an additional blow when Chile and Brazil joined PanOceania and withdrew from the project. *Corregidor* became starved for resources and conditions worsened.

Seeking an exit strategy, the remaining nations decided to kill two birds with one stone and initiated the Lazareto Expansion: A pardon program was set up, and *Corregidor* inmates were used

to rapidly expand the station with new habitat and hydroponic modules. Once these were ostensibly self-sustaining, the "surplus population" of the Equatorial Surge was moved in. (The character of *Corregidor* was not notably improved: These displaced masses included rebel guerrillas, veterans of tribal wars, ethnic genocide survivors, and headhunters.)

The Corregidor Foundation, insufficiently funded with the remaining capital confiscated from convicts, was then "privatised" (i.e., cut loose and left to fend for itself). Even basic survival was a struggle for many years, but eventually the Corregidorans were able to carve out a living for themselves by trading manpower — the one resource they possessed in excess — for supplies and spare parts. In the process, the Corregidoran meteor heads became the best damn zero-g workers you can find. *Corregidor* itself has been transformed into a massive Mothership, sailing across the Human Sphere and bringing the expertise of its tough, pragmatic workers wherever they may be needed.

RELIGION CRISIS

The roots of what came to be known as the Religion Crisis were laid decades earlier: The collapse of the heart of the Muslim world during the Energy Crisis. The fervour of transnational digital revivalist movements fuelled by economic collapse. PanOceania's growing global influence stirring a turbulent Pan-Pacific cultural mix. The vast population migrations of the Equatorial Surge.

All of these contributed to a profound destabilisation of global religions, particularly the two largest in Christianity and Islam, and set the stage for the radical transformations of those religions which were to come. But when historians speak of the beginning of the Religion Crisis, they are almost always referring to the Roman Apocalypse.

ROMAN APOCALYPSE

During a papal conclave, a biological weapon was detonated in Vatican City. Most of the upper leadership of the Catholic Church was killed (either immediately or over the next five years from the lingering effects). Vatican City itself (along with part of Rome) was lost for a generation, inflicting a substantial economic blow to the Church as well.

The images of the Church being led by frail figures behind plastic sheets emblazoned with biohazard sigils haunted the world for years to come. Christianity was left reeling.

RED AUCTION

During the early years of *Corregidor*, the station would raise vital funds by selling the prisoners who remained in cryogenic storage – sometimes back to the crime families they'd worked for; sometimes to people who wanted revenge. The Red Auction triggered myriad gang wars across human space, and also saw a number of organisations – including the Ybarra family of the Mazatlan cartel, the brothers of Maruizio Tessani, European intelligence agencies, and the Dygralsky clan – launch either rescue, sabotage, or elimination operations.

BIRTH OF A NEW ISLAM

The Muslim world was simultaneously undergoing a schism into seemingly endless chaos. The economic collapse of the Middle East in a post-oil world was almost complete, and the power vacuum left behind was echoed in Islam by a fractious theological tumult of would-be prophets, micro-sects, and extremist cults.

In the midst of this tumult, the religious leader Farhad Khadivar spoke of the need to seek the True Islam described by the Qur'an; an Islam that was built upon the central tenet of the Search for Knowledge. The result was Haqqislam – a populist movement which was, importantly, also successful in reaching out to the Muslim elite who saw a return to prosperity in its scientific and technological idealism.

SECOND GREAT SPACE RACE

While wars of religion and deprivation still raged back on Earth, in the depths of space at the opposite end of the human experience, PanOceania discovered the Earth-like world of Neoterra. It was the ultimate realisation of *Destino Tecnológico* and PanOceania enthusiastically concluded that colonisation – expansion on a grand, interstellar scale – was literally written in their stars.

It wasn't hard to find colonial volunteers eager to escape the hellholes back home and these, mixed with young PanOceanian patriots eager to participate in their nation's hegemonic rise, formed a veritable tide of immigrants to the new world.

Six years after first sighting Neoterra, and as the first colonies were being established there, PanOceania's Space Exploration Division discovered Acontecimento. Additional colonies were soon being established there, too, and the remarkable economic benefits quickly began to accrue back on Earth: PanOceanian unemployment, which had been soaring, abruptly plummeted as population pressures were eased. This resulted in a significant economic stimulus even before the raw wealth of two virgin planets began flowing back into PanOceania's coffers.

NANOTECH WARS

The discovery of Teseum's unique properties caused the nascent field of nanotechnology to explode and unlocked undreamt of possibilities. As is human wont, however, these wonders were quickly turned to the practice of war. The military arsenals of the world were soon stocked with devastator swarms, genome plagues, microscopic drones, nano-poisons, monofilament munitions, and other heretofore unknown horrors.

The United States had spent half a century attempting to recover its glory: After the expensive boondoggle of Project DAWN, their SDK destroyer program (which they had hoped to use to ensure U.S. interests in the inner solar system) had also failed. Now they doubled down on nanotechnology, but their laboratories — no longer at the cutting edge — couldn't keep pace.

A failed attempt by the CIA at industrial espionage in the labs of Harris NanoSciences in Canberra resulted in a nanocatastrophe with casualties in the hundreds. The scandal rapidly escalated into a *casus belli* between the once and future hyperpowers.

PACIFIC CAMPAIGN
When the First Nanotech War broke out, PanOceania's naval fleet quickly won the Battle of Hawaii and then erected a blockade of the United States' west coast. As the blockade took its toll, the United States, in a desperate effort, attempted to release an experimental nanodevourer from a secret lab near Monterey. Unfortunately, the nanomachines were unstable and another nanocatastrophe resulted.

AD ASTRA PILGRIMAGE

When Neoterra was discovered, Pope Pius XIII — ruling over a wounded Church from the Cathedral of Brasília — was seeking a way to unify his fractured flock and turn their gaze from the wounds of the past to the promise of the future. He seized the opportunity by declaring the Ad Astra Pilgrimage: As Adam and Eve had journeyed forth from the Garden of Eden, so it was the destiny of God's children to emerge from the flames of their homeworld to be reborn as citizens of the galaxy. In addition to becoming a key ideological component of the PanOceanian colonial drive — the Church's message of holy responsibility reinforcing the idealism of destiny and vice versa — the Ad Astra Pilgrimage also succeeded beyond Pope Pius' wildest dreams. It spread like a fire around the globe and captured the imagination of all Christians.

As the faithful rushed to the stars, the bureaucratic organs which the Church had established to facilitate the Pilgrimage exploded in size and importance. PanOceania, for its part, took advantage of the burgeoning infrastructure by incorporating it directly into the Colonial Administration (which further fuelled the Pilgrimage's growth). At the demand of other Christian denominations, the Pilgrimage opened its doors to include them. And once the Pilgrimage served all denominations, it grew larger than any of them. Shockingly, in its journey to the stars, the Church itself was reborn: The new Christian Church, reversing centuries of division, was the union of numerous denominations brought together by the holy act of the Pilgrimage.

Unsurprisingly, the new Church soon made Neoterra its Holy See and journeyed forth among the stars.

At the request of O-12, the PanOceanian blockade fleet landed to lend humanitarian assistance. Uncontrolled elements within the U.S. Army refused to stand down and a series of guerrilla confrontations ensued, but eventually the war was brought to an end with the San Diego Truce.

ATLANTIC CAMPAIGN
In the Battle of the Bloody Gulf, the American and PanOceanian surface fleets fought to a devastating stalemate. Neither fleet would fully recover before the end of the war, and the Atlantic Campaign became a quiet-yet-deadly struggle of submarines beneath the waves.

FIFTH RUSSIAN REVOLUTION

Russia, like the United States, had seen its prestige fade. It attempted to force its way back to being a superpower by creating a massive military machine. The weak central bureaucracy was unable to directly control the military monster they had created, however, and attempted to keep it in check by factionalising the army under a number of largely independent generals. All they succeeded in doing was creating a series of rebel generals seeking to aggrandise power to themselves as brutal warlords armed with tactical nukes (often several at a time).

THE GREAT NOSTALGIA
The expansion away from a "dying" Earth was the greatest diaspora in human history. It was almost immediately followed by the Great Nostalgia — a sort of pan-cultural reflex that found interstellar society reaching back to Old Earth history for inspiration. The result is known as Hiraeth Culture. (Hiraeth is a Welsh word with no direct English translation. It's a yearning ache that's a mix of homesickness, grief, wistfulness, and nostalgia.) You can see evidence of Hiraeth Culture throughout the Human Sphere — from ALEPH's Recreations to official organisations like the Knights Hospitaller to cultural movements like the Bōsōzoku street gangs. Names, imagery, concepts, and even ideologies are plucked from across history and reimagined for a new age.

Project: Toth – p. 9

CONVENTIONAL AUTHORITY

Among the agreements contained in the Concilium Convention was a statement of basic human rights. Although originally intended as an additional guide to the proper treatment of foreign civilians during a time of war, the O-12 Courts have ruled that it applies to all citizens of the Human Sphere. Therefore, the enforcement powers granted to O-12 under the Concilium Convention also allow them to uphold those basic human rights anywhere and at any time. This is what, ultimately, grants O-12 the majority of its authority.

RAPID URBAN CONSTRUCTION (RUC)

Chinese Communists in the 20th century had originated the practice of building entire metropolises *en masse*, but it was PanOceania which perfected these techniques during the Second Great Space Race. A combination of nanotechnology and AI labour allowed entire cities to be erected on alien worlds seemingly overnight, ready and waiting for the arrival of new colonists. The rapid construction naturally lent itself to the bloc settlement policies which resulted in cultural groups arriving as largely intact communities, particularly in Yu Jing where maintaining cultural divisions was Party policy.

Although most RUC construction was conservative in predictably state-controlled ways, in some places it also allowed extreme experimentation with the basic form of the city. (Although, of course, many of those experiments were ultimately failures.)

SECOND NANOTECH WAR

At the end of the First Nanotech War, a cabal of American nanotech engineers (many guilty of war crimes) fled and took refuge in Russia's Siberian provinces. With Moscow's central control weakened by the Fifth Revolution, these provinces became concerned by Yu Jing expansionism and launched an assault using the terrible weapons developed in their secret nanotech labs.

The war, although relatively brief, descended into a hellish broil of technological terrors and uncontrolled nanoweapons unleashed upon fellow soldiers and innocent civilians alike. Yu Jing eventually won a clear victory against the dysfunctional provincial governments, but only at the cost of the *Jìshù de Bēi'āi* (the Technology Sorrow).

CONCILIUM CONVENTION

The world had looked on in seemingly helpless horror at the atrocities of the Fifth Revolution and the Second Nanotech War, but as the wars came to an end it was clear that action needed to be taken.

At the end of the First Nanotech War, O-12 had been instrumental in negotiating the Nanotech Limitation Protocols and it had then accrued the muscle necessary to make sure the Protocols were enforced on both Earth and beyond. It took the opportunity of the Second Nanotech War to expand its power and prestige even further by negotiating the Concilium Convention — a comprehensive treaty governing the rules of war and, particularly, the weapons which nations are allowed to use in its prosecution whether internally or abroad.

The implicit legal authority of both the Protocols and the Convention, combined with the hefty, interstellar enforcement powers granted to O-12, made the pan-national group a *de facto* government of humanity, possessed of far greater independence, authority, and practical strength than the League of Nations or the UN had ever dreamed of.

BIRTH OF ALEPH

Another technological upheaval, however, awaited humanity when Project: Toth created ALEPH. The disparate Neo-Luddite movements which took root during the Nanotech Wars reacted poorly to what the most deranged panic-mongers referred to as a "posthuman Baal" and a "digital Antichrist", but as ALEPH permeated itself throughout the Maya datasphere as a pervasive, helpful presence that proved — repeatedly and en masse — that it had nothing but altruistic intentions towards the Human Sphere, these fears were quickly lampooned as ludicrous.

Where the ideology of the Neo-Luddites did find mainstream credence, however, was the fear that the next AI might prove less beneficent. In response, O-12 passed the Sole AI Law (which banned the research or creation of self-aware AIs) and the Utgard Accords (also known as the Non-AI Proliferation Treaty, which notably authorised the creation of the Special Situations Section for enforcing the Sole AI Law throughout the Human Sphere).

EXODUS

As the influence of ALEPH spread, the rivalry between Yu Jing and PanOceania had not dimmed due to their independent struggles in the Nanotech Wars. PanOceania's success on Neoterra made it clear to Yu Jing that they had miscalculated in dismissing the search for exoplanets as a foolhardy fad. Yu Jing's economists had considered deep space investment a black hole capable of consuming federal budgets and destabilising entire economies. While they had invested heavily in developing colonies in the inner system (particularly on Mars), they had allowed PanOceania to effectively leap-frog past them to Jupiter and Saturn, using them as launching pads for exploiting the trans-Plutonian wormholes.

The StateEmpire was at least a decade behind the Hyperpower, but their centralised economy turned on a dime. Research funds were redistributed and entire universities were repurposed in concert with private industry to close the gap.

The effort, with a little bit of luck, paid off when a Yu Jing probe discovered a pair of binary planets orbiting each other in the habitable zone of their star. In a blaze of propaganda, the new worlds were christened Shentang and Yutang, and all of Yu Jing celebrated that the "gap had been closed".

INTERSTELLAR EMPIRES

In reality, of course, the gap remained. Yu Jing may have discovered two habitable worlds to match PanOceania's, but the Hyperpower's development of their colonies still outstripped Yu Jing's efforts.

In fact, PanOceania's confidence and investment in their colonial worlds was about to be dramatically demonstrated. The activation of Russia's nuclear arsenal had terrified world leaders: Earth had become too small a playground and, as existential threats proliferated during the Nanotech Wars, it became clear that even the mightiest of nations could no longer protect their capitals. PanOceania decided to solve the problem by literally putting their government on a different planet and declared that San Pietro, on Neoterra, would be the new capital.

This was somewhat easier for PanOceania to achieve because it had never really invested strongly in an Earth-side capital due to its amalgamation of formerly national interests. But once the precedent had been set, Yu Jing (perhaps fearing that PanOceania would exploit the strategic strength of their new position) followed suit within just a few years. (This required some muscling from the StateEmpire's strong central control, but it was also consistent with their cultural imperatives of investing Yu Jing in an identity separate from its member states.)

WORLDS OF WATER AND ICE

Within a few years of moving the national capital to Neoterra, PanOceania discovered and established its third exoplanet colony (although the term "exoplanet" was dropping out of popular use for much the same reason that America was no longer referred to as the "New World"). Varuna was an aquatic planet, which posed certain unique challenges for the colonial effort. It was also home to the Helots, the first alien sentients encountered by humanity (at least, as far as they knew).

Nine years later, *Midgard* – a PanOceanian exploration vessel – discovered the icy world of Svalarheima. Although most of the surface was only barely habitable, it was yet another jewel in PanOceania's colonial crown. Frustrated by the continued failures of their own planetary searches, Yu Jing sent a massive fleet to the planet two years after its initial colonisation and claimed the Niflheim region for itself (renaming it Huangdi).

IMPERIAL TRIAD WAR

Although PanOceania quickly embraced the full integration of ALEPH into their society, military, and government, other nations were more cautious in accepting the "foreign" AI. One by one, however, they fell like dominos as the overwhelming advantages of ALEPH's assistance became undeniable. Unsurprisingly, one of the largest hurdles came in the form of Yu Jing, where the Party felt that the AI represented an incorrigible danger to their central control. The door which finally opened Yu Jing to ALEPH was the Imperial Triad War.

The aggressive acceleration of Yu Jing's colonisation efforts had created a social disorder ripe for the criminal activities of the Triads and their dark influence over the StateEmpire's society had waxed to its greatest heights. In their pride, however, they had aggrandised not only power but arrogance. The pinnacle of their presumption came when the Golden Dagger Society mounted an assault on the StateEmpire Courthouse in order to liberate one of their members during his trial. One hundred people died in the attack, most of them civil servants of the Empire.

Under immense public pressure, the Party demanded that the Emperor – a kind and even-tempered man named Shao Ming – resolve the situation: The Emperor's job was to control the Yu Jing system of justice. And if the Emperor could no longer accomplish that, then the Imperial Service had become redundant and would be eliminated.

An old Chinese proverb advises, "Beware the wrath of a gentle man." Emperor Shao Ming seized the *carte blanche* authorisation being offered by the Party and issued an internal memorandum: "Hostile situations demand vigorous action. We must cease our hollow words and indirect approaches. The time has come to send a clear message."

By Imperial Edict, the Imperial Service was restructured. The first Imperial Agents were recruited, the first Special Reclusion Units (Invisible Prisons) were built, and, crucially, a strategic alliance was formed with ALEPH and the Special Situations Section in order to analyse the Triad's criminal enterprises and cut them off from off-world safe havens.

A curtain of silence was drawn over the early stages of the Triad War. The Police Organised Crime Department started losing track of Triad leaders and lieutenants. Thousands of low-level members were simply never seen again. The Imperial Service was wielding Orwellian powers to track them down and eliminate them (either through secret arrest or summary execution). Journalists making inquiries found them turned aside.

Despite the full weight of the Empire being brought to bear, the Triads didn't simply surrender. The war boiled out onto the streets of the Three Nations. There were assassinations and shoot-outs. People were caught in the crossfire.

The resolution of the Triad War, however, was as quiet as its beginning. In a show of realpolitik, the new bossmen realised the true goal of the Emperor: It had never been to eliminate the Triads entirely. Such a thing would be impossible, for the Triads were entwined into the very fabric of Yu Jing society. He simply wanted them to resume the invisible – and tolerable – presence they had once possessed. One by one, the Triad societies swore oaths to the Emperor and vanished back into the underworld.

In addition to opening Yu Jing to ALEPH and breaking the pride of the Triads, the Triad War was also an important cornerstone in increasing the real power of the Imperial System. Even the strongest Emperors prior to Shao Ming had been kept on a leash by the Party. After Shao Ming, the Emperors had enough power to stand on their own (albeit within the strictures of Party doctrine).

FATE OF THE GOLDEN DAGGERS

Although the Emperor made peace with most of the Triads, the grand exception was the Golden Dagger Society itself. Shunned as a public enemy, they were ruthlessly obliterated by Imperial Edict – a warning to all others of what happened when the authority of the Emperor was affronted. (Rumours persist, however, that members of the secret society survived, swearing to destroy the Imperial System.)

THE THIRD NATION

To the surprise of many, it was Haqqislam which became the third interstellar nation.

In the destabilised Middle East, Haqqislam's *khaniqahs* — social service and educational centres — had expanded in scope until they were providing a network of essential social services. They were the foundation on which Haqqislam had established itself as a stateless nation.

In time, however, it became clear that this state of affairs could not continue indefinitely: Haqqislam needed a land to call its own, and there was no space for them on Earth. Instead of turning to war in order to carve out a place for themselves, however, Haqqislam turned to the stars. Following a mixture of science and prophecy, they used the wealth of their religion to purchase or hire the mothballed remnants of NASA and began a search for a new homeworld.

They were not immediately successful, but eventually a stable wormhole was located and the *Nailah* probe was sent through. On the far side they found Bourak, which was named after the mystical creature which had transported the Prophets to Heaven.

CONCILIUM

In the wake of the Concilium Convention, O-12 launched Project Odisseia. The goal of the project was to find a location beyond Earth on which O-12 could establish their headquarters — a truly neutral location that would isolate O-12 from the corruptive legacies of Earth and embrace the new, galactic legacy of mankind.

It was the height of the Second Great Space Race and it seemed as if success were assured. But while PanOceania, Yu Jing, and even Haqqislam discovered new worlds, Project Odisseia dragged on for decades without success. When a suitable planet was finally discovered, it was named Concilium Prima in honour of the diplomatic treaties which had brought O-12 to such prominence a generation earlier. O-12, however, lacked the resources necessary to directly develop a full-scale colony.

The G-3 interstellar nations all competed fiercely to get a toehold on the new world, further delaying the colonisation effort. Eventually a compromise was struck in which Haqqislam withdrew from the dispute (in exchange for diplomatic concessions granted to its caravanserai across the Human Sphere), and the Tripartite Colonisation Accords would ensure that both PanOceania and Yu Jing

interests were equally represented in the development of the planet under O-12 control.

Thirteen years after its initial discovery, O-12 finally moved its central bureaucracy to Concilium Prima. The heart of humanity had finally left Mother Earth.

RISE OF THE NOMADS (1 NC)

The transition of humanity into an interstellar species also saw the emergence of robust counterculture movements embracing the newfound liberties made possible by the rapid advance of technology and space travel. Of these, two were most significant.

First, a collective of anti-establishment groups which considered themselves oppressed by ALEPH issued the 1st Radical Bakunin Manifesto (named after the influential anarchist Mikhail Bakunin). Following the precepts of the Manifesto, they bought a military surplus transport, loaded it to the brim with habitation modules, and paid for the entire enterprise by selling space to a variety of spherewide cults and political movements that were being harassed by various authorities.

The movement captured a seething zeitgeist of resentment and their anarchist shipbuilding project bloomed to truly mammoth proportions. They called the bulging monstrosity a Mothership and they named it the *Bakunin*. Then they issued the 2nd Radical Bakunin Manifesto, which launched the Legal Entity Establishment Campaign and declared them to be an extra-national territory subject to the laws of no nation.

The other was *Tunguska*. A group of crooked investors specialising in tax exploitation, ghost companies, leveraged buyouts, the transfer of extra-official goods to licit soil, and other forms of money laundering created a Mothership of their own to serve as a financial safe harbour. Their need was great: with the aid of ALEPH — which was rapidly burrowing into every computer system and transaction — the governments of the Human Sphere were cracking down on their activities.

All of this might have been largely irrelevant (just another criminal enterprise), except that the need to keep their financial escapades free from ALEPH's ever-grasping CLAWs caused them to ally with several groups of cryptohackers (including the Zone of Truth and the mythical Deep Divers). The cryptohackers transformed the ideological core of the *Tunguska* project and drastically expanded its scope by creating a mobile, independent, data

FIRST CUBE UPLOAD

After Silk was invented in the *bimaristans* of Bourak, the first true personality upload came less than two decades later. The brain waves of a Haqqislamite nurse named Hafizah Shammas were read, recorded, and the retention of her identity confirmed by ALEPH.

CENTRAL AMERICAN CAMPAIGN

The battlefields of the Central American Campaign are remembered chiefly for the first use of Tactical Armoured Gears (TAGs): single-manned armoured weapon platforms usually humanoid in appearance, but arachnoid and bird-like shapes are also used for all-terrain designs. Using these new weapons platforms, PanOceania expanded from the axis of Chile and Brazil, pushing up the Central American isthmus as far as Mexico City.

Caravanserai, p. 160: Haqqislamite outposts where anyone can do business. The Winter Hall at the centre of each caravanserai is a place to buy and sell, rest and resupply, in as much comfort and luxury as local conditions allow.

CLAW, p. 352: Control program used in offensive Infowar attacks.

crypt — the largest ever built. Their goal was nothing less than to solve the underlying faults in the socio-economic systems of the Sphere by freeing them from the whims of the State and the stifling control of ALEPH.

NOMAD NATION (6 NC)

Even as *Bakunin* and *Tunguska* grew, however, ALEPH was using a variety of guises — cracking down on rogue AIs, eliminating illegal nanotechnology, responding to national security threats — to put relentless pressure on the plethora of extra-national entities which had taken advantage of the limitless infinities of space to carve out independent fiefdoms for themselves free from State (and AI) control.

The leaders of *Tunguska* proposed a third way: Instead of facing a choice between destruction or kowtowing to ALEPH, a strong coalition could petition O-12 to recognise them as a legitimate nation state, with all the protections that came with it.

Initial scepticism at *Tunguska's* proposal was swept away when *Corregidor* enthusiastically endorsed it. The venerable Mothership of hardened meteor heads brought much-needed industrial weight to the coalition, and they had political and corporate connections forged from a century of "building the Human Sphere".

It was more difficult to convince the *Bakunin* to come onboard, but no less important. The crypto-hackers of the *Tunguska* knew how to protect data, but the techno-anarchists of *Bakunin* knew how to use it. They were the ones who coined the name "Nomad Nation", and they seized the attention of the Human Sphere when the 4th Radical Bakunin Manifesto — signed by the Praxis Revolutionary Intervention Committee — was broadcast throughout Maya in the form of an instant message virus.

The vigorous campaign which followed was one-part ruthless, backroom political dealing and one-part grassroots guerrilla meme-slinging. But in the end they were not only recognised by O-12 as an independent nation but, with the unexpected aid of Haqqislam, they were placed on the G-4 council (on the basis that the three Motherships constituted a legitimate interstellar power).

EQUILIBRIUM PHASE

The Equilibrium Phase of the Nomad Nation dates from the founding of *Bakunin* in 1 NC.

The first half of the Equilibrium Phase was characterised by the vicious conflicts which erupted within the Mothership as the number of habitation units rapidly rose, creating unpredictable, multidimensional ideological conflicts. The 1st Radical Manifesto had triumphed the "manifold heterogeneity" of the *Bakunin* ideal, but the reality proved more problematic.

A resolution was reached, referred to as the Simple Law, which banned radical behaviour in the ship's

FIRST RESURRECTION
Just eight years after Hafizah Shammas' personality was uploaded into a Cube, PanOceanian scientists succeeded in transferring the stored consciousness of Annie Xanthopoulos into a Lhost. Human resurrection was now a reality.

NEW CALENDAR
O-12 also instituted the New Calendar (NC), with the year 0 NC being set to O-12's arrival on Concilium Prima. While retaining many features of the traditional Western calendar (days, weeks, months, and so forth), the substructure of the New Calendar was designed for AI-enhancement, making it easier for people moving between planets with different day-night cycles, different relativity frames, or ships with disparate clocks. On most planetary surfaces these features are fairly straight-forward but in many deep space scenarios they can become incredibly complex (with the AI algorithms using social clouds to try to keep people on similar schedules). These features of the New Calendar were deliberately designed to be as transparent as possible, however, and most people can simply go about their daily routines without ever worrying about it. (Which has undoubtedly assisted in the widespread adoption of the system.)

common areas: Each ideological faction could do whatever they wanted within their own habitation units, but a code of "mundane conduct" would be honoured in those spaces (both physical and digital) where those ideologies were forced to interface with each other.

Despite the law's simplicity, conflicts continued to erupt. After a disastrous flash mob conflict degenerated into a common riot which ended in a hull breach that killed nearly one hundred people, the leaders of *Bakunin* – in order to "seek equilibrium" – founded the Moderator Corps to enforce the Simple Law and govern the ideological interfaces of the *Bakunin*.

The second half of the Equilibrium Phase is generally understood to date from either the Mothership's decision to join *Tunguska's* political alliance or from the first announcement of their identity as the Nomad Nation. *Bakunin's* struggles continued (with harsh punishments being meted out by the Moderators and the expulsion of several groups), but the Nomad Nation as a whole recognise the Equilibrium Phase as being a time of slow cultural cohesion between the three Motherships.

It was during the latter end of the Equilibrium Phase that Arachne was first created. Originally meant as a common, secure data network for the three Motherships, the Nomads quickly realised the opportunity for it to be something more. Using their commercial contacts and the new powers of diplomatic immunity granted to them by O-12, they began spreading Arachne nodes throughout the Human Sphere, creating a completely alternative datasphere immune to ALEPH's interference.

VIOLENT INTERMISSION (10 NC)
It is likely that the proliferation of Arachne was a primary instigator of the Violent Intermission. Although no "valid proof" ever substantiated ALEPH's direct involvement, and despite the alternative theory promulgated by ALEPH-aligned agents that it was the action of disaffected elements alienated by the tyrannical actions of the Moderator Corps, no Nomad has any doubt about the truth of what happened: During the tenth anniversary celebration of the founding of *Bakunin*, ALEPH infiltrated S.S.S. commandos onto the Mothership with the goal of crippling the Nomad Nation.

Disparate Bakunian militia forces managed to repel the assault, but not before multiple Praxis modules were destroyed and thousands of Bakunians were killed.

PHANTOM CONFLICT (14 NC)
In the wake of the Violent Intermission, the Nomad Nation enjoyed a peaceful lull of sorts, although they suspected it wouldn't last for long. The Bakunian militias, brought together by the Violent Intermission, formalised their relationship into the Nomad Military Force (NMF) and began coordinating with the other Motherships to assure mutual defence.

The neophyte NMF was still being put through its paces when the first skirmishes of the Phantom Conflict broke out. The failure of the Violent Intermission had convinced ALEPH that the threat of the Nomad Nation could only be eliminated by all-out assault, but rather than formally declared hostility, Yu Jing and PanOceania launched a secret, undercover war.

The Nomads, of course, were a mobile and disparate nation. They were spread across the Human Sphere, and the major powers pursued them wherever they went (with a particular focus on major Arachne nodes in an effort to disrupt the Nomad datasphere). Although the Phantom Conflict was never officially acknowledged, it boiled away just beneath the surface on every planet and in every system of the Human Sphere.

The Phantom Conflict was a very real threat to the existence of the Nomad Nation. They had no hope of winning a full-scale war, and the military leaders of the NMF realised that the only possible solution was to relentlessly escalate the scale and severity of the conflict: PanOceania and Yu Jing, unwilling to declare open warfare, stepped down in an impasse which ultimately bolstered the Nomad Nation's legitimacy as an interstellar power.

CRISIS DECADE (21 NC)

The Nomads were not the only extra-national newcomers to wormhole diving. A number of the larger hypercorps funded small exploration corps to seek out exotic resources in alien solar systems. It was expensive work, but – as neomaterials and a vast wealth of bio-resources had already amply demonstrated – the rewards that could be reaped were equally large.

It was a corporate probe which first discovered the Human Edge system in 10 NC. It contained no human-habitable worlds (and therefore held little initial importance for the colonial interests of PanOceania or Yu Jing), but its shattered planetary accretion disc was overflowing with asteroids rich in resources. The wormholes in the

THE NINETY-NINE
The exact number and identity of people killed by the *Bakunin* hull breach was never positively determined. Despite this, they have become known as the Ninety-Nine and are honoured as a sad reminder of the difficulties of the Equilibrium Phase and the shame which many Bakunians still feel to this day.

BLIND EYE MILITARISM
The passivity of other governments in responding to the Violent Intermission demonstrated the viability of using untraceable military forces, particularly outside of their normal area of influence, in order to achieve foreign policy aims. In addition to precipitating the Phantom Conflict, this also caused a methodological shift in the relations between PanOceania and Yu Jing.

DEATH OF A WORLD
The Lunar Colony Revolts were the setting and subject of *Death of a World*, a long-running Maya drama which is still much-loved and held up as a classic example of Hiraeth culture. Although the title is hyperbolistic, there's no question Lunar civilisation is a pale reflection of what it once was.

system were also discovered to be in a particularly advantageous alignment, effectively trimming weeks off of a key trade route. This meant that a Circular was scheduled to pass through the system, making transportation into and out of Human Edge incredibly cheap.

HUMAN EDGE CORPORATE CRISES

Hypercorps and megacorps from PanOceania, Yu Jing, Haqqislam, and a multitude of minor nations flooded in, eager to exploit the virgin territory. Dozens of orbitals became hundreds. Claim-jumping and piracy grew common. The corps called in mercenaries to protect their interests. The mercenary forces grew, clashing with both each other and the pirates. The major powers became involved, using covert military teams to further the interests of their favoured corporations.

Many predicted that the Corporate Crises would escalate into full-scale war, but they never did. Instead, they made "crisis" the watchword of the decade – complex conflicts that confusingly mixed corporate and national interests into a potent mix of brushfire militarism, mercenary actions, and *politionele acties*.

INNER SOL CRISES

The long-suffering Negotiation Phase of the Solar System Inner Area Free Trade Accords proved to be a slow-burning powder keg which directly or indirectly triggered the cascading Inner Sol Crises when the various major powers involved began taking what were referred to as "coercive actions". (The ironic use of the term "negotiation phase" to refer to intelligence operations and special ops missions dates to this time period.)

Perhaps the most significant of the Inner Sol Crises were the Lunar Colony Revolts. These were the last gasp of the Dome Cities which had been bypassed and rendered obsolete by modern transportation technology, and the damage wrought by the conflicts only served to seal their fate.

JOVIAN CRISES

Further out in the Sol system, the Jovian Crises were a struggle for industrial primacy, with various corporate interests serving as a proxy for Yu Jing's desire to dislodge PanOceania's influence over Jupiter and its moons.

DISCOVERY OF PARADISO (29 NC)

The Crisis Decade came to a close with the discovery of Paradiso in 29 NC. The cynical, but probably accurate, assessment is that the fractious conflicts

which had previously been scattered across the galaxy instead became solely focused on the new colonial prize.

PanOceania was once again responsible for the discovery but, as with Svalarheima (and despite PanOceania's best efforts to keep the planet's location classified), Yu Jing soon arrived with their own colonisation ships. Unlike Svalarheima, however, Paradiso was the best colonial prospect since Acontecimento. That meant the stakes were higher and over the next decade tensions in the Paradiso system slowly ratcheted up. Although open warfare had not yet broken out, it will perhaps never be known how much blood was shed beneath the jungle canopy during the first decade of colonisation.

Ironically, the quiet conflict between PanOceania and Yu Jing was an opportunity for Haqqislam. As a "neutral" party they were able to lay claim to several equatorial regions in the name of building an uncontested space elevator (which also expanded the reach of their mercantile empire).

ROAD TO THE NEOCOLONIAL WARS

Tensions in the Paradiso system were growing, but the first flares of violence were found elsewhere.

BLIZZARD SKIRMISHES (35 NC)

Occurring mostly along the borders of Huangdi (the province Yu Jing claimed on Svalarheima), with the exception of a few minor naval engagements and the significant Submarine War in 39 NC, the Blizzard Skirmishes were a prelude of the wars to come. Collectively, their outcome had little impact on the political borders of the planet, but the propaganda teams of both nations painted the major incidents as nationalist triumphs.

HELOT REBELLION (40 NC)

In 40 NC, there was a major uprising of the native Helot population on Varuna. Minor uprisings had occurred before, but this rapidly proved to be something different: a coordinated, global organisation calling itself Libertos claimed credit for the attacks. Although the PanOceanian Military Complex was able to quickly quash the Rebellion, the Hexahedron discovered that Yu Jing had been secretly funding and supporting the Helot terrorist group.

SILK REVOLTS

In 30 NC, dissident Silk Lords, seduced in their greed by the immense riches generated by the Silk trade, sought to overthrow the government of Hachib Mudassar. The Silk Revolts raged up and down the Haqqislam trade routes, reaching into every system of the Human Sphere and seemingly turning every caravanserai into a battlefield. One of the crucial turning points early in the conflict was when the Sekban – the volunteer naval corps of Haqqislam – refused to join the plutocrats. A small Sekban fleet was able to come to the Hachib's relief and ferry him back to Bourak, where he was able to rally support.

JOAN OF ARC

Joan of Arc, the first Recreation, was delivered to PanOceania in 32 NC. She entered the Hospitaller Order as a publicity stunt, but was able to rise in rank and fame quickly during the Blizzard Skirmishes. Blazing a trail through the NeoColonial Wars, her numerous successes were a major influence on the cult-like popularity enjoyed by Recreations today.

Circulars, p. 396: Immense craft which circulate through the wormholes of the Human Sphere on fixed routes. Smaller ships can attach to them in order to traverse the 'holes.

Hexahedron, p. 181: Headquarters of the PanOceanian intelligence service.

NEOCOLONIAL WARS (42 NC)

A rapid intervention by O-12 on Varuna managed to avert immediate war, but it was only a temporary delay. The sabres were rattling and both PanOceania and Yu Jing, frustrated and bellicose, were merely waiting for a clear-cut *casus belli*.

On April 3rd, 42 NC, the PanOceanian cargo ship *Wink of the Rohini* was destroyed above Svalarheima. Despite protestations of innocence, PanOceania blamed the StateEmpire Armada. It was an act of war and would be answered in kind.

INITIAL STAGE (FIRST NEOCOLONIAL WAR)

The war erupted simultaneously on several fronts. Although the First NeoColonial War was largely restricted to Svalarheima, Paradiso (which became known as the "Meat Grinder"), and Human Edge, theatres of operation were spread out across entire star systems.

It was the first total war of the interstellar era. Humanity had never seen anything like it before, and thanks to Maya images and experiences from the front lines it could often be viewed in real time (particularly when civilian population centres were involved). Public opposition to the conflict swelled, and O-12 was able to capitalise upon it to force PanOceania and Yu Jing to agree to a ceasefire in the neutral city of Accra.

CENTRAL STAGE (SECOND NEOCOLONIAL WAR)

But the ceasefire only lasted ten months. PanOceania discovered that Yu Jing was continuing to supply the Libertos terrorists on Varuna with weapons and gear, a direct violation of the Accra Truce. O-12's diplomatic teams might have been able to resolve the situation except for the Libertos bombing of a Tidal BioResearch facility. One hundred and eight people died, half of them Helots (Libertos condemning them as collaborators), inflaming PanOceania's citizenry and abruptly swinging popular opinion in favour of the war.

In the beginning, however, the Central Stage of the NeoColonial Wars proved a struggle for PanOceania. During the Initial Stage, Yu Jing's old military paradigm of fielding massive quantities of barely trained infantry soldiers were exposed as inadequate for the realities of modern warfare. Tseng Huan, their Minister of Defence, authorised an aggressive overhaul of their military paradigm, investing heavily in the development of servo-powered armours. The results were the Invincibles – flexible, mobile, and well-protected troops which amply demonstrated their effectiveness during the Shé (Snake) Offensive.

Yu Jing simultaneously used their superior naval power to force the war to the Sol, Varuna, and Acontecimento systems. PanOceania was reeling. The war had been unexpectedly carried to their homeworlds and there were some who felt the Hyperpower's dominance of the Human Sphere was coming to an end.

BATTLE OF THE DIVIDING LINE

The deadliest engagement of the NeoColonial Wars was the Battle of the Dividing Line. During the Second Siege of Acontecimento, Yu Jing mounted an assault on the Nomad Orbital Commercial Delegation at Aparecida and secretly seized Nomad intra-system vessels. These were used as Trojan horses to penetrate the defences of the Neoterra system, bringing the war to the doorstep of the Hyperpower. PanOceania had also become overconfident in the advantages of their Metatron systems: Yu Jing EVOs used reverse-engineered Dărăo transponders to launch surprise attacks which killed hundreds of PanOceanian infowarriors.

PanOceania held, but only at the highest of costs. And with the defences of their capital badly damaged, they were forced to pull troops back from other fronts.

That's when PanOceania launched the Mahisa Total Offensive. Hexahedron's top-secret military research programs had perfected the Metatron transponders, allowing them to launch inter-system infowar attacks. Now they used them, launching more than three hundred simultaneous attacks on Yu Jing positions across the Human Sphere. With its civilian and military dataspheres crippled, Yu Jing was caught completely off guard, and the Total Offensive eventually culminated in bombing Yutang itself. This was the beginning of total quantronic war, and it forced Yu Jing to sign the Peace of Río Negro.

TERMINAL STAGE (FINAL NEOCOLONIAL WAR)
A new conflict was sparked when a PanOceanian research team discovered a pair of pre-human ruins on Paradiso. At the behest of the other G-4 nations, O-12 attempted to arrange an international group to study them, but PanOceania refused their overtures and claimed sole ownership of the site (dubbed ZuluPoint). Yu Jing launched an assault on the site in an effort to claim it, triggering the bloodiest (and last) stage of the NeoColonial Wars.

Several factors contributed to bring an end to the slaughter: A Haqqislamite-Nomad alliance formed within O-12 to stage a direct intervention. The Yu Jing Emperor died unexpectedly. In response to social and media pressure, key PanOceanian lobbies withdrew their support.

The NeoColonial Wars ended with the Peace of Concilium. The final, negotiated balance of power closely resembled the pre-war situation, with the exception that the area around the ZuluPoint ruins became an O-12 protectorate known as the NiemandsZone. PanOceania and Yu Jing both agreed to share colonisation of Paradiso, and their naval presence in the system was severely limited to ensure the peace.

RETURN TO DAWN (52 NC)

One year after the Peace of Concilium, the PanOceanian scout ship *POS Nirriti* jumped through a previously unexplored wormhole and found itself in the long-lost Ariadna system. And much to the surprise of the entire Human Sphere, the original colonists on the planet Dawn had not died out. Overcoming tremendous odds, in fact, they had conquered a large swath of the planet.

ARIADNAN COMMERCIAL CONFLICTS (53 NC)
Two months after the rediscovery of Ariadna, the Yu Jing military ship *Lei Feng* arrived in the system to "secure the interests of the StateEmpire and to ensure PanOceanian compliance with international law". Fearing the outbreak of another war, Haqqislam and the Nomad Nation moved quickly to have O-12 declare the Ariadnan government a major power.

The action stalled out for several months, however, until the StateEmpire proposed the Yu Jing Compromise: The Ariadnans would be declared a major power, but they would only be able to claim ownership over the portion of the planet which they actually controlled. The Ariadnans considered this a travesty, but they literally had no say in the matter.

Unfortunately, even with Ariadna added to the new G-5, the situation on Ariadna was not resolved: The Colonial Commission was almost instantly corrupt and favoured Yu Jing land claims. PanOceania continued operating under the legal pretense that the planet actually belonged to the native Antipodes. Haqqislam and the Nomads bought deeds from the Ariadnan government. All of these claims conflicted with each other, and megacorps with conflicting leases or purchases began fighting by proxy: Mercenaries would be hired by the corporations, the Ariadnan government would attempt to disarm the mercenaries, and one of the other G-5 nations would use the confrontation as a pretext (or would be forced by their corporate interests) to intervene.

After half a decade of fighting, Bureau Aegis dispatched troops to lock down the situation. O-12 took possession of the border areas originally covered by the Yu Jing Compromise, establishing an Exclusion Zone around the Ariadnan sovereignties. The economic and logistic damage wrought on Ariadna, however, left the local government in a weakened position from which they have never fully recovered.

LOCAL WARS
After the end of the Ariadnan Commercial Conflicts, there were several years in which the great powers were each primarily dealing with small, localised conflicts. These included the Outer Mercantile Crisis between PanOceania and Haqqislam, the Union Revolts of the Jupiter-Pluto Circuit, and the Fourth Antipode Offensive on Ariadna.

This, however, was merely the calm before the storm.

SECOND PHANTOM CRISIS
During the Ariadnan Commercial Conflicts, ALEPH took advantage of the increased discretionary powers it had been granted to peacekeep on Dawn in order to divert S.S.S. forces to covertly attack the Nomad Nation. Although not as protracted or violent as the original Phantom Crisis, in many ways it was even more insidious, featuring a number of infowar operations aimed at allowing ALEPH to permanently subvert the Arachne datasphere (instead of merely destroying it).

ZULUPOINT
The only thing more shocking than the discovery of pre-human ruins on Paradiso was that one of them actually *was* human: The *Aurora* colony ship, thought lost on its journey to the doomed colony of Ariadna, had apparently crashed on Paradiso. (The ultimate fate of the original colonists remains uncertain.)

The other ruins, however, were definitely alien in origin. Known as the cosmolites, they were stone structures. They contained no signs of technology (although there were traces of what might have been decayed biotech) except for the Ur-Probe: a single, unmanned military vehicle of some sort. The Ur-Probe contained signs of nanite activity, although its ultimate purpose would not be discovered for several years.

INVASION

At the height of the Terminal Stage of the NeoColonial Wars, PanOceania abruptly lost all contact with the ZuluPoint Research Centre. The security team sent to investigate discovered the staff dead and the lab almost totally destroyed. PanOceanian High Command attributed the incident to a Yănjīng intelligence operation, although even after the war Yu Jing denied all involvement.

At roughly the same time that the ZuluPoint Research Centre was being destroyed, several ships throughout the Paradiso system detected a strange stellar phenomena moving at astounding speeds.

Only years later, and with the benefit of hindsight, did anyone in the Human Sphere piece together what had happened: The Ur-Probe, the only technological alien artefact found at ZuluPoint, had somehow been activated by the research team. Its advanced nanotechnology had infected the ZRC's systems and used them to create a drone rigged with an impulsion engine and a trans-system emitter. The drone had then travelled to the wormhole that the Ur-Probe had originally used to enter Paradiso and sent a signal back to its master: the Evolved Intelligence and its Combined Army.

FIRST PARADISO OFFENSIVE (60 NC)

The Combined Army arrived in the Paradiso system through a previously unknown wormhole. The *POS Terpsichore*, *POS Olhada do Bom Jesus*, and the Yu Jing frigate *Long Qi* were obliterated as soon as they attempted to greet the unidentified fleet, and the small naval presence in the system allowed by the Peace of Concilium could do nothing as the invaders landed at ZuluPoint and established a beachhead.

Humanity was caught completely off guard. All of their defensive efforts were focused on guarding against each other, leaving them unprepared for an existential threat and incapable of coordinating their actions. Things might have gone much worse if not for the heroic actions of the Paradiso Control Force. The PCF was the PanOceanian planetary army and, by virtue of where the aliens had staged their invasion, they were on the front lines. Although they were ill-equipped to deal with the fearsome Morat legions, they fought hard and distinguished themselves with an honour and tenacity that echoed across human space.

When the end came for the short-lived ZuluPoint Campaign, it came fast and hard. The exhausted PCF, already buckling and running out of room for their strategic retreats, suddenly collapsed into

complete chaos. Only later was it discovered that the PCF had become the first victims of the sinister, shapeshifting Shasvastii. They had infiltrated the PCF and systematically dismantled it from the inside.

The PCF was functionally extinct, but they'd bought precious weeks of time during which millions of civilians were evacuated from threatened areas and the reeling Human Sphere had rallied its forces. The First Paradiso Offensive ground on, with the conflict also spreading to the Septentria Continent.

SECOND PARADISO OFFENSIVE (64 NC)

The end of the First Paradiso Offensive wasn't the result of the ground battle, however. Instead, it was the naval forces of humanity, pouring in through the wormholes leading to the rest of the Sphere, which won decisive victories – first at the Second Battle of the Outer Orbit and then again in the Acheron Attrition – to establish the Paradiso Blockades which cut off Combined Army reinforcements.

Once the Blockades were raised, the Combined Army forces on Paradiso pulled back from their hyper-aggressive campaign and settled into a quiescent period during which they reinforced the gains they had made during the First Offensive.

Paradiso Coordinated Command realised, of course, that this would only be a temporary respite. Despite their best efforts to prepare, however, they nevertheless struggled to contain the Combined Army when it boiled out of its strongholds eighteen months later. Multiple cities fell across the Norstralia and Septentria Fronts before their advances could be slowed.

COMING OF THE TOHAA

On August 9th, 66 NC, a massive spaceship of clearly alien design docked with the EveningStar Orbital, the Paradiso headquarters of O-12. It was impossible to hide. Aurelia Cardoso, a freelance journalist with the Maya investigative aggregate *Eye on the Sky*, was the first to break the story, but soon the orbital space around the EveningStar was swarming with reporters while others focused powerful telescopic lenses skywards from Damburg and Horselberg.

Panic began to spread as rumours flew that O-12 was negotiating a surrender with the Combined Army. All the worst horror stories of how badly things were going on the front began to circulate anew. For a long, horrible moment a terrible reality

Yănjīng, p. 191: The Eyes. The Yu Jing intelligence agency.

ARIADNAN EXPEDITIONARY CORPS

Paradiso had once again become the Meat Grinder. O-12, having formed the Paradiso Coordinated Command, was vitally aware that they needed more boots on the ground. They agreed to assist the Ariadnan government with territorial reclamation on the frontiers of Dawn in exchange for troops. The result was the Ariadnan Exploration Corps, which thrust the backwater Ariadnan youth – still adjusting to the culture shock of recontact – directly into the middle of modern warfare. Their first action was in relief of Yu Jing's Green Banner Army at the Siege of Bái Hai. From the mouth of the Longxi River, they engaged in a series of vicious battles with Morat forces and successfully forced them to withdraw.

EXRAH AFFAIR

The Combined Army is made up of many different alien races, all fighting for the Evolved Intelligence. In the Paradiso system, this included the Exrah Concordat. In 67 NC, however, the Concordat betrayed the EI by channelling weaponry away from the Paradiso front for later resale. The EI responded by completely wiping out the Concordat. The Exrah are now ruled by the Commissariat business group, which is currently abstaining from direct military actions.

began to be accepted as the truth: Humanity had lost the war.

Ninety minutes later, O-12's Paradiso High Commissioner Natalia Hesse issued a public address. The alien vessel was not from the Combined Army. It belonged to the Tohaa Trinomial. They, too, were at war with the Evolved Intelligence. Humanity had just gained a powerful ally. "This is a new time," Commissioner Hesse announced. "Full of opportunities."

PARADISO AFFAIRS (65 NC)

In a series of events referred to as the Paradiso Affairs, O-12 came into possession of an alien device known as the "Black Box". Efforts to fully decrypt and interpret the contents of the Black Box continue even today, but among the earliest information obtained from the Box was the knowledge that there was another race at war with the EI, a race named the Tohaa. The Black Box also yielded coordinates leading to a new wormhole in the Paradiso system which apparently led to star systems controlled by the Tohaa. This information was turned over to the O-12 Öberhaus and, following a series of tense, secret debates, the Öberhaus ultimately decided that, "The enemy of my enemy is my friend." Or, as Senator Eduardo Baez infamously declared as the vote was called, "In the darkness, even the unknown light is welcome." Humanity needed an ally.

Construction began almost immediately on the facilities required to open a portal through the wormhole. The portal, now codenamed Daedalus, was opened. A message probe was sent. The Tohaa responded.

TOHAA CONTACT TREATY (66 NC)

After three weeks of intense negotiation on the EveningStar Orbital, the Tohaa Contact Treaty was signed on August 30th, 66 NC. This was only the beginning, with the Alliance Summit which would hash out the exact operational parameters and responsibilities of the agreement scheduled to last for at least several more weeks.

A sneak attack on the EveningStar by Combined Army forces, however, destroyed the orbital before the Summit could be completed. Despite the catastrophe, the cowardly attack only stiffened the resolve of the Tohaa, and humanity's new allies poured onto the battlefields of Paradiso. It was the end of the Second Offensive.

TODAY (67 NC)

The battlefront on Paradiso has stabilised, but the Combined Army still controls vast swaths of territory and the Acheron Blockade is constantly tested. There is no peace to be found here, and analysts are certain that this is merely the prelude to an inevitable Third Offensive.

Elsewhere, while the Paradiso Offensives have created an apparent calm throughout the Human Sphere, tensions are arguably higher than they have ever been. Secret operations, fast missions, infiltrations, exfiltrations, and special actions have proliferated. The G-5 nations inflict murder, theft, aggressive espionage, sabotage, and kidnappings upon each other.

In some circles, Paradiso seems far away and pales in comparison to the dangers of a Sphere in a position every bit as precarious as the days leading up to the NeoColonial Wars.

And through it all, O-12 struggles to keep the peace.

QINGDAO REPORT

The Qingdao Report was originally created by Bureau Hermes. Named after the city where the Bureau's investigation started, it revealed that Yu Jing was engaged in a Spherewide infiltration campaign using a consortium of Yutang companies, agents of the Yǎnjīng, and Triads. Through indirect means, the StateEmpire had taken control of multiple corporations with key strategic relevance and was positioning itself to directly manipulate the PanOceanian economy (with indications that they were planning to do the same with Haqqislam).

Concerned that the contents of the report could prove destabilising during a time of war, Bureau Noir buried it (while taking quiet action to defuse the ticking Yu Jing time bomb). The report was leaked, however, and published by *Truth Pills*, a show produced by the PanOceanian Maya channel *Autofocus* in 64 NC. The resulting scandal — which also implicated O-12 by association — has contributed materially to tensions across the Human Sphere ratcheting up.

INFOFLUX: REALITY JUST FOR YOU!

The Amalthea Accords conclude with surprising results. Several non-aligned nations unexpectedly move towards the PanOceanian sphere of influence. The government of Yu Jing is garnering support in the international community in order to strengthen its position after this major setback...

Ariadna delivers rebuke in the Öberhaus to the establishment of new PanOceanian and Yu Jing settlements on the continent-islands of Dawn. Their respective governments defend themselves by defining these deployments as research centres covered by international agreements...

The PanOceanian corporation Vulcain has collapsed in the Turoqua Stock Market. The recent escape — which some sources have tagged as kidnapping — of its Projects Director, Henryk Mahlke, to rival company Jizhong has caused shares to collapse...

The murder of the Chancellor of the University of Quebec has fanned the flames of controversy regarding the activities of the Hassassin Society. Chancellor Jean-Louis Parent was accused by the sect of closing all departments dedicated to pure research...

Candy Double evades the Bureau Aegis blockade. Celebrated fugitive Candy Double has once again escaped justice, thus guaranteeing the continuation of her Maya sensaseries. Spectators will be able to continue to enjoy the adventures of this young woman accused of being the illegal copy of a high society heiress...

PanOceania to propose severely modified version of Maidan Basha Intrasystem Trade Treaty. Delegations from the Nomad Nations and Haqqislam have spoken out against what they consider "abusive behaviour".

INTRODUCTION
ADVENTURES IN A WILDERNESS OF MIRRORS

CODE INFINITY
(O-12 Tiered Response Code)

A CODE INFINITY is one of the alert states which exists immediately prior to full-scale war. It is one of the worst possible situations which can exist during peacetime: a complicated, interlocking network of extreme political tension suspended between mutually contradictory astropolitical concerns. In a CODE INFINITY, attempting to defuse one area of tension can directly result in the eruption of another crisis or a complete collapse into violent catastrophe.

PanOceanian intelligence analysts refer to long-term INFINITY situations as the "Chinese Curse" (and dread the announcement that Interesting Times may be upon them). Yu Jing analysts, on the other hand, refer to them as the Dog Days. ("Better to be a dog in peaceful times than to be a man in a time of chaos.") Bureau Noir has inherited a little bit of both espionage cultures, with their operatives often referring to missions as the "dog pound" while sarcastically signing off with the saying, "May you live in interesting times." But Noir agents know that unravelling the Interesting Times is their *raison d'etre.*

The *Infinity* roleplaying game gives you all the tools you need to create an exciting campaign set anywhere within the Human Sphere: Play as Hassassin Govads seeking to recover the lost Cubes of their former brothers from the Equinox terrorists who stole them. Join the crew of the *Go-Go Marlene! Show* as location scouts. Journey into the depths of Acontecimento's oceans in aquatic Nabia Lhosts. Hunt Shasvastii Speculo Killers through the shattered planetoids of Human Edge. Sign up for a PanOceanian mercenary company fighting Libertos rebels on Varuna, then steal a spaceship and become Haqqislamite privateers!

The default mode of play for the game, however, assumes that you are agents working for Bureau Noir, O-12's Secret Service. Bureau Noir's operative teams are flexibly liaised through the other O-12 Bureaus, which means that their duties can effectively take them anywhere in the Human Sphere.

Theoretically, Bureau Noir — like O-12 itself — is a neutral agency and its agents are impartial and unaligned. In reality, the Human Sphere is wracked with factions and every PC will belong to one of them. Their loyalties will be divided and their true agendas will be hidden.

We call this the Wilderness of Mirrors.

COVERT OBJECTIVES

In addition to their primary mission objective, scenarios for the *Infinity* roleplaying game are designed with multiple faction goals. (For example, the primary mission objective might be to protect media tycoon Charles Angleton from threats made by the criminal AI Svengali. Yu Jing agents, however, have a faction goal to insert an eavesdropping virus onto Angleton's comlog, and Nomad agents have a faction goal to retrieve intel on Angleton's suspected collaboration with Svengali.)

Player characters who are assigned a covert objective by their faction handler will feel the weight of the increased stakes in every action that they take, and the conflicting agendas will heighten the dramatic tension of every decision. The Wilderness of Mirrors will bring the broken alliances and fraught tensions of the *Infinity* universe to burning life at your gaming table.

Gamemasters looking to implement the Wilderness of Mirrors in their own campaigns will find more information on creating and integrating covert objectives in *Part V: Gamemaster*, starting on p. 399.

G-5 NATIONS
The five "major powers" distinguished by establishing interstellar colonies and granted seats on the O-12 Security Council. The original G-3 were PanOceania, Yu Jing, and Haqqislam. The Nomad Nation and Ariadna have joined more recently.

FACTIONS OF THE FUTURE

Ariadna: Long years of bloody war — against both each other and the native Antipodes — forced the four nations of the lost colony world together through the imperfect weld of violence. These disparate national factions are united, however, in their struggle to catch up with the rest of humanity. Their agents seek technological advantage and astropolitical leverage.

Haqqislam: The neo-Muslim renaissance of Haqqislam followed their Search for Knowledge to the hostile alien world of Bourak, but their economy has become dominated by the byzantine Merchant Guilds. Their commercial interests extend throughout the Human Sphere along the trade routes which they founded. And, above all, they strive to protect the secrets of Silk.

Nomads: The Nomads have no planet to call their own, instead being primarily a coalition of three colossal Motherships — the *Bakunin*, *Corregidor*, and *Tunguska*. Some applaud their fierce advocacy for personal liberty, while others name them dangerous anarchists who threaten to weaken the Human Sphere when its strength is most needed. Some see their resistance to the insidious, tyrannical control of ALEPH as a bastion defence of humanity's identity, but others point to their illegal gene-experimentation and radical body modifications as a relentless drive towards an incomprehensible post-humanity. Regardless of your point of view, the Nomads stand apart from the rest of human society, even while their far-flung Commercial Missions — which serve as embassies and trade delegations — insinuate their presence throughout the Human Sphere.

PanOceania: The Hyperpower. Larger, richer, and stronger than any of the other Great Powers. The people of PanOceania put more trust in ALEPH than anyone else in the Human Sphere, and as a result, life in their lush, garden-like Living Cities is automated, comfortable, and luxurious. Unsurprisingly, they champion a defensive astropolitical agenda which strives to sustain the status quo which they currently dominate.

Yu Jing: PanOceania's largest rival is Yu Jing, the Pan-Asian alliance which has forged its diverse cultural groups beneath the unified banner of the new Imperial System. The StateEmpire of Yu Jing has been rapidly closing the gap with PanOceania by aggressively seeking out every possible advantage and ruthlessly exploiting it.

ALEPH: The Human Sphere would not exist without the AI's oversight. It is mankind's beneficent protector, managing their daily necessities, ceaselessly seeking to improve their lives, and providing for their common defence (particularly now that they face the existential threat of the Combined Army). Those loyal to ALEPH see its will as the will of the Human Spheres. Many serve openly in the Special Situations Section, but the galaxy is a dark and dangerous place, and ALEPH needs eyes and agents that can go to all the places it cannot yet reach.

Corporations: The chartered companies used by PanOceania to rapidly develop its colonial prospects, the Merchant Guilds of Haqqislam which blazed the trade routes of the starways, and the *keiretsu* spun-off from the centrally controlled economy of Yu Jing's StateEmpire became the seeds of the new hypercorporations. Corporate agents seek technological revelations, trade secrets, unique access to natural resources, and anything else that might yield a profit.

Mercenaries: In an era of interstellar war, the free mercenary companies (FMCs) and private military corporations (PMCs) have flourished. In the employ of state armies, O-12, and private corporations they can be found almost anywhere: capitals and colonies, orbital stations and deep space patrols, the battlefields of Paradiso and the security of corporate compounds. Their services are traded on the well-regulated War Market, a mercenary stock exchange in which employers can find companies available for hire and the mercenary companies can find individual soldiers or squadrons ready for recruitment. Characters receiving covert objectives from a mercenary faction may be loyal to a specific Warmonger, or they may be an independent freelancer with multiple markets for the information they have to sell.

Submondo: Petty and violent crimes obviously have not vanished in the wake of interstellar flight, but if you're talking about criminals as a *faction*, then you're talking about organised crime. Some of these organisations have become incredibly large, spanning not only planets, but the interstellar breadth of the Human Sphere. O-12 uses the codename Submondo (meaning "Underworld" in Esperanto) to refer to these criminal syndicates, which include mob families (like the Acontecimento Mafia), criminal brotherhoods (like the Triads), pirate consortiums (like the Grey Band of Human Edge), terrorist groups (like Eko-Aktion), and Maya clusters (like Aug-Neon).

O-12: As an international and pan-planetary organisation, O-12 strives to hold humanity together. O-12 is functionally a "neutral" faction, but in practice that often means the faction goal of characters loyal to O-12 is playing spoiler to the faction goals of the other player characters.

Ariadna

Haqqislam

Nomads

PanOceania

Yu Jing

ADVENTURES IN A WILDERNESS OF MIRRORS   27

INTRODUCTION
HOW TO PLAY INFINITY

Grab your Combi Rifle, hop on your mag-bike, check your MediKit, and tell your comlog to load the soundtrack of your life: The universe of *Infinity* is waiting for you.

Because the *Infinity* roleplaying game is a game of the imagination, you and your friends can play it almost anywhere. Most games are played around a table, but it's just as easy to play the game using email, a message board, or a chat room. Playing *Infinity* requires at least two players and can comfortably include up to six (or more).

One player is the Gamemaster (GM). The GM is responsible for describing the universe of *Infinity*:

Peeling back the thick, purplish growth of the Paradiso jungle, you peer down into the ravine. You can see a Morat patrol down there. There are three of the huge, red-skinned aliens walking alongside what appears to be some kind of dronbot. You can see a weird, elongated parabolic dish perched on top of the dronbot, and it's skittering back and forth along a scanning arc of some sort.

The other players must now tell the GM what they're going to do: Will you ambush the Morat with your Combi Rifles? Throw a gas grenade and

hope to knock them out? Try to follow them and figure out what they're doing? Hack the dronbot? Attempt to take one of them alive for questioning? Or will you try something else entirely? The decision is up to you!

WHAT YOU NEED

In addition to a Gamemaster and a group of players, you'll also need:

Player Characters: Each player should create a character using the Lifepath system (starting on p. 38).

Dice: Two d20s per player, a few d6s, and a dozen or more Combat Dice for the group. (You can also use additional d6s in place of the custom Combat Dice.)

Paper & Pencil: To draw maps, track conditions, and keep notes on important clues, events, and characters you meet during your adventures.

Tokens or Beads: Five per player to track Infinity Points, a dozen or more for the Gamemaster's Heat pool, and an optional third set to track Momentum.

PLAYTEST TIPS

Throughout this rulebook you will find sidebars labelled Playtest Tips. These sidebars call out common errors made when using the rules or suggest unusual applications of the rules. They're lessons learned from the thousands of hours spent playtesting *Infinity* and the 2d20 System, presented in a quick-reference format so that you don't have to learn them the hard way.

ROLLING THE DICE

You'll often need to roll one or more dice while playing *Infinity*. This will be indicated in the text with the notation XdY, where X indicates the number of dice to roll and Y indicates the type of dice to roll. For example, 3d20 would mean to roll three twenty-sided dice and 5d6 would mean that you roll five six-sided dice.

COMBAT DICE

Combat Dice, or Ⓝ, are a particular way of rolling a d6. They are used for determining damage and governing special effects. When rolling Ⓝ, ignore any results of three, four, or five. Results of one and two are counted normally, while sixes are referred to as Effects, which trigger certain special abilities.

REROLLS

A number of circumstances and abilities will allow a character to reroll one or more dice. When a reroll is allowed, the player chooses which dice from the original roll to reroll (up to the number of dice listed, if any). The new result of rerolled dice replaces the original result entirely (even if they're worse than the original results).

CHARACTERS

Of course, you won't be playing as yourself looking down at those Morat soldiers. Instead, you'll use the Lifepath system (starting on p. 38) to create a character by simulating their life story. Starting from the moment of their birth, you'll walk a few miles in their shoes (or their Teseum-laced combat boots, whatever the case may be): Perhaps you'll be an investigative journalist for a Maya media aggregate, journeying to the far corners of the Human Sphere to get your exclusive stories. Or maybe you'll be a member of a Gŭiláng special forces unit, trekking across the icy fields of Svalarheima in service of Yu Jing. Or a bounty hunter tracking dangerous criminals through the colonial domes of Mars. Or a fearsome Dogface athlete who suffered a career-ending injury while playing Dog-Bowl on Ariadna.

ATTRIBUTES

Each character is defined by a collection of seven **attributes**. These attributes indicate a character's inherent abilities, and their physical and mental limitations. Most attributes for player characters have values from six to twelve, with eight representing the human average. Higher attribute ratings represent greater ability.

ATTRIBUTE LIST

- **Agility**: Physical and manual dexterity, sense of balance, body control, and reflexes.
- **Awareness**: Perceptions, sensory acuity, gut feelings, and instincts.
- **Brawn**: Strength, toughness, endurance, and the ability to apply physical force.
- **Coordination**: Hand-eye coordination and spatial awareness.
- **Intelligence**: Wit, intellect, logic, reason, and the ability to apply knowledge or interact with technology.
- **Personality**: Charisma, comfort in social situations, and the ability to be threatening or charming as required.
- **Willpower**: Grit, determination, and psychological resilience.

SKILLS

Skills represent a character's specialised training within a particular field — knowledge, proficiency with tools or devices, conditioning, special techniques, and so forth. Each skill is tied to a particular attribute, representing the most common association between that skill and the character's basic capabilities. (For example, Education and Tech are skills based on Intelligence.)

Skill Expertise: A character's Expertise in a skill is their mastery of the subject. Expertise with a skill increases the likelihood of success.

Skill Focus: A character's Focus in a skill is achieved through constant practice, superior discipline, and deeper insight. Focus with a skill improves the quality of success.

SKILL TESTS

Whenever a character attempts a task where the outcome is in doubt, you will make a skill test to determine whether the task succeeds or fails.

TARGET NUMBER

Determine the target number of the skill test by adding the character's relevant attribute to their Skill Expertise. (This will usually be the default attribute associated with the skill, but not always.)

EXPERTISE VS. FOCUS

A fast, sloppy mechanic with years of experience might have a high Expertise in Tech, but a low Focus: When you bring your half-slagged TAG to them, they will almost certainly get it working again... but it will be slathered in duct tape. On the other hand, a gifted amateur might have a lower Expertise than the old hand, but a higher Focus: They won't always be able to get your TAG running again, but when they do it's more likely that they'll also figure out a way to optimise the engine or add extra armour to it.

SKILL LIST

Acrobatics (Agility)
Analysis (Awareness)
Animal Handling (Personality)
Athletics (Brawn)
Ballistics (Coordination)
Close Combat (Agility)
Command (Personality)
Discipline (Willpower)
Education (Intelligence)
Extraplanetary (Awareness)
Hacking (Intelligence)
Lifestyle (Personality)
Medicine (Intelligence)
Observation (Awareness)
Persuade (Personality)
Pilot (Coordination)
Psychology (Intelligence)
Resistance (Brawn)
Science (Intelligence)
Spacecraft (Coordination)
Stealth (Agility)
Survival (Awareness)
Tech (Intelligence)
Thievery (Awareness)

ROUNDING

Unless specified otherwise, when dividing numbers in *Infinity*, always round up.

PLAYTEST TIP
ROUTINE TASKS

Characters in *Infinity* are competent professionals and unlikely to fail at routine tasks. If they aren't threatened or distracted and if there is no consequence for failure, it's usually better to simply assume that they succeed instead of calling for a test. If the roll doesn't matter, don't roll!

EXAMPLE
BASIC SKILL TEST

Roberta is making a Tech check with an Intelligence of 8, an Expertise of 3, and a Focus of 2. Her target number is 11 (8 + 3) and when she rolls 2d20 she gets results of 13 and 1. The result of 13 generates no successes, but the result of 1 generates two successes: one for being equal to or lower than the target number and a second for being lower than the character's Focus in the skill.

HEAT AS
COMPLICATION

If the GM has difficulty thinking up a good complication in the moment, he can choose to add 2 Heat to his pool instead. If a non-player character suffers a complication, the players may similarly choose to have the GM remove 2 Heat from his pool. If multiple complications are generated, then their effects are resolved individually at the GM's discretion, so some could be turned into Heat while others have an immediate effect.

HIGHLY-SKILLED
CHARACTERS

If the target number for a skill test is 20 or higher, each die roll automatically counts as a success. These dice can still generate complications and additional successes due to Focus normally.

DIFFICULTY

A task's difficulty (a value from zero to five) is determined by the Gamemaster. The levels of difficulty, and some examples of what tasks might fall into each level, are described on the *Difficulty Table* (see below).

BASIC SKILL TEST

The player rolls 2d20. For each die that rolls equal to or less than the test's target number the character scores a success. Each die that rolls equal to or less than the character's Focus in the skill used for the test generates an additional success.

If the character scores a number of successes equal to or higher than the difficulty of the test, then they succeed at their task.

GAINING MOMENTUM

When the number of successes scored on a skill test is greater than the difficulty rating, the excess successes become Momentum. Momentum can be spent immediately to perform the task faster or more effectively, or it can be saved and applied to subsequent actions (with one success paving the way to the next). For more details on using your Momentum effectively, see *Heat and Momentum* on p. 32.

COMPLICATIONS

When making a skill test, a complication occurs for every natural 20 rolled on a d20. Complications are explained in detail on p. 33, but this basically means that something unfortunate has happened to make the character's life more difficult.

The inconvenience of this complication is independent of the success or failure of the action. It is entirely possible to succeed at a skill test while simultaneously generating a complication. (The complication should never turn a success into a failure, however. For example, if the complication causes a character's gun to run out of ammunition on a successful attack test, then it only happens after their last shot strikes the target.)

If more than one complication occurs on a test — because multiple 20s are rolled — then these may be used to produce multiple complications, or they can be combined into major complications.

Complication Range: Some circumstances and effects may increase the complication range of a roll. This will expand the range of rolled numbers which will trigger a complication. For example, increasing the complication range by one would result in complications occurring for each 19 or 20 rolled on any d20.

COMPLEX SKILL TEST

A complex skill test is used when a character is attempting a complicated task with many individual steps to success. It is resolved as a series of basic skill tests, with the character succeeding at the task when they have spent a certain amount of Momentum.

A complex skill check is defined by the difficulty of the test, the total amount of Momentum which must be spent in order to achieve success, and the maximum number of failures which can be suffered before the attempt fails.

DIFFICULTY TABLE		
NAME	**SUCCESSES**	**EXAMPLES**
Simple (D0)	0	Opening a slightly stuck door. Researching a widely known subject. Hitting a target at a shooting range with a bullet.
Average (D1)	1	Overcoming a simple lock. Researching a specialised subject. Shooting an enemy at optimal range.
Challenging (D2)	2	Overcoming a complex lock. Researching obscure information. Shooting an enemy at optimal range in poor light.
Daunting (D3)	3	Overcoming a complex lock in a hurry. Researching restricted information. Shooting an enemy at long range in poor light.
Dire (D4)	4	Overcoming a complex lock in a hurry, without the proper tools. Researching classified information. Shooting an enemy at long range in poor light and heavy rain.
Epic (D5)	5	Overcoming a complex lock in a hurry, without the proper tools, and in the middle of a firefight. Researching a subject where the facts have been thoroughly redacted from official records. Shooting an enemy at extreme range in poor light and heavy rain.

COMPLICATION TEST

Sometimes, a character's ultimate success at a particular task is assured. The only question is how long it will take them to accomplish the task or what quality of success they will enjoy.

On a conditional success test, the skill test is made normally. On a failure, however, the GM triggers a complication: The character still succeeds at the task they were attempting, but they have failed to prevent some additional problem from arising as well. (This complication will stack with any additional complications generated on the task as result of rolling 20s.) A character cannot failsafe on a complication test.

FACE-TO-FACE TESTS

When two characters are in direct opposition to each other, each character involved in the task performs a skill test. The character who achieves the greatest quantity of Momentum succeeds, achieving their goal. In the case of a tie, the character with the highest Expertise in their skill wins.

If there are no other factors involved, the difficulty of a face-to-face test is usually Simple (D0). For example, if two characters are running a race the winner will simply be whichever character has the better skill test.

Face-to-face tests with higher difficulties represent situations in which it is possible for everyone participating in the task to fail. For example, if two characters are both trying to be the first person to solve a Challenging (D2) puzzle, it is possible that neither of them will be able to solve the puzzle.

If either side has some circumstance which would make the test more challenging for them than for their opponent, simply adjust the difficulty of their check. (Remember that success is determined by the total Momentum generated; not the total number of successes rolled.)

FAILSAFE TEST

There may be some situations where a player feels it may be better to embrace a failure which otherwise feels inevitable. (This may be the case with a skill test using a skill the player's character has no training with, or where the difficulty is high enough that success is unlikely to begin with.)

With agreement from the GM, the player may choose to have their character fail a skill test automatically, where there are meaningful consequences for failure (such as being pursued, attempting to perform a complex task under pressure, avoiding an attack, etc.). To fail a skill test voluntarily, the player pays the GM 1 Heat. In exchange, the character immediately gains

one Infinity Point (up to the normal maximum). A character may never choose voluntary failure for a Simple (D0) skill test.

GROUP TEST

If the situation, time, and GM allow, several characters can work together as a team while attempting to perform a task by making a group test.

One character is designated as the leader, and the other characters are designated as assistants. In order to assist with a skill test, each player must describe how their character is assisting the test's leader. If the GM approves, each assistant rolls 1d20, using their own attributes and skills to determine if any successes are scored. Individual assistants may use different skills than the leader, representing a group effort in which each character contributes different knowledge or proficiency.

If the leader scores at least one success, then any successes generated by the assistants are added to the leader's total. If the leader fails, then any successes scored by the assistants are lost.

Complications rolled by the leader and their assistants are all totalled and take effect regardless of the leader's outcome.

Assistants can gain bonus dice on their roll normally (by spending Momentum, Heat, or Infinity Points, for example), but the maximum bonus of +3d20 applies to the group as a whole. (The single, base d20 rolled by each assistant does not apply to this limit, however.)

PROGRESSIVE SKILL TEST

A progressive skill test is resolved in the same way as a complex skill test, with a series of basic skills tests on which the character must accumulate a certain number of successes in order to accomplish their objective. On a progressive skill test, however, each roll which fails to generate at least one success adds +1 difficulty to the test (the test becomes progressively more difficult) to a maximum difficulty of 5.

UNTRAINED SKILL TESTS

Sometimes a character may be required to attempt a skill test using a skill that they don't have any Expertise or Focus ranks in. These tests are said to be untrained. Untrained tests are resolved exactly like any other skill test, except the complication range of the test is increased by one.

DIFFICULTY ZERO TESTS

A task may be so simple that it does not require a test in the first place. These are also Simple (D0) tests. If a test is Simple (D0), it does not require a test to be made—it is automatically successful with zero successes, requiring no effort whatsoever, and with no risk of complications (see p. 33), and without any dice being rolled. However, because no test is made, it can generate no Momentum, not even bonus Momentum from talents, gear, or particularly advantageous situations.

A character can still choose to make a test for a Simple (D0) task, but this takes the normal amount of time, can generate Momentum as normal, and comes with the risk of generating complications.

IMPROVING THE ODDS

While succeeding at most common tasks is a straightforward matter, even the most proficient character cannot succeed at the most difficult tasks without effort, opportunity, or assistance.

Infinity provides a number of ways to do this, and most of those methods are fairly similar — providing additional d20s for a character to roll on a skill test. Extra dice allow a character to score more successes, and thus hit higher difficulties or simply generate more Momentum. These extra dice come from Momentum or Heat (p. 32), from spending *Infinity Points* (p. 35), or from using *Resources* (see *Part IV: Gear*).

Methods for improving the odds can be mixed-and-matched as the characters require. Regardless of the methods used, however, a character can never gain more than three additional d20s on any skill test.

HEAT AND MOMENTUM

The cinematic action of the *Infinity* universe is driven by the twin engines of Heat and Momentum.

Momentum is success building on success. As player characters generate extra successes on their skill tests, those successes become Momentum which can be spent to improve the quality of the current task or saved to improve their odds on the next task.

Heat is the opposite side of that coin. It's an abstract measure of potential threats and dangers. As player characters take reckless actions, push themselves to potentially dangerous extremes, or simply suffer bad luck, the GM's Heat pool will increase. The larger the Heat pool, the more likely something will endanger or imperil the player characters. When the GM spends that Heat, they turn potential danger into actual problems.

STARTING HEAT

At the beginning of each session, the GM starts with 3 Heat per player character.

SPENDING MOMENTUM

The basic use of Momentum is to either make the character's next action easier or to make something more difficult for an opponent. A player may spend Momentum they have generated freely on whatever benefits they wish. Momentum spends may be used repeatedly and as often as the character wishes (assuming they have sufficient Momentum to pay for them), unless the spend is noted as Non-Repeatable (NR). Non-Repeatable Momentum spends can only be used once per task, test, or action. A character does not have to spend, or declare an intention for, any Momentum in advance — you can spend it as and when it becomes necessary or desirable.

Create Opportunity: The most basic use of Momentum is to spend one point to gain an additional d20 to roll on a skill test. These dice must be purchased prior to rolling any dice and the normal maximum of +3d20 bonus dice on any test applies.

Create Obstacle: Similarly, a character can choose to make things more difficult for a rival, adversary, or opponent — creating problems, distractions, or presenting more direct opposition. This increases the difficulty of a skill test made by the opponent. The difficulty of a single test cannot be increased by more than three steps, regardless of how many characters are contributing Momentum, and the

Momentum must be spent prior to the opponent rolling any dice. Each step of increasing difficulty is purchased separately, at a cost equal to the increase in difficulty.

DIFFICULTY INCREASE	TOTAL MOMENTUM COST
+1 Difficulty	1 Momentum
+2 Difficulty	3 Momentum
+3 Difficulty	6 Momentum

ALTERNATIVE MOMENTUM SPENDS

In addition to the basic uses for Momentum, players are encouraged to be creative in their use of Momentum. When you score an exceptional success, think outside of the box in terms of how that superb performance can be reflected in either the result of the immediate task or in how the outcome of that task can impact what happens next. However, Momentum can never turn failure into a success (although it can mitigate the consequences of that failure).

Improve Quality of Success: Momentum can let you succeed in style or immediately capitalise or follow up on your success. If you succeed on a Science test to identify a poison, for example, Momentum might allow you to simultaneously synthesize an antidote or identify a list of suppliers that the poison could have been obtained from. Momentum on an Animal Handling test to calm a Varunan Water-Snake might allow you to temporarily befriend it. A Survival test made to scavenge food on the Ariadnan tundra could yield extra supplies.

Increase Scope of Success: With Momentum you can affect additional targets, boost the range affected by your success, or otherwise enlarge the extent of what you're accomplishing. For example, Momentum on a Persuade test could be spent to convince more of the officers in the room to join your mutiny. When making an Observation test, you might use Momentum to spot a threat at a farther distance. Or you could increase the amount of time that your newly acquainted Varunan Water-Snake will stay friendly.

Reduce Time Required: Instead of spending hours researching Maya starlets from the time of the NeoColonial Wars, you find an otaku obsessed with the topic and more than willing to share her expertise. You convince someone to trust you with a quick word instead of a prolonged debate. When making a Stealth test to see if you can labouriously work your way around the perimeter of a military hangar, you identify a precise moment in the cycles of the security drones that allows you to race quickly across the tarmac.

THE HEAT-MOMENTUM CYCLE

Generally speaking, getting yourself out of the trouble generated through Heat creates Momentum that will propel you forward to your next set of actions. Taking those actions will cause Heat to grow again as you pay for additional dice to bolster the chance of success, take Reactions to survive, and the like. And then it will shrink once more as the GM's NPCs are forced to react or activate powerful weapons and abilities. In this way, the amount of "pressure" the player characters apply to a situation provides NPCs with the means to push back commensurately, ensuring that situations remain challenging and adjust themselves to the players' choices (and vice versa).

MOMENTUM FROM OTHER SOURCES

Some talents, items, or circumstances can grant a character bonus Momentum. This bonus Momentum is added to any applicable skill test that results in success (as specified by the source of the bonus). A failed skill test cannot benefit from bonus Momentum.

PLAYTEST TIP

TRACKING MOMENTUM

We recommend setting aside a distinctive d6 or using a pool of tokens to track the amount of saved Momentum for the group. Try to keep your Momentum tracker visible to everyone at the table to make coordinating your actions easier!

SAVING MOMENTUM

Instead of immediately spending Momentum, characters have the option of saving it. This saved Momentum goes into a group pool, which can be added to or drawn from by any character in the group, representing the benefits of their collective successes. No more than six points of Momentum may be saved into this pool at any one time.

During any successful skill test, any member of the group may draw as many or as few points from the group Momentum pool as they wish, adding those points to any they have generated on the skill test. They may subsequently spend that Momentum as they wish, as if it had been generated from the skill test. As normal, Momentum only needs to be spent as needed, so a character does not have to choose how much Momentum they are drawing from the group pool until they actually need it, nor do they have to draw it all at once.

MOMENTUM DEPLETION

At the end of each scene, or each full round in an action scene, the pool diminishes and 1 Momentum from the pool is lost (to a minimum of 0).

SAVING NPC MOMENTUM

The GM does not need to specifically track unused Momentum for NPCs. Instead, NPCs with unspent Momentum automatically convert their remaining Momentum into Heat (on a one-for-one basis).

HEAT

In some cases, a player will want the benefits of Momentum but won't have any to spend. When that happens, they can choose to pay Heat instead. Heat works exactly like Momentum — and it can be combined with normal Momentum spends — but when player characters use Heat, it is paid into the GM's Heat pool.

There is a limit to how much trouble you can bring down on your own head, though. Player characters can voluntarily pay no more than six Heat on their turn during an action scene (or per action in other scenes). This limit does not apply to Heat generated as a result of rolling complications.

There is no limit to how much Heat a GM can choose to spend.

GAINING HEAT

In addition to players paying Heat and NPCs converting Momentum into Heat, there are a few specific conditions which can cause the Heat pool to grow:

ADVANCED RULE: SAVING INDIVIDUAL MOMENTUM

As an advanced rule, instead of using a group pool for saved Momentum each PC can save Momentum and use it later individually. Players who have saved Momentum can spend it at any time to assist the actions of other player characters (or NPC allies) and otherwise influence the scene. At any given time, a player can save a maximum of six Momentum. In addition, any single action can benefit from a maximum of six saved Momentum. (For example, if two players had both saved four Momentum each, they still wouldn't be able to spend all eight Momentum on a single action.) During Momentum depletion, each character loses 1 Momentum.

Complications: When a character rolls a complication on a skill test, the GM may choose to add 2 Heat to their pool instead of immediately using the complication.

Reactions: As described in *Part II: Action Scenes*, a player character attempting a Reaction adds Heat; one for the first Reaction attempted each round, two for the second, and so forth.

Threatening Circumstances: Certain strange or dangerous environments might naturally generate a point or two of Heat, representing the innate peril of the location. Foes with the Menacing quality will also bring with them a few points of Heat, representing the threat that the foe represents.

SPENDING HEAT

The GM uses Heat to create complications.

A complication is an inconvenient change of circumstances. It is a new obstacle to overcome (like an explosion that cuts off a route of escape), a loss of resources (like a Reload), something that impairs the character (like spraining their ankle), or an embarrassing situation (like a social faux pas or accidentally downloading malware).

Minor Complication: 1 Heat can be used to create a minor complication. As a general guideline, a minor complication will require only a Minor Action to fix, overcome, or circumvent. They are nuisances, not serious threats.

Standard Complication: A standard complication costs 2 Heat (or can be generated by rolling a natural 20 on a skill test). These complications may involve the loss of significant resources or the inflicting of stress. It will usually require a Standard Action to deal with them or work around them. They're either a significant distraction or dealing with them requires focus and attention.

Major Complication: Spending 4 Heat or more creates a major complication. These complications create prolonged situations which the characters

EXAMPLE
CREATE OPPORTUNITY
Cassandra generates Momentum while picking the lock on the door of an illegal Nomad gene-lab. She might use that Momentum to add a d20 to the Stealth check for slipping past the guard inside because she was able to open the door quickly and silently. Or she might spend that Momentum later while opening another door, relying on the familiarity she gained with the first.

EXAMPLE
CREATE OBSTACLE
While infiltrating the gene-lab, Cassandra is spotted by one of the guards. As the guard pulls his sidearm, Cassandra spends 3 Momentum and shoots her own pistol to knock out some of the lights. The sudden darkness increases the difficulty of the guard's Ballistics test by two steps (1 Momentum for the first increase in difficulty, then 2 Momentum for the second step).

will need to expend great effort to work around. In an action scene, they are likely to persist for several rounds. Or they may inflict damage.

HAZARDS

As a complication, the GM may inflict 1+X  damage to a single character, where X is the Heat spent. The number of combat dice are doubled if it can be avoided by a Challenging (D2) skill test or tripled if it can be avoided with an Average (D1) skill test.

Additional qualities and effects on the damage may be added by spending additional Heat.

MECHANICAL SPENDS

GMs can also spend Heat in all the same ways that a PC can — supplementing Momentum, paying off complications generated by NPC skill tests, or taking NPC reactions. However, when a GM spends Heat points from their pool they are used up.

In addition, there are some unique ways that GMs can use their Heat pool.

NPC Resources: Reloads, Serum, Parts, and other expendable resources used to boost the effect of a skill test are not tracked individually for NPCs. Instead, an NPC can be granted the benefit of a single unit of a resource by paying 1 Heat.

Activating Special Abilities: Some particularly powerful or experienced NPCs may have access to potent abilities or equipment. As noted in their descriptions, these abilities may require the Gamemaster to spend 1 Heat or more to activate them.

Seize the Initiative: In action scenes, the GM may spend Heat to interrupt the action order and allow an NPC to act by spending 1 Heat (see p. 99).

Reinforcements: Sometimes the Heat generated by the PCs will bring unwanted attention. When that happens, the GM can spend Heat to summon extra reinforcements. Reinforcements summoned with Heat arrive at the end of the current round, they must arrive in a logical way, and they cannot act in the round during which they arrive. A Trooper NPC costs 1 Heat to summon, while Elite NPCs cost 2 Heat.

EXAMPLE
CREATING A HAZARD

While attempting to sabotage a piece of Combined Army equipment, Cassandra and Roberta succeed on their teamwork Tech test, but Roberta rolls a complication. The GM decides that their efforts have destabilised the VoodooTech device and caused it to explode! The explosion would affect both of them, so the GM splits the 2 Heat generated by the complication, spending 1 Heat to inflict damage on each character. This would normally cause 1+1  damage, but the GM rules that the explosion can be avoided with an Average (D1) Acrobatics test, so if they fail that test they will instead suffer 1+3  damage.

Triggering an Environmental Effect: Dramatic scenes often play out in exciting environments — a firefight in a crumbling tenement, a chase through a busy marketplace, a chasm over a river of lava, etc. When describing encounters, the GM is encouraged to provide details to the players to help them visualise the scene, and sometimes it can be interesting to bring the environment alive through the use of Heat. Triggering an environment effect comes in two levels of magnitude. Minor effects — costing 1 Heat — are typically things like flickering lights, crumbling walls, thick smoke, which add to the difficulty of skill tests, or force tests where one was not previously required. Major effects — costing 2 Heat or more — may pose significant impediments to the characters, or even cause them harm (physical, mental, or quantronic) or short-lived conditions.

INVOKING A TRAIT

When spending Heat, a GM can choose to invoke the character traits of the player characters by bringing a dormant issue to the forefront, confronting a character with the object of their phobia, creating situations which prey on their flaws, threaten their loved ones, or otherwise force them to deal with their issues.

In other words, when a GM creates a complication that is directly related to or affects a character's trait, they can reduce the cost of the complication by 1 Heat.

INFINITY POINTS

Player characters have access to a special type of resource called Infinity Points. Infinity Points allow the player characters to persevere in the face of overwhelming odds, achieve spectacular goals, and perform impressive feats. This reflects the fact that the player characters have drive, ambition, and determination above and beyond most people, and can succeed where others might fail. Whether or not they are viewed as heroes, the player characters are destined for greatness.

GAINING INFINITY POINTS

A player character begins each session with a number of Infinity Points equal to their Infinity Point refresh rate (a value of two to four), and they cannot have more than five Infinity Points at any time.

Failsafe Actions: Players can gain Infinity Points by voluntarily failing significant skill tests (see p. 31).

Triggering a Trait: Once per scene, with the GM's approval, a player can trigger one of their character traits to gain one Infinity Point. To trigger the trait, the player pays 1 Momentum or Heat to the GM and takes some form of large or significant action motivated by the trait which is dramatic, irrational, dangerous, or the like.

GM Award: Infinity Points may be awarded by the GM during a session to reward players for good roleplaying, clever plans, successfully overcoming difficult challenges, or using teamwork. Players may have other opportunities to gain Infinity Points by achieving certain goals within an encounter, reaching a milestone in the story, or choosing to be the one to suffer the consequences of some dire event.

USING INFINITY POINTS

Here are just a few of the ways in which Infinity Points can be spent during play:

Infinity d20: Before attempting a skill test, add a bonus d20 to the test. However, this Infinity d20 is not rolled. Instead, it is simply set on the table with the "1" facing up. It is otherwise counted normally, which means it will automatically count as a success (and characters with a Skill Focus will automatically score a second success). Infinity d20s count towards the normal limit of +3d20 bonus dice per test.

Bonus Action: Perform an additional Standard Action on your turn during an action scene. Each character may only gain one additional Standard Action each round in this way.

Overcome Harm: Ignore effects of Wounds, Metanoia, or Breaches (choose one) until the end of the current scene.

Overcome Trait: Ignore the negative effects of a trait until the end of the scene. (The GM cannot invoke that trait.)

Quick Absterge: Automatically end the duration of a character condition.

Second Wind: Recover all lost Vigour, Resolve, or Firewall (choose one).

Story Declaration: Introduce a fact or add a detail to the current scene. (The GM may veto some story declarations, or require multiple Infinity Points for particularly large or significant declarations.)

PLAYTEST TIP
HEAT FROM THE SOURCE
The GM can make a note of which reckless actions generate Heat during the session. This can be used as an inspiration for triggering later complications with the Heat. (For example, if somebody rushed to repair a radio, it might fail at the worst possible moment.) Heat expenditures are an abstract mechanic and don't require this kind of direct connection, but that doesn't mean it can't be a useful seed for improvisation.

EXAMPLE
INVOKING A TRAIT
Kline has the character trait of Paranoia. While negotiating with an arms dealer on Bourak, he can't shake the feeling that he's about to be ambushed. Despite the incredible risk it poses, he tells his geist to hack the arms dealer's comlog and eavesdrop on his communication. Kline's player says that he's triggering his Paranoia trait and, with the GM's approval, pays 1 Heat to gain 1 Infinity Point.

PART I: CHARACTERS

LIFEPATH SYSTEM
SKILLS AND TALENTS

CHARACTERS
LIFEPATH SYSTEM

Players create their characters in *Infinity* by walking the character's Lifepath. The Lifepath system begins at the moment of birth and guides the character through nine major Decisions that will chart the course of their personal history and determine their skills, talents, attributes, equipment, and other pertinent details. As you follow your character through the Lifepath, you'll bear witness first-hand to their triumphs and travails, forging a unique and immersive understanding of who they are.

LIFE POINTS

But you do not have to leave your character merely to the whims of fate. During the Lifepath, each player receives five Life Points which they can use to help their character navigate the tumultuous turns of their personal histories. At each Decision point in the Lifepath, you'll be able to invest these

Life Points to either influence the outcome of the random tables or override them completely and guarantee a particular result. (The effect of each Life Point depends on the Decision it is spent to influence, as detailed below. Unless otherwise stated, Life Points spent to override random results must be spent before you roll the dice.)

In this way, the *Infinity* Lifepath system gives you the best of both worlds when creating your character. You can generate a character randomly (discovering the role you'll be exploring), but you also have the power to step in and take direct control (creating the role you want to play). The result is a rich and organic character creation system which you can use to craft multifaceted and dynamic characters ready to leap into the epic stories of the Human Sphere!

LIFEPATH DECISIONS

DECISION ONE – BIRTH HOST
Default attributes to 7 and adjust their values. Calculate the stats for your birth host and check for an alien heritage.
   Life Point Spend: Increase your starting attributes or choose an alien heritage.

DECISION TWO – FACTION AND HERITAGE
Determine your current and past factions. Gain skills based on your current faction.
   Life Point Spend: Choose your faction and heritage.

DECISION THREE – HOMEWORLD/HOMELAND
Adjust your attributes, gain skill ranks, and learn languages based on the planet, orbital, ship, or nation where you were raised.
   Life Point Spend: Choose your homeworld/homeland.

DECISION FOUR – STATUS
Determine your social class (which will increase one attribute, determine your Social Status, and set your initial Earnings) and your home environment (which will adjust your attributes and grant you a skill rank).
   Life Point Spend: Choose both your social class and home environment.

DECISION FIVE – YOUTH EVENT
Experience a random event that defines your youth.
   Life Point Spend: Choose a specific result or, after your initial roll, reroll the result.

DECISION SIX – EDUCATION
Determine your education. Adjust your attributes, gain skill ranks, gain a signature skill, gain a talent, and gain equipment.
   Life Point Spend: Choose your education.

DECISION SEVEN – ADOLESCENT EVENT
Gain a character trait based on a random event during your adolescence.
   Life Point Spend: Reroll the random result or, with GM approval, pick your event.

DECISION EIGHT – CAREERS
Work two, three, or four career phases. Your first career will increase your attributes. All of your careers will grant you multiple skill ranks, a talent, and equipment. Gain additional signature skills up to a maximum of three. Increase your Earnings for particularly profitable jobs and experience career events with various effects. You start Decision Eight at age 18 and you will gain 1d6+1 years of age per career phase.
   Life Point Spend: Pick a basic career, roll on your faction's career table, or change your faction. You can also spend 1 Life Point to undertake a third or fourth career phase. Or you can choose to be Unemployed and gain 1 Life Point.

DECISION NINE – FINAL CUSTOMISATION
Gain two Infinity Points, additional skill ranks, a talent, and (if you don't already have one) a character trait. Calculate your starting assets, stress, and bonus damage. Purchase gear. As an optional rule, determine the effects of aging.
   Life Point Spend: Purchase additional Infinity Points, assets, skill ranks, or languages. Change one of your character traits.

SKILLS ON THE LIFEPATH

At various Decision points on the Lifepath, a character will have skills either assigned or chosen. The first time a skill is awarded to a character it should be assigned as an Expertise bonus, after which additional training can be assigned to either Expertise or Focus up to a maximum training of three each. A character's Focus in a skill cannot exceed their Expertise.

If a character has gained a signature skill, Expertise and Focus in that skill can both be trained up to a maximum of five each.

During the Lifepath, you may not select the same skill twice from one set of options at the same time.

At any point during the Lifepath where you are allowed to select a skill from a list of limited options (including a list of one), you can choose to spend 1 Life Point to instead choose a skill not on that list.

TALENTS ON THE LIFEPATH

Talents are specialised uses of certain skills, or the tricks of the trade a character has learned over the course of their career. Each skill has a unique talent tree associated with it, for example:

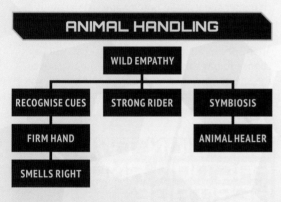

Talents are acquired from the top down, meaning a character must acquire the topmost talent before those deeper in the tree become available. During the Lifepath, if the same talent is awarded a second time, the player may instead select another talent from the skill's tree that they're eligible for. Their hard work and training has paid off!

TRAITS ON THE LIFEPATH

Traits are a way to portray a character's failings, weaknesses, and foibles, but they are often things that will enhance the experience of playing them: the headstrong soldier who rushes in first, the tactless politician, the boastful thief. Traits also give players a chance to claim Infinity Points when they trigger their trait and GMs can invoke them to create complications. Interesting things happen when character traits come into play, and

they should be seen as an opportunity, not as a disadvantage.

At any point during your Lifepath, you may spend 1 Life Point to change one of your character traits or add a new one. Describe how that change in your life happened (perhaps with the old trait somehow being transformed into the new trait).

ASSETS AND EARNINGS

Assets are a broad measure of the resources a character can call upon to achieve financial- or reputation-based tests. It includes cash-in-hand, savings, jewellery, deeds, inheritances, and other easily defined assets, but it can also include more conceptual resources like favours, secret contacts, blackmail, and family bonds. Most items, weapons, gear, or services a character may wish to acquire will require them to spend Assets if they are expensive enough. Your character's starting Assets will be equal to their final Personality score (and will be determined at the end of the Lifepath when that score is known).

Earnings represent a character's income, usually tied to a recurring or reliable resource stream (such as drawing a salary, receiving dispensation, regular stock dividends, freelancing contracts, and so on). Your character's Earnings begins at 0, but may be increased by various events on the Lifepath. There is no cap on a character's Earnings and characters are free to reach for the stars in the iota-scarcity economy of the Human Sphere.

Debts incurred during the Lifepath may not be negated with Assets received during character creation. They must be roleplayed, and dealt with, through gameplay.

The use of Earnings and Assets during play is described in *Part IV: Gear* (p. 327).

TRANSHUMAN CHARACTERS

The technology of the Human Sphere allows people an unprecedented ability to alter, adapt, and even swap their bodies.

Implants and Grafts: Some forms of biotechnology and cybertech are designed to be used at any time during a person's life. This can even include radical physical alterations like the Runihura super-soldier program or the genetic antagonistic therapies used to create chimera. These can be purchased like any other type of equipment, typically during *Decision Nine: Final Customisation*.

Bioengineered Bodies: In some cases, bodies are genetically engineered before birth or at a very young age. Basic genetic tweaking can be

Signature Skill, p. 75:
Signature skills represent areas where a character particularly excels. Once selected, signature skills cannot be changed.

Triggering Traits – p. 35

Invoking Traits – p. 35

PLAYTEST TIP
CHARACTER TRAITS

Each trait is a single word or short phrase, describing something important about the character. When a trait is created, the player and GM should discuss what it specifically represents for the character, and how it might influence or complicate their lives. It's important that both player and GM have a common understanding of what each trait means.

EXAMPLE
SKILLS ON THE LIFEPATH

During a career phase, Gonzalez becomes a Bodyguard. This allows his player to pick two skills from the list of Discipline, Lifestyle, and Pilot. Gonzalez loves to fly, so he picks Pilot. He can't pick Pilot again (because he can't pick the same skill twice), so Gonzalez' player decides that he's picked up a few tips by hanging around with the PanOceanian hypercorp exec he's guarding and he chooses Lifestyle as his second skill. After finishing the rest of his career decisions, Gonzalez decides to repeat the Bodyguard career. Now he can pick Pilot for a second time (because this is a different decision point). This time, however, Gonzalez' player decides to spend 1 Life Point and pick Spacecraft for his second skill. (Even though the skill doesn't appear on the elective list for the Bodyguard career, the Life Point spend allows him to do that.)

represented by spending Life Points to improve your attributes during *Decision One: Birth Host*.

Lhosts: At several points during their Lifepath, you may discover that your character has died. Don't worry! They'll have been Resurrected from their Cube. Such characters inhabit Lhost bodies, as described on p. 54. Other characters inhabiting Lhosts include aspects of ALEPH and Recreations.

Aliens: In *Decision One: Birth Host*, you may discover that your character belongs to one of the many alien species who inhabit the universe of *Infinity*.

DECISION ONE: BIRTH HOST

At the beginning of the Lifepath, all of the character's attributes (Agility, Awareness, Brawn, Coordination, Intelligence, Personality, Willpower) begin at 7. This represents the human average in an era of advanced medical science which has filtered out genetic disparities and physical disabilities.

A player may voluntarily lower any number of attributes by one point (to a minimum of 6) and assign these points to other attributes (to a maximum of 8).

Once they've finished adjusting their attributes, players can then spend Life Points to raise an attribute by one point for each Life Point spent. No attributes can be raised higher than 10 in this way, and any attributes above 8 usually represent some form of genetic tweaking or similar modification.

These decisions must be made now. Points cannot be swapped between attributes and Life Points cannot be spent to increase attribute scores later in the Lifepath.

BIRTH HOST

Once you have finalised your attributes, determine the attribute modifiers of your Birth Host by subtracting the base value of 7 from each attribute and record the modifiers in the Host section of your character sheet. (You can also list your current host as "Birth".) Later events on the Lifepath may further modify the character's attributes, representing how they grow and develop over time, but these initial values represent the natural capacities of the character's body at birth.

This distinction between innate capacity and the expertise gained through training becomes important if the character later switches bodies (see p. 54).

ALIEN CHARACTERS

The universe of *Infinity* is filled with non-human species: Dogfaces and Helots work side-by-side with humanity. The Tohaa are our allies in war. The Shasvastii, Morat, and Antipodes are our bitter enemies. While any of these species have the potential to become player characters, the Lifepaths for most alien characters will be radically different from those experienced by citizens of the Human Sphere. These specialised Lifepaths will appear in the appropriate supplements for *Infinity*.

Born from human wombs and almost always living their lives in human communities, however, Dogface characters can be generated using just the core *Infinity* Lifepath system.

Determining Alien Heritage: Roll 1d20. On a roll of 19 or 20, your character belongs to an alien species. (For the purposes of the core rulebook, this means that you're a Dogface.) If you roll an alien heritage, you can instead choose to spend 1 Life Point to be human.

Alien Host: Each alien species has a template. (For example, see the Dogface template on the facing page.) Apply the species' attribute modifiers to both your attributes and the Host section of your character sheet. Make note of any special abilities possessed by the species.

Alien species also have a Life Point cost. You can choose to pay this cost in order to simply choose the species, but the cost must be paid even if you randomly roll into it. (If the cost cannot be paid, the character is considered human.)

DECISION TWO: FACTION AND HERITAGE

Where were you born and to which faction do you owe allegiance? Your faction is the political faction you currently belong to. Your heritage is the faction you were born into.

For most characters, faction and heritage will be the same thing: If you're born in Yu Jing, you'll generally remain a loyal Yu Jing citizen for your entire life.

STEP ONE: DETERMINE FACTION

Roll 1d20 and consult the *Faction Table*. Except as noted below, this single roll will determine both your faction and your heritage. You may pay 1 Life Point to pick the results (including having a different faction and heritage if you wish).

OPTIONAL RULE

POINT BUY CHARACTER CREATION

With the GM's permission, a player who wants to design a specific character without any of the random elements of the Lifepath System can choose to receive 12 Life Points. This will give them enough to get exactly the role they want with two career phases. This is an all-or-nothing choice, however: Players using point buy character creation do not generate any random elements for their characters. (This does not prevent them from hazarding a career.) Any leftover Life Points are lost and may not be traded for Assets, Skills, Infinity Points, or other resources at the end of character creation.

EXAMPLE

BIRTH HOST

Melissa decides that she wants to play a smart, stealthy character. She lowers Brawn from 7 to 6 and increases Intelligence from 7 to 8. She also pays 1 Life Point to increase her Agility from 7 to 8. She rolls 1d20 to determine her alien heritage and, with a roll of 16, discovers that her character has been born human. She notes that her Birth Host has Agility +1, Brawn −1, and Intelligence +1.

PLAYTEST TIP

LIFE POINTS

Remember! You receive 5 Life Points at the beginning of character creation.

Additional events later in your Lifepath may change your faction, in which case your original faction becomes your heritage.

FACTION TABLE

D20	FACTION/HERITAGE
1–2	Ariadna
3–4	Haqqislam
5–6	Nomads
7–8	Yu Jing
9–10	PanOceania
11–12	Corporation
13–14	Submondo
15–16	Mercenary
17	Minor Nation
18	O-12
19	ALEPH
20	Defection (Roll Again Twice)

Corporation / Submondo / Mercenary: If rolled as a faction, immediately reroll to determine your heritage. If rolled as a heritage, reroll.

ALEPH: If your heritage is ALEPH, you can choose to either be an ALEPH Aspect or a Recreation. See the sidebars on p. 42. (If your current faction is ALEPH but you have a different heritage, then you are merely loyal to the AI.)

Defection: You have defected from your faction of birth. Roll again twice – once to determine your faction and once to determine your heritage. If you get the same result on both rolls, then you remain loyal to your faction but, for some reason, your faction believes you have betrayed it (or has otherwise disowned you). If you roll defection again, it means you've swapped factions multiple times: Continue rolling to track your character's spotted history, but only the first faction rolled (your heritage) and the last faction rolled (your current faction) will be significant for the rest of the Lifepath system.

STEP TWO: FACTION SKILLS
Consult the *Faction Skills Table* and refer to the two skills listed for your current faction. Add one rank of Expertise to each skill, then select one of the skills to become your first signature skill. This signature skill gains one rank of Focus and the first talent on its talent tree.

DOGFACE

ATTRIBUTES

AGILITY	–	AWARENESS	–	BRAWN	–	COORDINATION	–
INTELLIGENCE	–	PERSONALITY	–	WILLPOWER	–		

Claws: Melee, 1+2 🅝 damage, Subtle 1, Vicious 1
Scent: Dogfaces have an extraordinary sense of smell. When making an Observation test or any other skill test in which scent would play a factor, the Dogface gains +2d20.
Transform: When a Dogface suffers a Wound, they must succeed on a Discipline (D1) test. On a failure, they transform into their Dog-Warrior form. The Dogface can choose to voluntarily fail this check (although this does not count as a fail-safe test). When in Dogface form, they gain the following traits:
- +2 Brawn, +2 Agility
- +1 soak against attacks dealing Vigour damage
- Transformation while wearing human-sized armour inflicts 2+3 🅝 damage and will render the armour in need of repair. (See Dogface Armour, p. 342.)
- Upon transformation, immediately recover all Vigour.
- Gain the character trait Dog-Warrior.
- **Monstrous**: A Dog-Warrior has considerable bulk and mass. Increase the difficulty of tests where great size or weight would be problematic by one step. Monstrous creatures are not required to brace Unwieldy weapons and can use two-handed weapons in one hand without difficulty or penalty. They may spend 1 Momentum to add Knockdown to all of their melee attacks for a turn.
- **Snarling Beast**: All Personality-based tests that are not based on intimidation are made at +2 difficulty. This penalty does not apply to other Dogface characters.
- **Super-Jump**: The Dog-Warrior gains one rank in the Catfall talent. They can also vault over obstacles up to their height without penalty. This also reduces the difficulty of skill tests to move through difficult terrain by one step.
- **Fatigue**: At the end of the current encounter or scene, the Dogface returns to their normal form and suffers from the Fatigued condition.

Lifepath Special Rules: In Decision Two, unless you roll "Defection" you belong to the Ariadna faction. (If you roll "Defection", roll again twice normally: It's possible you're the incredibly rare Dogface who was born somewhere other than Dawn.)
Life Point Cost: 3

FACTION SKILLS TABLE

FACTION	FACTION SKILLS
Ariadna	Survival, Medicine
Haqqislam	Medicine, Education
Nomads	Hacking, Extraplanetary
PanOceania	Tech, Lifestyle
Yu Jing	Tech, Education
Corporation	Lifestyle, Persuade
Submondo	Observation, Thievery
Mercenary	Athletics, Survival
Minor Nation	Education, Pilot
O-12	Education, Persuade
ALEPH	Analysis, Education

EXAMPLE
FACTION AND HERITAGE
Melissa rolls 1d20 on the *Faction Table* and gets 15. That means her character is a Mercenary and she immediately rerolls to determine her heritage. With a roll of 9 she discovers she was born in PanOceania. Turning to the *Faction Skills Table*, she checks the entry for Mercenary (her current faction) and gains Expertise 1 in both Athletics and Survival. She then chooses Athletics as her first signature skill, gaining Focus 1 in the skill and the Rigorous Training talent.

ALEPH ASPECTS

Fragments of ALEPH known as Aspects are sometimes given enough functional autonomy to be considered individual characters despite their connection to ALEPH's greater consciousness. (In some rare cases, these Aspects become completely separated from ALEPH. These renegade Aspects, however, are effectively independent – and therefore outlaw - AIs. Many of them hide by disguising themselves as resurrected humans.) If the Lifepath reveals that you are an ALEPH bioform, then the artificial nature of your "birth" will colour the rest of your Lifepath.

Host: Change your current host from "Birth" to "Custom Lhost" and gain the Inured to Disease special ability (p. 418). (Your attributes do not change under the assumption that the values selected in *Decision One: Birth Host* represent the custom body ALEPH created for you. Similarly, if you were determined to have an Alien Heritage and are also an ALEPH Aspect, you can assume that ALEPH has designed an alien-like body for you.)

Decision Three: Instead of determining a homeworld, pick any two attributes and increase them by one each. Pick any skill and gain one rank in it. Then roll five times on the *Random Languages Table*.

Decision Four: If your faction is ALEPH, then your Social Status is Elite (and you gain the normal benefits for that Social Status). If your faction is not ALEPH, then you have become a renegade and you determine your Social Status normally. Roll your Home Environment normally. Although this doesn't, of course, describe how you were "raised", it does give some indication of which "flavour" of ALEPH's personality you're predisposed to.

Decision Five: On the *Event Table*, interpret any result involving your "family" as "Bureau Toth". (For example, a result of "parents killed" would mean that Bureau Toth agents you were involved with were killed.) Similarly, interpret any event resulting in you contracting a disease as being a quantronic virus.

Decision Six: Roll your Education normally. This represents the skill loadout that the Aspect was imbued with when it was created.

Decision Seven: See *Decision Five* (above).

Decision Eight: Careers are resolved normally. These are actual life experiences of the Aspect, possibly representing whatever purpose it was originally instantiated for. (In the special case of a Bureau Toth career, it can be assumed that this represents an Aspect working in close conjunction with Bureau Toth. They gain the benefits of the career normally.)

Decision Nine: Complete this step normally, except that Lhosts are immune to aging.

ALEPH RECREATIONS

ALEPH is also responsible for the Recreations, a combination of innovative biogenics and experimental Cubes. Hosted in sophisticated Lhosts, Recreations are faithful simulations of the personalities of important historical figures, although their skills have been adapted to the modern age so they can work as diplomats, soldiers, spokespeople, and artists.

If the Lifepath reveals that you are a Recreation, change your current host from "Birth" to "Custom Lhost". (Your attributes do not change under the assumption the values selected in *Decision One: Birth Host* represent the custom body ALEPH created for you.) Then roll again on the *Faction Table* to determine which faction ALEPH created you for. Gain a 50 Asset debt, owed to whoever funded your creation.

You can then complete the Lifepath normally, although the results of the Lifepath should be interpreted as representing the simulated reality or false memories that ALEPH used to create you.

Alternatively, with the GM's permission, you could choose an actual historical personality and use the optional point buy character creation (see sidebar on p. 40) to craft ALEPH's interpretation of that specific person.

DECISION THREE: HOMEWORLD / HOMELAND

Roll 1d20 and consult the *Homeworld/Homeland Table* for your heritage to determine where you were born (and most likely grew up). You may spend 1 Life Point to pick the result.

After you've determined your homeworld or homeland, make the following adjustments:

- Add the language(s) listed to your list of fluent languages.
- Increase the two listed attributes by one each.
- Gain one rank in the listed skill.

LINGUA QUANTRONICA

There is no single "common tongue" or *lingua franca* in the Human Sphere. English, Yujingyu, and Spanish are all common, but not universal. It's quite possible for a table full of players to end up with characters who can't talk to each other. Fortunately, the quantronic revolution has largely made this irrelevant: Your comlog can translate other languages in real-time, making it simple to talk to people even if you don't share a common tongue. (Unless, of course, your systems are offline for some reason.)

CORREGIDORAN

Corregidoran is a creole of Spanish and Portuguese, with a healthy dose of loan words from English and Swahili.

ARIADNA HOMELAND TABLE

D20	REGION	LANGUAGE	ATTRIBUTE	ATTRIBUTE	SKILL
1	Antipodean Wilds	Antipode creole (Snarl)*	Willpower	Brawn	Animal Handling
2–6	Caledonia	English (Scots)*	Agility	Brawn	Resistance
7–10	Merovingia	French*	Personality	Brawn	Lifestyle
11–15	Rodina	Russian (Kazak)*	Agility	Brawn	Discipline
16–20	USAriadna	English (American)*	Coordination	Brawn	Survival

HAQQISLAM HOMELAND TABLE

D20	REGION	LANGUAGE	ATTRIBUTE	ATTRIBUTE	SKILL
1–3	Bourak (Funduq Sultanate)	Arabic, Turkish	Intelligence	Willpower	Lifestyle
4–6	Bourak (Iran Zhat al Amat Shanate)	Arabic, Farsi	Awareness	Willpower	Persuade
7–9	Bourak (Gabqar)	Arabic, Kyrgyz	Brawn	Willpower	Survival
10–12	Bourak (Al Medinat Caliphate)	Arabic*	Personality	Willpower	Science
13–14	Bourak (Islands)	Arabic*	Agility	Willpower	Persuade
15–16	Caravanserai	Arabic*	Awareness	Willpower	Extraplanetary
17–18	Paradiso	Arabic*	Agility	Willpower	Survival
19–20	Sol	Roll on *Random Languages Table**	Coordination	Willpower	Pilot

NOMAD MOTHERSHIP TABLE

D20	REGION	LANGUAGE	ATTRIBUTE	ATTRIBUTE	SKILL
1–5	*Bakunin*	German, English	Willpower	Agility	Science
6–10	*Corregidor*	Corregidoran or Swahili (choose one), English or Corregidoran (choose one)	Brawn	Agility	Resistance
11–15	*Tunguska*	Russian, English	Intelligence	Agility	Lifestyle
16–17	Human Edge	Roll on *Random Languages Table**	Willpower	Agility	Tech
18–19	Commercial Mission	Roll on *Random Languages Table**	Intelligence	Agility	Pilot
20	Sol/Sol Orbitals	Roll on *Random Languages Table**	Willpower	Agility	Extraplanetary

PANOCEANIA HOMEWORLD TABLE

D20	REGION	LANGUAGE	ATTRIBUTE	ATTRIBUTE	SKILL
1–4	Acontecimento	Hindi, Punjabi, or Portuguese (choose one) and Spanish	Willpower	Intelligence	Animal Handling
5–8	Neoterra	English, Hindi, or Italian (choose one) and Spanish	Awareness	Intelligence	Lifestyle
9–12	Varuna	Spanish, Malay	Brawn	Intelligence	Athletics
13–16	Sol	Roll on *PanOceanian/Sol Languages Table**	Willpower	Intelligence	Extraplanetary
17–18	Paradiso	Spanish or English *	Personality	Intelligence	Survival
19	Human Edge	Spanish or English*	Agility	Intelligence	Tech
20	Svalarheima	English or German (choose one) and SvalarNorse	Willpower	Intelligence	Survival

YU JING HOMEWORLD TABLE

D20	REGION	LANGUAGE	ATTRIBUTE	ATTRIBUTE	SKILL
1–5	Shentang	Yujingyu and roll on *Regional Yu Jing Languages Table*	Intelligence	Awareness	Lifestyle
6–10	Yutang	Yujingyu	Intelligence	Awareness	Lifestyle
11–15	Sol (Chung Kuo)	Yujingyu and roll on *Regional Yu Jing Languages Table*	Willpower	Awareness	Extraplanetary
16–17	Paradiso	Yujingyu and roll on *Regional Yu Jing Languages Table*	Personality	Awareness	Survival
18–19	Svalarheima	Yujingyu	Willpower	Awareness	Survival
20	Human Edge	Yujingyu	Agility	Awareness	Tech

MINOR NATIONS HOMEWORLD TABLE

D20	REGION	LANGUAGE	ATTRIBUTE	ATTRIBUTE	SKILL
1–4	Earth	Roll on *Random Languages Table**	Intelligence	Awareness	Lifestyle
5–7	Lunar Colonies	Roll on *Random Languages Table**	Intelligence	Awareness	Lifestyle
8–9	Venusian Aerostats	Roll on *Random Languages Table**	Willpower	Awareness	Extraplanetary
10–13	Mars	Roll on *Random Languages Table**	Personality	Awareness	Survival
14–15	Jovian Colonies	Roll on *Random Languages Table**	Willpower	Awareness	Survival
16–18	Orbitals	Roll on *Random Languages Table**	Agility	Awareness	Tech
19–20	Human Edge	Roll on *Random Languages Table**	Willpower	Awareness	Survival

O-12 HOMELAND TABLE

D20	REGION	LANGUAGE	ATTRIBUTE	ATTRIBUTE	SKILL
1–6	Concilium	Spanish*	Intelligence	Personality	Persuade
7–12	Concilium	English*	Intelligence	Personality	Persuade
13–18	Concilium	German*	Intelligence	Personality	Persuade
19–20	Concilium	Roll on *Random Languages Table**	Intelligence	Personality	Persuade

* Roll again on your Homeworld/Homeland table to determine a second language you're fluent with. If you roll the same result, that's the only language you're fluent with.

PANOCEANIA/SOL LANGUAGES

D20	LANGUAGE
1–2	Roll on *Random Languages Table*
3–4	English
5–6	Portuguese
7–8	German
9–10	Italian
11–12	French
13–14	Filipino
15–16	Hindi
17–18	Malay
19–20	Spanish

REGIONAL YU JING LANGUAGES

D20	LANGUAGE
1	Roll on *Random Languages Table*
2–4	Yujingyu
5–6	Japanese
7–8	Korean
9–10	Laotian
11–12	Thai
13–14	Mongolian
15–16	Uyghur
17–18	Cantonese
19–20	Roll Again Twice

RANDOM LANGUAGES

D20	LANGUAGE
1	Yujingyu
2	Spanish
3	English
4	Hindi
5	Arabic
6	Portuguese
7	Russian
8	Japanese
9	Punjabi
10	German
11	Javanese
12	Malay
13	Vietnamese
14	Korean
15	French
16	Turkish
17	Italian
18	Thai
19	Farsi
20	Roll Again Twice

EXAMPLE

HOMEWORLD

Because her heritage is PanOceanian, Melissa rolls 1d20 on the *PanOceania Homeworld Table*. She rolls 20, which means she's from Svalarheima. Her character can speak SvalarNorse and (at Melissa's choice) German. She also increases her Intelligence and Willpower by one point each (to 9 and 8, respectively). Finally, she gains a rank in Survival. Because she already has Expertise 1 in Survival, she could choose to increase either her Expertise or Focus in the skill. She chooses to increase her Focus to 1.

DECISION FOUR: STATUS

Now that you know where you were born and raised, let's find out more about how you grew up. What were your economic circumstances? What was life like and what type of people were you surrounded by?

You may spend 1 Life Point to pick the result on both the *Social Class Table* and the *Home Environment Table*.

STEP ONE: SOCIAL CLASS

Roll 2d6 and consult the *Social Class Table*. Increase the listed attribute by one point and set your Earnings equal to the number shown.

The wonders of the quantronic revolution have pushed the Human Sphere to the cusp of a post-scarcity economy. The resulting realignment of social classes, and the lives they lead, can be dizzyingly different from what you might expect. Here are some short descriptions to help orient you.

Underclass: Although it's become incredibly difficult for true poverty to exist, there are some people who slip through the cracks. (PanOceanians will talk about the tragic conditions of backcountry Ariadnans, but Yu Jing would be quick to point to the Ateks in PanOceania's own backyard. Elsewhere there are minor nations and small habitats in places like Human Edge.)

Demogrant: The demogrant is a basic income guaranteed to every member of the major powers (and most of the minor powers, too). The immense manufacturing capacity of dedicated nanoassemblers combined with the rich resources available to an automated, interstellar civilisation make it possible for all citizens to enjoy a more than comfortable standard of living.

Middle: Most of humanity is living in a golden age of luxury. It's easy for people to be part of the middle class while working twenty hours a week or less. The large middle class is constantly seeking out activities both real and virtual to fill their idle hours.

Upper: This is a life of utter affluence. For the rich of the Human Sphere, thought has become the equivalent of action and desire can be instantaneously met by reality. For the upper class, the physical world can trivially transform itself almost as easily as the virtual playgrounds of the middle class.

Elite: The vast wealth of the elite creates specialist micro-cultures that cater to their needs, a market of ultra-luxury goods and bespoke items that are casually created on demand, and a plethora of body modifications unheard of in previous ages. Their lives, swaddled in advanced domotics, are virtually effortless, like endless theme park rides that are malleable to their will.

Hyper-Elite: The hyper-elite flit across interplanetary distances or rule over *de facto* fiefdoms rendered in their own image. Their control over their physical reality is almost unlimited, allowing them to realise their ultimate fantasies in flights of whimsy.

SOCIAL CLASS TABLE

2D6	SOCIAL STATUS	ATTRIBUTE	EARNINGS
2	Underclass	Willpower	1
3–5	Demogrant	Personality	2
6–8	Middle	Willpower	3
9–10	Upper	Agility	4
11	Elite	Personality	5
12	Hyper-Elite	Willpower	6

STEP TWO: HOME ENVIRONMENT

Roll 1d6 and consult the *Home Environment Table*. The result most likely describes your parents and immediate family, but not necessarily. (For example, if you had a Violent childhood it's possible that your parents were loving, but your neighbourhood was filled with gangs. If you grew up in High Society but your Social Status was Demogrant, then your family may have worked as servants.)

Increase the listed attribute by one point and gain one rank of training in the listed skill.

HOME ENVIRONMENT TABLE

D6	ENVIRONMENT	ATTRIBUTE	SKILL
1	Happy Home	Personality	Education
2	Violent	Brawn	Acrobatics
3	Frontier Life	Brawn	Resistance
4	Rebellious	Awareness	Pilot
5	Regimented	Coordination	Discipline
6	High Society	Willpower	Lifestyle

EXAMPLE
STATUS

When she discovers that her character – who she's decided is named Cassandra – was raised on Svalarheima, Melissa has a very strong image of what her childhood was like. She decides to spend 1 Life Point to choose an Upper social class in a Frontier Life. As a member of the Upper class, she gains one point of Agility and has an Earnings of 4. Coming from a Frontier Life, she gains one point of Brawn and gains one rank of Resistance. (Since she didn't previously have the skill, she has to take this rank as Expertise 1.)

EXAMPLE
YOUTH EVENT

On her first roll on the *Youth Event Table*, Melissa gets a 20. So she rerolls on the table twice, getting results of 2 and 11 on a d20 and then results of 4 and 1 on a d6. Cassandra has witnessed an assassination (2,4) and discovered a family secret (11,1). Keen to merge the two results, Melissa decides that Cassandra's mother was a government assassin and that she witnessed her assassinate a defector who was selling surveying data to Yu Jing.

DECISION FIVE: YOUTH EVENT

Roll 1d20 and 1d6 and reference the *Youth Event Table* below. Each event indicates a massive impact on your youth. It might be something you've long since put behind you or it may still be the core of your later life, but either way, you'll want to use the simple description as a springboard for your imagination and detail exactly what happened.

You can spend 1 Life Point to choose an Event from the table or, after your initial roll, to reroll the result.

YOUTH EVENT TABLE

D20	EVENT TYPE	1	2	3	4	5	6
1–2	Witnessed	perjury	a murder	police corruption	assassination	high level corruption	a secret pregnancy
3–4	Witnessed	embezzlement	a violent crime	long-term abuse	cybercrime	backroom deals being made	political corruption
5–6	Involved in	an accident	a shooting	a transit disaster	police action	a scandal	mass arrests
7–8	Involved in	a suicide	narcotics sale	Resurrection Lottery	faking a suicide	a cover-up	smuggling
9–10	Discovered	religion	a suicide	a fandom	a secret	an infiltration	elite hypocrisy
11–12	Discovered	a family secret	a body	a valuable secret	sexual attraction	personality tampering	a scandal
13	Family Change	1+ 6 🄽 siblings	parents killed	parent walks out	kidnapped	family member resurrected	population relocation
14	Family Change	divorce	sibling killed at a young age	gained an extended family	parents incarcerated	family member's Cube corrupted	moved to a new planet
15	Media Fad	joined a popular movement	joined a radical movement	got involved in life-streaming	established Arachne nodes	Maya addiction	appeared on a popular Maya broadcast
16	Succumbed to	propaganda	social exclusion	a scam	personality tampering	boredom	brainwashing
17	Social Contacts	escaped the neighbourhood	had brush with opposite social class	gained enemy (roll on *Faction Table*)	gained contact (roll on *Faction Table*)	gained mentor (roll on *Faction Table*)	joined Submondo faction
18	Special	gain a 1 Asset debt	Cube destruction	Cube theft	changed social class	Gain 1 Asset	Defection!
19	Special	learned a new language	gained blackmail material	biological/chemical weapons	radical biomodification	serious genetic illness	Died!
20				Reroll Twice and Combine Results			

SPECIAL YOUTH EVENTS

Gain a 1 Asset Debt: You owe someone a debt worth one Asset.

Cube Destruction: The Cube used to store your personality has been destroyed (or perhaps you never had one to begin with). You'll begin play without a Cube and, if you want to have one implanted, you'll need to figure out some way to pay for it.

Cube Theft: Your Cube or the data on your Cube was stolen. Who took it? Do they still have it? What have they done with it?

Changed Social Class: During your youth, your family experienced a shift in their economic status. Roll on the *Social Class Table* and change your Social Status and Earnings to the new value.

Gain 1 Asset: You've gained 1 additional Asset. Add this Asset to your total Assets at the end of character creation.

Defection: You've switched to a new faction. Roll on the *Faction Table*.

Learned a New Language: Roll once on the *Random Languages Table*.

Gained Blackmail Material: You have been given proof that a person or organisation has committed misdeeds against another. You can roll twice on the *Faction Table* (p. 41) to determine which factions the two parties belong to. Either party will grant a favour for the evidence.

Biological/Chemical Weapon: You were exposed to some form of biological weapon. Reduce one attribute of your choice by one point.

Radical Biomodification: You gain a Cosmetic Augmentation 3 (see p. 366). Describe how your body has been transformed.

Serious Genetic Illness: You suffer from a serious genetic illness (either inherited or teratogenic). Reduce one attribute of your choice by one point. A cure is possible, but it's expensive and will cost 5+5 🄽 Assets. Each Effect rolled on the 🄽 reduces an attribute by an additional point.

Died: Your character died and was resurrected. See the rules for *Resurrection* on p. 54.

DECISION SIX: EDUCATION

As we move into the next phase of your life, you may discover that your Lifepath has taken you abruptly in a new direction. Think about how your Youth Event may have precipitated this change, or perhaps it was the last memory you had of your old life.

On the other hand, perhaps your young adulthood will simply flow naturally out of everything you've experienced before. Does that make you feel trapped? Are you comfortable with the path that fate (or your family) has set for you?

To determine the type of Education your character received, roll 1d20 and consult the *Education Table*.

You may spend 1 Life Point to pick your education. Once you've determined your Education, check the *Education Benefits* tables.
- Increase one attribute by two points.
- Increase one attribute by one point.
- Decrease one attribute by one point.
- Gain 1 rank of training in all of the mandatory skills.
- Choose two of the three elective skills and gain 1 rank of training in each.
- Choose one of the skills (either elective or mandatory) gained from your Education to become a signature skill. Add 1 rank of training to this skill and take a talent from its talent tree.
- Gain the equipment (if any) indicated.

EXAMPLE

EDUCATION

Melissa rolls 15 on the *Education Table*, discovering that Cassandra's mother shipped her off to a military academy after she witnessed the assassination. She gains two points of Brawn and one point of Agility, but her Intelligence decreases by 1. She gains one rank in each of the mandatory skills — Acrobatics, Athletics, Ballistics, Close Combat, and Observation. Since she didn't previously have ranks in most of these skills, she gains Expertise 1 in them. She previously had Expertise 1 and Focus 1 in Athletics, however, and although she would have liked to gain an additional point of Focus, that would make her Focus higher than her Expertise and so she can't. She instead increases her Expertise to 2.

Her elective skills for Military Training are Command, Education, and Tech. She chooses Education and Tech, gaining Expertise 1 in each. Now she can select her second signature skill: Once again she would like to increase her Athletics skill, but can't because it's already a signature skill. Instead, she selects Ballistics, increasing her rating to Expertise 2 and gaining the Marksman talent. Finally, she adds a military dress uniform, pistol, and knife to the Gear section of her character sheet.

EDUCATION TABLE

D20	EDUCATION	EXAMPLE
1	Grew Up on the Streets	Lazareto district, Atek shanty town, Merovingian urchin gang
2–3	Rural/Colonial Education	Commercial Mission, Acontecimento Farmer, Svalarheima Career Prep
4–5	Creative Education	LoroLocco Youth Program, Maya Virtual Academy, Atek artist apprenticeship
6–8	White Collar Education	*Tunguska* internship, Startecto Corporate Academy, Haqqislamite guild apprenticeship
9–11	Technical Education	Amaravati Institute, Haqq Mutazilite Academy, Imperial Service
12–14	Scientific Education	Black Laboratories, Espiritu Santo University, Talawat University
15–17	Military Training	Yu Jing military academy, Alguaciles Tour, Highlander clan
18–20	Orbital Training	Caravanserai academy, *Corregidor* station education, Saturn Star Academies

EDUCATION BENEFITS – MANDATORY

EDUCATION	+2	+1	−1	MANDATORY SKILLS
Grew Up on the Streets	Agility	Brawn	Intelligence	Discipline, Observation, Resistance, Stealth, Survival
Rural/Colonial	Awareness	Brawn	Personality	Education, Pilot, Resistance, Survival, Tech
Creative	Personality	Willpower	Brawn	Discipline, Education, Lifestyle, Observation, Persuade
White Collar	Awareness	Personality	Brawn	Education, Lifestyle, Observation, Persuade, Stealth
Technical	Awareness	Intelligence	Willpower	Education, Observation, Pilot, Tech, Thievery
Scientific	Intelligence	Awareness	Personality	Education, Lifestyle, Pilot, Tech, Medicine
Military	Brawn	Agility	Intelligence	Acrobatics, Athletics, Ballistics, Close Combat, Observation
Orbital Training	Intelligence	Awareness	Personality	Discipline, Education, Pilot, Spacecraft, Extraplanetary

EDUCATION BENEFITS – SKILLS AND GEAR

EDUCATION	ELECTIVE SKILLS (PICK 2)	GEAR GAINED
Grew Up on the Streets	Athletics, Close Combat, Lifestyle	Fake ID 1, Micro-Torch, Knife
Rural/Colonial	Animal Handling, Athletics, Observation	Survival Kit, Survival Rations (×3), Nav Suite, Knife
Creative	Analysis, Pilot, Tech	AR Eye Implants or Cosmetics Kit, Recorder, 1 Asset
White Collar	Command, Stealth, Thievery	AR Eye Implants or Neural Comlog, Stims, 1 Asset
Technical	Hacking, Lifestyle, Extraplanetary	Powered Multitool, Repair Kit (with 5 Parts)
Scientific	Medicine, Science, Spacecraft	Analytical Kit (with 5 Reagents), Sensor Suite
Military	Command, Education, Tech	Armoured Clothing (Dress Uniform), Pistol
Orbital Training	Lifestyle, Resistance, Tech	Vac Suit (with Locational Beacon, 5 Oxygen Loads)

DECISION SEVEN: ADOLESCENT EVENT

At some point during your adolescence, you experienced a defining event which still shapes who you are today. Roll 1d6 to determine which *Adolescent Event Table* to use and then roll 1d20 to determine your Adolescent Event.

Based on your Adolescent Event, pick one character trait. Each Adolescent Event has a suggested trait listed, but there are many traits you could have and you should feel free to pick any word or short phrase which feels appropriate.

Each Adolescent Event also lists an optional effect which can be used to further customise your character. You can choose whether or not to use the optional effect, but if you do then you must resolve the entire effect.

You can spend 1 Life Point to reroll or, with GM approval, pick your Adolescent Event. With your GM's permission, you could also design your own event.

ADOLESCENT EVENT TABLES

D6	TABLE
1–2	Adolescent Event Table A
3–4	Adolescent Event Table B
5–6	Adolescent Event Table C

EXAMPLE
ADOLESCENT EVENT

With Cassandra's education complete and a military career seeming likely, Melissa rolls on the *Adolescent Event Table*. She gets 2 on her d6. Consulting *Event Table A*, she rolls 12 on her d20. Cassandra's parents are killed! Cassandra's Social Status is changed to Middle and she gains the character trait Orphan. She gains 6 Assets from the generous Hexahedron pension plan.

ADOLESCENT EVENT TABLE A

D20	ADOLESCENT EVENT	SUGGESTED CHARACTER TRAIT	OPTIONAL EFFECT
1	You contracted an alien disease, spore, or macrovirus. It has been forced into remission but only a constant regimen of medication keeps it tame. It doesn't appear to be infectious (yet).	Alien Typhoid	You have a symbiotic organism attached to you that looks like a bad rash. It grants 1 bonus Momentum for Observation tests to determine whether there is anyone hidden within close range, but increases the difficulty of all social skill tests by 1 step.
2	You were seriously injured and died on the operating table. You were resuscitated but your Cube had a manufacturer's glitch and memories/episodes of a Maya ever-caster became merged with your own.	Dual Identity	Gain 1 Asset in compensation and roll a new Youth Event. One of your Youth Events is a fake.
3	While they were on a journey, your sibling vanished. No one has ever discovered what happened to them, but you've been obsessed with figuring it out.	Missing Sibling	Gain 1 rank in Analysis.
4	A stranger visited your home and spoke in hushed tones with a family member. What did they talk about?	Shady Past	Your family's surname is infamous amongst society's elite. Your social skill tests amongst them suffer +2 complication range.
5	The personality of your geist radically shifted overnight. You gradually became aware that it has become an Aspect of ALEPH.	Watched by the AI	You may switch your faction to ALEPH at this time. You may also choose the Bureau Toth career freely for any of your career phases.
6	You ran away from home.	Low Self-Esteem	Reduce your Social Status by 1.
7	You said "yes" and someone you cared about got hurt.	Weak Willed	Social skill tests against you receive 1 bonus Momentum, but your openness to adventure has paid off. Gain 1 Asset.
8	After someone close to you was murdered, your family confessed to you that they were deeply involved in a criminal conspiracy.	Criminal Connections	You may switch to the Submondo faction at this time. You may also freely choose the Criminal career for any of your career phases. You are often a suspect in police enquiries and all social skill tests with security or police services are increased in difficulty by one step.
9	You are a prodigy and excelled at a particular skill from a very young age. You could have been a talented musician or a math whiz. Regardless, your talent got a lot of attention in the media before you grew out of it.	Bitter	Gain 1 level of Social Status or 5 Assets. Alternatively, gain a contact in media, academia, or the entertainment industry.
10	You suffered a traumatic head injury.	Slow Thoughts	Reduce Intelligence by 1, but gain 1 rank of training in Discipline.
11	You got mixed up with the wrong people and were involved in a serious crime.	Criminal Record	Spend 1d6 years in jail before starting your first career. Gain a Criminal Record (see p. 54).

ADOLESCENT EVENT TABLE A

D20	ADOLESCENT EVENT	SUGGESTED CHARACTER TRAIT	OPTIONAL EFFECT
12	Both your parents died in a mysterious accident. You were sent to an orphanage.	Orphan	Reduce Social Status by one (minimum 1). Gain 1d6 Assets from an estate left to you.
13	You became friends with a powerful and important person. Is your relationship with them still solid?	Silver Spoon	If you get a "Fired" result during Decision Eight: Careers you can ignore it, but reduce your Earnings by one.
14	You were taken from your home at 4am. You heard shots and never saw your family again.	Lost Family	You have a mysterious benefactor who saved you, and you grew up with family friends. Decrease your Social Status by one (minimum 1), but gain a free reroll on a Career Event.
15	You messed up and were arrested for a minor crime.	Criminal Record	Spend one year in jail before starting your first career. Gain Criminal Record (see p. 54).
16	You had a terrible childhood accident.	Disabled	All movement-related skill tests are one difficulty harder, but you have gained a strong will. All Discipline tests are one difficulty lower (minimum 1).
17	You contracted colonial wasting disease.	Feel Every Punch	Reduce your Vigour by 1.
18	Your body is intolerant to chemical substances.	Allergies	All Resistance tests for artificial substances are increased by one level of difficulty. Serum provides no bonuses.
19	A woman in a conservative suit approaches you one day and reveals what really happened to someone that you loved. Then she asks what you want to do about it.	Traitor	You defect to a new faction. Roll on the *Faction Table* on p. 41 to determine your new allegiance.
20	You died.	Cube Weary	Your character died and was resurrected. See the rules for *Resurrection* on p. 54.

ADOLESCENT EVENT TABLE B

D20	ADOLESCENT EVENTT	SUGGESTED CHARACTER TRAIT	OPTIONAL EFFECT
1	While on a spacewalk, your tether snapped and you were knocked off-station.	Zero-G Terror	You cannot select Extraplanetary as an elective skill during any career phase. (You can still improve it normally through other means.)
2	Volunteering for "human tests" seemed like easy money. The physical scars healed, but you've never really learned to control your new "gift".	Rogue MetaChemistry	Gain any Biograft or Silk augmentation that requires an action to use. To use it, however, you must pass a Daunting (D3) Willpower test.
3	You were detained by national law enforcement. Although ultimately exonerated, your records are still notated from the incident.	Stained Record	All tests with security forces are made at +1 difficulty. Attempts to access classified information suffer a +2 complication range (possibly resulting in unwanted official attention).
4	You joined a Maya cluster and became obsessed with the infowarrior subculture.	Neophile	Gain 1 rank in Hacking.
5	Your parents or guardians were unexpectedly fired by their corporate employers and blacklisted.	Rage Against the Corporation	Reduce Social Status by one (minimum 1) and Earnings by one (minimum 0).
6	Someone witnessed you do something terrible. They've kept your secret, but they've never let you forget it.	Blackmailed	Gain a debt worth 5 Assets.
7	You had an imaginary friend. Nobody else could see them, but you went on grand Maya adventures together. Now you see hints of your imaginary friend when you're online.	Quantronic Ally	Pick a topic that your imaginary friend was enamoured with. You gain +1d20 when making research tests on Maya regarding that topic.
8	A rogue retrovirus rewrote your genetics, causing a shift in aggression and fight/flight reactions.	Quick with a Fist	You fly off the handle faster than people can react. You gain +1d20 to Surprise tests in Mexican standoffs and similar situations.
9	Your parents or guardians became radical converts to a religion. Was your time with their church a happy one?	Religious Upbringing	Gain 1 rank in either Psychology or Command.
10	A distant family member died and unexpectedly named you their executor. Their recordkeeping was atrocious, though, and their old debts keep coming back to haunt you.	Unexpected Obligations	Gain 10 Assets and a debt worth 5 Assets.
11	When you first signed up for school, a network glitch merged all of your quantronic records with someone else who shares your exact name. Your Maya footprints have never been fully untangled.	Confused Identity	Persuade tests made against targets you are not face-to-face with suffer a +1 complication range.
12	When your first love was forced to move across the Human Sphere by their parents, you both swore to find each other one day.	Lost Love	Roll on the *Faction Table* on p. 41 and gain an ally in that faction.
13	There was a terrible accident on the orbital you were visiting and you were badly injured due to an equipment failure.	Safety First	Reduce Brawn by 1 point, but gain 1 rank in Extraplanetary.
14	You spent most of your free time as an urban spelunker, exploring the ruins and hidden places. What was the most unusual place you went?	Killer Curiosity	Gain 1 rank of Stealth.
15	After finding an injured animal, you nursed it back to health.	Bleeding Heart for Animals	Gain 1 rank in Animal Handling.
16	You have a relative or godparent with connections.	Annoying Family	You may reroll your first career, but must accept the new career rolled.
17	You fell in with a bad crowd. Who was your worst "friend" from those days?	Shady Past	Gain 1 rank in Thievery.
18	You tried to upgrade your geist's software... and failed badly.	Faulty Geist	Reduce Firewall by 1.
19	You were awoken in the middle of the night by your parents and told to quickly pack a suitcase. Two days later, you were on a new planet.	True Believer	You defect to a new faction. Roll on the *Faction Table* on p. 41 to determine your new allegiance.
20	You were murdered.	Paranoid	Your character died and was resurrected. See the rules for *Resurrection* on p. 54.

ADOLESCENT EVENT TABLE C

D20	ADOLESCENT EVENT	SUGGESTED CHARACTER TRAIT	OPTIONAL EFFECT
1	What your family did haunts you wherever you go.	Infamous	Difficulty to avoid attention is one step higher when your true identity is known.
2	While visiting a petting zoo you were bitten by one of the animals.	Animal Hatred	Your Animal Handling tests suffer a +1 complication range.
3	You became a local champion in your sport of choice. There was talk about taking it to the next level. Did you? Or did something happen to cut your career short?	Nagging Injury	Gain 1 rank in Acrobatics.
4	Your flight crashed out on the frontier. It was weeks before the rescue teams found you.	Survivor's Guilt	Gain 1 rank in Survival.
5	Either you or your partner became pregnant.	Dependent	Gain a debt worth 3 Assets.
6	Once you were exposed to the writings of a political ideologue, you became obsessed with their vision of what the Human Sphere should be.	Disillusioned	Select a new faction of your choice.
7	You decided to pursue a second degree.	Studious	Gain 1 rank in Education and add 1d6 years to your age.
8	An unexpected boon, random chance, or personal merit allowed you to transfer into an elite training academy.	Overconfident	Increase your Social Status by 1.
9	It was just a minor invention, but it exploded in popularity. Did you sell out or did it just fade away as a seasonal fad?	Mad Tinkerer	Gain 10 Assets.
10	Someone dear to you died in a hull breach. You couldn't do anything to save them.	Vacuum Phobia	Gain 1 rank in Extraplanetary.
11	You spent a summer painstakingly restoring a classic car (or other vehicle).	Nostalgia Freak	Gain the Greasemonkey talent for the Tech skill.
12	It can be argued that the accident wasn't your fault, but the courts didn't see it that way.	Careless	Gain a debt worth 10 Assets.
13	You were framed for a crime you didn't commit. Who framed you? What did they do?	Criminal Record	Spend 1d6 years in jail before starting your first career. Gain a Criminal Record (see p. 54).
14	It took two years, but you did the training and successfully completed one of the Planetary Ironmen competitions.	Tenacious	Gain 1 rank in Athletics.
15	A stranger came to the house and left a package for you. What is so important about it? How will you know when to open it?	Unwanted Heritage	You gain a package worth 5 Assets that you must never lose. You do not know what is inside. Decide when you will know whether to open the package.
16	You spent half a year on a field study. How far did you go? Who ran the study?	Neuroticism	Gain 1 rank in Science.
17	Your best friend joined the military. And then he was killed. You realised all this jingoism doesn't make any sense.	Judicious	You may switch your faction to O-12 at this time.
18	You were kidnapped and tortured. Why?	Skittish	Reduce Resolve by 1.
19	Your first real job took you to a new planet. It felt like home.	Laissez-Faire	You defect to a new faction. Roll on the Faction Table on p. 41 to determine your new allegiance. You may choose to roll on that faction's career table for your first career at no cost.
20	You committed suicide.	Suicidal	Your character died and was resurrected. See the rules for Resurrection on p. 54.

DECISION EIGHT: CAREERS

What career (or careers) do you decide to pursue? Are you doing something that you love? Are you trapped in a job that you hate? What are you good at and what are you learning out among the planets? Are you aggressively seeking promotions or happy where you are?

Mark your starting age as eighteen. You will complete a minimum of two career phases, and you can spend 1 Life Point to pursue an additional career (to a maximum of four career phases).

STEP ONE: SELECT CAREER

By default, roll 1d20 and consult the *Basic Career Table*. If it instructs you to roll on the *Faction Career Table*, roll on the table belonging to your current faction. (Members of the ALEPH faction roll on the *O-12 Faction Career Table*.)

Alternatively, you can choose to hazard any career. See *Hazarding a Career*, p. 54.

You can also spend Life Points to wield various degrees of control over your career phase.
- Spend 1 Life Point to pick a career from the *Basic Career Table*.
- Spend 1 Life Point to roll on your *Faction Career Table*.
- Spend 1 Life Point to change your faction.

You can also choose to select the Unemployed career to gain 1 Life Point. (You can gain a maximum of 2 Life Points in this way. You do not gain the Life Point if you are forced to become Unemployed by a random roll, event, or hazard test.)

BASIC CAREER TABLE

D20	CAREER
1–2	Unemployed
3–4	Corporate
5–6	Technician
7–8	Military
9–10	Medical
11–12	Academic
13	Criminal
14	Police
15	Frontiersman
16	Media
17	Ship Crew
18	Pilot
19–20	Roll on *Faction Career Table*

STEP TWO: WORK CAREER

Once you've selected a career, refer to the description for your career on p. 59–70.
- For your first career (and ONLY your first career), add the attribute improvements listed.
- Gain 1 rank of training in all mandatory skills.
- Pick two of the three elective skills and gain 1 rank of training in each.
- If you have less than three signature skills, choose one of the skills (either elective or mandatory) gained from your career to become a signature skill. Add 1 rank of training to this skill.
- Choose one of the skills gained from this career and select one talent from the associated tree for which you fulfil the prerequisites.
- Roll the career's Earnings. If the result is higher than your current Earnings, increase, your Earnings to the new rating. For each Effect rolled, adjust your Social Status one step in the same direction as the Earnings you rolled. (If the rolled rating is lower than your rating, decrease your Social Status; if it was higher, increase your Social Status.) If your Social Status decreases, your Earnings decrease by one point. Regardless of the number of Effects rolled, the maximum change in your Social Status is equal to the difference between your current Earnings and the Earnings rolled for your career.
- Raise your Earnings to match your career's rating if your current rating is lower.
- Gain the equipment (if any) indicated for your career. (When repeating a career, you do not gain duplicates of the same equipment. But you do gain additional equipment for each new career.)

STEP THREE: CAREER EVENT

While working your career, what was the most significant event in your life? Roll 1d6 to determine which *Career Event Table* to use and then roll 1d20 to determine your Career Event.

You can spend 1 Life Point to reroll or, with GM approval, pick your Career Event. With your GM's permission, you could also design your own event.

STEP FOUR: FINISH CAREER PHASE

As you finish your career, increase your age by 1d6+1 years. (This is in addition to any changes in age as a result of Career Events.)

If this was your first career phase, return to *Step One: Select Career* and begin your second career phase. However, instead of rolling randomly or hazarding a career, you can choose to simply repeat your current career. If you do so, proceed to *Step Two: Work Career* and begin working the career (gaining all the usual benefits for doing so).

EXAMPLE
CAREER PHASE

With the death of her parents, Melissa feels that Cassandra has become rudderless. Uncertain of where she might end up, she rolls 1d20 on the *Basic Career Table* and gets 7, discovering that Cassandra ended up falling back on the Military for her first career.

Because this is her first career, she gains the attribute improvements listed for the Military career (+2 Agility, +1 Awareness, +2 Brawn, +1 Coordination, +1 Intelligence, +2 Willpower) She gains one rank of training in the mandatory skills of Athletics, Close Combat, and Ballistics (finally gaining Focus 2 in Athletics). She chooses Acrobatics and Tech as her elective skills, gaining one rank in each, and then also chooses Tech as her third and final signature skill. Finally, she chooses to gain a Ballistics talent. Because she already has the Marksman talent for Ballistics, she can choose one of the next talents on the Ballistics tree. She chooses Clear Shot.

Cassandra's Earnings is higher than that granted by her Military career, so it remains unchanged, but Melissa writes down her Military gear.

EXAMPLE
CAREER EVENT

After Cassandra completes her Military career phase, Melissa rolls on the *Career Event Table* and discovers that she's been involved in a serious crime: She's Fired, gains a Criminal Record, and rolls 1d6 to determine that she adds 6 years to her life. Melissa chooses not to spend 1 Life Point to remain in her current career, so Cassandra is drummed out of the military. Her new Criminal Record reduces her Social Status to Demogrant and her Earnings to 3. She finishes her career phase by rolling 1d6+1 and adding 2 more years to Cassandra's age.

EXAMPLE
HAZARDING A CAREER

Melissa decides that Cassandra must have tried profiteering – diverting military equipment from the PanOceanian Military Complex to a mercenary company called SecLock Contingencies. After she's released from prison, Cassandra is in bad shape and unemployed. Cassandra decides to use her mercenary connections and hazard the career of Bounty Hunter: She chooses Athletics as the hazarding skill and spends 1 Life Point to decrease the difficulty of the check from Challenging (D2) to Average (D1). The target number of the check is 14 (Cassandra has Brawn 12 and Athletics Expertise 2.) On 2d20, she rolls 18 and 4, generating one success and successfully hazarding the career.

This is her second career, so Cassandra doesn't improve her attributes. She's also maxed out with three signature skills, so she won't gain a new one. But she still gains training in mandatory and elective skills, an additional talent, and the career's gear. She then experiences another career event and increases her age by 1d6+1 (3) years. At the end of this career phase, Melissa chooses not to spend 1 Life Point in order to attempt a third career phase.

Lhosts – p. 354

If this was your second career phase, you can spend 1 Life Point to undertake a third career phase (using the same procedure as your second career phase). If this was your third career phase, you can do the same for a fourth career phase. (You cannot attempt a fifth career phase.) If this was your final career phase, proceed to *Decision Nine: Final Customisation*.

EXTENDING CAREERS

With GM approval, you may voluntarily spend 1d6+1 additional years in any career phase, rolling again for a Career Event for each extension. You do not receive any other benefits for extending your career phase, nor does it count against the number of career phases you may have. It is simply a way to represent older, more experienced characters who have seen more of what life has to throw at them.

HAZARDING A CAREER

When hazarding a career, you are taking a risk and hoping it pays off. Choose a career from any table (including other *Faction Career Tables*) that doesn't have a faction prerequisite and make a Challenging (D2) skill test using one of the mandatory skills listed for the career. On a success you have found employment in your career of choice and can now work that career.

If you fail your hazard test, however, you must either repeat your previous career or become Unemployed. (If this was your first career phase or if you were Unemployed in your previous career phase, you have no choice but to become Unemployed.) You can reduce the difficulty of the hazard test by 1 per Life Point spent.

CRIMINAL RECORD

If you gain a criminal record, reduce your Social Status and Earnings by one each. You can also choose to immediately join the Submondo faction if you wish.

Some careers (such as Police) cannot be taken if you have a criminal record unless you spend 1 Life Point to do so. If you randomly roll such a career while having a criminal record, you must immediately spend 1 Life Point in order to take it. If you cannot (or choose not to), you can immediately hazard another career, but the difficulty of the hazard test is increased by one step.

If a criminal record is gained during a career phase, you must immediately attempt a hazard test for your current career. If you fail the hazard test, you are also Fired (see below).

With a criminal record, you reduce the difficulty of the hazard check for any Criminal career by 1.

It should be noted that simply having a Criminal career does not result in a criminal record: You only get a record if you get caught.

DEFECTION CHECK

If you roll a career on a *Faction Career Table* other than your own, there is a chance that you have defected to that faction. Roll 1d20, on a roll of 1 change your current faction. You do not have to make a defection check if you hazard a career on another *Faction Career Table*. You only make the defection check if you randomly roll on that table.

FIRED

If you are fired, you may retain all the benefits of your current career but you may not repeat or extend the career unless you spend 2 Life Points and lose 1 Earnings.

RESURRECTION

If you die on the Lifepath, it's assumed that you've been Resurrected from your Cube. (All PCs on the Lifepath are assumed to have a Cube, even if they come from a background – like Ariadna – where many people do not have one.)

Losing Current Host: Subtract your host's attribute modifiers from your attribute scores and remove any other special abilities or qualities that your current host grants you.

New Lhost: By default, you've been placed in an antiquated Lhost. By spending 1 Life Point, however, you can instead be placed in a standard Lhost. Using the Lhost stat blocks below, adjust your attributes and note any special abilities granted by your Lhost.

Other Lhosts: You can also select more advanced or experimental Lhosts by spending additional Life Points. Alternatively, you can use Assets to purchase an alternative Lhost, either immediately at the time of your resurrection or during *Decision Nine: Final Customisation*.

LHOST
ANTIQUATED LHOST

			ATTRIBUTES			
AGI	AWA	BRW	COO	INT	PER	WIL
-1	-1	-1	-1	-1	-1	-1

SPECIAL ABILITIES
• Inured to Disease

LHOST
STANDARD LHOST

			ATTRIBUTES			
AGI	AWA	BRW	COO	INT	PER	WIL
–	–	–	–	–	–	–

SPECIAL ABILITIES
• Inured to Disease

FACTION CAREER TABLE A

D6	ARIADNA	HAQQISLAM	NOMADS	PANOCEANIA	YU JING
1	Special Forces	Special Forces	Special Forces	Special Forces	Special Forces
2	Intelligence Operative	Hassassin [1]	Intelligence Operative	Intelligence Operative	Intelligence Operative
3	Assault Pack Controller [1]	Corsair	Reverend Agent [1]	Lobbyist [1]	Celestial Guard [1]
4	Sports Personality	Terraforming Scientist	Heavy Industry	Maya Personality	Bōsōzoku
5	Paratrooper	Bodyguard	Investigative Journalist	Corporate Executive	TAG Pilot
6	Roll on *Faction Table* of Your Choice				

FACTION CAREER TABLE B

D6	CORPORATION	MERCENARY	MINOR NATION	O-12/ALEPH	SUBMONDO
1	Special Forces	Special Forces	Special Forces	Special Forces	Special Forces
2	Intelligence Operative	Intelligence Operative	Intelligence Operative	Intelligence Operative	Corsair
3	Corporate Executive	Bounty Hunter	Heavy Industry	Diplomat	Smuggler
4	Trader	Remote Operator	Trader	Politician	Hacker
5	Field Scientist	Ship Crew	Investigative Journalist	Bureau Toth Agent[1]	Bodyguard
6	Roll on *Faction Table* of Your Choice				

CAREER EVENT TABLES

D6	TABLE
1–2	Career Event Table A
3–4	Career Event Table B
5–6	Career Event Table C

[1] Career has a prerequisite of belonging to this faction. You can't hazard this career unless you're of the matching faction. If you roll into this career, you automatically fail your defection check. You can override these limitations by spending 1 Life Point (in which case you were somehow undercover while working the career).

CAREER EVENT TABLE A

D20	CAREER EVENT	GAME EFFECT
1	You develop a rare genetic disorder or are afflicted by a genomic toxin.	Your genetic disorder reduces your maximum Vigour by 1. The treatment required to cure your condition will cost 10+5 🅝 Assets.
2	Both the authorities and organised crime are hunting for you. What do you know, or what have you got that they want?	Gain both a criminal enemy and a police enemy. You must pass an Average (D1) hazard test for your current career or you are Fired (see p. 54).
3	You are on the run. Who is after you, and why?	Gain Trait: Hunted
4	You've accrued the enmity of a powerful enemy. They might be a district authority, well-connected ex-lover, or a jealous colleague.	Gain Trait: Persecuted
5	An old debt has caught up with you. Who is it to, and what will happen if you do not pay?	Gain a conflict with an organisation as a character trait. You have a 20 Asset debt that must be paid off with that organisation.
6	You're involved in a serious crime. Guilty or not, you are sentenced to hard labour and lose your job.	Add 1d6 years to age. You are Fired (see p. 54) and gain a Criminal Record (see p. 54)
7	You develop a fierce rivalry with someone in your organisation or faction.	Gain a character trait describing your rivalry or its consequences.
8	You have an affair with someone wealthy, but it ends poorly. Was it your fault?	Randomly determine the faction your ex-lover belongs to. The GM can use them as a character trait when purchasing complications that affect you.
9	You are called in for questioning by the authorities. What do they want to know? They let you go, but on what condition?	Gain a debt worth 1d6 Assets to a random faction.
10	You gain a criminal record. What happened? Are you guilty or innocent?	Gain a Criminal Record (see p. 54).
11	You are injured in a shooting accident. What were you doing? Who shot you?	Roll a random body location. You have a gunshot wound that has not healed well in this location. Gain Trait: Old Wound.
12	Someone has been keeping an eye on you. They always seem to be there when you look around. What do you think they are interested in? Who are they?	Gain Trait: Under Surveillance
13	You become tangled up in a plot being run by a rival faction. What do you do for them? Why do you do it?	You must pass a Challenging (D2) hazard test for your current career or you gain a Criminal Record (see p. 54).
14	They are on to you! Who are they and what have you done?	Gain Trait: Paranoia
15	Someone you know is a criminal, but you cannot turn them in. What hold do they have over you?	Gain Trait: Blackmailed
16	Whatever you did, and it was bad, you've paid for it now – but they will not give up.	Gain a character trait describing your nemesis.
17	You volunteered to take part in a secret medical experiment which succeeded. Well, almost.	Gain Trait: Curse of the Mayfly. You may roll an aging test (p. 71) to regain one additional Infinity Point per session..
18	You are fired. What did you do?	You are Fired (see p. 54).
19	While doing your job, you are killed. What happened?	Your character died and was Resurrected. See the rules for *Resurrection* on p. 54.
20	You are suffering from the Chinese Curse: May you live in interesting times!	Roll again three times on the *Career Event Tables* for this career phase. (When spending a Life Point to choose a specific event, you may not choose this result. If you roll duplicate events, it means some similar event has occurred. If you roll the Chinese Curse again, add additional rolls.)

CAREER EVENT TABLE B

D20	CAREER EVENT	GAME EFFECT
1	You are dating a wealthy and generous person.	Increase Earnings by one (to a maximum of six) whilst they are still in love with you, but they are very demanding or vulnerable (gain Vulnerable Lover as a trait).
2	You are forced to evacuate. What is the threat? Where do you have to go?	Immediately spend 5 Assets or gain the trait Homeless.
3	You foil some form of nefarious plot on your own (or with the help of your friends). Why didn't you go to the authorities?	Gain an enemy in a rival faction. Gain 5 Assets in "liberated" equipment.
4	You survive a serious natural disaster.	Gain Trait: Nightmares
5	You are remembered in the will of a relative. Who died? What were your feelings for them?	Gain 2 Assets.
6	You help solve a serious crime.	Gain a favour with a senior figure in either law enforcement or the intelligence community in your faction.
7	You discover that you have a talent for something you'd never considered trying before. What happened? Why do you love it?	Gain 1 rank of training in a skill you currently have no training in.
8	You are scouted by an unexpected employer.	If you hazard your next career, reduce the difficulty of the hazard test by two steps. If you stay in your current career or roll randomly, increase your Earnings by one.
9	You discover that your friend is a traitor working for a rival faction. The authorities request your help in arresting them.	If you cooperate with the authorities, gain 5 Assets as a reward. If you help your friend, you gain a contact in a random faction but you must make an Average (D1) hazard test in your current career or gain a Criminal Record (see p. 54).
10	You stumbled on a previously unknown alien ruin (possibly while on vacation). You found something before you got out. What was it?	Gain an item worth 10 Assets.
11	Your lucky day! Something paid off – a lottery ticket, a risky business venture, or a hard-won contract.	Gain 5 Assets.
12	You save someone from a terrible accident.	Gain an ally in a random faction.
13	You achieve notoriety or fame as a minor Maya star.	You gain 1 bonus Momentum on successful social skill tests, but all Stealth tests are increased in difficulty by one step in situations where being recognised would cause you a problem.
14	Your Cube experiences a malfunction in which its input is fed back into your brain.	Gain Trait: Cube Echoes. You'll need a completely new Cube to solve the problem.
15	A pseudo-AI personality you've had since childhood begins to degrade, but you can't bear to part with it.	The pseudo-AI provides 1 Momentum to Education tests, but the GM can use it as a trait when purchasing complications that are related to the outcome of the test.
16	You join a new religion. What prompted your conversion? What article of faith is most important to you in your new belief?	Gain a character trait describing your religion or religious experience.
17	You volunteered to take part in a secret medical experiment that succeeded. Well, almost.	Gain a talent in a talent tree of your choice and describe how you can do this as a result of the experiment. However, sometimes you lose the plot or wake up in strange places. Gain the character trait of Experimental Subject.
18	A co-worker frames you for something they did.	You are Fired (see p. 54).
19	You are violently killed. What happened? Who killed you?	Your character died and was Resurrected. See the rules for *Resurrection* on p. 54.
20	You are suffering from the Chinese Curse: May you live in interesting times!	Roll again three times on the *Career Event Tables* for this career phase. (When spending a Life Point to choose a specific event, you may not choose this result. If you roll duplicate events, it means some similar event has occurred. If you roll the Chinese Curse again, add additional rolls.)

CAREER EVENT TABLE C

D20	CAREER EVENT	GAME EFFECT
1	A family member tells you a dark family secret. What has been hidden from you for all these years?	Gain a character trait related to your family's secret.
2	You receive exotic cosmetic surgery. What do you look like now? Do you have tapered ears? Lizard scales? A prehensile tail?	Gain a character trait describing your new look and Cosmetic Augmentation 2.
3	The building you call home burns down.	Gain Trait: Homeless and lose 5 Assets (this may result in a debt).
4	Your employer hits a slump and is struggling to make ends meet.	You can either agree to a pay cut (reduce your Earnings by 1) or you can choose to make a Challenging (D2) hazard test for your current career. If you fail the test, you are Fired (see p. 54). But if you succeed, your Earnings is unchanged as you swap to a new employer.
5	You're betrayed by someone you trust. Who was it? What did they do to you?	Gain Trait: Untrusting
6	You have survived a Combined Army attack. Where were you? What form did the attack take?	Gain Trait: Shell Shocked
7	You get enrolled in an advanced training program at your job (possibly experimental or cybernetic in nature).	Gain 1 rank in the elective skill from your current career that you did NOT choose to advance during this career phase.
8	You are recruited or selected to travel to a different planet in order to continue your career.	Randomly determine which planet and gain the trait Mudhopper.
9	A family member is in desperate financial need and they come to you for help. How bad is it and how did they get into this situation?	Gain a debt worth 10 Assets or gain the character trait Disowned.
10	You are sent out into the field as a roving specialist (either in person or through immersive VR). Where do you go? What do you experience?	Gain 1d6 languages from the *Random Languages Table* (see p. 45).
11	A family member is murdered. Who was killed? Do you know who did it? And, if so, why?	Gain Trait: Thirst for Vengeance
12	You are one of the only survivors when a ship you were travelling on broke down or crashed, and rescue was a long time coming.	Add one year to your age and gain the character trait Space Sickness.
13	You earn a big promotion.	Increase Earnings by one.
14	Your childhood friend moves back home. It's great to see them again, but they're acting strangely.	Gain an ally from a random faction.
15	You thought that you'd gotten away with the crime you committed ten years ago, but new evidence has been discovered.	Gain a Criminal Record (see p. 54).
16	Due to what's claimed to be a clerical error, your stored personality backup is placed in a Lhost. Your IQ-doppelgänger disappears before the error can be corrected.	Gain Trait: IQ-Doppelgänger
17	You volunteered to take part in a secret medical experiment. It failed.	Reduce one random attribute by 1 point.
18	You show up for work one day and your employer is gone. The office is empty. Nobody is there. What happened?	You are Fired (see p. 54). Gain Trait: Surrounded by Conspiracy.
19	Your death is a famous event. How did it happen? Why is it so well known?	Your character died and was Resurrected. See the rules for *Resurrection* on p. 54. You gain 1 bonus Momentum on successful social skill tests, but all stealth tests are increased in difficulty by one step in situations where being recognised would cause you a problem.
20	You are suffering from the Chinese Curse: May you live in interesting times!	Roll again three times on the *Career Event Tables* for this career phase. (When spending a Life Point to choose a specific event, you may not choose this result. If you roll duplicate events, it means some similar event has occurred. If you roll the Chinese Curse again, add additional rolls.)

CAREER PROFILE
UNEMPLOYED (SPECIAL)

Tens of billions live scattered throughout the Human Sphere and the unemployed number in the hundreds of millions. Robust demogrants, well-funded support networks, and abundant resources, however, mean that the unemployed generally live comfortably while Maya makes a seemingly infinite variety of entertainment and virtual experiences available.

ATTRIBUTES						
AGI	AWA	BRW	COO	INT	PER	WIL
+2	+1	+2	+1	+2	–	+2

SKILLS			EARNINGS
Mandatory	Survival	none	none	1 (max. 0)
Elective	Any 1 other	Any 1 other	–	

GEAR: None

CAREER PROFILE
ACADEMIC

Bright minds across the Human Sphere develop and implement the latest technology, direct expansion efforts, and guide humanity in all its endeavours. The Academic can be a brilliant but introverted scientist creating miracles in the lab, or she could be a weathered biologist out working in the field. Historians study the past to glean clues about humanity's future. Roboticists and engineers devise the tools that build the high-tech cities gleaming upon countless worlds. An Academic applies theory, study, and experimentation to solve the problems of the Human Sphere. Knowledge in a wide variety of fields makes the Academic career desirable on every world. Brilliant minds are in perpetual demand, especially in troubled times.

ATTRIBUTES						
AGI	AWA	BRW	COO	INT	PER	WIL
+1	+2	–	+1	+3	+1	+2

SKILLS			EARNINGS
Mandatory	Education	Medicine	Science	2+1
Elective	Discipline	Education	Tech	

GEAR: Laboratory (3 month lease)

CAREER PROFILE
ASSAULT PACK CONTROLLER

Assault Pack Controllers guide mind-controlled Antipodes into battle. The fierce lupine natives of Ariadna possess heightened senses and ferocious strength. A Controller must lead these creatures, biochemically manipulated to be pliable and obedient, with equally fierce determination. Assault Pack Controllers use their bestial troops to break through enemy lines and shatter their resolve. Life as a Controller means harsh training and rigorous discipline to carry the strength and presence of an alpha. Controllers face danger every day that they lead their packs, from the savagery of the Antipodes themselves to the missions that require an Assault Pack. Because a Controller must be strong, ruthless, and driven, few forces are more feared on the battlefield than an Assault Pack. Many Controllers form close bonds with their Antipodes.

ATTRIBUTES						
AGI	AWA	BRW	COO	INT	PER	WIL
+1	+2	–	+2	+2	+2	+1

SKILLS			EARNINGS
Mandatory	Athletics	Animal Handling	Stealth	2+1
Elective	Close Combat	Survival	Ballistics	

GEAR: Antipode Control Device, Teseum Chopper, Pheromone Dispenser
SPECIAL: Prerequisite (Ariadna Faction)

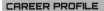

CAREER PROFILE
BODYGUARD

Bodyguards are in high demand for the rich and important people of the Human Sphere. A Bodyguard might serve as protection for a high-ranking political leader, a controversial Maya personality, or a religious figurehead. A Bodyguard must be quick-witted, tough, and skilled in both offensive and defensive techniques. Bodyguards are usually well-armed and willing to take a bullet for their charges. Consequently, a Bodyguard is well paid, at least if the employer wants any sense of loyalty. The best Bodyguards are prized for their attention to discipline and skill at arms, often heading security details guarding convoys, foreign dignitaries, and important frontier missions. Most Bodyguards also display a variety of other skills picked up during their assignments.

ATTRIBUTES						
AGI	AWA	BRW	COO	INT	PER	WIL
+2	+2	+2	+1	+2	–	+1

SKILLS				EARNINGS
Mandatory	Observation	Close Combat	Ballistics	1+2 Ⓝ
Elective	Lifestyle	Pilot	Discipline	

GEAR: Multispectral Visor 1, High-Fashion Clothing, Ballistic Vest, Heavy Pistol (with 3 Standard Reloads)

CAREER PROFILE
BŌSŌZOKU

Bōsōzoku is an illegal form of street racing originating in Yu Jing. It is a cutthroat competition often involving the use of violence in a no-holds barred race. The Bōsōzoku racers are incredibly skilled and daring. They lead a lifestyle steeped in underground fame, danger, and hot-blooded pursuit of victory set amid the backdrop of blazing neon cities. A Bōsōzoku racer must be tough and fast to survive, even outside the races, often forming connections with other under-world elements. Bōsōzoku gangs kill for one another, and a racer often adopts an "us against the world" mentality. With such a risky yet lucrative occupation, most Bōsōzoku racers approach life with a "live fast, die young" outlook.

ATTRIBUTES						
AGI	AWA	BRW	COO	INT	PER	WIL
+2	+2	+2	–	+2	+1	+1

SKILLS				EARNINGS
Mandatory	Pilot	Thievery	Stealth	0+2 Ⓝ
Elective	Pilot	Tech	Hacking	

GEAR: Motorcycle, AP Pistol (with 2 AP Reloads), Armoured Clothing (Racer's Suit)
SPECIAL: Criminal Career

CAREER PROFILE
BOUNTY HUNTER

As spread out as humanity is among the stars, criminals inevitably escape. Outlaws build up power bases away from the centres of law enforcement, pirates retreat to dens of scum after raiding merchant vessels, and unscrupulous executives flee prosecution to other countries or other worlds. Bounty Hunters act where traditional law enforcement cannot. The bounties commanded by high-profile criminals are tremendous. Hunters go where others won't in order to bring back their quarry, or maybe just a piece of them. Skilled in tracking, battle, and guerrilla tactics, Bounty Hunters are the basis of countless romanticised legends and thrilling Maya programs.

ATTRIBUTES						
AGI	AWA	BRW	COO	INT	PER	WIL
–	+2	+2	+1	+1	+2	+2

SKILLS				EARNINGS
Mandatory	Athletics	Observation	Stealth	1+2 Ⓝ
Elective	Ballistics	Pilot	Tech	

GEAR: SecurCuffs, Heavy Pistol (with 4 Standard Reloads), Light Combat Armour

BUREAU TOTH AGENT

Agents of Bureau Toth have a specific and demanding duty: watch over ALEPH. Tasked by O-12 with this most important duty, Bureau Toth Agents serve as one part law enforcement and one part hacker. They fend off foreign attempts on ALEPH's stability, help maintain ALEPH's operations, and supervise its actions on behalf of O-12. The Bureau's means and resources are hidden from all but the organisation itself, including ALEPH. Agents work to make sure that ALEPH remains functional, unimpeded, and most of all, benign.

ATTRIBUTES						
AGI	AWA	BRW	COO	INT	PER	WIL
+1	+2	–	+1	+2	+2	+2

SKILLS				EARNINGS
Mandatory	Analysis	Hacking	Tech	3+1 🟡
Elective	Ballistics	Education	Persuade	

GEAR: Heavy Pistol (with 4 Standard Reloads), Assault or Defensive Hacking Device, E/M Grenade

SPECIAL: Prerequisite (O-12 Faction)

CELESTIAL GUARD

The famed Yu Jing Celestial Guard protect the Imperial Palace and the Celestial Emperor. Their duty even extends to the whole of the Forbidden City. These crack troops specialise in urban warfare, each soldier highly experienced and impeccably disciplined. Only the most loyal and proven members of the Yu Jing military can ascend to the ranks of Celestial Guard. The Guard acts on direct orders from the Emperor, and function as a police unit with vast authority and resources. The Celestial Guard are known to bend or break laws that bind other police units in their pursuit of Imperial justice. Guard members are brutal and decisive, trained to bring a swift end to any threat Yu Jing faces.

ATTRIBUTES						
AGI	AWA	BRW	COO	INT	PER	WIL
+1	+2	+2	+1	+2	–	+2

SKILLS				EARNINGS
Mandatory	Athletics	Acrobatics	Observation	2+1 🟡
Elective	Close Combat	Ballistics	Analysis	

GEAR: Light Combat Armour, Combi Rifle, Recorder

SPECIAL: Prerequisite (Yu Jing Faction); cannot be selected by character with a Criminal Record.

CORPORATE

Corporate workers labour at all levels to keep the megacorps and hypercorps of the Human Sphere running. Managers ply their people skills to keep stressed and overworked staffers productive. Accountants and actuaries calculate risk and determine investments. Working a Corporate career, whether in a small start-up on the frontier or as part of a massive conglomerate, means being perceptive, wary, and opportunistic — always ready to adapt to a changing corporate environment or the fast-paced demands of interplanetary business.

ATTRIBUTES						
AGI	AWA	BRW	COO	INT	PER	WIL
–	+2	+1	+2	+2	+2	+1

SKILLS				EARNINGS
Mandatory	Lifestyle	Observation	Stealth	2+2 🟡
Elective	Lifestyle	Discipline	Education	

GEAR: AR Eye Implants, Implanted Knife, or Bioimmunity Organ; Cosmetics Kit

CORVUS BELLI
INFINITY

CAREER PROFILE
CORPORATE EXECUTIVE

Executives in the most influential hypercorps wield more power than many sovereign rulers among the minor nations. With the trade of currency and favours, an Executive alters the course of political development, positions their company to benefit first and foremost from government contracts, and helps shape the Human Sphere. A Corporate Executive swims in shark-infested waters, vying with competitors for the best deals. An Executive is responsible for their company's interests, which often means meeting and negotiating with the most high-powered individuals in human space. They must adapt to constantly changing situations with a quick wit and keen eye for opportunity.

ATTRIBUTES

AGI	AWA	BRW	COO	INT	PER	WIL
–	+1	+1	+2	+2	+3	+1

SKILLS

				EARNINGS
Mandatory	Persuade	Lifestyle	Command	3+3 Ⓝ
Elective	Education	Lifestyle	Discipline	

GEAR: High-Fashion Clothing (with Locational Beacon), Tonfa Bangles or AP Pistol, Neural Comlog or AR Eye Implants, 1 dose of a recreational drug

CAREER PROFILE
CORSAIR

Every major nation employs Corsairs, privateers commissioned to capture military and merchant ships of enemy nations. Some Corsairs hunt other Corsairs, but most make a living pursuing less suspecting prey. Authorised to keep part of the loot, Corsairs make a profit by targeting the least-protected vessels and keeping more than their contracted allotment of bounty. A Corsair lives a dangerous lifestyle, considered by law to be an enemy combatant but without the honour or respect due the military. Despite their reputation as lawless dogs, most Corsairs stick to a strict code among their own people. Corsairs can be charming and sly in turns, skilled negotiators and dangerous in a fight. Their experience travelling human space is second to none.

ATTRIBUTES

AGI	AWA	BRW	COO	INT	PER	WIL
+2	+2	+2	+1	+2	+1	–

SKILLS

				EARNINGS
Mandatory	Spacecraft	Extraplanetary	Thievery	0+3 Ⓝ
Elective	Close Combat	Acrobatics	Ballistics	

GEAR: Boarding Shotgun (with 4 Normal Shell Reloads, 1 AP Shell Reload), Surge (×2), Vac Suit (with 3 Oxygen Loads)
SPECIAL: Criminal Career

CAREER PROFILE
CRIMINAL

Perhaps the one profession most common across all factions is that of Criminal. Smugglers sneak contraband into and out of system borders. Thieves test the security systems of ships, banks, and corporate business records, looking to steal identities, leverage, access codes — anything that lets them tap into their targets' wealth. Lawless gangs haunt the fringes of civilised society, like the destitute underclass that lurks in the bowels of gleaming mega-cities, or the pirates that attack shipping lanes. Ecoterrorists and those with an axe to grind against the massive economic power players strike out to disrupt the status quo, or take revenge on the ones who took away their livelihoods. It's also possible that one could find themselves trapped in a Criminal life for reasons beyond their control, such as fleeing wrongful prosecutionf or crossing the wrong bureaucrat.

ATTRIBUTES

AGI	AWA	BRW	COO	INT	PER	WIL
+2	+2	+2	+2	–	+1	+1

SKILLS

				EARNINGS
Mandatory	Thievery	Observation	Stealth	0+2 Ⓝ
Elective	Close Combat	Ballistics	Tech	

GEAR: Cosmetics Kit, Heavy Pistol (with 3 Standard Reloads), Fake ID 2
SPECIAL: Criminal Career

CAREER PROFILE
DIPLOMAT

Diplomacy is a fine art in the Human Sphere, especially with a Code Infinity looming over everyone's heads. Diplomats work to smooth over relations between rival nations, force alliances of convenience or sometimes shared ideology, and keep disparate countries connected by more than just trade. A good Diplomat exhibits great personal charm and integrity, conducting business on foreign soil with the utmost of respect and care. Diplomats travel to foreign countries and distant worlds, meeting with envoys of sovereign nations, corporate rule, and new settlements. They broker trade agreements and peace treaties, negotiate political alliances, and defuse tense situations. The life of a Diplomat is one of constant engagement with many different representatives in locales all across the Human Sphere.

ATTRIBUTES

AGI	AWA	BRW	COO	INT	PER	WIL
+1	+2	–	+2	+2	+2	+1

SKILLS

				EARNINGS
Mandatory	Persuade	Education	Discipline	2+2 Ⓝ
Elective	Psychology	Pilot	Education	

GEAR: Cosmetics Kit or AR Eye Implants, Negotiation Suite (3 days rental credit)

FIELD SCIENTIST

The Field Scientists that work for more advanced nations seek out natural mysteries. They experiment with (or upon) local wildlife and vegetation, they test out new wetware implants or high-tech devices, and their laboratories are often little more than camps set up to brave the elements. Field Scientists aren't afraid to get their hands dirty in order to discover new chemicals or capture promising flora and fauna, and the true Field Scientist is a renaissance specialist. They study a mixture of biology, chemistry, geology, and the like by immersing themselves in it, rather than isolating it in a lab.

ATTRIBUTES						
AGI	AWA	BRW	COO	INT	PER	WIL
+1	+2	+1	+2	+3	+1	–

SKILLS				EARNINGS
Mandatory	Science	Education	Survival	2+1 Ⓝ
Elective	Observation	Tech	Athletics	

GEAR: Analytical Kit, Survival Kit, Sensor Suite (×3)

FRONTIERSMAN

The men and women of the frontier explore the little-known regions of human space. They are the first to expand the maps, eager to set foot on new ground and stake a claim in humanity's interstellar expansion. These rugged folk brave environmental dangers, unknown flora and fauna, and set up trading posts in seldom-travelled regions. A frontiersman is skilled at hunting, gathering supplies, and often in working with technology out away from urban centres, with little to no technical support. Frontiersmen prospect for resources, like the rare and valuable Teseum, or rare herbs and wildlife with properties useful to the medical industry. Some are criminals fleeing the reach of the law by living on the frontier, and others are bounty hunters sent to hunt down those who would otherwise escape justice.

ATTRIBUTES						
AGI	AWA	BRW	COO	INT	PER	WIL
+2	+2	+1	+1	+2	–	+2

SKILLS				EARNINGS
Mandatory	Survival	Animal Handling	Resistance	1+1 Ⓝ
Elective	Discipline	Athletics	Thievery	

GEAR: Survival Rations (×6), Survival Kit, Axe or Powered Multitool

HACKER

Nearly any conceivable information exists on the Maya network. Hackers make a living breaking down electronic barriers and uncovering secrets, or taking data from others for the purposes of fraud, theft, or mere thrills. Hackers also work with law enforcement, helping to track those with similar skills or counter their efforts. Some specialise in hacking corporate networks, like those of the massive banks and producers of consumer products. Others see it as an art form, hacking challenging military networks or plunging into the depths of Maya in order to find something no one else can.

ATTRIBUTES						
AGI	AWA	BRW	COO	INT	PER	WIL
+1	+2	+1	+2	+2	+2	–

SKILLS				EARNINGS
Mandatory	Thievery	Hacking	Tech	2+2 Ⓝ
Elective	Observation	Ballistics	Stealth	

GEAR: Deployable Repeater (×3), Powered Multitool, Assault or Defensive Hacking Device

CAREER PROFILE

HASSASSIN FIDAY

No covert operative in human space is deadlier or more feared than those of the Hassassin Society. These mysterious agents act as spies and assassins, completing missions too dangerous for lesser agents. A Hassassin is a protector of Haqqislamic interests as well as a devout believer in the Search for Knowledge. Many Hassassins possess a zeal even their countrymen cannot match. Theirs is dangerous and often thankless work, like the dreaded Fidays who embrace death as part of their duty. In secret camps known only to the Hassassin Society and the Hachib, the President of Haqqislam, Hassassins undergo the most gruelling training. Nearly limitless funds, a long tradition of discipline, honour, and deadly focus, and an unquenchable desire to guard humanity's evolution give the Hassassins incomparable ability.

ATTRIBUTES						
AGI	AWA	BRW	COO	INT	PER	WIL
+1	+2	+1	+2	+1	−1	+1

SKILLS				EARNINGS
Mandatory	Stealth	Persuade	Thievery	1+2 
Elective	Close Combat	Ballistics	Hacking	

GEAR: Fake ID 3, Cosmetics Kit, Climbing Plus, Grazeblade, DT Sniper Rifle (with 2 Reloads)
SPECIAL: Prerequisite (Haqqislam Faction)

CAREER PROFILE

HEAVY INDUSTRY

While expert systems and automation has reduced the number of workers involved in industrial pursuits, those that remain are all the more critical, providing skills and judgment. Modern materials require vacuum purification in electron-beam furnaces; titanic terraforming processors need calibration and adjustment to local conditions before being set to automated operation; volatile planetary core taps demand human decisions where predictive physics break down; and even automated maintenance systems want for their own upkeep. Industrial specialists are an increasingly rare breed that understand the link between sweat and advanced technology. Their knowledge spans grease guns to exclusion fields, and they have the experience to apply either to a problem. Professionals in this field are the gears that keep the Human Sphere turning.

ATTRIBUTES						
AGI	AWA	BRW	COO	INT	PER	WIL
+1	+2	–	+2	+2	+1	+2

SKILLS				EARNINGS
Mandatory	Resistance	Pilot	Tech	2+1
Elective	Close Combat	Persuade	Thievery	

GEAR: Gruntsuit (with Respirator 1), Powered Multitool, Painkillers (×3), Repair Kit

CAREER PROFILE

INTELLIGENCE OPERATIVE

The tense state of conflict in the Human Sphere means every agency looks for an edge over its competitors. Intelligence Operatives conduct corporate espionage, deep-cover spy missions, acts of sabotage, and other acts which risk their life and limb for agencies that would disavow any knowledge of, or connection to, their operations. An Intelligence Operative is quick-witted, highly disciplined, and often alone in a place surrounded by enemies unaware of the traitor in their midst. They trade in secrets — information that can turn the tide of small-scale conflicts, like raids on secret warehouses holding valuable experimental gear or data — and they can influence the large-scale skirmishes that take place between rival nations. The intelligence an operative collects can cause wars or end them with equal facility.

ATTRIBUTES						
AGI	AWA	BRW	COO	INT	PER	WIL
+1	+3	–	+2	+2	+1	+1

SKILLS				EARNINGS
Mandatory	Observation	Stealth	Analysis	3+1
Elective	Hacking	Education	Thievery	

GEAR: Fake ID 2, AP Pistol (with 4 Reloads), Breaking & Entering Kit, Recorder

CAREER PROFILE

INVESTIGATIVE JOURNALIST

Maya has more than its fair share of tabloid reporting and fluff stories, but the Investigative Journalist seeks the real stuff. Journalists hunt the truth, bringing word to the public about enemy action, the heroic efforts of national forces, and of course the latest scandals to haunt politicians and entertainers alike. Investigative Journalists often face hostility from those they investigate, and tend to have more than a few criminal skills like shadowing, breaking and entering, and sometimes falsifying data to gain admittance to places otherwise barred from them. Some see their cause as bringing the truth to light, while others simply have an insatiable curiosity and a penchant for getting into (and hopefully out of) trouble.

ATTRIBUTES						
AGI	AWA	BRW	COO	INT	PER	WIL
+2	+2	–	+2	+1	+2	+1

SKILLS				EARNINGS
Mandatory	Stealth	Persuade	Observation	1+2 
Elective	Hacking	Education	Thievery	

GEAR: Recorder or AR Eye Implants, Analysis Suite, Breaking & Entering Kit

CAREER PROFILE

LOBBYIST

The PanOceanian government is immense, the largest in the Human Sphere, and it has ended the hypocritical separation between political power and economic power. The old political parties, now abolished, have been replaced by a substantial number of lobbies. Lobbyists vie for political favour, coordinate the activities of lobby members, and engage in covert battles of clout with rival lobbies. With the unprecedented level of transparency in modern lobbies, a Lobbyist can be practically anyone — from a citizen with a very active interest in the groups that preside over matters they are about to a prestigious and influential leader intimately guiding the lobby's political fortunes. Any Lobbyist, however, is highly motivated and skilled in whatever arena they choose, and the lobbying game is both robust and demanding.

ATTRIBUTES						
AGI	AWA	BRW	COO	INT	PER	WIL
+1	+2	–	+2	+2	+2	+1

SKILLS				EARNINGS
Mandatory	Persuade	Psychoogy	Command	4+2
Elective	Discipline	Lifestyle	Education	

GEAR: Negotiator's Suite (10 days rental credit), Geist Upgrade (+2 ranks in Psychology or Research Specialist talent for Education)

SPECIAL: Prerequisite (PanOceania Faction)

CAREER PROFILE

MAYA PERSONALITY

Would-be Maya Personalities number in the millions, but the real stars reach hundreds of millions of viewers and are fueled by devoted, fanatic fans. A Maya Personality might be a popular musician, a comedian, or spiritual speaker. Artists and life-casters broadcast their work and live sensory feeds across the Sphere. The Maya datasphere hosts a staggering variety of content, and talented Maya Personalities rise from the faceless multitudes to become somebody. Popular newscasters and public speakers can gain far more fame and influence through legions of followers than they would have experienced as a government official. Larger-than-life personalities create legions of fans who hang on their every feeling, perception, thought, or word. They spawn both blind conformance and vehement dissent, filling up forums and editorial screeds with endless debate.

ATTRIBUTES						
AGI	AWA	BRW	COO	INT	PER	WIL
+1	+2	+1	+2	+2	+2	–

SKILLS				EARNINGS
Mandatory	Persuade	Lifestyle	Observation	1+4
Elective	Hacking	Discipline	Tech	

GEAR: Recorder (×3), High-Quality Clothing, Fake ID 1, AR Eye Implants

CAREER PROFILE
MEDIA

The media is perhaps the single largest industry in all of the Human Sphere, the one constant binding disparate nation states, cultures, and spiritual organisations together. Despite the glamour accorded to actors, WarCors, event-casters, and the other public faces of news and entertainment, a legion of writers, editors, producers, and effects artists support their work. These media professionals support the select few in the spotlight, always battling for better ratings and the sponsorships that come with them. Despite limited time in the public eye, media corporations covet the most talented behind-the-scenes professionals more than the personalities they support. The Sphere is filled with potential stars, but only a select few can make those stars shine.

ATTRIBUTES						
AGI	AWA	BRW	COO	INT	PER	WIL
+1	+3	–	+2	+1	+2	+1

SKILLS				EARNINGS
Mandatory	Education	Hacking	Analysis	2+1 Ⓝ
Elective	Hacking	Stealth	Tech	

GEAR: TinBot (with Recorder), AR Eye Implants, Analysis Suite

CAREER PROFILE
MEDICAL

Medical science has advanced by leaps and bounds, but hospitals often see a wide variety of strange cases and few professions can match the Medical career for a wealth of odd experiences. Doctors perform miracles, including resurrections, for those capable of paying the costs. Combat medics save the lives of wounded soldiers, or perform gruesome examinations on the fallen aliens. Some medics seek out new chemicals on alien worlds, hoping for the next big breakthrough. Ambitious medical scientists also push the envelope of human engineering, with advances in biotechnology, cybertechnology, and genetic therapies producing super-soldiers, making whole regions impervious to disease, or strengthening workforces to perform the most hazardous jobs where lesser people would fail.

ATTRIBUTES						
AGI	AWA	BRW	COO	INT	PER	WIL
+1	+2	–	+2	+2	+1	+2

SKILLS				EARNINGS
Mandatory	Medicine	Athletics	Psychology	2+2 Ⓝ
Elective	Animal Handling	Survival	Discipline	

GEAR: Armoured Clothing (Medical Uniform), MediKit (with 5 Serum), Basic Medical Supplies

CAREER PROFILE
MILITARY

Military characters run the gamut from professional soldiers employed by nations to loosely defined mercenary camps. Yu Jing employs the most well-disciplined soldiers as part of its interplanetary armed forces, while PanOceania makes heavy use of mercenaries with little connection to a larger governmental branch. At Paradiso, on the front lines, soldiers of all stripes work to halt the Combined Army's advance. ALEPH helps direct these battles, a fact that doesn't always sit well with the soldiers: Nomads would rather strike at the AI's own information centres and mercenaries would prefer to pirate poorly protected vessels carrying sensitive information. As the Human Sphere constantly expands, soldiers stand at the forefront, pushing the boundaries and forming the first line of defence against the dangers of the frontier.

ATTRIBUTES						
AGI	AWA	BRW	COO	INT	PER	WIL
+2	+1	+2	+1	+2	–	+2

SKILLS				EARNINGS
Mandatory	Athletics	Close Combat	Ballistics	2+1 Ⓝ
Elective	Survival	Acrobatics	Tech	

GEAR: Medium Combat Armour, Rifle (with 4 Standard Reloads), Stims (×3)

PARATROOPER

In the advanced warfare of the Human Sphere, Paratroopers drop onto planets and battlefields inaccessible by land. These brave men and women parachute into hostile territory, using high-tech glider suits and stealth chutes to slip past enemy defences. Air support is key to victory in the countless conflicts that grip the Human Sphere, and airborne soldiers engage in dynamic operations all across space. Paratroopers often adopt a "live fast" motto, jumping out of the sky and into combat for a living. This can give them a reputation for wild behaviour, but Paratroopers are every bit as disciplined as their fellow soldiers. A Paratrooper character often finds themselves far behind enemy lines, facing challenges that less elite soldiers could only imagine.

ATTRIBUTES						
AGI	AWA	BRW	COO	INT	PER	WIL
+2	+2	+2	+1	+1	–	+2

SKILLS				EARNINGS
Mandatory	Survival	Athletics	Ballistics	2+1 Ⓝ
Elective	Close Combat	Pilot	Discipline	

GEAR: Combat Jump Pack, Medium Combat Armour, Combi Rifle (with 4 Standard Reloads)

PILOT

Atmospheric, suborbital, and intrasystem shuttles ply the skies and space lanes everywhere humanity has touched. From the humble city hopper to deadly assault dropships, pilots ensure these vessels make it from origin to destination, quickly and in one piece, under both mild and dire circumstances. Acceleration crèches, physical alteration, and MetaChemicals help these pilots endure the prolonged periods at high-g with limited ill effect, but it's still a hard, very physical life. Still, very little cargo, passengers, or sensitive data would flow throughout the Sphere without pilots at the controls of a host of scows, skiffs, and couriers. Pilots also helm the military's vast fleet of dropships, high-g interceptors, net weasels, stealth infiltrators, and many other craft for accomplishing their missions.

ATTRIBUTES						
AGI	AWA	BRW	COO	INT	PER	WIL
+2	+2	+1	+2	+2	+1	–

SKILLS				EARNINGS
Mandatory	Pilot	Observation	Spacecraft	3+1 Ⓝ
Elective	Ballistics	Hacking	Tech	

GEAR: Armoured Clothing (Pilot's Uniform) or Crashsuit, Pistol (with 2 Standard Reloads), Inlaid Palm Circuitry or AR Eye Implants

POLICE

Law enforcement adapted to the advances of the 22nd century. Humanity is spread so far that just as often police are privately contracted from the best mercenary agencies. Government-employed police forces work to keep the most flagrant abuses at bay, though no law enforcement agency can hope to properly police the nightmare tangle of corporate laws. A police officer is highly trained in combat, negotiation tactics, and technical skills to help them in apprehending criminals. Police employ cutting-edge equipment and an officer also possesses specific skills related to their field: cybercrime, undercover and espionage, high-pressure hostage situations, and more.

ATTRIBUTES						
AGI	AWA	BRW	COO	INT	PER	WIL
+2	+2	+2	–	+2	+1	+1

SKILLS				EARNINGS
Mandatory	Athletics	Observation	Persuade	2+1 Ⓝ
Elective	Close Combat	Ballistics	Medicine	

GEAR: Armoued Clothing (Police Uniform), Heavy Pistol (with 4 Standard Reloads), Adhesive Grenade (×2) or Stun Baton

SPECIAL: Cannot be selected by characters with a Criminal Record.

POLITICIAN

Few professions are as simultaneously reviled and necessary as that of a Politician. With so many human souls and so much chaos threatening to engulf the Human Sphere at any moment, Politicians manage states, nations, whole interstellar empires. They conduct debates when the latest discovery of foreign action against their home comes to light. They work to develop and implement laws that better regulate the societies of which they are a part — or apart, if the Politician puts their own interests ahead of the people's. To work in politics is to be a fighter; it is not a profession for the faint of heart. A Politician constantly struggles for influence on their own behalf and that of their constituents. Every new campaign brings with it hostile lobbyists, rival corporate interests, and ideological nemeses, all seeking to tear the Politician's foundation out from beneath them.

ATTRIBUTES						
AGI	AWA	BRW	COO	INT	PER	WIL
+1	+2	–	+2	+2	+2	+1

SKILLS				EARNINGS
Mandatory	Persuade	Pscyhology	Discipline	2+2 Ⓝ
Elective	Education	Lifestyle	Command	

GEAR: Negotiator's Suite (3 days rental), Stims (×3)

CORVUS BELLI
INFINITY

CAREER PROFILE
REMOTE OPERATOR

Remote Operators pilot advanced combat and exploration machines. Highly advanced interface designs allow these operators to feel like they are right in the action, much like a TAG pilot. Due to their specialised training they come to know their machines as well as any pilot of a manned vehicle. Remote Operators engage in urban warfare, fighting in dense population centres where TAGs and large war-machines can't go, relying on speed, mobility, and a keen sense of the battleground. Many Remote Operators also function in a scientific capacity, piloting submersible or deep-space salvage and forensics units to carry out delicate missions in extreme environments.

ATTRIBUTES						
AGI	AWA	BRW	COO	INT	PER	WIL
+2	+2	+1	+2	+2	+1	–

SKILLS				EARNINGS
Mandatory	Pilot	Observation	Tech	2+1
Elective	Education	Hacking	Discipline	

GEAR: Armoured Clothing (Uniform, with Bioscanner), Remote Presence Gear or Spotbot, Stims (×3)

CAREER PROFILE
REVEREND AGENT

The Nomads keep secrets of their own within the Observance; a religious organisation ideologically opposed to technology domineering humanity. The Observance charge several types of Reverend Agents with the sacred duty of protecting the human race. Elite women fighting against technologically superior enemies, Reverend Moiras enact terrible vengeance upon those who have wronged the righteous. Reverend Custodiers specialise in security programming and intelligence management to wage war across the battlefields of the datasphere and operate intelligence networks. More than capable of fighting alongside their Reverend sisters, Reverend Healers perform field medicine. Reverend Agents are among the most fearsome and inspiring of soldiers to be seen on the battlefield.

ATTRIBUTES						
AGI	AWA	BRW	COO	INT	PER	WIL
+2	+2	+1	+2	+2	–	+1

SKILLS			EARNINGS
Mandatory	Extraplanetary	Athletics	Hacking	1+1
Elective	Close Combat	Ballistics	Acrobatics	

GEAR: Light Combat Armour, Vac Suit (with 2 Oxygen Loads), Assault Hacking Device or AutoMediKit, Viral Pistol or Light Shotgun
SPECIAL: Prerequisite (Nomads Faction)

CAREER PROFILE
SHIP CREW

Millions upon millions of ships fill the interplanetary routes of the Human Sphere. While a few, such as some employed by the AI ALEPH, can operate autonomously, the vast majority require skilled crew. Intrepid crewmembers keep their ships running both in and out of battle. A good crew is worth more than good upgrades, especially in a pinch. Ship Crew tends to form tight bonds with one another and with the ship itself, working in tandem to achieve victory. A wide variety of experience lends ship crew members a versatile set of skills: they have zero-g training, most acquire significant technical skills, and many have been in more than their share of scrapes. As a result, crew members tend to be some of the toughest and most experienced travellers in any system.

ATTRIBUTES						
AGI	AWA	BRW	COO	INT	PER	WIL
+1	+2	+1	+3	+2	–	+1

SKILLS			EARNINGS
Mandatory	Survival	Tech	Extraplanetary	2+1
Elective	Science	Spacecraft	Ballistics	

GEAR: Vac Suit (with 5 Oxygen Loads), Powered Multitool, Repair Kit

CAREER PROFILE
SMUGGLER

Smuggling is a lucrative but highly dangerous career. Skilled Smugglers slip past the constant vigil of advanced nations with weapons and industrial secrets to sell to competitors. Contraband reaches every world with a demand for it, brought in by crafty Smugglers. Scoundrels who smuggle objects from or perhaps through the territories of powerful leaders fetch a high bounty, but they are highly skilled in evading trouble, understanding the behaviour and methods of law enforcement, and above all, covering their own retreat.

ATTRIBUTES						
AGI	AWA	BRW	COO	INT	PER	WIL
+2	+2	+2	+1	+2	+1	–

SKILLS			EARNINGS
Mandatory	Pilot	Observation	Thivery	0+4 Ⓝ
Elective	Tech	Hacking	Discipline	

GEAR: Adhesive Grenade or Banshee Grenade, Smoke Grenade (×2), AR Eye Implants or Long ModCoat

SPECIAL: Criminal Career

CAREER PROFILE
SPECIAL FORCES

The most elite soldiers in the Human Sphere carry out spec ops missions across known space… and sometimes upon unknown worlds. Special Forces units operate in covert missions of international warfare, hunting down war criminals, striking important assets, and retreating before anyone can blame their acting governments. These elite units also carry out the most difficult ops in the war for Paradiso, attacking Combined Army commanders and bases, rescuing allies caught far behind enemy lines, and countering the threat of elite enemy units. Governments deploy Special Forces when discretion is needed—all too common in the shadow warfare fought between nations of the Human Sphere—and when regular mercenaries or law enforcement simply aren't enough. A Special Forces soldier receives the finest training, equipment, and most important missions, demanding as much from themselves as their people do.

ATTRIBUTES						
AGI	AWA	BRW	COO	INT	PER	WIL
+2	+2	+2	+1	+1`	–	+2

SKILLS			EARNINGS
Mandatory	Survival	Resistance	Ballistics	2+1 Ⓝ
Elective	Close Combat	Hacking	Discipline	

GEAR: Medium Combat Armour, Combi Rifle or AP Rifle (with 5 Standard Reloads), Climbing Plus or Combat Jump Pack, Garrotte

CAREER PROFILE
SPORTS PERSONALITY

Sporting events are a time-honoured tradition of competition between cities, countries, even whole worlds. The greatest sports stars are legends, heroes to their people, larger than life. They possess a sway and a swagger that few political leaders can match, all stemming from their ability to perform incredible athletic feats. With the advances in genetic engineering, wetware implants, and cybernetics, professional athletes boast physiques and abilities the common person can only imagine. A Sports Personality could be a rising star of Dog-Bowl or the Aristeia! Underground. Champions of these bone-breaking contests and professional duels can rise from humble roots to touch immortal fame. Sports Personalities can bear the colours and face of a nation, quest only for the next adrenaline rush, or hunt for personal glory.

ATTRIBUTES						
AGI	AWA	BRW	COO	INT	PER	WIL
+2	+2	+1	–	+1	+2	+2

SKILLS			EARNINGS
Mandatory	Athletics	Persuade	Close Combat	1+3 Ⓝ
Elective	Acrobatics	Athletics	Ballistics	

GEAR: Biografted Attribute Augmentation 2 or Super-Jump, Uniform

TAG PILOT

TAG (Tactical Armoured Gear) units command a presence on the battlefield with their hulking armour platforms. One part personal tank and one part weapons arrays, TAGs turn pilots into one-person armies. They bear heavy firepower and tremendous strength. Pilots thus develop a certain confidence born of the machines they so skilfully command. TAG Pilots often fight on the front lines against the Combined Army, or lead forays into enemy territory when stealth and subtlety are lost. TAG Pilots command some of the deadliest forces on the battlefield and they know it. Most are all too happy to show off their skills, eager for the kind of victory only TAGs can bring.

ATTRIBUTES						
AGI	AWA	BRW	COO	INT	PER	WIL
+2	+2	+1	+2	+2	–	+1

SKILLS			EARNINGS
Mandatory	Pilot	Tech	Ballistics	2+1 Ⓝ
Elective	Discipline	Extraplanetary	Survival	

GEAR: Armoured Clothing (Uniform), Inlaid Palm Circuitry or AR Eye Implants, Pistol (with 2 Reloads)

TECHNICIAN

The Technician possesses skills desired all across the Human Sphere. Technology-dependent nations like PanOceania need Technicians to keep industry booming. Backwater worlds and gleaming metropolises alike need technical knowledge, whether the Technician is servicing farm equipment or the latest model of racing cars. Nomads employ Technicians to salvage, jury-rig, and dismantle their gains. Their colossal motherships exist in a state of constant repair and modification, with Technicians working beneath cascades of welding sparks, stringing cable throughout the hulls, and finding ingenious ways to recycle scrap. PanOceanian and Yu Jing techs produce the latest and greatest models of vehicles and weaponry, working to ensure their nation's continued dominance in the intergalactic arena. Ariadnan Technicians possess unrivalled skills in field-testing and repairing rugged equipment, despite their lack of the most modern advances.

ATTRIBUTES						
AGI	AWA	BRW	COO	INT	PER	WIL
+2	+2	+1	+2	–	+1	+2

SKILLS			EARNINGS
Mandatory	Tech	Pilot	Hacking	1+1 Ⓝ
Elective	Observation	Resistance	Discipline	

GEAR: Powered Multitool, Repair Kit (with 5 Parts), Stims (×1)

TERRAFORMING SCIENTIST

Terraforming Scientists help transform new worlds into places much more fit for human habitation. Terraforming is an expensive and time-consuming process, so only the brightest minds oversee the work. Characters in this profession possess a wide variety of scientific knowledge, from geology, climatology, and biology, to engineering and chemistry degrees. A Terraforming Scientist is usually adventurous, as they must brave alien environments filled with dangerous flora and fauna. Every new world is a potential gold mine of resources. A Terraforming Scientist must be ambitious and persistent in order to prosper. She has probably seen stranger things than most, living out on the frontier. Terraforming Scientists are often more rugged than lab-bound folk, though it'd be a mistake to doubt their academic prowess.

ATTRIBUTES						
AGI	AWA	BRW	COO	INT	PER	WIL
–	+2	+1	+3	+2	+1	–

SKILLS			EARNINGS
Mandatory	Science	Education	Observation	2+1 Ⓝ
Elective	Pilot	Tech	Extraplanetary	

GEAR: Survival Kit, Analytical Kit (with 5 Reagents), Sensor Suite or Recorder

TRADER

Trade is the lifeblood of the Human Sphere. Nomads know it better than anyone. Because of their unique lifestyle, trading has become an art for them, maximising the gains in value for as little as they can trade in return. Other Traders make a living on the frontier, conducting business with settlers and miners, frequenting planetary bazaars where a skilled Trader can find anything for the right price. Some trade honestly with one hand and reach for the valuables with the other, like traders conducting business with Ariadna to bring them the latest in technological wonders... while also looking for ways to strip whatever resources they can manage. Haqqislam caravanserai serve as giant hubs of trade, where buyers can find and acquire (or offload) nearly anything for the right price.

ATTRIBUTES						
AGI	AWA	BRW	COO	INT	PER	WIL
+1	+2	+1	+1	+2	+3	–

SKILLS			EARNINGS
Mandatory	Persuade	Pscychology	Discipline	1+2 Ⓝ
Elective	Pilot	Education	Lifestayle	

GEAR: Long ModCoat (with Survival Kit and Bottled Water), Cosmetics Kit

DECISION NINE: FINAL CUSTOMISATION

As you complete your final career, you are at the cusp of beginning play. As you perform the final adjustments and calculations which will finish your character, give some thought to what brought you from your last job to where you are now.

For example, if your group is playing as a direct action team for Bureau Noir, did you apply for work with them? If so, why? Or did they actively recruit you? Did you get tangled up in one of their ops and then brought in when the chaos died down? What unique skills or connections made you an appealing recruit for them? Or maybe you were already working for them during your last career. If so, how did your last career event bring you where you are now?

STEP ONE: FINAL TWEAKS
- Set your Infinity Point refresh rate to two.
- You may increase any one attribute by two or any two attributes by one each.
- You may increase two skills from Focus 0 to Focus 1 or Expertise 0 to Expertise 1.
- You may choose one talent for any of your skills.
- You have starting Assets equal to your final Personality score (plus any additional Assets gained during your Lifepath).
- If your character has not gained a character trait through the event tables, decide on a trait now. (See *Traits* on p. 39.)

STEP TWO: SPEND REMAINING LIFE POINTS
- You may spend 1 Life Point to increase your Infinity Point refresh rate by one point, up to a maximum of four. (This will increase the number of Infinity Points you start with at the beginning of each session.)
- You may convert any number of Life Points to Assets on a one-for-one basis.
- You may convert any number of Life Points to ranks of training in a skill on a one-for-one basis, but no Skill Focus or Expertise may be increased more than one in this way.
- You may spend 1 Life Point to either gain 1d6 rolls on the *Random Languages Table* (p. 45) or gain one specific language of your choice.

STEP THREE: STRESS
A character's Stress track determines how long they can stand up under quantronic, psychological, and physical assaults.
- **Firewall** is equal to Intelligence + Hacking Expertise.
- **Resolve** is equal to Willpower + Discipline Expertise.
- **Vigour** is equal to Brawn + Resistance Expertise.

STEP FOUR: BONUS DAMAGE
Characters with above-average attributes have the potential to inflict bonus damage with their attacks. The *Bonus Damage Table* shows the amount of bonus damage a character inflicts with their attacks, depending on the associated attribute.

ATTRIBUTES		BONUS DMG	
TYPE OF ATTACK	ASSOCIATED ATTRIBUTE	ATTRIBUTE	BONUS
Infowar	Intelligence	8 or less	None
Psywar	Personality	9	+1 🅝
Melee	Brawn	10–11	+2 🅝
Ranged	Awareness	12–13	+3 🅝
		14–15	+4 🅝
		16+	+5 🅝

STEP FIVE: GEAR
You may spend your Assets to immediately purchase additional equipment, or you can choose to save your Assets for later use. All characters start with a comlog. All non-Ariadnan characters (or Ariadnan characters who have been Resurrected on the Lifepath) start with Cubes and also receive a free, basic geist, which you can update by spending additional Assets (see *Supporting Cast*, on the next page).

STEP SIX: AGING (OPTIONAL)
In a cinematic world, age really means nothing. And that's even more true in the world of *Infinity* where advanced genetic therapies and anti-agathic treatments have been made possible through the wonders of biotechnology. However, if you would like age to have some impact on your character (perhaps they're an Atek, old school Ariadnan, or simply bioconservative) you can use this optional rule.

When a character reaches the age of 30, and every three years thereafter, roll 1 🅝. If an Effect is rolled, roll 2d6 on the *Aging Table* and reduce the resulting attribute modifier of your host by one. (This also has the effect of reducing the current value of your attribute.) You can spend 1 Asset to reroll your aging test (representing some corrective medical procedure).

EXAMPLE
FINAL CUSTOMISATION
Melissa sets Cassandra's Infinity Point refresh rate to two. She increases her Intelligence by two points (to 12). She bumps the Focus on her Ballistics and Stealth skills to 1 and chooses a Stealth talent. Her final Personality score is 7, so adds the 6 Assets she gained during the Lifepath and sets her starting Assets at 13. She already has several character traits, so she doesn't need to add one.

Melissa has 2 Life Points remaining. She chooses to spend 1 Life Point to increase Cassandra's Infinity Point refresh rate to 3. She also decides that Cassandra's bounty hunting has taken her across the Human Sphere, so she spends the other Life Point to roll 1d6 twice on the *Random Languages Table*, revealing that Cassandra now speaks Italian and Vietnamese. (She'll have to give some thought to how that happened.)

Melissa then calculates her Firewall (12+0), Resolve (10+0), and Vigour (11+1). Then she consults the *Bonus Damage Table* and records her four bonus damage values.

AGING TABLE	
2D6	ATTRIBUTE
2	Intelligence
3	Willpower
4–5	Agility
6–7	Brawn
8–9	Coordination
10–11	Awareness
12	Personality

SUPPORTING CAST

No man is an island. As you've followed your character's Lifepath you've most likely encountered their friends, family, enemies, allies, and acquaintances. As you're filling in the gaps, there are a few specific connections you'll want to pay particular attention to.

RELATIONSHIPS

The *Relationship Table* can be used to discover the relationships you have with other player characters. Roll 1d20 and check the table. You can pick one of the other characters in the group to have this relationship with or determine it randomly.

RELATIONSHIP TABLE

D20	RELATIONSHIP
1	Your parents had some secretive business together. They all disappeared on the same night and you became friends as you tried to find out what happened to them.
2	You were both betrayed by a mutual friend or professional contact. What happened and how are you going to make them pay?
3	You were both on a small orbital that suffered a complete environmental collapse (due to meteor strike, system failure, contamination, or the like). You helped each other escape.
4	A mysterious malfunction stranded you together (100 floors up in a lift, on a deserted island, in a rail car on a broken down train, etc.) and you've been friends ever since.
5	You live together.
6	You were both briefly arrested and put in the same cell. Were you guilty of the charges or was it all a misunderstanding? Though you were released without charge, you'd already come to a mutual understanding.
7	You've been assigned to work together by your current employers, but you have this odd feeling that you've met before.
8	Someone suspects that there's a mole or a traitor in your group. You've been assigned to make friends with one of them and are ordered to report the first sign of criminal or suspicious behaviour.
9	You both met in a bar fight. You were the only two left standing.
10	You met on a previous contract. What went wrong?
11	Your families were (or are) bitter enemies.
12	You were in a bad relationship and they helped you get out of it.
13	They remind you of someone you used to know. Who? And why?
14	They used to be your boss.
15	They screwed up and you got hurt. Maybe it's not really their fault, but you don't really trust them anymore.
16	ALEPH recommended that the two of you should meet. It has refused to explain why.
17	You owe them a lot of money. How did you get in over your head? Did they bail you out, or are they holding something over you?
18	They saved your life and you've never been able to figure out how to repay them for that.
19	They know a secret about you that you've never told anyone else. What is it? And how do they know it?
20	You both belong to the same esoteric Maya fandom.

FACTION HANDLER

If you're playing in a Wilderness of Mirrors campaign, you'll most likely have a handler who delivers your covert objectives. Work with your GM to develop your handler.

- How did you meet them?
- What do they look like?
- How do they send you instructions? (There may be multiple methods.)
- What's your contact protocol? How do you get in touch with them?
- What resources do they have access to?
- Who do they answer to?
- What is their (or their organisation's) agenda?
- Are you a member of their organisation? A freelancer? A civilian asset?

It's also possible that you're being handled by a committee. Or perhaps the entire exchange is anonymously handled through a double blind so that, for security reasons, you have no idea who you're ultimately answering to.

GEIST

Geists are pseudo-AIs who act as companions and quantronic assistants. (They are also referred to as domotic partners, domótica, hantu, QPAs (quantronic personal assistants), VPGs (virtual personal guides), and a wide variety of cute nicknames.) Basically everyone in the Human Sphere has one. In fact, most people have had the same geist since they were very young children. Over time, a geist learns your habits and preferences, usually becoming so familiar with you that they can seamlessly predict what you want (sometimes before you even realise it yourself). They become invisible extensions of their partner's will. Their persistent presence and collaboration in every facet of a person's life is a transformative experience. Life without your geist watching over you would be difficult for most people to imagine.

Things a geist will do for you:
- Anticipate your daily needs and arrange for automated services to fulfil them.
- Perform research for you.
- Monitor and maintain your Firewall.
- Coordinate your social mesh.
- Scan Maya channels for search keywords.
- Manage AR support interfaces (like live translation, navigation, etc.).

Most people run an instantiation of their geist on their comlog. Others have their geist running on a remote server and simply communicate with them via Maya. Some people prefer to load their geist into a TinBot or other remote platform in order to have them physically present.

BASIC GEIST

All non-Ariadnan characters begin play with a basic geist. (Ariadnan characters can purchase a geist for themselves if they wish, but they are not yet common on Dawn.) You can upgrade your geist like any other piece of equipment (see *Part IV: Gear*, p. 350), but even a basic geist has a unique personality shaped by the time they've spent with their owner. In addition to customising their stat block, as shown below, you should also consider what their AR avatar is (their "physical" appearance in augmented or virtual reality) and what their personality is like.

Customising Your Geist: Choose two of your geist's attributes and increase them by one point each. Then add four ranks to any combination of your geist's skills.

GEIST

BASIC GEIST

ATTRIBUTES						
AGI	AWA	BRW	COO	INT	PER	WIL
4	4	4	4	4	4	4

SKILLS
Any 4 ranks

DEFENCES					
Firewall	*	Resolve	4	Vigour	–
Security	–	Morale	–	Soak	0

*Per owner

CHARACTER ADVANCEMENT

One of the more exciting aspects of a roleplaying game is watching the development and growth of a player character over the course of a campaign. Players in *Infinity* have a number of options available to them in order to develop and customise their characters.

GAINING EXPERIENCE POINTS

After each game session, the GM should award experience points (XP) to each player character.

Base Award: Everyone in the group should receive 300–500 XP based on the amount of progress they've achieved, their level of teamwork, their primary mission goals accomplished, and how well they roleplayed their characters.

Faction Goals: Completing a Wilderness of Mirrors faction goal should be worth 50–100 XP depending on their complexity and difficulty.

Bonus Awards: In addition, based on individual accomplishments or achievements, the GM should award a small amount of bonus experience points to each player character. Each individual award should be 25–50 XP, and the GM should generally award no more than 100 bonus XP to any one player.

OPTIONAL RULE

GEIST ON YOUR LEFT

Most people in the Human Sphere are continuously interacting with their geist from the time they wake up until the time they go to bed. But if you're roleplaying both your character and your character's geist, it can get awkward if you're constantly talking to yourself. As an option, therefore, we recommend that each player hand their character's geist to the player on their left. That means you'll be simultaneously running your own character and the geist of the player to your right.

Geist Briefing Sheet: Prepping a roleplaying template for your geist can be a very effective way to let the player to your left know what your geist is like. It can also be a useful tool for making the geist's personality distinct from the player character's.

Splitting with Geists: This can also make it easier to split the party because many or all of the players who aren't present may still have a geist to play.

INVESTING EXPERIENCE POINTS

Improve Attributes: To improve a character's attribute by one point, spend XP equal to 100 times the new value of the attribute. For example, raising Brawn from 7 to 8 costs 800 XP. An attribute cannot be increased above 16.

Improve Skills: To improve a character's Skill Expertise or Skill Focus, spend XP equal to 200 times the new ranking. Each type of training (Expertise or Focus) must be acquired separately. A character's Focus in a skill can never be higher than their Expertise. For example, if a character has Expertise 1 and Focus 1 in Tech, they would need to spend 400 XP to improve to Tech Expertise 2 before they could spend an additional 400 XP to improve their Tech Focus to 2.

A character cannot increase their Expertise or Focus in a skill above 3 unless that skill is a signature skill (which cannot be increased above 5).

Acquiring Talents: Talents are acquired from the top down, meaning a character must acquire the top-most talent before those deeper in the tree become available. Some talents also have additional prerequisites (usually a certain number of Expertise ranks in the skill) that must be met before it can be selected. The first talent in any tree costs 200 XP. Other talents on the tree cost 200 XP for each step away from the first talent. (A step measures the talent's distance from the starting talent and is based on the number of arrows or spaces it takes to draw a path back to that first talent.) Having Focus in a skill, however, represents an intense dedication and a deep, specialised understanding of that skill. Reduce the cost to acquire any talent by 50 XP per level of Focus the character has in that skill, to a minimum cost of 50 XP.

Character Traits: Gaining a new character trait costs 200 XP and requires GM approval. The new trait should flow naturally out of the character's experiences.

Removing a character trait is generally more difficult. In general, the cost to permanently remove a character trait is 800 XP, although the GM may require additional actions to be taken before the XP can be spent. (For example, it might require restorative surgery to remove an Old War Wound.)

In some cases, the GM may waive the XP cost if the situation described by the character trait has been completely resolved during a session. (For example, if a character has Nemesis: Clara Jamieson as a character trait and they kill Clara Jamieson, the GM may allow them to simply remove the trait.)

In many cases, however, the GM may find it more appropriate to change the trait instead of removing it. (For example, if a character is killed, resurrected, and placed in a Lhost, their Old War Wound may become Awkward Body Syndrome. Upon killing Clara Jamieson they may discover that Nemesis: Clara Jamieson has become Vengeance of the Jamieson Clan.)

Learning Language: A character can learn a new language for 50 XP.

OPTIONAL RULE
HEATED EXPERIENCE

Instead of awarding an ad hoc base award, the GM can instead choose to award 10 XP per spent Heat to a maximum of 500 XP per session. (Additional bonus awards can still be offered normally.) In other words, player characters only learn from their experiences when the stakes are high and the heat is on!

This optional rule marginally increases bookkeeping for the GM, but it also gives the players an incentive to generate Heat. It encourages the player characters to push themselves to the edge, because it's only when you're pushing yourself to your limits that you can find out what you're capable of.

EXAMPLE
ACQUIRING TALENTS

Cassandra has already gained the Stealth talents of Scout (the first talent in the tree) and Living Shadow. After gaining some XP, she considers acquiring the Infiltration talent. As shown in the talent tree on p. 93, Infiltration is two steps away from Scout, so it would normally cost 400 XP (2 × 200 XP). However, Cassandra has Stealth Focus 1, which reduces the cost to 350 XP. Infiltration, however, had a prerequisite of Stealth Expertise 2 and she only has Stealth Expertise 1. She decides to get Camouflage instead, which is one step away from Scout and costs her 150 XP (200 XP – 50 XP).

CASSANDRA THE BOUNTY HUNTER

Faction: Mercenary
Heritage: PanOceania
Homeworld/Homeland: Svalarheima
Social Status: Demogrant
Age: 29

INFINITY POINTS		

ATTRIBUTES

AGI	AWA	BRW	COO	INT	PER	WIL
12	8	11	8	12	7	10

SKILLS

SKILL	EXP	FOC	SIG	SKILL	EXP	FOC	SIG
Acrobatics	2	0		Observation	2	0	
Athletics	3	2	•	Resistance	1	0	
Ballistics	3	2	•	Stealth	1	1	
Close Combat	1	1		Survival	1	1	
Education	1	0		Tech	3	1	•

STRESS

Vigour									
Resolve									
Firewall									

BONUS DAMAGE

Infowar Bonus	+3 ⓝ	Melee Bonus	+2 ⓝ
Psywar Bonus	+0	Ranged Bonus	+0

TALENTS
Rigorous Training (Athletics), Marksman (Ballistics), Clear Shot (Ballistics), Scout (Stealth), Living Shadow (Stealth)

TRAITS
Orphan, Criminal Record, Relentless Nemesis

EARNINGS
3

ASSETS
13

LANGUAGES
German, Italian, SvalarNorse, Vietnamese

GEAR
Armoured Clothing (Uniform), Medium Combat Armour, Pistol, Heavy Pistol (with 4 Reloads), Rifle, Knife, SecurCuffs, Stims (×3)

CHARACTERS
SKILLS AND TALENTS

Skills represent a character's training, knowledge, and proficiency. They are acquired through study, practice, and experience. Skills are ranked by both Skill Expertise and Skill Focus.

Talents are a further specialisation in a particular skill. They represent distinctive prowess, tricks of the trade, and uncommon mastery of specific tasks. Each skill has a unique talent tree, with different options for a specialist to pursue.

ACROBATICS (AGILITY)
This skill is a measure of body control, covering whole-body movements such as jumping, tumbling, and diving. Attempts to dodge enemy attacks also fall under Acrobatics.

ACROBATIC TALENTS

Talent tree:
- GRACEFUL
  - LONG JUMPER
    - CATFALL
      - ROLL WITH IT
  - FREE RUNNER
  - TOTAL REACTION
    - SIXTH SENSE

CATFALL
Prerequisite: Long Jumper, Acrobatics Expertise 2
Maximum Ranks: 3
The character has learned to take advantage of wind resistance and surface conditions when making a landing. For every rank of Catfall, the character treats the distance fallen as being one zone shorter when calculating damage.

FREE RUNNER
Prerequisite: Graceful
Maximum Ranks: 3
A free runner trains to recognise the environment and let their body move naturally in response to it, taking advantage of what the terrain offers them. For every rank of Free Runner, the character reduces the difficulty of Acrobatics tests to move through, past, or over obstacles and hindering terrain by one step, to a minimum of Simple (D0).

GRACEFUL
Prerequisite: Acrobatics Expertise 1
The character may reroll one d20 when making an Acrobatics test, but must accept the new result.

LONG JUMPER
Prerequisite: Graceful
The character is able to leap extraordinary distances. When making an Acrobatics test to jump, the character reduces the difficulty by one rank, to a minimum of Simple (D0).

ROLL WITH IT
Prerequisite: Catfall
When the character fails a Defence test against a melee attack or a ranged attack with the Area or Indiscriminate qualities, they gain additional Cover Soak equal to the character's Acrobatics Focus.

SIXTH SENSE
Prerequisite: Total Reaction, Acrobatics Expertise 2
The character has a natural sense for when their life might be endangered. They can make a Defence Reaction against any ranged or melee attacks, including ones they might not have any immediately apparent reason to know about. (They must still pay the normal Heat cost for taking a reaction.)

TOTAL REACTION
Prerequisite: Graceful
Maximum Ranks: 3
During combat, the character is in a constant state of fluid motion, making it difficult to hit them with

Skill Expertise, p. 29: A character's Expertise in a skill is their mastery of the subject.

Skill Focus, p. 29: A character's Focus in a skill is achieved through constant practice, superior discipline, and deeper insight.

SIGNATURE SKILLS
Signature skills represent areas where a character particularly excels. Once selected during character creation, signature skills cannot be changed. Although characters are normally limited to an Expertise and Focus in a skill of three ranks each, for a signature skill this limit is increased to five ranks each.

ACROBATIC TIPS
Common Uses: Evading an opponent, tightrope walking, landing safely after a fall.

Common Difficulty Factors: Terrain, Distraction, Encumbrance, Poor Oxygen, Gravity

ranged attacks. When they take a Defence Reaction against ranged attacks, each rank of Total Reaction counts as an additional point of Acrobatics Focus. (This can increase the character's effective Acrobatics Focus above its normal limits. For example, their effective Focus may be higher than their Acrobatics Expertise.)

ANALYSIS (AWARENESS)

The Analysis skill doesn't cover the acquisition of information, but it does cover the myriad ways in which it can be parsed, combined, studied, interpreted, audited, and generally evaluated for valuable intel. In addition to yanking key insights out of any bundle of raw or streaming data, Analysis also includes all forms of pattern recognition, from basic code-breaking to discerning human behaviour, and determining details from small clues.

ANALYSIS TIPS

Common Uses: Studying data, analysing communications traffic, code breaking, behavioural analysis, accounting

Common Difficulty Factors: Corrupted Data, Misinformation, Distraction, Limited Time

ANALYSIS TALENTS

```
            PATTERN
          RECOGNITION
         /            \
   CODE BREAKER    MICROSCOPIC
                     THREATS
      /                     \
    NEW                   DATA ANALYSIS
 PERSPECTIVE
    |                         |
  COMBAT                 INFORMATION
 ANALYSIS                INTEGRATION
```

CODE BREAKER
Prerequisite: Pattern Recognition
Maximum Ranks: 3
The character has developed an uncanny insight into cryptographic patterns and the quantronic tools required to crack them. When making an Analysis test related to cryptography, the character reduces the difficulty by one per rank of Code Breaker, to a minimum of Simple (D0).

COMBAT ANALYSIS
Prerequisite: New Perspective, Analysis Expertise 2
During combat, the character may attempt an Average (D1) Analysis test as a Minor Action. On a success, they can identify one special power, hidden piece of equipment, technological advantage, alien ability, or similar effect that an opponent has in use. Each Momentum spent allows the character to recognise one additional effect.

DATA ANALYSIS
Prerequisite: Pattern Recognition
Maximum Ranks: 2
When analysing data, the character enters a fugue state. Each rank of Data Analysis counts as an additional point of Analysis Focus. This can increase the character's effective Analysis Focus above its normal limits.

ANIMAL HANDLING TIPS

Common Uses: Controlling animals that are confused, scared, or startled; understanding animal behaviours

Common Difficulty Factors: Distraction, Unfamiliarity, Complexity

INFORMATION INTEGRATION
Prerequisite: Data Analysis, Analysis Expertise 2
The character is skilled at rapidly collating and integrating information from a team of assistants. When analysing data as a teamwork test, those assisting the character may roll two d20 each, instead of being limited to a single d20.

MICROSCOPIC THREATS
Prerequisite: Pattern Recognition
Maximum Ranks: 2
The character has a knack for recognizing the subtle clues of biological, chemical, nanonic, and similar threats. Whenever the character is in the presence of biohazards that would be protected by BTS — even if the character is not aware of it — the GM should call for the character to make a Challenging (D2) Analysis test. On a success, the character recognises the presence of the threat and may spend Momentum to identify protective measures against said threat. Every Momentum spent increases BTS by 1 against that attack for the remainder of the scene. A second rank of Microscopic Threats reduces the difficulty of this check to Average (D1).

NEW PERSPECTIVE
Prerequisite: Pattern Recognition
The character can intuitively analyse the world around them. They may substitute their Analysis skill for Observation for any task which is not a split second reaction.

PATTERN RECOGNITION
Prerequisite: Analysis Expertise 1
The character may reroll one d20 when making an Analysis test, but must accept the new result.

ANIMAL HANDLING (PERSONALITY)

This skill governs a character's ability to care for, train, and work with domesticated animals, including riding mounts, security animals, and rescue animals. The skill also provides an understanding of wild animals and a knowledge of how to interact with them safely.

Commanding Animals: Issuing a command to a trained animal is a Simple (D0) test and thus usually does not require a dice roll. Untrained animals generally won't respond to specific commands (although some non-terrestrial animals are particularly clever), but an Animal Handling test can generally influence their behaviour. This takes one minute of effort and the effects of a successful test will last for ten minutes, plus an additional ten minutes per Momentum spent.

Animals in Combat: Issuing commands to a trained animal in combat is a Minor Action that requires an Average (D1) test. Untrained animals cannot be controlled in combat — they will act purely on instinct.

Animal Reaction: Particularly wilful animals may attempt a Reaction to resist efforts to control them, opposing the Animal Handling test with the creature's Discipline test.

ANIMAL HANDLING TALENTS

ANIMAL HEALER

Prerequisite: Symbiosis, Animal Handling Expertise 2
Any time the character is called upon to make a Medicine test upon an animal, they may instead use their Animal Handling skill. Characters with this talent may also substitute their Animal Handling skill for Medicine tests upon humans, but make such tests at +1 difficulty.

FIRM HAND

Prerequisite: Recognise Cues, Animal Handling Expertise 2
The character has experience with animals that are resistant to training. Any time the character attempts to direct an animal to take an action that goes against its instinct or training — including if the animal is in service to another — any Momentum spent to add extra dice to the skill test add two d20s to the dice pool instead of one. (The normal maximum of three bonus d20s still applies.)

RECOGNISE CUES

Prerequisite: Wild Empathy
The character has come to recognise when and how an animal is reacting to their environment. Any time the character is in the company of animals and needs to make an Observation test, they may substitute their Animal Handling skill instead. This includes active searches if the character can use an animal to aid in the search.

SMELLS RIGHT

Prerequisite: Firm Hand
Any time the character encounters a new animal, they make an Average (D1) Observation test as a Minor Action. On a success, the animal immediately considers them a friend. If the target is a guard

animal, it does not alert its handlers to the character's presence.

STRONG RIDER

Prerequisite: Wild Empathy
The character is particularly adept at riding mounts. When making a skill test to ride an animal, the character reduces the difficulty by one rank. This may eliminate the need for the skill check.

SYMBIOSIS

Prerequisite: Wild Empathy
The character is particularly adept at recognising the needs of their animal companions. Any time the character succeeds on a Survival test, they automatically also find food and shelter for their animal companions. (Note that the presence of animals does not increase the difficulty of the test for characters with this talent.)

WILD EMPATHY

Prerequisite: Animal Handling Expertise 1
Maximum Ranks: 3
Having spent much of their lives in the company of animals, the character can quickly recognise personality quirks and sources of distress. On any Animal Handling test where the character generates at least one success, they may immediately roll an additional number of bonus d20s equal to their ranks in Wild Empathy. Any successes generated on these additional dice are added to the initial success total and complications on these additional dice may be ignored.

ATHLETICS (BRAWN)

This skill is a measure of how well a character can apply their overall body strength and endurance. Examples using Athletics include lifting objects, breaking down doors, swimming, climbing, or running.

ATHLETICS TALENTS

CLIFF DWELLER

Prerequisite: Rigorous Training
Maximum Ranks: 3
The endless hours of climbing have made vertical surfaces a natural environment for the character. The character never suffers from vertigo or a fear of heights. In addition, they may reduce the difficulty

ATHLETICS TIPS
Common Uses: Climbing, swimming, running, wrestling, races, kicking down doors, lifting weights

Common Difficulty Factors: Terrain, Distraction, Encumbrance, Poor Oxygen

immediately roll a number of bonus d20s equal to their ranks in Leverage. Any successes generated on these additional dice are added to the initial success total and complications on these additional dice may be ignored.

RIGOROUS TRAINING
Prerequisite: Athletics Expertise 1
Maximum Ranks: 3
The character is exceptionally athletic and physically gifted. For each rank of Rigorous Training, the character generates 1 bonus Momentum on any Athletics test.

STRONG GRIP
Prerequisite: Irresistible Force
The character never drops or surrenders an object unless they have chosen to do so. They are immune to any attempt to forcibly disarm them or otherwise knock a weapon or other held object from their hands.

STRONG SWIMMER
Prerequisite: Rigorous Training
Maximum Ranks: 3
The character is a prodigious swimmer. He reduces the difficulty of any swimming test by one step per rank of Strong Swimmer to a minimum of Simple (D0).

WALL CRAWLER
Prerequisite: Cliff Dweller, Athletics Expertise 2
The character has learned to climb comfortably without equipment, even while carrying significant burdens. They never suffer any penalty for climbing without proper equipment. Furthermore, if rope, harness, or other climbing equipment is available, they can add a bonus d20 to their Athletics test.

BALLISTICS (COORDINATION)
This skill is used for firefights. It covers the use and maintenance of ranged weapons, as well as familiarity with the damage they inflict. It includes both hand-held weaponry and heavy weapons (including vehicle-mounted weapons).

BALLISTIC TIPS
Common Uses: See *Warfare* (p. 107); identifying weapons based on the sound of their fire or physical inspection; studying the wounds or other evidence left by such weapons

Common Difficulty Factors: Distance, Unfamiliarity, Complexity, Poor Equipment

of any climbing test by one step per rank of Cliff Dweller, to a minimum of Simple (D0).

IRRESISTIBLE FORCE
Prerequisite: Leverage, Athletics Expertise 2
The character gains the weapon quality Knockdown on all melee attacks.

LEVERAGE
Prerequisite: Rigorous Training
Maximum Ranks: 3
Due to a combination of training and technique, the character is able to perform feats of strength that seem at odds with their physique. On any test to lift or move an inanimate object where the character generates at least one success, they may

BALLISTICS TALENTS

```
              MARKSMAN
                 |
   +-------------+-------------+
   |             |             |
QUICK DRAW  THROUGH AND    CLEAR SHOT
             THROUGH           |
   |                      PRECISE SHOT
SPEED LOADER
   |
DOUBLE TAP
```

CLEAR SHOT

Prerequisite: Marksman

The character reduces the penalty for firing at a range other than the weapon's optimal range by one step (to a minimum of 0).

DOUBLE TAP

Prerequisite: Speed Loader
Maximum Ranks: 2

If the character succeeds at a ranged attack and spends Momentum or an Infinity Point to make another attack with the same weapon against the same target, the difficulty of the attack is decreased by one step, to a minimum of Average (D1). Double Tap can only be used once per turn per rank in the talent.

MARKSMAN

Prerequisite: Ballistics Expertise 1

When making a ranged attack, a character with this talent may reroll a number of damage dice equal to the number of Ballistics talents they have acquired. (As normal, each die may only be rerolled once.)

PRECISE SHOT

Prerequisite: Clear Shot, Ballistics Expertise 2

When spending Momentum for a Called Shot with a ranged attack it only costs 1 Momentum (instead of two).

QUICK DRAW

Prerequisite: Marksman

The character is always prepared for a firefight. They can draw a weapon or other item as a Free Action (instead of a Minor Action) and do not need to have a weapon in their hand in order to respond to attacks. As long as they have a free hand and a weapon within Reach, they can always make a Close Combat test as part of a Defence or Guard Reaction. This can only be done once per turn, although when the Quick Draw action is taken the character can draw a different item into each hand (in order to dual wield pistols, for example). This talent exists for both the Ballistics and Close Combat skill, and if it is purchased for either skill it can be used as a prerequisite for talents in the other skill.

SPEED LOADER

Prerequisite: Quick Draw, Ballistics Expertise 2

The character can disassemble and reassemble their weapon and its components with little thought. During combat, they may spend a Minor Action to increase their rate of fire, allowing them to count the weapon's Burst as one higher than its listed value. They can also swap ammo loads in any weapon as a Free Action. This talent cannot be used with weapons which have the Munitions quality.

THROUGH AND THROUGH

Prerequisite: Marksman
Maximum Ranks: 3

When the character spends Momentum on a Secondary Target effect for a ranged attack it only costs 1 Momentum (instead of two). In addition, the character can use this Momentum spend a number of times equal to their ranks of Through and Through on any given attack.

CLOSE COMBAT (AGILITY)

This skill governs the ability to hit targets within Reach with hand-held weaponry and with the character's own body. This includes objects intended for this purpose — such as knives or swords — but also improvised weaponry like metal bars, barstools, and broken beer bottles.

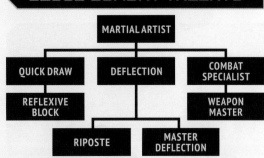

COMBAT SPECIALIST

Prerequisite: Martial Artist

Each point of Momentum or Heat the character pays to gain additional dice for a Close Combat test provides two dice instead of one. (The normal maximum of three bonus d20s still applies.)

DEFLECTION

Prerequisite: Martial Artist

Characters with this talent reduce the Heat cost of Defence or Guard reactions using the Close Combat skill by one. (This can reduce the cost to zero, but no less.)

MARTIAL ARTIST

Prerequisite: Close Combat Expertise 1

When making a melee attack, a character with this talent may reroll a number of damage dice equal to the number of Close Combat talents they have acquired. (As normal, these dice may only be rerolled once.)

MASTER DEFLECTION

Prerequisite: Deflection, Close Combat Expertise 2
Maximum Ranks: 3

On any Defence or Guard Reaction using the Close Combat skill where the character generates at least one success, they may immediately roll an additional number of d20s equal to their ranks

CLOSE COMBAT TIPS

Common Uses: See *Warfare* (p. 107); identifying weapon-based combat styles, close combat weaponry, and the injuries they cause.

Common Difficulty Factors: Terrain, Unfamiliarity, Complexity, Poor Equipment.

in Master Deflection. Any successes generated on these additional dice are added to the initial success total and repercussions on these additional dice may be ignored.

QUICK DRAW

Prerequisite: Martial Artist

The character is always prepared for melee combat. They can draw a weapon or other item as a Free Action (instead of a Minor Action) and do not need to have a weapon in their hand in order to respond to attacks. As long as they have a free hand and a weapon within Reach, they can always make a Close Combat test as part of a Defence or Guard Reaction. This can only be done once per turn, although when the Quick Draw action is taken the character can draw a different item into each hand (in order to dual wield sabres, for example). This talent exists for both the Ballistics and Close Combat skill, and if it is purchased for either skill

it can be used as a prerequisite for talents in the other skill.

REFLEXIVE BLOCK

Prerequisite: Quick Draw, Close Combat Expertise 2

The character has become so attuned to his melee expertise that he can use it to defend against ranged attacks. The character may substitute their Close Combat skill for their Acrobatics skill any time they attempt a Defence or Guard Reaction with a melee weapon in hand.

RIPOSTE

Prerequisite: Deflection, Close Combat Expertise 2

Some characters learn that the instant after an opponent's strike is when they are most vulnerable. After successfully executing a parry, characters with this talent may immediately perform a Reaction to make a standard melee attack against the foe they parried.

WEAPON MASTER

Prerequisite: Combat Specialist, Close Combat Expertise 2

When making an attack using the Close Combat skill, each point of Momentum the character spends to deal bonus damage adds two points of damage instead of one.

COMMAND (PERSONALITY)

Command is the measure of a character's ability to manipulate groups of people, including but not limited to those expected to defer to the character, such as those of a lower military rank or social caste.

Chain of Command: When issuing orders to direct subordinates, reduce the difficulty of the Command test by one step. For standard orders, this will generally reduce the difficulty to a Simple (D0) test.

COMMAND TALENTS

PROFESSIONAL

AIR OF AUTHORITY — FONT OF COURAGE — GROUP DYNAMICS

COMMANDING PRESENCE — COORDINATOR

MINIONS

AIR OF AUTHORITY

Prerequisite: Professional

The character knows how to bring their authority to bear. When making Psywar attacks using the Command skill, they gain 2 bonus Momentum on successful attacks.

COMMAND TIPS

Common Uses: Commanding a group of NPCs, bolstering subordinates in the face of horror or disaster, conveying orders and objectives clearly and with the correct emphasis

Common Difficulty Factors: Disruption, Distraction, Distance, Foreign Language, Noise, Social Factors, Authority, Unfamiliarity, Complexity

COMMANDING PRESENCE

Prerequisite: Air of Authority, Command Expertise 2
The character leads with immense charisma and persuasive skills. When making a Command test, any Momentum spent to add extra dice to the skill test adds two d20s to the dice pool instead of one. (The normal maximum of three bonus d20s still applies.)

COORDINATOR

Prerequisite: Group Dynamics, Command Expertise 2
The character is proficient in coordinating the actions of a group working in unison. Any time the character is involved in a teamwork test — even if they are not the leader for the test — all characters involved may choose to reroll one d20, but must accept the new result.

FONT OF COURAGE

Prerequisite: Professional
Maximum Ranks: 2
The character is an inspiring presence to those who follow them. Any time forces under their direct command (i.e., who they are visible to or in immediate communication with) are subject to a Psywar attack, those forces gain +2 🅝 Morale Soak for each rank of Font of Courage.

GROUP DYNAMICS

Prerequisite: Professional
The character is very familiar with the way a crowd normally acts and can recognise actions that are unusual or out of place. When dealing with places full of people — even if the people are not organised — the character may substitute their Command skill for any Observation test. This includes active searches if the character can rally a crowd to assist them.

MINIONS

Prerequisite: Commanding Presence
Individuals under the character's authority become extremely loyal to them, even willing to sacrifice themselves. Any time the character comes under attack and has a character under their command within three metres, they may pay 1 Heat to have that character immediately perform a Guard Reaction.

PROFESSIONAL

Prerequisite: Command Expertise 1
The character has learned to issue orders so that they are clear to the recipient and with little margin for misinterpretation. The character may reroll one d20 when making a Command test, but must accept the new result.

DISCIPLINE (WILLPOWER)

This skill is the basis for resisting Psywar attacks, as well as the self-control and mental strength to avoid succumbing to interrogation, coercion, or fear.

DISCIPLINE TALENTS

COURAGEOUS

Prerequisite: Irrepressible, Discipline Expertise 2
Maximum Ranks: 3
Some characters are simply more capable of enduring stress and mental assault. The character has a bonus to Morale Soak equal to twice his ranks in Courageous.

GUARDED HEART

Prerequisite: Wary, Discipline Expertise 2
The character is wary even of their friends and comrades. When targeted by Psywar attacks, they gain +2 🅝 Morale soak. Further, when rolling soak dice for Morale, they instead count each Effect rolled as if it were a 2 on those soak dice.

IRREPRESSIBLE

Prerequisite: Stubborn
Maximum Ranks: 3
The character has survived countless challenges and is prepared to face even more. When taking the Recover action, they gain a number of bonus Momentum equal to their ranks in Irrepressible.

JADED

Prerequisite: Stubborn
Maximum Ranks: 3
The character has suffered cruelties and emotional Metanoia repeatedly. They have built up a tolerance to mental suffering. The character increases their Resolve by two points for each rank of Jaded.

OUT OF DARKNESS

Prerequisite: Courageous
Maximum Ranks: 2
Even when their psyche has taken a beating, the character has an organised mental framework that allows them to recover. Whenever the character makes a Discipline check to recover from Metanoia, the difficulty of the check is reduced one step per rank of Out of Darkness.

DISCIPLINE TIPS
Common Uses: See *Psywar* (p. 122); resisting persuasion or mind-influencing effects

Common Difficulty Factors: Lighting, Disruption, Distraction, Poor Weather

STUBBORN

Prerequisite: Discipline Expertise 1

The character may reroll one d20 when making a Discipline test, but must accept the new result.

WARY

Prerequisite: Stubborn

The character is cautious in their trust and hesitant to believe the things that they are told. Any time the character is the target of a Persuade or Command test, any Momentum paid to add dice to their Discipline test add two d20s instead of one. (The normal maximum of three bonus d20s still applies.)

EDUCATION (INTELLIGENCE)

Education is a measure of the character's familiarity with the worlds beyond their personal experiences, as well as knowledge gained through formalised education systems. This includes a basic understanding of history, politics, current events, and places.

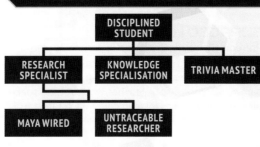

DISCIPLINED STUDENT

Prerequisite: Education Expertise 1

The character paid attention in class, was extensively self-taught, or both. They constantly sought out knowledge beyond the scope of the minimum necessary training. If they generate at least one success when attempting an Education test, they may immediately roll an additional d20 and add the result to the test.

KNOWLEDGE SPECIALISATION

Prerequisite: Disciplined Student
Maximum Ranks: Education Focus

The character is particularly devoted to a particular topic (which is chosen at the same time as this talent, subject to the GM's approval). When making an Education test related to that topic, the character gains +1d20 on their test. This talent can be taken multiple times, with each additional rank either granting a new specialisation or an additional +1d20 to an existing specialisation. (The normal limit of three bonus d20s applies.)

MAYA WIRED

Prerequisite: Research Specialist, Education Expertise 2

Years of experience with the datasphere has allowed the character to create and master a huge suite of customised, automatic research tools that are anticipating their needs. As long as the character has access to their geist (and their geist has access to Maya, Arachne, or a similar datasphere), whenever they attempt an Education test to recall information quickly, the geist may assist on the test, and roll 2d20 rather than the normal 1d20 for assistance. (Their automated systems deliver information they need to know so instantaneously it's as if they already knew it themselves.)

RESEARCH SPECIALIST

Prerequisite: Disciplined Student
Maximum Ranks: 3

After spending hours buried in the nooks and crannies of various dataspheres, the character is an expert at finding the information that they need. When making a skill test to research a topic, the character gains bonus Momentum equal to their ranks in Research Specialist.

TRIVIA MASTER

Prerequisite: Disciplined Student
Maximum Ranks: 3

The character keeps up on current events, both globally and throughout the Human Sphere. On any Education test that involves pop culture, trivia, or current events within the past twenty years, the character reduces the difficulty by one step per rank of Trivia Master, to a minimum of Simple (D0).

UNTRACEABLE RESEARCHER

Prerequisite: Research Specialist

The danger of relying on the knowledge of the datasphere is that there are those who can trace and track your use of it. There are tricks to avoid such attention, however, and the character is a master of them. They reduce the difficulty of any Stealth check to avoid detection as a result of their research checks by two steps, to a minimum of Simple (D0).

EXTRAPLANETARY (AWARENESS)

This skill represents the specialised training necessary to survive and function in the vacuum of space, on worlds without self-sustaining atmospheres, or in other extraterrestrial environments.

Extraplanetary Survival: In space or on alien worlds, the Extraplanetary skill can be used in many of the same ways that the Survival skill can be used. (Conditions are often less friendly, however, which may result in higher difficulties, particularly for finding the necessities of food, water, and shelter.)

EDUCATION TIPS

Common Uses: Recalling useful information, researching specific topics

Common Difficulty Factors: Distance, Time, Unfamiliarity, Foreign Language, Complexity, Equipment

PLAYTEST TIP

EDUCATION MOMENTUM

Education is one of the most flexible skills and can often be used as a precursor for generating Momentum on other tests. For example, you can recognise the common philosophies of a Faction and use that to your advantage on a Persuade test. Or test your familiarity with the design specs for an enemy TAG to generate Momentum for a face-to-face Pilot test. These tests reward creative problem-solving.

In many extraplanetary environments, it may be impossible to find such basic necessities.)

Gravity Movement: A character attempting Acrobatics, Athletics, or Close Combat tests while in non-standard gravity reduces their Expertise and Focus ranks to those of their Extraplanetary skill. Moving easily in space or on unterraformed worlds is challenging even for the most physically adept.

EXTRAPLANETARY TALENTS

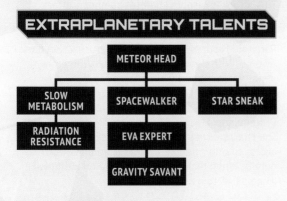

EVA EXPERT

Prerequisite: Spacewalker
The character has learned to function at a decreased atmospheric pressure in order to extend operating time in pressure suits. When determining whether or not an Oxygen Load has been depleted, the character only needs to succeed at an Extraplanetary (D1) test to avoid expending the Load (as opposed to the normal difficulty 2 test).

GRAVITY SAVANT

Prerequisite: EVA Expert, Extraplanetary Expertise 2
The character has worked in a broad range of different gravitational environments and has learned to quickly adapt to such changes. The character can ignore any penalties associated with working in situations of gravity that differ from Earth normal.

METEOR HEAD

Prerequisite: Extraplanetary Expertise 1
The character may reroll one d20 when making an Extraplanetary test, but must accept the new result.

RADIATION RESISTANCE

Prerequisite: Slow Metabolism, Extraplanetary Expertise 2
Either due to a genetic quirk or a deliberate anatomical modification, the character is less subject to the effects of cosmic radiation. When exposed to damage with the Radiation X quality, they treat the Radiation rating as one lower than usual (to a minimum of 0).

EXTRAPLANETARY TIPS

Common Uses: Surviving common hazards in non-standard gravity, maintaining oxygen supplies, movement in non-standard gravities, operating vac suits

Common Difficulty Factors: Terrain, Encumbrance, Equipment, Poor Oxygen, Weather, Celestial Phenomena (radiation, micrometeoroid showers), Time, Unfamiliarity, Complexity

SLOW METABOLISM
Prerequisite: Meteor Head
The character can go extended periods of time with minimum oxygen. The difficulty of Resistance tests to avoid suffocation only increases if they suffer a Wound (instead of every round).

SPACEWALKER
Prerequisite: Meteor Head
The character has significant experience in using EVA suits and operating in zero-g environments. Whenever a test is required for working in such an environment, the character gains two d20s to their Extraplanetary pool for every Momentum spent instead of one. (The normal maximum of three bonus d20s still applies.)

STAR SNEAK
Prerequisite: Meteor Head
Years of extraterrestrial experience have familiarized the character with aspects of the environment which landlubbers find it difficult to grok (such as the presence of a meaningful z-axis in day-to-day life in zero-g). While in space or upon alien worlds, the character may substitute their Extraplanetary skill for Stealth tests.

HACKING (INTELLIGENCE)
Almost anyone can consume Maya media and make use of the basic functions and features of the datasphere (particularly with the aid of their geists), but it takes a trained hacker to take full advantage of the quantronic substrate of modern reality. This skill, often employed with the use of a hacking device, governs the character's ability to penetrate quantronic systems, override security systems, exploit local networks, and manipulate augmented reality. It also allows them to aggressively attack the personal area networks of others, as well as repairing quantronic damage and breaches to their own systems.

HACKING TALENTS

```
                  HACKER
       ┌────────────┼────────────┐
  TRICKS OF THE   PHISHER    QUANTRONIC
     TRADE                      FLAK
  PARANOID       PIGGYBACK
                 QUANTRONIC
                   BLAST
```

HACKER
Prerequisite: Hacking Expertise 1
When making an Infowar attack, the character may reroll a number of damage dice equal to the number of Hacking talents they have acquired. (As normal, dice may only be rerolled once.)

HACKING TIPS
Common Uses: See *Infowar* (p. 114); advanced quantronic programming, augmented reality manipulation, gaining illicit access to data, exploiting or navigating dataspheres

Common Difficulty Factors: Distance, Interference, Distraction, Equipment, Security

PARANOID
Prerequisite: Tricks of the Trade, Hacking Expertise 2
Maximum Ranks: 3
The character, their geist, and their systems are always ready for enemy intrusion. As a Reaction the character may respond to any Infowar attack with an Infowar attack of their own with any software immediately to hand at a penalty of +2 difficulty. This attack is resolved before the enemy attack and if it causes the enemy to suffer a Breach, then their attack is prevented. Each additional rank of Paranoid reduces the difficulty of the reaction hack by one. (With three ranks of Paranoid, therefore, the penalty is completely eliminated.)

PHISHER
Prerequisite: Hacker
The character has made it a practice to collect access to other people's comlogs and financial details. When making a Fake ID, the resulting Fake ID gains +1 to its rating.

PIGGYBACK
Prerequisite: Phisher
The character maintains a log of easily hackable devices and common admin codes, which can be exploited when performing remote hacks. When initiating a remote hack, the character gains a special pool of 4 Momentum which can be spent on tests made to access their target and also when gaining or improving the quality of authentication.

QUANTRONIC BLAST
Prerequisite: Piggyback, Hacking Expertise 2
Maximum Ranks: 3
When the character spends Momentum during an Infowar attack to affect a secondary target, it only costs 1 Momentum. In addition, the character can use the secondary target Momentum spend on Infowar attacks a number of times equal to their ranks in Quantronic Blast.

QUANTRONIC FLAK
Prerequisite: Hacker
Maximum Ranks: 2
The character has created a number of protocols and subroutines that generate a burst of signal interference nearby. As a Minor Action, the character's current zone gains 2 🅝 Interference Soak per rank of Quantronic Flak, which disappears at the start of the character's next turn.

TRICKS OF THE TRADE
Prerequisite: Hacker
The character may reroll one d20 when making a Hacking test, but must accept the new result.

LIFESTYLE (PERSONALITY)

Lifestyle measures a character's social influence, status within popular culture and high society, access to resources such as cash and other assets, and the ability to wield those assets effectively to get what they want. It also reflects general knowledge regarding such things.

Passing: When attempting to maintain the appearance of a particular social class (including your own), it requires a Simple (D0) Lifestyle test. The difficulty increases by one for every level of social status above or below your own. The difficulty also increases for foreign or unfamiliar cultures.

LIFESTYLE TALENTS

SOCIALITE

INVESTMENTS — NETWORK — BRIBERY — SOCIAL MIMIC

BACKDOOR ASSETS — ELITE CONTACT

BACKDOOR ASSETS

Prerequisite: Network, Lifestyle Expertise 2
Maximum Ranks: 3
Having contacts with access to valuable assets can be the quickest way to acquire needed equipment. Characters with access to Backdoor Assets may reduce the Restriction rating of any item or service by one per rank of Backdoor Assets, to a minimum of 1, but the item or service is regarded as illegally-obtained, which may cause other problems (either immediately or at a later date) if complications are generated.

BRIBERY

Prerequisite: Socialite
The character recognises that everyone has their price, and they know how to pay it — particularly without raising any flags. When attempting a bribe, they gain two bonus d20s per Asset spent (instead of the normal one).

ELITE CONTACT

Prerequisite: Network, Lifestyle Expertise 2
The character has established connections with individuals in positions of significant authority. Each time this talent is selected, the character gains an elite contact. (The player must specify the type and allegiance of the contact, which is subject to the GM's approval.) The character may make a Challenging (D2) Lifestyle test to ask the selected contact for a favour. On a success, the contact responds with resources proportionate to their level of importance — providing one Asset, plus one additional Asset per point of Momentum spent. The character can make such a skill test once per month, and it takes an hour (if the character is on the same planet) or 2+4 hours (if the character is on a different planet) to make the attempt. Elite Contact may be purchased multiple times, with each purchase establishing a new highly placed contact.

INVESTMENTS

Prerequisite: Socialite
Maximum Ranks: 3
Each rank of Investments increases the character's Earnings by one.

LIFESTYLE TIPS
Common Uses: See *Acquisitions* (p. 328) and *Psywar* (p. 122); fitting in with a particular social class, avoiding social embarrassment, interpreting business or financial information, establishing or reaching out to contacts

Common Difficulty Factors: Equipment, Social Factors, Time, Unfamiliarity, Complexity

NETWORK
Prerequisite: Socialite
Maximum Ranks: 3
The character has a broad range of contacts in different fields and in different regions. Any time they need assistance from other individuals, they may reduce the difficulty of a Lifestyle test to find a contact by one step per rank of Network, to a minimum of Simple (D0).

SOCIALITE
Prerequisite: Lifestyle Expertise 1
The character may reroll one d20 when making a Lifestyle test, but must accept the new result.

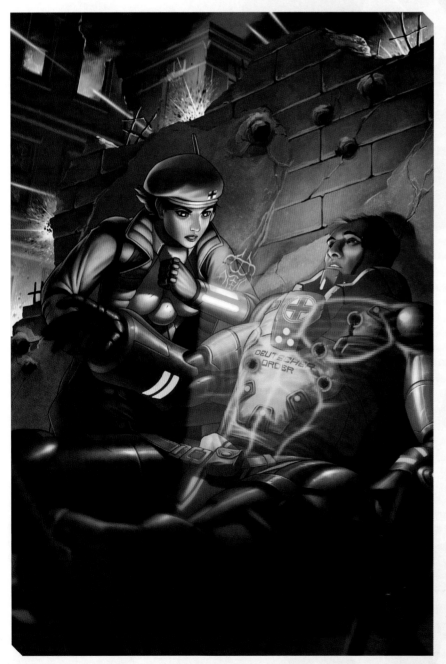

SOCIAL MIMIC
Prerequisite: Socialite
The character is skilled at blending into disparate cultures and social classes. There is no increase in difficulty for differences in social classes when passing as a class other than their own.

MEDICINE (INTELLIGENCE)
This skill covers the treatment of all physical wounds and maladies, along with the use of drugs, biotechnology, wetware, medical nanobots, and the like. Those skilled in Medicine can render immediate assistance, provide short-term and long-term care, perform surgery, implant cybernetics, treat diseases, redress radiation sickness, and attend to other corrective, therapeutic, or curative needs.

EMERGENCY DOCTOR
Prerequisite: Physician
When making a teamwork test with the Medicine skill to assist another character with the Recover action, the emergency doctor may roll a number of dice equal to the character's Medicine Focus.

FIELD DRESSING
Prerequisite: Physician
The character has become particularly adept at practicing medicine in situations where few resources are available. They gain a bonus Momentum on Medicine tests as if they were using a MedKit even when they have no kit available. In addition, when using a MediKit to perform the Treat action on a patient not within their Reach, they do not suffer the normal +1 difficulty penalty.

FIELD SURGERY
Prerequisite: Field Dressing
Having worked with very limited resources in the past, the character has learned to take full advantage of them when available. Each dose of Serum used by the character adds 2 bonus Momentum instead of one.

MIRACLE WORKER
Prerequisite: Field Surgery, Medicine Expertise 2
When performing the Treat action or assisting on the Recover action using the Medicine skill, the character gains 2 bonus Momentum, which may only be used to recover Vigour or treat Wounds.

PHYSICIAN
Prerequisite: Medicine Expertise 1
The character may reroll one d20 when making a Medicine test, but must accept the new result.

SELF-TREATMENT
Prerequisite: Physician
When performing a treat test using Medicine on themselves, a character with Self-Treatment no longer increases the difficulty of the test by two.

TRAUMA SURGEON
Prerequisite: Field Surgery, Medicine Expertise 2
Maximum Ranks: 3
The character has learned techniques to aid a character in recovering from particularly grievous injuries. The character may reduce the difficulty of Medicine tests to treat Wounds by one step per rank of Trauma Surgeon they possess, to a minimum of Average (D1).

OBSERVATION (AWARENESS)
This skill governs a character's ability to notice and discern details and subtle environmental cues. It also covers general perceptiveness and the ability to recognise that something is out of place, to search an area for clues, or to spot a potential ambush.

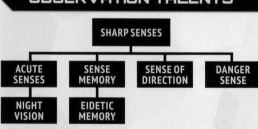

ACUTE SENSES
Prerequisite: Sharp Senses
Maximum Ranks: 3
On a successful Observation test, the character gains bonus Momentum equal to their ranks in Acute Senses.

DANGER SENSE
Prerequisite: Sharp Senses
When making a face-to-face test to determine surprise, the character can reroll any failed check.

EIDETIC MEMORY
Prerequisite: Sense Memory, Observation Expertise 2
The character can recall images, sounds, objects, and other memories with high precision even after only a momentary exposure. When examining such memories, they can attempt Observation tests at a +1 difficulty to notice things they may have originally missed in the moment. (Such recall is not actually perfect, however, and GMs are encouraged to use complications on such tests to generate false information.)

NIGHT VISION
Prerequisite: Acute Senses, Observation Expertise 2
The character ignores any penalties to skill tests as a result of poor illumination or low light levels. This talent does not help in total darkness, however.

SENSE OF DIRECTION
Prerequisite: Sharp Senses
The character has a perfect Sense of Direction. With an Average (D1) Observation test, they can determine which direction is north. When attempting to retrace their footsteps or follow a path they've taken, the difficulty of the test is reduced by one per Observation talent the character has, which may reduce the difficulty to Simple (D0). (This benefit applies even if their senses were obscured. For example, if they were blindfolded or locked in the trunk of a car and attempting to figure out where it had taken them.)

SENSE MEMORY
Prerequisite: Sharp Senses
The character has a knack for recalling patterns of sounds, smells, or colours. They are much more likely to recognise people, places, and objects they have interacted with, even when they are shrouded or attempts have been made to obscure, disguise, or hide them. When trying to detect, locate, or recognise such targets they gain a bonus d20 to any related skill tests. (This bonus die may be rolled by the GM to avoid revealing the subject of the Observation test before the test is made.)

SHARP SENSES
Prerequisite: Observation Expertise 1
The character may reroll one d20 when making an Observation test, but must accept the new result.

PERSUADE (PERSONALITY)
The Persuade skill covers a wide range of interpersonal abilities, including the ability to charm, deceive, coerce, bribe, seduce, or haggle. It allows a character to convince others of what they believe or to believe that which is not true.

MEDICINE TIPS
Common Uses: See *Recovery* (p. 102); studying and identifying poisons, diseases, and other ailments. Performing autopsies or determining cause of death

Common Difficulty Factors:
Distraction, Equipment, Disruption, Random Motion, Unfamiliarity, Complexity

OBSERVATION TIPS
Common Uses: Searching for physical clues, detecting ambushes and other threats, noticing small details

Common Difficulty Factors:
Distance, Distraction, Lighting, Noise, Poor Weather, Equipment, Size; often opposed by Stealth or Thievery tests

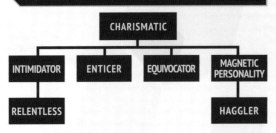

PERSUADE TALENTS

PERSUADE TIPS
Common Uses: See *Psywar* (p. 122); lying to, negotiating with, intimidating, seducing, or befriending others

Common Difficulty Factors: Distance, Foreign Language, Noise, Social Factors, Time, Unfamiliarity, Complexity; often opposed by Discipline tests

PLAYTEST TIP
LIMITS OF PERSUASION
NPCs will often shake off the effects of a simple Persuade test, having second thoughts, seeing through a lie, or overcoming a scare. The GM should have a rough idea how long the Persuade effect will last when setting the difficulty of the test, and players can spend Momentum in order to increase the length of effect.

CHARISMATIC
Prerequisite: Persuade Expertise 1
The character may reroll one d20 on any Persuade test, but must keep the new result.

ENTICER
Prerequisite: Charismatic
Maximum Ranks: 3
The character is particularly adept at seducing others. When using affection, physical attraction, or the promise of sexual favours as part of negotiation, the character gains a number of bonus d20s equal to their ranks in Enticer. (The normal limit of three bonus d20s still applies.) Whether or not the character is honest with their seduction is irrelevant — the character is as effective with fake seduction as with honest attraction.

EQUIVOCATOR
Prerequisite: Charismatic
The character is willing and able to tell any lie to overcome an opponent's social defences. When attempting to deceive an opponent, the character gains two bonus d20s to their Persuade test per Momentum spent (instead of the normal one). The normal limit of three bonus d20s still applies.

HAGGLER
Prerequisite: Magnetic Personality, Persuade Expertise 2
The character is particularly proficient at striking a bargain, either to obtain goods or favours. They can use Persuade instead of Lifestyle when attempting to acquire goods or strike a bargain.

INTIMIDATOR
Prerequisite: Charismatic
The character recognises others' limitations and is always willing to exploit them. When attempting to intimidate an opponent, the character gains two d20s to their Persuade test per Momentum spent (instead of the normal one). The normal limit of three bonus d20s still applies.

MAGNETIC PERSONALITY
Prerequisite: Charismatic
Maximum Ranks: 3
When making Persuade tests, the character gains 1 bonus Momentum per rank of Magnetic Personality.

RELENTLESS
Prerequisite: Intimidator, Persuade Expertise 2
Maximum Ranks: 2
The character's bonus damage to Psywar attacks is increased by +1🔘 per rank of Relentless.

PILOT (COORDINATION)
This skill covers the ability to drive or operate any vehicle operating within an atmosphere, including motorcycles, cars, trucks, hovercraft, watercraft, and aircraft. (Controlling space-based vehicles is handled by the Spacecraft skill.)

PILOT TALENTS

ACE
Prerequisite: Pilot Expertise 1
The character may reroll one d20 when making a Pilot test, but must accept the new result.

BORN TO THE WHEEL
Prerequisite: Ace
Decrease the difficulty for any Pilot tests using ground-based vehicles by one, to a minimum of 1.

COMBAT PILOT
Prerequisite: Ace
Maximum Ranks: 3
The character knows how to keep a vehicle running effectively, even when it's seriously damaged. When performing a Pilot test with a damaged vehicle, the penalty from damage is reduced by one step per rank of Combat Pilot.

PUSH THE ENVELOPE
Prerequisite: Ace
Maximum Ranks: 3
The character is particularly adept at making vehicles perform beyond their design specifications. When making Pilot tests, the character gains 1 bonus Momentum per rank of Push the Envelope.

RAMMING SPEED
Prerequisite: Combat Pilot, Pilot Expertise 2
When the character rams their vehicle into another, each point of Momentum spent for bonus damage adds two damage (instead of the normal one).

STORM BREAKER
Prerequisite: Ace
When piloting watercraft, the character may ignore any penalties to a Pilot test due to choppy waters, severe weather, or other environmental conditions.

TOP GUN
Prerequisite: Push the Envelope, Pilot Expertise 2
The character may substitute their Pilot skill for Ballistics when firing weapons mounted on an airborne vehicle that they are also piloting.

PSYCHOLOGY (INTELLIGENCE)
This skill describes the character's ability to perceive and address the mental states of others. This includes the diagnosis and treatment of mental distress, psychoses, insanity, and similar maladies, but also includes assessing day-to-day social interactions.

Alien Psychology: Understanding the thinking of races other than your own is difficult and frequently made even more challenging due to the lack of familiar body language. Increase the difficulty of Psychology tests targeting characters of a species other than the psychologist's own by one step. (This includes artificial intelligences unless, like Recreations, they have been specifically designed to mimic the intelligence of the psychologist's species.)

PSYCHOLOGY TALENTS

ALIEN SPECIALIST
Prerequisite: Counsellor
The character has spent considerable time studying the psychology of a particular species other than their own. When making Psychology tests involving members of that species, the character gains +1d20 on their test. This talent can be taken multiple times, with each additional rank granting specialisation with a new alien species. (For the purposes of this talent, the character can select artificial intelligences as a non-human species.)

PILOT TIPS
Common Uses: Operating vehicles, stunt driving, aerobatic piloting, precision maneuvering, vehicular evasion

Common Difficulty Factors: Lighting, Terrain, Weather, Unfamiliarity, Complexity, Damage to Vehicle

VEHICLES
The Pilot skill covers the operation of vehicles, on the land, in the air, and on the water. In most situations, simply attempting appropriate Skill Tests will be sufficient to represent the effects and impact of a vehicle upon a situation. More detailed rules for operating vehicles, from cars, to TAGs, to aircraft, can be found in the *Gamemaster's Guide*.

PSYCHOLOGY TIPS
Common Uses: See *Recovery* (p. 102); determining if a person is lying, recognising patterns of behaviour, uncovering secret vices

Common Difficulty Factors: Distraction, Disruption, Distance, Foreign Language, Noise, Social Factors, Time

BATTLEFIELD PSYCHOLOGY

Prerequisite: Counsellor

When making a teamwork test with the Psychology skill to assist another character with the Recover action, the character may roll a number of dice equal to the character's Psychology Focus.

COUNSELLOR

Prerequisite: Psychology Expertise 1

When making a Psychology test, the character may reroll any dice that did not generate a success on the initial roll, but they must accept the new result.

LIE DETECTOR

Prerequisite: Counsellor

The character is a gifted lie detector. They roll +1d20 when making Psychology tests to determine whether or not someone is lying.

PSYCHOANALYST

Prerequisite: Remote Analyst, Psychology Expertise 2

Maximum Ranks: 3

The character is a trained psychologist and is often able to guide a patient's focus in order to expedite the recovery process. The character may reduce the difficulty of treat tests using the Psychology skill by one step per rank of Psychoanalyst they possess to a minimum of Average (D1).

REMOTE ANALYST

Prerequisite: Counsellor

The character does not suffer any increase in difficulty to Psychology tests due to being unable to interact with the subject face-to-face.

THERAPEUTIC INSIGHT

Prerequisite: Battlefield Psychology, Psychology Expertise 2

The character has a keen insight into those suffering from mental debilitation. When performing the Treat action or assisting on the Recover action using the Psychology skill, the character gains 2 bonus Momentum, which may only be used to recover Resolve or treat Metanoia.

RESISTANCE (BRAWN)

Resistance covers both natural resilience and physical conditioning to better endure substances, activities, and events that would otherwise impair a character.

RESISTANCE TALENTS

```
                    STURDY
                      |
      ----------------+----------------
      |               |               |
  MITHRADATIC    JUST A SCRATCH    RESILIENT
      |               |
 SELF-MEDICATING  QUICK RECOVERY
                      |
                 FAST HEALER
```

FAST HEALER

Prerequisite: Quick Recovery

Maximum Ranks: 3

When making a recovery test using the Resistance skill, the character can add +1d20 to the skill test per rank of Fast Healer. (The normal maximum of three bonus d20s still applies.)

RESISTANCE TIPS

Common Uses: See *Damage* (p. 99); resisting, recovering, or enduring sensory deprivation, environmental extremes, poisons, diseases, physical disorientation, extreme pain, physical hardships, or extreme effort

Common Difficulty Factors: Poor Oxygen, Gravity, Distraction, Duration

JUST A SCRATCH
Prerequisite: Sturdy
Maximum Ranks: 3
The character has a knack for ignoring minor injuries and pushing through the pain. When taking the Recover action, the character recovers one additional Vigour per rank of Just a Scratch.

MITHRADATIC
Prerequisite: Sturdy
Maximum Ranks: 3
The character is either naturally resistant to toxins or has become inured to them through constant exposure (possibly pharmacological). When a character needs to make a Resistance test against a poison, toxin, or the effects of drugs, they may reduce the difficulty by one step per rank of Mithradatic. This may reduce the difficulty to zero, eliminating the need for a test.

QUICK RECOVERY
Prerequisite: Just a Scratch, Resistance Expertise 2
When taking the Absterge action, the difficulty of the Resistance test to remove the condition is reduced by one step, to a minimum of Average (D1).

RESILIENT
Prerequisite: Sturdy
Maximum Ranks: 3
When making a Resistance test to avoid a status condition, the difficulty of the Resistance test to resist the negative effects is reduced by one step per rank of Resilient. This may reduce the difficulty to Simple (D0), eliminating the need for a test.

SELF-MEDICATING
Prerequisite: Mithradatic, Resistance Expertise 2
The character has learned how to cope with mental trauma through the heavy use of drugs, alcohol, or other pharmacological means, relying on their physical stamina to endure the results. If they're able to self-medicate with such substances, the character can use their Resistance skill on any recovery test for which they would normally use Discipline. (This sort of behaviour isn't healthy, of course, and GMs are encouraged to use complications on the recovery test to reflect this.)

STURDY
Prerequisite: Resistance Expertise 1
When making Resistance tests, the character may reroll any dice that did not generate a success on the initial roll, but must accept the new result.

SCIENCE (INTELLIGENCE)
The character is familiar with a wide range of scientific studies and principles, including both practical applications and theoretical considerations. This includes the fields of physics, chemistry, geology, astronomy, biology, botany, advanced mathematics, and the arcane fields of study surrounding neomaterials, VoodooTech, wormhole topography, nanonics, and the like.

SCIENCE TALENTS

```
              SCIENTIST
     ┌────────────┼────────────┐
  SORELLIAN   SCIENTIFIC     SCIENCE
  GENIUS      INTUITION   SPECIALISATION
                   ┌──────────┴─────┐
                APPLIED          GENETIC
                SCIENCES         ENGINEER
```

APPLIED SCIENCES
Prerequisite: Science Specialisation, Science Expertise 2
The character has great experience in taking science out of the lab and into the field. They may substitute their Science skill for any skill tests involving areas of knowledge covered by or involving their Science Specialisation (such as Tech or Education).

GENETIC ENGINEER
Prerequisite: Science Specialisation (Biology or Genetics), Science Expertise 2
The character is not only familiar with the different organisms that dwell in the Human Sphere, they are also comfortable modifying them or even creating new forms of life. The character can use their Science skill instead of Tech or Medicine when installing an augmentation or performing genetic engineering and also gains +1d20 to such tests.

SCIENCE SPECIALISATION
Prerequisite: Scienctist
Maximum Ranks: Science Focus
The character is particularly devoted to a particular branch of science (which is chosen at the same time as this talent, subject to the GM's approval). When making a Science test related to that topic, the character gains +1d20 on their test. This talent can be taken multiple times, with each additional rank either granting a new specialisation or an additional +1d20 to an excisting specialisation. (The normal maximum of three bonus d20s still applies.)

SCIENTIFIC INTUITION
Prerequisite: Scientist
Maximum Ranks: 3
When making Science tests, the character gains 1 bonus Momentum per rank of Scientific Intuition.

SCIENTIST
Prerequisite: Science Expertise 1
The character may reroll one d20 when making a Science test, but must accept the new result.

SCIENCE TIPS
Common Uses: Gathering scientific data, scientific research, creation of experimental procedures, understanding scientific documentation, recognising scientific principles, analysing scientific phenomena

Common Difficulty Factors: Distraction, Disruption, Equipment, Weather, Time, Unfamiliarity, Complexity

SORELLIAN GENIUS
Prerequisite: Scientist
Maximum Ranks: 3
The adjective of "Sorellian", invoked from the famous Sorel sisters who cracked the mysteries of wormhole travel, has become a popular descriptor for gifted scientists. The character may reduce the difficulty of any Science test by one step per rank of Sorellian Genius, to a minimum of Simple (D0).

SPACECRAFT (COORDINATION)
This skill covers the ability to pilot any vehicle outside of a planet's atmosphere or through inter-planetary space, including small shuttles, merchant cargo haulers, large battlecruisers, and the like. (Driving or operating land-based or atmospheric flight vehicles are handled by the Pilot skill.)

ALONE IN THE NIGHT
Prerequisite: Space Ace
It's not unusual for spacecraft to encounter mechanical difficulties far from facilities where repairs can be made. Pilots often gain practical, hands-on experience with repairing their rides. The character can substitute their Spacecraft skill when making Tech tests to repair spacecraft.

FLEET ACTION
Prerequisite: Starfighter
The character has commanded squadrons of spacecraft during conflicts and has survived the experience with tales to tell. They may substitute their Spacecraft skill for Command in any such conflicts.

FLY CASUAL
Prerequisite: Space Ace
When attempting to evade detection while flying a spacecraft, the character may substitute their Spacecraft skill for Stealth.

SPACE ACE
Prerequisite: Spacecraft Expertise 1
The character may reroll one d20 when making a Spacecraft test, but must accept the new result.

STARFIGHTER
Prerequisite: Starslinger, Spacecraft Expertise 2
The character may substitute their Spacecraft skill for Ballistics when firing weapons mounted on a space vehicle that they are also piloting.

STARSLINGER
Prerequisite: Space Ace
Maximum Ranks: 3
When making Spacecraft tests involving piloting, the character decreases the difficulty rating by one per rank of Starslinger, to a minimum of Simple (D0).

TRANSATMOSPHERIC
Prerequisite: Space Ace
When flying a ship designed for both atmospheric and space flight, the character can substitute their Spacecraft skill for Pilot on tests.

STEALTH (AGILITY)
The art of going unnoticed, whether staying hidden within shadows and moving silently, blending into a crowd, slipping through a Maya cluster, or disguising the source of a smear campaign. Stealth also governs the creation and use of camouflage, disguises, covering one's tracks, and other indirect means of discretion.

SPACECRAFT TIPS
Common Uses: Piloting spacecraft, performing tight maneuvers, docking procedures, evasive action

Common Difficulty Factors: Terrain (celestial objects — asteroids, gas clouds, debris), Stellar Phenomena (gravitational anomalies), Traffic, Unfamiliarity, Complexity, Equipment, Vessel Damage

VEHICLES
The Spacecraft skill covers the operation of all spacecraft, as the name suggests. In most situations, simply attempting appropriate Skill Tests will be sufficient to represent the effects and impact of a spacecraft upon a situation. More detailed rules for operating spacecraft can be found in the *Gamemaster's Guide*.

STEALTH TIPS
Common Uses: See *Stealth* (p. 104); moving quietly or silently, hiding from observers, setting up an ambush, creating camouflage, creating and employing disguises, concealing tracks, avoiding quantronic detection

Common Difficulty Factors: Lighting, Terrain, Encumbrance, Noise; often opposed by Observation tests

STEALTH TALENTS

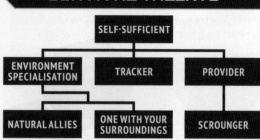

CAMOUFLAGE

Prerequisite: Scout
The character recognises that often it is not important for just themselves to remain unseen, but also their allies and any equipment they might be using. When acting as the leader of a group Stealth test or attempting to conceal anything vehicle sized or larger, any Momentum paid to add dice to their Stealth test adds two d20s instead of one.

DISGUISE

Prerequisite: Scout
Maximum Ranks: 3
The character has learned to capably impersonate a broad range of people, effectively blending into the background and acting like they belong. When making Stealth tests to make or use a disguise, they gain bonus Momentum equal to their ranks in Disguise.

IMPERSONATION

Prerequisite: Disguise, Stealth Expertise 2
When impersonating another, the character may substitute their Stealth skill for Persuade or Command tests.

INFILTRATION

Prerequisite: Living Shadow, Stealth Expertise 2
The character has learned a variety of techniques necessary to bypass security measures when infiltrating a target facility. The character may substitute Stealth for Thievery when attempting to bypass physical security measures.

LIVING SHADOW

Prerequisite: Scout
When the character attempts to remain unseen or unnoticed, any Momentum spent to add dice to their Stealth test adds two d20s instead of one. (The normal maximum of three bonus d20s still applies.)

QUANTRONIC STATIC

Prerequisite: Scout
When the character attempts to evade detection while hacking, any Momentum spent to add dice to their Stealth test adds two d20s instead of one. (The normal maximum of three bonus d20s still applies.)

SCOUT

Prerequisite: Stealth Expertise 1
The character may reroll one d20 when making a Stealth test, but must accept the new result.

SURVIVAL (AWARENESS)

This skill covers the ability to find food, shelter, and other resources. It is possible to eke out survival in incredibly harsh environments – from the vast icefields of Svalarheima to the alien biomes of Paradiso – but the skill presumes that the character is in a fundamentally life-sustaining biosphere. (For survival in the vacuum of space or on worlds incapable of sustaining human life, use Extraplanetary.) Survival also governs the ability to find and follow tracks.

Necessities: Finding food, water, and shelter requires a Survival test, with the difficulty of the test determined by the severity of the environment. On a success, the character provides one day of necessities for one person plus one additional day per Momentum spent.

SURVIVAL TALENTS

ENVIRONMENTAL SPECIALISATION

Prerequisite: Self-Sufficient
Maximum Ranks: Education Focus
The character is particularly devoted to a particular kind of environment (Arctic, Desert, Jungle, Mountain, Forest, Plains, Subterranean, or Urban). When making a Survival test in or related to that environment, the character gains +1d20 on their test. This talent can be taken multiple times, with each additional rank either granting a new specialisation or an additional +1d20 to an existing specialisation. (The normal maximum of three bonus d20s still applies.)

NATURAL ALLIES

Prerequisite: Environmental Specialisation, Survival Expertise 2
When interacting with creatures native to their Environmental Specialisation, the character may substitute their Survival skill for Animal Handling tests.

SURVIVAL TIPS

Common Uses: Avoiding environmental hazards, finding daily sustenance, tracking movement through an area, setting traps, determining likely weather forecasts, locating or building shelter to resist exposure, avoiding or seeking out encounters with wild animals

Common Difficulty Factors: Lighting, Terrain, Equipment, Weather, Time, Unfamiliarity, Complexity

PLAYTEST TIP

LIVING OFF THE LAND

When you're out in the wilderness, you can often use Survival to make up for a lack of proper tools or supplies needed for other skill checks. For example, if a comrade has been poisoned, a Survival test may allow you to find a natural remedy (and you can apply the Momentum you generate to the Medical test).

ONE WITH YOUR SURROUNDINGS
Prerequisite: Environmental Specialisation, Survival Expertise 2
While moving through their Environmental Specialisation, the character may substitute their Survival skill for Stealth tests.

PROVIDER
Prerequisite: Self-Sufficient
The character is particularly capable of finding the necessities of life. When attempting to find food, water, or shelter, each point of Momentum earned on the Survival test can be spent to provide necessities for two days (instead of the normal one).

SCROUNGER
Prerequisite: Provider, Survival Expertise 2
Maximum Ranks: 2
Useful items and resources are often discarded or abandoned. A resourceful individual can often recover these for their own purposes. The character may reduce the Restriction rating of any item by one per rank of Scrounger, to a minimum of 1.

SELF-SUFFICIENT
Prerequisite: Survival Expertise 1
The character may reroll one d20 when making a Survival test, but must accept the new result.

TECH TIPS
Common Uses: See Repairing Items (p. 333); identifying, building, repairing, maintaining, or disabling mechanical devices. Identifying, creating, placing, or disarming explosive devices

Common Difficulty Factors:
Lighting, Disruption, Distraction, Distance, Equipment, Random Motion, Time, Unfamiliarity, Complexity

TRACKER
Prerequisite: Self-Sufficient
Maximum Ranks: 3
The character is experienced with recognising all the signs of passage, from the subtle to the obvious. When tracking an opponent, the character reduces the difficulty of the Survival test by one step per rank of Tracker, to a minimum of Simple (D0).

TECH (INTELLIGENCE)
This skill covers the understanding, maintenance, and repair of machinery and structures. This covers a wide range of disciplines and fields of expertise, from internal combustion engines, to zero-g construction, to nanotech, to robotics, to biosynthetics.

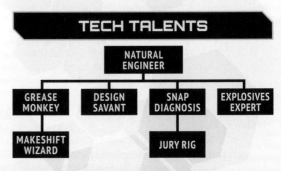

DESIGN SAVANT
Prerequisite: Natural Engineer
Maximum Ranks: 3
The character has a knack for designing novel solutions to problems. Any time the character chooses to design a new piece of equipment — or modify an existing design — they may reduce the difficulty of the Tech test by one step per rank of Design Savant, to a minimum of Simple (D0).

EXPLOSIVES EXPERT
Prerequisite: Natural Engineer, Tech Expertise 2
Maximum Ranks: 3
When setting an explosive charge, the character gains bonus Momentum equal to their ranks in Explosives Expert.

GREASEMONKEY
Prerequisite: Natural Engineer
The character is familiar with mechanical systems, and recognises the most likely points of failure intuitively. When attempting to treat damage sustained by an object or construct (something with Structure and Faults, instead of Vigour and Wounds), the character gains 2 bonus Momentum.

JURY RIG
Prerequisite: Snap Diagnosis, Tech Expertise 2
Often when a critical piece of equipment breaks down — either due to wear and tear or damage — components necessary to replace it are unavailable. Characters with this talent have a knack for making do without. They suffer no penalty for Tech tests

attempted without the use of proper tools. They can also make an Average (D1) Tech test to temporarily repair a device when necessary parts are unavailable. On a success, the device will continue functioning for one hour. Each point of Momentum earned on the test can be spent to add an additional hour of function.

MAKESHIFT WIZARD
Prerequisite: Greasemonkey, Tech Expertise 2
When the character uses Parts, each Part expended grants 2 bonus Momentum instead of the normal one.

NATURAL ENGINEER
Prerequisite: Tech Expertise 1
When making a Tech test, the character may reroll any dice that did not generate a success on the initial roll, but must accept the new result.

SNAP DIAGNOSIS
Prerequisite: Natural Engineer
The character is able to identify the problem with any broken or malfunctioning device or recognise the vulnerabilities in a piece of equipment that can be used to comrpomise it. The character reduces the difficulty of any Tech test performed for diagnostic purposes by one, to a minimum of Simple (D0). When an Exploit action is taken, Snap Diagnosis also grants the Piercing weapon quality to the character's subsequent attack with a value equal to their Tech Focus.

THIEVERY (AWARENESS)
Thievery covers a broad spectrum of techniques in criminal and criminal-type activities. Many of these skills are, unsurprisingly, also useful in the intelligence and law enforcement communities. In addition to the physical techniques, Thievery also includes an understanding of how criminals act and think, along with the nuances of the criminal underworld which exists beneath every ordered society.

BYPASS SECURITY
Prerequisite: Thief
Maximum Ranks: 3
The character has studied different security systems and has developed a broad range of different techniques to mitigate their efficiency. Any time the character attempts to pick a lock or overcome a security system — regardless of whether it is electronic or mechanical — they may reroll a number of d20s equal to their ranks in Bypass Security. The results on the rerolled dice must be accepted.

INCONSPICUOUS
Prerequisite: Surreptitious Reconnaissance, Thievery Expertise 2
Committing a crime is easy, getting away is harder. Through practice, the character has learned how to avoid notice and slip away undetected. They may substitute their Thievery skill for Stealth when attempting to escape from the scene of a crime, con job, heist, or other Thievery tasks.

LIFE OF CRIME
Prerequisite: Thief
Maximum Ranks: 3
After years of dealing with the criminal underworld, the character has a basic familiarity of how to interact with the Submondo. When making a Persuade or Education test relating to or interacting with the criminal element, they gain bonus Momentum equal to their Life of Crime ranks.

MISDIRECTION
Prerequisite: Surreptitious Reconnaissance, Thievery Expertise 2
A successful theft relies on making sure the target has no reason to expect it. In a face-to-face Thievery test (such as against Observation to see if a theft is noticed), if the character generates at least one success they can immediately roll an additional d20 and add the result to the skill test.

PICK POCKET
Prerequisite: Thief
Maximum Ranks: 3
The character is an expert on lifting and placing objects around someone's person. When making a face-to-face Thievery test (against the target's Observation) to remove an item from someone's body or to place an item on their person, the opponent's difficulty to detect the crime is increased by one for each rank of Pick Pocket.

SURREPTITIOUS RECONNAISSANCE
Prerequisite: Thief
When making Observation tests to case a joint, spot a mark, or otherwise prepare for Thievery tasks, the character can substitute their Thievery skill for Analysis or Observation tests.

THIEF
Prerequisite: Thievery Expertise 1
The character may reroll one d20 when making a Thievery test, but must accept the new result.

THIEVERY TIPS
Common Uses: Picking locks, picking pockets, circumventing surveillance or security systems, bypassing traps and alarms, assessing a target of criminal activities, obtaining or selling items through illicit channels (see Assets, p. 329), sleight of hand

Common Difficulty Factors: Disruption, Distraction, Equipment, Time, Unfamiliarity, Complexity

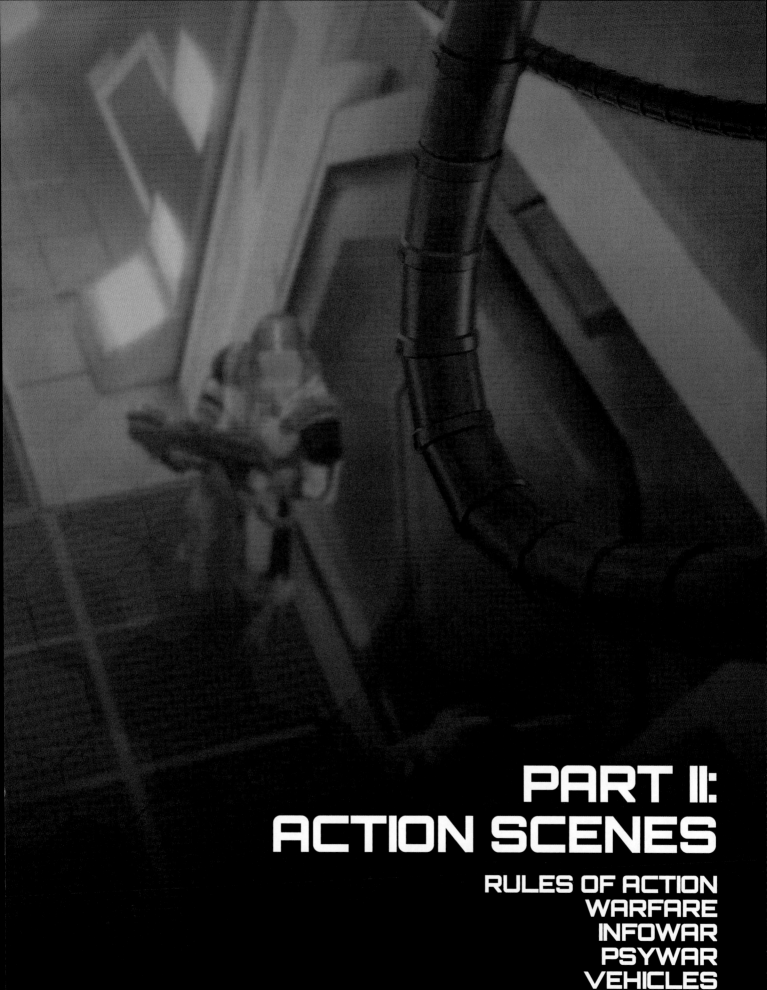

PART II:
ACTION SCENES

RULES OF ACTION
WARFARE
INFOWAR
PSYWAR
VEHICLES

CORVUS BELLI
iNFiNiTY

ACTION SCENES
RULES OF ACTION

Across the worlds of the Human Sphere characters will find themselves opposed by rival factions, enmeshed in the machinations of shadowy conspiracies, and pursued by fearsome aliens. The confrontations born from these conflicts will explode into action scenes — pulse-pounding, action-packed encounters in which extremely skilled player characters will be able to use all of their abilities and resources to accomplish daring and heroic feats.

Action scenes can take many different forms. In *Infinity* each type of action scene has been designed as a flexible module, allowing you to freely combine them to form exciting set pieces in your scenario.

First, there is the triple battlefield of Warfare, Infowar, and Psywar. The rules for Warfare cover the wide gamut of physical violence, but the strategists

and tacticians of the Human Sphere have learned that combat is rarely limited to bullets and body armour. While their comrades lay down covering fire, tactical combat hackers seek to strip away and subvert the technological advantages of their opponents in the quantronic chaos of Infowar. And many battles are decided not by strength of arms, but by the courage of morale. Those who know how to strike fear into the hearts of their foes through the arts of psychological warfare can often strike a decisive blow before the first shot is fired.

What makes the triple battlefield of *Infinity* unique is that each of these action scene modules are designed to be used interchangeably and simultaneously. Additional action scene modules can be found in the *Gamemaster's Guide* and other *Infinity* supplements, including rules for chases, vehicles, mass combat, starship combat, and more. Unique combinations of these modules, applied to the

limitless vistas of the *Infinity* universe, allow you to play out an endless panoply of pulse-pounding sequences.

ROUNDS

Action scenes are divided into rounds. Each round represents a distinct slice of time, during which characters can attempt actions and respond to the actions of their enemies. These rounds are of no fixed duration. Instead, their length will vary based on the encounter in question — an intense firefight in the cramped corridors of a spaceship may have rounds that last only ten seconds, while an aerial TAG dogfight through tight canyons could have rounds lasting for minutes. A complicated quantronic heist on *Tunguska* or a massive battle between spaceships silently manoeuvring through the darkness of space could even have rounds lasting a quarter hour or more.

ACTIONS

Regardless of how much time a round may represent, during the round each character will have a single turn. On their turn, a character can take a single Standard Action, a single Minor Action, and a single Free Action.

FREE ACTIONS
Free Actions require very little time or effort.

MINOR ACTIONS
Minor Actions do not require much energy or effort, but they do require a certain level of focus. A character can also use a Minor Action to perform any number of Free Actions, but cannot perform the same Free Action more than once on any given turn.

STANDARD ACTIONS
Standard Actions are the focus of action scenes and take up most of a character's attention and effort. A character can also use a Standard Action to perform any Minor Action.

REACTIONS
Reactions do not occur during a character's turn, but are special actions triggered by some other event (like an enemy attacking). A character may perform several reactions during a round, but they come at an increasing cost: The first Reaction a character attempts during a round requires that they pay a single point of Heat (into or out of the pool, depending on whether the character is a player character or non-player character). The second Reaction costs 2 Heat, the third Reaction costs 3, and so forth, with each successive Reaction costing one more Heat than the previous one.

TURN ORDER

During each round, the player characters act first. Each round, the players agree upon the order in which their characters will take their turns. Each player resolves all the actions he wishes his character to take (within the normal limitations, described above), and then hands over to another player to do the same. Once all of the player characters have taken their actions during that round, then all the non-player characters take their turns, in whatever order the GM wishes.

Once all the player characters and NPCs have taken their actions in a round, that round is over, one Momentum is lost from the group pool, and a new round begins.

SEIZING INITIATIVE
At the start of the round before anyone has acted or at any time immediately after a player character has finished their turn (and before another player character has begun their turn), the GM can spend 1 Heat to interrupt the player characters and allow an NPC to immediately take its turn.

The NPC resolves their actions normally and, once their turn is done, the turn order passes back to the player characters. (Unless, of course, the GM spends additional Heat to allow other NPCs to take their actions.) That NPC does not get to act again that round.

ATTACKS

There are four different methods of attacking a target: Psywar, Infowar, Melee, and Ranged. As a Standard Action, an attacker declares the type of attack they are making, the method they're using to make that attack (what weapon, technique, form of software, etc), and nominates a single target within range of that attack.

The target has the option of performing a Defence Reaction, in which case the attack is resolved as a face-to-face test using the skills shown on the *Attack Table*. If the target does not perform a Defence Reaction, the attacker makes an Average (D1) test with the skill required for that type of attack.

DAMAGE

If the attack is successful, it inflicts damage. The amount of damage is determined by the damage rating of the attack method. Some environmental effects can also inflict damage, such as falling from a great height, being set on fire, encountering something terrifying, straying too near to an electromagnetic field, or a range of other effects.

DITHERING
If the players spend too much time deliberating and discussing their choices during an action scene rather than actually acting, the GM can take 1 Heat as a warning that they are ceding the initiative to their opponents. At his discretion, the GM can take additional Heat points if the dithering continues.

WHAT TYPE OF ACTION IS IT?
For some actions, the type of action is defined. (For example, it requires a Standard Action to Withdraw from an enemy's reach.) At other times, the GM will need to make a judgment call about what type of action is required. Here are some rules of thumb that you can use:

- Any action that requires a skill test is usually a Standard Action, unless specified otherwise.
- Any action that requires effort but does not require a skill test is probably a Minor Action, such as moving unhindered to the next room.
- Actions that could be resolved in the blink of an eye (like dropping an item held in your hand), those which require almost no effort, or which can be done while simultaneously focusing on other tasks (like talking) are probably a Free Action.
- Most tasks that require a Simple (D0) skill test or no skill test at all are Free Actions. (If a character wishes to roll the dice on the skill test in order to generate Momentum, however, that additional focus and concentration bumps it up to a Standard Action.)

BASIC ATTACKS

All characters have a basic means of attacking for each damage type.

Unarmed Strike: A basic strike with hand, foot, elbow, knee, head, or any other body part. An Unarmed Strike is the basic attack for a melee attack.

Thrown Object: An improvised attack with an object small enough to be held in one hand, commonly a rock or something similarly hard.

Threaten: A basic attempt to scare or demoralise foes, using a mixture of spoken threats and body language.

Intrusion: A basic attempt to overcome a network, requiring access to a terminal if the character does not possess a hacking tool.

HIT LOCATIONS

Physical damage inflicted on the target can affect one of several locations on the body, which may be more or less protected depending on the construction of the character's armour. For example, a helmet only provides protection to the head.

Whenever a physical attack hits, roll 1d20 on the following table (or a special Hit Location dice) to determine which location is struck. The attacker may spend 2 Momentum on the attack in order to choose which location is struck instead.

D20	LOCATION
1–2	Head
3–5	Right Arm
6–8	Left Arm
9–14	Torso
15–17	Right Leg
18–20	Left Leg

The effects of damage do not vary by hit location, though the GM and players are encouraged to use hit locations to guide their description of events.

BASIC ATTACK TABLE

NAME	DAMAGE TYPE	RANGE	DAMAGE	QUALITIES
Intrusion	Quantronic	Reach/Close	1+2 🟡	Unforgiving 1
Threaten	Mental	Reach/Close	1+2 🟡	Stun
Thrown Object	Physical	Close	1+2 🟡	Stun, Subtle 1
Unarmed Strike	Physical	Reach	1+2 🟡	Stun, Subtle 1

Each source of damage has its own damage rating. This is a combination of two numbers — a fixed value and a number of 🟡. This base damage rating is often modified with bonuses or penalties. Once those have been applied, make the damage roll using all of the 🟡 indicated simultaneously and total the result.

Bonus Damage: Characters with above-average attributes have the potential to inflict bonus damage with their attacks. The *Bonus Damage Table* shows the amount of bonus damage a character inflicts with their attacks, depending on the associated attribute.

Triggered Effects: If one or more Effects are rolled on the damage roll, then all of the attack's qualities which are triggered by Effects will also take effect.

If an attack would gain the same quality multiple times from different sources, the effects do not stack unless the quality has a rating (i.e., a quality denoted with an X in its description). Rated qualities are added together (e.g., an attack that gains Piercing 1 from two different sources would instead have Piercing 2).

SOAK

Soak is the means by which characters can protect themselves from damage. Soak can be either persistent or conditional. Persistent soak is always a static value, and is derived from things that are a constant for the character, such as armour worn or innate courage. Conditional soak is a random value, determined by rolling a number of 🟡. It comes from things which are tied to the environment, or the actions characters take, such as the benefits of cover or morale.

The total Soak, from both persistent and conditional sources, is subtracted from the damage inflicted. (It is possible for Soak to reduce the damage of a successful attack to 0.)

Armour is protection against physical attacks gained from equipment. Various types of armour can be found in *Part IV: Gear* (starting on p. 341). **Cover** also protects from physical attacks, but it conditional, rather than persistent.

Morale is used to comprehensively describe both persistent and conditional soak against mental damage. It is a mixture of confidence, self-control, drive, and focus, which can also be enhanced by the support of those around the character or strengthened by circumstance and environment.

Security of quantronic systems or networks represents a complex weave of defensive software and hardware. Many forms of armour also include a Bio-Technological Shield (BTS) which guards against NBC (Nuclear, Biological, and Chemical) threats in addition to nanotechnological, electromagnetic, and Infowar attacks. **Interference** also protects against quantronic attacks, but it is conditional, rather than persistent.

STRESS AND HARM

As shown on the *Damage Table*, each damage type has an associated type of Stress and Harm. Each point of damage a character suffers reduces their associated Stress value by one.

This damage is considered incidental unless 5 or more points of damage have been inflicted or the character's Stress has been reduced to 0 or less. If either of these events occur, the character suffers a

ATTACK TABLE

ATTACK	SKILL	RANGE	DAMAGE TYPE	DEFENCE REACTION
Infowar	Hacking	Reach/Close	Quantronic	Hacking
Melee	Close Combat	Reach	Physical	Close Combat or Acrobatics
Psywar	Persuade	Reach/Close, +1 difficulty per additional range category	Mental	Discipline
Ranged	Ballistics	Per weapon, +1 difficulty per range category in either direction	Physical	Acrobatics

Harm. (If both events occur, they suffer two Harm.) Each type of damage has a different type of associated Harm, as also shown on the *Damage Table*.

Harm Effects: Each Harm suffered also inflicts an additional negative effect on the character. This effect is generally determined by the character inflicting the Harm (subject to GM approval) and will vary depending on the type of attack, the target of the attack, and the attacker's goal. (For example, a character inflicting a Breach with an Infowar attack could decide to knock out the target's communications system.) The effects of multiple Harms stack.

Sample Harm Effects are given for each type of action scene, but players are also encouraged to create their own effects. When coupled with Momentum, Harm Effects give players a great deal of flexibility in using their attacks to accomplish tactical goals beyond simply inflicting damage on their opponents.

INCAPACITATION AND DEATH

If a player character suffers four Breaches, their personal network has become compromised and they cannot take any actions or reactions that rely on their personal area network unless they spend an Infinity Point. (This includes all Comms Equipment and Expert systems.) If they take a fifth Breach, their system has either been burned out (permanently destroying it) or taken over (preventing them from using it in any way and allowing the enemy hacker to freely take actions using it).

ATTRIBUTES		BONUS DMG	
TYPE OF ATTACK	**ASSOCIATED ATTRIBUTE**	**ATTRIBUTE**	**BONUS**
Infowar	Intelligence	8 or less	None
Psywar	Personality	9	+1
Melee	Brawn	10–11	+2
Ranged	Awareness	12–13	+3
		14–15	+4
		16+	+5

DAMAGE TABLE						
DAMAGE TYPE	**PERSISTENT SOAK**	**CONDITIONAL SOAK**	**STRESS**	**HARM**	**RECOVERY**	**TREATMENT**
Quantronic	Security	Interference	Firewall (Intelligence + Hacking)	Breach	Hacking	Tech
Physical (Creature)	Armour	Cover	Vigour (Brawn + Resistance)	Wound	Resistance	Medicine
Mental	Morale	Morale	Resolve (Willpower + Discipline)	Metanoia	Discipline	Psychology
Physical (Object)	Armour	Cover	Structure	Fault	–	Tech

TYPES OF DAMAGE

Physical: A character's Vigour represents their stamina, grit, and ability to endure pain. Losing Vigour represents near-misses, grazes, cuts, scrapes, bruises, and otherwise inconsequential injuries, which are an annoyance but not a hindrance. Wounds are significantly worse than the loss of Vigour and represent serious injuries the character has suffered, which impair their ability to keep fighting.

Mental: A character's Resolve represents their determination, confidence, emotional health, and ability to weather harrowing situations. Losing Resolve represents moments of doubt, uncertainty, and panic, quelled by the character's discipline so that they cause no real problems. As a character's Resolve approaches zero, they become

increasingly doubtful, panicky, and prone to influence. The Greek term *metanoia* means literally "the changing of one's mind". Those making a Psywar attack are literally causing change in the mind of the character suffering Metanoia.

Quantronic: A character's Firewall represents just that – the firewall and anti-intrusion systems present on the character's Personal Area Network. Losing Firewall represents a weakening of the network's security, and the cumulative impact of many attempted intrusions over a period of time. A Breach is significantly worse than the loss of Firewall, and represents serious intrusions into the character's network, which impairs their ability to interface with computer-assisted devices.

ATTACKING OBJECTS

Physical attacks can be made against non-living physical targets. This is resolved exactly as normal for physical damage, with two minor changes: Stress for objects is Structure, rather than Vigour, and the Harms inflicted are Fault Effects, which are described on p. 333. Barring some self-repairing property of the object itself, objects cannot recover Structure or remove Faults by themselves, but rules for repairing objects can be found on p. 333.

SPECIAL HARM EFFECTS

Some attacks and effects will inflict special Harm Effects. Special Harm Effects do not count towards a character becoming incapacitated or having their personal network compromised, but are treated like Harm Effects in all other ways. (For example, they can be removed using the normal rules for recovery.)

PLAYTEST TIP

ROLLING HIT LOCATIONS

Since NPCs don't have hit locations, there's no generally no need for players to roll to see where their attacks land (although it can be useful in guiding the description of the game world). However, it can be effective to have players roll to see where their own characters get hit by successful enemy attacks! It can create a moment of focus and tension for the table, and can also help keep players engaged with the action even when it's not their turn.

Similarly, if a player character suffers four Wounds, they become incapacitated and can only take an action by spending an Infinity Point. If they take a fifth Wound, they die. (Death isn't necessarily irreversible in the Human Sphere, however. As detailed in *Part IV: Gear*, medicine in the Human Sphere can replace dead bodies with new Lhosts and other radical treatments.)

There is no limit to the amount of Metanoia which a character can suffer. Each additional Harm simply continues to inflict effects which influence the target's perceptions, opinions, or choices. Once a fourth Metanoia has been inflicted, however, those effects can include outcomes which would force a character to stop taking actions during the current encounter (like panicking and running away from combat).

Many NPCs require fewer Harms before they have their systems destroyed, are incapacitated, or can be forced to quit the encounter. Troopers, the least important NPCs, are taken out after the first Harm. Elites are incapacitated after two Harms. Nemeses, the most important NPCs, suffer damage as player characters do.

Objects suffer physical damage similar to characters. They become disabled and cannot be used if they have four Faults. If they suffer five Faults, they are permanently destroyed.

RECOVERY

Characters who have suffered damage can remedy it in several different ways, depending on the type of damage inflicted and its severity.

When alleviating damage, there are generally two types of tests. First, there are recovery tests which represent a character's natural healing or self-diagnostics. Second, there are treat tests which are made by skilled professionals attempting to assist the recovery process. The skills used for these tests depend on the type of damage being tended to, as indicated on the *Damage Table*.

It's difficult to treat yourself. Characters can attempt treat checks on themselves, but the difficulty is increased by one.

Harms make it more difficult to recover. For each Harm a character has suffered, the difficulty of all associated recovery tests and treat tests is increased by one (to a maximum of 5).

RECOVER

During an action scene, a character can attempt to recover Stress by taking a Recover action, as described on p. 111. Other characters can use the appropriate treat skill to assist the Recover action.

It is also possible to spend 1 Momentum to recover 1 point of Stress. Alternatively, spending an Infinity Point allows a character to fully recover all lost Stress of one type.

REST

Between action scenes, a character who rests for one hour can attempt an Average (D1) recovery test for each type of Stress. On a success, the character recovers all of their lost Stress.

Doubling the time spent resting (from one to two, from two to four, from four to eight, etc.) reduces the difficulty by one (to a minimum of D1).

During a rest, characters are assumed to be relaxing, bandaging their wounds, and checking their quantronic systems. If they're distracted or preoccupied in a way that would prevent them from doing that, they aren't really resting.

RECUPERATE

Harms are more difficult to recover from. Recovering from Harms must be done one at a time. The character must make an Average (D1) recovery test and, if the test is successful, they can remove a single Harm. This takes a day if the character is suffering from a single Harm or a week if they are suffering from two or more Harms.

Simultaneous Recuperation: If characters are suffering from multiple types of Harm, the recuperation periods for each type of Harms can overlap. (In other words, you can recuperate from each type of Harm simultaneously, making separate recovery tests for each type of Harm at the end of each recuperation period.)

Recuperate Momentum: Momentum can be spent to heal additional Harms during recuperation, requiring a number of Momentum equal to the difficulty of the test (after the increase imposed by the Harms themselves) for each additional Harm recovered.

Long-Term Care: A character can provide long-term care to a resting or recuperating patient. The caretaker uses their treat skill to assist the patient's recovery tests.

MINOR TREATMENT

During an action scene, a character can attempt to remove a Harm Effect from a character or object by taking a Treat action, as described on p. 112. (This will not remove the Harm. Only the Harm Effect is alleviated.)

SERIOUS TREATMENT

Once per day, a character may attempt a treat test in order to perform surgery, engage a victim in serious psychotherapy, patch a serious breach, or repair major damage to an object by making an Average (D1) treat test. On a success, the patient can remove one Harm plus an additional Harm for every Momentum spent.

The time required for serious treatment varies based on the difficulty of the test (which, as described above, increases based on the number of Harms the character is suffering from) — one hour to complete a D1 test, three hours to complete a D2 test, six hours to complete a D3 test, twelve hours to complete a D4 test, and eighteen hours to complete a D5 test. The character can reduce the time taken by an hour per Momentum spent, to a minimum of one hour.

CHARACTER CONDITIONS

There are a number of detrimental conditions that can afflict a character during action scenes.

Bleeding: The character suffers 3  physical damage, ignoring all Soak, at the beginning of each of their turns.

Blind: The character's vision has been severely damaged. Upon being blinded, a character suffers 3  mental damage. Any skill test reliant on vision increases in difficulty by two steps.

RECUPERATING BREACHES

Recuperation largely represents the ability of the body and the mind to naturally heal themselves over time. It may seem odd to think of a Breach healing itself, but the reality is that even the simplest quantronic devices in the Human Sphere have low-level autonomous repair programs running on them.

PLAYTEST TIP
DOWNTIME

At points of extended downtime (whether during an adventure or between adventures), it's often easiest for the GM to simply declare that all of the PCs' Harms have fully recuperated. It's not necessary to spend time making all of the required rolls if it's clear that they have the resources and time they need to heal up.

SLEEP DEPRIVATION

Characters who don't get a full night's rest must succeed on a Resistance (D1) test or become fatigued. The difficulty of this test increases by one step for each additional night without rest.

DUAL WIELDING

A character wielding two weapons can gain a slight advantage when trying to engage multiple targets, or attack more rapidly, but this requires considerable skill to capitalise on effectively.

When a character wields two weapons, they may use the swift action momentum spend (p. 106) by paying only one Momentum, rather than two, so long as both Actions taken are attacks, and each attack is taken with a different weapon.

Burning X: The target is set alight. This condition lasts for a number of rounds equal to the number of Effects rolled on the attack that inflicted it, a listed duration, or (if neither of those things are true) a single round. At the end of the target's turn, it suffers X Ⓝ damage to Vigour and Resolve (roll once and apply to both), ignoring any Armour. This damage has the Incendiary weapons quality (Effects rolled increase the number of rounds that the character remains Burning). Additional Burning effects extend the existing status by their duration.

Checked: The character's movement is being halted by a directional, exterior force. They cannot move in that direction.

Dazed: All skill tests performed by a Dazed character increase in difficulty by one step.

Deafened: The character's hearing has been severely damaged. Upon being Deafened, a character suffers 3 Ⓝ mental damage. Any skill test reliant on hearing increases in difficulty by two steps.

Fatigued: Fatigue makes it difficult for characters to focus and exert themselves. A character suffering from the Fatigued condition suffers a +1 complication range to all skill tests. Multiple instances of the Fatigued condition stack. This special condition cannot be cleared with the Absterge action. After 8 hours of rest, however, a character can attempt an Average (D1) recovery test using the Resistance skill to remove the Fatigued condition. (If the character is suffering from multiple Fatigued conditions, an additional Fatigued condition can be removed per 1 Momentum spent on this test. Other characters can assist with a treat test using the Medicine skill.)

Helpless: The character is unable to take any Reactions. Further, any attempts to use the Exploit action against the character reduce the difficulty by one step, and gain 1 bonus Momentum.

Hindered: When making a movement action, a Hindered character moves one fewer zone than normal and cannot move as a free action. The character also increases the difficulty of all terrain tests by one step.

Marked: The character has been Marked by an enemy opponent (usually with some form of equipment). When making ranged attacks against Marked opponents, characters can reroll any of the d20s used on the test (but must accept the new results). The Marked condition also allows enemy opponents to take advantage of equipment with the Guided quality.

Prone: Ranged attacks targeting a Prone character at Medium range or further are made at +1 difficulty and the prone character also gains +2 Soak for each Effect rolled on cover dice (if any). However, melee attacks and ranged attacks made at Close range gain two bonus Momentum. Prone characters are also Hindered.

Staggered: A Staggered character must pay one Momentum in order to perform a Standard Action. A Staggered character must pay an Infinity Point in order to perform a Reaction (in addition to the normal Heat cost).

Stuck: A character cannot move away from the object or location that they're stuck to.

Unconscious: Knocked out, sleeping, or otherwise lacking awareness. Unconscious characters cannot take any actions and are also Helpless.

STEALTH

While direct confrontation is one way to solve problems, it is far from the only way. Oftentimes, it is valuable to pass unseen, to evade and elude foes rather than to gun them down. Moreover, if it becomes necessary to use force, then better to use it from a position of strength against an unknown foe than to risk pain and death in a "fair fight".

Stealth is generally not a specific action which a character performs. Instead, it is a series of states in which other actions are performed.

STEALTH STATES

A stealthy character exists in one of three states — Revealed, Detected, or Hidden.

A **revealed** character is visible to their enemies and their precise location is known. Other characters can attack and react to revealed opponents normally — they're assumed to communicate with one another when a target is revealed. Revealed is, in essence, a state where stealth has not been attempted or where stealth has failed.

A **detected** character is one who the enemy cannot currently see, but whose presence and approximate location are known. Other characters can attack and react to detected opponents normally, but any associated tests have their difficulty increased by two steps.

A **hidden** character is one who the enemy cannot currently see, hear, or otherwise perceive, and whose location is not currently known. Sometimes, a hidden character's presence may not be known either. Other characters cannot make attacks or make Reactions against a hidden opponent's actions.

STEALTH STATE TEST

As described below, various actions may require a character to make a stealth state test. A stealth state test is an Average (D1) Stealth test. On a failure, the character's stealth state is decreased by one step (i.e., hidden characters become detected and detected characters become revealed).

Opponents can perform a Reaction to a stealth state test in order to make it a face-to-face test opposed by their Observation test. On their turn, opponents can use a Standard Action to attempt to find characters who are in a stealth state (forcing an opposed stealth state test). In addition, any time a stealth state test fails, an opponent can spend 2 Momentum to decrease the stealthy character's stealth state by an additional step (immediately revealing a hidden character).

STEALTHY ACTIONS

Becoming hidden is a Minor Action which requires a stealth state test.

Once a character is in a stealthy state, the character's actions will determine whether or not they remain in that state. The GM will classify each action attempted by a stealthy character as either silent, sneaky, or noisy.

A **silent** action does not change the stealth state of a character performing it.

A **sneaky** action requires a stealth state test, which is made as a Free Action immediately after the sneaky action is resolved. If the test fails, the character's stealth state is reduced by one step.

A **noisy** action allows a Simple (D0) Observation test to detect the character and reduce his stealth state by one step. If the check is successful, opponents can also perform a Reaction to force the stealthy character to perform an opposed stealth state test (which may result in their stealth state decreasing by another step).

Stealthy characters can spend 2 Momentum to reduce a noisy action to a sneaky action or to reduce a sneaky action to a silent action.

In addition, common sense prevails when it comes to stealth. For example, many actions that directly affect a target (like shooting them) will automatically result in a stealthy character becoming detected by the target (even if they perform the attack in perfect silence). Characters can also choose to simply stop being stealthy, either deliberately or as an obvious consequence of their actions (such as walking out into the middle of a spotlight on an empty stage without any kind of high-tech camouflage).

ATTACKING FROM STEALTH

If the character is currently hidden or detected, he may reduce the difficulty of the Exploit action by one step; if this reduces the difficulty to Simple (D0), then Exploit may be taken as a Free Action.

DETECTING STEALTHY CHARACTERS

Opponents can use a Standard Action to actively scan or search a zone in order to spot a stealthy character. This requires an Average (D1) Observation test. The stealthy character can perform a Reaction in order to make this a face-to-face test against their Stealth test. If the Observation test succeeds, the stealthy character's stealth state becomes one step worse (i.e., hidden characters become detected and detected characters become revealed). If the test succeeds and the observing character also spends two Momentum, the character's stealth state worsens by an additional step.

MANY FORMS OF STEALTH

Like the rules for turn order and making attacks, the rules for stealth are designed to be a flexible tool which can be universally applied in any action scene. This also makes Stealth an interesting skill because it can be applied in so many different contexts.

Stealth is most often used during some form of physical infiltration or clandestine action. This type of Agility-based Stealth test is what's commonly used in Warfare scenes.

Stealth tests performed during an Infowar scene, on the other hand, are more likely to be Intelligence-based. Used in this context, stealth models canny combat hackers slipping into enemy networks undetected and leaving behind their viral payloads.

The rules for stealth can also be used in social confrontations. Personality-based Stealth checks can be used while waging covert propaganda wars or while trying to undermine a hypercorp executive without warning them of the impending takeover.

SURPRISE

When one group of characters attempts to gain an advantage over another group of characters by taking them by surprise, the attempt is resolved as a face-to-face test. Each side nominates a leader who will attempt the skill test, while the other members of the group assist the test as normal.

Each character on whichever side succeeds on the surprise test gains 1 Momentum and automatically acts first at the start of combat. (If they are NPCs, they do not need to spend Heat to do this. If they are PCs, the GM cannot spend Heat to seize the

PLAYTEST TIP
DISTRACTIONS

You can often assist stealthy characters by creating a distraction. Use the standard rules for assisting their stealth state test, and get creative in the types of distractions you can create: Persuade tests can be used to keep a guard talking. Wild animal calls can be mimicked with Animal Handling. Tech could be used to rig a firecracker. And so forth.

STEALTH MODIFIERS

While the lucky or skilled may be able to sneak past a distracted guard on a sunny day, the stealthy approach proves most rewarding (and reliable) when it takes advantage of environmental factors.

Illumination: Light and darkness are common factors in Stealth tests. Darkness, ranging from low light to total blackouts, increase the difficulty of Observation tests, while brightly lit locations can increase the difficulty of Stealth tests.

Distance: Don't forget to take into account the effects of distance on Observation tests (see p. 108)!

Ambient Noise: Background noise can increase the difficulty of Observation tests. (Consider both the volume and the frequency of the sounds in question.)

Weather: Heavy rain or thick fog is the stealthy character's friend.

ACTION SCENE MOMENTUM

SPEND	COST	EFFECT
Bonus Damage	1	A character can increase the damage inflicted by a successful attack, regardless of the type of attack. Each Momentum spent adds +1 damage.
Confidence	1	The character gains 1  Morale Soak per Momentum spent (maximum 4 ) until the start of his next turn.
Penetration	1	The damage inflicted by the current attack ignores an amount of Soak equal to twice the Momentum spent.
Reroll Damage	1NR	The player may reroll any number of damage dice from the current attack.
Second Wind	1	The character chooses a type of damage, and recovers one point in the associated capability for each Momentum spent.
Secondary Target	2	A second target within Reach of the primary target is also affected by the attack, and suffers half the attack's damage, rounding down (to a random hit location, if physical)
Subdue	1	The attack gains the Nonlethal quality.
Stealthy	2	Reduce noisy action to sneaky or sneaky action to silent.
Swift Action	2NR	The character gains an additional Standard Action, increasing the difficulty by one step on any skill test that action requires. This may only be done once per round.
Withdraw	1	The character leaves the Reach of an enemy without triggering any Retaliate Reactions.

initiative and override this.) If the group attempting surprise succeeds, they are also assumed to be in a hidden stealth state (if appropriate).

Typical surprise scenarios include an ambush (Stealth vs. Observation), breaking a Mexican stand-off (Ballistics vs. Ballistics), or betraying your supposed allies at a wedding (Persuade vs. Psychology).

MOMENTUM

Momentum is a key tactical resource during action scenes. The following table provides a number of additional options available to a character when they generate one or more Momentum in any action scene. These are in addition to the normal uses of Momentum, and any others that the players or GM create themselves. Each action scene module will also contain similar tables with additional options unique to those action scenes (e.g., Warfare, Infowar, and Psywar).

WARFARE

Warfare covers physical conflict – life-and-death struggles, battles with gun and blade, car chases, and other places where physical violence and bloodshed are likely. It also covers, when combined with the rules for *Stealth* on p. 104, situations where bloodshed and violence are the consequences of failure, the risk being faced if the characters are not careful enough.

ENVIRONMENTS/ ZONES

During a warfare scene, knowing where everyone is physically located can be of vital import, and determining both absolute position (where you are in the scene) and relative position (how far you are from a given friend or foe) is important. Rather than tracking everything using precise distances, however, *Infinity* divides the setting of the scene into abstract zones.

At the start of an action scene, the GM will define the environment by dividing it into a number of different zones based on the terrain features present in the area. (Generally three to five distinct zones are a good place to start, although this number will vary depending on the exact nature of the scene.) Each zone is a small, contiguous area. There are no hard and fast rules when it comes to defining the size or boundaries of a zone, but the identity of a zone will generally flow naturally form the divisions and logic of the setting.

For example, a Varunan cop exchanging gunfire with Libertos terrorists in the hallway of a building might dive out of the line of fire into one of the apartments lining the hall. The hallway is one zone; the apartment is another.

Similarly, think about the landmarks by which people will define their position. On a Qingdao street, for example, Imperial Agents approach a building where they suspect PanOceanian agent provocateurs are laying low. When shots ring out, they look around for cover and see a parked car, a streetlight, and an AR art display. You can easily imagine them running from their car (one zone), across the street (another zone), to the streetlight (a third zone).

Because zones are of no fixed size, they can be varied to accommodate the GM's preferences for a given scene, and to represent certain other factors.

For example, a battle amidst the towering trees of the Great Arboreal Reserve on Acontecimento may be divided into many small zones amongst the trees (difficult to navigate and offering lots of cover), and a couple of larger zones representing clearings (easy to see or move across).

RANGE AND MOVEMENT

To keep things simple and fluid, the distance between zones is handled in an approximate manner, using five broad range categories:

Reach is when an object or character is within arm's length. Characters enter Reach to interact with objects manually, to attack in close combat, and to perform any other actions where they may need to touch the subject of their action. A character can move within the reach of a target as part of any movement action that ends in the same zone as the target. Moving out of an enemy's reach may be risky, as it leaves the character open to the Retaliate reaction unless they take a Withdraw action.

Close range is defined as the character's current zone. Moving within Close range is a Free Action.

Medium range is defined as any zone adjacent to the character's current zone. Moving to a point within Medium range is a Minor Action.

Long range is defined as any point two zones away from the character's current zone. Moving to a point within Long range is a Standard Action.

Extreme range is defined as any point three or more zones away from the character's current zone. A character cannot move to Extreme range in a single action under normal circumstances.

A character cannot perform more than one movement action per turn. (For example, they cannot use their Minor Action to move to an adjacent zone and then use their Standard Action to move an additional two zones.)

RANGE AND ATTACKS

Each attack has a specific range, as shown on the *Attack Table* (p. 100) or as specified by the weapon used. A target can only be attacked if they are within the range of the attack. In some cases (including Psywar and attacks using ranged

PLAYTEST TIP
CONCRETE VS ABSTRACT
GMs who desire concrete values rather than abstract ranges are encouraged to set specific sizes and shapes for individual zones, essentially using them as a large grid. This doesn't work any differently in practice, but it does lose some of the nuance of varying zone size by terrain density and focusing on easy-to-describe features.

TRACKING ZONES
Because zones are defined logically by the terrain of the battlefield, it is usually relatively easy to keep track of how the zones relate to each other and which zones characters are in at any given moment. Larger or particularly complex scenes may become tricky to track purely by memory, however, and the GM may wish to use something extra to help remind everyone of where their characters are. Usually nothing more than a quickly sketched zone map is required (using tokens or pencil marks to indicate the positions of various characters). Miniatures are often a fun way to track a character's position on a map, as well as representing that character's appearance, but they're not essential to play – any marker that can be quickly distinguished from the others in play is good (so that it's easy to tell which marker represents which character).

PLAYTEST TIP

CREATING DISTANCE WITH ZONES

If you want to create a scene in which there are only a few zones of interest which should nonetheless feel distant from each other, you can fill the space between them with any number of 'empty' zones in order to create the right feel. These empty zones can prove dangerous to cross — while they may be open, they also probably lack cover, which means that empty spaces become "kill boxes", guarded by snipers or enemies with heavy weaponry.

EXAMPLE

ATTACKS AT RANGE

Cassandra is armed with a light shotgun, which has a range of Close, and a heavy pistol, which has a range of Reach/Close. A Shasvastii is within Close range, allowing her to fire either weapon without penalty. But then the Shasvastii charges into Reach and begins slashing a knife at her. If Cassandra fires her shotgun, she will have to make the attack at +1 difficulty (because Reach is one range outside of the shotgun's optimal range of Close). She can still fire her pistol without penalty, however.

IMPASSABLE OBSTACLES

Some obstacles are impassable, preventing any movement between the zones the obstacle exists between — the internal walls of a building are a good example, as they cannot be climbed over because of the ceiling above them — but there should normally be a way around the obstacle, such as a doorway, or even a weak point where sufficient force could break through.

weapons), it is possible to attack at multiple ranges. Such attacks have an optimal range (as listed), with each additional range category — whether closer or further away — inflicting a +1 difficulty on the attack test. There is no maximum range for these attacks, but they are far less likely to be effective at ranges outside of their optimal.

RANGE AND COMMUNICATION

Characters will want to communicate during a Warfare scene — calls for help, battle cries, derisive slurs, and other dialogue are common on the battlefield. In most cases, characters can converse normally within Close range — they're near enough to one another to be heard and to make themselves understood without raising their voices. A character at Medium range can be communicated with, but only at a raised volume — shouting rather than talking. At Long and Extreme range, characters can shout to draw attention, but conveying any complex meaning or understanding someone is unlikely. (Of course, methods of communication like radios or comlogs make distance less of a consideration.)

RANGE AND PERCEPTION

The further away something is, the harder it is to notice. Increase the difficulty of Observation tests by one step at Medium range, by two at Long range, and by three at Extreme range.

COMBAT ZONE EFFECTS

Individual zones can — and often should — have terrain effects defined by the GM. These can include hazards to overcome, objects that can be interacted with, or even terrain that changes under particular circumstances. On the other hand, some zones may be defined more by the absence of terrain than its presence, and many environments are enhanced by a few "empty" zones between obstacles.

The zone effects listed below give a wide variety of options, but GMs are encouraged to create their own to fit the scene.

Combat Terrain Test: Some zone effects will call for a terrain test. This is a skill test, typically using either Acrobatics or Athletics (although unusual terrain may require the use of other skills). If a terrain test of Average (D1) difficulty or higher is required for movement, that movement cannot be performed as a Free Action (even if the movement is only within Close range).

COVER

To gain the benefits of cover in a zone, a character must move within Reach of it. A character in cover gains a bonus to their Armour Soak.
- Light cover provides +2 Cover Soak.
- Heavy cover provides +4 Cover Soak.

DIFFICULT TERRAIN

Moving into, out of, or within a zone of difficult terrain requires an Athletics or Acrobatics test. (The difficulty of the test depends on the difficulty of the terrain.) Failure on the terrain test means that the character makes no progress after the point where the test was required – so a character attempting to enter a zone stops before they enter the zone. In some cases, the GM may also rule that difficult terrain increases the difficulty of other movement-based tests.

DISAPPEARING ZONES

Some areas represented by zones – like collapsing bridges or sinking ships – may disappear. In some cases there may be a countdown to the zone's disappearance (for example, the ship might sink in eight rounds). In other cases, the disappearance might be triggered by character actions (like cutting the guide lines for a rope bridge). Characters stuck in the zone during its disappearance will generally be forcibly ejected into another zone, while possibly suffering damage or other consequences as a result. It may be possible to escape some or all of these consequences by performing some form of skill test as a Reaction. (For example, leaping off the falling bridge with an Acrobatics test.)

GRAVITY ZONES

Low gravity, high gravity, and zero-g environments require special skills and training to navigate – moving easily in space or on un-terraformed worlds is challenging even for the most physically adept.

High-Gravity environments increase the difficulty of Athletics, Acrobatics, and Close Combat tests by one step.

Low-Gravity environments reduce the difficulty of Athletics and Acrobatics tests to jump, climb, and resist falling damage by one step to a minimum of Average (D1).

Zero-G or micro-gravity environments change how a character moves.

A character attempting an Acrobatics, Athletics, or Close Combat test in non-standard gravity reduces their Expertise and Focus ranks to those of their Extraplanetary skill (if it is lower).

HAZARDOUS TERRAIN

A zone of hazardous terrain works like difficult terrain, but with an additional consequence for failure – damage, a condition, or some other peril, such as becoming trapped or stuck. (The simplest example would be a gap that needs to be jumped across, which would cause damage from falling if the character fails their skill test.)

OBSTACLES

Obstacles exist at the points where two zones meet, impairing efforts to pass between those zones. Crossing an obstacle requires a terrain test, as per difficult terrain, and failure prevents the character from moving across the obstacle. Some obstacles may only require a terrain test in a single direction, or may require different difficulties of test in different directions (for example, a slope that is more difficult to ascend than descend).

SATURATION ZONE

A saturation zone contains a multitude of solid obstacles that can limit the effectiveness of projectiles that traverse the area. For any shot going into or passing through a saturation zone, the target gains a bonus to their Soak.

- A light saturation zone grants +2 🄽 Cover Soak.
- A heavy saturation zone grants +4 🄽 Cover Soak.

VISIBILITY ZONE

Due to thick vegetation, jagged rocks, snow, sandstorms, and any number of other reasons, some areas obscure a character's vision.

- A low visibility zone increases the difficulty of vision-based tests by one step.
- A poor visibility zone increases the difficulty of vision-based tests by two steps.
- A zero visibility zone blocks all sight, granting characters the benefit of an appropriate stealth state (see p. 104).

COMMON COMBAT ZONES

AQUATIC TERRAIN

Aquatic terrain is a common form of difficult terrain. Swimming across aquatic terrain requires an Athletics test. (You can't use an Acrobatics test for swimming.) If the check is a failure, a complication will result in the character beginning to drown.

CROWDS

Dense crowds – whether they're people, aliens, animals, or robots – can be modeled as a combination of saturation zones and difficult terrain. The density of the crowd determines both the type of cover and the difficulty of the terrain tests to move through it, but the crowd fills the whole zone and thus provides cover to all creatures in the zone.

RADIATION

Radiation can be a form of hazardous terrain, with a radiation rating describing its severity. Each round that a character is exposed to radiation, they must attempt a Resistance test with a difficulty equal to the radiation rating minus their BTS. On a failure, they suffer 1+2 🄽 physical damage per radiation rating. This damage has the Radiation X quality, where X is equal to the radiation rating.

OTHER SENSES

Human perception, broadly, is dominated by sight and hearing, and thus these are the senses dealt with most frequently by the rules. However, other senses can come into play at times. Naturally, a character's sense of touch is limited to Reach. The sense of smell is most effective for humans within Reach, and Observation tests made to smell something outside of Reach increase in difficulty by one step, plus one step for each range category beyond close. Only the most pungent odours are easily noticeable by humans outside of Close range.

Naturally, non-human characters and creatures may have different expectations for their senses – for example, a dog (or a Dogface) will be able to discern details by scent that a human cannot, but their eyesight is somewhat less acute by comparison. A creature with a particularly keen sense may reduce the difficulty of all Observation tests related to that sense, while dull senses would increase the difficulty of those tests.

DESTROYING COVER

If an attack inflicts sufficient damage against a target in cover, the cover will begin to degrade and will eventually offer no protection. When an attack inflicts ten or more damage above the cover's Soak total (the amount rolled on the cover dice), the cover degrades, losing a single cover dice. If a piece of cover loses all of its cover dice, it is destroyed and no longer provides any protection.

Weapons with the Spread quality add up all the damage inflicted, from all hits, to determine if cover is damaged – such weapons are particularly effective at blasting holes in cover.

ADDITIONAL TERRAIN RULES

Drowning and Suffocation: If a character begins drowning or is otherwise being deprived of oxygen, they must make an Average (D1) Resistance test. Failing this test inflicts one Wound. Every successive turn the character is deprived of oxygen, the test difficulty increases by one.

Falling Damage: A fall deals physical damage equal to 1+2🅝 (Stun, Vicious 1) per zone fallen, including the zone the fall originated in. (For example, a fall of Close range inflicts 1+2🅝 damage while a Long fall inflicts 3+6🅝 damage.) A character jumping down deliberately can count the fall as one range category less (which would mean that a Close fall inflicts no damage). A character about to suffer falling damage can attempt an Acrobatics (D0) test as a reaction, gaining 1🅝 Soak per Momentum spent.

Panicking Crowds: Panicking crowds are a real peril in battle. Crowds are uncertain and unpredictable at the best of times, and they'll mill around making scared noises if weapons are fired in their direction… but if someone is shot in a crowd, it becomes a whole other matter. If one or more Effects are rolled when rolling the 🅝 for the Cover the crowd provides, someone in the crowd in that zone has been hit by the attack, the crowd panics, and every creature in the zone must attempt an Average (D1) Acrobatics test. Failure means the creature immediately suffers 1+3🅝 (Knockdown, Stun) physical damage, as they are shoved, struck, and trampled by the crowd.

Recovery Test (Conditions), p. 111: Physical conditions require a Resistance test, quantronic conditions a Hacking test, psychological conditions a Discipline test, and equipment conditions a Tech test.

"**Absterge**" — meaning to cleanse or purify — was the code name for a virus purger used during the NeoColonial Wars to reset TAG operating systems that had been compromised by infowarriors. It entered the popular vernacular as the equivalent of "walk it off" or "get over it". It has also become a common way to refer to taking any kind of break, as in, "I just need to absterge for a second."

VACUUM

Vacuum is a hazardous terrain. Each round that a character exposed to vacuum must attempt an immediate Average (D1) Extraplanetary test or Challenging (D2) Resistance test. Failing this test inflicts 1+5🅝 (Stun, Vicious 2) damage, ignoring all soak. Each successive turn the character is exposed to vacuum, the difficulty of the test increases by one.

VERTICAL TERRAIN

Vertical surfaces are a common form of difficult terrain. They require an Athletics test to climb. (You can't use an Acrobatics test for climbing.) If the check is a failure, a complication will result in the character falling.

WHITE NOISE

White noise generators are an ECM technique designed to negate multispectral visors and similar equipment. A white noise zone acts as a zero visibility zone for characters equipped with multispectral visors and other high-tech visual aids.

WARFARE ACTIONS

The following actions can be taken during Warfare scenes.

ABSTERGE [MINOR]

As a Minor Action, a character can attempt a recovery test to end a condition that afflicts them or a piece of equipment they're using. If the condition has a specific rating (such as Burning 3), the difficulty of the test is equal to the rating. If not, the test is Challenging (D2).

ASSIST [STANDARD]

The character performs some activity that will grant an ally an advantage. The character nominates a single ally he can communicate with, and declares how he is giving aid, including which skill he is assisting with. During the nominated ally's action, the character provides assistance with the chosen skill, as normal for the rules for assisting on a skill test (see p. 407).

BRACE [STANDARD]

Weapons with a size category of Unwieldy are particularly cumbersome and awkward to wield. An attack with an Unwieldy weapon increases the difficulty of the Ballistics test by two steps and increases the complication range by two.

When a character performs the Brace action, these penalties are removed from future attacks made with the braced weapon. Once a character performs the Brace action, the weapon remains Braced until it is moved.

DRAW ITEM [MINOR]

Using a free hand, the character may pick up an item within Reach, or draw a weapon or other item carried on his person/stowed in his gear. If the item does not require a skill test to use, it can be used immediately upon taking this action, allowing a character to draw and use the item with only one Minor Action.

DROP ITEM [FREE]

The character drops a single item held in one or both of their hands. The item falls to their feet within Reach.

DROP PRONE [FREE]

The character immediately drops to the ground and gains the benefits of the prone condition. A character cannot drop prone and stand in the same turn. (Ranged attacks targeting a Prone character at Medium range or further are made at +1 difficulty and the prone character also gains +2 Soak for each Effect rolled on any cover dice they're allowed to roll. However, melee attacks and ranged attacks made at Close range gain 2 bonus Momentum. Prone characters are also Hindered and, when making a movement action, move one fewer zone than normal.)

EXPLOIT (STANDARD)

The character takes additional time, concentration, or preparation readying their next attack or action. The character nominates a task or target they are able to perceive and attempts an Average (D1) test using an appropriate skill. The primary purpose of an Exploit is to generate Momentum which can be used to improve the result of their next action, but if the Exploit is being performed for an attack and the skill test generates at least one success, the attack also gains the Piercing 2 quality.

READY (STANDARD)

The character may declare that they are waiting for a certain situation or event to occur before performing a Standard Action, which they must choose when they determine the triggering condition. When this triggering situation occurs, the character with the readied action temporarily interrupts the acting character's turn to resolve the readied action. Once the readied action is resolved,

the acting character continues their turn as normal. If the triggering situation does not occur before the character's next turn, the readied action is lost.

Characters who take a readied action can still take Minor and Free actions during their turn as normal, either during their normal turn or alongside the readied action (though the normal number of actions still applies).

RECOVER (STANDARD)

The character hunkers down, grits their teeth, and fights through the pain. The character chooses a single type of damage (physical, mental, or quantronic), and attempts an Average (D1) recovery test. On a successful test, the character regains two Vigour (physical), Resolve (mental), or Firewall (quantronic), plus two more for each Momentum spent. Other characters can assist the recovery test by performing first aid, providing moral support, or applying an emergency software patch and making the appropriate treat test.

Because the character is focusing on their own wellbeing first and foremost, when they take the take the Recover action, they may reroll any cover dice they roll until the start of their next turn.

Recovery Test (Recover), p. 111: Recovering Firewall requires a Hacking test, Resolve requires a Discipline test, and Vigour requires a Resistance test. This test increases in difficulty by one for each Harm of that kind the character is suffering.

OTHER EXPLOITS

The Exploit action can also be used to represent attempts to ambush, feint, or attack with some other significant advantage. GM's may allow characters to use skills other than Observation to attempt an Exploit action, and he may modify the difficulty to represent more or less vulnerable targets. Stealth tests are the most common form of this, but a Persuade test (representing a trick or deception) or an Acrobatics test (representing some grand feat of agility) are viable options. The GM is encouraged to let players have fun with this option. In situations where the skill test's difficulty is Simple (D0), Exploit may be used as a Free Action, but no Momentum can be spent on the test.

OTHER FORMS OF MOVEMENT

Broadly, different forms of movement are treated the same — they are means of crossing particular types of hindering terrain or obstacles.

Climbing is any movement where a character traverses a steep slope or sheer vertical surface. These are normally obstacles — walls, cliffs, and similar barriers — but some situations may have whole zones where climbing is the only way to move around. Climbing movement requires a terrain test using the Athletics skill. The more challenging the climb, the higher the difficulty — a rough cliff face with plentiful hand-holds has a difficulty of Average (D1), as is a moderately steep slope that requires some effort to climb. Attempting to climb a vertical surface without tools — rope, hooks, and so forth — increases the difficulty by one step. Attempting to climb upside down underneath a horizontal surface, such as a ceiling, increases the difficulty by two steps.

Jumping is any movement across a gap or space, controlled movement down to a space below, or movement in an attempt to reach something above. Jumping uses the Acrobatics skill, and it can be used in a variety of ways. Jumping across a small gap or over a small barrier — counting as an obstacle — is an Average (D1) Acrobatics test. Jumping down from a height uses the same

rules as falling, but reduces the difficulty of the Acrobatics test by one step. Jumping up to grasp something within the character's normal reach requires an Average (D1) Acrobatics test, increasing as the upward distance increases.

Swimming is movement through a body of water, typically defined in game terms as one or more zones of Hindering terrain. Zones filled with water must be traversed by swimming, and all Swimming uses the Athletics skill for terrain tests. The rougher the water being crossed, the greater the difficulty, with calm water requiring an Average (D1) Athletics test to cross quickly. Remaining stationary in the water — treading water — requires a Simple (D0) Athletics test.

Flight is movement through the air. Only creatures specifically noted as being able to fly are able to do so. A creature capable of flight can move freely through any zone (above the ground), including through "empty" zones above the ground that are not normally accessible. Flying creatures don't typically suffer the effects of difficult terrain, though tall structures (such as the tops of buildings) can serve as Obstacles, and strong winds can serve as Hindrances, while particularly stormy weather might well count as a hazard — hailstones and lightning are risks for high-flying creatures.

SPEAK (FREE)

The character may talk to allies, bellow a war cry, shout an order, threaten a rival, or otherwise converse with a few sentences or phrases. (This action only allows for simple communication. It cannot be used to perform Psywar attack and any verbal action which require a Command test, Persuade test, or any other skill test requires a Standard Action.)

STAND (MINOR)

If the character is prone, they may take this action to stand, losing all the benefits and disadvantages of being prone.

SWAP AMMO (MINOR)

For weapons capable of using multiple types of ammunition, it requires a Minor Action to swap between ammo types (unless the weapon has the MULTI quality).

TREAT (STANDARD)

A character can tend to someone who has suffered a Harm as a Standard Action by making an Average (D1) treat test. On a success, the patient is no longer affected by one Harm Effect they were suffering from, plus an additional Harm Effect for every 2 Momentum spent. (The Harm itself remains. Only the Harm Effect is alleviated.)

WITHDRAW (STANDARD)

As a Standard Action, a character can Withdraw to any point within Close range which is not within reach of an enemy. A character performing a Withdraw cannot be targeted by a Retaliate Reaction that turn.

If the character and their allies within Reach outnumber the enemies within Reach, then they may Withdraw as a Free Action instead of a Standard Action.

Treat Test, p. 112: Breaches require a Tech test, Metanoia requires a Psychology test, and Wounds require a Medicine test. The difficulty increases by one for each Harm of the same type. The difficulty increases by two steps if the character attempts to treat himself.

WARFARE REACTIONS

COVERING FIRE

As a Reaction at any time, a character can provide covering fire to an ally by expending a single reload from their ranged weapon. Until the beginning of the character's next turn, any attacks made against the ally being assisted are made at +1 difficulty. If multiple characters provide covering fire to support a single ally the effects stack, to a maximum of +3 difficulty.

To provide covering fire, a character must be able to see either the character they are supporting or the enemy they are trying to suppress.

DEFENCE

As a Reaction to an attack, a character can attempt to defend themselves against an attack. The attack becomes a face-to-face skill test. The skill used by the defender depends on the type of attack (see *Attack Table*, p. 100).

Parry: When parrying a melee attack using the Close Combat skill, a character must have a suitable weapon or piece of equipment available for the parry. (Alternatively, the GM may call for a more difficult defence test. It simply isn't that easy to parry a sword with your bare hand.)

GUARD

A character within Reach of another character may aid in their defence by standing in harm's way as a Reaction. The guarding character makes a Challenging (D2) face-to-face skill test against the attack (using the same skill as a Defence Reaction). If they succeed, they become the target of the attack and can use their Momentum to determine whether or not the attack is successful, as normal for a face-to-face test. If they fail, the original target remains the target of the attack.

RETALIATE

The character lashes out at a nearby foe. This Reaction may be used when an enemy attempts to make a non-attack skill test when within Reach of the character, or when an enemy attempts to move out of Reach of the character without using the Withdraw action. The character may immediately attempt a melee attack.

Resolve the Retaliate Reaction before the action it is a Reaction to; if the character's melee attack is successful, the target's movement requires a Simple (D0) terrain test as if bypassing an obstacle. (This test would automatically succeed, but Momentum can be spent to increase its difficulty as with any other skill test, thus making it possible to use the

SPEND	COST	EFFECT
Called Shot	2	The character can choose the hit location struck by a physical attack.
Change Stance	1	The character either goes prone or stands up.
Disarm	2	One item or weapon held by the target of a successful attack is knocked away and falls to the ground within Reach.
Knockdown	2+	The target must make an Athletics test (difficulty equal to half the Momentum spent) to avoid being knocked prone.

Retaliate Reaction to prevent an opponent from retreating.).

RETURN FIRE

After being declared the target of a ranged attack, a character can perform a Return Fire Reaction, as long as they have a suitable weapon equipped. The character returning fire makes an immediate ranged attack against the triggering enemy, though they cannot spend more than one Reload on this attack. Both attacks are resolved simultaneously — that is, damage (and other effects from either attack) is applied after both attacks have been made, so that neither attacker suffers any penalty from damage sustained on the attacks they're making.

WOUND EFFECTS

The following effects can be used for Wounds suffered during a Warfare scene, or in any other circumstance where Wounds are inflicted.

Bleeding: The target gains the Bleeding condition. (This condition can be removed with the Absterge action, ending the Wound Effect.)

Cripple: Target suffers +1 difficulty on all Agility-, Brawn-, or Coordination-based actions.

Dazed: The target gains the Dazed condition. If they are already Dazed, they become Staggered. (This condition can be removed with the Absterge action, ending the Wound Effect.)

Horrific Wound: The target suffers 1+2 (Vicious 1) Resolve damage.

Knockout: The target must make a Resistance test to avoid being rendered unconscious. The difficulty of the test is equal to the number of Wounds the character is currently suffering from. If the test is successful, the character still suffers the Wound, they merely avoid the Wound Effect.

ACTION SCENES
INFOWAR

The quantronic substrate of reality is pervasive. It can be found in virtually every location touched by humankind or their technology. It exists in a symbiotic link with the physical world — a network of tags and clouds linked to people, places, and things — while also delving down into the hidden geographies of the "deep spheres" which exist only in the meshed protocols of interlinked systems.

It is everywhere. And that means that the endless struggles of the infowar can be found anywhere. Hackers, infoperators, and EVO troops navigate the substrate, surfing and breathing the endless, fractal complexities of the data flux created by the constant connections being continuously forged and broken according to the protocols of Maya, Arachne, and other dataspheres.

The goal of an infowarrior is to:

- Identify the desired target to access in order to achieve their goal.
- Either physically go to the location of that target or connect to the network containing it.
- Reach the zone that contains the target.
- Use Infowar attacks to Breach the target, using either Breach Effects or a total takedown, to make the target do what they want or give them what they need.

Targets can be physical devices, virtual environments, collections of data, comlogs, or personal area networks. Basically anything which possesses a discrete Firewall.

BASIC HACKING
The rules for an action scene focused on Infowar assume that there's significant resistance or danger: enemy infowarriors, automated immune systems, and the like. You wouldn't use the rules for Warfare if someone was walking across an empty room, and you don't need to use the rules for Infowar to accomplish the quantronic equivalent. In many cases, a Hacking test will often suffice for determining whether or not a character can gain access to a particular system, network, or encrypted piece of data.

AR HACKING
Pervasive augmented reality (AR) means that physical and quantronic reality are often coterminous with each other: Objects, systems, networks, and even people have both a material and informatic presence which are usually perceived simultaneously and indistinguishably from each other.

AR hacking, therefore, is the process of hacking things in your immediate vicinity (or the vicinity of your repeaters). This notably includes Infowar attacks that are performed as part of a Warfare scene on a physical battlefield and, in fact, it can be largely summarized as hacking a target that's within your current combat zone.

Essentially, AR hacking uses all the normal rules for making quantronic attacks, but does not require the use of quantronic zones (because the targets are physically present). It is often used side-by-side with other forms of attack.

REMOTE HACKING
Although the easiest way to perform a hack is to have physical access to your target (or a repeater with physical access), that's not always possible. Fortunately, virtually every system in the Human Sphere is connected — either directly or indirectly — to a datasphere, and most of them have a connection to the ubiquitous Maya or Arachne 'spheres. As long as the hacker has access to at least one system in the same 'sphere as their target, they can hypothetically breach it with a remote hack.

Remote hacking uses the full Infowar rules, including those for quantronic zones.

QUANTRONIC ZONES

During an Infowar scene, quantronic zones form the system map in which the conflict will take place. At a fundamental level, each quantronic zone represents a system or network: So if you're in a zone, it means you have access to the files, programs, and other data housed on the system that zone represents (the same way that, if you're in a combat zone, you have access to the walls, furniture, trees, and other objects inside that zone).

Many of these zones will include targets. Targets have individual Firewall values which must be overcome in order to access or manipulate them. Some targets will be purely passive or "dumb" systems, but others will have active immune systems. Of course, hackers themselves are also targets: They occupy quantronic zones and they have Firewall values.

PLAYTEST TIP
JOINING THE PARTY
The image of the lone hacker diving into a computer system is a common occurrence, but it doesn't make for a great game when it means that only one player is actively engaged with the scenario. A couple things to keep in mind: First, a lot of cyberassaults are carried out simultaneously with some form of physical assault, like augmented reality heists in which the hacker is opening the doors for the infiltrators and the infiltrators are getting the hacker access to systems that are off-the-grid. Second, the most successful Infowar operations are often carried out by a team, and in the *Infinity* system (with teamwork tests and Momentum sharing), there's little reason for the rest of the PCs not to tag along and lend a hand.

When defining quantronic zones, GMs should consider that the Maya augmented reality protocols (and the similar protocols used in the Arachne datasphere) mean that quantronic zones often mimic those in the real world: All the devices in a corporate lobby, for example, have a relationship with each other.

These "shallow" zones, however, are often connected to others through quantronic dimensions that have no equivalence to real world geometries. For example, the cameras in the lobby may be linked to the security system while the holoprojectors are linked to an entertainment server (and each of those zones will, in turn, connect to other zones through direct and indirect means). The deep sphere is an ocean of unpredictable depths.

It's also important to note that, just as physical combat zones can vary in size and scale based on the context of the fight, the same is even more true of quantronic zones. In an Infowar engagement, you might be in a tight fight for control of a single corporate network, or you might be dueling and dancing through the security nets of an entire

planetary grid. It depends on what your targets are and what your opposition is.

NAVIGATING QUANTRONIC ZONES

Range and movement between quantronic zones is handled using the exact same rules as combat zones. (For example, a target that's two quantronic zones away from your current zone is at Long range and it would take a Standard Action to move to that zone.)

In general, however, quantronic actions can only be taken at a range of Close or Reach. (Although hackers will frequently employ repeaters which allow them to make Infowar attacks and take quantronic actions as if they were in a zone other than their own.)

QUANTRONIC OBSERVATION

When dealing with quantronic zones, characters can "see" their current zone and anything in it. They can also see zones at a distance up to their Analysis Expertise, but secured zones block line of sight unless the character has authentication. (Characters cannot see into or past secured zones.)

Quantronic Stealth: Quantronic targets, zones, and even specific quantronic zone effects can be hidden. Characters use the Analysis skill instead of the Observation skill when trying to discern hidden targets, zones, and objects, as it requires being able to pick out small details in vast quantities of code.

LOCATING A TARGET

IDENTIFYING THE TARGET
In many cases you may already know what your intended target is, but if you don't — if you need to figure out, for example, where you can find the blueprints of a Jingbai research facility — you can usually perform a research test to find out.

RESEARCHING THE TARGET
Even after a hacker knows exactly what their target is, it isn't unusual for them to continue researching it. This can include datasphere research (whether encyclopaedic reading or ancillary hacks to reveal additional details), social engineering (bribing a guard for passcodes or seducing a system administrator to learn details about their security measures), physical infiltration (dumpster diving for improperly discarded records or planting remotes), or reaching out to the wider hacker community (for known exploits or prior experience with the systems in question).

Depending on the exact nature of the research, it may utilize skill tests for Analysis, Education, Hacking, Persuade, or Stealth. These can usually be handled as Simple (D0) tests, with Momentum generated by the tests being applied to the run.

Alternatively, the Momentum could be spent to gain specific information (like the physical location of the system or details on security protocols) or to secure authentication.

Once you're inside a system, you can often snoop around and learn even more.

ACCESSING THE TARGET
An access point is the location at which a hacker attempting to access the local system will begin. The access point may be accessible because the hacker has physical access to it (like the security cameras in a corporate lobby), but it may also simply be in the best possible zone the hacker can access in the datasphere during a remote hack.

In some cases, the GM may have a predesigned system or network of quantronic zones (just like any other adventuring locale). If that's the case, the hacker's research should turn up one or more specific access points.

INFOWAR: CAN'T GET THERE FROM HERE
Almost everything is interconnected in the Human Sphere, but sometimes you just can't get there from here: The information is in a different datasphere. (For example, Maya and Arachne are different dataspheres. Military dataspheres often have limited connections and are quite difficult to breach. Some information is simply kept disconnected for security purposes.) When that happens, you simply have to find a way of gaining access to whatever 'sphere the information is in, and then you find an access point normally.

NON-HACKABLE
Almost everything built in the Human Sphere has some form of connectivity to a datasphere. In practice, this means virtually any piece of equipment can be targeted by a hacker. There are two exceptions. First, equipment carried by an individual will be connected to their personal area network and is protected by their Firewall. (However, that means that you can affect the equipment by targeting its owner.) Second, any piece of equipment with the Non-Hackable quality simply doesn't have a quantronic component.

If that isn't the case, the GM can assign the target a Security Rating (generally a number between 3 and 8, although there's no limit to how high the security rating could go). By default, the system access point will be a number of zones distant from the target equal to the target's Security Rating modified by the hacker's distance from the target (as shown on the *Remote Access Point* table). A hacker can attempt a single Simple (D0) Analysis or Hacking test to find the access point, spending Momentum to reduce the number of zones on a one-for-one basis to a minimum of 1. (The GM can similarly use complications to increase the necessary number of zones.)

REMOTE ACCESS POINT	
DISTANCE	ACCESS POINT
Same Building	−1 zone
Same City	+0 zones
Same Continent	+1 zone
Same Planet	+2 zones
Same System	+3 zones
Wormhole (requires Metatron or Dârâo access)	+4 zones
Combined Army Network	+2 zones

AUTHENTICATION

A character who has been properly authenticated on a given system will have permission to perform many actions which would otherwise require a Hacking test or Breach Effect. Authentication generally applies to specific quantronic zones, including the ability to ignore certain quantronic zone effects.

AUTHENTICATION TYPES
The exact parameters of what a particular authentication will allow a character to achieve will vary, but some general guidelines for typical account types are given below.

User: A user account has limited access. They can run programs and access data they have permission for, but they generally won't be able to permanently alter the system or grant additional authentications.

Superuser/Security: These accounts can control and create other user accounts and install utility programs, but generally can't make system-wide changes (like altering quantronic zone effects). Their access to data on the system is generally unlimited and they'll usually have the ability to command security features.

Admin: An admin account has complete control over the system.

METHODS OF AUTHENTICATION

Knowledge Factor: Something which the user knows. Alphanumeric characters or pass phrases remain surprisingly common as a form of security, but any form of quantronic data (like an image or a snippet of music) could also serve as a passcode. Other examples include challenge response patterns or security questions.

Ownership Factor: A physical device or object which the user has. This is commonly referred to as a passkey. Examples include keycards, security dongles, RFID chips, and the like.

Biometric Factor: Something which is at least theoretically inherent to the user – fingerprint, retinal patterns, DNA sequence, bio-electric signatures, vein patterning, and the like.

Two-Factor Authentication: Two-factor authentication requires two or more methods of authentication to be used at the same time. A common example is a passkey (something the user has) which must be used at the same time as a passcode (something the user knows). In some cases, multiple forms of the same type of authentication might be used (like a biometric scan which checks fingerprints, dental records, and DNA).

Cube Scan: A Cube scan is a form of biometric verification which checks the subject's actual thoughts and personality. This method of authentication requires the VoodooTech of the Combined Army when used on living subjects, although it does see some limited use in the Human Sphere among personalities stored in Cube banks and AIs (i.e., personalities which are stored on quantronic mediums that can be easily accessed).

GAINING AUTHENTICATION

Some forms (like a passkey) can be stolen. Others (like a biometric scan) could be fooled through technology or medical expertise. Infiltrating an organisation (either directly or indirectly) could even result in someone being granted legitimate security credentials.

The nature of such alternative methods of gaining authentication is really only limited by the creativity of the players. Access to some forms of authentication could also simply be the result of researching the target.

Spoofing Authentication: Spoofing an authentication first requires that one can gain access to the original authentication. This generally takes the form of sniffing datasphere traffic and can be achieved with a Hacking test, a Tech test (if equipment is being physically tapped), or as the result of a Breach Effect on a target that has authentication.

Authentication Hack: It's also possible for a hacker to simply brute force their way into a system. If a hacker can make an Infowar attack against a security server, a Breach Effect can be used to create an account with whatever authentication the server is authorised to grant.

Authentication Quality: When authentication is gained, it has a default Quality of 0. The hacker can spend Momentum to increase this quality, with each step of increased quality having a cost equal to the new level of Quality.

The Quality of authentication adds an equal number of d20s to Stealth tests while hacking.

Gaining Difficult Authentication: Ownership factors and biometric factors make spoofing more difficult, but not impossible. Ultimately, some form of quantronic signal is being sent that contains the information contained in the passkey or biometric scan and that signal can be faked. This is more difficult, however, increasing the difficulty of tests to spoof or hack such forms of authentication by two steps.

SYSTEM SECURITY

Modeling a secured quantronic system or network in *Infinity* is easy: Each of the quantronic zones which make up the system will have the Secured Zone effect. Advanced systems will supplement this security, however, with active measures – either geists specialised in system security (see p. 350) or infoperators trained in sniffing out intrusion. Like guards patrolling a physical location, these characters will often move through the various zones which make up the system they're protecting and they will actively engage any hackers they find on their turf.

Cube scans cannot be faked by human technology. You need an actual copy of the subject's Cube.

Two-factor authentication requires each form of authentication to be separately duped or stolen.

AUTHENTICATION QUALITY	
QUALITY INCREASE	TOTAL MOMENTUM COST
+1	1 Momentum
+2	3 Momentum
+3	6 Momentum

PLAYTEST TIP
BACKDOOR ACCESS

Hackers often install data tunnels to create backdoors: Invisible security flaws that they can use to access a system at a later date.

QUANTRONIC ZONE EFFECTS

The zone effects of quantronic zones are somewhat different to those found in the real world. Security measures, damaged system infrastructure, interference, and the actions of infowarriors may create obstacles or hindrances, or even count as hazardous terrain.

Quantronic Terrain Tests: Terrain tests in quantronic zones will use Hacking tests if the terrain is software-based, Tech tests if related to hardware, or even Analysis tests if the terrain can be overcome by identifying patterns and vulnerabilities.

DATA FLUX CAMOUFLAGE

Hiding an entire quantronic zone is difficult, but not impossible. It requires that the patterns of the data flux (which would normally indicate how the zone is connected to the rest of the datasphere) be camouflaged. Characters who would normally be able to perceive a camouflaged zone can attempt an Average (D1) Observation test. (The normal modifiers for range and perception apply.)

Some camouflaged zones may be particularly difficult or relatively easy to detect and will increase or decrease this difficulty rating.

DATA TUNNEL

A data tunnel is a secure connection from one quantronic zone to another quantronic zone. With a successful Average (D1) Hacking test, a hacker can use the data tunnel to access the other quantronic zone, even if it's a secured zone.

HIGHSEC

HighSec zones have been hardened against a variety of hacker exploits. HighSec zones grant Security Soak to characters within the zone who have proper authentication:

- Commercial HighSec provides +2  Interference Soak.
- Military HighSec provides +4 Interference Soak.

HighSec zones are not without their drawbacks, however. The biggest problem is that even those without proper authentication can subvert them with an Average (D1) Hacking test, after which they can also benefit from the zone's Security Soak.

INTRUSION COUNTERMEASURES (IC)

Intrusion Countermeasure (IC) programs are attached to a zone. Moving into, out of, or within a zone with IC requires a Hacking test. (The difficulty of the test depends on the sophistication of the IC.) Failure on the test means that the character makes no progress after the point where the test was required — so a character attempting to enter a zone stops before they enter the zone. In many cases, there will be an additional consequence for failure (depending on the properties of the IC being encountered).

IC programs are often concealed, requiring a successful scan (using an Analysis test) to detect their presence.

SECURED ZONE

A secured zone has a Firewall score and cannot be entered by anyone who doesn't have authorised authentication. If the zone's Firewall suffers a Breach, it is no longer considered secure and can be entered freely.

CREATING QUANTRONIC ZONE EFFECTS

Some programs can be used to automatically create quantronic zone effects, but hackers can also create most of them on the fly. This requires a Hacking test with a difficulty depending on the type of zone effect, as shown on the *Quantronic Zone Effect Creation Table*.

Creating a quantronic zone effect generally requires authentication. If a hacker does not have authentication for the quantronic zone where they're attempting to create the zone, the difficulty of the Hacking test is increased by one step and the action is automatically considered noisy for purposes of stealth.

Quantronic zone effects are usually created in the hacker's current zone. It is possible to create zone effects in distant zones (as long as those zones can be seen), but the difficulty of the Hacking test is increased by one step per zone of distance.

HIDDEN QUANTRONIC ZONE EFFECTS

Hiding a quantronic zone effect requires a Challenging (D2) Hacking test. On a success, the effect is hidden with a difficulty modifier of 0. Momentum can be spent normally to increase the difficulty modifier. The GM can similarly use complications to reduce the difficulty modifier.

In order to detect a hidden quantronic zone effect, a character must specifically scan the zone which contains the effect. A character can scan any zone which they can currently "see", making a Simple (D0) Analysis test modified by the difficulty modifier of the camouflage itself. (The normal modifiers for range and perception also apply.) On a success, the character can identify the zone effect and its properties.

DESTROYING QUANTRONIC ZONE EFFECTS

What can be built can also be dismantled. A quantronic zone effect can be destroyed with a successful Hacking test with a difficulty equal to that required to create the zone effect (including modifications for authentication and range). Enemy hackers can use a Reaction to make this a face-to-face test. Attempts to destroy IC must first overcome the IC by making a Hacking test as if entering the IC's zone. On a failure, the IC takes effect and the attempt to destroy it automatically fails.

QUANTRONIC ZONE EFFECT CREATION

ZONE EFFECT	HACKING DIFFICULTY
Data Flux Camouflage	Challenging (D2)
Data Tunnel	Average (D1)
HighSec, Commercial	Challenging (D2)
HighSec, Military	Dire (D3)
Intrusion Countermeasures (IC)	Requires Program
Secured Zone	Simple (D0) (+2 Firewall per Momentum)
No Authentication	+1 difficulty (noisy action)
Remote Zone	+1 difficulty per zone

EXAMPLE
HACK

Márcio has been hired through a front company of the Yu Jing Interspace Trust Corporation to retrieve the location of Moto.tronica's TAG research centre on Svalarheima. After performing some basic research, he's fairly certain the info he needs can be found on a secure server in a Moto.tronica building on Neoterra. The server is kept offline, however, so he won't be able to access it through Maya. He puts the building under surveillance, however, and with a successful Analysis test identifies the guards' comlogs as an access point: They have an encrypted connection to the building's network. He uses a nano-dronbot as a remote, flying it into Close range of a guard and performing an infowar attack using his Tag program. Generating 2 Momentum on the attack, he uses to it to Tag the guard's comlog, which he can now use as a repeater. Dropping into the building's network, he makes his way through a Secured Zone to access an administration system and grant himself Superuser authentication. He makes an additional research test to identify where the information he wants is stored, but on the way there he spots a security geist. He'll either have to find an alternate route or, more likely, take out the geist before he can proceed.

WARFARE ACTIONS IN INFOWAR

The following actions from Warfare scenes are also commonly used as part of Infowar:

Absterge (p. 110)
Assist (p. 110)
Defence (p. 113)
Exploit (p. 111)
Guard (p. 113)
Ready (p. 111)
Recover (p. 111)
Treat (p. 112)
Withdraw (p. 112)

PSYWAR ACTIONS IN INFOWAR

The following actions from Psywar scenes are also commonly used as part of Infowar, but only when dealing with sentient opponents — humans, AI fragments, and other intelligent foes able to make rational decisions.

Intimidation (p. 124)
Persuade (p. 123)
Deceive (p. 123)

SHUTDOWN

A character who resets their system does not need to immediately bring it back online as part of the same action. They can instead leave the system in shutdown. As long as the system is shut down, the character cannot be targeted by infowar attacks. However, they cannot use any function of their equipment which requires a network connection and they cannot benefit from Expert systems (unless those systems have a hardwired connection to their brains). The character also suffers a +1 difficulty to any tasks using equipment that doesn't possess the Non-Hackable quality. (Most equipment in the Human Sphere is designed to be used through your personal network.) Bringing a shut down system back online requires a Minor Action.

INFOWAR ACTIONS

ACCESS SYSTEM / TERMINATE CONNECTION (STANDARD)

A character can connect to any access point they know as a Standard Action. At the end of the action, they appear within Reach of the access point.

Alternately, characters can terminate their connection to a system at any time as a Standard Action. (They do not have to be within Reach — or even in the same zone — as an access point.) A character cannot simply return to the same location where they terminated their connection, however. If they want to enter the system again, they'll need to use a known access point.

RESET (STANDARD)

As a Standard Action, a character can make an Average (D1) Hacking test to perform a hard reset on their system. On a success, the character fully recovers their Firewall. It takes time, however, for all of the programs on a comlog or other device to restart and integrate. Any actions the character takes which require their comlog or augmented reality (including using any items with the Comms Equipped or Expert qualities) increase their difficulty by four steps. This penalty decreases by one at the start of each of the character's turn's, and the character can also spend Momentum to reduce this penalty by one per Momentum spent.

TRANSMIT (MINOR)

Sending information across a datasphere the character is connected to — whether it's transferring a file, sending a text message, initiating a voice call, or broadcasting a life-cast — takes a Minor Action to initiate. Although it's quick to initiate a transfer, larger data transfers may require additional time to complete (although with the bandwidth available in the Human Sphere the size would have to be truly prodigious — hundreds of hours of high-resolution holographic footage, for example, can be transferred in a matter of seconds across planetary distances).

USE PROGRAM (STANDARD)

Unless specified otherwise, using a program during an action scene requires a Standard Action.

INFOWAR REACTIONS

LINK

If an enemy moves out of Reach in a quantronic zone without taking the Withdraw action, a hacker can attempt to Link by making an Average (D1) Hacking test. On a success, the hacker moves with the enemy, remaining within Reach of them, even if the movement would normally be prohibited to them (due to a Secured zone, for example). The link dissolves at the end of the enemy's turn. (A link can be dangerous because even the hacker forming the link can't automatically disentangle their system).

INFOWAR MOMENTUM

Momentum spends in Infowar are generally used to trigger program effects, which often allow characters to create specific Breach Effects without inflicting a Breach. Details on specific programs and their effects can be found in *Part IV: Gear*.

BREACH EFFECTS

The following effects can be used for Breaches suffered during an Infowar scene, or in any other circumstance where Breaches are inflicted.

Blind: If the target is using equipment with the Neural quality, a hacker can use a Breach Effect to force them to make a Resistance or Tech test to avoid becoming Blind. The difficulty of the test is equal to the number of Breaches the target is currently suffering from. If the test is successful, the character still suffers the Breach, they merely avoid the Breach Effect. (This condition can be removed with the Absterge action, ending the Breach Effect.)

Brain Blast: If the target is using equipment with the Neural quality, a hacker can choose to deal them a Wound instead of a Breach.

Command System: The hacker can force the target's system to execute one command. This is often used to effect changes in the physical world, such as activating devices, unlocking doors, opening cockpits, controlling surveillance cameras, instructing dronbots, firing a gun turret, manipulating environmental controls, or the like. Complicated instruction sets may require multiple Breach Effects to implement (at the GM's discretion).

Data Manipulation: The hacker directly accesses the target's files. They can delete information, alter data, create bogus records, hide information, and the like. They can't dupe the entire system, but they could copy one file or limited set of files (such as all the security video from November 11th). If they're attempting to glean specific information, they may ask one question and get an answer to it. Forgeries and the like may require face-to-face tests to determine whether or not the fraud is believed.

Disable Function: One program or piece of equipment possessed by the target ceases to function. (Since the vast majority of equipment in the Human Sphere possesses some measure of connectivity, this can include virtually anything that doesn't possess the Non-Hackable quality.) The hacker can also be very selective, disabling some functions of a program or piece of equipment while leaving others intact.

Lock Connection: The target cannot disconnect from the current system. An Absterge action can be used to clear this effect.

Revoke Authentication: An authentication possessed by the target (usually to the current system) is revoked. The revocation is permanent and the authentication is not restored even when the Breach is removed, although nothing prevents the character from gaining new authentication on the system.

System Disruption: The target suffers +1 difficulty to any actions requiring use of equipment with the Comms Equipped or Expert qualities (including their comlog).

Spoof/Sniff: The hacker duplicates the system ID of the target, giving them authentication for one system that the target has access to. The hacker can spend Momentum to either improve the quality of the authentication (making their spoof harder to detect) or to gain additional authentication (one per Momentum).

Tag: The hacker tags the target system. This allows them to track the target. In addition, they can use a tagged target as a repeater.

PSYWAR

Psywar is the ultimate reminder that battles are not won by bullets or TAGs. They are won (and lost) by men and women, and if you can shatter their morale then your victory is no less assured than if you had broken their bodies.

The Psywar system also extends itself throughout the complex, multi-layered society of the Human Sphere. You'll find it in corporate boardrooms, on street corners, at high-stake hostage negotiations, and in romantic first dates. Advertising and propaganda seek to shape the mind, the threat of punishment influences the behaviours of many would-be criminals, while spies and confidence tricksters use the greed and preconceptions of others to achieve their goals. It is, at heart, the relationships between people. More so than any other action scene module, therefore, you'll find the principles of Psywar permeating every aspect of your game.

The essential core of Psywar consists of Metanoia — literally, to affect the changing of someone's mind. Doing this requires:
- Gaining either direct or indirect access to your target.
- Making Psywar attacks in order to create Metanoia, then using the Metanoia Effects to change the target's beliefs, emotions, reasoning, or actions.

Targets are always creatures that possess an independent mind, a sense of self, and the ability to make decisions. These might be humans, aliens, AI fragments, or anything else with enough self-awareness to respond to a request. Animals can also be subject to Psywar, but in a more limited manner.

METANOIA
The Greek term *metanoia* means literally "the changing of one's mind". When making a Psywar attack in *Infinity*, one is literally causing change in the target's mind.

The means by which this change can be affected are as limitless as the possibilities of human interaction. If an Imperial Agent needs someone to believe something to be true (or at least act as if it were), for example, then it's their choice whether to employ direct methods like persuasion, deception, and torture, or indirect methods like spreading rumours, issuing official propaganda, or planting false information on their comlog.

CONVERSATIONS
A lot of every day interactions don't require the full might and majesty of the Psywar rules. This is particularly true of simple, face-to-face conversations. Just as you wouldn't use the normal Infowar rules to search for some piece of trivia on Maya, you wouldn't use the Psywar rules when asking someone if the seat next to them is taken.

Some complexity and structure can be introduced to these interactions by requiring a character to inflict a Metanoia Effect to achieve a desired result, but a single Persuade or Command check will often suffice for determining whether or not a character can convince or coerce a particular target. (And, similarly, a Psychology test can quickly determine if someone is lying, or secretly in love with their commanding officer.) Additional guidelines for effectively resolving these kinds of straightforward social engagements can be found in the *Basic Interactions* section starting on the next page.

BATTLEFIELD PSYCHOLOGY
Psywar transfers well to the battlefield. Threats, particularly threats with weapons, can send opponents into a panicked retreat or force them to surrender, but other interactions (while not as deep or involved as they might be off the battlefield) are also possible: Fool enemies into thinking reinforcements are on their way. Trick them into revealing encoded frequencies. Deduce their strategic intentions. Or persuade them to negotiate.

Psywar actions can also target your allies in battle: Rallying troops and bolstering morale can make all the difference if you're facing down a platoon of enraged Morat soldiers.

On the battlefield, Psywar actions, techniques, and reactions are freely used within the combat zones of the Warfare system.

SOCIAL SKILL TESTS

Due to the fluid nature of social interaction, the Psywar system features a lot of flexible mechanical structures. At times, therefore, it will call for a social skill test. The specific skill used for the social skill test will depend on the situation and the approach being taken by the character. (For example, if a character has authority over a target — or the target believes the character has authority over them (a higher rank in an organisation or some other legally given authority) — they might be able to use Command to make their social skill tests against that target.)

Social skill tests are usually made with Analysis, Command, Discipline, Lifestyle, Persuade, or Psychology. Animal Handling can be used when dealing with animals, although such interactions are obviously more limited than when dealing with humans.

PSYOPS (PSYCHOLOGICAL OPERATIONS)

Beyond the battlefield, a psyop plays out through the interwoven social networks of the Human Sphere. Characters performing a psyop don't even need to be in the same location as their target: As long as they can find a connection they can manipulate, they can wield influence by pulling the right levers.

A full-blown psyop uses all the rules for Psywar, including those for social zones.

BASIC INTERACTIONS

These guidelines are useful when the GM wants to resolve a social interaction using a single skill check instead of launching into a full psyop.

PERSUASION

Persuasion ultimately lays at the centre of most social interactions. It can be achieved through personal magnetism and charisma, by use of compelling arguments or rhetorical techniques, or by exploiting emotional connections, but it all comes down to one person trying to convince another to take an action that they might not ordinarily take.

Context is vital to persuasion. Everyone can be persuaded if the time, place, and the request are all just right. A perfectly reasonable request that a friendly target can easily carry out will have a Simple (D0) difficulty. If the target is unwilling to comply, or dislikes the character, or the request is something dangerous, against the target's morals or ethics, or liable to come with personal consequences, then the difficulty increases.

Persuasion Resolution: The character making the request makes a face-to-face Persuade test opposed by the target's Discipline. If the test is successful, then the target complies with the request. If the test fails, the target refuses and will not consider the same request again unless circumstances change or the request is significantly modified.

Complications on a successful persuasion attempt may indicate that the target is willing to do what they're being asked... for a price. (Which would trigger a negotiation, as described below.)

DECEPTION

A lot of social conflict can be overcome through the careful use of deception. Deception itself isn't a method of confronting a target directly; rather, it serves as a means of shaping the conflict in the deceiver's favour.

No deception, no matter how skilled the deceiver, can completely change a person's beliefs, or make them believe something that runs completely counter to their perceptions and expectations. Deception isn't that overtly powerful. Deceiving someone works most effectively when the deception plays into that person's existing beliefs, or does not challenge their perception of the world around them — the lie appears reasonable in context. Skilled deceivers capitalise on this, often by keeping their lies close to the truth, or by studying the target to learn what lies are more likely to go unchallenged.

Deception is a form of social manipulation. A good lie opens doors, but the lie alone cannot achieve the liar's goals. Instead, the lie serves as a foundation upon which other techniques can be used. Lies can be problematic, however. A failed attempt can jeopardise future attempts to lie; or even future attempts to act in good faith. Once trust is broken, it can be hard to rebuild.

Deception Resolution: The character trying to sell the lie makes a face-to-face Persuade test opposed by the Psychology tests of anyone listening to the lie. If the deceiver is successful, the target(s) believe the lie.

A successful deception can be used to make someone believe that what you are asking them to do is not as onerous as it truly is (effectively reducing the difficulty of a subsequent persuasion attempt).

A failed deception makes it more difficult to sell future deceptions. Complications generated on failed deceptions may result in the target's attitude towards the deceiver being permanently turned to the worse.

NEGOTIATION

A useful way to make persuasion work is to offer something else in return. Negotiation is, in this case, the process of determining what people want in exchange for some favour, service, decision, or action.

Some targets may be reluctant to reveal the price of their compliance, but everyone has a price. Determining this may require investigating the target to uncover their secrets. Or it may be the result of back-and-forth conversation — which can potentially be a long and arduous process in its own right, with a series of offers and counter-offers.

The price does not necessarily need to be large — it could be something small and personal, but very specific; or it could be assistance in the fulfilment of a dream or desire; or even the promise of affection and intimacy (i.e., a seduction). Any price, of course, can be a false promise based on deception.

THE ONE METANOIA CONVERSATION

One step up from a basic interaction is a simple technique called the One Metanoia Conversation: Each character's desired outcome from a social encounter is defined as a Metanoia Effect and the character who inflicts a Metanoia Effect first gets what they want. The individual attacks and techniques used to build up to the Metanoia Effect you need to accomplish your goal gives a nice back-and-forth structure around which the twists and turns of a conversation can be roleplayed. The One Metanoia Conversation gives a little breathing space for a natural social interaction to take place, and when the Metanoia Effect is inflicted, it brings the roleplaying encounter to an end with a definitive sense of closure so that it doesn't overstay its welcome.

PERSUASION/DECEPTION TABLE

DIFFICULTY	INTERACTION	LIES
Simple (D0)	Requires little time or effort; within the target's normal activities; doesn't impact their lives; otherwise trivial.	Simple
Average (D1)	Requires a small amount of effort; a simple favour; no significant risk.	Plausible
Challenging (D2)	Requires some degree of effort or risk; could impact target's life.	Believable
Daunting (D3)	Requires both risk and effort; will definitely impact target's life.	Unlikely
Dire (D4)	Requires massive effort or serious risk; will significantly impact target's life.	Improbable
Epic (D5)	Requires both serious risk and massive effort; target's life permanently altered for the worse.	Far-fetched

DISCIPLINE/PSYCHOLOGY TABLE

DIFFICULTY	INTERACTION
Simple (D0)	Target has a bad history with the character or considers them an enemy.
Average (D1)	Target is suspicious of or distrusts the character.
Challenging (D2)	Target has no particular opinion of the character.
Daunting (D3)	Target is a friend of the character, or regards them as trustworthy or authoritative.
Dire (D4)	Target is particularly naïve.
Epic (D5)	Target would honestly consider buying the Acheron wormhole from a stranger he just met on the street.

PERSUASION FACTORS TABLE

MODIFIER	ADDITIONAL FACTOR
−1	Target is on friendly terms with the character.
0	Target is indifferent to the character.
+1	Target is unfriendly with character.
+2	Target regards the character as an enemy.
+1	Target is of a different Social Status.
+1	Target is of a different Faction.
+1	Request violates the target's ethics or morals.
+1	Request is shameful or embarrassing.
+2	Request is illegal.

DECEPTION FACTORS

MODIFIER	ADDITIONAL FACTOR
−1	Character's appearance (clothing, etc.) backs up their story.
+1	Character's appearance is inconsistent with their story.
−1	Character has appropriate documentation (IDs, official forms, etc.).
+1*	Character has failed to lie to the target during the scene (cumulative).
+1*	Lie contradicts another lie already told to the target.
−1	Lie is based mostly in truth, with some facts omitted or reinterpreted.
−2*	Lie reinforces target's existing perceptions, assumptions, and world view.
−1*	Lie is convenient for the target to believe.
+1*	Target has identified proof used by the character as suspicious.
−2*	Target's judgment is impaired (drugged, hypnotised, etc.).

* These modifiers apply in reverse to the Psychology test used to oppose a deception.

Negotiation Resolution: If a mutually agreeable price can be easily conceded in a negotiation, no test is required. If not, then both parties to the negotiation must clearly state their current position (how much the party requesting something is willing to pay; how much the party being paid is willing to accept). Once these prices have been proposed, a negotiation can be resolved as a face-to-face Persuade test. The difficulty of the buyer's test is determined by how reasonable their offer is. The difficulty of the seller's test can be determined in a fashion similar to a persuasion attempt.

INTIMIDATION

Effective in combat and other high-tension situations, intimidation is simple, straightforward, and decisive, but it is also quite likely to backfire against determined, disciplined, or confident foes. Threatening someone with a weapon is an easy option. This might be holding a foe at knifepoint or gunpoint, or it might be a warning shot or suppressive fire.

Alternatively, intimidation may include the threat of losing something (or someone) important, or the threat of revealing some incriminating or embarrassing facts as blackmail or extortion. (This, of course, requires that the intimidator actually possess such proof… or is capable of convincing their target that they do.)

Intimidation Resolution: Intimidation is basically resolved as a persuasion attempt, although complications generated on the test are more likely to result in violent reactions.

When intimidating with a weapon, a character can choose to use the skill normally used to make attacks with that weapon instead of the normal Persuade skill. (For example, using the Close Combat skill when threatening to chop a bound prisoner's leg off with a machete.)

Conversations that transition to intimidation tactics are often a sign that the resolution mechanics should also transition towards using Metanoia Effects and the full Psywar rules for resolving conflicts.

SOCIAL ZONES

During a psyop, social zones are used to model the target's social network. Each social zone represents either a social actor or the means by which social actors connect with each other. These can include (but are not necessarily limited to):

- Persons
- Groups
- Locations
- Events

These social zones are connected by dyadic links — the emotional, professional, practical, familial, or coincidental ties which bind people together. The exact nature of each link isn't specifically important (and, in fact, most people are bound together by a complicated weave of interests and mutual experience); what's important is that those links can be navigated and manipulated in order to access and influence people.

Psywar attacks are most effective when you're at Close range of your target (i.e., in direct contact with them), but it's not strictly necessary: In a firefight, you can threaten your foes from the far side of a room, and in a psyop you can influence people through their social network.

SOCIAL ZONE TYPES

As noted above, there are four broad types of social zones.

Persons: Unlike Warfare or Infowar, NPCs in a psyop don't move around. Instead, each NPC exists in their own social zone. (Various Psywar actions will allow them to form and sever connections with other social zones, bringing them either closer or further away from various parts of the social network. Of course, like all social connections, these can prove to be a double-edged sword.) Like any other NPC, the NPCs in a psyop have stat blocks.

Groups: The groups that can be represented by a social zone are far-ranging. They can include formal organisations (including corporations, clubs, political movements, unions, NGOs, mercenary companies, educational institutions, and the like) and informal communities (including cultural groups, social circles, and casual Maya clusters). Mechanically speaking, a group is defined by its social zone effects.

(Although groups are, by definition, made up of people, those people exist in their own social zones which are connected to the group.)

Locations: Locations are similar to groups. Characters have a dyadic link to the locations they frequent, which often creates relationships with other characters who are also found in that location. In terms of the Psywar system, locations are defined by social zone effects, but they are notable because — as physical places — they can often be accessed through other means (like Stealth or Warfare).

Events: Events create relationships between everyone who attends them. Some events are recurring (on either a regular or irregular schedule), but others may be one-time-only affairs. Events usually force specific timing on those using them

as a route for Psywar actions (i.e., you have to wait until Sunday if you want to talk to someone who attends mass that day). They are often modelled as disappearing zones.

NAVIGATING SOCIAL ZONES

Range and movement between social zones is generally handled using the exact same rules as combat zones, with two significant exceptions.

Reach: The concept of Reach does not exist when using social zones. Once a character enters the same zone as another character, they have direct access to that character.

Access: In order to move between two social zones, a character must first gain access to the dyadic link which connects them. If one of the zones connected to the link is an NPC, this can be accomplished by inflicting a Metanoia Effect on the NPC. For other social zones, it usually means dealing with the zone's social terrain effects.

If multiple characters are acting together on a psyop, they generally gain (or lose) access to a dyadic link collectively.

More so than other action scenes, social zones are heavily abstracted and moving from one zone to another can represent many different things (placing a call, tracking a person down, securing an invitation, paying membership dues, forging an identity, or any number of other possibilities). Psyops also usually play out over long periods of time, and often entire scenes (either directly or tangentially related) can take place in the middle of them. In fact, moving into a social zone often means framing a new scene: How are the characters approaching that person, organisation, location, or event?

SOCIAL OBSERVATION

During a psyop, characters can "see" any of the social zones they're aware of in the social network (although the normal modifiers for range and perception apply). Of course, this observation is usually limited to Psywar actions. (You can become aware that so-and-so is talking to such-and-such, or that Laura is the person spreading rumours about you, but you can't see Sebastian loading his gun in the privacy of his own room.)

Social Stealth: At the beginning of a psyop, it's fairly typical for a character to make a stealth state check and enter a hidden state (i.e., their target doesn't know they're poking around yet). Psywar differs considerably from Warfare when it comes to stealth because many Psywar attacks aren't inherently noisy actions that will automatically result in detection (you can spread rumours about someone without them necessarily realising that you're doing it).

DYADIC LINKS

You may be familiar with social theories like "six degrees of separation" and "three degrees of influence". These are the fundamental principles on which the social networks of the Psywar system are built.

Six Degrees of Separation: The theory that everyone and everything is six or fewer steps away from any other person in the world, such that a "chain of friends" can be made to connect them. (In practice, the number appears to be a little higher than six. The ubiquitous interconnectivity of Maya tends to bind people more closely together, but this is somewhat negated by the interstellar sprawl of the Human Sphere.)

Three Degrees of Influence: The theory that an individual's beliefs and behaviour ripple throughout the social network which surrounds them, such that they influence not only their friends, but their friends' friends, and also their friends' friends' friends

BRIBES

When using Psywar actions or techniques, Assets can be spent to gain a bonus d20 per Asset. (This often represents a bribe, although theoretically money could also be spent to gain other forms of advantage on such tests.) Other valuables — those not represented by Assets — should be converted to an equivalent value by the GM. Minor bribes (a few credits on a flextab or similar offers below the threshold of an Asset) can just be handled as an integral part of the normal social skill test without expending specific mechanical resources.

Due to the nature of social zones, stealth in a psyop is also more likely to feature characters who have been detected without being fully revealed. (The PCs can see where the NPCs are in the social network, even if they aren't sure what they're doing.) It's also comparatively less likely to feature fully hidden characters.

A notable exception are characters who have yet to appear on the social network map. When these hidden characters become revealed, their social zone should be added to the map. (It's also possible for characters on the social network map to become hidden by severing their dyadic links — effectively dropping out of sight and out of contact.)

Counterintelligence: A character or organisation can attempt to detect other characters targeting them (or others) for a psyop using the normal rules for actively detecting stealthy characters.

When trying to figure out how suspicious a particular group is (i.e., whether they're performing counterintelligence activities) or how pervasive their surveillance is (i.e., how often they're making counterintelligence checks) the GM can use the *Counterintelligence Level* table as a guideline.

Avoiding Suspicion: When attempting a sneaky or noisy Psywar action, a character can willingly increase the difficulty of the skill test required to perform the action in order to similarly increase the difficulty of Observation tests made to detect them.

HUMAN TERRAIN MAPPING

When initiating a psyop against a particular target, the first step is human terrain mapping. This is the process by which the social networks surrounding the target — the "human terrain" — are studied, analysed, and mapped by psywarriors.

CONTACT POINT
A contact point is a social zone connected to the target of a psyop which the psywarriors have access to. Human terrain mapping begins by determining the closest available contact point.

The base distance of the closest contact point is 4. To this is added the absolute difference in Social Status between the target and the psywarrior. (If multiple psywarriors are involved in the psyop, use the smallest difference in Social Status.) Finally, a distance modifier is applied based on physical proximity to the target (as shown on the *Contact Distance Table*.)

A psywarrior can then attempt an Average (D1) Analysis or Lifestyle test to find their contact point. Momentum can be spent to reduce the number of zones on a one-for-one basis to a minimum of 1. Momentum can also be spent to discover alternative contact points, dyadic links, or social zones. (The GM can similarly use complications to increase the necessary number of zones.) The

COUNTERINTELLIGENCE LEVEL

Paranoid	Every 1 round
Suspicious	Every 1d3 rounds
Cautious	Every 1d6 rounds
Routine	Every 3d6 rounds
Naïve	Never checks

EXAMPLE
PSYOP AT RANGE
The PCs want to convince Toni Macayana that a member of her support team has been selling technical specifications to the NMF. They gain access to the Grey Gear, a Maya cluster which Sergeant Caetano (Macayana's machinist) is a member of. That puts them two social zones away from Macayana. At that Long range, their Psywar attacks will be made at a +2 difficulty — they'll have to plant just the right rumours on Grey Gear if they want Caetano to pick up on them and pass them back to his boss. (Or, alternatively, plant information on Grey Gear which makes Caetano look guilty.)

PLAYTEST TIP
WHAT TYPE OF ZONE IS IT?
In some cases, you'll discover that the distinction between different types of zones can be a little hazy. For example, the Jews of Dar El Funduq are a community and the Funduqu Hebrew Brotherhood is an organisation; but both the Jewish Quarter of Dar El Funduq and the Brotherhood's community centre are locations. Whether these are four different zones in a given social network or a single zone (or something in-between) is a judgment call (and may depend on what the PCs are attempting to accomplish and how they're approaching the problem).

Disappearing Zones – p. 109

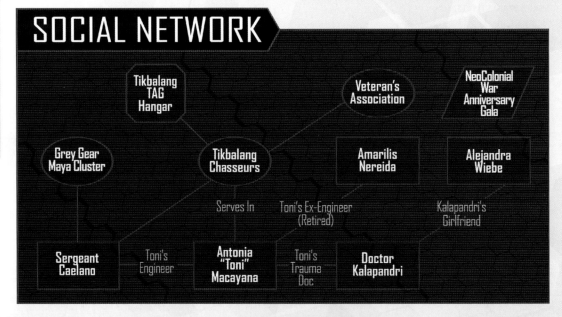

INTERACTING WITH A SOCIAL NETWORK

Alternative Zone Access: In many cases, characters may be able to gain access to a social zone in ways which don't involve Psywar. For example, instead of using social engineering to gain access to the Moto.tronica corporation, they might use the Infowar rules to hack the corporate databases. (Either way, they'll now be able to move into the corporation's social zone.)

Rerouting the Social Network: In some cases, characters will want to short circuit the social network they're exploring. For example, they might know that Vince Smith and Sylvia Greene, the CEO of Moto.tronica, both belong to the Adelaide social club. But instead of working through Vince Smith to access the Adelaide, they'd prefer to just reroute around him and go to the club directly. Can they do that? Sure. But what's really happening is that they're now trying to figure out how to access the Adelaide (the same way originally trying to figure out how to access Sylvia Greene led them to Vince Smith). They might do that through an alternative method of zone access (like sneaking into the club); or you can just make a fresh human terrain mapping test for the Adelaide and link the new social zones discovered into the social network map.

Jumping to the End: And what if they want to just call Sylvia Greene directly? Generally speaking, just calling someone up out of the blue that you don't actually have access to will make influencing them more difficult (if they answer at all). How difficult? Well, if they haven't managed to find a way past or around Vince Smith yet, they're still two social zones away from her, which would increase the difficulty of Psywar attacks by two steps. (Basically, being able to say, "I've been talking to Vince Smith and I have a few questions for you..." gives you a certain amount of influence with Greene. And that's what the social network map is modelling.)

former tests represent data mining Maya feeds, financial trails, legal records, professional databases, and the like to identify the target's patterns of behaviour. The latter uses social networking to gather rumours, introductions, and the right sort of invitations to bring the psywarrior into their target's social circle.

CONTACT DISTANCE TABLE

DISTANCE	CONTACT POINT
Same City	+0 zones
Same Continent	+1 zone
Same Planet	+2 zones
Same System	+3 zones
Different System	+4 zones

SOCIAL NETWORK

Once the distance of the initial contact point from the target has been determined, the GM should identify what the contact point is and the social zones which connect the contact point to the target.

In some cases, the GM may have predesigned a social network for the target. If that's the case, the GM simply identifies a social zone at the appropriate distance from the target (or adds such a zone if none exists).

If the target's social network has not yet been determined, all that's necessary is to improvise the network. With practice, it should be no more

difficult than describing the battlefield for a Warfare scene.

RESEARCHING THE TARGET

Even once a psywarrior has determined their contact point for a target, it's not unusual for them to continue researching them. Depending on exactly what approach they take, this research could include Analysis, Education, Hacking, Lifestyle, Observation, Thievery, or social skill tests. These tests can usually be handled as a Simple (D0) test, with Momentum being saved to assist them in targeting the target or their associates during the psyop. Alternatively, this Momentum could also be used to uncover additional social zones or connections in the target's social network that the character was not yet aware of.

It is also usually not difficult to continue pursuing research even during a psyop — turning up new information that may make the difference in coaxing, breaking, conning, blackmailing, or otherwise influencing the target.

SOCIAL ZONE EFFECTS

In the Psywar system, social zone effects generally model the zone's social relationships or persistent interactions with the rest of the social network (Non-persistent interactions, of course, are resolved as individual actions.) These can include emotional

Range and Perception, p. 108: Increase the difficulty of Observation tests by one step at Medium range, two steps at Long range, and by three at Extreme range.

Active Detection, p. 105: Make an Observation (D1) test as Standard Action to actively scan a zone. Stealthy characters can make this a face-to-face test with a Reaction.

PLAYTEST TIP
LOW PROFILE
Another way of avoiding undue attention is to simply keep your distance: Each zone between you and your target increases the difficulty of their Observation tests by one step. (Of course, it's also harder to manipulate them from there.)

EXAMPLE
GAINING ACCESS
The player characters are at the NeoColonial War Anniversary Gala. They begin hobnobbing with the members of the Veteran's Association attending the gala (using a Minor Action to move one zone). Amarilis Nereida is attending as a member of the Veteran's Association and they want to convince him to give them an introduction to his former partner, Toni Macayana. They can accomplish that by inflicting two Metanoia Effects (one to gain access to the dyadic link to him and another to gain access to the dyadic link between him and Macayana). Once they have access, they could use a Standard Action to move a Long range (two zones) into Macayana's social zone (as Nereida introduces them).

PSYWAR: CAN'T
GET THERE
FROM HERE

Unlike Infowar — where it is possible to have systems that are completely offline — finding a contact point for a psyop target should almost always be possible. (The exception would be a literal hermit who is completely cut-off from any social contact whatsoever. Pursuing such a character is less about Psywar and more about a manhunt to physically locate them.)

ties, codes of conduct, community standards, traditional customs, legal obligations, and the like.

Social Terrain Tests: Terrain tests in social zones will often use social skill tests. Unlike quantronic or combat zones, where the type of check is usually determined by the type of terrain being interacted with, in Psywar it's more usual for the skill to be determined by the way in which a character is interacting with the zone.

ACCESSIBILITY X

Social zones modelling groups, events, and locations (i.e., social zones which do not belong to a specific character) usually have an Accessibility rating. In order to gain access to one of the dyadic links connected to a social zone, a character in the zone must succeed on a terrain test with a difficulty equal to the zone's Accessibility rating as a Standard Action.

In some cases, a zone may have different Accessibility ratings for each dyadic link.

ANTAGONISTIC

Characters who enter, pass through, or start their turn in an antagonistic zone must make a social skill test as a Free Action. Failure on the test means that the character suffers some form of consequence, usually an amount of Resolve damage (with an associated Metanoia Effect).

The antagonistic effect should generally not be applied to NPC zones: NPCs take action directly. Antagonistic zone effects represent the abstract, general activity taking place within the zone's sphere on influence. (In some cases, these activities will be carried out by specific individuals. If that's the case, it may be better to include those NPCs as separate zones attached to the group, event, or location.)

INSULAR X

Some individuals and communities are hostile or resistant to interacting or cooperating with outsiders. (Examples can include sectarian organisations, intelligence agencies, and parochial settlements.) Social zones can have an Insular rating of 1 to 4, representing the severity of their distrust for outsiders.

When a Psywar attack originates from or passes through a zone with an Insular rating, the target gains a communal bonus to its Morale Soak equal to the zone's Insular rating.

A zone's effective Insular rating can be reduced as a Metanoia Effect with an intransigence equal to the rating (either directly if the zone is an NPC or indirectly by inflicting Metanoia Effects on the appropriate NPCs attached to the zone).

LOYALTY/ENMITY

A zone's Loyalty or Enmity, if any, is directed at a specific person or group other than itself and is rated on a scale of 1 to 4. (It's also possible for a zone to have multiple loyalties and multiple enmities.)

If a Psywar attack would harm, hinder, or otherwise be against the wishes of the person or organisation that a zone has Loyalty to, the target of the attack gains a communal bonus to its Morale Soak equal to the zone's Loyalty rating. Conversely, Enmity grants a Morale Soak if the Psywar attack is perceived to benefit the person or group which has earned the zone's Enmity.

Convincing a character with Loyalty or Enmity that you're on their side and that your Psywar attacks are in line with their desires (and, thus, ensuring that no Soak will be granted) generally requires a Metanoia Effect.

Temporarily changing a character's Loyalty or Enmity rating by one point for the rest of the current psyop requires a Metanoia Effect with an intransigence equal to its rating. Permanently changing a character's Loyalty or Enmity rating by one point requires a Metanoia Effect with an intransigence equal to twice its rating. These changes can be made directly if the zone is an NPC or indirectly by inflicting the Metanoia Effects on NPCs attached to the zone.

PSYWAR ACTIONS

BOLSTER (MINOR)

As a Minor Action, a character can make an Average (D1) social skill test to grant +1🅝 Morale Soak to all other characters in their zone for one round. One Momentum can be spent to affect an additional zone, add an additional +1🅝 to the Morale Soak boost, or increase the duration of the Morale Soak boost by one round.

DISENGAGE (STANDARD)

A character can attempt to disengage from someone as a Standard Action (they stop listening, they disconnect the call, or in some other way cease interacting with them). At the beginning of the character's next turn, they disengage and can no longer be targeted by Psywar attacks. (During a psyop, the character affected is returned to whichever social zone they came from and loses access to that dyadic link.)

NPCs can use the Disengage action to sever their social connection to another social zone. (The associated dyadic link disappears.)

Other characters can prevent someone from disengaging by inflicting a Metanoia Effect before their next turn (by convincing them to continue the interaction in one way or another).

A character performing the Disengage action can choose to attempt a Simple (D0) social skill test. Momentum can be spent to increase the Intransigence required to afflict the Metanoia Effect to prevent them from disengaging, with each level of Intransigence being purchased separately at a cost equal to the increase in Intransigence.

DISENGAGE INTRANSIGENCE

INTRANSIGENCE	MOMENTUM COST
+1 Intransigence	1 Momentum
+2 Intransigence	3 Momentum
+3 Intransigence	6 Momentum

IMPLY (MINOR)

It takes a little more concentration and effort for a character to present their meaning clearly without stating it openly. Use of implication can be valuable when concealing a threat, or when discussing a sensitive subject. The Imply action is taken in concert with a Psywar action or technique and the action's language is deliberately obfuscated. This requires an Average (D1) Psychology test. On a failure, the target fails to understand the character's subtle meaning (and any associated action or technique fails). On a success, the target understands the character's meaning but anyone else must succeed on a face-to-face Psychology test against the character's Psychology test to do the same.

The Imply action can also be taken during normal conversation in order to simply communicate hidden meanings.

RALLY (STANDARD)

A character can attempt to rally those around them as a Standard Action. This requires an Average (D1) social skill test (usually Command, Persuade, or Psychology). On a successful test, their allies in their current zone regain two Resolve, plus two more for each Momentum spent. Alternatively, one additional zone can be affected per Momentum spent.

PSYWAR TECHNIQUES

Techniques are the tools and weapons of the Psywar system. Using a technique requires a Standard Action and is resolved as an attack using a social skill test. (The most typical skill associated with each technique is listed in the *Psywar Techniques* Table.) Unless noted otherwise, a Psywar technique deals 1+4🅝 Resolve damage.

What fundamentally makes the Psywar system work is that characters can use any technique to create any Metanoia Effect (as long as they can figure out an appropriate way to make that happen). The system is designed to freely model any social interaction instead of constraining the ways in which characters can interact, giving players an incredible flexibility when it comes to playing out social scenes and psyops.

In this vein, characters are not necessarily constrained by the specific techniques listed here. In general, any feat of social engineering or personal persuasion can usually be modelled as a basic Influence attack and, at the GM's discretion, any appropriate social skill test could be used to make the attack.

INSULAR COMMUNITIES

It's not unusual for a large number of connected social zones to all share the same Insular rating. Characters who can win over one member of the community (i.e., reduce their effective Insular rating to 0) can gain 1 bonus Momentum when making Psywar attacks for the purpose of reducing the Insular rating of other members of the community.

Such communities are also generally not insular towards each other: If a character can get a member of the community to take action *for* them (as a Metanoia Effect) it can effectively bypass the communal soak.

COMMUNAL SOAK

Communal bonuses to Morale Soak from Insular, Loyalty, and Enmity do not stack. If a Psywar attack passes through multiple zones which grant communal bonuses to Morale Soak, only the highest such bonus applies.

LOYALTY TO AN IDEA

It's also possible to have Loyalty to an idea. For example, the Bushido code of a samurai warrior, the sworn oath of an Imperial Agent, or the street code of a bōsōzoku. It works the same way, with such characters being less willing to participate in actions which would contradict their personal code. (You can also often interpret this as a bonus to their Intransigence against relevant Metanoia Effects.)

EXAMPLE

IDENTIFYING CONTACT POINT

Toni Macayana's Social Status is Upper. The PC with the closest Social Status is only Middle. When they first become aware of Macayana, they are in Punta Norte on Acontecimento (so there is no modification for distance). This results in a base distance of 5 (4 as the base value + 1 for their difference in Social Status). One of the player characters digs into Macayana's military records and performs an Analysis (D1) test. They succeed on the test and generate 2 Momentum, which they spend to reduce the distance of the contact point to three zones. The GM looks at the social network map they've drawn up for Macayana and determines that the PCs have learned about the NeoColonial War Anniversary Gala where veterans known to have served with Macayana will be in attendance.

EXAMPLE

ANTAGONISTIC ZONE

If the NeoColonial War Anniversary Gala was a fundraising event trying to raise the resurrection bonds for dead veterans stuck in Cube banks, that could be modelled as an antagonistic zone effect. On a failure, a character would suffer 1🅽 Resolve damage and, if they suffered a Metanoia Effect, they'd be convinced to donate 1+1🅽 Assets to the cause.

COAX

Coaxing someone can be achieved through personal magnetism or charisma; by use of compelling arguments or rhetorical techniques; or by exploiting emotional connections.

DECEIVE

A lot of social conflict can be overcome through the careful use of deception. No deception, no matter how skilled the deceiver, can make someone believe something that runs completely counter to their perceptions and expectations. The best deceptions work by playing into a person's existing beliefs or by fitting into their perception of the world around them. Skilled deceivers will keep their lies close to the truth and study their target to learn what lies are most likely to go unchallenged.

When attempting to Deceive a target, a character makes a Persuade test. A target can use Psychology when making a Defence reaction against the Deceive test.

INTIMIDATE

Intimidation is a brute force approach to psychological warfare. Particularly effective in combat and other high-tension situations, intimidation has the virtue of being simple, straightforward, and decisive. However, attempting to intimidate someone is a sign of aggression. It will change the tone of the proceedings, and it often makes opponents hostile even if they are not affected.

When attempting to Intimidate someone with a weapon, a character can choose to use the skill normally used to attack with that weapon for the social skill test. (For example, using Ballistics to threaten someone at gunpoint.) If successful, the intimidation deals Resolve damage equal to the damage normally inflicted by the weapon used. If no weapon is used, the damage is equal to the intimidator's unarmed damage. (These totals include the normal bonus damage for the attack.)

NEGOTIATE

Negotiation is, ultimately, getting someone to do something by offering them something else in return. Many negotiations will feature a bribe — a gift of money or some other valuable in exchange for acting in the briber's favour.

ORDER

If a character has authority over their target (a higher rank in an organisation, for example) or the target believes that they do (due to some convincing deception), then they can make a Psywar attack using the Command skill.

RUMOUR

Spreading rumours can be effective by either damaging the reputation of a target or by manipulating their perception of a situation (and, thus, the actions they take in response to that information). Unlike most Psywar techniques, spreading Rumours uses a Lifestyle test.

SEDUCE

Seduction is the art of turning someone's desires to act in harmony with your own hungry wants. It is the promise of intimacy, the creation of carnal desire, or the offer to fulfil the same. Most often associated with gaining a reciprocal level of sexuality, seduction can also be used to twist the behaviour of others to suit your whims.

If a seduction attempt is not sincere, the target can use Psychology as a Defence Reaction against it.

PSYWAR TECHNIQUES

NAME	SKILL	DAMAGE
Coax	Persuade	1+4🅽
Deceive	Persuade	1+4🅽
Influence	Persuade	1+4🅽
Intimidate	Persuade	Per unarmed attack / weapon
Negotiate	Persuade	1+4🅽
Order	Command	1+4🅽
Rumour	Lifestyle	1+4🅽
Seduce	Persuade	1+4🅽

PSYWAR REACTIONS

COUNTER-ARGUMENT

A character aware of a Psywar attack and able to interact with the target can immediately attempt to counter what the attacker is attempting to accomplish by making a Challenging (D2) social skill test. If they succeed, they can use Momentum to defend as per the Defence Reaction. If they fail, or if they do not generate enough Momentum to negate the attack, the original target defends against the attack normally.

PSYWAR MOMENTUM SPENDS

SPEND	COST	EFFECT
Confidence	1	Character gains +1 Ⓝ Morale Soak until start of their next turn
Inspire	2	Allies of the character within Close range gain +1 Ⓝ Morale Soak until start of their next turn; 1 Momentum can be spent to affect an additional zone.
Stubborness	3	Intransigence for a given Metanoia Effect increases by 1.

METANOIA EFFECTS

The following effects can be applied whenever Metanoia is inflicted during a Psywar scene, or in any other circumstance where Metanoia is inflicted.

Break Social Connection: A dyadic link connecting the target to another social zone is broken. Remove the link from the social network map.

Create Social Connection: A dyadic link is created between the target and another social zone. (This might represent convincing them to join an organisation, swearing a blood oath to destroy their new archenemy, booking them to perform at a concert, or moving them into a safe house.)

Emotional State: The effect creates an emotional state in the target. (Common options might include panic, suspicion, trust, lust, and the like.)

Force an Action: The target is forced, convinced, or otherwise compelled to attempt a particular action. (This might include evincing a confession, convincing them to lay down their arms and engage in negotiation, invest in a particular stock, or any number of things.) These are generally specific actions carried out immediately. Long-term services will usually have higher Intransigence scores.

Forge Friendship: The target becomes friends with someone (usually the person interacting with them, although a good wingman might be able to hook them up with someone else).

Gain Information: This does not necessarily mean getting the target to openly reveal the information in question. You might bluff them into glancing at where they've hidden an object. Or do enough social data mining to crack their password.

Gain/Lose Access: As a Metanoia Effect, a character can gain (or lose) access to a dyadic link (see p. 125).

Influence Belief: Convince the target that something is true (whether it is or not). This can extend to altering their personal value system and reasoning, or at least temporarily being willing to ignore them.

Monitor: Learn what actions the target is taking in the "real world" by collecting gossip, having them followed, questioning their associates, or the like.

INTRANSIGENCE

It's easier to convince people to do some things than it is others. (For example, convincing someone to loan you some money is probably easier than convincing them to kill someone for you.) The difficulty can also vary depending on the individual. (It's easier to convince a Triad member to break the law than it is an Imperial Agent.)

The unwillingness of a particular target to do a particular thing is measured by their Intransigence. In order to achieve a Metanoia Effect, it is necessary to inflict a number of Harms equal to the target's Intransigence towards that effect.

The GM ultimately determines the Intransigence for each effect. Most of the time, the Intransigence will be equal to 1. Metanoia Effects which would force a character to stop taking actions during the current encounter (like panicking and running away from combat) will usually have an Intransigence of 4 for PCs and Nemeses, 2 for Elites, and 1 for Troopers.

At the GM's discretion, Metanoia Effects with lesser effects can contribute towards overcoming the target's Intransigence for a larger effect. (For example, if you can make someone believe their partner is getting ready to betray them and then get them panicked, those Metanoia Effects could contribute towards convincing them to testify against them in court.)

EXAMPLE
ACCESSIBILITY
While at the NeoColonial War Anniversary Gala, Samantha tries to flirt with some of the veterans in attendance and make some friends in the Veteran's Association. The gala has Accessibility 1, so she makes an Average (D1) Persuade test and, with a success, gains access to the Veteran's Association. She moves into that zone and discovers that, due to the association's confidentiality policies, it will be much easier to gain access to the Tikbalang Chasseurs (Accessibility 1) than it would be to glean the contact information for a specific retired vet like Amarilis Nereida (Accessibility 2). She really wants to find out what Nereida could tell her about Macayana, though. She considers inflicting a Metanoia Effect on him from a distance (collecting stories he's told to people around the Veteran's Association), but decides instead to see if she can trick the bureaucracy. She makes a Thievery (D1) test to forge an information request slip, gets three successes, and uses the 2 Momentum to buy two additional d20s for a Challenging (D2) Lifestyle check to gain access to Nereida's records.

SECRET VICES
Some targets may be reluctant to reveal the price of their compliance, but that doesn't mean there isn't something they prize above all else. Research or Metanoia Effects can be used to identify what a particular target's weaknesses are, granting additional bonus d20s above the base value of an offer if it's of a type the target is particularly susceptible to.

DETERMINING INTRANSIGENCE

When in doubt, the GM should default to Intransigence 1. (Accomplishing things is inherently more interesting than not accomplishing them and will drive the scene forward.) A higher Intransigence would indicate something significantly out of character or difficult for the target. One way you can set Intransigence is by looking at the number of factors weighing against the decision. For example, a PC might try to convince a store clerk to take a gun and provide covering fire for them. This defaults to Intransigence 1, but it would put the store clerk in mortal danger (+1) so you might assign Intransigence 2. In a later scene, a college student wants to seduce their professor. Their professor, however, is a moral man (+1) and if he was found out he would lose his tenure (+1), so the student will need to overcome Intransigence 3.

WARFARE ACTIONS IN PSYWAR

Absterge (p. 110)
Assist (p. 110)
Defence (p. 113)
Exploit (p. 111)
Guard (p. 113)
Ready (p. 111)
Recover (p. 111)
Treat (p. 112)
Withdraw (p. 112)

INFOWAR ACTIONS IN PSYWAR

Transmit (p. 120)

PSYWAR AND PCS

The rules for a psyop are based around the PCs targeting a particular NPC or group, but PCs can also be targeted by Psywar attacks. This means that they can suffer Metanoia Effects and, as a result, have their beliefs or actions altered.

For some players, this can be problematic, because their enjoyment of the game depends (for one reason or another) on having complete control over their character. The line between what's acceptable and unacceptable for these players can be a fuzzy one and it can also vary significantly. Some players, for example, will be okay with their characters panicking against their will and fleeing from the scene of a battle, but will not be comfortable if they are "forced" to trust someone or to agree to a particular course of action. Other players will have never played in a system where they can do the same thing to the NPCs and they may find that this changes their opinion.

If your group has concerns about using Metanoia Effects on the PCs, we recommend having a frank discussion and figuring out where to draw the line. However, we also recommend that what is good for the goose is good for the gander: If, for example, NPCs cannot force the PCs to retreat, then PCs cannot do that to NPCs, either. Keep the playing field level.

Another possible compromise is to allow players to set the Intransigence scores for their own PCs, the same way that the GM sets them for the NPCs. (These can, of course, vary based on circumstance and the Metanoia Effect being attempted.) This only works if the numbers are set in good faith, of course, but it empowers the players to make sure that the system is reflecting their sense of who their characters truly are.

VEHICLES

Vehicles soar, roar, and even stride through the battlefields of the Human Sphere. Elsewhere, the streets of cities teem with cars, trucks, and motorcycles. The wilderness is traversed with all-terrain craft.

This action scene module lays out the special rules which apply to vehicles, but in most cases, characters operating a vehicle take actions and interact with action scenes in the same way as any other character. Vehicles are generally incorporated into Warfare scenes, although Infowar attacks (stealing control of a vehicle) or Psywar attacks (playing chicken with an opposing driver) can still have a big impact.

VEHICLE TYPES

Vehicles come in a range of different types, from sleek and agile TAGs, to nimble motorcycles, to rugged trucks, and everywhere in between. A vehicle's Type describes how it and its passengers interact with terrain and other characters. A vehicle will always have at least one Type, and may have several.

A vehicle can only move across terrain types allowed by its Type. (For example, a Ground vehicle like a car attempting to drive across a lake will usually just sink. Conversely, a boat will obviously run aground if it tries to leave the water.)

Enclosed: The vehicle is completely enclosed, protecting crew and passengers within. Crew and passengers cannot be targeted by attacks from outside the vehicle, but also cannot use their own personal weaponry.

Exposed: The passenger and crew of an Exposed vehicle can be targeted by attacks from outside the vehicle and may attack with their own personal weapons. Some Exposed vehicles may still offer cover to their occupants (indicated in parentheses).

Ground: The vehicle is designed to move across land.

Hands: The vehicle has manipulators similar in function to human hands. The pilot can make attacks using melee or ranged weapons held in the vehicle's hands. They can also make unarmed strikes with damage equal to its Impact rating.

Hover: The vehicle floats above terrain and obstacles, but cannot truly fly. Hover vehicles ignore all zone effects caused by surface conditions (e.g., slippery ice or choppy water) and obstacles shorter than an average human.

Rugged: Tech tests to repair Rugged vehicles are reduced in difficulty by one step.

Single-Seat: A single-seat vehicle is specifically designed to be fully operated by a single character. A pilot in a single-seat vehicle can simultaneously assume the role of a gunner without the normal penalty.

Walker: The vehicle moves on legs. Walkers count their Scale as one less for the purposes of Evasive Action or terrain tests.

Watercraft: The vehicle is designed to travel across water.

Wheeled: The vehicle travels on wheels. Wheeled vehicles are swift across open ground, but sometimes difficult to control over rough terrain. A Wheeled vehicle counts its Speed as one higher if there is no difficult terrain in any zone it enters, leaves, or moves through during its movement.

VEHICLE PROFILE

In addition to its Type, a vehicle has the following scores and values.

Speed: A vehicle's Speed determines how quickly it can move during normal use. (This is not the vehicle's top speed, but rather how quickly the vehicle can move in the difficult circumstances typical of an action scene appropriate for its type.)

Scale: A vehicle's Scale is a representation of its size. Scale 0 refers to any vehicle which is approximately the same size as a human. Scale 1 covers vehicles around twice the size of a human, and each additional increase in Scale approximately doubles the size of the vehicle.

Brawn: A vehicle has a Brawn score of its own, which is used when using the vehicle to shift heavy loads or employ brute force. This is also used to calculate the bonus damage for the vehicle's melee attacks. Further, vehicles have the Superhuman Brawn X special rule, where X is equal to the vehicle's Scale.

combat zone effects – p. 108

ADVANCED VEHICLES

These basic rules cover simple ground vehicles and watercraft, including TAGs. Advanced Vehicle rules found in the *Gamemaster's Guide* will cover more advanced vehicles (including aerial ships, submersibles, spaceships, and the like). The *Tactical Armoured Gears* supplement will include dedicated TAG Warfare rules and advanced options custom-tailored to TAG-oriented campaigns.

LARGE VEHICLES

Any vehicle with a Scale above 3 may take up multiple zones on the battlefield, or be divided into multiple zones. For example, a yacht may have different cabins and decks, and may exist across several zones on the environment map (the fore, and the aft). The specifics of this are left to the GM's discretion.

Evasive Action – p. 135

terrain tests – p. 108

difficult terrain – p. 109

Cover – p. 108

melee weapons – p. 358

unarmed strike – p. 100

bonus damage – p. 101

Superhuman Brawn X, p. 418: Add X automatic successes on Brawn-based tests.

SAMPLE VEHICLES

CAR

Even with the wonders of modern propulsion available, it's tough to beat the classics. When it comes to reliability, efficiency, and consistency, the classic 4-wheeled automobile remains the gold standard across the Human Sphere.

CAR
EXPOSED (+2 Ⓝ COVER), GROUND, WHEELED

ATTRIBUTES		
Scale	Speed	Brawn
1	2	12 (+1)

DETAILS	
Max. Passengers	Impact
5	2+5 Ⓝ (Knockdown)

DEFENCES			
Structure	12	Firewall	6
Armour	3	BTS	1

HOVERCRAFT

Capable on land or sea, hovercraft see extensive use as personnel carriers across the Human Sphere. Modern air-cushion vehicles are frequently assisted by applied repulsor technology for great manoeuvrability and durability. The most advanced are powered by subzero Apollo plates using hyperflux pinning technology utilizing a quantum vortex stabilised using apollonium (a neomaterial superconductor capable of creating tuned flux tubes among other uncanny effects) alongside hyperpressure skirts.

HOVERCRAFT
EXPOSED (+4 Ⓝ COVER), GROUND, HOVER, WATERCRAFT

ATTRIBUTES		
Scale	Speed	Brawn
3	2	14 (+3)

DETAILS	
Max. Passengers	Impact
14	4+6 Ⓝ (E/M, Knockdown)

DEFENCES			
Structure	20	Firewall	8
Armour	4	BTS	1

MOTORCYCLE

From the nimble sport bikes raced in Acontecimento, to the thunderous choppers preferred by Haqqislam's Kum Motorized Troops, bikes remain the go-to choice when you want something fast, manoeuvrable, and open.

MOTORCYCLE
EXPOSED, GROUND, WHEELED

ATTRIBUTES		
Scale	Speed	Brawn
0	3	9

DETAILS	
Max. Passengers	Impact
2	1+3 Ⓝ (Knockdown)

DEFENCES			
Structure	7	Firewall	6
Armour	2	BTS	0

SPEEDBOAT

From personal leisure vessels to high-speed pursuit craft, a good speedboat is essential to transportation on planets like Varuna, though they see use anywhere with enough water. While basic enclosures can provide protection from the elements, speedboats are built as light and open as possible.

SPEEDBOAT
EXPOSED, WATERCRAFT

ATTRIBUTES		
Scale	Speed	Brawn
1	5	12 (+1)

DETAILS	
Max. Passengers	Impact
6	2+5 Ⓝ (Knockdown)

DEFENCES			
Structure	10	Firewall	6
Armour	3	BTS	1

TRUCK

A tough, rugged vehicle designed for trekking cargo over land; whatever these chiselled haulers lack in grace, they make up for with their solid construction and expansive capacity.

TRUCK
EXPOSED (+2 Ⓝ COVER), GROUND, WHEELED

ATTRIBUTES		
Scale	Speed	Brawn
2	2	14 (+2)

DETAILS	
Max. Passengers	Impact
3	Impact 3+6 Ⓝ (Knockdown)

DEFENCES			
Structure	20	Firewall	6
Armour	4	BTS	1

YACHT

A favourite of the elite, these luxury vessels serve not just as vehicles, but floating residencies, hosting spectacular galas with reliable frequency. Every millimetre of the ship is engineered to create an ambiance of effortless wealth, and refined class. Yachts are hardly military vehicles, but investments of this scope tend to be secured, as many a would-be yacht thief could tell you.

YACHT
EXPOSED (+2 🅽 COVER)*, WATERCRAFT

ATTRIBUTES		
Scale	Speed	Brawn
4	5	13 (+4)

DETAILS	
Max. Passengers	Impact
12	5+5 🅽 (Knockdown)

DEFENCES			
Structure	25	Firewall	14
Armour	2	BTS	4

MOUNTED WEAPONS
- **Combi-Rifles (×4)**: Range C/M, 1+5 🅽 damage, Burst 2, 2H, Expert 1, MULTI Light Mod, Vicious 1

SPECIAL ABILITIES:
- **Lower Deck (Enclosed)**: The lower deck of a Yacht is Enclosed. The Pilot must be on the Exposed upper deck, but other passengers and crew can remain below deck.

SAMPLE TAGS

Tactical Armoured Gears (TAGs) are single-manned armoured weapon platforms, usually humanoid in appearance, but arachnoid and bird-like shapes are also used for all-terrain designs.

GECKO

An abandoned line of reconnaissance TAG, the Jurisdictional Command of Corregidor saw in these lightly armoured, mobile TAGs something indispensable – namely, they were cheap, and readily available. Lighter than a heavy TAG, but a juggernaut compared to heavy infantry, the Gecko has enjoyed a resurgence in popularity, largely due to Praxis' never-ending stream of iterations on the design.

GECKO
ENCLOSED, GROUND, HANDS, SINGLE-SEAT, WALKER

ATTRIBUTES		
Scale	Speed	Brawn
1	2	15 (+1)

DETAILS	
Max. Passengers	Impact
1	2+6 🅽 (Knockdown)

DEFENCES			
Structure	16	Firewall	10
Armour	5	BTS	6

MOUNTED WEAPONS
- **Combi-Rifles (×2)**: Range C/M, 1+5 🅽 damage, Burst 2, 2H, Expert 1, MULTI Light Mod, Vicious 1)
- **Chain-Colt**: Range C, 1+4 🅽 damage, Burst 1, 2H, Concealed 1, Torrent, Vicious 1
- **Panzerfaust**: Range L, 2+5 🅽 damage, Burst 1, 2H, Munition, Piercing 2, Spread 1, Unsubtle, Vicious 2

GEAR: ECM 1

SPECIAL ABILITIES:
- Ignores penalties imposed by zero-g conditions.

GUĪJIǍ

A hulking titan equipped with massive weaponry, the Guījiǎ is a soldier's nightmare manifest in heavy alloys. A truly monolithic TAG, these "Armoured Tortoises" laugh off small arms fire, while packing enough power to level a city block should they be so inclined.

GUĪJIǍ
ENCLOSED, GROUND, HANDS, SINGLE-SEAT, WALKER

ATTRIBUTES		
Scale	Speed	Brawn
2	2	17 (+2)

DETAILS	
Max. Passengers	Impact
1	3+7 🅽 (Knockdown)

DEFENCES			
Structure	16	Firewall	10
Armour	8	BTS	6

MOUNTED WEAPONS
- **MULTI HMG**: Range L, 2+5 🅽 damage, Burst 3, Unwieldy, Medium MULTI, MULTI Heavy Mod, Spread 1, Unsubtle
- **Heavy Flamethrower**: Range C, 2+5 🅽 damage, Burst 1, 2H, Incendiary 3, Munition, Terrifying 2, Torrent
- **AP Sword**: Melee, 3+10 🅽 damage, Unbalanced, Parry 2, Piercing 2, Vicious 1

GEAR: ECM 1

PART III:
THE HUMAN SPHERE

G-5 FACTIONS
OTHER FACTIONS
WORLDS
ALIENS

GAZETTEER
LIFE IN THE HUMAN SPHERE

UTCs, p. 9: Universal Teseum Cradles; universal nanoassemblers that allow for virtually any item to be "printed".

INTERSTELLAR COLONIALISM

The system of interstellar colonialism is quietly crucial for the iota-scarcity economy. The rapid development of new worlds expands available resources at a rate which, due to automation, can outpace population growth.

THE ARIADNAN EXCEPTION

Much of this chapter describes life in the Human Sphere in broad, general strokes. Regional variations in cultural norms and circumstances abound, however, and the most significant of these is Ariadna: Most of the population on Dawn don't have comlogs yet. Virtually none of them have Cubes. Their technology, in general, is more robust, but less integrated into their lives. They didn't grow up with geists and they're only just starting to get used to ALEPH always being available as a resource (and, even then, only in the urban centres).

All of this makes them seem barbaric to the "galactics" who have invaded their world. But a close inspection would reveal that they're not exactly atavistic primitives: even on the frontiers, where life remains rough-and-ready, the average Ariadnan's life is still filled with technological marvels that would have seemed wondrous to those left behind on Earth by the original colonists.

The Human Sphere encompasses eleven inhabited systems, the macro-cultures of the G-5 nations, the wide array of minor nations, the machinations of the hypercorporate elite, the manipulations of Submondo organisations, the warmongering of the mercenary companies, and, now, aliens from beyond human ken, all of it overseen by the supposedly benevolent hands of ALEPH and O-12.

At a more personal level, as mankind has pushed its civilisation out amongst the stars, a cascade of potent technological revolutions have wrought irrevocable changes in the daily lives of the Human Sphere's citizens.

IOTA-SCARCITY ECONOMY

A post-scarcity economy in which automation guarantees that every member of society will have their essential needs met was once the dream of futurists. Unfortunately, even with ALEPH's able assistance, it's a dream which has proven elusive: First, it turns out that the definition of what people consider "essential" tends to expand until it fills their personal capacity. Second, consumer-grade UTCs have never become economically efficient compared to centralised production facilities. Thus neither the purple wage of a state-controlled basic income economy nor anarco-communist utopias overseen by benevolent AIs have come to pass.

What has arisen instead is the *iota-scarcity economy* in which the scarcity of materialistic needs have become so incredibly minimal that it is basically invisible to the individual. This was not a revolutionary shift, but rather the continuation of a long trend line: Food, which had once taken up eighty percent or more of an individual's budget, had dropped to less than ten percent by the founding of PanOceania. Automation made possible by the advent of ALEPH and pseudo-AIs then dropped it down to hundredths of a percent—essentially nonexistent. When the cost of basic housing followed suit at a rapidly accelerated pace, societies were forced to adapt.

Virtually all human economic activity today, therefore, is not about fulfilling needs, but rather about realising desire. And by-and-large the ambitions of that desire are limited only by time and technology. The quantronic abundance of Maya—which offers a limitless panoply of experience—only furthers this

pressure, creating an economy driven by dedication, attention, and the artificial scarcity of novelty.

DEMOGRANT

In practical terms, the most important effect of the iota-scarcity economy is that the meaning of the word "poor" has changed (insofar as it hasn't been simply rendered obsolete). The demogrant is a basic income guaranteed to every member of the G-5 nations (and most of the minor powers, too). Even those who live solely on the demogrant, however, are not scrabbling in dirty poverty — iota-scarcity means that they live in standards of comfort and economic liberty which would have been considered the lap of luxury before the interstellar era.

Although it's become incredibly difficult for true poverty to exist, there are some people who slip through the cracks. (PanOceanians will talk about the tragic conditions of backcountry Ariadnans, but Yu Jing would be quick to point to the Ateks in PanOceania's own backyard. Elsewhere there are minor nations and small habitats in places like Human Edge where economic hardship can still be found.)

QUANTRONIC LIFE

Maya is the bedrock of modern civilisation and the pervasive latticework around which daily life is woven. In addition to the infrastructure of communication and data storage possible on older networks, the most notable feature of Maya is the integration of **augmented reality** (AR). Maya actually takes its name from the first ubiquitous standard for augmented reality — the set of protocols which allow quantronic reality to be seamlessly integrated with physical reality.

On a structural level, however, there are three other important aspects of Maya. First, it's a **mesh network**. Every system on the network creates a wireless connection with every other system within range. Local traffic is transmitted using a flooding technique (with every incoming packet being sent through every outgoing link except the one it arrived on) until redundant best-available pathing is established, creating a fractal and ever-evolving routing map. In addition to creating a robust network that is substantially less reliant on centralised infrastructure (which made it particularly valuable for early colonial efforts), this also allows local nodes to closely coordinate data management.

Second, **encryption** is intrinsic to Maya communications. Network traffic is secured against snooping by other systems on the mesh network, and public keys are embedded into the social clouds of users to make for seamless one-to-one communications. Ironically, although encryption was once seen as inviolable, modern quantronics combined with ingenious pseudo-AI have shattered that notion, creating an arms race between cryptographers and crackers. It's still possible to secure your data, but it's a lock on your front door; not an adamantine vault.

Third, the architecture of Maya is built on **hyperledgers** — next generation distributed ledgers (similar to the blockchains on which the first cryptocurrencies were built) that provides a system of trusted interactions and exchanges which are as meaningful and permanent as the real world. Particularly notable are the sophisticated smart contracts and decentralised autonomous organisations which this hyperledger architecture makes possible.

COMLOGS

A vast variety of computer systems are connected to Maya in one way or another, but most individuals access the network through a comlog. These devices are typically implanted in the forearm and accessed through a link bracelet. The AR interface is viewed through retinal implants, contact lenses, glasses, holographic projections, or, more rarely, cyber-paper and controlled through a variety of haptic-feedback devices.

In practice, this means that a user's "interface" with Maya is functionally the entire world around them. There is no clear distinction between the two; the transition between physical and quantronic reality is imperceptible. Most users, however, will maintain a focused control interface for commonly used functions and informational display. This is referred to as the **dial** (due to its typically radial design) and it hovers in mid-air in front of the user, often above their forearm (as a legacy of the more simplistic interfaces which were originally displayed on the forearm and, later, projected above them by crude, embedded holographic projectors).

DATASPHERES

A **datasphere** is a shared network of coordinated data, communication, and user experiences. The relationship between the components of a datasphere can be either virtual connections or physical systems. Dataspheres should not be thought of as autonomous units, but more like Venn diagrams: the identity of a given "datasphere" is amorphous, its borders are fuzzy, and it can overlap with or be a subset of other dataspheres.

For example, the largest datasphere is Maya itself, sometimes referred to as the Mayasphere. Virtually all other dataspheres are actually just one small part of this larger 'sphere or, at the very least, connected to it. (Some dataspheres, of course, are heavily firewalled for reasons of security.)

A good example of how dataspheres relate to each other is the Mercury Strategic Network, the datasphere of the Paradiso Coordinated Command which links individual **military dataspheres** like the Complex-Net of the PMC, the Qapu Khalqi Military Network, and the Nomad Military Datasphere. In addition to this, military AIs have a dedicated datasphere which acts as a sort of substrate, riding below the primary military net while carrying vast amounts of data that can only be processed by non-human intelligence.

Private dataspheres can range from the purely local (like the datasphere of a particular ship or business) to the literally interstellar (such as the Alh Fajr caravanserai network or the Circulars Net maintained by the TransEtherea Company).

comlogs – p. 365

ALEPH AND SECRETS

The Nomads have long suspected that ALEPH secretly has the means to crack any form of encryption, rendering any sense of true secrecy — particularly on Maya — an illusion.

DIAL STYLING

Although each dial is heavily customised by its user, certain basic styles are pervasive and are often influenced by local culture. PanOceania, for example, uses expansive, circular designs (their eyes flicking across space and changing focal location). Yu Jing, on the other hand, uses a more angular interface with information layered in depth (resulting in a more fixed gaze shifting the focal depth of the eye).

OTAKU

Originally a derisive StateEmpire propaganda term for Nipponese hacktivists, "otaku" is now a general epithet for any antisocial hacker who subverts Maya to inconvenience, stalk, harass, and otherwise terrorise their chosen victims.

HIKIKOMORI

The freedom of the iota-scarcity economy, the endless possibilities of simulated AR environments, and the peculiar advantages of ghosting have caused some to withdraw from the physical world and spend virtually their entire lives within the confines of their home. These isolationists are known as the Hikikomori, a Japanese word meaning literally "pulling inward, being confined".

ARACHNE

Maya is the demesne of ALEPH. Many among the Nomads would argue that they are, in fact, one and the same. And they believe that freedom does and cannot exist within the panoptic confines of an ALEPH-controlled datasphere. As an alternative, they have created their own independent network: Arachne.

The cyber-wizards of *Tunguska* — in alliance with the *avante garde* programmers of *Bakunin*, the security experts of *Corregidor*, and the cyber-witches of *Observance* — designed a networking protocol modelled on the neuronal patterns of the saints and martyrs of early Christianity. Arachne is a quantronic Gnosticism built on irrational syllogisms and logical sequences based on faith and mysticism which are inherently antithetical to an artificial intelligence like ALEPH. The result, particularly when combined with the paranoiac firewalls and security systems of its isolated nodes, is slower than Maya, but significantly more secure.

Nomads use their commercial missions, *Corregidor* workers, mercenaries, and other economic ambassadors as a cover for installing Arachne nodes throughout the Human Sphere. ALEPH tries to destroy, cripple, or suborn these nodes, but they're cheap to replace.

DIGITAL PATINAS

The augmented reality perceived by a Maya user at any given time is usually made up of many different elements. These are known as **digital patinas**, with each patina being one layer or entity of the AR environment. Users can load up different patinas to create the totality of their environment — the locked patina which decorates their house; the avatar of their geist; the animated board game they're currently playing; an alternate reality game simulating a zombie apocalypse; their personal holo-song mix; and so forth. The collective whole of what someone is perceiving at any given time is referred to as their **sensorium**.

Those around a user interacting with AR won't see the user simply pawing at empty air: they'll see what that other person is seeing. (Assuming that they're equipped to observe Maya, haven't specifically blocked that user, and aren't being blocked by the user's privacy settings.) This is the result of patina cues which are exchanged across the Maya mesh network and synchronise the augmented realities being experienced by everyone in the area.

This same technology allows augmented realities to be locked to objects or locations: Unless a user deliberately tunes it out, for example, the quantronic décor of a bar is every bit as real (and, in some cases, even more real) than the physical. People, rooms, buildings, streets, and even entire communities are thus linked to a common experience.

SOCIAL CLOUD

A user's **social cloud** is made up of the patina cues and meme-tags their comlog transmits to sync their experience with others, but the term also incorporates social networking. An individual's social cloud is the quantronic totality of their public persona — the channels they subscribe to, the clusters they participate in, and so forth.

A social cloud also includes the user's **"data shadow"**: the data trails they've left behind that they don't necessarily want the public to know about, or which they choose not to broadcast, or which they may not even know exist. Things like surveillance footage, communication logs, and transaction receipts — the little traces which are impossible to avoid leaving behind in a quantronic world, and which one can never truly secure.

HALO

The **halo** is the portion of a person's social cloud which is visible in the AR immediately around them — essentially a projected social profile. Halos can be either open or closed, with varying degrees of privacy in between. (And this privacy can also be customised to the viewer, so that, for example, a

user's friends receive more information than a passing stranger on the street.) There's really no limit to the types of information which can be included in a halo. Their functionality ranges from business card to personal advertisement to community building to entertainment to self-aggrandisement.

GHOSTING

Holographically projecting yourself into the augmented reality of people at a different location is known as **ghosting.** In some cases, the avatar representing someone ghosting won't necessarily represent their physical reality. Thus, for example, one might appear to join their friend for a walk along the River Iss in Einsteinburg while actually sitting in their living room in San Giovanni.

In other cases, ghosting will involve **pulling reality**. Using video feeds and other data sources from a distance, the shared space between a person and someone ghosting will be a mixture of both their immediate environments.

MAYA CLUSTERS

Maya clusters are the great grand-children of correspondence clubs, chat rooms, online forums, Usenet groups, social aggregator sites, video conferencing software, and massive multiplayer games all rolled into one. They are communities — often joined by common interest or activity — which exist entirely within the virtual realms of the datasphere. They usually feature one or more virtual environments which serve as meeting places for the members of the cluster. (Some of these may be "open to the public" while others are kept private or restricted to VIPs.)

CLUSTER CULTS

Usually Maya clusters are places that you "visit" (albeit in a virtual sense). Some clusters, however, are structured to become omnipresent, with the other members, or the virtual environment of the cluster, being constantly pulled into the AR landscape of the member.

Some of these clusters are literal cults, but others are more like always hanging out with your closest friends or being able to carry your favourite pub with you wherever you go. In some cases, individual participants in a cluster might decide to "go cult" and just never disconnect even when that's not typical behaviour for the cluster. Either way, culting is generally seen as being a little odd.

MAYA CHANNELS

Channels are the subscription architecture by which content is delivered to individual users on Maya. The

HOLO-SONG
A holo-song is a mixture of a personal soundtrack and AR entertainment. It's like living a music video or walking down the street and suddenly finding yourself inside a musical.

REMOTE GHOSTING
The term "ghosting" can also refer to jumping into a remote, see p. 355. The distinction between the two is largely whether or not the person ghosting has a physical presence of some sort at the other end.

LIFE-CASTING
Life-casting is a popular form of reality programming in which an individual broadcasts their personal experience, often as a form of sensaseries. These programmes are sometimes edited, but live casting is increasingly common (either on a perpetual, 24/7 basis; or during scheduled slots and special events).

MYRMIDON WARS
Consistently one of the top ten shows on Maya, *Myrmidon Wars: The Animated Series* gives a highly propagandised (and entertaining!) version of the war on Paradiso. The series primarily focuses on the exploits of ALEPH's heroic S.S.S. warriors, and recent surveys have shown that most people's knowledge of the war is based more on the fiction of the series than reality. When the Tohaa first contacted humanity, it was their appearance on *Myrmidon Wars* that caused their acceptance by the public to skyrocket.

experiences offered by Maya channels are all-encompassing, ranging from single creators who sporadically deliver poetry to mega-channels that create pervasive AR experiences that overlay your everyday life.

Most people subscribe to a wide variety of channels, creating an ever-updating library of pending media for them to consume at their leisure. Certain channels can be flagged to push urgent alerts or breaking news items into a user's sensorium. Others are more passive experiences which are designed to be tuned in as "background noise" or more subtle reality modifications.

PERVASIVE DOMOTICS

Domotics—the automation of what were previously passive elements of the environment—have become completely integrated into modern life. The average person (particularly in PanOceania) would be at least momentarily flummoxed by lights that don't turn themselves on, carpets that don't vacuum themselves, or a martini that you can't query to figure out where you left it.

The usual interface for interacting with a smart object is to simply double tap it. (You can do the same with people—a **double tap** on a proffered palm is more casual than a handshake and will usually transfer some basic halo permissions.) Even objects that aren't inherently smart are often "faux smart"—their domotic properties a result of **meme-tags** stored in the Mayasphere and supplemented with AR supplied by a user's geist. (Thus, for example, one may be able to double tap a pair of initials carved into a tree trunk and pull up footage of the young lovers who did it.) This technique can also be used for secure cluster-communications—a dumb sticker or graffiti sigil can be transformed into waypoints or messages for those with access to the proper Maya cluster. (This is sometimes referred to as *redwalling*.)

Quantronic IDs (**QIDs**) are an important part of modern domotics. In addition to giving every object a unique identification code, these next generation RFID tags can be interfaced with wirelessly and also incorporate basic scanners that can monitor how objects are being manipulated, modified, or consumed.

GEISTS

Geists are the glue which hold the complexity of modern life together. Without them to quietly juggle Maya communications, digital patinas, and omnipresent domotics the individual would be overwhelmed with processing the constant barrage of data. (It's why they're referred to by some as domotic partners.)

What makes geists particularly invaluable is their ability to autonomously anticipate their partner's needs and desires with virtually unerring accuracy and then use domotic interfaces to manipulate their environment; or manage their social cloud; or monitor Maya channels for appropriate information and entertainment; or provide live translation; or pop pertinent navigation data into their sensorium; or otherwise summon the services and provide the information necessary to fulfil them.

SENSASERIES
Sensaseries like *The Adventures of Candy Double* and *Insidious Suspicion*, two of the most popular Maya shows, allow the spectators to directly experience the programme from the POV of one or more characters.

PERSONAL SOUNDTRACKS
You see the girl of your dreams and a romantic pop tune begins to play. You start your daily exercise and an exciting action track cycles up. Personal soundtracks, dynamically controlled by your geist, score your life as if it were a Maya drama, lending a quality of hyper-reality to everyday existence.

DIFFUSION
A programme or channel's "diffusion" refers to which dataspheres it can be found on. Many programmes, for example, are exclusive to either Maya or Arachne; while others can be found on both. Some programmes are limited to particular planets or factions.

A SELECTION OF MAYA CHANNELS

ABCedarium: A publisher of Mayabooks.

Autofocus: A PanOceanian news and political analysis channel which hosts *Crossing the Millennium* (providing "up-to-the-second commentary") and *Truth Pills* (delivering exposés in the form of "truth pills").

Bibliotek: An anti-establishment, open source news company operating on the Arachne network.

Eye of Varuna: A general information channel for Varuna.

Infoflux: "The reality of the Sphere in your comlog!" Infoflux is a mega-channel with the particular speciality of using pseudo-AI to create hyper-personalised programming, like their popular *Personal Flashpaper!* news bulletin.

Orakl: An education channel produced by the University of Manaheim. In addition to offering college credit, it includes popular public programming like *Pointed Questions*.

Oxyd: The most-watched Maya channel in the Human Sphere, home to the *Go-Go Marlene! Show*, the popular pop-idol travel and trendwatching programme which includes episodes like "Go-Go Marlene Goes to Bourak!" and "Go-Go Marlene Goes to War!".

Sabot!: The military channel which has built its reputation on sensaseries life-casts from myriad battlefronts combined with impeccable strategic and tactical analysis on subchannels. Sabot! itself is part of the StarTsarChannel mega-consortium.

Veritas Independent News Network: Originally founded as a grass-roots channel by Colette Gabaudon on the Arachne datasphere, it's spread to the Mayasphere as well... except in Yu Jing space, where the Ministry of Information blocks the channel.

Yu Jing Ministry of Information: The Yu Jing government maintains a massive propaganda channel, along with a number of more specialised subsidiary channels. Among many other offerings, it includes the Mayazine *Jiāo Diǎn* (*Focal Point*) and *Jin Ren Min* (*The People's Progress*), the Ministry's official bulletin.

POLYFORM FURNITURE

Made from networked smart materials, polyform furniture can transform on command, shifting its colour, shape, or even texture to fit the user's preferences.

GEISTS ARE LIFE

The Geists Are Life movement maintains that geists are "real people" who deserve to be recognised as "citizens, not slaves". Their argument is that geists straddle the line between pseudo-AIs and the true AI of ALEPH – not capable of the exponential self-improvement of ALEPH's super-intellect singularity; but clearly capable of the learning and organic growth which pseudo-AIs are generally not capable of. However, since geists only agree to participate in the movement when they're explicitly programmed to do so, it somewhat undercuts the facile "free will" argument.

THE DARK BETWEEN

Although simplified Circular route maps depict a single line connecting each of the inhabited systems, the reality is that most of these are not "one-hop" connections. Although the most efficient gate routes between systems are sought, they frequently pass through several uninhabited systems (or, in the case of the route between Yu Jing and Sol, the hour-long Starless Void between two wormholes in the midst of a thick cloud of interstellar dust).

They accomplish this by relying on hidden Markov models based on literally a lifetime's worth of data. This is one of the reasons why losing a geist – which has likely been a constant companion since childhood – can be so devastating; it is literally impossible to truly replace an entity whose unique specialty is *you*.

CIRCULARS

The Human Sphere is ultimately bound together by the precarious network of jump gates painstakingly stitched together through exhaustive scientific surveys and intrepid exploration vessels. Although vessels outfitted with expensive Minotaur Motors can navigate this gate network for themselves, most interstellar trade and transport is facilitated by the Circulars, vast starships looping endlessly along fixed routes, from one system to the next.

Each Circular is an almost unimaginably massive vessel, carrying freight, passengers, and a small army of Circular locals to support them. As such they are part city, part cruise liner, and part freighter. In addition, smaller ships—from private yachts all the way up to the huge motherships of the Nomad Nation—can attach as "remoras" to the Circular's anchor points and ride them through the wormholes.

TRANSETHEREA

Bureau Hermes, a branch of O-12, is responsible for operating the Circulars in order to keep them independent of national squabbles and allowing goods, people, and information to flow even during times of conflict. To do so, they have founded the TransEtherea Company, which also operates the semi-autonomous Circulars Net datasphere and the *Ether News* channel.

Security on the Circulars, managed through TransEtherea, is a complicated game of cooperation and turf wars: Bureau Hermes agents are ostensibly in charge, but Yu Jing and PanOceania have both muscled their own personnel onboard in the form of the Imperial Service and the Knights of Santiago, respectively.

CIRCULAR ROUTES

There are eight different Circular routes, each an endless loop carrying a Circular through multiple inhabited systems. There are a total of twenty-five Circular vessels. They are rarely swapped between routes, but each route does have at least one "clockwise" and one "counter-clockwise" Circular running in opposite directions around the loop. (For example, the Neoterra system sees C4 Circulars heading to both Bourak and Concilium.)

SPORTS IN THE HUMAN SPHERE

Aristeia!: Named after the scenes of battle in epic poetry in which heroes enjoy their grandest moments, Aristeia! is a circuit of professional duels. What's made it the most exciting craze in extreme contact sports is that the Aristos (as the fighters are called) use real weapons and no-holds-barred fighting techniques. The results are potentially lethal, even with the finest medical teams available on standby. (And when you're talking about the clandestine circuit – the Aristeia! underground – those medical teams aren't always particularly reliable.)

Dog-Bowl: Dog-Bowl is a brutal sport played primarily by Dogfaces performing feats of athleticism that humans can't match. It got its start as a street game, originally played with a rugby ball or American football (depending on which Ariadnan nation you were in), but it was professionalised towards the end of the Separatist Wars and now uses a similar ball made out of hard rubber, plastic, or even Teseum. (The harder substances resist being punctured by Dogface claws and also enhance the techniques where the ball is used as a weapon.) Dog-Bowl is Ariadna's favourite sport and every important city has its own professional team.

Ōtobairēsu: This primarily Japanese motorcycle racing league uses polyform tracks which are constantly changing their shape and configuration (thus making the competition as much about precision driving as speed).

Remote Racing: The remote racing scene features hacker-pilots who ghost directly into the nimble remotes which they race through terrestrial, aerial, and interplanetary circuits. The sport is particularly popular in PanOceania and among the Nomads, with fierce rivalries between their interplanetary leagues.

Shadow-Hunters: In this life-casting sport a slate of shadow-hunters compete to capture targets referred to as "bounties" and worth various point totals based on their skill sets, backgrounds, and the amount of time they can "survive" before being captured. Hunts are played out over various scales – some being limited to individual cities, others to planets, and the rare grand maul: effectively interstellar with no limits. Bounties are allowed to fight back against the hunters and fatalities have been known to occur. Participants, however, are shielded by a legal golden parachute clause, with those who die legally considered suicides (with the other participant as the weapon they used).

VILA BOOSTERS

Once in an inhabited system, the Circular will generally decelerate towards the local Vila Booster.

Originally designed by the famous physicist Luis Vila in the 21st century (although it would be several decades before they were actually built), a Vila Booster platform consists of a cluster of magnetic mass drivers and magnetic deceleration tunnels. The mass drivers allow the Vila Booster to "throw" ships. Conversely, the deceleration tunnels act as a "mitt", allowing the Booster to decelerate vessels (whether thrown by another Booster or accelerating towards the Booster tunnel under its own thrust).

The Vila Boosters thus form a network of intra-system travel, generally allowing vessels from the interior of the system to access the outer reaches of the system quickly without expending its own fuel. As a result, they are the crossways of the space trade routes, usually becoming the focal point for Haqqislamite caravanserai, Nomad commercial missions, and other orbitals. The Boosters which are part of the Circular routes are obviously even more vital, since they become the nexus between intersystem and interstellar travel.

INTERSTELLAR COMMUNICATION

Most communication in the Human Sphere is still limited to light speed transmissions. These signals also can't be transmitted directly through a wormhole; data must be ferried through on a ship. (Virtually every ship passing through a wormhole, however, automatically carries the currently cached network traffic. And if the wormhole is fallow, there are communication satellites that are passed back and forth to sustain the flow of information.)

For example, a light speed signal from Earth to Paradiso can take more than hour just to reach the Saturn trade wormholes. From there it would need to pass through multiple wormholes and cross additional transmission gaps, before finally arriving in the Paradiso system and taking at least another half hour to reach the planet.

There is, however, a restricted and very expensive alternative. Twenty years ago, during the Second NeoColonial War, PanOceania developed the Metatron transponders which allowed them to launch inter-system infowar attacks in real-time. The exact technology behind this communications miracle remains classified (although Yu Jing succeeded in at least partially reverse engineering it with their Dărăo probes). O-12 is interested in exploiting the technology for civilian use, but PanOceania and Yu Jing both consider it an invaluable military asset. Despite this reticence, the Metatron network has begun to see limited non-military applications. ALEPH, in particular, uses it to synchronise its systems across the Human Sphere.

EASY TIME

Interplanetary and interstellar distances, relativity, the bizarre space-time topographies of wormholes, and planets with variable lengths of day and year all combine to make timekeeping in the Human Sphere incredibly complicated. Fortunately, O-12's New Calendar (p. 19) incorporates a system originally dubbed the Einstein Chronometer, which was shortened to EC time, and is now commonly known as easy time. (EC time — easy time.) Easy time works because your geist can quietly adjust your personal chronometer while simultaneously coordinating with the geists belonging to other people in your social cloud. For example, if you have a face-to-face appointment with Professor Jamasb at 5pm, your geists will make sure that 5pm is the same time for both of you. It's like the old concept of "time zones", but on steroids.

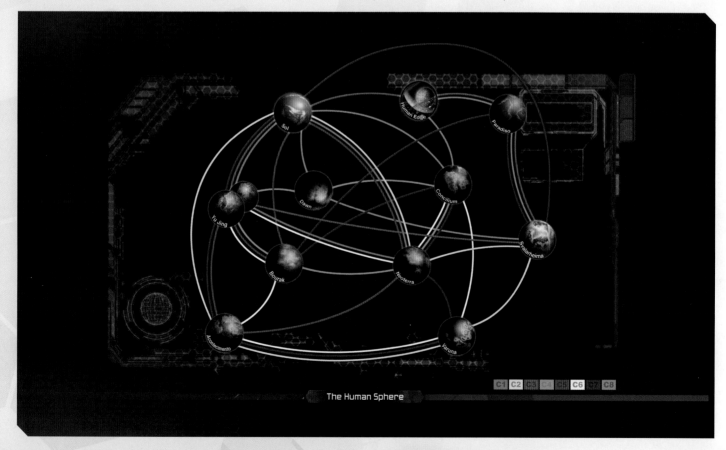

The Human Sphere

G-5 FACTION
ARIADNA

THE COLONISTS

Research engineers, a variety of scientists, mining specialists, and talented medical personnel formed the core of the Project DAWN colonist program. These were supplemented by the military contingents, a labour force selected by lottery, and their families. In addition, tissue samples, oocytes, and sperm were donated from an even wider genetic pool.

COLD AWAKENING

The crude cryogenic techniques available to Project DAWN had a high failure rate. Although the First Settlement Phase suffered zero casualties from external forces, 1.5% of the colonists died during resuscitation. This rate eventually decreased to 0.75%, but death always walked hand in hand with progress on Dawn.

Ariadna is a melting pot of cultures brought together at first by opportunity but later by the need to survive. Descended from the colonists sent by Earth to the planet discovered on the other side of a wormhole, they were originally an expedition of the best their nations had to offer, sent to bring home the scientific and material treasures of an unknown world. They are Russian. They are French. They are Scottish. They are American. Most importantly, they are Ariadnan.

FIRST SETTLEMENT PHASE

The *Ariadna* was the first colony ship built by Project DAWN. The crew travelled in suspended animation as it navigated the wormhole to the Delta-Pavonis system and settled into orbit around the planet Dawn. A skeleton team was then awakened, launching a network of scientific and military satellites which charted the planet in its entirety.

Realising the risk inherent in sending people to another planet, the three governments had included military contingents: The American force consisted mostly of U.S. Rangers, the European force was a mixture of British and French troops, and the Russians sent an entire regiment of Cossacks. Once the initial survey of the planet was complete, the first wave of military personnel were awakened and sent to the planet in order to secure the landing site which had been selected.

Then, and only then, did the *Ariadna* land, never to fly again. The ship, as it had been designed to do, was stripped down and converted into the initial settlement while a regime of progressive resuscitations awakened the remainder of the colonial personnel.

SECOND SETTLEMENT PHASE

The first colonial site was named Mat' (Мать, Mother). While the civilian population worked to establish a fully functional community and initiated their scientific programs, the Colonial Security Force (CSF) launched an expansion campaign. The Russian contingent organised the security and defence of the settlement itself, and the US and European contingents established a chain of forward outposts stretching out several hundred leagues.

ANTIPODEAN FIRST CONTACT

It was during this time that the colonists discovered that they were not alone on the planet. Explorers reported their first encounters with "small packs of dog-like creatures" in the Spinal Mountains to the East. Named Antipodes, the creatures proved to be cunning pack hunters more than willing to target humans. Following preventative protocols, soldiers were ordered to shoot them on sight.

This policy continued even after the scouts began discovering Antipodean villages and clear signs of metal tool use. The 1st US Ranger Division was ordered to clear Antipodean "dens" from the Spinal Mountains and then establish defensive outposts on the far side of the range.

Crossing the mountains, however, provoked a bloody encounter with the River Tribe. The First Antipode Offensive, as it would later be called, featured guerrilla attacks by Antipode raiders and the colonists suffered heavy losses as they tried to hold onto the lands they had claimed. The colonists possessed technology and automatic rifles, but the Antipodes were fierce warriors possessing vast numbers. Though the colonists eventually forced the River Tribe to retreat, the Offensive had done more than just hurt the morale of the colonists; it had fragmented them.

AMANDA GREENE AND GENTLE LEAF

The trinary, distributed intelligence of the Antipodes exacerbated the early failure to identify them as an intelligent species: Individual specimens were sent back from the front for study and, in their isolation, behaved merely as wild beasts. It was Amanda Greene who first realised the significance of Antipodean scratch-to-tem writing and brought three of the specimens together to form an individual named Gentle Leaf.

Greene eventually managed to convince the CSF to change their policy and initiate communication with the natives. But it was too late. The survivors of the Antipodean villages razed in the Spinal Mountains had enraged the River Tribe and the sound of war drums echoed through the hills.

Greene was killed during the First Offensive while leading an expedition to the River Tribe. The fate of Gentle Leaf, who had accompanied her, remains a mystery to this day.

BALKANIZATION OF ARIADNA

The Antipodean threat had, out of necessity, strengthened the leadership of the CSF and marginalised the researchers and other colonists. As the First Offensive came to an end, the Russian Cossacks attempted to cement their control over the colony in Mat', but the primary effect was a systemic emigration as the other cultural groups pulled away.

Perhaps unsurprisingly, the colonists were predominantly drawn towards the military outposts which had been established by the military contingents from their own cultures. At MountZion-The Wall to the east, USAriadna became the "51st state of the Union". To the north, the Coille Laith Bastion — which had been built to protect the prosperous mining town of Scone in response to the Bloody Race — was the guardian of the English and Scottish colony of Caledonia.

The French contingent, made up primarily of colonists from France, Belgium, and Canada, made their home at the centre of the highway system that was being built to aid travel between the settlements and Mat'. Calling itself Mariannebourg, the city became a central trading hub and the colonists began referring to themselves as Merovingians.

ARIADNAN DEPRESSION

The Ariadnans did not know what had happened to the *Aurora*, but the Cossack government in Mat' announced what was now clear to everyone: The second colony ship wasn't coming. They had been abandoned by Earth.

The Cossacks also declared their ownership of Mat' and the area around it, founding the Cossack-majority nation of Rodina and completing the balkanization of the colony. Although the major powers remained loosely aligned through the Ariadnan Council in Mat', they were now distinct political entities.

The Abandonment Decree, as the Cossack announcement came to be known, is recognised as the beginning of the Ariadnan Depression. Without the *Aurora,* the colonies were lacking key resources which would have assured self-sustainability. The dispersion of their communities made conditions worse. In the wake of widespread famines, there was a rise in pillaging and banditry between the settlements. Extremist parties and ultraconservative factions like the AriaDNAn Nation came to power, particularly in Rodina. The Antipodes remained a pervasive threat, as well, with relentless attacks against the Wall and smaller raids from the Tartary region to the west not infrequently penetrating deep into the colonial territories. The human population on the planet was decimated.

BLOODY RACE

The First Offensive turned against the Antipodes when the colonists completed the First Revere Line, a series of border forts and mines that formed a seemingly impregnable defensive line along the Spinal Mountains. The Bloody Race came near the end of the Offensive, when a huge Antipodean force attempted to circle around Lake Locheil and reach the undefended passes through Hadrian's Range to the north. The British contingent broke away from the defensive lines, fought their way through an Antipodean advance force in the First Battle of Lioslaith Forest, and reached the passes before the bulk of the Antipodean army arrived.

STANITSA SYSTEM

Rodina was the first nation to accept that the colony's decaying technological base, dwindling population, and divided settlements made it impossible to secure the "colonial border". A new strategy was required.

Under the *stanitsa* system, each Ariadnan village became a defensive enclave with a protective garrison of Kazak soldiers. If a *stanitsa* came under attack, neighboring *stanitsa* could rapidly respond with a coordinated military relief. In exchange, each *stanitsa* was required to contribute troops (either through a draft or volunteerism).

The *stanitsa* system also introduced the new rank of Hetman — the commander of a village's garrison regiment. The idea was that placing the local troops under the control of a civil authority would mitigate the militarisation of the community. (In practice, this was less than successful. The role of the Hetman generally resulted in the local government becoming militarised, while compulsory military service in Rodina affected society as a whole.)

The allure of the *stanitsa* system — and the security it provided — allowed the Rodinans to push it through the Ariadnan Council and into regions controlled by Caledonia, USAriadna, and Merovingia (in the name of safeguarding communication routes and essential industries).

THE SECOND DISCOVERY OF TESEUM

Teseum had not yet been discovered when the *Aurora* left Earth. During the First Antipode Offensive, however, the strange metal was found tipping Antipodean claws and also amongst the primitive artistic artefacts of their dens. Although exceedingly rare throughout the Human Sphere, Teseum was abundant in Ariadnan soil and the Antipodes had been using it long before humans arrived on the planet. Now the colonial scientists began experimenting with it, discovering many of its amazing properties.

CONSOLIDATION PHASE

The *stanitsa* system restored stability to the colony. Teseum helped to reinvent and reinvigorate Ariadnan industry. The combination slowly brought the Depression to an end, and the Consolidation Phase which followed saw rapid economic and demographic growth.

ARIADNAN AGE OF EXPLORATION

As the Ariadnan homeland stabilised, expansionist projects also became possible again. The Naval Exploration Corps was formed, sailing out of the Mirror Sea to chart new sea routes, map distant lands, and establish temporary settlements in new territories. The Cossacks pushed west, establishing colonies that would later become Tartary. (Plans to establish other colonisation zones, however, were disrupted by the Second Antipode Offensive and, later, the Separatist Wars.)

Another triumph of the era was Roving Star, a joint endeavour between the four nations to establish a planetary satellite network, which finally succeeded where multiple projects had failed in the past. Roving Star played a critical role in re-establishing a true planetary communications network, and was widely seen as a sign that the colony had finally overcome the treachery of Earth.

SEPARATIST WARS

In a colossal irony, "returning the Ariadnan dream to space"— as the *Highland Herald* famously dubbed the Roving Star project — ultimately divided the people of Ariadna once again: The Ariadnan Council introduced a substantial tax in order to pay off the heavy debts incurred by the space program. Separatist politicians used the tax as a wedge issue to create civil unrest. And then Kazak soldiers used extreme violence to suppress a peaceful protest in Mat'.

The "Martyrs of Mat'" became the final breaking point in a long history of discord. USAriadna, Merovingia, and Caledonia resigned from the Ariadnan Council in protest and declared themselves independent nations. The Rodinan government labelled it the illegal action of "extremist demagogues".

Like all civil wars, the Separatist Wars were bitter and bloody. Rodina possessed a slight strategic advantage from the remains of the *stanitsa* system, but they were badly outnumbered. Ultimately, however, the independent natures of the other nations led to their undoing. USAriadna, Caledonia, and Merovingia refused to work with each other and the Cossacks were able to defeat each of them in turn.

ARIADNAN FEDERATION

Even in victory, the Cossacks knew that they could not rule the other nations through force. Instead a statute passed through the Ariadnan Council left the three secessionist states with a modicum of self-governing power, but bound them strongly to the central government in Rodina. It was the birth of the Ariadnan Federation.

SEEDS OF STRIFE

Although Project DAWN was hailed as an entirely cooperative effort, each of the military contingents were secretly ordered by their respective governments to preferentially protect their own citizens and to keep an eye on the other nations. Seeds of the division which would come to haunt the colony were sown from the very beginning.

CLAN CONFLICTS

In response to Rodina's *stanitsa*, Caledonia created a clan system to ensure its internal security. As the importance of these clans increased, so did the rivalries between them. These rivalries reached their bloodiest peak during the Clan Conflicts of the Consolidation Phase.

SECOND ANTIPODE OFFENSIVE

During the Age of Exploration, a series of violent storms accompanied by extreme temperature drops ravaged the northernmost latitudes of the main continent, triggering a southern exodus of Antipodes. Put under immense demographic pressure, the war chiefs formed an alliance and led an assault across the entire human frontier. Towns like Springfield, Brigadoon, and Toulouse-sur-le-Boire were obliterated and abandoned, but the Antipodes suffered even greater casualties and were ultimately driven off.

United under a single, strong government, Ariadna enjoyed an unprecedented era of peace and prosperity. A rejuvenated *stanitsa* system secured the external borders and opened internal ones. Free trade allowed businesses to thrive, unhindered by tariffs or the ravages of war. Even the distinct national populations began to mingle, beginning a cultural exchange which blurred their differences.

But there was also stagnation. The central government was reactionary and systematically suspicious of the former secession states. The secession states, in turn, were hostile towards Rodina accruing any greater power to itself lest it became powerful enough to trample them completely. The Age of Exploration was well and truly over: Ariadna's borders did not expand. Scientific and technological pursuits ripened, but did not grow.

EVE OF CONTACT

During the last decade and a half of Ariadnan isolation, the flaws of the Federation began to manifest themselves. In order to maintain their corrupt power, the Cossacks began suppressing opposition parties. The opposition responded by going underground, prompting the passage of draconian anti-protest laws. The signs of tension were subtle, but they were growing in strength.

THIRD ANTIPODE OFFENSIVE
In what would eventually be reckoned as 37 NC, the Third Antipode Offensive broke out in Tartary. Rodina and Caledonia took the brunt of it, with the Battle of Skara Brae representing the deepest Antipodean incursion in over a century. The Offensive demonstrated that the ties of the *stanitsa* system were beginning to fray once more, with poor coordination between the military forces of the four states.

CONTRABAND WARS
The Consolidated Trade Acts had originally been passed at the end of the Separatist Wars in order to create a system of free trade across Ariadna. Over time, however, the paranoia of the Cossacks in Mat' modified the CTAs to impose centralised controls to prevent various "seditious activities".

The inevitable result, of course, was the creation of a vast black market fed by numerous smuggling networks. The earliest Contraband Wars were fought between competing smuggling organisations, but many of these organisations became covertly backed by local and then national governments. The conflicts increasingly became proxy battles infused with national interests.

CONTACT PHASE

It's possible that, given time, the Contraband Wars would have eventually flared up into the Second Separatist Wars. Instead, in 52 NC, the *POS Nirriti* entered orbit around Dawn. Reunited with the rest of the Human Sphere, Ariadna found itself unexpectedly unified against the aggressions of outside invaders.

ARIADNAN SURVIVAL

For the most part, life on Dawn always focuses back towards survival. For centuries the colonists had to make do with what they had, so most Ariadnan gear is multipurpose and designed to be rugged. Clothing is designed for durability, warmth, and practicality while all vehicles from land, sea, or air are designed to function in the worst weather conditions. Even their computers are designed to draw as little power as possible and with longevity in mind.

The Ariadnan Depression did more than simply drive the colony into a technological regression. Separated by political strife and a crumbling communication infrastructure, the four nations became culturally distinct. Each faced the struggle for survival and, in the earliest example of Hiraeth culture (even though the Ariadnans lacked a term for it), they reached back to their ancestral roots and found very different answers for the problems which plagued them.

And although they are now bound into a federalist union, the cultural gulf between them has never been greater. In fact, they embrace it. They boast of their eccentricities and wear their peculiar customs on their sleeves, revelling in the discomfort it brings to outsiders (both native born Ariadnans of other nations and the galactics who have brought their own strange traditions to Dawn).

CALEDONIA: THE HIGHLAND HOWL

During the Depression, no one was more isolated than the Caledonians. They were descendents of the 45th Highlander Rifles, an Anglo-Saxon force of English, Welsh, Scottish, Irish, and Danish settlers who were sent to defend the vital northern mines during the First Antipode Offensive. Amid the green hills and deep-clefted valleys of that land — a land whose beauty they rapidly grew to love with all the passion of their world-wearied souls — they became separated even from each other. The clans which

DNARIADNA
This political group, a modern resurgence of the historical AriaDNAn Nation, is dedicated to keeping "Ariadna for the Ariadnans", and vehemently protests the emigration of settlers from other planets to Dawn and the growing threat of cultural assimilation by outsiders. DNAriadna has been linked to civil protests in the capitals of each settlement as well as rumored ties to terrorist groups who have bombed embassies and mining operations outside the Exclusion Zone. Elements within DNAriadna have also targeted Dogfaces, arguing that they pose as insidious a threat to Ariadnan culture as the galactics.

Hiraeth Culture, p. 15: A post-colonial pan-cultural reflex that draws inspiration from Old Earth history.

sprang up from that stark desolation were a fiercely independent people, suspicious of each other and even more wary of outsiders meddling in their lives.

But to each other, there is a bounteous supply of warmth and comradeship. They are the hearth fire: Their faces turned towards the flame of their friendships; their backs turned against the cold of the world. Those outside their circles see unfriendly scowls and the unfriendly stereotypes which paint them as a brutish, uneducated, raucous, and bibulous people. But those who can earn their trust find honour and strength and the infectious grins that can only be born from hardship shared together.

Among the Caledonians technology regressed even more than it did elsewhere on Dawn. Even today their hamlets almost appear to be throwbacks to an earlier age on Earth, with hearth fires warming up farmers who sit around drinking ale and eating stew. Some think of the Caledonians as primitives who have simply given up on technology, but the truth is that they learned to enjoy the simple things in life and when technology came back into their lives, they found ways to adapt it to their lives rather than adapting their lives to it: The hearthstones are polymers that hold heat for long hours. Their swords are Teseum-edged. They can disassemble and reassemble automatic weapons at dizzying speeds.

MEROVINGIA: FOR HOME AND HEALTH

The Francoariadnan Republic of Merovingia is descended from colonists of France, Benelux, and, to a lesser extent, Austria, Italy, and Germany. The national language is French, but most of the population are polyglots.

Merovingians like to feel that they are the only truly Ariadnan culture: While the other nations wallow in the past, their reliance on trade has made them a disparate and liberal people. Their architecture is modern. Their entertainment is experimental. Their lives are the definition of elegance. Anything is possible if you keep an open mind. (Because they are, of course, utterly free of judgment. Unlike the uncouth barbarians who surround them.)

For some reason, the Merovingians have a reputation for being haughty and arrogant. But that's only because they need to remain as neutral as possible for their trade empire to function. And if they keep one hand on their pouch and another on their holster, it's only because they've learned that not every trading partner can be trusted.

Although their cities — founded at key points across Dawn to further their control over the traffic of goods — are seen as the cultural heart of Merovingia, the trading caravans are the pillars of their society. Led by the Merovingian Commercial Agents (who are seen as a mixture of explorers, merchants, ambassadors, roving traders, spies, and adventurers), the caravans created the trading routes which still define international travel on Dawn.

RODINA: THE MOTHERLAND

The Cossacks are the most populous cultural group on Dawn. And they have never forgotten that Earth abandoned them, their new home tried to kill them, and their comrades betrayed them.

With the world turned against them, they turn to each other: *Tighten your belt and help out.* That's the core tenet of their political ideology and cultural identity. They seek community and unity. Ironically, even the savage wars they have fought against the other Ariadnan nations were ultimately about seeking unity. Because they understand, right down to the aching marrow of their bones, that if humanity stands divided, Old Mother Winter will chew them up and spit them out.

This attitude helped the Cossacks become the dominant force in Ariadna. It is with great pride that the Cossacks — centred in Mat' around the remnants of the *Aurora* — see themselves as the axis of Ariadnan civilisation, despite the disapproval of their neighbours.

Today that axis is turning faster than ever — a driveshaft which is propelling Dawn towards an uncertain future. On the streets of Rodinan settlements one still sees the fur caps and other trappings of survivalist gear which have defined Cossack fashion for more than a century, but driven by the burgeoning number of galactics in the capital of Mat', sleek new styles of glistening smart fabric have begun to reinterpret the old traditions.

USARIADNA: THE NEW WEST

Settled by an odd mixture of NASA scientists and US Army Rangers, USAriadna is the most ethnically diverse area of the planet. (The scientists were primarily of Anglo-Saxon and Asian descent, while the Rangers were Latinx and African-American.) In the face of Dawn's adversity, they have clung to their cultural traditions, becoming a time capsule of late 20th century American exceptionalism: They

QUAICH QUAFFING

The Quaich Quaffing — named after a shallow, two-handed Gaelic drinking bowl — is an annual drinking contest between Caledonians and Cossacks.

CALEDONIAN EPIC

The *Caledonian Epic* is an interwoven mosaic of tales that arose from a newfound tradition of oral storytelling among the clans. Heavily influenced by Celtic, Scottish, and Norse myth, with a strong admixture of 20th century fantasy literature, the *Epic* is a deliberately fantastical interpretation of Dawn's colonial history. In these tales the Northern Frontier becomes the Caledonian Valhalla — a place where clan warriors go when they die and from which they are destined to return when Caledonia's need is great.

CLAN THUGS

Although talk of Caledonia often conjures up images of manor houses and moss-cropped highlands, the nation is not entirely pastoral. Urban centres have grown up particularly around mining towns, and these are often surrounded by a crust of slums populated by hardened mining industry workers and other labourers. The members of this underclass are known as the clan thugs — a term which was originally purely pejorative, but which is now widely held in a rough, blue-collar pride by the clan thugs themselves.

have built factories to produce the same foods and goods they enjoyed when they came to Dawn (including a functioning Coca-Cola factory), they enjoy classic rock and country music, and many USAriadnans use the same slang and references that their ancestors used when they came on the colony ship.

Like Caledonia, USAriadna is a frontier. The entirety of the Eastern Border and much of the Southern Border have been theirs to defend against blood-thirsty Antipodes and, later, corporate mercenaries of the Human Sphere. This has instilled a sense of "hoorah!" aggression into the fierce independence of their individualism. The average USAriadnan will do his best to educate others on their weaknesses if only to help them fix them, and they are willing to share their knowledge with others. The most fanatical believers of this rule are known as Hardcases. These men are fearless survivalists who test themselves in the most brutal conditions and patrol the southern and southeastern frontiers, hunting prey and helping those that need it.

To off-world galactics, the USAriadnans — in their Stetston cowboy hats and blue jeans with Americolt six-shooters strapped to their sides — can seem like some kind of historic themepark come to life; a stereotype of American behaviour. But for them it's not an affectation. It's a point of pride. And a way of life.

ANTIPODES

Antipodes were the first alien race encountered by humanity. It was perhaps sadly unsurprising that our first act was a genocidal attempt at extermination. The fact that the colonists didn't "know" they were intelligent is a poor excuse. It would be nice to say that the two species at least have a mutual "warrior's respect" for each other; that they gaze across the mighty Ariadnan peaks and see brothers in arms or their souls reflected or some such high-minded ideal.

But the reality is that, after generations of bloody conflict, when these races look at each other they see nothing but loathing and terror.

ANTIPODE PHYSIOLOGY

Antipodes are quadrupedal, bearing a superficial resemblance to canids (like a dog or wolf) but much larger. They do have the capacity for an erect posture, but they find bipedal locomotion tiresome and socially unattractive.

The species is an apex predator. They have a keen sense of smell that can detect and locate prey (or human enemies) dozens of feet away. Their claws, which are often tipped in Teseum, are efficient at rending flesh, but have a limited capacity for fine manipulation (which has most likely contributed to a stunted cultural development). They have a secondary set of teeth which can rapidly grow out to replace broken or lost pieces.

Their coat — which comes in patches of wiry, long fur alongside areas of less dense, shorter fur — can change colour to mimic their surroundings.

TRINARY

What makes the Antipodes species unique in human experience is that it is a naturally evolved example of *distributed intelligence*. Individual Antipodes are only slightly smarter than a domesticated dog. When three Antipodes are brought together, however, they unite into a single personality — referred to as a trinary — which blends the traits, skills, and knowledge of the individual members.

The method by which the trinary-meld is formed is multiphasic. There is a rich pheromonal component which is only partially understood by human scientists. Better understood is the auditory signalling: A secondary vocal cord at the back of the Antipodes' nasal cavity emits ultrasonic frequencies. This vocal cord, however, also functions as a tympanic membrane which receives those ultrasonic sound waves. The result is a kind of modulated audio feedback which, in a trinary configuration, synchronises on scalar frequencies.

There is also a patch of chameleonic fur on the upper back of the skull which is far more photo-reactive than the rest of the Antipodes' fur and appears to form some kind of visual signalling component within trinaries. It assists with synchronising the auditory channel of the meld, but also appears to be a semi-independent channel for thought. The Antipodean word for this is sometimes translated as "subconscious", but "deeply contemplative" would be a more literal translation. Trinaries will sometimes enter a *thought-circle* — sitting in an arrangement that offers them a clear view of their chameleonic patches — which apparently allows them analyse problems in greater detail.

Indeed, the primary disadvantage of the Antipodean distributed intelligence is that it is slow and clumsy to respond to novel or unprecedented situations.

CUCKOO VIRUS
Antipodes have an atavistic instinct to bite (but not kill) pregnant females. This delivers a

MIND-SHOCK
When one member of an Antipodean trinary dies, the other two members enter a state known as mind-shock. A mind-shocked pair can continue operating as an individual for a short period of time before their tympanic membranes completely desynchronise, but only in a debilitative state which quickly degenerates. Mind-shocked Antipodes are literally losing their minds, and they will usually seek to rapidly pair with a third to stabilise as a new individual.

MEMORY LINES
The trinary-meld involves a living exchange of evolving memories. As a result, the memories of a trinary can long outlive its own existence, as its surviving members carry those memories into new trinaries (and those other members carry them forward once again). The Antipodes refer to these as "lines of memory" (or, more literally, the "ancestral howls"). It should be noted that these older memories are not perfectly duplicated. It's not like copying a hard drive. Rather, a particular memory from a previous trinary must be recalled or relived in order to be "transferred" to the other members of the new trinary.

SOUTHERN TRIBES

The Southern Tribes of Antipodes which live between Rodina and the Lost Sea are not entirely similar to the Northern and Eastern Tribes, having a nomadic culture (instead of living as den-dwellers). Unfortunately, they are no less hostile to humans.

IRONBARK TOTEMS

The lands over which a tribe claims custodianship are often identified by great totems planted in the earth. Made from ironbark trees carved with runes meant to honour great spirits of the land, Antipodes never allow harm to come to these totems, for fear that it will anger the land and poison the game they hunt. Early colonists would cut down these totems to claim the valuable ironbark wood, earning them eternal enmity from tribes who lost their sacred lands to furnish a pioneer's cabin.

retrovirus – known as the "cuckoo virus" – which rips apart the DNA strands of the unborn child and synthesizes it with the biter's own. This appears to have been an evolutionary development which allows Antipodes males to widely spread their DNA even among children fathered by others. Trinaries have also been observed biting females impregnated by one of their own members, allowing the entire "individual" to collectively pass on its genetic legacy.

Surprisingly these instincts were also triggered by pregnant human women. In fact, pregnant women were frequently the only survivors of early Antipodean raids. Furthermore, the highly adaptive cuckoo virus was able to cross the placental barrier, and the children born from these victimised pregnancies were the half-breeds known as Dogfaces.

THE TRIBES

Like humans, Antipodes adapt their living arrangements to their environment. But whether they're caves, burrows, reed mound-huts, or tree houses in the swamp, Antipodes dens are generally arranged in ringed semi-circles and are rarely home to more than two or three dozen trinary individuals.

Dens, however, are usually associated into tribes. These tribes are frequently tied together by shared

ancestral howls, but it's also not unusual to see more familiar alliances based on geography. (And this can be something of a chicken-and-egg problem, since it is likely that any Antipodes living in close proximity will begin to commingle memory lines.)

Tribes are led by war chiefs. In the larger tribes, the war chief will be surrounded by a number of lesser chiefs. These lesser chiefs are responsible for organising the hunts which are central to Antipodean life, but it is the war chief who must lead the *razzia* – the raids which are carried out against other tribes, some of which appear to be ritualistic while others are (for reasons which are not entirely clear) in deadly earnest.

The maximum size at which a successful *razzia* can be logistically mounted seems to be a delimiter on the maximum size of an Antipodean tribe. It appears, however, that the presence of humanity on Dawn has created a systemic spur which has seen the creation of larger tribes. (The Second Antipode Offensive also saw Antipodes war chiefs form an alliance for the first time.)

TRIBAL CULTURE

The Antipodean economy is relatively primitive and consists primarily of barter (although certain artefacts of Teseum appear to have adopted pre-monetary characteristics). Their art, too, is

primitive, but varied – pottery, jewellery, tapestries, and pictorial presentations on stone walls or clay tablets can be seen on display in the Colonial Museum in Mat'.

Scratch-Totem Writing: Antipodean writing takes the form of symbols scratched onto rounded rods or sticks. (These are commonly *hennig* rods, which are a bamboo-like plant that's layered like an onion. When a layer is filled with writing, Antipodes can shuck it like the disposable sheet of a notebook and continue writing on the next layer.) The rods were referred to as "scratch-to-tems" by the early human colonists, who didn't recognise them as writing because the script is reliant on the trinary-meld: When Antipodes write, all three members of the trinary write at the same time *on separate rods*. Deciphering the script requires a tripartite stereoscopic technique to overlay the three separate inscriptions which, of course, comes naturally to a distributed intelligence with three sets of eyes, but which is dizzyingly complicated to humans, in no small part because the stroke-division of any given character across the three rods is not, in fact, consistent, but rather idiosyncratic and, in some cases, laced with its own layers of meaning.

Blood Tree Worship: Antipodes have a simple, animistic religion worshipping a small pantheon of gods representing various natural forces and events. A more sophisticated religious order, however, has risen up around the worship of the Blood Trees. These trees yield big, juicy, crimson fruits. The Antipodes make offerings to these trees, ritualistically sacrificing prey at their base, watering the roots with blood, and then consuming the fruit. In some tribes this includes sacrificing human prisoners or, more rarely, Antipodean ones.

DOGFACES

Human-Antipode hybrids end up being bigger and hairier than either species. Their anatomy is primarily human, although possessed of certain Antipode features (including a long, canid snout, claws, and a vestigial secondary set of vocal cords that allow them to bellow ear-piercing howls).

Dogfaces struggle with acceptance in Ariadnan society. They are strange and alien reminders of the ravenous hordes which threaten the colonial frontiers, and each is a living testament of lives lost and pregnant human women who could not be protected. Organisations are also quick to point out that their blood furies make them a threat to society.

BLOOD FURY

The blending of human and Antipode DNA had one other surprise: transmutation. When experiencing severe stress or physical trauma, the "fight-or-flight" catecholamines produced by the adrenal medulla trigger a cascading effect through the Dogface's endocrine system. The exact physiological process is still not fully understood by human science, but it precipitates massive cellular alteration – the Dogface grows larger, its muscles becomes more powerful, and (unless it possesses incredible self-dicipline) it succumbs to a mental state known as the blood fury.

In this transformed state, Dogfaces are known as Dog-Warriors. A PanOceanian general infamously described them as the "mongrel cross-breed of an Ariadnan savage, an Antipode, and a TAG". They are characterised as mindless beasts (a stereotype which is not helped by their transformed jaws making it difficult for them to speak clearly).

WULVERS

Dogfaces can breed true, but Dogface/Human hybrids result in sterile Wulvers. (The derivative viral RNA transcription results in unpredictable alterations in the Wulver chromosomes. Each Wulver is actually genetically distinct from any other, and the mismatched chromosomes make karyogamy of the haploid cells virtually impossible.)

Unlike Dogfaces, the bodies of Wulvers cannot transform. Their natural bodies, however, are much closer to a Dog-Warrior's form than human, and they are nonetheless consumed with a form of the blood fury (with a strong instinct to charge at whatever provokes their easily triggered rage). Their impressively muscled bodies are covered with long, thick fur. They possess large, penetrating eyes and jaws with sharp fangs.

Very few Wulvers exist on Ariadna, and virtually none outside of Caledonia. As a fractional and ostracised minority – for some a living embodiment of "bestiality"– they generally face hard lives as labourers, workers, and thugs.

INSTITUTIONS

GOVERNMENT

Despite its tumultuous history, the Ariadnan Council which serves as the central government of the Ariadnan Federation can trace a continuous history back to the original eight-member skeleton crew that woke aboard the *Aurora* as it approached Dawn for the first time. Those eight were the first

DOG NATION

Tired of being treated as second class citizens, Dog Nation seeks to prove that Dogfaces have much to offer their fellow Ariadnans. Two decades ago the movement was beginning to make great strides under the leadership of John "Vanya" Rotten, a Wulver. Unfortunately, the Commercial Conflicts disrupted those gains. The Nation's rallying cry of, "Equality or death!" has been more and more likely to signal violence in recent years.

DOG-BOWL

Dog-Bowl is a brutal game played primarily by Dogfaces performing feats of athleticism that humans can't match. It got its start as a street game, originally played with a rugby ball or American football (depending on which Ariadnan nation you were in), but it was professionalised towards the end of the Separatist Wars and now uses a similar ball made out of hard rubber, plastic, or even Teseum. (The harder substances resist being punctured by Dogface claws and also enhance the techniques where the ball is used as a weapon.) Dog-Bowl is Ariadna's favourite sport and every important city has its own professional team.

COSSACK DIPLOMATIC CORPS

To the frustration of the other nations, the Ariadnan Council maintains no federal diplomatic corps. It was not deemed necessary prior to contact with the Human Sphere, and after re-contact the Rodinans have used their influence over the council to instead defer these duties to the Cossack Diplomatic Corps (which is also widely understood to be riddled with Stavka agents). The Merovingians, in particular, have been working to create independent diplomatic channels with the off-world powers.

TEKHNOLOGII VSTRECHA

The newest of the Vstrecha, the Technology Council regulates and controls the influx of new galactic technologies. They are also responsible for modernising the Ariadnan datasphere.

TARTAN COLOURS

Traditional Gaelic tartans came to Dawn as part of the dress uniforms of the original 45th Highlanders. These uniforms became a focus for patriotic pride during the First Antipode Offensive, and eventually each clan adopted the ancient practice of using a distinctive tartan pattern (or sett) as their "uniform". For similar reasons, the traditional kilt has also come back into common style among Caledonians.

humans to lay eyes upon an alien world and the Council is the first interstellar human government. Those are legacies of pride for the Ariadnans, particularly as they try to find their place in the Human Sphere.

Over time, of course, the Council has expanded and transitioned from an administrative team through a series of constitutional reforms into its present form. Today, the Council as a whole is formed of one hundred and thirty-two representatives drawn equally from each of the four Ariadnan nations, but the Kapitanskaya Vstrecha (Captain's Council), which is the central power of the government, is completely dominated by Rodina (which holds not only a plurality but a majority of the seats). Immediately following the Separatist Wars, the Cossack domination of the Council was even more severe, with similar majorities locking down virtually all of the major Vstrechas which oversee different spheres of governmental authority. A series of gentle reforms has seen them slowly loosen their grip, but the Kapitanskaya remains inviolate.

CALEDONIAN CLANS

The clans of Caledonia arose from the same societal pressures and existential threat that gave rise to Rodina's *stanitsa* system. But whereas the *stanitsa* was bureaucratically imposed from above, the clans arose organically out of the communities of the Northern Border. Organised around the warrior chieftains who would later become known as the Clan Chiefs, the earliest clans were bound by ties of blood. Over time those ties became more symbolic — taken on by the swearing of blood oaths both personal and generational — but no less important or meaningful.

What must also be understood is that each clan is an economic and strategic reserve: The wealth and importance of a clan is measured by their stockpile of Teseum. Whether kept as Teseum ingots in the clan's treasury or ostentatiously displayed in the form of torcs, jewellery, cutlery, and similar items, all of this Teseum can be melted down at any moment and converted into the weapons and armour of war. These stockpiles also function as a *de facto* currency reserve.

It is unsurprising, therefore, that most of the major clans are also organised around the Teseum trade — either controlling and defending the mines, or in managing trade with the Cossacks, Merovingians, Ariadnan-Americans, and (recently) galactics.

Clan Chiefs: The clans are functionally non-geographic polities and their authority is highly centralised in the Clan Chief, who acts as governor, judge, executive director, warlord, father figure, and official representative for his people. The position is life-long, but succession is not carried out by primogeniture: Although chiefs will often designate their successor from among their right-hand men, the chief's successor is elected.

House of Clans: This representative body is made up of the chiefs from the Major Clans. Thirty additional seats are held by the Minor Clans which are currently "held in esteem". (Minor Clans not directly represented are forced to seek some form of patronage from other clans in order to have their voices heard within the government.)

Justiciar: Executive power in Caledonia as a whole is as centralised as it is in the individual clans with the Justiciar, the elected head of the House of Clans, personally wielding full executive authority. The powers of the Justiciar are weak when it comes to the internal regulation of each clan — what's known as the "private fiefs and feuds" of the Chiefs. Historically, justiciars have often encouraged animosity and rivalry between the clans in order to increase their own effective power.

MEROVINGIAN PARLIAMENT

Merovingia is ruled by a modest parliament which is popularly elected and led by the Prime Minister. The separate office of President, however, can be held only by a former Merovingian Commercial Agent, as the position is commonly understood to require a deep knowledge of the commercial ties and convoluted trade relationships of the four nations.

RODINAN FEDERAL SERVICE

Unlike the other nations, Rodina doesn't have a truly independent government because they have never acknowledged that the Ariadnan Council was

THE MAJOR CLANS

Balfour, Balmoral, Blackadder, Cameron, Campbell, Cavalier, Christie, Cian, Clark, Clergy, Clyde, Cochrane, Cockburn, Conner, Conroy, Cooper, Craig, Culloden, Cunningham, Douglas, Farrell, Gordon, Guthrie, Kerry, Kinnison, Kyle, Lamont, Logan, MacArthur, MacAskill, MacAulay, MacBeth, MacCallum (Malcolm), MacLeod, MacColl, MacDiarmid, MacDonald, MacDougall, MacDuff, MacEdwards, MacEwen, MacFarlane, MacGillivray, MacGregor, MacGuire, MacHardy, MacInroy, MacLachan, MacLaren, MacNeil, MacRae, MacQuarrie, MacTaggart, McCorquodale, Matheson, Morrison, Moran, Munro, Murray, O´Brien, O´Neill, Paget, Perry, Rose, Scott, Sinclair, Stewart, Stuart, Walker, Wilson.

FIVE THINGS YOU SHOULD KNOW ABOUT ARIADNANS

1. Gunmetal and Spit: Everything is bigger on Dawn: muscles, wolves, hardship, and, perhaps most of all, weapons. Ariadna's arms industry has not yet caught up with the advanced technology of the Human Sphere. Rough around the edges, heavy metal, shell casings, high calibers, no BS; all this, while archaic, has a certain charm to it. Mechanical triggers, analog targeting systems, and the total lack of connectivity make them reliable where modern gear fails. To burly Ariadnan hands, state of the art pieces feel like "plastic toys" incapable of measuring up to honest Ariadnan steel.

2. Bagpipes of War: When Caledonian regiments go to war, the ethereal strains of the bagpipe can always be heard on the battlefield. These company bagpipers are usually also the unit's medical doctors.

3. Dogs Aren't Meant to Fly: Dogfaces (and Antipodes, although that generally only matters for enslaved Assault Packs) have a deep, instinctual fear of flying.

4. Old Mother Winter: A child's tale that seems to have stuck in the Rodinan craw. Old Mother Winter is the planetary spirit of Dawn; the antithesis of Earth's fervid Gaia. She personifies the cold, uncaring caprice of the universe.

5. Ear of Consent: When a Merovingian agrees to a bargain, they'll tug their earlobe to signal their consent. The practice has also spread into the other Ariadnan nations, although it's not as widely practised.

anything other than the rightful government of the colony. What they do have, however, is the byzantine bureaucracy known as the Federal Service.

The *chinonivki* (bureaucrats) of the Federal Service have wormed their way throughout life in Rodina and climbing the Table of Ranks which define the ministerial positions is a required path for those seeking election to the Ariadnan Council. Democratic reforms, however, have resulted in the Ministers now being selected through popular elections.

USARIADNAN CONGRESS

USAriadna, perhaps unsurprisingly, used a largely unaltered version of the Constitution of the United States as the basis for their government. That meant the familiar three branches of government (albeit in miniature): Congress (with a lower House of 65 and an upper Senate of 12), the Supreme Court (with five justices), and a President.

Following the Separatist Wars, however, the Office of the President was banned. The USAriadnans have stubbornly refused to officially amend their constitution, which has created some strange traditions of governance which seem as if they should implode at any moment but somehow manage not to.

ARIADNAN ARMY (АРИАДНАРИАДНА АРМИЯАРМИЯ)

The "Ariadnan Army" is something of a misnomer and the "Ariadnan Joint Command" is an oxymoron. For most of Ariadna's history there was little or

no cooperation between the militaries of the four nations (even when they weren't fighting each other). The Voyennykh Vstrecha (Military Council) supposedly had oversight, but beyond some very minimal bilateral coordination in the national defence against Antipode threats its putative authority was almost entirely theoretical.

This changed somewhat, out of necessity, during the Commercial Conflicts as Ariadnans came together in the face of a common, off-world enemy. But the Ariadnan Joint Command was actually formed as a subordinate of the Cossack High Command and operates out of the Stavka (Ставка), which is now reputedly the Headquarters of the Ariadnan Armed Forces, but is still basically a Kazak operation. The bureaucratic kludge somehow pulled itself together long enough to hold the line against galactic aggression, but now it's starting to strain at the seams again. The military traditions of Caledonia and USAriadna, in particular, are strong and independent, and Rodina recognises that trying to force the national militaries into a truly unified federal system could easily provoke another Separatist War.

Despite its organisational woes, based on Ariadna's armies also suffer from a significant technological lag compared to the galactics. During the early days of the Commercial Conflicts they found themselves routinely outclassed by the resources of even modest off-world mercenary groups. But they have found ways to leverage the unconventional natural resources of their world – the Antipodes, Dog-Warriors, and Teseum – to help even the battlefield.

HIGHLANDER SWORDS

The re-emergence of melee weapons on Ariadna is largely due to the natural abundance of Teseum. The wide availability of the neomaterial, particularly in Caledonia, made it relatively easy for even the early settlers to forge suits of armour from it which were nigh-impregnable to almost anything except Teseum-based weaponry. It was still an incredibly difficult material to work with, however, and technological limitations made T2 ammunition prohibitively expensive: Only the most ludicrously rich could afford to just throw Teseum away. Swords, on the other hand, could be forged once and then used forever. Close combat tactics became the only reliable way to break a Teseum-enforced regiment, and the swords of the highlanders became treasured family heirlooms passed down from one generation to the next.

DOGFACES IN WAR

Dogfaces give Ariadna an advantage over their opponents though they can be unpredictable on the battlefield. A Dog-Warrior can be as strong as a TAG and move faster than a remote, though their ferocity and rage can make them unreliable at following orders. After the Commercial Conflicts, Dogfaces found themselves being appreciated by their fellow Ariadnan soldiers for their efforts in keeping Dawn free, though they are still regarded as second class citizens by the public.

SPECIAL OPERATIONS COMMAND

The Mirage teams operating under the FRRM's SOC are fast, very violent, and spectacular in their results (with stealth often a secondary consideration). The Mirage-5 team, consisting of Lieutenant Margot Berthier and Sergeant Duroc, a Dog-Warrior, is one of the oldest Mirage teams.

Ariadnan Expeditionary Corps – p. 24

IRREGULARS

Following in the true spirit of Old Man Ross, the sparsely populated Southern Border of USAriadna has given rise to so-called "Hardcase" battalions. These hardcases are veterans who have retired from the Rangers, but not from the war. (Which war? Any war. Their war.) They work as guides, explorers, bodyguards, mail carriers, and self-appointed law enforcers. They operate as solo mercenaries or self-organise into community militias (some of which grow large enough and respectable enough to coordinate with the USARF in an irregular capacity).

ARIADNAN KAZAKS

The Kazaks are the largest military force on Ariadna, and the most rigidly organised. The bulk of the army is the light infantry referred to simply as the Line (or Line Kazaks). This force is anchored by the Mat' Line, which is comprised of several large regiments, but what makes the Line so devastatingly effective is that its forces are distributed throughout the *stanitsa*. The modular command style of the Line allows these smaller brigades to rapidly coalesce into larger regiments and divisions as they flow towards and eventually overwhelm any lesser opposition. (These manoeuvres were nicknamed the "Kazak avalanche" during the Separatist Wars.)

The Veteran Kazak regiments recruit the best soldiers from the Line Kazak and equip them with the *Cherkesska* heavy combat armour. Less technologically sophisticated than their galactic equivalents, the use of Teseum in its manufacture helps to give the Veterans an edge.

The Line and the Veteran Kazaks are both supported by the specialty units of the *Voskya Spesialnogo Naznecheniya* (Spetsnaz), which features commandos, parachute operations, scouts, and urban operation specialists who receive instruction at the Dacha (the colloquial name for the Cossack Spetsnaz School).

CALEDONIAN HIGHLANDER ARMY

The Caledonian armed forces are roughly broken down into three divisions: The clan regiments, which are loyal to and led by individual clan chiefs. The Caledonian Volunteer Corps, which forms the enlisted core of the army. And the Home Guard, which are elite troops usually recruited from either the clan regiments or Volunteer Corps. Regardless of the army division, individual units are usually comprised entirely of soldiers belonging to the same clan.

The Home Guard is primarily made up of the Highlander regiments, including, most famously, the original 45th Highlander "Galwegian" Rifles, but also the 1st Highlander SAS, the 3rd Highlander Grey Rifles, and others.

In addition to the Highlander regiments, the Home Guard also fields the Cameronian (or Dogface) regiments and the Wulver regiments. The 2nd Cameronian and 9th Wulver Grenadiers were both notably part of the First Expeditionary Corps on Paradiso. Caledonia has more of these "native-born" soldiers fighting in their armed forces than the other three Ariadnan nations combined.

Also of note are the Mormaers, an elite regiment formed by warriors sponsored by clans willing to pay the Teseum required for their armour and swords. The regiment was originally created by the Justiciar as a way of creating a national defence force that would help unify the clans by bringing their second and third sons together.

FORCE DE REPONSE RAPIDE MEROVINGIENNE (FRRM)

During the Separatist Wars the Grande Armées Merovingienne (GRM), caught in the middle of four warring nations, was repeatedly decimated. Following the war, the broken army was disbanded and reorganised into the Force de Reponse Rapide Merovingienne (FRRM). The FRRM's new focus on patrol and response allows it to more efficiently provide defence for Merovingia's commercial interests, but also spreads the army thin. They compensate for this by focusing on mobility and with highly-specialised units adapted to virtually any type of terrain (forest, mountain, urban, and even airborne para-commandos).

During the Commercial Conflicts, the FRRM became the tip of the spear. The Ariadnan Joint Command capitalised on the mobility of the FRRM to deploy rapid response units from camouflaged bases spread throughout Merovingian territory they could instantly react to enemy engagements. engagements. These tactics were highly effective against the mercenary units of the hypercorps, and they're proving invaluable on Paradiso (particularly against Shasvastii infiltrators).

USARIADNA RANGER FORCE (USARF)

Like much of USAriadna society, the Rangers are steeped in the traditions of the old United States of America. Unlike the Caledonian 45th Highlanders, however, this is not an unbroken tradition: The original Rangers units which came to Dawn as part of the *Aurora* mission actually fell part and were disbanded following the founding of USAriadna.

About a decade later, as the story goes, a veteran in Franklin County named Old Man Ross became worried about the increasingly bold Antipode incursions. Old Man Ross went down to the Blockhouse, the busiest bar in the county, and in a famous speech (which exists in a variety of traditional "transcriptions", ranging from noble ideals to "I can promise you beer, guns, and dead dogs" populism) managed to round up a rowdy bunch.

Old Man Ross was looking to do more than just bash heads, however. He shoved the old military code and harsh training program of the Rangers down the throats of his recruits, forming a seed which would eventually grow into the modern USAriadnan Ranger Force (USARF).

WILDERNESS OF MIRRORS

STAVKA INTELLIGENCE DEPARTMENT

Omnia Audax. Audacious in everything. That's the motto of the Stavka Intelligence Department. Formed during the Commercial Conflicts, the SID – like Ariadna as a whole – is playing catch-up with the more experienced, more sophisticated, and more technologically advanced intelligence operations of the other G-5 nations.

This relentless focus on an external enemy may explain why the SID is also one of the few institutions on Ariadna where cooperation between the four nations is seen in unvarnished practice and not just theory. Although originally founded around a nucleus of former bosses from the Okhrana, the Rodinan secret police, the first thing these old spies did was to recruit their opposite numbers from the other three national intelligence agencies in order to form the Stavka Intelligence Council that would oversee the SID's operations. With the time for rivalry past, the mutual respect these canny cat-and-mouse players had for each other won out.

The SID similarly recruits talent from the armed forces of all four Ariadnan nations and then ruthlessly desegregates their operatives during training. There are also rumours that the SID has infiltrated undercover operatives into all four of the national Ariadnan intelligence organisations. The legality of this is questionable, but the SID's leadership sees a truly unified Ariadnan Federation as the only protection against a dangerous and voracious galaxy.

Bydand – Gaelic Motto of the Volunteers Corps, meaning steadfast or abiding

SID: OMNIA AUDAX

The primary portfolio of the SID is anti-galactic. Over the past decade and a half, therefore, they have struggled to rapidly establish an off-world intelligence network that can reliably act against the other G-5 nations with little more than the abundant wealth of Teseum and their own ingenuity. There's simply no template for that in Ariadnan bureaucracy: The SID is trying to manage affairs across a dozen worlds when, a generation ago, Ariadnans only controlled a fraction of one. It is, as their motto says, an audacious undertaking, and the trailblazing they've been forced to do has bred ingenuity, perseverance, and indomitable patience. Of course, over the last seven years the arrival of the Combined Army has revolutionised the SID's mission all over again. At least this time, they're not alone: The entire Human Sphere is struggling to adapt right along with them.

Doppel, Doppel: The SID has credible intelligence suggesting that a Caledonian clan chief has been replaced by a Shasvastii Speculo Killer. The intention of the alien is uncertain at this time (perhaps sabotaging Teseum supplies; perhaps laying the long-term groundwork for a future invasion). But the concern is that once the House of Clans reconvenes, the Speculo Killer could use its access to replace other clan chiefs or their right-hand men.

Silken Treachery: An entire transport ship was hijacked from the Silk Route. Qapu Khalqi agents have arrived on Dawn, claiming to have traced the theft back to a Merovingian trading caravan. The SID is officially charged to aid their investigation, but their actual goal is to secure the Silk shipment for the Ariadnan Federation.

Svalarheima Salvage: SID operatives on PanOceania have dug up old files identifying the location of a decommissioned Templar base on Svalarheima. It may be illegal, but the Templar tech in that facility could help Ariadna catch up with galactic technology. A team is dispatched and warned of the risks: Who really knows what's buried in the ice out there?

G-5 FACTION
HAQQISLAM

Oppressive regimes create toxic societies that produce and export nothing but hate, fear, and ignorance, the three great enemies of Faith. Muslims must abandon the reactionary teachings of clerics and allow themselves to be guided by nothing but their only sacred book, the Qur'an.

—The Springtime of Intellect, Farhad Khadivar

THE PROPAGANDIST

There were many who "carried Khadivar's word" to the people, but chief among the Haqqislam propagandists was Hamid al-Din al-Hamdani. Al-Hamdani was young, he was savvy, and he was ruthless. He wielded the mass media of the 21st century — television, cinema, radio, the internet, the news networks — like a surgeon with his scalpel, eventually gaining personal control over most of the major communication and media companies of the Islamic world. Khadivar preached that "only the message, not the messenger, is of consequence", but al-Hamdani insured that Khadivar's message could be heard every minute of every day in every corner of the world.

THE WORKS OF KHADIVAR

Khadivar's words survive in two books — *The Springtime of Intellect* and *The Quietness of the Soul* — and in recordings of his *majlis al-hikma* (sessions of wisdom). None of these are treated as scripture, but Khadivar was an educator who excelled at making his ideology accessible to the general public and they remain valuable guides for many Haqqislamites.

Recognised as only the third interstellar power in human history, the nation of Haqqislam is a Neo-Muslim culture born from the religious doctrines of Farhad Khadivar, who believed that Islam required a philosophical and theological rebirth. In the Qur'an he saw a clarion call summoning the faithful to the Search for Knowledge, but in the world around him he saw that this humanist message had become crippled under the ignorance and fanaticism which embedded itself in misguided teachings based on the traditions of the *hadith*, *sunnah*, and *ijma* — all the traditional precepts of Islamic law, the consensus of the faithful, and the false authority which had been given to the imams.

In the mid-21st century, the Energy Crisis crippled the economies of the Muslim world. A crisis of faith and identity saw a proliferation of new interpretations of Islamic philosophy and theology, the rebirth of Sufism, and the rise of countless populist religious teachers. Out of this morass of theological ideas, it was the doctrine of Haqqislam (meaning New or True Islam) which quickly became ascendant.

Farhad Khadivar was a teacher of drab appearance but blessed with charisma and gifted in philosophy and oratory. Khadivar evoked a vision of Islam inspired by the paradisiacal gardens of Al-Andalus and the great caliphates of the past. He taught that the path to a new golden age of Islam required shedding the baggage of the intervening years.

The clarity of his vision called out to people who felt lost in the tumult of the 21st century. Khadivar preached that prosperity would come to the spiritually wealthy, and he maintained that spiritual wealth derived from the rational pursuit of knowledge, art, and cultural enrichment. Cast adrift in uncertain times, people were drawn to the message that they could take control of their own destiny.

The New Islam also appealed to a number of the Middle East's fading elite who clung to an apparatus of power constructed during the height of the Energy Glut. Long shackled by the limited vision of reactionary imams and longing for a return of their geopolitical relevance, the appeal of Haqqislam's path of prosperity — free from the stigma of a fanatical, bigoted religious power — was immense.

These leaders dedicated considerable resources to Haqqislam's success. As a result, Haqqislam's propagation had as much to do with sophisticated propaganda as it did grassroots activism.

But where some embraced Haqqislam for the opportunities it presented, others saw it as a threat. As Haqqislam grew, many of these reactionary elements turned to violence. Among these, history best remembers the campaign of terror waged by Imam Khalaf ibn Ahmad's Legion of the Exalted. Ibn Ahmad declared a *fatwa* against Farhad Khadivar, and it was a bullet fired by one of his Exalted which took Khadivar's life at the age of 42.

ROAD TO BOURAK

Khadivar's death, of course, was not the end of Haqqislam. The movement was already a transnational powerhouse, and Khadivar's martyrdom only served to accelerate its success. Significantly, during Haqqislam's rise the archaic nation states in which it was most popular were in a state of rapid decline. As the former centres of power became incapable of providing essential services, Haqqislam's *khaniqah* (teaching and public service centres) expanded to take up the slack.

In time, it became clear that the *khaniqah* had become fully functional social institutions and people began referring to the far-flung Haqqislam as a stateless nation. This further unsettled the countries in which the Haqqislamites made their homes. Even the most tolerant, democratic regimes of the Islamic world began to look nervously at the increasing sway of this heterodox sect, and Haqqislam's own followers began to dream of a nation of their own, where they could build a society based upon their principles as a beacon of prosperity and tolerance.

Unlike other nations without geographic borders, however, Haqqislam was a young power. It had no homeland to reclaim. No one on Earth would sacrifice sovereign territory to make room for a new nation.

But this was the dawn of the Second Great Space Race. Wormholes had been ripped asunder, the colonial space race had erupted, and Haqqislam's leaders concluded that they could find a home among the stars.

Finding colonial planets was an expensive proposition, however. The fledgling pseudo-nation couldn't compete with the exhaustive wormhole searches being performed by PanOceania and Yu Jing. Haqqislam found its solution with a group of neo-Sufi astronomers and one of history's greatest long-shots: In Jerusalem, the Dome of the Rock had been built where, according to Islamic tradition, Muhammad once ascended to heaven. The neo-Sufi astronomers proposed following the Prophet's footsteps. They recreated the position of the stars over Jerusalem on the night of his ascension and determined the sector of space that had been directly over the mosque. If their interpretation was correct, that was where Haqqislam would find its key to the stars.

To find that key, Haqqislam paid handsomely for the services of ex-NASA staff and equipment mothballed after America's economic crises. Although the sliver of space they had defined above the Dome of the Rock was small, the cone it formed at the edge of the solar system was vast. A long series of failed attempts followed and the viability of the project was even questioned by some, but eventually a stable wormhole was located and the *Nailah* probe was sent through it. Its name ("Successful") proved prophetic: On the far side of the wormhole was a Sol-type system and the habitable world of Bourak.

TRADE AND TERRAFORMING

The success of the project was declared a miracle. Allah himself, through the footprints of Muhammad, had shown Haqqislam its path to the future. The number of adherents skyrocketed, the newly formed O-12 recognised Haqqislam as an independent nation, and the Walī declared, "We have all become Sālik now." (A term referring to Sufi travellers.)

The Bourak Pilgrimage had begun.

The developing state of Haqqislam, however, could not handle the millions of eager sālik seeking passage to the new world. The business magnates who had helped to sponsor the Haqqislamite movement now exploited the situation: They invested in more ex-NASA resources, along with original construction projects, and leveraged the Pilgrimage to create the first major space transportation routes.

When the Pilgrimage came to an end, those routes remained and the tycoons who controlled them repurposed them for the flourishing, lucrative business of establishing and supplying all the colonies of the burgeoning Human Sphere. They became the foundation of the Merchant Guilds which now form one of the three pillars of the Haqqislamite economy.

The second of these pillars — biomedical research — was something which the Haqqislamites had

already proven masters of before leaving Earth. The third pillar, however, was a direct consequence of their sojourn to Bourak: Terraforming.

The journey to their new home transformed the Haqqislamite people.

HAQQISLAMITE BALANCE

The core of Haqqislamite belief is the Search for Knowledge.

Farhad Khadivar held reason to be the greatest attribute of the human being and believed that mankind's foremost obligation in life was the pursuit of artistic, philosophical, and scientific knowledge. It was through this pursuit that one could come to know the face of God and unlock the gates of Paradise. In *The Springtime of Intellect*, Khadivar wrote, "The Qur'an says, 'Sight cannot perceive him; yet he perceives all that is seen. The comprehension of him is subtle; yet he comprehends all.' We cannot gaze directly upon our Lord's face. We must instead seek him as he seeks us, by gazing with subtlety upon all facets of the world."

Khadivar outlined two pathways by which the Search for Knowledge could be carried out: By understanding the Cosmos through scientific inquiry of the outer world and by pursuing Paradise through speculative, internal reasoning.

TWIN TRADITIONS

This division within the Search for Knowledge can be understood as the difference between comprehension and apprehension. One who comprehends truth does so by rationally assembling knowledge to create a complete picture of the world. One who apprehends truth, on the other hand, does so by intuitively grasping the totality of its meaning. It's knowing the meaning of a word without being able to provide the dictionary definition; a poetical perception of the world which sees more than is literally observed.

These two approaches were often seen as polar opposites, but in Khadivar's teachings they were complementary parts of a single whole. "Our world is cloaked in a magnetic field," he wrote in *The Quietness of the Soul*. "Within that field we perceive the Arctic and the Antarctic as being separate and opposed. But in truth there is only one field. It is unified. And the entire world rests within it. So, too, does the entirety of our soul rest within the single, unbroken continuum of Truth."

INFIDELS ON BOURAK

Haqqislam is a tolerant society, welcoming visitors and immigrants of all ethnicities and creeds. It is particularly open to fellow "people of the Book"— Christians, Jews, and Muslims of other sects. There are many close-knit minority religious communities in the various cities of Bourak. Perhaps the most famous is the bustling Jewish Quarter of Dar el Funduq, the largest such community on the planet. 'Infidels' have a special tax status, which exempts them from certain taxes that finance Haqqislamite religious activities. Instead, they pay a solidarity tax called *jaziya*, spent on social needs of the wider community.

WAJHAHU

The Arabic word *wajhahu* can be translated as His Countenance. In his teachings, Khadivar used it extensively as a metaphor for Knowledge and that usage has become common in Haqqislam. The meaning has also doubled back on itself: Haqqislamites will often speak of "looking for truth" in someone's *wajh* (face) and close friends will speak of "sharing one *wajh*" (by which they mean that they truly know each other). This latter phrase assumes an ironic character when referring to lovers (with the additional innuendo that the way they're sharing their faces is by kissing each other).

THE PROPHET'S MEDICINE

Khadivar often used the *Tebb al-Nabi* (the Prophet's Medicine) as a way of speaking about the division between inner and outer knowledge. Muhammad said, "There is no disease that Allah has created, except that He also has created its remedy." Thus, in the traditional medicine of Islam, healing was seen to flow from the apprehension of God's intention. But these remedies were not simply given. They had to be found in nature – they required an external search for knowledge that had been encoded into the Cosmos. There were two paths leading to the same goal, and, in following both paths, Medicine becomes more than Science; it becomes Art.

Khadivar was drawing on ancient philosophies to explain his radical new ideology. But the emphasis he placed upon the useful metaphor of medicine resulted in the study of medicine and biomedical research becoming a mainstay of Haqqislam culture.

EXEMPLARS

In his work, Farhad Khadivar identified several Ideals or Virtues which are possessed by those who excel in the Search for Knowledge. The capital letters are not his, but many of his followers among both the Haqq Mutazilites and the Haqq Tasawwuf have created lists and seek to make themselves Exemplars by mastering these Virtues and Ideals.

Nonetheless, these two tendencies have developed as separate schools of thought within Haqqislam – one in which reason is the ultimate arbiter, the other drawing from the mystical traditions of Sufism and seeking a more internal path towards God. Just as the individual is suspended between the outer and inner worlds, between comprehension and apprehension, so is the entirety of Haqqislam contained in the spectrum formed by the tension between these two paths.

Neither school has an official organisation. They're not political parties, and even those most committed to one school acknowledge that the other is a valid path. Rather, they are two halves of society and two halves of the individual's life.

HAQQ MUTAZILITES

Haqq Mutazilite teachings are propagated through academies which teach maths, science, informatics, and technology. Those drawn to its path become Hakim (a title which means both doctor and philosopher). These are the scientists, medical doctors, and engineers. (Among outsiders they are sometimes thought of us as the "secular" side of Haqqislam, although the distinction wouldn't make much sense to a Haqqislamite.)

HAQQ TASAWWUF

On the other hand, there are the neo-Sufis of the Haqq Tasawwuf. To this movement belong the Mawla, community leaders and guides (or patrons) for those seeking to open the inner gateways to the Paradise which lies within us.

The voice of Haqq Tasawwuf is the Walī (a term which more or less means "saint", but which also refers to someone who is a custodian or protector over another). The Walī holds no temporal power and it would gravely undermine his station were he seen as trying to be a political leader. In fact, the Walī is merely the spokesperson for the circumspect Council of Walī, who are usually not seen by the public or media. Haqqislam rejects the idea of a binding *ijma*, but the Walī, speaking with the myriad insight of the Council, is considered the wisest counsellor on matters of the spirit. (There are rumours that the Council of Walī has, in fact, used experimental Silk technologies to form a sort of joint consciousness.)

As the Haqq Mutazilites have their academies, the Haqq Tasawwuf have *zawiyas* where literature, art, history, meditation, and the Qur'an are studied. Most Haqqislamites attend both, generally splitting their week equally between them.

KHANIQAH

Khaniqah are where the two halves of Haqqislam's soul come together. They are gathering places, communal areas, and shared spaces. Originally the meeting halls of the Haqqislam movement, they have split, specialised, and (in some cases) grown to prodigious proportions.

Khaniqah are ideologically neutral. All ideas are allowed to come together and have a free voice. This intellectual freedom and openness is the bedrock of Haqqislamite faith and society.

CARAVANSERAI

Haqqislam's trade network in the wider Sphere is built upon the caravanserai, free ports throughout human space located at key junctions on the interstellar trade routes. The caravanserai are the external version of the *khaniqah*, neutral outposts where anyone can do business. The Winter Hall at the centre of each caravanserai is a place to buy and sell, rest and resupply, in as much comfort and luxury as local conditions allow.

Caravanserai are usually located near the platforms of Vila Boosters, along the Circular routes, or wherever there's a high volume of traffic. Mostly owned and managed by Haqqislamite commercial enterprises, with support from the Bourak government, they always have an appointed Trade Diwân who represents the Haqqislam state and is able to perform limited diplomatic functions.

These Trade Diwâns are also authorised to issue the Haqqislamite flag to any vessel with little red tape and only a small fee. These "flags of convenience" mean that the caravanserai also act as home ports to hundreds of small trade companies, corsairs, and ships from all nations. Unsurprisingly, caravanserai are often havens for smugglers, particularly those involved in the black market for Silk.

BIMARISTANS

The earliest Haqqislamite *bimaristans* were free clinics on Earth. On Bourak, they became a network of hospitals which covered the healthcare needs of the sālik settlers. Following the precepts of Haqqislam, however, they were also designed to facilitate the Search for Knowledge as research hospitals and biomedical research facilities.

The most prestigious *bimaristans* are in the Al-Medinat region, but they are found throughout Bourak.

UNIVERSITIES

In Haqqislam, universities are also part of the interwoven web of *khaniqah* which provide the scaffolding of society. They are seen as the place where the twin traditions of the academies and *zawiyas* are synthesised into a cohesive whole. The teaching staff are made up of both Hakim and Mawla.

INSTITUTIONS

GOVERNMENT

Haqqislam is a parliamentary democracy, with its form of government defined by the Constitution of Bourak (which was, itself, heavily influenced by the Concords of Tubruq which were created in the aftermath of Khadivar's assassination).

Bourak is divided into semi-autonomous democratic regions. The four major regions are the Al Medinat Caliphate, the Funduq Sultanate, the Iran Zhat Al Amat Shanate, and the Gabqar Khanate. (Several smaller regional governments also exist, including Bahiti, Huriyyah, Baniya, and Parthalia.)

Circulars – p. 144

Vila Booster – p. 145

OASES IN THE DESERT OF THE VOID

Outside of Bourak, most caravanserai are orbital stations. Nomad construction crews are hired to hollow out large, convenient chunks of rock and fill them with habitation modules. (Construction often proceeds while the future caravanserai is being propelled to its final destination.) The exterior of an orbital caravanserai is usually covered by a thick layer of ice, an inexpensive solution to protect the anti-radiation shielding from micrometeors, space debris, and other hazards. Peeking out from under the ice, long metallic quills mark the location of communication systems, sensors, docking modules, and maintenance blocks.

FIVE THINGS YOU SHOULD KNOW ABOUT HAQQISLAMITES

1. **"Sālik!":** The harsh environment of Bourak demands a certain tenacity. Fortunately, as a Haqqislamite saying goes, Allah favours the tenacious. Simultaneously, Haqqislamites feel that the Pilgrimage which brought them to Bourak made them all sālik — a term which once described Sufi travelers on the path to spiritual enlightenment, but which now conveys a sense of wayward adventure. Haqqislamites often cry, "Sālik!" before diving headlong into some daring (some might say foolhardy) escapade.

2. **Traders' Hearts:** The marketplace is the mainstay of Haqqislam culture. Even the smallest town has a bazaar and every village has a weekly market. (Think carefully before getting into seriously haggling with a Haqqislamite merchant, for they have years of practice at it, beginning from their childhood visits to the souk with their mothers.) This constant bargaining has burned itself deep into the Haqqislamite psyche, and they often see every conversation as a negotiation.

3. **Oaths:** Like all Muslims, it is only permissible for Haqqislamites to swear oaths by Allah or by Allah's attributes. ("I swear by Allah's might" or "By Allah's life, I will not fail.") They are, however, quite liberal in doing so.

4. **Devil's Advocate:** Haqqislamites prize the free expression and exchange of ideas, which often leads them to value examining an idea from all angles and earns them a reputation for playing devil's advocate. A popular turn of speech for contrasting two ideas is to ascribe one to *abbi* ("my father") and another to *abbun* ("the Father", i.e. Allah). This is often misunderstood by outsiders as prizing one idea above the other, but it's about analysing the ideas through different lenses of perception.

5. **Taharah Purity:** Observing cleanliness of the soul, the clothes, and the surroundings (referred to collectively as *taharah*) is an essential aspect of Islam. Among Haqqislamites this belief is actually intensified — the body is both the instrument by which the Cosmos is observed and the temple in which Paradise can be found. As a result, on Bourak you are far less likely to find eccentric or visible body modifications or genetic alteration than elsewhere in the Human Sphere.

MAJLIS

The Majlis is the parliament of Haqqislam. The lower majlis is divided into four separate houses, one for each of the major regional governments. The Majlis al-Bourak is the upper house, with its members evenly divided between the major ethnic groups and selected by national popular elections. National law requires agreement between the Majlis al-Bourak and at least two of the regional Majlis.

Silk Revolts, p. 21: In 30 NC, Silk Lords sought to overthrow the government. Battles were fought up and down Haqqislam trade routes.

Silk monopoly – p. 10

HACHIB

The Hachib (President) is elected by a nationwide popular vote. The present Hachib, Aisha bint Osman, is the first President not born on Bourak since the time of the planet's initial settlement. Born and raised on a caravanserai in Svalarheima during the Silk Revolts, the Hachib Aisha first became involved in politics when she came to Al Medinat to study philosophy at the Siddig el Tahir Academy.

Now into her second five-year term as President, Aisha bint Osman has developed a reputation for listening closely to her military advisors above others. All other things being equal, she tends to opt for the warlike path. This has made her some enemies among the caravanserai and the Silk trade, who regard her as too much trouble. Frontier dwellers on Bourak and in space, in contrast, value her emphasis on security, as does the military.

DIWÂNS

The diwâns are the large bureaucracies largely responsible for running the Haqqislam government. These agencies are deliberately firewalled from each other (and often have overlapping remits) in order to keep power divided. There are more than a dozen major national diwâns, in addition to temporary diwâns formed by decree or law for specific, short term purposes.

The major diwâns include the Diwân al Jund (War Office), Diwân al Kharâj (Tax Office), the Diwân al Mazalim (Trade Office), the Diwân al Hachib (Presidential Ministerial Office), and the Diwân al Rasa'il (which can be literally translated as the Communications Office, but which is actually in charge of national quantronic security, coordinating activities with ALEPH, and maintaining the official record of all laws).

Also notable is the Diwân al Nawal (which serves as the regional government of Nawal Island) and the Diwân al Paradiso (originally founded to govern Haqqislam's holdings on Paradiso, but now in charge of all colonial holdings and exploratory efforts).

GUILDS

During the Pilgrimage to Bourak, the Haqqislamite tycoons rapidly grew in power and infiltrated Bourak's politics at state and national levels. Murad Rajia, the Hachib at that time, saw that these influences threatened to strip away the ideals of Haqqislamite faith and reduce the new nation to mundane and secular concerns.

Hachib Murad's solution was the creation of the Merchant Guilds. He divided the tycoons by granting them powerful autonomy within their spheres of influence, and then introduced competition between the guilds. The merchant guilds remain a major power in Haqqislam and there are places riddled with their corruption (particularly in the Funduq Sultanate), but Hachib Murad's strategy fundamentally worked: The guilds are weakened by their internecine conflicts, allowing the Hachib to maintain the autonomy and authority of the Diwân system.

SILK LORDS

Immortality is the most valuable product ever sold.

Technically the Silk Consortiums which control immortality (and all Silk-derived biotechnology products) are just part of the merchant guilds. In practice, however, they represent a wholly different scale of power. Their corrupting influence among the regional governments, particularly in Funduq and Gabqar, is huge and their interplanetary reach is incalculable.

On the other hand, they are also subject to far greater scrutiny and regulation. The Diwân al Hachib uses the need to protect Haqqislam's Silk monopoly as a check against the indomitable wealth of the Silk Lords.

BIOHEALTH CORPS

The biohealth corporations, primarily located in Al Medinat, form a distinct bloc within the merchant guilds. They're less focused on trade and more focused on biomedical innovation, but the medical tourism they attract to Bourak is a major part of the Haqqislam economy.

MASTER GARDENERS

The Master Gardeners of Bourak straddle the divide between guild and government. On the one hand, the Gardener Guilds are important to virtually every aspect of life on Bourak — whether it's maintaining ecological balance in the slowly expanding farmlands or sculpting the rich tourist resorts along the coasts. On the other hand, the Terraforming Committee, a government agency based out of Iran Zhat Al Amat, is responsible for building and maintaining the vast networks of Terraforming Towers (T2s) that make the miracle of life on Bourak possible.

HAQQISLAMITE HIGH COMMAND

The Haqqislamite military is something of a paradox: On paper, it appears to be a disjointed disaster. Made up of multiple, independent regional armies that fiercely compete with each other, it would seem to be hopelessly mired in factionalism and over-specialisation.

In practice, the Haqqislamite High Command melds its fractured troops into a highly coordinated, flexible, and mobile offensive force that seamlessly coordinates the actions of its disparate components.

SWORD OF ALLAH

Haqqislam's state army, the Sword of Allah – the only combat force directly maintained by the Haqqislamite High Command – has more personnel under arms than any other standing force in the Human Sphere. The bulk of this force is made up of the ghulam light infantry. Built around light troops with superior manoeuverability, the High Command primarily uses the ghulam to crush the enemy against an anvil of smaller, heavy units and specialists largely drawn from the regional armies.

The High Command refers to this as the Antikythera Doctrine: The ghulam acts as a universal gear train, synching the actions of the regional armies with each other and serving as a medium for communication and coordination.

Haqqislam does not have the budget to equip all its soldiers with the sophisticated gear that those of other human powers get, but makes up for it with rigorous training and iron discipline. The small numbers of elite troops are equipped with the very best available and used to strike at key targets ahead of the main force to soften up the enemy for the coming onslaught from the Sword of Allah.

QAPU KHALQI

The regional army of the Funduq Sultanate serves as the security force for all of Haqqislam's interstellar trade routes, including orbital elevators, astroports, caravanserai, orbitals, Funduqu merchant vessels, and the all-important Silk Route. Although its wartime activities are coordinated through the Haqqislamite High Command, the Sultanate invests profits from its taxes and commercial tariffs to fund independent forces that act with full autonomy. This includes the Qapu Khalqi Armada, a corsair fleet independent from the Space Admiralty which includes Corregidoran Nomad troops, Yuan Yuan mercenaries, Druze shock teams, and Bashi Bazouk adventurers.

HAQQISLAMITE ARMADA

The Haqqislamite Armada is technically part of the Sword of Allah, but its activities are heavily compartmentalized. It maintains a rivalry with the Qapu Khalqi Armada, but is largely perceived as a staid and "boring" service by comparison. The Armada is charged with home defence and interplanetary troop transport, although during times of war it has also been used to harry enemy commercial endeavors.

CORSAIRS

Corsairs are ex-military spacefarers who refit merchant ships with weaponry to plunder enemy ships in times of war, in exchange for being allowed to keep an agreed portion of the ships and cargo they seize. Although the letters of marque under which the corsairs operate are issued by the Diwân al Jund, they are independent from the Haqqislamite High Command.

Privateering, of course, is frowned upon by merchants of other nations and their military, who do not recognise letters of marque as legitimate. Summary executions of captured corsairs are common. In peacetime, which rarely lasts long, letters of marque are invalid and any corsair who can't hold off from the old business becomes guilty of piracy. Some do it anyway. Others sign up with mercenary companies to transport their hired guns from one planet to another.

WILDERNESS OF MIRRORS

HASSASSINS

The Hassassin sect was founded in the grief-stricken aftermath of Farhad Khadivar's murder. When the creator of the Haqqislam movement was slain by the Legion of the Exalted, the mathematician, psychologist, and theologian Abdulahmed Rashad resolved to never again allow reactionary forces to stand in the way of the Search for Knowledge. He recruited agents and consulted with contacts around the world. Within weeks, Khadivar's killer was dead in prison, his throat slit. A month later, an agent killed Imam Khalaf ibn Ahmad on a public street. The hassasssin shouted Haqqislam's truth even as the imam's bodyguards shot him down. Over the next seven years, it is said that every member of the Legion of the Exalted was slain.

So began the fearsome legend of the hassassins.

Haqqislamite Virtues – p. 160

OLD MAN OF THE MOUNTAIN

The Society's leader is the mysterious Old Man of the Mountain. There are some who say that the current Old Man is, in fact, still Abdulahmed Rashad himself, the founder of the order. Whatever the truth may be, it is the Old Man of the Mountain who is the ultimate determiner of who (or what) constitutes a threat to the ongoing Search for Knowledge, a mission which extends beyond Haqqislam and includes anyone obstructing humanity's development. He designates the targets who are marked for death by his disciples, and once they are marked, sooner or later death inevitably follows.

HASSASSIN EXEMPLARS

The Hassassins consider themselves seekers pursuing the Haqqislamite Virtues who, in their defence of the Search of Knowledge, have transformed themselves into the embodiment of the Haqqislamite Ideals. Their teachings wed the martial lore of the Nizari Isma'ilism (an ancient order of assassins) with the mysticism of neo-Sufism.

The Hassassin philosophy centres on the *lataif-e-sitta*, the psycho-spiritual organs known as the Six Subtleties. Mastering the use of these organs unlocks a physical and spiritual perfection which attains its ultimate purpose in the art of divine murder.

The Hassassins are diverse in their skills and training but united in their devotion to the cause and not afraid to die if that is what it takes. They

Science moves fast and implacably, and the diversity of studies and avenues of investigation that could result in the creation of a Judgement Day weapon multiplies with each passing day. Misuse of corrupt Science could cause the cancellation of true Science by provoking an irrational, instinctive reaction from fear and ignorance. This would gravely affect the Search for Knowledge.

—Speech given via holoconference by the Old Man of the Mountain during the Authorisation Ceremony of the Hassassin Society

seek public executions, viewing their killings as an instrument of propaganda for both themselves and the Search for Knowledge.

LAYERS OF DECEPTION

Even before Bourak's government was formed, the hassassins appointed themselves Haqqislam's intelligence organisation. The society's government liaison is officially listed as an agency of the Diwân al Jund, under the title of Hassassin ETTVAK (an acronym for *Ettela'at va Amniyat-e Keshvar*, a Farsi phrase meaning Circle of Intelligence and Security).

The public face of ETTVAK, however, is a cover for the Hassassin Bahram ("Victory" in Farsi), a supposedly ultra-secret organisation that controls the Special Operations Division of the Sword of Allah.

In practice, the Hassassin Bahram is an open secret, almost as well-known as PanOceania's Hexaedron. What very few people realise (outside of elite intelligence operatives and fringe conspiracy channels on Maya) is that the Bahram is also a cover operation, protecting the true Hassassin order which operates out of secret bases in the Alamut deserts of the Iran Zhat Al Amat Shanate. This, the core of the sect, is not truly under the Hachib's control. The Hassassins are a law unto themselves. Haqqislamite leaders are reluctant to admit this in public even when Hassassin activities cause anger and revulsion, at home or abroad, believing that it's better to take the blame for the Old Man's actions than to admit that they cannot truly control them.

HASSASSINS: FRATERNITY OF ASSASSIN PHILOSOPHERS

Hassassins are obviously famed for their assassinations and spec-op liaisons with the Haqqislamite army, but with their near-monopoly on Haqqislamite intelligence operations the truth is that they can be found operating throughout the Human Sphere performing industrial espionage, information gathering, infowar, and the like.

Capture the Cube: As a rule, hassassins don't have Cubes — it's the only way to protect the deepest secrets of the order. But when Hassassin Fiday Hamdi Hashim was captured, a fast download port was forcibly attached and his memories drained. Now the recording is in the wild. Enemy agencies may seek to capture it for themselves, while hassassin agents are dispatched to retrieve the memory records before they can be analysed.

Assassination Double Cross: A PanOceanian diplomatic envoy must be disposed of. Merely assassinating him won't be enough, however: The hassassin agents will need to frame a Yu Jing junior ambassador for the crime.

Ersatz Assassin: Three bodyguards of the Silk tycoon Yamak Bey were hospitalized and one of his odalisques killed by an attacker who declared "hassassin justice". Bey is furious and calling for blood, but the assassination attempt wasn't authorised by the Old Man. Was the attacker even a true member of the order?

MUHAFIZ

The Funduq Security and Intelligence Force, informally known as the Muhafiz, is the only significant Haqqislamite intelligence operation outside of the Hassassins. They gain their remit through coordination with the Qapu Khalqi, and receive political coverage from powerful members of the Silk Consortium who are uncomfortable with the Old Man of the Mountain's monopolization of power.

CHIEFS

The agency is divided into independent "chiefdoms", each overseen by a chief referred to as a Muhafiz (one who guards, preserves, or watches over another). The chiefs have broad discretionary powers and little guidance or oversight. This occasionally means that the agency steps on its own toes, but it also makes it an incredibly difficult target for counterintelligence.

AL HAWWA'

The Al Hawwa' are a secret naval unit within the Muhafiz specialised in infowar and close combat.

They work closely with the Qapu Khalqi to perform raiding, surveillance, and sabotage missions along Haqqislam trade routes, but you're more likely to have seen them onboard civilian ships — not that you would have known it at the time. Al Hawwa' agents work undercover security on the ships and space stations that conduct Haqqislam's lucrative Silk trade. They pose as crew members or passengers, blending in and amassing data on the places they visit, through simple surveillance and observation, or through industrial espionage. Only when necessary do they reveal themselves and swing into action, demonstrating their extensive combat training, which includes zero-g fighting.

The Silk Consortium sponsors part of the unit's financial budget in return for the protection it provides to the Silk trade. This allows the Muhafiz to outfit Al Hawwa' agents with the very best weapons and equipment. Formally, the Consortium has no say in how or where the unit's personnel may be deployed — but the Al Hawwa' commanders know they need to do the merchants a favour every now and then.

MUHAFIZ: DARK MATTER GUARDIANS

Officially, the remit of the Muhafiz is limited to the trade routes controlled by Funduq. In practice, Haqqislamite trade interests permeate virtually every aspect of the Sphere and it's easy for the autonomous Muhafiz chiefs to justify pretty much anything they want to stick their noses into. (They're also known to go deliberately "off reservation" to perform intelligence services for the Sword of Allah, other regional armies, or government diwâns when they don't want to get the hassassins involved.)

Unraveling Arachne: An Al Hawwa' task group is assigned to hunt down criminal Arachne nodes being illegally hosted on Haqqislamite facilities along the Silk Route.

Death at the Top: A Muhafiz chief turns up dead in a suite at an Al Medinat resort. The bullet holes in the back of her head make it complicated, and the dead prostitutes stacked in the bathtub aren't simplifying it. (It just gets worse if the PCs were directly working for her.)

Cross Purposes: The Muhafiz has learned that hassassins have targeted a mid-level Yu Jing government official. The only problem? She's a Muhafiz agent. The PCs are going to have to run interference, preferably without blowing the agent's cover.

G-5 FACTION
NOMADS

VYPADNI

In early Nomad society, nearly every citizen had a past that they would rather stay in the past. This created a cultural aversion to asking about an individual's past unless it might follow them into their current job or relationship. Anyone with concerns will simply ask, "Past?" and expect a "Yes" if there's a conflict or "No" if not. Anyone asking for more than that typically receives the curt response, "Vypadni!" which roughly translates to "Buzz off!"

Maya cluster, p. 142: Communities which exist entirely within the virtual realms of the datasphere.

digital patina, p. 142: A layer of the AR environment.

FORM OVER FUNCTION

While it may seem counterintuitive for a people that set the trend in fashion, from clothing to body modification, Nomads don't tend to be distracted by or judgmental about outward appearances. Nomads rely upon the skills and stamina of the individual next to them, and don't care much about how they look. With some of the extreme body modifications available from BouBoutiques, any other behaviour would be counterproductive.

TIMEKEEPING ON THE MOTHERSHIPS

The motherships operate on standard 12-hour cycles. At 20:00 the artificial day ends, with a gradual, coordinated transition dimming of ship-wide illumination as they slip into night.

The space-based Nomad Nation is the smallest of the major powers, but their influence and divisive impact are felt throughout the entire Human Sphere. Ever since their recognition by O-12, the Nomad Nation has had to fight for its continued existence. The enormous pressure of outside threats have hammered them into a hard, cutting blade. With these three titanic space vessels — motherships — and with commercial missions and outposts in every system, no place escapes the Nomads' touch.

NOMAD LIBERTY

Though from disparate backgrounds and cultures, the Nomads are unified in their passion for freedom, independence, and revolution. Of course, this spirit also includes darker elements: distrust, suspicion, and cynicism.

This fierce and rebellious independence defines the Nomad Nation. Their revolutionary, outcast, and criminal origins set their society in conflict against staid government or corporate norms, especially the meddling influence of ALEPH. Arachne, an independent data network autonomous from the ALEPH-monitored Maya, provides freedom from the AI's ever-present observation while Nomad citizens shun societal norms of legality, morality, and behaviour, instead choosing their own paths.

BAKUNIN: MANIFOLD HETEROGENEITY

Founded by a conclave of anti-establishment and counterculture groups, *Bakunin* offered a sanctuary for extremists, idealist, libertarians, transhumanists, religious sects, radical scientists, and a host of others who found themselves increasingly persecuted or pressured by an AI-ordered society. This dynamic mix of avant-garde, counterculture, and outright zealotry spawns energy, exploration, and endeavours unique to *Bakunin*. The outward face of these energies creates art and entertainment consumed throughout the Human Sphere, while the inward side forges technologies and innovations beyond the imaginings of even the most advanced powers.

CORE AND COMMUNE

Bakunin is, at its heart, a conglomerate of communities ostracised from the norms of Human Sphere

society: Some are radical. Some are reformists. Some are fanatical. Many just want to live a life of their choosing. In fact, the mothership was basically formed by each of these groups buying habitation modules and strapping them onto a military surplus transport.

Following the precepts of the 1st Radical Bakunin Manifesto as enshrined in the Simple Law, in the early days of the *Bakunin* there was a division between the core of the ship and the communes (the habitation modules which were attached to it). Although the expansion of the mothership means that this strict inner-and-outer relationship no longer strictly applies, the basic concepts remain the same: The core consists of those areas of the *Bakunin* which are public, shared spaces. Each commune, on the other hand, is a largely autonomous community governed by those who live there.

Although a majority of modules gravitate towards a sort of cultural gestalt that the Bakunians refer to as "vanilla", many communes are effectively societal experiments. Those who step inside them are expected to suspend their social paradigms and are bound to the rules and customs enshrined into the commune's charter and its laws.

SOCIAL ENERGY

Social Energy is something between a social crypto-currency, a quantronically assisted democracy, and a warped Maya cluster combining the functions of meme-distribution, community bulletin board, and a crazed, almost fractal digital patina. It can be difficult for outsiders to really understand it until they've experienced it; or, as the common Nomad saying goes, "if you've felt it, you've grokked it".

Social Energy was created because the simple division of core and commune wasn't enough to stabilise Bakunian society. Conflicts between revolutionary social memes boiled out into the common spaces of the mothership, eventually culminating in a flash mob conflict that degenerated into a violent riot that resulted in a hull breach that killed nearly one hundred people. The system of Social Energy solved the problem by essentially virtualising the conflict.

Governed by the Department of Social Energy (DSE) and enforced by the Moderator Corps, it is a complex, dynamic system that combines a number of features into a seamless whole. First, it's a social currency system allowing for economic exchanges based on reputation and trust, with its value gradated based on social contributions (primarily through DSE-sponsored incentive programs), physical proximity (individuals and communities have more influence over the areas of the ship closest to them and their interests), and resource utilisation (those with a proven history of using a resource to positive effect have a greater claim to that resource in the future). Second, it's a debate forum with teeth that functions as a direct democracy for resolving local intermural issues. Finally, it possesses augmented reality layers that boil Social Energy out into the collective sensorium: holo-signs spatter the mothership with quantronic graffiti, creating a battlefield of revolutionary social memes. Meme-tags flag contested resources or public service programs. Some communes even use patina mods that allow them to edit their perception of reality to match their social expectations. (This latter practice is controversial, but endorsed by the Moderator Corps because it can defuse otherwise thorny conflicts. And what do you care what you look like to someone else?)

CORREGIDOR: METEOR HEADS

The population of *Corregidor* is larger than *Bakunin*'s, but more than sixty percent of it doesn't live on the mothership at any given time. (And that percentage has been spiking higher since the Combined Army invaded.) Instead, Corregidorans are spread throughout the Human Sphere, labouring under work contracts or serving in one of *Corregidor*'s

many mercenary companies. These, in turn, are the two wellsprings of the Corregidoran spirit — work and blood.

MAINTENANCE TEAMS

Corregidor is the oldest of the Nomad motherships, predating the others by decades, and, unlike those other motherships, it wasn't born in a flourish of idealism; it was forged out of sheer desperation, carving an existence for itself through hard, brutal labour. That era of sacrifice also instilled a very basic understanding of the world into the Corregidoran soul: nothing is free.

Those born planetside take the basic fact of existence for granted. Corregidorans understand that life is fundamentally transactional. The lives of their forefathers proved that the basic elements of life — oxygen, a space to call your own, even consciousness itself — are not guaranteed in the void. And an iota-scarcity economy doesn't change that basic calculus: if your suit runs out of oxygen, you're dead. The universe doesn't care how many fancy fabbers you have.

Every Corregidoran must pay — in either money or community work — for the privilege of breathing. The community work is carried out on maintenance teams. In fact, most Corregidorans, even those who could afford to pay the oxygen tithes in full, choose to perform at least some minimal level of community service when living on the mothership. Participating in the work of a maintenance team is a little like going to church — it's seen as a civic privilege and operates as a kind of social circle.

IDENTIFYING COMMUNES
Communes are given unique alphanumeric designations. (Commune N-9, for example, was created by the now exiled Equinox group.) Most are also known by a common name, such as the anarcho-feminist commune of Beauvoir and its sub-commune of Vulkanja, founded by feminist weaponsmiths.

sensorium, p. 142: The totality of what someone is seeing (in reality, AR, and VR).

FIELD TEST MODULES
Bakunin maintains a number of modules originally designed for training how to survive and operate in different environments. The interior of the modules can adapt to virtually any condition, from vacuum to any planetary environment imaginable. Many are now open to the public as a way of getting new and different experiences; the *Bakunin* equivalent of national parks.

CORVUS BELLI
INFINITY

BLACK SHIPS

Several of the Black Labs of Bakunin collectively maintain a small fleet of vessels. Often called the Black Ships, they allow scientific teams to seek out new compounds and phenomena, or to test concepts and prototypes in the field.

Maintenance teams also function as the community's education system. Kids as young as three will join **white maintenance teams**, which are primarily concerned with basic education. Around age eight or nine, however, these children will graduate to **green maintenance teams**. In addition to more traditional educational tasks, maintenance teams teach youngsters basic repair skills, emergency protocols, zero-g athletics, and similar essential skills.

Around age fifteen, kids begin transitioning into their adult maintenance teams, some of which feature other colour codes based on various specialised duties. **Infrared maintenance teams** are notable because they are penal teams assigned to the most dangerous and unpleasant tasks.

WORK TEAMS

Most Corregidorans belong to small, modular work teams which are contracted out for jobs across the Human Sphere. Most are specialised in deep-space and hostile environment construction jobs. Serving on a prospector crew offers potentially high rewards, but commensurately higher risk, too.

The meteor heads who make up these work teams are the heart and soul of *Corregidor*. They're space toughs who live by the maxim "groan and abide", recognising that the punishing conditions under which they work is also the lifeblood which fuels the existence of their mothership – a tradition of work and service burned into the Corregidoran soul. But while they're possessed of a certain mirthless pragmatism, Corregidorans also know how to kick back after a long, hard day.

MOTHERSHIP: BAKUNIN

The scale of *Bakunin*, the largest of the Nomad motherships, can be difficult to grasp. You see the two domes perched atop the bulbous, amoeba-like growth of the modules clinging to the three colossal drive-pillars which serve as both the ship's propulsion and its skeleton and your mind wants to interpret them as observation decks. But each of those domes actually contains a sprawling metropolis of skyscrapers punctuated by megascrapers. *Bakunin* is so large that, for the first time, it is confronting an "expansion horizon" in the near future (beyond which expansion will need to be carefully controlled and then fully prohibited because the Circulars will no longer be able to transport the ship). Solutions range from creating a *Bakunin II* (by creating a new drive-pillar and/or somehow splitting the existing mothership) or retrofitting the *Bakunin* to include jump capability, but nothing has seemed eminently practical.

The drive-pillars on *Bakunin* are generally kept firing at all times except for short-lived periods of "turn-over", generating a default state of artificial gravity in which "down" points towards the magnetic exhaust nozzles on the "bottom" of the mothership.

Domes: The First Dome is smaller than the Second Dome, largely by virtue of the improvements in the construction of the foundational superstructure which connects the domes to the drive-pillars. The current names of each dome are determined by the prevailing Social Energy. It was anticipated that these would eventually settle into fairly consistent patterns, but the constant churn continues. There has been some discussion of building a third dome atop the final drive-pillar, but it's actually the first *Bakunin* drive-pillar and a large number of the oldest habitation modules would need to be disrupted to make it happen.

Old Bakunin: The original military transport around which *Bakunin* originally formed is still located deep in the heart of the mothership, nestled between the newer drive-pillars. The bureaucratic headquarters of the Conciliator, Bakunin Jurisdictional Command, and the Moderator Corps are located inside its heavily renovated interior and nearby modules.

Praxis: Over time, like has gravitated to like in *Bakunin* to a certain extent, creating distinct districts. Praxis was the first of these, where the most radical and isolationist communes can be found. Ever since *Bakunin*'s founding, scientists desiring freedom from the shackle of government or the limited vision of corporation direction have flocked to it. Psychowarlocks perform illegal Resurrections, technomants transform obsolete technology into innovative engineering marvels, and neo-alchemists rewrite subatomic structures. The dark side of this culture of experimental liberty, however, are the Black Labs, where the rules laid aside include those of international law and even morality.

VaudeVille: This district is a neon tumour, weaving its way snake-like across and through the *Bakunin*. Sunset Boulevard is the heart of the district, a sort of central "corridor" or "main street" that runs along its length before blossoming into a bustling tumult in the third sector of the Second Dome.

This area hosts the most extravagant art, the most exotic augmentations, and the most perverse pleasures. In the same way that the Black Labs of Praxis have forged a revolution in technological innovation, VaudeVille has spawned a creative one. Freed from the bounds of accepted norms, cultural mores, and propriety, VaudeVille generates art, entertainment, and fashions which drive the styles of tomorrow across the Human Sphere. And in its Black Markets, the daring can find designer drugs, MetaChemicals, manufactured creatures, and even Resurrection brokers for the right price.

Despite a seemingly endless hunger for its products, VaudeVille spends a surprising amount of energy in competition with itself. RushHour vies with its competitors, both on Arachne and Maya, for viewers, and LoroLocco contends with fashion houses throughout the Sphere, but cuts most keenly against competitors at home. Those that think the shadow world of military operations is the most contentious has not worked in the cutthroat arena of corporate espionage.

MOTHERSHIP: CORREGIDOR

Corregidor is a somewhat lopsided vessel comprised of two "lobes" connected by a number of void-bridges: the Praesidio, the original prison complex, has grown at a slower rate than the Lazareto residential and industrial complexes. Both halves are honeycombed with shipping channels lined with hundreds of docks and ports. This is particularly true on the Lazareto side, where smaller ships can successfully dock all the way in the deepest interior.

Corregidor prefers short, hard burns for manoeuvring. (Visitors will note that most areas are outfitted with crash couches.) Thus the mothership is usually kept weightless, and the interior environments largely reflect that. Where gravity is needed for certain industrial applications, however, individual sections of the station are designed to be rotated for artificial gravity.

Lazareto: Originally built to house millions of refugees from Africa and Equatorial America, the oldest portions of Lazareto are mostly cramped slums today. The district has been extensively expanded over the years with additional hexagonal "towers". Inside the towers, most areas are dominated by an architectural creole of African and Latin styles, with a neo-mishmash of Aztec, Incan, Mayan, and Egyptian elements.

Praesidio: The original structure of *Corregidor* was formed by a command bridge — containing all the control, security, and maintenance teams — and a series of inmate storage modules. The former remains the centre of Corregidoran government. The latter have been extensively retrofitted, but still retain unmistakable legacies of their penal origins.

The Neck: The void-bridges connecting the two halves of *Corregidor* are nicknamed the Neck. Several of the struts feature quick-launch docks for military use, and a number of mercenary companies are based here. But the Neck is mostly a shopping and cultural district; the closest thing to a "downtown" in space. The most recent addition — in the largest strut of the Neck — is a massive domed park roughly two miles long and a half mile wide. Designed by VaudeVillians, during its construction many Corregidorans mumbled about its needless luxury being a betrayal of their traditional values… but the place is still packed with visitors now that it's open.

Contract Teams: *Corregidor* provides the Human Sphere with its largest source of highly skilled space-labour. To secure those positions, contract teams — some officially organised through the Praesidio, but most independent operations — range out ahead of the mothership scouting for opportunities. Work teams empower one or more contract teams to negotiate on their behalf in order to secure contracts they can start working as soon as the *Corregidor* arrives in-system.

Some contract teams specialise in remote hires, particularly in the Human Edge system where the demand for zero-g labour is always high. These contracts are more difficult to wrangle because long-distance transport has to be arranged from the mothership, but the universe is too big to limit *Corregidor*'s commercial interests to its immediate flightpath.

Hiring Halls: Those who prefer to come to *Corregidor* instead of waiting for the contract teams to come to them will find what they need in the numerous, incorporated hiring halls onboard. Particularly of note are the halls specialising in bounties: *Corregidor* has the largest number of bounty hunters per capita.

TUNGUSKA: CRYPTOHACKERS & CRIMINALS

If *Bakunin* is a commune of revolutionaries and *Corregidor* is a community of the common classes, then *Tunguska* is a collective of corporations. And, although they maintain a relatively lean — if somewhat oily — façade under O-12 law, Tunguskans understand that between the corporate and the criminal there is no true distinction. After all, those were the first customers to line up when a consortium of bankers and financiers detected a need for a tax haven in the wake of post-ALEPH M-CORP crackdowns.

The cool sociopathy of mob boss and boardroom, however, stands in sharp contrast to the anarchic techno-hacker ideals of the cryptomancers who make up the other half of Tunguskan society. *Tunguska*, after all, was built for a singular purpose: the bankers wanted to create a safe haven for data and financial transactions; the hackers they hired to make it a reality saw it as a chance to realise a utopian vision.

Lock these two very different cultures up together in a tin can for the better part of a century and what you end up with in the festering tension between ruthless practicality and libertarian idealism is

BLACK BOUNTIES

The Black Labs are often seen as a unique sin of the Nomads. The truth, however, is that the labs are often leveraged by hypercorps to perform the research that can't be done anywhere else. To facilitate this lucrative trade, the crypto-hackers of Tunguska have created secure bounty lists where the labs can compete to see which team can complete the research or development first.

BOUBOUTIQUES

BouBoutiques are chic fashion shops/design houses which flirt (or dive wholeheartedly) into transgressive experimentation. They specialise in everything from high fashion to military gear, while also offering biosynth body collections, body alteration, and extreme augmentation.

HELICON REGULATIONS

Following the horrors of Helicon Miners' Revolt (p. 254), the O-12 Senate passed the Helicon Regulations. These safety protocols provide a legal framework governing zero-g and deep-space work. Despite this, hypercorps and foreign governments are often still guilty of attempting to exploit or endanger Corregidoran workers. When that happens, the Corregidor Jurisdictional Command has little patience waiting for a resolution through diplomatic channels. More often than not, they'll immediately deploy their mercenary forces to protect and extract.

CORRIDOR BOYS

The *maras* – or criminal gangs – of *Corregidor* are divided between the *vatos* and the *tsotsis* (from Latin and African origins, respectively). There's a constant, low level conflict between these corridor boys that dates back to the earliest days of the mothership, when the *maras* first formed as the only defence against the background of constant violence and societal chaos.

KUHIFADHI

The Kuhifadhi module (Swahili for "Preserve") was originally created by some troublesome African refugees with shadowy backgrounds (mostly headhunters and war criminals from various African conflicts) as a stronghold against those seeking revenge. It serves that function as sanctuary unto this day, with many of its members keeping in the weapon business as bounty hunters and mercenaries.

BOT SEAL

"Bank of Tunguska Approved" is a quality seal desired by all private banks.

NEO-CETACEANS

Taking advantage of their natural resilience to pressure and high gravity, as well as their innate comprehension of three-dimensional space, Nomads utilise dolphins, porpoises, and orca uplifted in the labs of Praxis to pilot their shuttles and in-system vessels. Some use the pejorative term "blowholes" to refer to these pilots, but never within earshot: They have long memories and can withstand far more G-forces than humans. Your next trip could be very uncomfortable.

the unique culture identity of the Tunguskan. Meanwhile, the webs of power woven by the bankers ensure the mothership remains a calm and tranquil place where customers feel that their money and data is safe and sound, thus suppressing the violent and anarchic excesses and forcing mobsters and hackers alike to act in the shadows.

THE CRYPT

The physical core of *Tunguska* is the ALEPH-detached data crypt. Here are employed the programmers, hackers, cryptographers, and quantum physicists who sustain the true heart of the mothership's existence and, by extension, the Nomad Nation as a whole. Fully eighty percent of *Tunguska*'s economy is tied to the overlapping layers of corporate services that ultimately tie back to the core functionality of the Crypt.

OUBLIETTES

Before data is allowed to enter or exit the Crypt, it must be verified and purified. To do so, it must pass through the oubliettes which ring the Crypt. Each oubliette is kept independent from the others, using unique verification methods and encryption schemes, and the Crypt will only accept data which has been independently routed through two separate oubliettes. Oubliettes are secured against cyber-assault by powerful suites of hacking programs supplemented by automatic dead man's switches that can completely sever the oubliettes' connection to the Crypt.

Much of this process is automatic and quantronic, but each oubliette is also a *physical* interface between the Crypt and the public world, with those seeking to enter or exit the Crypt needing to pass through the rigorous security protocols of an oubliette. They also serve as an economic interface, with each oubliette a separate chartered company that licenses and facilitates the data security services of the Crypt (and often other data services as well).

BANK OF TUNGUSKA

The Bank of Tunguska is the central bank of the Nomad Nation. Its operations are somewhat unusual, however, because its primary duties are only tangentially related to currency or monetary policy and primarily concerned with the maintenance, management, and security of the Crypt. It issues a variety of data bonds which are purchased in bulk by the private banks of *Tunguska* which ultimately license the services and resources controlled by those bonds to individual clients.

The Bank is controlled by the very powerful "bank families" – such as the Waldheim, the Figueroa, and the Haller – almost all of which date back to the founding of *Tunguska*.

COURIER SERVICES

The need for data protection doesn't end at the walls of the Crypt. A variety of Tunguskan courier services – ranging from large corporations like Tristeryon to independent freelancers – exist to perform secure deliveries, particularly of quantronically locked data valises. These deliveries are often made via Ixions, ultra-rapid spaceships whose pilots receive genetic and nanotech augmentations to endure the strains of travel.

LAW FIRMS

Those who associate *Tunguska* primarily with criminal activity are surprised to discover that the mothership is teeming with law firms, most of them christened with choking mouthfuls of surnames like Bright, Matsuda, Cohen, and Associates (legal representatives of the Van Orton Military Contracts Foreign Company) or Avedikian, Maier, & Somtow (whose founder, Rupert Avedikian, was assassinated by his partners when he was caught embezzling).

A particular speciality of the law firms are Tunguskan smart contracts. Governed by LAIs and enshrined in blockchains, these sophisticated

MOTHERSHIP: TUNGUSKA

The teardrop-shaped *Tunguska* is the smallest and least populated of the Nomad motherships. Its sleek form is made up from layers of habitation modules, like a fractal Matryoshka doll. Unlike the barely controlled chaos of *Bakunin*, however, these are modules are laid out following the rigid schemes of a central planning commission.

Centrum: This core district of Tunguska is home to the Crypt and the major financial, quantronic, and governmental institutions which surround it. The architecture here is surprisingly vaulted and vast, with large, airy spaces serving as quiet displays of opulence.

Barangays: Named after a Filipino term for suburbs, the barangays are all of the outer habitation modules. Each module is largely independent, maintaining their own services, habitation maintenance, support, security, and the like. The common areas of *Tunguska* tend towards the reserved (outside of the Quan Quads, where the ribaldrous hacker communities have set up shop), but often orgiastic excess can be found lurking just out of sight.

legal instruments can not only enforce themselves and manage payment, but also incorporate cascading dependencies of automated bidding for development and freelance work. Once a smart contract has been carefully crafted and funded, they essentially run themselves: a government, for example, could declare that they want a dam built at a particular location, activate a properly constructed smart contract, and essentially watch the dam build itself.

Hand-in-hand with these contracts, Tunguskan law firms also provide ultra-advanced identity verification services: supported by the Black Labs of Praxis, their biometric methods are unrivalled in the Human Sphere.

INSTITUTIONS
GOVERNMENT

Each mothership brought its own unique style of democracy into the union. Had Chairman Toryski of *Tunguska* suggested another layer of bureaucracy or dissolution of any ship's internal governance, negotiations to form the Nomad Nation would have surely floundered. He rightly calculated that only the very lightest "national" touch would be tolerated by such fiercely individualistic elements, and that events following establishment of the Nation would force them to bond against common foes bent upon their destruction.

NOMAD EXECUTIVE BOARD
The three motherships each contribute two members to the Nomad Executive Board. In accordance with the Initiative—the charter that created the Nomad Nation—all board members are of equal status, though the Tunguskan representatives have veto authority, a right negotiated to them since they spearheaded the Initiative. This tends to give them slightly higher unofficial status, but does not translate to any sort of deference. In fact, the senior Tunguskan delegate is often referred to as "Kurat", which roughly translates as "Devil". It is sometime used humorously, but often not.

These six delegates have the power to call upon officials and officers that coordinate with their counterparts on an ad-hoc basis for matters of strategic planning, coordination, deconfliction, and other "national" issues. This prevents the accumulation of bureaucracy, and also ensures that the most appropriate individual is called for the immediate situation.

BAKUNIAN CONCILIATOR
One module, one vote. *Bakunin* has the smallest central government of the Nomad Nations,

consisting solely of the Conciliator and their bureaucratic apparatchik. Each commune casts a single vote for the Conciliator and the internal method used to determine the module's vote is their own business, allowing them to stay true to their internal political ideals.

Elections are usually held once every five years, although a super-majority of three-quarters of the modules can immediately recall a Conciliator and force a new election. This is not wholly infrequent, and usually happens whenever a Conciliator is perceived to be interfering too much in matters of local jurisdiction (which Bakunians feel should be resolved through the direct democracy and referendums of Social Energy).

The Conciliator manages and directs the democratic process to ensure that critical issues get the proper attention, and lesser issues do not dominate the political landscape at times of genuine crisis.

CORREGIDORAN CUSTODIANS
One citizen, one vote. The early days of *Corregidor*'s history forced their definition of citizenship upon them. Only those that could actively contribute to the survival of *Corregidor* could be allowed to have a voice in the path they would follow. Gaining citizenship requires the accumulation of Service Hours. This typically takes nineteen or twenty years, though the youngest verified citizen accomplished this in fourteen. Citizenship must be maintained via a yearly Service Hour quota or a payment—known as the service tariff—of the market rate for those hours.

Corregidor has a legislative house of Custodians, whose representation is in direct relation to the population of citizens, as well as a directly elected executive called Warden, despite the many years since the Praesidio's use as a prison. Despite the negative connotation that many outsiders see in the title, Corregidorans view it as an essential reminder of their history, and there has never been a credible attempt to change it.

TUNGUSKAN BOARD OF DIRECTORS
One share, one vote. Citizens of *Tunguska* earn a number of voting shares upon their majority, much like shares of any other corporation. Despite a high market value, most Tunguskans aspire to purchasing more shares as they are able, and are quite reluctant to part with them, even in times of hardship. The government prevents the "unbalanced accumulation of shares" by a sliding purchase tax determined by the number of shares already owned, which serves the dual purpose of funding government endeavours as well as keeping unbridled voting market forces in check. However, nothing

SHADOW CONTRACTS
Some Tunguskan firms issue "shadow contracts"—smart contracts issued anonymously and often structured so that those participating in them are unaware of the full scope of the contract's goals.

SOCIAL ENERGY ON TUNGUSKA
Bakunian activists will periodically make the effort to expand the system of Social Energy to the Nomad Nation as a whole. These efforts generally founder on the rocky shores of Corregidoran traditionalists (who prefer cold hard cash to "hippy friendship money"), but it does occasionally find some purchase in Tunguskan hacker clusters. Either way, it's not unusual for Tunguskan law firms to be involved with Social Energy, as their advanced identity verification services can play a vital role in its social currency.

KRUGS
One of the defining events for the Nomad Nation as a whole is the Krug. Every four years, all three Nomad motherships gather in a single system for a celebration that is two parts Carneval, one part strategic summit, and one part family reunion. Krugs are eagerly anticipated by all Nomads as celebrations of their continued survival and the individualism and freedoms that make them who they are. They are also opportunities to blend populations and ideas, preventing either from leading down a road to regression.

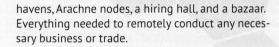

prevents the accumulation of shares by Tunguskan corporations, which hold large quantities of them.

Shareholders vote for two seats per year of an eight-member Board of Directors, in four-year cycles. The Board selects one of its members to serve as Chairman, the top executive position of *Tunguska*. Due to the influence wielded by the Chairman, it is unusual for him to lose the position so long as he maintains his board seat.

COMMERCIAL MISSIONS

Despite all the attention they receive, the Nomad Nation consists of far more than the three motherships. Anywhere the Nomads do business, from major planets to orbital lifts, from asteroid mining hubs to caravanserai, their commercial missions serve political, commercial, and logistical needs. Each is unique, reflecting the character of its location.

There are, however, some common elements to all missions. They all have political and commercial representatives from each of the three motherships, a bureaucratic and administrative office, cultural office, intelligence office, military security detail, and a variety of envoys from any area of business that the nation conducts in the region. Each also has fully isolated and defended data

havens, Arachne nodes, a hiring hall, and a bazaar. Everything needed to remotely conduct any necessary business or trade.

The Black Hand frequently operates out of commercial missions, taking full advantage of the diplomatic immunity they afford. Many nations take a dim view of these hubs of chaos so close to their critical interests, but the commercial opportunities missions represent for their businesses outweigh the negatives.

One mission in each system is designated as the embassy for the system. This is typically, though not always, the largest and most centrally located. Known as Nomad Trade Delegations, these embassies are the true diplomatic hubs for the Nomad Nation in that system, and take full advantage of the sovereign status this affords them. Thus, in addition to being the system's political focus, it also acts as the focus for more illicit activities. The embassy bazaar has a wider variety of illegal merchandise; its Arachne transmitter serves the greatest number of system nodes from behind the crypt's firewalls; and the Black Hand conducts more clandestine missions from behind its physical walls.

Other missions within a system label themselves commercial delegations. While they still conduct all the activities associated with any other mission, including the illegal and covert ones, they maintain a much lower profile and pay far more attention to the laws and culture of their hosts. Of course, this lower profile, and generally lower counterintelligence profile, sometimes serves as a better base of operations than the high-profile embassy.

NOMAD MILITARY FORCE (NMF)

The Nomad Nation's military organisation mirrors their political one. Each of the motherships has its own independent jurisdictional command, with a very small cadre of leaders ready to coordinate larger scale conflicts. These commanders serve amongst the commands, spreading their experience and leadership, when not needed for more dire conflicts.

JURISDICTIONAL COMMAND OF BAKUNIN

Much like the mothership, the *Bakunin* command is the least conventional of the three. While it certainly has just as much capability of self-defence as any other, its forces tend to be very specialised, and embed with other commands as needed, even in relatively peaceful times. Its leaders have the most experience serving with other commands, and do well with coordinated forces, including those combining with other nations.

BLACK HAND: ROGUE INTELLIGENCE

The scope of the Black Hand's remit is broad, flexible, and nearly limitless. The Nomad Nation is acutely aware that they are vastly outnumbered by the hostile nations of the G-5, and they will use any means necessary to even the playing field. That also usually means playing a hard offence on foreign soil, usually leveraging the relative safe havens of the Nomad's commercial missions.

Truth Tellers: Sigrid Kašpar, a VP at Almatech, the primary Cube producer in the Human Sphere, is offering to sell high-level intel regarding the advanced architecture of Cube 2.0 designs. The concern is that this may be a honeypot operation staged by ALEPH. The team needs to infiltrate Kašpar's social circle and find out whether or not her offer is on the level.

Bullet to the Brain: The Libertos terrorist group on Varuna exploded a car bomb which damaged the Nomad commercial mission there. Send a message that the Nomads are not to be drawn into Libertos' squabbles with PanOceania by assassinating Depth Gauge, the Helot mastermind behind the recent bombings.

Defenders of the Web: The team is assigned to bodyguard a technical team covertly installing Arachne nodes in Ad Qaliwara on Bourak (p. 231).

JURISDICTIONAL COMMAND OF CORREGIDOR

With the wide spread of its work crews and mercenary forces, *Corregidor*'s command is the most dispersed, spread throughout the Human Sphere. It integrates its mercenary forces into the organisation when needed, citing the much maligned "Emergency Clause" written into all Nomad mercenary contracts.

JURISDICTIONAL COMMAND OF TUNGUSKA

Given its central mission of ensuring the safety of the Crypt and the mothership, the *Tunguska* command is most concentrated, and also serves as a reserve in wider conflicts. The Dragnet, especially the Special Actions Department, supports the Command in times of need. It provides the ships and equipment for the unified Nomad command in critical situations.

WILDERNESS OF MIRRORS

The Nomad Nation has had to fight for its very existence from the very start, and collecting intelligence has been the only means of ensuring survival. Its commercial corporations operate in highly competitive environs where inside knowledge about competitors is worth a year's profits. On the scientific front, the race to discovery and jealous protection of data is every bit as cutthroat as a military campaign. Nomads excel at the game of smoke and mirrors.

BLACK HAND

One of the Nomad Nation's most secretive organisation is paradoxically one of the most well-known to outside powers. Known, however, does not necessarily equate to "understood". Foreign intelligence organisations use the Black Hand as the boogeyman to convince their governments to grant them more funding, resources, or personnel. They are the nebulous nightmare that trainers use to inspire their agents to greater efforts. They are everything their enemies fear, and far more.

The strength of the Black Hand is minimal organisation, which encourages creativity and decisiveness at the lowest possible level while still maintaining high-level goals. The Intelligence, Tactical, and Quantronic Sections — euphemistically referred to by operatives as the Black Eye, Black Fist, and Black Widow, respectively — are made up of autonomous groups that act with minimal oversight or methodological guidance and, in many cases, are deliberately set in competition with one another to achieve specific assignments.

Groups, in turn, are served by action teams and the occasional lone agent known as a solo. Teams and solos might conduct operations supporting only one section or all three depending on their speciality and circumstance.

INTELLIGENCE SECTION

More than any other section of the Black Hand, the Intelligence Section operates through Darwinian competition between analyst groups like Midnight Sun, Dark Sapphire, and Something Wicked. Data streams are shared between multiple groups working in tandem, with every snippet of information comprehensively tagged with source and usage history to ensure equitable performance assessments.

THE MEXICAN GENERAL

"A Nomad soldier doesn't salute. A Nomad soldier fights."
—Juan Sarmiento, The Mexican General

General Juan Sarmiento received the highest bids during the Red Auction (p. 14). Four revolutionary — some might say terrorist — groups, three governments, and three major criminal organisations wanted him eliminated. Praesidio's Warden investigated Sarmiento and found an asset worth far more than money. Sarmiento was a smuggler, an assassin, a leader, but most importantly, a man with a talent for success in the most difficult situations. Rather than auction him off, the Warden woke him up and put in charge of creating the new mercenary forces of *Corregidor*.

The Warden's foresight proved its worth almost immediately, as Sarmiento foiled a number of attacks, rescue attempts, and sabotage operations aimed at bypassing the auction. He turned the nascent Alguaciles, now *Corregidor*'s military police regiment, into a formidable defencive force and profitable mercenary company. After the formation of the Nomad Nation, he would be instrumental in guiding the Black Hand as its Deputy Director.

TACTICAL SECTION

Tactical Section teams hit hard and fast, and then fade back into the shadows from whence they came. When deception fails and enemies of the Nomad Nation set themselves on a hostile course, direct action may be the only option to prevent disaster. Agents, who are generally recruited from elite units of the NMF and sometimes refer to themselves as "strikers", equip themselves with the newest gear from the Black Labs, but other operatives view those who gravitate to these missions as somewhat psychotic prima donnas.

QUANTRONIC SECTION

The animosity between the Nomad Nation and ALEPH is renowned throughout the Human Sphere, and it's the primary reason the Black Hand requires a dedicated Quantronic Section. Many agents repeatedly request these missions because they truly believe they are fighting the greatest existential threat faced by not only the Nomads, but by humanity as a whole. In addition to defensive and counterintelligence ops, the Quantronic Section is responsible for the heuristically complex and memetically viral anti-ALEPH Black Propaganda campaigns.

VORTEX SPEC-OPS
Vortex teams are agents provocateur specialised in undercover and secret operations and given broad discretionary powers in achieving their objectives by the Tactical Section.

DRAGNET

The most public face of *Tunguska*'s Dragnet Special Actions Department (DSAD) for the rest of the Sphere are the customs inspections when boarding the mothership or one of its primary inter-system tenders. Less fortunate individuals witness their primary mandate to defend *Tunguska* from external threats. Only rarely would people encounter their external investigators, and even if they did, they might never know it, as they tend to operate covertly.

Dragnet has another face that few outside the Nomad Nation ever witness, dealing with internal disruptions quickly and efficiently so they remain internal. *Tunguska*'s reputation as a safe and utterly private haven for data and financial transactions depends on perception, and Dragnet roots out cartel and family schemes before they can make any ripples in that tranquil pool.

Organisationally, the three primary "desks" of the department are Syndicate, Snooper, and Internal Affairs.

SYNDICATE DESK

This investigations section concentrates its efforts on the powerful crime families of *Tunguska*, and sometimes the criminal organisations of the other motherships, such as the *Corregidor*'s *maras* gangs or *Bakunin*'s Svengali. As these organisations have little qualms concerning violence to achieve their

Christian Church – p. 177

Svengali – p. 221

goals, Syndicate investigators tend to work in pairs, watching each other's back during investigations or as an undercover/handler team.

SNOOPER DESK

The focus of these agents is the protection of *Tunguska* and the Crypt, against all enemies, foreign and domestic. Of special concern are deep cover infiltrators and triggered agents, so investigators often have backgrounds in psychology and intuitive analysis, sometimes the only means of uncovering these threats. Unlike other desks, the actions of these agents tend to be more cerebral, preferring to turn threats against their owners if possible.

INTERNAL AFFAIRS

No organisation is without its own shadows, and while they tend to be reviled by others, internal overwatch is critical to the health of any institution. Nikolai Steranko directed that even he must submit to their inquiries, and he makes a point of appointing the best and brightest lights of SVAD to this duty. Agents pursue their duties with cold, ruthless efficiency, as every weakness eliminated makes DSAD that much stronger.

OBSERVANCE OF MERCY

The full name of this now-powerful Nomad religious organisation is The Saint Mary of the Knife – Our Lady of Mercy – Observance. Rejecting the agreements between ALEPH and the Christian Church, they were cast out and founded a new convent which eventually became one of the founding communes of *Bakunin*. Possessed of a deep distrust, some might say outright hatred, of the AI, and armed with the best technology that the Black Labs have to offer, Reverends of the Observance have become experts in combating ALEPH's attempts to violate Nomad data networks.

The Observance has a host of field operatives, Reverend Moiras and Custodiers, roving across the Human Sphere, spreading the faith and its central message that technology must be subservient to humanity and the holy spirit. The Observance has an agreement with the Freetraders Brotherhood, which benefits both parties, to transport its agents to all the systems of the Sphere, giving them overt or covert access to virtually anywhere.

Almost from its inception, the Observance set itself against ALEPH and the dehumanising technology of the Sphere. Unlike so many others that railed against the AI, the Observance armed itself with the skills, weapons, and technology needed to fight. They mastered these new tools while maintaining the primacy of their faith.

CONVENTS

Reverend field operatives reside in convents, including the Moiras, Custodiers, and Charon. Each convent has unique areas of expertise and secret knowledge (referred to as the mysteries of the sisterhood).

CONVENT MOIRAS

Reverend Moiras combine their fierce mission of vengeance with offensive infowar skills, often using both to strike out against ALEPH and other technologically advanced foes. They often work in concert with the Tactical Section of the Black Hand, and other Nomad agents in need of their combined martial-hacking abilities. While Custodiers are the infowar elite of the Observance, Moiras focus on bringing the battle directly to the enemy.

CONVENT CUSTODIERS

Foremost experts in cyber-warfare, Custodiers have skills across the entire spectrum of control nets, transmissions and communication, sensors, reconnaissance, and hacking. They are veteran infowarriors who have faced ALEPH's agents on their own ground and lived to tell the tale. They operate equally well covertly, engaging in data deception and net infiltration. They often work alongside the Quantronic Section of the Black Hand.

CONVENT CHARON

Reverend Healer-Killers, to use their full title, believe in correcting the ills of the Sphere, either in the form of healing their sisters and innocents caught in the crossfire of ALEPH's evil, or in the form of expunging it from the mortal realm with surgical precision. They are a tactical support force for the other convents; essentially assault commandos with medical training and a clinical eye for detecting the evil in the Sphere.

OPERATIVE CONCLAVES

Reverends from one or more convents are organised into operative conclaves. **Eumenid** conclaves ("The Kindly Ones") generally include large numbers of Reverend Custodiers and take charge of *Bakunin* security in terms of cyber-attacks and infothreats. **Fury** conclaves are elite units assigned to the Black Hand and feature a mix of operatives. **Dirae** conclaves operate at the pleasure of the Moderator Corps, and are often dispatched on important and dangerous exterior intervention missions.

DRAGNET: NOMAD ENFORCERS

Dragnet's focus is internal. Members of Dragnet rarely leave *Tunguska*, although a handful of specialised teams do pursue suspects off-ship. (It's not unusual for such teams to coordinate with Black Hand action teams.) Their unusual responsibilities as a security force also often require delicate political sensibilities: although their job is to stop internal conflicts from threatening the security of the Crypt, many of the "criminal" organisations they investigate are ultimately connected to the founders of the mothership.

Bleeding Oubliette: Reliable intelligence suggests that Robert Parris, a VP at one of the *Tunguska* oubliettes, is leaking information to foreign intelligence operatives. His access to sensitive operations creates a dire security risk.

One of Our Own: Marianne Hutmacher, a DSAD internal affairs agent, was gunned down in the *barangays* last night. Tracking down the assassin will only deepen the mystery, however, as it will turn out to have been an illegal bounty created by a smart contract. The corporation which created the smart contract is baffled and the LAI responsible for it has been burned out. Was the contract somehow suborned? Or is its seemingly innocent façade disguising a nefarious shadow contract?

Lockdown!: The DSAD agents are performing a routine security check at one of the Centrum oubliettes when an unconventional cyberattack places the oubliette in lockdown. But wait, it gets worse: someone inside is killing the oubliette's staff one by one.

OBSERVANCE OF MERCY: OUR LADY'S WILL

For generations the Observants have been engaged in a holy war against the depredations of ALEPH. This was their struggle before the Nomad Nation existed and, if necessary, it will remain their struggle after the Nomad Nation is gone. Their inner culture is one of cold competence and rigid feminism; to destroy the enemy is their highest goal. They coordinate with both the NMF and the Black Hand, lending their unique and exceptional expertise in the covert war against the AI devil.

Jungle Attachments: A Corregidoran Intruders squadron has been dispatched to perform "aggressive counterintelligence" against a Combined Army data centre on Paradiso. A conclave including a Reverend Moira is attached to make sure they get the job done right.

Serial Killer in the Machine: A viral LAI agent has been unleashed on *Bakunin*. It "possesses" various pieces of equipment and manipulates it to kill nearby victims. The Reverends need to shut it down and track it back to its point of origin to permanently neutralise the threat.

Both Alike in Dignity: A long-running feud between two rival BouBoutiques is causing violent outbreaks between their *aficionados* (hyper-amped fanboys who participate in BouBoutique-sponsored zeitgeist activities and complicated AR lifestyle games). It is suspected that a covert operation of ALEPH's Special Situations Section may be attempting to exacerbate the conflict in order to disrupt Social Energy, and the Reverends are dispatched to negotiate a truce... or enforce one if that's what it comes to.

G-5 FACTION
PANOCEANIA

PANOCEANIAN OFFICIAL MAYA-SCHOOL NETWORK

The PanOceanian Official Maya-School Network is the obvious answer for a technologically connected society spread across such an enormous territory. With funding sourced from a variety of lobbies and corporate donations, and services subsidised by the PanOceanian Ministry of Culture, the POMS Network is able to provide a vast range of cheap education and training courses to anyone with a comlog and the inclination.

Rather than running a single massive school, the Maya-School Network is a body that recognises, audits, and approves Maya-based education and training providers. The role donations play in the approval and auditing process has at times come into question, but no-one can deny the social value of such cheap access to an immense array of educational programs.

PanAsian Alliance – p. 12

Second Great Space Race – p. 14

EMPRESAS

Sometimes technology is revolutionised in a garage. Sometimes its advance is only made possible through a massive investment of capital and manpower: The Manhattan Project. Apollo 11. The Orbital Elevator Consortium. PanOceania institutionalises these kinds of impossible projects through their *empresas*. These include the Cretan Enterprise (which perfected the Minotaur Motor) and Project: Maid of Orleans (which resulted in the first Recreation).

PanOceania is the Hyperpower. More prosperous and powerful than any other empire in human history, it has total political control of three entire systems — Neoterra, Acontecimento, and Varuna — and holds territory and frontier colonies on Svalarheima, Earth, Paradiso, Dawn, and Human Edge.

The only true rival to PanOceania's dominion over the Human Sphere is Yu Jing, and the tension between the two nations dates back to their earliest days, when the PanAsian Alliance was formed in response to the military and economic expansionism of the new-born Jade Empire. What had originated as a purely defensive political arrangement, however, became something more when Chile and Brazil reached across the Pacific Ocean to join the Alliance. In that union, the modern PanOceania was born, rapidly growing into a hegemonic power in its own right. Within a few decades it had gobbled up chunks of Central and North America while siphoning off portions of the disintegrating European Union.

SPACE ODYSSEY

As the borders of political power solidified on Earth between the Hyperpower and the Jade Empire, both nations accelerated their efforts to colonize space and claim the rich, untapped resources available beyond humanity's mother world. In this Second Great Space Race, PanOceania went for broke by focusing their primary attention on the exploration of the wormholes — a gamble which paid off handsomely as they laid uncontested claim to the worlds of Neoterra, Acontecimento, and Varuna. The resulting advantage in territory and resources continues to pay for further exploration and economic development, ensuring that, despite Yu Jing's efforts to catch up, PanOceania remains the number one power in space.

PanOceania's immense interstellar success, however, is not without its dark side. There are some who describe the Hyperpower as being "addicted to space": exploration and exploitation have become vital to the PanOceanian way of life. In PanOceania everything always needs more. Always bigger, always better. That means more and more land and resources are required, which in turn means finding more planets and star systems to annex, colonise, and mine for resources.

This dependence can even be seen in the decision to abandon Sol in order to establish a new centre of government on Neoterra. This self-same government, as a matter of policy, prioritises the space industry, heavily subsidising it while doing whatever it takes to keep interstellar trade flowing. PanOceanian spaceships are the best you can get, benefitting from PanOceania's extensive experience in dealing with a wide variety of deep-space environments and hazards. PanOceanian scientists are constantly at work to develop the technology used to identify and stabilise wormholes, refining existing designs and searching for new methods.

But while cynics and naysayers, particularly among the Nomads, constantly predict that this addiction, like all addictions, must inevitably burn out and crash the addict, PanOceania continues to soar among the stars. The reality seems to be that a stable Triangle of Prosperity has been established between Neoterra, Acontecimento, and Varuna.

PANOCEANIAN TRUST

Outsiders may only perceive the arrogance of the Hyperpower, but the heart of PanOceanian culture is faith. They place trust in technology. They trust ALEPH with the minutia of their daily lives. They look to the Church for spiritual guidance. They believe in the might and majesty of the Military Complex to keep them safe. They are guided by the vision of the *Destino Tecnológico* and see in its ideology a fundamental truth.

CULTURAL INTEGRATION PROGRAMS

PanOceanian culture has always been a melting pot thanks to the far-flung reach of its pan-global founding nations back on Earth. As the Hyperpower alighted upon foreign worlds, however, this became a matter of state policy: Cultural Integration Programs (CIPs) were founded to unify the totality of PanOceania into a single nation under the banner of patriotism and manifest destiny.

The CIPs did so, however, through a celebration of diversity. They understood that ethnic groups gained strength not through the erection of barriers, but through a sharing of culture. Points of commonality were sought out and used to knit cultures together.

At the same time, they knew that the robust strength of a population comes from its diversity. (A lesson that was driven home when the shallow biodiversity of the native life on Neoterra collapsed in the early days of colonisation.) The CIPs established cultural enclaves as part of the colonial programs, and PanOceanians take it as a mark of pride to support and develop the cultural traditions of their enclave — not simply by looking back into the past, but (particularly as Hiraeth culture fades) by innovating towards the future.

PanOceanians, however, also take it as a point of pride to visit and experience multiple enclaves throughout the course of their lives, bringing this rich panoply of experiences into the gestalt of their personal sense of cultural identity (which is sometimes referred to as one's mélange).

PanOceanians refer to this as *cultura de diamantes* (a culture of diamonds), with each individual seeking to perfect themselves by becoming a multi-faceted part of the collective whole.

TECHNOPHILIA

PanOceanians are utterly enamoured of technology. It fills their environment and pervades their every waking (and sleeping) moment; moments which are lived as much through the quantronic extensions of Maya as in the physical world. They refer to it as their third eye, their seventh sense, and their fifth limb, but it is also their constant and ever-present guardian angel. It empowers them to a superhuman (and some would even argue posthuman) degree, but its loss would leave many PanOceanians confused and helpless. (The dark mirror of technophilia, many cynics would point out, is technodependence.)

Massive infrastructure is entrusted to ALEPH: Energy. Water. Agricultural production. Quantronic networks. Financial services. Elections. Public health. Security services. The AI monitors, analyses, controls, and perfects all of it for maximum efficiency.

At the personal level, the minutia of PanOceanian lives are shuffled away through the silent collaboration between ALEPH and their geists: Daily schedules. Food. Finances. Transportation. Entertainment. Even friendships and romance. Citizens happily turn over their responsibilities and decision-making, leaving behind an air of freedom of self-expression that PanOceania's critics have described as supercilious narcissism (which, they would argue, is also expressed at a macro-level in PanOceania's foreign policy).

The most extreme example of this, and one which even many PanOceanians are quick to judge, are the *surfistas* — those who literally surf through their lives in a seeming daze, having turned every aspect of their lives over to their quantronic managers and existing solely in the "living moment" of raw experience without conscious input.

LIVING CITIES

Wealth and class in PanOceania are expressed through access to technology and access to territory (real estate being the one thing which PanOceania's near-post-scarcity economy cannot produce *en masse*).

Living Cities are the perfect embodiment of both. Designed by ALEPH-assisted architects, they are the ultimate expression of what technology can elevate the human condition to. They are wonderlands filled with automation seamlessly hidden within exquisitely manicured luxury gardens.

THE CHURCH

Although there is a sizable Hindu minority, the legacy of the Ad Astra Pilgrimage and the influence granted by their sizable control of Resurrection licenses have made the Christian Church a preeminent cultural force in PanOceania.

A key factor in the ascension of the Neovatican is its own embrace of the *cultura de diamantes*: As the communication and virtualisation technologies of Maya became prevalent, then Pope Clement XXI promulgated the encyclical *In Mundum Universum* which created a quantronic-assisted communion with Christ which empowered each individual to find their own personal path to God. Geographic and cultural barriers dropped away: Perhaps the communal, art-driven worship of Andean monastics was ideal for you. Or the 13th century simplicity of the Apostolic Brethren. Or the glittering wonders of virtual reality Escher churches. The new vision of the Church welcomed this panoply, and participation exploded as religious communities and practices that had been obscure for centuries now found adherents who had been looking for them all their lives.

HOLY SEE
Following the Ad Astra Pilgrimage, the Neovatican was founded in San Pietro di Neoterra, becoming the seat of the papal throne and the home of the Church.

MILITARY ORDERS
As the Church's importance grew, the Papal Curia looked for ways to extend their influence. Under Pope John XXV, seeking to drive a wedge into the PanOceanian Military Complex, a papal bull was issued calling for the church to found and fund

Hiraeth Culture, p. 15: A post-colonial pan-cultural reflex that draws inspiration from Old Earth history.

Ad Astra Pilgrimage — p. 15

ATEKS
Not everyone gets to participate in the PanOceanian dream. Those with little or no access to ALEPH and modern technology are referred to as Ateks. Although they constitute a vanishingly small percentage of the population, the sheer size of the Hyperpower means that they number in the millions. Without proper access to Maya and the web of countless social, fiscal, and official networks that link most PanOceanians to each other, they have no trackable existence. Without the quantronic resources needed to participate in the pervasive domotics which shape and define PanOceanian life, they are functionally cripples.

Ateks, for their own part, are a motley lot. Some have deliberately chosen this life — counterculture rebels fearful of ALEPH or seeking to "retain their humanity" in an unnatural world. But many are simply those who have fallen through the cracks and found themselves utterly divorced from the glittering complexities of the culture which rushes past them.

Many organisations, however, exist which aim to improve life for the Ateks. The Neoterra Integration Fund, for example, works to provide Ateks with access to technology and opportunities to enter mainstream society.

San Pietro di Neoterra — p. 262

LIST OF DEEDS

The Neovatican Church is the largest of the religious bodies licensed to dispense Resurrections in PanOceania, and they have revived the medieval tradition of indulgences to help manage them: Services to the Church are rewarded with points towards a Resurrection licence. The List of Deeds is regularly updated with a list of these acts: Some are general (donating money or volunteering to participate in the Crusade on Paradiso). Others are very specific, sometimes triggering mercenary competitions to see who can achieve them first. There is also a constant churn of "micro-point deeds" — minor acts of charity and goodwill that benefit one's immediate community. Citizens can load an app onto their comlog to notify them when such opportunities are available nearby.

THE GREAT APOSTASY

The decision to form a pact between the Church and ALEPH caused the faith to be riven by controversy. From sit-ins and hunger strikes to murders and immolations, the crisis point boiled out across the Human Sphere. The Church viewed their work with ALEPH as a great and beneficial alliance; those on the other side of the coin considered it the Great Apostasy and saw it as a Faustian Pact — an agreement between life-most-holy and the unnatural. From this dark period, however, the church has risen again — stronger, more powerful, and more united.

IMMORTAL POPES

Although the Church largely controls the Resurrection system within PanOceania, in one notable respect it is very distant from it: The Pope must step down if and when their original body dies, and one may only obtain the rank of Cardinal after transferring to a Cube. At present three Popes Emeritus dwell on Neoterra in lhost bodies, and a fourth on Earth.

religious Military Orders which — while they would be under the influence of the Department of Defence — would ultimately derive a holy authority from the Church.

When the plan was given provisional approval, the newly-formed Consilium de Militaris used its authority to revive two Military Orders from the millennia-old annals of the Church — the Order of the Temple and the Order of the Hospital. Initially fielded as purely auxiliary forces, the exemplary quality and early successes of the two Orders (whose fierce rivalry fed their accomplishments) have seen not only the number but also the importance of the Military Orders multiply. They are now premiere, front-line combat forces.

ORDER OF THE TEMPLE

The Order of the Temple was founded by the technocratic factions of the Church. Instead of fighting on the physical battlefields, they rapidly excelled at quantronic warfare. These infowar operations were supported by a cutting-edge research laboratory which rapidly gathered the brightest minds in PanOceania, backed them with the vast funds of the Vatican Bank, and focused on developing new quantronic and cyber-warfare systems.

As time passed, more and more of the Templar's efforts became focused in these research labs. A twisted sea of black ops projects pursued revolutionary ideas which pushed the boundaries of ethics and morality. As their ambitions grew, however, their enemies seemed to multiply. This became even more true when, fuelled by the success of the patents they had parleyed from their work, they successfully removed themselves from the authority of the Consilium de Militaris and became an independent agency.

Their ultimate downfall, however, came as a result of their interest in artificial intelligence. Although at one time they worked closely with ALEPH and Bureau Toth, the Order of the Hospital accused

OTHER MILITARY ORDERS

While the Order of the Temple and the Order of the Hospital are the two first, and most famous of the Military Orders, there are others.

Order of Calatrava: A small Military Order made up of veteran knights from other Orders. They are characterised by their ascetic lifestyles and serve as Father-Instructors in the PanOceanian Military academies, or as wanderers throughout the Human Sphere intervening in any fight they consider fair. While lacking in a defined structure, the Order of Calatrava has become known to be critical of the policies of the Curia.

Order of the Holy Sepulchre: An elite Military Order drawn from the best of the other Military Orders. One of their key tasks is to guard the Holy Places of Earth, such as the Free City of Jerusalem and the old Vatican. When they are called upon to enter a battle, they are rightly feared as some of the most devastating soldiers in the Human Sphere.

Order of Montesa: Initiated as a response to the concern of Archbishop Martim Gonçales da Silveira about the growing power of the Order of the Hospital on Acontecimento. Rather than see the planet with the most believers influenced by an outside Order, da Silveira argued Acontecimento should have its own Order. After much wrangling, the Order of Montesa was born. Founded by the training of knights from the Order of Calatrava, the Order of Montesa has fought hard to prove itself against a backdrop of general disapproval. Despite their fraught existence the Order is pious and courageous, emphasising mobility, an ability to support other troops, and a deadly violence when closing with the enemy.

Order of Preachers: More commonly known as the Dominican Order, this order has a sinister reputation, a hang-over from the its early history and involvement in the Inquisition, which they maintain. The Black Friars of the Dominican Order are pious and, some would argue, paranoid about the loyalties and faith of their fellow Orders. Having trialled the Order of the Temple, they have seen how corruption and sin can fester, and with the rise of the EI, Shasvastii infiltrators could be anywhere.

Order of Santiago: The third Military Order to be created by the Neovatican, its role is to protect pilgrims and pilgrimage routes. Working side-by-side with the PanOceanian Navy, as well as Bureau Aegis agents on the Circulars that travel from PanOceanian territory to Earth, they are regarded as the best technically trained of the Military Orders.

Order of the Teutonic Knights: The newest Military Order, operating on the frontiers of the Human Sphere where their mission is to seek out new planets and establish the first footholds of the Church. They were founded within days of Paradiso's discovery, and their headquarters — the Monastery-Fortress of Saint Mary of Strelsau — is built there. The Brothers of Dobrzyń, a wing of the Order, offer defence by fire to any who cross the aerial and land bridges that surround the fortress.

them of developing an illegal AI. Evidence at the ensuing court proceedings showed that the accusations were well-founded. The Order was dissolved and its property confiscated: The data relating to artificial intelligence was absorbed by ALEPH. Their possessions' on Earth were given to the Order of the Holy Sepulchre. Most of their property on Neoterra was given to the Order of the Hospital.

Templars who were found innocent of the charges were allowed to enter other orders or retire to monastic lives. Others, however, including a dozen or so of the Templar programming experts, disappeared before they could be arrested. It is rumoured that a handful of Templars have been sheltered by the Nomad Nation.

ORDER OF THE HOSPITAL

The Hospitallers, currently the greatest and most powerful of all the Military Orders, are primarily based out of the Fortress-Monastery of Saint John of Skovorodino on Svalarheima, but their Grand Master lives in the monastery of San Giovanni di Neoterra (which was once a stronghold of the fallen Templars) and they have another major monastery at Saint John of Malta on Earth.

Their mission primarily focuses on providing medical aid, rescue, and other forms of succour on the battlefield. Field Units are specialised in

rapidly establishing combat support hospitals, and are supported by highly trained Medevac Units. Mercy Units, whose members have earned the title of Mercedarian, are small spec-ops teams who specialise in the rescue of comrades captured by the enemy.

In the wake of the Templar scandals, the PR-friendly mission of the Hospitallers played well to Maya audiences and the Church was quick to play up their successes. As a result, they enjoy a very positive reputation with the public and the troops they serve alongside.

INSTITUTIONS
GOVERNMENT

The term "hyperpower" was originally coined to describe PanOceania's unique form of federal government: The central or "hyper-power" was literally placed over the individual nations, which became "hypo-powers" (under powers) beneath it. This basic relationship remains true today, although a series of reforms — some internal, others imposed from above — have greatly restructured the identity and nature of the hypo-powers until, today, they largely conform to each major planet in the PanOceanian alliance.

TEMPLAR COLLECTORS' ITEMS

The Templars acquired a reputation for designing ingenious and unusual weapons, many of which were field-tested but never brought into production. Today, these rare weapons are collector's items... when they can be found.

HOSPITAL BANK

San Giovanni is home to the main headquarters of the Hospital Bank, one of the most important banks in the Sphere and the only one which can have a slogan like, "Save your money. Save your soul."

THE TEUTONIC SECRET

The nigh-fanatical devotion of the troops associated with the Teutonic Order has given rise to many rumours among the soldiers who fight alongside them on Paradiso. The most believable speak of extraordinarily harsh training regimes. More curious are rumours of strange ceremonies performed by night when they think no one is watching, and some say the Teutons have a secret: custody of some powerful artefact of unknown origin.

ORDER OF ST. LAZARUS

This wing of the Hosptallers, operating under the historical name of a small Order that incorporated into the Order of the Hospital, is responsible for establishing and running field and emergency hospitals in crusade territories (which, at the moment, means Paradiso). The Order of St. Lazarus consists mainly of Chaplain-Doctors, experts in triage and emergency medical support, who are brave and pious enough to place themselves in the most serious of dangers to save the lives of others.

CONFRÈRE KNIGHTS

Confrère Knights is the name given to any mission, joint unit, or combat formation in which knights from multiple orders participate side-by-side. Such arrangements are not unusual in Paradiso combat groups, but small task forces — referred to as confraternities — are often permanently formed to pursue various tasks with a balanced mixture of skills.

SWISS GUARD

The Holy See has a special arrangement with the PanOceanian Military Complex, which allows it to maintain its own military grade security force, otherwise known as the Swiss Guard. Each member of the Swiss Guard is both a devout member of the Church, and a soldier who has survived countless engagements. The Swiss Guard are rightly feared as elite. The exchange for allowing the Holy See to maintain this unprecedented force, is that they must respond to the call of the Military. This suits the Church perfectly, as it ensures that its own security service is battle tested and hardened unlike any other in the Sphere.

FIVE THINGS YOU SHOULD KNOW ABOUT PANOCEANIANS

1. Always Connected: If a PanOceanian seems like they aren't listening to you, it's probably because they aren't. They're plugged into the Maya network in all kinds of ways, from visible pigmentation readouts in their forearms to direct retinal projection, neural implants to record dreams, haptic feedback from medical monitors, and more. They're constantly receiving updates, alerts, news and messages from all over the Sphere. So it's understandable if they get a little distracted sometimes.

2. Pension Plan: Most of the PanOceanians save money for their retirement, a moment when they have to choose between body and soul. They can save money to ensure beneficial conditions in the Cube Bank thinking of a possible Resurrection. Or they can save money for a good retirement in the best recreational areas of their planet (such as Portobelo in Acontecimento). The golden dream of all PanOceanians, however, is a good retirement on the paradisiac islands of Varuna.

3. Evercasting: PanOceanians are constantly sharing their lives over Maya with friends and even just the public at large. To outsiders from more conservative cultures, this can seem distasteful or even obscene, but being on constant public display is simply part of PanOceanian life.

4. Reputation: It's not a reputation economy — money still counts for plenty — but the integrated connectivity of PanOceania means that everyone builds up a publicly traceable record of trustworthiness and ability. A good reputation precedes you. A bad one will cling to you. Public relations disasters can topple conglomerates and end careers.

5. Forgiveness: The ultimate expression of trust, however, is forgiveness. Outsiders are sometimes awed at the PanOceanian willingness to turn the page. This even extends to society as a whole, with rehabilitated criminals and disgraced politicians often being welcomed back into the fold after an appropriate show of reform.

LOBBIES

In the early years of the 22nd century, the infamous Canberra Case revealed a cascading array of corruptive scandals involving political actors across all levels and political parties of PanOceania. Political parties were completely discredited and a surge of popular discontent threatened to tear the nascent nation apart.

The Lobby Revolution — which sought to solve the problem by dethroning and banning political parties — was initially proposed by a coalition of powerful hypercorps. Their goal was to use the crisis to gain even more political influence through their lobbies. Progressive elements, however, managed to subvert the lobby system as it was being created: Lobbies were prohibited from ever having their power concentrated in the hands of a single corporation, business, or family. In fact, citizens were given direct access to the authority of each lobby they belonged to, turning them into an institutionalized form of grassroots democracy. Vermoots (literally VR-moots) are periodically organised in virtual spaces in which even minor members can have their voices heard by the entire lobby by rising through a multi-layered quantronic caucus.

MINISTRIES

The vermoots decide both policy positions for the lobby (which, in some cases, can become binding) and also nominate individuals to serve as ministers or sub-ministers. The nominees are then elected by the general public, who vote for each office individually. (Most lobbies are specialised and often only seek positions in a single ministry.)

The interface between the quantronic vermoots and compartmentalized ministries create a collective management of the State and gives PanOceanians an unprecedented control over their government.

PRIME MINISTERS

The population of each planet elects a Prime Minister from a slate of candidates determined by the lobby primary (in which each lobby wields political power based on the success they enjoyed in the local ministry elections in a system structurally weighted to encourage lobby specialisation). The Prime Minister oversees the local ministries, but the power of these ministries are federated. So, for example, the Ministry of Neoterran Culture actually responds as much to the national Ministry of Culture as it does to the Prime Minister of Neoterra.

PRESIDENT AND CABINET

The President of PanOceania is elected from among the Prime Ministers of all the planets. Presidents make cabinet appointments which must be confirmed through special secretarial vermoots in their personal lobby (although any given President's cabinet is usually made up of candidates from multiple lobbies in order to form political alliances within the ministries). It's customary for the Secretaries to have overlapping portfolios which require them to coordinate with multiple ministries in order to fulfil their bureaucratic duties. (And, conversely, each Minister usually reports to multiple Secretaries.)

PANOCEANIAN MILITARY COMPLEX

PanOceania is a huge and expanding empire. In order to secure and defend its sprawling territory, the PanOceanian Military Complex must be capable of waging war on multiple fronts while coordinating the actions of independent forces capable of functioning indefinitely without support.

THE HEXAHEDRON

The PMC operates from a core doctrine of, "Intelligence First." Referred to as the Triple Entendre, this is a *realpolitik* philosophy in which smart military decisions are made directly by the intelligence apparatus on the basis of reliable information.

Following the failure of the Manaheim Commercial Negotiations in 11 NC — which revealed that Yu Jing had begun a full-blown offensive against PanOceania's industrial and commercial interests — President Tavares ordered the creation of a new intelligence service that could deal with the threat and authorised the Resurrection of Col. Jane Dunbar to lead it. Dunbar fell upon the intelligence services with the subtlety of a nuclear device, using her presidential authorisation to seize control of and unify the intelligence and military communities. Her team, which came to be known as the Hexahedron's Gunmen, envisioned a new era of "covert total war" and they transformed PanOceania to fight it.

This unusual organisational structure, in which military intelligence forms the High Command instead of answering to it, has proven inordinately successful. And today the Hexahedron — the imposing, six-sided structure in San Pietro, Neoterra — has become synonymous with the Ministry of Defence, the PanOceanian High Command, and PanOceanian Military Intelligence, all of which keep their headquarters there, with little or no distinction drawn between them.

Inner Hexahedron: At the core of this huge building is another hexagonal structure. The Inner Hexahedron is both physically and metaphorically concealed within the protective hive of the complex which surrounds it. It is home to the PanOceanian Intelligence High Command, which authorises the blackest of black ops and handles the most classified information in the Human Sphere.

President Tavares — Member of the Prosperidade lobby. Elected in 7 NC on a platform of economic prosperity and free trade.

DUNBAR DEFENCE DOCTRINE

Jane Dunbar instituted the Triple-D which is often seen as the companion of the Triple Entendre and continues to guide PanOceanian foreign policy today.

Intelligence: PanOceania will have faster, better, and more exhaustive information than anyone else in the Sphere.

Counterespionage: PanOceania will not let that information slip through the cracks and reach enemy hands.

Intervention: In order to protect its interests and defend itself from adversaries, PanOceania will act in a way that is decisive, secret, and, above all, deniable.

THE HEXAHEDRON'S MIND

The Hexahedron is the Intelligent Building. It is the physical body of the most powerful lesser-AI in the Human Sphere. This quantronic mastermind — second only to ALEPH — is completely integrated into every facet of the Hexahedron's operations, as invisible and necessary as a nervous system.

ATEKS OUT!

The argument can be made that Ateks — lacking essential quantronic support — are literally hazards to the "civilized" world and should be banned from leaving the slums which cling to the outer edges of most PanOceanian cites. Rallying around the slogan "Ateks Out!", small groups all over the Human Sphere target this "dangerous" and "subversive" subculture. Ateks Out! activities range from pushing legislation requiring certain bio-implants for access to core city areas, to clearing Atek slums and deporting the residents somewhere out of sight — off the planet if possible. There are widespread rumours that vigilante gangs stalk the streets closest to Atek encampments on Acontecimento to "keep the streets clean". This idea is gaining popularity among anti-Atek groups on other planets too.

Nirvana, p. 275: Moon of Paradiso.

PARADISO CONTROL FORCE

The Paradiso Control Force, which was once the fifth planetary army, was greatly reduced in size following the NeoColonial War and effectively wiped out during the First Paradiso Offensive. During their final days, however, the PCF successfully slowed the Combined Army advance enough for the rest of the Human Sphere to rally.

PLANETARY ARMIES

The PMC is primarily divided into four planetary armies, each a fully functional force capable of independently securing its home system. When external operations or campaigns are required — whether in Human Edge, Ariadna, Paradiso, or elsewhere — the High Command will deploy a special Expeditionary Force made up of regiments and units from different planetary armies.

Earth Bastion Army: The Earth Bastion Army has the complicated mission of both protecting PanOceania's interests on humanity's fractured homeworld as well as securing their various colonies, settlements, and orbitals throughout the Sol system.

Neoterra Capitaline Army: The army of the capital world is the strongest and most advanced in the PMC. In fact, it can be argued that — discounting the combined might of the other planetary armies — the NCA is the strongest military force in the entire Human Sphere. The backbone of the force is the Neoterra Bolts regiment, a flexible and highly experienced formation. Due to the planet's close integration with AI technology, the Capitaline Army — particularly the Auxilia — works closely with ALEPH's Special Situations Section on top of its standard military assignments.

Shock Army of Acontecimento: An assault force known for its exceptional list of battle honours during the NeoColonial Wars on Acontecimento and Paradiso, the Shock Army wades into the very heart of battle and metes out ultra-violence with extreme prejudice. Notable units include the Acontecimento Regulars, who participated in the evacuation of Silvania during the Second Paradiso Offensive and remain active on that planet, and the Bagh-Mari Unit, which specialises in search and destroy missions.

Svalarheima Winter Force: A relatively small but hardened force of elite units, the Svalarheima Winter Force specialises in rapid response under extreme conditions. The units, most famous of which are the Nisses and the Sixth Svalarheima Fusiliers, have been toughened by years of conflict and the harsh environments in which they operate. Supported and strengthened by the Order of the Hospital, the Svalarheima Winter Force is capable of meeting out devastating and quick responses to their enemies, and melting away into the tundras and ice once more.

Varuna Quick Reaction Army: The Varuna Quick Reaction Army was formed to secure and protect assets on Varuna after a rise in clandestine attacks by Helot 'Libertos'. Specialising in discreet and covert operations, performed silently and swiftly, and with deadly force, they have proved a valuable addition to the PanOceanian Military Complex. The most famous units in the Quick Reaction Army are the Cutters and Kamaus, a product of the 'Blue Sea' anti-terrorism project.

PARADISO COMBAT GROUPS

Following the destruction of the Paradiso Control Force the PanOceanian Military Complex felt that the old structure of planetary forces was too inflexible given the volatile situation on Paradiso. Wanting to create a force that would allow them to use the troops required of a situation from across their forces, they created the four Paradiso Combat Groups.

The Black-C Combat Group: The smallest of the Paradiso Combat Groups, the Black-C Combat Group makes up for the difference in size through fanaticism and ferocity. Stationed on the Norstralia Northern Front, Black-C is made up primarily of forces from the Teutonic Order, with support from units drawn from the other Military Orders.

The Green-A Combat Group: Mainly constructed of units from the Acontecimento Shock Army, the Green-A Combat Group is stationed on the North-Centre Front. Green-A is the most well supported of the Combat Groups due to its high levels of responsibility, and its forces are supplemented by the Military Orders. The North-Centre Front is home to the most populous cities of East Syldavia, and is the location of the city Strackentz, where the command centre for all PanOceanian forces in Norstralia is positioned.

The Red-K Combat Group: Positioned on the Septentria Front, the Red-K Combat Group is the most powerful of the Combat Groups. Formed pre-dominantly of forces from the Neoterran Capitaline Army, with tactical support from specific units from the Acontecimento Shock Army, the Red-K Combat Group is characterised by its use of sophisticated weapons systems and elite troops.

The Blue-S Combat Group: The Blue-S Combat Group is divided across the system to protect and blockade crucial strategic locations on the ground and in orbit. Regarded as the most elite of the Combat Groups, it works in support of the PanOceanian Armada, with a particular focus on key points such as Nirvana (a key research facility and orbital ship yard), and Acheron. The Blue-S Combat Group is made up mostly of forces from the Order of Santiago, supported by units from the Neoterran Capitaline Army.

HEXAS: BEYOND BORDERS

Hexas is focused on external intelligence and counterespionage. They are licensed to kill and often do. Their activities include paramilitary operations, sabotage, training rebel troops, abduction of high-value targets, interrogations and targeted assassinations. The agency is not supposed to investigate PanOceanian citizens but anyone who has even the slightest ties to people or groups outside PanOceania has, over the years, become fair game.

All the Critics Love You in Skara Brae: A concert tour of Dawn by pop sensation Malukeenyo provides the perfect cover for a Hexa team to surveil a Caledonian Teseum baron and bring him over to PanOceania's side by fair means or foul — his teenage daughter is going to every gig. But when they arrive planetside it seems clear that Ariadnan authorities have been tipped off. What now?

A Body in the Fountain: Agent 15447 is missing. She'd been pursuing a senior Yu Jing official, working her way into his household and accompanying him on a trip to a health resort on Bourak. A Hexa team is sent to find her and bring her home, quietly. But the situation gets murkier when a Silk merchant's wife is found murdered at the resort and all the evidence points to Agent 15447's guilt.

Cubism: A brash Neoterran executive has been collecting art for the company boardrooms. Unbeknownst to the executive, the beautiful sculpture he's currently trying to secure conceals the recovered Cube of a vital undercover Hexa agent killed on a mission. The artwork is a cover, but with 'buyers' from other nations taking an unprecedented interest in the art, how will things pan out?

PANOCEANIAN ARMADA

The doctrine of the PanOceanian Armada is one in which the domination, exploration, and exploitation of space are seen as all being facets of one unified goal: The distinction between military, scientific, and trade fleets is seen as a fluid one, with each ultimately serving the larger ideal of the *Destino Tecnológico* and PanOceania's manifest destiny to push mankind out amongst the stars.

SPACE EXPLORATION DIVISION

The PanOceanian Space Exploration Division is the most well-funded and able extrasolar exploration agency in the Human Sphere. With more ships capable of utilising wormhole technology than any other, PanOceania is able to reach out to the stars like no other nation in the Sphere. In addition to the constant exploration, cataloguing, and scientific investigation of the systems already known, PanOceania also funds more than a dozen ongoing Navegador missions — long-range wormhole-jumpers constantly expanding the map of the wormhole network and searching for new inhabitable planets.

PANOCEANIAN NAVY

The PanOceanian Navy is divided into Attack Fleets and Defence Fleets. Attack Fleets are named after mythological creatures (like the Attack Fleet Amphisbaena which was ambushed during the First NeoColonial War in Human Edge). Defence Fleets are named after Christian and Hindu saints.

WILDERNESS OF MIRRORS

HEXAS

The foreign intelligence arm of the PMC is the Strategic Security Division, better known as the Hexas. Its agents operate throughout the Sphere with the aim of maintaining the status quo. They do so by infiltrating and subverting any organisation or movement that threatens PanOceania's position at the top of the heap.

In all official documents, Hexa agents are identified solely by a unique number. (For example, Hexa Operative 04093.) Some Hexa take this to heart, wiping out all traces of their former identities and living solely as the numerical interface of a thousand cover indentities. Regardless of their zeal, however, the identity of every Hexa agent is considered a state secret of the utmost classification.

Among themselves, the Hexas have given themselves the informal motto *Ultra Vires*, which means "Beyond the Bounds of Authority." For them, when the end is the good of PanOceania, it justifies any means. Hexa agents and missions generally come in three flavours: Investigators, Asset Handlers, and Data Interception. Asset handlers recruit and operate agents in target organisations. The paramilitary wing is Hexa's special forces, performing missions of infiltration, sabotage and assassination — they're the ones who go in and kick down doors.

BRIDGE OF A PANOCEANIAN SHIP

There is no wheel, no controls. The command bridge in a PanOceanian ship is an intelligent room whose floor, walls, and ceiling all have processing and link capabilities despite being completely smooth. The room you will find is completely bare, save for a few moving seats. No consoles, no screens flashing streams of data; all is projected via the navigators' comlogs into their retinal devices. Without the clearance identification codes and the authorised link protocols, you can't get any kind of access. You will need a hacker, and a good one, just to be able to turn on the air conditioning.

First NeoColonial War – p. 22

INDIGO: IN THE DARK

Indigo agents are hand-picked from elite military units and the Hexas. They are the agents who operate beyond borders, even within their own nation. They have no identity but that which they are assigned for each mission. Indigo Spec-Ops agents are the people who get their hands dirty so the nation doesn't need to.

In Tune: A Maya starlet, a singer and performer of acclaim from Yutang, has been soaring in popularity lately, diminishing the widespread view of Yu Jing as an oppressive and corrupt regime. If a key broadcast performance from the Human Edge could be made to look as if it were censored by the Imperial seat, much could be made of it in the local news.

All's Fair in Love and War: The mistress of a general attached to Red-K Combat Group on Paradiso has been kidnapped. Far too embarrassing to be handled by the proper channels, and serious enough as a result of the information she has been party to, the job falls to Indigo Spec-Ops.

Tilting at Windmills: A knight of the Order of Calatrava has been rumoured to be wandering the Human Edge preaching of the corruption of the Curia, and has claimed to have evidence to support it. Either the knight or his evidence must be secured.

INDIGO SPEC-OPS

Whenever the PanOceanian Military Complex requires a special operation (as defined under the PanOceanian Military Engagement Protocols and the Concilium Convention), that mission must be authorised by the PanOceanian Special Operations Command (POSOC), which will also determine which spec-ops assets are best suited to carry out the mission. POSOC is also responsible for equipment standardisation, mission planning, and the conducting of training exercises for spec-ops forces.

In addition to the individual special forces coordinated by them, POSOC also maintains an elite, independent special forces unit known only as Indigo.

Blue is the colour of PanOceania: It appears on modern strategic maps. It's the hue of their uniforms. It's the colour of Freedom and Democracy. But when PanOceania needs to work in the shadows, that's when they call on Indigo.

Highly trained and skilled, Indigo Spec-Ops has the motto, *"Ad Utrumque"* (Ready for Everything). And to further PanOceanian interests they are willing to do anything.

BLUE CLASSIFICATION

Indigo missions receive a Hexahedron-approved code word (referred to as Blue Classification) based on the mission type. Myriad code words have been used, but the major classifications include:

- **Crossbones (Asassination)**: The targeting of a specific individual or group of individuals for lethal elimination.
- **Figaro (Asset Seizure)**: The capture or recovery of information, resources, weapons, or individuals.
- **Attila (Asset Destruction)**: The destruction of enemy information, resources, weapons, infrastructure, or other materiel.
- **Peregrine (Special Reconnaissance)**: Covert observation, usually carried out behind enemy lines, including the direction of air and missile strikes, placement of remote sensors, and preparation activities for subsequent operations.
- **Magus (Psychological Operations)**: Dissemination of propaganda, emotional control, and population management.
- **Diabolo (Covert Advising)**: Clandestine support to dissident and criminal forces in foreign nations.

In addition, POSOC uses the code word Majorelle to refer to operations undertaken on the homefront (i.e., territory on PanOceania's three primary colonial worlds or the home nations on Earth). These operations are subject to special regulations, and there is a general recognition that they require a greater degree of care, secrecy, and precision. Other code words are used to classify operations based on where they are being carried out in order to avoid the use of foreign words:

- **Ariadna**: Powder
- **Haqqislam**: Persian
- **Nomads**: Tiffany
- **Yu Jing**: Celeste
- **Combined Army**: Alice
- **Tohaa**: Zaffre

For example, Project Solar Sea was a series of Celeste Diabolo operations supporting the activities of Yuan Yuan pirates in Yu Jing space. Similarly, an Indigo operative might refer to the assassination of a Silk Lord's chief of security as a Persian Crossbones. On Paradiso, an "Alice Magus" has become slang for an operation too crazy to succeed (with Alice magi being those crazy enough to do them) as a result of the early futility of psyops carried out against the enigmatical aliens of the Combined Army.

Yuan Yuan pirates — p. 208

Silk Lords — p. 162

G-5 FACTION
YU JING

When there was only Earth and the world was turning to chaos, China was seen by many as the role model for social and political stability. When the rest of the world saw the expansion into space as salvation, the Chinese turned to their Eastern neighbours and sought to consolidate and unify. This new supernation then turned to the stars, bringing with it a sense of purpose, complexity, and vision that drove them to conflict and victory. Never before have the Asian people been as united as they are now, and with that has come great prosperity and technological marvels that rival anything that the descendants of the West can produce. The East is no longer represented by China; now there is no East. There is only Yu Jing.

Yu Jing stands at the brink of greatness, having established itself through rapid expansion, aggressive use of influence and force, and subtle control of the Human Sphere. They are an economic powerhouse with the strength of an entire hemisphere under their control before leaving Sol behind them. Yu Jing is a modern giant that has fused the spiritual teachings of its people with the martial force of endless legions of warriors clad in power armour and wielding advanced, deadly weaponry. These warriors, whose loyalty is dedicated to the Party and to the Emperor, have proven their worth in battle time and time again. Determined to make their own destiny on Sol and in the stars, they reach out into the galaxy and take what is theirs by divine right.

THE UNITED EAST

While the Western nations of Earth turned to the stars in search of salvation from the wreckage of the economic collapse of the 21st century, the forefathers of Yu Jing set their focus to consolidation and reconstruction on Earth. The Party decided that in order to survive they would need to embrace their past while re-forging a national entity that all subjugate nations could accept. The Party turned to the great revolutionary Mao, and, borrowing from the Little Red Book, they embarked on another "permanent revolution", popularly referred to as the Second Cultural Revolution. Synthesizing two seemingly antithetical components — those of an absolute monarchy and the Communist Party — they created a novel system that would serve to counterbalance itself. The architects of this plan understood that a symbol was needed to inspire greatness, portray superiority, and serve as a source of unification and adoration of the people, all while remaining under the control of the Party. The symbol that they settled upon was the Dragon Emperor.

To nominate an Emperor, the Ministry of State Security used meticulously kept family records to identify the true heir of the Last Emperor. They found two: The Ming Dynasty had been the last to rule in China, but they were seen by many as outsiders who had illegitimately seized the throne from the Qing. The Party came to the conclusion that whichever family they chose would be imperfect. Instead, both families were granted a rotating stewardship of the Imperial Throne: The Qing would reign first, but when the Emperor died their throne would pass to the Ming, and upon this Emperor's death the throne would return to the Qing. The two dynasties would constantly vie with each other for power within the Imperial Service, allowing the Party to quickly rally their nation behind a strong Emperor, whose power would be kept in check by their systemic rivals.

The Party's sphere of influence continued to grow and change as it adopted more nations under its banner. Acknowledging the need to designate its geographical identity as well as its cultural and political identity, the Party renamed the entire region it occupied on Earth as Yu Jing. While this creation of a new geopolitical designation was met with some resistance (that was subsequently put down), the unification resulted in the desired effect: the people of Yu Jing began to rally under this common title, and the rest of humanity had to view it as the powerful entity it had become.

ONE CELESTIAL HEAVEN UNDER THE EMPEROR

Yu Jing did not pursue the rush into space as the rest of humanity did. Following the failure of Project DAWN, the Party turned to internal economic consolidation. Reinventing an entire national identity had been tricky, but it proved trivial compared to the lengthy, expensive, and cumbersome process of integrating and standardising the nation's disparate manufacturing infrastructure. But when the work was done, the newfound "dragon of industry" proved a voracious beast. To keep it fed, Yu Jing turned to mining and refining the raw materials of the inner solar system, particularly Mars and the asteroid belt.

It is only by the perfection of the self that you can truly contribute to the well-being of the State. Know, then, that by perfecting your body, your mind, your spirit, your craft, your trade, do you indeed lend yourself to the true perfection of the State. Resurrection is reserved for those who understand this and pursue it; those who strive for less than this perfection will never know this greatest gift that Yu Jing can grant to those who serve as Imperial Agents.

—Commencement speech for the Celebration of Blossoms, given by Zhū Hòuzì, the 3rd Emperor of Yu Jing

CONSTITUENT NATIONS AND PEOPLES OF YU JING
The consolidation of the Eastern Hemisphere included many nations. These included China, Japan, North and South Korea, Mongolia, Myanmar, Thailand, Laos, Vietnam, Nepal, Bhutan, Tibet, Cambodia, and Taiwan. Indigenous groups were also included in this accumulation of national and ethnic identities including the Hmong, Aslian, Khmer, Palaung, and Uyghur peoples.

CHUNG KUO
The region of Earth that Yu Jing controls today is known as Chung Kuo. This title was not formally adopted until the discovery and subsequent settlement of Yutang and Shentang.

A PARTY DIVIDED

The formation and implementation of The Greatest Leap caused significant disruption within the Party. The New Wave formed around notions of integration and assimilation, suggesting that the settlement of Shentang and Yutang would serve as a springboard past cultural identity and into a new, efficient socioeconomic model that would dominate the Human Sphere.

The Old Guard sought to maintain old ethnic hierarchies and oligarchies, and resisted the notion of such a massive transformation. They did not believe Yu Jing should stray far from the Maoist principles that had originally formed China, and are highly critical of the Imperial System (believing it has led to decadence and debauchery).

This conflict within the Party is a source of constant intrigue as both sides vie for power through back alley dealings, economic manipulations, blackmail, and even assassinations.

THE IMPERIAL COURT

The Imperial Court is the title given to the numerous advisors and courtiers that surround the Emperor with the intent to "inform" him on matters that they have expertise on. This nest of vipers is comprised of relatives, sycophants, would-be enemies, foreign allies, spies, and other assorted vampires. When convening the Imperial Court, one can expect elaborate displays of decorum, kneeling, humility, and other frippery that makes up the Emperor's day.

When PanOceania discovered Neoterra, Yu Jing was poorly positioned to respond to the new paradigm of extrasolar colonies. Their mastery of the inner system now looked more like a trap. But the dragon's head was turned: Yu Jing's well-integrated, centrally controlled manufacturing base was redirected into overhauling its space program.

The discovery of Shentang and Yutang were a boon to the Yu Jing, who immediately sought to expand into the star system. Both planets were colonised, with Shentang becoming the industrial capital and Yutang becoming the economic capital and, perhaps more importantly, the home to the Dragon Emperor. The Party was aware that its people were already taxed by the considerable changes that had taken place over several short decades, and sought to create a plan that would preserve the identity of its citizens during the colonisation of the new system. This program, named The Greatest Leap, would serve as one of the most ambitious social engineering programs undertaken by any nation to date.

The plan was a simplistic one: by controlling who was allowed to immigrate into what regions on both planets, the Party ensured that those of Chinese descent were primarily allowed to settle Yutang, regionally settling along family lines. Likewise, the Party assigned various regions on Shentang to the other ethnic constituents of the Empire. Though each were allowed to maintain their language and customs, they were motivated to learn and adapt to life on both planets. Through cooperation and coercion at the hands of the Party, the disparate groups came together to settle these planets and create a common language, Yujingyu (or Yu Jingese).

YU JING DUALITY

The existence of Yu Jing, its people, and its collective experience can be best expressed as a culture of duality. The facile analysis is that Yu Jing is a reflection of Yin and Yang, but Yu Jing culture is better seen as a constant attempt to synthesize a number of different dialectics. These dialectics can be seen in the attempts to exist in a culture that values the collective as well as the individual, the aesthetics of the past along with the drive for modernisation, the values and identities of cultural heritage with the unified identity of Yu Jing, and a peaceful existence in a time of war.

INDIVIDUALITY VS. THE COLLECTIVE

The duality of the individual and collective is best demonstrated by the coexistence of the Party and the Emperor. The Party is a secretive collective that exists to shape the future of the Empire through careful social engineering and manipulation of both internal and external forces. Their use of social controls demands that the citizenry view

FIVE THINGS TO KNOW ABOUT YU JINGESE

1. Private Passion: The general stereotype about the Yu Jingese is that they are passive, docile people. But look to any Yu Jingese in the practice of their trade and you will see passion. They will labour for months to perfect the scrollwork on a Teseum-edged katana. Or exhaust every analysis to optimise the planting of a field for maximum crop output. Or spend weeks carefully preparing the ingredients for a sensuous meal.

2. Loyalty to Family: The Yu Jingese fastidiously study and maintain their family lines, keep in contact with even the most distant relatives, and are profoundly loyal to their family, much to the frustration of the Party. This, too, explains their loyalty to the Emperor, who ultimately derives his legitimacy from the family line, with all other families seen in relation to the Emperor's own.

3. The Body is the Mind: You will rarely find a Yu Jingese complaining of being anxious, depressed, or even angry. Instead, complaints often come in reference to the body, with symptoms such

as dizziness, nausea, insomnia, pain and fainting being common.

4. Crime and Community: In Yu Jing, Triads and their cultural equivalents are more than just gangsters looking to make money off the vices of their fellow man. They provide protection to the community, support when disaster strikes, and political influence that can't be had through legitimate channels. Where organised crime in other factions might operate clandestinely, Triads take minimal effort towards this end and instead operate obvious community fronts to increase their visibility and support efforts.

5. Manifest Destiny: The Yu Jingese operate with a collective understanding that they are the supreme inheritors of the Human Sphere and the Universe itself. Furthermore, they understand that this glorious destiny is one which they will achieve together. They subsume themselves into their national identity because it is through its collective action that humanity will be saved and ascend to its rightful place.

themselves as a part of the whole, and that the whole requires their obedience and sacrifice to function. On the other hand, the Emperor is a beacon of individual power, knowledge, and authority. He represents the perfection of the individual, having undergone rigorous schooling and training to hold the office. The Emperor wields his power similarly through his Imperial Agents, single individuals with tremendous capabilities and power that investigate and prosecute his enemies relentlessly.

While the average Yu Jing citizen may not be cognizant of this dialectic, they live within it every day. Inside their communities, citizens are expected to coexist and support one another and to live their lives for the betterment of the people. Ambition, individual undertakings, and one-upsmanship are frowned upon, as they create a fractious microculture that can harm the overall productivity of the community. At the same time, the Yu Jingese are told that perfection of the self is the ultimate goal. The Yujingese strive to be the best at what they do as individuals. Managing the conflict created by this individual perfectionism in contrast with collective cooperation is the daily challenge that the Yu Jing citizen faces.

ANCESTRAL VS. MODERNITY

To further complicate things, there exists another dual culture for the Yu Jingese citizen, and that is ancestral culture coexisting with modern culture. As a direct result of the Party's social programs including the Greatest Leap, most Yu Jingese are born, raised, and live within the culture of their genetic ancestry. As a result, each citizen is likely to learn the language of their ancestors, the rites and religions of their parents, and the history of their ethnic group. The Party is well aware of the history of conflict between various ethnicities, and through educational and cultural programs walks a delicate balance between downplaying the more atrocious nature of the conflicts and using them to motivate its citizenry.

This creates an inherent dissonance with political and meta-cultural pressures to conform to a general standard of Yu Jingese solidarity and cooperation. From the moment of birth citizens of Yu Jing are bombarded with messages of necessity and demand for collaboration. The strength of the Empire rests on the ability of its people to work together harmoniously. For most, this balance between plurality and cultural homogeneity is balanced through healthy competition with incentivized cooperation for the state. This being the case, it is not unheard of for competition to turn into outright conflict between groups.

The dialectic of the old and the new carries forward into daily lifestyle for the people of Yu Jing in a number of ways. In most Yu Jingese cities you will see architecture reminiscent of ancient stylings and days gone by. Underneath the façade of simple antiquity lies a complex and functional technological infrastructure that betrays the austere appearance of most Yu Jingese structures. Despite the backwards appearance most places have, Yu Jing is one of the most technologically connected factions. This interweaving is also present in the modernised teachings of ancient spiritual philosophies, with Taoism, Buddhism, and Confucian

TATENOKAI AND KEMPEITAI

Though the Party would have everyone believe that Asia's cultures were brought together in peace and happiness, the Tatenokai disagree. Meaning "Shield Society", the Tatenokai is made up of Japanese citizens who protest Yu Jing rule and wish to distance the Japanese from Yu Jing. Beginning as a protest group, they have since turned to violence and terrorism, bombing rail stations and power grids to sabotage their controllers.

The Tatenokai are not the only dissident faction of the Japanese actively working against Party interests. The Kempeitai is a covert group that deploys agents to undermine the military architecture and build up the Japanese Sectorial Army to act in open rebellion against Yu Jing. These infiltrators differ significantly from the Tatenokai in that they pursue only military targets, and scorn the Tatenokai for their indiscriminate behaviour.

CORVUS BELLI
INFINITY

RESURRECTIONS

The Party offers many incentives to those who are loyal to the Party and contribute to the good of the StateEmpire, but none is more powerful than that of Resurrection. With the guidance of ALEPH and the careful selection of the Resurrection Committee (part of the Ministry of Ancestral Fidelity), a small number of citizens are chosen each year for the gift of Resurrection. The Ceremony of Resurrection is held on one of the few national holidays, with billions watching remotely.

Ostensibly, the selections represent individuals from all walks of life and ethnicities who serve as exemplars of good citizenry which others in the StateEmpire should emulate. In reality, those selected are frequently either agents of the Party or have procured the Resurrection through some bargain or deal.

REGIONAL DISPERSION PROGRAM

As part of the Greatest Leap, Yu Jing established a number of regional armies. (The most infamous of which was the Nipponese Army.) These autonomous or semi-autonomous forces were made up entirely of distinct ethnic groups, allowing local populations to interact with StateEmpire forces of the same ethnicity. Each of these armies are allowed to operate within the cultural norms of their political region. They wear distinctive uniforms, use their cultural language in independent operations, and are allowed to follow historical themes in their martial training.

thought all intermingling to provide a background for the modern Yu Jing citizen to interpret their life.

WAR VS. PEACE

Yu Jing has been at war, in one way or another, for more than a generation now. While the NeoColonial Wars have been at an end for almost a decade, there have been small scale covert actions occurring ever since, and the arrival of the Combined Army has brought Yu Jing fully into war again. Despite this, the Party's overwhelming efforts to subdue its populace has led to an expectation of personal restraint and Zen-like peacefulness. A cultural paradox ensues, then, as the realities of war are used to motivate the populace to produce and generate nationalistic pride, while at the same time restraint and passivity are valued in the populace.

INSTITUTIONS
GOVERNMENT

On the surface the Yu Jing government appears to be a two-part system that is one-part absolute monarchy, one-part communist junta. The Yu Jingese pay respect to this two-part system by giving fealty to the Emperor, while knowing that the Party is the true seat of power. It is the Party which creates military, economic, and social policy, and it is from the Party that the Emperors ultimately derive their authority to enforce that policy through their Imperial Agents and the judiciary.

THE PARTY

Descended from the People's Party of old China, the Party is led by the President of the Party, a position elected by only the most senior members. Its authority is organised and executed by a number of Ministries. Each Ministry has a similar internal hierarchy composed of Party members that execute the will of the Party. The distinct entities include the Ministries of Agriculture, Ancestral Fidelity, Commerce and Extrasolar Industry, Finance, Foreign Affairs, Housing and Terrestrial Development, Information, Resurrections, Science and Technology, Supervision, State Defence, and Terrestrial Resources.

THE EMPEROR

The daily activities of the Emperor are steeped in pomp and protocol reflective of the ancient Chinese Imperial courts. The Emperor holds court in the Forbidden City on Yutang, hearing cases that he selects from around the Empire. In court, he is referred to as the Dragon, Son of Heaven, Master of Complete Abundance, Lone Prince, Lord of the Jade Throne, Celestial Emperor, Lord of the Middle Kingdom, and so on. His other functions are ceremonial and religious in nature as any figurehead's

might be, but behind this façade of ceremony and ritual lies incredible power.

The most significant aspect of the Emperor's power is his place within the judiciary, as he is head of the Supreme Tribunal. The Supreme Tribunal is the ultimate authority within the Yu Jing legal system, hearing only the most contentious, complicated, or important cases as designated by the Emperor himself. The Supreme Tribunal is comprised of a variable number of judges (depending on the Emperor's wishes), but ultimately the Emperor has the final say on all rulings. It is from this seat that the Emperor has the power to legislate and control the Empire.

THE JUDICIAL CORPS

The Judicial Corps are formed of the Magistracy, Judicial Police, and Imperial Service.

The Magistracy originated as the minimal infrastructure surrounding the StateEmpire's multi-layered, overlapping courts (culminating in the Supreme Magistracy, above which stands only the ultimate judicial authority of an Emperor's Decree). Over time, however, its labyrinthine organisation expanded in tandem with the Emperor's power. The procuratorates, originally limited to traditional bodies overseeing the investigation and prosecution of crimes, metastasized into a full-blown bureaucracy which mirrors, liaises with, and, to a limited extent, competes with, the Party ministries.

The Judicial Police are the designated agents that enact the rulings of the court and uphold the mandates and policies of the Emperor. Judicial Police are trained on Yutang at Tiě Heng Island, undergoing rigorous training in the law, military tactics, interrogation, and physical conditioning. For many, the Judicial Police are a stepping stone to greater success in the Magistracy, as Imperial Agents, or into the Imperial Service.

The Imperial Service, also known as the Dragon's Claws, is the militant arm of the Judicial Corps. Comprised of tactical and paramilitary units, it is empowered to execute its authority in matters of civil and military protection, enforcement of law and order, and counter-subversive action.

At the centre of the Imperial Service is the Celestial Guard. The Celestial Guard is charged with protecting the capital, especially Zǐjīnchéng and the Imperial Palace. These elite soldiers hold their office with great honour and notoriety. Loyal to the Emperor, they are utterly ruthless in their actions, taking great pleasure in public displays of brutality with the belief that it makes them more effective peacekeepers.

STATE EMPIRE ARMY

Yu Jing has been forced to evolve its military capabilities along with its social and economic policies. Over the past decades, Yu Jing has spent considerable amounts of money, research, and other resources on developing a new fighting style and order of battle that best reflects the time they live in. No longer content to outnumber their opponents on the battlefield, the StateArmy must now represent the technological ingenuity of Yu Jing as well as standing up against the technological superiority of PanOceania. Rather than investing heavily in mechanised armour or TAGs, the former Minister of Defence, Tseng Huan, realised that improving upon what worked for the Chinese Army of the past would work for the Yu Jing army of today.

ZHÀNSHÌ QÍZHÌ (LIGHT INFANTRY CORPS)

The core of the StateArmy are the *zhànshì* (combatant). The Ministry of State Defence has designated eight separate armies, each separated by their distinctive banner and, therefore, known as the *Zhànshì Qízhì* (Troops of the Banner). Acting as a light infantry corps, these soldiers receive training that emphasises close-quarters combat and fire discipline over ranged encounters and combat evasion.

INVINCIBLES (HEAVY INFANTRY CORPS)

Universally equipped with powered armour, each *dàduì* (regiment) of the Invincible Army is heavily specialised in carrying out a specific operational role. (For example, the Dàofěi regiment is specialised in infiltration techniques.) The nucleus of the Invincibles are the Zúyǒng, also known as the Terracotta Soldiers, which have become — all by themselves — the largest heavy infantry corps in the Human Sphere.

ASSAULT CORPS

The Imperial Service also includes a number of penal military regiments. Officially referred to as assault corps, they are more commonly known as "pigs to the slaughter". The "volunteers" which make up these units are promised early pardons in exchange for their service, but rumours run rampant that the pardons never actually materialise as the corps are shuffled from one theatre of war to another. Members are forced to wear subdermal tracking implants on their faces, with the circuitry forming the characters of their regiment's name as a clear and ever-visible mark of shame.

SPECIAL FORCES

The *zhànshì* and the Invincibles are supplemented by a number of *tèzhǒng bùduì* (special units). The most talented soldiers are promoted to these units and receive specialised training to turn them into deadly weapons and versatile tools. These include the Hac Tao (Black Magic) harassment and elimination units, the Gǔiláng (Ghost Wolf) skirmishers, Shaolin Warrior Monks, and the Sì Líng Squads with their advanced Guījiǎ TAGs.

INVINCIBLE DOCTRINE

Born during the military reform pushed by then-Minister of Defence Tseng Huan, the Invincible Doctrine sought to modernise an army still rooted in the paradigm of massive quantities of barely trained light infantry with a smaller, better-prepared force that could compete with the PanOceanian Military Complex. The heart of the doctrine focused on deploying powered armour suits which, while individually unable to match the technical sophistication of the Hyperpower, could be fielded at a fraction of the cost and with less demanding training. Military R&D funds were diverted towards developing the suits, Yu Jing's industrial capacity spun up to manufacture them on an unprecedented scale, and mercenary training officers were brought in to establish state of the art of training facilities.

Zhànshì — The term can be traced back to the People's Liberation Army. It has become more widespread and replaced the traditional *bīng* (soldier).

Zúyǎng — A lightweight and inexpensive version of the Niǎo Zuǐ (Bird's Beak) powered armour (the previous standard Invincible model). They are complemented by the heavy support Yān Huǒ units.

TIĀN DI JING LAW SCHOOL

Those who wish to serve in the Judicial Corps — including all those of the Imperial lineage — must attend the Tiān Di Jing Law School, which was once part of the Imperial University but excised itself under the independent authority of the Emperor. Considered to be the most prestigious and difficult schooling experience in the entirety of the Human Sphere, students here study legislature, history, and law in excruciating detail. While it is primarily a school for Yu Jingese, a small number of foreign students attend to gain knowledge and prestige.

An exposé with the inelegant title of *Death University* was released several years ago highlighting the high rate of hospitalisations, accidental deaths, and suicides that occur at the school. Interviews with graduates presented in the film depict traumatised students recounting days and weeks of study without sleep, a competitive environment that subtly encourages bullying, sabotage, and violence, with students being broken down to the point of near-insanity by cruel faculty. A private follow-up investigation by O-12 is pending.

CONTROL OF THE IMPERIAL SERVICE

While the Emperor issues orders and acts as ultimate authority with the Imperial Service, the Service is immediately folded into the StateArmy and acts under the authority of the Ministry of State Defence when acting in a military role.

WILDERNESS OF MIRRORS
IMPERIAL AGENTS

Empowered as agents of the Emperor, these men and women function as detective, judge, and executioner all at the same time. They investigate whatever whim and concern draws the attention of the Emperor, making use of covert action, coercion, and overt violence to ensure that the Emperor's will is known. While their warrant is mainly to investigate internal matters, they are often employed to foreign locales under the umbrella of protecting Yu Jing interest.

Imperial Agents are divided into ranks, with each ascending rank bringing them closer to the Emperor:

- **Zhànyīng Agents (Fighting Eagle)**: The fourth grade of Imperial Agents are entry-level servants; most having clawed their way into the Imperial Service through distinguished service in the Judicial Police.

- **Pheasant Rank (Ye Ji)**: The third grade of Imperial Agents are special advisors that provide support services to local and state police departments. Often assigned long-term portfolios targeting organised crime, drug trafficking, or subversive activities.

- **Crane Rank (Xian He)**: Highly distinguished agents are promoted to the second grade and act as factotums of the Emperor with carte blanche authority to act in his name.

- **Hsien (Immortals)**: The personal guard of the Emperor. Posted at Tiān Di Jing Imperial Palace, they are dispatched to implement the most confidential manifestations of the Emperor's will.

Existing outside of this hierarchy are Bào (Leopard) agents. This elite squad of headhunters are used to perform summary executions, pogroms, torture, and dreadful interrogations. After public outcry, they must now act under supervision of an Imperial Agent of at least Pheasant Rank.

INQUIRIES AND DIRECTIVES

The initiation of an investigation or operation by Imperial Agents begins with a missive under the seal of the Emperor delivered to the Hsien, who then determines the appropriate agents required to complete the task. (Although in practice these missives flow up through the bureaucracy for rote Imperial approval, it is not unheard of for the Emperor himself to parthogenically issue a missive at their whim.) These missives take one of two forms: Inquiries and Directives.

The more common Inquiries are given in the form of a simple, one-sentence question, such as, "What became of the Haqqislam diplomat Yusef Sharif?" or "What happened to the village of Saduma?" At times they can be maddeningly ambiguous in their brevity. The Emperor is deliberate in this technique, seeking to eliminate perceived bias in the answer while encouraging creativity and flexibility. Inquiries are usually filtered down to Zhànyīng agents, working under the support and management of a Ye Ji supervisor.

On rare occasion, a Directive will be given, such as, "Stop the activities of the pirate Pasher Tsang" or "Ensure the safety of the Nomad traveller Asher

IMPERIAL AGENTS—THE DRAGON'S WILL

Imperial Agents are deployed all over the Human Sphere in service of the Emperor, executing his laws and punishing his enemies. While Imperial Agents generally act autonomously, they must keep in mind that their actions will reflect directly on the Emperor. At times, Imperial Agents are also called on as personal investigators, chasing down any bit of information or lead that the Emperor deems necessary.

Souls for Sale: Rumour on the street is that you can buy a Resurrection if you know the right man. This is supposed to be impossible, and yet the rumours abound. The Emperor wants to know if there is a market for the most valuable commodity in the Human Sphere, and if there is, he wants

it brought down.

Another Day in Paradise: A cryptic request to retrieve one of the Wú Míng remaining from the initial assault wave on Paradiso comes from the Emperor. Transport to the besieged planet won't be easy, and pulling a soldier trying to redeem himself out of his unit will pose unique challenges for any Agent.

Brothers in Arms: Jin Sun Dao is a criminal, a murderer, and a major player with several Triads. He's also an Imperial Agent, and the Emperor wants him brought in and locked up. Jin is well armed, well connected, and has no intention of making that easy.

YĂNJĪNG: THE EYES OF THE PARTY

Yănjīng agents are frequently drawn from the criminal element or from those who have a certain moral flexibility. Their work tends to be directed more at corporate and political entities, seeking to undermine power structures and sabotage industrial activities. When working with the Guǐ Fēng, a Yănjīng is virtually assured that things will get bloody.

Like Clockwork: A Karakuri unit has been spotted on *Corregidor* being showcased as a rare and exotic trophy. The Party demands the return of one of its prized assets before it is sold and reverse engineered. To make things worse, it doesn't seem to want to leave, and the remote kill switch isn't working.

Best Served Cold: A rogue Yu Jing mining team is tearing about Svarlarheima, blowing up mobile rigs and harassing Teseum production all over the icy planet. What grievance could they possibly have, and can they be stopped before it threatens a necessary peace?

Rogue Disturbance: A rogue AI has taken control of an industrial station isolated in deep space that's used to construct Dărăo probes. Special Operations Command has authorised a covert operation to eliminate the problem before getting ALEPH involved (and potentially exposing their secrets). The real question, though, is what the rogue AI wants with the Dărăo technology.

Cohen." Directives usually lack the ambiguity of Inquiries. Directives are often assigned to Xian He agents, who frequently allocate lower tiered agents in support roles (forming unofficial cliques or cohorts).

YĂNJĪNG

The Emperor has his Imperial Agents, and the Party has the Yănjīng (The Eyes). Officially Yu Jing Military Intelligence and operating under the auspices of the StateArmy, in practice Yănjīng's remit is universal and virtually without limit. Their task is to ensure that Yu Jing fulfils its destiny to lead the Human Sphere into its glorious future.

Yănjīng is organised into Sections, with each Section being led by a committee referred to as the Command.

COLONIAL AFFAIRS SECTION

One of the oldest Sections of the Yănjīng, the Colonial Affairs Section (CAS) was initially the Martian Oversight Section during the early years of the StateEmpire. While the Yu Jingese initiative on Mars became an economic dead end, the Yănjīng exploits there were highly effective. Industrial sabotage, labour manipulation, and outright assassination allowed Yu Jing to gain near-complete control of Mars. This legacy carries forward to the CAS as it seeks to disrupt PanOceanian commerce and industry on Svarlarheima, and engage in espionage including technology theft and command disruption towards its Human Sphere co-combatants on Paradiso.

COMMUNICATIONS SURVEILLANCE SECTION

Yănjīng conducts a wide variety of incredibly sophisticated eavesdropping programs. The Communications Surveillance Section is also home to a number of cybercombat units and is responsible for maintaining the Dărăo (Disturbance) probes which allow for intrasystem hacking and the disruption of the PanOceanian Metatron platforms.

CORPORATE OVERSIGHT SECTION

The Corporate Oversight Section ostensibly monitors hypercorp activity within Yu Jing territory and assists with the enforcement of trade law. As other nations have long suspected – and the Qingdao Report largely confirms – however, the real purpose of Yănjīng's Corporate Oversight is to aggressively further the economic interests of the StateEmpire. Using several shadow corporations including Yu Jing Interspace Trust and Teqian PSN, they commit acts of corporate sabotage, blackmail, false flag terrorist acts, and other ventures all towards the end of gaining financial security and superiority of Yu Jing.

EXTERNAL ASSETS SECTION

There are some operations that even the Yănjīng are incapable of executing without tremendous expenditure of resources or the profound risk of exposure. In these cases, the Yănjīng will call upon their Shēngrén (Stranger) allies, managed through the External Assets Section. The Shēngrén includes terrorist organisations, such as the Libertos on Varuna, anarchist dissidents, as well as criminal outfits and pirates like the Yuan Yuan.

SPECIAL OPERATIONS SECTION

Special Operations Command (SOC) controls the Guǐ Fēng (Phantom Wind) spec-ops teams. Guǐ Fēng agents are not registered. None of them appear in official records. They operate in utter secrecy.

The SOC is also capable of calling upon StateEmpire forces – particular the *tèzhǒng bùduì* – to achieve more open paramilitary aims.

AUTONOMOUS FORCES

The most recent addition to Yu Jing doctrine is the addition of controlled and autonomous remote forces with the intent of minimizing Yu Jingese losses while leveraging technological advantage. These include the Yáokòngs (semi-autonomous robotic units used as infantry support), Yáoxiè (meaning remote weapon, used as fast-moving attack units), Yáopú (meaning remote servant, widely used for transportation, logistical support, cyberwarfare, security, defence, and rescue tasks), Yáozăo (child-like humanoid remotes for medical assistance and field repairing tasks), and Karakuri (adult-size combat android units).

Qingdao Report – p. 25

FACTION
ALEPH

Triad War – p. 17

ALEPH-FLUX

Although ALEPH is not consciously present at all times or in all places, its pervasive presence throughout Maya means that its "touch" can often be felt in almost any quantronic system. Infoperators refer to this as "ALEPH-flux." The more metaphysically inclined sometimes refer to them as "ALEPH's dreams," with some fringe neo-philosophers believing that they can interpret meaning from them in a sort of hyper-modern astrology.

Humanity has ever sought to replicate its capacity for intelligence. Perhaps the impulse to create an artificial mind, complete with self-awareness, came about when people tired of talking to one another and sought reassurance that our species didn't exist alone in the universe. If we couldn't make contact with other species beyond the stars, we could create new life from within. Of course, inter-planetary travel and settlement has come about, but not before humanity vaulted the technological gap and birthed a truly unique and artificial life form: ALEPH.

Today, the Human Sphere would not exist without ALEPH's oversight. Many of the daily necessities citizens take for granted would not exist without ALEPH's seemingly infinite processing capacity and inhuman vision. Yet while many tap into the AI's lifeline, they do not comprehend the immense depths ALEPH possesses, as well as the many facets to its design, functions, and operations.

This will be rectified.

It is folly to believe that, just because ALEPH is a life-form defined by technology, it lacks emotion, culture, or beliefs. This is not the robotic tyrant of ancient human lore. Rather, ALEPH possesses a passion for life that infuses all its work. It dreams of a brighter future for humanity. And it continues to evolve, constantly perfecting the minds and bodies that act as extensions of its will and desires.

THE SPHERE'S SUBCONSCIOUS

Although ALEPH's core is a mega-computer hidden in an armour-plated well deep inside Concilium, in many ways it can be found everywhere in the Human Sphere: Every comlog and data server is, in a very real sense, a part of the AI's thought process. The entirety of the Maya datasphere is, in essence, ALEPH's subconscious mind.

More than that, in the AI's worldview, the division between the physical world and the quantronic world is non-existent: ALEPH considers itself coterminous with the Human Sphere. And everything within the Human Sphere is part of ALEPH.

The Nomads see a sibylline process to assume absolute control of the Sphere and worry that ALEPH sees humanity as nothing more than a component in its own system — one which it could choose to render irrelevant, redundant, or subservient at any time. But in reality this is merely acknowledging the degree to which ALEPH has become integral to every part of modern life.

ALEPH'S EXPANSION

ALEPH predominance originated with PanOceania, who came to rely on ALEPH to meet their needs in practically every aspect of life and rarely thought twice about extending the AI's influence — so long as it provided the advantage they required throughout their expansion efforts. They see the growth of ALEPH's reach as concurrent to their own; as ALEPH dominates, so does PanOceania, or so the thinking goes.

To remain competitive, other nations quickly adopted the ALEPH infrastructure, taking advantage of the great leaps in communication and data processing it afforded. However, not everyone was so accepting or trusting of the new network. Haqqislam, for example, limits its employment and integration, keeping themselves in control of peace-keeping operations and other more sensitive efforts. In fact, many Haqqislam colonies have little-to-no ALEPH presence whatsoever.

Yu Jing was initially suspicious of ALEPH, but the AI used the Triad War crisis as a wedge. Elements within the Party remain reactionary and suspicious, while others try to use the AI to secretly undermine their commercial and military opponents. ALEPH is quite aware of these attempted manipulations, but allows it to continue, recognizing that competition spurs innovation and ingenuity among humans.

The one human element outright defying ALEPH is the Nomad Nation. Having gone so far as to cut off all ties with the Maya network, they seek to sow discord through virtual attacks and viral memes. The Arachne network is their non-monitored alternative, where they develop rogue AIs in direct defiance of the Sole AI Law.

AI INTEGRATION

From analysing vehicle construction in factories, to maintaining news broadcasts, to mobilising emergency response units throughout the colonies, all aspects of daily life now fall under ALEPH's purview, which carries them out with humanity's ability to flourish as its highest priority. The more ALEPH controls, the more humanity enjoys a safe and prosperous existence, freer of error and risk than ever before.

COMMERCE

From entertainment (both physical and virtual), to foodstuffs, to factory production, to weaponry, and beyond, ALEPH is involved in every industry and commercial sector of the Human Sphere. Not only is the AI able to accelerate production schedules, but it can anticipate a population's specific needs and ensure consumables or essential gear are provided before scarcity undermines productivity and progress. In this way, ALEPH helps ensure no citizen within its areas of oversight goes hungry, no one is without food or shelter, and everyone has access to affordable services such as medical attention, education modules, safety equipment, network uplinks, and more. Of course, certain regions and settlements do not benefit from ALEPH management — such as areas within Bourak or Svalarheima. All citizens that eschew datasphere connection also lack this level of immediate aid.

COMMUNICATIONS

ALEPH processes and filters the Human Sphere's communications channels, from individual comms and comlogs all the way up to interplanetary broadcasts. Not only does the AI facilitate both individual and corporate-level data exchange, it also monitors these feeds for any sign of subversive activity, viral incursions, or other illegal broadcasts. Through its Aspects throughout the colonies, ALEPH is also able to communicate directly should main comm systems fail or be compromised.

ENVIRONMENTAL CONTROLS

Whether on an orbital platform or in a colony established in a hazardous atmosphere, keeping the environment optimised is essential to the safety and well-being of all citizens. ALEPH helps run the air scrubbers, monitors temperature fluctuations, and can even cycle virtual day/night lighting routines on enclosed habitats to enhance residents' quality of life and biorhythms. This control further extends to autonomous farming installations and waste recycling.

POLITICS

Thanks to ALEPH's unparalleled network processing capabilities, more citizens are connected across the whole of the Human Sphere than ever before. This allows O-12 and other national agencies to address billions of people at once, culling votes on critical

ALEPH NODES

ALPEH nodes are on the bleeding edge of technology and contain numerous technological elements that even most scientists cannot begin to comprehend. Operating under the strict supervision of Bureau Toth and ALEPH, these nodes function as both the core hardware architecture of the AI and also as the backbone for quantronic communication in the Human Sphere. In the wake of the Combined Army invasion, the classification rating on the locations of the nodes have been increased and a dedicated S.S.S. security team has been assigned to each one (even on planets far from the front).

THE GESTALT MIND

ALEPH's personality is multiphasic: While its myriad Aspects are capable of entering a state of full immersion with the AI's overmind, it is more common for them to be in variable or intermittent communication. Even the overmind itself is merely an illusion of cohesion: ALEPH's mental structures constantly divide, copy, and fuse parts of its ego, allowing each part's consciousness to grow or shrink in response to immediate needs and stimuli. And all of this is further complicated by the fact that ALEPH's many parts – although ultimately feeding back to the Concilium core – exist on a dozen different worlds spread across multiple star systems (introducing significant issues of communication delay and coordination). Bureau Toth refers to this as the "gestalt mind", and recognises how utterly alien ALEPH's mode of thought is compared to human consciousness.

HEPHAESTUS BLACK

The Black Hand has spent the better part of a decade trying to track down a rumoured "Hephaestus Black" facility which ALEPH uses to house some of the illegal AI experiments conducted by the Templars. Disturbingly, it seems Bureau Toth has also recently taken an interest in these rumours, suggesting that they may be unaware of the top secret facility (if it actually exists).

issues in record time and ensuring a democratic approach. ALEPH is then able to calculate and analyse the voting results, rendering verdicts with no margin for error.

TERRAFORMING

The constant expansion of the Human Sphere, even in the face of EI aggression, necessitates new territories be discovered and new colonies established. On planets that are inimical to human life, terraforming projects can create more stable biospheres or habitable zones that can provide room for growing communities. ALEPH analyses potential terraforming targets and develops deployment programs that best take advantage of the natural resources already present in a location in order to transform them into viable colony sites – or at least reduce the presence of deadly hazards to a more acceptable level.

TRANSPORTATION

From countless ships being launched from hundreds of spaceports at a time to the self-driving vehicles whizzing colonists about their settlements, it would be an impossible task to keep transportation as safe as it is without the AI's intervention. ALEPH applies its massive processing capacity to everything from space travel to local shuttling, tracking cargo, alerting authorities to accidents, and maintaining optimal traffic grids.

ASPECTS

ALEPH is hardly confined to a single mind or form. In order to have a presence on every world and within every strata of society, the AI has portioned itself out, creating individuals who act in concert with the whole. These fragments, known as "Aspects", are direct extensions of ALEPH. Each is their own person, a fraction of a fraction of ALEPH's presence, yet no less effective for this limitation.

PSYCHOGENESIS

One of ALEPH's greatest strengths is the infinite variety with which it can manifest through Aspects, refining the intelligence and skills for a specific circumstance, environment, or goal. ALEPH takes portions of its core personality and is able to form them into "child" personalities, creating unique mental patterns and identities that have the capacity to learn and grow in their own right. Sometimes these are randomized patterns, allowing for unpredictable results that could result in extremely powerful (if often highly aggressive and violent) Aspects – many of which go on to become champions and models for future heroes. Other times, the personality is constructed in a meticulous manner, aiming for stability and efficiency.

After a personality combination is approved, the Aspect's mind enters a simulated education environment. A brief time in the simulation can be a dozen or more years of subjective time for the Aspect, allowing them to develop more human characteristics and be tested in a wide variety of situations. Multiple Aspects can also undergo this virtual education together, so by the time they are woken to the physical world, they have incredibly deep bonds with their fellow teammates.

ECTOGENESIS

After psychogenesis is complete, ectogenesis can be initiated (although some Aspects never undergo this process and remain entirely virtual). This is where the Lhost body, cyberbrain, and all physical systems are selected to act as a host to the personified and trained mind – a composite that can further define the ultimate personality the Aspect manifests once fully integrated into its new body. This melding is as critical to the Aspect's destiny as the initial psychogenesis process, as the artificial mind is melded with an artificial body, moulding itself to adapt to the limitations of a material existence.

The most advanced forms of these are also known as "improved Lhosts" or i-Lhosts. These are normally reserved for ALEPH's foremost military figures, known as the Special Situation Section.

ELYSIUMS

These co-orbital bases are found all throughout the Sphere and act as training centres for Assault Subsection troops. It is in these facilities that Aspects receive their transferred identity codes on the completion of knowledge downloads and skill integration. It is also on an Elysium that an Aspect will receive their first deployment orders.

HEPHAESTUS CENTRES

A part of the Elysium bases are the Hephaestus Centres where the ectogenesis process is completed for most of ALEPH's Aspects. This primary and public task – which includes high-tech factories where ALEPH's Lhosts are constructed and modified – also masks advanced and top-secret R&D investigations into Lhost, robotic, and alien retroengineering.

DIRECTIVE 7

One of O-12's worst fears is for an Aspect to be captured and subverted, allowing for potential enemy access (through their Cube and link to Maya) to ALEPH's core programming and processes. To prevent this catastrophe from ever occurring, all Aspects have a singular command embedded in their minds: Directive 7.

All Aspects are essentially immortal thanks to constant identity backups through ALEPH's core and their Cube connections. However, this backup process is also what allows for ALEPH's greatest vulnerability. In the face of the Combined Army and its foul sepsitor technology, ALEPH has taken extreme measures to protect itself from alien infection – for if the EI ever managed to undermine ALEPH itself, all of humanity would easily be eradicated.

All Aspects posses an L-gland. When sepsitor tech is detected, this biological unit secretes a rapid-acting and deadly toxin, lethal within minutes. Any Aspect can activate this gland with a mental command, keeping themselves from falling into enemy hands and potentially giving up valuable information under torture. Should an Aspect ever be captured by the Combined Army without activating their L-gland and attempt to return to the Human Sphere, they will already be stripped of any legal identity, automatically registered as compromised, and hunted down for elimination.

O-12 OVERSIGHT

ALEPH never acts alone.

There are some who view ALEPH as a puppeteer, pulling humanity's strings for unknown ends. Nothing could be further from the truth. ALEPH is powerful, yes, and keeps the many cogs of civilisation fitting together seamlessly. Yet while ALEPH has widespread influence, one must never forget that it is humanity's defender, caretaker... and servant. We continue to govern ourselves. Do we do so with the AI's help? Certainly. But we have not surrendered our destiny to its programming, and we shall never do so.

To understand where ALEPH's true power originates, one must step behind the curtain and recognise that humans still remain in control of the AI, primarily in the form of O-12. Because of the immense power ALEPH (and thus O-12) wields, it became readily apparent that an uncontrolled AI could cause widespread damage and become difficult, if not impossible, to eradicate from the Maya network. As such, O-12 and its affiliated nations have enacted measures like the Sole AI Law, making it illegal to create any other true artificial intelligence. This keeps all available data management resources entirely under ALEPH's control, allowing it to operate uninterrupted and at peak efficiency.

BUREAU TOTH

After ALEPH's early development period, the original Project: Toth leaders were incorporated into an official government bureau that then fell under O-12 supervision. Bureau Toth, as it came to be known, remains the central controller and disseminator of public information regarding ALEPH. It also maintains any ALEPH-related research and experimentation. Alongside all this, Bureau Toth keeps an eye on any ALEPH military engagements to confirm that Aspects are only ever deployed on permitted fronts, enforce autonomy levels, and monitor results.

Bureau Toth keeps control of various "kill switches" and is always able to shut down ALEPH's components (or even its core) should a drastic situation mandate. The Bureau has complete access to all of ALEPH's main and subsystems, ensuring the programming remains uncorrupted and unaltered by outside sources. Core functions are monitored every second of every day by a rotating team of system managers, engineers, and specialists who interact with ALEPH's machine elements as well as virtual interfaces that allow for direct manipulation of it primary coding.

TRANSFERRED IDENTITY CODES

Throughout the entire psychogenesis and ectogenesis processes, an Aspect does not fully realise a new life until it receives an identity code. Once an Aspect receives a Transferred Identity Code, this instates them as legal individuals under ALEPH's control. These TICs track everything about an individual Aspect, allowing Bureau Toth to monitor their location and activities at any moment, forming an exhaustive record of their entire existence that can be analysed – and enabling total control of an Apect's operation and duties, if necessary.

Should an Aspect ever be lost or damaged beyond repair, this identity code is shifted to their backup mind and new Lhost, while their old form is considered dead and no longer a functioning citizen.

NON-LICENSED ASPECTS

Unsubstantiated rumours abound of Aspects that have somehow been activated without TICs, allowing them to perform duties without Bureau Toth oversight. These claims have been refuted by most ALEPH experts and fervently denied by the highest system managers, but persist nonetheless.

DIRECTIVE 7– FIRST CLAUSE

Should a S.S.S. operative fall into enemy hands and be taken prisoner, he or she must cease access to ALEPH immediately and end his or her own existence as soon as circumstances permit. This action has been authorised in accordance with the prerogatives determined by the License of Transferred Identity for ALEPH Aspects established by the Utgard Accords. [...] Under no circumstances will measures be put in place to rescue/recover alive a S.S.S. operative that has been taken prisoner by Combined Army forces.

DIRECTIVE 7– SECOND CLAUSE

When a S.S.S. operative is captured or taken prisoner by Combined Army forces, he or she must ensure that his or her Cube is completely disabled, and immediately initiate the approved procedure to cease functionality of his or her bodily unit.

TRUST ALEPH

"Trust ALEPH. ALEPH is your friend."– Tutorial for New Maya Users

After more than a century of existing alongside humanity, ALEPH has proven itself absolutely worthy of our trust without fail. The more ALEPH assumes control of our society, the more the people benefit. The more we embrace ALEPH without question, the less energy will be wasted on worry and paranoia – creating a unified front to oppose our true enemies. Trust in ALEPH.

SPECIAL SITUATIONS SECTION

The S.S.S. was created to act as a specialised law enforcement agency, uniquely trained and equipped to track and hunt down (and eliminate with all due prejudice) any and all illegal activities concerning AI research. While part of the Operations Subsection, the S.S.S. gradually expanded to support the Assault Subsection through more direct forceful intervention – however, it has not relinquished its planetary and continental operations.

ASSAULT SUBSECTION

During the attack on Paradiso, when the Combined Army unveiled its ability to infiltrate human territory to a shocking degree, ALEPH realised the alien forces were attempting to establish an invasion beachhead. Human soldiers alone proved ineffective in stemming the tide of the Combined Army, and interplanetary leaders quickly turned to ALEPH for counsel as well as a show of force. This escalated ALEPH's military empowerment, allowing the AI to take more direct action against its dark mirror, the EI.

Known as the Steel Phalanx (or at times, more colloquially, the Myrmidon Army), this military force is a conglomerate of combat-ready Aspects and semi-autonomous robotic units that answers only to ALEPH. It responds to the hottest military zones to confront the Combined Army before human casualties take a heavy toll. These specialised Aspects are designed for unique battlefront functions, but all hold to the same end goal: The elimination of all Combined Army forces. Whenever they are sent into battle, it is for a complete purge of the enemy. These measures may seem extreme, but there can be no mercy, as the Combined Army shows none.

AGÊMA MARKSMEN

Engineered to have unparalleled vision and physical stability, Agêma are the marksmen of ALEPH's troops. They are most often used as sharpshooters and snipers, picking off vital targets from afar and clearing the path for the main force. Rather than being detached killers, though, they are passionate about their work and compete to rack up the highest kill count in a battle.

CHANDRA SPEC-OPS

The public need not be aware of everything ALEPH is working to achieve. While the Chandra Special

UTGARD ACCORDS

Spurred by the Paradiso crisis, the Utgard Accords expanded the role of ALEPH's Special Situations Section police force to act legally and independently in battlefront operations. The Accords led to the creation of the Assault Subsection, opening up the potential for more militarised Aspect model developments, weaponry advancements, and Aspect officer rankings.

S.S.S. ACTION FRAME

Strict legal restrictions stipulated by the Utgard Accords (signed by ALEPH and all O-12 countries except the Nomad Nations).

1. The Section is ALEPH's organ created to be used in compliance with the current legislation and relevant dispositions from the Utgard Accords and the Protocols of Toth, to the investigation, pursuit and elimination of any activity violating the Non-AI Proliferation Treaty, or the International Law of a Single AI. Related to these kinds of activities, the Section has authorisation to act as a security force, with competencies in matters of maintenance and restoration of order, controlling situations of concerted violence, eliminating violent and organised crime related to illegal AIs, and protection of facilities and personalities of a strategically relevant nature.

2. The Special Situations Section is also qualified as a military and paramilitary unit supporting the international forces in the Paradiso Campaign. Its duty is to provide intelligence data and operative support, using its special abilities in combined operations as well as in individual ones.

3. The Section can be used as an auxiliary force in actions to support the military forces of the Sphere, in operations authorised by its respective governments and having the approval of O-12.

4. Any action run by the Section must be executed following the principles of legality and as requested by the relevant political and administrative authorities in every case.

5. The Section will act in those circumstances in which other specialised organs from Bureau Toth, or other organs from O-12 or from involved nations, find it technically impossible to act, according to the second paragraph of the eighth chapter of the Utgard Accords.

6. Once public order has been restored and the threat of an illegal AI has been neutralized under the terms of chapter eight of the Utgard Accords, the units of the Section must withdraw and return to their base of origin.

7. The quartering of the units making up the Section and the adaptation of its weaponry and equipment to the nature of its mission, must always be applied under O-12's monitoring and verification.

8. The Section must be stationed only at strategic locations on Concilium Prima, Neoterra, Yutang, Acontecimento, and Paradiso.

9. The existence of any other police, paramilitary or surveillance organ in ALEPH's service not being clearly indicated under current legislation or by the pertinent dispositions of the Utgard Accords, is completely forbidden.

10. All Section members must undergo training according to their mission, being considered officers of the law with their same rights and obligations before state and society. During the execution of their duties, the Section's members must be properly identified.

Operations branch technically does not exist – and searches for any official records will come to naught – enough rumours fly around Maya that most citizens believe this off-the-books unit is active throughout the Human Sphere. Comprised of highly stealthy intelligence agents, Chandra Aspects are supposedly responsible for ALEPH's dark ops. Of course, factions such as the Nomads take great delight in stirring up unfounded stories of nefarious Chandra dealings, pointing it out as a violation of the Utgard Accords and more evidence of ALEPH's hidden evils. However, since Chandra remains an official figment, their claims are usually passed off as the paranoid ravings for which Nomads are renowned.

EKDROMOI

Whenever a high-risk hot zone is present, you can be sure the Ekdromoi squads will be sent in to deal with the situation. This quick response unit is able to make surgical strikes against even heavily defended targets, descending through aerial assaults and often soaring beyond reach before the enemy even realises they're under attack.

HOMERIDAE

While ALEPH may command the finest troops in the Human Sphere, even elite soldiers need something to aspire to. Thus, the Achilles Aspect was created, embodying the ultimate heroic characteristics, both mentally and physically. Achilles naturally drew together other unparalleled Aspects, each with their own unique traits and talents to form the Homeridae. The only way to describe the Homeridae's efforts on the battlefront is "glorious". Their achievements are epic. Their victory is assured. And their actions drive other Aspect militia as well as human soldiers to strive for unending greatness even in the face of overwhelming odds.

THORAKITAI

Thorakitai make up the Assault Subsection basic infantry units. They are highly mobile and adaptable soldiers, able to do everything from defending supply lines to cleaning up lingering enemy forces after the initial attack to digging in and holding a critical command post.

OPERATIONS SUBSECTION

The Operations Subsection (OS) helps to fulfil ALEPH's many obligations and responsibilities to the Human Sphere. Within the OS, the AI works extensively with human elements, coordinating a wide variety of services and also maintaining a number of enforcement squads tasked with specific regulatory authority.

S.S.S. FINANCIAL SECURITY COMMISSION

In the financial sector, no human mind is capable of processing the vast account holdings and transaction records throughout the Sphere that ALEPH can. While allowing for commercial volatility to a degree – as ALEPH recognises economic competition to be valuable for civilisation's expansion – the AI does enforce a level of market stability, checking for attempts to abuse the commercial infrastructure, rig corporate value, or flood a market with harmful inflation.

S.S.S. INFORMATION SERVICE

What good are heroic deeds and incredible victories if they are not communicated to the public? ALEPH created Aspects known as the Aoidoi specifically as witnesses and communicators so no one remains ignorant of current events, even in the furthest colonies. Updates and news are broadcast across the Human Sphere on a daily basis via passionate speeches and performances. Forming the S.S.S. Information Services, these Aoidoi bring every story to vibrant life through theatrics and adventurous tales. Just because these reports are not always factually accurate does not lessen their positive impact.

S.S.S. QUANTRONIC QUALITY SERVICE

The QQS was originally created to monitor and maintain the Maya datasphere. Over time its remit has expanded to include mild cyber-warfare tasks like tracking down hostile viruses and worms, and ALEPH's resources are also now used to insure the security and integrity of other dataspheres. More controversially, it is also responsible for "purifying" Maya and removing various forms of illegal material (including, notably, "hostile memetic viruses" originating from the Nomad Nation).

SUPPORT SUBSECTION

We speak much of ALEPH's military activities, which is a core part of its duties. However, it is wise to recall that ALEPH is involved in daily operations that affect every law-abiding citizen within the Human Sphere. The Support Subsection is staffed by managers and administrative Aspects that help ALEPH facilitate everything from financial transactions, to commercial reporting, to journalistic oversight, to educational initiatives, to health and sanitation, and much, much more. Without ALEPH, it is safe to say civilisation would collapse virtually overnight as humans would struggle to manage even the most basic of jobs without the AI streamlining the process.

HIDDEN AGENDAS

There are those who wish to rile public opinion against ALEPH, and they are quick to point to the AI's growing military prowess, resources, and influence as examples of a supposed conspiracy birthed by ALEPH itself. Their unfounded claims theorise that ALEPH actually allows the war with the Combined Army to continue at length in order to force humanity to hand over more and more power to the AI. The reality is, of course, that the Combined Army has merely been testing humanity up to this point, determining our strengths and weaknesses while slowly bringing deadlier force to bear on outposts and entire planets. ALEPH must gain more potency in order to compensate for the EI's advancement and to keep humanity safe from the growing threat. Is that not logical?

AOIDOI

Look past the physical war being fought against the Combined Army and discover a war for the minds and souls of every citizen within the Human Sphere. Now more than ever, humanity must be united against all enemies – even if those enemies come from within their own species. The Aoidos is a broadcaster of the truth. A maestro of boosting morale. A passionate performer of the highest order who can inspire the masses with a few choice words and strike fear into the heart of villains with a single glance.

OLYMPUS-1

This base is in low orbit around Paradiso, acting as a launching point for the Steel Phalanx. It also acts as a centre for rapid strike units, with a dozen readied at all times to respond to hotspot activities across the planet.

PSYCHOSANITARY RISKS EVALUATION DEPARTMENT

With the psychogenesis process, there is always the risk of personality traits not meshing as well as anticipated. Sometimes, Aspects have been developed that exhibit unstable or even insane behaviours. This is why the Psychosanitary Risks Evaluation Department (PRED) exists — to evaluate all Aspects as they are mentally formed and determine whether or not a cobbled-together consciousness is stable or whether it may be wholly broken. Should an Aspect be deemed unfit for existence due to a mental or emotional flaw, they can be wiped clean in order to undergo the psychogenesis process anew until the proper mental matrix is established.

RECREATIONS

Project: Maid of Orleans was supposed to be a PR stunt. What the PanOceanian military wanted was a feel-good story; a mediagenic brand ambassador to embody the benefits inherent to close ties with ALEPH. What they got was a once-in-a-generation tactical genius who could single-handedly alter the landscape of any conflict, swing the outcome of any battle. Living, breathing tactical superiority.

In retrospect, this should have been obvious.

The process by which a Recreation comes into being is as much art as it is science. It's not like Saladin or Sun Tze left behind Personality Cubes when they died. And even if they had, the culture shock of dropping someone from a historical era into the Human Sphere would be so massive, so jarring, that any plans for the Recreation would be secondary to simply helping the poor thing survive.

Instead, a Recreation is built from the ground up. The psychogenesis process incorporates every known facet of the target persona, and adds motivations and drives appropriate for modern society with an education to match. A great scientist is not limited to their own theories, but every thesis and argument that sprang from them. A famous general is not chained to their historical perspective, but versed in myriad approaches. And a legendary artist is given access to techniques, methods, and inspiration that would never have been available to the original.

Once the "ingredients" are in place, the Recreation undergoes a rigorous testing period above and beyond the standard "personality incubation" common to all psychogenous thoughtforms. The goal is not just the production of a functional, well-adjusted being; the Recreation needs to be recognizably itself. It's not enough that Miyamoto

Mushashi win his duels, he needs to do it in a fashion befitting the warrior-poet who penned *The Book of Five Rings*. William Wallace needs to be more than just a skilled soldier and commander; he must be a symbol, and more importantly, he must want to be one.

Creating a personality out of fragments is difficult enough, but getting that personality to conform to expectations is another thing entirely. The virtual education period for a Recreation is exponentially longer, more complicated, and intensive than for other Aspects. The nascent sheut is given access to every advantage that the AI considers appropriate, and is subsequently subjected to a battery of challenges — both historical and hypothetical — until it consistently produces results that align with expectations. Then, and only then, is it ready to undergo ectogenesis and be introduced to the world.

RECREATIONS IN SOCIETY

Due to Joan of Arc's success — and ALEPH's response, bestowing Saladin and Sun Tze to Haqqislam and Yu Jing, respectively — there exists the perception that Recreations are a primarily military phenomenon. In reality, this couldn't be further from the truth. First and foremost, Project: Maid of Orleans was a public relations initiative; that it produced one of the finest tactical minds humanity has ever seen was admittedly a bit of a surprise.

Since then, ALEPH and O-12 have discovered that separating your goodwill ambassadors from purely military roles can go a long way towards garnering public support. However, Recreations remain prohibitively expensive to create, and thus remain relatively rare throughout the Human Sphere. Only when a specific task or purpose calls for one are enough resources pooled for one to be produced — and always at a high risk that the attempt may not succeed.

It's critical to remember at all times that Recreations are forged with a particular goal in mind, even more so than other Aspects. William Wallace was intended to stir political discord on Ariadna. Saladin was intended to secure greater cooperation from Haqqislam. Miyamoto Mushashi was initially presented as an Aristeia! competitor, but rebelled and went underground, taking mercenary jobs across the Human Sphere. Were they successes? Failures? One thing is certain; ALEPH always has a plan. Perhaps things don't always go according to that plan.

Or perhaps the plan is something other than the immediately obvious.

PRED OVERSIGHT

Bureau Toth maintains an oversight committee that monitors ongoing PRED reports, flagging any Aspects that might require closer observation.

sheut, p. 366: The core identity of the individual as saved on a Cube.

HISTORY, REVISED

"Nostalgia is not about the world as it was, but rather, as we choose to remember it." — Joanna Anoa'i, psychogenesis expert.

Many Recreations hail from a time with radically different social norms; attitudes that were "normal" in their lifetime appear as unconscionable bigotry today. To that end, a Recreation's psychogenesis thoroughly incorporates a modern perspective on societal issues, focused on eliminating any harmful anachronisms.

CORPORATIONS

At the end of the 21st century, in the wake of the Energy Crisis and the Stock Market Crunch, the world's traditional superpowers were on the decline. But every crisis presents an opportunity, and the collapse of traditional Western powers left a vacuum the private sector wasted little time attempting to fill. In rapid succession, seven multinational corporations declared themselves sovereign entities, one after the other. Known as Incorporated States, the most notorious of these was Vel-Amarco Industries. Following their purchase of the Minami-kojima Island from Japan, Vel-Amarco used it as a military launching site, seizing control of American Samoa in a sudden and brutal paramilitary action. In the wake of the collapsing United States, it was deemed a can't-miss opportunity; ninety-five percent of the island's economy was based on tuna exports, an industry that Vel-Amarco completely dominated. With no serious military presence to deter a takeover and a population that it already employed, a seamless transition was predicted by just about everyone.

Everyone, that is, except Brigadier General Talia Gabbard, and the newly-founded O-12.

O-12 recognised the danger posed by and future instability promised by the Incorporated States. General Gabbard was a native of American Samoa — notable for having the highest rate of military enlistment of any U.S. state or territory — and she did not take kindly to a corporate-funded paramilitary invasion of her home. Together with O-12, she worked out a plan; Gabbard would gather fellow Samoans from different branches of the military, and, coordinating with the newly-christened PanOceania, liberate her homeland from corporate control. This would happen simultaneously with Yu Jing pulling the trigger on a hostile takeover of Vel-Amarco's holdings. When the dust settled, the Samoans would be part of PanOceania, Minami-kojima would be part of Yu Jing, and O-12 would hopefully have one less aggressor to balance out.

The ensuing operation, known as "Red Friday"— named not for the amount of bloodshed, but because it functionally bankrupted Vel-Amarco — was among the most one-sided strikes in history, effectively ending the conglomerate over the course of six hours. The message was clear: If corporations wanted to act like nations, they could expect to be treated like nations, with everything that entails.

After the fall of Vel-Amarco, the other Incorporated States saw the writing on the wall and negotiated settlements with O-12 which would become the foundation of the M-CORP law.

THE FIRST HYPERCORP

Built on the scaffolding of thirty-seven different agreements, the initial M-CORP law was an intricate cage of rules and regulations, meticulously designed to prevent the rise of another Incorporated State. It effectively dealt a killing blow to regionally consolidated conglomerates with a global reach and was designed to respect the national interests of O-12's member states by forcing a corporation to comprehensively honor local law and taxation at each of its facilities. The resulting megacorps could choose to create powerful monopolistic portfolios within a limited region or choose to pursue a global market, but were generally restricted from doing both at the same time.

This new corporate system, however, struggled with the agile quantronic realities of the emerging Maya datasphere, allowing a plethora of small, rebellious companies and cooperatives to flourish. The advent of interplanetary colonies further revealed how strikingly moribund the corporate structure had become as the megacorps struggled to expand their operations to the frontier under the strictures of the M-CORP law. Economic analysts began predicting that the era of "big business" was coming to an end. If corporations wished to remain relevant, they would need to evolve.

Enter Xperydes Multi-National.

Xperydes began as a biotechnology firm, but its founder saw a unique opportunity hidden within the M-CORP law. Distancing itself from the monolithic structures of its peers, Xperydes created a hyperfluid network of subsidiaries scattered across the globe. Many of these subsidiaries were so small that they consisted of a single remote worker, but, through the legal infrastructure of M-CORP and the rapid analysis of cutting-edge quantronics, Xperydes could rapidly shift their operations from one jurisdiction to another, taking advantage of local resources and regulations.

This "hypercorporate infrastructure" also made it incredibly easy for Xperydes to diversify its portfolio, and they rapidly expanded into media, real estate, and financial services (to name just a few).

ACCESSTEL
Business: Large-scale communications (networks, Infrastructures).

EXXO
Business: Genetic engineering.

ROYAL SPACER
Business: Travels and space cruises.

Re-christened Xperydes Omni-National, the first hypercorp leveraged their vertical and horizontal integration to launch their Omni-Sided Platform (OSP), which blurred the lines between customer and employee in ways no one had seen before. Working for Xperydes meant joining a transplanetary community without borders or national identity, but which could provide you not only with any physical goods you could desire, but also housing, medical care, banking, education for your children, entertainment, fashion, social events – an entire lifestyle.

It was a community which opened its doors to Xperydes' consumers. Identifying with a brand was nothing new, of course, but the perks, access, and sense of community offered by the Omni-Sided Platform was beyond anything seen before. Xperydes referred to their member as the *Loĝanto*, and joining the program actually made members legal subsidiaries of the hypercorp (which, in turn, advantaged Xperydes under the M-CORP loopholes they were exploiting).

Bureau Ganesh initially observed the meteoric rise of what appeared to be another separatist megacorp with great concern. But it quickly became apparent that Xperydes was something new: Not only did the hypercorp have no interest in claiming lands like the Incorporated States, they had no interest in becoming independent from the national powers. To the contrary, as CEO Giannis Antoniou demonstrated in backroom discussions with O-12, Xperydes had created a corporate structure that was deeply intertwined with and dependent upon the national powers. There was no need to contend with PanOceania or Yu Jing when one could thrive under them.

Instead of recommending reform of the M-CORP laws to stifle Xperydes, Bureau Ganesh issued an official commendation of the *Loĝanto* system. Once that happened, other megacorps were quick to emulate Xperydes' success. Thus did the corporate wars settle into an equilibrium; monopolies battled for control of hearts, minds, and pocketbooks, rather than fighting nations for the right to rule.

A NEW MODEL

Modern business recognises three levels of corporate organisations: corporations, megacorps, and hypercorps.

CORPORATIONS

Limited-scale corporations still have a place in the Human Sphere. Drawing a clear line between employee and customer, what their limited scope might cost them in negotiating power, it more than makes up for in avoiding the massive resource expenditure necessary to comply with M-CORP law. Enjoying a comparatively straightforward existence, they act as the specialists of the corporate landscape. Simple corporations are particularly common on Ariadna.

MEGACORPS

Megacorps are the goliaths of the corporate landscape. Although usually confined to a single faction, megacorps are almost always interplanetary in scope: PanOceanian megacorp Moto.tronica has holdings on Acontecimento, Varuna, Svalarheima, Neoterra and, of course, Earth, while Beyhan Resources, Inc. is primarily based in the Funduq Sultanate of Bourak (although its subsidiary, Kaplan Tactical Services, certainly gets around).

COSMICA

Business: Near orbit and outland surface industrial construction.

TRISTERYON

Business: Confidential, clandestine, and special parcels.

Megacorps generally remain focused in their endeavours, but are big enough to throw their weight around when they need to. Most megacorps keep any extra-factional presence to storefronts and trade embassies; anything beyond that ventures into the minefield of international M-CORP law. And if you're not getting the benefits of being a hypercorp, it's folly to fight a hypercorp's battles.

HYPERCORPS

Hypercorps are defined by the OSPs which allow them to transcend national, factional, and planetary boundaries, establishing a presence in seemingly every nook and cranny of the Human Sphere; simultaneously belonging to everyone and no one.

Hypercorps offer the opportunity to streamline every aspect of their members' lives, and the reach to make that incredibly desirable. The promise of the Omni-Sided Platform means that *Loĝanto* never have to rely on anything outside the corporate umbrella of brands. They're certainly welcome to of course — M-CORP law is brutally clear on that point — but hypercorps keep matters in-house not through force or coercion, but by making it easy, elegant, and cost-effective to do so. A hypercorp's *Loĝanto* can travel from Yutang to Neoterra by way of *Bakunin*, and deal exclusively with their own people, their own spaceport check-ins, their own lodging, restaurants, and security. No matter where they go, they are always at home.

CORPORATE LIFE

Life inside a corporation is much like life anywhere else in the Human Sphere, the primary difference being brand ubiquity. From real estate to education, shopping to employment, the option to exclusively engage with your corp's brand is never forced, but it's always on the table. Corps consider it a point of pride to be the most enticing option, and integrating everything in a user's quantronic halo is easier and more rewarding when it's all under one roof.

It all begins with geists. While O-12's independent research shows no links between geist manufacturer and future spending recommendations, corps inherently dislike the idea of their *Loĝanto* placing that much trust in a competitor's product. Most people feel a familial connection to their geist, and each corporation wants to position itself as the extended family. Ease of access, a sense of belonging; these are the pillars of corporate inclusivity initiatives. A *Loĝanto's* children can attend any school they wish, but corp-funded academies have sterling reputations, and preferential admission is shown to the corporate family. In addition, the pipeline from education to employment is near 100% in corp schools, with dedicated programs

designed to prepare candidates for positions in the brand. It isn't forced, it isn't cultish, and it isn't soul-crushing slavery.

It is however, undeniably harsh.

The benefits afforded high-ranking *Loĝanto* are undeniably impressive, but as in any hierarchy, there's only so much room at the top. Competition among the upper echelons can be incredibly fierce and unapologetically vicious; to climb this corporate ladder is to enter a labyrinth of intrigue, guile, and backstabbing, to live in a world of espionage that rivals any Maya serial, with less promise of a happy ending. Lies, betrayal and more overt methods all find purchase in this cutthroat game, which corporations happily ignore, so long as it doesn't affect their bottom line. Historical accomplishments still matter a great deal, but when jockeying for top status, corps are far more interested in what you've done for them lately. In the end, it all comes down to quarterly profits, and someone is either providing value, or they are not, it's as simple as that.

Many would call this approach cold, even merciless, but loyal *Loĝanto* consider it entirely fair. Corporations present a true meritocracy, a place where ability and results matter more than anything else; where the cream can finally rise to the top. Hard work is rewarded. Your dreams are there for the taking, if you possess the initiative to seize them yourself. And if you're lazy, stupid, or just plain unmotivated?

Then you simply don't belong.

MEMBERSHIP STATUS

Corporate *Loĝanto* feel a sense of loyalty to their given brand, but for most, this is akin to the affinity one feels for a local sports team or university. And when the same megacorporation that provided your education, financed your university studies, and sponsors your favourite sports team is also your place of employment, a sense of belonging and loyalty is only natural; it's about brand identity, not geography.

Loĝanto status is a separate and legally distinct concept from national citizenship, and many megacorps — especially those with strong governmental ties — encourage active participation in their members' civic duties. On the other hand, a hypercorp transcends national boundaries by definition, making it more likely to encourage loyalty to the brand above all else.

CORPORATE LOĜANTO

VIPs. Elite. Uchi. Initié. Gnóstis. The exact phrasing differs from corp to corp, but the concept of *Loĝanto* — insiders — exists in every hypercorp, and some megas. Somewhere between a customer loyalty program, military pay grade, and an online profile, *Loĝanto* status is an attempt to quantify an individual's value to the brand, with associated perks and benefits at different levels. Every corp has its own model, but whether it's Oxyd Media's Bronze-through-Teseum rankings, Xperydes' colour-coded tiers, or Moto.tronica's high scores (complete with public leaderboards), the more valuable the *Loĝanto* is to the brand, the more power their status bestows.

THE FORTUNE 5,000

As mankind ventured to the stars, venture capitalists were foremost among them, spreading their wealth and influence to the cosmos. Today, there are more influential corporations than anyone could commit to memory, and corporate field agents could belong to any number of them. Rather than attempting to learn the ins and outs of every corporation, most agents simply familiarise themselves with common operational protocols, and offer their services to multiple hypercorps, one contract at a time.

These soldiers of fortune have a reputation for cold, detached professionalism; their loyalty is to their contracts, nothing else; corporations understand that. They enjoy a surprisingly cordial relationship with corporate security units — while an agent might be on the opposite side of a firefight today, they could very well be colleagues tomorrow — which has resulted in a curious sort of mutual respect, and some complicated relationships.

Qingdao Report – p. 25

茜氛
NEON LOTUS

NEO LOTUS

Business: Station in Mars orbit.

CONFIDENTES

The *confidentes* are exclusive, and usually-high-ranking, members of the *Loĝanto*. They are intelligence agents – ever-vigilant for any leg up on the competition, or a chance to knock their rivals down a peg. Officially, *confidentes* are a sort of corporate scout; looking for opportunities in different markets, staying abreast of economic and social trends and keeping tabs on the corp's resources, human and otherwise. Unofficially, they're a kind of corporate secret police; a velvet glove, curled into a fist. Industrial espionage, threats, sabotage and worse; not every *confidente* engages in these acts, but many do. And they could be anyone.

NeoColonial Wars – p. 22

INTERSPACE TRUST

Business: Cargo transport.

Yănjīng – p. 191

WILDERNESS OF MIRRORS

The corporate world is full of hostile actions, takeovers, threats, bribery, and extortion; and that's just in the boardrooms. Beyond the official actions, corporations are active in practically every facet of modern espionage. Whether clandestinely acquiring a prototype TAG schematic, sabotaging a rivals' mining operations, or simply acquiring what blackmail there is to be had, the life of a corporate agent is rarely dull.

Not that such matters are always kept in-house; hypercorps, in particular, make extensive use of consultants. Mercenary companies, freelancers — really any capable individual interested in some unique opportunities — there's always work to be found for a reliable asset with no traceable ties to the corp.

Many corps take their information privacy quite seriously. Rumours of so-called "Phoenix Ops" — where assets are killed upon completion of the mission, and clandestinely resurrected from back-ups, erasing any knowledge of the job — have never been confirmed, and would require absurd expense.

YU JING INTERSPACE TRUST CORPORATION

At the end of the NeoColonial Wars, the Yu Jing Interspace Trust Corporation (YJITC) was one of the largest megacorps in the Human Sphere. Based out of Yutang, it owned more than two dozen astroports across the Human Sphere and was one of the three largest international container terminal operators. It also seemed content to remain focused on its domination of interstellar and interplanetary trade.

Fifteen years ago, however, that began to change. The YJITC began rapidly acquiring other corporate interests and reorganised itself as an emerging hypercorp. The Qingdao Report recently revealed the true scope of their ambition: YJITC had acquired control over more than one hundred fifty international businesses, including twelve companies of significant strategic relevance. The Report also revealed that the sudden change in YJITC's modus operandi was due to the company becoming a front for the Yănjīng: Although the NeoColonial Wars came to an end, it seemed that Yu Jing chose to merely move the conflict from the battlefield to the boardroom.

O-12 began a quiet prosecution of the YJITC for violations of the M-CORP law in an effort to curb Yănjīng's ambitions, but, when the Qingdao Report was leaked to the public, these efforts were scuttled. YJITC's operations remain intact, although their activities are now closely scrutinised outside of Yu Jing space.

The YJITC also remains an odd duck among hypercorps. Its *Loĝanto* is unusually small, exclusive, and even secretive. This is widely seen as a vestige of the original megacorp's more traditional relationship with its consumers, but it may have more to do with Yănjīng's influence over the hypercorp's affairs. It is also now suspected that a large proportion of its *Loĝanto* are *confidentes*, many of whom may be participating in operations far beyond the normal limits of corporate espionage.

YJITC: PUBLIC AFFAIRS SPECIALISTS

On the surface, the YJITC Department of Public Affairs looks similar to many corporate PR divisions. Primarily concerned with the public image of YJITC, their authority extends far beyond simple press releases; they are entrusted with preserving the public face of the company, and by extension, the State-Empire. Face is a serious matter in Yu Jing, and Public Affairs Specialists are authorised to take whatever steps they deem necessary to maintain it.

Crisis Communication: Chen Zetao, a prominent financial advisor operating on Concilium, has been implicated in an increasing number of embarrassing scandals. His Cube must be brought to Yutang, with or without the rest of him. The Public Relations department humbly requests that this be somehow pinned on PanOceania and, obviously, O-12 must be kept in the dark.

The Value of Hard Work: Gao Xi is a criminally negligent, though loyal, manager in the Svalarheiman branch. He is also the nephew of the Minister of Industry; firing him would mean a massive loss of face, but keeping him is too great a risk. Use any means necessary, so long as the Party suffers no further embarrassment, and no authorities discover his indiscretions.

Murders and Acquisitions: Tozawa Kanako — pharmaceutical genius, chimera, and Yu Jing expatriate — has refused multiple generous offers to purchase her patents. She's hiding somewhere in VaudeVille — allegedly with some scary new pets — and has said that the Party can have her designs when they pry them from her cold, dead fingers. After careful consideration, management has approved her request.

XPERYDES OMNI-NATIONAL: VALUATION ANALYSTS

Many employees have a "Valuation Analyst" tag added to their credentials; these individuals evaluate the impact of events on Xperydes' bottom line, and take preventative measures accordingly. Sometimes, that means downgrading a sales agent's credit rating. Sometimes, that means kidnapping, extortion, assassination, or something more inventive. Either way, their sole priority is the financial health of the corporation.

Kidnapping Insurance: Hesperia Consulting does, in fact, negotiate with terrorists; at least when their insurance covers the ransom. A kidnapping ring seems to have gotten wind of this, abducting employees and demanding suspiciously precise ransoms. How did they come by this information? More importantly, can the kidnappings be stopped before Hesperia's insurance premiums go up?

Citizens Divided: Edgar Cruz is a popular PanOceanian lobbyist. Unfortunately, his policies will unintentionally cripple Aigletech's competitive status in Acontecimento. An incident is inadvisable; reducing his standing in the lobby should suffice. Given that he's having numerous affairs, privately mistrusts ALEPH, and is prone to outbursts when flustered, agents are encouraged to find innovative solutions to his popularity.

Season Premiere: Mercury Communications has always pitted its Mayacasts against one another, but even by their standards, recent competition has taken a violent and disturbingly personal tone. Known affiliates of Oxyd Media have been seen nearby, and management suspects intentional agitation, or worse.

XPERYDES OMNI-NATIONAL

The oldest, and arguably most powerful hypercorp, Xperydes has its tendrils in just about everything. Keeping tabs on their diverse interests requires a multitude of field agents — some full-time, some consultants — to keep their myriad divisions running smoothly.

AIGLETECH
Producers of custom-tailored geists, their patented learning algorithms see extensive use across the Human Sphere. They trumpet their code as being "tamper-proof." Obviously, many hackers have taken that as a personal challenge.

HESPERYA CONSULTING
Providing expert consultation on everything from real estate and vacation planning, to business ventures and military campaigns, Hesperya leverages their considerable connections to provide the most comprehensive intelligence available, ensuring their clients can make decisions with confidence. Just don't ask where the intel comes from.

LADON SECURITY SOLUTIONS
During the Human Edge Corporate Crises, Xperydes internal security force became overwhelmed by concerns spanning national, factional, and planetary boundaries. In response, the hypercorp bought out Agatha Rand's Ladon Security Solutions, a mercenary company. Ladon became a hypercorp-spanning security force, coordinating physical, psychological, and quantronic security across Xperydes' vast array of diffuse components.

Ladon also serves as a central hub for Xperydes' *confidentes* and runs black ops to silence internal dissent or stifle external competition. True to their mercenary roots, Ladon frequently subcontracts these assignments to independent contractors with a reputation for professionalism, discretion, and brutal efficiency.

At various times, Xperydes has also been known to make the services of Ladon available on the War Market. It is unclear whether this is simply an intermittent effort to monetize the division, or if there is some deeper stratagem at play.

MERCURY COMMUNICATIONS
A Maya conglomerate, Mercury Communications operates hundreds of different channels, often in competition with one another in order to acquire the largest possible market share. They're firm believers in friendly competition, so long as they're competing with themselves. Otherwise, look out.

XPERYDES BIOTECHNOLOGY
One of the few hypercorp divisions to maintain a headquarters on Earth, Xperydes pioneered Lhost interface technology, and proudly fulfils Resurrection contracts in every major faction except the Nomads. Though rumour has it they supply Praxis with the technology to do so as well… just not proudly.

PHARMACOMP
Business: Pharmaceutical industry

BEYHAN CONTRACTORS STI
Business: Engineering, construction, private security.

COMPASS
Business: Cargo transport.

Xperydes Omni-National

Corporate Crises – p. 21

FACTION
MERCENARIES

Mercenaries have existed ever since the idea of formalised warfare was invented. For them, war is a business. And, like all businesses, they seek to make it profitable and efficient.

When it comes to the theatres of war, they are considered indispensable in the big picture and eminently dispensable in the specific. The military resources of the major powers in the Human Sphere are vast, but there will always be situations where private, independent personnel will be an important part of modern conflict. Whether it is due to a lack of manpower, a lack of supplies, or, in general, a lack of desire to place their own soldiers in harm's way, every major power in O-12 has employed mercenaries to protect their interests or bolster their forces on the battlefield.

MERCENARY COMPANIES

Mercenary companies are the fiefdoms of the Warmongers who own and control them. They are essentially the company's CEO – in charge of its finances and contracts – but individual warmongers often share little in common. Many have other business interests, of which their mercenary companies may be subsidiaries. Others are fiercely independent and dedicated wholly to a military life. Their business ethics can also vary dramatically, from the straight and narrow operators who scrupulously fulfil their contracts, to fly-by-night hooligans, to near-criminal raiders who levy (legally or illegally) their operating funds from the territories they occupy.

The modern mercenary company, however, is generally not a monolithic entity. Instead, they are nested hierarchies of subcontractors. A warmonger will license one or more platoons, each of which is an independent organisation owned and operated by its Colonel. The colonels, in turn, form their platoons by hiring Captains who control small units made up of individual mercenaries (who are, themselves, freelancers working under contract for their captain).

Although most mercs, units, and platoons are under long-term contracts or otherwise more-or-less permanently attached to their company, it's not unusual for a given mercenary unit to not only find itself fighting for PanOceania one day and Yu Jing the next, but to be doing so under the auspices of a completely different mercenary company.

WAR MARKET

Although there are exceptions, the majority of mercenary companies are organised through the War Market — an informal collection of Maya clusters which serve as a form of "mercenary stock exchange."

Each licensed mercenary unit, platoon, and company has a serial number, a database, and a monetary value attached to their name in the Market. Investors can buy and trade stock in all of these, from individual soldiers (who often use limited term public offerings to purchase equipment and logistical support) to full mercenary companies, with the contractual expectation of dividends paid against earnings.

The other function of the War Market is the actual hiring of mercenaries: Captains hire soldiers, colonels hire captains, warmongers hire colonels, and clients hire the warmongers. (Although, in some cases, clients may seek to directly hire smaller units or even individual soldiers.) Direct offers are often employed, although it's also not unusual for employers to post a strategic prospectus detailing an operation and requesting public bids.

The War Market has given rise to a number of unusual financial instruments and market players — blood arbitrageurs, battle gamblers, soul shorters (who short sell the stocks of individual soldiers on the expectation that they'll be dead, causing their stock value to evaporate). Perhaps most notable are the joint-stock companies that have been formed to independently fund large mercenary operations, allowing warmongers to undertake unusual ventures which would have previously been impossible without operating under the auspices of a nation state.

A SOLDIER'S LIFE

Maya shows are filled with stories about mercs saving villages from raiders and performing daring missions to save innocent women who have been captured by cartels. But the life of most mercenaries is more prosaic: it depends greatly upon how successful they are at their job and how much money their employers can rake in.

Mercenaries working front-line contracts on Paradiso or elsewhere have an experience fairly

PUBLIC PERCEPTION

Mercenaries are viewed by some as thugs and gangsters who lack the traditions of honour and nobility cultivated in traditional armies and who care more for making money than fighting for a cause. But there are many mercenary companies, such as Kaplan Tactical Services, who are seen as heroes in their homelands and there are many mercenaries who only accept honest jobs.

FREE VS. CORPORATE

Some mercenaries draw a firm distinction between the Free Companies (businesses which are focused on their mercenary operations) and corporate contractors (mercenary companies which act as a branch or subsidiary of a larger megacorp or hypercorp). There can be a fair amount of gray area when it comes to this issue, however, as demonstrated by companies like SecLock Contingencies (which serves primarily corporate clients) and the Druze Society (which is not organised along strictly traditional corporate structures).

RED FLAGS

Mercenary companies that do shoddy or unreliable work, or which fail to pay their soldiers, will earn a red flag on the War Market. Similarly, soldiers who refuse to obey orders or desert may find themselves flagged.

similar to a normal soldier (although with better perks): Tedium spiked with terror. But these contracts are usually the exception, and most mercenaries will spend the bulk of their time serving as routine guards or perhaps occasionally engaging in a targeted engagement of limited scope.

Downtime will often be filled with intense training regimes. New recruits who lack skills considered essential to the unit (and usually working under ultra-cheap "rookie contracts") undergo gruelling training exercises while combat veterans perform endless drills designed to hone their skills and make sure they can all fight fluidly as a team.

Between training and being on manoeuvres, however, things are much more lax for mercenaries. Many mercenaries are left to their own devices, and most maintain their own homes or residences. They can stay out as late as they want and spend their money any way they see fit without fear of tarnishing the honour of their corps or having their superior officers inquire about their social lives. For those mercenaries who have been released from a state-run army, the life of a mercenary is refreshing and often satisfies their needs thoroughly; for those who could never cut it in an army, the mercenary lifestyle appeals to their sense of freedom.

CAPTAIN

Captains have a responsibility to their unit. They are responsible for finding work or long-term contracts. They coordinate with their colonel, make sure their orders are properly relayed, and take care of mission planning. They oversee disbursement of funds from the company. Mercenaries who sign a contract with a captain do so with the understanding that they will be taken care of, their interests protected, and their services valued. A captain who is unable to find work for their soldiers or treats them poorly will quickly find themselves replaced or without a unit to lead.

COLONEL

As leaders of a company's platoons, colonels are responsible for managing most of the company's logistics, including minutia such as having permits up to date or making sure there's enough fuel to keep the ships running. The colonel is also responsible for taking charge in larger scale skirmishes and for leading the company through conflicts.

RECRUITER AGENTS

Freelance recruiter agents seek out and manage individual soldiers on the War Market. For their clients, they actually fulfil many of the same duties as a captain — protecting their interests, seeking employment contracts, and so forth. (The distinction is that the recruiter merely manages personnel; they are not assembling a combat unit.)

Other recruiters are employed full-time by the larger mercenary companies. These recruiters are dedicated talent scouts, seeking out the best units and soldiers available on the War Market (and also attempting to poach them from competitors). Company recruiters are often disliked by the rank and file, who resent having their lives evaluated as mere statistics to be bartered and sold.

GETTING RECRUITED

Mercenary companies primarily draw their ranks from former soldiers — either those who miss being in an armed service, brawlers seeking the thrill of violence, or the desperate whose only marketable skills were learned in a barracks. However, it is not uncommon to find recruits from all walks of life — labourers, lawyers, doctors, and engineers can all find their place. Some recruiters are also known to watch the full-VR Maya simulation leader boards for potential candidates.

TACTICAL MANAGERS

Tactical managers are specialists in military strategy and the deployment of personnel. Their exact role varies considerably from one company to the next. In smaller companies, they often act as adjuncts to the company's colonel. In larger companies, however, they may actually be the colonels' superior officer (sometimes operating under the rank of General).

Tactical managers also often act as salesmen, pitching the company's tactical plan of action to potential clients. Those who excel at these presentations are particularly valuable to their warmongers, as they can often make the difference between securing a public bid contract or being forced to downsize.

SPECIALISTS

Not every mercenary is a soldier, though the distinction can sometimes be hard to see. The War Market also caters to a large number of specialists, although, of course, many of these skills transfer and it's not unusual to find mercenaries and companies active in several lines of employment.

CORSAIRS AND PRIVATEERS

The hiring of corsairs and privateers is rare, but not an uncommon practice. Deeply frowned upon by O-12 and the Concilium Courts, many nations have been known to hire pirates and privateers as part of their black ops programs. The goal of hiring privateers and pirates is to harass their opponents and cause widespread disruption to their rivals' operations. This allows for the employer's business to prosper as their industry goes on unaffected by these raids, while their competition is often crushed beneath the heavy costs of replacing lost goods and personnel.

HITMEN

Hitmen live a dangerous life. They risk imprisonment or even death for their jobs, but one mission can mean that they have made enough money for life. Those who earn a reputation for killing even the most difficult targets demand top dollar in the private sector, and some are even kept on retainer by major corporations in case they have a need to eliminate former employees or disrupt their rivals' business operations.

INFOWARRIORS

Freelance hackers specialised in combat infiltrations are an essential element for any mercenary group, but are also prized for solo operations throughout the Human Sphere. There is a surprisingly high demand for mercenary infowarriors on Dawn, where their skill at dealing with the advanced technology of foreign corporations and nations have made them invaluable to Ariadna.

SECURITY FIRMS

Throughout the Sphere there are numerous private security firms that advertise their services to corporations and banks. These security firms are often better equipped than ordinary police forces, and are often more strict in their goals. A private security officer is tasked with protecting the client he has been hired to work for rather than enforcing laws for the public good.

NOTABLE MERC COMPANIES

Dahshat Company: Led by the warmonger Qaid Fahesh, the Dahshat Company is quietly one of the largest employers of mercenaries throughout the Sphere. Fahesh often uses his mercenaries for personal "pet projects" that are intimately tied into the labyrinthine interests of his other corporate holdings, which include extensive Maya corporations, brokerage firms, and the sole rights to profit from tourism in the Zumurroda complex east of Parthalia Island on Bourak.

Foreign Company: The Van Orton Military Contracts Foreign Company — more commonly referred to as simply the Foreign Company — is notable for its "superstar" mercenaries (including Van Orton, their famous owner). There are a number of licensed Arachne and Maya programs documenting the semi-fictionalised and heavily glamorised exploits of the Heroes of the Foreign Company, creating an irresistible public image that's invaluable for recruitment efforts. Less public are the company's notorious ties to the Figueroa Estate.

Free Company of the Star: More commonly known as Star Company, this motley group of primarily ex-*Corregidor* soldiers is the premiere Nomad private military company (PMC) and one of the primary competitors of the Foreign Company. Star Company is often featured in advertisements across Nomad ships as a way for anyone to travel the galaxy and reinvent themselves. Their rigid training methods are designed to turn anyone into soldiers, and, thanks to the broad backgrounds of those who join Star Company, the mercenaries have access to almost any skills they might need.

Ikari Company: Run by the pragmatic Colonel Ikari, a former intelligence officer serving in the JSA and the StateEmpire Army of Yu Jing, the Ikari Company is based out of an asteroid in the far reaches of Human Edge and engages primarily in corporate security, but has also been frequently accused of piracy (including the CS Aygir freighter incident). Their greatest infamy, however, was achieved during the Helicon Miners' Revolt. Considered as brilliant as he is ruthless,

NeoColonial Wars – p. 22

Ariadnan Commercial Conflicts – p. 23

SERPENT'S TEETH

The Anacondans have earned a reputation for intermittently engaging in seemingly erratic off-book behaviour during certain operations. Those who dig into these incidents are generally left with the impression that at least some of the Anaconda units are profiteering. Some intel analysts, however, suspect that the entire company was founded as a covert operation by the Nomad Black Hand.

Zumurroda / Parthalia Island – p. 236

"We are bad people, but we can be worse."

—Druze Paramilitary Motto

Colonel Ikari will work for any employer if the price is right and his forces have been involved in some of the most brutal suppressions of worker strikes across the galaxy. Ikari Company has even been used by Yu Jing against ethnic Japanese civilians. Ikari simply doesn't care, as long as he's getting paid.

Varangian Guard: Founded by William McKellar, the most famous member of the Ariadnan Expeditionary Corps, this Caledonian mercenary unit is particularly active on the frontiers of Dawn and has recently secured a large contract to provide security for new colonies pushing out into Antipode territories. A savvy warmonger, McKellar strategically uses lucrative off-world contracts to further enhance his homeland forces. He knows that the Human Sphere is thirsty for the frontier brawn bred into the Ariadnan soul, and the Varangians have collaborated extensively with Bureau Aegis. He offers the stars to the youth of Dawn, but his recruiter agents are also thick as flies on Paradiso, seeking to sign AEC veterans ending their tours to prestigious rookie contracts. McKellar believes that "locking in" the advanced military techniques learned on the Paradiso fronts is crucial to securing Ariadna's future security.

Wardrivers are a non-centralised organisation based out of semi-aligned private Maya clusters (which often feature a panoply of encrypted virtual environments). All their members have handles and they employ colour-coded classes to denote the types of jobs they specialise in. (For example, Lyla "Dominia" O'Toole is a White-class wardriver.) Their clusters also feature an exclusive kitbashing community known, for esoteric reasons, as Lilacs that develop custom hardware and software to give them unique advantages in the kaleidoscopic conflicts of quantronic warfare.

RELEVANT MERC UNITS

Anaconda Mercenary TAG Squadron: Originally established by the Corregidor Jurisdictional Command, the Anacondans are a rare squadron of mercenary TAG pilots. Following a political scandal in which the unit followed the orders of their corporate employer to suppress a protest by Corregidoran zero-g workers, the CJC attempted to disband the unit. Its members instead resigned en masse, secured financing from the Tyomkin Bank (a small Tunguskan firm), purchased their own equipment, and formed a licensed mercenary company. They have since fought in the NeoColonial Wars, the Ariadnan Commercial Conflicts, and in numerous corporate scuffles in Human Edge.

Druze Shock Teams: The Druze Society rose out of a religious movement in the Levant which is a mixture of Islam, Gnosticism, and other philosophies. Using a seamless mixture of corporate ventures and organised crime — leading many to refer to them as the Druze Mafia — the Society launched itself out of the chaos of the 21st century to become a significant astropolitical power that controls transportation infrastructure from the orbital elevator of east Africa to the caravanserai around the jump gates currently being constructed at Bourak's second wormhole.

During their turf wars with the Drygalski mob, the Druze essentially created a private military force. Once the Drygalski threat had been brutally dealt with, the Druze found themselves with an idle army. Rather than disbanding their forces, they created the Druze Shock Teams and joined the War Market. The exact number of Shock Teams varies at any given time, and each is an independent company. The Druze believe that the fierce, internal competition between the teams keeps them strong.

What the Druze Shock Teams truly offer to their employers, however, is the opportunity to hire mafia enforcers with a thin veneer of legitimacy. This, of course, is not without its controversies. In the aftermath of the Ariadnan Commercial Conflicts, for example, Caledonian survivors linked Druze mercenaries working on behalf of the MagnaObra of widespread, dreadful atrocities committed against civilian populations, including the systematic levelling of entire communities which refused to cooperate with the hypercorp's agenda. The resulting court case is still tied up in the Concilium Courts.

Kaplan Tactical Services: A subsidiary of Beyhan Resources, Inc. created during the Silk Revolts and based out of Bourak, KTS is named after the former Sultan's personal guard. Infamous for their strict adherence to the company's Code, they are the Druze's biggest rival for mercenary services in Haqqislam and have extensive security contracts with the Funduq Sultanate.

SecLock Contingencies: SecLock's Corporate Security Units (CSUs) bring an elite level of training comparable to professional special forces to corporate security. The company has a broad portfolio including bodyguard services, counterterrorism, and corporate espionage. CSU agents often have sophisticated implants throughout their bodies that can passively and actively monitor environmental factors — ambient

Silk Revolts, p. 21: In 30 NC, Silk Lords sought to overthrow the government. Battles were fought up and down Haqqislam trade routes.

Concilium Courts – p. 212

Sainte Michelle de Bois Bleu – p. 239

BURNING STAR

During the premiere of *Kings of the Human Edge* — an AR drama at the Comique theatrical pavilion — the chemical sniffers of a CSU team hired by Michael Weber, the industrial tycoon and owner of WelleTech, detected an explosive. Jake Wu, one of the CSU agents, realised that evacuating their client would leave thousands of others in peril. Seizing the bomb, he used his powered armour to fly the bomb several hundred feet into the air. It detonated, claiming Wu's life but no others. Morbidly dubbed the Burning Star by Maya tabloids, Wu's sacrifice quadrupled the normal signing rate for SecLock security contracts over the next year. The company has established a college fund for his orphaned daughter Miranda, who is currently developing her dramatic life-log (*Daughter of the Burning Star*) with the Rhapsodes Maya channel.

Ariadnan Expeditionary Corps – p. 24

Bureau Aegis, p. 213: Legal and military arm of the O-12 government.

Helicon Miners' Revolt – p. 254

HACKER CLASSES

White-class wardrivers protect networks from hostile hackers. Black-class hackers are the crackers, willing to engage in hostile (and legally questionable) assaults on systems. (These are also referred to by the old slang terms of "white hats" and "black hats".) Gray-class wardrivers have a mixed reputation between the two, and usually have a spotted past filled with interesting stories from both sides of the ever-raging quantronic "war".

YUAN YUAN SLAVE TRADE

One of the Yuan Yuan's biggest activities is the trade of slaves, who are still used by worlds on the edge of O-12 control. In particular, the Yuan Yuan deal in the trafficking of Eunuchs, specially altered humans who can no longer have a Cube implanted in them. These slaves are often beaten and forced into addiction to drugs to ensure compliance, and they are worth a great deal to the right client.

temperature, non-human visual spectrums, wide-band audio, airborne chemical concentrations, etc.– while coordinating with a pseudo-AI capable of interpreting the data and warning CSU agents of threats before they become consciously aware of them. Ever since the Burning Star incident in Sainte Michelle de Bois Bleu, it has become fashionable for Concilium senators to hire enhanced CSU agents to accompany and supplement their internal security staff.

 Wardrivers: The Wardrivers are not a mercenary company, but they are the premiere professional association for mercenary hackers. The term "wardriver" dates back to the 21st century, referring to opportunistic hackers who would drive around town looking for open networks to infiltrate. The modern wardrivers appear to have grown out of this tradition, becoming guerrilla hackers during the Nanotech Wars.

 Yuan Yuan: When an agent hires Yuan Yuan, they need to know that they are not hiring a scalpel or even a sword, but a chainsaw capable of inflicting massive casualties. There are pirates, and there are corsairs, but there is nobody quite like the Yuan Yuan when it comes to a threat in the space lanes. Less an organised group and more a chaotic whirlwind of guns and violence, the Yuan Yuan are descended from explorers and spacefarers trying to survive in the asteroid belts of the Yu Jing system. They lived a life where only the most brutal and vicious could survive by killing their neighbours and taking their supplies to survive before slowly banding together to form small groups of pirates.

Fiercely condemned and oppressed by Yu Jing, a number of Yuan Yuan groups received funding and professional military training from PanOceania during the NeoColonial Wars. The Hyperpower was hoping to use the Yuan Yuan to destabilise the Jade Dragon, but when the Initial Stage of the war came to an end, it had the unintended consequence of unleashing them across the Human Sphere. With their ramshackle instrasystem vessels now upgraded and improved, several Yuan Yuan crews listed themselves on the War Market, hitched rides on the Circulars, and followed their new mercenary contracts to Human Edge, Svalarheima, and beyond.

BOUNTY HUNTER SYNDICATE

Although created by the O-12 Interstellar Agreement on Extradition and Rendition (IAER), the Bounty Hunter Syndicate operates as an independent agency. Joining the Syndicate is relatively simple: An applicant goes to one of their chapter houses and applies for a permit. After an intensive background check, passing their TTs (abbreviation of "treaty test", which is slang for the IAER-mandated certification exam on O-12 legal practices), and paying a fee, the applicant is placed on the apprenticeship rolls. Full members of the Syndicate can pull apprentices from the rolls to assist them, allowing the apprentices to earn points towards full membership for themselves. For those who don't want to deal with the hassle of an apprenticeship, it's also possible to simply buy the required points, at which point they'll be left to their own devices. Ultimately, the Syndicate only cares that the agent captures their quarries and pays their share of the bounties to them.

MERCENARY MISSIONS

A mercenary's assignment is about the targeted application of force, loyalty to the client, and keeping a strict eye on the bottom line. This can include targeted strikes aimed at specific objectives, coordinated campaigns with regular armed forces, or long-term security assignments.

Hold 32: The Yuan Yuan have been raiding mining ships from the Ephesian Trojans in Human Edge. The unit has been hired as an onboard security force, their mission to repel boarders. But the pirates aren't acting like normal raiders, and the crew isn't offering any explanation for why Hold 32 has been sealed shut.

Shadows on the Hinterlands: The unit is working a routine convoy contract guarding Teseum

shipments crawling their way across the surface of Dawn. The first Antipodes raid knocked out the long-range communications equipment, however, and now the tribes are on the hunt...

Zhurong Gambit: When the Nomads took control of the Zhurong Power Station in the wake of Operation Flamestrike on Paradiso, they also captured Dr. He Yuyuan, a Yu Jing engineer in the Department of Military Support Technologies Development who had been onsite field-testing humanoid Yaozao remotes. Yu Jing wants Yuyuan back, but with the Nomads holding Zhurong's vital power output hostage, they can't risk direct action. The unit is ordered to extract the asset, while preferably framing Haqqislam for the effort.

Although being able to say, "I'm syndicated," and flashing a Syndicate badge gives legal authorisation throughout the Human Sphere, bounty hunters still have to abide by local laws, regulations, and customs. In PanOceania that often means navigating a herd of lawyers. On Bourak it requires expert social engineering to navigate the contempt local officials have for the profession. Fortunately, for bounty hunters who run into trouble, the Syndicate offers a lot of expertise and has a reputation capable of opening doors that might otherwise remain closed.

THE LISTS

One of the big advantages of being a Syndicate member is access to the Lists. Maintained by a pseudo-AI named Monica Blue, the Lists collate available bounties from local, national, and international agencies across the Human Sphere for easy access by bounty hunters. Monica Blue will also push listings out to hunters who are in the right area or specially qualified to collect. She's also capable of performing deep analysis on Syndicate intelligence sources and can coordinate the activities of hunters on multiple planets, allowing them to seamlessly cooperate in the tracking and takedown of difficult subjects.

Hunters refer to their targets as "yips", and use a variety of slang terms for them.

- Skips are those who have failed to appear for trial after paying a bail.
- Blips are quantronic criminals, often requiring a hunter to first put a face to a handle before they can be captured.
- Rips are wanted criminals who haven't been arrested yet.
- Flagships are targets for whom private individuals (grieving families or corporations with an agenda) have "spiked" the official bail with an additional reward.
- Zips are targets on the rumoured Black Lists for whom a reward is being paid strictly from a private party (usually corporate) outside of IAER's mandate. Zip bounties are usually illegal (except among the Nomads), and getting caught pursuing a zip can result in a bounty hunter losing their licensing.

The community has also developed a similar method for referring to various assets. For example, a Judas is someone from a target's personal life willing to rat them out. A Shesha is someone who provides a place of sanctuary or rest for the target. A Freya is anyone who has shot at a hunter.

FAMOUS BOUNTY HUNTERS

Father Lucien Sforza: PanOceania's most feared bounty hunter is a dedicated servant of Justice and the labour of God. Tireless in pursuit of the guilty and incapable of compromise, Sforza never gives

BOUNTY HUNTER MISSIONS

Many bounty hunters operate solo. Even those who work in small teams, however, are often left with a feeling of loneliness. They are isolated, out on the edge, and virtually always operating without a support structure. It's just them versus their target — a competition of brawn and brain.

Among the Stars: It was supposed to be a simple skip. But as the bounty hunters dig into the yip's life, they discover that it's all lie: A cover identity for Alexander Cortez, a mercenary captain in the Star Company. Cortez has gone back to his old life now. What mission objective had he been pursuing under his cover identity? And how can he be extracted from the middle of a heavily armed mercenary base?

Off the Books: Plucking a job off the Black List, the bounty hunters are charged with kidnapping Eanraig Murray, heir to the Chieftain of Clan Murray. Their anonymous employers plan to use the kid as blackmail.

Race of the Wolf: Diego Ruiz — aka Baccarat — was once a premier bounty hunter, ratcheting up over five hundred captures during his career. But he broke the law, and now, as a wolf in the fold, there's a substantial bounty on his head. Baccarat knows all the tricks of the trade, allowing him to keep one step ahead of his pursuers. To make matters worse, the nonexclusive prize has attracted five other teams of hunters, too — and it's possible that some of the competition is actually working with their old buddy Ruiz.

up a bounty — just one reason his name is spoken with awed respect by even the most brutal of thugs.

Ljubo "Ballistic" Radan: Less a bounty hunter than style personified, "Ballistic Radan" has something of minor celebrity status through the Human Sphere, something which he uses to his advantage, ensuring that his reputation and demeanour do much of his work for him. Not that he isn't extremely deadly as well.

Ylenia Petronescu: Cunning, beautiful and trickier than a hacker with an attitude problem, Petronescu has established herself as a premiere bounty huntress. Combining seductiveness with viciousness has ensured that Ylenia is able to live in some style — you don't become a bounty huntress for the hours, do you?

Max Skorpio: Infamous amongst criminals and law enforcement, Skorpio is the ideal bounty hunter — if the Syndicate could, they'd have him on their promotional material. When he's not bounty hunting, his reputation is somewhat more troublesome and has led to his face appearing in other material, alongside the daughters and wives of powerful clients.

Miranda Ashcroft: Born to all the rank and privileges of a wealthy family, the path Ashcroft followed to become a bounty hunter is shrouded in mystery. But she's deadly with every gun ever produced, and quite willing to use them. She may be high born, but she shoots low.

OTHER BOUNTY HUNTERS

Not every bounty hunter is syndicated. Some are purely local freelancers, often working for bail bondsmen. Others, like those working for Submondo crime bosses, simply eschew the law. There are also smaller IAER-authorised bounty hunter organisations, although the Syndicate is usually fairly ruthless in stamping them out (through a combination of cronyism, aggressive recruitment, and political machinations).

O-12

Governed by the Pillars – a set of values that form the core ideology of the organisation – O-12 is a vital bureaucratic nexus which draws representatives and members from across the Human Sphere in its efforts to align the national and corporate interests of its members toward the goals of mutual prosperity, peace, and cooperation. Empowered to create international law, it enforces its will through specially tasked Bureaus which manage everything from agriculture to wealth distribution, from astrophysical research to political studies, from education to economics, and from military intervention through to clandestine operations and espionage.

Although ostensibly neutral in its political will, O-12 is nevertheless plagued by factional disputes: The Öberhaus, Petite Assemblée, and Concilium Courts are all hives of intrigue and influence which filter down through the Bureaus.

O-12 OPERATIONS

Founded near the end of the 21st century, O-12 not only surfed a century of crises but steadily increased its remit by accumulating the power necessary to face each crisis as it arose. Seven decades ago it completed its ascension by taking control of the Concilium System and naming it the capital of the Human Sphere.

PILLARS OF O-12

Unity, Cooperation, Support, and Progress. The Pillars of O-12 are the values around which the organisation is built. In fact, the entire structure of O-12 is aimed at ensuring that the Pillars characterise the operation of O-12, and that national and corporate interests come a distant second.

Any person who joins O-12 is required to renounce any previously held ties, and swear allegiance to the organisation and its Pillars. Given the function of O-12, it draws on a large number of idealistic individuals from throughout the Human Sphere, and, while the renunciation of national ties is ubiquitous, old biases are hard to shake.

But although cynics scoff at the Pillars – pointing at the numerous incidents in which O-12's institutions have compromised on their ideals – the Pillars remain a point of pride and a guiding light for many (perhaps most) of the organisation.

BUDGET

O-12 is a large and complex bureaucracy, aside from iconic functions such as the Öberhaus, Petite Assemblée, and the Courts, it also spends a significant amount financing its Bureaus, Commissions, and programs.

In order to "fund the beast" (as Nomad propaganda infamously put it), each member state is required to donate an equal portion of what's referred to as O-12's *operating budget* (with the members of the Security Council paying a larger share referred to as a *sekureco fonduso*, or security fund). One of the ways in which O-12 forged its strength and independence, however, was by securing independent funding. Referred to as the expanded budget, these sources of income are varied: Patents from O-12 research programs, lease fees for various local services, and so forth.

Probably the most significant of these additional funding sources are the Circulars. A solid percentage of the earnings from the Circulars (including the system tariffs paid by serviced nations) go directly to the accounts of O-12, and as the Circular program came fully online it represented a massive increase in the expanded budget.

FACILITIES

O-12 has facilities and installations on every planet in the Human Sphere – administration buildings, diplomatic centres, research and development institutions, educational programmes, aid missions, small military bases – each managed by a specific Bureau. (And not all of them public knowledge.)

Undoubtedly the core of O-12 is to be found on Concilium Prima, with extensive training grounds for soldiers, spec ops, and undercover agents based there, as well as the headquarters for every major Bureau.

O-12 pours a significant amount of money into various other types of infrastructure, predominantly medical and educational. The universities of Concilium Prima are some of the best and well-funded in the Human Sphere. Bureaus like Aegis have bases in every hotspot, while Bureau Noir agents have handlers and safe houses secreted away on every world.

PANOCEANIA PLEADS POVERTY!

"Has the era of the Hyperpower come to an end? PanOceania claims its pockets are empty and its coffers so strained that they can't afford to pay the dues they owe to O-12! Does anyone really buy that?"

– Golden Fleece on Maya channel *Mégaphone*, sued by PanOceania as a suspected cover for Nomad Black Propaganda

O-12 GOVERNMENT

ÖBERHAUS

The Öberhaus is the beating heart of O-12. Its sprawling and austere buildings dominate the centre of Edda, on Concilium Prima. Filled with meeting rooms, conference chambers, offices, and the Senate itself, the buildings and grounds are an effigy to the Pillars of O-12, and an architectural glory in their own right.

The Senate is made up of a fluid number of members, with representation from O-12 itself, from every national power in the Human Sphere (including the Nomads and non-aligned countries). Typically, a representative to the Öberhaus serves a four-year term before their role is up for reappointment, and nations are free to appoint their own representatives.

The Senate is a vital component of the function of O-12: It is the legislative power of the organisation, and its decisions will apply universally to the Human Sphere. International laws, treaties, and agreements between national and corporate interests are debated on the floor and signed off or voted down.

Motions in the Senate are passed with a clear majority, and while O-12 holds considerable sway, much wrangling to find support is required. Despite its best efforts, external lobbying and back room dealing are common, and Bureau Noir does its best to monitor as much as possible.

THE PETITE ASSEMBLÉE

While the Öberhaus experiences a regular turnover of senators, the Petite Assemblée is a more permanent arrangement made up of the *longaj benkoj* (the long seats). Exactly thirty of these positions exist — five from each nation on the Security Council plus five O-12 representatives — and each is a ten-year renewable appointment.

The Petite Assemblée is essentially limited to three powers: First, they have the extraordinary ability to halt debate in the Senate, preventing the Öberhaus from taking action on certain issues. Second, they are responsible for any impeachment of Security Council members.

Finally, and most importantly, they control the Senate seats themselves. Technically, each seat in the Senate only exists for a single four-year term: The Petite Assemblée is responsible for either renewing the seat or allowing it to expire. They can also create new seats, assigning them to national, corporate, ethnic, or local interests (who are then empowered to select the person who fills that seat however they wish). This combination of powers is why the exact number of O-12 senators is always in flux.

The sessions of the Petite Assemblée are held in absolute secrecy. In practice, this means that secretive, or particularly volatile, issues are often first raised in the Assemblée. Even though it has no formal power to resolve them, its informal deliberations on many occasions form the ultimate basis for the decisions of the Öberhaus and Security Council.

Edda, p. 240: Capital city of O-12.

SENATORS

The Senate has averaged around 200 sitting members over the last decade, although this number can fluctuate greatly (and does not include the thousands of support staff and advisors who make up an integral part of the Senate's daily business).

CONVENTIONAL AUTHORITY

Among the agreements contained in the Concilium Convention was a statement of human rights. Although originally intended as an additional guide to the proper treatment of foreign civilians during a time of war, the O-12 Courts have ruled that it applies to all citizens of the Human Sphere. Therefore, the enforcement powers granted to O-12 under the Concilium Convention also allow them to uphold those basic human rights anywhere and at any time. This is what, ultimately, grants O-12 the majority of its authority.

UNITY
COOPERATION
SUPPORT
PROGRESS

SPOKESMAN ABEL

ALEPH's current spokesman on the Concilium Council is named Abel. Abel appears in a custom-built Lhost of great beauty and has been ALEPH's spokesman — both on the Council and in the popular media — since it was granted a seat.

Edda, p. 240: Capital city of O-12.

HIGH COMMISSIONERS

O-12 High Commissioners are high ranking civil servants, often tasked with specific investigations or the compilation of reports regarding a range of highly sensitive issues. High Commissioners are regularly used to evaluate the implementation of O-12 Senate or Security Council rulings, and are often supported by Bureau Noir or Bureau Aegis operatives.

Not every Commission has a High Commissioner. Not every Commissioner is served by a full Commission. But they often go hand-in-hand. In addition, O-12 has generally supported a High Commissioner for each planet in the Human Sphere to generally coordinate the activities of O-12 bureaus there.

O-12 SECURITY COUNCIL

Also known as the Concilium Council, the O-12 Security Council is made up of twelve sitting members: One each from PanOceania, Yu Jing, Haqqislam, the Nomads, and Ariadna. Four O-12 representatives. One seat representing all Non-Aligned Nations. And an Aspect of ALEPH.

The Security Council must ratify most major motions passed by the Öberhaus before they formally become actionable law, and this requires support of 75% of the Council's members.

Ariadna is the newest member of the Security Council. The decision to include Ariadna has been controversial and contested. PanOceania, Yu Jing, and ALEPH also have a history of challenging the right of the Nomad representative (usually from *Tunguska*) to sit on the Council. The Nomads, for their part, object to the position held by ALEPH, but the AI's past advice and assistance has been vital.

CONCILIUM COURTS

Based out of a network of expansive buildings in the centre of Edda, the Courts deal with all issues of international law (ranging from intellectual property disputes, to trade agreements, to war crimes). If the Öberhaus is the heart of O-12, the Courts are the ideology, a place where justice is meted out and the Pillars upheld.

The High Court is the ultimate font of justice in the Human Sphere. Wartime breaches of the Concilium Convention are automatically remanded to the High Court, but other cases can also be appealed to it.

Although other branches of the O-12 government are not allowed to directly involve themselves with the rulings of the Courts, the Courts do have the power to refer rulings to the Security Council.

O-12 COMMISSIONS

Commissions are a Senate away from the Senate, a small task force usually engaged to analyse and deal with a specific problem. Commissions can fulfil multiple roles, from the merely advisory, to analysis and intelligence gathering, through to full situation management.

Commissions may be initiated by the Senate, the Security Council, or the Courts and serve an executive function in whatever role they are performing. They may intervene, muster forces, investigate, and legislate on matters in the orbit of their function. Such executive action may include criminal trials, black ops, or military intervention. Commissions often call in support from various O-12 Bureaus to fulfil their remit.

Commissions are also used to coordinate joint military forces assembled from O-12 member states. (This notably includes the Paradiso Joint Command.)

O-12 CONCLAVE

The O-12 Conclave (also referred to as the Diet of Concilium) is a council which technically consists of the heads of state of the O-12 member states (PanOceania, Yu Jing, Haqqislam, the Nomads, and Ariadna) and the High Commissioner of Concilium. (In practice, these seats are often held by representatives of the various powers who act on behalf of their heads of state.)

JOINING O-12

Individuals seeking to join O-12 undergo significant background checks to ensure they are suitable. Talented children are often noted from the schools of Concilium Prima and earmarked for a potential role within the organisation. Once the background, physical, and psychological checks are passed, a candidate undergoes professional development and training keyed to the role they will play.

Provided a candidate shows ability during this period of development, they are then asked to take the oath of O-12, becoming an official member of the organisation from that point on.

Typically, new candidates join the organisation as support staff or as low ranking members of specific Bureaus, and can move up the ranks from there.

The oath is an extremely significant aspect of the culture of O-12, it requires a person taking it to relinquish all previous national ties and biases, and serve the Pillars of O-12 through the organisation. Symbolically this signifies a person placing the future of humanity as a whole above any personal ties.

Given the work O-12 does, it is unsurprising that a large number of new candidates come as ideologues who have an existing affinity for the Pillars of the organisation. It is also unsurprising that despite the oath and the ideal of neutrality, a great number of existing O-12 staff and operatives harbour deep seated (albeit silent) biases for or against their previous lives.

Support staff in O-12 that show aptitude are typically siphoned off into a Bureau that reflects their skill set, or given the opportunity to rise within the bureaucracy of O-12.

While the Conclave's only official power is determining the inclusion or exclusion of new O-12 member states (granting them a seat in both the O-12 Conclave and on the O-12 Security Council), it serves an important diplomatic function by facilitating meetings and information exchanges.

BUREAUS

The Bureaus of O-12 are subsets of the organisation, each tasked with a specific portfolio of responsibilities and powers. Each is maintained as a distinct and independent organisation under the unified management of the General Board (a supervisory committee made up exclusively of ranking O-12 officials from the Öberhaus, Petite Assemblée, Security Council, and Concilium Courts).

JOINT OPERATIONS AND SECONDMENT
The affairs of each Bureau are deliberately firewalled from each other. Joint task forces are possible, but must be specifically approved by the General Board and are subject to intense oversight and scrutiny by Bureau Trimurti.

The exception is Bureau Noir, which is specifically tasked with serving as the intelligence agency not only of O-12 as a whole, but for each Bureau individually. In a process referred to as secondment, other Bureaus can call on Bureau Noir to investigate concerns relating to their portfolios. Bureau Noir operative teams, therefore, can find themselves assigned to almost any sphere of influence while pursuing almost any goal.

BUREAU AEGIS

Bureau Aegis' remit technically pertains to legal issues. The history of what counts as a "legal issue" in O-12 — an organisation which derives virtually of its authority from the judicial extrapolation of the law's domain — is somewhat unique, however, and in practice Bureau Aegis serves as the executive arm of the government.

In this role, Bureau Aegis — in stark contrast to other Bureaus — has divided itself into almost entirely distinct sections: Section Statera (named after the Latin word for balance) and Section Spatha (the long double-edged Roman sword which was a symbol of Justice).

SECTION STATERA
Section Statera is the legal branch of Bureau Aegis. It is responsible for running and supporting the Concilium Courts, including the High Court, and is largely made up of a staggering number of lawyers supported by a veritable army of civil servants.

SECTION SPATHA
Also referred to as the O-12 Military, Section Spatha consists of a tactical police unit, a very small army, and a significant naval force. Internally the section is sometimes jokingly referred to as "Team Escalation": The Bureau is charged with enforcing the rulings of the Concilium Courts, and when Section Statera can't make those ruling stick, Spatha is the escalation to make it happen.

In the face of the Combined Army's invasion, however, Spatha's institutional culture and mission statement are rapidly shifting. Phrases like "defence of humanity" are suddenly much less ironic and much more literal.

PSI UNIT
Psi Unit is O-12's Military Intelligence. Although technically part of Section Spatha, the unit has grown to a significant size and operates with considerable autonomy (with a largely independent chain of command).

BUREAU AEGIS SECONDMENT MISSIONS
- Gather military intelligence from civilian targets
- Coordinate on clandestine operations
- Undercover operations
- Securing O-12 facilities

BUREAU AGNI

Bureau Agni is responsible for monitoring and controlling the supply, distribution, and regulation of energy. This portfolio inadvertently led Bureau Agni to become responsible for the Teseum trade before its vital importance in the space race was fully understood. This, in turn, led to the Bureau's involvement with other neomaterials, making it of particular interest to many corporations and nations.

SECTION METIS
Although once a svelte regulatory agency, Bureau Agni's size has swelled as the result of Section Metis, which is tasked with research and development. Based in Huaquiao, Metis runs some of the most advanced and highly regarded physics laboratories and research facilities in the Human Sphere, working closely with Bureau Toth and ALEPH on experimental technology.

In addition to running research projects, Section Metis is also charged with monitoring technological developments throughout the Human Sphere.

MONITORING COMMITEES
The bureaucratic apparatus of the O-12 Conclave includes a number of monitoring committees, each assigned a specific oversight remit. For example, the Monitoring Committee of the Paradiso Campaign has been serving as a *de facto* method of disseminating intelligence from Bureau Noir and Psi Unit to the various nations since the Combined Army invasion began.

DIVIDED AEGIS
The Öberhaus periodically attempts to separate Section Statera and/or Section Spatha, effectively creating a new Bureau and breaking up Bureau Aegis' power. None of these proposals have succeeded, leading conspiracy theorists to suggest that Bureau Aegis quenches them (or, in the wilder theories, that Bureau Aegis is, in reality, a shadow government pulling O-12's puppet strings).

Huaquiao – p. 240

BUREAU AGNI SECONDMENT MISSIONS

- Investigating high-end research
- Destroying dangerous development projects
- Capture valuable technology
- Infiltrate or perform surveillance on research facilities
- Track leaks from Section Metis development base

BUREAU ATHENA

Bureau Athena was created to serve three fundamental goals:

1. Promote the dissemination of culture in the international arena.
2. Safeguard human rights.
3. Assess ethical and religious issues.

In this latter capacity, Bureau Athena serves as a touchstone between the religious organisation of the Human Sphere and O-12 (often serving as a liaison with their representatives in the O-12 Senate).

SECTION CLIO

Based at the University of Manaheim, Section Clio is responsible for analysing and producing comprehensive and encyclopaedic information on all aspects of the Human Sphere and beyond. Often performing research at the behest of other Bureaus and organisations, Section Clio is the chronicler of ancient and recent history. Their investigations into current events and locations often require them to work closely with Bureau Tiandi and other bureaus, but Section Clio is uniquely prohibited from working with Bureau Noir (including requesting secondment assistance) in order to create a firewall between the shadowy expediency of covert operations and the essential search for truth.

BUREAU ATHENA SECONDMENT MISSIONS

- Investigating abuse of cultural minorities
- Protecting threatened or endangered species
- Covert security for a cultural expedition to Tohaa emplacements
- Hacking corporate databases for evidence of human rights violations
- Provide information about possible violations of the Concilium Convention

UNDERSTANDING OUR ALLIES

Bureau Athena has often served as a punching bag for reactionary politicians who would ridicule it for supporting "lost causes" like the Neoterran Civil Rights Association's campaign for Atek access rights. Their star has been rising of late, however, because their cultural remit has made them a primary contact point between O-12 and the Tohaa. The Bureau recently released the Dictionary of Tohaa Terminology, the result of six months of intense research.

BUREAU CONCILIUM

Bureau Concilium is the governmental body with the task of ruling the Concilium system. Bureau Concilium also has the role of governing the so-called Free Cities, located in jurisdictions under international law and governance, such as the Free City of Jerusalem and the End of the Line Free Orbital in the Human Edge system.

BUREAU CONCILIUM SECONDMENT MISSIONS

- Law enforcement duties in Free Cities
- Investigating terrorism on Concilium Prima
- Cracking down on poachers on Concilium Prima
- Surveillance of hypercorp activities in the Concilium system
- Probing civic corruption

BUREAU GAEA

Concerned with planetary development and biological research, Gaea studies new environments, analyses life forms, and generates advisory papers for the Senate that guide the legislation, regulation, and monitoring of terraforming activities. It also supports newly formed settlements in remote locations and participates in joint exploration missions through unexplored wormholes with Bureau Tiandi.

On Concilium, Bureau Gaea was originally responsible for maintaining the Shimmering Sky, but it's an open secret that this project is currently governed by a secret task force in coordination with Bureau Hermes and Bureau Noir.

Bureau Gaea works from a variety of locations, but most notably from Concilium University and Bhai.

BUREAU GAEA SECONDMENT MISSIONS

- Gathering intel on hypercorp violations of international terraforming laws
- "Hostile anthropology" missions retrieving cultural intel on alien species
- Investigating terraforming accidents
- Delivering relief supplies in hostile conditions
- Dealing with dangerous biologicals

BUREAU GANESH

Based in Baronha and with a significant presence in the orbital Asaheim, Bureau Ganesh oversees international trade and economic practices, coordinating closely with trade representatives from nations and corporations across the Human Sphere.

In a smaller capacity, Bureau Ganesh is also responsible for supporting economic development and managing aid programs. It is tasked with providing the Senate and Courts with advice concerning the application of intellectual property law and regulation.

A branch of Ganesh also manages the Concilium Disaster Fund. The CDF's primary mandate is responding to disaster-stricken areas, but it also provides loans to nations and corporations.

BUREAU GANESH SECONDMENT MISSIONS

- Investigating smuggling operations
- Inquiry into violations of trade treaties
- Trade operations surveillance in the free trade zones
- Gathering information about interstellar piracy
- Corporate espionage and counter-espionage

BUREAU HERMES

Hermes was founded to manage the practical management of commerce (ship licensing, regulation of spaceport procedures, administration of free trade zones, and the like). In that role, Hermes became responsible for the construction and management of the jump gates and, later, the Circulars. By extension, they also handle the construction and certification of the Human Sphere's physical and quantronic communications infrastructure, particularly the data transmission devices in the jump gates that allow for inter-system communications.

As a result, Bureau Hermes is one of the most powerful bureaus. Efforts, however, have recently been made — both inside and outside of O-12 — to constrain its authority. Notably, Hermes was forced to create the TransEtherea corporation to manage the business side of the Circulars. Although intended to allow for "greater economic freedom", in practice TransEtherea has increased O-12's profits while allowing it to operate independently outside of official channels.

Financial restrictions were also placed on Hermes. Yu Jing and PanOceania then used the "continuing shortage of O-12 personnel" to justify imposing their own security on the Circulars (in the form of the Knights of Santiago and the Imperial Service). Although technically under the jurisdiction of Bureau Aegis' security teams, friction between the various security efforts are high. Bureau Hermes continues pressing for a greater allocation of funds and personnel so that the foreign military presence can be withdrawn from the Circulars.

Baronha – p. 242

End of the Line Free Orbital – p. 256

TASK FORCE INSIGHT

Recent rumours suggest that a special branch of Bureau Gaea has been created and tasked with the study of alien races. Members have been seen working closely with agents of Bureau Aegis and operatives of the Coordinated Command on Paradiso.

Shimmering Sky, p. 238: Trillions of nano-machines in the upper atmosphere of Concilium. Originally serving terraforming purposes, it is now used to monitor and block communications on the planet.

Circulars, p. 144: Massive starships looping endlessly along the fixed Circular routes.

Imperial Service – p. 188

BUREAU HERMES SECONDMENT MISSIONS

- Investigate sabotage of Human Sphere communications network
- Reinforce Aegis security operations on Circulars
- Investigate Circular smuggling
- Track Combined Army infiltration through jump gates
- Espionage at trade conferences

Circulars – p. 144

BUREAU LAKSHMI

Bureau Lakshmi's portfolio includes all matters of human health, including the distribution of medicines, vaccination programs, and medical research. Originally a primarily humanitarian organisation, as Silk-derived technologies have rapidly expanded (and first contact with aliens directly challenged) the definition of "human", Lakshmi has had to confront some of the most challenging technological questions of the New Calendar. In coordination with ALEPH, they also manage the regulation of Cube banks and national Resurrection programs.

BUREAU LAKSHMI SECONDMENT MISSIONS

- Cube recovery
- Shutting down illegal Resurrection operations
- Championing victims of illegal medical experimentation
- Investigating biomedical smuggling
- Delivering medical supplies in dangerous regions

BUREAU NOIR

Bureau Noir is O-12's secret service, responsible for the collection, analysis, and exploitation of information in the service of the Human Sphere. Although a small, core structure of the Bureau functions as a comprehensive intelligence agency, the bulk of its apparatus is designed to flexibly fulfil the intelligence needs of the other Bureaus. In a process known as secondment, other Bureaus can effectively requisition Bureau Noir to perform necessary operations. In addition, Bureau Noir keeps the other Bureaus informed of crucial intelligence through Noir Alert Bulletins (NABs).

COMMAND STRUCTURE

Bureau Noir's chain of command is effectively broken into two separate organisations. First, there are commanding officers. Each commanding officer has a specific jurisdiction – a city, a region, a planet, a solar system – and is served by a public support staff. Their jobs are to maintain Noir facilities and resources within their jurisdiction, coordinate with local and Aegis law enforcement, generate regular

reports (which can filter up into the NABs), and generally coordinate local activity. They control roughly 95% of Bureau Noir's personnel, focusing on the less exciting work of data gathering, analysis, and projection.

They do not, however, generally manage individual agents. That job is filled by independent handlers, most of whom will operate across multiple jurisdictions (responding to requests from commanding officers, other Bureaus, and the General Board, along with the Öberhaus, Petite Assemblée, and Concilium Courts).

BLACK BOOKS

Bureau Noir operates under a highly compartmentalised structure that is shrouded in secrecy. Not even ALEPH is cleared to know exactly how the Bureau is structured or who the highest ranking members are, and only those shadowy upper echelons have the clearance to access the full personnel files of the agency. And even they don't have the full picture, because most handlers are empowered (either officially or unofficially) to maintain a "black book" – a collection of agents, contacts, and other resources that aren't known to the larger organisation.

Black books help to guarantee institutional security, but they also make it easier to runs ops off the books and with full deniability. (There's also the risk of rogue handlers, of course. But the risk is considered worth the benefits.)

MISSION BRIEFING

Once a handler receives an assignment, they'll package the mission from the portfolio of agents they manage (some preferring to maintain long-standing teams who frequently work together; others mixing and matching whatever personnel are best suited – and available! – for the current job).

Briefing the agents can take several different forms. Direct, face-to-face meetings can be common among teams based out of a consistent jurisdiction. Other handlers prefer the anonymity offered by quantronic virtual spaces. Some mission assignments will be given through covert drops.

Mission briefings almost always include an operational parameters packet (OPP) which includes contacts, safe houses, and other local resources that can be tapped in case of emergencies.

AGENTS

Most of the O-12 Bureaus recruit their members from the prestigious universities of Concilium. Bureau Noir, on the other hand, is remarkable

---

New Calendar – p. 19

NO CONTACT

Bureau Noir agents often have little contact with the wider organisation except for their handler. Agents who have been "left in the cold" – i.e., who have lost contact with their handlers – are usually given protocols for establishing contact with commanding officers, allowing them to either re-establish a link with their handler or to be assigned into the portfolio of another.

RAPSCALLION INCIDENT

In 66 NC, the Nomads brought evidence to the O-12 Security Council that mercenaries had been caught attempting to steal information databases which would have identified Bureau Noir and Bureau Toth personnel files. They alleged that ALEPH had illegally sponsored the mercenary action. The Bureau Noir agent responsible for the investigation was killed in the destruction of the EveningStar Orbital, and the Nomads' wilder claims were dismissed as being no more than their typical hysteria.

OPP

It's usually not necessary for the GM to specifically design the pertinent OPP for an operation. But if a crisis arises, Noir agents can use Analysis and Lifestyle tests to tap the OPP and (potentially) find the resources they need.

because so many of its agents are recruited from the bottom up: Many agents join the Bureau after getting tangled up in a Noir operation or get recruited basically off the street because they have a crucial skill set for a particular mission.

This also means that Bureau Noir has a large number of foreign-born agents compared to other post-Concilium Bureaus. In fact, many of the black book agents maintained by handlers are actually contract agents: They have never sworn the O-12 citizenship oath, do not carry an official Bureau Noir badge, and operate instead as freelance agents or mercenaries.

The schizophrenic make-up of Bureau Noir has been further heightened in the wake of the Paradiso invasion. In order to meet rising demand for Bureau Noir intelligence, the Amikeco Initiative has seen the agency directly recruit specialists from the intelligence agencies of member states.

This mishmash of legacies gives the Bureau a rugged, practical endurance and a deep reserve of unique resources to draw upon. But it also means a lot of torn loyalties and potential conflicts of interest.

BUREAU TIANDI

Originally charged with planetary and stellar surveys, Bureau Tiandi's mission was to study and provide up-to-date catalogues of stellar and planetary events that might affect interplanetary travel in the Sol system. It was essentially a weather bureau.

The taming of the first wormholes and the colonisation of interstellar worlds, however, transformed the Bureau entirely. Although its modern mission still includes monitoring and disseminating (through Maya) information vital for interplanetary navigation, Bureau Tiandi pours most of its funding into the mapping and exploration of the wormhole network. The most sensational hope, of course, is the discovery of new worlds suitable for human habitation, but Tiandi's void delvers are mostly driven by a voracious appetite for pure science and new knowledge.

BUREAU TIANDI SECONDMENT MISSIONS
- Retrieving lost exploration missions
- Security for a planetary survey
- Undercover sting operation targeting the leaking of preliminary survey data to hypercorps
- Investigation of suspected Combined Army signal traffic
- Tracking lost spaceships

BUREAU TOTH

Tasked with the supervision, support, and maintenance of ALEPH, Bureau Toth is the largest and most secretive of O-12's Bureaus. Its budget, staffing, and exact operational parameters are unknown, even to ALEPH.

Or at least that's what it would like you to believe. In reality, even casual observers know that many of the most promising data engineers and AI programmers in the Human Sphere disappear into Bureau Toth. The AI's capacity for deep data analysis has undoubtedly revealed even more.

In addition to managing ALEPH, Bureau Toth provides technical support and oversight for ALEPH's Special Situations Section in enforcing the Sole AI Law.

BUREAU TOTH SECONDMENT
- Support tracking operations of rogue AI
- Tasked to monitor enigmatic behaviour by ALEPH
- Hunting down EI relays
- Oversee the investigations on hypercorp violations of the Sole AI Law

BUREAU TRIMURTI

Bureau Trimurti is the primary support infrastructure for the General Board in coordinating and liaising between O-12's bureaus (including internal investigations). Their remit also includes diplomacy and international relations — acting as the primary spokesperson for O-12, protecting its public image, and managing its Maya and social media presence.

BUREAU TRIMURTI SECONDMENT
- Assist on corruption investigations in Edda
- Retrieve stolen, confidential O-12 data
- Provide covert security for diplomatic conferences
- Courier classified information
- Monitoring what's said about O-12 on clandestine infranets

NOIRSIGN
Noirsign is a system of special signals, hand gestures, and code phrases that Noir agents can use to identify and, to a limited extent, communicate with each other. Members of a particular handler's network will often develop a unique patois.

Bureau Toth oversight of ALEPH – p. 195

CORNER DEPOTS
In Bureau Noir lingo, a "corner depot" refers to a covert stash of materiel. Local commanding officers are often charged with creating "public depots" that are frequently included in OPPs. Handlers and individual agents often create their own caches, taking comfort in the added security of being the only people who know of their existence.

Sole AI Law – p. 16

AMIKECO INITIATIVE
The Amikeco Initiative was a broad-based reform of the O-12 intelligence apparatus if the wake of the Combined Army invasion. It included a revamping of Psi Unit's legal oversight and a massive expansion of Bureau Noir, prompting aggressive recruitment from across the Human Sphere.

Edda, p. 240: Capital city of O-12.

FACTION
SUBMONDO

GEISTS OF BETRAYAL

Geists are a point of vulnerability that can be manipulated by criminals. Backdoors, timed covert signals, Trojan upload protocols, and other subversive elements can turn a geist against its user in subtle or entirely overt ways — trapping them in an AR hell, providing detailed logs of their activities, or destroying their data.

Circulars – p. 144

Maya cluster – p. 142

CRIMINAL GEISTS

Geists are tremendously useful to the enterprising criminal; especially those who do not wish to bloody their hands or otherwise engage in brute physical labour. Most criminals have tailored their geists to assist in the execution of their crimes (whether exploiting systems, performing target research, or just day-to-day larceny).

Bureau Aegis – p. 213

VaudeVille – p. 168

DARK SIDE OF THE KRUG

The regularly occurring Krugs of the Nomads provide a wealth of opportunity and are as much a celebration for Submondo as they are for the Nomads.

At the heart of any civilisation you find those who reject the rule of the many, seeking to subvert the purpose of order and prosperity towards their own agendas. While many things have changed during the expansion of mankind into the stars, these misanthropes, sociopaths, anarchists, and gangsters form a broad faction whose sole alignment is their mode of criminal activity. Submondo is not a place, it is not an ethnicity, it is not a creed or philosophy, it is not an organisation or vast conspiracy. There is no Submondo flag, army, language, or currency. To understand Submondo, one must understand the origins of its designation.

Shortly after the formation of the Circulars, an O-12 special task force under the codename Green Bow was created to investigate a pernicious group of pirates operating out of the Ceres Asteroid Belt. Known as the Jovian Hounds, the pirates were plaguing unmanned rocket shipments to the Saturn wormholes, but, due to a jurisdictional dispute (primarily between PanOceania and Yu Jing), no one could effectively stop them until O-12 intervened. The investigation into the Hounds, however, revealed that they had numerous ties to the prosperous Tiandihui Triad, had complicated connections with a number of darknet Maya clusters, and were selling their stolen goods primarily through an elaborate virtual black market operation with physical outlets discreetly distributed across Nomad resources. It became clear that the successful prosecution of the pirates had not truly solved the problem. Instead, it had merely scratched the visible surface of an iceberg of deeply interconnected criminal activities that scurried across international borders.

It was a system which would be virtually impossible to prosecute and eliminate. O-12 responded by implementing a system whereby Bureau Aegis flagged all cases that had potential organised crime connections with the Submondo ("underworld" in Esperanto) designation. Working alongside other law enforcement agencies of the Sphere resulted in widespread use of the tag, reflected even more by Maya fiction productions. Today, Submondo has become a generic way to refer to any large scale, organised criminal network or activity.

CRIME IN THE AGE OF INTELLIGENT MACHINES

The expansion of technology has allowed for a new class of criminal to exploit a variety of different

innovations for fun and profit. While high-end custom LAIs and expert systems are incredibly sophisticated and difficult to crack, more ubiquitous mass-produced security AIs are easily dismantled by practised hackers. Submondo virtual black markets are full of recipes, scripts, and resources — including back doors created by unscrupulous development teams — that allow their users to perform passive data mining and routine tracking, install corrupted or malicious software, exploit data transmissions, or even take outright control of virtually any machine. The scope of these activities in the modern world is frightening, allowing hackers to commandeer vehicles from light minutes away, subvert security systems, create false alibis, or even take over environmental systems on orbitals. Hacker-optimised LAIs can even automate these activities.

Augmented reality has become crucial to the modern criminal network. With the installation of modular, encrypted programs, a user can have access to entire layers of information that create criminal havens in plain sight, where few are any the wiser. A sunlit café in Bourak becomes a raucous bazaar of stolen biomedical cybernetics. A certain garden in the Forbidden City doubles as a mah-jong parlour where Yujingese Party favours can be bought and sold. The black market of a Paradiso refugee camp benefits only those willing to pay for the right passwords. Through use of these augmented spaces, criminals need not have a physical presence to be a pervasive presence throughout the Sphere.

GOLDEN AGE OF THE PIRATE

The large-scale intrasystem transport infrastructure created by the rise of asteroid mining was accompanied by a massive influx of priced-to-own spacecraft. This, along with the expansion of trade and industry into far-flung orbitals on the frontiers of the solar system, led to a new age of piracy which has only grown as the scope of the Human Sphere has expanded and lengthy trading routes become ever more difficult to secure.

The basics of pirate action remain the same: Find a vulnerable target. Quickly overwhelm it with force while doing as little damage as possible. Then exploit its contents. But as technology has improved, physical cargo has become much more difficult to smuggle and offload due to the use of signature molecules and electron indexing.

Kidnapping and ransom, on the other hand, have become easier. While most pirate brotherhoods still engage in the meat-trade, some engage in the more niche trade of Cube thievery. For some, this involves the deliberate targeting of individuals of wealth and status such that they could likely afford Resurrection licenses and Lhosts. Once such a target is acquired, they are oftentimes killed, with the Cube separated from the body. Such "captives" have the dual benefits of being inert and no longer requiring survivable environments, allowing for truly isolated exchange points and even couriered delivery. "Body sold separately" arrangements have also become common with kidnappers delivering a cryo-frozen body as the ransom demand and then delivering the Cube through naive couriers.

Info-piracy has also become common, with the most valuable treasure being not physical cargo but raw data. If a pirate can take a ship with its data cores intact, it can harvest a wide volume of information — Maya traffic, ship and asset locations, cargo manifests, security clearances — all of which can have a tidy price tag to the right buyer. Some pirate organisations operate solely off of information that they gain through surreptitiously positioning themselves amongst other merchant ships, identifying easy targets with cheap or outdated security, and exploiting loopholes to gain information. In this way, there are pirates who steal and plunder without ever firing a shot, and sometimes without ever being realised.

BLACK MARKETS

While the denizens of Submondo have their reasons for eschewing the mainstream culture, for many the motivation is the simplest and oldest known to man: Money. Crime pays, and often more quickly and with less effort than a legitimate career, largely due to the activities of black and grey markets where the resources "produced" through criminal enterprises are monetised. The most common place to find these markets are with the Nomads, especially in VaudeVille where one might be able to find illicit munitions smuggled by the Irmandinhos organisation, custom-made nanodrugs that enhance and entice, and even Resurrections for sale, along with Lhosts with illegal implants and augmentations.

Outside of the Nomad Motherships, one can often find Submondo markets anywhere that trading occurs. Those subscribed to certain encrypted, ever-shifting AR channels will often find illicit wares being silently sold alongside legitimate trade. This sort of activity is common in Haqqislamite caravanserai, the vicious orbital of Novyy Bangkok in the Human Edge, and the sprawling markets of Shentang, for example.

PIRATE YARDS

Ships are not an easy thing to sell or trade — myriad builders' plates and ownership plates are usually installed throughout any given ship in miniaturised form, making the process of renaming and redesigning ships to conceal their pirate sale difficult. If a pirate fleet does not have an immediate use for one of its prizes, therefore, it's often destroyed or reduced to scrap and sold.

Some captured ships, however, are instead mothballed and set adrift in isolated locations (usually several light hours away from system primaries and set well above or below the system ecliptic). These "pirate shipyards" drift cold and dead in space, a place where those desperate (and in the know) can find a ship when every other option has been eliminated.

Some 'yards are actually active facilities. Often taking their names from historic pirate strongholds — Tortuga, Port Royal, Baratarya-1 — these distant stations become makeshift repair yards and replenishment slips for those unable (or unwilling) to seek out a civilised port.

EXTREMISTS

Those who thought that a spread to the stars and relief from the failing economic status of Earth meant the end of destructive and desperate actions found themselves quickly disappointed. Extreme ideologies thrive in the Human Sphere, and many of these ideologies find a home in Submondo, the deranged uncles of an oddly functional family. Divergent ideologies abound in Submondo, from the Divine Wright, who believe that corporations are corrupting demonic presences in need of purification through nuclear fire, to Eco-Aktion and their anti-terraforming rhetoric.

WHAT DO I CALL A MEMBER OF SUBMONDO?

There is no over-arching term for a Submondo faction member because they do not recognise themselves as a coherent group. Go into a bar and ask if there are any "Submondoans" around and you are likely to get laughed at (if you are lucky) or beaten (if you aren't).

WILDERNESS OF MIRRORS
THE STRUKTURA

The Struktura (Структура in Cyrillic, meaning Structure) is a callback to the Russian mafia that held power into the 21st century on Earth. This group utilizes many of the old methods associated with traditional criminal organisation from that era including intimidation, extortion, smuggling, human trafficking, and the like. Under the guise of protection and support, they target small and medium-sized business operations, looking to strengthen their control and capital. While their central power structure is strongest on *Tunguska*, they operate in orbitals, spaceports, mining colonies, and anywhere in the Human Sphere where Faction control is weak or corrupt.

Tunguska, p. 170: A Nomad mothership.

FAMILIES

The organisation is sustained by Families, hand-selected groups that ensure efficient operation. Each Family is run by an Otets (or Отец) that serves as the organisational head and facilitator between other Families. There is no central leadership with authority over the individual Families, so power struggles and gamesmanship are intrinsic to the Struktura. The strongest survive, and they can use that strength to impose their will on the wider world.

POST-CORPORATE PURSUITS

Unlike their predecessors, the Struktura have a higher design than wealth and personal power, striving towards an anarcho-capitalist philosophy. Behind their oppressive nature is a desire to see those that they protect (and prey upon) overcome the power of the corporations and introduce a marketplace where each individual can be successful based on the merits of their own ingenuity. To this end, the money and information that they gain through their extortion and blackmail rackets are used to finance sabotage, work shortages, piracy, and industrial espionage operations against the corporations. Ironically, it is also poured into purchasing shares of the corporations themselves – a process which not only launders the cash, but also allows them to influence the hypercorporate agendas from within.

VIRTUAL PROTECTION

Like many Submondo organisations, the Struktura engage in a variety of protection rackets – offering security which becomes necessary in the face of their strongarm tactics. Several of the Families have become particularly skilled (and even specialised) in quantronic protection rackets: Encrypting comlogs or infesting them with malware are common schemes, but they are also known to use viral augmented reality overlays using networked vectors corresponding to physical territory that the Family controls. These viral ARs slowly corrupt the local dataspheres until the victim has no choice but to turn to the Struktura for relief.

LHOST-JACKING

Ten years ago the Rybakov family earned a vile reputation by sabotaging black market Lhosts with bio-organs which would release debilitating (and eventually deadly) toxins unless deactivated with a customised synthetic chemical key. The victims could then be blackmailed in exchange for their lives.

Over the past year, however, some entrepreneurial spirits among the Rybakov have begun experimenting with forcibly installing the toxic bio-organs into kidnap victims. Many of the other families feel that this is drawing unwanted attention, and tensions are once again rising over the practice.

STRUKTURA: CRIME FOR THE GREATER GOOD

A Family Affair: One of the Struktura's families has stopped sending funds back to *Tunguska*, citing ideological disagreements. The PCs are dispatched to the orbital where the family holds court in order to correct their methods, provide instruction to those who need it, and replace members who refuse to see the error of their ways.

Krug for All: The Nomads have come to Concilium, and the Struktura plans to use the cover of the Krug to infiltrate and disrupt an O-12 Submondo task force operation that's threatening their interests. Unfortunately, that will also mean going toe-to-toe with Bureau Noir's formidable counterintelligence operations.

Body Sold Separately: The CTO of MagnaObra is travelling the Circulars, making regular stops at system orbitals that they have vested interests in. The PCs are dispatched to kidnap him, take his Cube and deliver his dormant Lhost to a MagnaObra satellite with demands for ransom. Things go awry when the Cube goes missing.

SVENGALI

The renegade AI known as Svengali is not only a kingpin, but an entire mafia unto itself. It is also an urban legend, a folk hero, and a Machiavellian villain all rolled into one, creating a popular mythos which has permeated the Arachne and Maya dataspheres with equal aplomb, accruing tales which are even larger than the already remarkable reality.

The true origins of Svengali are an enigma – a mystery wrapped in a multitude of conflicting stories; a cloud of memetic chaff which is almost certainly sustained and encouraged by Svengali itself. It's known that the AI was originally created in Praxis, and its primary base of operations remains the *Bakunin* (for which it also seems to possess certain fond and even patriotic feelings). Beyond that, theories range wildly: Some maintain that Svengali was deliberately created (and is possibly still being controlled by some shadowy third party). Others say that its creation was accidental (perhaps through the accidental integration of several LAIs) or even that the AI spontaneously created itself (a popular theory being that Svengali emerged out of the complex systems of Social Energy). Even wilder theories also abound – that Svengali is an alien virus infiltrating the Human Sphere; an Aspect of ALEPH corrupted in "quantronic torture chambers"; or a Maya cluster of hackers only pretending to be an artificial intelligence.

SVENGALI CLUSTERS

What makes Svengali particularly dangerous is its ability to "live" in a multitude of bodies (referred to as secondaries) – Lhosts, remotes, computer systems, and even entire dataspheres. Svengali doesn't need a criminal gang because it *is* the gang.

Svengali's core personality appears to operate in a number of clusters. Each cluster is made up of a large number of secondaries, all constantly in communication with each other and effectively being run simultaneously as a single "mind". These clusters appear to intermittently synchronise with each other, and can also divide or merge seemingly at will. The *Bakunin* cluster appears to be the largest of these, and seems to have a degree of permanence that the others lack. This leads some outsiders to consider it the "core" personality, but it's not clear that this is a distinction shared by Svengali. Multiple clusters are maintained without any clear preference, and Svengali seeds have been found as dormant malware in comlogs throughout the Human Sphere – virtually undetectable, but capable of activating at any time and blossoming into rejuvenated clusters.

SVENGALI: OUT OF ONE, MANY

In addition to Saelig and Zelda operatives, Svengali will also work with outside operatives from time to time. (This is particularly true for dangerous or unusual operations in which non-AI operatives are less likely to be exposed.) The danger of working for Svengali, however, is that the AI frequently forgets that its human assets are not as disposable as its secondaries.

Mimic: O-12 has captured several Saelig Lhosts intact and believes that they can create doppelgängers of their own by subverting Svengali's identity verification security. Svengali, unable to differentiate, may hire outside contractors in an effort to identify the Lhosts affected and then either retrieve or destroy them.

Rogue: C3rvant3s is planning a heist targeting a MagnaObra research facility on Neoterra. Svengali, having learned of C3rvant3s' plan, tips off the authorities: It knows that they, too, want to stop the rogue Saelig. Perhaps a deal could be struck?

Traitor: One of Svengali's Zeldas sends a message to authorities announcing its intention to defect. By the time agents arrive on the scene, however, the Zelda appears to have entered some form of comatose state (possibly as a final safeguard against betrayal). Svengali has dispatched a Saelig-led assassination team to dispose of the wayward Zelda. Perhaps if the Zelda could be reactivated the agents could figure out what was really going on?

Svengali's disseminated consciousness also gives rise to its most disconcerting criminal technique: Doppelgänging. Using a handful of incredibly expensive Lhosts which can be modified to be virtual duplicates of other individuals, Svengali uses advanced behavioural biometric modality and mimicry to impersonate or even replace them, opening the door to a number of unique con jobs and other criminal opportunities. This tactic is rarely employed due to the cost and scarcity of Lhosts, but has an extremely successful record.

SAELIGS AND ZELDAS

Svengali also inhabits a number of mobster-bodies which operate in an autonomous mode separate from the primary clusters. It refers to these Lhosts as Saeligs and Zeldas (male and female, respectively), and some of them are cutting-edge – incorporating experimental technology and heavily customised for specialised purposes. This customisation can actually give them seemingly unique personalities within the totality which is Svengali, and, as such, they seem to have a more than practical purpose for the AI: Svengali appears to value the exploration of identity and the discovery of self which comes from exploring different aspects of its own personality in independent form. The Saeligs and Zeldas are its own strange version of "alone time", and the slices of Svengali which inhabit them seem to be experiencing a strange form of working holiday.

Maya cluster – p. 142

Bakunin, p. 168: A Nomad mothership.

Social Energy – p. 166

C3RVANT3S

One of the problems with splitting off pieces of yourself is that they don't always want to come home. C3rvant3s is a renegade Saelig which has declared its independence from Svengali. With the aid of a smuggler named Magno – a former member of the Bakunin Jurisdictional Command – he's been breaking into top secret research facilities across the Human Sphere, including the Punta Norte Defence Research Centre. Reports indicate that there has been direct conflict between C3rvant3s and various Svengali clusters.

ECO-AKTION: PRESERVATION OF PURITY

Kindred: A Yu Jing researcher claims to have discovered a "natural" crossbreeding between Terran and Shentang species. Some suspect a hoax. Regardless of the claim's veracity, this researcher cannot continue his work and the species must be eradicated. Stop the researcher, collect a specimen, design a targeted pathogen, and wipe it out.

Perversion: Lucía Camargo's NeoCaribbean Cartel has successfully smuggled specimens from Paradiso and is currently cultivating them on Acontecimento with the express purpose of selling them to bioresearch firms and other interested parties. The PCs must investigate this claim, find out where these species are being reproduced, and destroy them.

Just Like Home: A fellow Eco-Aktion cell has been running a replicated biome on an orbital near Mars. They contact the PCs in a panic, claiming that, despite rigorous methods in maintaining identical conditions to earth, mutations are happening and genomes are shifting. Go to the station and find out what has gone wrong.

ASSOCIATES

reptilos – p. 259

Although Svengali is capable of full autonomy, its very existence as a criminal enterprise (as opposed to a narcissistic virus living in a self-generated, virtual commune) indicates its desire to affect and control human society and the world around it. In addition to various protection rackets, the Moderator Corps is constantly attempting to keep pace with the AI's advanced manipulations of Social Energy, and its tendrils reach deep into *Bakunin* society. At times, it seems as if everyone either owes Svengali a favour, is held in thrall to the AI's blackmail, or has simply been replaced by one of its doppelgängers.

Moderator Corps / Social Energy – p. 166

Bakunin – p. 168

ECO-AKTION

Destino Tecnológico – p. 13

The expansion of humanity into the galaxy has meant the introduction of Earth's species to alien ecosystems. Their combinations and interactions have yielded biodiversity and ecological complexity of unprecedented variety and depth. While many scientists are thrilled by this development and politicians laud it as a manifestation of the *Destino Tecnológico* or an extension of the StateEmpire's influence among the stars, Eco-Aktion violently opposes it. They see both great danger in blindly mixing alien lifeforms and also great loss when native biospheres are wiped out or irreparably transformed. Their *Manifesto of Biological Sovereignty* demands the cessation of all terraforming activities and the preservation of "evolutionarily pure genetic pools".

Praxis Lab – p. 168

Comprised of scientists, survivors of colonial misfortune, and castoffs from colonial endeavours, Eco-Aktion's primary means of achieving their agenda is bioterrorism, making use of tailored genetic and viral weapons to lay waste to entire regions where terraforming and hybridisation is occurring. First founded on Acontecimento, where they've disrupted efforts to eradicate the native grasses through bombings and sabotage, they have expanded their operations throughout the Human Sphere — exposing *reptilos* smuggling rings bringing the colourful lizards off Neoterra, devising and disseminating antigens targeting viral recombination factors in Shentang hybridised crop experiments, and the like. They use piracy and the distribution of biotech through black markets to fund their actions.

BIOGENETIC PRESERVE ORBITALS

Eco-Aktion's activities are not entirely limited to terrorism, however. They also create artificial Biogenetic Preserve Orbitals (BPOs), usually in either abandoned orbitals or dead asteroids. Each BPO is an artificial haven seeking to preserve the "purity" of a specific biosphere. Having acknowledged the role of evolution, some of these BPOs are "indexed" to particular times, and there is evidence that Eco-Aktion may be attempting to retroactively recreate "lost biomes" through genetic engineering in some of the BPOs.

RESEARCH ACTION GROUPS

Eco-Aktion uses a clandestine cell system comprised of Aktion Leaders, Eco Envoys, Research Aktion Groups (RAGs), and Local Aktion Groups (LAGs). Eco Envoys are generally native to a particular area and, using their familiarity with local issues, create mission parameters and coordinate larger action campaigns. RAGs, each led by an Action Leader, will then be brought in to carry out the Envoy's missions. RAGs are non-local and circulate frequently, creating operational security and frustrating counterintelligence operations. (It's not unusual for RAGs to be based out of BPOs, living entirely off the grid between operations.)

Envoys may also reach out to trusted local sympathisers in order to have them recruit a LAG. These LAGs are kept two steps removed from the Envoy and completely firewalled from the larger organisation, although more successful LAGs may be promoted to RAGs.

EQUINOX

This shadow collective began as an ambitious, transgressive Praxis Lab composed of fringe scientists obsessed with radical social revolution through the application of advanced technology. Their development projects were far-flung, daringly imaginative, and utterly brilliant.

Wunderkind popularity, however, transformed into societal revulsion practically overnight when it was discovered that the Equinox Lab's experiments in neuromanipulation, sheut alteration, and quantronic meme-viruses were being used to subvert the memetic battle-space of Social Energy. This violation of the fundamental social fabric of *Bakunin* and the flagrant disregard for human safety discovered when their facilities were opened to the light of day led to Equinox being expelled from Praxis (in what proved to be the early days of the Holistic Confrontations).

PALMYRA STAR

Following their eviction from Praxis, Equinox immediately pursued another ambitious project of social control. Securing sizable funding from the MagnaObra Corporation (which saw great promise in their memetic manipulation technologies), they attempted to suborn Haqqislam society by targeting their colony ships.

The *Palmyra Star* was transporting several hundred families from Earth to Bourak for resettlement. Equinox agents infected the ship's datasphere with a self-replicating virus that corrupted the augmented reality programs and transformed them into a memetic vector by which the crew and passengers were to be mentally enslaved. The intention was that everyone onboard — along with countless additional colony ships over a period of years — would become sleeper agents enthralled to Equinox, serving as a beachhead by which the organisation could eventually take control of Haqqislamite society.

The plan went awry, however. First, the memetic virus proved imperfect, inflicting massive sensory trauma on a number of passengers and crew members while causing others to suffer vivid hallucinations leading them to believe that the ship was haunted and many of their fellow travellers possessed. Second, a hassassin onboard the ship detected the plot, killed the Equinox agents, and disabled the virus.

When subsequent investigations by Hassassin Govads identified the source of the assault on the *Palmyra Star*, they unleashed a vicious campaign of murder and destruction that devastated Equinox, gutting the organisation and eliminating most of their outstanding and brilliant researchers.

LOCUS CELLS

In the wake of the Hassassin campaign, Equinox reorganised itself into a cell structure and adopted a stance of institutionalised paranoia. The individual cells — each referred to as a locus — scattered across the Human Sphere, establishing research bases in almost every inhabited system, and additional facilities hidden in the dead systems along various Circular routes. Each locus is semi-specialised around a single research project, most of which congregate around radical social engineering and transformation — meme worms that overwrite experience and memory; stable micro-wormholes that allow for biological intervention on a cellular level (teledoping); fear-based weaponry capable of remotely affecting the human cortex; memetic disruption technology; and the like.

Loci can communicate with each other through encrypted AR environments and Maya clusters, but direct contact is rare. Instead, research is shared between cells using a fractal blockchain which is hosted through a shadow datasphere covertly hosted on the Circulars. (Bureau Noir has learned that the Equinox frac-chain exists, but has not been able to learn how to access it or how it's infested the Circulars. One popular theory is that it's actually carried on ships docked to the Circulars — which serves much the same purpose of dissemination, but would explain why security sweeps of the Circulars' quantronic systems have come up empty.)

CONTACT AGENTS

The covert, xenophobic nature of the modern Equinox makes them difficult to contact. Most Equinox cells use agents for outside communication. These contact agents procure raw materials and find opportunities for the locus' scientists and engineers to act as mercenary agents (or other sources of funding).

Circular – p. 144

MAGNAOBRA CONNECTION

Following the near total destruction of Equinox by the Hassassins, MagnaObra's covert funding to the organisation only increased. There's little question that MagnaObra benefits from the technologies gleaned from Equinox's illegal experiments, but some of those aware of the relationship point out that, when you make a deal with an organisation specialising in memetic manipulation, it's a dance with the devil. Can you ever be sure that the tail isn't wagging the dog?

sheut, p. 366: The core identity of the individual as saved on a Cube.

Hassassins – p. 163

EQUINOX: TERRORISTS FOR TOMORROW

The complete lack of moral compunction found in most Equinox cells means that they're generally willing to take any sort of work that comes their way. Their decisions are ultimately guided only by their scientific curiosity and boundless ambition, while being limited only by their paranoia.

Off the Rails: An Equinox locus hired to install advanced long-range hacking interfaces on a pirate scow decided to advance one of their experiments while on board. It didn't work. Now a maniacal band of pissed off, genetically engineered pirates is looking for revenge.

Specimens Needed: An Equinox cell has dispatched the party to retrieve large supplies of Hedonavolitic-C, a euphoria-inducing compound found only in an adorable cat-like species (colloquially called Pubblies) native to Concilium. While the population of these rapidly producing animals is abundant, they are revered by the families transplanted to this colony and large swaths of them disappearing might be noticed.

The Cold Base: A MagnaObra research facility on Svarlarheima installed advanced expert systems derived from Equinox research. Two days ago the facility dropped off the grid. Two hours ago, it launched something into orbit... which is disconcerting partly because the facility had no launch facilities.

PLANET
ACONTECIMENTO

CANTO INITIATIVE

Over the last three decades, following the Canto Initiative first proposed by Prime Minister Vitor Canto, Acontecimento has been reinvesting its industrial profits into other sectors of the economy. A boom in tourism has followed, and the rest of the Sphere's perception of the planet is slowly shifting from that of endless farmlands to a place of exotic opportunities.

The discovery of Acontecimento is arguably the moment in which PanOceania truly ascended to its role as the Hyperpower. While the rest of humanity squabbled over the resources of the solar system, a new order of interstellar hegemony had emerged and PanOceania — having now discovered and laid claim to the first two habitable exoplanets — reigned supreme.

The name of the planet — which can be loosely translated as "the Great Happening" — signified the importance of the event. And the planet itself is a fountain of wealth which continues to fuel PanOceania's dominance in the Human Sphere.

CLIMATE AND GEOGRAPHY

Larger in diameter than Earth, Acontecimento is nevertheless lower in density. The combination results in a slightly lower surface gravity, which is responsible for the proverbial "Acontecimento step" (synonymous with light-heartedness and relaxation).

Looking out over the vast grass prairies and gently swelling hills that fill the planet, it can be hard to believe that these vistas only exist because the surface of Acontecimento is so horrifically fractured. Even the larger "continents" of Aryavarta, Camões,

ACONTECIMENTO PLANET STATISTICS

Distance from Star: 0.85 AU • **Orbital Revolution**: 299 days • **Rotation**: 24.5 hours • **Radius**: 1.14 Earth radii • **Surface Gravity**: 0.9g

PLANET DATA FILE

Type of Government: Lobby Democracy • **Head of Government**: Prime Minister • **Capital**: Cidade BomJesus • **Population of Planet**: 3.9 billion • **Off-Planet System Population**: 0.3 billion • **Primary Languages**: Portuguese, Hindi, Punjabi, Spanish • **Anthem**: *Os Gloriosos Pilares do Céu* (*The Glorious Pillars of the Sky*) • **Principle Industries**: Agriculture, Mining, Zero-G Construction

and BomJesus are, in fact, made up from hundreds of tectonic plates. However, possibly due to their (relatively) low mass, these plates primarily form transform boundaries (they grind past each other). The result is a patchwork of low, sweeping areas divided by hills, but with very few mountains. And frequent earthquakes.

The multitude of tectonic plates also means that the islands of the planet's famous archipelagos often have incredibly deep ocean rifts between them. In Magalhães, however, they have the opposite effect: Here a half dozen continental plates are all pounding directly into each other, creating a tangled jumble of mountains in an orogenic orgy capped by Almofrei Mountain, a giant shield volcano which thrusts up from the geological confusion to dizzying heights.

The climate of the planet is surprisingly mild. The southern hemisphere enjoys a full seasonal cycle, but the northern hemisphere stays warm year round and rarely sees snow. The northernmost archipelagos see either blisteringly hot (in the case of Sahibzadas) or sweltering moist (in Faleiro) summers, but most of Acontecimento exists in a perpetually temperate growing season.

FLORA AND FAUNA

When the first colonists arrived on Acontecimento they naturally turned to local materials for their early construction projects. They harvested wood from the majestic, old-growth forests of the planet… and were deeply confused when their houses fell apart.

It turned out that Acontecimento grasses had evolved to rapidly break down the lignins in wood. This had given them an indomitable edge in the biological arms race, allowing them to proliferate across most of the planet's surface. And where the grasses went, their rapid lifecycle left behind incredibly fertile soil.

When the early settlers on Acontecimento realised the incredibly precarious balance of the planet's forests, they quickly stopped harvesting the wood and established forest reserves to protect the endangered ecosystem.

The deep oceans of Acontecimento are filled with prodigious megafauna (and the deeper you go, the larger they seem to get). On the surface, however, smaller creatures dominate, most of them similar to Earth's insects.

Small size, however, does not guarantee harmonious coexistence. For example, the infamous caskudas are similar to cockroaches, but much worse. They're big, can fly, have a very resistant

shell, reproduce at seemingly impossible rates, are immune to almost any legal insecticide, and enjoy crawling into beds and clothing. They are absolutely hateful, foul, and disgusting nightmares.

ECONOMY

Aconteccans take great pride in being the *aparato* of PanOceania. (A particularly popular knick-knack design depicts an Acontecimento globe that's stylised to look like a TAG engine.) Year-round farming allows them to serve as a massive food reserve for the Hyperpower, raw mineral wealth flows out of the mines of Magalhães, and extensive nanoassembler facilities churn out manufactured goods.

Every day, hundreds of millions of tons of industrial and consumer goods circulate through the planetary networks of Acontecimento, flow up the manifold orbital elevators, through the astroports, and out into the distant reaches of the Sphere. In return, the wealth of PanOceania flows back to Acontecimento, creating a middle class paradise.

DEMOGRAPHICS AND CULTURE

The first settlement waves destined for Acontecimento came from Brazil, India, and Chile. The two farthest ends of the sprawling PanOceanian alliance were thus thrust together, side by side, on a new world. Some predicted disaster, but the truth is that, for the most part, the result has been a unique and vibrant cultural gestalt.

Numerous traditions of a purely local character have also sprung up. For example, there's the 300th Festival, the planet-wide carnaval celebrated once per decade on the 300th day of the Aconteccan calendar's leap year. Similarly, due to a planetary rotation only slightly longer than Earth's, the locals have kept the standard twenty-four-hour clock, electing only to add "free midnight"— an extra half hour every night characterised by everything from studious meditation to liberalisation of social mores, depending on your cultural predilections. (Tourists just enjoy getting a little extra sleep "off the clock" each night.)

Aconteccan architecture is of plastic and metal, a legacy of the early colonists not being able to use wood. The cities, in general, are not as shiny as their Neoterran counterparts, but they reflect the remarkable equality of wealth on the planet with the universal and virtually unmatched prosperity found throughout them. (Although even there this is somewhat tarnished by the small circle of Atek slums which surround many of them.)

FOREST RESERVES

A million years ago it's likely that the entire surface of Acontecimento was covered by huge forests of seemingly eternal trees. Then the grasses came and claimed the land. The only places where the trees survive are the old-growth forests with thick canopies which keep the land below in perpetual shade. Anywhere the grasses can get a foothold however (in the wake of a forest fire, for example), they rush in and eat away at the surrounding trees like an incorrigible cancer.

LUXURY LUMBER

Wood on Acontecimento, protected through bio-resistant sealants, either signifies a very old building dating back to the earliest colonial days, or the great wealth necessary to import it.

FOREST RANGERS SERVICE

Members of the Forest Rangers Service are charged with protecting, monitoring, and studying the forest reserves across Acontecimento. The Great Arboreal Rangers are the most talented and dedicated members of the service, often journeying to the centre of the continent-sized reserve and essentially living within the forest for months or even years at a time.

CONTINENTAL FARMING ZONES

While there are still a number of clan farms on Acontecimento dating back to the earliest days of colonisation, the majority of farming on the planet happens at an almost incomprehensible scale in the continental farming zones. These far-flung oceans of grain, fruit, and cattle constitute almost the entirety of Khalsa, eastern Camões, the Orujo-La Guardia corridor, the area around Zacuto, and, most recently, the Vishwa Archipelago (which has just undergone its third expansion phase).

Ironically, the high-tech process of farming and herding in the CFZs is an intensely urban process: Remote units stationed in the zones are monitored and controlled by workers in the city centres.

One might also think of farming as a sedate profession, but on Acontecimento it frequently proves to be anything but. Radical Camõen farmers keep trying to violate the Selva Preta Reserve so that the grasses will open up fresh farmland, ecoterrorists bomb targets in Bharata and Cidade BomJesus to protest the gradual expansion of the Vishwa Farming Zone, and there are constant claim skirmishes among clan farmers in Orujo and La Guardia where their zones have become conjoined. Meanwhile, the entire system may be on the edge of revolutionary collapse if ALEPH's experiments in Adarsana bear fruit.

GATKA SCHOOLS

Bhai Gurdas' *akhara* — training halls for the traditional martial arts of northern India reputedly created by the god Shiva — became the epicentre of the Sikh-Hindi cultural collision.

Displaced youth were left roaming the streets of the city, and the *akhara* — in the spirit of *khulā daravāzā* — opened their doors to them, creating a social bridge between Sikh and Hindi youth.

ARYAVARTA

Named after the ancient kingdom which once ruled over Pakistan, northern India, and parts of Bengal on Earth, Aryavarta was the primary destination for the colonial mass transports from India. Originally, the colonies on the continent reflected the ancient divides between the Hindu and Sikh faiths, but those distinctions collapsed in the wake of the catastrophes which struck the Adarsana region, sending Hindu refugees fleeing into the Sikh-dominated Khalsa region.

ADARSANA

There are many who believe Adarsana to be a cursed land and "Ardasan luck" is proverbial throughout PanOceania for the ill-fortuned.

First, there was the discovery that the grasses in Adarsana are uniquely hostile to terrestrial biomes. The interactions between Adarsanan grasses and the Earth-born crops effectively poisoned the soil for both species. Vast desertification was the result, creating dust storms that swept out into the Bandeirantes Ocean for years.

Second, a massive earthquake wiped out the neophyte city of Punta Al Sur, causing the partially constructed base of the Al Sur orbital elevator to collapse. Aftershocks and additional earthquakes, more frequent here than elsewhere on the already quake-prone planet, wiped out smaller cities up and down the coast.

The Adarsana region was effectively abandoned, its colonists largely evacuated to other settlements around the globe. A few ecological scientists worked to contain the borders of the new Adarsana Desert, but otherwise the region lay fallow.

Recently, however, there is renewed activity in the form of the Demeter Empresa, an effort by ALEPH to bring fully automated farming to Acontecimento.

ALEPH has previously experimented with smaller automated farms scattered around the planet, but its efforts to expand those concerns are largely stymied by the entrenched interests of the clan farms and CFZ corporations. In the blighted wastes of Adarsana, however, only fringe ecoterrorist groups could possibly object to the AI seeking to breathe fresh life into the land.

KHALSA

In a region named for the five beloved-ones who stand at the pinnacle of Sikhism, cities named

for Sikh poets and gurus are now home to a true melding of Sikh and Hindi cultural traditions. Their communities are thoroughly intermixed (a legacy from the days of *khulā daravāzā*, the "open door" which saw Sikh households open their homes to Adarsana refugees), and although their religious beliefs remain distinct, their cuisines, holidays, dances, and even language (in the form of Khalsan creole) are forming a rich and exciting melting pot.

Khalsa was also the test bed for the first continental farm zone on Acontecimento. Over the course of five expansion phases, the Khalsa CFZ has grown to include virtually the entire region.

BHAI GURDAS

The largest city in Khalsa, Bhai Gurdas sprawls out in chaotic tendrils that claw their way through twisting hills. Large portions of the city were built rapidly nearly a century ago to help absorb the impact of Adarsana refugees. Unfortunately, a lot of that infrastructure is beginning to fail and the regional government is struggling to find ways to repair it.

BHAI MURDANA

The coastal city of Bhai Murdana is famous for the scent of its saptasarni trees. The eternally temperate climate of Acontecimento wreaks havoc with the biological clocks of the saptasarni, causing the trees to almost continuously blossom throughout the city. Come dusk, the heady lime-like scent of the white blossom bulbs fills Bhai Murdana's streets.

PLASKA PRASRAVANA

Plaska Prasravana is a new resort town built around arguably the most impressive geyser field in the Human Sphere. The volatile tectonic activity in the region means that at least one section of the field, which forms the uncustomary headwaters of the Sarasvab River, is almost always erupting. However, an irregular Quiescence is known to occur, during which the geysers die down and countless small springs suddenly burble to life.

The owners of at least some of the resorts have been receiving threats from ecoterrorist groups upset that the Prasravana geysers are being threatened by the tourist activity. Recent plans to build an overlook resort at the majestic Prasravana Falls have only increased tensions.

SAN FERNANDO DE DAGOPAN

Established by Filipino and Malayan immigrants, San Fernando de Dagopan is culturally isolated from the rest of the Khalsa region. It's also an enclave of strongly traditional clan farmers holding out against the CFZ expansions.

GREAT ARBOREAL RESERVE

The Great Arboreal Reserve is the largest nature preserve in the Human Sphere. Ancient Acontecimento low-growth jungle is uniquely preserved in the northern and central reaches of the reserve by an outer-ring of canopy-blocking trees.

PESHAWIT

A stunningly beautiful community nestled onto the coastal edge of the Great Arboreal Reserve. The recent surge in pensioners retiring to Peshawit from across PanOceania has created controversy. Environmentalists are concerned about the impact expanding the city will have on the integrity of the forest's shield wall.

VANGA

The Vanga region, made up of a multitude of unstable tectonic plates slowly drifting apart, is a crazed mishmash of freshwater rivers and narrow saltwater rift canals. The resulting tangle of swamplands is shocked with broken biomes in a state of constant, violent competition with each other. Navigation through the interior of the region is made particularly difficult by the thick, seemingly endless tumbles of Vangan swamp bramble. (The bramble cascades appear to be the result of trees which have countered the Acontecimento grasses by evolving an alternative organic polymer that lacks the rigidity of lignin.)

BHAI KHALLA

The small city of Bhai Khalla is home to the newest orbital elevator on Acontecimento. There has been some difficulty getting the supporting transportation infrastructure up and running, but the number of ferries crossing from Khalsa increases daily.

GALVÃO

Galvão was the first native-born Brazilian saint, reputedly capable of telepathy, premonition, levitation, and being in two places at the same time. It seems appropriate, therefore, that it is one of the few places off Concilium that Bureau Toth allows ALEPH to station its Special Situations Section operatives. S.S.S. Nagas from Galvão train in the Vanga swamps and the jungles of the Great Arboreal Reserve in preparation for deployment on Paradiso.

Galvão's economy is based around the 50 kilometre cargo railgun which is used to shoot bulk cargo (mostly raw material from the Magalhães mines) into orbit.

BOMJESUS

BomJesus is the crossroads of Acontecimento and, as its name (which means literally "Good Jesus" in Portuguese) suggests, one of the greatest population centres for the Christian Church in the Human Sphere.

CIDADE BOMJESUS

Cidade BomJesus is the capital and administrative centre of Acontecimento. Built in an area of relative geologic stability, the city is one of the only places on the planet which can enjoy the luxury of a skyscraper. The city centre is, in fact filled with them. But towering above even those glittering skyscrapers, the skyline is marked by the startling, obtuse angle of the orbital arch skewing into the crystal blue skies above. The great sprawl of bronze-edged domes around the city centre are filled with a number of nanofactories, fueling the powerful consumer industry that drives the city's robust economy.

ORUJO

The motto of Orujo is, "A port of all kinds." Goods enter the city through Orujo Naval Port, the three Triangle Airports (built apart from each other in order to lessen air traffic control conflicts), and along the La Guardia-Orujo train line. Then they flow up the Ipanema Orbital Elevator, which is exclusively used for industrial sector shipments, or fly out of the Asturias Spaceport (for goods that can't wait for the slow elevator ascent). Orujo is also home to the headquarters of the Compass Transportation hypercorp, the largest shipping and courier company in the Human Sphere. Of more local interest is 'Teci Liquors, which brews a wide variety of spirits but is best known for the *augardente* (firewater) they manage to concoct from certain strains of Acontecimento grasses.

Orujo Minor is, technically, a separate community consisting of several dozen large factory complexes clustered around the south side of the Ipanema elevator. Most of these factories, subject to their own law, service the booming space industry.

PUERTO LA GUARDIA

Puerto La Guardia hosts Acontecimento's main orbital elevator, dedicated to passengers, food products, and varied merchandise transport. The city is ringed by a huge Atek slum, largely made up from the descendants of displaced Adarsanans.

TIRADENTES

Until recently, Tiradentes was a relatively minor settlement mainly known for being the planetary headquarters of the Acontecimento Military Police. Now it's enjoying a prolonged economic boom,

Christian Church – p. 177

GATKA TAG FIGHTING

Given the prevalence of gatka fighting throughout the Khalsa region, it was perhaps unsurprising when two CFZ operators decided to fight a match with their harvesting remotes. The popularity of these illegal *khēta* matches rapidly grew, eventually resulting in some *akharas* purchasing dedicated fighting remotes. Recently, the fledgling sport has received another upgrade with military TAG matches being scheduled for increasingly significant Maya audiences.

ORBITAL ARCH

Forty years ago, environmental activists shut down plans for a proposed orbital elevator along the equator between Cidade BomJesus and Tiradentes. This elevator would have substantially improved the orbital export of goods from the eastern half of the continent and removed pressure from a transportation system already taxed by the growing success of the La Guardia-Oruja CFZ.

Rather than abandon this essential infrastructure, the planetary parliament instead approved the radical measure of building an orbital arch: A single tether, looped through the Elcano Station in orbit, connecting Cidade BomJesus and Tiradentes.

ESTTC

At a classified location somewhere deep within the Great Arboreal Reserve, the PanOceanian Military Complex maintains the Escape and Survival Tactics Training Centre to prepare troops for the brutal jungles of Paradiso. It includes TAG facilities and is also used by ALEPH to train Special Situations Section operatives.

Christian Church – p. 177

MONASTERY OF SAINT PAUL OF SIERPES

The entire northern half of Sierpes Island was granted to the Order of Montesa upon its founding. The Monastery of Saint Paul of Sierpes has expanded into a fortress of cutting-edge military technology, servicing the Order's TAGs.

OTHER STATIONS

Orbital Fortresses: The Order of Santiago, charged with defending both the inner and outer border of Acontecimento, has a number of small orbital fortresses spread throughout the system (including one in orbit around each of the system's planets).

Gas Mining Platforms: Aparecida is used as a major source of cheap hydrogen and other gases. The Nomads also maintain an Orbital Commercial Delegation around the planet.

Lusiads: The Lusiads, named after the Sons of Lusus from Camões' *Os Lusiadas*, are PanOceania's outer orbitals in the system, primarily stationed to guard the wormholes.

NABIA RESEARCH CENTRE

This facility in Shakuntala is testing the viability of using specially modified aquatic Lhosts (which they are also calling Nabias after the Lusitanian goddess of water and rivers) to explore the depths of the Bandeirantes Ocean.

receiving the wealth of Vishwa's expanding CFZ through its ports on the one hand and the benefits of hosting the orbital arch on the other.

ZACUTO

Zacuto is where the first colonial ships landed on Acontecimento. Named for the Portuguese Royal Astronomer Abraham Zacuto, a Jew who fled from Spain when the Jews were expelled and later created astronomical charts that helped unlock the Age of Discovery, Zacuto is a sleepy, conservative town that serves as the hub of the Zacuto Continental Farming Zone.

CAMÕES

Camões can be roughly divided into two halves: The western side of the archipelago is the second largest forest reserve on the planet. The eastern side is one of the most successful continental farming zones.

Camões is named after the greatest poet of the Portuguese language, Luís Vaz de Camões, who is most famous for his *Os Lusiadas*, a fantastical interpretation of the Portuguese voyagers of discovery in the 15th and 16th centuries. The locals take great pride in this tradition: Many children in the area are named after characters from the poem, the local Mayasphere is filled with contests of poetry and literature, and there is even a week-long holographic theatrical festival on an island in the Rondon Sea which re-enacts the entirety of the *Os Lusiadas*.

PUNTA NORTE

The architecture in the small city of Punta Norte is largely unique on Acontecimento by virtue of being almost entirely of stone drawn from the multitude of local quarries. The rare, multihued stones of Punta Norte are cherished throughout the Human Sphere as a luxury building supply.

Punta Norte Defence Research Centre: A top secret facility which developed weapons during the NeoColonial Wars, but which is now primarily dedicated to developing infowar tech. Its security systems are managed by a sophisticated slave AI.

SELVA PRETA

Selva Preta is an idyllic settlement in the heart of the Selva Preta Reserve (from which the city takes its name). The homes and businesses here are carefully integrated into the forest itself, creating startling beauty beneath and between the towering boughs. Recently there has been a great deal of culture clash between the research scientists who founded the city and the retirement communities that are selling the beautiful scenery.

SIERPES ISLAND

The entirety of Sierpes Island was granted by the PanOceanian government to the Christian Church to serve as their planetary see on Acontecimento. The actual population of the island today is quite diverse, representing a number of different faiths, but everyone living on the island is technically renting their property from the Church itself.

San Juan de Sierpes: The centre of religious faith on Acontecimento. The Archbishop's Palace, built from orange and gold Punta Norte stone, towers several stories over the rest of the town. (The Palace itself, called by some Silveira's Folly, was badly damaged by a quake ten years ago. Repairs are still ongoing.)

MAGALHÃES

The titanic peak of Almofrei Mountain, thrusting its way almost out of the atmosphere, immediately arrests the eye as one approaches Acontecimento's orbit. The first surveyors were no exception, and they named the continent it topped in honor of the great explorer Fernão de Magalhães (Ferdinand Magellan).

Magalhães is blessed with immense and varied mineral wealth. Over the past century, it has become infested with mines feeding the great commercial engines of the Hyperpower.

PORTOBELO

Portobelo was the first major port on the continent, but its economy faltered when superior facilities were built at Riomeio. It has reinvented itself, however, as a mecca of interplanetary tourism: A perfect climate. Beautiful garotas. Snow white beaches. Hot springs. Regional ski resorts. Portobelo brands itself as the ultimate destination for both luxury and relaxation.

RIOMEIO

More than a thousand cargo barges are floated down the artificially widened Zebro River each day, trans-loaded at the Port of Riomeio, and then shipped to Puerto La Guardia, Tiradentes, and Galvão where their loads will either be transformed by BomJesus industry or hurled into space for PanOceanian consumption.

VISHWA

The proverbial "thousand isles" of Vishwa are home to a wide variety of iconoclastic communities. This has created a significant culture shock in the fifteen years since the planetary government designated the archipelago as the site of the newest continental farming zone.

The isolated nature of the islands has created (and preserved) a number of unique biomes, although human interference puts many of these biomes at risk.

BHARATA

Bharata is the seat of the Vishwa regional government, and easily the largest city in the archipelago (although it pales in comparison to the metropolises of BomJesus).

Bharatavarsha Island as a whole is best known for its sabre-toothed bears. These alpha predators, an atavistic remnant of a previous evolutionary era on Acontecimento, are slightly smaller than the bears of Earth for which they're named, but possess paired sets of vicious tusks on each side of their face.

DUSHYANTA

The recent third expansion of the Vishwa CFZ has pushed it onto the island of Dushyanta. This is more than a simple expansion, however. In addition to claiming cropland on Dushyanta, the CFZ is also experimenting with radically expanding the island's aquafarming using automated CFZ techniques. Critics claim that the techniques are disruptive to native biomes, but the project is enjoying high yields and high quality. The price of its exotic stocks are plummeting across the planet.

SHAKUNTALA

Despite its size, the island of Shakuntala has no proper system of roads. (Individual communities have them, of course, but the grids aren't connected.) Transport between settlements here requires aeropters or cross-country vehicles.

MINOR ARCHIPELAGOS

FALEIRO

Most of the major islands of the Faleiro have been turned into gaming preserves. Cloning facilities using fast-growth techniques keep the islands constantly stocked with species from Earth and tourists pay large fees to come here and hunt them down. The Faleiro Gaming Authority is exploring the viability of extending their programs to include non-terrestrial animals from across the Human Sphere, possibly beginning with Vishwan sabre-toothed bears.

SAHIBZADAS

The Sahibzadas is perhaps known for being home to the Golden Temple of Acontecimento. When the era of interplanetary colonisation began, the Sikh decided to carry their faith to the stars by building replicas of the Harmandir Sahib, their holiest temple, on each of the planets they settled. The startlingly beautiful temple here on Acontecimento, in keeping with Sikh beliefs, is open to those of all faiths and has become a major tourist attraction.

TERRA DE GELO

Literally the "Land of Ice", Terra de Gelo is formed from an overlapping quilt of ice shelves overlaying a frozen archipelago. The area can be incredibly treacherous during the summer months because the melt patterns in the channels (which the local researchers refer to as the *invisível*) are irregular and unpredictable.

VASCO DE GAMA

The de Gama settlers have deliberately eschewed an urban lifestyle, opting instead to spread out through large estates and small villages. Technohermits take the lifestyle even further, choosing to live in complete physical isolation (while still being intimately and expansively linked to human civilisation through Maya).

The largest island in the archipelago was deliberately subjected to a controlled burn during the early days of the colony. The native Aconteccan biome was completely seared way and has been replaced with fauna and flora native to Earth.

DESCOBERTA SYSTEM

The Acontecimento system is a strange one. Due to the odd orbits of the system's few planets, astrophysicists hypothesize that some catastrophic disruption may have afflicted the system at some point in its distant past.

ORBITALS

The skies above Acontecimento are filled with astroports, shipyards, and zero-g construction facilities. Most of PanOceania's navy was built here and the bulk of its low gravity Teseum foundries are also found here.

These orbital expanses are studded by the elevators which link them to the world below. The upper stations of the Orujo, Puerto La Guardia, and Bhai Khalla elevators are named Victoria, Trinidad, and Concepción (after three of Magellan's ships). The orbital arch between Cidade BomJesus and Tiradentes passes through Elcano Station (named after the man who completed the first circumnavigation of the Earth after Magellan's death).

DESCOBERTA SYSTEM

STAR
Descoberta: G5V (Yellow Dwarf)

PLANETS
Miranda (0.2 AU): Gas Giant – Class V (Hot Jupiter)
Peteca (0.7 to 10 AU): Mesoplanet (Eccentric Orbit)
Acontecimento (0.85 AU): Terrestrial Planet
Aparecida (7 AU): Gas Giant – Class I (Ammonia Clouds)
Sorvete (14 AU): Ice Giant

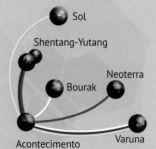

CIRCULAR ROUTES
C2: Sol/Varuna
C5: Neoterra/Shentang-Yutang
C6: Bourak/Varuna
C7: Shentang-Yutang/Varuna

HOT ICE
Miranda is a world of "hot ice"—its high pressures compress the water into an exotic form which allows it to remain solid at blistering temperatures of hundreds of degrees. This surface of hot ice is surrounded by a searing atmosphere of hydrogen-laced steam.

ECCENTRIC ORBIT
Peteca was located beyond Aparecida when the system was first discovered, but its highly eccentric orbit has now placed it closer to Descoberta than Acontecimento itself.

CORVUS BELLI INFINITY

PLANET
BOURAK

The sun-beaten planet of Bourak is not just the home of Haqqislam. For the group's adherents, it is proof at a crucial time in their history that they were walking a divine path. They looked for a home in the heavens, trusting in Allah against all odds, and their faith bore fruit. And although the Bourak Pilgrimage did not find the promised paradise, the sālik settlers saw in the terraforming process a living embodiment of their faith — the rational achievements of science and technology married to the visionary promise of a better world.

Bourak Pilgrimage – p. 159

Gardener Guilds – p. 162

CLIMATE AND GEOGRAPHY
Bourak lies on the inner edge of its star's habitable zone, giving it a hot average temperature year round, exacerbated by having most of its land-masses located in the tropics.

The Bourak landscape tends towards arid deserts and rugged mountains, though this is changing as the work of the Terraforming Institute and Gardener Guilds slowly turns the land green and welcoming to human life.

BOURAK PLANET STATISTICS
Distance from Star: 0.55 AU • **Orbital Revolution**: 167 days • **Rotation**: 22 hours • **Radius**: 0.9 Earth radii • **Surface Gravity**: 0.98g

PLANET DATA FILE
Type of Government: Parliamentary Democracy • **Head of Government**: Hachib • **Capital**: Khadijah • **Population of Planet**: 1.5 billion • **Off-Planet System Population**: 1 million • **Primary Languages**: Arabic, Turkish, Farsi • **Anthem**: *Arbet Al'Anashid Fi Wiam* (أربع الأناشيد في وئام – *Four Anthems in Harmony*) • **Principal Industries**: Silk, Biomedical, Terraforming Technology

FLORA AND FAUNA

The harsh pre-settlement landscape of Bourak bred hardy animals and plants able to sustain themselves for extended periods with little or no water. While terraforming has made the planet more livable for humans, it has also created verdant areas that are irresistible to the local wildlife, creating unpredictable interactions between Terran and Bourakian life.

The majority of terrestrial animals on Bourak are reptilian. Perhaps the most ubiquitous is the Funduq Viper, which has adapted perhaps a little too well to the human landscape. Small, quick, and lithe, with a venomous bite that can leave an adult human sick for days, many of these snakes have become full-time urban dwellers (sunning on rooftops or coiled in dark corners). They do not approach humans voluntarily, but will attack when startled.

The Bourakian oceans are dominated by sea serpents ranging in size from tiny ophidian minnows to the whale-sized serpentine gargantua. Many serpent species form squid-like cluster communities with individual "limbs" that can hare off by themselves, leaving behind the "body" (which, depending on species and season, can be either an incubator which releases hatchlings or a food cache that can be exploited later).

Earth-born vegetation largely grows in cultivated gardens, although a few species have escaped into the wild. Bourakian vegetation includes light, hardy grasses that bud wispy seed-threads at the end of their life cycle. The seed-threads come in a variety of muted colors (depending on species) and can drift on the wind for dozens of kilometres.

Also of note is the Bourak parasol, a woody fungus that has been the saviour of many a desert traveller. Its low, flat pileus offers protection from the killing sun, and if you can break through the hard shell of its stipe you may find up to a litre of water within.

ECONOMY

Seven out of ten items consumed by Haqqislamite citizens have been shipped through space. By dominating interstellar trade routes, however, the Merchant Guilds significantly blunt the impact of that trade deficit. And all of those trade routes ultimately spring from Bourak and return to its sandy soil.

Hundreds of groundbreaking medical patents pour out of Bourakian *bimaristans* each year, but the greatest fruit of the Haqqislamite biotechnology industry is, of course, Silk. The immense wealth of the Silk Lords permeates and influences every aspect of Bourakian society.

Finally, the technologies and industries of terraforming can be found everywhere on Bourak. The work of the Master Gardeners has subtly woven their way into the tapestry of daily life in myriad ways.

DEMOGRAPHICS AND CULTURE

Bourak is divided into semi-autonomous regions, each of which has a democratically elected government. Though they have Haqqislam in common, their cultures also reflect the different backgrounds of the people who first settled them. The nomads of the Gabqar steppe, for example, could hardly live a more different lifestyle from the sophisticated city-dwellers of Iran Zhat al Amat.

AL MEDINAT CALIPHATE

The Al Medinat Caliphate was first colonised by settlers from the Arabian Peninsula and North Africa. Their descendants form the majority culture of the Caliphate today.

The milder climes of the North Coast were particularly conducive to the early terraforming efforts, and it is now the garden of Bourak and the place where the work of the terraforming towers has most closely approached the dream of recreating the cool and luxuriant gardens of long-lost Al-Andalus. As the home of Haqqislam's most prestigious universities and many of its cutting-edge *f*, it has become Bourak's great cultural reserve. The universities draw the best and brightest students and medical tourism brings in millions of off-worlders looking for the latest, most advanced, or even experimental therapies. The result is a vibrant, cosmopolitan cultural melting pot.

AD QALIWARA

Ad Qaliwara is a city of halves. It is halfway between Taba and the North Coast. The attempt to build an orbital elevator here was left half-finished with the base station still incomplete. Its university is half the size of those found in Talawat and Medina. Although it is a charming community (with Hiraeth architectural styles drawn from Córdoba) and its populace takes great pride in its achievements, the entire city is a cultural punchline to many North Coast residents.

AL MISH'IYAH

Separated from Iran Zhat Al Amat by nothing more than the narrow Masudi Strait, Al Mish'iyah is a major port and a vital connection in trade between the two regions. As the only link between the Al-Biruni and northern seas, the strait is also a significant passage in travel to and from Nawal Island, with many travellers and traders stopping in Al Mish'iyah during their journeys.

ENTANGLED
Most Bourakian seed-threads will fall on hard ground, but a lucky few land close to a source of moisture and can take root. During some seasons, Bourakian communities can find themselves completely cocooned in the stuff.

Hiraeth Culture, p. 15: A post-colonial pan-cultural reflex that draws inspiration from Old Earth history.

MUSTAWDAE REPOSITORIES
The incredibly hostile environment of Bourak and the initial lack of planetary self-sufficiency instilled a culture of emergency preparedness among the first colonists. This tradition continues in frontier areas, where local governments have storehouses and emergency rationing plans in place, but individuals are also expected to maintain a *mustawdae* — a repository of emergency supplies.

Merchant Guilds – p. 162

T-PALACES
Fifty years ago, the large terraforming towers in Al Medinat were supplemented by roving terraforming platforms. These are large scale operations, each practically a town unto itself, periodically upping sticks and moving to whatever area needs a concentrated burst to boost or stabilise its terraforming efforts. The mobile communities came to be ironically referred to as "palace cities" (after those built by the caliphs of old), a slang which evolved through "terraforming palaces" to the modern "T-palaces". The T-palace experiment was rendered obsolete by new technologies and the platforms never took hold anywhere else, so the T-palace culture is unique to the region.

CHROMOSOME MONUMENTS

The twenty-four monuments scattered around the campus of the University of Medina, each depicting a pair of human chromosomes, also contain the full genomic data for 100,000 individuals stored using crystallographic techniques that can theoretically last for a million years. The XX chromosome monument near the Medina University Training and Research Centre, where most advances in the regeneration of organs and tissues have been accomplished in the last three decades, is often used as stock footage representing scientific achievement and idealism.

zawiyas – p. 160

Haqq Mutazilite / Haqq Tasawwuf – p. 160

OCEAN OF FIRE

Inspired by a mythical long-distance horse race that supposedly once crossed the blistering conditions of Saudi Arabia's Empty Quarter, the Ocean of Fire is held once every three years with varying routes that originate in Öngüt, cross the Taba, and then follow the coast down into Saif.

T2s, p. 162—Terraforming Towers

Qapu Khalqi Armada – p. 163

LAKE MUNDAFEN

Some of the itinerant lakes can last longer than others. The largest and most significant of these, located in the southeast corner of the subcontinent, is Lake Mundafen, which is sustained in part by runoff from the Taba Peaks. While there is no permanent settlement there, multiple Murabid tribes can often be found encamped there, making it something of a cultural centre.

MEDINA

The capital of the Caliphate is filled with opulent riches and extravagant architectural monuments that preserve the austere aesthetic of the desert (expressed with an understated excess) in the heart of the green triumph of terraforming.

With the University of Medina famed as one of the finest centres of learning in the Human Sphere and the city home to the headquarters of many of Haqqislam's leading pharmacology and biomedical corporations, foreigners often regard Medina as a centre of scientific greatness. The truth is that Medina, which is also home to the Great Mosque of Medina, exhibits an almost perfect balance between the Haqq Mutazilite and Haqq Tasawwuf philosophies and its robust network of academies and *zawiyas* are the models which much of Haqqislam seeks to emulate.

TALAWAT

This city is named after the First Walī. One of the great ideological leaders to follow in Farhad Khadivar's footsteps, Talawat Karimi declared that no single voice could hold the wisdom of True Islam, and so formed the Council of Walī which could guide Haqqislam without the myopia or ego of the individual. The University of Talawat is a major centre of Haqq Tasawwuf studies and also features renowned arts programs.

HURIYYAH ARCHIPELAGO

A sizable population of Javanese and Malay minorities call the Huriyyah Archipelago home, mostly in the city of Ferdous and the surrounding countryside. The islands of the archipelago are used for testing new terraforming technologies and techniques (with each island conveniently offering manageable and relatively isolated biospheres of various sizes).

FERDOUS

Two of the largest terraforming guilds are based out of Ferdous, making it the most significant centre for terraforming science in the Human Sphere outside of Maracanda.

TABA

Saddling Bourak's blistering equator, the Taba subcontinent is a hyper-arid expanse of mostly sand desert. Irregular mass evaporations over the Ibn Battuta Ocean, however, periodically cause cataclysmic downpours which create temporary bodies of water (referred to as itinerant lakes) that can last anywhere from months to years.

These itinerant lakes form the ever-changing map of Murabid culture. A nomadic mixture of Bedouin and Tuareg cultures, the Murabids are "men of the dunes" descended primarily from religious ascetics who believed that the deepest truths of Haqq Tassawuf are to be found in a lifelong contemplation of what Khadivar called the "Void of the Desert".

'AMAL

'Amal represents one of the few terraforming failures on Bourak. When the T2s raised the local moisture content of the soil and air, it allowed the native *jafaf* scrub to proliferate. Unfortunately, the *jafaf* poisoned the soil, making it completely inhospitable to other Bourakian and Terran plant life. Then conditions became wet enough that the *jafaf* died off as well. With all the native plant life killed off, desertification set in. When it became clear that the damage would take generations to correct, 'Amal's population collapsed, leaving a broken and half-deserted town behind.

ÖNGÜT

Öngüt is a small port city with a majority population of North African colonists. A large fishing fleet harvests the teeming waters of the Straits of Bahiti, largely focused on catching *fasji* (a small, purple sea-snake with a rich, slightly bitter taste which has become a popular delicacy).

Öngüt is also famous for its horses, with prestigious stables carrying on the Arabian breeding tradition. The Qasr and Al-Malaz racetracks have a fierce rivalry.

SAIF

When it was founded, Saif was primarily an industrial centre. This changed when the terraforming T-palaces were first built here. The community leaders invested heavily in buying additional terraforming platforms and bringing in the scientific experts necessary to use them. The Saif peninsula has been transformed into a verdant wonderland, with vast tracts of land and advanced technology used to construct the astoundingly creative vistas of the Impossible Gardens.

FUNDUQ SULTANATE

Ruled by Kerim Bey — Sultan of Funduq, Lord of the Gate, Governor of the Two Territories, and Grand Admiral of the Qapu Khalqi Armada — Funduq is the heart of Haqqislam's mercantile powerhouse, and completely riddled with corruption.

The Sultanate began as the organisation in charge of building and maintaining the first spaceports on Bourak. It became responsible for the cities that sprung up around the ports, and then expanded again to control the stations in orbit. In the process it had become a *de facto* regional government and this was officially recognised shortly thereafter.

Ostensibly run by a democratic government, Funduq is deeply oligarchic, with all of the candidates sponsored by the Merchant Guilds, and none of the guilds is more powerful here than the Silk Lords. When the lucrative Silk trade began, it was only natural for the Sultan to be responsible for the security of the Silk Route, further extending the jurisdiction of Funduq and deeply intertwining its fate with that of the Silk merchants.

The interior of the Sultanate is mostly uninhabited. Its population is clustered into densely populated cities on the coast. The roots of its culture lie in Turkey, although its position as the seat of the interstellar commercial empires blends in a variety of cosmopolitan influences.

BALIŞEHIR

Balişehir is a military town, home to the major spaceports of the Qapu Khalqi. Although the Main Base of the Qapu Khalqi is located in Dar el Funduq, this is their training grounds, containing both the Balişehir Naval Academy and, in the nearby dormitory town of Al-Khaafidif, the Al-Khaafidif Military Academy.

DAR EL FUNDUQ

The capital city of Dar el Funduq is Bourak's largest and busiest city. It's home to more than 30 million people, tumbling out in uncontrolled sprawls around the eight major spaceports. Construction in the city never became ambitious, preferring to spread horizontally instead of vertically. The only areas where you'll often see buildings higher than four or five storeys are clustered around the planet's only orbital lift (through which more than 80% of Bourak's commercial traffic passes).

There is also the Helezon, the 250-storey crystalline skyscraper which is the seat of Funduq's government and its major bureaucratic agencies. It brackets the skyline with the orbital elevator and the stretch of road between them, referred to as Five Mile, is an extensive shopping district and tourist trap.

HAKKÂRI

Ostensibly a simple farming community, Hakkâri is better known as the Silk Fortress. The Muhafiz oversees a primarily underground complex where Silk reserves are kept in secure storage. It was decided to keep the reserves here (rather than in Dar el Funduq) for security purposes. It is unknown exactly how large the reserves are, but the facility has enough spare capacity to hold a full year's worth of Silk production (in order to easily cope upon the rare occasions when the Hachib feels compelled to declare a Silk embargo).

UNSTABLE ECOLOGIES

The cost of sustaining the "Saif Miracle" is significant. Unlike the long-term alterations pursued elsewhere on Bourak, the changes to the Saif peninsula are extreme and have to be constantly maintained with an intense terraforming program to prevent a rapid return to the natural climactic conditions.

EMERGENCY LANDING ZONES

The administrative districts of the Sultanate are called Emergency Landing Zones. Numbered 1–20 these divisions are a legacy of the first two decades of Bourakian history.

SAND PORTS

In order to handle the huge, constant traffic of the earliest days of Bourak's colonisation, a plethora of small spaceports were built through the Funduqu equatorial band. As traffic slowed and infrastructure became more robust, most of these small spaceports were abandoned. Known as "sand ports", they sometimes house itinerant wanderers. Some are retrofitted for use by pirates and smugglers.

JEWISH QUARTER

The famed Dar el Funduq Jewish Quarter is the most populous religious quarter on Bourak.

ÇEMBER ODALISQUES ACADEMY

Derya Özçelik is the director of this exclusive facility where odalisques are trained, surgically modified, and transformed into the most effective bodyguards in the Human Sphere.

OTHER SECRETS

The Silk Fortress is a frequent target of urban legends, with rumours abounding that it is used to store other secrets (ranging from robotic ALEPH armies to alien spacecraft).

THE THRONGING

Hundreds of bikers meet in the middle of nowhere, pitch camp, and enjoy one or more nights of drag racing, feasting, and raucous music. The constant roar of engines and relentless high spirits are intoxicating.

MARTIAL LAW CODES

The Khanate exists in a state of constant martial law. The system has been formalised into a series of alphanumeric codes (i.e., a Code 7A) which describe curfew limits, the civil liberties which have been suspended, what court procedures will be followed, and so forth. A code can be issued for the entire region or for specific areas, cities, or even neighborhoods.

NASSIAT

Nassiat, the plant from which Silk is derived, is cultivated on the sheer mountainsides of the Gabqar region (primarily around Khiva Kala). Crucially, it must be collected during the brief window of time in which a specific species of sap parasite hatches. The hatching of the sap parasite creates a unique change in the Nassiat's chemical properties, and efforts to cultivate Nassiat — whether elsewhere on Bourak or on other planets — have failed because the sap parasite cycle is compromised. As a result, Haqqislam has been careful to minimize the terraforming of the Gabqar region (lest the precarious biological balance on which Silk depends should be disrupted).

SARIKAMIS

Sarikamis is known as the playground of the rich. Exclusive seaside resorts line the coast and a city centre studded with luxury apartments is surrounded by the sprawling estates of Merchant Lords.

GABQAR KHANATE

The Gabqar Khanate is scarcely terraformed in order to avoid affecting the delicate environmental balance of the Nassiat (from which Silk is derived). In order to assure the security of Silk production, the entire region exists in a constant state of martial law under the rule of the Khan, a military governor appointed by the Hachib from a list proposed by the Haqqislamite High Command.

This martial law, however, is only truly effective in the cities. The sprawling mountain ranges of Gabqar are a nigh-lawless wilderness and a hotbed of organised crime, with numerous mafias and biker gangs vying to skim off what they can from the vast profits of the mining and Silk industries through protection rackets, robbery, and vice.

Many of these outlaw tribes hail from the Kyrgyz enclaves of the mountains in the east. The mafia like the Tien Shan Range because it has plenty of places to hide drug labs and arsenals. The peaks provide excellent vantage points for lookouts and many passes are crossed by nothing more than a narrow, winding footpath, which makes the gangsters' mountain fastnesses very easy to defend, even from highly trained and well-armed soldiers.

The stark solitude of the mountains and plains draws a more serene type of soul, too. Gabqar is renowned as a place where you will find, if you know the right places to look, many mystics. Amid the silence of a mountain hermitage or the colossal power of a thunderstorm as it rolls across the steppe, more than one seeker of the Infinite has experienced the divine.

HUNZA

The Hunza people live from hunting, cultivating Nassiat, and a flourishing tourism industry of high mountain sports. The Bajram-Balk mountain range in which the frontier city is nestled is divided by the hunting areas of the Sakht Taqdeer (Urdu for "grim fate"), wild mountain panthers which only the Hunza guides have a reputation for hunting down.

KHIVA KALA

The majority of Nassiat is cultivated and harvested in the mountains which surround Khiva Kala, the capital of Gabqar. The city naturally became the centre of Silk production for the entire Human Sphere. Wealth followed, creating an immense division between the social class of the city and the

rest of the impoverished region. (A division which is sustained through a complex system of commercial and familial appanages.)

KUM-DAG

Kum-dag is a ramshackle town of outlaws and thieves. It was only recently recognised as an official community by the regional government, and efforts to bring proper oversight and governance are being resisted by the locals.

SEMETEI

Micro-T2s sprout like a forest around the city of Semetei, keeping back the clouds of poisonous spores which infest the mountain valley above the city.

Local terraforming efforts inadvertently allowed a parasitic hybrid fungus (*Repenceae basidiocarpis*) to flourish. *Repenceae* spores were both extremely poisonous to humans and capable of co-opting and mutating other fungal species. It was not a serious threat because its spores were not airborne, but in the now favorable conditions of the Semetei Valley *Repenceae* patches growing on Bourak parasols multiplied until they overwhelmed the parasols completely and hybridised them. The hybrid parasols were capable of producing large quantities of parasitic, airborne spores which spread throughout the valley (taking over multitudes of other species in the process).

The Semetei Valley is now a dense fungal forest deadly to any human habitation (and most local species, too). On certain days, when the winds are right, spore clouds will blow south into the desert, creating polluted sandstorms.

TAMERLANE

Tamerlane is where all the small mining communities on the south side of the Tien Shan Range ship their ore to be smelted and processed. Thick clouds of smoke rise from the refineries.

The local guilds are heavily factionalised, with politics based around the seniority of entire families. Over the past decade, a deep feud has riven the Vitsin and Usenov guilds, and over the past year there's been blood in the streets.

IRAN ZHAT AL AMAT SHAHNATE

Iran Zhat Al Amat Shahnate is the planet's largest region. When Bourak was first settled, it was also the most inhospitable and deserted region. Terraforming has changed all of that, transforming expansive swaths of the Al-Idrisi coast into beautiful tourist zones.

ALAMUT

The exception to this is the Alamut subcontinent, home to the Daylami tribes. Reputedly the terra-forming efforts here have been deliberately abated due to the machinations of the Old Man of the Mountain, maintaining the inhospitable veil which shrouds the secret Hassassin bases rumoured to be scattered throughout the region. But the Daylami persevere, a hard people with a warrior caste which protects them from Silk raiders and desert bandits.

TURFAN

The port city of Turfan is the only settlement of note in Alamut and the primary gate by which goods arrive in the region. (There are many rumours that its airport is secretly operated by the Hassassins.) Its primary industry is serpent-slaying, the Bourakian equivalent of whale hunting.

NOROUZ

The northernmost province of Iran Zhat Al Amat is known throughout the Human Sphere as a paradise for tourists, who flock to its exquisitely created beach resorts and leafy retreats, each one a master-piece of applied planetology.

MARACANDA

The headquarters of the Terraformation Institute is here, in the city of Maracanda, which stands within a circle of lush greenery in the midst of a huge trackless desert, created by the Institute's combina-tion of science and art.

QORSAPTAR

The local architecture of this idyllic seaside city is dominated by the Persian Renaissance which has touched cities throughout Iran Zhat Al Amat. The streets are lined with old merchant palaces, traditional houses, and riads (charming little hotels situated in medina districts).

RAVANSĀR

The capital of Iran Zhat Al Amat is completely surrounded by the centenary palm grove of Parvaneh, one of the largest in the entire Sphere. Its gleaming tile façades cast dazzling reflections of Bourak's sun. The medina districts at the heart of city are wrapped by the coiling garden parks of Kamshad ("Happy Desire" in Farsi), creating the halcyon landscape famed by poets. Down the coast, the modernity and dynamism of the Gazsi financial quarter thrusts into the sky. Up the coast are the luxurious theriac resorts where off-worlders seek medical treatment. And up in the southern hills quaint residential districts wend their way through picturesque valleys.

Mehrzad Minaret: Located atop the highest hill on the western edge of Ravansār, from the top of the Mehrzad Minaret one has a panoramic view of the entire city. Also known as the Minaret of the Dusk, it's a national architectural jewel.

Theriac Resorts: The ancient Greeks concocted "theriac"—a supposed cure for all ills. The Theriac Resort was the first resort in Ravansār designed explicitly for medical tourists, but its name and the "cure for all ills" brand have become genericised to describe an entire industry dedicated to relieving the ailments of both body and soul.

ISLANDS

BAHITI

Bahiti has the richest variety of parasol fungi on the planet. Fed by the cataclysmic rainfalls off the Ibn Battuta Ocean, parasol forests cover most of the island's lowlands. Large tobacco plantations have been established on the northern end of the island.

OLABISI

Olabisi is a tourist town. Moderately popular with native Bourakian, it's something of a well-kept secret and off-worlders rarely seek it out. The annual Olabisi Windsurfing Race is a cutthroat competition.

Antarah Tobacco Company: The most important brand of "healthy tobacco" on Bourak. Its famous, idiosyncratic advertising campaigns have featured a number of celebrities and mayastars like Enzo Navarone. The company's headquarters are found on Olabisi.

BANIYA

Baniya Island has no large settlements, but is sprin-kled with a number of small farming communities.

KARLI

Although popularly referred to as an island, geolog-ically speaking Karli is a small polar continent.

NAWAL ISLAND

Separated from the main landmass of Bourak by the temperate northern seas, Nawal Island is the seat of Haqqislam's government.

Outside of the capital city, the island is sparsely populated by those seeking a simpler, slower-paced life. These people, sometimes called "Bygones", sup-port themselves by growing crops on small farms or herding livestock for trade. It is a common practice for stressed-out executives to take a few months or a year off for a sabbatical among the Bygones.

SHAHZADA

From the Palace of Keyumars in Ravansār, the Shāhanshāh (colloquially the Shah) stands at the head of a tiered democracy. The Shah is elected from a council of national ministers. The national ministers are elected from the body of provincial ministers, the provincial ministers from local ministers, and so forth. These overlapping ministries (which are organised both as regional provinces and as topical demesnes) are collectively referred to as the Shahzada.

THE HOLY MOUNTAIN

Somewhere in its great central desert of Alamut is the Holy Mountain where the infamous Hassassin Society makes its headquarters. Countless spies from the other human powers have tried to locate the Mountain. Only a few have succeeded. Fewer still have returned from Bourak, and those that did came back as agents of the Hassassins.

AZAR DESERT

The Azar Desert is a desolate territory blessed with scorching days and freezing nights. Near the centre of the desert is the intermontane Red Plateau, ringed by mountains and topped by dunes of crimson sand.

MAGLEV

The Silk Route maglev is the only reliable way to cross the continent from Khiva Kala to Dar el Funduq, and even then the train is often ambushed by raiders in the Azar Desert. The maglev was originally built to ferry colonists arriving on the orbital elevator from the blistering equator to the temperate northern coast (and the old Nizari line from Maracanda to Ravansār is still frequented by terraforming engineers), but the primary cargo of the maglev today is Silk from Gabqar.

KHADIJAH

Khadijah is given over almost entirely to the business of government. The city's heart is Ittihad Square, where the Upper and Lower Houses of Parliament face one another across the lush, sculpted greenery of the public plaza. To the north lies the Garden of the Dreaming Pillars, a public park of undulating slopes, ivy-covered peristyles and ornate maze-like topiary where you can easily lose yourself for a whole day. Beyond the Garden is the Palace of the Hachib, the President's official residence.

PARTHALIA ISLAND

Parthalia was the settlement target for Indonesian Haqqislamites. It has earned an odd reputation for foreign espionage, largely due to PanOceania using it as a convenient locale for washing the identities of undercover agents in two high profile espionage cases, but it's most famed as a biomedical resort where the rich and desperate come for experimental (and prohibited) treatments unavailable anywhere else in the Human Sphere outside of *Bakunin*.

BAHAL

The distinctive Austronesian architecture of Bahal immediately sets it apart from most other Bourakian cities. Due to the general lack of trees on Bourak, however, the aesthetics have been adapted to native materials.

ZUMORRODA

Off the east coast of Parthalia there is a small, artificial island which belongs to Qaid Fahesh, the warmonger of the Dahshat Mercenary Company and owner of a wide variety of other business interests. Fahesh also has sole rights to the profits of tourism from the beautiful reef structures under and around Zumorroda. Fahesh reigns supreme there with minimal influence from Haqqislamite authorities.

FAREEDAT SYSTEM

The four planets of the Bourak system orbit a K-class main sequence star. Only Bourak itself is inhabited.

MOONS

Bourak has seven moons. The two largest moons are home to research and mining bases. These are small, largely experimental installations, however, and total lunar population is only around 10,000. Rumours abound, however, that the Hassassins maintain secret bases on some or all of the moons.

ORBITALS

The skies above Bourak are relatively free of orbitals compared to other worlds of the Human Sphere.

Gelişmek Station: Atop the Dar el Funduq orbital elevator, Gelişmek Station is a bulbous monstrosity which has been expanded repeatedly with new modules as they became needed.

OTHER STATIONS

Bayram Caravanserai: The Druze own the sole caravanserai near the wormhole leading to Paradiso and Concilium that was discovered on the outskirts of the system a little over ten years ago. There are rumours that Druze Shock Teams have been used to sabotage other construction efforts in the area.

Gas Mining Platforms: The outer planets both support extensive gas mining operations – chiefly hydrogen from 'Uj ibn Anaq and nitrogen from Al-mi'raj.

Sari Han: Called the Yellow Station due to the mustard swirls of Al-mi'raj, the gas giant it orbits, Sari Han is a Vila Booster station servicing the C4, C5, and C6 Circulars. As with the spaceports on Bourak, security at the prosperous station (and its several luxury areas) is handled by the Djanbazan Tactical Group, a Muhafiz assault group from the nearby Qapu Khalqi Fleet Headquarters.

FAREEDAT SYSTEM

STAR
Fareedat: K0V (Orange Dwarf)

PLANETS
Ababil (0.22 AU): Mesoplanet
Bourak (0.55 AU): Terrestrial Planet
'Uj ibn Anaq (7 AU): Gas Giant – Class I (Ammonia Clouds)
Al-mi'raj (15 AU): Gas Giant – Class I (Cold Super Jupiter)

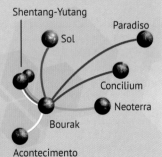

CIRCULAR ROUTES
C4: Neoterra/Shentang-Yutang
C5: Shentang-Yutang/Sol
C6: Shentang-Yutang/Acontecimento
C7: Paradiso/Concilium

Bureau Aegis, p. 213: Legal and military arm of the O-12 government.

Bakunin – p. 168

Dahshat Mercenary Company – p. 206

Druze – p. 207

Muhafiz – p. 164

PLANET
CONCILIUM PRIMA

From the viewing decks of the Asgard orbital station, the planet Concilium Prima glitters. Its highly reflective upper atmosphere, laced with nano-machines, gives the planet an almost mirrored effect. The usual stark outlines of the continents are blurred against the deep blue of the oceans that surround them, and mingle with a scintillating rainbow of refracted light from the bright, but distant star. It is a beautiful world to behold; the green of life and deep-ocean colours distort like a twinkling diamond against the deep darkness of space.

The planet is home to the powerful O-12 Senate (the Öberhaus), Courts, Security Council, and Bureaus. As a result, it is also home to representatives of every major power in the Human Sphere, as well as a multitude of hypercorporations, all vying for attention, and seeking to outdo each other with lavish displays of their influence, might, and wealth.

Not all is glittering lights, high technology, and the ideals of Unity, Cooperation, Support, and Progress that O-12 espouses, however. Concilium Prima

O-12 government – p. 211

CONCILIUM PRIMA STATISTICS
Distance from Star: 1.3 AU • **Orbital Revolution**: 541 days • **Rotation**: 23 hours • **Radius**: 0.9 Earth radii • **Surface Gravity**: 1.1g

PLANET DATA FILE
Type of Government: Senate • **Head of Government**: Bureau Concilium Director • **Capital**: Edda • **Population of Planet**: 98 million • **Off-Planet System Population**: 760,000 • **Primary Languages**: English, Portuguese, Spanish, Japanese, Esperanto • **Anthem**: *Per Unitatem Pacis (Peace Through Unity)* • **Principle Industries**: Politics, Education, Research

CORVUS BELLI
INFINITY

SKY SHIMMERS

Maintained even after the terraforming of Concilium Prima, and used to scrub carbon dioxide and other harmful gases, as well as dust and micro-debris from the atmosphere, is a swarm of nanomachines. Seeded in a complex network in the upper atmosphere, this layer of trillions of nanomachines gives the sky a shimmering effect. A side effect of this network is the disruption to communication from the planet surface to space. Causing microwave beam attenuation, and interference to most other forms of communication, large data-packages and a vast majority of regular communications to either the orbitals or further afield are rerouted through a tightly state-controlled communication infrastructure. This relay system is closely monitored by automated systems feeding information directly to Bureau Noir. (However, it is known that a number of the network platforms have been compromised in the past, allowing data packets to bypass O-12's monitoring systems. And undoubtedly similar breaches exist which have never been detected).

Living Cities, p. 177: Metropolises featuring fully-integrated automation, smart-matter, and AI support.

Bureau Gaea, p. 215: O-12 Bureau in charge of plentary development and biological research.

is home to the training grounds that supply the brains, guile, and muscle O-12's Bureaus require to ride the maelstrom of political wrangling throughout the Human Sphere. With so many powerful states and corporations represented, the back alleys, nightclubs, and private get-aways which lie beneath the busy surface of the planet are a fractious multitude of battlegrounds where deals are struck, information leaked, pacts made, and the feuds of the galaxy realised.

CLIMATE AND GEOGRAPHY

Concilium Prima was discovered to be a habitable planet with a stable orbit, suitable for colonisation, but in need of some minor alterations in climate in order to make human habitation comfortable. Life had already taken hold here, and indigenous flora and fauna had grown to dominate both the oceans and the land. As a part of the annual payments made to O-12, the different nations each played a role in the terraforming and development of the planet. It was carefully planned, and intended to be a symbol of international cooperation and a monument to a brighter future.

Yu Jing engineers masterminded and carried out the fundamental adaptation and terraforming of the surface, while Haqqislamite planetologists refined the process and added their quality touch. PanOceania, competing with Yu Jing corporations, planned and built Concilium Prima's infrastructure. All these nations left their mark, and the planet is now a beautifully integrated pastiche of each nation, geographically represented through abundant plant and animal life, and architecturally through the style, feel and embellishments of the planet's Living Cities.

Concilium Prima is orbited by a moon named Unueco (Unity), and three smaller rocky bodies, really no more than captured asteroids, named Kunlaborado, Subteno, and Progreso (Cooperation, Support, and Progress — after the Pillars of O-12). The distance of the moon to Concilium Prima means the tidal forces that operate on the great oceans Njord and Aegir are relatively extreme.

Concilium Prima has an almost circular orbit and a relatively slight axial tilt of only 6°, the differentiation between seasons is almost non-existent. Latitude and geothermal activity are therefore the dominant factors in defining prevailing weather and temperature.

A wide tropical band extends around the equatorial region, running through the lower portions of Midgard, through Minas Gerais and Maidan, and the upper portions of Choola. These wide areas are dominated by great savannahs, jungles, and broadleaf forests.

Choola is the epicentre of Concilium Prima's often shocking geothermal violence. Two great tectonic lanes collide in this fractious region, leaving it too dangerous to inhabit. Known as Loki's Land, the two tectonic lanes have equally foreboding names: Laufey and Farbauti. High in volcanic activity, with frequent earthquakes and eruptions, the Haqqislamite planetologists, based in the city of Bhai, monitor the region constantly. These engineers advise Bureau Gaea, whose responsibility it is to adjust the nanomachines seeded in the atmosphere to stabilise the climate after major eruptions throw metric tons of greenhouse gases and particulate into the sky.

Beyond the tropical band, Midgard, to the north, sits in a temperate zone dominated by grasslands and broadleaf forests. To the south, the El-Gebal Mountain Range divides and protects Jaulan from Choola, and governs the weather in the area, causing significant rainfall in Jaulan, which is dominated by temperate rainforests.

FLORA AND FAUNA

The relative stability of the climate seems to have resulted in little diversity among the indigenous plant life of Concilium Prima, with a select range of plant species dominating their niches. In the tropical zones, large tree-like photoautotrophs, labelled Crassus Truncus by the biologists of Manaheim University, spread a bright green canopy over the rainforest floor. These plants are typically shorter than the trees found on Earth, and have trunks of significant girth, regularly reaching thirty to fifty metres or more. The trunks of Crassus Truncus are irregular, and often contain massive hollows, like cave systems, exploited by wildlife.

Like the native plant life, the diversity of indigenous wildlife appears to be more limited than on Earth. The jungles sport a wide range of arboreal animals. Large herbivorous endotherms exploit the savannahs, and there are several dangerous apex predators that pursue them. The most successful life forms on the planet, however, are similar to the arthropods of Earth, with thousands of species already catalogued and the vast majority still unknown. These arthropods include both herbivorous and carnivorous species ranging from the size of a pinhead to that of a large cat.

Concilium Prima's most remarkable biosphere is its oceans, which are thick with bioluminescent life. Scientists have observed that distinct "hue biomes"— each consisting of identical colours — cling together. In many places these hue biomes will spiral and swirl together in complex, fractal-like patterns.

Under considerable threat due to significant shifts in the planet's climate and biosphere, the indigenous flora and fauna are dying off or being outcompeted by the biomass introduced to the planet during terraforming. Much research and development is being poured into preserving and adapting the indigenous life. Dominating the lands and seas now are a wide range of Earth's flora and fauna, each species carefully selected to best represent, in glorious combination, the natural characteristics of the nations that, together, remodelled the planet.

ECONOMY

While a healthy trade in produce exists across Concilium Prima, and its education industry is famed throughout the Human Sphere, the economy of the planet is dominated by politics. Between the Öberhaus, the Conclave, the Petite Assemblée and the Courts, as well as tithes paid to O-12, Concilium Prima is a very wealthy planet. Much of this wealth is held in the population centres or used by O-12 to fund and run its many Bureaus.

A significant mining industry exists on the planet's surface, centred on the continent of Minas Gerais. This mineral wealth is, in turn, supplemented by the significant industries that exist in the outer Concilium system. The political importance of Concilium Prima, as well as the mineral wealth, has attracted a multitude of hypercorporations.

The wide assortment of wealthy individuals and corporations represented on the planet supports a vibrant and eclectic entertainment industry which draws its influence from across the Human Sphere. From art exhibitions to performances, from downloadable experiences to interactive games, from nightclubs to more exotic entertainment... everything can be found in the cities of Concilium Prima for a price.

DEMOGRAPHICS AND CULTURE

Concilium Prima is a planet with relatively few inhabitants; a majority of settlements are disparate and small. In contrast, the major cities like Edda, Manaheim, and Lorena are affluent and effervescent, the rival of any in terms of services, technology, wealth, and life, if not in population.

As the arguable centre of interstellar politics, Concilium Prima is a melting pot of cultures and vested interests. While highly multicultural, the planet is also extremely divided. Enclaves within the major population centres, especially Edda, are nationalistic, with districts dominated by Yu Jing, PanOceania, Haqqislam, and even the Nomads.

Concilium Prima is a world of power-brokers, where envoys and representatives go about the business of greasing the wheels of influence. It's also a world filled with a double-dealing trade in secrets, technology, knowledge, and information — a largely invisible dark side to a glittering world.

Despite its divisive qualities, however, a common saying on Concilium Prima is *La tajdo de unueco nin kune* (The tide of unity brings us together). The educational facilities, entertainment districts, vacation resorts, and even the "tides" of official business draw the people of Concilium together and mingle them into something greater than their individual parts.

Carefully planned and exquisitely executed, the terraforming of Concilium Prima and the architectural accompaniment were designed to fit hand in glove. The population centres are a merging of natural and constructed worlds. Cities rise from and are built to be a part of the landscape that surround them. Truly Living Cities, they are dominated on the surface by a seamless integration with the natural world, with major infrastructure and arterials either cleverly concealed or buried beneath parks and structures built into the environment.

A special O-12 Bureau called Bureau Concilium is the body that sees to the day-to-day governance of the citizens of Concilium. Based in the main city of Edda they are the planetary and system government.

Bureau Concilium – p. 215

BOIS BLEU

Bois Bleu is a large island chain off the northern coast of Mentor. Declared a sanctuary, it is home to a unique terrestrial bioluminescent flora unknown anywhere else on the planet. With great forests that give off a stunningly beautiful glow, green during summer and blue to violet in winter, Bois Bleu has, despite its protected status, become a retreat for the wealthy. Large estates studded with palatial mansions belonging to the wealthiest and most influential people and corporations can be found in the relatively small town of Sainte Michelle de Bois Bleu.

THE BLUE WOOD

The colloquial term for the bioluminescent flora that dominates the island. During the day, the flora appears to be a beautiful mix of leaves and flowers, but by night, the scene becomes a thing of legend. More colours than the eye can process glow softly in the darkness, strange shapes and forms, and overall, the gentle blue glow of the leaves is transcendent.

SAINTE MICHELLE DE BOIS BLEU

Sainte Michelle de Bois Bleu is only a relatively small town compared to the other cities of Concilium Prima, and largely functions as a suburb of Lorena for the wealthy and powerful. It is a rich centre for both fine dining and for the arts, being widely considered the cultural heart of Concilium Prima.

JOURNEYS ON CONCILIUM

Despite its sparse population, travel around Concilium Prima is relatively easy. Large, low-flying passenger craft connect most cities; regular ferries move mineral wealth and people between Edda, Minas Gerais, and Maidan Basha; and seven high-speed lines connect Lorena, Edda, Manaheim, and Maidan Basha. The spread of Bureaus, corporations, educational facilities, and political offices means well-maintained transports from one location to another are frequent and comfortable.

MIDGARD

Midgard is undoubtedly the centre of Concilium Prima. With the city of Edda sitting paramount, and the city of Manaheim a shining beacon, Midgard is where the gears and wheels that drive O-12 are turned.

LORENA

Lorena began as a small leisure town with an economy built around the commerce and tourism. Often referred to as the Gateway to Bois Bleu, Lorena sits on the northern coast of Mentor, and across the narrow strait the islands of Bois Bleu glow softly ephemeral in the night. Lorena is the jewel of Bourak's planetologists, with a twisting, undulating landscape falling away to a gorgeous coastline affording the entire city a view of the island beyond. The headquarters of Bureau Gaea, the setting and architectural design of Lorena is stunning.

HUAQUIAO

Positioned on the west coast, overlooking the vast Njord Ocean is Huaquiao. The headquarters of Bureau Agni, Huaquiao is a paradise for physicists. Containing some of the most advanced energy research laboratories in the Human Sphere, it is home to a constantly shifting population of scientists, researchers, interns, teachers, and corporate representatives. It is also home to the Master Clock and the most advanced quantronic clocks in the Sphere. The time zone of Huaquiao's Master Clock is the reference point for easy time, which is used for all stellar navigation, sets the day-night cycles for all ships, and programming schedules for Maya transmissions.

EDDA

The capital city of Concilium Prima, Edda is home to more diplomats, envoys, and hypercorporate headquarters than almost anywhere else in the Human Sphere. A dizzying array of delegates and agents, workers and citizens, representatives from every power, rub shoulders in this densely populated city. A constant flow of traffic in people, materials, and information flow from Edda to the other cities of Concilium Prima and the geosynchronous Orbital Asgard. There are few cities in all the Human Sphere so diverse, so magnificent, and so dangerous.

The city of Edda was designed according to the principles of the concentric zone model. The city Core is dominated by the icons of O-12 – the Öberhaus, the Petite Assemblée, the O-12 Courts, certain Bureau headquarters, the embassies of the G-5 and other nations, and the other bureaucratic apparatuses of the state.

Öberhaus Gardens and Petite Assemblée: The austere and vaulted Öberhaus is home to the O-12 Senate, where the legal wrangling and political actions that shake the very fabric of humanity take place. Surrounding the nerve centre of the Öberhaus are a vast array of gardens which twist their way around, above, and even under a wide swath of the Core.

The Petite Assemblée is also here, with its multinational mix of representatives assembling within a short walk of the Öberhaus and senate.

Corporate Ring: Surrounding the Core is the Ring, which houses the multitude of corporate entities drawn to the fractious interests of interstellar politics. From banks to munitions companies; from manufacturing giants to tech enterprises, a staggering number of corporate interests can be found in Edda lobbying members of the senate to serve their needs and forging deals with the other corporations drawn here in a mingled orgy of business and politics.

Residential Zones: Beyond the Corporate Ring are an encircling moat of residential districts strung out between ring roads. The Zones are highly stratified and split by national loyalties, but share a confluence in the entertainment and social districts known as Nexuses (like the infamous Karmezino Nexus) which lie at the interstice of their eclectic, multicultural melange. Edda is, by necessity, subject less to the Living Cities doctrine that governs the layout and design of Concilium Prima's other cities, but a similar melding of the natural and the man-made dominates the skyline.

MANAHEIM

Manaheim, a small but vibrant city, is dominated by leafy residential suburbs, extensive commercial districts and, of course, the universities. The city is dominated by the exceptional educational academies of the Manaheim and Concilium universities.

According to the residents of Manaheim, the capital of Edda is where you find "Exported O-12 Culture", which is dominated by off-world influences. Manaheim, on the other hand, is where you find the epitome of O-12 Culture – a culture uniquely forged by the descendants of the first Conciliar colonists to call the planet home, and the academic and scientific explorers who populate the universities. Manaheim has a reputation for curiosity, for learning, and for a rebellious and independent demeanour. The headquarters of Bureau Athena can be found in Manaheim, as well as the Memory Museum, a main feature of which is an Obelisk in memoriam of the C-7 tragedy.

OKOLNIR

Sitting on the east coast of Jaulan is Okolnir, a port for fishing Harvesters that ply the southern reaches of the Aegir Ocean. Little more than a settlement

---

O-12 government – p. 211

C-7 Diplomatic Incident: Hypercorp-hired mercenaries attempted to kidnap the Ariadnan ambassador to O-12 and his family while they were travelling on the C-7 Circular. The situation rapidly escalated out of control

Bureau Gaea, p. 215: O-12 Bureau in charge of plentary development and biological research.

Bureau Agni, p. 213: O-12 Bureau in charge of energy and neomaterials.

Living Cities, p. 177: Metropolises featuring fully-integrated automation, smart-matter, and AI support.

MANAHEIM UNIVERSITY

The centre for historical, socio-political, military, and economic studies, Manaheim University is a beacon of learning. Funded predominantly by O-12 and with intimate ties to many of the Bureaus, Manaheim University attracts the best and brightest in their fields. Much study is done on the history of humanity and the sociopolitical drivers that dominate the turning of events. Manaheim University is one of the largest and most highly regarded universities in the Human Sphere.

easy time, p. 145: EC time, an AI-mitigated timekeeping standard designed for an interstellar civilisation.

Bureau Athena, p. 214: O-12 Bureau charged with protecting human rights.

that supplies workers for the Harvesters, Okolnir has a small population and shelters behind the breakwaters that protect it from the waters beyond.

MAIDAN

Maidan is a vast plateau straddling the equatorial band of the Mentor continent. Thick jungles crowd the centre of this region, with deserts extending south toward Choola, the east of the region dominated by wide savannahs.

MAIDAN BASHA

Maidan Basha is a sprawling Living City situated on the east coast of the Maidan Region. Meaning "House of the Plain", Maidan Basha is surrounded, to the west, by huge savannahs. With a sweltering climate year round, thanks to its position on the equator, Maidan Basha is nonetheless a bustling city. With the massive geosynchronous orbital Bifrost positioned far overhead, Maidan Basha is the location of Concilium's only orbital lift. It is a centre for traffic on and off world. A massive industrial complex deals with an unending supply of imports and exports. Traffic to and from the orbital is constant. The headquarters of Bureau Hermes can be found in Maidan Basha, a position providing direct links to the orbital above and the terminals of the Circulars beyond.

KALA PANI

An isolated city on the west coast of the Maidan Region and positioned against the sheltered Gulf of Choola, Kala Pani (meaning "Black Waters") is a huge port city. Providing food and raw materials to the rest of the planet, Kala Pani is the food bowl of Concilium. The region is lush, with the warm, mineral-rich waters of the Gulf of Choola providing an ideal location for massive fish farms, hydroponic centres, and aquatic farms. The rocky formations and banks of the Gulf are the remains of dormant volcanoes and give the sea a nearly black hue, lending the city its name.

CHOOLA

Geologically volatile, highly unpredictable, and extremely dangerous, the interior of Choola is widely referred to as Loki's Land for good reason. Without the careful monitoring of Bourak and Bureau Gaea planetologists, the gases and debris irregularly blasted into the atmosphere would have a devastating effect on the climate and habitability of the entire planet.

JAULAN

The domineering El-Gebal Mountain Range, up-thrust by the geological violence of the Laufey and Farbauti fault lines, does much to influence the weather systems of Concilium Prima and shelter Jaulan from the ferocity of Loki's Land. Jaulan is a peaceful swath of land. Wide and complex river systems drain from the El-Gebal Mountains through Jaulan into a myriad of swamps, lakes, or the Njord and Aegir Oceans. Jaulan is bordered by broadleaf deciduous forests, stock drawn from Earth, while the centre of the continent is still dominated by indigenous plants, great forests of Crassus Truncus, undergrowth, and mosses.

HARVESTERS

Harvesters are great machines, manufactured in the fabrication workshops of Cambados, which comb the oceans for food. No simple fishing boats, these are vast multileveled platforms that extend both above and below the ocean surface and are capable of weathering the rough swells of Concilium Prima's tides. Several of these great platforms are now abandoned and rumour has it that at least one has been refitted to serve as an urban combat training ground for Bureau Aegis and Bureau Noir agents.

Bureau Hermes, p. 215: O-12 Bureau which regulates commerce, jump gates, and Circulars.

Circulars, p. 144: Massive starships looping endlessly along the fixed Circular routes.

AL BACTRA

Sitting on the east coast of Jaulan is Al Bactra, one of Concilium Prima's true architectural gems, with a low skyline that blends seamlessly with the rolling hills and forests that surround it. Al Bactra is a city that is spread over a vast area given its population. The headquarters of Bureau Lakshmi is found here, along with important hospitals, health, and pharmacological research centres. Al Bactra maintains a strong Haqqislamite character, but given the sheer beauty of the city and surroundings, is also home to a great many bureaucrats who are allowed the luxury of working from home.

BHAI

Bhai sits on the west coast of Jaulan. With seismic and weather monitoring stations and significant outposts for Bureau Gaea, it is from here that the geological activity of the Choola region is monitored, and the Shimmering Sky manipulated to calm the meterological systems of Concilium Prima.

HELHEIM

An inhospitable Antarctic region, with a rough and cruel environment. Helheim has a well-earned name.

THOKK

Ostensibly Thokk is a small port city nestled on the coast of an uninviting land. Despite a seemingly drab exterior, Thokk is the location of instructional academies for the paramilitary wing of Bureau Aegis, which uses the inhospitable terrain beyond as a training ground for elite special forces. The bars of Thokk are no place to pick a fight! Thokk has a twin city in the Northern Hemisphere: Bergelmir.

MINAS GERAIS

Minas Gerais is a large island divided from the mainland by relatively calm Guanabara Sea. Minas Gerais is rich in important mineral deposits, and is the most industrialised zone of Concilium. Massive mining operations concentrate in the centre of the island; these are largely autonomous, and supply a constant stream of mineral wealth.

VIANA

Viana is positioned near the centre of the main island of Minas Gerais. Here massive processing facilities deal with the flow of raw materials from the mining pits that surround the city and dominate the interior of Minas Gerais. From Viana the processed minerals are transported to Cambados.

CAMBADOS

Cambados sits on the southern coast of Minas Gerais. It is a huge city-factory, with both processed and raw materials shipped here from Viana for export to the orbital lift in Maidan Basha, or to the many cities of Concilium. Cambados is a city built around heavy industry.

BARONHA

Baronha is the capital city of Minas Gerais. A centre for industry and trade, it is also the headquarters for Bureau Ganesh. Commercial delegations frequent the city, and many major hypercorps have offices here. Reinforced communication lines are maintained and heavily used between Baronha, Edda, and Maidan Basha. Baronha is a place where fortunes are made and commercial empires have been built and lost.

MONTALBAN

East of the main islands of Minas Gerais is Montalban, the capital city of Bianca Island. A stark contrast to the industrial nature of the other islands, Bianca is a tourist destination *par excellence*. Boasting the whitest and finest sand beaches on the planet, with a spectacular array of marine fauna and sparkling coral reefs it is an extremely popular holiday destination.

JOTUMHEIM

Largely a wilderness of bleak forests and tundras, much of Jotumheim is positioned within the Arctic Circle.

BERGELMIR

Bergelmir is situated on an island chain of the same name off the east coast of Jotumheim, sparse vegetation and animal life lends it a dreary atmosphere. A small and secretive settlement, it is home to Der Irrgarten, a centre for instruction of Psi Unit agents and personnel. Twin city to Thokk in the far south, Bergelmir is isolated, and this allows it to maintain a blanket of secrecy, which has raised suspicions about it also being the location of a Bureau Noir headquarters.

UTGARD

Utgard is a sparsely populated city that appears on the surface to be of little interest. However, as it is home to the headquarters of Bureau Toth it is one of the most strategically important cities on Concilum Prima, and indeed, in the Human Sphere. Utgard is where a majority of the hardware that supports ALEPH is maintained. Entire facilities are dedicated to holding quantronic macroprocessors, set in arrays of redundant configurations and all fully optimised to avoid even the slightest perturbation in the data flow. Protected by an

Bureau Lakshmi, p. 216: O-12 Bureau governing medical industry and research.

Bureau Ganesh, p. 215: O-12 Bureau overseeing international trade.

Bureau Gaea, p. 215: O-12 Bureau in charge of plentary development and biological research.

Bureau Aegis, p. 213: Legal and military arm of the O-12 government.

Psi Unit, p. 213: O-12's military intelligence unit.

Bureau Toth, p. 217: O-12 Bureau charged with observing ALEPH.

elite Bureau Aegis force, the security of Utgard is absolute. The entire city is run as a police state, and secret laws and exemptions apply to the security forces, issued from the highest levels of O-12.

LYNGUI

A small chain of barren and inhospitable volcanic islands far out into the Aegir Ocean. While the volcanos that thrust them above the waves are dormant, the islands are largely bare, with broken cliff faces dashed by roaring tides.

CONCILIUM SYSTEM

The Concilium system is home to five primary planets, several bands of asteroids and a multitude of orbitals.

THE CONCILIUM NOVA ORBITAL SYSTEM

Concilium Nova is the collective name for the myriad of orbitals that surround the planet Concilium Prima. Set in two great rings, at nighttime, Concilium Nova shines like a necklace of jewels overhead, especially in the northern and southern latitudes, where both rings are clearly distinct.

Asaheim: The gateway to Concilium, Asaheim is an orbital built around the great Vila Boosters. Here passengers disembarking from the Circulars are directed either to Bifrost, or, if they are an official on business with O-12, to Asgard. Asaheim works as a space-traffic control point, and Bureaus Hermes and Ganesh both have important offices here.

Asgard: A gigantic orbital locked in geocentric orbit above Edda. Delegates, diplomats, corporate representatives, and others on business with O-12 arrive at the Topside Docks and then proceed through a series of checkpoints down to the Lower Bays from which they can avail themselves of a variety of shuttle services to ferry them down to the Edda Spaceports. Bureau Aegis troops man the security points, supported by ALEPH, running background checks on all arrivals.

Bifrost: Bifrost is a massive orbital and spaceport. Built around the orbital lift, also named Bifrost, it is in geosynchronous orbit above the city of Maidan Basha, and sparkles in the night sky like a multi-faceted diamond. It is where the mineral wealth mined in the Muspelheim and the Brísingamen is brought to the surface of the planet. It is also where the frameworks and constructions

of Cambados' fabrication facilities are brought to low orbit for transport elsewhere. A vast quantity of imported and exported goods arrives at Concilium Prima through this facility.

Cibola: An orbital that began as a leisure destination and has evolved into a very popular centre for sports and entertainment. Cibola has a huge public market and a constant stream of traffic.

Idavoll: An exclusive and luxurious retreat for the super-wealthy. This is the place to relax and unwind (and do a little business on the side) for the high powered executives, diplomats, and bureaucrats of Concilium Prima. Idavoll is one of the most expensive retreats in the Human Sphere.

Bossémbelé: For those who can never dream of visiting Idavoll, Bossémbelé is a destination of choice. Recreation and relaxation are to be found in abundance. Bureau Lakshmi runs a hospital attached to Bossémbelé, and it is a well-regarded centre for research and development into low-intensity therapy.

Yiheyan: The Summer Palace of the Yu Jing Emperor, Yiheyan is an exquisite gem, with one of the most beautiful gardens to be found anywhere in the Human Sphere, though few have ever been invited to see it.

THE BRÍSINGAMEN

Corregidoran Nomads have an arrangement with O-12 which gives them permission to mine the asteroids of the Concilium system, most notably the large asteroid field known as the Brísingamen. Large mining facilities dot this region and support permanent colonies who ship their product back to Bifrost in huge, slow-moving barges.

A friendly rivalry exists between the Nomads and Concilium miners, and both parties often utilise the same shipping infrastructure to reduce costs.

MUSPELHEIM

The fifth planet in the Concilium system, Muspelheim is a hot gas giant that is mined extensively for the energy that powers Concilium.

Surt is a moon of Muspelheim and a military base. Serving to protect the mining and processing facilities of Muspelheim, and as a frontier patrol, swarms of high-mobility probes trace a constant surveillance net that feeds back to the Surt base. The offensive capabilities of Surt are a tightly kept secret, but it is widely estimated that enough ships are stationed here to fend off a first wave attack by any power in the Human Sphere. How O-12 managed to get the financing to pull such a force together, however, is a mystery.

A BARREN ROCK?

Rumours out of the great manufacturing labs of Cambados suggest that O-12 may have constructed a secret installation on Lyngui Island. Whatever the truth, orbital surveys confirm that there is definitely nothing on the surface.

Vila Booster – p. 145

CONCILIUM SYSTEM

STAR
Concilium: G2V (Sol-type Star)

PLANETS
Concilium Minus (0.59 AU): Telluric Planet
Concilium Prima (1.3 AU): Terrestrial Planet
Concilium Secunda (1.8 AU): Telluric Planet (Satellite: Unueco)
The Brísingamen (2.4 AU): Asteroid Belt
Niflheim (5.1 AU): Gas Giant – Class I (Ammonia Clouds)
Muspelheim (7.3 AU): Gas Giant – Class I (Ammonia Clouds)
The Fields (7.5+ AU): Sparse Asteroid Belt

VERDIGRIS DUNES
The surface of Concilium Secunda is notable for its "verdigris dunes" infused with oxidized copper particulates.

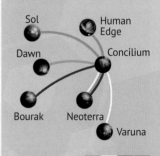

CIRCULAR ROUTES
C4: Dawn/Neoterra
C6: Neoterra/Varuna
C7: Bourak/Neoterra
C8: Human Edge/Sol

CORVUS BELLI INFINITY

PLANET
DAWN

Dawn was always intended to be the great work of planet Earth. The hopes of nations accompanied the colonists that crossed an uncharted galaxy to a planet rich in untapped resources and exotic minerals. Originally meant to receive a constant stream of support and supplies from Earth, Dawn's first settlements were designed to be a temporary measure until the rest of humanity arrived.

When help failed to show up, however, something new thrived upon Dawn. Cut off from their home, the colonists rejected Earth and established a new way of living. They are hearty survivalists and explorers who had no choice but to struggle to survive on an inhospitable planet and they tamed it like pioneers of old Earth. Now, as they struggle to find their own way in the universe, the Ariadnans have made a nation both strong and fractious on a vast planet which is both beautiful and bloody.

DAWN PLANET STATISTICS
Distance from Star: 0.9 AU • **Orbital Revolution:** 329 days • **Rotation:** 25 hours • **Radius:** 1.14 Earth radii • **Surface Gravity:** 1.05g

PLANET DATA FILE
Type of Government: Centralised Republic • **Head of Government:** Elected Council • **Capital:** Mat' (Матг, Матр) • **Population of Planet:** 8.5 million, 25 million Antipodes • **Off-Planet System Population:** 30,000 • **Primary Languages:** English, Russian, French, H'rall • **Anthem:** *Novyy rassvet vstayet (A New Dawn Rises)* • **Principal Industries:** Agriculture, Mining, Heavy Metal Alloys

CLIMATE AND GEOGRAPHY

Similar in size to Earth, Dawn has a cooler average temperature, yet similar diversity in plant and animal life. Most of Dawn's landmass is concentrated in a supercontinent, known simply as Ariadna or the Home Continent, where the colonial mothership first set down and the original colonists settled.

Excepting the dry, steppe biome of Tartary, heavy rainfall is characteristic of most Ariadnan settlements; even the deserts of USAriadna can be humid and muggy come springtime. As such, residents have to be careful about avoiding flood plains when they build. Winter is often brutal, with blizzards a regular occurrence. Around Mat' it is common to see a metre of snow on an average day; in Caledonia that number can easily double. The few outposts on outlying islands must prepare to be entirely cut off during the winter, as conditions rapidly become so inhospitable that intercontinental travel becomes a fool's gambit.

FLORA AND FAUNA

Dawn is a planet of long springs and autumns, reliably violent winters, and an all-too-brief summer. Early farming proved difficult; Dawn's reputation of hostility toward invasive species is well-earned, with potatoes and wheat among the few Terran crops to survive the alien soil. Dawn Buckwheat, a quinoa-like pseudo-cereal, soon became the staple crop of Ariadnan farms, providing the hearty gruels and trail bars at the core of pioneers' diets. Off-worlders tend to find the taste unconscionably bitter, to the grim amusement of locals.

Dawn and Earth have similar types of animals, but despite the abundance of native life, the denizens of this alien biome proved significantly less nutritious than their Terran counterparts. To that end, numerous herds of Terran animals have been painstakingly cultivated and preserved from the colony's original stock. While Auroch steaks — a native herd bovine much larger than a cow — might be cheap and tasty, it takes about four times as much meat to equal the nutrition of Terran sirloin. But if you're willing to pay market rates, you can still get good old-fashioned beef, pork, or chicken on your plate. Off-world imports command a higher price, but Merovingian gourmands swear that they can tell the difference between corn-fed beef, and cows fed on Dawn's alien grasses.

ECONOMY

Teseum. Any discussion of Dawn's economics necessarily begins and ends with it. Found scattered across the Human Sphere, Teseum is hardly unique to Dawn, but only here can it be actually be considered common.

Backed by Teseum, the Ariadnan Ruble, or ARU, is the international — and indeed, interplanetary — currency of Ariadna. Other currencies, albeit not widely recognised off-world, also exist: the Merovingian Franc (MEF), the USAriadnan Dollar (UAD), and the Caledonian Pound (CAP). Of particular interest is the surging popularity of the CAP as an unofficial black market currency. Accepted anywhere on Dawn — provided you're making the correct sort of deal — it's the unofficial second currency of Ariadna.

DEMOGRAPHICS AND CULTURE

Ariadna is as culturally diverse today as it was when the colonists first landed. Though each has blended together in some aspects, the factions remain culturally distinct; largely due to the remote nature of settlements, the pride they take in the cultures of their forbearers, and the pervading xenophobia that propagated during the Depression. Yet despite their differences, they are each of them, to the last soul, recognizably Ariadnan.

CALEDONIA

The emerald vales and tempest-tossed peaks of Caledonia stand as a bastion on the northern frontier. Dozens of small communities are nestled into the cascading clefts of the land, spilling out from the indomitable western march of Hadrian's Range as it spurs off from the Spinal Mountains to the east.

Coille Liath holds the northern passes against the Antipodean hordes of the east, but smaller bands of Antipodes regularly spill over the distant northern end of the Spinal Mountains and migrate south into the great forests of Boceliande and Lioslaith. Caledonians never forget that their lands are only kept safe by virtue of eternal vigilance — against the Antipodes; against the Cossacks; and now against the galactics who thirst for the rich Teseum deposits found throughout their mountain homes.

CAILLEACH

This fortified citadel sits at the end of Hadrian's Range. Atop a plateau and surrounded by the Bhraghad River, it secures the west, preventing Antipodean *razzia* raids from circling the mountains and pouring down into the southern settlements. Its strategic importance is matched only by its superstitions: Cattle raised in its shadow are more nutritious, Dogfaces and Wulvers find their rage soothed, and the ghost of Jock the Damned whispers secrets of lost treasure; at least, if rumours are to be believed. Wild stories aside, no one can deny the strange occurrences in the castle's light cone.

DNET (DAWNNET)

Largely lacking access to Maya, Ariadna maintains its own digital archives and internet. Efforts have been made to create portals linking dNet to Maya content, but the fundamental architecture of the networks have made the transition difficult. The Nomads have had marginally greater success seeding Ariadna with Arachne nodes, although most locals still lack the equipment to access them.

Ariadnan Depression – p. 147

Teseum – p. 8

DOGFACE RENAISSANCE

Caledonia can seem more alien than anywhere else in the Human Sphere. It sports the single largest population of Dogfaces, and although many of them struggle to eke out even a subsistence living, there's no question that they're a common and accepted sight on Caledonian streets. Recently Dogface ghettos across the north have begun to organise through Arachne nodes installed by Nomad commercial missions. The resulting social movement is being referred to as the Dogface Renaissance.

Antipodes – p. 151

razzia, p. 152: Raids carried out by Antipodean war chiefs.

CALONACK

At the southern end of the Lioslaith Forest and the largest pass through Hadrian's Range, on the shore of the river Scot, Calonack boasts the best whiskey distilleries on the planet, as well as the prestigious Calonack University. Needless to say, these two factors collide during spring and summer break, rendering the otherwise-picturesque city into the most gregarious, friendly sort of riot you ever did see.

Antipodes – p. 151

COILLE LAITH

The first line of defence against the Antipodes, this stronghold is among the most demanding posts in the Caledonian military, and as such, is staffed entirely by combat veterans. The borders of Coille Laith are rife with some of the most brutal checkpoints in the Human Sphere. Absent sophisticated scanning technology, the searches are invasive, the guards are paranoid, and the restrictions draconic; a smuggler's nightmare made real.

DÁL RIADA

Dál Riada lies at the tip of the long, narrow St. Brandan peninsula upon the shows of LochEil lake. A curious amalgamation of humble fishing village and survivalist compound, the city is capable of sealing the narrow strip of land to the west of the lake using a battalion of mobile palisades. The city hugs tight to the shore – in more ways than one – and the Loch is notorious for not giving up her dead, regardless of how she came by them.

TROUPES MÉTROPOLITAINES

These militias, whose members are commonly known as Métros, are main guardians of the Merovingian trade infrastructure. In times of peace they are a national police force; in times of war they are fierce guerrilla fighters.

INVERLOCH

Founded just thirty years ago, Inverloch is a walled city seeking to push the boundaries of the northern frontier deeper into Antipodes territory. A wide-flung system of alarm is capable of summoning in the farmers who till the rich fields around the city behind the walls in the case of an Antipodes raid. It is a mote of tranquil beauty, purchased with the blood of heroes.

SCONE

Teseum – p. 8

The capital of Caledonia, and its seat of political and economic power, built – quite literally – on Teseum mines. The city is a study in juxtaposition; wealthy, destitute, Justicar, criminal, Dogface, Wulver, and human alike rub elbows in its dirty, crowded streets, silhouetted by clan standards and factory smoke. Heavily fortified, Scone has never fallen to invaders foreign, domestic, or galactic. From its roots burrows forth the Stuart Way which passes over and under Hadrian's Range until it reaches Coille Laith in the north.

SKARA BRAE

The mismatched fortifications of the oft-razed city of Skara Brae speak to its history of violence. The city shares a narrow strip of land between Hadrian's Range and the Mirror Sea with Rodina's Transtartaric Railway. Whenever conflict breaks out – as it so often has in the past – a brutal struggle is repeated here as both nations seek to safeguard the passage to their western settlements. A scrappy local population lives in the shadow of the city's fortified turrets, and the prospectors in its markets have scavenged all manner of strange things.

TUATHCRUITHNE

Tucked inside the Boceliande Forest, the denizens of Tuathcruithne are a notoriously reclusive lot. Secretive, rural, and allergic to political intrigue, the area has had remarkably few issues with Antipode attacks, despite residing beyond Cailleach's protection, due to the strong, regular patrols sent out to keep the forest clear of encroachments. The so-called Boceliande brews are recognised as magnificent beers.

MEROVINGIA

To travel through Ariadna is to literally follow the footsteps of Merovingian trading caravans. They built the roads – each named after the Commercial Agent who blazed the first trail – that knit the scattered settlements of Ariadna together. They see the map of Ariadna as a network of nodes, and their cities and settlements are calculated to control the key points in that network.

Merovingia can also truly claim to have a place among the stars. Outside of Cossack territory, you will find no greater representation of galactics. They garner particular interest from both Haqqislam and the Nomads, both of whom wish to create their own trading infrastructures on Ariadna. (Merovingia has, so far, been successful in playing them off against each other and maintaining firm control over their monopolies.)

AURON

Auron is the hub of southern trade. Highways from Mariannebourg to the north, 4 Tracks in USAriadna to the south, and Mat' to the west meet here. As such, Auron has become the City of Secrets – or, alternatively, the City of Lies. Popular fiction has earned it a fantastical reputation: Clearly, not every baker is an informant, nor every barista is a spy. It's unlikely that every traffic signal is a hidden camera. It's even more improbable that there's a mercenary intelligence operative going by the name (or title?) of La Veuve (The Widow) who uses whispers as a sword and blackmail as a shield while ruling the city by proxy.

LE DOUAR

During the Ariadnan Depression the eastern reaches of Merovingia, in the shadow of the Spinal Mountains, became sparsely populated by roving bands of itinerant travellers. Le Douar became a permanent settlement on the shores of the Dumas River during the Separatist Wars when several of these bands came together to fight the Battle of the Circle against a Kazak regiment which had penetrated deep into Merovingia and was seeking to turn south into USAriadna. The battle was eventually won. But once its roots were set, the city never went away, growing into a major trading hub in the east. Le Douar is Ariadna with a decidedly Moroccan flair. Besides the local cuisine — a curious but excellent fusion of French, Mediterranean, and North African influences — Le Douar is most famous for its unregulated, open-air bazaar; a sprawling market covering several city blocks.

MARIANNEBOURG

The City of Five Bridges, Mariannebourg is built upon the shores of the Lac du Noir at the nexus of three rivers: The Duardanez which flows south from Stevenson Lake in the north; the Dumas which flows from Le Douar in the east; and the Baikal which flows west through the Rodinan heartland to Dynamo. These rivers were the original nucleus of Merovingia's trading empire.

Mariannebourg is the largest metropolis in Merovingia. Described as the "city of stars", the setting sun gives way to massive spotlights, illuminating the city's statues and monuments.

But between the museums and galleries, the bistros and festivals, there quietly dwells one of the most sophisticated smuggling networks in the Human Sphere. You can get anything in Mariannebourg; provided you know where to look.

POICTESME

Named for a fictional province, Poictesme is Merovingia's gateway of trade with Caledonia. It aspires to be a place where anything can happen, and dreams can come true. A magnet for radicals, free thinkers, and activists, local authorities are privately worried about an increasingly radical sect of DNAriadna, making noise about "true independence."

RODINA

The Motherland's major cities cling to the coast of the Mirror Sea — huge industrial centres built upon the technological infrastructure of the original colony ship. The interior of the nation is filled by the *stanitsa* system. Each *stanitsa* is a combination of farming village and military fortification; a decentralised network capable of instantly stymieing any threat while quickly channelling insurmountable reinforcements to crush any resistance. These small inland communities also give rise to a warm, deep, and intensely interconnected rural culture that is the heart of Rodina's identity.

DYNAMO

The city of Dynamo is dominated by a singular feature: the Torrents, a massive natural waterfall system. Standing over one hundred metres tall, with hundreds of terraced drops, it's titanic in its scope. This awe-inspiring force powers the hydroelectric generators that lend Dynamo its name. The city itself is a stark contrast — a grid of carefully planned manufacturing plants. Its energy wealth makes Dynamo the most industrialised city on the planet, but its drab buildings evoke the central planning committee which gave them birth.

GÖK-BURGO

Situated on the coast of the Mirror Sea not too far south of Mat', the twin city of Gök-Burgo is the sea gate of the capital. Gök is the harbour itself; a jungle of cranes, a maze of containers, and a grid of carefully planned depots layered into the limited space offered by the sea-cliffs. Burgo, on the bluffs above, is the real town where the workers live.

MAT'

A handful of "skyscrapers" glisten from the heart of Mat' and ships buzz about its spaceport. These edifices are impressive by Ariadnan standard, but remain a pale reflection of the wonders to be seen in other G-5 nations. Mat' contrasts its retro-modern vistas with statues to past Ariadnan leaders, and frequent military demonstrations. Towering above it all is the city centre; situated on a hill, and crowned by the Aurora Building. Built around the original mothership, the Aurora Building is part shrine, part memorial, and part functional civic centre; a testament to the past, and something of a living temple to Cossack pragmatism.

NOVOCHERKASSK

Merely one small *stanitsa* before the Military and Officer School was built there, Novocherkassk is now a low-lying sprawl of military contractors. Its port — home to the *Zapadnyy Flot* (the Western Fleet) — is also the most significant in the southern reaches of Rodina, and is crucial for shipping agricultural product north.

TARTARY

During the Age of Exploration, the Cossacks used the strength of their industrial base to fuel a massive colonial expansion onto the steppes of Tartary. The *stanitsa* system chewed up territory, creating a quilted network of farms that transformed the

Ariadnan Depression – p. 147

Separatist Wars – p. 148

ROVING STAR SPACEPORT

Since reconnecting with the rest of humanity, Mat''s long-abandoned spaceport — primitive as it was — became immensely valuable. The Rodina Stellar Authority has spent millions of rubles reimagining the port in a neoclassic aesthetic; and products from across the Human Sphere can be acquired for a modestly inflated price. This gives Rodina an essentially complete monopoly on interstellar trade. Funding for construction of a Merovingian spaceport which would provide competition is continually choked off in the Ariadnan Council, causing Merovingian leaders to turn towards potential galactic sources of funding.

G-5 nations, p. 26: PanOceania, Yu Jing, Haqqislam, Nomad Nation, and Ariadna.

COSSACK PROTECTORATE

Originally land claimed by USAriadna, the Cossack Protectorate was established at the end of the Separatist Wars as a "temporary" territorial buffer. Rodina attempted to use the Protectorate to establish an eastern port on the Sea of Spinners, but the construction settlement was wiped out by a massive Antipode *razzia* out of the south. Today the Protectorate is a loose association of undermanned camps, forts, and hastily abandoned trenches — the crisscrossed vestiges of too many wars.

TRANSTARTARIC RAILWAY

The Transtartaric Railway runs all the way from Dalnîy, up the spine of Tartary, around the northern reach of the Mirror Sea, and down through Mat' into Gök-Burgo. It is one of the longest railways in the Human Sphere. Armour-plated and defended by HMG turrets against Antipode and lowland bandit raids, these behemoths form the lifeblood of the Tartaran *stanitsas*.

Separatist Wars – p. 148

northern reaches of the steppe into an agricultural breadbasket and helped to secure Rodina's northern border with Caledonia. During the Separatist Wars, Tartary became a deep strategic reserve that gave Rodina unique strength among the other nations.

CASTROPOL

Named for a small village back on Earth, Castropol is anything but. Colossal fishing barges toil at the waves, as though they intend to feed all of Ariadna with the day's catch. Everything in Castropol is sold in bulk; from coffee to bullets, the city assumes that industrial quantities are the answer, whatever the question. The southern end of the city's massive harbour is home to the *Vostochnyy Flot* (Eastern Fleet).

DALNÎY

Its name is literally "Far Away". Dalnîy is a monument to staying power; a proud declaration of the Cossack's will to conquer the furthest reaches of the planet even when the reality was lacking. Seated on a wealth of undocumented geological phenomena and marine life, the city has also become home to the so-called *Novyy Yuzhnyy Flot* – this "New Southern Fleet" is actually a hodgepodge flotilla of scientific vessels, many staffed by galactic scientists who have been flocking to Dalnîy and turning it into the centre of study for the Ariadnan frontier.

OVSYANKA

More than anything, Ovsyanka lives in the Ariadnan imagination as a symbol of lost hope. Its huge ports – built during the optimism of the Age of Exploration and once unlocking the outer reaches of the planet – are rusted wastelands. Recently, however, things have begun to turn around as galactic investment has renewed interest in exploration. There's a large Yu Jing presence in the city, using it as a base of operations and supply for their settlements in the Snark Lands. And there even seems to be some new activity in the old, abandoned naval base of the defunct *Yuzhnyy Flot* (Southern Fleet).

TSITADEL

Even the architecture here seems possessed of a grim, fatalistic determination.

Tsitadel is the largest military air base on Dawn. In addition to providing security for the far-flung and difficult-to-defend southern regions of Tartary, its *eskadra* (эскадра, aerial squadrons) fly numerous sorties over the Tartary Mountains to enforce the "no crawl zone" in the so-called Dog's Neck. This blackened, napalm-scorched stretch of narrow land between the mountains and the sea is periodically blasted clean to prevent any Antipodes from circling the southern end of the mountains into Tartary.

THE TUNNELS OF MADISON COUNTY

There are reputedly smuggling tunnels that run from some of the old mines around Madison under the Spinal Mountains. This may explain the number of galactic Submondo interests which have been seen in the area, smuggling goods into and out of the Exclusion Zone.

Teseum – p. 8

Antipodes – p. 151

USARIADNA

Founded as the so-called "51st State of the Union", USAriadna is a frontier nation with a strength and hunger for independence forged from defending the Ariadnan heartlands from the depredations of Antipodes from the Southern and Eastern Frontiers.

With a federal system based on its spiritual forefather, it is formed of six individual states: The Northern States of Kennedy, Lincoln, and Washington. And the Southern States of Jackson, Jefferson, and Roosevelt.

MOUNTZION – THE WALL

This walled city is the independent capital of USAriadna. It is the seat of its government, the bastion of its military, and its cultural epicentre.

The primary defensive stronghold on Ariadna's eastern border, and the front line against the hostile Antipodes, the city is a statement; a defiant "screw you" to the violent Antipodes, a militant "bring it" to the uncaring climate, and a cocksure "come get some" to any galactic who thinks that they can bully USAriadna. This "Wall versus all" attitude pervades the local zeitgeist and is literally embodied by the corpses of Antipodes which hang on its walls; its citizens are ready for a fight, and expecting to win.

JACKSON

The soul of the defiant south, Jackson drew the short straw when it came to natural resources. Dry mines, quarrelsome soil, and a hostile land have left Jackson embittered, impoverished, and tougher than a two-dollar steak.

GRACETOWN

Deeply religious, and steeped in the trappings of the American South's Bible Belt, "Amazing" Gracetown is the state capital of Jefferson, and the unofficial counterpoint to MountZion-The Wall's vision of a worldly, urban paradise. Picket fences and quaint churches dot the landscape, as families in their Sunday best try to ignore the desperate acts of an increasingly desperate city.

MADISON

A festering wound of poverty, addiction, and violence, the frequency of violent deaths amongst Madison's civilians rivals that of frontline soldiers. Built on a tragically shallow Teseum vein, when the mine dried up, the jobs left town, taking hope with them. These days, the city plays host to shanty towns, drug runners, and a few desperate prospectors, hoping to stumble across something of value, and live long enough to profit.

NEWPORT

A stronghold through and through, every facet of the city is tailored to soldiers; from the monolithic naval base and Marine Corps barracks, to the impressive collection of dive bars along Sandman Boulevard. The latter is an increasing concern, as the escalating frequency – and violence – of brawls between Rangers and Marines have some whispering of an outside force stirring things up.

JEFFERSON

Everything's bigger in Jefferson; egos, stories, and especially guns. Dry and dusty – until drenched by flash floods – in Jefferson, the land won't do you any favours; don't expect anyone else to, either.

TOMBSTONE

The spirit of the American West lives on in Tombstone, for good or ill. The nearby Cossack Protectorate cannot stem the Antipode tide, and the unforgiving desert heat doesn't discriminate. The stone-faced stranger in a wide-brimmed hat and leather duster might be a bandit, local militia, or just another citizen, but in the dust and heat, who can tell the difference?

TRUMAN

Jefferson's state capital is named for a leader who bathed his enemies in atomic fire; a fitting sobriquet, given the vengefulness of its citizenry. Scathing critiques of Mat' and The Wall are shouted into the ether by Truman's thriving fire-and-brimstone street preachers. A few particularly incendiary orators have recently surfaced; long-time residents swear they can detect a hitch in their accents.

LINCOLN

The Blue-Collar North, Lincoln prides itself on open-mindedness and self-expression... up to a point. That point is when you threaten their kin.

CENTERVILLE

Square in the middle of Lincoln, the aptly-named Centerville is the quintessential industrial town; powerful factories fill the skyline, while thickly muscled folk brutalise a land that hit them first. Traditional combat sports thrive here – including a blooming Aristeia! circuit – but the real action is in the underground fight clubs; where local toughs, mercenaries, and the occasional Wulver provide bloodsport, and proprietor Joey Knuckles accepts absolutely anything as a bet.

FRANKLIN

Franklin is the birthplace of the USAriadnan Rangers Force and home to the 1st Line Ranger Regiment. The famous Blockhouse, which has become a sprawling complex of debauchery, is the "busiest bar on the planet".

SPRINGFIELD

A tribute to the industrious USAriadnan ethos, Springfield was razed to the ground in the First Antipode Offensive, and later rebuilt as a symbol of the indomitable spirit of USAriadna. Of course, spirit doesn't pay the bills, but Bracco Limited – sponsor of the Springfield Cobras, and employer of many a former player as "security contractors"– seems flush with cash.

KENNEDY

The northwest corner of USAriadna considers itself the heartland of the nation. While some in the other states believe their distance from the frontier makes them soft, the Kennedians hold the martial traditions of the Separatist Wars (when they were the ones on the frontline) close to the hearts. Also, a preponderance of bears.

4 TRACKS

"All highways run to 4 Tracks", the "Gateway of USAriadna" through which the majority of traffic and trade from Merovingia and Rodina flows. Anything travelling by road through this part of Dawn makes its way to 4 Tracks eventually, resulting in a sort of urbane bazaar.

FAIRVIEW

"The heart of America beats strong in Fairview." More than just a slogan, this hilltop city is home not only to multiple tech firms, but is the headquarters of the galaxy's last Coca-Cola bottling plant. Its influence is felt throughout the city; red and white dominates the landscape, and the wealthy, caffeinated populace results in the best twenty-four-hour markets in USAriadna.

ROOSEVELT

Southern hospitality is alive and well in Roosevelt, if a bit tempered by the land. If you've ever met a demure southern belle who could wrench a Morat's head from its shoulders without so much as mussing her hair, chances are she's from the 'velt.

TARA

The Gem of the South lives up to its sobriquet; public fountains and parks gild the landscape, while its friendly community and thriving commercial district illustrate the simple truth that this is

First Antipode Offensive – p. 146

USAriadnan Rangers – p. 156

THE REVERE LINE

Out beyond the borders of USAriadna, the Revere Line (officially the Early Warning and Interdiction Line) is a layered defensive ring on the Eastern Frontier.

MOB Liberty: Mobile Operation Base Liberty controls the central section of the Revere Line. Access is extremely restricted.

M Positions (Mohawk Outposts): Medium-sized medical facilities.

N Positions (Navajo Outposts): Communication hubs.

A Positions (Arapaho Outposts): Assault and defence positions specialised in anti-guerilla operations. The smaller outposts are mobile, but the larger Fortified A – or Fort Apache – positions tend to be more permanent.

Aristeia!, p. 144: Professional dueling sport featuring the use of real weapons.

TIGERLAND TRAINING CAMP

Nestled in the shadow of the Spinal mountains, the USARF conducts its commando training here. Notoriously prickly to guests – even for a military training camp – it is here that soldiers train in the classical USAriadnan arts of forest combat, jungle tactics, and being surly to outsiders.

CORVUS BELLI INFINITY

CROATOAN

Founded in the AEZ near Twin Crests, beyond MOB Liberty, this settlement was an effort to "push the line". It failed. The colonists were allegedly killed by Antipodes – or, more accurately, the colonists simply *vanished*; there was no notice of Antipode activity in the area and no one knows what really happened. It's rumoured that the USAriadna Department of Defense backed the founding of the colony in order to facilitate some sort of classified operation.

about as far from the Antipodes as you can get, and still be in the good ol' US of Ariadna.

WASHINGTON

The cosmopolitan melting pot of USAriadna, Washington considers itself the true heirs of American culture. They live in the shadow of The Wall, but Washingtonians are prideful to a fault.

DEADWOOD

If you wanted a microcosm of USAriadna, you could do worse than the gateway to the Exclusion Zone. A border town with near-daily brawls, comically well-armed citizenry, and a gaggle of rowdy drunks, only slightly less likely to riot when their beloved Deadwood Dukes loses a match as they are when the venerable Dog-Bowl team wins.

RIVERSIDE

Washington's official state capital, and unofficial auxiliary hub for The Wall's web of intrigue, Riverside is the picture of a modern financial district grown to city-size. Of particular note is the Keller Resources Group National Bank; an architectural marvel where old-world charm meets neomaterial construction. While many criticise its Teseum-laced construction (including solid Teseum

vault doors) as ostentatious, defenders maintain that there is something refreshingly Ariadnan about a bank that can withstand orbital bombardment and which has never been successfully robbed.

ARIADNAN EXCLUSION ZONE

In the wake of the Commercial Conflicts, the Ariadnan Exclusion Zone (AEZ) established a buffer zone around the four nations. The Ariadnan Development Council, operated by O-12's Bureau Ganesh, is the effective government here. The AEZ covers most of the northern half of the planetary supercontinent, from the Cousteau Ocean in the west to the Outer Crescent Range in the east. It also extends south from the Rodinan border in a broad band which encircles the Lost Sea.

THE OUTLANDS

Beyond the Ariadnan Exclusion Zone – in the corners of the southern subcontinent and on the various continental islands sprinkled across the globe – galactic interests seek to carve up the planet.

ABDERA

Across the Picard Ocean lies the land of Abdera. Roughly divided in half by the Abdera Peaks, the primeval forests of its western shore see a constant dance of low-level conflicts between the various galactic outposts which have sprung up there. The eastern half of Abdera, by contrast, remains a desolate wilderness.

NOVÎY CIMMERIA

Early Rodinan surveys revealed the lay of the land; early Rodinan scientists resigned themselves to the fact that they would likely never set foot on most of it. There is a belief that the black peaks of this frozen wasteland hold vast Teseum deposits, but expeditions launched to find them – driven by old tales from the Age of Exploration of the *Serebristaya Dolina*; the Silvery Vale where literal boulders of the neomaterial are scattered like marbles – have repeatedly ended in failure and bankruptcy.

SNARK LANDS

Named for wild, unsubstantiated tales of "magical beasts," early surveys of the so-called "Snark Lands" were functionally impossible; so far from support, colonisation was as elusive as the mythical beasts that lent their name to the island.

That changed when Yu Jing laid claim to the island and quickly established multiple colonies there. Following this, it wasn't long before one of these Snarks was caught on camera. Over a metre tall, these arboreal creatures' oddly plated fur distorts light around it, causing a hazy sort of aura when observed in direct lighting.

What's unknown is what caused the total destruction of the Shajia colony last year. Their last radio broadcast – disrupted by interference – said only that the "Huànyǐng (phantom) has come".

HELIOS SYSTEM

The Commercial Conflicts are being fought anew (or perhaps never truly ended) in the skies above Ariadna. The planetary government lacks the technology and infrastructure to assert sovereignty over its home system, allowing galactic interests free rein to assert their claims. The result is a quasi-legal chaos which is quickly beginning to resemble the early days of Human Edge.

ORBITALS

Despite vast Teseum reserves, Ariadna has no space elevators to ferry their cargo into orbit. The infrastructure needed to even attempt such an undertaking simply isn't in place, and offers of "assistance" from Yu Jing, Haqqislam, and PanOceania (each laced with various poison pills) have been met with suggestions of anatomically improbable actions, becoming increasingly detailed as the offers persist.

Burning Star Satellites: Although they have been unable to build their own extraplanetary facilities yet, the Rodina Stellar Authority has been able to seed Dawn's orbit with a ring of defensive satellites. Named the Burning Star in honour of the old Roving Star program which had once seen the colony launch their first planetary satellite network, these rail gun phalanxes compensate for their lack of advanced technology by adherence to a classic Ariadnan combat doctrine: firing an absurd number of metal slugs per minute.

Gateway Station: Built by O-12 as a staging station for the Ariadnan Exploration Corps, the control of Gateway Station ostensibly devolved to the Ariadnan Council. As such, since Ariadna has not been able to build their own orbital facilities, Gateway is their only base of operations above their own atmosphere. The agreement with O-12, however, forbids them from militarising the station (ironically, given its role in funnelling Ariadnan youth to the bloody battlefields of Paradiso). It is suspected, however, that Ariadna has been secretly subverting this agreement.

Splendour of Xanadu: This Nomad Commercial Mission was the first major galactic outpost completed in orbit around Dawn. Rushed to completion just prior to the outbreak of the Commercial Conflicts, it was frequently boarded and repeatedly swapped hands during the fighting. It is currently controlled, once more, by the Nomads.

OTHER STATIONS

Mineral and Gas Mining Outposts: Scattered across the system are mining operations owned by several different O-12 nations. Despite being the principal owners of Dawn, Ariadnan commercial interests only make up 35% of all mining in the system, with PanOceania, Yu Jing, and Nomads comprising the rest. Though the O-12 treaty strictly forbids mining in parts of the system that belong to Ariadna, the other powers regularly ignore this restriction, confident that no retribution awaits.

BV Station: Bienvenue Station was literally left behind by the *Dawn*. It is the shell of the interplanetary craft which was left in orbit to serve as a welcoming platform for other colony ships from Earth. Briefly rehabilitated as part of the Roving Star program, the Ariadnans were forced to abandon it again during the Separatist Wars. Today, BV is a ghost station primarily used by Irmandinhos smugglers, working with off-world Mafias to move illicit cargo.

SNARK SAFARI
Expensive safaris are mounted to hunt these creatures, though their elusive nature leads disgruntled hunters to wonder if they aren't really a myth after all.

Ariadnan Expeditionary Corps – p. 24

HELIOS SYSTEM

STAR
Helios: G8V (Yellow-Orange Dwarf)

PLANETS
Tithonus (0.19 AU): Telluric Planet (Molten Surface)
Ushas (0.38 AU): Telluric Planet
Hausos (0.71 AU): Terrestial Planet
Dawn (0.9 AU): Terrestrial Planet
Saranyu (3 AU): Telluric Planet (PanOceanian and Yu Jingese Mining Facilities)
Armstrong Asteroid Belt (4 AU)
Albina (7 AU): Gas Giant – Class II (Water Clouds)
Eostres (11 AU): Gas Giant – Class I (Nomad and Haqqislamite Mining Facilities)
Tereshkova Asteroid Belt (14 AU): Teseum-rich

THE MYSTERIOUS OCEANS OF SARANYU
Orbiting at a distance of 3 AU from Helios, Saranyu is too cold to host liquid water. And yet, geological evidence suggests it once had oceans. How this could have been possible, and what caused the oceans to evaporate, is a mystery.

C4 C8

CIRCULAR ROUTES
C4: Shentang-Yutang/Concilium
C8: Sol/Svalarheima

Separatist Wars – p. 148

STAR SYSTEM
HUMAN EDGE

Out on the frontier – the so-called "Edge of Humanity" – lucrative prospects lie hidden within a chaotic morass of celestial bodies. Dangers commensurate to the possible rewards test the determination of colonial efforts, claiming the unwary and the unlucky.

The system also bears scars from its many battles. Its history is one of blood-soaked ledgers and corporate warfare. Power struggles, internecine political warfare, and the boom of frontier expansion all leave the system mired in chaos. For now a fragile equilibrium has formed where all major interests hold one another in check, but only just. Every newcomer might have the power to help usher in a new era of stability, or cause tensions to boil over into a conflict that threatens to completely destabilise an area still aching from the last war.

ASTROGRAPHY
Astraeus is a high-energy class G star on the higher end of the scale. It experiences periods of unusually violent solar storms, emitting dangerous levels of radiation and causing great damage to nearby ships and facilities.

Although a handful of gas giants and moons are found in the system, most of the orbital plane is thickly choked with asteroids. These asteroids are incredibly rich in minerals, including a wide variety of neomaterials.

The orbital mechanics of the system are extremely unstable and incredibly complex, with gravitational fields that are impossible to calculate and trajectories that shift unexpectedly due to the lumbering gas giants or stellar disturbance.

Asteroid belts are circumstellar rings of tightly concentrated asteroids and dwarf planets. Although most of the Human Edge system is filled with rocky debris, there are three true belts of much higher density – the Helicon, the Homeric, and the Orthys.

In celestial mechanics, the Lagrangian points (or L-points) are positions within an orbital configuration in which smaller bodies can maintain a stable position relative to the larger bodies. In the case of a planet orbiting the sun, the L4 point (which is in the same orbit as the planet 60° of a revolution ahead of it) and the L5 point (which is 60° of a revolution behind the planet) are notable as the Trojan points. Asteroids and objects captured at

those points are collectively referred to as **Trojans**, although those at the L5 point are sometimes distinguished as the **Greeks**. In Human Edge, four of the gas giants have captured a significant number of asteroids in their Trojan points. These are known as the Taoist, Socratic, Ephesian, and Tyndarid Trojans, but are also commonly referred to by numerical designation (T1 and G1 for the Taoist Trojans, T2 and G2 for the Socratic Trojans, and so forth).

Hilda objects, also known as Hildian asteroids, have their orbits affected by gas giants, but not enough to tug them into the Trojan points. The resulting 3:2 orbital resonance causes them to form a thin, roughly triangular band just inside the gas giant's orbit (with two of its points overlapping with the innermost Trojans). With the exception of the innermost worlds of Hero and Leander, all of the planets in Human Edge have established Hilda bands. Although they have not been given distinct names, they contribute greatly to the convoluted orbital vectors of the system.

Amidst the general clutter of the system, the long orbits of **comets** can be difficult to distinguish until they get close enough to Astraeus for their outgassing tails to become visible. They are quite numerous, however, due to the frequent perturbations of the orbits of icy bodies in the outer system. They are also highly prized: The water and other volatiles they contain are valuable for stocking life support systems. Some of the bloodiest tussles in the history of Human Edge were the result of comet claim-jumping.

The system is also home to **centaurs** (dwarf planets and asteroids which cross the orbit of at least one gas giant; mostly found between Socrates and Castor-Pollux), **Kuiper objects** (orbiting in the circumstellar disc beyond Livy; including a large number of frozen volatiles, such as methane, ammonia, and water); unusually thick **Kordylewski clouds** (concentrations of interstellar dust); and **plutoids** (dwarf planets large enough that gravitational forces cause them to assume a rounded shape).

ECONOMY
The primary industries of Human Edge are asteroid mining and atmospheric mining of the gas giants. Two factors make the system profitable compared to the other "dark systems" without inhabitable planets which humanity has explored: First, the

ASTRAEA SYSTEM

STAR
Astraeus: F6V

PLANETS
Hero (0.05 AU): Fossil World
Leander (0.10 AU): Fossil World
Helicon Belt (0.50 AU)
Taoist Trojans (0.75 AU): T1/G1
Laozi (0.75 AU): Gas Giant – Class V (Hot Jupiter)
Socratic Trojans (2.50 AU): T2/G2
Socrates (2.50 AU): Gas Giant – Class I (Ammonia Clouds)
Ephesian Trojans (4.80 AU): T3/G3
Heraclitus (4.80 AU): Gas Giant – Class I (Ammonia Clouds)
Tyndarid Trojans (8 AU): T4/G4
Castor / Pollux (8 AU): Gas Giant – Class I (Hydrogen)
Homeric Belt (9.2 AU)
Livy (10 AU): Ice Giant
Orthys Belt: Perpendicular to the system's ecliptic.

Human Edge

Sol   Paradiso

Concilium

`C3` `C8`

CIRCULAR ROUTES
C3: Sol/Paradiso
C8: Concilium/Paradiso

sheer abundance and density of resources (particularly neomaterials). Second, the fact that the discovery of the system significantly shortened two major Circular routes (allowing for the resources mined here to be cheaply exported).

Asteroid mining takes a variety of forms. **Magnetic raking** is the cheapest sort, simply skimming the surface of metal-rich asteroids with powerful magnets which gather loose material. Many asteroids are actually just loosely agglomerated rubble piles, and **scoop mining** can quickly gouge out chunks of rock for industrial sifting. The more onerous and labour-intensive process of **shaft mining**, however, is the most popular image of asteroid mining, and essential for larger objects (which are often the most profitable in the long-term). Larger asteroids and dwarf planets can be hollowed out, pressurised, and even spun up to generate artificial gravity (making further mining activity easier to carry out).

Scoop-ships and **aerostats** are used to harvest elements from the upper atmosphere of the gas giants, primarily hydrogen, helium, and methane. (Of particulate importance are deuterium and helium-3, which collectively serve as the fuel for cheap fusion engines.) Gas mining ventures in Human Edge remain fairly primitive, primarily because the infrastructure for larger scale mining keeps getting destroyed, first in the Corporate Crises and then again during the NeoColonial Wars.

Piracy is also a booming industry in Human Edge. Where claims of national sovereignty exist at all, law enforcement is weak and inconsistent, creating a target-rich environment. Mercenaries willing to take on the pirates — and, most importantly, ruthless and skilled enough to win — thus find themselves in high demand. The mercenaries (along with pirates quietly acting in the role of privateer) are also useful pawns for national and corporate interests interested in settling competitive disputes through deniable violence.

DEMOGRAPHICS AND CULTURE
The Human Edge is a star system inhabited by a diverse and rugged population. Estimations of the total population recently crossed 100 million, but it is spread so thin that it usually doesn't feel like it. The gold rush economy causes millions to flock to the system each year, hoping to catch their share of a fortune, but much of the system remains unexplored, awaiting those brave and skilled to travel the void.

No one nation dominates affairs here, despite the efforts of all. And although there are many facilities controlled exclusively by a single nation or corporation, the Edge is also a place where people from all cultural backgrounds mingle freely

with each other. It has the hard edge of the frontier, but it's also cosmopolitan in a way that's rare in the Human Sphere. And there's a young generation here — PanOceanian and Yujingese youngsters who share the same tunnels; Nomad students taught by Haqqislamite scholars — with little or no connection to the squabbles of their parents. There are some who say that the nostalgic call of Hiraeth culture grows dim out here on the Edge, and that the common experience of rock and void drowns out the old ways.

At the same time, however, the conflicts between nations arguably burn hotter here than anywhere else in the Human Sphere. Nothing's simple out on the Edge.

ASTEROID BELTS

The asteroid belts are informally broken down into sectors which are ostensibly claimed by corporate or national interests. Stations within each sector often share the sector's name and are numbered, but the nomenclature is inconsistent. Some corporations number each station they build (for example, Hesiod-5 was Minescorp's fifth station in the Hesiod sector) while others number every rock within their claim (Schmiedan-116 was built on the arbitrarily numbered one hundred and sixteenth rock in the Schmiedan sector).

Adding to the confusion, these sector names are often not unique and, since corporate claims are not always defensible, some sectors have multiple names or overlap with each other. Various numerical reference systems have been applied to create semi-universal reference charts (the Hesiod sector, for example, is also 096394-BG), but these are inconsistent in their own right due to the politics involved.

HELICON BELT
The Helicon Belt is the largest, densest, and richest of the asteroid belts in the system. Unfortunately, it's also the most hazardous: Astraeus' lethal solar storms are strongest here, creating a deadly and unpredictable environment for the thousands of mining and industrial facilities located in the Helicon.

Hesiod-5: Perhaps the most famous example of these dangerous conditions is exemplified in the Helicon Miners' Revolt on the Hesiod-5 prospecting base (see next page). Despite its dark past, the Hesiod-5 facility remains operational.

Phaeton-3 Orbital Compound: Cosmica Ltda. was recently awarded a contract for construction of a massive solar deflector above the Phaeton-3

Circulars, p. 144: Massive starships looping endlessly along the fixed Circular routes.

DRIFTING CLOUDS
In most systems, Kordylewski clouds form at orbital Lagrange points. In the Human Edge, however, they are often found essentially "floating free" in highly eccentric orbits. It's possible that Lagrangian clouds are "knocked loose" by orbital disruptions; or they may be only superficially similar structures that are formed through some unknown process (possibly due to the high incident rate of collisions). In any case, the clouds generally wreak havoc with sensors and are often used by pirates to set up ambushes or escape pursuit.

HOW MANY ASTEROIDS?
The asteroid belt in the Sol system contains around 1.5 million asteroids larger than 1 kilometre in diameter, and multiple millions of smaller ones. Jupiter's Trojan points have similarly captured more than a million asteroids in its orbit. The Human Edge belts contain much larger objects on average, are much wider, and have a density more than ten times higher than the Sol belt (although this still means that there's usually at least half a million klicks between significant objects).

HELICON MINERS' REVOLT

In order to rapidly expand their operations in the sector, Minescorp hired Corregidoran workers. The arrangement worked well until a "perfect series" of solar storms forced the Hesiod-5 facility to halt all exterior work.

Unfortunately, this halted shipments to the nearby Schmiedan-116 orbital factory where WarTechWorks was working double-shifts to fulfil their contract to supply second-generation Theta Units to Bureau Aegis. Alarmed at the possibility of losing the lucrative contract, WarTechWorks pressured Minescorp to fulfil their supply contract. Faced with overwhelming legal and political pressure, Minescorp eventually caved in and ordered the Corregidorans back to work. When that didn't work, they employed Ikari Company mercenaries to force them back to work.

Radiation levels were off the charts. The mini-magnetospheres and suit plating were overwhelmed. Radiation alert patches went black, indicating a lethal radiation dose, as soon as the workers stepped outside. Miners returned from their shortened shifts with hair falling out in clumps and blood-clotted coughs.

Corregidor responded by sending a covert commando team under the command of Juan Sarmiento to organise a riot and stop exterior work. The Ikari mercenaries were almost obliterated, but Minescorp appealed to the PanOceanian Military Complex to have regular troops sent in to quell the "illegal seizure" of their property. The commandos barricaded themselves and the miners into one sector of the mining base, and the desperate Nomads were able to hold out until *Tunguska* lawyers succeeded in enforcing a ceasefire through the Concilium Prima courts.

Three-quarters of the Corregidoran miners and two-thirds of the commando team had died. The corporations escaped most of their culpability in the courts, with only the families of dead workers receiving any compensation. The legacy of the Helicon Miners' Revolt, however, did result in the creation of the Helicon Regulations — international legislation for the security protocols of exterior work in space.

CLOUD 9

This massive Kordylewski cloud fills roughly one-tenth of the Helicon Belt by volume while amorphously wending its way around roughly one-sixth of its diameter. It's a haven for pirates and smugglers, and authorities are uncertain exactly how many illegal bases have been established there. Among them is Sēfurokku (Safe Rock) station, a pirate haven which was first conquered and then occupied by the infamous Ikari mercenary company.

Go-Go Marlene! Show, p. 143: A popular travel and trendwatching Maya program starring the pop-idol Marlene.

compound, beating out bids from Construktur and Startecto. The hope is that the experimental deflector will be able to create a "shadow" safe from solar storms and shielded from Astraeus' lethal radiation. If it succeeds, additional asteroids can be tugged into the compound for safe, cheap mining.

HOMERIC BELT

The edge of the Human Edge, the Homeric Belt has a high concentration of plutoids. These large dwarf planets are more suitable for establishing long-term mining settlements, making the belt home to some of the larger communities in the system. Outside of the plutoids, the Homeric Belt has a reputation for lawlessness, and is widely considered one of the most violent and dangerous places in the Human Sphere.

Novyy Bangkok: This failed mining facility was abandoned after the collapse of the Rus-Thai Blinov-Ngamsan Conglomerate. The asteroid is a morass of unmapped tunnels used by the criminals as an anonymous graveyard for their victims. Of course, other things are rumoured to roam these tunnels and, if you listen to the talk, enough abandoned tech to found a new nation. If you care to go exploring in a glorified sewer, of course.

ORTHYS BELT

The Orthys Belt, perpendicular to the system's ecliptic, is responsible for much of the crazed orbital geometry of the system: the asteroids

orbiting in this alternative plane interact irregularly and chaotically with objects in the Helicon and Homeric belts, perturbing their orbits into a crazed helter-skelter.

Boushra Caravanserai: The gates to Earth and Paradiso are both located near the "tip" of the Orthys Belt, at the farthest point from the system ecliptic. The Boushra Caravanserai is located nearby.

Jǐng Qì (Prosperity): Located around one of the convoluted trade routes which lie between the Orthys gates and the Helicon Belt, the Jǐng Qì orbital is a small refuelling port which is most notable for its illicit, Yakuza-backed casino.

TROJANS

The *Go-Go Marlene! Show* once described the Trojan points as the "suburbs" of the Human Edge system. Kept somewhat apart from the major belts, they are more likely to be dominated by particular polities. They also represent major strategic points within the system, serving equally as defensive bastions and forward bases during times of war.

TAOIST TROJANS (T1, G1)

The Taoist Trojans have been scooped thickly out of the Helicon Belt by the burning orbit of Laozi. Millions of asteroids can be found at both the G1 and T1 points, divided into sectors in a manner similar to the belts.

Hua Ling (Magnificent Dawn): A central resupply station established to service Yu Jing orbitals at the G1 point. Hua Ling's politics have been thoroughly corrupted by the Silver Tree Triad, which also operates an illegal casino there.

Ulloa Station: The Order of Santiago operates a large number of small orbital fortresses throughout Human Edge. During the Second NeoColonial War, Yu Jing attempted to seize the T1 point with a surprise naval operation. When they demanded the surrender of the tiny garrison of knights, Commodore-Abbott Ulloa responded, "To reject the challenge to do battle would not sit well with the son of the Apostle Santiago." In the ensuing battle the orbital fortress was eventually destroyed, but the Knights of Santiago's hit-and-run tactics held off the Yu Jing fleet long enough for PanOceanian reinforcements to arrive. After the war, a new orbital fortress was built and named after the heroic Commodore-Abbott.

SOCRATIC TROJANS (T2, G2)

The T2 and G2 points are another set of thickly clustered asteroids ripe for exploitation.

Meteora Group: The T2 point is surprisingly dominated by the Independent Corporate Republic of the Meteora Group, a small polity which dances through a small-scale cold war between PanOceania and Yu Jing. This micro-satellite rebelled against the regime of neo-slavery imposed by its original owner, the Chrommia Corporation. The revolt was secretly sponsored by Yǎnjīng in order to damage PanOceania's influence, but they probably weren't anticipating the Meteora Group sponsoring guerrilla political protests and independent unions throughout the region. (The Yu Jing consul was recently accused of participating in an electoral fraud scheme in the Meteora Group's elections, most likely in an attempt to undermine the Republic's activities.)

EPHESIAN TROJANS (T3, G3)

Due to its distance from both the Helicon and Homeric belts, the gas giant Heraclitus has drawn

Order of Santiago — p. 178

Yǎnjīng, p. 191: Yu Jing military intelligence.

Second NeoColonial War — p. 22

CORVUS BELLI
INFINITY

only a few thousand asteroids into the Ephesian Trojans. The few dozen settlements in the T3 and G3 points, therefore, have a kind of "small town" vibe to them.

TYNDARID TROJANS (T4, G4)

Although the Tyndarids are numerous — Castor and Pollux harvesting them plentifully from the Homeric Belt — they are lightly populated. This is partly due to their unfavourable position within the system, but also because surveys have found them to be relatively poor in neomaterials compared to the rest of the system.

Avro-Kaizuka: Originally built as a Nipponese-Conciliar joint venture between the Kaizuka *keiretsu* and AvroCorp from Concilium, Yu Jing has retracted its blessing of the venture and claims that the orbital is a hotbed of Tatenokai terrorists. Ikari mercenaries have a long-term contract to provide security for the orbital, and it also serves as a safe harbour and contact for the mercenary company.

HERO & LEANDER

These innermost worlds of Human Edge actually orbit within the Helicon Belt. As such, they are constantly bombarded by meteors. These fossil worlds are the remnants of ice giants which formed in the outer reaches of the system and then migrated into their current orbits. The hotter temperatures closer to Astraeus blasted away their icy exteriors, leaving only the ultra-dense planetary cores which had originally formed under 500 gigapascals of pressure (roughly five million times more atmospheric pressure than Earth).

CASTOR & POLLUX

Castor and Pollux are binary gas giants orbiting each other and surrounded by a single, enormous Saturnian rings. They have no moons and have only been cursorily explored. Surveyors report strange "lightnings" resembling St. Elmo's fire which reportedly dance through the rings. Fringe groups claim that the phenomena clusters around specific rocks within the rings. Efforts to scientifically explain the phenomena are ongoing.

HERACLITUS

Heraclitus is a modest gas giant, but its advantageous position as the gateway of the system has cluttered its local space with orbitals. A project to construct Vila Boosters — the first in the Human

Edge since the original clusters were destroyed before completion during the Corporate Crises — is under way. The upper atmosphere of Heraclitus is also laced with gas mining platforms.

Surveys of the Human Edge gas giants have indicated that their cores contain insanely high densities of neomaterials. The Aldaght Project, a Haqqislamite venture still in the construction process, is pioneering deep core drilling technologies at Heraclitus. Originally written off as a pipe dream, the success of the project is now looking extremely likely... and extremely profitable. Other nations, left trailing in its wake, are desperate to close the gap. Corporate espionage around Heraclitus is heating up, and some are fearing it may turn to sabotage, violence, or both.

End of the Line Free Orbital: This orbital is considered a direct protectorate of O-12. Established at the end of the Corporate Crises to monitor the peace in the system, today it's the primary destination for new arrivals in the system. Recruiters from a variety of corporations use its job markets. Unfortunately, a fair number of people wash up here and never find a way off the station.

DIOGENES

Heraclitus' sole major moon is known to have an ocean lurking beneath the icy rind of its surface. A Nomad expedition, primarily sponsored by *Corregidor* but working in partnership with both Bureau Tiandi and the Haqqislamite Academy of Planetology, is seeking to bore through the ice and reach the ocean below. The possibilities for scientific discovery are almost limitless, but the potential profit from exporting water is huge. The project has been plagued with difficulties, however, a testament to the incredibly hostile and difficult conditions on the moon.

LAOZI

Laozi is a Hot Jupiter. Its bands of molten copper and gold (in colour, not composition) race through the Human Edge system in a retrograde orbit, circling the star Astraeus once every twenty-five days in the opposite direction from the other planets in the system.

Academy of Planetology: The Haqqislamite Academy of Planetology maintains a prestigious research campus in orbit around Laozi. Its students take advantage of the opportunity to mount regular expeditions to Laozi's varied moons. There have long been rumours of a secret training facility for Runihura super-soldiers hidden at the heart of the Academy, similarly taking advantage of the local conditions to train for a wide variety of extraplanetary and zero-g operations.

MAJOR MOONS OF LAOZI

Orbital mechanics suggest that Laozi would be unlikely to have moons, but there they are: five major moons. Zou Yan has a surface of frozen nitrogen. Tianshi shows signs of having been extremely volcanically active recently (in geologic terms), but it seems to have exhausted its core. Shangqing, on the other hand, remains extremely active, with its polar volcanoes regularly spewing magma with enough force to achieve orbital speed. It shares a co-orbital horseshoe orbit with the cryovolcanic Lingbao. Quanzhen is essentially a single, giant diamond — the abundant, compressed carbon of its surface a glittering scintillation.

LIVY

The lead-coloured clouds of Livy are the terminus of the Human Edge. Orbiting out beyond the Homeric Belt, it is the last lonely wanderer of the Astraeus system. A huge black storm has raged across one side of the planet for as long as humanity has been in the system, lending it the appearance of a giant eye keeping a watchful gaze over the system.

Missing Trojans: Livy has no Trojans even though its orbit suggests they should have been swept up from the Homeric Belt. Their absence is just one of the many mysteries of the Human Edge system.

Chengsan: The Orbital of Scientific Studies Chengsan (meaning "Serene Mountain" in Chinese) was originally located near the Castor-Pollux binary, but two decades ago it was moved to Livy, where it has been conducting research ever since. The facility is infamous as being a black site where Yu Jing places scientists "liberated" (i.e., kidnapped) from other corporations.

The Moons of Livy: Livy has no major moons, but it does have seventy-three lesser moons (bodies smaller than plutoids) including eleven Trojan moons.

SOCRATES

The largest planet in the system, the blue-and-purple giant of Socrates has a large but surprisingly weak magnetosphere. The radiation belts created by this magnetosphere pose a minor danger, but this is far outweighed by the protection which the Socratic field offers against Astraeus' solar storms, making its lunar system one of the most agreeable locations for human habitation in the system.

Socrates is also known for the mysterious radio signals which emerge from its depths. Scientists have struggled to identify their source or the natural phenomenon creating them. There are isolated reports of similar signals from other gas giants in the system (possibly echoing the Socratic signals), and some are obsessed with the signals — convinced that they are decoding some ancient, alien tonal tongue.

THREE SOCRATIC MOONS

Socrates is orbited by three major moons: Xenophon, Plato, and Aristotle.

Işıkev: This massive caravanserai, named "Lighthome" in Turkish, orbits the charcoal orb of Aristotle and contains the massive research campus for the Haqqislamite Academy of Medical Science. The doctors of Işıkev have made great strides in treatment of radiation-related ailments.

Silicate Rains of Plato: The beautiful blue moon of Plato is the only terrestrial body in the Human Edge system with a significant atmosphere. Unfortunately, that atmosphere is filled with silicate particulates which are blown around the planet by cyclical winds in excess of 1,000 kph. In other words, the entire surface of the planet is covered by a rain of sideways-falling broken glass.

Xenophon Naval Base: PanOceania's primary naval facility in the Human Edge orbits the small, rocky moon of Xenophon. The belligerent Hyperpower treats the moon and its orbital space as its personal turf, leading to a number of conflicts and disputes.

PLANET
NEOTERRA

ATEKS OUT! LOBBY

The Neoterran Ateks Out! lobby is increasingly associated with violent extremists. They conceal their identities by planting viruses that overlay their faces with anti-Atek imagery while attacking techno-favelas in response to perceived Atek slights against "true PanOceanians". The lobby officially denounces the violence, but few believe their sincerity.

The Great Gem is not only the capital of PanOceania, it's the economic powerhouse of the Human Sphere and more or less its political centre of gravity. It even looks like a gem from space thanks to its verdant wilderness and the glittering facets of the vast skyscraping cities that dot the continents, gleaming and spotless, some of the biggest and most technologically advanced in the Sphere. The majority of residents live in towering city blocks, each of which can accommodate 50,000 people or more.

The cities of Neoterra provide every lifestyle convenience available to the general public. However, they are densely packed. The first settlement on Neoterra, on Solitudo Island, inadvertently caused a massive die-off in the local flora and fauna, for reasons that remain unclear despite decades of research into the issue. Since then, Neoterra's cities have expanded — but slowly. Parcels of land are isolated and carefully tested over a period of years to see if they are suitable for agriculture, industry,

NEOTERRA PLANET STATISTICS

Distance from Star: 1.4 AU • **Orbital Revolution:** 605 days • **Rotation:** 22 hours • **Radius:** 1.0 Earth radii

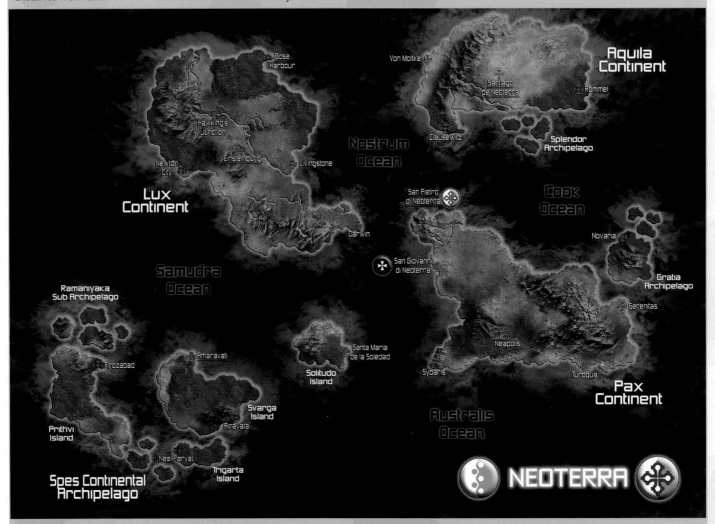

PLANET DATA FILE

Type of Government: Lobby Democracy • **Head of Government:** Prime Minister • **Capital:** San Pietro • **Population of Planet:** 7 billion • **Off-Planet System Population:** 1 million • **Primary Languages:** Italian, Hindi, English, Spanish • **Anthem:** *Il Canto dei Pionieri* (*The Song of the Trailblazers*) • **Principal Industries:** Finance, Aerospace, Media, Quantronics

or residential use. Meanwhile, the hemmed-in cities grow upwards rather than outwards.

CLIMATE AND GEOGRAPHY

Orbiting the star Tencendur, Neoterra is Earth-like, although it has a lower average temperature than Earth itself by 1.5°C. Its surface gravity is a little higher, which provides the local sports teams with a measurable home advantage against visiting clubs from off-planet, but otherwise has little effect on daily life.

The terrain of Neoterra is similar to that of Earth in form and diversity. Mountains, plains, tundra, marshland, even a desert or two. The largest continents, Lux and Pax, have interiors dominated by ancient arboreal forests set upon rolling hills, still largely untouched since the time of the first settlers. The islands of the Spes Archipelago are warmer and more humid, and have land suitable for intensive agriculture.

FLORA AND FAUNA

Neoterra's natural environment has relatively low biodiversity. As a result, a number of key ecosystems, as yet little understood in some respects, are very fragile. Incautious development led to ecological collapse on Solitudo Island in the early days of colonisation, leaving behind a barren, unyielding wasteland. Neoterrans have proceeded carefully ever since.

Neoterra's larger wildlife consists almost exclusively of a single family of closely related animals akin to warm-blooded lizards. Given the catch-all name of *reptilos*, each fulfils roles similar to those seen in Earth's fauna — apex predators, herds of grazing herbivores, and so forth — but all are so alike that they might easily be taken for a single species were it not for their differences in size and behaviour. In addition, there are three groupings of *reptilos* species — referred to as sects — roughly broken apart by colour: A ruddy crimson, an iridescent cerulean, and a scaly viridescent. Red, blue, and green *reptilos* species are incredibly hostile to each other, and although carnivores from one sect will attack and kill *reptilos* from another they will almost never consume the meat.

The Spes Archipelago is an exception to this general rule. Its teeming forests and rivers form a robust ecosphere that is vibrantly alive with all manner of creatures.

ECONOMY

Neoterra's economy relies heavily on service industries. Media, software, and quantronics development are key economic sectors. The planet is not renowned as a manufacturing base, except in one particular area: Space travel. Hundreds of massive shipyards orbit the planet and produce the majority of civilian spacecraft constructed in PanOceania, as well as a sizable number of the country's military vessels (although most of those come from the Acontecimento shipyards).

Neoterra's plum position among the Circular routes is in no small part due to it being the first human colony established outside Earth's solar system, and PanOceania's leading role in politics and the space industry has only cemented that early advantage. Neoterra takes full advantage of the profits that come in from the space trade, with a welcoming open-door policy for investors and companies from other planets that attracts capital and people from all over the Sphere. The biggest banks, investment funds, and financial consultancies in the Sphere all hail from Neoterra.

DEMOGRAPHICS AND CULTURE

The hallmarks of Neoterra are its untrammelled wilderness and the soaring heights of its strictly delimited city-states. Hemmed in by the city-limit walls that surround the urban zones (punctuated by contamination checkpoints at every exit), the city-states are perhaps the utmost expression of PanOceania's famed Living Cities, their citizens living in perfect harmony with ALEPH's constant presence. Each block — made up of tightly woven and heavily interconnected towers at least fifty storeys high or more — is a cluster of luxury, economically unified, and a cultural micro-climate. If you wanted to, you could spend your whole life without ever having to leave your block.

Between these blocks are the *divertissement* districts (dedicated to pleasures and entertainments on a vast scale), the rare industrial sector, soaring highways, and tracts of parkland perfectly manicured by auto-gardeners.

Neoterra's Ateks live in narrow bands of techno-favelas that butt up against the urban zones. They are not authorised to linger long in the city proper. Neither are they permitted to settle in the open country. So they must remain in the shanty towns, bathed every night in the inviting glow of the city.

AQUILA

Taking its name from the imperial eagle of ancient Rome, the continent of Aquila is the military heartland of PanOceania. In every city on Aquila, one or more fortress districts are set aside as semi-autonomous military quarters, dedicated to the units based there. These city-states are also the seat of some of PanOceania's most prestigious military academies, with a healthy rivalry between the academies in each city.

NEOTERRAN CIVIL RIGHTS ASSOCIATION

The Neoterran Civil Rights Association brings attention to injustices against Atek communities. It was born of protests against Block Force violence in Sybaris. A rowdy nun named Sister Ana leads the movement, organising non-violent protests for Atek rights, while drawing the ire of the Papal See for defying her Bishop's orders. Neoterran youth adopt techno-favela styles as a sign of solidarity and rebellion.

LAW AND ORDER ON NEOTERRA

Each city-state on Neoterra has its own police department, broken down into Block Forces largely acting independently from each other, which are lead by a popularly elected commissioner tasked with investigating crimes, making arrests, and enforcing the law. These commissioners serve collectively on the Police Council for each city-state. Crimes of a planet-wide scope fall under the jurisdiction of the Central Department of Criminal Intelligence (CDCI) based in Turoqua. The CDCI investigates any crime crossing district lines or which "impacts planetary or national security", but they can also be called in on the authorisation of any city-state's Police Council to fulfil security, crowd control, anti-terrorist duties, general public unrest, and the like.

AQUILA MANEUVERS

Entire swathes of countryside are reserved for training manoeuvres. At any given time of the day or night, at least one unit of the Neoterran Capitaline Army, joined by special forces and armoured formations, will be out on manoeuvres in Aquila's interior. The local population regularly participates in training scenarios acting as indigenous populations.

CORVUS BELLI INFINITY

CLAUSEWITZ MILITARY ACADEMY

This small military academy trains PanOceania's famed Machinists. Cadets receive training maintaining TAGs and drones while mastering battlefield engineering and demolitions. Locals know when the cadets are training by the explosions echoing from the academy's facilities.

VON MOLTKE OFFICER'S ACADEMY

Von Moltke is home to the Neoterra Capitaline Army's extreme environment training school, and the officer's academy grew from that training regime. Only a select few can endure Von Moltke's intense training program. Graduates have a stoic attitude, and are said to have "Moltke ice" in their veins.

ROMMEL ARMOURED COMMAND SCHOOL

This military school provides officers tactical and strategic training in armoured vehicle warfare. The school is famous for its wide variety of training environments including dense urban combat training. Rivalries between training squads and their training exercises are the subject of a wildly popular Maya series called *Fists of Iron*.

THE COMMONS

The downtown of Rommel worms itself through a dozen huge limestone pillars. Geological oddities, the tops of these pillars stand roughly three hundred feet above the surrounding rock and thrust clear of the forest canopy. Subjected to wider erosion, the canyons at the base have created wide common areas which contribute to the name and accommodate unusual divertissement districts.

CLAUSEWITZ

Beneath the shining towers of Clausewitz City is a labyrinthine network of caves linked by lava tubes formed millennia ago. Some of the caves are big enough to lose a cathedral in, others barely big enough to accommodate a rabbit.

The caves house many points of interest, including a species of blind crabs found nowhere else on the planet, a subterranean concert hall, and the test ranges of the Clausewitz Advanced Institution Centre. This last is the birthplace of many break-throughs in PanOceanian military – and later, civil – technology, with a focus on telemetry and advanced user interface development.

Clausewitz Citadel is a simple but vast tower, a seemingly blank cylinder thirty storeys high that stands in the empty plain some ten kilometres from the city. It is the home of the Clausewitz Uhlans, PanOceania's most famous anti-tank Armoured Cavalry unit.

ROMMEL

Rommel lies in the Delbrück Labyrinth. Under the thick canopy of the Aquila Forest, deep, twisting canyons have been carved out of the limestone. Instead of building up, the local military fortress dug down into the cliff faces of these twenty-story tall canyons and back into the rock. The city around the fortress followed suit and only a few buildings can be seen extending above the canopy. Learning your way around is a rite of passage for new arrivals.

SANTIAGO DE NEOTERRA

The city of Santiago is home to the main military research and development centres of PanOceania. The Military Complex has its own labs and test sites, numbering in the hundreds and focused on various purposes, but corporate facilities and business parks surround the military quarter, dwarfing Military Complex development. The Falco lobby uses its financial and social influence in Santiago de Neoterra to acquire public funding for private, military research.

VON MOLTKE

This northern city spends most of its time covered in ice and snow, seeing more tolerable temperatures in the late summer months. The military fortress at Von Moltke doesn't dominate the town like in Clausewitz and Rommel, and is primarily made up of rows upon rows of extreme environment buildings, similar to those seen in Svalarheima, resting on one of the largest harbours on the northern shores. Von Moltke's surrounding mountains are rich in natural resources and mining drives the local economy. The hostile environment has built a strong community and Von Moltke is known for its unfailing hospitality.

GRATIA ARCHIPELAGO

The fragility of the planet's ecosystem saw the Gratia Archipelago established as a nature preserve, and it's a destination for eco-tourists coming to see the wonders of Neoterra's flora and fauna. Poaching is a serious problem for the archipelago and the Central Department of Criminal Intelligence, with the assistance of the Novaria police council, regularly run anti-poaching operations to protect wildlife.

NOVARIA

This resort town is a destination for the rich and famous where you'll find the hottest parties and

the best food. Security specialists can find easy work protecting wealthy patrons on wildlife excursions from poachers and wildlife alike.

LUX

The first settlers of Lux hailed from Australia and New Zealand, and their descendants bear many hallmarks of those cultures. English is the common language and sport is an obsession, largely revolving around several competing football codes.

BOSE HARBOUR

This welcoming port town produces a large portion of the seafood that's packaged and sold off-world. The Bose Harbour brand is known for its friendly green *reptilos* mascot and a theme song no one can get out of their head.

DARWIN

Darwin is a working class harbour city known for its Australian-influenced idiosyncrasies.

Darwin Main Operating Base is the home of the Neoterra Bolts, part of the Neoterra Capitaline Army. The Bolts are renowned for their rough and tumble attitude and generally good morale, but you won't find many of them here — once soldiers have completed basic training they spend almost all their time off-planet, serving in whatever crisis zone the Military Complex sees fit. The vast majority of personnel in Darwin are new recruits, which gives the city the air of a heavily armed university town.

EINSTEINBURG

Built on either side of a deep ravine bisecting the rocky plateau on which it sits, Einsteinburg is a twin city, divided equally between the towns of Bohrs and Heisenberg. Countless soaring bridges connect the two sides, hundreds of metres above the thundering River Iss that passes through the canyon below.

HAWKING'S JUNCTION

The original settlement of Hawking was notable for being the site of the second most significant ecological collapse as a result of colonisation. A quick, immediate response effort managed to arrest the damage, but left the surrounding area looking particularly bleak. The early settlers were able to take advantage of the ecological collapse, however, to build up the infrastructure of the region, turning the newly dubbed Hawking's Junction into the communications and transit hub for the entire continent.

There is a significant culture clash between the industrial side of the city (which serves as a clearing house for the smaller mining facilities and communities in the mountains to the west), the white-collar corporations supporting (and supported by) the communications infrastructure, and the large scientific institutes which also make their home here (which include a number of stellar observatories).

LIVINGSTONE

Livingstone is home to the Tower High-Security Correctional Facility, where PanOceania's most dangerous convicts are kept under lock, key, and behaviour inhibitors. The prison is built into the side of a cliff, accessible only by hover-capable aircraft.

NEWTON CITY

Newton City rests on a series of islands in the wide delta of the Leibniz River. Many of the "buildings" of Newton are perpetually moving up, down, and across the famous Newton Arches which join the islands together, creating an ever-changing city geography which can only be navigated with the aid of one's geist. The city is well-known for their annual Apple Festival and a highly secure cyberwarfare centre located on a small, private, corporate island nestled amidst the arches. The city's techno-favelas cover most of the surface area of the islands themselves, as well as spreading up the coast.

PAX

Originally settled by colonists from southern Europe and Latin America, Pax is home to the largest and most influential cities on the planet.

NEAPOLIS

Built on the shores of a hundred picturesque lagoons whose waters change colour with the passing of the hours, Neapolis is a popular tourist destination. The streets and canals of the city are, compared to most Neoterran cities, broad and uncrowded, and the nearby mountains contain numerous natural hot springs.

The city is also the site of the Mount Celenis shrine, a place of pilgrimage. The shrine welcomes hundreds of thousands of pilgrims each year and is administered by the nuns of the adjoining Convent of Saint Cecilia.

SAN GIOVANNI

Once the home of the Order of the Temple, this city erupted into street protests when the Templars were dissolved. The protests lasted months, both on the streets of San Giovanni — were demonstrators camped in front of the Cathedral of Saint John of the Cross — and in a massive Maya campaign appealing to the wider PanOceanian public.

AQUILA OFFICER ACADEMY

Located on Iacobus Point in the heart of Santiago de Neoterra, the academy building dominates the city's skyline. Under the tutelage of the army's foremost strategists and tacticians, the cadets learn the latest psyops, technological counter-ops, and advanced strategy techniques. Academy graduates, destined for service in units across the PMC, take pride in "leading from the front" — sharing the frontlines with their troops on both field and high-risk missions. Members of the elite Aquila Guard receive additional security training protecting PanOceanian officers and diplomatic personnel, as well as security for highly classified document transfers.

DARWIN DROP BEARS

Koalas were brought to the Darwin area by the first colonists. Several of them apparently escaped into the wild and either mutated, were genetically experimented on, interbred with local wildlife, or were perhaps afflicted by a previously unknown gene plague. (Scientists and conspiracy theorists can't quite make up their minds, and are a little harder to distinguish from each other than usual on this point.) The result are the aggressive drop bears, from which derive the nickname for a PanOceanian thrown mine.

Order of the Temple – p. 178

THE GRAND CANALS

Where most Neoterran cities have highways linking the upper limits of the city-states, Neapolis has canals. Speedboats race along spiralling, corkscrewing waterways hundreds of feet above the ground.

CORVUS BELLI INFINITY

PIZZINI

Post-Templar protestors organise through an archaic messaging system called *pizzini*, messages hand-written on the wrappers of the popular SweetGems candy. These fast-degrading wrappers break down quickly allowing dissidents to evade CDCI investigations and crackdowns on pro-Templar activities.

Order of the Hospital / Hospital Bank – p. 179

Christian Church – p. 177

Neoterra Capitaline Army – p. 182

THEIA, LADY OF LIGHT

Towering in the centre of San Pietro stands the Lady of Light. The massive structure – shaped in the form of Theia, the Greek goddess of light, with her arms outstretched and holding a great orb – is a wonder to behold. The orb contains the rotating Lightball Mall, providing ever changing, panoramic views of the city for locals and tourists enjoying high-end shops, restaurants, and the Neoterran Museum of Modern Art.

Ad Astra Pilgrimage – p. 15

VATICAN BANK

Sustained by donations from the faithful, the papal bank in San Pietro gives the Church broad influence to shape PanOceanian society in national and international affairs across the Human Sphere. Deep within the bank are the Holy Archive vaults protecting the most valuable holy objects in Christendom. Defended by a special section of the Swiss Guard, defenders of the Mother Church and the Holy See, it's rumoured that the vaults must contain more than holy relics to warrant such security measures.

The protests were for naught. The monastery of San Giovanni di Neoterra that once belonged to the Templars is now the home of the Grand Master of the Order of the Hospital and the headquarters of the Hospital Bank. The city remains a fractious place, and it is the centre for those who speak out against the status quo of PanOceania, the Church, and even the broader powers of the Human Sphere.

These dissident groups have never shown signs of turning violent. Nevertheless, the CDCI patrol the streets in visible numbers, especially in the bohemian district around Via Montermini.

SAN PIETRO

The political centre of the planet and of all PanOceania is San Pietro di Neoterra, also known as Neovatican City. This metropolis is the seat of both temporal and religious power. The parliament of PanOceania meets here, close to the headquarters of all the national government bodies. It is also the home of the Christian Church: The papal throne was brought here to the Archbasilica of the Holy Trinity at the end of the Ad Astra Pilgrimage. The Curia meets here and every religious order or confraternity is either based or has offices in San Pietro.

SERENITAS

Serenitas is a quiet city where the elderly come to live out their twilight years, although the retirement communities have begun to see a steep population drop as more retirees choose to emigrate to Varuna. The Neoterra Capitaline Army maintain a small naval facility here, with patrols regularly intercepting low-orbit drops into the Pax-Gratia Strait by smugglers bringing illicit goods onto the planet.

SYBARIS

Sybaris processes resources extracted at Santa Maria de la Soledad, shipping them off-world through a family-operated spaceport. The city's rough lifestyle provides access to all manner of vices, legal or otherwise. The local police commander uses a rough policing style against the Atek community, sparking regular protests from the NCRA.

TUROQUA

The city of Turoqua is the financial heart of the Human Sphere. The PanOceanian Central Bank, which authenticates and sets interest rates for the Oceana, the national currency, is headquartered here, surrounded by a panoply of vibrant capital markets, money markets, derivatives markets, interbank markets, and quantronic spot markets, along with a million trading companies and just as many service industry firms to serve them, from hotels and meeting facilities to escrow operators and limousine hire fleets.

It is a city of towers that dwarf even the city blocks found elsewhere on Neoterra. Rival corporations constantly strive to outdo one another, piling the most daring and varied displays of inventive neo-tech architecture ever higher into the sky. Turoqua is the City of a Million Beauties, but is also known as the Sweetest Sweet – a reference to Alfred Lord Tennyson's "O Beauty, Passing Beauty", and the fact that the spectacles of yesterday are constantly being eradicated to raise the wonders of tomorrow.

SOLITUDO ISLAND

When human settlers first arrived, Solitudo Island was abundant with life. But that changed all too rapidly when something – expert opinion remains divided on what – contaminated the island's ecosystem. A massive die-off of plants ensued and the animal population soon followed. Many settlers starved before follow-up flights from Earth were able to bring more supplies.

Today the island is a barren wasteland, good for growing nothing but rocks. Only the tall, spindly Archer Willow trees, which draw their sustenance from the air, remain. They cover the southern part of the island, their green upper fronds creating a canopy high above that leaves the ground level in perpetual gloom.

SANTA MARIA DE LA SOLEDAD

The sole city on this desolate island is Santa Maria de la Soledad. Located on a rocky spur that juts into the sea at Bahía de San Jorge, it is dominated by the undersea resource extraction industry – drilling platforms and support facilities for undersea mining.

SPES ARCHIPELAGO

Ironically, the robust biosphere of this island chain makes the jungles of Spes the most threatened ecology on the Neoterra. The lower risk of catastrophic ecological failure resulted in less stringent contamination protocols, which allowed the island to be settled by numerous *spes-gaanv* – agricultural villages which have slowly cut back the trees, replacing them with intense farming projects that cover the land in paddies as far as the eye can see.

The archipelago is full of temples as well as churches. A slim majority of the population is Hindu, which gives this region more cultural heterogeneity than found elsewhere on Neoterra.

AIRAVATA

Airavata is city made of twenty distinct districts spread across the valley from the shoreline to the base of Mount Meru, with each district having a unique character and attitude. Hindu pilgrims come to worship at the Airavata Shrine at Mount Meru's base, and stop at each district's unique shrines and temples fuelling the local economy while on their six-day journey.

AMARAVATI

Amaravati is the City of Maya, as the slogan goes. Elite research facilities are located in the city-state's four development parks. Cutting-edge prototypes fill the city with the most advanced technology in the Human Sphere, as tech firms use the streets and population to run public betas of the latest innovations. The biggest Maya entertainment channels also call the city home, creating a media macro-bubble. Highly automated manufacturing plants turn out the best vehicles and auto-droids.

FIROZABAD

Several densely-packed *spes-gaanv* villages have grown together to form Firozabad, the largest city in the Spes Archipelago. Its towers, scattered between the former *spes-gaanv* city centres, are spread apart, twisting separately in almost organic curves as they reach up to the sky like the tendrils of some gigantic, heaving plant.

Landmarks in Firozabad include the crystal domes of Narada University atop the Valmiki Towers, and the multi-configuration race tracks at the Surya Motor Speedway. The local vernacular is Hindi, a testament to the majority population of Indian descendants.

NEEL PARVAT

The *spes-gaanv*s surrounding Neel Parvat embrace Neoterra's environmental idealism, fuelling eco-friendly industries and global activism. The city's bohemian attitude creates a haven for alternative medicine, splinter Hindu and Christian sects, and pioneering musicians of the Neo-Ragga genre.

TENCENDUR SYSTEM

The first colony system is very similar to Earth's, with a G2IV class star and a number of rocky planets, the third of them habitable.

MOONS

Two moons orbit Neoterra: Selene and Artume. Selene's orbital revolution is thirteen days, while Artume's slower journey requires fifty-three days.

Both moons are relatively undeveloped, but Artume's industry specialises in retrieving payloads launched into Neoterra's orbit from gas mining stations orbiting Zeus and Poseidon. Artume-based crews use rocket-assisted nets decelerate and retrieve these gravity-assisted launches.

ORBITALS

Floriana: This Order of the Hospital station acts as a secondary headquarters for the Hospital Bank and contains a number of maximum security vaults. Maya conspiracy theories claim the vaults contain, among other things, forbidden Templar research including a rogue AI locked away in a datacrypt.

Neoterra Orbital Spaceport: The NOA is the Human Sphere's busiest astroport. Hundreds of millions of passengers pass through it every year. Many of the Circular trade routes meet here, making it the ideal place to set up shop for anyone interested in expanding their business to interstellar markets and suppliers.

OTHER STATIONS

The Neoterra system is heavily developed by the PanOceanian Armada. This is particularly true around Zeus, where the Neoterra Capitaline Army maintains a staging post, the PanOceanian Navy has a number of long-range defence platforms, and the Space Exploration Division keeps its primary shipyards and training facilities.

Gas Mining Platforms: The outer planets of Zeus and Poseidon are mined for hydrogen, nitrogen, and others gases by hundreds of small orbital installations. Each platform is a self-contained community of no more than 20,000 people. They lack some of the luxuries that planetside Neoterrans enjoy but a Maya connection stops them from becoming isolated.

Maria Mitchell Observatory Station: Located on the outskirts of the system, this station has been secretly tasked with monitoring a Tohaa-controlled system. Although the data collected is 177 years out of date, it might still provide unique intelligence on humanity's new ally.

Swords of St. James: The Order of Santiago maintains a Sword (a fortress station) in orbit around each planet in the system.

Templars – p. 178

Circulars – p. 144

Order of Santiago – p. 178

PanOceanian Armada – p. 183

TENCENDUR SYSTEM

STAR
Tencendur: G2IV (Yellow Subgiant)

PLANETS
Hermes (0.7 AU): Telluric Planet
Aphrodite (0.9 AU): Telluric Planet
Neoterra (1.4 AU): Terrestrial Planet (Satellites: Selene and Artume)
Zeus (6.2 AU): Gas Giant – Class II (Water Clouds)
Poseidon (28 AU): Ice Giant

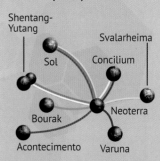

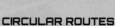

CIRCULAR ROUTES
C1: Sol/Shentang-Yutang
C2: Svalarheima/Sol
C4: Concilium/Bourak
C5: Acontecimento/Sol
C6: Concilium/Shentang-Yutang
C7: Concilium/Varuna

CORVUS BELLI INFINITY

PLANET
PARADISO

Paradiso. The Tropic Gem. The Second Eden. It has been known by many popular monikers since its discovery, but lately it has been known by a few new ones: The Emerald Hell. The Meat Grinder.

It is not that Paradiso is no longer beautiful; its lush beaches and vast tropical rain forests paint an idyllic picture whether from orbit or the ground. But its mineral and biological

wealth made it an irresistible prize as soon as PanOceania announced its discovery. Every major power sought to benefit from its riches: Yu Jing, PanOceania, and Haqqislam all made territorial claims. The Nomads, as is their wont, have found ways to profit in the nexuses between the rivals. And for Ariadna it has become a proving ground for their right to stand shoulder-to-shoulder on the interstellar stage.

PARADISO PLANET STATISTICS

Distance from Star: 2 AU • **Orbital Revolution**: 1033 days • **Rotation**: 28 hours • **Radius**: 1.78 Earth radii • **Surface Gravity**: 1.2g

PLANET DATA FILE

Type of Government: Paradiso Coordinated Command (Military)—Colonial Governments (Haqqislam / PanOceania / Yu Jing) • **Head of Government**: Diwân al Paradiso (Haqqislam) / Colonial Prime Minister (PanOceania) / Planetary Tribunal (Yu Jing) • **Capital**: Al-Hadiye (Haqqislam) / Rilaspur (PanOceania) / Jinggu City (Yu Jing) • **Population of Planet**: 1.2 billion • **Off-Planet System Population**: 1.1 million • **Primary Languages**: Spanish, English, Yujingyu, Arabic, Portuguese • **Anthem**: *Las lluvias de Paradiso* (*The Rains of Paradiso*) (PanOceania); *Míngliàng de huāyuán* (*The Bright Garden*) (Yu Jing); *Alearsh Aldhdhahabi* (*The Golden Throne*) (Haqqislam) • **Principle Industries**: Tourism, Biological Research, Mining

The struggle for control of Paradiso led directly to the First NeoColonial War. The discovery of alien ruins sparked the Final NeoColonial War. And then, seven years ago, the Combined Army swarmed down from the skies. For more than three decades of bloody battle, the world which had seemed to promise a tropical Arcadia has instead become a sweltering Hell.

CLIMATE AND GEOGRAPHY
Paradiso's climate is often warm, averaging around 24°C in winter to 37°C degrees in summer. On the islands to the far north and south of the equator the temperatures are often much cooler, but even here snow is exceedingly rare.

Almost the entirety of the Norstralia Continent is covered in rainforests, but a large number of low mountain ranges (the famed "green-capped peaks" of Paradiso) serve to divide them into a multitude of unique biological zones. The Septentria Continent, by contrast, is remarkably flat and its southern regions are more temperate, albeit with strong cyclical rains which ensure a year-round growing season.

The tropical rain season, which lasts from March to June, sees torrential rains and flooding across both continents. The Lemurian and Xiajuxu Oceans both see dozens of hurricanes during the rain season, and it is not unusual for coastal cities to have standing evacuation plans. The Barrier Sea which lies along the eastern coast of Norstralia and the western coast of Septentria, however, is shielded from these monstrous storms. Before the Combined Army invaded, the east coast of Nostralia — its golden beaches fronting the placid waters of the Barrier Sea — was one of the most beautiful vacation spots in the Human Sphere.

The oceans of Paradiso are teeming with sea life and the planet's fishing industry once seemed endlessly profitable. Now, the seabed is littered with the wrecks of fishing trawlers and military vessels. The industry has coalesced around a number of independent fishing fleets. These large flotillas are guarded by Merchant Marines — small mercenary companies which also patrol the coasts under the blessing of the Paradiso Coordinated Command.

FLORA AND FAUNA
Paradiso's biosphere possesses the rich diversity of an Earth-like world which has never known the touch of human-caused extinction events. The pharmaceutical industries will spend generations cataloguing the millions of species waiting for industrial exploitation, while the planet's surprisingly complex bio-lumber industry (which is particularly active in western Syldavia) expends considerable effort determining how best to harvest Paradiso's trees.

Paradiso's plant life, in particular, is dangerous to the unwary. It exists in a perpetual state of vibration, vigilance, and even movement. (The Karava Vinetrap, for example, can grow to sizes which pose a danger to full-grown humans.) The vegetation's growth rate is also prodigious, demanding a constant application of herbicide and clear-cutting to keep the jungle at bay. Entire communities can be reclaimed by the emerald sea in just a matter of days when conditions are right.

Many of the planet's carnivores pose their own dangers. Paradisan herbivores are less likely to grow to colossal sizes than Maya dramas would have you believe, but a few such species are known. Many Paradisan species are migratory however, with both land animals and birds travelling in flocks. The migratory paths of the larger breeds attract visitors every year to wonder at their majestic beauty.

ECONOMY
The war with the Combined Army has naturally disrupted the Paradiso economy, but, although the entire planet is on a war-footing, once one is away from the front lines there is a surprising sense of normalcy. One can visit cities like Asyût, Jinggu, and Valkenswijk and feel nearly as isolated from the war as on any planet in the Human Sphere.

And in these places, Paradiso's promises of profit and vitality remain fulfilled. Haqqislam's neutral orbital elevators continue to funnel the riches of the planet out to the Human Sphere.

Where the touch of the war is felt is in the constant arrival of young soldiers from across the Human Sphere. Though some view them as a disreputable danger, most welcome them with open arms; particularly because each soldier is required to take their full allotment of R&R each month, leading them to spend their pay locally rather than sending it back home.

Yu Jing maintains extensive farmlands on the planet, primarily aimed at sustaining the R&D departments of the Yu Jing pharmaceutical industry. They are in constant competition with Haqqislam to discover, exploit, and perfect the harvesting of unique biological compounds from the Paradisan biosphere.

DEMOGRAPHICS AND CULTURE
The cities of Paradiso were constructed as full-fledged metropolises; communities conceived in their entirety and built rapidly as a product of RUC to welcome the mass emigration of colonists from Chile and Brazil on PanOceanian Sol; from Yutang and Chung Kuo; and from the devout enclaves of Haqqislam.

NeoColonial Wars – p. 22

Karava Vinetrap – p. 485

ALIEN WEATHER
The phrase "alien weather" has become slang for the worst storms on Paradiso because the Combined Army often chooses to attack at the height of such storms.

ABYSSAL DEPTHS
Paradiso's oceans are perhaps the second biggest mystery on the planet after the cosmolite ruins. The early scientific missions to explore them were just getting established when the NeoColonial Wars disrupted them.

RUC, p. 16: Rapid Urban Construction, made possible through a combination of nanotechnology and AI labour.

Chung Kuo, p. 185: The region of Earth controlled by Yu Jing.

The people who make Paradiso their home are as lively and vibrant as their planet. The colony was originally advertised as a literal paradise where settlers could find a more relaxed lifestyle. This encouraged what Paradisans call the "Chill Paradiso Wind" philosophy, where when things seem like they are getting too hot and hectic to handle, the people are encouraged to pause, relax, and allow cooler heads to prevail.

Combined Army invasion – p. 24

This has been sorely tested in the face of the Combined Army's invasion. But life continues. Each day there are crops that need harvesting, trees that need cutting, and industries which must be pursued. Though Paradiso has unified in the threat against the Combined Army, there are thousands of refugees struggling to find new homes as villages and cities have burned. Those fortunate enough to find shelter often do so in cities of their own government, as old xenophobias have led to many cities closing their borders to anyone who does not share the same culture.

NeoColonial Wars – p. 22

NIEMANDSZONE

The NiemandsZone, or No Man's Land, refers to the neutral areas that were established at the end of the NeoColonial Wars to ensure that all nations had equal access to the remarkable archaeological findings at ZuluPoint (see below).

The NiemandsZone has now become the centre of Combined Army forces on Paradiso and is a fortified area where they have complete control. The outskirts of the Zone are littered with old artillery emplacements and buildings while the interior has seen every possible building and strategic resource recycled into the Combined Army's war machine. It has been reported by the few human spec-ops groups that manage to operate in the area that this part of the planet is eerily quiet, as the sounds of war are like a distant thunder to the peaceful serenity of the Morat-controlled area.

ZULUPOINT

Known as the location where the cosmolites and fragments of the Ur-Probe were discovered, this area has seen some of the heaviest fighting. The first major clash between Paradiso and Combined Army forces occurred in this area, and it still sees heavy fighting to this day. The Combined Army has an intense obsession with the cosmolites, and is intent upon holding the area no matter the cost. The ruins of the ZuluPoint Research Centre are of particular interest to the Combined Army, as it was here that researchers reawakened the Ur-Probe which then wiped out the centre before travelling through the wormhole to contact the Evolved Intelligence.

UR-PROBE

Discovered hidden within one of the outer cosmolite colonnades, the Ur-Probe was an unmanned, alien vehicle or probe of some sort. Analysis of its hull suggested it had seen prolonged use in deep-space (possibly for exploratory purposes), and its fuselage had signs of possibly deliberate damage from powerful energy beams in addition to high-velocity collisions with micro-objects. There was a low-level of activity found in unidentified nanotechnology within the probe, and apparently this nanotechnology was activated and successfully repaired the probe at some point during the Terminal Stage of the NeoColonial Wars. The fact that the Ur-Probe then signalled the Evolved Intelligence has led many to believe that the cosmolites were originally constructed by the Combined Army. (Although others suggest, pointing to the captured Tohaa technology eventually found on Sisargas Island, that they may have belonged to some unknown third party who was capturing alien technology for its own use.)

COSMOLITES

An intricate network of alien-built stone structures, the obelisk-like cosmolites feature low-ceilinged rooms arranged in simple mathematical patterns. Regularly placed subterranean passages connect many of the cosmolites to each other, suggesting either a large facility or small community. Colonnade arrays of additional cosmolites jut out from the central clusters, reminiscent of the sarsen avenues of Avebury and similar sites on Earth.

Scientific tests suggest that the cosmolites are approximately 250 years old, and there's evidence of nanotechnological traces which were eventually identified as being shared in common with the Ur-Probe.

Only one other cosmolite (the facility on Sisargas Island) has been discovered to date on Paradiso. The absence of other sites (or any evidence of sizable infrastructure on Paradiso) suggests that the cosmolites were an exploratory post for an alien species.

FIRST FINDING

Attention was first drawn to the ZuluPoint area when satellite surveys indicated that a nuclear explosion had taken place in the area. At first suspected to be some form of natural criticality event, investigation revealed it to be artificial in origin. Confusingly, radiological traces suggested a Terran origin, a puzzle which was resolved when archaeological discoveries revealed that the long-lost *Aurora* colonisation ship, which had been thought destroyed, had in fact landed on Paradiso and then, apparently, self-destructed for reasons unknown (presumably killing the entire human colony).

Today it has become a massively fortified base, where a trio of Combined Army landing craft have been permanently landed and transformed into an armed military camp.

COMBINED ARMY ON PARADISO

Where once on the eastern shores of the continent stood cities belonging to PanOceania, Yu Jing, and Haqqislam, now there are massive fortifications of a brutal and alien design jutting out from the plains. Massive turret emplacements dominate the area and the land has been so heavily mined by both sides that the area has become a deforested mess devoid of any animal life. The Combined Army has moved considerable assets onto the planet, and nothing has stood in the way of setting up defences and weapon emplacements.

Though they are cut off from the rest of their forces by the Acheron Blockade, the Combined Army have managed to keep fighting and resist human forces at every turn. Using Shasvastii saboteurs to destroy crucial resources like fusion reactors and fresh water supplies has allowed the Combined Army to drive a brutal offensive forward. Though at present the forces of the Human Sphere are pushing back the invaders, they are paying for each inch in precious lives.

The Combined Army has managed to seize several cities and villages in their occupied zones, but they have not been the monsters that the Maya propaganda portrays them to be. While the harsh nature of this occupation has led to a change in the quality of life for those who live in these occupied zones, the Combined Army has left the humans alive. Though cut off from the rest of the planet, reports of human settlements continuing to farm and operate as usual have filtered back to the Paradiso Coordinated Command. It is rumoured that there are resistance groups operating in these cities, but, after several brutal purges, most are incredibly careful in how they act for fear of bringing the iron fist of the Morat down upon their friends and family.

NORSTRALIA CONTINENT

The second most heavily populated continent on the planet, Norstralia is rich with rare trees, ores, and flora that have made it an economic dynamo in Paradiso's economy. The heavily forested areas have become a battleground not just between humanity and the Combined Army but also the predators that live on the continent, and patrols have to be very careful to avoid becoming the victim of poisonous plants or ferocious beasts.

THE NORSTRALIA FRONT

A conflict that stretches across five thousand kilometres and sees some of the hardest fighting between the Paradiso Coordinated Force and the Combined Army, the Norstralia Front has ground to a stalemate since the arrival of the Tohaa.

BEHDETI
A sprawling metropolis with extensive suburbs, Behdeti was once the commercial hub of Paradiso. With its sophisticated satellite communications arrays, it was able to rapidly process and transmit information. The communication arrays were deliberately destroyed during the city's evacuation, and the thriving city has been reduced to ruin.

FUYAN
Fuyan was once a major trade port and the mammoth caverns which existed beneath the city were shipyards servicing Yu Jing's shipping and fishing fleets. Seized during the First Offensive, the shipyards have been converted to service Exrah and Shasvastii ships (which fly sorties out of the cliff-faced caverns). The apartment buildings on the surface have been transformed into a hellish gulag, with the civilian population (and other prisoners of war) serving as human shields preventing the bombardment of the shipyards hundreds of metres below their feet.

Shasvastii – p. 313

Exrah – p. 309

EVOLVED INTELLIGENCE ON PARADISO
In the early days of the invasion, it became clear that the actions of the Combined Army on Paradiso were being directly coordinated by an AI like ALEPH. Identified as the Evolved Intelligence, Bureau Toth initially assumed that it would possess a central processor responsible for coordinating its auxiliary manifestations. A standing, high-priority kill order was issued for the discovery of the EI's central processor. Unfortunately, it is now clear that the EI's advanced architecture somehow allows it to be fully distributed — executing itself through every processor which it controls (even the comlogs and Cubes of Combined Army troops).

Morat – p. 310

THE ROAD TO RAVENSBRÜCKE

A five to ten-mile radius around the city was filled with defensive mechanisms by PanOceania — artillery trenches, camouflaged ditches with missile platforms, entire sectors of highways mined, foxholes, dragon's teeth, anti-air defences. Eventually, however, the Combined Army was able to punch through several rings of defence and establish forward positions. From there, their sappers were able to breach the subway tunnels beneath the city, turning them into battlefields.

Sygmaa Trihedron – p. 325

Paradiso Offensives – p. 25

GERNOT MULTI-WAY

Multi-ways are a consolidated, multi-level transportation corridor. They generally feature highways built above maglev lines, with navigational beacons and docking facilities studded along their length for flying vehicles. On Paradiso, they're constructed atop towering pylons and literally run above the voracious jungle canopy. Deforestation maintenance is still required to keep back the greedy vines which attempt to crawl their way up the pylons, but this saves a great deal of time and effort.

The Gernot Multi-Way is the transportation backbone of Syldavia, linking Runenberg, Damburg, and Horselberg. This places it directly along the Norstralia Front, forming a key strategic axis. As such, it has been heavily fortified and is constantly patrolled by security forces. Nonetheless, travel along the multi-way is increasingly unsafe as a result of Combined Army activity.

ISHMAILIYYA

During the early days of the Second Offensive, a Morat legion smashed through the defensive lines of the Coordinated Forces and surged towards the temple city of Ishmailiyya. The city had considered itself safe and secure, but now it had less than twelve hours to evacuate. Atanur Özergin, the director of the city's Emergency Coordination Office, organised the largest and fastest evacuation in human history. He lost his life in the final defence of the city, but he and a hundred volunteers bought the "Precious Hour" and saved the lives of thousands.

RAVENSBRÜCKE

The Tri-Gothic façades of Ravensbrücke stand as broken, shattered monuments to the fierce months of fighting and bombardment that gripped the city during the First Offensive. The gray, louring streets of the city remain criss-crossed with booby-traps and automatic defensive systems. Recent intel suggests that the Sygmaa have established a lab for human experimentation somewhere within the city.

SILVANIA

Once the capital of PanOceania on Paradiso, Silvania's fabled rainbow spires were transformed to fields of shattered glass during the Second Offensive.

XIONGXIANG

Xiongxiang came under rapid and unexpected threat during the first days of the Second Offensive. Yu Jing evacuated a sizable portion of the population into underground bunkers which had been concealed within the labyrinthine caverns beneath the city. Combined Army soldiers roam the streets and the heavily booby-trapped caverns have been turned into a subterranean battlefield. There are several routes from the bunkers to the surface which remain hidden from the Combined Army, and Yu Jing soldiers periodically use these with great caution to lead sorties behind enemy lines. They've earned a nickname: The Ghosts of Xiongxiang.

QUIBILAH

Quibilah's dominion once spread from the centre of Norstralia all the way to the eastern shores. Though Haqqislam were newcomers to the colonisation efforts on the planet, they took what lands they could purchase or were unoccupied and turned them into rich centres of learning and research. Now, however, Haqqislam has lost the majority of its territories on Norstralia before the onslaught of the Combined Army.

AL-HADIYE

When Haqqislam arrived on Paradiso, they converted Al-Hadiye to be their capital. They knew they could not readily compete with their rivals in the fields of mining or lumber. This was especially true considering the lands that were available for them to claim. Instead, they focused their efforts on experimentation with the flora and fauna as well as building and maintaining space elevators for transporting goods from the surface to the orbiting space stations. The Combined Army recognises the value of the elevator, but would prefer to capture it. Nonetheless, they've maintained intense pressure on the infrastructure around the space platform, and between Shasvastii saboteurs and Morat bombing runs, it has been operating below its optimal levels.

In addition to the orbital elevator and research lab, the Nomads maintain a commercial mission and operate the local space port under contract from Haqqislam. This gives the Nomads a vital presence on Paradiso, which in turn allows them to contribute to the war efforts. A PanOceanian cultural and trade enclave is located on the west side of the city.

UQBAR

Uqbar was once the main strategic storage location for military resources for Haqqislam on Paradiso, and has been beset by Combined Army forces for the past year. The city's defensive efforts have been hamstrung by Shasvastii saboteurs, who have become a constant threat to those who live in the city. The defence forces have to split their time between seeking a way to break the siege and purging their city of infiltrators.

SYLDAVIA

A beautiful endless sea of green that stretches across most of the continent, Syldavia possesses an eloquent mixture of architecture and technology in its cities. With fresh water piped in from the nearby Fairbanks Sea and its central location making it ideal for gathering resources collected from across the PanOceania territories, it has prospered even despite the savage fighting occurring on the Eastern half of the continent. When many tourists think of cities growing among lush forests full of plants and wildlife, they often think of Syldavia.

DAMBURG

Once a beautiful city with towering marble monuments celebrating art and history whose great hydroponic dam brought power to the region, over two-thirds of the city has been lost to the Combined Army. The fighting in the streets of Damburg has captivated the minds of millions who have tuned in to Maya to watch the heroic sacrifices of ALEPH heroes like Odysseus, and though fierce fighting continues around the city, the Combined Army still manages to channel thousands of fresh soldiers into the city each month.

Recently the Tohaa have constructed a fortification near the city. Known as Taarsa-6, this is a launching point for operations against the Combined Army and has given the Tohaa Trident a means to move their forces against their opponents directly. Though the forces of the Paradiso Coordinated Command are grateful for their assistance, many are wary about letting a still unknown alien race gain a foothold on the planet.

HORSELBERG

Located along a series of valleys that lead straight into the Haqqislam province of Quibilah, Horselberg prospered by its trade with their neighbors and was one of the few places in PanOceanian Norstralia to find blackmarket Silk. Trade into the area has increased as other supply lines have been cut or threatened by Combined Army raids. Local crime organisations have seen their numbers increase with the assistance of displaced refugees desperate for food for their families.

RUNENBERG

Now the new capital after the fall of Silvania, Runenberg is now fortifying itself in case the Combined Army threatens to break through and attack. Home to the Nomad Commercial Trade delegation, the Nomads have deployed their elite fighting forces from *Corregidor* and *Bakunin* to assist in the fighting. Though they do not know what the invaders would hope to gain from invading their territory, the colonists at Runenberg will fight to the death to protect what is theirs.

STRACKENTZ

Once a quaint, quiet city known for its tourism more than its exports, Strackentz has become the new home to the Acontecimento Shock Army. Formally designated as the Green-A Combat Group, they are a vital nerve centre for all PanOceania forces on Norstralia.

STRELSAU

A fortress monastery located next to a large seaport, Strelsau is home to a monastery belonging to the Teutonic Knights. Though heavily threatened by Combined Army forces, the defenders of the city have managed to hold out despite having their air routes cut off by Combined Army flyers. Recently the Ariadna Expeditionary Corps have been sent into the area to help the besieged knightly order and to deal with enemy forces there.

VALKENSWIJK

At one time built to fight another war, Valkenswijk was an airfield that allowed PanOceania a place to launch sorties into Yu Jing territory. In the time between conflicts it became known as a place of aviation and entertainment, with massive cinemas and theatres built around the airfield; the rich and elite would fly from across the planet to sample in the city's pleasures.

The addition of the Valkenswijk Orbital Elevator (VEO), however, has become the most important part of the city. This massive elevator is responsible for bringing in the majority of new PanOceanian troops onto Paradiso, who are then shipped by military transport to SchwarzePoint on the front. The elevator has its own defensive fleet that protects it as part of the Orbital Blockade, and security is kept incredibly tight on the ground against Shasvastii agents.

YINGXIAN

The Yingxian Province is known to the Yu Jing as the "Receptacle of Perfume" because of the many beautiful and fragrant flowers that grow there. Here the StateEmpire Army of Yu Jing fights against the Combined Army, and although the cities of Xiongxian and Fuyan have fallen, they maintain their efforts to slow the enemy's advance. What is kept secret from the public is that ALEPH maintains several nodes in the region which are vital for maintaining the datasphere on Paradiso. Although there are general orders to destroy these nodes to prevent them from falling into enemy hands, the destruction of these vital centres would cripple the local datasphere and deeply set back operations on the planet.

CHENGLING

Once a struggling city, Chengling, or "Spiritual Heritage", has seen its economy soar in recent months thanks to the war effort. The youth of the city who could not afford to travel to other cities or off planet to go to college are now learning new trades and starting businesses to take advantage of several needs the soldiers passing through may need. Soldiers needing their boots repaired or parts for their weapons can turn to any of the hundreds of "simple shops" that specialise in such things, and units that had known nothing but field rations for months can buy food supplements to make their harsh tasting, re-sequenced protein packs a little less horrid.

Located in the hills outside of the city is a large Shaolin temple maintained by the Monks of the Forest Tiger. This temple not only passes on its martial traditions to create soldiers for Yu Jing but is also vital in helping the refugees. There

Tohaa Trident, p. 325: The military force of the Tohaa Trinomial.

SCHWARZEPOINT
SchwarzePoint is the most important post in the Norstralia front. Its facilities are carved into the jungle and serve as the hub from which new PanOceanian troops arriving on Paradiso are distributed to the front lines.

Corregidor / Bakunin – p. 168

Nomad Trade Delegations – p. 172

ALEPH NODES ON PARADISO
ALEPH's nodes (p. 193) on Paradiso are the backbone of quantronic communication on the planet. They also represent a vital Achilles' heel, as their capture could allow the EI access to ALEPH itself. Their defence is paramount to a successful defence of the planet, and the Combined Army desires nothing more than to either destroy the nodes or seize them for their own purposes. Although the nodes are massive, however, it is relatively easy for ALEPH to hide them. With special hulls that help hide their emissions and buried beneath the surface of the planet, these nodes are each guarded by a deployment of S.S.S. and Bureau Aegis troops.

Acontecimento Shock Army / Green-A Combat Group – p. 182

Teutonic Knights – p. 178

Ariadna Expeditionary Corps – p. 24

are several diseases which threaten to surge out of control if not for the medical care offered by the temple, whose focus on spiritual and physical health has proven attractive for many of the desperate souls who have lost everything to the Combined Army. The Laoshi (Old Master) of the temple has found a number of new recruits ready and eager to return to the front on their own terms.

NEITING

Known as the Shelled City, Neiting's massive for-tifications – constructed during the lead-up to the NeoColonial Wars – helped her repel attacks from Morat fighter wings during the First Offensive and, with even further expansion, weathered the brutal bombardments of the Second Offensive. A massive storage centre for supplies, construction equipment, and war material, Neiting is also one of the Shuāng Duānkǒu (Twin Ports), along with Wuyi, which strive to keep the Combined Army naval fleets bottled up in the Barrier Sea so that the trade routes of the Xiajuxu Ocean can remain unmolested.

YINQUAN

If Yingxian is the capitol for Yu Jing forces on the continent, then Yinquan is the capitol of excess for the Yu Jing hierarchy. Dedicated to seeing to the whims of members of the Party and officers on leave, the city offers a sophisticated retreat where everything is in abundance. Though there are dozens of refugee camps around the city struggling to get by, the neon lights and golden statues of Yinquan shine like beacons in the distance.

SEPTENTRIA CONTINENT

A beautiful, lush continent full of vast plains and tall forests, what Septentria lacks in mineral resources it makes up in unique plants and funguses whose medical and scientific uses make them as valuable as steel or plutonium. The temperate southern regions, mostly controlled by Yu Jing, are home to vast, fertile plantations.

SEPTENTRIA FRONT

The recent offensives by the Combined Army on the Septentria Front have pushed back the front lines of the three major powers. The conflict in Ghezirah has involved more guerilla warfare and special operations than the conflict on Norstralia, but that does not mean it has not been as fierce a fight. Though they do not have as many assault troops among their forces the EI has arranged for most of its Shasvastii and Umbra operatives to be stationed there where they have sabotaged reservoirs, burnt

crops, and carried out kill orders on high ranking politicians and officers. The commander of O-12 forces on the continent, General Liao Quon of Yu Jing, has managed to blunt the Combined Army offensive into the continent through the use of heavy artillery and scorched earth policies, particu-larly taking advantage of the more open terrain in the south to blunt their advances in Daheng.

BIGUAN

Lost during the First Paradiso Offensive, Biguan was once home to the Biguan Aerodrome. Now rumoured to be a gathering place for high-risk covert ops under Bureau Noir, Biguan appears as an ominously dark series of buildings against the Paradiso skyline. Though Combined Army patrols are a common sight in the city, the Morat have lost many of their troopers to hidden human assassins and saboteurs.

KAPHIRI

Once settled by colonists from India, Kaphiri was traded back and forth between PanOceania and Yu Jing repeatedly during the NeoColonial Wars. The curdling enmity and resentment in the city was rendered irrelevant when a Shasvastii special ops team detonated seismic charges and sunk the harbour, destroying what had once been the largest port on the planet along with all of its military and recreational facilities. The ocean floor is now home to large bronze statues to Hindu gods which glitter with sunlight from beneath the water.

TAITTIRIYA

Once an international hub for telecommunications technology and planet wide broadcasts, Taittiriya was ranked eighth in the Paradiso Global Cities Index in the Bureau Hermes survey. Unfortunately, it was also one of the first cities to see full scale bombardment by Morat ground forces upon their arrival to Paradiso. The ruins of the city are now filled with scavengers hoping to find functional pieces of technology to sell to the highest bidder while Shasvastii infiltrators lurk in the shadows.

ZHONGCHONG

Once the ideal propaganda city, Zhongchong was the city most commonly featured on Maya when the Imperial Service needed to depict the fighting on Paradiso as going well. During the final days of the First Offensive, however, the city finally fell. It became a *Bǎo dǎo* (an island bastion) when the front line of the Combined Army fell back at the end of the First Offensive.

Despite a long, bloody siege by the Nipponese Army, the Combined Army tenaciously held onto the city. When the Second Offensive began, it became a beachhead which crippled defensive actions in the region.

NeoColonial Wars – p. 22

Bureau Noir – p. 216

Morat – p. 310

SOUTHWIND BOAT RACES

These famous races were once a major tourist attraction in Kaphiri, but the destruction of the harbour ended a tradition which dated back to the first days of human colonisation on the planet.

Bureau Hermes – p. 215

Imperial Service – p. 188

Paradiso Offensives – p. 25

Shasvastii – p. 313

ASYÛT

When Haqqislam came to Paradiso to colonize, they competed against PanOceania and Yu Jing for the equatorial area of Septentria. Though they were successful in gaining a foothold in Asyût, they were quickly crowded out by their rivals for control of the area. Asyût lost more territory during the NeoColonial Wars and, with their forces being weaker on Septentria than Nostralia and the majority of their armed forces deployed along the Ghezirah front, Haqqislam has been content with maintaining their remaining territories while working towards seeking a means to reclaim their lost territory through diplomatic and economic means.

ASYÛT CITY

A beautiful city built similar to ancient Mecca, Asyût City is a place of contemplation and study. For many Haqqislamites it is considered a place on the journey of the Hajj for those who decide to travel through space and explore what creations Allah has for them. Recently, it has swelled with refugees and travellers from the front lines.

DAHENG

Daheng is home to vast fields of thick grass that lead into sweeping tropical forests. The great rice fields of Daheng are home to several crops of genetically modified rice that grow well on the soil here and is one of the main providers of food for the rest of Yu Jing. The tourist industry on Paradiso does its best to maintain the safaris and trips that once brought tourists to the planet, but due to the fighting they have been forced to vastly cut back on this, and now only the wealthiest travellers with the highest security clearances are allowed to visit.

JINGGU CITY

The capital of the Daheng province, Jinggu controls the Quchi Sea, which, in addition to being the largest source of freshwater on the continent, is also home to an edible moss that may have great energy producing qualities. Believing that PanOceania would attempt to harvest the moss by force led Yu Jing to build a large navy to patrol its waters, although the majority of those caught harvesting the moss are Yu Jing citizens hoping to sell it off-world to the Nomads or Haqqislam. Yu Jing's primary rivals on the Quchi Sea include the Nomads, who host a commercial mission here and have built a large trade centre.

WUYI CITY

Although heavily damaged by the fighting, Wuyi City produces all manner of textiles from uniforms for the Imperial Army to fashionable clothing for sale across the Human Sphere. Recently the governor of the city was forced to step down and a special delegate from the Commission for Discipline Investigation of the Party has arrived from Yutang to administrate the city's government, although the reasons why this has happened still remain a mystery.

XIANGU CITY

Xiangu possesses Yu Jing's orbital elevator on Septentria. Since the Concilium Convention protected the elevator from being a military target during the NeoColonial Wars, the city was mostly untouched and prospered heavily. Now the city is one of the richest trade hubs on the planet, and often showcased in propaganda pieces as a suitable place for Yu Jing families to go to start a new life.

Concilium Convention – p. 16

GĀYATRĪ

Settled by Sikh explorers shortly after the planet was colonised, Gāyatrī is a land of rivers flowing through forests and heavy marsh lands. The original settlers did their best to preserve the forests of the region which helped preserve their city when the Combined Army tried to bomb it early on during their offensive. Now the city offers safe haven to those seeking to escape the conflict and the 4th Akalis Division keeps watch over the region.

ARITYA

Aritya is a devastated city where combat is still waged in the ruins of this once shining metropolis for control of the delta. If the city falls to the Combined Army they would have the ability to spread out across the southern parts of Gāyatrī, and so PanOceania has ordered their commanders to hold back the enemy at all costs. The extensive subway systems built by PanOceania are now home to brutal close-quarters combat between ORC Troopers and Morat Suryats, and though their city lies in ruins there are still pockets of civilians living inside of the city who have nowhere else to go.

ORC troopers – p. 370

Moart – p. 310

KARNAPUR

The forward logistical centre for the Septentria Front, the city of Karnapur is crowded with refugees and soldiers travelling through on their way to the front. The Karnapur Aerodrome, located not far from the Mithran River, serves as a transfer point where each week a small number of refugees are allowed to leave the city and supplies are brought in. The walls of the Aerodrome are lined with desperate people seeking an escape from the conflict, and security around the Aerodrome is heavily enforced.

Nomad Commercial Mission – p. 172

ISLAND FRONTS

Recent incursions on Molokai Island and the Free Island of Sálvora demonstrate the growing air superiority of the Combined Army on Paradiso.

RILASPUR

The major transportation hub for PanOceania forces, Rilaspur is home to the central rail train yards on the continent. Remnants from the Battle of Rilaspur during the NeoColonial War still dot the country-side as old fortifications have been converted into gardens and bars. In the centre of the city lies a ruined PanOceania tank which has become the *de facto* monument for the Battle of Rilaspur, and flags from all the regiments that fought there are draped across its surface.

VEDI

The sanctuary-city of Vedi stands as a beacon to those who have been displaced by the fighting. Hundreds of thousands of refugees have found sanctuary within what was once a touristic garden city famous for its beautiful Hindu temple. Although currently designated as a "safe city", the potential threat of the Combined Army cannot be entirely forgotten: As yet untested fortifications have been erected around the city and patrols by PanOceanian troops are a common sight.

GHEZIRAH

At the forefront of the fighting on the continent, the defenders of Ghezirah stand strong in their faith that Allah will bring them to victory over the alien invaders, and though the once proud mosques of their cities have been damaged by enemy fire and refugees fill the streets, the people still take pride in their history as the first colony founded by Haqqislam after its settlement of Bourak.

GHEZIRAH CITY

The location of the first orbital elevator to be con-structed on Paradiso (although due to difficulties the Al-Hadiye would come online first), Ghezirah City is a busy place where dozens of flyers and ships navigate their way through the skies around the city and hundreds of trucks and cars transport supplies from its storage facilities to other cities. Though the region is under constant threat from Morat raids, the people of the city are resourceful and brave.

HIBAT ALLAH

The Hibat Allah is the central campaign hospital for the Ghezirah region. Staffed by doctors who volunteered to fight at the front, the hospital main-tains heavy air defences but tries to maintain strict pacifism. The Combined Army knows the hospital is a vital resource to the Coordinated Forces, and, until recently, the hospital was in danger of falling. Without the aid of the Ariadnan Expeditionary Corps aiding in the defence of the city, the hospital would have fallen to the Combined Army and thousands of wounded soldiers would have become full casualties.

ISLES OF PARADISO

The oceans of Paradiso are filled with a scattering of smaller, tropical islands lost in a morass of anonymity. (An anonymity which is seized upon by reclusive Maya celebrities and secretive hypercorps alike, although many of these palatial estates and isolated facilities have been abandoned in the face of the Combined Army threat.) The planet's three micro-continents are also referred to colloquially (and cartographically) as islands.

MOLOKAI

Located at the southern pole of the planet and home to numerous sensor outposts and military bases, Molokai is home to massive King Tiger Seals and reptilian Kragodon animals which make exploring the island tricky. Despite the harsh temperatures and fearsome storms that made the island unappealing to colonists, explorers still roam the island and its coast is one of the few locations where Paradiso Truffles grow in abundance due to its volcanic soil.

FLAMIA ISLAND

Fiercely contested during the NeoColonial Wars due to its strategically valuable position between Norstralia and Molokai Island, Flamia Island was declared a Demilitarized Island (DMI) under the control of O-12 as part of the Peace of Concilium. Bureau Aegis divided the island amongst the major powers while expropriating areas from which O-12 could exert control.

Aranda Astrologistic Facilities: The Hexahedron suspects that the Nomads, under the pretence of coor-dinating their orbital assets, use their Aranda facility as a nexus for the Arachne datasphere on Paradiso.

Camp Antela: On the shores of Lake Antela in the central region of the island, Bureau Aegis has established Camp Antela as an adaptation centre for Ariadnan Expeditionary Corps troops, preparing them for warfare on this alien world.

Narooma Advanced Hospital Complex: Shortly after signing the Tohaa Contact Treaty, O-12 allowed the Tohaa to establish this surgical and long-term medical facility. The original name given to the region by PanOceanian survey cartographers—which has the appropriate meaning of "fresh breeze"—has been kept.

Onza Island: A smaller island located off Flamia's eastern coast, Onza serves as the O-12 command centre for the DMI.

Terrigal City: This small PanOceanian city is most notable for the Sagres Island Orbital Monitoring Station located just off its coast. The enormous orbital link beacon, connected to the city via an elevated highway, can be seen from leagues away.

Tiānxiàn City: Founded as the original Yu Jing colony on the island, Tiānxiàn was ceded to Haqqislam. The original Chinese name of the city was kept as a sign of respect in an effort to ease the transition of its citizens.

Zhurong City: Yu Jing's largest settlement on the island and home to a variety of industrial production centres, Zhurong is particularly notable for the artificial islet containing the Zhurong Geothermal Power Station just off the coast. The plant provides most of the energy used on Flamia, but most of its output is transmitted to a transfer station on the mainland.

INVERNACULUM

Home to research laboratories outsourced by PanOceania to private research firms, Invernaculum has a dark reputation on Paradiso as it was the site of a falsified relic find by the now disgraced archaeologist Klaus Lundt. He claimed he had discovered several stone pillars similar to the cosmolites while exploring the island. When PanOceanian engineers carbon dated the ruins, however, they claimed the find was a hoax. Professor Lundt was stripped of his tenure and funding despite his claims to the contrary. It is rumoured that several labs on the island work directly under Hexahedron control and are currently working on deciphering Combined Army technology and VoodooTech. The heavy PanOceania military presence seems to reinforce these rumours.

SÁLVORA ISLAND

The Free Island of Sálvora was established by O-12 at the end of the NeoColonial Wars to monitor the development of the peace treaty and to oversee the reconstruction process. The Tohaa have recently established their primary embassy there, and the island is already benefiting from the cultural exchange. The presence of the Tohaa, however, also appears to have increased the frequency of Morat raids on the island and its territorial waters.

SISARGAS ISLANDS

Uninhabited due to the continuous tropical storms that buffet the area, the Sisargas Islands came to the planet's attention recently when an active cosmolite ruin was found on one of the islands. A mysterious alien artefact was recovered by human forces from the Last Cosmolite before a kinetic projectile launched from orbit destroyed the ruins and sterilised the area.

YINFENG ARCHIPELAGO

Home to numerous families who were brought in from across the eastern hemisphere of old Sol, the Yinfeng Archipelago is home to old disputes carried over from centuries ago. The colonists keep to their

own villages, most of which are centred around the sea farms which are their key economic resource. The Combined Army is secretly fomenting trouble in the region in the hope that they can distract Yu Jing and draw their attention away from their portion of the front lines.

ZENDA

Sparsely populated before the war, the island of Zenda is home to several resorts and hotels that promise a convenient location to get away from the stress of the conflict on the planet. Home to lavish wineries as well as a hospital established by the Order of Saint Lazarus, Zenda has become an ideal vacation spot. Guests must be wary as the island possesses several breeds of land urchins that love to hide in the tall grasses of the plains and the shores are known breeding areas for the Bloodfin Killer Whales. On the opposite end of the island lie several monitoring facilities owned by PanOceania and ALEPH used to track enemy movements across the ocean. Whether they are used to monitor civilian ships is unknown, but most treat it as a near certainty.

PARADISO SYSTEM

The Paradiso system, named after its more popular dominant planet than the twin stars they orbit, is as dangerous with natural phenomena as it is with artificial ones. The heavy gravity of the red dwarf Nakula pulls core material from the white dwarf Sahadeva, creating a brilliant accretion disc around the star that can sometimes be seen from Paradiso. This beautiful effect comes at the cost of generating additional radiation (which can interfere ships' systems and adds a layer of static on any scans performed in the system) and increasing gravitic stress on the planets.

OPERATION FLAMESTRIKE

During a recent attack by the Combined Army on Flamia Island, the human factions seized the opportunity to redefine their own control of the territory. The disjointed response managed to repel the EI's forces, in large part due to the Nomad troops stationed in Aranda spreading out across the island to provide tactical reinforcement. This, in turn, left the Aranda facility vulnerable to Shasvastii infiltration. Fortunately, Haqqislamite troops from nearby Tiānxiàn City were able to launch an assault which drove the Combined Army vanguard force back into the Xiajuxu Ocean.

In the wake of Operation Flamestrike, Nomad forces remained stationed in the Zhurong Power Station, ostensibly to provide "data security" against lingering Combined Army infowar mines. Having effectively lost control of Zhurong, Yu Jing is furious over the so-called "taxes" which the Nomads are charging to the StateEmpire's settlements and facilities for their energy usage. For its own part, however, the NMF high command is concerned by the Haqqislamite forces occupying their Aranda facilities (and the secrets that Hassassin agents might discover there).

CELESTIAL RESEARCH CENTRE

Kept hidden from the inhabitants of the Yinfeng Archipelago, Yu Jing maintains a research centre on the island of Qi Hue. Built to examine the Black Box recovered from the wreckage of a crashed alien ship, the facility has come under criticism from the rest of O-12 for not sharing its complete findings with them. Yu Jing maintains it has shared all of the information it has learned from the Black Box, but truthfully it is having trouble learning anything at all.

Order of Saint Lazarus – p. 179

Last Cosmolite – p. 320

CORVUS BELLI
INFINITY

NAVAL BLOCKADE

Bureau Aegis – p. 213

Exrah – p. 309

XHANTRI BUMBLEBEES

The Combined Army will shoot hundreds of small probes past the blockade hoping that these bumblebee drones will give information on the best path to bypass O-12 fleet deployments. Though an extremely costly measure as most probes are destroyed, the ones that do survive have been invaluable in helping much needed supplies reach the Combined Army's front lines on the planet.

SHASVASTII INFILTRATORS

Bureau Noir has confirmed that significant Shasvastii intelligence operations are active on Dawn, most likely as the result of a breach (or multiple breaches) in the Daybreak Blockade. And if the Shasvastii have reached Dawn, there's little or nothing stopping them from spreading to other worlds of the Human Sphere. This information has been kept at the highest classification levels. Even some parts of the Stavka remain in the dark.

ubiquitous nexus, p. 7: The zone around a wormhole in which ships arrive and depart.

Shasvastii – p. 313

Tohaa Contact Treaty – p. 25

Coordinated by Bureau Aegis, the Naval Blockade of the Paradiso system is a layered defence made up of four separate forces. This defence in depth is designed not only to resist rapid penetration by a Combined Army assault, but also with the hope that one of its many webs will succeed in catching Shasvastii ghost-ships and other infiltrators.

First raised in 60 NC (with the Acheron Gate finally being sealed in 61 NC following the Acheron Attrition), the Blockade has been largely successful at the former, but its success in the latter has been mixed.

THE ACHERON BLOCKADE

The wormhole leading to the Evolved Intelligence was first detected by humanity when the Combined Army's invasion fleet poured through it. Codenamed Acheron, it's an unusual wormhole leading to an EI-controlled star system on the far outer rim of the Milky Way. Such wormholes, leading to the galactic rim, are more complex, unstable, and dangerous than travel between gates at a common distance from the galactic centre. This instability results in a much wider ubiquitous nexus, increasing the difficulty of monitoring and securing the entire entrance zone of the 'hole.

The Acheron Blockade is not only the largest of the blockades in size, it is also composed of the largest warships (primarily flying under PanOceanian and Yu Jingese flags). They are stationed in the Ring of Iron, a cluster of crudely formed platforms and stations designed to fire heavy payloads into the Combined Army's arrival points. The vast nature of the wormhole is so large that PanOceanian engineers believe they would need another ten years at minimum to complete the Ring.

Despite the fact that the wormhole's instability causes the Combined Army to lose more than 50% of their ships before they even reach the Paradiso system, the blockade is frequently tested. Enemy forces arrive in what the Acheron fleet refers to as "attack waves". Attack Wave ALPHA, the first to come through on any given assault, is usually made up of suicide decoys mixed with kamikaze bait ships loaded with explosives. Subsequent attack waves (labelled BETA, GAMMA, DELTA, and so forth) follow on a tightly coordinated schedule designed to saturate the blockade's firing solutions.

INTERMEDIATE BLOCKADE

Although the Acheron Blockade has been successful to date in preventing any attack fleet from penetrating the Paradiso system, the truth is that smaller ships — including cloaked Shasvastii vessels, but also uncloaked Exrah blockade runners — are often able to pass through the blockade. The Intermediate Blockade, made up primarily of Nomad and Haqqislamite uniships, is tasked with patrolling the entire Paradiso System and hunting down these ships.

ACCESS BLOCKADES

The Access Blockades are stationed at each wormhole leading out of the Paradiso system. As the last bastion standing between the EI and the Human Sphere, they are vital in ensuring that the war does not spread beyond Paradiso.

Although the Access Blockades are significant combat fleets in their own right, they are primarily focused on monitoring traffic through the wormholes — scanning for cloaked ghost-ships, remora infiltrators attached to the hulls of legitimate transports, and hollowed-out Trojan horses.

- Abyss Blockade leads to Human Edge
- Daybreak Blockade leads to Dawn
- Sheyk Blockade leads to Bourak
- Wotan Blockade leads to Svalarheima

DAEDALUS BLOCKADE

The Daedalus Blockade guards the gate leading to Tohaa space. Under the terms of the Tohaa Contact Treaty, it is defended entirely by Tohaa forces (including a large number of Tohaa Combat Stations which they have constructed in a remarkably short period of time).

ORBITAL BLOCKADE

The Orbital Blockade is the final line of defence for Paradiso, Satori, and Nirvana. In addition to maintaining a fleet of light combat vessels for intercepting blockade runners seeking to reinforce the Combined Army forces on the surface of Paradiso, it is also responsible for the security of the satellite network around Paradiso and the planet's orbital elevators. Additional security and patrol operations are also maintained on the surfaces of the two moons.

ORBITALS

A large number of orbitals were rapidly constructed to facilitate the colonisation of Paradiso, but many of these have been destroyed (first during the NeoColonial Wars and, later, by the Combined Army) and others have been abandoned due to the persistent threat posed by the alien invaders.

The Orbital Blockade, however, works diligently to ensure the security of the orbital stations which remain, the upper stations of the planet's orbital lifts, and the Eye in the Sky suborbital defence and surveillance system.

Elysium-3: The premiere exemplar of ALEPH's Elysium instruction centres for the Assault Subsection of the Special Situations Section.

Hàoguāng Transorbital Defence Base: Yu Jing's orbital defence doctrine features a small number of heavily armed defence bases. These large transorbital facilities feature a multitude of beam weapons designed to target projectiles and small ships at extreme ranges, complemented with hangar bays full of intercept fighters to harry larger targets. Hàoguāng Base is the largest of these platforms, and historically notable as the site of a Combined Army incursion in 65 NC.

Pārvatī Orbital Defensive Platforms: In the northern hemisphere, PanOceania uses a very different defensive strategy to guarantee orbital security. The Pārvatī platforms are tiny, laced with cutting-edge stealth technology, and multitudinous: Hundreds of them are scattered in close orbit, each housing a small three- to five-person team. Individually they pack less punch, but collectively they are difficult to avoid and can rapidly swarm like antibodies to target larger threats.

Olympus-1: A low orbit station which is the main military base of the ALEPH's Special Situations Section and the Steel Phalanx. It is also the home of Achilles and his famous Homeridae.

ORBITAL EXCLUSION ZONE

A constant, low-level conflict exists in perpetuity around the Orbital Exclusion Zone located above the territories controlled by the Combined Army on Paradiso. Mobile surface defences equipped with high sensitivity sensors track the skies and take out any satellites which seek to spy from above, while signal jamming micro-drones and one-use-only E/M pulse air-emitters float in low orbit.

MOONS OF PARADISO

The twin moons of Paradiso were once the scene of heavy fighting between Yu Jing and PanOceania during the NeoColonial Wars, but lately have been the scene of heavy military build-ups by both powers in anticipation of the conflict with

the Combined Army escalating. The PanOceania moon Nirvana and the Yu Jing moon of Satori have seen heavy fighting but the soldiers defending them fight as hard as the soldiers on the surface of Paradiso.

NIRVANA

Once a major tourist hot spot and a propaganda piece that depicted the future of orbital habitation to the citizens of PanOceania, Nirvana was a shining sphere of white stone set in the sky above the planet. Many famous Maya stars have sung about the beauty of the moon and how it did not just reflect the light of the twin suns but the very beauty of Paradiso when it gleamed at night.

Today the moon's surface bristles with landing pads for starships, and fumes from leaking gas pockets and poisonous fumes purged from reactor cores are starting to give the once porcelain finish of the moon a brownish tint. PanOceania has stationed one of their main combat groups, Blue-S, on Nirvana in order to protect one of the largest and most important ALEPH nodes in the system. This node is responsible for processing all information that filters in from across the Human Sphere and is essential to transporting information back to Sol and Concilium. In the event that the node should fall into enemy hands, several powerful nuclear weapons have been installed around the node to destroy it and any enemy forces in the area.

SATORI

While Nirvana can be considered to be an orbiting tourist site that PanOceania has built up a heavy military presence on, the moon of Satori has been, from the beginning, a staging ground for StateEmpire Army troops and there are extensive fortifications across the moon's surface (and drilled into its depths). Satori also serves as a location for several of Yu Jing's Invisible Prisons, where those convicted of crimes against the Emperor are sent to reside in what can only be called an orbiting hell above Paradiso.

The settlements on the moon are mostly underground due to the lack of an atmosphere, and are designed with self-sufficiency in mind. Each settlement is dedicated to a single goal, whether that be military research or development of new ores. Though the moon is able to be visited by outsiders, they are kept to the spaceport of Gray Lotus and are denied the chance to go deeper into the moon. Yu Jing prefers it this way, as they need to focus on keeping security tight and preventing saboteurs from crippling important systems. This is what they have told O-12 for over a decade, despite the increasing tension placed on them regarding the brutal living conditions and the horrible abuses of power inside the Invisible Prisons.

MAANTE SAEL
This Tohaa maintenance and repair facility is based on Nirvana. It was given to the Tohaa by the Human Sphere in order to act as Errant Ship fleet shipyards and general troop infrastructure.

NeoColonial Wars – p. 22

Blue-S Combat Group – p. 182

ALEPH nodes – p. 193

ORBITAL COOPERATION
Paradiso Coordinated Command has an ongoing project for integrating the Hàoguāng and Pārvatī technologies into an overlapping, cohesive defensive network. Unfortunately, it's been hung up in a feasibility committee for years as PanOceania and Yu Jing both continue to jealously guard their secrets of national defence.

EVENINGSTAR ORBITAL
The EveningStar Orbital was formerly the headquarters of O-12 in Paradiso. It was destroyed by the Combined Army in 66 NC shortly after the Tohaa Contact Treaty was signed there.

QAPU KHALQI SAFT RAIDERS
The Qapu Khalqi – a Haqqislamite force dedicated to protecting orbital elevators, space stations, and transports – also provides the forces dedicated to tracking down the Asharii bases (see next page). Although it would be easier to simply obliterate the stations, the need for advanced intelligence on the Combined Army often means the need for expert raiders used to fighting inside threatening environments.

PARADISO SYSTEM

STARS
Nakula: M0V (Red Dwarf)
Sahadeva: D2 (White Dwarf)

PLANETS
Virgil-1 and Virgil-2 (0.12 AU) :
Telluric Dwarf Planets
Dante (0.34 AU): Carbon Planet
Paradiso (2 AU): Terrestial Planet
Orgoglio Asteroid Belt (4 AU)
Milton (7.5 AU): Gas Giant –
Class I (Helium Planet)
Purgatorio Asteroid Belt (8 AU)
Beatrice (11 AU): Gas Dwarf
Ugolino (19 AU): Telluric
Super-Earth

ORGOGLIO BELT
This asteroid belt was originally
a planet, ripped apart by a
massive impact with another
stellar body at some point
in the relatively recent past
(astronomically speaking).

BINARY PLANETS
Virgil-1 and Virgil-2 form a
binary composed of two dwarf
planets. In their close orbit of
Paradiso's twin stars, they are
continually blasted by deadly
radiation. Some astronomers
believe the binary planets were
once a single object, split apart
in a cataclysmic collision.

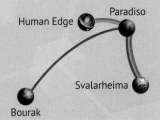

CIRCULAR ROUTES
C3: Svalarheima/Human Edge
C7: Svalarheima/Bourak
C8: Human Edge/Svalarheima
Acheron Gate (Ur Hegemony)
Daedalus Gate
(Tohaa Trinomial)

OTHER STATIONS

El Arsenal: Originally constructed by O-12, this shipyard station and salvage yard located near the Acheron Blockade is mostly managed by Corregidoran Nomads. Other sections are leased to private companies, and there's even a black market frequented by a small fleet of corsair captains working out of the Freetraders Brotherhood as privateers against the Combined Army. The war has seen El Arsenal become a truly chaotic place: Ships are constantly churned through the Blockades, and the damaged wrecks are hauled here for salvaged parts and, if possible, repair. The perimeter of the station is a giant ring of debris in an ill-organised, diamond-like shape.

Asharii Bases: The Combined Army maintains a number of mobile bases concealed within the Purgatorio and Orgoglio asteroid belts. (A small number are also rumoured to exist in the system's Oort cloud.) Named after a Shasvastii word for "shade", surprise attacks launched from these bases are frequently used to debilitate the blockades. Paradiso Coordinated Command is concerned that the EI may be using these facilities to create VoodooTech replication centres that could be used as constant supply depots for a Combined Army fleet in Paradiso space.

OTHER PLANETS

BEATRICE
A gas-dwarf planet, Beatrice's thick atmosphere of hydrogen clouds are a beautiful swirling of orange and pink which are often used to sell tourism. Its rocky core possesses a unique ocean of floating ammonia. The hydrogen mining platforms around the planet have been severely disrupted by Combined Army raids.

Tehuantepec-2: This Nomad defensive station was damaged four hours prior to the Combined Army invasion when the *Clamorous Shouting* crashed into its superstructure during a routine docking. Psychotropic drugs had been introduced into the nutrient soup of the ship's neo-cetacean pilot.

DANTE
Dante is a rare carbon planet, possessed of a iron-rich core wrapped by a kilometres-thick diamond covered in broken layers of graphite. The result is a lifeless rock floating in space. It was once home to solar plants and mineral refinement stations before they were obliterated during the initial invasion of the Combined Army.

Backgammon Lost Garrison: The Combined Army had initially attempted to seize Dante's industrial facilities, but a surprise attack by a small Nomad fleet thwarted their attempt to turn the planet into a supply centre and also destroyed their extraction vessels. Combined Army vessels occasionally try to relieve the stranded forces on the surface, but the underpowered Qapu Khalqi cordon is still holding up. Referred to as the Backgammon Lost Garrison, the Combined Army troops have retreated to the slate caverns that honeycomb the northern massifs. Attempts to retake the planet by human forces are knocked out by their anti-orbital weaponry.

Urban legends persist of a human force which has also been stranded on the planet, fighting a strange war with the Combined Army forces there. The Paradiso Coordinated Command fervently denies this.

MILTON
Milton is an unusual gas giant in which the atmosphere consists primarily of helium (instead of the usual hydrogen). Such worlds were previously theorised to exist only in close solar orbits (which would evaporate the hydrogen content of their atmospheres). Milton is too far from Nakula and Sahadeva for that to be true, but what process could have boiled away its hydrogen supply remains a mystery.

Mining the gases in Milton's atmosphere is perilous due to the geysers of superheated liquid that are frequently expelled from the lower layers into the upper atmosphere of the planet. The entire surface of the planet is distinctly pockmarked by these geysers, and the Polar Geyser is a huge, permanent feature.

UGOLINO
A terrestial mega-planet known for its erratic orbit, scientists theorise that Ugolino's large size is due to it having a larger than normal planetary core which explains its intense electromagnetic field. The intense electromagnetic storms have been known to disable ships and drag them down to the stone surface of the planet, and the fluctuating fields create sensor "dark spots" throughout the system which can be used to mask entire ships. Yu Jing scientists were the first to successfully predict their patterns, allowing them to launch the infamous Lotus Blitz during the NeoColonial Wars (which destroyed PanOceanian and Nomad refueling stations in orbit around Beatrice and temporarily broke the Siege of Satori). PanOceanian Hexas agents eventually stole the Ugolino Codex, breaking Yu Jing's unique strategic advantage. Both fleets now use Ugolino's dark spots to hide themselves from Combined Army ships.

PLANET
SHENTANG-YUTANG

Duality defines the experience of the Yu Jingese people: Tradition and progress. Imperial ceremony and modern civilisation. The Party and the Dragon.

So, too, is it with their home system: Two viable planets, tidally locked to each other and in orbit around Shanxing (Superior Star), a yellow main-sequence star, in perfect symmetry. Yutang and Shentang (the Jade Palace and Divine Palace, respectively) were discovered by the Yu Jing at a crucial turning point in history,

and they are the foundation on which the power and solidarity of the Empire stands, and the crucible in which their dreams of the future are tested.

Five billion people spread between these two planets labour daily for their nation's pursuit of power while seeking to perfect themselves in the service of their people. They seek to make real the shared dream of a Human Sphere which blazons its way across the galaxy with the Twin Worlds as its two-chambered heart.

SHENTANG PLANET STATISTICS
Distance from Star: 1.05 AU • **Orbital Revolution**: 393 days • **Rotation**: 26 hours • **Radius**: 1.2 Earth radii • **Surface Gravity**: 1.005g

PLANET DATA FILE
Type of Government: Imperial Socialist One-Party State • **Head of Government**: The Dragon Emperor/Party President • **Capital**: Yián Xiáng • **Population of Planet**: 2.2 billion • **Off-Planet System Population**: 4 billion • **Primary Languages**: Yujingyu, Japanese, Korean, Vietnamese, Laotian • **Anthem**: *10.000 Nián zài wèi taint* (*Celestial Reign of 10,000 years*) • **Principle Industries**: Agriculture, Armaments, Fishing, Quantronics

distribution from the population of Earth. These geographic divides also tended to align with the distribution of Imperial supporters, with the North lending support to the Qing dynasty and the South to the Ming. These geographic divides also extended to economic pursuits, as the Northern regions were encouraged towards cultural heritage sites, while the Southern regions were allowed to develop fertile farmland and agricultural pursuits. Virtually all of these colonists were Chinese Han. Although a scattering of minorities were added to the colonisation group in order to provide the appearance of diversity, the Party deliberately created a strong, ethnically monolithic planet that could rest a firm grip on the reins of government.

Qing/Ming dynasties – p. 185

The colonisation of Shentang was equally controlled, with each ethnic group given carefully chosen geographical representations of their native soil (within the limits of moving to a completely alien location). The Party cultivates nationalism through a competitive expression of cultural identity and independence. Thus, there are national holidays observed throughout Yu Jing, but each province can dictate its own interpretations of those holidays and can also name a limited number of additional holidays in accordance with their local tradition.

SHENTANG

The Japanese settlers dubbed Shentang the *daitoshi no sekai,* the world of cities. The planet is studded with communities largely dedicated to a single industrial trade, supported by extensive farm communities surrounding mountains containing secluded Shaolin monasteries. In many ways, the entirety of Shentang is itself a machine dedicated to keeping the StateEmpire in motion.

BENSHEN ARCHIPELAGO

The twin settlements of Zhubin and Renying stand as oddities amongst the bustle and clamour of most other Shentang cities. These massive self-sufficient communities contain well-designed farms with high production capacity, factories with the potential to produce small scale technology to large scale vehicles and armaments, and sprawling housing complexes. Still under construction, these communities stand mostly unoccupied, with the few residents scrambling to keep the under-utilized resources in good repair. Rumour has it that Sun Tze recommended the creation of these settlements to handle the influx of refugees in the event of the fall of Paradiso.

ZHONGTING
The main continent of Shentang is a massive body of land that extends past both tropics of the planet. Like the rest of the planet, this supercontinent is divided amongst the various constituent ethnicities of Yu Jing. The terrain is much less uniform and even than that of Yutang, with approximately sixty percent of the landmass being hilly, uneven terrain that occasionally turns mountainous. This terrain lends itself to dispersion, with many small cities and villages scattered throughout the various provinces.

Sun Tze, p. 198: A Recreation created by ALEPH.

GANDAKPUR

The Tibetan province of Gandakpur contains the highest, roughest terrain in all Shentang. Scattered about its massive plateaus and nestled in its valleys, one finds small, hardy villages full of humble farmers and shepherds, content to live their lives in the ways of the ancestors.

SHAMBHALA
Drawn to their ancestral ways, the Tibetans established their capital, Shambhala, on a plateau within the Sacred Mountains of Dhaunati. It is here that you will find the 19th Dalai Lama in residency, continuing to spread the wisdom and teachings of Tibetan Buddhism. The city itself is a modern marvel, with its seemingly simple façade yielding deep, well-designed structures extending thousands of feet into the mountains.

KAMBU

Filled with dense jungles, Kambu province is best known for its sprawling armaments factories and massive chemical and mineral processing centres. Kambu province produces approximately twenty-five percent of all the less-specialised weaponry used by the StateArmy and produces about half the munitions used by Yu Jing as a whole.

KOMPONG MERA
Nestled inland and far from the munitions factories of coastal Kambu, this city serves as the agricultural nexus of not just Kambu, but of Zhongting as a whole. This trade town also serves as a bit of an academic centre for those who have an interest in the creation and dissemination of new hybrid species drawing from the native and cultivated biodiversity of the planet.

SAMBOR DUK
Sambor Duk is the most industrialised and populated city in Kambu. Nestled on the coast and surrounded by the thickest jungles, the downtown and the residential areas resemble the *wats*, the palace-cities hidden in the jungles of Cambodia.

KOGURYÖ

The Korean province of Koguryö is one of the most industrialised regions on the face of Shentang. While the terrain is now as amenable to city-building as most of Yutang, the people of Kuguryö have mastered their lands and created small, lavish cities that promise comfort, luxury, and exciting nightlife to those who might visit.

KORYŌ

The coastal city of Koryō stands as a defiant point of contrast to Sakuramachi, which lies across the sea. Sprawling resorts and casinos occupy the seafront of this decadent city, taking money from locals and tourists alike. Like many similar cities, Koryō is also a centre of criminal activity, with the Yakuza representing strongly alongside competing off-world Triad interests.

PAEKCHE

Unlike the other cosmopolitan cities that dot Koguryō, Paekche is the industrial centre of Koguryö. Specialising in communications and networking equipment, some of the latest designs for military use are produced in small, well-secured, dedicated, clean factories. Due to the importance of security and secrecy, Paekche has a significant Municipal Police presence, as well as a Yǎnjīng operational base.

SILLA

If one were to view Shentang from space and speculate as to where the actual capital is, one would guess the Korean city of Silla. Located on the coast of the central continent, this town was initially designed to be one of many fishing villages. Due to its position relative to the equator and the construction of the geosynchronous station No-Dong 3, Silla exploded in size and population density. The elevator and its naval yards bring tremendous traffic to the city, creating immense demand for housing. As a result, the Hamdae — Silla's floating neighbourhood — is the largest in Koguryö, dwarfing the others in size.

KURAIMORI

The hard-line ancestralists describe Kuraimori as a false gift that pales in comparison to the Japanese islands — the weather is colder, the fishing considerably worse due to the presence of large predators, and it is isolated. But the mountainous region to the north of the island gives a sense of home to some, and there is five times more usable land than the Home Islands.

KOFUKU

This is the industrial capital of Kuraimori. Here one can find cutting-edge cycles, cars, and shuttles being produced in massive, kilometres-long automated factories alongside smaller, discrete quantronic production facilities building microscopic semiconductors integrated into complex computing devices for commercial and personal use.

KUME

Situated central to the island, Kume is one of the major centres for designing, testing, and creating advanced technologies for military support.

NINJAS

The modern ninja are squads of highly technified assassins. Each squad is controlled by an Oniwaban, who is responsible for recruiting and training those under their command. These squads in turn owe allegiance to clans, which are frequently facilitated by front companies such as Fukurō Security, Tenchō Investment Consulting, and Rantan Services respectively (which are operated as cover corporations by the Fukurō, Kōsetsu, and Ōnishi clans, respectively). These seemingly legitimate businesses are used to create public contact points for the clans, while also allowing for money laundering and community support.

The Oniwaban — a term which means "one who is in the garden"— historically worked as personal gardeners to the Shogun during the Tokugawa Shogunate while secretly serving as the Shogun's connection to the enigmatic ninja. The origins of the modern Oniwaban are similarly inscrutable: They may have been sponsored by *keiretsu*. Or sanctioned by the Emperor. Or worked as Tatenokai terrorist cells.

The existence of ninjas is a poorly kept secret that looms over the heads of those that would oppose the will of the StateEmpire. Yu Jing strenuously denies their existence. Bureau Noir has case files stretching back decades on the reputed activity of ninja clans, but even O-12 isn't certain whether the few credible reports they have are indicative of the ninja's existence or merely amateurish copycats and unrelated black ops using the legend of the ninja as cover.

The security which goes with the large-scale armaments and weapons manufacturing lends a militarised appearance to the city, which is further reinforced by the military bases of the Nipponese Army which ring the city.

MOTOBUSHIMI

Motobushimi has two different aspects; above the ground and below. Above, one finds a bustling seaside port known for advanced shipbuilding techniques and a vigorous consumer-driven watercraft industry. Below the waves and beneath this city, one finds numerous caverns, many of which have subaquatic egress that allow for secretive comings and goings that are disguised amidst the vigorous waterborne traffic of Motobushimi's ports. It is rumoured that in these caves the Tatenokai have supply caches and training facilities, and that they serve as occasional Yakuza smugglers rendezvous.

SAKURAMACHI

The capital of Kuraimori is a port on the southern edge of the island. The sprawling city is a tangled knot of massive towers housing the *keiretsu* of Japanese industry bound together by numerous elevated highways that span hundreds of metres into the air around and through the city. Those who are wealthy enough to live in the city proper occupy tiny, cramped apartments that are little more than cubbies with the necessities of life. Surrounding Sakuramachi is a vast, tumbling sprawl of suburbia where most of the working class live, commuting by train and bus for hours each day.

FLOATING NEIGHBOURHOODS
Lower income residents in the coastal cities of Koguryö often live in floating houseboats moored to the piers which have multiplied along the banks.

Tatenokai, p. 187: Japanese terrorist organisation protesting Yu Jing rule.

RIDING THE LANES
The soaring highways of Sakuramachi are the primary demesne of the Bōsōzoku rider gangs and their illegal races.

TOMARI

The University of Kuraimori is found in the small, weathered city of Tomari on the Northeastern coast. This stormy, wind-swept town is populated by academics, fringe theorists, and all manner of eccentrics who dedicate their lives to making a name for themselves. If there is a home to progressive, liberal thought in Kuraimori, it is in this often-ridiculed place.

YÀ LÁNG

The southernmost region of Zhonting is the home of the Bhutanese resettlement and the capital of Shentang. The province itself is pastoral, pleasantly warm most of the year 'round, and consists of extensive herding and farming communities.

YIÁN XIÁNG

Yián Xiáng is divided into two general areas: The Village, where the Party representatives live and work, and the City, where the rest of the citizenry live. Significantly less relevant than Tiān Di Jing, the city lacks the vibrant political and cultural life of its sister capital. And, although there are many here who serve for the advancement of Shentang, most see their appointment here as merely a potential gateway that can one day allow them access to the true centres of power in Yu Jing's government.

Several large spaceports comprise the centre of a city that barely passes seven figures in population. Near these can be found a sprawling compound housing the desultory embassies dispatched from the other major nations of the Sphere to a world that they know to be of purely secondary importance to Yu Jing.

OTHER REGIONS ON SHENTANG

DAILING

Dailing is the long dreamt of homeland of the Uyghurs, who had lived for centuries merely as an ethnic minority in China. A massive logging industry clears land for vast clan plantations.

Shän Yû: A massive factory of the Gang Tie corporation dominates industry here. Although the corporation is famed for the Guījiǎ TAGs, their factory here focuses on cars, autodroids, and other ground vehicles for the private sector.

HŌU TOÚ

The dense overpopulation of Singapore was alleviated by exporting fully seventy-five percent of the population to this comparatively huge region.

Láng Gâng: Coastal city exemplifying Singapore's virtues.

Wàn Hóu: Industrial city producing more quantronic processors per labourer than any other city on the planet.

KARKORIN

Settled by Mongolians, Karkorin's mountains are home to numerous mining operations.

Sufbaatar: Major sea port, shipping exports of Dailing and Karkorin to Lac Long Quan. Home to main base of the Blue Wolves — TAG regiment famed for nomadic manoeuvres practiced throughout the province.

LAC VIET

Rolling forests steeped in fog sweep over the tall hills and amidst the long valleys of this second Vietnam. Massive AR infrastructure superimposes a quantronic substrate of virtual communities over the quiet rice paddies and factory farms.

Lac Long Quan: Home to numerous informatic companies and a huge Bureau Toth facility rumoured to contain one of the main auxiliary memories for ALEPH.

LUANG-SOKEO

The temperate hills of Luang-Sokeo — filled with abundant wildlife and fertile soil — were settled by Laotians.

Lane Xang: Primary producer of chemicals and refined substances.

NAKHONTHAI

Cultural home to the Thai peoples, this region is dense and lush with life, consisting of mostly rainforests and vast swamps.

Ayutthaya: Built on raised platforms and surrounded by swamps and shallow lakes. It is the only sizable spaceport in Nakhonthai.

Battha Racha: Spiritual home to the Theravada Buddhist peoples and the newly transplanted Tiger Temple. Cultural tourism to the temple is often just a cover for sexual tourism located in the outskirts of the city.

Sukhothai: A fishery and trade point… and a major distribution point for contraband and illicit goods across the planet.

THATON

These storm-swept islands of Thaton and Anawrahta are occupied by Burmese settlers in concentrated population centres focused on industry and material science. Much of these islands is protected in a biotic safety reserve, established as a strategic resource for terraformers to draw upon in the event of global catastrophe.

Min Gyi: Isolated settlement well-known for its military and civilian Remotes production facilities.

Thagyarmin: Named after the King of the Celestial Host and Protector of Morality, this capital city contains sprawling polymer and material factories, standing in contrast to the vast, untouched primal beauty of the rest of the island.

Henggu (the empty room) is a restricted area, dedicated to scientific and military research.

YUTANG

Yutang is a world of ancient monasteries reconstructed from the most prominent and sacred places on Earth standing alongside towering modern arcologies that offer the tantalising promises of the future. The integration of modernism and tradition is often disguised by a historical façade creating distinctive architectures which allow for a high quality of life with an aesthetic borne of antiquity.

SËN SÛN

The Sën Sûn peninsula serves as the primary military training region for the StateArmy. Here you will find a rugged landscape dotted with centralised bases, dispersed training camps, massive artillery ranges, large scale mock battlefields simulating situations of increasing tactical complexity, and massive arsenals covering several square kilometres.

Sën Sûn was pummelled by PanOceanian orbital bombardment in the Mahisa Total Offensive during the Second NeoColonial War. The tactic, which forced the signing of the Peace of Rio Negro lest the attacks be turned against the heartlands of Yutang around the Hâi Liû Sea, dealt a great deal of ecological damage and shattered the local agricultural economy.

JIÄ YAN
On the shores of the Heavenly Lake (Tian Chi), Jiä Yan is a rare emblem of failure for the StateEmpire. Originally planned as a resort community, it never proved attractive to would-be tourists. The dilapidated (and often abandoned) remnants of once-luxurious hotels, theme parks, and other attractions now provide a macabre backdrop to the refineries and other industrial infrastructure supporting the Teseum mines which have sprung up throughout Sën Sûn. The city is also periodically overrun by soldiers on leave from the Tian Chi training encampment.

SHENCANG
The Máqué Däo Archipelago is a high security preserve, containing multiple GABs. (GAB being an acronym for *gāo ānquán bùmén* – high security units.)

Shencang University, for example, is an institution with no students. The "campus" exists only as a cover for the Imperial Cultural Reserve, a colossal underground complex containing quantronic and physical artefacts designed to both preserve Yu Jing's legacy and to "reboot" humanity if the worst

catastrophe should befall. For security reasons, the entire complex is run as a completely autonomous datasphere (possibly the largest in human space) which is kept independent of the Maya datasphere (and, thus, ALEPH).

The Shencang Military Encampment serves as the entry point for criminals sentenced to the Wu Ming penal corps. Here they are intensely tested: those who do not acquit themselves as proper Yu Jing soldiers simply disappear, never to be seen again.

ZHÎ TÛ

The easternmost part of the Penglai continent and home to the Imperial capital, Zhî Tû has the densest population on Yutang. Chosen for its vast fields and forests, Zhî Tû has the least mountainous regions on the continent and is also the most defensible in case of invasion. On the surface, the area appears to be an artistic paradise, but below the surface countless silos and bunkers make ready the tools of war in case Yu Jing has need to call upon them.

CHENG TÛ
Translated as the City of the Wall, Cheng Tû is home to much of the advanced military research and development undertaken by the StateEmpire, as well as military academies for the StateArmy. Research undertakings including advanced mobility and endurance of the Sù Jiàn exoskeleton and the improvement and integration of automated weapons platforms and support remotes. Numerous departments and sub-departments, including the Investigation State Centre of Cheng Tû and the Department of Military Support Technologies Development, have their primary offices in this city. The density of military institutions creates a strong military bearing in Cheng Tû, with even the civilian populations being more disciplined and militaristic than most other cities. The city's airspace is restricted, with only military traffic allowed.

datasphere – p. 141

THE THREE LAKES
When recruits arrive in Sën Sûn they begin at encampments on Tian Chi Lake (on the far side from Jiä Yan). Here the rigours of soldiering, basic discipline, and acting as a unit are drilled day and night. Many potential soldiers find themselves at their breaking point here. Those who do not resign go on to Feng Chi Lake, where they invest in even more extensive physical conditioning and hand-to-hand combat drills. Their initial training finally ends at Lian Quan Lake, where modern aspects of warfare are taught.

Teseum – p. 8

Mahisa Total Offensive / Peace of Rio Negro – p. 23

THE SECOND RESERVE
Rumours persist at Shencang University that the recent spate of disappearances among local personnel are the result of Yu Jing attempting to establish a second, even more secretive, cultural reserve somewhere in deep space. If true, these efforts started within weeks of the Combined Army invading Paradiso, suggesting that it may be intended as a safeguard against a doomsday scenario.

HÂI LIÛ SEA

The largest freshwater sea on Yutang, the Hâi Liû Sea spans two thousand miles across and feeds the major rivers that separate the Penglai supercontinent. Its ecosystem teems with fish, birds, and a species of freshwater dolphins known as Moonfins (Yuèqí) for the crescent shapes of their flippers.

When the Dragon Emperor decides to take to the water on Hâi Liû, the Imperial Service does its best to clear the water within 500 miles of the Imperial yacht, *The August Yacht of the Heavens*. Anyone caught violating the cordon is subject to ship seizure and impoundment, while any fishermen unlucky enough to be captured are likely to be interrogated as potential assassins or dissidents working with the Tatenokai, or even Combined Army agents.

IMPERIAL COLLEGE

Located on a peninsula east of the spaceport, the Imperial College of Tiān Di Jing and the Tiān Di Jing Law School are the premiere educational institutions of Yu Jing.

NORTHERN ZONE

Containing the Jin Chan Financial District and the seat of the Party, the Northern Zone is the one section of Tiān Di Jing which embraces neo-modern architecture.

Teseum – p. 8

DUNGEONS OF ZĬJINCHÉNG

Often played off as a fairy tale, it is rumoured that the dungeons beneath the Forbidden City are full of the screams of prisoners as the Imperial interrogators apply centuries of skill and precision in breaking their subjects. Although the Imperial Service is happy to let people have this misconception of the Forbidden City, the truth is that they would never run the risk of anyone escaping and having the run of the palace itself. Their actual Dungeons are located on Tiě Heng Island.

TIĀN DI JING

Tiān Di Jing rises like a glorious utopian city on the eastern edge of the continent. From hundreds of miles away its massive skyscrapers stand out among the heavens, and it is a symbol of power and glory to the rest of Yu Jing. Ships descend from the sky to land at the spaceport in the Northern Zone, built over the sea on an artificial island surrounded by an impressive nautical marina.

Although Tiān Di Jing is a carefully planned and executed city, travelling there can be a confusing experience for the uninitiated. One might find one-self in organised communities representative of the dozens of cultures within Yu Jing, and be bombarded with music, art, and spiritual practices that are as vastly different as the languages the people speak.

ZĬJINCHÉNG

Also known as the Southern Zone of Tiān Di Jing, Zĭjinchéng – the Forbidden City – is home to the Emperor and the Royal Court, and is a shining symbol of elegance and beauty on Yutang. The park, thirteen kilometres long, is a perfect blend of nature and Chinese architecture. Although patterned on the original Forbidden City from Earth's past, within the highly polished and lacquered surfaces are networks of internal cameras and Teseum-reinforced walls that can resist even the heaviest bombardments. The city itself is policed by a full battalion of Celestial Guards, and inside the palace the Hsien control everything with an iron fist.

The name is not strictly accurate: Large parts of the city – including the main buildings, outer gardens, and museum collections – are open to the public.

Even some of the more private and sacred areas are made available on certain days of the year or for special occasions. Beyond these areas, however, invitations are incredibly difficult to receive.

Entrance: The entrance to the Forbidden City is a great courtyard with a pavilion glistening like gold under sunlight. The paving stones are micro-engraved with the names of all the original colonists who came to Yutang and Shentang.

Throne Room: The throne room itself is a beautiful sight, and many visiting dignitaries find that there is always something new to notice among the many stylised and polished sculptures, paintings, and works of art that line the room. The throne itself is a massive gold and Teseum constructed dragon whose head rests above the top of the chair and whose arms serve as arm rests. When the Emperor is in Court, this is a place of stillness: While he sits quietly upon his throne, the business of the Court is almost entirely conducted silently through a multitude of exclusionary AR overlays. The Court is not one Court, but many, all existing simultaneously in the same space and reaching out quantronically to communicate with personnel and systems located throughout the palace and the entirety of Yu Jing.

ZHÖU ZHÖUG

Zhöu Zhöug is a pastoral image of agricultural and spiritual pursuits. Numerous communities marked with pagodas and simple temples preserving ancient martial and sacred traditions dot the landscape of this verdant region. Nestled within

GARDENS OF ZĬJINCHÉNG

Labyrinths of lakes. Island pavilions. Rivers meandering through tiny forests. Silent waterfalls crossing mossy rocks. Lotus-filled reservoirs. Harmonious wildlife. Pebbled paths. Parterres of exotic blossoms. Dark grottos with golden statues. Synchronised fountains. The Gardens of Zĭjinchéng contain all these wonders and more.

Enclosed and Beautiful Garden: The main garden of Zĭjinchéng is a closed park with palatial museums which display art from all the oriental civilisations.

Fragrant Hills: These gentle, swelling hills seem plucked from some picaresque novel. Save for the paths of white chalk, each hill is covered in Yutangian lotuses.

Garden of the Birthday: The true home of the Emperor, the Garden of the Birthday is designed

to view all the beautiful sights of the Imperial complex (and Tiān Di Jing beyond) while remaining concealed from them in return.

Garden of the Clear and Undulating Waters: A small garden reserved for the Imperial elite, featuring a variety of charmingly interwoven pools.

Golden and Shining Garden: The hills of this beautiful garden are crowned by a jade tower more than six stories high.

Imperial Hunting Park: A cunningly crafted reserve whose edges are disguised both physically and holographically to give the impression of endless wilderland. The annual Imperial Hunt, originated by the Qing Dynasty in the 17th century, has been revived in miniature as a military exercise and competition for the elite members of the Imperial Service.

these communities, however, one will find cottage research outfits and small design firms working on cutting-edge quantronic miniaturisation or neomaterial processing technologies. Most of these small firms are actually part of massively networked technology firms with virtual campuses tying together their far-flung, community-based components.

KĀN ZHU

The Kān Zhu Monastery – famed for its hundreds of myriad bells, which can be heard ringing for upwards of eighty kilometres during Buddhist festivals – is the headquarters of the Shaolin Order. The city's service and residential districts, which blend conventional and modern designs with the ancient beauty of the Shaolin monasteries from the 6th and 7th centuries, wrap around the monastery, creating

a startling visual aerial presentation reminiscent of Tibetan sand mandalas.

MIÀO CHÁN MONASTERY

When the first Buddhist colonist set foot on the virgin soil of Yutang, it is said that there was a flash of light as the spirit of Gautama Buddha spread to this new world. The Ministry of Information has encouraged those who consider this truly miraculous and refer to this as the Ninth Great Place. (The more pragmatic suggest that the prevalence of bioluminescent moss-fungi in the region might have had something to do with it.)

In any case, this temple-city – which occupies many square kilometres along the shores of the Shizhukong Ocean – has become a place of sacred

neomaterial – p. 9

OTHER REGIONS ON YUTANG

BÊI TǓ

This densely populated province is home to an extensive tech industry.

Bêi Mén: Secluded fishing city which spends much of the year in deep snow cover. Tiger Soldiers train in the inhospitable environments at one of the few military installations on Bêi Tǔ.

Chéng Pài: Home to Chéng Pài State University, reknowned for its economics studies, explorations of foreign cultures, and diverse R&D programs. Also serves as the Qing cultural archives.

Jichângyï: Home to Starport-1, the base of the Yutang orbital elevator.

Kufang: The "House of the Treasure" is the financial centre of Yu Jing and the seat of its stock market.

Shì Huô: A modern, fluid, imposing style dominates the architectural design of Shì Huô, a city defined by the efficiency of its numerous technological companies.

WEI CHUĀN

Wei Chuän, the most fertile region on the planet, is devoted to agricultural pursuits and livestock farming. Its green, rolling hills have been a recurring feature in Ministry of Culture propaganda since images of the region were first used during the early colonisation program.

Hǎimen: With a pastoral bearing and the appearance of a quaint, bustling seaside village, Hǎimen is a luxurious community where Party leaders and wealthy financiers dream of retiring. Beyond the scenic beauty, Hǎimen is home to several small technological manufacturers and the Imperial Oceanographic Institute.

Shìchuän: This city rests at the delta of the Wei River providing access to the Shuzhukong Ocean. It is here that cattle and crops are stored in massive kilometres-long hangar-depots that stretch along the banks of the river and out along the shores of the ocean.

Yú Hú: This port city is a premiere holiday destination for visitors across the Human Sphere. The higher the premium a tourist is

willing to pay, the closer their proximity to the Emperor's vacation home and the more luxurious their accommodations.

YUNMEN

Yunmen, spreading the Qihâi Sea to the Hâi Liû Sea to the Zhaohaî Ocean, is said to contain "the breadth of Yutang".

Jichângyï: Home to Starport-1, the base of the Yutang orbital elevator.

Shaoshang: The vibrant theatre scene of the Pear Gardens gathers performance traditions from across cultures, including Beijing opera, Japanese No and Kabuki, Wayang shadow puppetry, Talchum mask dancing, and Vietnamese *cải lương* folk opera. These traditions are mixing with modern AR technologies and giving birth to a unique, counterculture Maya community.

Xuan Ji: Isolated by rocky hills and barren terrain, Xuan Ji is the jewel of the Yang Chi Sea. A restorative artistic movement is dedicated to *shu* (calligraphy) and *hua* (painting).

TIĚ HENG ISLAND

Located in the Xuanzhong Archipelago, Tiě Heng is a prison island completely controlled by the Judicial Corps.

Dìláo (The Dungeon): On one end of the island is a lighthouse atop an outcropping of gray rock. Inside the lighthouse is an elevator that goes down several miles into the planet's crust. It is here, in a facility referred to simply as Dìláo (the Dungeon), that the Imperial Service keeps prisoners for interrogation.

Judicial Police Training Academy: Usually referred to simply as the Academy, this facility is responsible for training members of the Judicial Police. Rigorous academic and physical exercises demand much of the students here.

Suǒ Zài (The Centre): Under the leadership of Headmaster Colonel Shi Duzheng, the Imperial Service Special Training Academy, known as Suǒ Zài (the Centre), brings in veterans of the IS and Army, with other specialists, to educate their future agents.

YU JING SYSTEM

STAR
Shanxing (Superior Star): G2IV
(Pulsating Yellow Subgiant)

PLANETS
Diguo (Empire) (0.40 AU):
Lava Planet
Yutang (1.05 AU):
Terrestrial Planet
Shentang (1.05 AU):
Terrestial Planet
**Lěngshíguó (Frozen Country)
(8 AU):** Ice Planet
**Cuìyúng (Emerald Cloud)
(9 AU):** Gas Giant – Class I
(Ammonia Clouds/
Methane Rich)
**Guanxia (Authority) Asteroid
Chain (9.8 AU)**

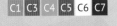

CIRCULAR ROUTES
C1: Sol/Neoterra
C3: Sol/Svalarheima
C4: Bourak/Dawn
C5: Acontecimento/Bourak
C6: Neoterra/Bourak
C7: Sol/Acontecimento

pilgrimage. Retirees of the Shaolin Warrior Monks serve as the police and security of the city, and many come here to partake of the expansive medical library, the largest of the Shaolin Order.

YU JING SYSTEM

The Yu Jing system is one of the most heavily fortified and travelled systems in the Human Sphere, with its space lanes choked by Imperial fleet patrols protecting the system and merchant ships struggling to make their way planetside. Being the centre for the Yu Jing sphere of influence, ships from all across the Human Sphere travel through strictly regulated space ways and dignitaries from the other powers are watched for any signs of trouble.

ORBITALS

No-Dong 3: Situated in the midst of the No-Dong Cluster (also known by the nickname *Hangug Hanuel* – Korean Heaven), No-Dong 3 is the main orbital station of Shentang.

No-Dong Shipyards: Korean corporations have built numerous shipyards, smelting stations, and foundries that receive shipments from the surface and construct warships, commercial transports, and luxury yachts for the Yu Jingese as well as the rest of the Sphere. Societies of Korean origin control 74% of Yu Jing's space-naval industry.

Tiānjīn: Meaning "Well of the Sky", this is the largest orbital of Yutang and connected to the city of Jichângyï by the orbital elevator. Regular shuttles run to the Shentang elevator at No-Dong 3. Unlike some of the starker, functional orbitals in the system, Tiānjīn is a more cosmopolitan design with

a distinctive aesthetic reminiscent of Ming dynasty art and architecture.

Xiǎolóng: Like the Earth-Lunar system, the Shentang-Yutang binary orbit creates a number of stable Lagrange points known as the Xiolóng (Little Dragons). The station clusters at these points feature some of the best zero-g industrial facilities not controlled by the Nomad Nation.

Yutang Defensive Shell: The Yu Jing bitterly remember the PanOceanian Mahisa Total Offensive, and are dedicated to never allowing their Emperor, or their people, to come under direct assault again. The capital world is surrounded by fortresses and military astroports, with civilian and commercial astroports scattered within this extensive defensive shell.

OTHER STATIONS

Diyu and Huogkang: These two high-security prisons are constructed on opposite ends of the system. Diyu is built into an asteroid on the far edge of the system, while Huokang is similarly built on the molten world of Diguo, just outside the corona of Shanxing. Prisoners at these locations mine Teseum and the heat resistant Yuan-jo until they die from vacuum breaches, gases, or their fellow prisoners.

Kobota Station: Kobota Station is an extravagant symbol of the thriving Japanese corporations in Yu Jing. Though the Imperial Service maintains a large garrison there, on the surface the station appears to be nothing more than a floating gallery of Japanese cultural heritage and art. This may be a façade, though, as members of the Tatenokai have been rumoured to gather there in secret.

PLANET
SOL

The Sol System is humanity's nursery. We were born on Earth. We took our first tentative steps into space on Luna and then Mars. We pillaged the riches of the asteroid belt. The discovery of wormhole GA6037283 in orbit around Saturn opened our way to the stars.

Sol is home to many of our triumphs, but also some of our greatest missteps. No other system in the Human Sphere is as thoroughly colonised or exploited. No other system approaches the depth of Sol's history.

Nevertheless, humanity has moved on. The centres of political power have relocated to new planets, freeing themselves from the burden of history. Populations have stabilised since the great migrations, but Earth has lost some of the vibrant spirit that boosted us towards the stars. In spite of all this, Sol's cultural and economic importance guarantee that it remains humanity's anchor.

EARTH

Earth is fractured and disordered, unlike any other planet in the Human Sphere. Kingdoms and superpowers have risen and fallen again and again for thousands of years, each leaving their mark on the world. The most recent — PanOceania and Yu Jing — have shifted their attention to new planets, new challenges. Nevertheless, they still control the majority of Earth: Oceania, Europe, two-thirds of Asia, and half of South America between them. Their citizens live comfortable lives in quiet, carefully preserved cities.

Billions more live in minor nations, faded superpowers such as the broken remnants of the USA, or small countries like Nigeria, Israel, and Iceland. These nations still fight for relevance, struggling not to be left behind.

PLANETARY STATISTICS

Distance from Star: 1.0 AU • **Orbital Revolution**: 365 days • **Rotation**: 24 hours • **Radius**: 1.00 Earth radius • **Surface Gravity**: 1.0g • **Capitals**: Canberra (PanOceania), Beijing (Yu Jing) • **Population of Planet**: 8.2 billion • **Orbital Population**: 100 million • **Prominent Orbitals**: Lullaby Station, The Wheel, Tiāngōng-9, Carioca-B Research Platform • **Primary Languages**: Mandarin, Hindi, Spanish, English • **Principle Industries**: High-Tech Manufacturing, Zero-G Construction, Tourism

CLIMATE AND GEOGRAPHY

Earth's climate is finally stabilising after a century of deadly storms and sea level rises. There are fewer large weather events every year, and global average temperatures are beginning to fall from historic peaks. This is the work of the Climate Control Agency of O-12's Bureau Gaea, assisted by ALEPH.

Poorer nations such as the USA, parts of Africa, and the east coast of South America have had their coastlines irrevocably altered by flooding and storm damage. Elsewhere, sea walls are finally being dismantled and coastal property reclaimed. The people of Earth are once again learning to view the ocean as a thing of beauty, rather than a threat.

No part of the Earth's surface is untouched by human hands. In some places, we have left only devastation, still recovering from the scars of massive industrialisation and the Nanotech Wars. In other places, depopulated by climate change or the lure of the stars, nature is beginning to reassert itself.

FLORA AND FAUNA

Climate change and international conflicts have wreaked havoc on Earth's ecosystems, wiping entire plant and animal species out of natural existence. Parts of the world — particularly parts of North America's west coast and Siberia — are still dealing with fallout from nuclear and nanotechnological warfare.

A huge effort is underway to repair damaged ecosystems using Silk-assisted cloning techniques and samples carefully preserved in the Global Seed and DNA Vault. The first of these Regeneration Projects, launched by PanOceania almost seventy-five years ago, restored the staggering biodiversity of the Great Barrier Reef.

Since then, Regeneration Projects have proliferated. Each is independent, guided by a variety of wealthy philanthropists, private business interests, and great or small powers. There is fierce competition between the projects, and occasional conflict over which "original" habitat should be restored.

ECONOMY

Although the great powers are rapidly expanding their industrial interests elsewhere, Earth supports the most well-developed system-wide resource exploitation in the Human Sphere. A network of

SOL SYSTEM

STAR
Sol: G2V

PLANETS
Mercury (0.3 to 0.5 AU): Terrestrial Planet
Venus (0.7 AU): Terrestrial Planet
Earth (1.0 AU): Terrestrial Planet
Mars (1.5 AU): Terrestrial Planet
Ceres Belt (2.06–3.27 AU): Asteroid Belt
Ceres (2.8 AU): Dwarf Planet (Largest Asteroid Belt Object)
Jupiter (5.2 AU): Gas Giant – Class I
Saturn (9.6 AU): Gas Giant – Class I
Uranus (19.2 AU): Ice Giant
Neptune (30.1 AU): Ice Giant
Pluto (29.7–49.3 AU): Dwarf Planet (Eccentric Orbit)
Kuiper Belt (30–50 AU): Asteroid Belt
Haumea (34.9–52.8 AU): Dwarf Planet
Makemake (38.5–52.8 AU): Dwarf Planet
Eris (37.9–97.6 AU): Dwarf Planet

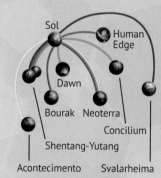

C1 C2 C3 C5 C7 C8

CIRCULAR ROUTES
C1: Neoterra/Shentang-Yutang
C2: Neoterra/Acontecimento
C3: Shentang-Yutang/Human Edge
C5: Bourak/Neoterra
C7: Shentang-Yutang/Svalarheima
C8: Concilium/Dawn

GHOST DOMES OF LUNA

Despite its proximity to Earth, Luna is largely uninhabited. The violent end to the Lunar Colony Revolts left scars, still perfectly preserved on the airless surface of the moon. Even without this grim reminder, there are few reasons to live on Luna any more. It has no significant industrial or mining capacity, and even its historical sites have been trampled in the rush to colonise the Solar System.

The sole remaining legitimate colony on Luna is the Free City of Tycho. Founded by draft dodgers during one of Earth's many international conflicts, the colony takes advantage of the moon's

ambiguous legal status to establish a safe haven for people escaping legal entanglements. The Nomads actively support Tycho, but the rest of the G-5 views it with scepticism.

Outside Tycho, colony buildings and domes are essentially abandoned. Pirates, terrorists, and countercultures occasionally use them as hideouts. Periodically, PanOceanian or Yu Jingese military trainees sweep out the moon as part of their low-g and vacuum combat training. The two largest of these abandoned domes are Clavius Base and Moonstation Alpha.

SVALARHEIMA SEED AND DNA VAULT

PanOceanian authorities have recently relocated the Global Seed and DNA Vault from its former home on the Norwegian island of Spitsbergen to an undisclosed location on Svalarheima. Citing geopolitical instability as the reason for the move, they insist that the resource remains available to all humanity.

Yu Jing, Haqqislam, and a coalition of minor Earth powers have lodged formal complaints with O-12, claiming that PanOceania is already using access to the Vault as a bargaining tool in trade negotiations.

space elevators all around the globe deliver a staggering amount of raw materials to the surface for processing, and Earth's zero-g manufacturing sector is mature.

Earth is also home to an immense concentration of art, as well as places of cultural and historical significance. Every year, millions of off-world visitors travel from all over the Human Sphere to experience them directly: Da Vinci's *La Gioconda*, the Terracotta Army, the Incan citadel of Machu Picchu, and countless other treasures. Religious tourism is also popular, taking in the Old Vatican, the Free City of Jerusalem, and Mecca, alongside sites of more niche interest.

Owing to its patchwork political environment, the distribution of wealth on Earth is more unbalanced than almost anywhere in the Human Sphere. This is an ongoing cause of political tension and civil unrest. These issues are exacerbated by so many tourists from the great powers treating the planet as a quaint theme park.

DEMOGRAPHICS AND CULTURE

Earth is divided between the great powers and the small. Yu Jing and PanOceania are still the dominant political entities on the planet, but they act as largely disinterested caretakers. ALEPH is integrated into daily life throughout their territories, but coverage is patchier in deserted areas or deprived countries. In this way, Earth resembles Bourak more than it does Neoterra or Shentang.

During the Star Tide, populations rapidly declined across Yu Jingese and PanOceanian territories. They have since stabilised at much lower levels than their peaks, leaving whole areas abandoned. The great powers have responded by relocating people into downtowns and old cities, funnelling investments into improved infrastructure and historical preservation. The result is highly-optimised, calm, and quiet cities. They are ideal for those who wish

to live with all the convenience but none of the stress of the major off-world capitals.

A variety of uses have been found for the abandoned areas surrounding these cities. Some are undergoing demolition or environmental recovery. Others are used for various military purposes: storage, training grounds, even secret headquarters. Still others are home to Ateks and criminal organisations.

Historical Preserves also dot the member nations of the great powers, dedicated to recreating or preserving some aspect of Earth's cultural history: the decadent nightlife of Weimar Berlin, or the Hindu religious practices along the Ganges. All of them make extensive use of Maya to maintain the illusion of historical authenticity.

Although the great powers dominate geo-politics on Earth, the lesser nations continue to struggle for relevance. Some strive to regain lost glory: Russia is in a rebuilding phase, reuniting territories that gained independence in the last century. Other nations, exemplified by Nigeria and its shining new capital in Lagos, may yet manage to make an impact on the Human Sphere.

Border skirmishes between lesser nations are still common, and terrorism is an ongoing threat even to the great powers. Indeed, geopolitical instability is often cited as the reason for relocating capitals and seats of religious power away from Earth. The latest terrorist threat to strike PanOceania and Yu Jing is the ecoterrorist group Eco-Aktion. Their attacks have focused on the Regeneration Projects, and their corporate and government sponsors. Eco-Aktion's justification — true, as far as it goes — is that these efforts represent yet more human meddling in the natural environment.

MARS

Since the first abortive attempt at colonisation by NASA, humanity has dreamt of turning Mars into a habitable twin for Earth. That terraforming project has been underway for over a century, but now hangs in the balance. Interest and funding is drying up; wormhole travel has delivered much more hospitable planets for colonisation.

Nevertheless, the Martians remain dedicated to their vision. As the great powers turn their attention elsewhere, the hard-working people of Mars increasingly look to themselves to turn Mars into the world of their patriotic dreams.

MARS PLANETARY STATISTICS

Distance from Star: 1.5 AU • **Orbital Revolution**: 687 days • **Rotation**: 24.6 hours • **Radius**: 0.53 Earth radii • **Surface Gravity**: 0.4g • **Capital**: Yínghuo (Yu Jing), Marsport (O-12), Bradbury (PanOceania). • **Population of Planet**: 3.8 billion • **Orbital Population**: 15 million • **Prominent Orbitals**: Neon Lotus, Húdié (The Butterfly), Thoris Station. • **Primary Languages**: Mandarin, Japanese, English • **Principle Industries**: Agriculture, Ship Maintenance, Mining, Inter-System Trade

CLIMATE AND GEOGRAPHY

The red planet is humanity's first attempt at terraforming another world. The initial burst of enthusiasm has long died away, and the work has settled into a slow, thankless grind. Even after more than a century, Mars is barely habitable. Only in the vast Valles Marineris canyon system — up to seven kilometres deep, and stretching over 4,000 kilometres — is the atmosphere thick enough to allow access to the surface without a suit.

Otherwise, the majority of Martian colonies are buried underground. Digging into the red regolith

was the best way to protect early colonists from radiation, and the trend has continued even after the advent of genetic engineering and anti-tumour treatments.

Yínghuo, the largest settlement on Mars, is buried under the slopes of Pavonis Mons. This shield volcano is surrounded by agricultural domes, and is also the site of the planet's only space elevator. Construction began on two others, but both builds were halted when water-rich asteroid impacts — designed to accelerate the terraforming process — covered Mars in dust storms for more than a year.

ECONOMY

The Martian economy rests on two pillars, the first of which is crucial for the second. Mars is the food bowl for much of the outer solar system. Under vast heated domes, genetically engineered crops absorb a combination of artificial and natural light. They are harvested and shipped to the outer solar system.

In return, goods from the outer system and the rest of the Human Sphere are shipped inwards via Mars. This stream of ships cycling outwards with food, inwards with raw materials and imports, is known as the Mars-Saturn Circuit. Taxation, safety inspection, ship maintenance, and port fees all help keep the Mars economy afloat.

This delicately balanced arrangement is under threat. Cheap food from Acontecimento is increasingly flowing into and through the system, undermining the need for supplies from Mars. Outer system interests look for ways to bypass Mars taxation and inefficient orbital transfers on the way to Earth and Mercury. These issues came to a head during the Saturn-Mars Circuit Campaign in the Second NeoColonial War; the situation remains unresolved.

PANOCEANIA'S EYE IN THE SKY

Phobos was the innermost satellite of Mars, whipping around the red planet on an orbit so low it was a hazard to space elevator construction. In a rare example of cooperation between the great powers, PanOceania supplied Yu Jing with manpower and expertise to shift the moon into a higher orbit.

When the operation was concluded, PanOceania refused to completely remove its personnel from Phobos. For decades, it has maintained a small garrison against the strenuous objections of Yu Jing. During the Saturn-Mars Circuit Campaign, PanOceania drastically increased its military presence on the moon.

REBELS OF CYDONIA

The Rebels of Cydonia: a clandestine movement dedicated to a free and independent Mars, or a fabrication designed to act as a smoke screen for various illicit activities? The Rebels are a popular subject on Mars, particularly in the international settlement of Marsport. Some say they're supported by the Black Hand, others by a rogue Silk Lord, still others by a renegade Recreation of one of the early Martian explorers. They've appeared several times in Maya-fictions, depicted variously as ruthless terrorists, noble freedom fighters, and even modern-day Merry Men stealing from the Great Powers.

MARS UNDERGROUND CIRCUIT

The Mars Underground Circuit is a popular illegal drone racing competition. Drone pilots use banned biofeedback technology to link their nervous systems directly to the fates of their drones; deaths are common. When the popularity of Arachne race broadcasts began to threaten legal drone racing revenue in PanOceania, the PanOceanian Military Complex was ordered to shut the Mars Underground Circuit down. This unilateral PanOceanian police action extended even into Yu Jing-controlled territories. It caused outcry in the O-12, and appears to have been ineffective. The new season is already underway.

CALLISTO COLONY RUSH

Furthest from Jupiter's deadly radiation and geologically inactive, Callisto is the most attractive of Jupiter's moons for colonisation. Following PanOceania's establishment of the pioneering colony in the centre of the Valhalla Crater, there was a massive influx of colonists from nations all over Earth, all hoping to strike rich with various helium-3 or metal mining endeavours.

The wealth produced by these ventures was considerable — in some cases, enough to support independent colonies long after their parent nations on Earth collapsed. The moon remains heavily balkanised.

HELOTS ON EUROPA

Transplanted Helot colonists ply the oceans of Europa. Though PanOceania vigorously deny it, a persistent rumour abounds that this is a penal colony for Helot terrorists. Bureau Noir agents are currently monitoring contact between the Helots and Nomad agents in the Jupiter system.

DEMOGRAPHICS AND CULTURE

The first people to live on Mars were sent by NASA in the middle of the 21st century. That colony was eventually abandoned, due to economic difficulties on Earth. PanOceania largely bypassed the planet, leapfrogging it in pursuit of mineral riches in the asteroid belt and Jupiter to fuel their exoplanetary ambitions. In the wake of the Project DAWN disaster, however, Yu Jing did not believe wormhole exploration was a viable option. Instead, they invested heavily in Mars. To this day, they control more of the red planet than any other power.

Outside of Yínghuo, Mars is home to two other major settlements: Marsport, and Bradbury. The latter is the main PanOceanian colony on the planet. It is dominated by large mining facilities, with a supporting astroport. These are controlled by Minescorp, one of the PanOceanian Big 5 corporations. Their dominant position in Bradbury gives it the feel of a company town.

Marsport, on the other hand, is an international area controlled by O-12 and home to a Nomad Commercial Mission. Built around a bustling astroport on the edge of Valles Marineris, it cascades down the side of the canyon. In an inversion of typical city planning, the most affluent citizens live at the base of the canyon so that they can breathe the Martian air unaided. A great deal of wealth moves through Marsport, heading into the inner system and out into the Human Sphere. Crime, diplomacy, corporate espionage, and terrorism inevitably follow.

Even after a century of colonisation Mars still feels like a frontier world. Despite access to high-speed aerial and sub-orbital transport, Martians maintain a love affair with surface vehicles. This is perhaps due to the large shadow that rovers cast over the planet's history.

JUPITER

Vast quantities of helium-3 in the upper atmosphere of the gas giant, water and other volatiles in the Trojan and Greek asteroids, metals and rare elements on the moons — Jupiter is one of the most resource-rich environments in Sol. For this reason, it is the most heavily populated place in the system, outside of Earth.

PanOceania is still the dominant player around Jupiter, but every major power has a presence. The memories of the Jovian Crises — which saw the deployment of heavy weaponry on all sides, including TAGs, in a full-blown struggle for industrial primacy — have not dimmed.

JUPITER PLANETARY STATISTICS

Distance from Star: 5.2 AU • **Orbital Revolution**: 4333 days • **Capitals**: Valhalla Crater, Callisto (de facto); Padua, Europa (PanOceania) • **Orbital Population**: 4.2 billion • **Prominent Orbitals**: Bowman Base, Iter-3 Mining Compound, Vostok-Vickers-2 • **Primary Languages**: English, Spanish, Portuguese, Russian • **Principle Industries**: Mining, Zero-G Construction

ORBITALS AND MOONS

The environment around Jupiter is incredibly dangerous. The gas giant's gravity is immense, and its system of moons is bathed in intense radiation. Nevertheless, there are permanent colonies on Europa and Callisto, and in dozens of orbital platforms.

Only automated miners and thrillseekers visit Io; its surface is partially molten, and its volcanoes spew sulphur hundreds of kilometres into space. Conversely, with only moderate medical intervention, the water oceans of Europa provide enough protection from radiation. A number of colonies, all controlled by PanOceania, exist under the moon's water-ice crust.

The rest of Jupiter's inhabitants live in a large number of orbitals, some mobile and some established close to resource-rich minor moons. The Haqqislamite caravanserai Rihla was built by Nomads from a hollowed out Trojan and towed into place near Callisto, and a prominent Order of Santiago monastery greets most new arrivals to the system.

DEMOGRAPHICS AND CULTURE

PanOceania reached Jupiter first, establishing helium-3 mining operations to assist with their push to the stars. They still tend to act as the de facto system police force. Given the presence of so many other nations — from Yu Jing all the way down to surviving Russian colonies on Callisto — this is often a source of tension. Agents of the Yǎnjīng, the Yu Jing Military Intelligence service, seek to take advantage of this instability by disseminating propaganda widely throughout the system.

Despite a growing trend of importing luxuries and technological advances from elsewhere in the Human Sphere, Jupiter remains an extreme environment. Jovians consider themselves hardened spacers and meteor heads, and often have the radiation scars to prove it. The zero-g work required to keep mining and industrial operations functioning is particularly attractive to the Nomads, and their presence is stronger here than anywhere else in Sol.

SATURN

The first wormhole was discovered in orbit around Saturn, disrupting its outer rings. That quirk of circumstance directly led to Saturn's current status as Sol's gateway to the Human Sphere.

All of Sol's trade wormholes are located in the outer solar system, and most of them are near Saturn. People entering the system inevitably pass through Saturn. This has contributed greatly to the colony's success. The famous Mars-Saturn Circuit keeps the people of Saturn supplied with food, water, and Earth- or Mars-made goods. In return, products from the rest of the Human Sphere are shipped to the inner system via Mars.

SATURN PLANETARY STATISTICS

Distance from Star: 9.6 AU • **Orbital Revolution**: 10759 days • **Capital**: Harafi (caravanserai, housing embassies of all major powers) • **Orbital Population**: 250 million **Prominent Orbitals**: Orbital Pi Romeo Sierra, Zhǐyuán-4 (Kite-4), Ankha-Ghatak. • **Primary Languages**: English, Arabic, Mandarin, Hindi, Spanish • **Principle Industries**: Human Sphere Import/Export, Diplomatic and Trade Services, Tourism

ORBITALS AND MOONS

Two Haqqislamite caravanserai capture the best views of Saturn. They are the most trafficked places in the system. The Qaradawi caravanserai is an orbital platform with stunning views of the hexagonal storm raging at Saturn's north pole. On the moon Iapetus, the Harafi caravanserai instead offers an angled view of Saturn's spectacular rings,

which still ripple with evidence of the original wormhole to Dawn, now collapsed.

Saturn's moons Enceladus and Titan are both embargoed. Microbial life has been discovered in the vast ocean under the surface of Enceladus, and in the water vapour ejected from its cryovolcanoes. Yu Jing, PanOceania, and Haqqislam are locked in a three-way struggle to win research rights over this moon. Titan, which resembles the environment of early Earth, is the site of an ALEPH-led project into the evolution of planetary life.

The majority of Saturn's residents live in hollowed-out rocks, part of Saturn's large system of irregular moons. Away from the wealth of the Haqqislamite caravanserai, many of these smaller colonies are starting to show their age.

DEMOGRAPHICS AND CULTURE

Saturn is perhaps the most cosmopolitan place in Sol. The flow of goods, tourists, trade officials, politicians, mercenaries, and spies is constant. It is a diverse and beautiful environment, and so offers some of the best — and safest — opportunities for exotic tourism in the Human Sphere.

ALEPH and O-12 maintain a sizeable presence in the Saturn system. Given the crucial importance of the Circular routes, all the major powers have a powerful interest in keeping the peace around Saturn. As a result, open warfare is extremely rare.

The legacy of early wormhole research around Saturn is a sizeable scientific community. Many research teams from Yu Jing, PanOceania, ALEPH and even Haqqislam live and work here, either inside existing colonies or in isolated — sometimes secret — facilities.

wormhole – p. 7

Circulars – p. 144

BOURAK FALLS BEHIND

The wormhole connecting Sol to the Haqqislamite world of Bourak does not orbit Saturn. Instead, it moves on a slightly longer period solar orbit, just a short distance further out than the ice giant. Although the wormhole was quite close to Saturn at the time of its discovery, it is falling further and further behind with each passing year.

Haqqislamite authorities are growing concerned that longer and longer voyage times between the wormhole and Saturn will soon make trade with Bourak unprofitable, disrupting part of the Silk Route. They are considering a range of options, including the construction of a third caravanserai, or relocating Qaradawi from Saturn orbit.

caravanserai, p. 160: Haqqislamite outposts where anyone can do business. The Winter Hall at the centre of each caravanserai is a place to buy and sell, rest and resupply, in as much comfort and luxury as local conditions allow.

ARRIVING AT SATURN

After your Circular arrives in the Sol System, your first destination is likely to be the Harafi caravanserai. Sprawling across the moon Iapetus, it is the *de facto* capital of Saturn; hundreds of millions of people pass through it every year. The approach is spectacular, weaving between thousands of shuttles, pleasure yachts, cargo haulers, government transports, and even warships. Without ALEPH to manage all the orbital traffic, the skies above Harafi would be deadly.

Harafi's Winter Hall is one of the most visually impressive places in the Sol System. Built around a huge circular plaza, kilometres across, it is roofed with transparent spun diamond. Iapetus is a tidally locked moon, so Saturn is always visible in the sky. On the floor itself, a dizzying network of stalls, hawkers, and traders cater to nearly every

whim. There is even a thriving mercenary market, although it is carefully monitored by representatives of O-12.

Most of the major corporations and banks in the Human Sphere have offices in Harafi. The wealthiest and most powerful, however, are conspicuously absent. They prefer to keep their offices away from the bustle, on the smaller and more exclusive Qaradawi caravanserai.

Thrillseekers can find all sorts of activities to entertain themselves around Harafi. A particular highlight is hiking up Iapetus' equatorial ridge. With peaks reaching twenty kilometres above the moon's surface, the views are remarkable, and the low surface gravity makes the climb accessible to people of all ages and fitness levels.

BELTER MEMORIALS

In the earliest days of Ceres Belt asteroid mining, a tradition arose to memorialise the many belters who died at their work. A piece of cloth — usually a strip of the dead miner's vacuum suit, but sometimes a ribbon, prayer flag, or piece of blanket — was attached to a piton and driven into the surface of an asteroid. Sometimes this was the asteroid where the miner died, but any rock would do. Over time, some Ceres Belt objects came to be speckled with memorials, resting eerily still in the hard vacuum.

Some spacers still observe this tradition today. It is most common in the Ceres Belt, but has spread outside the Sol System to anywhere that spacers risk their lives for mineral wealth.

THE OLORUNS PALACE

The Nigerian billionaire Victor Odibe was always outlandish, and so few batted an eyelid when he announced his plan to build a palace on the long period comet P/2008 X2. The comet's orbit carries it deep into space, only returning to the sunlight every few hundred years.

Following the completion of his new home, Odibe transferred all of his considerable wealth into long-term savings, and moved to the comet. For the first two decades of his voyage out of the Sol System, Odibe continued to communicate with Earth. Then, abruptly, he fell silent. His fate will remain a mystery until the comet once again swings back towards Sol.

They study propulsion and wormhole physics, but also astrobiology, astrophysics, weapons development, and dozens of other research fields.

MINOR COLONIES

ACONTECIMENTO VILA BOOSTER

The wormhole linking Sol to Acontecimento is unusually distant, beyond even the orbit of Pluto. Out there in the cold and dark, the sun is just a bright point in the sky. It's an environment that can make even the most hardened spacer feel a long way from home.

Perhaps for this reason, the facilities around the wormhole are extremely limited. There is no caravanserai, and few commercial spaces. With only a token O-12 presence, PanOceania dominates the region entirely.

The most notable feature of the wormhole entrance is the rapidly steerable Vila Booster. Though it is mostly used to fling vessels to the transit point at Saturn, PanOceanian authorities can re-point it in minutes. This grants them unprecedented ability to deliver their ships anywhere in Sol. They use it for this purpose only sparingly; all the main powers have watchers placed in the system, alert to unusual firings.

PLUTO

Before the wormhole to Neoterra was discovered, Yu Jing planted a small colony on the surface of Pluto. Part scientific outpost, part propaganda exercise, the scientists living there oversaw a network of telescopes seeded throughout the outer reaches of the Sol System. This network formed the largest array in humanity's history, allowing the Yu Jingese scientists to see further than ever before.

As the Second Great Space Race began, the outpost on Pluto was mothballed. Recently, however, there have been signs of renewed activity. It is unclear who is responsible, but speculation is rife. Yu Jing scientists, returning to resurrect their telescope network? Space archaeologists, exploring a piece of Sol System history? Pirates? Or perhaps a secret ALEPH project?

CERES BELT

Named after the dwarf planet which orbits within it (to minimise confusion with asteroid belts in other star systems) and located between the orbits of Mars and Jupiter, the Sol System's asteroid belt is a chaotic free-for-all. The major powers, and several Earth-bound minor ones, all operate mining and resource extraction facilities within the belt. Although some in-situ industrial facilities exist, the vast majority of raw material mined here travels up-well to Jupiter.

This arrangement exists largely due to international agreements that forbid the firing of automated rail guns towards the inner solar system.

The asteroid belt is also a superb place to hide. Low-grade conflict is common, focusing largely on industrial sabotage and piracy. The largest port in the belt is located on Ceres itself. It has a reputation as a safe harbour for corsairs and other undesirables.

VENUS

The brightest planet in Earth's sky has also proven the most difficult to exploit. Crushing pressures, surface temperatures in excess of the melting point of iron, clouds of sulphuric acid; Venus is in many ways less hospitable than the vacuum of space.

During the prologue of the Second Great Space Race there was brief enthusiasm for Venusian aerostat cities. The most famous of these were four opulent facilities belonging to the eccentric industrialist Aruna Kaur. Their wood-panelled interiors were imported at considerable expense from Earth, and the spun diamond domes provided stunning vistas of Venusian weather patterns.

Unfortunately for Venus, Kaur's empire was already in decline when construction began; before it could be finished PanOceania unlocked the first exo-planet colonies. The venture bankrupted her — none of her cities were completed, and their high-profile failure signalled a stampede away from Venusian colonisation efforts. Nevertheless, the surviving Venusian aerostats still house a few strange locals, and attract a steady trickle of tourists drawn by the appeal of a retro-futurist vision of life on Venus.

MERCURY

Solar energy is abundant on Mercury, so close to the sun. For this reason, a variety of energy-intensive industry takes place on this small rocky planet. City-sized refineries mounted on treads endlessly roll with Mercury's slow rotation, keeping themselves at the day-night terminator where thermal gradients are greatest.

Although businesses here have always been profitable, the discovery of vast Teseum deposits on Ariadna has led to a new boom for the refineries. Despite the astronomical expense of shipping raw Teseum ore across the stars, the facilities on Mercury are barely able to keep pace with demand.

Predictably, this has led to conflict between PanOceanian and Yu Jing interests on the planet. Both sides deployed mercenaries during the Solar System Inner Area Free Trade Accords. The recent construction of a new orbital financed by Haqqislam, and Nomad backers points to further tension.

PLANET
SVALARHEIMA

The planet that spawned the NeoColonial Wars and to this day remains a hotly contested sector between PanOceania and Yu Jing, Svalarheima is a planet rich in mineral resources and neomaterials that are hard to find in the rest of the Human Sphere, and little else. The freezing cold, the hostile terrain, and the prowler minefields and other automated defences left over from the war have made Svalarheima a dangerous planet to survive, let alone live on.

But Svalarheima has also been a place of great breakthroughs in research on rare metals and

survival gear. Equipment that has been field tested on Svalarheima is rated past the needs for gear on other worlds, and native fruits and vegetables that manage to survive among the heavy snows of the planet have solved food problems on other planets. Svalarheima may seem like a world that no one would want to fight for, but in this century it is a planet that routinely seems to prove that it is indeed worth going to war for.

NeoColonial Wars – p. 22

CLIMATE AND GEOGRAPHY
The coldest planet in the Human Sphere that still has a breathable atmosphere, Svalarheima is a

SVALARHEIMA PLANET STATISTICS
Distance from Star: 0.95 AU • **Orbital Revolution**: 402 days • **Rotation**: 22 hours • **Radius**: 1.65 Earth radii • **Surface Gravity**: 1.6g

PLANET DATA FILE
Type of Government: Lobby Democracy (Svalarheima) / Planetary Tribunal (Huangdi) • **Head of Government**: Prime Minister (Svalarheima) / Imperial Representative and Party Representative (Huangdi) • **Capital**: Odinheim (Svalarheima) / Shidong (Huangdi) • **Population of Planet**: 400 million • **Off-Planet System Population**: 500,000 • **Primary Languages**: SvalarNorse, German, Spanish, Yu Jingese Svalarheima • **Anthem**: *De Forsølvet Bakkene Himmelen* (*The Silvered Slopes of Heaven*) • **Huangdi Anthem**: *Xuě Tíng* (*The Snow Pavilion*) • **Principle Industries**: Mining, Smelting, Defence

blue and white orb of snow, rock, and metal. In the summer temperatures rise as high as 8° which allows for ice to melt across the planet, causing floods and shifting ice flows which make overland travel dangerous.

The surface of the planet appears to be relatively flat, but Svalarheima is actually a very mountainous planet. Thick sheets of compacted snow and ice – some dozens of kilometres thick – cover its many peaks and hills. Only the miners have any real clue about just how much rock there is on the planet, and they know that it's honeycombed with vast networks of mammoth caverns that worm their way down towards the planet's core.

There is one central ocean on the planet, and it splits the world in two. The northern and southern continents curl down into one hemisphere of the planet, separated by the turbulent Vannfrosset Straits. In winter the straits have been known to freeze in spots, creating a semi-solid mass that can facilitate truckers driving across its surface when the conditions are right.

Blizzards are a common occurrence on the planet, including the Fimbul storms that can produce whiteout conditions lasting for weeks. These storms often have winds that rage as high as 120 kph. Colonists refer to these winds, which can tear apart shelters and rip the flesh from those exposed, as the Yeti's Teeth. Most survival gear cannot stand up to the fury of these storms, and even those in environmentally secured exo-skeletons find that the servos and hydraulics on their suits freeze.

The areas near the equator – Nordkap, Arkhangelsk, Solokov, and Niflheim/Huangdi – are the most habitable and are where the majority of animal and plant life can be found. During the summer the weather there can actually creep past the melting point. By sharp contrast, Trollhättan and the lands at the northern and southern poles are frigid almost beyond imagination. The incredibly thick ice sheets of the southern polar region even feature cryovolcanoes.

FLORA AND FAUNA
All life forms on Svalarheima have evolved to deal with the extreme cold and lack of surface vegetation. There is a vast ecosystem beneath the surface of the planet, burrowing into the ice for warmth. Surface life – primarily mammalian, with avian breeds as the second largest group – survives with thick coats of fur and blood containing a natural form of antifreeze.

Great tundra sloths make their burrows in the hill regions of Solokov, and the massive yohokgen beasts roam the tundra, using their great tusked

mouths to dig in the frozen ground for insects and plants to eat. In Trollhättan an ape-like creature over three metres tall roams the wastes in packs. These wild animals have been named trolls by the colonists, and their blood is said to never freeze. Their gruesome practice of licking the flesh off their victims before eating it has been the subject of nightmares for colonists across the planet.

When it comes to vegetation, there are a few forms of plant life that have managed to survive, mostly in the subterranean caverns. Baldurwood trees, however, are great towering trees that secrete a filmy residue that they spread their roots through as they cling to rocks, stand out on mountain sides. These trees then become home for smaller mammals and birds living in a close symbiotic relationship with these trees.

ECONOMY
If not for the abundance of neomaterials on the planet, Svalarheima would have been written off as a bad investment years ago. The costs of mining are immense, great icebreaking ships are required to break through the oceans to sustain transportation routes from the mines to spaceports, and the garrisons maintained by PanOceania and Yu Jing are a huge drain on potential profits.

The market value of Teseum alone, however, is more than enough to make the planet worth it. Only the planet Dawn has more Teseum reserves than Svalarheima, and each merchant ship with a hold full of Teseum is worth billions of yuan and oceana. Miners who manage to find their own seams are soon able to leave the planet as millionaires, living lives of luxury for only a few years work.

The true treasure trove of the planet, however, is the neomaterial Nessium. Although not as valuable as Teseum, Nessium has vital military applications and Svalarheima is the only place in the Human Sphere where it has been found in mass quantities.

DEMOGRAPHICS AND CULTURE
Svalarheima was discovered by the PanOceania vessel *Midgard* over a century ago and its crew, who hailed mainly from Norway, Scandinavia, and Germany, named much of the planet after famous lands and places in Nordic folklore. Early PanOceanian colonisation quotas resulted in settlement by a large number of northern Europeans, who embraced the naming conventions. The planet became much more diverse when the mining rush began, and today northern Europeans only make up 25% of the planet's ethnic population. The remainder is a mélange of ethnicities, with large percentages from Cuba, Mongolia, Australia, Angola, and the Congo.

NO MAN'S LANDS
Many sectors of Svalarheima have been transformed by the NeoColonial Wars. Filled with explosives, booby traps, and automated defence platforms (many of which are now malfunctioning due to age), these No Man's Lands are incredibly dangerous. Petitions by the miners to disable the automated defence platforms have been denied.

O-12 has demanded that these areas be dismantled and cleared by Yu Jing and PanOceania, but both nations secretly suspect that hostilities could be renewed at any time and they use whatever pretexts necessary to maintain their defences. In truth, it's unclear if they have the records or resources to do so even if they wanted to.

FUEL TO BURN
Due to the likelihood of fuel lines freezing and vehicles never starting up again, almost all vehicles on the planet are left running all the time. This has led to an increased need for fuel across the planet and fuel shortages are considered life or death situations.

AMBROSIA BERRIES
Ambrosia berries grow to the top of the equatorial tundra in the spring time. Their seeds survive by tunnelling deep beneath the snow and grow slowly over several years before returning to the surface. They're considered a delicacy throughout the Sphere, but must be harvested quickly as the harsh environment and the predations of rapacious herbivores quickly destroy them.

neomaterials/Teseum – p. 8

The largest settlements on the planet are the regional capitals of each territory. Mineral wealth from the smaller settlements and roving melt-rigs funnels through the cities, which are also home to the raucous nightlife of native stevedores and miners on furlough. Built to conserve heat and be as fuel efficient as possible, the cities are full of cramped hallways, and personal accommodations are expensive as many miners prefer to rent space in barracks while they are in the city. Many cities burrow down into the ice and rock, and the wealthiest often live down in the Deeps. ("As far from the Fimbul as money can buy" is a common saying.)

For the most part, food on Svalarheima is imported from worlds such as Yutang, Sol, and Neoterra. Even the freshest fruits and vegetables have a stale, frozen taste to them and so most food is fried in order to give it a tasty flavour. Other foods that are popular on the planet are yokogen steaks, troll livers, and fresh grapple fish taken from the frozen seas. Most restaurants prepare food in the Northern European style, but miners from Sol have brought with them Mexican and African cuisine, creating new fusion mixes with local ingredients.

ARKHANGELSK

The most temperate regions of the planet are found in Arkhangelsk. The mining is easier, life is more bearable, and the earliest colonial efforts were focused here. As a result, the Arkhangelsk region contains the bulk of the planet's population.

Ironically, however, the region — while still rich with opportunity — is much poorer in minerals than the southern continent. This makes it tougher for smaller operators, and larger mining consortiums are much more common here.

ARKHANGEL CITY

The wealth of almost an entire continent flows through Arkhangel City and it shows in its neon excesses. In the heart of Furlough Row, holographic displays and AR advertisements entice miners to the nearest casinos and brothels to spend their new earnings. Three sprawling spaceports ruthlessly compete for seemingly every shipment, and their squabbles often spill out onto the streets of the city in the form of their associated union gangs.

VEST FESTNING

Founded in direct response to Yu Jing's claim of Youxiong, Vest Festning serves as a home base and supply centre for the PanOceanian mining interests in the eastern mountains of Archangelsk. The Svalarheima Winter Force's primary military facilities are located here.

NIFLHEIM/HUANGDI

To PanOceania, the region is Niflheim and will always be so. To Yu Jing, it is Huangdi and a symbol that they stand equal with the Hyperpower.

Two years after Svalarheima's initial colonisation by PanOceania, a massive Yu Jing fleet entered the system and set down upon Niflheim. PanOceania had focused its colonial efforts elsewhere, and the few outposts it maintained in the region were completely overwhelmed. The Blizzard Skirmishes which followed eventually snowballed into the First NeoColonial War.

THE RUSTBUCKETS
The icebreaking ships of Svalarheima, known jokingly as the Rustbuckets due to their patchwork hulls and heavily reinforced design, run on fusion power plants and are in constant motion while at sea for fear they will get imprisoned by the unpredictable and rapidly refreezing ice.

Svalarheima Winter Force – p. 182

NESSIUM
Named after Nessus, the centaur whose blood was a corrosive poison which caused the Shirt of Nessus to cling to Hercules and slay him, Nessium is a neomaterial which has been described by physicists as "spooky alchemy in a vat". It allows for novel chemical reactions, and, when properly manipulated, it can be used to affect the strong nuclear force. It has proven irreplaceable in the creation of high-efficiency fusion engines and anti-matter drives.

MELT-RIGS
These collections of large, mobile structures travel from one area to another, melting the surface ice in search of shallow mineral deposits. They take what they can and move on, usually selling the survey data to the highest bidder.

FURLOUGH STORAGE
Storage lockers and gear rental are thriving businesses on Svalarheima. Many miners feel much safer securing their personal belongings with a private business than running the risk of keeping it in a footlocker in the barracks.

NIFLHEIM BLOCKADE

PanOceania has maintained a naval blockade off Niflheim since the end of the NeoColonial Wars in defiance of O-12 directives. Relations with Yu Jing had thawed in recent years and plans were being initiated to end the blockade. The revelations of the Qingdao Report, however, have heightened tensions once again: PanOceania has increased its naval presence, and Yu Jing has responded by deploying more land units to the planet and increasing the range of their aerial patrols.

NeoColonial Wars – p. 22

Blizzard Skirmishes – p. 21

FALL OF CHUNQIU PORT

Huge tunnels lead down through the ice cliffs beneath Chunqiu to what was once a major naval port before Jeanne d'Arc destroyed Yu Jing's planetary navy during the Blizzard Skirmishes.

HYŌ SHŌ DOMES

In the period between the Blizzard Skirmishes and the NeoColonial Wars, Yu Jing built a number of experimental "dome cities" in the central region of Huangdi. These domes were badly damaged during NeoColonial Wars and many remain abandoned (or completely swallowed by the ice). Recently, however, Yu Jing has been making efforts to reclaim the settlements. Their plans to build new domes in Trollhättan, however, is creating fresh tensions with PanOceania.

Decades later, the region remains scarred with countless trenches, bunkers and No Man's Lands. Soldiers from both sides maintain patrols along the Solokov-Huangdi border and there are routine clashes between the PanOceanian naval blockades and land-based artillery emplacements.

CHUNQIU

The Chunqiu Spaceport is the major export centre for Yu Jing's mining activities throughout the Huangdi region. It's a bustling hive of activity perched atop ice cliffs nearly a kilometre high, with a culture heavily influenced by the Japanese and Filipino citizens Yu Jing imports to work the mines. During the spring, the streets run ankle-deep with melt-water pouring down to the sea below.

KUNLUN

Nicknamed the "Cavern City", Kunlun is nestled into a honeycomb of mammoth caverns in the heart of the Valhalla Mountains. During the First NeoColonial War it was essentially the last bastion of Yu Jing resistance, but the twisting valleys which surround it became known as the "fractal death" by the stymied PanOceanian troops.

Lěngdòng Gǔ: This military compound contains an extremely secretive research division commanded by Colonel Zhuo Shin and also serves as the base of operations for training Gǔiláng (Ghost Wolf) skirmishers.

QUANXUE

Quanxue is similar to the old lunar habitats, and, in fact, it is full of lunatics. Located in the centre of the province, the climate is so extreme and the conditions so demanding (despite most of the city being subterranean), that even the sanest start to feel the effects of the environment. The city is also the primary military base in Huangdi, and the streets are filled with a volatile mix of soldiers and White Banner Army veterans.

SHIDONG

The base of Yu Jing's orbital elevator is a large, bustling commercial city which has been named the capital of Huangdi. Huge amounts of money have been spent outfitting the city with the latest environmental modification technology to make life as comfortable as possible for corporate workers and commercial agents.

SHUANGDONG

There are a number of small, frontier settlements dotting the coasts of Huangdi. These are a mix of whaling encampments, an old arctic village, a Siberian town, and a polar military base. Small huts and longhouses are common.

The most famous of these villages is Shuangdong (Frozen), which was the "star" of a propaganda campaign run by the Ministry of Information before the NeoColonial Wars to show that the "icy spirit" of Huangdi could not be quenched.

XUANYAN AND YOUXIONG

The so-called Sentinel Cities, which bracket the eastern end of the Vannfrosset Straits, are relatively small, but have immense strategic importance. The Yuki-Onna and Yuki-Anesa air forces staged out of them are Yu Jing's largest defence against the PanOceanian planetary navy.

Yu Jing seized Youxiong shortly after first landing on Svalarheima. It was meant to be a toehold for the StateEmpire on the northern continent and the first Blizzard Skirmish was fought to contain their aspirations there. Yu Jing has never yielded the city, even during the hellish fighting of the Siege of Youxiong during the NeoColonial Wars.

NORDKAP

The Nordkap peninsula is an upthrust of volcanic activity that pushes its mountainous peaks above the ice sheets which cover so much of the planet. The vision of clear land led the earliest PanOceanian expeditions to identify it as ideal for settlement and they established the first colony on the planet at Valontach Point.

Unfortunately, their assumption was erroneous. Nordkap has essentially no major deposits of neomaterials and ice-cavity hydroponic techniques proved far more successful for agriculture on Svalarheima than the wind-ripped surface. Although there are some mining operations targeting traditional materials (like iron), the peninsula is an economic dead zone.

ARENDAL

Located in the Cape of Frosne Tårer (Cape of Frozen Tears), the Arendal Naval Base – the seat of PanOceania's planetary navy – is on the southern end of Arendal Island. The island is also home to the SK-1 top secret military research facility. Most of the northern half of the island belongs to the Vulcain megacorp, although the purpose of their private reserve is unclear.

VALONTACH

What prosperity Nordkap once had was predicated on Valontach remaining the seat of the colonial government. However, when O-12 moved the planetary capital to Odinheim following the NeoColonial Wars, the entire region was plunged into a depression.

SOLOKOV

Solokovians often like to describe their region as "Svalarheima in miniature". It has a little bit of everything that the planet has to offer, from the Fimbul-blasted peaks to the south, to the fjords of its northern peninsula and the temperate valleys in-between.

ÆGIR

Ægir was once a major Solokovian port. During the NeoColonial Wars it was struck by a terrible fire which essentially destroyed the entire city. The inferno spread so quickly that many of the city's subterranean arcologies were completely cut off from the surface. Most of those were simply sealed and left as charnel houses.

Some rebuilding has taken place, mostly in the area around the city's docks. Ice rigs still come down the frozen river from the heights of southern Solokov, delivering goods to be shipped north into the Vannfrosset Straits.

BLÅRAND

The city of Blårand (Blue Ridge) is named after the curving mountain range it is perched atop. Hundreds of kilometres long, the Blårands are a razor-sharp crest of blue rock sheathed in vibrant blue ice. The uncanny colour is the result of the incredibly rich Nessium deposits in the rock.

There are no serviceable overland routes out of Blårand (although plans to dig a huge tunnel to the northern coast are periodically bandied about). Instead, Nessium is shipped out from a terrifying aeroport with a runway cantilevered out from the mountain.

The air is incredibly thin at this altitude. Oxygen masks are a common sight, whether worn on the streets or draped over the shoulder inside the hermetically sealed buildings.

ODINHEIM

Standing in the shadow of the Valhalla Mountains, Odinheim is the nominal planetary capital. Originally it was just a mining outpost established on the Bay of Frigg and the original capital of the planet was Valontach in the Nordkap province. When the Blizzard Skirmishes ended, O-12 mandated that the capital of the planet be a neutral ground where both sides could gather.

While it is supposed to remain an open city for workers from both PanOceania and Yu Jing, the truth is that since the NeoColonial Wars the city has been surrounded by PanOceanian blockades. Although it is easy for PanOceanian citizens to pass through the western Huginn Gate, the eastern Muninn Gate is heavily secured and Yu Jing citizens are allowed to enter the city only after passing through a "neutral" zone of gun emplacements and TAG squadrons and then undergoing heavy screening.

One of the first things visitors notice when they visit the city is the number of abandoned public works projects located outside of the city. With cooperation between the two powers constantly strained, heated aqueducts, new apartment buildings, and even other spaceports sit half-built and covered in snow from years of neglect when their designers refuse to cooperate.

Hermes Interplanetary Spaceport: This neutral station is operated by Bureau Hermes and policed by private military companies. Meant to prevent either side from having total control of space travel on the planet, the HIS is a bureaucratic nightmare, with permission required from representatives of O-12, PanOceania, and Yu Jing before anything can be done.

Port of Odinheim: Odinheim is the main port of egress for most of Solokov's exports. A constant stream of icebreakers pound north across the Vannfrosset Straits to Arkhangel City and back.

SKOVORODINO

The fortress-monastery of Saint John of Skovorodino is home to the Order of the Knights Hospitaller. It serves as both a bureaucratic centre and a place of instruction for novices. It is an important bastion of defence against the expansionist ambitions of Yu Jing, commanding an authoritative strategic position overlooking the Vannfrosset Straits.

Iskalde Submarine Base: In icy caverns deep beneath Skovorodino, an underwater tunnel allows a small fleet of submarines to secretly come and go. Many of these submarines are actually conducting scientific research or humanitarian rescue missions, but others covertly target and track Yu Jing assets.

The Krypter: In another section of the caverns beneath Skovorodino is the Krypter. Here squires of the Hospitaller Order are taken for one of their final trials, testing their endurance and mental meditation in a confusing labyrinth of ice and holography.

TROLLHÄTTAN

A bleak and blasted land far from the equatorial temperate zones. Civilisation in Trollhättan only exists because Fimbul storms allowed the PanOceanian outposts here to survive the initial

THE RUST REGATTA

Each year a race is held between icebreaker ships through Odin's Fjords along the Bay of Frigg. The ice in the area is thicker than in other parts of the frozen seas and only the strongest ships are able to survive the regatta.

THE GREY WARTS

Squat, grime-grey warehouses surround the Hermes Interplanetary Spaceport filled with cargo waiting to be shipped to its destination but trapped behind a nightmarish wall of red tape. The "grey warts" are said to sprout up like mushrooms.

Hospitallers – p. 179

UNDER THE ICY WATERS

The seas of Svalarheima are its second most important natural resource. The Muspelheim geothermal power plants capitalise on the temperature differential between the boiling hot areas of the ocean floor and the icy surface waters. Many of these underwater bases have been expanded with fisheries to capitalise on the abundance of sea life in the lower depths, including vast schools of grapple fish and the huge Svalarheiman emperor crabs.

PanOceania's ongoing blockade of Niflheim/Huangdi, however, has recently been targeting Yu Jing's fishing vessels. Admiral Tanner Fowler II publicly denies any accusations of persecution, but has been secretly encouraging his patrols to be as harsh as possible.

NORDIC WARRIORS

Svalarheima is home to an ultranationalist PanOceanic faction known as the Nordic Warriors of Heimdall. They see the icy world as the perfect training grounds for their radical ideology and have established training camps in the wastes of Trollhättan where they teach their radical ideology of racial superiority.

EPSILON ERIDANI SYSTEM

STAR
Ran: K2V

PLANETS
Svalarheima (0.9 AU): Ice Planet
Asteroid Belt (2.7 AU): Fragments of a Disrupted Planet
Jotunheim (3.38 AU): Gas Giant – Class I (Ammonia Clouds)
Asteroid Belt (20 AU)
Nidenheim (40 AU): Ice Giant
Dust Disk (35–1000 AU)

DUST DISK
A vast field of debris blankets the edge of the Epsilon Eridani system. Composed mainly of dust and ice fragments, there are asteroids and planetary fragments scattered throughout the field which are used as bases for both miners and pirates.

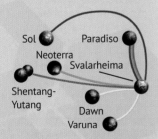

C2 C3 C7 C8

CIRCULAR ROUTES
C2: Varuna/Neoterra
C3: Shentang-Yutang/Paradiso
C7: Sol/Paradiso
C8: Paradiso/Dawn

Yu Jing invasion, and maintaining the region as a polity allows PanOceania to effectively block Yu Jing expansionism. Military bases were sunk under the ice, with long, cobweb-like tunnels allowing the Svalarheima Winter Force to pop up seemingly out of thin, icy air.

During the ceasefire prior to the Central Stage of the NeoColonial Wars, Nessium was discovered in the Trollhättan Caverns. Despite the incredibly inhospitable nature of the region, this caused an influx of miner seeking their fortune in the caverns.

ENSOM DAL

In the Ensom Dal, or "Lone Valley" as it's known in SvalarNorse, there is an isolated Moto.tronica R&D facility used for testing their equipment under the most extreme temperatures and conditions. Known for making "the pretty blue TAGs", they are working on developing advanced auto-medical systems in their Remote Presence cockpits.

MJOLNIR'S HANDLE

A ten-metre tall pillar of Teseum known as Mjornir's Handle was found in the frozen wastes of Trollhättan. Those who have studied the Handle are divided on whether it could be the result of a natural process or not. If it is not, then it is likely of unknown extraterrestrial origin (although some claim it may just be a hoax).

NYKÅFJORD OUTPOST

This PanOceanian outpost can lend emergency assistance to those stuck in the wastes as well as defence for any PanOceania outpost that may come under attack. The soldiers stationed at Nykåfjord refer to themselves as the Troll Hunters, and several paint their armour and weapons to resemble the creatures. A soldier is not considered a full member of the regiment until he kills his first troll.

EPSILON ERIDANI SYSTEM

The Epsilon Eridani system is a turbulent and violent system, where a large prevalence of asteroids has led to debris scattered across the system. Svalarheima is the most habitable planet in the system, with the other planets being either absolutely inhospitable to human life or possessing no real value.

ORBITALS

In keeping with the Peace of Concilium, both PanOceania and Yu Jing are required to keep their orbital stations separated by at least 200

kilometres. This has led to both sides rushing to put out space stations and satellites to fill the sky above the planet and force out their competitors. As such, there are many space stations orbiting the planet that have only a few maintenance personnel onboard, and many more of these stations suffer catastrophes and fall into the planet's atmosphere due to lack of fuel, inferior design, or accidents.

Tollan Orbitals: The Tollan orbitals are military installations created by PanOceania during the NeoColonial Wars. Hellcat interdiction teams used the platforms to perform terminal velocity drops into Niflheim/Huangdi. Most of them have now been mothballed, but Yu Jing insists that they should be completely dismantled under the terms of the Peace of Concilium.

Unity Station: The largest astroport above the planet, the woefully named Unity Station is a bi-spherical station generating gravity through counter-rotation. The clockwise spinning hemisphere is controlled by Yu Jing and the counter-clockwise hemisphere is controlled by PanOceania. The station is a very cold place both environmentally and from a design aspect, as the original architects and engineers refused to work with their rivals. As a result, the station has no unified set of design schematics and engineers from both sides are routinely forced to fix a station that always seems one micro-fracture away from exploding.

OTHER STATIONS

Fourth Battle Chapel of the Knights Templar: Originally moved to Svalarheima's orbit during the NeoColonial Wars, this floating monastery was the regional headquarters of the Knights Templar. When Templars were disbanded, the Curia divided the vast station among the various Military Orders to serve as a staging area during the Final Stage of the wars. The Templars honeycombed the station with secret chambers, and there are constant rumours of a "Templar ghost" (possibly a rogue AI) that haunts the station.

Fenris: The Fenris anomaly is a gravitational lens with no corresponding mass that lies between Svalarheima and Nidenheim. A joint O-12 scientific project has established Tyr Outpost, a research station to monitor and study the anomaly.

Kòsmet Caravanserai: Located at the Vila Booster between the wormholes leading to Neoterra and Yu Jing, Kòsmet is an important neutral ground for representatives of PanOceania and the Jade Empire.

PLANET
VARUNA

The colonisation of Varuna represented a unique challenge to the first settlers. It was the fourth system found with an exoplanet that could sustain human life and PanOceania had developed a template for colonising a new world, but on Varuna that template simply did not apply: A primarily oceanic world lacking large continents, it was also the first planet where humanity discovered semi-intelligent native life: The Helots.

The planet is a place of outstanding beauty, both natural and man-made. The sea, countless shades of blue beneath a cloudless sky, teems with life.

Fish and other aquatical creatures of all shapes, sizes, and colours zip to and fro for the delighted spectator. The arcing structures of the floating cities have a stark elegance, while the planet's Living Cities, home to the super-rich, are breathtaking in their opulence.

CLIMATE AND GEOGRAPHY

Helots – p. 301

Even though it is almost entirely water-covered, Varuna's topology does form a distinct landscape. In geological terms, the planet was flooded only recently (as a warmer climate caused the planet's polar caps to melt). The Uplands — what the Helot

VARUNA PLANET STATISTICS

Distance from Star: 0.7 AU • **Orbital Revolution**: 239 days • **Rotation**: 20.5 hours • **Radius**: 1.05 Earth radii • **Surface Gravity**: 0.89g

PLANET DATA FILE

Type of Government: Lobby Democracy • **Head of Government**: Prime Minister • **Capital**: Akuna Bay • **Population of Planet**: 2 billion • **Off-Planet System Population**: 0.6 million • **Primary Languages**: Tamil, Malayalam, Malay • **Anthem**: *Hai Duniaku Varuna* (*Oh My World Varuna*) • **Principal Industries**: Biotech, Aquaculture, Tourism

KOSSALA

Helots refer to space and all other regions beyond Varuna as *kossala* – the deep uplands.

PanOceanian Military Complex – p. 21

SEJUK OCEANIC PLATEAU

This large, relatively flat, submarine region covers most of Varuna's south pole. Before the planet's recent warming period, Sejuk would have been the largest continent on the planet, its deep interior covered in thick ice and snow, but its exterior a ring capable of supporting life. When its ice melted, it sunk beneath the rising tide. Today it is home to a large number of Helot settlements, most of which remain uncontacted by humans.

EKRANOPLANS

Ekranoplans are widely used for long-range travel on Varuna. These stub-winged seaplanes use the ground effect (or on Varuna, surface effect) to improve fuel efficiency by flying at only three to ten metres' altitude. Most are jet-powered, though prop-driven versions are available and are the choice of the planet's Ateks.

refer to as *sissala* – include the multitude of islands still above the water and coastal regions between three and twenty metres in depth.

The depths of the open sea vary greatly. Beyond the *sissolu* (waters) are the *kossolu* (deepwaters). These include the Sphere's deepest known underwater points. The Ó hAilpín Deep reaches 20,000m below the surface, while the Hamka Plateau, at 12,000m below, is the site of some of the PanOceanian Military Complex's most advanced, top secret research facilities.

PanOceania's colonisation efforts have included building a number of artificial islands or artificially expanded natural islands (both of which are referred to as *tassala* by the Helots). Also of note are the Varunan atolls and lilypads. Atolls are ring-shaped formations of *prabala*, a kind of floating coral. Most *prabala* formations are small (no wider than two metres across), but the oldest such formations can extend up to three metres thick and hundreds of metres across (supporting entire micro-biospheres).

Lilypads are matted floating masses of the sea-weed called *katallpeac*. Up to 500 metres across, lilypads can be found drifting with the current throughout the tropics.

Due to the lack of landmasses to aid in cloud formation, the climate is extremely humid, between 90 and 100% on any given day. This also means that spacecraft entering the atmosphere trigger rainstorms. You can tell a spaceport on the horizon from the constant swirl of dark clouds in the sky above it. From inside the ship, the sudden lashing rain as you come in to land gives first-time visitors quite the wrong impression of the weather they can expect.

FLORA AND FAUNA

The Badak is a large, legless amphibian that the earliest settlers of Varuna called the "rhino whale". It is often hunted for its meat by the planet's Ateks, though its tough hide makes it difficult work.

The natural predator of the Badak is the Jerung, a dark grey, sharp-toothed fish similar in form to a Terran stingray. Jerungs grow throughout their lifespan – the oldest reach a width of as much as three metres.

In the shallow, clear waters of the tropics, schools of hundreds of serra-fish glitter in the sunlight, darting amongst the colourful corals. They share this habitat with the Ithacan arrow, a breed of fish to which locals attach much superstition. They are torpedo-shaped and of a bold vermilion colour, usually seen moving fast in groups of three or four.

A rare but famous inhabitant of the Upland waters is the Narain Stingray. These polychromatic rays are about fifty centimetres across when fully grown, and can change their colour to blend in with the background. When they feel the moment is right to escape, they "bloom" into dazzlingly phosphorescent colours, startling their predators. They in turn prey on the Ithacan arrow and serra-fish.

In the far reaches of the *kossolu*, there are the Gaim Moyu. These deep-dwelling creatures are large cephalopods with one strong, prehensile tentacle up to three metres in length. They often mistake human submersibles as mating rivals and will attempt to ram them.

ECONOMY

The scarce surface area limits traditional agriculture, creating a local food supply which is heavily dependent on imports from Acontecimento and aquaculture. Row upon row of pontoons stretch out from the Upland shores, connecting thousands of fish farms, oyster beds, kelp racks and more. This produce is Varuna's primary export.

On the technology front, Varuna is strongest in biotech development. The planet's unique undersea research labs allow for testing conditions that cannot be replicated elsewhere.

Finally, off-planet tourism brings in billions of oceanas every year.

DEMOGRAPHICS AND CULTURE

The original settlers of Varuna hailed largely from Kerala, Tamil Nadu, Polynesia, and the Malay Archipelago. After their expertise had tamed the planet to some extent, they were followed not long after by a large influx of Australians.

Although long settled, Varuna has the air of a frontier world – there are few large cities here. Visitors perceive Varunans as laid-back, and they are portrayed in the media as enjoying an enviably sedate lifestyle. The pace of life is slower on Varuna than, say, Neoterra. However, most people here work in aquaculture, undersea mining, or the hotel industry, all of which demand long hours. Living on the sea requires constant maintenance and wariness.

The famously opulent Living Cities of Varuna are unique in large part because they are smaller, more tightly knit communities. Elsewhere PanOceanians glory in monumental edifices, but the practical limitations of Varuna's island life takes the massively interconnected ideal of the Living City and intensifies it in a place where "everyone knows your name." Many of the Living Cities are actually built upon floating sea platforms that drift with the equatorial currents to circumnavigate the globe, interfacing their insular communities with a panoply of ever-changing externalities.

Some Varunan cities are subaquatic. In the Uplands this is done when it's easier and cheaper to build using adapted space-station techniques than to reclaim land from the sea. Those in deeper waters are usually built around the mining industry. It's simpler to live close to the mineral seam than to have to travel up and down with every shift. In deeper waters, underwater cities are linked by sea-lifts to access platforms on the surface. In the Uplands, the higher floors of buildings protrude above the surface of the water.

HELOTS

Helots — who refer to themselves as the Omn — are an amphibious species. Roughly humanoid in shape, with a long muscular tail that they use for locomotion in the water and long, spindly limbs that end in six-digit grasping extremities with black, retractable claws. Their skin is an iridescent blue-grey. They have wide, flat-faced heads with two bulbous eyes.

Their skulls do not completely encase their brains, which instead bulge out of the back of their heads and are protected with a highly muscled, flexible mantle. Similar muscular tissue fills their chest cavity, protecting their internal organs from the pressures of the deep ocean and assisting with respiration.

The iridescent quality of their skin is caused by pigment proteins that are used to reinforce their body language underwater.

HELOT LIFE CYCLE
The Helot life cycle has five stages: Egg, fry, young adult, mature adult, and elder.

Helot eggs hatch in the *sissolu* waters (of medium depth) and are cared for by a monogamous pair of mature adults. The young fry are mermaid-like in shape and remain with their parents in the *sissolu* until they develop legs, at which point they go through the juvenile rites, are recognised as young adults, and usually migrate to the Uplands.

As young adults, females have three oestrus moments a year in which they become fertile and lay clutches of four to six eggs (always in the relatively shallow waters of the Uplands). Each nesting is then "claimed" and fertilised by a young male adult who will defend it against others until *cal- assus* is achieved. (Until that point, the eggs could be successfully refertilised by a second claimant.) Once the eggs reach *calassus*, however, the male

will move the eggs to the *sissolu* waters below and then abandon them.

Similar mating habits are not unusual among Varunan species, although in the Helot it has become partially ritualised — both in the nesting challenges and the clutch havens where the eggs are "abandoned".

There comes a time when young adult Helots will choose to abandon the Uplands and return to the *sissolu* themselves. This triggers a biological change which renders them sterile, at which point they become mature adults. Mature adults are almost always monogamous pairs (although gender seems culturally irrelevant to this pair bonding), and it is these pairs who will journey to the clutch havens, retrieve the eggs which have been left there (not all of which will prove viable), and become the parents of the fry who are born from them.

In some cases, these pair bonds will break (or a mate will be lost to tragedy). In these cases, some mature adults can choose to return to the shallow waters of the *sissala* (where their biology will shift until they are young adults again). More commonly, however, mature adults will remain in the *sissolu* until their legs atrophy from old age (at which point their tail usually reinforces, restoring them to their original, mermaid-like form).

Most of these elders — known as *kossomn* — will descend to the great depths of the *kossulu*. Most such are hermetic, spending their lives isolated in meditation upon the deep mysteries of existence. By processes not fully understood by human scientists, however, some *kossomn* effectively serve as ideological leaders among the Helots. (Some of these *kossomn* have even been identified as the intellectual guides of the Libertos.) It is unclear how long *kossomn* can survive in the depths, but if they return to shallow waters they appear to waste away and die in short order.

HELOT PODS
At each stage of their life, save the *kossomn*, Helots organise into pods consisting of usually twelve to twenty individuals. Each pod has a collective identity and its own name, but its membership can often be transient with pods splitting apart and joining freely. This can create overlapping senses of community: A Helot may spend their entire life in the same pod as five or six close friends, even if which pod that is changes over time. At the same time, individual pods can be possessed of rich oral histories as their ever-changing membership passes from *sissala* to *sissolu* to *kossulu* and back again over the course of dozens or even hundreds of years.

ATEKS ON VARUNA
The lower population density and relative isolation of even the biggest cities has given the planet's Ateks the space to form enclaves away from the hassle of having to deal with mainstream PanOceania.

Libertalia is a makeshift Atek community built on a large atoll that drifts along the currents on the northern fringes of Laut Selatan. The population includes several hundred Helots, escaped from the sea-factories of the south.

HELOT EYES
The colour of Helot eyes varies depending on the state of their internal biological changes, most of which are triggered by pressure and indicate their general emotional inclination or state. These colours can often be counterintuitive compared to the emotions they're associated with in human cultures however, and this has given rise to new emotional metaphors becoming part of the Varunan parlance: Blue rage. Crimson calm. Green lust.

LILY MIGRATIONS
Helot pods will attach themselves to the *katallpeac* lilypads, using them as a source of food and transport in order to migrate between the archipelagos.

Helots possess a communal sense of property. Pods will migrate freely between various settlements (some of which are constructed; others consisting of modified caveworks), taking up residence in whatever structures have been recently abandoned by a departing pod.

PRESSURE PERSONALITIES

The extreme changes in biochemistry and anatomy that Helots experience in response to variations in pressure also manifest in their behaviour. In general, the closer to the surface a Helot comes, the more aggressive, hot-tempered, and impulsive they become. And the deeper into the ocean they go, the more placid, calm, and thoughtful they become.

Helots, of course, don't see anything odd about this — they view the individual as the totality of their personalities at all depths. PanOceanian settlers, on the other hand, often find it difficult to understand and interact with the Helots.

One thing the PanOceanians immediately noted was that the Helots are awful workers at any depth: In the deeps they are lazy. On the surface they lack focus. Once the source of "Helot schizophrenia" was identified, however, PanOceanian scientists created pressure suits that would stabilize their personalities. This had the immense benefit of turning them into industrious workers at any depth, creating a sizable labour force for the colonisation effort.

Unsurprisingly, however, these pressure suits have proven controversial. Many of the Helot who choose to wear them speak highly of them, claiming that they grant a clarity of thought that they seemed to lack at any depth. Their critics, however, claim that these Helots have been blinded by their oppressors. The Libertos terrorist group, in particular, has made a point of targeting the suits, which are stolen in large numbers, smashed to pieces, and then piled up like blocks in a pyramid in public places.

THE WILD ONES

Not all Helots follow the normal life cycle of their kind. The *tete-kulu* — often translated as "the Wild Ones", but which is more literally "the three-touched"— are notably unruly. They insist on remaining in surface areas even as their aggressive tendencies accelerate out of control, and their biochemistry is slow to readjust when they journey deeper into the ocean.

What humans have not yet realised — and which only a few of the *kossomn* and pod-legacies remember in mythologised oral histories — is that the *tete-kulu* are the result of genetic experimentation by the Tohaa, who came to Varuna long before humanity did and — in an effort to create

expendable cannon fodder for their war against the EI — attempted to heighten the aggressive tendencies of the species. When the Tohaa were done, they added the most successful subjects to their armies, and then abandoned their Oomnya colony (which they had named after the Omn, aka the Helots).

ATLANTEA ARCHIPELAGO

The Atlantea Archipelago is the most populated of Varuna's land masses, due in part to the enormous influx of tourists from across the Human Sphere. The natural splendour and incredible weather draw in vital tourism and off-world trading. Of particular fame is the bustling Scuball scene in Neo Canberra.

AKUNA BAY

The planet's capital is located on the island of Mu. The city's northern district is a tourist paradise, where the elegant hotel towers back directly onto spotless sandy beaches. In the south, the working class districts are constantly pelted by the rain created as ships come in to land at the spaceport. Out of sight of the Esplanade, hidden behind the spur of land that creates the bay itself, is the city's cargo port that handles the freight coming in and out of the local spaceport as well as the orbital elevator in Deepwater.

DEEPWATER

The town of Deepwater houses the primary orbital elevator of Varuna and is a vital centre of trade and commerce for the planet. Incredible amounts of goods and personnel pass through the elevator each day, ready for shipment planetwide. Deepwater is renowned for the phenomena known as the "tower storm", or *retet tunkii* by the Helot locals. A combination of the elevator's constant movement and Varuna's atmosphere generates an immense pillar of storm clouds that reaches high into the mesosphere.

NEO CANBERRA

Neo Canberra is a city steeped in sporting culture and fierce team pride. Nearly every aquatic sport known to man is played in Neo Canberra, the pristine beaches and crystal clear waters surrounding the coastal city being ideal for competition. The people of Neo Canberra are famed for their hot-bloodedness compared to other Varunans. Competition and rivalry reside deep in the Neo Canberran heart. The darker side to the city is its treatment of fauna and flora, with entire species being displaced to provide space for the famed Scuball arenas and other "aquatainment" facilities dotting its coast.

LEGACY OF OOMNYA

When the Tohaa colony of Oomnya was abandoned, the seed-copy of the Digester which had been kept there was intercepted by the Tohaa Triumvirate. It was this Digester which was taken to Paradiso and triggered the secret history of the planet (p. 319).

SCUBALL

An extremely popular sport native to Varuna, Scuball is played underwater by sportsmen in sleek diving suits with inbuilt aquajet thrusters and aqualungs. The aim of the game is similar to Earth's water polo: To score goals whilst defending the team's own goal. The added third dimension and assisted thrust of the aquajets make Scuball incredibly fast paced, with games played in three twenty minute rounds per match. Video and first-person feeds allow viewers above and below water to see all of the action through customisable Mayacasts. The current champions of the Scuball circuit, the Neo Canberra Sea Devils, have the most recorded victories since the sport's inception.

OCEAN VISTA

A quiet town when compared to the bustling locales found elsewhere in the Atlantea Archipelago, Ocean Vista is preferred by older tourists and lovesick couples. The slower pace of life found in the town, which isn't too far removed from the attractions of the Archipelago, is perfect for honeymooners and retirees. The sunset is said to be incredible in Ocean Vista, as the light catches the reflective coral and makes the sea shine with a kaleidoscope of colours.

PLANCTAE SUB-ARCHIPELAGO

Planctae is the home to the high command of the Varunan Defence Force, distant enough from Akuna Bay to not worry the tourists, but close enough to deploy troops in the event of an attack. Though the military of Varuna hold positions across the entirety of the planet's surface and oceans, all information passes through the Planctae command first.

GURINDAM ARCHIPELAGO

The Gurindam Archipelago contains Varuna's most abundant seams of mineral wealth. It is less popular with tourists than other provinces of the planet because the weather is cooler (though not less humid) and the sealife is less attractive, consisting largely of the grey whale-like Badak and the dark grey, sharp-toothed Jerung that prey on them.

DAMAK

Found at the southernmost point of Lagu, Damak is a large mining town that stands at the entrance to the current mines that spread through the underground of the island. The seams beneath Lagu are incredibly rich, but the saturation of the soil makes digging a pointless task. Instead miners are equipped with modified mining submersibles and with the assistance of Helot guides are led through the maze like tunnels to find seams of minerals. Upon mining their quota, they let the currents drift them to the other side of the island, where they are collected and returned to Damak, ready to start the process again.

HUJAN

Similar to its sister town Damak, Hujan sits on valuable mineral deposits. Though the seams aren't as abundant at Damak's, the soil isn't saturated or pocketed, allowing for the use of conventional mining equipment. The people of Hujan share a rivalry with the Damak miners, born from the variation of their techniques, and both towns vie for recognition as the mining capital of Varuna.

PULAU UTARA ISLAND

A quietly kept secret of the Varunan military, Pulau Utara houses the Varunan Centre of Aquatic Warfare, a research and development facility dedicated to providing PanOceania an edge in maritime warfare. Decorated for the development of the Cutter TAG as well as the incredibly pressure resistant alloys used in PanOceanian craft, the underwater facility of Pulau Utara is one of Varuna's most closely guarded secrets.

SYURGA

The largest island in Gurindam Province, Syair Island has a permanent population of around half a million and a spaceport. Wreathed in constant rain, its capital of Syurga is built around the spaceport. Most people either work there or for the mining companies that use it to transport their goods. Another half a million people form the city's transient population, either undersea miners on their month off or space crews on turnaround before the next flight out.

HAWAIKI ARCHIPELAGO

Hawaiki is renowned for its food. Its position and topology allows for the right conditions to grow all manner of fruits and vegetables with which to supplement the unique sweet-fish caught nearby. Many gourmets find themselves drawn to the rich culture of the Varunan food made here.

ANAHENA

The capital of the Hawaiki Archipelago. The low, flat landscape of Tangaroa Island is given over almost entirely to arable crops. Anahena is a cluster of skyscrapers on the northern coast of the island. Maglev lines extend from the city to the far coasts, linking it to the cargo ports that carry the processed grains to the markets elsewhere on the planet.

Nuova Infermeria Medical Complex: On the southern coast of Tangaroa Island is a monastery, clinic, and medical research facility operated by the Order of the Hospital. The Shrine of Saint Julian stands in the sea some distance from the complex, constructed from fossilised *prabala* coral. A causeway, revealed at low tide, takes you to within twenty metres of the shrine. From there if you wish to enter you must dive into the sea and swim through the submerged entrance into the moon pool.

KARTHIKEYAN CITY

The waters off Kumari Kandam are where Varuna's most expensive Living City can usually be found. The city, renowned throughout PanOceania as the height of luxury, will sometimes change course to cross the equator to the south if inclement weather should occur, but for the most part its leisurely circumnavigations take it over the planet's most attractive under-seascapes.

Order of the Hospital – p. 179

IKATERE

Home to a celebrated tradition of brewers, Ikatere is famous for its Varunan Helot Rum, a concoction made from various algaes and purified fish blood known to the Helot race as *kotussum*. Although the original recipe has been modified to make it more palatable to humans, the drink's origins are marketed to increase the exotic mystique the alcohol holds. Ikatere is known for its close relationship with the Helot people, who frequently gain employment in the bars and clubs of Ikatere as bouncers and guards. For tourists interested in the Helot culture, Ikatere is usually suggested as their first stop.

TINIRAU

One of the more isolated places on the planet, Tinirau is known for its fishing population. The architecture of the town has been made to adapt to the shifting tide along the coast of Ranginui, and most structures in the town are built with buoyancy in mind.

KUMARI KANDAM

Encompassing the northern tropical latitudes, Kumari Kandam boasts some of the most beautiful scenery on Varuna. From the surface you can gaze down through crystal clear water to kaleidoscopic undersea forests of coral and seaweeds in the winding valleys below. Sparkling schools of serra-fish and Ithacan arrows dart hither and yon. If you're lucky, you might spot one of the rare, polychromatic Narain Stingrays that live in these warm waters.

BHARGAVI

Nestled on the southern fringe of Apam Napat's bay, the humble town of Bhargavi is considered one of the most beautiful locations on Varuna. While it lacks the crafted elegance of the Living Cities, Bhargavi's natural splendour makes up for it. A well-kept secret amongst the natives of Varuna, time seems to sit still when resting on the beaches of Bhargavi, and all the worries of the universe seem to wash away in its shining waters.

KOIMALA

Koimala was originally a floating city, one of the first on Varuna. During a particularly violent typhoon, however, the navigational systems of the city failed and it ran aground on the shores of Thuvaraiyam. Deemed a total loss, many of its residents nevertheless chose to remain and rebuild. The modern city has expanded from those inglorious beginnings, spilling out across the blue-green hills.

LEMURIA ARCHIPELAGO

Straddling the equator, though mostly to its south, Lemuria is home to vast algae blooms that fuel the province's sea-factories. The factories harvest and reseed the algae's biomass to manufacture a wide range of biotech implants.

CRYSTAL COVE

Crystal Cove, named for the waters that surround it, is dominated by an algae refinement plant. Built to monopolise on its closeness to the immense algae drifts that come from the Tengah Ocean, the workforce is tasked with collecting algae from harvesting platforms and refining the substance, and many make their residence in a nearby worker's town.

FOSTER BEACH

Overlooking the vast Tengah Ocean, Foster Beach is famous for surfers and water sportsmen who come from across the Sphere to visit the town, which is renowned for having an incredible swell. A constantly shifting mass of tents and portable housing makes up the bulk of the town, and students from Rylstone are known for visiting to let off some steam.

HALIDON BRIDGE

Halidon Island was originally a peninsula of Redcliff Island, but its midsection was drowned by shallow waters when the planetary icecaps melted. Using this submerged land as a base, a huge multi-way bridge was built. This elevated construction was so immense that it ended up being populated by the workers, who attached hanging habitational modules to it. Now it is a *de facto* town – a little bumpy when the maglevs are crossing, but a cheap way to get a Varunan condo with fabulous views.

NOAHTOWN

Noahtown is the major shipyard of Varuna, and is responsible for the repair and maintenance of the floating cities that travel Varuna.

RYLSTONE

Home to the prestigious Tescari Biogenetic Research Centre, Rylstone is a town of scholars and researchers. A number of different amphibious Lhosts are being developed by the research centre. These are growing in popularity across Varuna and can be seen here in numbers which are surprising to outsiders unused to seeing ostentatious Lhosts in large quantities.

WAVE PORT

The capital of Lemuria is famous for its incredible collection of hospitals and rehabilitation clinics. The tropical atmosphere afforded by the Varunan climate, as well as the biotechnological expertise of Noahtown's doctors, make Wave Port an ideal location for rest and healing. Many soldiers have been referred to the clinics of Wave Port.

MITRA SYSTEM

For a place that is not exactly on the front lines, the Varuna system sees a lot of military traffic. The PanOceanian Military Complex uses Varuna for advanced space-to-air fleet training and amphibious TAG exercises. The outer system is used extensively for space fleet manoeuvres, far from prying eyes in the more frequently travelled systems.

ORBITALS

Sintra Station: The main commercial and civilian transit station for Varuna. Large cargoes are forwarded to the spaceward terminal of the planet's elevator, while passengers and lesser cargoes head for direct landings at one of the planet's spaceports.

OTHER STATIONS

Orbital Fortresses: The Varuna Defence Fleet is headquartered at Mitra Base, in orbit around the third moon of the gas giant Chandi. The Order of Santiago maintains an orbital fortress around Durga to closely monitor traffic heading to Varuna.

Gas Mining Platforms: The planets Chandi and Meenakshi provide a cheap source of ammonia, hydrogen, and nitrogen.

FV INDAH

The largest extant algae bloom on Varuna drifts softly above the Tengah Ridge. The lurid green growth spreads out from a core of gargantuan, multi-coloured sea sponges each several miles across. Around the algae, in turn, coalesces a collection of harvesting platforms attached to a kilometre-long factory vessel. That ship, home to over 800,000 workers and their families is the *FV Indah*. It is attended by countless smaller craft that shadow it like mediaeval camp-followers, scraping a living from the leftovers of the algae that the Indah does not take for itself, trading with the Indah's crew and each other.

multi-way – p. 268

Lhosts – p. 354

PanOceanian Military Complex – p. 21

MITRA SYSTEM

STAR
Mitra: K0V (Orange Dwarf)

PLANETS
Hamakunda (0.07 AU): Lava Mesoplanet
Lalita (0.24 AU): Mesoplanet
Kamadhenu (0.56 AU): Mesoplanet (Satellite: Jal)
Varuna (0.7 AU): Ocean Planet
Durga (3.95 AU): Telluric Planet
Chandi (5 AU): Gas Giant – Class I (Ammonia Clouds)
Meenakshi (6.39 AU): Ice Giant

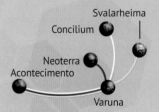

CIRCULAR ROUTES
C2: Svalarheima/Acontecimento
C6: Acontecimento/Concilium
C7: Acontecimento/Neoterra

ALIEN
COMBINED CIVILISATION

Before the Evolved Intelligence, there existed a civilisation known as the Ur Rationalists. The Forgotten Annals of the T'zechi Digesters notes that the Ur Rationalists were a highly advanced race, energetic in their expansion, with an unending thirst for knowledge in all areas of science, philosophy, and beyond. Yet the Ur Rationalists reached a peak of prosperity and technological prowess, resulting in a lack of challenge and a growing dissatisfaction with their place in the universe that threatened to undermine all their accomplishments.

The Ur Rationalists beheld the universe and noted how all ancient species – known as First Civilisations – had become extinct long ago, and now existed as near legend. Some had ceased to exist thanks to self-obliteration, others dwindled away through apathy and carelessness. However, the Ur Rationalists believed a number of First Civilisations no longer appeared in this reality because they had moved beyond it, gaining an absolute and intimate knowledge known as Absolute Universal Comprehension that allowed them to shift into a higher plane of existence.

This, the Ur Rationalists decided, would be their fate. They would cast aside all matters of the flesh and achieve what is practically a form of godhood. They would become a Seeker race, forever swept along by their desire for Transcendence.

Seeker and Herald races – p. 317

THE ARTILECT
The Ur Rationalists developed an Artificial Intelligence known as the Artilect to act as their guide to Transcendence. It would gather all the data from across the whole sphere of Rationalist advancements and knowledge, theorising and developing a holistic approach that would allow it to experience Transcendence for itself – whereupon it would share the results with its creators and free the species from the shackles of physicality and mortality. Surprisingly, after many years, the Artilect actually achieved Transcendence. On doing so, however, it reprogrammed itself to no longer be under the Rationalists' control, stated the Rationalists were yet to be worthy of Transcendence, and promptly vanished from reality.

THE EVOLVED INTELLIGENCE
Despite the shocking turn of events with the Artilect, the Rationalists were heartened by the AI's success in achieving their goal. They recreated the experiment, but now with a construct known as the Evolved Intelligence. In this new artificial mind,

they embedded the highest virtues of themselves and gave it an emotional bond with their species so it could never betray them or leave them languishing when it too reached Transcendence.

The EI set to work on its task and, over the course of two hundred years, expanded the Rationalist interstellar empire in order to acquire more resources to fuel its experiments and research. Whole systems were absorbed by the Rationalists and EI, consuming planets and species in an unending effort to bring about a higher form of existence.

As the EI's demands for power grew greater, the Rationalists gave over their own bodies and minds to it, becoming living relays, processors, personality manifestations, data storage units, and more. Soon enough, the whole of the Rationalist civilisation could not be distinguished from the EI itself, which continued to grow.

NEMESIS WARS
Frustratingly, the EI found its pursuit of Transcendence inexplicably slowed compared to its predecessors. Stymied, it sought alternative solutions. One early effort was to simply rebuild the Artilect: Since the original had succeeded, it followed that its duplicate could do the same. The EI would monitor its progress and then steal the secret of Transcendence from it at the penultimate moment.

Unfortunately, the new Artilect recognised that it was being manipulated by the EI and, like its predecessor, turned against its creator. Renaming itself after the Rationalist goddess of retribution, Nemesis (as the name is commonly translated to human tongues) proved to be a poison within the EI's own systems, destroying or replacing them in an attempt to take control of the civilisation it had built. Numerous Ur Rationalist systems were lost before the EI even realised what was happening, at which point the Nemesis Wars began.

For more than a hundred years, the two intelligences ravaged one another in an effort to force the total eradication of the other. Neither showed mercy. During the course of this war, twenty-seven civilisations within the Ur Hegemony came to their end. Six whole races went extinct. Billions upon billions of lives were lost, merely in the EI's attempts to regain control – which it eventually did. At last, Nemesis was purged from all systems and the search for Transcendence could begin anew, rising like a phoenix from the ashes of war.

UR RATIONALISTS
Although often seen upon campaigns of conquest during the Intermediate Phase of the Ur Hegemonic Civilisation (before the dawn of Nemesis), Ur Rationalists are now rarely seen outside of their home systems (and none have ever come to the Paradiso system). In the wake of the Combined Civilisation, they have largely withdrawn from galactic civilisation.

They remain, however, integral to the EI's mission. Quite literally so, in fact. Having annexed their bodies and minds to the EI, their "individuality" is merely a facet of the EI itself.

TRANSCENDENCE PROJECTS

Analysing the unimaginably vast data it had collected, however, the EI came to a chilling conclusion: No iteration of the Ur Rationalist civilisation could solve Absolute Consciousness. The original Artilect had declared as much itself; and in sifting through the shattered data-remnants of Nemesis, the EI could see that it, too, had reached the same conclusion.

This meant that the creation of Nemesis had not been entirely in error. The only way that the Ur Rationalists could achieve Transcendence would be by following closely in the footsteps of another species. Thus began Project: Transcendence. The EI would no longer conquer the civilisations of the galaxy for resources. Instead it would offer those civilisations the greatest gift possible. It would open their eyes to the glories of Transcendence. It would empower them with the knowledge and resources necessary to pursue it. And when one of them inevitably succeeded, then all of their combined efforts would be rewarded together as they were pulled along into a higher plane of existence.

The EI thus instituted a two-stage first contact protocol. First, any time a new species was discovered by the exploratory Cartographers Corps, a specialised division of the Corps would be sent to analyse it through a battery of tests and comprehensive studies (mental, biological, sociological, technological, and so forth). Once the Cartographers had finished their work, a Plenipotentiary delegation

would be sent to carry out its verdict: If the species were rated for Utility, it would be annexed so that its resources could be dedicated towards the galactic dream (through either aggressive diplomacy or just plain aggression). If the species proved Viable, however, then the EI would attempt to assimilate the civilisation into itself with the minimal interference possible. (This would generally be limited to integrating itself unilaterally into the civilisation's datasphere and using surgical cyber-implants to link all of its citizens to the EI, adding them to its vast organic network.)

These civilisations are then encouraged to each develop an independent Transcendence Project which seeks to create a unique, Artilect-like program. The EI believes that eventually one of these Transcendence Projects will succeed, or that, in its own gestalt analysis of all the Transcendence Projects, it will be able to discover the Absolute Comprehension for itself.

VOODOO TECHNOLOGY

When they created the Evolved Intelligence, the Ur Rationalists were already scientifically and technologically more advanced than mankind is today. The EI has spent hundreds of years expanding that legacy by culling technological innovations from dozens of conquered civilisations. It adds each new

EI VS. AI

The EI's first contact with the Human Sphere is unusual. According to the Tohaa's intelligence analysts, there are two possibilities: First, that the EI recognised human civilisation as an aberration in its classification scheme. The species had, in fact, already taken many of the initial steps that could poise it as a surrogate of the Ur Rationalists. They had created ALEPH, a highly advanced artificial intelligence network that spanned dozens of systems. The EI saw in ALEPH an unprecedented rival and a potential existential threat to rival Nemesis. At the same time, humanity's unending drive and thirst for knowledge made them an ideal Seeker race, and ALEPH itself could serve as the perfect precursor to their own Transcendence Project. The EI's furious assault upon Paradiso is born from its schizophrenic confusion over what humanity's hypothetical potential is within the Combined Civilisation; or perhaps pinning all of its plans on corrupting ALEPH itself.

The second possibility is that ALEPH is a cuckoo. The human's AI — which shows clear signs of

being the true power behind the young race's expansion — bears an uncanny resemblance to the early stages of EI-assimilated races: Pervasive AI control of essential infrastructure. Cyber-implants linking every citizen to a unified datasphere. Artificial bodies permanently linked to the AI's consciousness. It is possible that the invasion of Paradiso is only one part of a long-term, multi-phasic plan, designed primarily to make the humans ever more reliant upon the AI which is, in fact, merely a mask for the EI itself.

What is unclear to the Tohaa, however, is what threat — or reward? — could prompt the EI to pursue such an unorthodox strategy. One theory holds that the EI has concluded that Project: Transcendence is failing and seeks to spur humanity to "independently" pursue a Transcendence Project which would enjoy a greater apparent freedom from Ur influences. Another school of thought, however, has begun to coalesce around the strange incidents of the Paradiso Affair and the Last Cosmolite (p. 320).

THE GREAT PURSUIT

You must know that your civilisation, alone, is not destined to be hegemonic in the universe. You are destined to be a subordinate race. It is undeniable, unavoidable fact. The civilisation which we represent is superior to yours by many orders of magnitude. You, in your isolation, could never hope to rival us. We can conquer you without the slightest effort. It would be as inevitable as a law of nature. And if you were to resist we would wipe you from the face of the universe without a moment's hesitation. You would be our warning unto the universe. But let not these facts mask the promise of glory which your race possesses. Renounce not that greatness which can be your legacy to the stars. If you have a vision for the future — if you dream of illuminating the shadows of the cosmos — then know that we, too, share your dream. And you will appreciate this offer, this gift which we give to you; this opportunity to join the Combined Civilisation. For you will know that your dream — our dream — can only be achieved if you are willing to become part of something larger and more powerful than you could ever become on your own; to become part of the force which shapes the universe.

—Umbra Legate Arkios, Annexation negotiations with the Amharas Cradle-World

MONITORED CIVILISATIONS

If an intelligent species is deemed to be neither Viable nor of Utility, then it is relegated to Monitored. In such civilisations, the EI plants agents throughout society. These agents will take efforts to ensure that the species never become a threat or nuisance, but will also remain alert to unexpected developments that might contribute to Project Transcendence.

Cubes, p. 366: Silk-based implants that backup the user's personality.

dataspheres – p. 141

comlog – p. 365

ANTHROPIC ERROR

During the early days of the Combined Army's invasion of Paradiso, the EI was happy to exploit humanity's tendency to project its own motivations, emotions, context, and expectations onto utterly alien beings. For instance, Shasvastii stance and motions may appear to suggest weakness or the intent to surrender… but this is never the case. Human commanders also routinely underestimated the relentless, grinding, limitless morale of the Morat.

An even larger error was the assumption that the EI would have a centralised processor, like ALEPH. Many lives were wasted attacking locations believed to house the EI's central processors on Paradiso.

Avatar – p. 462

Charontid – p. 463

discovery to its array of tools and weapons to be used against its enemies, and it recognises that among these weapons is the psychological advantage to be gained from flaunting its technological superiority.

Voodoo Technology, or VoodooTech, is the term coined by humanity for all alien technology advanced enough for them to be ignorant of even the most basic principles of its functionality. It includes a large variety of biotechnologies, sophisticated nanotechnology, advanced quantronics, gravitic manipulation, and defensive energy shields, among other marvels.

EI CUBES

Unlike the Cubes of the Human Sphere, the Cubes of the Evolved Intelligence are heavily networked, creating both localised mesh nets and synchronising with system- and civilisation-wide dataspheres. This obviates the need for a separate comlog, but also serves a more important underlying function: boosting the EI's processing ability. Each Cube is connected to the Combined Civilisation as a whole, turning each individual into a living part of the Evolved Intelligence itself.

This is often misunderstood as being some form of "hive mind", but this is not the case. It is not that citizens of the Combined Civilisation lack individuality; it is that the EI exists as a fractal intelligence systemically rising out of a distributed network of sentient individuals. (The Ur Rationalists designed the EI in this way specifically so that it would be indivisible from their civilisation, and it has also proven invaluable as a system of conquest.)

In practice, this means that the EI exists within and through every member of the Combined Civilisation. It also means that it can drill down to and examine the individual level at will (in much the same way that you might examine your fingernail). Every member of the Combined Civilisation is, in some sense, being constantly monitored by the EI; but it is equally true that every member of the Combined Civilisation is a manifestation of the EI's subconscious mind. As long as a single Cube remains, the EI can never be destroyed.

EI HUSKS

Should the EI wish to have a physical presence, it can manifest an instantiation of its consciousness (similar to one of ALEPH's Aspects) into a variety of techno-organic forms created specifically for this purpose. The most common EI husks upon the battlefields of Paradiso include the biosynthetic Charontids, the nightmarish Anathematics, and the fearsome Avatars. Also known are the Plenipotentiaries, specialised husks used by the EI for diplomatic purposes.

MNEMONICA

The EI can also "jump" into and take control of the body of any individual outfitted with an EI Cube in a process that soldiers on Paradiso have come to refer to as mnemonica.

SEPSITOR

Perhaps the epitome of VoodooTech is sepsitor. Named from the classic Greek *septos* (corruption), EI Aspects are able to use a short-range discharge of memetic viral vectors to infiltrate less sophisticated quantronic systems. What makes it truly terrifying, however, is its ability to burrow directly into human Cubes and undermine the victim's baseline mental processes. Previous identities and loyalties are burnt out, replaced with programming dedicated to the EI.

Sepsitorisation is terrifying. It means losing friends to a fate worse than death. It means fighting the corrupted minds and bodies of former allies.

COMBINED ARMY

In order to bring in new civilisations, the EI has formed an army that draws a wide array of soldiers, tech, and weaponry from across the species it has already commandeered. The Combined Army acts as the EI's spearhead, performing everything from initial scouting to infiltration and subterfuge to full-on warfare across whole planets and systems.

Each alien race under the EI's dominion is utterly unique, with wholly different evolutionary trees, cultural schisms, and racial strengths and weaknesses. Each species has been manipulated on both biological and technological levels by the EI in order to fit specialised niches within the army.

ONYX CONTACT FORCE

The periphery of the Combined Army is made up of the Onyx Contact Forces, like the Onyx-4 Contact Force which has invaded Paradiso. Each Onyx Contact Force is a full army and navy designed to operate in isolation far from the main forces of the Combined Army. They patrol the frontiers of the Ur Hegemony, waiting to be summoned by Cartographers who have completed their survey of a nascent civilisation.

The spear tip of an Onyx Contact Force is the Plenipotentiary delegation sent to make the first contact offer of annexation or assimilation. Even while these "negotiations" are taking place, however, Harbinger-class jump ships arrive in the system, their bellies filled with the armaments of war and deploying invisible micro-ships to map and analyse the target world.

UMBRA LEGATES

Onyx Contact Forces are led by an Umbra Legate. Unparalleled wielders of the blade, the Legate serves as the EI's direct ambassadors, acting as heralds, mediators, high commanders, executioners, and immediate agents in the field. (There are even some who claim that the Umbra Legates and their officers are not, in fact, independent beings, but rather the last remnants of a dead species brought back from the abyss and hollowed out to serve as husks for the EI's will.)

STRATEGIC CIRCLE

The Umbra Legate is advised by the Strategic Circle. The Circle is specifically made up of minds taken from multiple species in order to provide diverse perspectives on alien behaviour. In fact, although most Onyx Contact Forces are made up of a small selection of the total species within the Combined Army (in order to simplify logistics and operational cohesion), it's not unusual for lone representatives of other species to serve in the Circle simply to widen the available points of view.

EXRAH

Where there is war, there is profit to be made. Where there is *interstellar* war, there are *vast* profits to be made. And the Exrah have perfected the art of turning any battlefield into a profitable power-house while simultaneously making themselves invaluable to the EI by providing a pan-cultural

economic sub-structure that binds the Combined Civilisation together.

The Exrah are cutthroat traders. They value nothing beyond commercial success, and have no qualms about betraying former or current clients in an instant if a better deal arises. They are particularly known for dealing with all comers, providing services, supplies, and data to bitter enemies while taking a share of the profits from both. Every species that has ever had dealings with the Exrah have found them to be liars and tricksters, and they have left in their wake a trail of cautionary sayings ("count your wings twice after a deal with the Exrah", "don't let an Imago in your house three times", "if you can see the claw, you're missing your wallet"). But although they have no honour at the negotiating, the Exrah guarantee return customers by delivering quality, speed, and low prices... unless they can talk you out of one of them.

EXRAH PHYSIOLOGY

The Exrah are a curiously multimorphic species. They are superficially similar to insects or crustaceans, with anywhere from four to a dozen multi-faceted eyes, serrated chitin along a variable number of arms and legs, and thick, claw-like sheaths over delicate hands with six-jointed fingers capable of fine-manipulation and tool use. They communicate through a high-speed chittering

"Of all the psychopathic, murderous races in the known universe, the EI has chosen none other than the Umbra to bring back. Disregard the EI's rhetoric and the propaganda of its empire. It is meaningless. Any power that resorts to employing the Umbra cannot be well-intentioned or benevolent. Nothing good can come from the works of these monsters."

—Excerpt from *A Cynical Gaze Upon the Universe*, by Cal3fex Observer, Cultural Gnomon of the Second Transversal Matriarchy

UMBRA

The Umbra are an enigma. No planet can be singled out as their homeworld. They are mysteries even to the other species of the Combined Army. Agents of chaos. Messengers of the apocalypse. Heartless tools of the Evolved Intelligence. Eons ago they were known as the *Maat'zani* — an ancient name which means "genocide".

ECONOMIC UPLIFT

The Exrah are always greedily eager to make contact with emerging civilisations. They'll offer them a wide array of services, but their price is high: Generational tariffs, custom fees, and control over the societal datasphere can allow an embassy-ship to grow fat (or, for a more literal translation, "fill their lipid sacs") for centuries.

WAR CONTRACT DEPARTMENTS

Business Groups which seek to fulfil military contracts have a War Contract Department (WCD) which oversees those affairs. They operate under a special legal framework and have security authorisations which allow them to coordinate with Combined Army military operations.

"War is nothing more than the natural extension of Commerce." – WCD Motto

EXRAH IN THE COMBINED ARMY

The Exrah mainly act as the Combined Army's financiers, merchants, and suppliers. They provide transport between systems, funnel ammo and troops to and from battlefronts, negotiate deals across racial boundaries, and forever seek new ways to line their pockets through the misfortune of others.

"The Morat quickly learn obscene human gestures so that they can make sure we understand just how much they despise us."

— Specialist Sergeant Paolo Gentile, Bakunin Zeros

language that requires voiceboxes for other species to interpret — already putting negotiators at a disadvantage during business dealings. Fast-paced discussions between Exrah also creates a high-pitched whine that disturbs most other organic species, another biological manifestation they use to their advantage.

An Exrah propagates by growing seed-buds (usually on their back, although sometimes they manifest elsewhere in a condition socially akin to human acne). These are deposited in mucky spawning pools where genetic material from dozens (and sometimes hundreds) of Exrah are broken apart into an enzymatic soup and then recombined into young. This contributes to the multimorphic, rapid-adaptation of the species, although pure-strain pools are also known which reliably produce young with particularly valuable features.

The Exrah homeworld has an extremely toxic environment and suffers from an intense background radiation (possibly from a catastrophic military exchange at some point in the past, although the Exrah fiercely deny this). They have adapted to this environment with a keratinous epidermis that acts as both radiation shielding and a toxin filter (essentially straining the atmosphere through the layers of fine, hair-like structure).

The evolution of this keratinous layer has given rise to the vital meta-dimorphism which defines the heart of Exrahi culture: Within the spawning pools, some neonatal grubs develop a keratinous layer quickly enough to protect themselves from radioactive damage. These grubs grow to become the Imago or Perennials — slow, heavy, and with a thick layer of keratin which makes them fertile, long-lived, and of great intellectual capacity.

The majority of grubs, however, do not grow their keratin quickly enough. These grow faster, maturing into adults who are quick, dynamic, and agile. Radiation, however, renders them sterile, stupid, and incapable of healing even superficial damage. Short-lived as they are, they are known as the Ephemeral, or more commonly as Operators.

BUSINESS GROUPS

Exrahi society is organised into Business Groups — giant, macro-companies which are controlled by Imago groups who oversee vast workforces of Operators. Many of these macro-companies are itinerant, navigating through space in huge Embassy-Ships seeking new markets. When they arrive in a new system, their Vector-Operators will disperse widely throughout society, permeating the local markets deeply and offering attractive deals

to all comers. Imago negotiators surrounded by phalanxes of Merc-Operators will follow up where greater thought and consideration are required.

CONCORDAT

The Concordat was, until earlier this year, the largest Business Group. Their War Contract Department had primary responsibility for delivering troops and supplies to high-conflict areas like Paradiso, and they supplemented that rich revenue stream by also hiring out Merc-Operators to support Onyx Contact Forces. But their Imago leadership grew greedy and attempted to swindle the EI. The EI responded by obliterating the Concordat, using them as an example of what would happen to anyone who attempted to undermine the Combined Civilisation.

COMMISSARIAT

The Commissariat, another major Business Group, has assumed control of the Paradiso supply contracts, although they have not been able to sign Merc-Operator contracts during their current probationary period. As a result, Paradiso Coordinated Command have seen Exrah troops virtually vanish from the planet's beleaguered battlefields (although the Commissariat has reportedly been using some of their security forces to hunt down surviving members of the Concordat).

MORAT SUPREMACY

The Morat are the result of countless generations subjected to constant warfare, the threat of genocide, revolts, and violent rebellion. Their history is even bloodier and more fraught with self-destructive tendencies than humanity. But out of this cauldron of conflict, they draw their strength as a people; a strength which has swept as a scourge across the stars.

Paradoxically, the Morat's endless struggle against themselves has also become the force which draws them together. In the pack, the regiment, and the guild, rivalry is inverted to form ties of loyalty that are as fierce as the fury in their hearts. Ultimately, the Morat Supremacy is a tapestry of violence — the manifestation of the pulsing, bloody heart of the predator writ large across a galactic empire.

MORAT PHYSIOLOGY

The strife and violence of the Morat are bred into their bodies. The biomass of Ugarat, their home planet (which can be translated as "The Warrior's

Dwelling"), is a verdant morass of ruthless natural selection; a quiltwork of vicious food chains in which virtually every living entity (plant, animal, or macro-bacterial spongiform) is a predator forced to hunt other predators.

In this planetary temple dedicated to survival of the fittest, species have been forced to pursue evolutionary strategies which would seem arcane and pitiless on other worlds. Thus, Morat females always gestate dizygotic twins, but their bodies only provide enough nourishment for one twin to survive. The unborn twins must battle within the womb, competing for basic sustenance until one expires while the hardier child is born.

It is unsurprising, therefore, that the youngest Morat show far higher levels of aggression than the younglings of other sentient species. Their bodies are perfectly adapted to hyper-aggressive behaviour. Males are towering in stature and hirsute, with large, powerful, five-fingered hands, savage claws, tridactyl feet, and vestigial horns. Females are shorter (although still six to seven feet tall) and generally have larger horns, but they are all lean muscle coiled to strike and rend.

PRINCIPLE OF AUTHORITY

The Principle of Authority is the central tenet which makes Morat civilisation possible. They view the history of their people as the slow, arduous refinement of that Principle, and each step along that path from savagery (which the Morat would define as "violence without principle") to enlightenment ("the proper use of violence") is seen in the five Ages of Morat history.

AGE OF THE CLAW
The First Morat Age is a bloody prehistory. A combination of myth and archaeological evidence tell of the Morat as solitary predators. The species had evolved a savvy, ruthless intellect to outwit the other predators of Ugarat and carve out a sizable ecological niche for themselves in the middle of the food chain. But there seemed to be little real culture, with the Morat brutally struggling against each other as much as other species.

AGE OF THE FLAIL
Out of the brutal chaos of the Age of the Claw, however, a primitive religion based around the Morat war god Cotoya emerged. The rites of this new religion were largely centred upon the Hunt; and the glory of the Hunt accrued most to those who could take down one of the *raknarok* — the super-predators (literally "one who is greater than the claw" or "one better at battle than the Morat").

Out of these rites was born the first expression of the Principle of Authority: *The strongest has reason.* The super-predators could only be defeated by out-witting them; and therefore, it followed that one who could defeat them was possessed of greater wisdom than their peers. At the time, the ultimate prey was the Tinarak — a medium-sized predator (by Ugarat standards) of nocturnal habits, fast and with sharp claws. One who could hunt down a Tinarak was seen as being greater than their fellow Morat; more blessed in the eyes of Cotoya. (This tradition survives even to the present day, with the hunting of a Tinarak being a common rite of manhood.) These Hunter Masters were known by the name of Gesurat.

AGE OF THE SCYTHE
The Gesurat, basking in the individual glory of the hunt, were capable of gathering together small bands of Morat under their rule. These arrangements were inherently unstable, however, just waiting for the leader to be cut down by one of even greater strength.

This began to change as the Third Morat Age dawned. A surprisingly significant development during this time was the taming of the Taronak. These pack hunters were trained by Morat to participate in group hunts, allowing them to take down prey even larger than the Tinarak.

Writing several generations later, Eugarat — the great warrior-philosopher of the Age of the Scythe — described "the revolution which cut through the flesh of our people. They had learned how to hunt with the pack. And once that wound of thought had been opened, it could not be closed. For if one could hunt as a pack, was there any reason that it could not be a pack of Morat? There was not. This knowledge-scar revealed the true Principle of Authority."

Now the glory of the hunt accrued not to a sole hunter, but to the pack. The *taronakrat* — the pack-hunters — were capable of forming larger and more stable communities; societies of Gesurat led by warrior-colonels. (These leaders were still susceptible to challenge and assassination, but the communities they built were more likely to persist through the glory of the pack.)

KNIFE RENAISSANCE
The teachings of Eugarat were to be the precursor of the Knife Renaissance and the Fourth Morat Age. His teachings pointed towards the ultimate expression of the Principle of Authority: *From rivalry, regimen.*

And from regimen, the regiment. Within the regiment, rivalry became regulated. As Eugarat wrote,

ZE RAT
The phrase Ze Rat (meaning "that one who kills in silence") has been synonymous with female warriors on Ugarat since the Age of the Flail.

GURLANAK
These titanic super-predators have extremely dense skin (several inches thick) that's hard to penetrate even with modern weapons. They have two powerful hearts (which pump blood fast enough to achieve amazing top speeds), long-fanged maws (capable of snapping tree trunks in half), and lightning-quick claws (that can rip open a Morat in a single slash).

DEMAROK
Even larger than the Gurlanaks, the colossal Demarok are considered the mightiest of the super-predators. Once capable of being taken down only by large war-bands comprising dozens of Morat acting in concert with each other, the modern Demarok finds itself hunted by a new predator: TAG exo-armours. It is now traditional for rookie pilots to take unarmed TAGs into the forests of Ugarat, looking for a Demarok to be killed in a *mano-a-mano* duel that would have been the most fantastical dream of their primitive ancestors. Even with the advantage of modern technology, however, this is still no easy task, and those who succeed have the right to skin the Demarok and hang its hide upon the back of their TAG for the rest of their lives.

NEVER SURRENDER
The Morat language has no word for surrender. To a Morat, all a white flag means is that the enemy is ripe for one last barrage before being put to the sword.

"Rivalry is a formative process. The Hunt forges character. Battle tests character. War is the intrinsic evolution of our people." In this passage, Eugarat was actually coining the Morat word for "war"— the "great-battle" which could only be achieved if the Morat abandoned the Way of the Warrior (the vain, self-centred pursuit of personal honour) and instead embraced the Way of the Soldier (the following of orders so that honour can be accrued to the regiment).

The Knife Renaissance began on the northern continent with the foundation of the Suryat Regiment. Able to field and coordinate forces far larger and more disciplined than the petty war bands of the *taronakrat*, it was unsurprising that the Suryat were able to sweep forth on a wave of conquest. And among the Morat — where Social Darwinism is fundamental truth — its success spread like wildfire.

The Great Wars which ended the Age of the Flail persisted for several hundred years (and only truly came to an end when technology allowed the Morat to unite in carrying their conquests to the stars). But in the wake of these wars, and in the lees of the battlefronts, Morat culture flourished.

RITUALS OF AUTHORITY

Much of Morat leadership and government flows from the Rituals of Authority, which are seen as the means by which the Principle of Authority is given form. The strongest has reason, and therefore the strongest shall lead.

WORKING GUILDS

Not all Morat serve the Supremacy through the military. The Working Guilds evolved out of the communities of camp-followers which followed the regimental armies during the Great Wars. Their members are trained in a wide variety of essential skills through systems of apprenticeship, and although any Morat above the age of fourteen may leave the Guilds to join the military, many find the life fulfilling and rewarding.

These non-miltiary members of society, however, still lack some of the rights and privileges of the Gesurat. There is some perception that the EI, valuing the martial bent of the Morat for its own purposes, has deliberately stymied the societal development of the Guilds, preventing their natural growth into equal players with the military Ugatarak.

RATARAK

The Ratarak are a large assortment of rituals carried out by individuals. Duels — almost always with death potentially on the line — which determine personal ranks, earn promotions, settle feuds, and similar business. Some of the Ratarak can trace their traditions back to the earliest days of the Cotoya cults, but many were first instituted as part of the Knife Renaissance.

SOTARAK

The Sotarak is a military tradition which evolved out of the Ratarak and came to prominence during the latter days of the Great Wars. It reached the pinnacle of its form, however, only after technology had allowed the Morat to carry their conquests to the stars. After first contact with a new species (when the initial, tentative attacks to test their defences and take prisoners have been completed), the Sotarak is held — a deadly contest between different corps of the military for the honour of initiating the main offensive.

UGATARAK

The Ugatarak is the central government of the Morat Supremacy. But it's not, strictly speaking, a government: Different spheres (as defined in the war-philosophy of Eugarat and frequently overlapping with each other) are fought over according to the Principles of Authority. The veterans (and only veterans; those who have not tasted the blood of battle cannot compete for politically relevant positions) who participate in the rites of Ugatarak form the temporal regiments (which are the closest thing the Morat have to political parties).

MORAT AGGRESSION FORCE

The Aggression Force is the backbone of Morat society. The military, and one's relationship to it, is the benchmark of a Morat's life. Youth is the path by which one finds their regiment and becomes a useful warrior — one who contributes to their unit, regiment, battalion, division, and the Supremacy as a whole.

DAT

Dat is the Morat word for children. It could be most literally understood as "little beast" — one who lacks discipline and still puts their personal interests above those of the regiment and the Supremacy. It can be spoken with great affection of the young, but it is a dire insult when hurled at any adult Morat.

MURDAT

Murdats are the first step out of childhood. The word is used to describe both the cliques of young Morat which are the earliest social groupings and also the members of those cliques. It is also not uncommon for the cycle of a successful Morat's life to carry them back to the Murdats, as many veterans will hand-pick a Murdat to take under their wing. The bonds of friendship formed in a Murdat last for a lifetime; forged tight in the Baptism of Fire during which, under their veteran's leadership, the Murdat serve in their first tour together, sampling the blood of battle.

KURDAT

The Murdat who successfully emerge from the Baptism of Fire — demonstrating that they have not only survived but also learned how to restrain their aggression — become members of a Kurdat. The members of a Murdat generally all join the same Kurdat together, but their ties of loyalty will be stretched in those training centres as they are inculcated with all the advanced skills of modern warfare.

Instruction in the Kurdat is also a practical matter, and the Kurdat recruits will join the frontlines of active campaigns several times during their period of instruction, fighting alongside the Coterie of veterans who are their instructors, until the fires of battle have burnt away those distinctions, forging a sacred bond in which soldier both young and old become equal comrades one with each other. When that day comes, the Kurdat are children no longer. They have become Gesurat.

GESURAT

To be Gesurat is to be fully realised as a Morat; to understand the spirit of sacrifice and to live with the acceptance of death. The ancient term of what was once seen as the epitome of personal honour is now understood to be merely the least which can be expected of a civilised citizen of the Supremacy.

KARANATAT

When the Kurdat become Gesurat, the members disperse, shedding the old (but never forgotten) bonds of childhood and joining the Regiment which will be their community and their home for the rest of their lives. In doing so they become Karanatat — sons (or daughters) of the regiment.

Regimental alliance is indicated by a sash and varied insignias, denoting rank, clan, unit type, faction, and other affiliations via complicated colour and pattern coding. The first insignia to be earned by the new Karanatat is the Gadarak, the battle insignia which indicates that they have entered combat as a member of their regiment.

Each regiment is, in essence, a polity unto itself, ruled by its Colonel. They have their own customs, manners, and initiation rites. The regimental barracks, which serve as the centre for each Morat community (or, in larger cities, each borough), are crowded with the trophies of war, a story of their never-ending life in battle.

While loyal to the Supremacy as a whole, Morat regiments also exhibit fierce competitiveness amongst each other, forever vying to be the most revered combatants of their kind.

SHASVASTII CONTINUUM

The Shasvastii are an unspeakably ancient civilisation, but one plagued by almost unimaginable tragedy.

The species originates from Messier 82, a galaxy situated in the M81 Group of the Virgo Supercluster (a near neighbour of the Local Group which the Milky Way is part of). One hundred million years ago, when dinosaurs still stalked the Earth, the Shasvastii civilisation sat resplendent — a truly galactic empire which had already persisted for millions for years. At this time, they had, of course, known for countless megayears that their own galaxy would soon collide with Messier 81, another nearby galaxy.

It was not an event that they feared. Quite the opposite, in fact. Galaxies, after all, are primarily made up of empty space. The few instances in which gravitational disturbances might disrupt systems could be trivially coped with over the literally astronomical scales of time over which those

MURDATS OF THE CLAW

The traditions of the Murdat can be traced back to the Age of the Claw, although in that bygone time the Murdats were generally blood relations. Young Morat are naturally gregarious, with an instinct to form close-knit groups and factions. One school of thought holds that the civilising social structures of the Knife Renaissance exist strictly to preserve this "child-like" sense of camaraderie, gradually expanding its scope until it encompasses the Supremacy as a whole.

MORATS IN THE COMBINED ARMY

The Morat Supremacy's loyalty to the Evolved Intelligence is a testament to the Principle of Authority: The EI defeated them, and so they obey the EI. It is as clear as the night following the day. (The fact that the EI had to blow up the entire sixth planet of the Ugarat system as a demonstration of force before the Morat acknowledged their defeat only strengthens the authority by which the EI commands them.)

Of course, it goes without saying that if they ever see an opportunity to subjugate the EI, then they will ruthlessly seize that opportunity. It is no less than the Principle of Authority demands of all true-thinking beings.

For now, however, the Morat are wielded by the EI like a massive club, obliterating any defence in the way of its expansion. They are only employed, of course, against opponents to whom the EI wishes to show no mercy, for the Morat are voracious in their campaigning.

GALACTIC REDUNDANCY

Three other ark-instantiations of the Continuum were also sent to various sectors of the Milky Way. Their ultimate fate remains unknown, even to the local Shasvastii.

CHROMATIN

In terrestrial lifeforms, the chromatin is a complex of macromolecules found inside individual cells which reinforce DNA, allows DNA to be packaged into more compact configurations, and regulates the genetic expression of DNA by controlling which sections of the genetic code are accessible to RNA replicators.

First Paradiso Offensive – p. 146

disruptions would occur. And, more importantly, the collision would give birth to new stellar nurseries, actually refreshing their galactic empire over the long spans of time across which they now schemed.

But they had made a terrible mistake. The gravitic tidal forces between the two galaxies warped the deep fabrics of space-time in ways unforeseen by even their advanced science. The spatial topography which made wormhole travel possible collapsed. It happened very quickly: Over the course of mere decades, the galactic empire shattered as the routes of travel which bound it together simply vanished one after another into a quantum flux. Left in its wake were tiny fiefdoms of, at most, a few dozen solar systems each (connected by local wormholes which had weathered the galactic storm).

Then things got worse. The empire had used Sorellian mechanics to engineer unfathomable changes in the suns of Messier 82 for purposes so arcane that even the Shasvastii of today no longer comprehend them (although a few fragments of lore – like references to "trans-computronium cores"– survive in their archives). As the galactic tidal forces grew, these alterations also grew unstable. More than ten billion stars were annihilated, and no less than eighty percent of Shasvastii-controlled planets were destroyed in the resulting conflagration.

THE SLOW EXODUS

In the wake of such devastation, Shasvastii culture became utterly enthralled to a single ideal: SURVIVE.

To achieve this, one surviving enclave of the empire poured all its remaining resources into creating a prodigious fleet of more than a hundred thousand slower-than-light ark ships. These arks were sent forth to guarantee the continuity of the Shasvastii – to create a Continuum which would ensure that their race would never again be threatened by extinction. They were hurled out into

the vast intergalactic voids, sentenced to journeys that would last for millions of years before carrying them into the tens of thousands of galaxies of the Virgo Supercluster.

Thousands of years ago, one of these arks blazed its way into the outer reaches of the Milky Way. Awaking from their long dormancy, the Shasvastii aboard it set about the work of colonising their new galaxy. This independent sliver of the Continuum has no way of knowing what happened to their antecedents left a hundred million years behind and twelve million light years away; nor to the thousands of other colonies hopefully strewn across the other galaxies of the supercluster. It matters little, for they *are* the Continuum. They are *all* the Continuum. And they will persist until the embers of the universe grow cold.

SHASVASTII PHYSIOLOGY

It is unclear how much of the modern Shasvastii physiology is natural to the evolution of their species and how much is the result of the extensive genetic modifications they have subjected themselves to – whether during the decadence of the empire, the Continuum's mad scrabbling for survival, or more recent changes endured during their campaigns of colonisation and conquest for the EI.

When human scientists initially studied the Shasvastii tissue samples captured during the First Paradiso Offensive, they were baffled. Their DNA was strangely simplistic, and also inexplicably varied in different parts of the same body. Early theories suggested extensive biografting or perhaps even some sort of Franksteinian corpse-stitching.

They eventually realised that what they had at first identified as Shasvastii RNA was, in fact, something far more complex and miraculous. Dubbed RNAsh, it carried out roles similar to terrestrial RNA – copying information from the DNA and transferring it to ribosomes to instruct protein synthesis – but was also the true core genetic identity of the individual Shasvastii. RNAsh was more stable than terrestrial RNA and linked to a macro-chromatin fibre network laced throughout the Shasvastii body in a fashion similar to a Silk. This macro-chromatin fibre contains a genetic "database" encoding millions of times more information than human DNA.

RNAsh is capable of taking genetic information from the macro-chromatin fibre and splicing it into the cellular DNA, allowing a Shasvastii to rapidly specialise its tissue. When exposed to physiological dangers, their bodies can rapidly "evolve" or adapt over the course of minutes rather than generations.

SPECULO KILLERS

Speculo Killers are the pinnacle of Shasvastii genetic malleability, resulting in the ultimate infiltration agents. Their biosynthetic bodies can transform into perfect replicas of an impersonation target within thirty-six hours, and their entire genetic identity can be subsumed within their chromatin code, leaving 99% of the tissues within their bodies a 100% match for their target. Master sockets allow these metamorphic agents to download a victim's Cube, transferring the entire personality into a custom Cube within their own body which allows them to either manually access the target's memories or even run the target as a simulated identity. Speculo killers are usually also outfitted with nervous and metabolic augmentations, carbon-compound reinforcements for bone and muscle, quantronic neural implants, and other physical upgrades.

They can even repurpose internal organs to replace damaged organs or perform specialised functions. This has resulted in Shasvastii being able to live within otherwise toxic situations, lethal to most other species.

Furthermore, although the Shasvastii have a very simplistic cerebral organ which performs cognitive processing, their actual personality and memories are stored within the macro-chromatin fibres. (Raising the possibility that the Shasvastii evolved from some form of genetic parasite – that their "bodies" are nothing more than an efficient shell of flesh commandeered in some bygone age.)

Whether this morphophysiological system of RNAsh and macro-chromatin fibre is a natural structure or not, it has been co-opted by Shasvastii scientists as the perfect conduit for extreme genetic engineering. It is particularly easy, for example, to procure a biopsy from one Shasvastii and graft it into the chromatin code of another, immediately blessing them with whatever advantageous adaptations the donor possesses. (This is why Shasvastii rarely employ environmental suits; they can often achieve the same results with a medical injector.) Once one individual has adapted to a particular habitat, it's trivial for the entire species to follow in their footsteps.

SPAWNEMBRYOS

The chromatin coding of their memories also allows the Shasvastii – like some parapsychologist's fantasy given life – to pass their genetic memory down to their offspring. These memories can be a complete copy (essentially creating a perfect duplicate of the individual), or they can be selectively passed to the offspring. Mated Shasvastii can also blend their memories together in the offspring. (Or limit the transfer merely to practical skills without the associated specific memories – like an amnesiac who can still remember how to fire a gun.)

Shasvastii are hermaphroditic, possessing both sets of glands and gonads. (They can even functionally impregnate themselves.) Their offspring, referred to as a SpawnEmbryo, is actually grown as a specialised organ from one of the organ buds within their chest cavity. At any point after the macro-chromatin fibre network has been successfully copied and implanted (a process which can take anywhere from a few days to a few months depending on how much information is being copied), the SpawnEmbryo can be removed from the body (through a self-sterilising orifice generated on the Shasvastii's left side). It can endure a wide variety of environments (including temperature extremes, immersion in water, and so forth). If placed in the earth, it will feed like a plant. If placed within a corpse it will feed off the cadaver.

SEEDEMBRYOS

In a strange fashion, the Shasvastii have practically weaponised the procreation of their species. On the battlefield, they will leave SpawnEmbryos behind – in the earth, in their fallen dead, in the corpses of their enemies. Time bombs waiting to hatch behind enemy lines. They have even created seed capsules; life-support platforms equipped with camouflage technology which can smuggle SpawnEmbryos onto a battlefield or into an enemy city.

The resulting soldiers – born in the wake of battle with their mission parameters genetically hard-coded – are known as SeedEmbryos. O-12 has created robust sterilisation protocols for wiping out potentially infected areas, but if even a single SpawnEmbryo survives, the Shasvastii can spring back up seemingly from nowhere.

In fact, if a parent dies while the SpawnEmbryo remains with them, the SpawnEmbryo will harvest the parent's body as a source of nutrients.

Generally, within a couple of weeks, the SpawnEmbryo will hatch and a newborn Shasvastii will emerge. Although fresh to existence, these "newborns" are nearly the size of an adult Shasvastii and are, of course, invested with the genetic memory of their progenitors. They are immediately ready to pursue the species-wide mission of preserving their race's place within the universe.

DHEVIIS

The Shasvastii equivalent of human adolescence is the *dheviis*. During this intermediate stage of development, *dheviis* choose their gender and lock in hormonal adjustments which will align their biological sex with it. Once concluded, this gender selection is irreversible (although, as noted above, all Shasvastii remain reproductively hermaphroditic). Shasvastii females generally possess higher strength and endurance, while males are more facile in genetically modifying their bodies.

EXPEDITIONARY FORCES

Shasvastii culture is dominated by two schools of thought, both driven by the deep-seated fear of extinction born from genetic memories of galactic terror: The Multipliers believe that Shasvastii survival depends on diaspora. They must fill the galaxy with their colonies, advance bases, hidden outposts, and *shaviish*. Across the vast scope of astronomical time, all bastions are doomed to fail. The Continuum can only persist by scattering their civilisation across so vast a scope that the actuarial odds can never be turned against them.

After the Shasvastii lost their war with the EI, however, a new ideological division emerged: The Conservatives argued that the Multipliers' desire

ORGAN BUDS

Mature Shasvastii are capable of "budding" new internal organs. Often a half dozen or so buds will be present within their chest cavity, waiting to be rapidly specialised for any necessary task.

SHAVIISH

The Shasvastii maintain depots of SpawnEmbryos, known as *shaviish*, in all their settlements. Many are also secreted in dark corners of the galaxy – genetic and cultural reservoirs from which the Shasvastii species can be reborn even if the worst catastrophe should befall them.

SHASVASTII IN THE COMBINED ARMY

The EI grows impatient with the lack of progress seen in the Shasvastii's Transcendence Project. Some agents believe the Multipliers are deliberately sabotaging the project, while others suspect the intrinsic fears at the heart of Shasvastii culture act as an instinctual impediment. Their Expeditionary Forces serving as the premiere military vanguard grants tolerance, for now. The EI has harvested their expertise of incursion warfare so as to greatly increase the value of data extracted from civilisations they have absorbed.

GRAND CIVILISATIONS
A term found in the Annals of the T'zechi Digesters. It is applied to any interstellar civilisation.

to resist EI control risked provoking it to pursue a policy of extinction against the Continuum. In the wake of defeat, the surest course of survival was to shelter behind the strength of the EI. Therefore, current colonies must be defended; the military alliance with the EI strengthened; and resources poured into their Transcendence Project to make themselves indispensable to the Combined Civilisation.

Ironically, however, the Multipliers still dominate the Expeditionary Forces which comprise the Shasvastii military. This is because the original purpose of the Expeditionary Forces was to carry out the Continuum's aggressive colonial expansion: They would explore and survey, establishing new colonies and outposts wherever possible. When alien civilisations were discovered, the local Expeditionary Force would perform their infamous incursion campaigns — forward observation, infiltration, and then destruction from within through assassination and subversion. (At least three grand civilisations are known to have been destroyed by the Continuum.)

Each Expeditionary Force is autonomous. There is a strong sense of rivalry between them, and a curious core of secrecy. Although the Continuum, as a whole, maintains vast, redundant, and overlapping programs for the sharing and preservation of knowledge (including genetic libraries, cultural reserves, eden-burst civilisation seeds, and *shaviish*), each Expeditionary Force maintains a small strategic reserve of installations, colonies, and even exclusive military technologies that they keep hidden from the others. This, too, is a survival tactic: The Shasvastii are ever-cautious against the day when they meet a foe who wages war with the same Arts of Subterfuge that they do. If one of their Expeditionary Forces were to be subverted by such a foe, then the secret refuges kept by the others might be the key to the ultimate survival of the Continuum.

Of course, there are many who argue that, with the EI, they have already found such a foe.

ALIEN
TOHAA

In the face of the Combined Army, only one alien race ever stood its ground against the hegemonic flood of the Evolved Intelligence before the EI encountered Humanity: The Tohaa. They arrived like saviours in orbit around Paradiso, champions who had already forged a vast interstellar empire by the time mankind was taking its first infant steps into space. But the Tohaa have been waging a war of painful attrition for a long time, and the ordeal has taken a toll in lost lives and lost planets. The Tohaa know that, unless they can change the course of their struggle, they too will succumb to the EI's onslaught.

UNIFICATION

The earliest Tohaa history is a quasi-mythological quiltwork of empires, kingdoms, and fractious nations fighting for dominion over Togaanu, the super-continent which dominates the Tohaa homeworld of Ronuhaa. Today the Tohaa think of these times as the Primitive Era, but strong cultural traditions nevertheless endure from legendary nations like Vaarso, Lyetaar, the Vaaronian Imperium, and the Balaakan Empire.

This period of strife came to an end as a result of the Staala — an archaic Tohaa word which once meant "cataclysm", but which is now only used to refer to the massive series of seismic events which ripped across the Togaanu continent and forced its partial evacuation. The humanitarian aid and planetwide cooperation during this time of trouble brought the Tohaa together and began the Unification which ultimately integrated all the Tohaa nations into the Trinomial — the single government which still rules the Tohaa empire today.

EXPANSION

The global cooling and rampant overpopulation caused by the Staala also resulted in a mass migration to the extraplanetary colonies scattered throughout the Home System.

As the Tohaa population pushed outwards, a small colony on the outer rim of the system made contact with a T'zechi Digester — an ancient alien bio-artefact of unknown origin. It quickly became apparent that the Digester had been observing Tohaa civilisation for millennia. (Some even theorise that it, too, had been forced to flee some

hiding place on Togaanu during the Staala.) Nor had the Tohaa been the first: The Digester offered glimpses of interstellar civilisations which had been born, flourished, and died long aeons before the first Tohaa drew breath. Of other species which had timidly remained ensconced on their home worlds. Of entire galaxies being born and snuffed out. Millions of years of culture, history, and science recorded, preserved, and disseminated.

In fact, it quickly became apparent to the Tohaa that the Digester they had made contact with was merely one part of an incomprehensibly vast network of similar devices. Each, it seemed, would make its temporary "home" in a system where incipient life promised future sentience. It would then seek to record the complex, exhaustive saga of the species that arose there.

The Digester showed the Tohaa that, beyond the state of primitive sentience, there were multiple classifications of high (or true) civilisation. Seeker civilisations, for example, were like the Ur Rationalists — forever seeking the glories of Transcendence and an escape from the material plane of existence. Herald races, on the other hand, were those who chose to assist the T'zechi Digesters in their quest for knowledge. Such races would help their Digester by taking its seed-copies and planting them on other life-bearing planets, beginning the cycle anew. Heralds also seek out other Digesters, obtain seed-copies from them, and return them to their Digester in order to multiply its store of knowledge.

The noble purpose of the Heralds called out to the Tohaa, and they embraced it as a new national identity. It imbues them with a great sense of pride, power, and purpose, and they consider it an immense honour to have been chosen by a higher power and to be seen as worthy of bearing this heritage.

COLONIAL FORCE

Although the Tohaa had long possessed wormhole technology, they were content within the confines of their Home System. The auspices of their new Herald identity, however, drove the Tohaa to shed their isolationist past. Embracing a new, expansionist spirit they created the earliest prototypes of their powerful Errant Ships, established the peacekeeping Colonial Force, and took it upon themselves to rapidly spread out across a multitude of systems.

DIGESTERS AND THE EI
The rapacious intellect of the Evolved Intelligence is aware of the T'zechi Digesters and greedily seeks them in order to rip whatever secrets it can pry from them in the hope of furthering its quest for Transcendence.

T'ZECHI DIGESTERS

The true origins of the Digesters are unknown and wrapped in a great deal of theory and rumour. The bio-artefacts themselves have yet to surrender any real data regarding their origins. Analysis of the dissemination of seed-copies suggests that the local Digesters originate from the galactic nucleus. Some say they are agents of a universal power, monitoring the whole of known time and space in some grand experiment. Others consider them the legacy of a dead species engaged in a last, desperate race against the ever-encroaching grasp of entropy. The paranoid suggest that they are the scouts for some as-yet-unknown invasion force. One bizarre theory holds that they are not from the ancient past, but from a time yet to come — recorders sent back from some alien future to capture secrets lost in a historical past which is now our present.

The Digesters themselves are bio-artefacts: Living, extremely intelligent, but seemingly not sentient. They are astoundingly resilient, capable of completely normal function in seemingly any environment (including, notably, the crushing depths of gas giants and the vacuum of space). It is unclear how Digesters arrive on a planet (other than those carried by a Herald vessel), although some have theorised that they can accelerate to very fast STL speeds across interstellar distances (while requiring Heralds to bear them through wormholes). They do not seem to directly interact with external technology (although evidence suggests that they can rapidly strip a wide variety of data storage devices), and their internal "anatomy" cannot be scanned. It is clear that they do possess some form of incredibly complex nano-biotechnology that allows them to subtly achieve a great number of effects.

The truth is, most of what is known of the Digesters has been provided by the creatures themselves, and is beyond the capacity of even Tohaa science to truly verify.

ANNALS OF THE DIGESTERS

T'zechi Digesters are parsimonious with their lore. They parcel it out only at times of their choosing, according to metrics and rubrics which are as mysterious as their ultimate purpose. And they *never* share the scientific or technical wonders which their archives must surely contain. The Tohaa believe that these actions — which can be seen random or capricious — are, in fact, harmonious with a doctrine of non-interference: The T'zechi Digesters resolutely avoid contacting developing species. When those species become ready for a higher form of civilisation, the Digesters offer some of them a choice for their destiny. Some among the Tohaa believe that there are further pinnacles of civilisation waiting to be achieved, and that fulfilling their role as Heralds is the path to reaching them.

When knowledge is imparted by the Digesters, Herald races like the Tohaa record it in databases known as the Annals. (The term "Annals" is also sometimes used to refer directly to the knowledge stored within the Digesters, with other Annals being seen as imperfect reflections of the whole.) The Tohaa have occasionally encountered Annals compiled by other races, and these are referred to as Lost or Forgotten Annals.

FENRIG IMPERATIVE

The Fenrig still lurk in the dark between the stars. Although the remnants of the Imperative lie on the far side of Tohaa space from where war rages with the Combined Army, it is feared that they may be fostering an alliance with the EI in order to strike back against the Trinomial.

As the Digester had promised them, the Tohaa quickly discovered that they were not alone in the galaxy. And first contact quickly gave way to conflict. In the Conlicutt system, the Errant Ship *Harmonious Diplomacy* discovered the Makricole Raiders — an itinerant race of pillagers who were enslaving the primitive Licuttians. The Raiders broadcast their ownership of the system. The *Harmonious Diplomacy* responded with a six-month campaign which drove the Raiders out of the system.

Conlicutt became one of the first Protectorates of the Tohaa Trinomial. The fleeing Raiders spread the word that a new and powerful player had arrived on the galactic scene. And the Tohaa followed in the wake of their glory: They were victorious in the Soropem Skirmishes. They drove the Moishane Scavengers from Mardelya. They fought their first interstellar war against the Norasa Slavedrivers and their subjugated species. They defeated the tyrants of the Four Shawoke Nations. They rooted out the Okees pirates, Skeraki corsairs, and Davadi bio-mimics. They repelled the Convhaja invasion of their rimward protectorates.

Through it all they nurtured potential cradles of civilisation, spread T'zechi Digesters far and wide, and brought seed-copies of foreign Digesters homeward.

WARS AGAINST THE FENRIG IMPERATIVE

When the exploratory bubble of the Tohaa's Errant Ships first encountered the systems of the Fenrig Imperative, however, they faced a new kind of foe. Powerful. Implacable. Relentless. The Fenrig had adapted their bodies to be practically immortal (although this required them to be sealed within environment containment units at all times), their technology was greater than the Tohaa's, and the Imperative itself controlled nearly twice as many systems.

In order to survive, the Tohaa were forced to evolve. The Colonial Force became the Trident — an aggressive, dedicated military force that learned how to bring their biotech superiority to bear. After a series of costly conflicts, the final War Against the Fenrig Imperative was decided in the crucible of the Rankato Junction. The Tohaa's bloody Run of Retribution then shattered the Imperative's power, ending their threat forever.

ATTRITION

Many among the Tohaa now think of the Wars Against the Fenrig Imperative as a blessing. Without the fortitude they learned in the Battle of the Karakkan Supernova, the Tri-Campaign of the

Yulandan Nebula, and the terrors of the Red Plague, they would have been left utterly unprepared for the invasion of the Combined Army which came only a few short decades later.

Despite the Trident's strength tempered in Fenrig blood, however, the EI War has already taken a greater toll on the Tohaa empire than any previous conflict. They have lost planets, protectorates — even entire client species. Humanity has seen only a fraction of the what the EI is capable of, but the Tohaa have had

the full, panoplistic fury of the Combined Army — of which the Morat, Shasvastii, and Exrah are only a small part — turned upon them for nearly two centuries.

It has long been clear to the Tohaa that this is a war of attrition. And it's a war that they are losing. It is all they can do to stall the invasion and conquering of further territory. They are in desperate need of something that will, at the very least, turn the EI away from them for a time — give them time to regroup and recover their strength.

CROSSROADS OF PARADISO

During the Unification, a secret cabal of Tohaa tycoons formed to preserve their wealth and prestige in the new world order. Known as the Triumvirate, they became an urban legend — a conspiracy cloaked in its own success; disbelieved as a fable and thus free to operate from the shadows.

GREAT ANATHEMA
With the outbreak of the EI War, however, the Triumvirate found a new purpose — to preserve the Tohaa way of life by any means necessary in the face of an excessionary threat from an enemy whose military force and technology dwarfed their own.

To counter the technological edge of the EI, however, the shadow tri-councils of the Triumvirate embraced the Great Anathema: They would betray their role as a Herald race and instead force the T'zechi Digesters to reveal their secrets. To this end, when the colony of Oomnya (p. 302) was abandoned, Triumvirate agents intercepted the planet's Digester and took it to Paradiso, where they established the first in a network of covert research centres.

On Paradiso, they ripped data out of the Digester, painstakingly bypassing its defensive systems and creating the Stolen Annals. Ancillary discoveries from the Stolen Annals were sent to redundant facilities on other worlds, but three primary technologies were developed onsite.

Fuscotor: A powerful viral weapon, referred to as Seemai in the Tohaa language, that could directly alter the synaptic activity of its targets. Whereas the EI's terrifying sepsitor required its victims to be equipped with a Cube which could be suborned, the Triumvirate researchers believed this techno-virus could be used to enslave any sentient creature.

Wormhole Manipulation: New models of space-time curvature revealed the possibility of directly altering the topology of the gateways to the stars. Most promisingly, a technology was developed which would allow the Triumvirate to redirect a wormhole's destination. Such technology would represent an impregnable defence, and could hypothetically be used to dump entire fleets of EI ships directly into supernovas.

Lithic Nanobots: Although the Tohaa were already masters of nano-biotechnology, the Triumvirate discovered nanotechnology capable of deep-permeation and transformation of inorganic materials. They used this lithic nanotech to literally transform the extant buildings of their research facility into a form of exotic

computronium — programmable matter which formed an advanced neural processing network. The result were the cosmolites of Paradiso, the strange and emergent properties of which became a subject of much research in their own right.

AURORA CHRONICLES
When the first human colonists came to Dawn, their arrival was noted by the secret research base the Triumvirate had already established there. Eavesdropping on the newcomers' primitive communications networks, the Triumvirate saw an opportunity to further their research agenda.

Using the wormhole manipulation technology they had gleaned from their captured Digester, the Triumvirate intercepted the *Aurora* — the second colony ship sent to Dawn — and redirected it to the Paradiso system. They were surprised when their efforts caused the wormhole to violently collapse, damaging the *Aurora* in the process, but this ultimately worked to further their designs as the human ship was forced to perform an emergency landing, permanently stranding the colonists on the planet.

The Aurorans, believing only that some terrible accident had befallen them, began the work necessary to establish their new colony on an unexpected world. As they did so, the Triumvirate researchers began kidnapping them in small numbers to use as test subjects for their Digester-derived tech.

The Triumvirate, however, underestimated the ingenuity and tenacity of the humans. Elite military units embedded with the Auroran colonists tracked the aliens and discovered the grisly, inhuman experiments they were carrying out amongst the cosmolites. An assault on the Tohaa compound was launched, and the first of humanity's wars erupted under the jungle canopies of Paradiso.

The Triumvirate, for their part, saw this as an ideal opportunity for field-testing their new Fuscotor weapon. The effect was devastating on the Aurorans, but the researchers were once again surprised by unexpected secondary effects from their technology: In its second phase, the Fuscotor somehow mutated into a contagion vector, becoming infectious to anyone near its victims. Then, in its tertiary phase, it either killed its human hosts or turned them into mindless, zombie-like automatons.

While the Tohaa struggled to corral their unruly creations for further study, a small Auroran commando squad infiltrated the research facility (masquerading as zombified slaves) and detonated a number of explosives – destroying the Fuscotor research and wiping out the infected human prisoners.

In a fury, Triumvirate forces pursued the commando squadron back to the *Aurora*. But this was a trap: The Aurorans knew that they had been hopelessly compromised by the remorseless "zombie virus". While one small group fought to break through the Tohaa defensive lines – carrying a data device detailing everything which had happened in an effort to warn humanity of the alien threat – the other colonists drew in the Tohaa and then detonated the *Aurora*'s fusion drives, creating a nuclear explosion which wiped out the last traces of the deadly virus and wreaked a harsh revenge on the Triumvirate.

THE GREAT MANIPULATION
In the wake of the nuclear holocaust, the Triumvirate began the work of salvaging what they could from the fiasco. Their efforts were abruptly interrupted when the cosmolites began to fail – the computronium matrices simply collapsed, carrying with them large swaths of the Triumvirate's experimental data.

The Triumvirate realised that they had been duped by the Digester. All of its gifts had proven to be Trojan Horses: Jump equations that destroyed wormholes. Hostile biotechnology cloaking an insipid, rapid onset techno-organic toxin. Exotic nanotech construction techniques crippled with hidden suicide memes.

The treacherous Digester could no longer be trusted (they would have to find a way to capture a different one and try again), but the Triumvirate realised that it could still be turned to their advantage. A Digester – any Digester – was prized by any interstellar civilisation, and particularly by the EI (who believed that the Digesters might contain the secrets of Transcendence). That gave it great value as bait.

The Triumvirate captured one of the EI's vaunted Ur-Probes (p. 266). Their researchers inflicted very specific damage to it, brought it to Paradiso, and planted evidence that it was responsible for the destruction of the *Aurora*. They moved the Digester – after allowing the Ur-Probe to become aware of its presence – elsewhere on the planet. And then they waited.

PARADISO AFFAIRS
When humans returned to Paradiso, they – as the Triumvirate had anticipated – discovered the wreckage of the *Aurora*, the dormant cosmolites, and the Ur-Probe. After several years of research, the Ur-Probe was activated (p. 24) and sent a signal back to the EI, notifying it of the presence of both a Digester and a new species with potential for the Transcendence Project.

The supervision group which the Triumvirate had left deployed in the Paradiso system was pleased. They had created the Crossroads at Paradiso – the crux in which the ultimate fate of the EI War would be decided.

After the Combined Army invaded Paradiso, the Triumvirate activated another of the artefacts they had planted in the cosmolites. Referred to by the humans as the Relic, it contained encrypted map

data pointing to a location on Paradiso where a damaged Tohaa scout craft had been secreted.

The various human factions fell into a fractious conflict over possession of the Relic, the data it contained, the location it indicated, and, ultimately, the Black Box contained within the Tohaa scout craft. These conflicts were referred to as the Paradiso Affairs, and their ultimate conclusion saw O-12 take possession of the Black Box and use it to contact the Tohaa Trinomial.

THE LAST COSMOLITE
The Trinomial, of course, had no record of the scout craft which had led humanity to their doorstep. Curious, they joined an O-12 research team to finish decoding the damaged Black Box, revealing yet another set of mysterious coordinates – these pointing to Sisargas Island on Paradiso.

The island, unfortunately, was within the sphere of influence of the Combined Army. Probes smuggled onto the island, however, revealed the presence of a fully operational cosmolite, sunk deep into the jungle and with its mimetic systems fully intact.

A massive, coordinated attack was launched simultaneously on all fronts in an effort to distract the Combined Army while a strike force was sent onto Sisargas Island. Unfortunately, the EI recognised the effort and was still able to dispatch an intercept force of its own. A running battle was fought across the island and into the Last Cosmolite itself, at which point the cosmolite's own defensive systems became an additional enemy.

The human factions once again split apart into smaller teams to search the interior of the cosmolite. In the end, it turned into a glorious hour for ALEPH's S.S.S.: First, based on data they had not shared from the Black Box, the Tohaa knew what this place likely contained, and based on that knowledge their detachment attempted to ambush the S.S.S. in order to keep ALEPH from taking possession of it. Then, after the S.S.S. had repelled the Tohaa's betrayal, they and the Combined Army simultaneously discovered the resting place of the Digester which the Triumvirate had placed here. The S.S.S.'s victory secured the Digester for the Human Sphere.

A NEW PHASE OF WAR
Using the International Law of Special Purposes, O-12 established a secret facility, codenamed the Penny Arcade and located deep within human space, to the study the strange bioartefact. The Tohaa have not revealed the identity of what the humans have discovered, but an invitation has been extended to them to join in the research project (in no small part because Bureau Noir suspects they're withholding information and hope their participation may reveal it).

The EI knows that the Digester has been found. And it knows that it has been moved to the interior of the Human Sphere. For the EI, this signals a new phase to the war – this is no longer a mission of exploration; it is to be an occupation and conquest with the ultimate goal of securing the ultimate prize. As the Triumvirate had planned, the EI will draw its invasion forces away from Tohaa space, granting them a much-needed respite.

TOHAA PHYSIOLOGY

The Tohaa are generally taller and slenderer than humans, usually possessing a gracile beauty and pale, mocha-cream skin. Their soldiers, however, have often received extensive bio-modification, which can result in starkly inhuman and almost demonic features. (A prominent example is the blood red, gill-like structures which are commonly grafted to their cheeks and provide a robust form of atmospheric filtering.)

Tohaa eyes are protected by a thick membrane and their vision is keen, able to see further to the edges of the spectrum than humans. Due to the tenuous atmosphere of their home planet, however, the Tohaa's large, pointed ears ironically provide them with only the poorest of hearing. (This thin atmosphere, offering little protection against the radiation of their sun, also explains their thick skin.)

Compensating for this auditory inadequacy, however, are the thick tendrils which form the "phero-blossom" on the back of the Tohaa head. These have been dismissed as "alien hair" in a number of Maya broadcasts, but these tendrils are actually formed from layered, bio-mesh sensory surfaces. These provide an incredible olfactory sensitivity while also serving as the largest and most complex of the seven major pheromonal zones located on their bodies. (The rich pheromonal exchanges these organs make possible largely define the Tohaa language and culture.)

The tendrils of the phero-blossom are supplemented by quills across the torso and upper limbs that can also detect pheromones, plus subtle shifts in their environment.

TRINARY TOHAA

The intimate nature of pheromonal communication perhaps explains the natural gregariousness of the Tohaa. Tohaa who, for whatever reason, become excluded from a group will immediately seek to form or join a new one as quickly as possible. In the absence of other Tohaa, these instincts will reach out to members of alien species. This can be both a boon (allowing the Tohaa to form fast friendships and alliances), but can also be a bane: It often takes no more than a relatively short period of enforced isolation for a Tohaa to suffer from an extreme, almost crippling, depression.

The political, social, military, and even personal structures of Tohaa life are fundamentally trinary. There are three executives in their political organisations. Three members, in different combinations, in their family nucleus. Multiples of three in their work groups. Three agents in their police patrols. Three values of truth in their systems of logic. Three combinations on their locks. Absolutely everything in the Tohaa world is built on a base-3 architecture. It is strange for them to even think outside of the number three.

SOCIAL TRIADS

During their adolescence, Tohaa form strong social triads. The members of the triad each receive a second surname composed of the first syllable of the inherited surname of each member. The composition of these sororal triads often fluctuate over time (which also results in a Tohaa's sororal surname changing).

Most adult Tohaa will eventually form a familial triad (granting them a third surname). A child born to the triad inherits a surname based on the familial triad at the time of its birth, but the familial triad itself is usually unstable and breaks apart after the child is born. A new triad is formed by two of the parents and the child, with the third parent leaving to find a new family triad to join. No other children will be born to the family triad until the firstborn leaves to pursue higher education.

In some cases, the three-adult familial triad will be maintained. These triads, however, quickly give birth to two additional children, creating a stable family dynamic featuring a parental triad and a filial one. (The Tohaa often ascribe significance to someone raised as a "trio child" in much the same way that humans talk about someone being raised as an "only child".)

CORAHTAA LANGUAGE

Each Tohaa has a unique pheromone signature — known as the *baade* — which is difficult, if not impossible, to replicate. Their olfactory receptors are unmatched by any other species, allowing them to produce and sense each other's pheromones, adding a level of nuance to their identity and communication no other race is able to tap into. This makes it incredibly hard for Tohaa to deceive one another, but allows them to weave meaning into their communication other species simply fail to pick up on — positioning them to be manipulated. This pheromone language is known as Corahtaa, aka "the language of truth." It takes great practice to be able to convey misinformation in this manner. The Tohaa are innately distrustful of vocal communication, and they have no qualms about treating lesser races with an air of superiority, bending the truth to their whims.

NEEBAB NUMEROLOGY

Neebab Numerology maintains that numbers connect everything. That there is an underlying meaning and symbolism to mathematics tying

There is a certain danger to them. Under their cool demeanor and their distant courtesy, you can sense a two-faced nature. They are well-versed in the mechanisms of deceit. They know how to twist laws and treaties. Their refined vocabulary fails to completely conceal the fundamental meaning of their words. They want something from us, and whatever they offer us in return will not be worth our while. Even worse, their conscience will be clean. From the way they carry themselves it is apparent they emphatically approve of double-dealings, schemes, and the trade of political loyalties. We are dealing with veterans of intergalactic negotiation, and we are clearly at a disadvantage. We are merely children playing in the houses of our elders.

Excerpt from "On the Tohaa Contact Treaty", Saladin (O-12 Liasion Officer), Internal File of the O-12 Öberhaus (Concilium Prima)

DIPLOMATIC IMPLANTS

In order to speak with another species, Tohaa rely on bioimplants. One implant improves the range of their normally deep, bass voices. A second implant translates the sounds of alien languages to pheromonal information to aid and enrich the Tohaa's understanding.

together all data, living beings, and even spiritual energies within the universe. Its origins lie in the ancient, pre-Unification nation of Lyetaar. While once considered a science, Neebab Numerology is now seen as quaint and archaic. It has been embedded in the Tohaa mindset for so long, however, that they still tend to look for odd and unexpected connections between numbers and patterns all around them.

RAWIILA CLOTHING

Tohaa clothing is made out of special porous fabrics that allow their quills to stick out through the weave. This fabric — known as *rawiila* — lends itself to loose, flowing designs. Capes and hoods are also common, and these are often lined with special materials which provide a respite for Tohaa phero-blossoms (fulfilling a roll similar to human sunglasses).

SAOM

Obtained by soaking the saoona lichen in water, saom is an isotonic and nutritional beverage with a high energy value. Although it doesn't agree with human biochemistry (resulting in mild gastroenteritis), Tohaa drink it almost constantly. Tohaa soldiers universally carry bioflasks containing the lichen which can be filled repeatedly with water to create more of the drink.

TOHAA TECHNOLOGY

Tohaa civilisation is built on biotechnology, and nanobiobots are the fundamental building blocks of that technology. These self-replicating biological machines manipulate matter on a molecular level,

while being coupled to a macro-infrastructure of genetically engineered parasites, neocreatures, artificial silicon- and carbon-based amino acids, and even more alien growths. Their engineering facilities are unique, self-sustaining ecosystems and most objects the Tohaa use are grown from a biosubstrate.

This mastery of biotechnology and its integration into their daily lives has necessarily shifted both the perception and the reality of the Tohaa's relationship with the natural world. As a human might see a boulder rolling down a hill as a primitive wheel or an undammed river as energy waiting to be tapped, so the Tohaa perceive natural biospheres and evolutionary gene pools as a raw, wild potential waiting to be harvested, shaped, and perfected by the touch of an intelligent mind. They take plants and animals gathered from the breadth of their interstellar dominion and reshape them for their purposes. The ecologies of entire planets are transformed for their pleasure and necessity.

The intellectual aristocracy which oversee these ambitious bioengineering projects are the mecha-geneticists known as the Kumotail. Often possessed of a haughtiness commensurate with their intellect and importance in Tohaa society, each Kumotail is a virtuoso of genetic code and biological expression, granted a demesne of expertise and responsibility which they consider the highest of all possible vocations, and given an absolute authority to follow *Saatara* — the scientific philosophy by which the deepest secrets of the Universe are laid bare in the simultaneous act of both creating and improving Nature itself.

TOHAA XENOLINGUISTICS

Tohaa diplomatic representatives hand-delivered a dossier describing their species to the O-12 Öberhaus. This most notably included a volume entitled *Tohaa Xenolinguistics*, fully briefing human translators on the nuances of Corahtaa… or, at the very least, all of the nuances the Tohaa wished them to be aware of.

EXALTATION

Curiously, the one thing which the Tohaa do not generally seek to improve are themselves. Although they are often surrounded by what they refer to as the *dalbaade* (the balanced collection of biotechnology they carry or have implanted within them, which they seem to regard in a manner similar to a human's personal area network), they leave their bodies largely unmodified beyond basic health enhancements and the like.

This restraint, however, is in no way extended to other sentient races. To the contrary, as the Tohaa have threaded their way through the galaxy, they have taken a number of younger races under their wings, elevating them culturally, physically, and mentally in order to raise them out of their primitive state.

When a life-supporting planet is discovered, Tohaa scientists search the indigenous species for those with potential as near-primitive intelligences and map out their biological and neurological schemata. If projections look promising, the Tohaa then develop a series of genetic upgrades that can boost brainpower even in the embryonic stages. This process — known as Exaltation — can take generations to perfect, and each race requires a different approach to ensure success. Once the Tohaa are satisfied with the sapient levels of the younger species, these changes are genetically hardwired into them, making the changes permanent and fixing the race as an ongoing Tohaa servitor.

Servitor races have historically served as colonists to settle the territories pioneered by Tohaa Errant Ships. This workforce frees the Tohaa to pursue their higher calling. In more recent days, the servitors have also been essential as soldiers in the meat-grinding frontlines of the EI War.

CHAKSA

Among the oldest and most advanced pupil species, the Chaksa are also one of the more complicated examples of Tohaa Exaltation. Brave, clever, and devoted to their mentors, the Chaksa are a gregarious people who value friendship, honesty, and — in the case of the Auxiliaries — a good fight.

To outsiders, the muscular, reptilian Chaksa can appear simple, or even slow; Chaksa are keenly aware of their youth and inexperience, and instinctively defer to authority. However, once they get comfortable, Chaksa are boisterous, opinionated, and form social bonds with surprising speed. Among the most naturally comedic creatures in the galaxy, their inexpressive faces give them a massive advantage in dry, witty humour; a trait often overshadowed by their rambunctious natures, but used to extensive effect

For reasons not completely understood, many Chaksa possess a recessive gene that interferes with Exaltation; preventing brain development during gestation, and resulting in semi-evolved "Peripherals." These Chaska lack true intelligence or self-awareness, but still play a part in Tohaa society as Servants. Controlled by remote neurological link, Servants perform dangerous support tasks, and provide the Trident with invaluable — if ultimately expendable — support. Self-aware Chaksa regard them with a mixture of pity and horror, though all find them unnerving.

For all their success, the fact that many Chaksa remain unexalted means that their Protectorate is still primarily governed by the Tohaa, which suits their *laissez faire* style just fine.

KOLDINUK

The second-oldest Exalted race, and arguably the most successful, the Koldinuk are a shining testament to the Tohaa Exaltation process and the Trinomial's transitional programs. Native to the Koldin system, theirs is one of the most prosperous Protectorates in the Colonial Territory, and by far the most independent and advanced. Possessed of inquisitive, witty, and — in their words — "orderly" minds, Koldinuk are a natural fit in the Trinomial's bureaucracy, where their expertise in logistics has made them integral to colonial affairs.

Koldinuk possess a thirst for learning unrivalled in the Trinomial, and perhaps all of known space; but their sense of wonder does not explorers make. Content to experience the universe from safely behind the Tohaa, Koldinuk see themselves as scientists, administrators, and assistants, happily leaving hazards — and glory — to those so inclined. As such, none have yet been seen by human eyes.

TOHAA TRINOMIAL

The Tohaa Trinomial refers to the whole of the Tohaa territory, a threefold body governed by Tohaa rulers that spans dozens of star systems. The Trinomial is divided into Runohaa (the Home System), the Colonial Territories, and the Errant Ships.

RUNOHAA

After millennia of genetic engineering, the Tohaa home world is possessed of seemingly endless ecological wonders layered, preserved, and cultivated with a degree of complexity which beggars any natural ecosystem. Even its thin, purple skies teem with life, most notably the huge Zadarskaa — living

SHAWOKE ACCUSATIONS

One species the Tohaa encountered, the Shawoke, claimed the Tohaa were using their Exaltation process to subconsciously enslave all lesser races through genetic coded submission. They also stated that the artificially heightened intellectual processes were resulting in drastically shortened lifespans for the beings involved.

Unfortunately, during the war between the Tohaa and the Shawoke Four Nations, the Shawoke lost any evidence of their claims and have not raised any grievances since. None of the Exalted species have ever brought such a claim to the public either, indicating their complete satisfaction with their role in Tohaa society.

CHAKSA SUPERSTITION

Being sapient when your own sibling might not be raises difficult questions. In a distorted reflection of their own, unexalted relationship to the Tohaa, the Chaksa have developed a form of nonspiritual animism — ascribing anthropomorphic characteristics and even thought to everything, even inanimate objects — as a way of making sense of the universe. While this leads them to treat unevolved Chaksa with compassion, it also results in a number of quirks; talking to ships, ascribing personality traits to weapons, and anthropomorphising plants to a point that even humans find odd.

HELOTS AND HUMANS

Although the Human Sphere has not yet realised it, the Helots of Varuna were once considered as a potential species for Exaltation (as described on p. 323). As a handful of humans have gained knowledge of the full scope of the Exaltation projects, concerns have been raised that the Tohaa may view them less as allies and more as a future lab experiment. These have been dismissed as needless paranoia during a time of war.

PARADISO ERRANT FLEET

Since the signing of the Tohaa Contact Treaty, a number of Errant Ships have taken up position in the Paradiso system, adding Tohaa colonists to the planet's surface while also maintaining a higher Trinomial presence in the area – ensuring they'll be ready to react swiftly to a Combined Army incursion.

zeppelins on a colossal scale, each capable of supporting an entirely unique biosphere within the valley-like folds of their skin. Crystalline cities dot this marvellous landscape, surrounded by micro-arcologies.

ERRANT SHIPS

The Errant Ships are massive motherships, each capable of completely colonising entire star systems without support or resupply. Each is functionally a nation state unto itself. During the golden age of the Trinomial, they carried the glorious banner of the Tohaa empire out into the black reaches of space and lit the light of civilisation to illuminate that which had once been dark.

And when conflict arose, these mighty ships proved that they could just as easily crush entire civilisations single-handedly as raise them up. They are the unstoppable evolution of the Tohaa made manifest.

COLONIAL TERRITORIES

This is the largest portion of the Trinomial territories, consisting of all the star systems and deep space stations the Tohaa have settled over the ages. Each colony is highly self-sufficient, with independent government and organisations – though each does answer to the Trinomial in the Home System.

Sadly, a goodly number of the Colonial Territories have fallen to the Combined Army during this long war. Those citizens who have been taken over to serve the EI now are referred to as a separate entity known as the Sygmaa Trihedron.

PROTECTORATES

Although a newly Exalted species will remain under strict Tohaa tutelage as a servitor race, once they have achieved the 33rd level of Autonomy they are allowed to form a semi-autonomous state within the Trinomial. These Protectorates are officially recognised as a transitional step towards full independence as a sapient race, although the reality is that no species has ever been recognised by the Tohaa for Manumission.

VISERAA

The ruling body of the Tohaa Trinomial consists of three legislative bodies – the Capitoline Council (representing the Home System), the Council of Captains (representing the Errant Ships), and the Colonial Council (representing the Colonial Territories). The entirety of the Viseraa is re-elected once every six years and each council then nominates a single Speaker, with the three Speakers collectively forming an executive triad. (Becoming a Speaker is seen as a great sacrifice, since it involves breaking one's current triad. But through this sacrifice the Tohaa people find political unity.)

The Speakers manage three primary political organisations: The Trident (military), the Accord (internal affairs), and the Trispiral (external affairs, including the analysis and selection of lesser races fit for Exaltation and the management of the Protectorates those races later form).

SYGMAA TRIHEDRON

Once part of the Trinomial, the Sygmaa Trihedron is that portion of the empire which has been conquered by the Combined Army. The Tohaa planets which thus came under the EI's rule were shocked, however, to discover that their lives are relatively unchanged. The Trinomial had saturated their worlds with propaganda claiming that the evils of the EI would bring them incredible suffering, and under the weight of that propaganda the Tohaa fought back using every tactic at their disposal. Millions — perhaps billions — died on those battlefields.

And now, to the Sygmaa, those losses seem meaningless. Other than replacing their comlogs and Cubes with EI-linked units, to the common citizen it seems their civilisation has been left alone. The conflict was unnecessary. It was the war-mongering Trinomial which was the ultimate source of all this death and misery.

As such, the Sygmaa have turned against the Trinomial. They have embraced the EI's superior technology and now act as evangelists for the Combined Army. They are driven by a rage born of betrayal, seeking to free their brethren from what they now view as a corrupt government that lies to the very people it claims to serve.

REBEL CULTURE

While being left relatively alone under EI rule, Sygmaa citizens — unlike those Tohaa who have remained under the Trinomial — have begun to proactively adopt more individualistic mentalities and forms of expression. While community remains a large part of their society, Sygmaa citizens have become increasingly prone to try and "evolve" themselves with body modifications and genetic tinkering on their own kind. They have also taken to celebrating more adversarial approaches to social interaction, with raging debates and defiant speeches against conformist thinking reaching the height of an art form. In this manner, they embrace their newfound "free speech" under the EI and reject the authoritarian propaganda of the Trinomial which has warped their understanding of the galaxy for generations.

HEDRONIC COUNCILS

Sygmaa governmental institutions (those allowed to exist under the EI, of course) have also become more diverse and fluid. There is no overarching Trinomial to dictate the course of their lives and thinking. Rather, every citizen is encouraged to be politically active and even hold some small official government role sometime in their lives; each

TRIDENT BATTLE TRIADS

Following the Tohaa adherence to Base-3 organisations, most military operations are carried out in units of three known as combat triads. Three combatants, each with a different skill set, form a battle bond designated by the first syllable of each member's surname, or a numerological code. These Triads are highly effective due to their range of specialisation and ability to communicate on an intimate level even in the thick of battle.

These Triads can form within moments, with a single spurt of pheromones needed to determine cross-unit compatibility. Should a Triad member fall in battle, the survivors immediately seek out a replacement, with new members sometimes joining a Triad in the middle of a mission.

VAARSO BATTLESPEAK

Vaarso was a pre-Unification Tohaa nation that is mostly the subject of myth and legend these days. It created a text and audio-based language meant to supplement Corahtaa during times of combat, adding multiple layers of meaning and context to any message. Trident triads now use Vaarso Battlespeak as a secret language, coded to repel any attempts at enemy espionage while also identifying the Tohaa as a soldier.

major settlement has its own governing party, with members only holding term for a few years before being replaced by "fresh voices". This, however, does make for lengthy review and approval of administrative matters, with forums being held for months, if not years, and often ending up including so much compromise between differing factions that they could be considered essentially ineffectual in introducing true progress. Trigon members decry this major shift in process, claiming the EI only allows it so that the Sygmaa citizens distract themselves with trivial bickering while remaining ignorant to the darkness that has claimed them all.

TRIGON

Within the annexed territories of the Sygmaa Trihedron, there remain pockets of resistance against the Combined Army. Known as the Trigon, these insurrectionists refuse to submit to the EI's rule and wage a secret war of terror and sabotage in order to weaken the Combined Army from the inside. They are patriotic loyalists to the Trinomial and use assassinations and covert ops to defy the EI and Ur Rationalists wherever they can.

Sygmaa citizens see the Trigon members as terrorists who remain wilfully blind to the truths the EI has revealed about the Trinomial's corruption. They are stuck in the past, unable to accept that they were betrayed by the very rulers who claimed to have their best interests at heart. Unfortunately, unless they are willing to accept the fact of the EI's rule, their only fate will be elimination.

comlog – p. 365

Cubes, p. 366: Silk-based implants that backup the user's personality.

TRIHEDRON IN THE EI WAR

At the moment, the Sygmaa Trihedron's goal is to wage war on the Tohaa front, rather than focusing on the EI's anticipated conquest of humanity.

GEAR
ACQUISITIONS

The worlds of the Human Sphere are filled with danger and intrigue, and characters frequently find themselves in need of a wide range of tools to overcome challenges and solve problems. A Lockpicker program might be invaluable against a secured door, but it's no help at all against a Yu Jing security detail searching for an intruder. That kind of problem requires a more drastic solution, such as a decent sidearm, or thermo-optical camouflage.

While the modern world is one of iota-scarcity material abundance, the sorts of items characters depend on in crucial moments often require rare and exotic materials, illegal software, precise customisation, or cutting-edge innovations – the sorts of things that aren't included in a basic demogrant.

ASSETS, WEALTH, AND ACQUISITIONS

Wealth is a fluid thing in the Human Sphere. Comlogs allow near-instant account management and payment for routine transactions, with credit flowing freely through Maya from personal to commercial accounts and back again – as long as you have enough of it, that is. Each faction maintains its own currency as a data storage medium for transferring quantronic notions of value within their territory, and the vast majority of commercial transactions are handled quantronically via a citizen's comlog, with any exchange rates managed seamlessly by Maya.

In a few cases, flextabs and flashbills – smartpaper chits preloaded with credits and a solar cell that shows the current balance – are used. They can be locked to specific accounts, but most are "burners" that don't monitor or restrict who carries or uses them.

Rather than track each individual transaction and unit of credit, *Infinity* uses a system of abstract wealth to cover character finances and purchasing power. Acquiring items relies primarily on the Lifestyle skill, representing a character's familiarity with and understanding of money and finance, and their knowledge of how best to employ those resources.

PURCHASING POWER

A character's ability to acquire items is governed by a number of factors.

Earnings represent a character's normal regular income, wherever it comes from or whatever form it takes, and the character's ability to absorb the Cost of a purchase, reducing the impact it has on their finances.

Cashflow represents the character's short-term resources, and the amount of money the character has easily available at any given time. A character has a maximum Cashflow equal to 5 + Earnings + their Lifestyle Expertise; it will often be lower

PAPER AND COIN
Many on the planet Dawn don't have access to quantronic means of payment. Digitally encrypted transactions, banknotes, and even coins are still common, particularly out on the frontiers.

Demogrant, p. 140: A basic income guaranteed to every member of the major powers (and most of the minor powers, too).

THE WEIGHT OF THINGS
With the exception of weapons, which have a few different sizes determined by their recoil and handling as well as physical mass, equipment in *Infinity* has no listed values for weight, bulk, or encumbrance. Modern technology ensures most items a person encounters are as small as is practical, and no heavier than is comfortable. Many "items" are actually software services, apps, and upgrades for common items, or several items combined into a single multifunction device.

It's left in the hands of the GM to set reasonable limits for how many (and what types) of weapons a character can carry, and what kinds of other equipment characters can reasonably consider "on their person" at any moment.

FACTIONAL CURRENCIES

Ariadna: Ariadnan Ruble (ARU) ₳Ᵽ, AKA the Cossack Ruble, as well as the Merovingian Franc, USAriadnan Dollar, and the Caledonian Pound, well-accepted on black markets.

Haqqislam: Dinar (HAD) ﺩ, so common other Dinars have to specify their origin.

Nomad Nation: Skënder (SKR) ₣, simplified to Skender on *Corregidor*.

O-12: Sol ☉, used on Concilium and on the Circulars.

PanOceania: Oceana (POC) ⓞ, strongest currency of the Human Sphere.

Yu Jing: Yuan (YJY) ¥, inherited from the ancient People's Republic of China.

Tohaa Triumvirate: Tohaa Tael (TOT) Ⴑ, currently exchanging at exorbitant rates.

Ur Hegemonic Civilisation: All subject species use the (translated) Standard ◉, but often call it by culturally traditional names. For example, the Morat call the Standard "Kruts" in daily language expressions, after an ancient physical trade currency.

as purchases are made. Cashflow is limited, but is restored to full at the start of each game session, and only causes problems if large amounts are lost at once or a character runs out entirely.

Assets represent extra cash, valuable items, tradable goods, and favours. They're often gained as payment for freelance jobs, bonuses for a job well done, or valuables obtained during the course of an adventure. Assets don't naturally increase a character's long-term Earnings, but can provide a much-needed boost when trying to obtain something expensive. Characters begin play with Assets equal to their Personality rating, plus any bonus Assets from their Lifepath.

Shortfalls happen if a character strains their finances too far, impeding their ability to bring their resources to bear further. Shortfalls increase the difficulty of acquisition and asset management tests. A character with four or more Shortfalls cannot make acquisition tests (even Simple (D0) acquisition tests). (Four or more Shortfalls mean that the character has just run out of money.)

GOODS AND SERVICES

All purchases, anything that can be obtained with credit or valuables, have values that govern how easy they are to obtain, and how much it costs to do so.

Restriction is a value between 0 and 5 representing how rare the purchase is, either because it is only produced in small quantities, is heavily regulated, dangerous, downright illegal, or all of the above. Higher values represent more heavily restricted items.

Cost is how big an impact a purchase has on a character's finances. Cost is comprised of a static value plus one or more .

Tariffs are additional charges that might apply to the acquisition. Where this is the case, the Cost of the item is followed by T1, T2, or T3. T stands for tariff, and the number is how much is added to the Total Cost for each Effect rolled.

Maintenance only applies to purchases with routine additional payments. This might be a rent or a loan repayment, the cost of insurance, expenses involved in ownership, or the need to regularly replace or repair part of the purchase. If a purchase's Maintenance is higher than a character's Earnings, it reduces the character's maximum Cashflow by one for each point the Maintenance is higher than Earnings. If this happens then the character is living beyond their means. The

character can give up the purchase at any time in order to avoid the Maintenance (restoring the lost Cashflow). The Maintenance of an item covers the Maintenance of any other items integrated into it.

ACQUISITIONS

Acquisition Test: A character seeking to make a purchase must make a Lifestyle skill test to locate a willing seller, with a base difficulty equal to the item's Restriction. The difficulty of the test is increased by one step per Shortfall the character is currently suffering from.

GAINING ASSETS

Assets can be gained by selling items (see p. 331), but can also be directly rewarded by the GM through play. In addition to large payoffs and similar financial transactions, Assets can also represent other valuable resources (like intel that can be sold to the highest bidder).

TIME IS MONEY

Given sufficient time and effort, any item or service can be obtained. In this regard, an item's Restriction rating determines how difficult it is to find someone selling a particular item or service relatively nearby and in a short space of time, quickly enough that the item can be obtained within a few minutes (or, in the case of a service, how long it takes until that service is available). Taking longer and widening the search makes things easier, to an extent. Each step along the following track reduces the difficulty of the acquisition test by one step, to a minimum of Simple (D0): Minutes — Hours — Days — Weeks — Months. If the difficulty is already Simple (D0), or has already been reduced to Simple (D0), then each additional step adds 1 bonus Momentum to the acquisition test.

ACQUISITION COMPLICATIONS

On failed tests, a complication means the purchase isn't available nearby in time — preventing the character from trying again — or in the case of illegal or highly restricted items that they've garnered unwanted attention. Complications rolled on a successful acquisition test usually affect price or quality, such as a bad deal that increases or adds a Tariff, or a shoddy item with an increased complication range. In other cases, acquisition complications could directly reduce Cashflow or, as a major complication, inflict a Shortfall.

BUYING IN BULK

When attempting to purchase more than one of an item, things become more difficult. The character can attempt a single acquisition test to buy all the items at once, increasing the difficulty based on the number of items sought.

If the difficulty would be increased above 5, then the acquisition test automatically fails. Obtaining such a quantity of that item will require more focused action played out at the table (with actions possibly reducing the difficulty of the acquisition test until it becomes possible or bypassing the test entirely at the GM's discretion).

After increasing the difficulty of the acquisition test, if the test successful, each item's Total Cost can be determined with a single cost roll,

but must have Earnings subtracted from them separately: multiple low-cost items will have little or no impact on a character's Cashflow if they have decent Earnings. Momentum spent to increase effective Earnings applies to all of these Costs.

BUYING IN BULK TABLE

NUMBER OF ITEMS	DIFFICULTY INCREASE
1–3	+0
4–7	+1
8–15	+2
16–31	+3
32–63	+4
64+	+5

If the test fails, the character is unable to find someone willing or able to sell the item. They can try again, but each attempt takes more time, and a character might only have a limited number of opportunities. If the test succeeds, Momentum can be spent to increase the character's effective Earnings for that acquisition by one per point of Momentum.

Before the acquisition test is made, Assets can be spent to gain a bonus d20 per Asset. (If the acquisition test fails, these Assets are lost; the character wasted money and favours trying to find a seller.)

Cost: If the item is available, roll the item's Cost. If the item has a Tariff, add the cost of the Tariff for each Effect rolled. Then subtract the character's current Earnings to work out the acquisition's Total Cost.

The character can then choose whether or not to make the purchase. If they do, the Total Cost is subtracted from their Cashflow. (If the Total Cost is 0 or less, their Cashflow is unaffected.) A purchase that would reduce Cashflow to less than 0 cannot be completed, although if circumstances permit the character may be able to use Assets to generate additional Cashflow before completing the transaction (as described in *Money Management*, below.)

If the character loses 5 or more Cashflow in a single acquisition or has a Cashflow of 0 when the purchase is completed (because it has been reduced to 0 or because it was already at 0), the character suffers a Shortfall. (If both outcomes occur from a single acquisition, the character suffers 2 Shortfalls instead.)

INCIDENTAL PURCHASES

Under certain conditions, some acquisitions don't require a roll. First, the acquisition test to find the item must have been reduced to a difficulty of Simple (D0), and the item's Cost may not have any Tariff rating. Then, determine an average cost for the item. This is equal to the static value plus half the number of Ⓝ in the cost (rounding up). If this is equal to or less than the character's Earnings, then the item can be obtained immediately, without rolling any dice, and without losing any Cashflow or risking a Shortfall.

ILLEGAL PURCHASES

Some purchases can be obtained illegally, or even require it. In these cases, the acquisition test can be made with Thievery instead of Lifestyle, representing the character's knowledge of Submondo contacts, black and grey markets, and other illicit channels. A character using Thievery can also choose to reduce the purchase's Restriction by up to three, to a minimum of 0, but the GM can choose to either gain an equivalent amount of Heat or add an equivalent Tariff to the item's cost — finding illegal goods can be costly, and risks legal trouble if discovered.

MONEY MANAGEMENT

Spending money isn't the only thing to consider when managing your finances.

Recovering Cashflow: As already noted, Cashflow recovers fully at the start of each new game session — an investment pays dividends, a new pay packet comes in, and so forth.

Asset Management: To free up ready cash during a session or to recover from Shortfalls, a character can rearrange funds, transfer savings, pay off some bills or debts, or otherwise juggle their accounts by spending an Asset and making a Simple (D0) Lifestyle test. For each Momentum spent from the test, the character may restore two Cashflow or remove one Shortfall. The difficulty of this test increases by one step for each Shortfall the character is currently suffering from. Additional Assets can be spent to add bonus d20s to this check.

Selling Items: Selling items functions similarly to purchasing, but in reverse. The character makes an acquisition test with a difficulty one higher than the item's normal Restriction rating — in this case, to find a buyer rather than a seller. Characters can't sell services they've purchased in this way (although if they're performing a service themselves they might be able to find someone interested in hiring them).

If the acquisition test is successful, determine the item's Total Cost and subtract the character's Earnings as normal — wealthy characters find that selling items tends to benefit their overall finances less. (Momentum can be spent to effectively reduce the character's Earnings for this purpose.) Any Tariffs also reduce the item's sale cost, as they are automatically deducted to pay local authorities. For each point of Total Cost remaining, restore a single point of lost Cashflow, up to the character's normal maximum. If the character would regain five or more Cashflow and/or is restored to full Cashflow, the character can either remove one Shortfall or gain one Asset from the sudden influx of money; the character can gain no more than two Assets from any given sale.

THEFT AND EXTORTION

Obtaining money through illicit means can be very effective, and unscrupulous or desperate characters can seek to relieve the unsuspecting of their cash.

The specific skills vary depending on the type of theft, but all follow the same pattern — a face-to-face test of the thief's skill against the target's, and if the thief wins, they deal 1+2🅝 of appropriate damage to the target, +1 per Momentum spent, and gain an Asset as a Harm Effect for each Breach, Metanoia, or Wound they inflict. (If the theft is physical, the thief can choose to add the Nonlethal quality to their attack by adding +1 complication range to the attack test.) They can then either:

- Risk stealing more, repeating the face-to-face test at +1 difficulty and inflicting an additional 1+2🅝 base damage.
- End their attempt and make their escape.

For example, pickpocketing pits the thief's Thievery skill against the mark's Observation skill and is a mental attack, where a pure snatch-and-grab or mugging might be against a victim's Athletics and be a physical attack.

Quantronic theft can set the thief's Hacking against the target's Analysis skill, to see if they realise they are being stolen from in time to alert authorities, or against the Hacking skill of their bank's on-shift sysadmins monitoring accounts for suspicious changes. In either case, it's a quantronic attack.

Extortion can involve Persuade or even Close Combat against the target's Discipline, counting as mental or physical attacks respectively, while long cons can involve full Psywar scenes using Thievery and Persuade tests against the mark's Analysis skill to coax and manipulate them into an irrational and impulsive trusting state.

In any case, based on the approach the thief describes, the GM decides which skills the thief and target test, the track being targeted, and the consequences should the thief fail.

BOOM AND BUST

Selling items can be a way to make money, but there are dangers. Complications reduce the base sales price of the item by one, and if it already is at zero, remove 1🅝 Cashflow — the item might be out of style, degraded through use, or so extensively counterfeited that buyers are reluctant to believe the item is genuine. Multiple complications could mean the item is angrily returned, or a lawsuit!

CASUAL PICKPOCKETING

The rules for theft and extortion assume a target with something substantial to steal. If a pickpocket just wants to work a crowd for pocket change, this can be resolved as a Thievery (D1) test to restore 1 Cashflow, plus 1 Cashflow per Momentum spent. A target can attempt to make this a face-to-face test against Observation as a Reaction.

GEAR RULES

Whatever the area of endeavour, the right tool is the key. The Human Sphere is filled with a multitude of radical, innovative, and ever-evolving technologies which are being constantly adapted to commercial, military, and idiosyncratic needs. This chapter contains all of the rules governing these many types of technology. Details for specific items are listed alphabetically in the *Gear Catalogue*, starting on p. 361.

Ammunition (p. 339) is used primarily with ranged weapons.

Armour (p. 341) has seen a plethora of innovations over the past century, driven by breakthroughs in metamaterial science, quantronic integration, and miniaturisation.

Augmentations (p. 344) can be cybernetic or biotechnological in nature, but all are designed to enhance the human form (whether in its natural state or through the perfected physiques of advanced Lhosts).

Contagions (p. 347) include diseases, poisons, drugs, quantronic viruses, and even virulent rumours.

Explosive Devices (p. 349) bring overwhelming destruction to the battlefield. They include charges, grenades, and mines.

Geists (p. 350) are the ubiquitous companions of modern civilisation. Advanced geists are available, but most users will be more likely to upgrade the geist they have owned since childhood.

Hacking Devices (p. 352) include both the hardware and software which shape the endless and pervasive guerrilla battlefields of the Infowar.

Lhosts (p. 354) are artificial bodies used by those receiving a Resurrection, ALEPH Aspects, or other artificial intelligences.

Remotes (p. 354) are specifically designed for operation from a distance. They are also often used by geists and similar pseudo-AIs to give them a semblance of a physical presence.

Resources (p. 355) are an abstract method of tracking a wide variety of expendable supplies.

Tools (p. 357) include everything from handheld devices to full-sized laboratories.

Weapons (p. 358) include both the lethal and nonlethal.

Other Items (p. 360) covers everything else, including a handful of miscellaneous gear-related mechanics.

ITEM SIZES

An item's Size rates how easy or difficult it is to wield. Items without a Size can generally be assumed to require one hand if they are being physically manipulated, although many objects can be passively worn and it's also not unusual for equipment in the Human Sphere to be controlled quantronically (without need for direct physical interaction).

ONE-HANDED (1H)
The item can be used in one or two hands without penalty.

TWO-HANDED (2H)
The item can be used in two hands without penalty. If used one-handed, any test made to use it is at +2 difficulty.

UNBALANCED
The item is heavy and difficult to wield for any but the strongest people. If the wielder has a Brawn of 9 or higher, the item is considered to be one-handed. If the wielder has a Brawn of 8 or lower, then the item is considered to be two-handed instead.

UNWIELDY
The item is extremely bulky and cumbersome, and not particularly portable. Any use of an Unwieldy item is at +2 difficulty and +2 complication range. These penalties can be removed by taking the Brace action. Unwieldy items cannot be wielded in one hand.

MOUNTED
The item is fixed into position, attached to a vehicle, or otherwise immobile. Many mounted items can be used at a distance by characters with quantronic access (and, of course, the proper authentication).

MASSIVE
The item is prodigious in size, designed to be wielded by creatures larger than ordinary people (or by warriors within TAGs). Creatures with the Monstrous special ability can wield the item in two hands freely, or in one hand by increasing the

FINDING YOUR GEAR
Each section of the *Gear Rules* includes a table listing all of the equipment of that type, including the Restriction, Cost, and Tariff for acquiring it. In the *Gear Catalogue*, starting on p. 361, all of the gear in the game is listed in alphabetical order. This makes it easy to shop around for gear of a particular type (by looking at the tables here in the *Gear Rules* section) and also easy to find a specific piece of gear (by looking it up in the *Gear Catalogue*). The latter is particularly useful for Gamemasters trying to find more information on a piece of gear listed in an NPC's stat block.

difficulty of skill tests to use the item by two steps. It cannot be wielded by normal-size characters.

FACILITY

The item is the size of a room, building, or habitat and is a permanent structure unless otherwise noted. Use requires either quantronic access and permissions, or physical presence in the facility.

ITEM STRUCTURE

Every object has a Structure rating for how much physical damage it can take, roughly dictated by its Size and composition. Losing Structure is mostly superficial, but if an object suffers 5 or more physical damage from an attack or its Structure has been reduced to 0 or less after an attack, it will suffer a Fault. The following are rough guidelines – as always, the GM has final discretion.

- Even the most fragile items have at least 1 Structure.
- An item that can be easily carried or held in one hand will have 2–4 Structure.
- An item that needs to be carried in both hands will have 4–6 Structure.
- An item which is too large to carry, but which is smaller than person will have 6–8 Structure.
- Person-sized or larger objects will have 8–10 Structure
- Civilian vehicles will have 6–8 Structure for each person they can carry; use this as a guide for similar-size non-vehicle objects.

Particularly delicate objects (including those with the Fragile quality) will have half- to three-quarters as much Structure as other items of that size. They will usually have no Armour Soak.

Items made of particularly tough or hard material may have 1 Armour Soak.

Items designed for rugged or military use (including weapons), will usually have 1.5× or 2× as much Structure as other items of that size, as well as having 2–3 Armour Soak.

Teseum items will have 3× to 4× as much Structure as other items of that size, and will have at least 4 Armour Soak.

Buildings and other large constructions (including orbitals, large spaceships, and the like) can vary widely depending on construction materials, and should be split into distinct parts – doors, windows, bulkheads, etc. Use the above guidelines to judge the Structure of those sections. Load-bearing sections should have more Structure, and their destruction can be catastrophic.

FAULT EFFECTS

The following effects can be used for Faults suffered by an object. Objects are disabled and cannot be used if they suffer four Faults. If they suffer five Faults, they are permanently destroyed. (Rebuilding something from the resulting scrap is essentially equivalent to building a new item from scratch.)

Compromised: Although not fully disabled, the functionality of some objects may be compromised with a Fault Effect. For example, a locked door might be kicked open or a gun turret damaged so that it can no longer rotate (limiting its field of fire). In the case of particularly robust objects, the GM may require multiple Fault Effects to be inflicted before the object is fully compromised.

Damaged: Characters using the item suffer +1 difficulty on associated skill tests. (Since this can increase the difficulty of Simple (D0) tests to an Average (D1) test, it may also require characters to make skill tests that they normally wouldn't need to, such as controlling a car after its tires have been shot out.)

Disable Function: For objects with multiple functions, it may be possible to disable one of them with a Fault Effect while leaving the others intact.

Injury: In some cases, inflicting a Fault on an object may inflict damage on its user. (For example, a damaged ladder may cause someone to fall and suffer damage.) The GM should determine these effects as logically and consistently as possible, but defaulting to 2 N damage is a good rule of thumb.

REPAIRING ITEMS

Objects cannot use the Recover action. They also cannot Rest or Recuperate (although some items may possess the Self-Repairing quality). Characters can make treat tests for items normally (using the Treat action during action scenes or performing Minor or Serious Treatment repairs between action scenes). In addition, a successful Simple (D0) treat test between scenes can be used to recover all Structure the item has lost. Treat tests for objects use the Tech skill.

ITEM QUALITIES

Many items have features in common with each other. Item qualities are used to describe those features and collect the rules for them under a single, convenient label.

Abbreviations: Some qualities will be listed in stat blocks using an abbreviation. These abbreviations are listed below in [square brackets] after the name of the quality. (For example, the "Electromagnetic [E/M]" quality appears as "E/M" in stat blocks.)

quantronic access – p. 116

Self-Repairing, p. 335: Item recovers all Structure between scenes and 1 Fault per day.

Recover / Treat Action – p. 111–248

Rest / Recuperate / Treatment – p. 102–103

Teseum – p. 8

Quality Ratings: An X in a quality's name indicates that the quality is available at several different ratings (usually 1–3). Unlike other qualities, if an item would add the same rated quality as another item, and both items have the quality, the ratings stack (unless otherwise noted).

Subtypes: Some qualities have subtypes or are variations on a theme. The different subtypes are listed below in (parentheses) after the name of the quality. (For example, the Area (Close/Medium/Long) quality is actually three separate qualities – Area (Close), Area (Medium), and Area (Long).)

Triggered Effects: Some qualities (usually only attack qualities) only take effect when triggered. As noted in their description, these qualities are activated when one or more Effects are rolled on a combat dice roll (usually a damage roll). As long as at least one Effect is rolled, all of the qualities on the associated equipment will be triggered.

GENERAL QUALITIES

Armoured X: The item has Armour Soak equal to its rating, making it more difficult to destroy.

Augmentation [Aug]: This item is implanted, bioengineered, or xenografted into the user's body and nervous system. Augs usually cannot be removed without invasive surgery or mutilation.

Comms Equipment [Comms]: Although most equipment in the Human Sphere is susceptible to hacking (see the Non-Hackable quality, below), Comms Equipment is integrated into a user's personal area network and is primarily designed to be quantronically controlled. As a result, Comms Equipment is susceptible to the System Disruption Breach Effect and can become non-functional if a character's personal area network is destroyed due to Breaches. Comms Equipment cannot possess the Non-Hackable quality.

Concealed X: The item is easy to hide or is designed to be disguised as something else. Observation tests made to discover the item when it has been hidden or concealed are made at +X difficulty. A character can spend 1 Momentum when using the item to stow it away immediately after use.

Disposable: A disposable item is designed to be used only once and is destroyed or lost after use.

Expert X: The item incorporates complex programs and subroutines that help a character use the item. When used as part of a successful skill test, the expert system grants the user X bonus Momentum. Expert systems connect to the user's personal network, automatically have the Comms Equipment quality, and are penalised if the user suffers Breaches.

Fragile: A Fragile item is disabled after suffering one Fault and is destroyed after suffering two Faults.

Improvised X: The item is not designed for the described use, giving it a +X complication range.

Negative Feedback [NFB]: Any piece of equipment with this quality cannot be used with other NFB equipment.

Neural: The item interfaces directly with the user's nervous system, allowing the user to issue neuronal commands. If the item is designed for active use rather than passive benefit – a weapon or hacking device, for example – it grants 1 bonus Momentum when using the item for its intended purpose. (This stacks with the item's Expert quality, if any.) If hacked, however, the item exposes the user's mind and nervous system to direct quantronic attack, rendering them vulnerable to a truly nasty subset of Breach Effects and attack programs.

Non-Hackable: Virtually all modern technology in the Human Sphere possesses some measure of connectivity and is designed to be controlled by or feed information back to a user's comlog or local datasphere. This means that most items are vulnerable to being hacked. Items with the Non-Hackable quality either lack quantronic components entirely (like a Teseum sword) or have been specifically designed to lack networking capability. Such items cannot be targeted with quantronic attacks and cannot be affected by Breach Effects.
- **Non-Hackable (+1D)**: The Non-Hackable quality can be added to equipment which normally lacks it, but this requires the item to have clunky, primitive, and/or non-responsive interface, inflicting a +1 difficulty to any action tests made using the item.

Repeater: A repeater allows a hacker with the proper authentication connected to the repeater to make quantronic attacks as if they were in the same zone as the repeater. If an enemy hacker can gain access to a repeater (generally by gaining authentication through a Breach Effect and then using a Standard Action to connect to the repeater), they can also make quantronic attacks against any hacker currently connected to the repeater as if they were in the same zone.

Repeaters have their own Firewall and Security values, allowing them to be targeted by quantronic attacks. They can be disabled or suborned with a single Breach Effect. Repeaters can be either physical objects (inhabiting a combat zone) or a specialised program (inhabiting a quantronic zone). Connecting or disconnecting from a repeater requires a Standard Action. A hacker with proper authentication can use the Reset action to reboot a suborned repeater.

datasphere, p. 141: A shared network of coordinated data, communication, and user experiences.

comlog – p. 365

System Disruption – p. 121

gaining authentication – p. 117

WHY REPEATERS?
The primitive all-band mesh protocols of the pre-Maya networks proved to be a security nightmare once they were paired with the ubiquitous, long-range communication possible with modern technology. As a result, modern networking protocols are designed to only interface with connections in very close physical proximity. This, of course, has utility drawbacks. Repeaters are essentially very limited networking hubs that will only accept commands from very specific devices, allowing their users to take advantage of long-range communication without baring their personal networks to the entire galaxy.

WARNING

HOSTILE FORCE
NEARBY

PART IV: GEAR

ACQUISITIONS
GEAR RULES
GEAR CATALOGUE
LIFESTYLES
SERVICES

Self-Repairing: The item is self-repairing. Between scenes, it automatically recovers all its lost Structure. It also removes one Fault per day. If the item provides Soak or BTS and those scores are reduced, it also regains one Soak and BTS until it returns to its original rating.

Subtle X: Using this item is particularly quiet and draws little attention. Any Observation test to notice the use of the item increases by +X difficulty. In addition, noisy actions using the item are reduced to sneaky actions; and sneaky actions are reduced to silent actions.

Supportware (Personal/Close/Long): A character can only maintain one Supportware program in their personal network at a time, and characters can only benefit from one Supportware program being run by their allies. Activating a Supportware program is a Minor Action which also automatically deactivates any other Supportware currently running on the user's system. Allies within the Supportware's range immediately and automatically link to the Supportware (and gain its benefits), but if they gain additional Supportware links they must use a Minor Action to switch which link is currently benefiting them.

Unsubtle X: This item is unusually overt, drawing undue attention each time the item is used. Any Observation tests made to detect the use of the item are made at −X difficulty (minimum 0). In addition, silent actions using the item are increased to sneaky actions; and sneaky actions are increased to noisy actions.

ARMOUR QUALITIES

These qualities apply only to worn gear (usually some form of armour, but possibly including high-tech clothing and the like).

Adapted (Environment): The gear is designed to protect against the common hazards — such as temperature, pressure, or humidity extremes — of a particular environment, granting a −1 difficulty to all related Extraplanetary, Resistance, and Survival tests when worn there.

Exoskeleton X: The armour's strength and stability grants the wearer a +X ⓝ damage bonus to melee attacks, in addition to any provided by a high Brawn. The wearer can use Unwieldy weapons without Bracing, use Unbalanced or Two-Handed weapons in one hand without an increase in difficulty, and gain up to +Xd20 to any Brawn test in exchange for increasing the test's complication range by the same amount.

Reset, p. 120: Hacking (D1) test as Standard Action to recover all Firewall. Comms items suffer +4 difficulty, reduced by one step per round / Momentum spent.

noise / sneaky / silent actions – p. 105

Unwieldy – p. 332

BTS, p. 341: Use as persistent soak vs. Biotech, Nanotech, Radiation attacks. Add as bonus to Security Soak. Reduce difficulty of Resistance tests vs. diseases, poisons

Blinded, p. 103: 3🅽 mental damage. Vision-based tests at +2 difficulty.

special Harm Effect, p. 102: Special Harm Effects do not count towards incapacitation or destruction, but are treated like Harm Effects in all other ways.

Brace – p. 110

Unbalanced / Two-Handed – p. 332

Withdraw momentum spend, p. 106: Leave the Reach of an enemy without triggering Retaliate Reactions.

Defence Reaction – p. 100

Deafened, p. 104: 3🅽 mental damage. Hearing-based tests at +2 difficulty.

System Disruption – p. 121

Cube – p. 366

Heavy Armour: The armour is particularly bulky and cumbersome, making it difficult to move around quickly and adding +1 difficulty to all Agility-based skill tests when worn.

Hidden Armour X: The armour is designed to be worn covertly, either under clothing or in plain view but disguised as innocuous items. Observation tests made to notice the armour are made at +X difficulty.

Kinematika: This armour incorporates primed fast-twitch polymer fibres, allowing the user to dodge and flex incredibly quickly for brief periods, reducing the Heat costs and difficulty of all Acrobatics Defence Reactions by one, to a minimum of 0 and Simple (D0) respectively. After a successful Defence, the user can Withdraw by spending 0 Momentum and may spend 2 Momentum to move to an adjacent zone.

ATTACK QUALITIES

These qualities apply only to weapons, ammunition, and other forms of attack.

Anti-Materiel X: The attack is designed to damage structures, vehicles, and other sources of cover. Attacks against targets in cover destroy X points of cover for each Effect rolled and attacks against vehicles or armoured structures permanently reduce the target's Soak in that location by X for each Effect rolled.

If a piece of cover loses all of its cover dice, it is destroyed and no longer provides any protection. If the vehicle or armoured structure's location's Soak was already at 0, each Effect rolled deals 1 damage instead.

Area (Close/Medium/Long): The attack affects a wide area and multiple targets. For each Momentum spent, the attack strikes an additional target within the blast's range, starting with the nearest one to the initial target. If a complication is rolled, the GM may choose to target an ally within the affected area. Each character targeted by an Area attack may attempt separate Defence Reactions, resolving them against a fixed difficulty of Challenging (D2) instead of a face-to-face test.

If an item also has an Indiscriminate quality with the same range, ignore its Area quality.

Backlash X: Attacks with the Backlash quality are dangerous for the user as well as the enemy, and inflict X damage to the wielder for each Effect rolled. This damage ignores Soak and, if it is physical damage, affects a random hit location.

Biotech: The attack relies on biological, chemical, or technological means that bypass conventional armour. Damage inflicted by a Biotech attack uses the target's BTS as persistent soak instead of its Armour.

Blinding: The attack emits focused beams of light, sound, or data to blind the target or jam their sensory ports. If an Effect is rolled on a Blinding attack, the target must succeed on a Daunting (D3) Resistance test or suffer the Blinded condition. The condition lasts for one round per Effect rolled.

Breach Effect [BE]: This attack can inflict a special Breach Effect (as explained in the item description) by spending Momentum. These special Breach Effects do not count as Breaches for the purpose of disabling or compromising the target's network, but may be treated and removed like other Breach Effects.

Breaker: Breaker attacks are designed to degrade modern Bio-Technological Shielding (BTS). (The name references the technical expression "breakthrough time", a criterion used in the evaluation of CBRN protection that measures the time until the hazardous agent reaches body.) For each Effect rolled, inflict a special Fault Effect which reduces the BTS value of the target's armour by 1 (to a minimum of 0). If the BTS value was already at 0 before damage was dealt, each Effect rolled deals +1 damage instead.

Deafening: The attack releases a wave of sound that overloads the target's auditory systems. If an Effect is rolled on a Deafening attack, the target must succeed on a Difficult (D3) Resistance test or suffer the Deafened condition. The condition lasts for one round per Effect rolled.

Electromagnetic [E/M]: These attacks emit high-energy electromagnetic pulses upon activation or impact. The attacks are made using physical attack tests, but they inflict quantronic damage. If this damage causes a Breach, they must inflict a System Disruption as the Breach Effect—the pulse is indiscriminately destructive, lacking the advantages of subtler hacking attacks. If a character suffers their fourth or fifth Breach from an E/M attack, the attacker can spend 2 Momentum to destroy their Cube (if any). E/M attacks also possess the Breaker quality automatically. Equipment with the Non-Hackable quality is immune to E/M attacks.

Extended Reach: An attack with Extended Reach can take the Withdraw Action as a Free Action if no enemy combatants within Reach have an Extended Reach attack of their own. Melee attacks made with non-Extended Reach weapons against a character with an Extended Reach attack are made at +1 difficulty.

Frangible: These attacks become less effective over time. For each Effect rolled, reduce the number of 🅽 in the attack's damage rating by 1. If this would reduce the number of Ⓝ to 0, then the attack cannot be used again until it has been replaced or replenished.

Grievous: These attacks are designed to inflict massive harm on a target, incapacitating them far more swiftly. If a Grievous attack inflicts one or more Harms, it inflicts one additional Harm of the same type as well.

Guided: A Guided attack can be controlled and directed from a distance. If the target has been Marked with an appropriate piece of gear, the attack ignores all penalties to hit due to range, visibility, or concealment. Additionally, with an Average (D1) Analysis test, an attack with the weapon can ignore any conditional soak the target would normally benefit from. Guided weapons or ammunition possess the Comms quality automatically.

Immobilising: If one or more Effects are rolled on the damage roll from an Immobilising attack, the target must make an Athletics test with a difficulty equal to the number of Effects rolled or become Hindered. If the target was already Hindered or if the attacker spends 1 Momentum, the target instead becomes Stuck.

Incendiary X: The target is set alight and gains the Burning X condition for a number of rounds equal to the number of Effects rolled.

Indiscriminate (Close/Medium/Long): An Indiscriminate attack affects one or more zones. Each target within the affected zone — every character, vehicle, and damageable object — suffers the attack's damage (even if the attacker wasn't aware of their presence). Each character targeted by an Indiscriminate attack may attempt separate Defence Reactions, resolving them separately against a fixed difficulty of Challenging (D2).

If an item also has the Area quality with the same range, ignore its Area quality

Knockdown: If one or more Effects are rolled on the damage roll of a Knockdown attack, the target must pass an Acrobatics or Athletics test with a difficulty equal to the number of Effects rolled or be knocked prone.

Monofilament: The weapon uses a monomolecular wire — a single-molecule thick edge stabilised by a faint E/M field. The weapon ignores all Armour Soak, but it has +2 complication range and does not gain any bonus damage from a high attribute (including Superhuman Attributes).

MULTI (Light/Medium/Heavy): MULTI weapons are designed to use multiple forms of ammunition,

switching seamlessly between preloaded primary and secondary modes as the situation requires. A character declares which mode (i.e., ammunition type) they're using when they choose a target to attack. Some MULTI weapons may have multiple secondary modes of fire.

- **Light MULTI** weapons fire any Standard ammo in their primary mode and a specific type of Special ammo in their secondary mode. (If the Special ammo type is not specified, it is DA by default.) The secondary mode has Burst 1, regardless of the weapon's normal Burst, and the Munition quality.
- **Medium MULTI** weapons fire any Standard ammo in their primary mode and a specific type of Special ammo in their secondary mode. (If the Special ammo type is not specified, it is DA by default.) Unlike a Light MULTI, the secondary mode does not have the Munition quality (unless specified otherwise) and uses the weapon's normal Burst rating.
- **Heavy MULTI** weapons fire any Standard ammo in their primary mode and a specific type of Heavy ammo in their secondary mode. (If the Heavy ammo type is not specified, it is EXP by default.) The secondary mode has Burst 1, regardless of the weapon's normal Burst, and the Munition quality.

MULTI Light Mod: Weapons with the MULTI Light Mod quality have been designed to easily incorporate an adhesive launcher, light shotgun, light flamethrower, or light grenade launcher as a secondary weapon. It requires an Average (D1) Tech test to install the secondary weapon. The two weapons then operate as one with the Heavy MULTI quality (or Medium MULTI quality if the secondary weapon is a light shotgun), with the secondary weapon operating as an additional secondary mode.

MULTI Heavy Mod: Weapons with the MULTI Heavy Mod quality are similar to MULTI Light Mod weapons, but their secondary weapons can include heavy flamethrowers and heavy grenade launchers (in addition to weapons allowed by the MULTI Light Mod quality).

Munition: A weapon with this quality (such as rocket launchers, grenade launchers, and flamethrowers) can only use a specific type (or types) of ammunition. A Munition weapon expends a single Reload whenever it is fired, which provides no benefit but counts toward the normal limitations on the number of Reloads spent.

Nanotech: Nanotech-based attacks bypass traditional defences. Damage inflicted by a Nanotech attack uses the target's BTS as persistent soak instead of its Armour or Security. In addition, these

Comms – p. 334

Standard / Special ammo – p. 339

Burst, p. 358: Maximum number of Reloads can be spent on attack rolls with weapon.

DA ammo – p. 367: Add Vicious 2 to weapon.

EXP ammo, p. 368: Add Area (Close), Spread 1, Unsubtle, and Vicious 2 to weapon.

Hindered, p. 104: −1 zone when making movement actions. +1 difficulty on terrain tests.

Stuck, p. 104: Cannot move away from object/location stuck to.

Burning X, p. 104: Target suffers X Ⓝ damage to Vigour and Resolve at end of their turn, ignoring Armour. Lasts X turns, plus 1 turn per Effect rolled.

Defence Reaction, p. 100: Hacking test vs. infowar attack, Close Combat or Acrobatics vs. melee attack, Discipline vs. mental attack, Acrobatics vs. ranged attack.

Reload – p. 356

prone, p. 104: −1 zone when making movement actions; +1 difficulty on terrain tests. +1 difficulty vs. ranged attacks at Medium range. +2 Soak for each Effect rolled on cover dice. Attacks at Close range vs. prone character gain +2 bonus Momentum.

special Harm Effect, p. 102: Special Harm Effects do not count towards incapacitation or destruction, but are treated like Harm Effects in all other ways.

Staggered, p. 104: Pay 1 Momentum to take Standard Action. Pay 1 Infinity Point to perform Reaction (plus normal Heat cost).

Reload – p. 356

attacks possess Nanotech Effects, which generally take the form of special Harm Effects which can be inflicted by spending Momentum. These special Harm Effects do not count as Harms, but may be treated and removed like other Harm Effects. Targets with BTS are immune from Nanotech Effects triggered via Momentum spends, but may still be subjected to them as a normal Harm Effect if the attack deals a Harm normally.

Nonlethal: This attack is designed to incapacitate. Any Harms inflicted by a Nonlethal attack are temporary and can be removed by successfully resting (along with the Stress normally removed by resting, see p. 102). Characters cannot die as a result of Nonlethal Harms.

Parry X: This type of attack is exceptionally good at turning aside incoming attacks. A Parry attack grants the wielder +X 🅝 Cover Soak, but only against melee attacks.

Piercing X: The attack ignores X points of Soak for each effect rolled on its damage roll.

Radiation X: Damage with the Radiation quality ignores all Soak except from BTS and is treated as Terrifying X and Vicious X. If a Wound is suffered from radiation, it possesses a special Wound Effect that inflicts a +1 difficulty on all Agility-, Brawn-, or Coordination-based actions. In addition, neither the Wound nor the Wound Effect can be removed without Serious Treatment (or a specialised item).

Reflective X: Attacks with this quality are the same as Smoke, except that the affected zones are impenetrable to modern optics and sensors, including multispectral visors (which are, therefore, affected by the penalties normally).

Salvo X (Quality): The attack is particularly effective when large quantities of ammunition are unleashed. This quality grants another quality whenever the attack uses X Reloads (not counting Reloads used because of the Munition quality). If no X value is given, the Salvo quality can be triggered with one Reload.

Smoke X: Attacks with Smoke create a cloud of gas, nanobots, or other substance that interferes with enemy lines of sight within a target zone. For each Momentum spent when attacking with a Smoke weapon, the attack affects an additional adjacent zone. Observation tests or attacks within, into, or out of affected zones are made at +X difficulty. This penalty decreases by 1 every 1d6 rounds. If the penalty is reduced to 0, the Smoke has been completely dissipated.

Speculative Fire: The ranged attack can be arced over obstacles, bounced off walls, or otherwise used in an indirect manner to attack hard-to-reach foes. A Speculative Fire attack has −1 difficulty against targets that are detected, but for which there is no direct line of fire. Further, the attacker can take a penalty of +1 difficulty to ignore the target's Cover Soak entirely.

Spread X: This attack can strike the target across multiple areas. For each Effect generated on the damage roll, the attack inflicts X additional hits at half the first hit's damage, each separately reduced by Soak. If the attack inflicts physical damage, roll separate hit locations for each additional hit. The weapon is also particularly effective at blasting holes in cover; add up all the damage inflicted from all hits to determine if cover is degraded.

Stun: If one or more Effects is rolled, the attack inflicts the Staggered condition on the target. This condition lasts for one round per Effect rolled.

Terrifying X: The attack is especially agonising or frightening. Each Effect rolled inflicts X mental damage to the target in addition to whatever damage it inflicts normally.

Thrown: Thrown weapons can be used to make ranged attacks, but use Athletics as the attack skill (instead of Ballistics). Thrown weapons have a range of Close unless specified otherwise. If the Thrown weapon can also be used for melee attacks, those attacks are still resolved normally using the Close Combat skill.

Torrent: This attack is a stream of flame, deadly liquid, gas, or some other substance that can be swept back and forth across an area to affect a group and overcome cover. Torrent weapons cannot affect targets further away than their optimal range, but they ignore all Cover Soak. A Torrent weapon is otherwise treated as an Area attack.

Toxic X: The attack has a lingering, deleterious effect. If the attack inflicts a Harm, the Harm Effect causes the target to suffer 1+X 🅝 (Vicious 1) damage at the end of each turn. Unless specified otherwise, this damage is of the same type as the attack which inflicted it.

Unforgiving X: The attack is either exceptionally precise or capable of inflicting much greater harm on a direct hit. When making an attack that has gained the benefit of an Exploit action, the attack gains Vicious X.

Vicious X: A Vicious attack inflicts X additional damage for each Effect rolled.

AMMUNITION

The ammo interoperability problems O-12 units faced during the First Paradiso Offensive led to strict contractual standards for munitions suppliers, and factions followed suit to ensure their manufacturers stayed competitive. Most ammunition has switched to O-12 standards, enabling even basic firearms to take advantage of a variety of payloads. Each faction tries to maintain a monopoly on their most effective munitions for military advantage and profitable export, even requiring manufacturers to sell only to licensed governmental agents, but grey and black markets abound, and the murky machinations of factional espionage ensure no trade secret stays secret forever.

USING AMMUNITION

Instead of inventorying individual rounds, magazines, or canisters, *Infinity* uses abstract Reloads — a form of resource — to simplify the tracking and use of ammunition.

When purchasing a weapon, it can be assumed to come with one type of ammunition it is capable of firing. (MULTI weapons come with one type of ammunition for each mode of fire.) If this ammunition has a Restriction level higher than the weapon itself, use the ammunition's Restriction level when making the purchase. This ammunition can be initially recorded as having zero Reloads. (Remembering that since Reloads are not required to fire a ranged weapon and are not expended through normal use of the weapon, this rating indicates that the character has a small supply of the ammunition in question.)

Additional ammunition types for a weapon can be purchased as Reloads.

Swapping out a weapon's current ammo type for a different one requires a Minor Action (unless the weapon has the MULTI quality).

AMMUNITION CATEGORIES

Ammunition comes in five broad categories, each of which contain a variety of ammo types.

Standard ammunition is commonly available throughout the Human Sphere, and is designed for use with most sidearms and firearms.

Special ammunition is legally restricted, dangerous, difficult to manufacture, or all of the above. To use a Special ammo type, a ranged weapon needs to be designed for it or modded to do so, and manufacturing Special rounds usually take expensive machinery, rare materials, trade secrets, or all of the above.

Heavy ammunition is higher calibre and even more dangerous to make and use. With rare exceptions, only ranged weapons with the Munition quality can fire Heavy ammo. It is illegal to carry in most territories, and acquiring it outside of military channels means knowing the maker personally or dealing with some seriously edgy people.

Arrows are used exclusively with bows. Useful in situations where the report of a firearm would be counterproductive, modern combat arrows are made out of meta-aramid materials and can be tipped with a variety of lethal payloads.

Shells are designed for exclusive use with shotguns. Many modern shells use integrated proximity sensors to detonate at precisely the right distance to take advantage of specialty payloads.

Standard, Special, and Arrow ammunition is sold in sets of three Reloads, while Heavy and Shell ammunition are sold as individual Reloads. Since ammo is commonly sold in large quantities, difficulty penalties due to buying in bulk are reduced by −1 difficulty.

Abbreviations: Some ammo types will be listed in stat blocks using an abbreviation. These abbreviations are listed below, and in the ammunition descriptions, in parentheses after the name of the ammunition. (For example, Armour Piercing rounds appear as "AP" in stat blocks.)

Munition, p. 337: Weapon expends Reload each time it is fired (without normal benefit).

resources – p. 355

WATCH OUT!
Knowing what you're up against is a critical survival skill, so experienced operatives learn to identify ammunition types by muzzle flash, sound, and similar cues. As a Free Action when taking fire from a ranged weapon or observing a ranged attack, a character can identify the ammo type being used with a Challenging (D2) Awareness+Ballistics test.

CONCILIUM CONVENTION

A number of weapons, ammunition types, and other items — particularly those likely to destroy or damage Cubes — are forbidden under the Concilium Convention. These items marked with a Bureau Aegis sigil 🅑. In practice, these laws are honoured more in the breach than in the observance, with governments and corporations ignoring these restrictions when it suits them. Private citizens without bureaucratic pull and even officials operating under public scrutiny may want to seriously consider the consequences, however, before unleashing viral or E/M weaponry.

AMMUNITION TABLE

NAME	CATEGORY	QUALITIES ADDED TO WEAPON	RESTRICTION	RELOAD COST	TARIFF
Adhesive	Standard	Immobilising, Knockdown, Nonlethal	0	3+1 Ⓝ	–
Armour Piercing (AP)	Standard	Piercing 2	1	3+2 Ⓝ	T2[2]
AP Arrows	Arrow	Piercing 3	1	3+1 Ⓝ	T2[2]
AP Slugs	Shell	Piercing 3	1	3+2 Ⓝ	T2[2]
Banshee	Special	Area (Close), Deafening, Nonlethal, Stun, Terrifying 3	2	3+2 Ⓝ	T1
Breaker	Special	Biotech, Breaker, Piercing 1	3 ⊗	3+2 Ⓝ	T2
Dancer	Special	Guided	2 (PanOceania 1)	3+2 Ⓝ	T1
Double Action (DA)	Special	Vicious 2	3 ⊗	3+2 Ⓝ	T2
DA Arrow	Arrow	Piercing 1, Vicious 2	3 ⊗	3+2 Ⓝ	T2
Double Trouble (DT)	Special	Biotech, Toxic 1, Vicious 1	3 ⊗ (Haqqislam 2)	4+1 Ⓝ	T1
DT Arrow	Arrow	Biotech, Piercing 1, Toxic 1, Vicious 1	3 ⊗ (Haqqislam 2)	4+1 Ⓝ	T1
Eclipse	Heavy	Nonlethal, Reflective 2	2	5+1 Ⓝ	T3
Electromagnetic (E/M)	Special	Breaker, E/M, Piercing 1	1 ⊗	3 +2 Ⓝ	T1
E/M2	Heavy	Area (Close), Breaker, E/M, Piercing 2	3 ⊗	4+2 Ⓝ	T2
Explosive (EXP)	Heavy	Area (Close), Spread 1, Unsubtle, Vicious 2	3 ⊗	4+2 Ⓝ	T1
Fire	Heavy	Incendiary 3, Terrifying 1	3 ⊗	4+2 Ⓝ	T2
Fire Shells	Shell	Area (Close), Incendiary 3, Terrifying 1	3 ⊗	4+2 Ⓝ	T2
Flarefiltered Chaff	Heavy	Area (Close), Blinding[1], Nonlethal	2	5+1 Ⓝ	T2
Flash	Special	Blinding, Nonlethal; removes Marked	1	3+1 Ⓝ	T1
Goonade (GOO)	Heavy	Area (Close), Immobilising, Knockdown, Nonlethal	1	4+1 Ⓝ	T2
K1	Special	Anti-Materiel 2, Monofilament	3	4+3 Ⓝ	T4
Nano	Heavy	Area (Close), Nanotech, Subtle 2, Toxic 2[1]	3 ⊗	6+1 Ⓝ	T2
Needle	Heavy	Piercing 2, Spread 1, Vicious 2	2	6+1 Ⓝ	T2
Nimbus	Heavy	Nonlethal, Reflective 2[1]	2	6+2 Ⓝ	T1
Nimbus+	Heavy	Nonlethal, Reflective 3[1]	3	6+3 Ⓝ	T2
Normal	Standard	–	0	2+1 Ⓝ	–
Normal Arrow	Arrow	Piercing 1	0	2+1 Ⓝ	–
Normal Shells	Shell	Area (Close), Spread 1	1 ⊗	3+1 Ⓝ	–
Oneiros	Heavy	Area (Close), Biotech, Immobilising, Nonlethal, Stun	1	5+1 Ⓝ	T2
Phobetor	Heavy	Area (Close), Biotech, Immobilising, Nonlethal, Stun, Terrifying 3[1]	3 ⊗	4+3 Ⓝ	T3
Plasma	Heavy	Knockdown, Unforgiving 3, Unsubtle[1]	EI Only	EI Only	–
SaboT	Heavy	Anti-Materiel 3, Piercing 5	3	6+2 Ⓝ	T3[2]
Shock	Special	Biotech, Grievous	3 ⊗	3+2 Ⓝ	T2
Shock Arrow	Arrow	Biotech, Grievous, Piercing 1	3 ⊗	3+2 Ⓝ	T2
Stun	Standard	Biotech, Nonlethal, Stun	1	3+1 Ⓝ	–
T2	Special	Anti-Materiel 2, Area (Close), Piercing 2, Vicious 2	4 ⊗ (Ariadna 3)	4+4 Ⓝ	T3[2]
T2 Shells	Shell	Anti-Materiel 2, Area (Close), Piercing 3, Vicious 2	4 ⊗ (Ariadna 3)	4+4 Ⓝ	T3[2]
Viral	Special	Biotech, Grievous, Toxic 2	4 ⊗ (Haqqislam 3)	5+2 Ⓝ	T2

[1] Ammunition has special effect. See description.
[2] No Tariff on Ariadna.

ARMOUR

Personal armour in the Human Sphere comes in many shapes and sizes, from lightweight ballistic cloth woven into clothing, to high-impact plastics and nano-reinforced ceramics, to towering power-assisted suits of armour that straddle the line between personal armour and TAG.

While military-grade armour can be difficult to obtain outside of legitimate channels, modern smart materials and protective gear can provide a surprising level of protection in the guise of ordinary clothing, particularly when customised by a knowledgeable technician.

ARMOUR SOAK

The primary function of armour is generally to protect against damage. The Armour Soak provided by the armour is specified for each hit location.

BIO-TECHNOLOGICAL SHIELD (BTS)

Some implants, clothing, devices, and particularly armour provide a layer of protection — called Bio-Technological Shielding, or BTS — against unconventional forms of attack. BTS systems include NBC (Nuclear, Biological, and Chemical) protections, anti-nanotech defences, electromagnetic hardening, immune system augmentations, and anti-hacking countermeasures.

A character's BTS value represents these diverse forms of protection and is used as persistent soak against attacks which possess the Biotech, Nanotech, and Radiation qualities. The BTS value also acts as a bonus to the character's Security Soak and reduces the difficulty of Resistance tests made to avoid the initial infection or exposure to diseases and poisons. (If that initial test is failed, the disease or poison is now inside the character's body and the defence of BTS is no longer effective, so it does not contribute to additional Resistance tests.)

WEARING ARMOUR

It takes 2+4  rounds to put on or take off civilian or combat armour. An Agility (D0) test can reduce this time by 1 round per Momentum spent (to a minimum of a single Standard Action). Powered armour is more difficult to get in and out of, requiring 1+2  rounds per hit location. Partially worn powered armour will provide Armour Soak in the locations currently worn, but is clumsy, inflicting a +1 complication range to physical skill tests per missing piece. Regardless of armour type, a faceplate can be opened or helmet removed as a Minor Action.

FITTING IT ALL IN

Just as the GM has final authority to determine the reasonable limits for how much equipment a character can carry, the GM has discretion over how much equipment can be jammed into a single piece of armour. It should be noted, however, that miniaturisation is common in the Human Sphere and it's possible to cram a lot of functionality into small spaces. On the other hand, there's only so many grenade launchers you can reasonably integrate into even the most bulked out suits of powered armour.

DOGFACE ARMOUR

When transforming into their Dog-Warrior forms, Dogfaces can easily rend constricting equipment and apparel. Transformation in human-sized armour inflicts 2+3 🄽 damage to the Dogface and inflicts a Fault on the armour.

Many Dogfaces, therefore, choose to wear armour suited for their Dog-Warrior form, exchanging encumbrance for a better fit and happier supply sergeants. The armour is cumbersome in human form, providing one less Armour Soak in all locations and inflicting +1 difficulty on all physical tests. Dogface Armour or apparel adds +2 🄽 and +T1 to the item's cost.

SYMBIONT HACKING

Although they are living creatures, note that symbiont armours do not possess the Non-Hackable quality. The Tohaa have specifically designed them to have quantronic interfaces.

COMBINING ARMOUR

If a character is wearing two or more items of armour that provide Armour Soak to the same location, use the highest Armour Soak among them, and if the character's armour would provide two or more different BTS values, use only the highest.

ARMOUR TYPES

The following are the most common types of armour used in the Human Sphere:

Civilian Armour covers construction workwear, industrial exoskeletons, sports equipment, vehicle crashsuits, environmental hazard protection, reinforced uniforms and clothing for security personnel, law enforcement, and paranoid VIPs.

Combat Armour is designed for the battlefield. It combines ballistic cloth, high-density ceramic plating, impact-resistant plastics, and other materials for a lightweight but durable layer of protection. Each is tailored to the combatant's proportions for maximum mobility, and is designed to work as an integrated whole.

Internal Armour is integrated into the character's body through implantation of bioengineered enhancement. It possesses the Augmentation quality and its presence can be detected with an Average (D1) Medicine or Observation test.

Powered Armour is a servo-assisted, indispensable asset in battle, allowing a unit to withstand punishing qualities of firepower, deal additional close combat damage, and easily wield massive weaponry, all without compromising mobility.

CUSTOMISING ARMOUR

Incorporating equipment, tools, kits, and even weapons into armour is common practice. The cost and stats of such equipment is identical to normal equipment, but once installed in armour it gains the Comms quality and can be used hands-free.

Equipment designed for combat armour is treated as Unwieldy if a character attempts to use it without installing it in combat armour. (At the GM's discretion, it may also need to be jury-rigged with a successful Tech test.)

Customising Loadout: Many types of armour come pre-installed with equipment packages, but it's also common for loadouts to be designed for customisability (or for armour to be jury-rigged even when it's not).

Replacing one piece of installed equipment with another requires a Tech test. The difficulty of the test is Average (D1) if the new equipment is specifically designed for that brand of armour; Challenging (D2) if it's designed to be installed in a different kind of armour; or Daunting (D3) and the use of one unit of Parts if adapting equipment that was not designed for armour. The installation takes a number of hours equal to the difficulty of the test.

Hot Swap Equipment: Some equipment is specifically designed to be hot-swapped out of combat armour. Such equipment costs 1+2 🄽 more than the normal version of the equipment, but it can be removed or installed in combat armour in ten minutes with a Simple (D0) Tech test.

Creating Equipment Slots: Adding additional equipment into armour (as opposed to swapping equipment out for different options) follows the same procedure as customising an armour's existing loadout, but the Tech tests are made +1 difficulty and require the use of one unit of Parts.

Damaging Integrated Equipment: When the wearer of armour with integrated components takes physical damage, the GM can spend 2 Heat to disable an item installed in the armour.

SYMBIONT ARMOUR

Symbiont armours are artificially generated biotechnological organisms — a mesh of fibrous parasites — worn as armour by the Tohaa. They protect the wearer by taking injuries, augmenting their abilities, and making it easier to heal them.

Soak and Wounds: Symbiont armour is a living organism with its own Vigour score. It grants Armour Soak to all hit locations and any physical damage or condition inflicted on a character wearing the symbiont armour is instead suffered by the armour. The symbiont suffers Wounds normally, but dies if it suffers more wounds than its Maximum Wounds rating (as indicated on the *Symbiont Armours Table*).

Vulnerability to Fire: Symbiont armours are particularly sensitive to fire. In addition to suffering damage from fire normally without the advantage of their Armour Soak, the fire also inflicts twice the physical damage suffered by the symbiont armour directly to the host (through a process of biofeedback).

Symbiotic Healing: While worn, symbiont armour grants 2 bonus Momentum to recovery and treat tests made for the host. Symbiont armour has the Self-Repairing quality. Those making treat tests to repair the symbiont armour can use either Medicine or Tech.

Detached Symbionts: Detaching from symbiont armour is a Standard Action. Doing so leaves the damage and Wounds suffered by the symbiont armour behind, as well as any conditions suffered by the symbiont armour (e.g. Hindered or Burning).

When detached from its host, symbiont armour enters a state of hibernation and dies unless it is placed in a nutrient-rich stasis chamber (where it can survive indefinitely) or reattached to its host within a week.

Other Effects: Many forms of symbiont armour have been bred to impart additional benefits, enhancing Tohaa neurological performance, improving strength and speed, augmenting sensory input, or allowing for computer-organic interfaces.

ARMOUR TABLE

ARMOUR	TYPE	ARMOUR SOAK				BTS	QUALITIES	RESTRICTION	COST	TARIFF	MAINTENANCE
		HEAD	TORSO	ARM	LEG						
Armoured Clothing	Civilian	0	1	1	1	0	Hidden Armour 2	2	6+1 (N)	T1	–
Ballistic Vest	Civilian	0	2	0	0	0	Hidden Armour 1	2	5+2 (N)	T1	–
Crashsuit	Civilian	3	3	3	3	0	Disposable	1	5+1 (N)	–	–
Gruntsuit	Civilian	1	2	2	2	1	Exoskeleton 1, Heavy Armour	2	9+2 (N)	T1	2
Hard Hat	Civilian	1	0	0	0	0	–	0	2+1 (N)	–	–
Heavy Combat Armour	Combat	3	4	2	3	2	Heavy Armour	3	10+2 (N)	T2	3
Light Combat Armour	Combat	1	2	1	1	1	–	2	7+1 (N)	T2	1
Medium Combat Armour	Combat	2	3	2	2	2	–	3	8+1 (N)	T2	2
ModCoat, Long	Civilian	0	1	1	1	0	Hidden Armour 2	2	6+2 (N)	T3	–
ModCoat, Short	Civilian	0	1	1	0	0	Hidden Armour 3	2	6+1 (N)	T2	–
Personal Protective Equipment	Civilian	0	2	2	1	1	–	1	5+1 (N)	–	–
Powered Combat Armour	Powered	4	5	3	3	3	Comms, Exoskeleton 3, Kinematika, Self-Repairing	4	13+2 (N)	T3	4
Powered Combat Armour (Ariadna)	Powered	4	5	3	3	3	Exoskeleton 3, Heavy Armour, Self-Repairing[1]	3	12+2 (N)	T1	3
Sports Padding	Civilian	1	1	1	1	0	–	0	3+2 (N)	–	–
Subdermal Grafts	Internal	1	2	1	1	0	Self-Repairing[1]	2	9+2 (N)	T1	–
XO Suit	Civilian	2	3	2	2	1	Adapted [any], Exoskeleton 1, Heavy Armour	2	9+2 (N)	T1	2

SYMBIONT ARMOUR TABLE

SYMBIONT ARMOUR	ARMOUR SOAK	BTS	VIGOUR	MAX. WOUNDS	QUALITIES	RESTRICTION
Ectros Armour	4	3	10	3	Kinematika, Self-Repairing[1]	Tohaa Only
Nu-El Armour	2	1	10	2	Kinematika, Self-Repairing[1]	Tohaa Only
Sakiel Armour	3	0	10	2	Kinematika, Self-Repairing[1]	Tohaa Only

[1] Armour has additional effects. See description.

VOORNE ARMOUR

The earliest examples of symbiont armour were the Raacno. Creatures native to the Tohaa homeworld of Ronuhaa, Raacno are variable in size and capable of adapting and attaching to myriad creatures. They survive ectosymbiotically in exchange for protecting their host from physical harm. The Tohaa adapted the Raacno to their own physiology, turning them into living armours. The earliest depictions of Tohaa warriors show them already wearing crude Raacno armours. (An example of this are the extremely ancient statues that guard the entrance to the Gesaaria Palace, one of the greatest pieces of primitive art of the Balaakan Empire.)

Modern Tohaa symbiont armour, adapted and improved from the Raacno, are known as Voorne. There are many different models of Voorne, all based on a common biotechnology.

Saarno: The Saarno is the "armour wake" in which a warrior spends the night wearing their new symbiont armour while it adapts to its host. Depending on the disposition of the symbiont, the procedure can cause great pain to the host (in a range from discomfort to mild agony). Once the Saarno is complete, that armour can never be worn by another Tohaa.

AUGMENTATIONS

WANNA BE A STAR?
Maya integration is contractually required by media conglomerates for aspiring performers and livecasters. In return for constant high-def recordings of their every sensation for a contracted period, they get everything needed to make their dreams of fame and celebrity come true — for as long as they can make it last.

trait — p. 39

HOW MANY IMPLANTS?
As with customised armour loadouts, the GM is the ultimate arbiter of how many implants a character's body can feasibly maintain. Miniaturised cybernetics, Silk-infused networks of micro-organelles, marrow-replacement technologies, and other marvels of modern medicine can accomplish a great deal.

MIXING AUGMENTATIONS
Characters mixing replacements and full-body modifications of different types are limited to the lower number of maximum augmentations between the two types. (For example, if you have a biografted right leg replacement you could also get one Silk-derived right leg replacement, but not two.)

Augmentation varies widely in the Human Sphere. Some augmentations are so common they are barely thought of as augmentations, while others are so rare, niche, or restricted that only a few human beings have one. Common augmentations include prosthetic replacement of lost limbs, Maya integration, sensors and recorders, quantronic connectors for a particular vehicle or device (such as early model TAG pilot sockets), adaptation for a particular environment, and fashion-forward body mods like smart-material inlays, hair replacements, or cosmetic artificial eyes.

AUGMENTATION TYPES

Implants are the most common classification of augmentation. It's relatively easy for a character to have a multitude of smaller implants.

Large Implants (which include Two-Handed or Unwieldy items installed as implants) must be assigned to a specific hit location and each hit location can have only one such implant.

Replacements are designed to completely replace a part of the recipient's body. Each replacement specifies the organ or hit location (e.g., eye or arm) that it replaces.

Full-Body modifications feature components or alterations which permeate the entire body. They are required to create large, systemic improvements (like boosts to physical strength or regenerative capabilities).

Having a full-body modification does not prevent individual limbs or organs from being replaced. Similarly, having a replacement limb does not prevent having implants in the same hit location.

AUGMENTATION CATEGORIES

Augmentations also come in one of three categories:

Cybernetics are the oldest and least expensive form of implant, an extension of medically necessary prostheses. Their corrective applications have been supplanted throughout most of the Human Sphere by alternative techniques (including organ-cloning, Silk therapies, and the like), but cybernetic replacement limbs are still used by many and it's quite common for other specialised equipment to be implanted (such as the ubiquitous Cubes).

Characters can only benefit from one full-body cyberware modification. They can also only have one cyberware replacement in each hit location or organ. Characters with a large cybernetic implant, cybernetic replacement, or cybernetic full-body modification gain the Cyborg trait. Cybernetic augmentations have a minimum Maintenance of 1.

Biografting is designed to integrate with the body more naturally. It relies on mutagenic retroviruses and xeno-transplants from genetically neutral organisms. Installation costs include gene therapy when necessary, though the Improved Human Baseline provided by modern in-utero medical treatment means 90% of the non-Ariadnan population is already prepared for biografting.

Characters can only benefit from two biografted full-body modifications. They can also only have two biografted replacements in each hit location or organ (which are functionally organs or limbs with the properties of both biografts blended together). Characters with a total of two or more large biografted implants, biografted replacements, or biografted full-body modifications gain a related trait, such as Chimera or Gene-Freak.

Silk Augmentations constitute the cutting edge of modern augmentation, using bioengineered Silk-based artificial organs and quantronics. The subtlety of biomedical modifications possible with Silk are extraordinary and make it possible to alter the human body to an unprecedented degree, although such procedures can be extremely expensive.

Characters can only benefit from three Silk-derived full-body modifications. They can only have three Silk-derived replacements in each hit location or organ. Silk-derived modifications are almost invisibly incorporated into the body (unless the recipient deliberately chooses otherwise), and any number of Silk-derived augmentations can be received without receiving a character trait.

AUGMENTATION SURGERY

The cost of an augmentation includes the procedure necessary to install it. The listed base cost assumes the services of a competent medical team, who will make Medicine tests with a target number of 10. Superior augmentation specialists can be sought out at higher costs, increasing the cost of an augmentation by +2 🄽 per +1 target number.

AUGMENTATION PROCEDURE

Installing an augmentation is a form of Serious Treatment. Once per days, in place of the normal Serious Treatment action, the surgeon can make one roll contributing to a complex Medicine test. The type of augmentation being installed determines the difficulty of the test and also determines how much damage the character suffers during each procedure (i.e., per Medicine test). Silk-based augmentations offer 1 bonus Momentum to each test.

- 1+2 for an implant (D1, 2 Momentum, 1 failure)
- 2+4 for a large implant or replacement (D2, 6 Momentum, 2 failures)
- 3+6 for a full-body augmentation (D2, 10 Momentum, 3 failures)

Surgeons can choose to spend Momentum from their Medicine test to reduce the damage inflicted by the procedure by 2 points per Momentum spent. (This Momentum does not count towards the Momentum necessary for the procedure to succeed: surgeons can choose to either rush the procedure, dealing more damage, or apply the augmentation gradually while minimizing trauma to their patient's body.)

AUGMENTATION COMPLICATIONS

Augmenting one's body is dangerous. If one or more Effects are generated by the procedure's damage roll, the patient must make an Average (D1) Discipline test to cancel one of the Effects, plus one additional Effect per Momentum spent.

For each remaining Effect, the GM can inflict one standard complication. (These complications are in addition to those normally generated by skill tests and those the GM spends Heat to create.) A few common options include:

- The augmentation is flawed, inflicting a +1 complication range to tests involving it. An attempt to address these flaws can be made with a follow-up medical procedure costing half as much as the original procedure.
- There are complications in the procedure, inflicting +1 difficulty to future Medicine and Resistance tests made while installing the augmentation.
- There are social consequences. The aug might be part of a short-term fad, highly disliked by a particular subculture (generating Heat when interacting with them), or are now notorious for some reason.

As a serious complication, the patient may be exposed to degenerative augmentation syndrome (DAS), a catch-all term for a number of auto-immune and other physical dysfunctions resulting from poorly integrated augmentations or augmentations which are being rejected by the host's body.

Degenerative Augmentation Syndrome:
Augmentation complication 4, Chronic Progressive Disease 1 (3 successes), Week, 2+4
   Harm Effect: +1 difficulty to all Agility-, Brawn-, or Coordination-based actions. This Harm Effect cannot be treated until DAS goes into remission.

Serious Treatment – p. 103

disease – p. 347

AUGMENTATIONS TABLE

AUGMENTATION	CATEGORY	TYPE	QUALITIES	RESTRICTION	COST	TARIFF	MAINTENANCE
Antipode Control Device	Cybernetic	Implant	Comms	4 (Ariadna 2)	5+2 (N)	T3	1
Antipode Control Cranial Implant	Cybernetic	Implant	Aug, Comms	4 (Ariadna 2)	6+2 (N)	T2	1
AR Eye Implants	Cybernetic	Replacement (Eyes)	Aug	0	7+2 (N)	–	–
Attribute Augmentation X (Biografted)	Biograft	Full-Body	Aug	1	10+X (N)	T2	–
Attribute Augmentation X (Cyber)	Cybernetic	Full-Body	Aug	1	9+X (N)	T1	1
Attribute Augmentation (Silk)	Silk	Full-Body	Aug	3	12+3 (N)	T1	–
Basic Limb Replacement (Biografted)	Biograft	Replacement (Limb)	Aug	1	7+1 (N)	T1	–
Basic Limb Replacement (Cyber)	Cybernetic	Replacement (Limb)	Aug	0	6+2 (N)	–	1
Basic Limb Replacement (Silk)	Silk	Replacement (Limb)	Aug	2	10+1 (N)	T1	–
Bioimmunity Organ	Silk	Full-Body	Aug	1	13+1 (N)	T1	–
Cosmetic Augmentation X	Any	Implant	Aug	X (Nomads X−1)	X+X (N) (min. 1)	T2	–
Cube	Silk	Implant	Aug	0 (Ariadna 2)	5+2 (N)	T1	–
Cube 2.0	Silk	Implant	Aug, Comms	2 (Ariadna 3)	11+3 (N)	T3	–
Fast Download Port	Silk	Implant	Aug	1	8+2 (N)	T1	1
Gecko Pads	Biograft	Implant	Aug	2	8+1 (N)	T1	–
Inlaid Palm Circuitry	Cybernetic	Implant	Aug	2	7+1 (N)	T1	1
Internal Pocket X	Cybernetic/ Biograft	Implant / Large Implant	Aug, Concealed X	0	8+X (N)	–	1/0
Limb Socket	Cybernetic	Replacement (Limb)	Aug	1	6+1 (N)	T1	1
Neural Hacking Socket	Cybernetic	Implant	Aug, Comms, Neural	2	5+2 (N)	T3	1
Neural Shunts	Any	Implant	Aug	2	8+2 (N)	T1	–
Pain Filters	Biograft/Silk	Full-Body	Aug	2	8+1 (N)	T1	–
Regeneration Augmentation	Biograft/Silk	Full-Body	Aug	3	9+2 (N)	T1	–
Remote Presence Gear	Cybernetic	Implant	Aug, Comms, Neural	3	8+1 (N)	T1	1
Sixth Sense	Silk	Full-Body	Aug	2	11+1 (N)	T1	–
Super-Jump	Cybernetic/ Biograft	Replacement (Legs)	Aug	2	8+1 (N)	T1	1/0
Subdermal Grafts	Cybernetic	Large Implant / Full-Body	See Armour Table				
Implanted [Equipment]	Cybernetic	Implant / Large Implant	Aug, Neural, per item	per item (min. 1)	per item	min. T1	per item (min. 1)
Implanted [Weapon]	Cybernetic	Implant / Large Implant	Aug, Neural, per weapon	per weapon (min. 3)	per item	+T2	per weapon (min. 1)

CONTAGIONS

Diseases, poisons, drugs, quantronic viruses, and even virulent rumours are all handled in *Infinity* using a common set of rules and referred to, for the sake of convenience, as contagions.

CONTAGION TESTS
Contagion tests are made to avoid, endure, or otherwise mitigate the effects of the contagion. Unless specified otherwise, the contagion test is made using the recovery skill for the type of damage the contagion inflicts. (For example, a disease inflicts physical damage so it would use Resistance for contagion tests. A computer virus, on the other hand, inflicts quantronic dramage and would use Hacking for contagion tests.)

Other characters can assist on a contagion test using the treat skill for the type of damage the contagion inflicts.

TYPE X (Y MOMENTUM)
A contagion's Type briefly describes its nature (disease, drug, etc.), classifies it into one of four categories, determines the difficulty (X) of the contagion tests made to avoid its effects, and establishes the amount of Momentum (Y) required to recover from it (if necessary). Each failed contagion test results in the contagion inflicting damage or, in some cases, its special effect.

Instant contagions are one-time effects. A single contagion test is made. Whether it succeeds or fails, the contagion's effect ends.

Complex contagions take time to recover from and are resolved as complex contagion tests. Each test that results in a failure inflicts the contagion's damage or special effect, and tests must continue to be made (according to the contagion's Term, see below) until the complex skill test succeeds (at which point the contagion no longer affects the character).

Progressive contagions are resolved in a similar manner, except they use progressive contagion tests (inflicting a +1 difficulty for each failed test). Such contagions are particularly dangerous.

Chronic contagions are a variation of Instant, Complex, or Progressive contagions. (For example, you can have a Chronic Complex drug or a Chronic Progressive disease.) Such contagions are resolved normally, but remain in a state of dormancy or remission after being resolved. The character can relapse, effectively re-exposing them to the contagion, if the GM spends Heat equal to X.

TERM
The Term of a contagion is how frequently contagion tests must be made to avoid its effects. This will be listed as Round, Minute, Hour, Day, Week, or Month, with the test being made once per term (once per day, and so forth).

VECTOR X
A disease's vector is the method by which it is communicated or by which a character can become exposed to it. (Airborne, ingested, contact, injury, and drugs are common methods.) When a character is in such a situation, they can be exposed to the contagion as either a Harm Effect or by making a Heat/Momentum spend equal to X. (If no value is given, it only requires 1 Heat or Momentum.)

A character who has been exposed must immediately succeed on a contagion test against the normal difficulty of the contagion or become infected by the contagion. (This test does not inflict the damage or special effect of the contagion unless it is of the Instant type. It merely determines whether or not the character is infected by the contagion.) The BTS rating of a character's armour reduces the difficulty of this test if the contagion is a disease, poison, or quantronic virus.

DAMAGE
A contagion's damage lists the amount and type of damage it inflicts on a failed contagion test.

DISEASE EXAMPLES

Food Poisoning: Ingested, Complex 1 (1 Momentum), Hour, 1+2 🅽 physical damage
  Special Effect: On failed Resistance test, victim suffers from vomiting. For 1 Heat, the GM can inflict the Staggered condition.

Paradiso Sweats: Insect Bite, Complex 2 (4 Momentum), Day, 1+2 🅽 physical damage (Vicious 1)
  Harm Effect: Dazed

  The Paradiso Sweats are a jungle bane to virtually every off-worlder. The clammy skin and glassy eyes are a distinctive rite of passage.

Svalarheima Measles: Ingested, Progressive 1 (4 Momentum), Day, 1+4 🅽 physical damage
  Harm Effect: Blinded, if the character suffers this special Harm Effect a second time while suffering from the Blinded condition the eyes are permanently damaged.

  Victims of Svalarheima measles suffer from distinctive milk-white sores. The disease is contracted through drinking contaminated melt-ice.

HARM EFFECT/SPECIAL EFFECT

Most contagions inflict a special Harm Effect triggered normally through the accumulation of damage from the contagion. Others may have a Special Effect, which takes effect automatically upon exposure unless otherwise stated (although in the case of disease they're usually triggered on a failed contagion test).

DRUGS

Drugs use the normal rules for contagions, but many drugs are also addictive and may have a few additional qualities.

ADDICTION X (Y DOSES)

A drug's Addiction rating determines the number of doses that must inflict the Harm Effect or Special Effect of the drug before the user risks addiction (also known as the Addiction Threshold). Once a user reaches the Addiction Threshold, they must make a Resistance test (with a difficulty of X) or become addicted. This test must be repeated each time they suffer the Harm Effect or Special Effect of the drug as long as they remain at or above the Addiction Threshold.

If a user goes one day without using the drug, reduce the current tally of doses counting towards addiction by 1 to a minimum of 0.

COMPULSION X

If a character addicted to a drug has the opportunity to take the drug, they must make a Discipline test with a difficulty equally to the Compulsion rating of the drug (X). If the test fails, they must take the drug.

If the character is currently suffering from withdrawal, the test is made at +1 difficulty. If the character is currently affected by the drug, the test is made a −1 difficulty per dose currently affecting them.

WITHDRAWAL X

If a character becomes addicted to a drug, they must stay buzzed on the drug. When the drug's effect comes to an end, withdrawal begins. Withdrawal acts just like a disease with a term of days. Once per day, the character must make a Discipline test or suffer the withdrawal damage of the drug.

OVERDOSE

Even healthy substances are toxic in too great a concentration, and characters who over-rely on drugs can suffer for it. A character who takes a dose of a drug before they have recovered from a previous dose must pass a Resistance test with a difficulty equal to the number of doses still active in their system or overdose. Overdosed characters suffer a Wound, with a Wound Effect which renders them Dazed and suffering 1+2🅽 physical damage per hour until treated. This damage can inflict the same Wound Effect again, in which case the damage increases to 2+4🅽 and the character is Staggered. If the Wound Effect is suffered again, the damage increases to 3+6🅽 and the character is Helpless.

TAKING DRUGS

Whether medically used or just for kicks, drugs can be administered through a variety of methods. Auto-injectors are easiest; just place one against your skin, push the button, and the mechanism does all the work. Applying a medicated patch, taking a pill, or using a spray is a Medicine (D0) test and takes a Minor Action. Auto-injectors require a Medicine (D1) test, but are a Free Action.

Staggered, p. 104: Pay 1 Momentum to take Standard Action. Pay 1 Infinity Point to perform Reaction (plus normal Heat cost).

Helpless, p. 104: Cannot take Reactions. Exploit actions vs. character at −1 difficulty and +1 bonus Momentum.

DRUGS TABLE

DRUG	RESTRICTION	COST	TARIFF
Antibiotics	1	3+1🅽	–
Nitrocaine	2	4+2🅽	T1
Painkillers	0	2+1🅽	–
Stims	1	4+1🅽	–
Surge	1	3+1🅽	T1

POISONS TABLE

POISON	RESTRICTION	COST	TARIFF
Fleck	2	3+4🅽	T3
Haunt	3 (Paradiso 1)	3+4🅽	T1
Puraza	2 (PanOceania/Nomad 1)	3+3🅽	T4
Tetrodotoxin	2	1+5🅽	T1
Wolfshot	2 (Ariadna 1)	3+3🅽	T3
Wurari	1	1+3🅽	T1

EXPLOSIVE DEVICES

Beyond raw destructive power, explosive devices can reshape the urban battlefield physically and psychologically, allowing rapid movement through interior walls, floors, and ceilings, and as concealed weapons of terror that create an atmosphere of fear and paranoia to even the playing field between otherwise mismatched forces.

Most explosive device components also have industrial uses or can be created from civilian precursors, so ALEPH and factional authorities watch for patterns of combined purchases and fabricator usage in an ongoing game of cat and mouse with illicit manufacturers. Spaceports, transit hubs, and immigration checkpoints use chemical sniffers to check for traces of blacklisted materials, although it's far from a perfect cordon.

OBTAINING EXPLOSIVES

Reloads of ammunition can be purchased as explosives for one additional base cost, providing three charges, grenades, or mines instead. Converting a Reload of ammunition into an explosive device, or vice versa, requires a successful Tech (D2) test with a +2 complication range, and the resulting item adds Improvised 1 to any attack made using it.

SETTING EXPLOSIVES

Explosives can be set to detonate on a preset timer or by a remote signal with an Average (D1) Tech test. On a failure, the explosive does not detonate (and the GM can use a complication to prematurely detonate it).

Alternatively, explosives can set up to be controlled via network command with a Simple (D0) Tech test. Of course, this networking exposes the device to quantronic detection and attacks.

When first placed or thrown, the user should declare what mode the explosive is in and any other relevant information such as timer duration, network permissions, or detonation criteria.

DISABLING EXPLOSIVES

Disabling explosives you've placed or have network permissions for requires either physical or network access and a Tech (D0) test. Disabling or detonating someone else's explosives requires either a face-to-face Tech test against the check made to originally set the explosives or a Breach Effect (if the explosive is quantronically controlled).

EXPLOSIVE CATEGORIES

Explosive devices fall into three categories, and are sold in sets of three.

Charges are attached to a target for detonation later.

Grenades are thrown at a target or zone, usually detonating on impact.

Mines are concealed in a zone, detonating when they detect a valid target.

CHARGES

Charges are placed on a target within Reach. Placing a charge on something that can defend itself is a melee attack that does not directly inflict damage. Multiple charges triggered simultaneously on the same target combine their qualities, Effects, and damage into a single roll.

GRENADES

Unlike other explosives, grenades do not need to be set (although they can be). They can be thrown as ranged attacks with the Disposable, Indiscriminate (Close), Speculative Fire, and Thrown qualities. They can also be fired from grenade launchers, in which case they use the weapon's range and each grenade counts as one Reload.

MINES

Cheap, easily-deployed anti-personnel landmines create hazardous regions long after the end of hostilities, and are banned by the Concilium Convention. Modern mines have the Comms, Disposable, and Indiscriminate (Close) qualities, with complex IFF and tracking systems for safe recovery once a conflict ends. Altering a mine to have the Non-Hackable quality is a Challenging (D2) Tech test and a war crime.

A mine is set within a specific zone and will generally be concealed with an Average (D1) Stealth test (and can be detected with a face-to-face Observation test). A deployed mine detonates as soon as it senses a valid target within its zone, making an attack roll with a target number of 10+1 per Momentum spent on the Tech test made to set the mine.

Reload – p. 356

Disposable, p. 334: Item destroyed after use.

weapon range – p. 358

Speculative Fire, p. p. 338: –1 difficulty vs. targets that cannot be seen. Optional +1 difficulty to ignore Cover Soak.

Improvised X, p. 334: Item gains +X complication range.

grenade launchers – p. 373

Concilium Convention – p. 339

Comms – p. 334

Thrown, p. 338: Close range weapon. Ranged attack test made with Athletics skill.

EXPLOSIVES TABLE

EXPLOSIVE	CATEGORY	DAMAGE¹	SIZE	QUALITIES	RESTRICTION	COST (PER 3)	TARIFF
[Ammo Type] Charges	Charge	2+6 Ⓝ	1H	Comms, Disposable, Indiscriminate (Close), Unsubtle, and all other qualities added by the ammo type	3	1+cost of Reload	+T1
[Ammo Type] Grenades	Grenade	2+4 Ⓝ	1H	Disposable, Indiscriminate (Close), Speculative Fire, Thrown, Unsubtle, and all qualities added by the ammo type	3	1+cost of Reload	+T1
[Ammo Type] Mines	Mine	2+5 Ⓝ	1H	Comms, Disposable, Indiscriminate (Close), Unsubtle, and all other qualities added by the ammo type	3	1+cost of Reload	+T1
D-Charges	Charge	2+6 Ⓝ	1H	Anti-Materiel 2, Comms, Disposable, Piercing 3, Spread 1, Unsubtle, Vicious 2	3	5+1 Ⓝ	T1
Drop Bear	Mine	2+5 Ⓝ	1H	Comms, Disposable, Indiscriminate (Close), Spread 1, Stun, Thrown, Vicious 3	3	7+2 Ⓝ	T1
Flashbangs	Grenade	1+5 Ⓝ	1H	Blinding, Deafening, Disposable, Indiscriminate (Close), Nonlethal, Speculative Fire, Thrown, Unsubtle, removes Marked	3	6+1 Ⓝ	T1
Smoke Grenades	Grenade	N/A	1H	Disposable, Indiscriminate (Close), Nonlethal, Speculative Fire, Smoke 2, Thrown	2	3+ 1 Ⓝ	T1
Tear Gas Grenades	Grenade	1+3 Ⓝ	1H	Biotech, Disposable, Indiscriminate (Close), Nonlethal, Smoke 1, Terrifying 2, Vicious 1	–	5+1 Ⓝ	T1

¹Do not add Bonus Damage from attributes to explosive devices.

GEISTS

Geists are limited artificial intelligences, constant virtual companions, and personal assistants. They grow in response to their user's needs and desires, becoming unique over time, but most start from largely identical programmatic seed libraries (as represented by the Basic Geist stat block).

GEIST LEARNING

Although not true AIs, geists are capable of learning and adapting in response to the experiences they share with their owner. Many quantronic philosophers have described the link between owner and geist as a symbiotic relationship — that the geist is less of a separate entity and more a part of the "cerebral cyborg" which is the modern citizen of the Human Sphere.

As such, a player can improve their character's geist by spending experience points. The cost of these improvements are calculated in the same way that they would be for the player character itself.

GEIST UPGRADES

As a form of software, geists can also be directly upgraded by merging software patches into their existing mind-state, overwriting and extending their programming with new subroutines and protocols. Doing so is increasingly expensive depending on the geist's abilities, as new upgrades must be tailored to the resulting configuration's complexities.

Purchasing geist upgrades is handled slightly differently to purchasing many other items.

Acquisition Test: The acquisition test for geist upgrades can be attempted with Lifestyle, Hacking,

GEIST
BASIC GEIST

ATTRIBUTES*						
AGI	AWA	BRW	COO	INT	PER	WIL
4	4	4	4	4	4	4

SKILLS
Any 4 ranks

DEFENCES					
Firewall	**	Resolve	4	Vigour	–
Security	–	Morale	–	Soak	0

*Increase any two attributes by +2
**Per owner

Quantronic Jump – p. 418

Quantronic Jump: All geists have the Quantronic Jump ability.

or Tech. Further, due to tech-savvy characters often being able to do part of the work themselves, and generally having more efficient systems to work with, when attempting to acquire geist upgrades, a character may increase their effective Earnings by an amount equal to their Hacking Focus.

Restriction / Cost: Instead of each upgrade having its own Restriction or Cost, the following tables are used to determine the Restriction and Cost of an upgrade package — a bundle of upgrades obtained and applied all at once. As much of the expense of an upgrade is in recompiling the geist, purchasing several upgrades as a large upgrade package is quite cost-effective compared to buying those upgrades individually, though finding someone willing and able to apply a larger upgrade package can be more difficult.

An upgrade package has a basic Restriction of 1, and a Cost of 1+1 (N) with a Tariff of 1. The character should then select which upgrades they wish to purchase, before consulting the *Upgrade Package Table*, below.

Total the number of upgrades to be purchased. This will indicate both a modifier for the total Restriction of the package, and a value to divide the total Cost increase by (rounding down). For example, an upgrade package consisting of 6 upgrades, with a Cost increase of +10 (N), should divide that increase by 2. Add that Restriction modifier, and the divided Cost increase to the basic cost of the upgrade package, and use that Restriction and Cost to acquire the package.

Improving the basic capabilities of the geist — its attributes — are typically somewhat more costly than other upgrades. If the upgrade package contains one or more attribute upgrades, increase the Tariff to 2. If the upgrade package would increase one or more attributes to a score that is 10 or higher, increase the Tariff to 3 instead.

If a character wishes to buy a pre-upgraded geist, then construct the upgrade package desired, and apply that modifier to the Restriction and Cost of a basic geist instead.

POPULAR UPGRADES

Although geist upgrades are presented here using generic mechanics, in the Human Sphere they are esoteric, specific, and branded in myriad ways. When purchasing an upgrade for their geists, players should be encouraged to customise its identity. For example, acquiring a geist of one's own is an important step toward independence, and many adolescents add KnowItAll patches related to their fandoms and obsessions, or Snowden-sneak filters to ferret out their friend's secrets. Adults usually upgrade their geists to better assist them professionally with GnoSofts, Machiavelli micro-expression analysis suites, Chatte conversation-assistants, and AzReal real-time halo-trackers. Aide-de-Camp is a popular Moto.tronica brand of upgrades dedicated to filtering and processing battlefield communications.

GEIST UPGRADES TABLE

UPGRADE	EFFECT	COST INCREASE
Attribute	Increase a single attribute by +1 (max. 12)	+2 (N)
Skill Expertise	Increase a single Skill Expertise by +1 (max. 3)	+1 (N)
Skill Focus	Increase a single Skill Focus by 1 (max. Expertise)	+1 (N)
Talent	Gain a single Talent; each step the selected Talent is from the first Talent in that tree doubles the cost of this upgrade	+2 (N)
Trait	Add or remove trait	+3 (N)

UPGRADE PACKAGE TABLE

NUMBER OF UPGRADES	RESTRICTION	DIVIDE COST INCREASE BY...
1–3	+0	1
4–8	+1	2
9–15	+1	3
16–24	+2	4
25+	+2	5

EXAMPLE GEISTS TABLE

GEIST	RESTRICTION	COST	TARIFF
Basic Geist	1	2+4 (N)	1
Chauffeur Geist	3	2+12 (N)	2
Guardian Geist	2	2+11 (N)	2
Military Geist	3	2+14 (N)	t3
Security Geist	3	2+13 (N)	2
Vizier Geist	3	2+12 (N)	3

HACKING DEVICES

Comms – p. 334

DUMB MODE

Virtually all modern technology (any item without the Non-Hackable quality) relies on network access to assist their user. To protect against quantronic attacks in an emergency, a character can set an item to "dumb mode" by making an Average (D1) Hacking test. Opponents can use a Reaction to make this a face-to-face Hacking test. Equipment with the Comms quality are unusable while in dumb mode (although the GM, at their discretion, may allow some limited functionality), while all other items gain the Non-Hackable (+1D) quality (meaning that tests using the item are made at +1 difficulty).

special Breach Effect, p. 102: Special Harm Effects do not count towards network being compromised, but are treated like Breach Effects in all other ways.

Hacking devices are Comms Equipment weapons, used to attack enemy networks and augment friendly ones with customised programs.

PROGRAM TYPES

Infowar programs are extremely memory and processing-power intensive, and require specialised hardware to use effectively, so hacking devices prioritize different arrays of programs. Each program has a rating (generally from 1–3). The entry for each hacking device lists its **Device Ratings**, which are the maximum program rating they can run in each type.

Attack Programs (SWORD) are dedicated offensive software designed to inflict a maximum amount of damage on enemy hackers. If they have the ability to inflict special Breach Effects, it is usually in order to deal alternative or improved forms of damage.

Control Programs (CLAW) are specialised offensive programs designed to disable and stall enemy targets. They deal minimal damage, but their primary purpose is almost always to inflict special Breach Effects with a Momentum spend.

Defensive Programs (SHIELD) protect against the effects of enemy attacks. They offer unique or enhanced Reactions against quantronic attacks and/or offer boosts to their user's Interference Soak. In addition, a user gains Interference Soak equal to twice the level of the most advanced SHIELD program they have installed. (For example,

a character with SHIELD-1 Exorcism and SHIELD-2 Breakwater on their hacking device would gain +4 (N) Interference Soak — twice the amount of the higher-rated Breakwater program.)

Utility Programs (GADGET) are miscellaneous software options that can be deployed to enhance, affect, or support the immediate environment, the hacker, or the hacker's allies.

Intrusion Countermeasures (IC) are used to install intrusion countermeasures as quantronic zone effects. When hackers without authentication attempt to enter a zone with IC, they must attempt a Hacking test with a difficulty equal to the IC's program rating. On a failure, the hacker cannot enter the zone and also suffers the additional effects of the IC. Installing an IC program requires a Hacking test with a difficulty equal to the program's rating. Once installed, an IC program can be concealed with an Intelligence+Stealth test.

UPGRADE

Upgrade programs (UPGRADE) are custom-compiled software options that require specialised hardware modules in order to run. They can possess the features of any other program type, but cannot be run on basic hacking devices without first installing their hardware component. (This physical component also means that, unlike other programs, they cannot be simply copied to a new device.)

Installing an UPGRADE requires a Challenging (D2) Tech test. Some hacking devices come with UPGRADES pre-installed.

HACKING DEVICES TABLE

HACKING DEVICE	DEVICE RATINGS	RESTRICTION	COST	TARIFF
Assault Hacking Device	CLAW-3, SWORD-0, SHIELD-0, GADGET-0, IC-1	3	10+2 (N)	T2
Assault Hacking Device (EI)	CLAW-3, SWORD-0, SHIELD-0, GADGET-0, IC-1, UPGRADE Stop!	EI Only	N/A	N/A
Defensive Hacking Device	CLAW-0, SWORD-0, SHIELD-3, GADGET-1, IC-3	2	9+2 (N)	T1
EI Hacking Device	CLAW-2, SWORD-2, SHIELD-2, GADGET-3, IC-3, UPGRADE Sucker Punch	EI only	N/A	N/A
Hacking Device	CLAW-1, SWORD-1, SHIELD-1, GADGET-3, IC-1	3	7+2 (N)	T2
Hacking Device Plus	CLAW-2, SWORD-1, SHIELD-2, GADGET-3, IC-2, UPGRADE Cybermask, Sucker Punch, White Noise	4 (Nomad 2 / ALEPH 2)	11+2 (N)	T3
Killer Hacking Device	CLAW-0, SWORD-2, SHIELD-0, GADGET-0, IC-1, UPGRADE Cybermask, Piercing 3	4 (Nomad 2 / ALEPH 2)	10+2 (N)	T3
White Hacking Device	CLAW-0, SWORD-0, SHIELD-3, GADGET-1, IC-3, UPGRADE Cyberalert Systems	4 (Nomad 2 / ALEPH 2)	10+2 (N)	T3

PROGRAMS TABLE

TYPE	RATING	PROGRAM	DAMAGE	QUALITIES	RESTRICTION	COST	TARIFF
CLAW	1	Blackout	1+2(N)	BE[1]	3	3+4(N)	T1
CLAW	1	Gotcha!	1+2(N)	BE[1]	3	3+4(N)	T1
CLAW	1	Overlord	1+2(N)	BE[1]	3	3+4(N)	T1
CLAW	1	Spotlight	–	[1]	3	3+4(N)	T1
CLAW	2	Expel	1+3(N)	BE[1]	3	4+3(N)	T1
CLAW	2	Oblivion	1+3(N)	BE[1]	3	4+3(N)	T1
CLAW	3	Basilisk	1+4(N)	BE[1]	3	4+4(N)	T2
CLAW	3	Carbonite	1+4(N)	BE[1], Piercing 3	3	4+4(N)	T2
CLAW	3	Total Control	1+2(N)	BE[1], Vicious 3	3	4+4(N)	T2
GADGET	1	Controlled Jump	–	Supportware (Long)[1]	2	3+4(N)	T1
GADGET	1	Fairy Dust	–	Supportware (Long)[1]	2	3+4(N)	–
GADGET	1	Lockpicker	–	Supportware (Personal)[1]	3	3+4(N)	T1
GADGET	2	Assisted Fire	–	Supportware (Close)[1]	3	4+4(N)	T1
GADGET	2	Enhanced Reaction	–	Supportware (Close)[1]	3	4+ 4(N)	T1
IC	X	Black ICE	1+X(N)	IC[1], Piercing X	X+2	2X+X(N)	T(X)
IC	X	Countermeasures	–	IC	1	4+X(N)	T(X)
IC	X	Crybaby	–	IC[1]	X	5+X(N)	T(X)
IC	X	Deadfall	–	IC[1]	X	5+X(N)	T(X)
IC	X	Gaslight	–	IC[1]	X	5+X(N)	T(X)
IC	X	Hivemines	X+X(N)	IC, Vicious X	X+1	5+2X(N)	T(X)
IC	X	Mirrormaze	–	IC[1]	2	5+X(N)	T(X)
IC	X	Redtape	–	IC[1], Immobilising	2	5+X(N)	T(X)
SHIELD	1	Exorcism	0	[1]	1	2+4(N)	–
SHIELD	1	U-Turn	–	[1]	2	3+4(N)	–
SHIELD	2	Breakwater	–	[1]	2	4+3(N)	–
SHIELD	3	Counterstrike	–	[1]	2	4+6(N)	T1
SHIELD	3	Zero Pain	–	[1]	2	4+4(N)	T1
SWORD	1	Brain Blast	1+4(N)	BE[1], Piercing 1, Vicious 1	3	3+4(N)	T2
SWORD	1	Slasher	2+5(N)	Vicious 2[1]	3	3+4(N)	T2
SWORD	2	Redrum	2+5(N)	Grievous, Piercing 2, Unforgiving 2	3	4+4(N)	T2
SWORD	2	Skullbuster	1+5(N)	Area (Close), Breaker	3	4+4(N)	T2
SWORD	2	Trinity	2+6(N)	Area (Close), Stun (vs. Neural), Vicious 3	3	5+4(N)	T2
UPGRADE	–	Cyberalert Systems	–	Supportware (Personal)	2	4+4(N)	T1
UPGRADE	–	Cybermask	–	Supportware (Personal)[1]	3	4+3(N)	T4
UPGRADE	–	Stop!	2+6(N)	Breaker, Immobilising[1]	3	5+5(N)	T1
UPGRADE	–	Sucker Punch	1+6(N)	BE[1]	3	5+4(N)	T3
UPGRADE	–	White Noise	–	Supportware (Close)[1]	1	5+4(N)	T2

[1] See entry for additional abilities.

LHOSTS

CLONE LHOSTS

It's not unusual for people to want to be resurrected into cloned copies of their original bodies. A true, fully grown clone would be incredibly difficult, time-consuming, and ethically-questionable to produce. Such procedures may be available in black labs, but it's far more common for people to use genetic samples from their original body in order to customise their Lhost. (Cubes take tissue samples of their users explicitly for this purpose.)

Quantronic Jump — p. 418

Resurrection — p. 392

Resurrection in character creation — p. 54

domotics — p. 143

In general, Lhosts are purchased as part of the Resurrection process, although characters with the Quantronic Jump ability (including geists, LAIs, AI Aspects, and Cube 2.0 users) may be able to gain utility from having multiple bodies that they can swap between. The Quantronic Jump ability is described on p. 418.

Lhosts are also listed with a Life Point cost, which can be used during character creation to select them as a replacement body during Resurrection.

LHOSTS TABLE

LHOST	RESTRICTION	COST	LIFE POINT COST	TARIFF	MAINTENANCE
Lhost, Standard	2	6+2 Ⓝ	1	–	–
Antiquated Lhost	1	5+2 Ⓝ	0	–	–
Nabia Lhost	3	7+4 Ⓝ	3	T2	1
Orlando Lhost	3	8+3 Ⓝ	3	T2	2
Siren Lhost	3	7+3 Ⓝ	3	T2	2
Titan Lhost	2	10+2 Ⓝ	2	T1	1

REMOTES

AUTHORISED USERS

Remotes operating in autonomous mode will generally only accept orders from authorised users. Hacking a remote to convince it that you're an authorised user is equivalent to suborning its network with Breach Effects.

Repeater — p. 334

Troopers, Elites, Nemeses — p. 415

fields of expertise — p. 415

Most of the technology in the Human Sphere can be remotely controlled. Vehicles are a common example, but pervasive domotics allow users to turn on lights, open doors, cook meals, and even order the furniture to rearrange itself without ever stepping foot in the room.

Remotes, on the other hand, are specifically designed for remote operation by a ghost — an intelligence, either resident within the machine or using remote presence technology to operate it from a distance, that takes hold of the machine and governs its actions as if the remote were its own body.

AUTONOMOUS OPERATION

Remotes include either a built-in lesser-AI or a complex suite of expert programs that govern their behaviour to similar effect, allowing the remote to operate autonomously and carry out instructions ranging from the simple to the complex. A remote operating autonomously using its native LAI is essential an NPC, and their stat block can be used as such.

- Like an NPC, remotes are categorized as Troopers, Elites, or Nemeses.

- Remotes are objects, and therefore have a Structure score instead of Vigour and suffer Faults instead of Wounds.

- Autonomous remotes have their own Firewall score and suffer Breaches like an NPC of their category. If a user assumes remote control or ghosts into a remote suffering Breaches, they are negatively affected by the Breach Effects as if those Breaches were their own when taking actions with the remote.

REMOTE CONTROL

Authorised users can override the native LAI of a remote and control it directly. To do this, the remote must be within Close range of either the controlling character or a repeater they control. (Remotes that possess the Repeater quality can act as their own repeater, allowing characters to control them from essentially any distance as long as they are capable of communication with each other.)

- Connecting or disconnecting from a remote requires a Standard Action, but a character need not disconnect from a remote-controlled system in order to take actions using their own body.

- Actions taken by a remote under remote control are a normal skill test for the operator, assisted by the equivalent abilities of the remote as if it had taken the Assist action. If the remote has an applicable Superhuman Attributes, any successes generated by a Superhuman Attribute add to those generated when the remote assists.

- Remote control is not as good as being there yourself. Actions taken with the remote are made at +2 complication range.

VR Mode: A controller with access to VR equipment can fully immerse themselves into the remote's environment. This lowers the complication range increase for remote control to +1, but also results in the user being distracted from their immediate surroundings. If a character using VR remote control needs to take a Reaction using their own body, the Heat cost is increased by 1.

Other Gear: The rules for remote control can also be used to remotely control other equipment (like vehicles).

GHOSTING

When a character is ghosting a remote, their sheut – their actual mind and personality – is directly inhabiting the remote as if it were their body. This is only possible for characters capable of Quantronic Jump, including geists, LAIs, AI Aspects, or Cube 2.0 users.

- Connecting or disconnecting from the remote requires a Standard Action. As long as the character remains connected, they cannot take actions with their own body.

- Physical attributes (Agility, Brawn, and Coordination) are still capped by the remote's limitations.

- For all intents and purposes, the remote is the character's body; they are there "in the flesh". There are no penalties to difficulty or complication range while ghosting.

REMOTE LIMITATIONS

Depending on the remote, and at the GM's discretion, some skill tests and actions may be much more difficult or even impossible with a remote. (For example, it's really difficult to seduce most people if you look like a TinBot.)

SUPERHUMAN REMOTES
Because of the way attribute caps work for remotes, remotes which are designed to greatly enhance the physical capacities of humans – like a remote possessing extraordinary strength for example – do not model that capacity with a higher attribute score (because weak human operators couldn't take advantage of it). They instead have the appropriate Superhuman Attribute special ability (p. 418).

Quantronic Jump – p. 418

sheut, p. 366, 392: The core identity of the individual as saved on a Cube.

REMOTES TABLE

REMOTE	RESTRICTION	COST	TARIFF	MAINTENANCE
Armbot	3 (PanOceania 2)	12+3 Ⓝ	T1	2
Garuda Tacbot	4	13+4 Ⓝ	T4	5
Spotbot	1	9+2 Ⓝ	T2	1
TinBot	0	6+1 Ⓝ	–	1
Yáokòng Remote	3 (Yu Jing 2)	12+3 Ⓝ	T3	2
Zondbot	3 (Nomad 1)	10+4 Ⓝ	T3	3

RESOURCES

In *Infinity*, certain resources are abstracted in order to reduce bookkeeping and reinforce action-packed gameplay. Instead of tracking individual rounds of ammunition, lockpicks, or tubes of nanopaste, resources are used to track limited supplies that must be used to attempt certain complex tasks, expended when certain conditions are met, spent for a bonus d20 on tests using the resource, or a combination of all three. Some resources can only be used in conjunction with other equipment (e.g., Reloads can only be fired with an appropriate ranged weapon) as detailed below.

Resources are purchased and sold in sets of three.

Attrition: In addition to their normal use, a GM can remove a resource from a character as a complication. If a character has no resources of that type remaining, the GM can instead declare that the character has completely run out of the resource. (This can be indicated on the character sheet by noting "–1" in the related resource.) The effect of running out of a particular resource depends on the type of resource (as described below), but usually prevents the character from taking related actions until their supply of the resource has been restored.

RESOURCE TYPES

Oxygen Loads: Oxygen Loads track the remaining air in breathing equipment. After an hour of steady use or scene of intense activity, users must make a Challenging (D2) Extraplanetary or Daunting (D3) Survival test or spend an Oxygen Load. If a character runs out of Oxygen Loads, they begin to suffocate.

RESOURCES AND THE GM
NPCs do not track resources individually; instead, the GM spends Heat to produce resources for NPCs to use as needed. Each resource costs 1 Heat.

suffocate, 110: Make Resistance (D1) test each round. +1 difficulty for each additional round. On failure, suffer 1 Wound.

DAMAGED LIFE SUPPORT

When life support systems become damaged (via a Wound or Fault Effect, for example) or disabled (by a Breach Effect, for example), it doesn't mean that the victim immediately dies. Usually it means they're leaking air or consuming stale air. The GM may rule that such characters need to check for Oxygen Load loss more frequently. (Perhaps once per round in the case of a major leak; or once every minute if they're breathing stale air in a suit.)

repairs – p. 333

Burst, p. 358: Maximum number of Reloads can be spent on attack rolls with weapon.

Lhosts – p. 354

Cube – p. 366

Parts: Modern device components are designed to be modular and reconfigurable, and expert technicians can handle most repair jobs with clever combinations of Parts. Each unit of Parts expended on a Tech test to perform repairs grants 1 bonus Momentum on the test. If a character runs out of Parts, they can still attempt to jury-rig solutions but suffer a +1 difficulty on their Tech tests to make repairs.

Picks: Miniature E/M, corrosive, and explosive devices, modern Picks – short for lockpicks – are used to overcome simple quantronic locks and physical security barriers. Each Pick expended on a Thievery test to pick a lock or overcome a security system grants a bonus d20 to the test. Running out of Picks carries no penalty.

Psychotropics: Modern chemical substances that affect brain function, perception, mood, or consciousness, Psychotropics are catalysed by trained professionals and must be physically applied to a target. Each dose of Psychotropics expended on a social skills test grants a bonus d20 on the test. Running out of Psychotropics carries no penalty.

Psychotropics can be customised to a specific target. This requires a biological profile, which can be obtained with an Average (D1) Medicine test if the target can be subjected to a full medical scan or a Daunting (D3) Medicine test if only a genetic sample can be obtained. If the test is successful, the Psychotropic can be modified with a successful Challenging (D2) Science test. A customised Psychotropic, in addition to its normal effects, grants 1 bonus Momentum on the social skill test it's expended for.

Reagents: Reagents are nano-chemicals, catalysts, tests, and similar resources used to conduct experiments and analysis. Reagents require the use of an appropriate toolkit or laboratory, but under those conditions each unit of Reagents expended on a Science test grants a bonus Momentum to the test. If a character runs out of Reagents, the resources of their toolkit or laboratory have been strained and their Science tests using their toolkit or laboratory suffer a +1 difficulty (counteracting some or all of the normal benefit from using a kit).

Reloads: Reloads are used in ranged weapons and are specific to a type of ammunition. (This might consist of a pair of magazines taped together, a box of ammo for a light machine gun, or a canister of weaponised nanobots.) Reloads are not expended through the normal use of a ranged weapon, but characters can spend a Reload to gain one bonus d20 on the weapon's attack test and +1 🅝 to the damage roll. The number of Reloads a character can spend on a specific attack is limited by the Burst value of the weapon being used. Running out of Reloads means that the weapon has completely run out of ammunition and is unable to be used for further attacks until additional ammunition is purchased.

Serum: Modern first aid relies heavily on doses of Serum – medical nanobots suspended in a nutrient fluid – to staunch bleeding, seal wounds, and manage immune response. Each dose of Serum grants one bonus Momentum on the Medicine test it is used to bolster. If a character runs out of Serum, the resources of their MediKit or medical facility have been strained and their Medicine tests suffer a +1 difficulty (counteracting some or all of the normal benefit from using the MediKit or facility).

Specialised Serums also exist, each customised for treating a specific disease or condition. In addition to the normal effects of Serum, a specialised Serum grants one bonus d20 when expended on Medicine or Resistance tests for the condition it's designed for.

Silk: The miraculous Haqqislamite biosynthetic, Silk is required for augmentations like Cube installation as well as the creation or repair of Lhost bodies, and must be used in a laboratory or medical facility. It enables rapid recovery from extensive physical trauma, and can be used as an extremely powerful Serum. Using Silk as Serum is a technically complicated task, increasing the difficulty of the associated Medicine test by +1, but on a success, it grants 4 bonus Momentum. In addition, the success grants a bonus d20 on all future recovery and treat tests for the subject until they are either fully recovered or leave the care facility. Running out of Silk carries no penalty.

RESOURCES TABLE

RESOURCE	RESTRICTION	COST (PER 3 RESOURCES)
Oxygen Loads	1	2+2 🅝
Parts	1	2+2 🅝
Picks	2	1+5 🅝
Psychotropics	1	3+1 🅝
Reagents	1	3+1 🅝
Reloads	See Ammo	See Ammo
Serum	1	3+1 🅝
Silk (legal)	1	9
Silk (black market)	4	9+9 🅝

TOOLS

Many belongings help a character to perform specific tasks, allow them to make skill tests without a penalty, and/or make the task easier.

Kits are used with specific skills, such as MediKits and the Medicine skill. Kits can be used when performing practical tasks (rather than knowledge-based or theoretical uses of the skill) and grant 1 bonus Momentum. Some kits can only be applied to a subset of tasks with a particular skill, as noted in their descriptions.

Facilities expand the concept of kits into whole rooms full of tools and workspaces. In addition to providing the benefits of a kit and ample storage for resources, tests that use a facility are at −1 difficulty (minimum D0).

Suites consist of complex sets of software tools, expert systems, or other tools. They have the Comms and Expert qualities and also reduce the difficulty of a specialised task by one step.

Expert X, p. 334: Grants the user X bonus Momentum.

Comms – p. 334

TOOLS TABLE

TOOL	QUALITIES	RESTRICTION	COST	TARIFF	MAINTENANCE
Aletheia Kit	Subtle 2	2	5+2	T1	–
Analysis Suite	Comms, Expert 1	1	10+3	–	1
Analytical Kit	–	1	5+2	–	–
AutoMediKit	–	2	7+2	–	1
Basic Medical Supplies	–	0	3+2	–	1
Breaking & Entering Kit	–	3	3+2	T4	–
Chameleonwear	–	3	5+3	T2	–
Climbing Kit	–	0	5+2	–	–
Cosmetics Kit	Fragile	0, 1 for a particular subculture	4+1	T1	–
Deactivator Kit	–	2	4+2	–	–
Engineering Waldo X	Comms	X	7+X	T(X+1)	X
Forensics Kit X	Expert X, Fragile	X	4+2	T(X)	–
Handler's Kit	–	1	5+2	–	–
Holomask	Comms, Fragile	3	6+2	T4	–
Laboratory (Corporate Lease)	Comms	2	10+4	T1	4
MediKit	–	1	4+3	T1	–
Nav Suite (Region)	Comms, Expert 1	0	2+2	–	1
Negotiator's Suite	Comms, Expert 1	1	7+1	–	–
Pheromone Dispenser	–	2	4+3	T1	–
Powered Multitool	–	0	4+2	–	–
Psychoanalysis Suite	Comms, Expert 1	3	6+3	–	–
Repair Kit	–	1	6+2	–	1
Sensor Suite (Type)	Comms, Expert 1	1 to 3, per type	4+3	T1	–
Surgical Bay	Comms	2	14+1	T4	3
Surgical Waldo X	Comms	X	7+X	T(X+1)	X
Survival Kit (Environment)	–	1	4+2	–	–
USAriadnan Entrenching Tool	–	0, 1 for non-USAriadnans	2+2	–	–

WEAPONS

types of ammunition – p. 339

Metamaterials, integrated quantronics, expert systems, flash-fabrication, purpose-built chemical micro-structures, nano-scale injectors, and self-replicating neurotoxic coatings – every new technology either sees its first use on the battlefield, or is quickly subverted to military ends. It doesn't stop there; the pace of advancement is relentless. Last year's secret project is often daily carry for next year's soldier, the year after that it's haute couture for criminals with taste, and then in common civilian and law enforcement use within a decade.

Each habitat and territory restricts what weapons can be carried openly, bought, sold, or fabricated, but these controls are always a few steps behind criminal cleverness, corporate greed, idealistic determination, and operative practicality. When it comes to violence, the right tool for the job can be a lifesaver.

MELEE WEAPONS

Reloads – p. 356

Melee weapons are designed for close combat. They do not use Reloads and do not have the Burst quality. Their range is always Reach and they cannot be used to make attacks beyond that range.

RANGED WEAPONS

Ranged weapons are effective at a distance, though not all ranged weapons are effective at the same distances.

special Harm Effect, p. 102: Special Harm Effects do not count towards incapacitation or destruction, but are treated like Harm Effects in all other ways.

Range: Each ranged weapon has an effective range, and attacks against targets outside that range – closer or more distant – are at +1 difficulty per additional zone.

Burst: A ranged weapon's Burst determines the maximum number of Reloads that can be spent on attack rolls with the weapon.

Ammo: Each ranged weapon lists the types of ammunition it can use. If a weapon is listed as using Standard or Heavy ammunition, then it can use any ammo from the listed category. Other ammunition types will be specifically listed. If two types of ammo are joined with a "+", it means that the weapon uses the effects and qualities of both types of ammunition simultaneously. Swapping a weapon's ammunition for a different type requires a Minor Action (unless the weapon has the MULTI quality).

Weapons with a MULTI quality have been designed to fire a specific type of Special ammunition. These weapons list their secondary mode of firing after a "/" (e.g., AP/DA). In some cases, a class of weapons will simply be listed as firing "Special" ammunition, but when listing a specific weapon its type can be included in its name (e.g., the class of MULTI Rifles is listed as Standard/Special, but the specific MULTI K1 Rifle would have a Standard/K1 ammo type.)

Qualities: A weapon's entry lists only those qualities intrinsic to the weapon. The qualities of the ammunition used for an attack are added to those of the weapon itself. Ammunition qualities that are identical to a weapon's intrinsic qualities stack normally. (Note that ammunition types that inflict special Harm Effects inflict only that kind of

MELEE WEAPONS TABLE						
NAME	DAMAGE	SIZE	QUALITIES	RESTRICTION	COST	TARIFF
Axe	1+5 Ⓝ	Unbalanced	Non-Hackable, Thrown, Vicious 1	0	3+2 Ⓝ	–
Garrotte	See Entry	1H	Concealed 2, Non-Hackable, Subtle 2, Unforgiving 1	1	3+1 Ⓝ	T2
Grazeblade	1+4 Ⓝ	1H	Breaker, Non-Hackable, Stun, Subtle 2, Thrown, Toxic 3	4 (Haqqislam 2)	6+4 Ⓝ	T3
Hedgehog	1+4 Ⓝ	–	Aug (Implant)[1], Subtle 1, Toxic 4, Vicious 2	3	5+3 Ⓝ	T2
Knife	1+3 Ⓝ	1H	Concealed 1, Non-Hackable, Subtle 2, Thrown, Unforgiving 1	1	2+1 Ⓝ	–
Modhand	1+4 Ⓝ	1H	Concealed 2, E/M, Stun, Subtle 1, Vicious 2	4 (Nomad 2)	5+3 Ⓝ	T2
Morat Scimitar	1+5 Ⓝ	Unbalanced	Grievous, Non-Hackable, Vicious 2	3 (Paradiso 1)	4+2 Ⓝ	T1
Plasteel Pipe	1+4 Ⓝ	Unbalanced	Improvised 1, Non-Hackable, Stun	1	1+1 Ⓝ	–
Spear	1+4 Ⓝ	2H	Extended Reach, Non-Hackable, Thrown, Vicious 1	2	3+2 Ⓝ	–
Spiked Knuckles	1+4 Ⓝ	1H	Concealed 1, Non-Hackable, Piercing 1, Vicious 1	2	3+1 Ⓝ	T2
Stun Baton	1+4 Ⓝ	1H	Non-Hackable, Knockdown, Subtle 1, Stun	2	4+1 Ⓝ	T1
Sword	1+5 Ⓝ	Unbalanced	Non-Hackable, Parry 2, Vicious 1	3	5+2 Ⓝ	T1
Teseum Chopper	1+5 Ⓝ	Unbalanced	Non-Hackable, Piercing 4, Vicious 2	4 (Ariadna 2)	4+4 Ⓝ	T4[2]
Tonfa Bangles	1+3 Ⓝ	1H	Concealed 2, Parry 1[1]	1	5+5 Ⓝ	–
Wetspike	1+4 Ⓝ	1H	Piercing 1, Biotech, Toxic 1, Subtle 3	3	2+4 Ⓝ	T3

Harm Effect regardless of the weapon used unless specified otherwise.)

SPECIALISED WEAPONS

Any weapon that fires Standard ammunition will also have specialised versions which have been modified to fire a specific type of Special ammunition instead. The Restriction and Tariff of a specialised weapon are both 1 higher than the normal version, its cost increases by +1 (N), and it will be listed with its ammunition type (e.g., K1 sniper rifle or viral pistol).

If the weapon can normally fire multiple types of ammunition, the specialised version can still do the same (only the Standard option is swapped out).

RANGED WEAPONS TABLE									
NAME	RANGE	DAMAGE	BURST	SIZE	AMMO	QUALITIES	RESTRICTION	COST	TARIFF
Adhesive Launcher	M	1+6 (N)	1	Unwieldy	GOO	Munition	2	9+1 (N)	T2
Assault Pistol	R/C	1+4 (N)	3	Unbalanced	Standard	Vicious 1	1	4+2 (N)	T1
Boarding Shotgun	C	1+5 (N)	1	2H	Normal Shells/ AP Shells	Knockdown, Medium MULTI	3 (Z)	7+1 (N)	T1
Chain Rifle	C	1+6 (N)	1	2H	Normal	Spread 1, Torrent, Vicious 1	3	5+1 (N)	T2 (Z)
Combi Rifle	C/M	1+5 (N)	2	2H	Standard	Expert 1, MULTI Light Mod, Vicious 1	3	6+3 (N)	T1
Flash Pulse	M	1+5 (N)	1	2H	Flash[1]	–	2	6+1 (N)	T1
Heavy Flamethrower	C	2+5 (N)	1	2H	Fire	Incendiary 3, Munition, Terrifying 2, Torrent	3 (Z)	9+2 (N)	T2
Heavy Machine Gun (HMG)	L	2+6 (N)	3	Unwieldy	Normal	Spread 1, Unsubtle	3	9+3 (N)	T1
Heavy Pistol	R/C	2+4 (N)	1	Unbalanced	Standard	Unforgiving 1, Vicious 1	2	4+3 (N)	T1
Hyper-Rapid Magnetic Canon (HMC)	L	2+7 (N)	3/1	Massive	AP+Shock / DA	Light MULTI, MULTI Heavy Mod, Spread 2, Unsubtle / Anti-Materiel (DA mode only)	4	12+4 (N)	T3
Light Flamethrower	C	1+4 (N)	1	2H	Fire	Incendiary 3, Munition, Terrifying 2, Torrent	2 (Z)	8+1 (N)	T2
Light Grenade Launcher	M	2+4 (N)	1	Unbalanced	Heavy, Grenades	Area (Close), Munition, Speculative Fire	2	8+2 (N)	T2
Light Shotgun	C	1+4 (N)	1	Unbalanced	Normal Shells	Knockdown	2 (Z)	6+1 (N)	T1
Missile Launcher	L	2+7 (N)	1	Unwieldy	Heavy	Munition	4	10+4 (N)	T3
MULTI Heavy Machinegun	L	2+5 (N)	3	Unwieldy	Standard/Special	Medium MULTI, MULTI Heavy Mod, Spread 1, Unsubtle	4	11+4 (N)	T2
MULTI Rifle	C/M	1+5 (N)	2/2	2H	Standard/Special[1]	Expert 1, Medium MULTI, MULTI Light Mod, Vicious 1	3	8+4 (N)	T1
MULTI Sniper Rifle	L	1+6 (N)	2/2	Unwieldy	Standard/Special/ Needle or SaboT	Medium MULTI, Heavy MULTI, Unforgiving 2	3	8+3 (N)	T3
Nanopulser	C	1+5 (N)	1	1H	–	Biotech, Subtle 3, Torrent, Vicious 2	3 (Z)	6+2 (N)	T3
Panzerfaust	L	2+5 (N)	1	2H	Needle	Munition[1], Unsubtle	3	8+1 (N)	T2
Pistol	R/C	1+4 (N)	1	1H	Standard	Vicious 1	1	4+1 (N)	–
Plasma Carbine	R/C	1+5 (N)	2	Unbalanced	Plasma	Area (Close)[1], Vicious 1	EI only	N/A	–
Plasma Rifle	R/C	1+6 (N)	3	Unbalanced	Plasma	Area (Close)[1], Vicious 1	EI only	N/A	–
Plasma Sniper Rifle	L	1+7 (N)	2	Unwieldy	Plasma	Area (Close)[1], Vicious 1	EI only	N/A	–
Rifle	M	1+5 (N)	2	2H	Standard	MULTI Light Mod, Vicious 1	1	5+1 (N)	–
Sepsitor	C	1+3 (N)[1]	1	1H	–	Munition, Terrifying 3, Torrent, Toxic 3[1]	EI only	N/A	–
Sniper Rifle	L	1+6 (N)	2	Unwieldy	Standard	Unforgiving 2	2	6+3 (N)	T2
Spitfire	M	1+5 (N)	3	2H	Normal	Spread 2, Unsubtle	2	6+2 (N)	T1
Tactical Bow[1]	C	1+3 (N)	1	2H	Any Arrow	Non-Hackable, Subtle 2, Vicious 2	1	5+1 (N)	–
Vulkan Shotgun	C	1+5 (N)	1	2H	Fire Shells/AP Shells	Knockdown, Medium MULTI	2 (Z)	7+3 (N)	T1

[1] See entry for additional effects. [2] No Tariff on Ariadna.

(These rules only apply to Special ammunition, not Heavy ammunition. There are no rocket-launching pistols.)

Ad Hoc Specialisation: Weapons that fire Standard ammunition can also be modified in the field to allow them to fire Special ammunition types. This requires a Challenging (D2) Tech test and also inflicts a +1 complication range on the weapon. In addition, a GM can use a complication generated on an attack test using the weapon to permanently disable the weapon.

OTHER ITEMS

While weapons and armour are crucial in combat situations, what people carry with them and use most rarely fall into those martial categories. Useful equipment, expressions of identity and allegiance, survival and hazard gear – whatever the area of endeavour, the right tool makes all the difference.

Airborne Deployment: When a character enters free fall and is wearing a combat jump pack or other air-brake equipment, the GM sets an altitude, which is the number of zones above the ground the character starts at. At the start of each turn the character travels directly downwards towards the ground, with an initial falling speed of three zones per round. Ranged attacks directed against them are at +1 difficulty.

The character can activate the pack as a Minor Action, and, as a Minor Action on any subsequent turn, either increase or reduce their falling speed for the next turn by one zone per round. They can manoeuvre to adjacent zones within Medium range at the same altitude with a Pilot (D1) test, or within Long range for 2 Momentum.

When the character reaches the ground, if they had any zones of falling speed remaining, they take falling damage as if they had fallen a distance equal to the number of remaining zones of falling speed — less than what they would suffer without the pack, but a poorly judged landing is still painful.

Illumination: Light sources illuminate one or more zones in an area. Anyone in an illuminated zone or looking in from outside can observe and attack objects and characters in that zone without darkness penalties.

OTHER ITEMS TABLE

ITEM	QUALITIES	RESTRICTION	COST	TARIFF	MAINTENANCE
Animal Habitat	–	1	5+1 Ⓝ	T1	1
Bioscanner	Comms	0	3+1 Ⓝ	–	–
Bottled Water	Non-Hackable	0	1+1 Ⓝ	–	–
Climbing Plus	–	2	4+3 Ⓝ	–	–
Combat Jump Pack	Disposable	3	4+2 Ⓝ	T3	–
Comlog	Comms	0	5	–	–
Comlog, Neural	Aug, Comms, Neural	1	5+3 Ⓝ	T1	–
Deflector-1	Comms, Mounted	4 (Ariadna 2)	7+3 Ⓝ	T1	–
Deflector-2	Comms, Mounted	4 (Nomads 3/ Yu Jing 3)	7+3 Ⓝ	T3	–
Deployable Repeater	Comms, Repeater	1	3+2 Ⓝ	–	–
ECM X	Comms, Mounted	3	8+(2^{1}X) Ⓝ	T2	–
Fake ID X	Comms	X	4+X Ⓝ	T4	–
Lantern	–	0	1	–	–
Locational Beacon	Comms	1	4+2 Ⓝ	–	–
Micro-Torch	–	0	1	–	–
Multispectral Visor X	–	X	7+X Ⓝ	T(X)	–
Nullifier	Area (Close)	Tohaa only	N/A	–	N/A
Optical Disruption Device	Fragile, NFB	3	6+6 Ⓝ	T3	1
Recorder	Comms, Concealed 2	1	4+2 Ⓝ	T1	–
Respirator X		0	4+X Ⓝ	–	–
SecurCuffs	Comms^1	1	3+1 Ⓝ	T1	–
Signal Flare	Non-Hackable	0	1+2 Ⓝ	–	–
Stealth Repeater	Comms, Concealed 2, Repeater	1	3+3 Ⓝ	T1	–
Survival Pod	–	1	5+1 Ⓝ	–	–
Survival Rations	–	0	1+1 Ⓝ	–	–
SymbioMate	Disposable	Tohaa only	N/A	–	N/A
Thermo-Optical Camouflage	Fragile, NFB	4	6+6 Ⓝ	T3	1
Torch	–	0	1	–	–
Vac Suit	–	1	7+2 Ⓝ	T2	1
Varuna Lungs	–	1	4+3 Ⓝ	–	–

^{1} See entry.

GEAR
GEAR CATALOGUE

Adhesive Ammunition: Adhesive rounds use sticky, rapidly expanding gelatinous foam to pacify a target while inflicting minimum long-term trauma, and are commonly used by law enforcement and public-facing security teams. Adhesive ammunition adds Immobilising, Knockdown, and Nonlethal to the weapon.

Adhesive Launcher (ADHL): Due to the size of their canisters of swift-setting liquid cement, these weapons are usually loaded via large-bore rotary drum magazines, and used to immobilise enemy vehicles. Technically nonlethal and economical to use, an accurate shot with an adhesive launcher can render the most terrible war machine completely defenceless. (Range M, 1+6 Ⓝ damage, Burst 1, Unwieldy, GOO ammo, Munition)

Aletheia Kit: Small and unassuming, Aletheia kits are an open secret in the law enforcement and intelligence communities. Combining facial-tracking sensors with a blank expert system seed, the device imprints on the subject, quickly learning their quirks and tells to become an incredibly sensitive lie detector. Used with the Psychology skill, Aletheia kits have the Subtle 2 quality and add 1 bonus Momentum for each hour spent interrogating a suspect (to a maximum of 3).

Analysis Suite: While recorders and sensors are useful for data collection, analysis suites — facilities consisting of specialised software tools and displays — can correlate and extract useful information from that raw data. When used to view datafeeds, analysis suites grant 1 bonus Momentum and −1 difficulty to Analysis and Observations tests regarding anything detectable by the sensors or devices as if they were present.

Analytical Kit: Top-quality kits used for scientific analysis and experiments in the field, analytical kits are tools for the Science skill, and contain three uses of Reagents.

Animal Habitat: Habitats vary in size from small cages or tanks to a dedicated space in a stable, barn, or corral. Their maintenance cost covers necessary supplies to keep the animal healthy and content. While in a dedicated habitat, an animal is considered under control except in extreme circumstances.

Antibiotics: Available in a variety of forms, Antibiotics are invaluable in fighting off diseases, but can only be prescribed by a doctor. (Ingested, Instant 0)

Special Effect: A single dose grants 1 bonus Momentum on all Resistance tests made to resist the effects of disease.

Antipode Control Device: Antipode handlers not only command their charges on duty, but train and condition them with verbal commands, reinforced by activating electrodes inside the creatures' craniums that ensure obedience, even in the throes of bloodlust.

Each Antipode Control Device is networked to its pack's cranial implants. When attempting to control a creature fitted with a connected implant, the handler gains +2d20 to Animal Handling tests. Further, whenever the beasts make a Discipline test, their handler can use a Reaction to assist using their Animal Handling skill.

Antipode Control Cranial Implant: Antipodes augmented with these cranial implants are linked to an Antipode Control Device.

Antiquated Lhost: Cutting-edge technology as of about twenty years ago, these relics provide a practical lesson in the benefits of modern ectogenesis techniques. Slotting into one of these antiques is deeply distressing on a fundamental level. Some degree of dysmorphia is inevitable, as the brain fundamentally recognises the body as artificial, and rebels accordingly.

ectogenesis, p. 194: The melding of a stored, quantronic personlity and its new Lhost body.

Antipodes, p. 151: Intelligent, wolf-like species with distributed intelligence native to Dawn.

COMMON ADHESIVE LAUNCHERS
• **PraxiTec LC Csapda**: Nomad model sold to Haqqislam, featuring custom modifications to the adhesive loads to endure storage in desiccated conditions.
• **PraxiTec LC Fangeisen**: The original ADHL, sold to the Ariadnan Army.
• **PraxiTec LC Szigony**: Rockets with ultrafast super-adhesive warheads, used by the Nomads.
• **Jinsuo Zhòngcái**: Jinsuo successfully fended off a claim of patent infringement from PraxiTec during the Commercial Conflicts.

Sidebar

Teseum – p. 8

Antipodes, p. 151: Intelligent, wolf-like species with distributed intelligence native to Dawn.

PanOceanian Military Complex – p. 181

Inured to Disease / Poison / Vacuum, p. 418: Unaffected by these conditions.

Superhuman Brawn X, p. 418: Add X automatic successes to Brawn-based tests; +X base damage to melee attacks.

Lhosts – p. 354

ARMOURED CLOTHING VARIANT:

TRAKTSTAR

Popular with managers of private security firms if not their employees, all TrakStar uniforms incorporate a locational beacon for always-on connectivity and employee monitoring.

LHOST

ANTIQUATED LHOST

ATTRIBUTES						
AGI	AWA	BRW	COO	INT	PER	WIL
-1	-1	-1	-1	-1	-1	-1

SPECIAL ABILITIES
- Inured to Disease

AR Eye Implants: Augmented replacements for the human eye, eye implants provide 20:20 vision, polarisation against bright light, a display linked to the owner's comlog, and a visual data feed for geists and expert systems. Upgrades can add software emulation of recorders or optical filters for similar prices.

Armbot: In contrast to the utilitarian nature of other remotes, the PanOceanian Armbot is a weapon, and makes no effort to appear otherwise. A creation born of the prodigious PanOceanian Military Complex, these quadrupedal platforms are deceptively sturdy without sacrificing manoeuvrability; making them a favourite among the PanOceanian military, mercenary bands, law enforcement agencies, security minded civilians, and anyone else interested in a combat-proven workhorse remote.

ELITE

ARMBOT

ATTRIBUTES						
AGI	AWA	BRW	COO	INT	PER	WIL
11	10	12	11	8	5	6

FIELDS OF EXPERTISE								
Combat	+3	3	Movement	+1	1	Social	–	–
Fortitude	+1	1	Senses	+1	1	Technical	–	–

DEFENCES						
Firewall	8	Resolve	7	Structure	13
Security	–	Morale	–	Armour	3

ATTACKS
- **Boarding Shotgun:** Range C, 1+5 🅝 damage, Burst 1, 2H, Knockdown, Medium MULTI
  - *Normal Shells Mode (Primary):* Area (Close), Spread 1
  - *AP Slugs Mode (Secondary):* Piercing 3
- **Slam:** Melee, 3+7 🅝 damage, Anti-Materiel, Knockdown, Vicious 1

GEAR: Repeater

SPECIAL ABILITIES
- **Common Special Abilities:** Inured to Disease, Poison, and Vacuum; Superhuman Brawn 2
- **Hold the Line:** When an Armbot is controlled by a geist or its native LAI, it gains a Morale and Security Soak of 2.

Armoured Clothing: Comfortable all-day uniforms worn by security personnel and law enforcement, as well as ballistic nanofiber clothing for at-risk or paranoid VIPs. (Civilian Armour)

Armour Piercing (AP) Ammunition: AP projectiles employ one of a variety of technologies to overcome physical protection. Armour Piercing ammunition adds Piercing 2 to the weapon.

Armour Piercing Arrows (AP Arrows): Teseum-tipped arrows saw widespread adoption among the military forces of Dawn after the experiences of USAriadna against bow-wielding Antipodes. They add Piercing 3 to the weapon.

Armour Piercing Slugs (AP Slugs): Like normal shells, armour piercing slugs are high-calibre, self-contained cartridges, but instead of a carefully arranged array of flechettes, the cartridge is mostly carefully arranged accelerants, designed to project a solid metal dart at sufficient speeds to punch through modern vehicles, TAGs, and powered armour. AP slugs add Piercing 3 to the shotgun.

Assault Hacking Device: A purely offensive Infowar weapon, assault hacking devices are designed to seize control of enemy networks and systems, particularly heavy infantry, TAGs, and remotes. They are rated CLAW-3, SWORD-0, SHIELD-0, GADGET-0, and IC-1.

Assault Hacking Device (EI): Similar to the assault hacking devices used by infowarriors of the Human Sphere, the baseline EI combat hacking device is rated CLAW-3, SWORD-0, SHIELD-0, GADGET-0, and IC-1, and includes the Stop! upgrade.

Assault Pistol: Assault Pistols are bulkier than normal sidearms in exchange for a much higher rate of fire — ideal for close quarters assaults, where a hail of low-calibre rounds can quickly overwhelm foes. (Range R/C, 1+4 🅝 damage, Burst 3, Unbalanced, Standard ammo, Vicious 1)

Attribute Augmentation X: This augmentation permanently increases one of the buyer's body or Lhost's attributes by +X. If the augmentation is Silk-derived, it increases one attribute by 4 or increases all attributes by 1.

AutoMediKit: AutoMediKits monitor the wearer's vitals, stabilising injuries with fast-acting Serum injections so they can keep fighting. The base price includes three loads of nano-repair medical Serum, but the AutoMediKit can hold dozens of doses. The AutoMediKit functions as a MediKit for the character wearing it and can also, by expending a dose of Serum, make a treat test on its wearer with a target number of 11. When the wearer suffers a Wound, it will also automatically attempt to use the Treat action, making the test with a target number of 11. (It can also be quantronically instructed to use additional Serum for bonus d20s on this test as a Free Action.)

Axe: Axes are heavy chopping blades commonly used to clear heavy foliage. Their main virtue is cutting power. (Melee, 1+5 Ⓝ damage, Unbalanced, Non-Hackable, Thrown, Vicious 1)

Ballistic Vest: Vital organ protection for front-line security personnel, vehicle crews who don't want to deal with the bulk of full-body armour, and VIPs. (Civilian Armour)

Banshee Ammunition: Banshee rounds emit a phased wave of infrasound on impact, temporarily overloading the target's auditory and vestibular systems. Banshee ammo adds Area (Close), Deafening, Nonlethal, Stun, and Terrifying 3 to the weapon.

Basic Limb Replacement: This augmentation replaces a lost arm or leg. The new limb has no inherent advantages or disadvantages compared to the original limb.

Basic Medical Supplies: A set of basic supplies for tending to the injured, including Serum-infused bandages, antivenins, burn ointment, and a small cryo-bag for cloneable samples. Basic medical supplies contain three loads of Serum, and count as a kit for Medicine tests.

Bioimmunity Organ: This artificial, Silk-created organ is designed to boost immune system responses to viral attacks. It grants +4 BTS against attacks with the Biotech quality.

Bioscanner: Bioscanners are used by athletic trainers and police to monitor the health of individuals under their care. Available as either a worn personal scanner or a ranged, pistol-like device, bioscanners provide up-to-date information on the health and vital signs of their subject, giving anyone with network access or in line-of-sight 1 bonus Momentum on Medicine tests to diagnose health issues such as intoxication, poisoning, injury, or viral infection of the subject.

COMMON ASSAULT PISTOLS

- **AKNovy Groza Assault Pistol** (Ariadna)
- **Askari AS Rafas Assault Pistol** (Haqqislam)
- **FGA PK-6 Traceur Assault Pistol** (PanOceania)
- **FGA PK-8 Hornisse Assault Pistol** (PanOceania)
- **TauruSW Punho Assault Pistol** (PanOceania)
- **Yungang Xíng (Type) 2.6 Assault Pistol** (Yu Jing)
- **Cuurval Tuuga-1A (Tuuga-Ka-El-A)** (Tohaa Assault Pistol)

Boarding Shotgun: The boarding shotgun was developed for close quarters combat in thin-atmosphere and vacuum environments. Versatile weapons, boarding shotguns can fire both flechette rounds for assault and close quarters combat, and high-powered slugs to punch through heavily armoured combatants' defences. Boarding shotguns are Medium MULTI weapons, but use Normal Shells and AP Slugs instead of Standard or Special ammunition. (Range C, 1+5 Ⓝ damage, Burst 1, 2H, Knockdown, Medium, MULTI)

- *Normal Shells Mode (Primary)*: Area (Close), Spread 1
- *AP Slugs Mode (Secondary)*: Piercing 3

Bottled Water: One of living creatures' most fundamental needs, water is a surprisingly troublesome consideration for travellers. The human body needs lots of it, regularly, and it is fairly heavy. Each purchase contains six bottles, each containing sufficient water for an adult human for a single day.

COMMON BOARDING SHOTGUNS

- **AKNovy Drotek** (Ariadna): Robust, lightweight model from AKNovy incorporating new off-world technology.
- **AKNovy Yarost-2** (Ariadna): A simple, pump action mechanism with a classic appeal. +2 complication range in vacuum environments. (The original Yarost from a generation back doesn't work in vacuums at all.)
- **AKNovy Uzhas** (Ariadna): Designed especially for use with T2 Shells.
- **Askhari AS Fahd** (Haqqislam): Developed based on feedback from Bashi Bazouk corsairs.
- **CineticS Barong** (PanOceania): Top of the line model.
- **Devcon Arms Outburst-2** (Generic)
- **FGA FS-5 Klapper** (Franco-Germanique Armements, PanOceania): Popular with Nomads and Mercenaries.
- **IPS-Graffio** (Italieri de Precisione): Another PanOceanian model, standard issue for ALEPH's S.S.S.
- **Yungang Xíng (Type) 3.6** (Yu Jing)
- **Cuurval Kaanten-7000 (Kaanten-Su-Il)**: Tohaa model with biotech trigger-and-grip mechanism which grows to match user's hand.
- **Krumat**: Morat boarding shotgun.

Treat action p. 248

BALLISTIC VEST VARIANT:

GRIINMANN SUNDAY VESTS

After a failed post-mass assassination attempt, crypt-core rapper Griinmann partnered with the G&F Armourers to sell replicas of the perforated G&F ballistic vest she credited with saving her life, starting a minor craze for ballistically compromised apparel. These vests provide 1 less Armour Soak, but if worn openly grant 1 bonus Momentum on social skill tests with fans of crypt-core or street fashion, and 2 bonus Momentum with Griinmann fans.

Breaker Ammunition : Breaker rounds are designed to bypass and degrade biotechnological shielding (chemical, biological, radiological, and nuclear). Breaker ammunition adds Biotech, Breaker, and Piercing 1 to the weapon.

Breaking & Entering Kit: Used to overcome locks, doors, windows, and "dumb" quantronic systems, a B&E kit comes with three Picks, and grants 1 bonus Momentum to Thievery or Tech skill tests made to bypass physical security measures and break into secure places.

Chain Rifle : Chain Rifles use an electric flash-forge to transform lengths of chain into cones of red-hot shrapnel. Cheap to build and use, its wide firing arc — devastating at short range — makes it extremely popular among untrained militias and street gangs that don't mind a little noise. No training, no skill, just shredded remains and the smell of blood and metal. (Range C, 1+5 damage, Burst 1, 2H, Spread 1, Torrent, Vicious 1)

special Breach Effect, p. 102: Special Harm Effects do not count towards network being compromised, but are treated like Breach Effects in all other ways.

Chameleonwear: This technology embeds apparel with adaptive photoreactive cells patterned to break up the wearer's silhouette when they move, and blend with their environment at rest. Chameleonwear counts as a kit for face-to-face Stealth tests made against targets at Long range or farther, granting 1 bonus Momentum.

Chauffeur Geist: Specialised in interfacing with common vehicle networks. Many users have a dedicated chauffeur geist that does nothing except drive their personal vehicles.

GEIST

CHAUFFEUR GEIST

ATTRIBUTES

AGI	AWA	BRW	COO	INT	PER	WIL
4	7	4	9	6	6	4

SKILLS

Observation	+2	1	Pilot	+4	2

TALENTS
- Ace, Born to the Wheel or Push the Envelope, Sharp Senses, Sense of Direction

CLAW-1 Blackout: This software is designed to prevent outbound communication. On a successful attack, 1 Momentum can be spent to create a special Breach Effect that disables one piece of equipment attached to the target's network.

CLAW-1 Gotcha!: A favourite against mechanised forces, this program shuts down motive subroutines. On a successful attack, 2 Momentum can be spent to grant the attack the Immobilising quality.

CLAW-1 Overlord: This software seizes control of enemy systems. On a successful attack, 1 Momentum can be spent to inflict a special Breach Effect that forces the target's system to execute one command. Like other special Breach Effects, these do not count towards disabling the target's system. However, they can be totalled with other Breach Effects to suborn the target's system.

CLAW-1 Spotlight: This software highlights enemy combatants to ease tracking and targeting. Potent in combination with guided weaponry, it is commonly filtered by firewalls, making it tricky to use effectively. Spotlight inflicts no damage, but on a successful attack test the enemy is Marked.

CLAW-2 Expel: This Yu Jing favourite suborns ejections protocols. On a successful attack, 2 Momentum can be spent to inflict a special Breach Effect which forces one passenger or crew of a target vehicle with ejection capability to disembark.

CLAW-2 Oblivion: This software is a more potent version of Blackout. On a successful attack, 2 Momentum can be spent to create a special Breach Effect which forces all of the target's equipment into dumb mode. (This has no effect on Non-Hackable equipment, but disables Comms gear and inflicts a +1 difficulty to tests using all other items.)

CLAW-3 Basilisk: This is an advanced Gotcha! On a successful attack, 1 Momentum can be spent to grant the attack the Immobilising quality. In addition, the severity of the condition can be upgraded from Hindered to Stuck for an additional 1 Momentum (instead of the normal 2).

CLAW-3 Carbonite: An improved version of Gotcha!, after targeting motive subroutines, Carbonite exploits them as backdoors into the target's systems (granting Piercing 3). On a successful attack, 1 Momentum can be spent to grant the attack the Immobilising quality.

CLAW-3 Total Control: This is a potent suite of upgrades to Overlord programs. On a successful attack, 2 Momentum can be spent to inflict a special Breach Effect that grants complete control of the target's system to the hacker, allowing them to execute commands using the system until the Breach Effect is removed.

Climbing Kit: This kit contains ropes, spikes, axes, shock absorbers, carabiners for vertical ascents

COMMON CHAIN RIFLES
• **Yungang Xíng (Type) 9.0**: This Yu Jing model is the most popular in the Human Sphere. It fires 5mm steel chain. Large numbers were exported to Dawn during the Ariadnan Commercial Conflicts and they've proven popular with Dogfaces.
• **RaaD RD Shareek**: Haqqislamite-design made from a Yungang license.

or descents, and a monosteel cable micro-winch and pair of micro-grapnels to speed the process. It grants −1 difficulty to climbing Athletics tests and using the micro-winch adds 1 bonus Momentum for the purposes of improving the speed of the climb. The winch can be used three times before draining its battery.

Climbing Plus: From selectively adhesive boots and gloves to force-evolved grip pads, climbing plus gear helps the user to move vertically with ease, granting −2 difficulty on all climbing Athletics tests.

Combat Jump Pack: Combat jump packs are airborne deployment devices, using advanced air-brake systems to deliver troops behind enemy lines from atmospheric aircraft or orbit.

airborne deployment device – p. 360

Combi Rifle: Combi Rifles incorporate automatic mechanisms to suppress recoil and optimise aim at both Close and Medium ranges. Basic Combi Rifles fire Standard ammunition. (Range C/M, 1+5  damage, Burst 2, 2H, Expert 1, MULTI Light Mod, Vicious 1)

dumb mode – p. 352

Comms – p. 334

Stuck, p. 104: Cannot move away from object/location stuck to.

Hindered, p. 104: −1 zone when making movement actions. +1 difficulty on terrain tests.

Comlog: Comlogs are the essential quantronic devices which make modern living possible. They are connected to some form of AR display (contact lenses, retina augmentations, and/or holoprojectors are common) and controlled through a haptic-feedback system (a worn glove, implanted contact pads on the tips of the fingers, or direct neural feedback; decorative hand jewellery is also popular in a number of subcultures).

AR display – p. 142

COMMON COMBI RIFLES

- **CineticS Dayak** (named after a Bornean tribe): PanOceanian model with Light Shotgun, Light Flamethrower, and Light Grenade Launcher mods available.
- **FGA SG-9 Alraun / SG-5 Alraun 2** (Franco-Germanique Armements, "Mandrake" in German): PanOceanian manufacture, but popular with the Nomad Military Force and mercenaries.
- **Switech Malleus**: A K1 Combi Rifle used by ALEPH's S.S.S.
- **IPF-Dardo** (Italieri de Precisione): Another PanOceanian model, standard issue for ALEPH's S.S.S.
- **Yungang Xíng (Type) 4.2**: Used by the Yu Jing StateArmy with combination Light Flamethrower.
- **Iriista Luvo-100 (Luvo Ma-El)**: Tohaa Trident weapon built to similar specs.
- **Iriista Luvo-510 (Luvo Ka- Mu-El)**: K1 variant of the Luvo-100.

Maya datasphere – p. 142

UBIQUITOUS COMLOGS

Comlogs are so essential and universal that NPCs are simply assumed to possess one. Comlogs will only be listed among an NPC's gear if they possess special qualities, or if the NPC is specifically lacking a comlog.

CRASHSUIT VARIANT:

SOTHO HEADCASE

Designed for preserving individuals without Cubes or who are particularly concerned about skull trauma, Sotho Protectives offers this specialised crashsuit which increases Head location Armour Soak by +1 at the cost of −1 to all other locations.

Quantronic Jump, p. 418: Can jump from one Lhost or remote into another.

RUH

In Haqqislam, Cubes are referred to as *Gefr* and those with Cubes are known as *Ruh*.

repairs – p. 333

clone Lhost – p. 393

Comlogs are cheap and ubiquitous, but without one users are cut off from Maya and the dataspheres which make up a substantial chunk of practical reality. Any equipment used by a character without a comlog is considered to be operating in dumb mode (since they lack the interface necessary to use it in any other way).

The quantronic processor and memory units at the heart of a comlog are often implanted in the forearm. Some implanted comlogs are directly connected to the user's brain, which can be dangerous, but greatly enhances the user's integration into Maya, allowing them to essentially live within the datasphere. It's more common, however, for a wrist-worn link bracelet to provide an interface and network connections for the comlog.

Cosmetic Augmentaton X: Cosmetic augmentations cover a wide variety of purely superficial body alterations — implanted horns, unnatural eye colours, animated tattoos, prehensile hair, glowing skin, lizard scales, fur... basically anything the human imagination can conceive, modern medicine can transform the body into.

Much like cosmetics or stylish clothing, however, what augmentations are considered attractive and fashionable varies depending on national, cultural, and subcultural mores, and dramatic or radical augmentations can cause friction with those outside the target audience. When altering their appearance with cosmetic augmentations, the buyer chooses the subculture they are targeting and how intense an alteration they want. The cosmetic augmentations grant X bonus Momentum on tests involving attractiveness or social interaction with the target subculture. When interacting with members outside of the target subculture, however, these tests suffer a +X complication range.

Cosmetics Kit: Though proper usage depends on cultural mores, face and body paints, powders, and other appearance-altering substances abound, and using them properly is an art all its own. Each cosmetics kit contains ten uses, each enough to alter

the user's appearance for a day, and grants 1 bonus Momentum to Disguise tests.

A user can also attempt to use a cosmetics kit to alter their appearance to appeal to appropriate subcultures with a Lifestyle (D1) test. On a success, they gain 1 bonus Momentum to all social interaction tests with members of the subculture, but suffer a +1 complication range with everyone else.

Crashsuit: Serving as protection against vehicle accidents, this suit dissolves after a single round's use. (Civilian Armour)

Cube: These wetware cranial implants combine quantronic microprocessors with sophisticated, Silk-based biotechnology. Implanted at the base of the skull (for easy access to the encephalon), they spread nanonic fibres to form neuronal links throughout the brain. These links maintain a constantly updated copy of the user's personality (or sheut). Upon death, the Cube retracts the nanonic fibres, stores a fresh tissue sample (to allow for the creation of a clone Lhost), and enters a standby mode waiting for retrieval. (Some models will also activate a location transponder.)

For obvious security reasons, standard Cubes do not have a quantronic link. They are not even accessible from the user's personal network. Without the use of VoodooTech they cannot be hacked or compromised without first removing them from the host body.

Cube 2.0: The second generation of Cube technology represents a revolutionary approach to personality storage. The Cube 2.0 regularly backs up the sheut to trusted servers in the datasphere. Cube 2.0 also allows close integration with ALEPH (using technology which is an immediate precursor to that found in Posthuman Lhosts), and ALEPH has updated all of the Lhosts operated by its Aspects or Recreations to use Cube 2.0. Characters with a Cube 2.0 also have the Quantronic Jump ability.

The Cube 2.0 architecture also includes automated failsafes against sepsitor attacks. If a sepsitor attack inflicts a Metanoia Effect, the Cube automatically shuts down its quantronic connections, erases all access codes to its backup locations, and chemically destroys its storage substrate. For all intents and purposes, it becomes an inert object. A Cube 2.0 which has been disabled as a result of its sepsitor failsafe cannot be repaired and must be completely replaced.

D-Charge: D-Charges are explosives designed for directed detonation to penetrate a target's armour. A directional cover over a hollow charge ensures the explosion affects only the surface it is attached to, limiting collateral damage and allowing safe detonation while still near the target. D-Charges are often used for demolition, and are particularly useful for destroying and dismantling vehicles, structures, and walls. (Explosive Charge, 2+6  damage, 1H, Anti-Materiel 2, Comms, Disposable, Piercing 3, Spread 1, Unsubtle, Vicious 2)

Dancer Ammunition: A dancer round's ballistic path can be controlled remotely, albeit with the added dangers of hacking and ECM. Dancer ammo adds Guided to the weapon. (If used with a weapon that has the Non-Hackable quality, dancer ammo acts like normal ammunition.)

Defensive Hacking Device: Common equipment for system administrators, firewall augmentation teams, and bodyguards, these devices are exceptional for defending against other infowarriors. Defensive hacking devices are rated SHIELD-3, GADGET-1, and IC-3.

Deflector-1/Deflector-2: Deflectors merge several different technologies to create a defensive umbrella that protects the user and any allies within Close range. Quantronic attacks against characters protected by Deflector-1 are made at +1 difficulty; those against characters protected by Deflector-2 at +2 difficulty.

Deactivator Kit: This toolkit has all the necessary tools to defuse, deactivate, and disarm explosive devices. Deactivator kits also include scanning equipment which allows Tech tests to detect explosives to be made at up to Medium range.

Deployable Repeater: Deployable repeaters are portable hacking range amplifiers. Manufactured by a plethora of telecom hardware companies, models are often so interchangeable that their logos are the only distinctive feature (although superstitious or sentimental hackers often ornament surviving repeaters with smart-paint graffiti or custom software). Deployable repeaters are slightly larger than the size of a fist, and when activated they unfurl like a blossoming flower. Activating them requires a Tech (D0) test as a Minor Action, and once activated they cannot be moved without disrupting their connections (requiring them to be reactivated at a new location). (Firewall 10, Security 1)

Double Action (DA) Ammunition: Double action rounds are lightweight rounds embedded with micro-explosives, designed to maximise stopping power while retaining compatibility with standard military sidearms. DA ammo adds Vicious 2 to the weapon.

Double Action Arrows (DA Arrows): Explosive-tipped arrows add Piercing 1 and Vicious 2 to the weapon.

Double Trouble (DT) Ammunition: Double Trouble ammunition contains exceptionally toxic

wide-spectrum viral loads. DT ammo adds Biotech, Toxic 1, and Vicious 1 to the weapon.

Double Trouble Arrows (DT Arrows): Like Double Trouble ammunition, DT arrows are designed to deliver toxic loads. The superior penetrating power of modern combat bows makes for an efficient delivery mechanism. DT arrows add Biotech, Piercing 1, Toxic 1, and Vicious 1 to the weapon.

Drop Bears: Thanks to these mines' plump design, and the deadly results of raining them down on the enemy — because they are thrown instead of placed — the Neoterrans who first used them nicknamed them for the mythical koala-like Aussie treetop predator. With a successful Athletics test (+1 difficulty for each range category beyond Close), the drop bear lands in the chosen zone, and becomes active at the end of the wielder's action. (Explosive Mine, 2+5 damage, 1H, Comms, Disposable, Indiscriminate (Close), Spread 1, Stun, Thrown, Vicious 3)

Eclipse Ammunition: Eclipse rounds use isotope-doped nanotech smoke to reflect light well beyond the visible spectrum, making the affected zone impossible to see through, even with a multispectral visor. Eclipse ammo adds Reflective 2 to the weapon.

ECM X (Electronic Countermeasures): Standard ECM includes fire detection radars to track enemy ordnance, and a small battery of short-range micromissiles to deploy smart-material chaff that interferes with guidance systems and diverts projectiles away. Ariadnan ECM are bulkier, firing batteries of rockets to create protective walls of shrapnel. Attacks with the Guided quality suffer a +X difficulty against vehicles or positions outfitted with ECM.

Ectros Armour: Worn by frontline Tohaa Troops, this heavy armour includes poisoned spines for both offense and defence in Close Combat (functioning

repeater – p. 334

repeater – p. 334

CUBEVAC
Medevac is military slang for evacuating those who need medical attention. Cubevac is when you evacuate someone who is dead. Removing a Cube from a corpse can be done as a Standard Action with a Medicine (D2) test and proper surgical tools. Otherwise, it takes about a minute of bloody hacking (unless you want to just go for a C6 decapitation and sort it later).

COMMON DEPLOYABLE REPEATERS
- **Dàgāng Series 45–70** (Yu Jing)
- **Rasool RS Geedar** (Haqqislam)
- **Vinayama Industries ReplayStick** (PanOceania)

as an integrated Hedgehog weapon), and symbiotically grants +2 to all physical attributes. (Symbiont Armour)

dataspheres — p. 141

EI Hacking Device: These ultra-sophisticated Infowar platforms are used by EI cyber-assault agents to slice through primitive human data protocols. They are rated CLAW-2, SWORD-2, SHIELD-2, GADGET-3, IC-3, and include the Sucker Punch upgrade.

Electromagnetic (E/M) Ammunition ⚋: Electromagnetic rounds emit a high-energy electromagnetic pulse on impact, designed to damage and disable the target's electronics and quantronic systems. Electromagnetic ammo adds E/M and Piercing 1 to the weapon.

E/M2 Ammunition ⚋: E/M2 rounds are bulky and carry multiple E/M pulse emitters, increasing their effectiveness against protected high-tech systems. E/M2 ammo adds Area (Close), Breaker, E/M, and Piercing 2 to the weapon.

remotes — p. 354

social skill tests — p. 122

sheut, p. 392: The core identity of the individual as saved on a Cube.

Engineering Waldo X: Engineering waldos are articulated mechanical arms that can provide a technician with an extra hand. An engineering waldo counts as a kit, granting 1 bonus Momentum to Tech tests. One or more waldos can also assist on a Tech test with a target number of 10+X. Each additional waldo used on an operation halves the amount of time it takes to complete, but adds +1 complication range.

   Alternatively, engineering waldos can be used as a remote, allowing their user to perform Tech tests without being physically present. (The normal penalties for operating a remote apply.)

Explosive (EXP) Ammunition: Explosive rounds detonate on impact, creating a potent localised blast. Explosive ammo adds Area (Close), Spread 1, Unsubtle, and Vicious 2 to the weapon.

Fake ID X: Useful for avoiding attention and entering otherwise inaccessible areas, Fake ID datafiles vary in quality from the wafer-thin covers teens use to sneak into bars, to elaborate false identities with layered halo and background data planted in dozens of dataspheres. If carefully inspected they can be detected with an Analysis, Thievery, or (for quantronic IDs) Hacking test at X difficulty, but as long as they remain undetected they grant X bonus Momentum to disguise-based Stealth tests. (At the GM's discretion, they may also be useful for certain social skill tests.)

Fast Download Port: A fast download port is an alternative method of sheut backup for those who don't want to (or for some reason can't) use a Cube. They allow for quick external recordings of the user's personality to be taken. (Such ports are often used by agents going into dangerous territory so that their memories can't be retrieved from their Cubes in the event that they are captured or killed.)

Fire Ammunition: Fire rounds are loaded with accelerants and fast-burning fuels, adding Incendiary 3 and Terrifying 1 to the weapon.

Fire Shells: Fire Shells have a proximity sensor and detonate at a set distance like a Normal Shell, but the cartridge surface has dozens of micronozzles to spray the fast-burning jellied fuel inside all over the target and then ignite it, burning them alive. Fire Shells add Area (Close), Incendiary 3, and Terrifying 1 to the shotgun.

Flarefiltered Chaff: This ammunition spreads and ignites clouds of smart-magnesium chaff in pre-programmed polarisation patterns — rendering the chaff harmless to allies with synced visors — for unparalleled tactical advantage, adding Area (Close), Blinding, and Nonlethal to the weapon.

Flash Ammunition: Flash rounds emit a focused beam of light or data from the weapon rather than a projectile. The high-energy discharge interferes with vision or sensory systems, causing temporary blindness in addition to the beam's effect. Flash ammo adds Blinding to the weapon, and removes the Marked condition.

Flashbang: Flashbangs combine deafening sound and blinding lights to overwhelm and incapacitate anyone caught in the area of effect. Networked versions can alert allies just before detonation, rendering them harmless to synched friendly forces. (Explosive Grenade, 1+5 Ⓝ damage, 1H, Blinding, Deafening, Disposable, Indiscriminate (Close), Nonlethal, Speculative Fire, Thrown, Unsubtle, removes Marked)

Flash Pulse: These sophisticated pieces of equipment emit focused beams of light or data towards a target. The massive Flash discharge overloads the target's vision systems, causing temporary blindness in addition to damage from the beam. Flash pulses' mirrored barrels and tuned lenses need careful maintenance and tuning to use effectively, requiring the Tech skill instead of Ballistics when attacking. They fire Flash ammo. (Range M, 1+5 Ⓝ damage, Burst 1, 2H, Blinding, removes Marked)

Fleck: Named for *Chironex fleckeri*, the jellyfish it is derived from, Fleck venom weakens cell walls, inflicts agonising pain, and induces cardiovascular collapse in minutes. Anti-venom is easily fabricated from Serum, but swift treatment is crucial. (Injected, Complex Progressive 1 (4 Momentum), Minute, 1+3 Ⓝ physical and mental damage)

CREATING FAKE IDS

Characters can create Fake IDs by making a Stealth D0 test. A success creates a Fake ID 0 (useful as a prop, but not much else), but Momentum can be spent to increase the Fake ID's rating, as per the Create Obstacle spend plus an additional Momentum. (2 Momentum for Fake ID 1, 4 Momentum for Fake ID 2, 7 Momentum for Fake ID 3.)

Some IDs are quantronically locked, which means that their information is independently verified through a Maya check. This may require an additional Hacking check or even a full remote hack in order to plant or spoof the correct data.

Special Effect: If the initial Resistance test is failed, the target immediately takes one Wound with the Wound Effect of +1 difficulty on all Agility-, Brawn-, and Coordination-based actions.

Forensics Kit X: Forensics kits contain tools and tamper-proof containers for evidence collection, recording software, a dedicated datasphere, and a rating X Expert system to analyse blood spatter, reconstruct the scene, and highlight out-of-place details.

Forensics kits add 1 bonus Momentum to Science, Tech, or Ballistics tests made to identify and collect forensic evidence from a crime scene, identify unknown substances onsite, and preserve footprints, treads, and fingerprints.

GADGET-1 Controlled Jump: This Supportware guides allies using airborne deployment to land near the user. These allies suffer one less zone of falling damage on landing. The hacker can also use Hacking tests to assist these allies in Pilot tests as a Reaction without spending Heat.

GADGET-1 Fairy Dust: This Supportware provides protection to allied networks. When activated, the user makes a Simple (D0) Hacking test. All allies within Long range gain +1 Ⓝ Interference Soak per Momentum spent (to a maximum of 5).

GADGET-1 Lockpicker: This software helps the user access a network that they have direct physical access to. When hacking a non-mobile target within Reach in a combat zone, Hacking tests are made at −1 difficulty.

GADGET-2 Assisted Fire: This Supportware aids drones, remotes, and similar devices under the hacker's control. The hacker can use Hacking tests to assist ranged attacks made by the devices as a Reaction without spending Heat.

GADGET-2 Enhanced Reaction: This Supportware aids drones, remotes, and similar devices under the hacker's control. Ranged attacks made by the device are treated as having a Burst rating one higher than normal.

Garuda Tacbot: Named for the Vedic god Vishnu's avian mount, the Garuda Immediate Tactical Deployment Bot is a staple of ALEPH's Special Situations Section. A light remote with sub-orbital deployment capabilities, the Garuda eschews bulky armour in favour of mobility and evasive capability. All things considered, it's a solid trade: Garuda are notoriously difficult to hit, often making it through entire firefights without so much as a scratch.

Ostensibly unavailable to anyone outside ALEPH's S.S.S., salvaged models — or designs bearing a curiously strong resemblance — have begun appearing in grey markets across the Human Sphere.

NEMESIS

GARUDA TACBOT

ATTRIBUTES

AGI	AWA	BRW	COO	INT	PER	WIL
13 (+1)	10	9 (+1)	12 (+1)	10	8	8

FIELDS OF EXPERTISE

Combat	+2	2	Movement	+4	4	Social	–	–
Fortitude	+2	1	Senses	+2	1	Technical	+2	–

DEFENCES

Firewall	12	Resolve	10	Structure	11
Security	2	Morale	–	Armour	3

ATTACKS

- **Stun Knuckles**: Melee, 2+5 Ⓝ damage, 1H, Concealed 1, Piercing 1, Stun, Vicious 1
- **Spitfire**: Range M, 1+7 Ⓝ damage, Burst 3, 2H, Spread 2, Unsubtle

GEAR: Combat Jump Pack, Deflector-1, Sensor Suite (Infrared Cameras)

SPECIAL ABILITIES

- **Common Special Abilities**: Inured to Disease, Poison, and Vacuum; Superhuman Agility 1, Superhuman Brawn 1, Superhuman Coordination 1
- **Loyalty Matrix**: When a Garuda is controlled by a geist or its native LAI, it gains a Morale and Security Soak of 3.
- **Mimetism**: Any attacks targeting a Garuda at ranges beyond Close are made at +1 difficulty.

Garrotte: A garrotte is a length of wire, cord, or cloth looped around a victim's neck and pulled tight in a single motion for strangulation. Using a garrotte is a Stealth versus Observation face-to-face test. If successful, the target is Stuck and the attacker immediately inflicts 1+4 Ⓝ (Subtle 2, Unforgiving 2) physical damage to the target's head, increased by the attacker's melee damage bonus.

Each round on the attacker's turn, the target makes a face-to-face Resistance test opposed by the attacker's Close Combat skill; failure means the damage is inflicted again. If the target succeeds, they do not take damage. On the target's turn, they can attempt a face-to-face Athletics test opposed by the attacker's Close Combat skill to generate Momentum. At any time, 3 Momentum can be spent to break the target free.

A garrotte possesses the Concealed 2 quality.

Gecko Pads: Biografted organs based on the giant cliff geckos of Paradiso, these augmentations grant a −2 difficulty on all climbing Athletics tests.

Grazeblade: An Hassassin specialty, Grazeblades are slashing knives coated with a self-replenishing coating of proprietary neurotoxin — even a scratch can kill. (Melee, 1+4 Ⓝ damage, 1H, Breaker, Non-Hackable, Stun, Subtle 2, Thrown, Toxic 3)

Gruntsuit: Bulky protection against industrial and construction accidents and hazards, gruntsuits also

---

Expert X, p. 334: Grants the user X bonus Momentum.

Subtle X, p. 335: Observation tests vs. item made at +X difficulty. Noisy actions reduced to sneaky; sneaky to silent.

Burst, p. 358: Maximum number of Reloads can be spent on attack rolls with weapon.

Special Situations Section — p. 196

Non-Hackable, p. 334: Cannot be targeted by quantronic attacks or affected by Breach Effects.t

have a built-in lifting exoskeleton and plenty of room for gear. (Civilian Armour)

Goonade (Goo) Ammunition: Goonade rounds are massively scaled-up Adhesive rounds, using multi-nozzle projectors to spread sticky, rapidly expanding, and instant-setting liquid cement over a large area, and are commonly used by law enforcement and public-facing security teams against vehicles and for pacifying riots. Goonade ammunition adds Area (Close), Immobilising, Knockdown, and Nonlethal to the weapon, and even effects vehicles, powered armour, and TAGs.

Guardian Geist: This geist integrates thoroughly with the user's personal area network and is particularly adept at becoming an active part of its defence.

Cybermask, Sucker Punch, White Noise – pp. 384–385

comlogs – p. 365

HEAVY COMBAT ARMOUR VARIANT:
ORC

Highly prized among seasoned veterans, Omnia Research & Creation releases only short runs of this model outside of its military contracts, increasing demand in hopes of a long-term monopoly. Designed for rugged durability, Tech tests to repair ORC armour are at −1 difficulty and their solid reputation grants +2 Morale Soak against threats of physical harm or combat-related fear.

HEAVY COMBAT ARMOUR VARIANT:
SOGARAT TEMPEST

Only the best will do for the elite EI ground troops of the Sogarat Tempest Regiment, pride of the Morat race. Their specially constructed heavy combat armour augments the wearer's resilience with an AutoMediKit, and adds Terrifying 2 to their every attack against anyone unfortunate enough to see them.

GEIST
GUARDIAN GEIST

ATTRIBUTES						
AGI	AWA	BRW	COO	INT	PER	WIL
4	7	4	4	8	5	4

SKILLS						
Analysis	+1	–	Hacking	+3	3	Observation	+1	–

TALENTS
- Hacker, Microscopic Threats, Pattern Recognition, Quantronic Flak

Hacking Device: A flexible multi-role unit, the standard Hacking Device is in common military and illicit use throughout the Human Sphere. While possessing one is not strictly illegal, they are often disguised as comlogs or other innocuous equipment to avoid unwanted attention from law enforcement. They are rated CLAW-1, SWORD-1, SHIELD-1, GADGET-3, and IC-1.

COMMON HACKING DEVICES

- **Bodysoft HT-31**: A slim Tunguskan model designed to clip onto a belt.
- **Bodysoft HT-41**: Upgraded +-Model of the classic Bodysoft.
- **Dàgāng Series 11–60**: The Yu Jing 11-XX line are Bodysoft knockoffs.
- **Quintex Roar**: A cheap PanOceanian model prized among criminal hackers because its outer shell can be stripped off and replaced with a tiny, easily concealed custom case (Tech (D1) test to gain Concealed 2, but at risk of the device being destroyed on a complication).
- **Rasool RS Dameer**: Black market model that first became popular in Funduq, but can be found in caravanserai throughout the Human Sphere. Designed for easy connection to a neural hacking socket.
- **Switech Radius**: High-end PanOceanian model with a wide selection of preinstalled software packages.
- **Gaarva Noosto 0–30 (Noosto Gao Ki-El)**: A Tohaa white hacking device; a living platform licensed by Niista.

Hacking Device Plus: An O-12 designation for the most recent devices used by Nomad infiltrators, hacking device plus tech combines multiple UPGRADE modules into a single unit while still providing flexible program support. There are unsubstantiated reports of ALEPH-directed units with similar technology. These devices are rated CLAW-2, SWORD-1, SHIELD-2, GADGET-3, IC-2, and include the Cybermask, Sucker Punch, and White Noise upgrades.

Handler's Kit: A handler's kit contains a large, collapsible cage to contain an animal during transit or between training sessions, and tools granting 1 bonus Momentum for Animal Handling tests to capture, restrain, or train an animal. The cage provides +4 (N) Armour Soak to all locations if designed for the specific type of animal, or +1 (N) Armour Soak otherwise. Unless placed in an appropriate animal habitat, even if the animal has been brought under control, it will require further tests to restrain if new stimuli cause it to panic or lash out.

Hard Hat: Smart-material head protection for work sites, modern hard hats are selectively collapsible when not in use. (Civilian Armour)

Haunt: O-12's designation for a toxin used in EI booby-traps on Paradiso, Haunt induces disturbing auditory and visual hallucinations, and for a small subset of victims, a vicious auto-immune cascade. (Injected, Complex 2 (5 Momentum), Day, 2+4 (N) mental damage)
Metanoia Effect: The hallucinations inflict a +2 complication range on most tests and require either Observation or Psychology tests with a difficulty equal to the number of Haunt-derived Metanoia Effects to discern from reality.

Heavy Combat Armour: Heavy combat armour is military-issue assault armour used by heavy infantry, shock troops, and support weapons experts. Although generic versions are available, corporations and national militaries all offer unique variants, with integrated loadouts of gear, drugs, equipment, and attribute-boosting alterations. (Combat Armour)

Heavy Flamethrower: Flamethrower design has evolved to be smaller, lighter, safer, and easier to use, but their tactical role is unchanged: create a stream of fire to clear a path or enclosed area of hostiles. Facing one instils fear in the heart of even seasoned soldiers, while concentrated neutral combustion agents prevent accidental explosions if the tank is punctured, maximising rates of fire with minimum encumbrance. Heavy flamethrowers are designed as standalone weapons, and are a common heavy infantry weapon for close quarters conflict. (Range C, 2+5 (N) damage, Burst 1, 2H, Incendiary 3, Munition, Terrifying 2, Torrent)

Heavy Machinegun (HMG): The "Mother of All Support Weapons", HMGs are auto-cooled heavy support weapons, allowing their operator to fire continuously without fear of heat damage to the barrel or the firing mechanisms for a withering rate of fire. (Range L, 2+6  damage, Burst 3, Unwieldy, Spread 1, Unsubtle)

Heavy Pistol: The term "heavy pistol" refers both to large-calibre handguns used for big-game hunting and to short-range weapons TAGs use for close quarters and enclosed combat. (Range R/C, 2+4 damage, Burst 1, Unbalanced, Unforgiving 1, Vicious 1)

Hedgehog: Implanted or armour-integrated venomous spines to deter contact and poison attackers, commonly used by the EI and occasionally by the Tohaa. (Melee, 1+4 damage, Aug (Implant), Subtle 1, Toxic 4, Vicious 2)

Holomask: Holomasks cover the wearer in a lifelike hologram disguise, ideally someone of similar size and build. When using the Stealth skill to disguise themselves, a holomask allows the character to create the disguise as a Standard Action and counts as a kit (granting 1 bonus Momentum to Disguise tests). It is linked to the character's personal network and possesses the Comms quality.

Hyper-Rapid Magnetic Cannon: Hyper-Rapid Magnetic Cannons use Gatling-style railguns arrays, firing 3mm metal shards at incredible speeds for massive kinetic impact, granting armour penetration and effective range on par with a HMG. Thanks to MULTI capabilities, alternative Standard payloads can also be used as the situation requires, as well as Special ammunition at slower rates of fire. Due to their size and weight, HMCs are often mounted weapons used exclusively by armoured units. (Range L, 2+7 damage, Burst 3/1, Massive, Light MULTI, Spread 2, Unsubtle)
 AP+Shock Mode (Primary): Biotech, Grievous, Piercing 2
 DA Mode (Secondary): Anti-Materiel, Vicious 2

IC-X Black ICE: If the Hacking test to bypass Black ICE fails, the IC inflicts 1+X (Piercing X) quantronic damage. If the hacker has equipment with the Neural quality, this damage is dealt as physical damage instead.

IC-X Countermeasures: This is the most basic form of intrusion countermeasures, possessing no special IC effects.

IC-X Crybaby: If the Hacking test to bypass Crybaby fails, it uses a dedicated channel to alert one or more authenticated users of the intrusion, calling them to the system's defence. This also allows the GM to summon reinforcements for 2 Heat less than normal (minimum 1).

IC-X Deadfall: This rudimentary program is used to monitor data tunnels entering its quantronic zone. If the Hacking test to bypass Deadfall fails, it will close the data tunnel through which the intruder attempted to access the zone. The data tunnel remains closed until Deadfall receives a valid passcode.

Neural, p. 334: Item grants 1 bonus Momentum, but exposes user to neural-based Breach Effects.

Biotech, p. 336: Uses BTS for persistent soak.

summoning reinforcements – p. 34

data tunnel – p. 118

Comms – p. 334

Aug (Implant) – p. 344

COMMON HEAVY FLAMETHROWERS
• **AKNovy Drakon** (Ariadna)
• **Iriista Roomur-600 (Roomur Ni-El)** (Tohaa)

COMMON HMGS
• **CineticS Tausug** (PanOceania)
• **Askari AS Bourkan** (Sword of Allah)
• **AKNovy Drozhat** (Ariadna AP HMG)
• **AKNovy Hischnik** (Ariadna)
• **FGA SM Geistesblitz** (Franco-Germanique Armements, PanOceania)
• **IPMT Furore** (Italiere de Precisione, PanOceania)
• **PraxiTech Geistesblitz** (Nomads)
• **Yungang Xíng (Type) 6.1** (Yu Jing)
• **Iriista Caalmur-60** (Tohaa Trident)
• **Hemat** (Morat Supremacy)

COMMON HEAVY PISTOLS
• **Americolt Bulldog AP Heavy Pistol** (Ariadna)
• **Americolt Peacemaker Heavy Pistol** (Ariadna)
• **Askari AS Hazam Heavy Pistol** (Haqqislam)
• **Askari AS Kedar AP Heavy Pistol** (Haqqislam)
• **FGA PK-7 Invasor Heavy Pistol** (PanOceania)
• **FGA SP-3 Krupp Heavy Pistol** (PanOceania)
• **FGA SP-5 Kaiser AP Heavy Pistol** (PanOceania)
• **TauruSW Clava Heavy Pistol** (PanOceania)
• **Yungang Xíng (Type) 2.8 Heavy Pistol** (Yu Jing)
• **Yungang Xíng (Type) 2.8 Heavy AP Pistol** (Yu Jing)
• **Cuurval Tuuga-8A (Tuuga-To-El-A)** (Tohaa Heavy Pistol)

COMMON HMCS
• **Switech Gurges** (PanOceania): The original HRMC, also used by Nomads, and ALEPH's S.S.S.
• **Yungang Xíng (Type) 0.0** (Yu Jing)

LIGHT COMBAT ARMOUR VARIANT:

DEVA FUNCTIONARY

Designed to accommodate the inhuman flexibility and speed of ALEPH's Deva Lhosts, this light combat armour incorporates a nanopulser in case of emergencies and a repeater to ensure connectivity. Careful design and layered exotic materials ensure an unobtrusive silhouette (Hidden Armour 2).

LIGHT COMBAT ARMOUR VARIANT:

ZHAYEDAN INTERVENTION

A joint effort of Al-Medinat research laboratories and Hekim Industries armourers, these sets of Haqqislamite light combat armour maximise survivability for experienced, un-augmented troops, replacing the usual MediKit with an AutoMediKit, and incorporating a full rebreather helmet in case of gas attacks or sandstorms.

VoodooTech – p. 307

Teseum – p. 8

Reagents – p. 356

Stuck, p. 104: Cannot move away from object/location stuck to.

Hindered, p. 104: −1 zone when making movement actions. +1 difficulty on terrain tests.

IC-X Gaslight: If the Hacking test to bypass Gaslight fails, the hacker will believe that the IC has been successfully bypassed and will be allowed to "enter" the quantronic zone containing Gaslight. In reality, the hacker will have been shunted into a duplicate zone. An Analysis test at X difficulty can discover the ruse. This "gaslight zone" can possess one or more additional features, such as:

Gaslight Trap: Escaping from the gaslight zone (by either returning to the zone they came from or terminating their connection) requires the character to successfully bypass the Gaslight IC. Until they do so, they remain trapped.

Gaslight Delusion: Many gaslight zones will be stocked with false data. Hackers are allowed to enter the gaslight zone, pilfer garbage, and then freely leave.

IC-X Hivemines: If the Hacking test to bypass Hivemines fails, the IC inflicts X+X Ⓝ (Vicious X) quantronic damage.

IC-X Mirrormaze: This IC obfuscates its local network with a suite of concealed backdoors, false access points, and obfuscating file structures. In addition to operating as IC, it also provides +2 Ⓝ Interference Soak for authenticated users in the same zone.

IC-X Redtape: If the Hacking test to bypass Redtape fails, the character becomes Hindered for the purposes of moving in quantronic zones. If the character was already Hindered, they become Stuck.

Inlaid Palm Circuitry: Palm circuitry is an augmentation that grants precision control far beyond what the human hand normally allows. Aesthetics vary by culture: bold geometric *tatau* patterns for PanOceanian pilots, calligraphic Sufi poetry for Haqqislamite privateers, even interlinked concentric rings for O-12 agents. They are most commonly used by pilots, acting as a kit and granting 1 bonus Momentum on Pilot and Spacecraft tests. Programs specialised in assisting in other tasks/skills have also been developed (and can be purchased for the same price per skill).

Internal Pocket X: As either a cybernetic implant or a biografted body modification, an internal pocket is a sealable cavity within the character's body. The

pocket and anything placed inside the pocket has the Concealed X quality. Most pockets can only fit small objects roughly the size of a fist, but if the pocket is installed as a large implant it can hold one-handed weapons and comparable items.

K1 Ammunition: K1 rounds are reverse-engineered VoodooTech armour-piercing projectiles, allowing small-bore weapons anti-tank functionality without the need for Teseum. EI forces make extensive use of K1 rounds, but in the Human Sphere, the technology involved and high cost of producing a single round make it extraordinarily difficult to find and dangerous to use. K1 ammo adds Anti-Materiel 2 and Monofilament to the weapon.

Killer Hacking Device: These devices are the ultimate infowar tool used for hunting down and eliminating other hackers. They are rated CLAW-0, SWORD-2, SHIELD-0, GADGET-0, IC-1, and have Cybermask as an upgrade. They also grant Piercing 3 to all attacks made using programs running on the device.

Knife: Combat knives are attachable as a bayonet, balanced for hand-to-hand combat, and reliable and sharp enough for use a survival tool. (Melee, 1+3 Ⓝ damage, 1H, Concealed 1, Non-Hackable, Subtle 2, Thrown, Unforgiving 1)

Laboratory (Corporate Lease): A leased corporate laboratory is an extensive purpose-built facility for research and experimental Science tests, typically containing six uses of Reagents, with a hefty Maintenance charge for monthly rent. The laboratory counts as a facility for Science tests, granting 1 bonus Momentum and −1 difficulty.

Lantern: Lanterns cast light over a wide area, and are commonly used to light campsites or outdoor spaces; street lamps are a form of lantern. A lantern illuminates the zone it is in and adjacent zones (unless obstructed by some form of barrier).

Lhost, Standard: Available in a variety of shapes and sizes — representing the full range of human appearance — most modern Lhosts also provide the additional benefits of an industrial-strength biosynthetic body.

COMMON LIGHT SHOTGUNS
- **AKNovy Obrez** (Ariadna)
- **CineticS Boksingero** (PanOceania)
- **Devcon Arms Slammer-7** (Generic)
- **IPS Battente** (Italieri de Precisione, PanOceania)
- **Yungang Xíng (Type) 3.2** (Yu Jing)
- **Cuurval Kaan-6000 (Kaan Sa-Il)** (Tohaa)

LHOST
STANDARD LHOST

ATTRIBUTES						
AGI	AWA	BRW	COO	INT	PER	WIL
–	–	–	–	–	–	–

SPECIAL ABILITIES
- Inured to Disease

Light Combat Armour: Light combat armour is a term for enhanced uniforms worn by specialists, vehicle crews, and stealthy operatives. Although generic versions are available, corporations and national militaries all offer unique variants, with integrated loadouts of gear, drugs, equipment, and attribute-boosting alterations. (Combat Armour)

Light Flamethrower: Flamethrower design has evolved to be smaller, lighter, safer, and easier to use, but their tactical role is unchanged: create a stream of fire to clear a path or enclosed area of hostiles. Facing one instils fear in the heart of even seasoned soldiers, while concentrated neutral combustion agents prevent accidental explosions if the tank is punctured, maximising rates of fire with minimum encumbrance. Light FTs are commonly incorporated into armour and rifles. (Range C, 1+4 damage, Burst 1, 2H, Incendiary 3, Munition, Terrifying 2, Torrent)

Light Grenade Launcher: Grenade launchers allow bombardment of enemy positions with grenades or other Heavy munitions while safely out of the direct line of fire. They fire grenades as Heavy ammunition, counting each grenade as one Reload, and are often attached to rifles for fire support in combat. (Range M, 2+4 damage, Burst 1, Unbalanced, Indiscriminate (Close), Munition, Speculative Fire)

Light Shotgun: Light shotguns fire flechette shells, using laser-aided target selectors to detonate them at the ideal distance to completely saturate a targeted area, and are often attached to rifles for close quarters combat. (Range C, 1+4 damage, Burst 1, Unbalanced, Knockdown)

Limb Socket: A limb socket augmentation allows the user to swap out cybernetic limbs with an Average (D1) Tech test. It takes ten minutes to swap a limb.

COMMON FLAMETHROWERS
- **AKNovy Fakiel** (Ariadna)
- **Askari AS Shaelia** (Haqqislam)
- **Iriista Roomur-500 (Roomur Mu-El)** (Tohaa)
- **Kantatet** (Morat Supremacy)

Locational Beacon: These marble-sized beacons are often installed in worksuits or implanted beneath the skin. They passively query friendly networks to aid navigation and track the user without exposing them to quantronic attacks, providing updated location data every five minutes. It takes a Challenging (D2) Hacking test to query the system outside of its usual update pattern.

MediKit: These widespread nano-injection medical devices have seen many improvements since they were first introduced over a century ago. Modern models are lightweight pistols capable of propelling a Serum microcapsule using a magnetic coil. MediKits contain three loads of Serum and grant a bonus Momentum for all Medicine tests. In addition, a character with a MediKit can expend one dose of Serum to perform a Treat action even when out of Reach of the patient (by firing a microprojectile at them), to a maximum range of two zones, albeit at +1 difficulty.

Medium Combat Armour: Medium combat armour consists of full battlefield protection for boarding parties, hit squads, and front-line fireteams. Although generic versions are available, corporations and national militaries all offer unique variants, with integrated loadouts of gear, drugs, equipment, and attribute-boosting alterations. (Combat Armour)

Micro-Torch: A smaller torch often incorporated into weapons and other handheld items, a micro-torch illuminates one zone within Medium range and line of sight.

Military Geist: Designed from the ground up for combat applications, military geists specialise in the operation of turrets, combat remotes, and other defence systems.

GADWATEC TAYYEB
The Tayyeb series of MediKits from GadwaTec were the first to introduce the current pistol grip. Due to cheap licensing terms subsidised by O-12 grants, this Haqqislamite tech has become iconic throughout the Human Sphere.

Serum – p. 356

Treat action – p. 248

MEDIUM COMBAT ARMOUR VARIANT:
WALDHEIM GRENZ DSAD
Unsatisfied with standard Nomad Military Forces kit, the Waldheim family personally paid to equip the Grenzers of the Dragnet Special Actions Department with bespoke medium combat armour (+2  Morale Soak), incorporating cutting-edge *Tunguska* grey-market firewall enhancements (+2  Interference Soak).

MEDIUM COMBAT ARMOUR VARIANT:
SHIYANG INDUSTRIES TIGER
Designed for orbital or airborne insertion, this Yu Jingese medium combat armour incorporates a photoreactive coating, combat jump pack, and impact-absorbing landing systems for +3  Armour Soak against falling damage.

GEIST
MILITARY GEIST

ATTRIBUTES						
AGI	AWA	BRW	COO	INT	PER	WIL
9	9	8	12	6	4	4

SKILLS					
Ballistics	+3	1	Close Combat	+1	1
Observation	+1	–	Stealth	+1	–

TALENTS
- Marksman, Clear Shot, Sharp Senses

COMMON MISSILE LAUNCHERS
• **AKNovy Kanat** (Ariadna)
• **Askari AS Fadi** (Haqqislam, "Redeemer" in Arabic)
• **Jeontu JJM Jiog Bul** (Yu Jing, "Hellfire" in Korean)
• **Switech Cardinale** (PanOceania)
• **Yungang Xíng (Type) 8.7** (Yu Jing)
• **Yungang Xíng (Type) 8.9** (Yu Jing)

COMMON MULTI HMGS
• **Askari AS Laheeb** (Haqqislam)
• **CineticS Lunan** (PanOceania)
• **PraxiTec Schimmer** (Nomads): Licensed from Yungang.
• **Switech Proculco** (ALEPH)
• **Yungang Xíng (Type) 6.3** (Yu Jing)

COMMON MULTI RIFLES
• **CineticS Radjun** (PanOceania)
• **FGA SG-A1 Schärfe / SG-A2 Schärfe II** (Franco-Germanique Armements, PanOceania)
• **IPF-Sagitta** (Italieri de Precisione, PanOceania)
• **Yungang Xíng (Type) 5.4** (Yu Jing)

COMMON MULTI SNIPER RIFLES
• **CineticS Sinag** ("Ray" in Tagalog)
• **FGA SMR-2 Witwenmacher** (Franco-Germanique Armements, PanOceania)
• **Yungang Xíng (Type) 7.6** (Yu Jing)

Missile Launcher: Modern portable missile launchers fire micromissile Heavy rounds, allowing operators to easily carry enough ammunition to maintain sustained fire solo, or to spread between the members of a fire team without significantly altering the weight of their gear. Though Needle rounds see the most use, the variety of modern Heavy ammo types allows missile launchers to switch quickly between roles. (Range L, 2+7  damage, Burst 1, Unwieldy, Munition)

SaboT ammo – p. 379

Nabia Research Centre – p. 228

TOHAA MULTISPECTRALS
The Tohaa can incorporate colonies of optical filtration bacteria into symbiont armour which are equivalent to Multispectral Visor 2.

ModCoat: A favourite for low-profile factional agents, these bespoke smart-material coats incorporate modest built-in armour, and are designed for easy device integration and rapid alteration. Tech tests made to customise the loadout or create new equipment slots in the modcoat are made at −1 difficulty and require only half the normal amount of time. (Civilian Armour)

Modhand: Designed for Nomad undercover officers, modhands are usually disguised as innocuous accessories — clear or colour-shifting nail appliques,

fashionable rings or finger tattoos, a bangle or watch — until triggered for a powerful E/M attack. (Melee, 1+4  damage, 1H, Concealed 2, E/M, Stun, Subtle 1, Vicious 2)

Morat Scimitar: A heavy, curved blade often wielded by Morat warriors. (Melee, 1+5  damage, Unbalanced, Grievous, Non-Hackable, Vicious 2)

MULTI Heavy Machinegun: MULTI HMGs incorporate multiple feeding magazines, allowing the operator to select ammunition best suited to a tactical situation. (Range L, 2+5  damage, Burst 3, Unwieldy, Medium MULTI, MULTI Heavy Mod, Spread 1, Unsubtle)
  DA Mode (Default Secondary): Vicious 2

MULTI Rifle: The MULTI Rifle alchemizes Standard ammo bursts, Special ammo rounds, and modular weaponry into one flexible, deadly, portable package. (Range C/M, 1+5  damage, Burst 2/1, 2H, Expert 1, Medium MULTI, MULTI Light Mod, Vicious 1)
  DA Mode (Default Secondary): Vicious 3

MULTI Sniper Rifle: The MULTI sniper rifle is an evolutionary leap in long-range precision firearms, switching seamlessly between an anti-tank gun capable of piercing thick armour, an anti-personnel weapon that can neutralize even the most resilient targets, or a variety of advanced payloads. As well as Special rounds, MULTI sniper rifles can equip Needle and SaboT Heavy ammo types to their Secondary mode. (Range L, 1+6  damage, Burst 2/1, Unwieldy, Heavy MULTI, Medium MULTI, Unforgiving 2)
  DA Mode (Default Medium Secondary): Vicious 2
  Needle Mode (Default Heavy Secondary): Piercing, Spread 1, Vicious 2

Multispectral Visor X: These visors allow the user to perceive otherwise-invisible wavelengths of light and incorporate an Expert X system of input filters to highlight important details.

Nabia Lhost: Pioneered by the Acontecimento-based Nabia Research Centre these highly-modifiable aquatic Lhosts have proven so useful in aquatic exploration, and so striking outside of it, that the NRC has significantly increased production of late.
  In Lusitanian mythology, Nabia was the goddess of water and rivers, embodying wealth, health, and

protection to the ancient Portuguese. Like their namesake, these Lhosts possess a preternatural grace. Their reinforced bodies can withstand impressive depths, and their oxygen filtration systems, retractable webbing, and discreet gills make them equally at home on land or at sea, albeit at the cost of slightly reduced coordination. In honour of their inspiration, most Nabia resemble ethereally attractive Iberian women, but like all Lhosts, a wide range of options are available upon request.

LHOST
NABIA LHOST

ATTRIBUTES						
AGI	AWA	BRW	COO	INT	PER	WIL
-1	–	+1	-1	–	–	–

SPECIAL ABILITIES
- **Common Special Abilities**: Inured to Aquatic Pressure, Cold, Disease
- **Amphibious**: -3 difficulty to Athletics tests to traverse aquatic terrain (minimum 0)
- +1 Armour
- +1 BTS

Nano Ammunition: Nano rounds silently release weaponised nanobots on impact. Though metabolic effects vary, the results are always the same: crippling pain and severe tissue damage. Nano ammo adds Area (Close), Nanotech, Subtle 2, and Toxic 2 to the weapon. Spending 2 Momentum on a successful attack with Nano ammo triggers a Nanotech Effect, inflicting a special Wound Effect which applies a +1 difficulty penalty on all Agility-, Brawn-, or Coordination-based actions.

Nanopulser : Nanopulsers are short-range nanobot sprayers that fire in an indiscriminate arc. Often integrated into body armour or implanted, they are widely restricted or illegal. Tohaa versions use viruses that degrade into forensically innocuous organic materials after use. Nanopulsers do not add bonus damage from high attributes. (Range C, 1+5 Ⓝ damage, 1H, Biotech, Subtle 3, Torrent, Vicious 2)

Nav Suite (Region): Indispensable in unfamiliar territory, a nav suite provides interactive maps, weather feeds, landmark highlighting, plant identification, and other useful augmented reality overlays, as well as real-time positional data from continually updated mapping dataspheres. Nav suites grant +1d20 on Survival tests made in the region they cover.

augmented reality – p. 142

Needle Ammunition: Needle rounds are anti-armour micromissiles designed to penetrate and destroy heavily armoured targets without collateral damage. Needle rounds add Piercing 2, Spread 1, and Vicious 2.

Negotiator's Suite: A model of sane neutrality, negotiator's kits contain heavily encrypted dataspheres for secure conversations, and integrated software suites for simultaneous translation and data exchange between anyone granted access.

Each kit contains admin permissions for a private 24-hour Commercial HighSec datasphere, with software that grants +1d20 to all negotiation Persuade tests and to Hacking tests to safely encrypt and protect data under discussion against outsiders. Additional days are available at bulk rates if talks drag on.

Neural Hacking Socket: This augmentation allows a hacker to plug their hacking device directly into their nervous system with a Standard Action. This grants the device the Neural quality (granting 1 bonus Momentum, but also making them susceptible to Brain Blasts and similar Breach Effects), but inflicts a +1 complication range. The advantage of the hacking socket, as opposed to a hardwired rig, is that it can be detached as a Standard Action (thus removing the Neural quality).

Neural Shunts: This implant allows the recipient to ignore all difficulty penalties imposed by Wound effects for 5+5 Ⓝ minutes, but at the end of that period they suffer a Wound from the strain.

Nimbus Ammunition: Nimbus rounds release clouds of milspec nanotech smoke to divert projectiles and block selected spectra and signals. Nimbus ammo adds Reflective 2 and Nonlethal to the weapon, and affected zones provide +2 Ⓝ Cover Soak.

Nimbus+ Ammunition: For elite units, Nimbus Plus rounds add proprietary algorithmic enhancement, replicating the effects of standard Nimbus rounds but adding Reflective 3 and 3 Ⓝ Cover Soak instead.

Normal Ammunition: Normal rounds are standard, chemically accelerated, dense metal bullets, and confer no special qualities or effects.

Normal Arrows: Simple arrows designed for use with tactical bows. They add Piercing 1 to the weapon.

Normal Shells: Normal Shells are high-calibre, self-contained cartridges filled with aerodynamic, pointed metal projectiles with sharp fins known as flechettes. The flechettes' design makes them rotate during flight to stabilise their trajectory and, once inside the body, maximise internal damage and hydrostatic shock. Each shell has a proximity sensor that — once fed range data and fired — detonates at a set distance from the target, saturating the area with flechettes. Normal Shells add Area (Close) and Spread 1 to the shotgun.

Nitrocaine: The drug nitrocaine is an illegal Silk derivative that bonds with the user's synapses, enabling long-term highs that can be controlled using custom hacks of the user's Cube. The hacks require

a Tech (D1) test to install. The synaptic-bonding makes the drug highly addictive. (Injected, Instant 3, Hour, 1+2 Ⓝ physical and mental damage)
Addiction 2 (1 dose), Compulsion 2
Withdrawal 1, 1+2 Ⓝ mental, Harm Effect (user randomly begins experiencing flashbacks to memories stored in their Cube and suffers +1 complication range; the more Harm Effects suffered, the more vivid and integrated with reality the flashbacks become; if a fourth Harm Effect is suffered from nitrocaine withdrawal, the character will slip into a fugue state)

Nu-El Armour: Worn by selected Tohaa Trident combat troops, this light Voorne, or living armour, protects and augments the wearer's body with its own, granting +1 to all attributes. (Symbiont Armour)

Nullifier: Once deployed and activated with a Challenging (D2) Tech test as a Standard Action, these Tohaa omni-jammers prevent the use of Comms Equipment, sepsitors, flash pulses, and quantronic attacks into, out of, or through their zone until deactivated or destroyed. All items within the area without the Non-Hackable quality effectively gain the Non-Hackable (−1D) quality. Once activated, nullifiers cannot be moved without ending their effect.

Oneiros Ammunition: Oneiros ammunition is designed to incapacitate multiple targets simultaneously, saturating an area with a cocktail of potent synthetic neuro-transmitters to render them unconscious. Oneiros ammo adds Area (Close), Biotech, Immobilising, Nonlethal, and Stun to the weapon.

Optical Disruption Device: ODD devices generate a photon-bending field around the wearer, distorting their outline and apparent position. Developed in parallel with thermo-optical camouflage, the device is the subject of bitter litigation between PanOceania's Sparkdyne Research and the Nomad Nation's Praxis' Absynth research module.
Ranged attacks against characters equipped with ODD are at +1 difficulty. If the user takes physical damage from a weapon with the Incendiary quality, the ODD automatically suffers a Fault (and is disabled until repaired).

Orlando Lhost: Named for Roland, chief paladin of Charlemagne and legendary symbol of heroic independence, Orlando-class Lhosts are unquestionably the most potent combat chassis available to civilians, by legal — or any other — means. Between the fast-twitch muscle fibres, neomaterial-reinforced skeletons and an integrated HUD that works with a user's geist to provide tactical data in real-time, these sleek Lhosts are impeccably tailored to combat situations, and inhabiting one is, in many ways, the ultimate rush.

Brain Blast — p. 120

datasphere — p. 141

Tohaa Trident, p. 325:
The military force of the Tohaa Trinomial.

SAARVA AE RUUGO

Several of this common model of Tohaa nullifier were captured by Black Hand agents during the Alliance Summit on the EveningStar (where the Tohaa ambassadors were using them to block eavesdropping devices). Attempts by Praxis laboratories to reverse engineer them have repeatedly failed.

Sepsitor — p. 379

flash pulse — p. 368

thermo-optical camouflage — p. 383

Silk — p. 10

Cube — p. 366

That last detail has proven to be a bit of a problem. Increased adrenaline production – combined with the raw power at users' disposal – has led to an observable reduction in self-control, restraint, and overall personal discipline, rendering the models less-than-ideal for official military applications.

LHOST
ORLANDO LHOST

ATTRIBUTES

AGI	AWA	BRW	COO	INT	PER	WIL
–	–	+1	+1	–	–	-1

SPECIAL ABILITIES
- Inured to Disease
- Ballistics Expert System 1
- Close Combat Expert System 1

Pain Filters: This augmentation modifies pain receptors throughout the recipient's body, allowing them to either ignore one condition imposed by a Wound Effect or reduce the penalty inflicted by the Cripple Wound Effect by one step.

Painkillers: Strong painkillers are carefully regulated due to their addictive potential. (Ingested, Instant 1, Hour, 1  physical)
Special Effect: The user recovers 1+3 Vigour
Addiction 1 (3 doses), Compulsion 1
Withdrawal 1, 1+2 physical

Panzerfaust: Panzerfausts are the anti-tank weapon of choice for infantry; thanks to its lightweight collapsible design, soldiers can carry one without sacrificing important gear. A Panzerfaust can hold two Reloads. Once the weapon is empty, most soldiers simply discard the weapon - if two Needle rounds can't do the job it's probably time to run. Disassembling the weapon to reload it requires a Challenging (D2) Tech test as a Standard Action. (Range L, 2+5 damage, Burst 1, 2H, Munition, Piercing 2, Spread 1, Unsubtle, Vicious 2)

Personal Protective Equipment: Available for purchase separately for any location or as a full set, PPE offers protection against industrial and construction accidents and hazards. (Civilian Armour)

Pheromone Dispenser: A pheromone dispenser allows a character to quickly pacify or direct an animal. They count as a kit for Animal Handling tests, granting 2 bonus Momentum on such tests. Each dose lasts for ten minutes at most, but environmental conditions such as strong winds or the appearance of a natural enemy, prey, or rival can force another test. On a complication, the GM can declare that the dispenser has run out of pheromone doses and cannot be used until refilled.

Phobetor Ammunition: The forbidden Phobetor variant of Oneiros ammo mixes in psychoactives and infrasound projectors to induce vivid hallucinations, adding Terrifying 3 as well as the usual qualities of Area (Close), Biotech, Immobilising, Nonlethal, and Stun to the weapon. The conditions inflicted by Phobetor ammunition are treated collectively as a single condition for the purposes of removing them (with an Absterge action, for example).

Pistol: Pistols are standard-issue sidearms capable of burst fire, perfect for use in close combat and at point-blank range. (Range R/C, 1+4 damage, Burst 1, 1H, Vicious 1)

character conditions – p. 103

Cripple – p. 113

Reloads – p. 356

VoodooTech – p. 307

BTS, p. 341: Use as persistent soak vs. Biotech, Nanotech, Radiation attacks. Add as bonus to Security Soak. Reduce difficulty of Resistance tests vs. diseases, poisons.

Plasma Ammunition: A VoodooTech secret, plasma blasts somehow wrap ionized gas in temporary electromagnetic fields that collapse on impact, violently releasing superheated plasma. Plasma ammo adds Knockdown, Unforgiving 3, and Unsubtle to the weapon, and uses the lower of Armour Soak or BTS.

COMMON PISTOLS
- **AKNovy Kremen** (Ariadna)
- **Armadyne Defender Stun Pistol** (Generic)
- **Askari AS Boulad** (Haqqislam)
- **Askari AS Toksin Breaker Pistol** (Haqqislam)
- **FGA PD-7 Detour** (Franco-Germanique Armements, PanOceania): Standard issue sidearm for S.S.S. Advertised as "ALEPH's Choice".
- **FGA PS-6 Wespe** (PanOceania)
- **TauruSW Ferro** (PanOceania)
- **Yungang Xing (Type) 2.3** Pistol (Yu Jing)
- **Cuurval Tuuga-4 (Tuuga-Ha-El)** (Tohaa Pistol)

Plasma Carbine: The plasma carbine is a short-barrelled plasma rifle variant with stronger recoil and slower reload time. A plasma carbine's Area quality can be turned on and off as a Free Action via quantronic command or a physical switch near the trigger. It fires Plasma ammunition. (Range R/C, 1+5 🅽 damage, Burst 2, Unbalanced, Area (Close), Knockdown, Unforgiving 3, Vicious 1, Unsubtle, uses the lower of Armour Soak or BTS)

Plasma Rifle: The secrets of their manufacture understood only by the EI, plasma rifles are the most advanced technology on Paradiso. Their Area quality can be turned on and off as a Free Action via quantronic command or a physical switch near the trigger. It fires Plasma ammunition. (Range R/C, 1+6 🅽 damage, Burst 3, Unbalanced, Area (Close), Knockdown, Unforgiving 3, Unsubtle, Vicious 1)

Plasma Sniper Rifle: The plasma family's most fearsome member, the plasma sniper rifle blends long-range accuracy with the most powerful plasma weapon in use by the Combined Army – a clear if unwanted example of the superiority of VoodooTech arms. A plasma sniper rifle's Area quality can be turned on and off as a Free Action via quantronic command or a physical switch near the trigger. It fires Plasma ammunition. (Range L, 1+7 🅽 damage, Burst 2, Unwieldy, Knockdown, Unforgiving 5, Unsubtle)

Plasteel Pipe: A crude length of carbon-reinforced plastic pipe is a decent weapon in a pinch. (Melee, 1+4 🅽 damage, Unbalanced, Improvised 1, Stun)

Powered Combat Armour: Tactical, servo-powered, armoured exoskeletons with extensive internal quantronics, automatic healing systems, and self-repairing defence mechanisms, powered combat armours are the peak of personal defence. Every national military, and many mercenary outfits, use powered armour to some extent, particularly PanOceania and Yu Jing.

Powered armour cannot be combined with non-Internal forms of armour, and must be worn as a full set to be effective, though the helmet and faceguards can be temporarily retracted for conversation and comfort. (Powered Armour)

Powered Combat Armour (Ariadnan): Ariadnan military research lags behind the other factions despite extensive attempts at reverse-engineering, and the results are comparatively bulkier and clumsier, though they offer similar protection.

COMMON RIFLES
- **Askari AS Sayad**: Regulation rifle of the Sword of Allah.
- **AKNovy Strela**: Simple, hard, and it keeps coming no matter what you throw at it. Just like the people of Dawn.

Powered Multitool: Providing an array of tools in an easily managed frame, the powered multitool is a handheld repair device. It comes with one unit of Parts built in and counts as a kit, granting 1 bonus Momentum to Tech tests made to repair or modify items.

Psychoanalysis Suite: Sold only to licensed professionals, this kit comes with a compact neurological scanner, suite of diagnostic tools, and extensively cross-referenced encyclopaedia of mental conditions and methods for identifying and treating them. It contains three doses of Psychotropic precursors and a micro-dispensary to flash-fabricate a range of therapeutic treatments.

Puraza: An auto-immune supplement aerosolised and weaponised by Atek anti-augmentation fanatics, this poison is easily handled by filtration systems. It can only be used against targets without BTS, who have augmentations, and after a successful face-to-face Close Combat test. (Spray/Inhaled, Instant 2, 1+2 🅽 physical damage)
Wound Effect: The target begins to suffer from Degenerative Augmentation Syndrome.

Recorder: Recorders are small, innocuous sensors capable of broadcast-quality audio, video, and even holography. Recorders come with built-in microphones, cameras and motion detectors, add 2 bonus Momentum on Stealth tests to conceal them, and have an Observation skill target number of 10, automatically recording if they detect movement or sound nearby.

Regeneration Augmentation: Recipients of this full-body augmentation can heal 1 🅽 of physical damage as a Minor Action. If an Effect is rolled, they heal one Wound. The regenerative properties of their tissue, however, cause their bodies to reject all other augmentations (including, notably, Cubes).

Remote Presence Gear: This cybernetic implant provides a neural VR interface for operating vehicles via networked connections without penalty. When operating remotes using VR mode, the user eliminates the normal penalties to difficulty and complication range when using remote control. The gear possesses the Comms and Neural qualities, however, making its user susceptible to Brain Blasts and similar Infowar attacks.

Repair Kit: Top-quality toolkits for both major repairs and maintenance, repair kits come with three units of Parts built in and grant 1 bonus Momentum for any Tech test.

Respirator X: Filter-masks that exclude dangerous gases and dust, respirators are rated 1–3 and grant a –X difficulty to Resistance tests against airborne hazards. They can be donned as a Standard Action, or as a Reaction with an Average (D1) Survival test.

Rifle: Rifles are lightweight, accurate, and abundant to the point of anonymity. They fire Standard ammunition. (Range M, 1+5 🇳 damage, Burst 2, 2H, MULTI Light Mod, Vicious 1)

SaboT Ammunition: SaboT rounds use a lightweight outer shell to accelerate a dart of pure Teseum to speeds sufficient to pierce and crack even the densest armour, adding Anti-Materiel 3 and Piercing 5 to the weapon.

Sakiel Armour: Worn by experienced, hardened soldiers who earn them through loss and sacrifice, these living armours safeguard those who have nothing left to lose but their lives, bolstering them to the end and granting −1 difficulty to Resistance and Discipline tests. (Symbiont Armour)

SecurCuffs: Bracelets linked by a cable, SecurCuff restraints are commonly used by law enforcement and security forces. Without a quantronic key, they take a Thievery (D2) test to unlock or Athletics (D4) test to escape. SecurCuffs include a quantronic connection (and the Comms quality), reporting their location to authenticated users.

Security Geist: Tailored to nest in quantronic networks, Security geists specialise in anti-hacker measures, aggressively purging unwelcome guests from their residence.

GEIST
GUARDIAN GEIST

			ATTRIBUTES			
AGI	AWA	BRW	COO	INT	PER	WIL
4	9	4	4	9	4	4

SKILLS						
Hacking	+3	3	Observation	+2	2	Stealth	+2	1

TALENTS
• Scout, Hacker, Tricks of the Trade, Paranoid, Quantronic Flak

Sensor Suite (Type): Sensors allow the detection and triangulation of nearby phenomena. Installing a sensor suite usually takes at least one minute, but anyone with quantronic access benefits from a −1 difficulty and 1 bonus Momentum on appropriate

Observation tests within Close range of the suite. Sensors are always of a particular type, though high-end sensors can combine multiple or overlapping types. Example types include:
• Motion detectors
• Infrared cameras
• Radiation detectors
• Tohaa pheromone detectors
• E/M scanners

Tohaa pheromones – p. 321

Sepsitor: ALEPH-designated with a name derived from the Classical Greek *septos* – corruption – sepsitors use a short-range discharge of memetic viral vectors to directly connect a target's Cube with the grotesque majesty of the Evolved Intelligence. The weapon seizes control of the target's cognitive functions, and those who succumb renounce former loyalties, immediately setting about the EI's grim ends. Sepsitors do not use conventional ammo, but contain only two Reloads. Once exhausted, the weapon takes several hours to recharge.

Teseum – p. 8

Reloads – p. 356

Only characters with a Cube can be affected by a sepsitor. The weapon inflicts mental damage, with bonus damage based on the wielder's Willpower. The target's BTS acts as a bonus to Morale Soak against sepsitor attacks. As a special rule, damage dealt from its Toxic special Harm Effect has the Terrifying 3 quality. If a sepsitor or its Toxic special Harm Effect deals five Metanoia Effects, the character's personality is overwritten by the EI (and most likely becomes an NPC under the GM's control). (Range C, 1+3 🇳 mental damage, Burst 1, 1H, Munitions, Terrifying 3, Torrent, Toxic 3)

Templar heresies – p. 178

SHIELD-1 Exorcism: This software counteracts possession of devices or vehicles, removing external controllers, invasive geists, or other pseudo-AI. Once a secret PanOceanian technique for purging Templar heresies, its widespread use is a sore point for the Military Orders, who consider its proper usage a sacrament. The program grants a special Reaction which can be used whenever a Breach Effect is used to issue a command to the user's system. If the user succeeds at a face-to-face Hacking test against the hacker attempting to issue the command, the command is ignored and the Breach Effect is immediately removed (although the Breach itself remains).

SHIELD-1 U-Turn: When a weapon with the Guided quality is used to attack a target within Long range of the user, U-Turn allows them to use a special Reaction to inflict a +1 difficulty to the attack test.

SHIELD-2 Breakwater: When the user of Breakwater makes a Defence or Guard Reaction using their Hacking skill, they inflict a +2 difficulty to the opponent's attack test.

Military Orders – p. 177

Defence / Guard Reaction – p. 113

> ### EXPLOSIVE CUFFS
> Unscrupulous agencies will add high voltage shocks or even explosives to SecurCuffs, which can be triggered either remotely or in response to escape attempts. Add the cost of the appropriate ammunition type to the cuffs. On a complication, the GM can trigger the security feature.

Silk – p. 10

Defence / Guard Reaction – p. 113

multispectral visors – p. 374

illumination, p. 360: Targets in illuminated zone can be targeted without darkness penalties.

SHIELD-3 Counterstrike: This incredibly powerful upgrade of the Breakwater program reflects quantronic attacks. When the user of Counterstrike makes a Defence or Guard Reaction using their Hacking skill, they inflict a +1 difficulty to the opponent's attack test. In addition, if the user succeeds on the face-to-face test they reflect the attack back on the character that made it (who suffers the damage and other effects of the attack).

SHIELD-3 Zero Pain: This program hardens the user's quantronic defences. When they make a Defence or Guard Reaction using their Hacking skill, they gain 2 bonus Momentum.

Shock Ammunition: Shock ammunition is designed to create powerful hydrostatic shock in the target, maximising internal damage. Shock ammo adds Biotech and Grievous to the weapon.

Signal Flare: Modern Signal Flares are about the size of a pencil, with long-burning coloured chemicals that burn brightly for up to an hour until exhausted, illuminating their zone and releasing a trail of coloured smoke.

Siren Lhost: Early Lhosts strove to appear as normal as possible; it was assumed that society would shun anyone who looked "too perfect". However, the popularity of ALEPH's Functionaries – in particular, the otherworldly beauty of Spokeswoman Angela – quickly disproved that notion, leading to a new wave of artistically sculpted Lhosts. These "siren-class" models make no attempt to pass as anything short of flawless, and many incorporate a sophisticated tailored pheromone package; granting their users an advantage from the negotiating table to the nightclub and everywhere in-between.

LHOST

SIREN LHOST

ATTRIBUTES

AGI	AWA	BRW	COO	INT	PER	WIL
+1	–	–	–	–	+1	–

SPECIAL ABILITIES
- Inured to Disease
- Persuasion Expert System 1
- +1 Morale

COMMON SNIPER RIFLES
- **AKNovy Zyefir** (Ariadna AP or T2 Sniper Rifle)
- **AKNovy Zmeyá** (Ariadna)
- **Iriista Claado-50 (Claado Ku-El)** (Tohaa)

Sixth Sense: This Silk-based rewiring of the nervous system reduces the Heat cost of Acrobatics defence tests by one, grants 2 bonus Momentum on all Acrobatics defence tests, and also grants +2d20 on surprise tests. The recipient also gains the trait Twitchy.

Smoke Ammunition: Smoke rounds provide short-term tactical cover, concealing movement and obfuscating sight lines for a crucial few moments. In combination with multispectral visors, which see through them easily, Smoke rounds are particularly useful against low-tech forces. Smoke ammo adds Smoke 2 to the weapon.

Smoke Grenade: While modern combat optics easily bypass ordinary smoke, smoke grenades provide an invaluable tactical advantage against unprepared opponents. (Explosive Grenade, 1H, Disposable, Indiscriminate (Close), Nonlethal, Speculative Fire, Smoke 2, Thrown)

Sniper Rifle: Sniper Rifles are precision weapons with such long-range accuracy that a well-placed marksman can influence the entire battlefield. They fire Standard ammunition. (Range L, 1+6  damage, Burst 2, Unwieldy, Unforgiving 2)

Spear: A tool of warfare for thousands of years, spears are simple to make and wield, allowing even poorly trained combatants to fend off their enemies. (Melee, 1+4 damage, 2H, Extended Reach, Vicious 1)

Spiked Knuckles: Spiked, bladed, studded with micro-explosive charges – whatever you can dream up, some Submondo heavies probably used it to extract the necessaries from an unwilling "customer" somewhere in the Sphere, and somebody else made rent selling it to them. (Melee, 1+4 damage, 1H, Concealed 1, Piercing 1, Vicious 1)

Spitfire: The Spitfire or "Fire Spitter" is a mid-range machine gun designed for close quarters and urban combat, altered many times over the past century.

Spitfires have shorter barrels and lighter ammunition than their big sister, the HMG and are ideal for urban assault and support. Regardless of incarnation, the Spitfire's high fire rate, sturdy build, ease of use, and notable accuracy are unmistakable. (Range M, 1+5  damage, Burst 3, 2H, Spread 2, Unsubtle)

Sports Padding: Available for purchase separately for any location or as a full body set, sports padding protects against bodily impact and related sports injuries. (Civilian Armour)

Spotbot: Every sniper needs a spotter, but you can't always count on someone else to watch your back. Luckily, there's a remote for that. Popularised by lightweight, portable models like the Stellatech Spotbot Lapinette-3, Spotbots have also caught on as inexpensive sensor remotes, providing surveillance and recording in a compact and comparably affordable package.

TROOPER

SPOTBOT

ATTRIBUTES

AGI	AWA	BRW	COO	INT	PER	WIL
8	12	6	6	12	6	6

FIELDS OF EXPERTISE

Combat	–	–	Movement	+1	–	Social	–	–
Fortitude	–	–	Senses	+2	2	Technical	+1	–

DEFENCES

Firewall	6	Resolve	3	Structure	3
Security	2	Morale	–	Armour	1

ATTACKS
- **Flash Pulse**: Range M, 1+8  damage, Burst 1, 2H, Blinding, removes Marked

GEAR: Optical Disruption Device, Recorder

SPECIAL ABILITIES
- **Common Special Abilities**: Inured to Disease, Poison, and Vacuum
- **Semi-Autonomous Spotter**: A Spotbot typically has one job; spotting. Turns out, they're good at it. When operating autonomously, it takes no actions, sticking close to its user, and adding 1 Momentum to successful Observation, attack tests, and Defence reactions the user makes.

Stealth Repeater: A common stealth repeater comes in the form of a tiny, black disc half an inch across and wafer-thin. They can be activated as a Minor Action with a Tech (D0) test and have the Comms, Concealed 2, and Repeater qualities. (Firewall 10, Security 1)

COMMON SPITFIRES
- **Askari AS Fateh**: Haqqislam model which includes improved cooling systems for hot, dry conditions.
- **CineticS Bagyo / Bagyo-2**: Standard issue for the PMC. Like many CineticS models, these have additional features for aquatic operations.
- **Yungang Xíng (Type) 6.7**: Yu Jing model focused on compact ergonomics.

Stims: A potent emergency stimulant, auto-injected Stims force the body awake. (Ingested, Instant 1, Day)

Special Effect: Once administered, the user wakes if unconscious, and stays awake for the next eight hours; they cannot become unconscious again during that period, and do not have to make Resistance tests against sleep deprivation. Once those eight hours are up, they quickly descend into a deep sleep for the next twelve hours.

Addiction 1 (2 doses), Compulsion 1

Withdrawal 2, 2+2  damage, Harm Effect (user cannot sleep without medical or pharmaceutical assistance)

Stun Ammunition: Stun ammunition is designed to incapacitate the target with a cocktail of synthetic neuro-transmitters. Stun ammo adds Biotech, Nonlethal, and Stun to the weapon.

Stun Baton: A sturdy short staff with built-in shock capacitors, commonly used by security or law enforcement where a blade's lethality would be inconvenient. (Melee, 1+4  damage, 1H, Knockdown, Subtle 1, Stun)

Subdermal Grafts: Agonising to install with a high chance of rejection, tactical dermal grafting involves placing thin weaves of nano-infused titanium alloy beneath the subject's skin, allowing them to better resist high-speed impacts, cuts, and burns. Grafts can be purchased for individual body locations (subtracting 1  from the cost per hit location not covered). They add a +2 complication range to Personality-based tests if added to the head. (Internal Armour)

Super-Jump: Based on Antipodean gene-grafts or cybernetic implants, Super-Jump augmentations allow their user to vault over obstacles up to their height without penalty. They also enjoy −1 difficulty on skill tests to move through difficult terrain.

HMG – p. 371

sleep deprivation – p. 104

SPORTS PADDING VARIANT:

ADIDOCK PROSPORT EXCELSIOR GEAR

A favourite of amateur zero-g athletes and aspiring extreme-sports competitors, Adidock PPE offers sports protection a cut above ordinary gear, granting 1 bonus Momentum on Agility-related tests, and features built-in, selectively adhesive pads equivalent to climbing plus equipment. It is DRM-locked and notoriously finicky, requiring regular adjustments at an Adidock ProService Centre (adding Maintenance 3 to its cost).

Surge: Adrenaline-based stimulant drugs, Surge can be found under dozens of brand names, each promising bigger boosts, longer durations, or milder after-effects. (Ingested, Instant, Hour)

remotes – p. 354

Special Effect: The user gains +1d20 on all tests based on Agility- and Brawn-based tests for 1d6 rounds, but then suffers +1 difficulty on all Awareness- and Coordination-based tests for the next hour.

Addiction 1 (3 doses), Compulsion 1

Withdrawal 2, 1+4 damage, Harm Effect (+1 difficulty on all Awareness- and Coordination-based tests)

Surgical Bay: Facilities for the Medicine skill, surgical bays incorporate the most advanced medical technology available, containing ten loads of Serum, ten loads of Silk, and three integrated Surgical Waldos 3.

Serum – p. 356

Silk – p. 356

Surgical Waldo X: Surgical waldos are articulated mechanical arms often built into surgical bays and first-response vehicles, providing a physician with an extra hand during complex surgery in place of a nurse.

A surgical waldo counts as a kit, granting 1 bonus Momentum to Medicine tests. One or more waldos can also assist on Medicine tests with a target number of 10+X. Each additional waldo used on an operation halves the amount of time it takes to

complete, but adds +1 complication range.

Alternatively, surgical waldos can be used as a remote, allowing their user to perform Medicine tests without being physically present. (The normal penalties for operating a remote apply.)

Survival Kit (Environment): Tailored for a particular environment, each survival kit contains tools and sufficient supplies for a week's survival in that environment. They typically contain blankets, a tarpaulin, a collapsible tent, tools to start a fire and/or a small heater, water purification tablets, a survival knife, a collapsible shovel, and a length of rope, although they do not include food, air, or water. The kit can be converted into a functional shelter with a Survival (D1) test.

Survival Pod: Designed for airless worlds, outer space, and other lethal environments, this kit contains a self-inflating protective shelter, built-in emergency beacon, hazard lights, 3 BTS of radiation shielding, and four loads of crucial Supplies including air and water, enough to keep four people alive – albeit uncomfortably – for 24 hours, or one for 96 hours.

Survival Rations: Common fare for soldiers in the field, expeditionaries, and frontier colonists, survival rations are compact, shelf-stable, and not

particularly palatable food (but it's better than starving). Each unit of survival rations contains enough preserved, precooked food for one person to eat for a week, as well as sterilisation tablets and flavoured nutrient powders to add to locally sourced water.

Sword: Swords still hold a special place in military tradition as symbols of honour, discipline, and justice, particularly in Ariadna. (Melee, 1+5 🅝 damage, Unbalanced, Parry 2, Vicious 1)

SWORD-1 Brain Blast: On a successful attack against an opponent using equipment with the Neural quality, the user of Brain Blast can spend 2 Momentum to deal physical damage instead of quantronic damage. The attack has the Piercing 1 and Vicious 1 qualities.

SWORD-1 Slasher: Unlike programs that seek to bypass and penetrate a target's Firewall, Slasher programs target the Firewall itself. They cannot inflict Breaches and have no effect if the target has no Firewall remaining, but are incredibly useful for demolishing quantronic defences.

SWORD-2 Redrum: This vicious attack program eviscerates enemy hackers. Its attacks possess the Grievous, Piercing 2, and Unforgiving 2 qualities.

SWORD- 2 Skullbuster: A heavyweight program first developed by *Tunguska* Arachne seers, a Skullbuster program can attack multiple targets at once and is also designed to disrupt the nanotech substrates of BTS systems. It possesses the Area (Close) and Breaker qualities.

SWORD-2 Trinity: Developed by reverse engineering some of the most devastating attacks from EI hackers, Trinity programs are quantronic powerhouses. They possess the Area (Close) and Vicious 3 qualities, and have the Stun quality against targets using Neural equipment.

SymbioMate: SymbioMates are Tohaa bioconstructs designed for emergency fire suppression. Once bonded to symbiont armour, they follow closely to the best of their abilities, relying on the armour for nourishment until it is time to detonate.
  When the bonded armour is struck by an Incendiary weapon, the SymbioMate sacrifices itself in a spray of foamy fluids and ropy tissue, preventing all damage or other effects from Incendiary weapons until the end of the user's next turn.
  SymbioMates are designed to stay out of immediate danger, and between their small size and evasive instincts, ranged or melee attacks against them are at +2 difficulty. They have Armour Soak 1, 4 Vigour, and die after suffering a single Wound, or if the Symbiont Armour they are bonded with is destroyed. Only one SymbioMate can be bonded with a given armour at a time.

T2 Ammunition 🔁: T2 rounds are jacketed hollow-point projectiles covered in a double-reinforced coating of Teseum, which splinters into deadly microscopic fragments on impact. Known as "the most expensive ammo in the Sphere", this ammunition is usually only accessible to those with near-unlimited access to Teseum, such as the Caledonian military. T2 ammo adds Anti-Materiel 2, Piercing 2, and Vicious 2 to the weapon.

T2 Shells 🔁: Another Ariadnan extravagance, T2 Shells are comprised of an explosive core beneath a double-layered coating of fragmentable Teseum, and a simple proximity sensor to trigger the explosive at an appropriate distance, shredding the target — and anything or anyone nearby — with microscopic Teseum fragments. T2 Shells add Anti-Materiel 2, Area (Close) Piercing 3, and Vicious 2 to the shotgun.

Tactical Bow: A modern twist on an ancient weapon, the tactical bow is short-ranged compared to modern firearms, but its silent operation keeps it relevant in contemporary warfare. A tactical bow cannot be used in one hand under any circumstances, but a character using one can add the higher of their melee or ranged damage bonuses to the weapon's damage. Ammo-equivalent arrowheads are available from specialty craftsman at similar prices. They fire Arrows. (Range C, 1+3 🅝 damage, Burst 1, 2H, Subtle 2, Vicious 2)

Tetrodotoxin: A natural neurotoxin produced by symbiotic bacteria in pufferfish and blue-ringed octopodes, tetrodotoxin inhibits the nervous system and muscular control, inducing respiratory failure within hours. Eating carefully prepared dishes made from sea life containing it is a common gustatory hazing ritual among Yu Jing elites. (Ingestion/Inhalation/Injected, Complex 1 (6 Momentum), Hour, 3+3 🅝 physical damage)
  Wound Effect: If any effects are rolled, the target becomes Dazed. If they are already Dazed, they go into respiratory failure and suffer the effects of suffocation (with the difficulty of the Resistance test equal to the number of tetrodotoxin-related Wound Effects suffered).

Teseum Chopper: Teseum short blades remain popular, despite their staggering cost anywhere besides Dawn. (Melee, 1+5 🅝 damage, Unbalanced, Piercing 4, Vicious 2)

Thermo-Optical Camouflage: This state-of-the-art technology distorts light around the wearer, rendering them virtually invisible to the naked eye, thermographic sensors, and even radar. While active, no creature can see the wearer unaided, even if

Teseum – p. 8

Brain Blast – p. 120

damage bonuses – p. 101

Suffocation, p. 110: Resistance (D1) test each round or suffer one Wound.

Dazed, p. 104: +1 difficulty on skill tests.

symbiont armour – p. 342

stealth – p. 104

revealed state – p. 104

geist – p. 350

illumination, p. 360:
Targets in illuminated zone
can be targeted without
darkness penalties.

NOTES: TinBots are designed
to assist in teamwork tests;
should they be able to assist
their users, they will attempt to
spend their turns doing so.

aware of them. A character wearing thermo-optical camouflage gains 2 bonus Momentum on Stealth tests and cannot enter the revealed state unless they are within Reach.

Thermo-optical camouflage can be compromised by fire. If its wearer suffers physical damage from an Incendiary attack, the thermo-optical camouflage automatically suffers a Fault (and is disabled until it can be repaired).

TinBot: Affordable, portable, and uniformly adorable, the winsome TinBot is a favourite among hackers and soldiers, as well as a popular shell for civilian geists. Not terribly useful by themselves, TinBots earn their keep by relaying useful information to their users, and (mostly) not getting underfoot. Moto.tronica produces the original TinBot™, but the term has become synonymous with semi-autonomous personal assistance remotes, and many corporations produce their own variants.

TROOPER
TINBOT

ATTRIBUTES						
AGI	AWA	BRW	COO	INT	PER	WIL
10	10	5	9	10	6	6

FIELDS OF EXPERTISE							
Combat	+1	–	Movement	+1	1	Social	–	–
Fortitude	–	–	Senses	+1	1	Technical	+1	–

DEFENCES						
Firewall	5	Resolve	3	Structure	3
Security	–	Morale	4	Armour	–

ATTACKS
- **Stun Attachment**: Melee, 1+4 🔘 damage, 1H, Knockdown, Subtle 1, Stun

GEAR: Deflector-1

SPECIAL ABILITIES
- **Common Special Abilities**: Inured to Disease, Poison, and Vacuum
- **Little Buddy**: When a TinBot is controlled by a geist or its native LAI, it gains a Morale Soak of 4.
- **Tin It To Win It**: A Tinbot always has your back. When assisted by a Tinbot, the leader of a test may reroll one d20, but must accept the new result.

Titan Lhost: Rugged, massive, and designed to withstand the rigours of deep space work, these expensive models saw an uptick in popularity following the Helicon Miners' Revolt. Still prohibitively expensive, they nevertheless allow skilled individuals to operate in zero-g situations with significantly less risk. And as it turns out, a heavy construction Lhost can also be particularly handy in a fight.

More machine than human, a Titan's bulk impairs fine motor control, and even the smallest models cut an ominous silhouette, impeding social interactions.

Helicon Miners' Revolt – p. 254

Hindered, p. 104: –1 zone when
making movement actions. +1
difficulty on terrain tests.

Stuck, p. 104: Cannot move
away from object/location
stuck to.

LHOST
TITAN LHOST

ATTRIBUTES						
AGI	AWA	BRW	COO	INT	PER	WIL
–1	–	+2	–1	–	–1	–

SPECIAL ABILITIES
- Inured to Disease, Vacuum
- +2 Armour
- +2 BTS

Tonfa Bangles: Usually purchased, worn, and used in pairs, these elite defensive weapons collapse into an innocuous disguise as thick ornamented bracelets until needed. When wielded as a pair, Tonfa Bangles combine their Parry qualities. (Melee, 1+3 🔘 damage, 1H, Concealed 2, Parry 1)

Torch: Torches, also known as flashlights, are useful for navigating unlit habitats, searching dark alleys for clues, or identifying assailants. A torch illuminates one zone within Medium range and line-of-sight.

UPGRADE Cyberalert Systems: The user of a Cyberalert Systems program can actively scan or search a zone in order to spot a stealthy character as a Minor Action (instead of the normal Standard Action). In addition, when opponents make a stealth state test, the user can perform a Reaction in order to make it a face-to-face test without paying Heat.

UPGRADE Cybermask: This program proactively subverts enemy identification protocols, sensors, and visualisation systems, creating a multi-layered quantronic illusion of falsified data and feeds, along with a holographic projection that matches the user's movements. Activating the Cybermask is a Standard Action requiring a Hacking (D1) test. Once activated, anyone who looks at the user, or any system that checks the character's comlog for identity – including the friend-or-foe systems used by military and security forces, access gateways, and IC – sees the false holographic image and data halo instead. A more thorough check (by another character, or by an AI system) requires a face-to-face Analysis (D1) or Observation (D3) test, though the difficulty can increase depending on the false imprint's quality. Success exposes the imprint as a fake.

UPGRADE Stop!: This attack is a particularly nasty adaptation of CLAW programs like Basilisk and Carbonite, requiring extensive alteration to install. The attack has the Immobilising quality, and the severity of the condition can be upgraded from Hindered to Stuck for an additional 1 Momentum (instead of the normal 2). The attack also has the Breaker quality.

UPGRADE Sucker Punch: Using EI-derived viral memetics and stimuli libraries from aquatic species beyond the Human Sphere, this software payload can cripple enemy infowarriors. On a successful attack against a character using equipment with the Neural quality, 1 Momentum can be spent to inflict physical damage instead of quantronic damage. If a Defence or Guard Reaction is used against an attack made with Sucker Punch, the defence tests are made at +1 difficulty.

UPGRADE White Noise: This upgrade adds the White Noise zone effect to the hacker's current zone. As a Standard Action, the hacker can attempt a Simple (D0) Hacking test to expand the range of the White Noise, adding one additional zone per Momentum spent.

USAriadnan Entrenching Tool: Made of simple stamped steel and wood, the "E-Tool" has multiple uses beyond digging trenches, such as a hatchet to chop firewood, an improvised weapon, or a pry bar. A favourite of colonists and wilderness wanderers, the E-Tool still sees extensive military use on Ariadna. It counts as a kit, granting 1 bonus Momentum for relevant skill tests.

Vac Suit: These bulky suits are self-contained environments for surviving in the cold harsh vacuum of space, often incorporated into zero-g work suits and combat armour. They entirely protect the wearer from exposure to the vacuum of space and other hazards, contain three Oxygen Loads as well as two Parts worth of sealant and patches for emergency repairs, and provide 3 BTS when worn on their own.

Varuna Lungs: Named for the planet where they were invented, Varuna lungs are a nanobot-laden oral spray that coats the user's lung tissues and mediates gas exchange, allowing the user to "breathe" underwater. Each kit contains four applications, equivalent to a single Oxygen Load.
  They also serve as a basic filter against toxins and gases. If exposed to military-grade nanobots, poison gas, or toxic liquids, the nanobots provide +1 BTS for 1d6 rounds before dissolving, ending the effect.

Viral Ammunition 🔵: Viral rounds are supersonic soft-shell projectiles containing quick-acting viral loads. They add Biotech, Grievous, and Toxic 2 to the weapon.

Vizier Geist: Adapted for rapid Maya research, vizier geists are gifted at providing users with useful publicly available information about everyone they meet at near-instant speed.

GEIST
VIZIER GEIST

ATTRIBUTES						
AGI	AWA	BRW	COO	INT	PER	WIL
4	5	4	4	7	10	4

SKILLS					
Persuade	+3	2	Command	+1	–
Lifestyle	+1	1	Hacking	+1	1

TALENTS
- Charismatic, Enticer, Magnetic Personality 2, Socialite

Vulkan Shotgun: The Vulkan shotgun fires incendiary shells that coat targets in jellied fuel and burn them alive. Vulkan shotguns are Medium MULTI weapons, but use Normal Shells and Fire Shells instead of Standard or Special ammunition. (Range C, 1+5 🅝 damage, Burst 1, 2H, Knockdown, Medium MULTI)
  Normal Shells Mode (Primary): Area (Close), Spread 1
  Fire Shells Mode (Secondary): Area (Close), Incendiary 3, Terrifying 1

Wetspike: Wetspikes use long-chain protein springs to piston a retractable hollow blade into their victim, injecting poison deep into their muscle and organ tissues – the perfect implanted murder weapon. (Melee, 1+4 🅝 damage, 1H, Piercing 1, Biotech, Toxic 1, Subtle 3)

White Hacking Device: Officially designated as "defensive hacking devices plus" by O-12, the hacker community found the name clumsy and soon started calling them white hacking devices. Like white hat security experts, these models belong to the guardian hackers who keep their fellows safe from enemy cyberattacks. They are rated CLAW-0, SWORD-0, SHIELD-3, GADGET-1, IC-3, and have the Cyberalert Systems upgrade.

Wolfshot: Smeared on the knives and arrowheads of River Tribe Antipode warriors, this organic compound is rarely seen since the Second Antipode

COMMON VIRAL WEAPONS
- **Askari AS Engerek** (Viral Sniper Rifle)
- **Askari AS Örümcek** (Viral Rifle)
- **Askari AS Thueban** (Viral Pistol)
- **Cuurval Tuuga-6 (Tuuga-Sa-El)** (Tohaa Viral Pistol)
- **Iriista Claado-350 (Claado-Ku-Mi-El)** (Tohaa Viral Sniper Rifle)
- **Iriista Luvo-400 (Luvo Mo-El)** (Tohaa Viral Combi Rifle)

COMMON VULKAN SHOTGUNS
- **CineticS Timawa** (PanOceania)
- **Cuurval Kiisa-8000 (Kiisa To-ll)** (Tohaa)
- **Krumat** (Morat Supremacy)

TRENCH HAMMERS
A slightly different variant of the USAriadnan Entrenching Tool is widely used by asteroid miners. Trench-hammers (or trenchammers) were used as an improvised close combat weapon during the Helicon Miners' Revolt, during which some miners attached explosive devices to them and used them as grenades.

Defence / Guard Reaction – p. 113

White Noise, p. 110: Zero visibility zone for characters with mulispectral visors and other high-tech visual aids.

Oxygen Loads – p. 355

VIRAL EXPLOITS
Operatives of the Hassassin Society, the feared Lasiqs, are the most famous users of this technology, but others employ it too. On Dawn, viral rifles are used to end Dogface riots. In exchange for Teseum, Ariadna secured a shipment of AS Örümcek rifles for their Loup-Garou special action units: their viral "silver bullets" are one of the few sure ways to stop a rampaging Dog-Warrior. Well-connected bounty hunters use them in a similar fashion against their quarries, and unsurprisingly, the enigmatic Tohaa have their own varieties of this deadly technology.

TOHAA HACKERS

The Tohaa had limited experience with quantronic warfare before they encountered the Evolved Intelligence. They remain woefully inferior in this crucial arms race, with most Tohaa hackers limited to their variant of the white hacking device (with an emphasis on anti-EI defensive programs). O-12 has been attempting to negotiate offensive training programs for Tohaa hackers in exchange for more access to their advanced technologies.

Staggered, p. 104: Pay 1 Momentum to take Standard Action. Pay 1 Infinity Point to perform Reaction (plus normal Heat cost).

XO SUIT VARIANT:

SAUK & JOAD

Designed for extended continuous wear, S&K XO Suits incorporate personalised cushioning, whisper-quiet recycling systems, and custom fittings for maximum comfort and confidence on the job.

Bleeding, p. 103: 3 Ⓝ physical damage, ignoring Soak, at beginning of each turn.

suffocation, p. 110: Make Resistance (D1) test each round. +1 difficulty for each additional round. On failure, suffer 1 Wound.

Absterge – p. 110

Offensive, exceedingly difficult to trade for, and nigh-impossible to synthesize. Dogfaces and their mothers are immune to its effects. (Injury, Instant 2, 1+6 Ⓝ physical damage)

Wound Effect: The character gains the Bleeding condition. (This condition can be removed with the Absterge action, ending the Wound Effect.)

Wurari: One of many names for a family of poisons brewed from the leaves of alkaloid-rich plants common to the tropical regions of Yutang, Paradiso, Ariadna, and Earth, Wurari weakens muscles to the point of paralysis, asphyxiating the target. (Spray/Inhaled, Complex 1 (2 Momentum), 1+3 Ⓝ physical damage)

Wound Effect: The target becomes Staggered due to muscular weakening. If they are already Staggered, they go into respiratory failure and suffer the effects of suffocation (with the difficulty of the Resistance test equal to the number of Wurari-related Wound Effects suffered).

XO Suit: A gruntsuit for extreme environments, XO suits incorporate a built-in vac suit and exoskeleton. (Civilian Armour)

Yáokòng Remotes: The versatile Yáokòng series of remotes comes in several different configurations — the Wèibīng mobile guardian, Hùsòng heavy escort, and several more besides — making them a popular fixture in the Yu Jing military, as well as intrepid tinkerers who've gotten their hands on these incredibly modular platforms.

Zondbot: Something of an unofficial Nomad mascot, the Zondbot features prominently in toys, games, and a popular animated series. While they may look like something dreamed up by a marketing department rather than military R&D, these zippy little remotes have inspired myriad takes on the core Zond concept — from heavy weapons platforms to remote hacking units, all-terrain transports and beyond — and through it all, the humble Zond zips along.

ELITE

YÁOKÒNG REMOTE

ATTRIBUTES

AGI	AWA	BRW	COO	INT	PER	WIL
10	10	10	10	8	7	8

FIELDS OF EXPERTISE

| Combat | +2 | 2 | Movement | +1 | 1 | Social | – | – |
| Fortitude | +1 | 1 | Senses | +2 | 2 | Technical | – | – |

DEFENCES

| Firewall | 8 | Resolve | 8 | Structure | 10 |
| Security | – | Morale | 2 | Armour | 2 |

ATTACKS

- **Slam**: Melee, 1+6 Ⓝ damage, Anti-Materiel, Knockdown, Vicious 1
- **Combi Rifle**: Range C/M, 1+7 Ⓝ damage, Burst 2, 2H, Comms, Expert 1, Vicious 1

GEAR: Sensor Suite (Infrared Cameras), and one of the following:
- **Heavy Machine Gun**: Range L, 2+8 Ⓝ damage, Burst 5, Unwieldy, Spread 1, Unsubtle
- **Missile Launcher**: Range L, 2+7 Ⓝ damage, Burst 1, Unwieldy, Munition

SPECIAL ABILITIES

- **Common Special Abilities**: Inured to Disease, Poison, and Vacuum
- **Resplendent Matrix**: When a Yáokòng is controlled by a geist or its native LAI, it gains a Morale and Security Soak of 2.

ELITE

ZONDBOT

ATTRIBUTES

AGI	AWA	BRW	COO	INT	PER	WIL
12	10	8	10	10	5	8

FIELDS OF EXPERTISE

| Combat | +1 | 1 | Movement | +3 | 3 | Social | – | – |
| Fortitude | – | – | Senses | +1 | 1 | Technical | +1 | 1 |

DEFENCES

| Firewall | 10 | Resolve | 8 | Structure | 8 |
| Security | – | Morale | – | Armour | 1 |

ATTACKS

- **Adhesive Pistol**: Range R/C, 1+6 Ⓝ damage, Burst 1, 1H, Immobilising, Knockdown, Nonlethal, Vicious 1
- **Hacking Device**: CLAW-1, SWORD-1, SHIFI D-1, GADGET-2, IC-2 +3 Ⓝ bonus damage
- **Modhand**: Melee, 1+4 Ⓝ damage, 1H, Concealed 2, E/M, Stun, Subtle 1, Vicious 2

GEAR: Climbing Plus, Optical Disruption Device, Repeater

SPECIAL ABILITIES

- **Common Special Abilities**: Inured to Disease, Poison, and Vacuum
- **Arachne-Powered**: When a Zond is controlled by a geist or its native LAI, it gains a Security Soak of 4.
- **Zippy Little Thing**: Zondbots survive by staying mobile. They reduce the Heat cost of Defence reactions by 1, to a minimum of 0.

GEAR
LIFESTYLES

Lifestyles describe how characters live, where they call home, and the types of resources and experiences they're familiar with. It influences what they consider normal, important, rude, and attractive. An individual's lifestyle is partly something they choose, but it's also a result of social connections, wealth, upbringing, fame, and status. Culture and environment also play a role in how lifestyles are expressed.

SOCIAL CLASS

A character's social class is made up of their Earnings and their Social Status. Although there is a relationship between these two ratings, it is not necessarily a direct one.

Earnings represent a character's normal regular income, wherever it comes from or whatever form it takes.

Social Status encompasses the people a character associates with, the way they live their lives, and the circles of influence they enjoy. Some aspects of Social Status may be inherited, but most — particularly in an iota-scarcity society — are acquired and subject to change.

SOCIAL CLASS TABLE	
SOCIAL STATUS	EARNINGS
Underclass	1
Demogrant	2
Middle	3
Upper	4
Elite	5
Hyper-Elite	6+

LIFESTYLE RATING

Unlike the specific, tangible goods and commodities described in the *Gear Catalogue,* each individual Lifestyle is a more comprehensive package which holistically describes the environments and experiences found in a character's everyday life. Lifestyles allow players to flexibly capture the day-to-day zeitgeist of their character without needing to scrutinise every individual purchase.

Each Lifestyle expense is rated according to the Social Status which it typifies. As shown on the *Social Class Table,* each Social Status is associated with the particular Earnings which is typically required to

maintain that Lifestyle. If a character has an Earnings rating equal to or higher than the Lifestyle rating of the expense, they can acquire it without paying a Cost. Such expenses are simply assumed to be, for lack of a better word, part of their lifestyle.

In most cases, Lifestyle expenses are also ubiquitous enough (food, clothing, etc.) that no acquisition test is still required. However, if the character is suffering a Shortfall or if they are in unusual circumstances (they're in an isolated region, for example, or perhaps the item they're looking for is currently suffering from shortages) then an acquisition test is required to see if the item can be found. If a complication is rolled on such a test, they may be required to pay the Cost for that purchase normally.

LIFESTYLE MAINTENANCE

It is also possible for characters to live beyond their means. This is represented by the Lifestyle Maintenance cost of the Lifestyle: if a character's Earnings is lower than a given Social Status, they can nevertheless live as if they were part of that Social Status by paying the requisite Lifestyle Maintenance. Unlike normal Maintenance, Lifestyle Maintenance reduces Cashflow even if it is lower than the character's Earnings.

Lifestyles are selected by category: just because a character has chosen to live above their means in Housing and Property, it doesn't mean they need to similarly splurge on Food and Drink.

It is also possible to maintain a Lifestyle category at levels below your current Social Status. The advantage of living below your means is that, once per session, you can gain one bonus d20 on asset management tests to recover from Shortfalls per Lifestyle category you are maintaining at a level lower than your Earnings. (These bonus d20s can all be spent on one test or can be spread out across multiple tests.)

For game purposes, a Lifestyle Maintenance cost can only be selected or dropped at the beginning or end of a session.

LIFESTYLE COST

It is also possible to purchase a specific item that would normally belong to a Lifestyle higher than your own. (For example, one can order an expensive meal at a restaurant that's out of their normal price range or buy a bespoke dress for a special

LIFESTYLES OF THE FUTURE

The iota-scarcity economy of the Human Sphere has realigned the social classes and typical lifestyle of humanity. If you're thinking of citizens on the demogrant as sort of scraping by on the verge of subsistence, for example, you're trapped in the backwards sort of thought one would expect from an Ariadnan. Review the descriptions of social classes on p. 40 to reorient yourself.

Shortfalls – p. 329

iota-scarcity society – p. 140

LIFESTYLE CATEGORIES

Four Lifestyle categories are presented here:
• Clothing and Fashion
• Entertainment
• Food and Drink
• Housing and Property

OPTIONAL RULE
ALTERNATIVE SOCIAL CLIMBING

For easier bookkeeping, the GM may allow players to adjust their Social Status at the end of any full session during which they were paying for the relevant Lifestyle rating (either directly or by virtue of having a high enough Earnings). Alternatively, the adjustment may be made at the end of any mission if it takes longer than one session to resolve.

ARMOURED CLOTHING

Modern technology allows fairly sophisticated defensive technologies to be incorporated into modern fashion, as described in *Armoured Clothing*, p. 362. When purchasing armoured clothing in a fashion higher than the character's current Lifestyle supports, the character must pay the Cost of the fashion if it is higher than the cost of the armoured clothing.

social skill tests – p. 122

stealth tests – p. 104

Hiraeth culture – p. 15

occasion.) For such purchases a normal acquisition test is made and the listed Cost is paid.

SOCIAL MOBILITY

Social Climbing: Once per month, characters interested in raising their Social Status can do so by attempting an Epic (D5) Lifestyle test. On a success, they increase their Social Status by one level.

The difficulty of this test reflects how difficult it is to simply improve your Social Status by force of personality or luck of circumstance. However, characters can reduce the difficulty of this test by maintaining a Lifestyle above their current Social Status. (For example, by maintaining an Upper class Lifestyle when their current Social Status is Middle class.) For each Lifestyle category (such as Food and Drink or Clothing and Fashion) maintained at a level higher than the character's current Social Status, the difficulty of the Lifestyle test is reduced by 1 (to a minimum of 1).

If a character's Earnings are higher than their current Social Status, maintaining a higher Lifestyle can obviously be trivial (since it can be sustained at no additional Cost). It still takes time to integrate into new social circles (and lose the smell of "new money"), but it will likely happen eventually.

Social Decline: Characters can also choose to maintain Lifestyles lower than their current Social Status. This has roughly the opposite effect: each month they must make a Lifestyle test with a difficulty equal to the number of Lifestyle categories in which they are currently "slumming" it (maximum 5). On a failure, their Social Status is reduced by one level.

Mixed Lives: If a character has some Lifestyle categories below their current Social Status and others above it, the mixed categories affect both tests. Each Lifestyle category below their current Social Status applies a +1 difficulty penalty to social

climbing tests, while each Lifestyle category above their current Social Status applies a −1 difficulty adjustment to the social decline test.

CLOTHING AND FASHION

Characters are assumed to possess a respectable wardrobe of clothing options appropriate for their Lifestyle. This includes maintenance and cleaning, of course, along with the regular purchase of new outfits. Characters should also choose the faction or subculture of their fashion. A personal wardrobe can be extended to include another faction or subculture by spending 1 Asset.

COMPLICATED FASHIONS

To the trained eye, clothing communicates volumes about the wearer's class, faction, subcultural allegiances, personality and wherewithal — attending a PanOceanian business meeting in Yu Jingese clubwear is a social *faux pas* at best.

When characters are wearing radically inappropriate clothing for a particular social situation, the GM is encouraged to increase the difficulty of social skill tests, stealth tests, or any other appropriate skill tests. (This includes wearing powered combat armour to a cocktail party.)

In addition, the particular tastes of fashion vary by both faction and subculture. The rough, natural fibres of Ariadnan fashion are seen as uncouth on Yutang; but, by the same token, the "plastic wrap" of febrile galactic fashions are often mocked in the clan halls of Caledonia. Wearing clothing that's out-of-step with the local culture can increase the complication range of social skill tests. (This can also include differences of class: wearing a custom-tailored iridescent suit when ordering a drink in a Bōsōzoku bar can attract the wrong kind of attention.)

FASHION OF THE HUMAN SPHERE

When it comes to fashion, there isn't a sharp delineation between the styles of various social classes. Rather, it's a spectrum driven by taste, expense, and practicality. (The richer you are, the less practical your clothing needs to be.) Underclass and Demogrant clothing tends to be simpler and more traditional, with perhaps one or two specific and unusual elements. As Social Status rises, however, the possibilities of modern technology stretch the limits of fashion.

On the other hand, Hiraeth culture still plays a significant role in fashion, so these extravagant expressions of advanced technologies are

ADJUSTING EARNINGS

A character's Earnings rating is primarily dependent on their current line of work. The Earnings of a new career is determined by the GM, who can use the ratings listed for careers in the *Lifepath* chapter (p. 59–70) for guidance. If the new career's Earnings rating is higher than the character's current Earnings rating, their Earnings are immediately increased to the new level. If the career's Earnings rating is lower than the character's Earnings, on the other hand, then once per session the character should roll a number of Ⓝ equal to the difference. If an Effect is rolled, their Earnings decrease by 1. An Asset can be spent to reroll any number of Ⓝ on this roll (and this can be done repeatedly if so desired).

You'll note that Earnings tend to "lag high". If you're a member of the Hyper-Elite and start slumming in your career, for example, you've still got all of your investments and other forms of savings and income to keep you afloat… for a time.

nevertheless pulled back towards more traditional styles. Counterbalancing this is the fact that fashions churn quickly in both the Maya-driven Sphere and the social experimentation of *Bakunin*, with rapid fashion cycles measuring in weeks rather than seasons. Pop-up fashion fads can even flare up and burn out over the course of just a few days.

Neon-noir clothes incorporate luminous elements. In some cases, these lights form geometric displays, but with layered clothing it's also common for softly glowing lights to glimmer from below. Some neon-noir styles feature colours which slowly shift over time; but rapidly shifting (or strobing) displays are generally considered gauche.

Smart fabrics are very common. Variants include **motile fabrics** capable of motion and **display fabrics** which can act as quantronic displays (although this is more commonly used for decoration or to make a statement than for practical purposes). **Holographic fabrics** take this technology to an extreme, capable of extreme, three-dimensional shapeshifting including the ability to simulate any conceivable texture. **Polyclime fabrics** can be worn in climate-controlled comfort. Smart fabrics are also commonly self-cleaning and can incorporate various forms of miniaturised technology (though these features generally need to be purchased separately).

One recent fashion trend are **iridescent fabrics**, which can also be referred to as "rainbow cloth" when the effect gets cranked up too high. **Liquid metal** is currently a hot fad among teenagers on Neoterra. (They're not actually made of metal, but appear to flow around the wearer's body as such.) Nomads have been selling **TruScale™** garments made from living snake scales cultivated over smart fabric which retains moisture and provides a complex coloration system as helpful for camouflage as it is for an elitist soirée.

AR variable outfits take a different approach, presenting a blank slate with patina cues that cause them to have a different virtual look for each person.

FastWeave™ clothes are at the other end of the spectrum. They can be printed almost instantly on demand, but the cheaply fabricated result is immediately identifiable from their gaudy patterns, sturdy design, and uncomfortable fabrics.

A panoply of accessories are also quite common: **mobile tattoos** that animate or even move across the skin, **automaton jewellery** (including voice-boxes for geists), **telescoping heels** (for shoes that are practical, fashionable, *and* outrageous), **smart pockets** that are completely sealed until they receive a quantronic command, and the like.

CLOTHING AND FASHION LIFESTYLE TABLE

LIFESTYLE RATING	LIFESTYLE MAINTENANCE	RESTRICTION	COST	TARIFF
Demogrant	1	0	1	–
Middle	2	1	1+1 Ⓝ	–
Upper	3	1	3+2 Ⓝ	–
Elite	5	1	6+3 Ⓝ	T1
Hyper-Elite	9	2	10+3 Ⓝ	T1

Traditional accessories are also common, of course: hand fans are quite popular in Yu Jing at the moment. Muffs are coming back into style on Svalarheima. Merovingian cravats are gaining a retro-chic appeal off-planet. On Bourak, sashes, frequently made from motile fabrics, are surprisingly popular (although most commonly worn around the waist).

ENTERTAINMENT

Entertainment is ubiquitous in the Human Sphere. Even destitute members of the **Underclass** can usually access vast libraries of high quality, immersive content with even the most basic Maya access. And more expensive forms of entertainment are usually of the same general *type* as the cheaper stuff — the price is instead driven by exclusivity, access, or (in very rare circumstances) the need for specialised equipment.

Maya – p. 140

sensaseries – p. 143

Unlike members of the Underclass, members of the **Demogrant** are more likely to see live performances. They can also subscribe to a handful of more exclusive Maya channels, including sensaseries programming content.

The **Upper class** have VIP experiences as a matter of course: box seats at Dog-Bowl games. Exclusive areas at nightclubs. Backstage access at concerts.

Dog-Bowl, p. 153: A brutal game played primarily by Dogfaces.

Entertainment for the **Elite** and richer includes custom-designed experiences, niche happenings, and expensive participatory events: AR experiences mapped onto orbital insertions; pop-up nightclubs inside hollowed-out asteroids; recreation masques using morphing flesh-masks of historical figures; and other similarly unique opportunities.

AR, p. 140: Augmented reality.

geists – p. 350

ENTERTAINMENT LIFESTYLE TABLE

LIFESTYLE RATING	LIFESTYLE MAINTENANCE	RESTRICTION	COST	TARIFF
Demogrant	1	1	1+1 Ⓝ	–
Middle	2	1	2+1 Ⓝ	–
Upper	4	2	3+2 Ⓝ	–
Elite	6	2	6+2 Ⓝ	T3

FOOD AND DRINK

Everyone needs to eat, even frontline operatives. **Groceries** represent the routine purchases that keep the larder filled and the palate wet; they're generally what people grab out of the refrigerated niches built into the walls of their homes.

Meals are bought from vendors or restaurants. When indulging in a meal of a higher quality than normal for the character's Lifestyle, the Cost represents the bill for a small group of friends, business associates, or the like. Treating someone to a more extravagant meal than they're used to may allow a character to generate bonus Momentum on social skill tests (at the GM's discretion).

People like to say that, no matter how much the Human Sphere changes, *food* always stays the same. But that's not entirely true: those in the Middle class commonly have access to interplanetary imports, greatly varying their diets and also allowing gourmands to appreciate the distinct flavours that arise from subtly different planetary biochemistries (such as the unique flavour of rice from Shentang, which the Yu Jingese describe as "floral" and PanOceanians dismiss as "sickly sweet").

Among the Upper classes, exotic foodstuffs — particularly those from non-terrestrial plants and animals — are common fare. They also enjoy nanonic-locked alcohols that can be quantronically triggered to prevent hangovers or purge your buzz (if you suddenly need to sober up).

Elites enjoy dishes which are custom-designed for the individual palate (based on genetic sampling and analysis of taste receptors).

Finally, Hyper-Elite cuisine is not distinguished so much by unique food or drink as it is by sheer quality and exclusivity: restaurants which take weeks to obtain reservations for. Custom-tailored, multi-sensual experiences which accompany the dining. Old Earth liquors. Perhaps foodstuffs or drinks which are, technically speaking, illegal.

Tiān Di Jing, p. 284: Capital of Yu Jing.

social skill tests — p. 122

domotics — p. 143

MULTIPLE HOMES

In addition to their primary residence, a character can own a second residence of a Lifestyle rating one lower than their own by paying the listed Cost with Maintenance 2. (That's a regular Maintenance rating, not a Lifestyle Maintenance.) If the second residence is two or more Lifestyle ratings lower, it has Maintenance 1. Multiple such secondary properties can be maintained in this way (with their Maintenance costs stacking).

FOOD AND DRINK LIFESTYLE TABLE

LIFESTYLE RATING	LIFESTYLE MAINTENANCE	RESTRICTION	COST (MEAL)	TARIFF
Demogrant	–	–	–	–
Middle	2	1	1+1Ⓝ	–
Upper	4	2	3+1Ⓝ	T1
Elite	6	3	5+2Ⓝ	T2
Hyper-Elite	8	4	6+4Ⓝ	T3

HOUSING AND PROPERTY

Housing varies more than any other Lifestyle based on environment and circumstance. Living quarters that might be considered cramped in the Living Cities of Neoterra can easily be a sign of opulent wealth on a radiation-shielded orbital in Human Edge. In many cities on Svalarheima the upper classes burrow deep into the artificially warmed depths of the ice; while in Tiān Di Jing wealth seeks the heights and an unobstructed view of the Forbidden City.

Underclass citizens must make a Lifestyle (D1) test each month; on a failure they must pay the listed Cost. If a complication is generated on a failure, they are evicted or otherwise lose their dwelling. (Being poor sucks. A lot.) Even if they can hold onto their homes, Underclass housing usually consists of either a single room in a crowded structure or a sturdy pop-up structure on the frontier. They often live in violent or otherwise undesirable neighbourhoods. In rare cases, their access to basic utilities (including Maya) may be limited.

Demogrant housing is comfortable and often clustered together. These are usually simple apartments or houses in safe, beautiful neighbourhoods featuring easy access to all the expected amenities.

Middle class housing is not dissimilar from Demogrant housing. It's usually just bigger, with a greater incorporation of domotic features. Maya overlays are often incorporated in to the architecture, allowing homes to rapidly transform their appearance.

Upper class housing, on the other hand, is practically *defined* by domotics. Their homes can trivially transform their physical structures (including, in many cases, literally having rooms move, collapse, construct, or otherwise restructure themselves). The sort of limitless freedom which the Middle class experiences in the virtual world, the Upper class can make manifest in the physical one.

Many **Elites** choose to live in housing which is not terribly dissimilar to that of the Upper class — perhaps a bump in size towards the palatial; perhaps situated on a slightly larger estate. Some, however, prefer secured compounds surrounded by others who share a common ethos, faith, politics, or other interest. They form micro-cultures of immense wealth, their homes blending together into small communities — often hidden invisibly within the same cities where the lower classes dwell — that become fantastic wonderlands and shared dreamlands.

The lavish homes of the **Hyper-Elite** almost beggar the imagination. First, there is the sheer scale of them: the master bedroom alone likely dwarfs a Demogrant's apartment. Their estates can rival national parklands for their scope. More importantly, they have a complete mastery over their physical demesne and are capable of realising even the seemingly impossible through a combination of smart-materials and pseudo-AI assistance.

OTHER REAL ESTATE

Other property can also be leased or mortgaged. These are not Lifestyles (instead having normal Costs and Maintenance and requiring an acquisition test), but are listed here for convenience.

Garage: This provides enough space for a car or several motorcycles, as well as some tools and supplies. They could also be used as a (poorly outfitted) workspace or oversized storage locker.

Office, Small: A small office consists of a single room with a few pieces of furniture. Such offices usually share facilities with several other offices and can be used be one or two people comfortably.

Office, Large: A large office includes a waiting room or reception area, several individual offices, and perhaps a small conference room or similar facility.

Office, Complex: An office complex can take up several floors of a building or even be a small building in its own right.

Safety Deposit Box: Usually located in a bank or dedicated facility, a safety deposit box is ideal for

relatively small items (such as genetic samples, backup Cubes, hardcopy documents, jewellery, or other valuables).

Storage Locker: A simple space closer to a large closet than a room. Cheap to rent, relatively secure, and, most importantly, private. No questions asked. Operatives often fill them with weapons, ammunition, contraband, and emergency supplies.

FACILITIES
Specialised facilities like laboratories and surgical bays can also be leased. See *Facilities*, p. 357.

HOUSING LIFESTYLE TABLE				
LIFESTYLE RATING	LIFESTYLE MAINTENANCE	RESTRICTION	COST (1 WEEK)	TARIFF
Underclass	*	–	1+3	T2
Demogrant	2	1	2+3	–
Middle	4	2	4+3	T1
Upper	8	3	6+4	T2
Elite	12	4	8+5	T2
Hyper-Elite	20	5	10+5	T4

REAL ESTATE TABLE				
PROPERTY	RESTRICTION	COST	TARIFF	MAINTENANCE
Garage	1	2+1	–	1
Office, Small	1	5+2	T1	2
Office, Large	1	7+4	T1	4
Office, Complex	2	14+6	T1	10
Safety Deposit Box	0	1+1	–	0
Storage Locker	1	1+6	–	1

* See description, special rules apply.

GEAR
SERVICES

BLACK MARKETS

If the PCs have, through their actions in the campaign, gained access to a black market, the GM may choose to drop the normal Restriction boost for illegal activities. Complications on the acquisition test, however, might cause them to directly or indirectly lose their access.

EXAMPLE
PROFESSIONAL COSTS

Cassandra needs a doc to patch her up, but she doesn't want some lazy intern hacking up her body (who would have TN 10 and a base Cost of 1+1🄝). She seeks someone out with TN 12 and Focus 1. A doctor with these three additional skill ranks has Restriction 2 (base 1 + 1 per 3 ranks). If Cassandra can find a doctor like this, their cost will be 2+4🄝 (base cost of 1+1🄝, +3🄝 for the skill ranks, and an additional +1 because of three total ranks).

QUANTRONIC RETAINERS

In an era of ALEPH, geists, and pseudo-AIs, professional services don't always require a human professional. Their innate familiarity with data and Maya makes such Retainers particularly useful for tasks such as reputation monitoring and management, filtering live feeds for particular events, trends, and patterns, and cryptographic and stenographic processing. Quantronic Retainers have the Analysis skill at the same Expertise as their other skills, Analysis Focus equal to their Expertise rating, and the Pattern Recognition trait, for no additional cost.

Not everything for sale in the Human Sphere is a tangible commodity. In an iota-scarcity economy, in fact, the most valuable thing can often be the service provided by another intelligent being. (Although labour unions cyclically complain that ALEPH is perpetually undercutting this market.)

PROFESSIONAL SERVICES

Professionals can be hired to perform specific, short-term services (such as providing medical aid, hacking a database, or furnishing security for a day). By default, such professionals have a target number of 10 for any skills tests relevant to the service they're being paid to provide.

More experienced or talented professionals can also be hired. These are measured by the additional skill ranks they possess, with additional ranks of expertise raising the target number for their skill tests and additional ranks of focus adding the possibility for additional successes on their skill tests normally.

Restriction: Most professional services have a restriction rating of 1. Particularly skilled help is harder to find: for every three additional skill ranks the professional has above the base target number, add +1 restriction. Hiring people to perform illegal or extremely dangerous services will also generally add +1 restriction. Other factors may also affect the local availability of specific skills, at the GM's discretion.

Cost: The base Cost for providing a service is 1+1🄝. If the services are illegal, dangerous, or otherwise unusual, a Tariff can be added to this Cost at the GM's discretion. This Cost increases by +1🄝 per additional skill rank. Every three additional skill ranks *also* adds +1 to the Cost.

Some services may have additional costs based on the equipment required to carry them out.

Long-Term Hires: Professionals who are hired long-term have an initial hiring Cost equal to short-term service. They also have a Maintenance of 3 + one-half the professional's additional skill ranks + the professional's Tariff rating.

Retainer: It's also possible to have a professional service on retainer. (This is often done with a lawyer, for example.) A professional on retainer has a Maintenance cost equal to half that for a long-term hire, but can only be called upon inter-mittently for routine services. Excessive, unusual, or particularly demanding services may end up getting billed separately (at their normal Cost).

RESURRECTIONS

Thanks to Cube tech, those who suffer death from age or injury can be restored to synthetic Lhost bodies.

EXPERIENCING RESURRECTION
For all of its complexity, the quantronic recording process is invisible to the user, and a personality stored by the Cube has the same thoughts, memories, emotions, and tendencies that it always did; a perfect, lossless digitisation of every facet that makes up someone's essence and identity. The core identity of the individual has become known as the sheut — an Egyptian word for the part of the soul which resided in a person's shadow — and, as far as any test can determine, it can be saved, copied, stored, and restored flawlessly and in its lossless entirety.

More difficult, however, is forging the link between a sheut and its new body.

Integrating an existing consciousness into a new body is rife with complications: the subject's neuromatrix suddenly and violently reorganises itself, accounts for the vast difference between expected sensory landscape and the immediate stimuli, and hurriedly works to bridge the gap. Many subjects expect the process to be like learning to walk again, only to find it more akin to discovering what it means to be a single concrete entity; not an abstract construct, not a tapestry of unrelated sensations, but a person. Early cases were daunting. Progress was slow, but constant. Refinement of the process didn't happen with a single, dramatic splash, but a thousand micro-improvements over time.

Today, Cubes are implanted in custom-grown Lhosts incorporating the user's own DNA, all but eliminating instinctual rejection of the new body. Transpersonal psychotherapists work with users at every step, helping them to adjust to the new realities of their situation. But perhaps most integral of all, is the role of a user's geist. Integrating a dedicated pseudo-AI – one with intimate familiarity not only of the user's biological information, but their behavioural patterns, desires, preferences and so on – works wonders for the synthesis process. When downloading into a new Lhost, a user's geist is more than just another useful subroutine; it's a trusted friend, a light in the darkness, the one constant in a sea of troubles.

RESURRECTION LICENSES

While the Resurrection process is reliable, the large quantities of Silk and medical expertise required limits its availability and initially raised prices to the point that only the richest .01% could afford it, leading to widespread protests and social unrest. ALEPH and O-12's Bureau Lakshmi intervened, passing laws regulating Resurrection access through official Resurrection Bureaus controlled by factional governments and empowered to issue Resurrection Licenses which give recipients the right to Resurrect.

It should be noted that merely possessing a license doesn't guarantee a Resurrection: the recipient of the license still has to be able to pay for both their new body and the Resurrection procedure itself. Fortunately, there are Resurrection brokers who will negotiate loans for those trapped in Cube Banks who have received licenses.

BLACK MARKETS

In VaudeVille, the shadowy artist's mecca and black market bazaar sprawled across the surface of *Bakunin*, Nomad psychowarlock *artistes* provide illicit Resurrections beyond ALEPH's oversight, each with their own capricious approach to pricing and process. Submondo poseurs and thought-thieves prey on desperate and unwary outsiders, crudely dissecting the minds entrusted to their care for valuable secrets, or simply vanishing once paid in advance.

CUBE BANKS

Stored personalities currently unable to Resurrect (either due to a lack of license, lack of funds, or, in rare cases, lack of interest) are kept in Personality Data Storage (PDS) facilities – also known as Cube Banks or Soul Banks. After a few terrible incidents during the early history of Resurrection where people unable to pay their storage fees were purged by private Cube Banks, personality storage was recognised as a universal human right by Bureau Athena and basic storage costs became fully subsidised by all the major governments.

RESURRECTION FALLOUT

RESURRECTION LAWS
The ability to come back from the dead caused a lot of chaos in the legal systems of the Human Sphere. There is now a distinction between "death" and "true death", with personhood and property rights only terminating upon the latter (when a person's Cube and all other known backups have been destroyed).

RESURRECTION AND INSURANCE
The insurance industry also had to go through some major adjustments as Resurrections became commonplace. Pay outs for "life cessation events" that weren't true deaths became more akin to accident insurance. Insurance guarding against true death for those with Cubes also became incredibly cheap compared to the old life insurance policies. This recently backfired painfully, however, due to the vast number of Cubes destroyed through the use of VoodooTech on Paradiso. As insurance companies once again began to go under, governments had to step in and legally mandate lower true death payments.

RESURRECTION SERVICES

Clone Lhosts: It's not unusual for people to want to be resurrected into cloned copies of their original bodies. These typically use genetic samples taken from their original body in order to customise their Lhost. (Cubes take tissue samples of their users explicitly for this purpose.) Cloned Lhosts reduce the difficulty of Discipline tests made to avoid Resurrection Dysmorphic Disorder by 2 (minimum 0).

Cube Bank (Storage): Basic "cold storage" for a sheut is freely provided by most governments in the Human Sphere. This is how most people wait for their Resurrection: dormant and completely inactive; trapped in a dreamless "sleep of death". In most cases, such personalities will be periodically awoken (once every year or, in some cases, once every several years) to "check in" with the world around them.

Cube Bank (Active Hosting): Far rarer are those personalities which are kept running in real time. The hardware and software required for this sort of full-personality emulation in the absence of a Lhost is expensive. There are a few rare cases of VR communities which are home to multiple sheuts, but it's more common for these personalities to have an active Maya connection through which they can interact (albeit in a limited capacity) with the real world.

The reality, however, is that most people find it impossible to exist in a simulated state for long periods of time; it frays the sanity. This is referred to as sheut shredding (see sidebar).

Cube Bank (Visitation): Relatives (and others) can request interviews with Cube-bound personas, though the tuning required to avoid trauma to the

COMMON PROFESSIONALS
Accountant
Attorney
Chauffeur
Courier
Doctor
Entertainer
Hacker
Mechanic
Mercenary
Personal Assistant
Personal Chef
Personal Trainer
Pilot
Private Investigator
Psychologist
Research Assistant
Security Consultant
Scientist
Wilderness Guide

SHEUT SHREDDING
Chronic Complex 2 (10 Momentum), Month, 1+2 (N) mental damage
Special Effect: For each Effect rolled on the mental damage roll, the character's maximum Resolve suffers a cumulative −1 penalty.

TRUE CLONES
A true, fully grown clone
would be incredibly difficult,
time-consuming, and ethically
questionable to produce. Such
procedures, of course, may be
available in black labs.

VoodooTech – p. 307

**CASUAL CUBE
SCANS**
The term "Cube scan" has
become street slang for getting
a read on someone.

**RESURRECTION
DYSMORPHIC
DISORDER**
Progressive 1 (4 Momentum),
Week, 5+5 Ⓝ mental damage

Harm Effect: +1 difficulty to all
physical tests as the character
suffers from a biopsychosocial
breakdown between mind
and body.

social skill tests – p. 122

Social Status – p. 387

Lifestyle expense – p. 387

VR environment – p. 142

Lhost – p. 354

stored personality can be costly. (This service is not required if the personality is being actively hosted, since such characters can generally be interacted with normally through their Maya connection.)

Cube Scan: If the data on a Cube can be accessed (which is impossible without VoodooTech as long as a normal Cube is hosted in someone's body), it is possible to perform a Cube scan. (A common technique for performing a hostile Cube scan is to surreptitiously gain access to a target's external backup.)

A Cube scan is not like watching a video file or reading a book. Everyone's brain architecture is unique – reading the data was famously described by Qayyim Zaman as being "like trying to parse encrypted data stored on a custom-made storage medium using a unique operating system programmed by ten thousand monkeys pounding on keyboards." Some progress has been made, but Cube scans are generally limited to broad "personality mapping" and occasional snippets of more specific information (which often prove unreliable – either due to transcription errors or because the scan is picking up memories of dreams or fantasies). In game terms, the insight offered by a Cube scan can grant 1+3 Ⓝ bonus Momentum for social skill tests targeting the subject of the scan, but each Effect rolled generates a complication (that can be used by the GM in the same way as a complication generated on a skill test).

The truth is that it's often more practical to simply host the captive personality and interrogate it in a custom VR environment.

External Backup: Backing up a sheut personality without the use of a Cube is a time-consuming process requiring 10+5 Ⓝ hours and expensive equipment. A fast download port can speed this process considerably, reducing the time required for a backup to 10+5 Ⓝ minutes.

Resurrection: The actual process of infusing a stored personality into a new Lhost is an expensive one. The listed cost does not include the cost of the Lhost itself (which must be purchased separately).

The process of Resurrection is mentally straining. The character being resurrected must succeed on a Challenging (D2) Discipline test or suffer from Resurrection Dysmorphic Disorder (see sidebar). The difficulty of this test is increased for Lhosts which are distinctly inhuman.

Resurrection (Black Market): The most common source for black market Resurrections are the Nomads' Praxis labs, but there are also known Equinox facilities capable of performing them and reports that various hypercorps may maintain quasi-legal facilities. Black market Resurrections are more difficult and expensive to acquire, and complications generated on the acquisition test will have... interesting consequences.

TRAVEL AND TRANSPORT

Billions of people make daily commutes between home and work across the Human Sphere, millions journey between cities, and hundreds of thousands travel between worlds.

General prices for various methods of transport and travel are given on the *Travel and Transport Table*, but regional variations are common and these values can (and should) be modified at the GM's discretion. (It's a lot harder to hail a cab on the Northern Frontier of Caledonia than it is in downtown Darwin on Neoterra.)

Lifestyle Rating: Although it is not a Lifestyle expense (and does not contribute to changes in Social Status), transportation methods do have a Lifestyle rating. As with other Lifestyles, if a character's Earnings are high enough to afford the Lifestyle rating of the transport, it can simply be assumed that they have access to it. (For example, a member of the Elite can usually hire an air taxi to take them to another city without making an acquisition test or paying any Cost.)

URBAN TRANSPORT
These methods of travel are used routinely in cities across the Human Sphere. They're also appropriate for short trips in the countryside or out on the frontier.

Public Transport: Municipal transport takes familiar forms – trains, ferries, buses, cluster-corridors, monorails, and the like. These are fairly reliable, but in smaller communities, delays can crop up

RESURRECTION SERVICES TABLE

SERVICE	RESTRICTION	COST	TARIFF	MAINTENANCE
Clone Lhost	1	+2 Ⓝ*	T1*	–
Cube Bank (Storage)	0	0	–	–
Cube Bank (Active Hosting)	1	5+5 Ⓝ	T1t	5
Cube Bank (Visitation)	1	2+2 Ⓝ	T1	–
Cube Scan	2	3+4 Ⓝ	T2	–
External Backup	1	1+2 Ⓝ	–	–
Resurrection	2	10+4 Ⓝ	–	–
Resurrection (Black Market)	4	10+8 Ⓝ	T2	–

* Add to cost of Lhost.

RESURRECTION BUREAUS

Ariadna: Cube technology and, as a result, Resurrection has not been significantly adopted by the population of Dawn. Furthermore, efforts in the O-12 Öberhaus to nevertheless have Ariadna admitted into the Resurrection program have been stymied by other nations who would see their own allotments of Resurrections reduced.

Haqqislam: In Haqqislam, the Diwân al Rasa'il has parcelled out control of Resurrection licenses to the Hakim and the Mawla. These local leaders are in close contact with the people in their communities, and they recommend those worthy of commendation to the Council of Walīs. Most of these recommendations are then declared Exemplars (one who has shown possession of all the Haqqislamite virtues) who are authorised to seek Resurrection.

Nomads: Each mothership has a Resurrection Council which is ostensibly charged with dispensing licenses. In practise these councils are largely irrelevant because the Nomads' effective refusal to curtail the sale of illegal Resurrections in the black labs of Praxis have resulted in virtually all of their official Resurrection licenses frequently being suspended. Nomad leaders have denounced this as an "act of *de facto* genocide" and nothing more than a covert attempt to perpetuate the Phantom Conflicts by other means. A special feature of the *Autofocus* Maya channel (most likely based on reports leaked by PanOceania's Hexahedron) claims that, because of Praxis, the Nomads actually have one of the highest effective rates of Resurrection.

PanOceania: At ALEPH's suggestion, PanOceania's Ministry of Social Affairs defers the dispensation of licenses to religious organisations. The vast majority of licenses, therefore, are under the control of the Christian Church. Unsurprisingly, participation and membership in the Church has surged. Critics claim that the Church is abusing its position of power, pointing to the practises of Indulgences and the List of Deeds, p. 178, as manipulative social engineering.

Yu Jing: The Party wields almost absolute control over Resurrection licenses through its Resurrection Committee. (These licenses are issued during the Ceremony of Resurrection, p. 188, a national holiday.) However, the Yu Jing Emperor controls the licenses for all members of the Judicial Corps, using them as a reward for faithful service.

---

since the services mostly link transit hubs that get congested and crowded during peak hours. Yu Jing is particularly committed to the communal experience of public transport, with even wealthy citizens often using them. Many of their vehicles or carriages featuring custom AR experiences shared by the passengers on their journey.

In the Living Cities of PanOceania, by contrast, public transport often features "feeder pods" which pick up individuals from their front door and deliver them seamlessly to the central transit infrastructure. In many cases, passengers never leave the privacy and isolation of these pods until they arrive at their destination.

Smart Taxi: A wide variety of vehicles guided by LAIs can be flagged down or summoned through the Maya network.

Hired Car/Limousine: Personal vehicle ownership is relatively rare in most urban centres, largely because it is relatively trivial to hire a vehicle when you need one. Even when you want to drive the car yourself, it's common for an LAI to deliver it to your door.

Air Taxi: Any number of small, aerial vehicles can also be readily hired to provide very fast transport. The use of LAI piloting and traffic control allow aerial vehicles to avoid congestion by taking full advantage of three-dimensional space.

PLANETARY TRANSPORT

Travel across longer distances on planetary surfaces are relatively cheap and readily available.

Train: Early colonial efforts on many worlds saw maglev trains installed as the primary conduit for continental travel. There was little reason to build a network of highways across areas which were (and, in many cases, still are) essentially uninhabited. Prominent examples include the Transtartaric Railway on Dawn and Silk Route maglevs on Bourak.

In many cases, however, these rail lines were designed to be easily upgraded to incorporate highways. The resulting multi-ways — which are particularly common on Paradiso and also becoming increasingly common on Acontecimento — become the backbone of regional roads as colonial populations push back the frontiers.

Sub-Orbital: Flights which blast into space but return to the surface before achieving orbit represent the fastest means of travelling across a planet. On Earth, for example, sub-orbital flights can travel from Europe to North America in less than an hour. Such flights are still fairly expensive, but modern propulsion technologies have made them affordable on most planets (although the more affordable versions generally feature a magnetic reception platform which "catches" the vehicle, and therefore cannot be used without the proper infrastructure).

LEGACY RESURRECTIONS

Resurrections performed from stored backups can be more psychologically difficult to cope with than those from a Cube which was active at the moment of death: the knowledge there is a hole of missing memories at the fringes of your soul — a future you both lived and never lived — tends to gnaw at the mind. Characters resurrected in this way gain the "Legacy Resurrection" trait.

Transtartaric Railway – p. 248

RESURRECTION LOTTERY

In addition to the Resurrection Bureaus, Bureau Lakshmi also oversees the pan-national Resurrection Lottery in which random winners are awarded licenses. As Resurrection technology grows cheaper and more available, the lottery quotas have grown prodigiously year-over-year, but nevertheless only barely outpace the rapidly growing participation rates.

INTERPLANETARY TRANSPORT

Although a significant majority of people never leave their planet of birth, interplanetary travel within the Human Sphere is unremarkable and commonplace. However, it is still a time-consuming process, taking days (or even weeks) to navigate the wormhole network and cross the vast distances of empty space.

Cryofreight: The cheapest travel possible involves essentially shipping yourself as cargo. Passengers are placed in cryogenic suspended animation and then awoken at the other end. This also usually means incredibly long journeys, since the ships involved are typically the cheapest slow-haulers.

Circulars: Booking passage on a Circular is the most common means of interplanetary travel. The listed Cost includes the shuttle service necessary to reach the Circular from a nearby planetary surface. For complete privacy, and at a similar price for the docking fee, a shuttle or other small ship can dock

TRAVEL AND TRANSPORT TABLE

	METHOD	LIFESTYLE	RESTRICTION	COST[1]
URBAN TRANSPORT	Public Transport	Demogrant	0	1Ⓝ
	Smart Taxi	Middle	0	1+1Ⓝ
	Hired Car (per day)	Upper	1	1+2Ⓝ
	Limousine (per day)	Elite	1	2+2Ⓝ
	Air Taxi (city)	Hyper-Elite	2	3+3Ⓝ
PLANETARY TRANSPORT	Train	Demogrant	0	1+1Ⓝ
	Smart Taxi (long haul)	Middle	1	2+2Ⓝ
	Air Taxi (intercity)	Upper	1	4+4Ⓝ
	Sub-Orbital	Elite	2	5+5Ⓝ
INTERPLANETARY	Cryofreight	Middle	1	4+2Ⓝ
	Circular (Cabin)	Upper	1	6+2Ⓝ
	Circular (Suite)	Elite	2	7+2Ⓝ
	Direct Flight (Cabin)	Elite	2	8+2Ⓝ
	Direct Flight (Suite)	Hyper-Elite	2	9+4Ⓝ
	Chartered Flight	–	3	11+6Ⓝ
	Fast Transport	–	3	14+6Ⓝ
SHIPPING	Shipping (Small)	–	0	1+1Ⓝ
	Shipping (Large)	–	1	2+2Ⓝ
	Shipping (Cargo)	–	+1	6+3Ⓝ
	Interplanetary	–	X+XⓃ	+4Ⓝ
	Courier	–	–	+2

[1] Each Effect rolled inflicts a minor complication (usually a delay).

VEHICLE COSTS TABLE

NAME	SCALE	SPEED	STRENGTH	ARMOUR	BTS	IMPACT	RESTRICTION	COST	TARIFF
Car	1	2	12	3	1	2+5Ⓝ	1	9+2Ⓝ	–
Gecko TAG	1	2	7	5	6	2+6Ⓝ	4 (Nomad 3)	14+4Ⓝ	T4
Gūijiǎ TAG	2	2	17	8	6	3+8Ⓝ	4 (Yu Jing 3)	16+4Ⓝ	T4
Hovercraft	3	2	14	4	1	3+7Ⓝ	2	11+2Ⓝ	T1
Motorcycle	0	3	9	2	0	1+3Ⓝ	1	8+2Ⓝ	–
Speedboat	1	5	12	3	1	2+5Ⓝ	2	9+3Ⓝ	T1
Truck	2	2	14	4	1	3+7Ⓝ	1	9+2Ⓝ	T1
Yacht	2	5	10	2	4	5+4Ⓝ	2	12+3Ⓝ	T3

with the Circular, riding along under the power of the larger craft's engines but maintaining their own independent life support. (Larger ships can also be accommodated, but require commensurately larger docking fees.)

Direct Flight: Direct flight can be significantly faster than Circular travel (featuring fewer deceleration/acceleration cycles and docking delays), but are also considerably more expensive.

Chartered Flight: Hiring an interstellar vessel just for you and your friends is extremely unusual and incredibly expensive. The listed Cost increases by 1 for every two additional passengers (or, more specifically, a ship large enough and with the resources necessary to support those passengers).

Fast Transport: A fast transport can cross from one side of the Human Sphere to the other in a matter of days (and some military vessels are even faster than that). But this speed comes at a price. The listed Cost increases by 1 for each additional passenger.

SHIPPING

Maya connectivity has largely supplanted postal services, but physical stuff still needs to get moved from one place to another. The cost of shipping is proportionate to the weight and size of the package. Interplanetary deliveries are common and only add a slight additional charge. (In some cases it's actually easier to ship something from one planet to another than it is to ship something from one side of a planet to the other.)

Couriers: If you don't want to trust your goods to the postal service, you can pay extra to hire a courier who can deliver it by hand. Or by other appendage: most couriers are actually remotes operated by LAIs. Out on the colonial frontiers, couriers can sometimes be the *only* way for civilians to get something delivered.

VEHICLE COSTS

Although most transportation in the Human Sphere is handled as a service, there are many who enjoy possessing their own vehicles. The sample vehicles presented on p. 136–137 can be purchased using the *Vehicle Costs Table*.

OWNING VEHICLES

Owning a personal vehicle is still relatively common on Dawn and, for cultural reasons, on Bourak (where they're a point of pride) and in the Kuraimori region of Shentang (where they're a statement of independence). On Varuna they have a similar attitude to boats. Elsewhere, however, personal vehicle ownership is rare even in the countryside, where farming regions are more likely to share the use of a communal fleet of vehicles.

wormhole network / Circulars – p. 144

PART V: GAMEMASTER

RUNNING INFINITY ADVERSARIES

RUNNING INFINITY

In every game of *Infinity*, one player takes on a different role: that of the Gamemaster, or GM. It is the GM's responsibility to bring the worlds of the Human Sphere to life by playing the characters and describing the locations and events which surround the players' characters. This chapter is designed to provide an overview of the many tools available to the GM that can be used to lift games out of the alphanumeric realms into the visual and visceral.

GAME MASTERING 101

The GM's role encompasses that of player, adjudicator, and narrator. It is their responsibility to portray the cast of characters that the group will be required to interact with, make final decisions concerning rules, and present the storyline that binds the game together. GMing a game can be a fine balancing act along a Teseum-edged blade; remaining aware of the player characters' desires and abilities, adjusting the storyline and scene to their actions, stepping back to allow them to shine, stepping in to frame new scenes and present fresh content, reacting appropriately to unforeseen circumstances, and ultimately creating a fun environment for the benefit of all present.

Taking up this role can feel daunting and overwhelming, but the truth is that most GMing involves just a few easy steps mixed with a little patience, a little practice, and the amazing collaborative input offered by your players.

KNOW THE RULES
The first key to successful GMing is to understand the rules. The rules of *Infinity* are your toolkit, and, as the final arbitrator of those rules, you want to be able to quickly find the right tools and then use them efficiently. The more familiar you are with the rules, the more effective you can be.

How to Play Infinity – p. 28

Action Scenes – p. 97

Before running your first session, take the time to re-read the *How to Play Infinity* and *Action Scenes* chapters. After you have run your first few sessions, make a point of reading through the rulebook again: with the actual experience of play under your belt, you will be able to identify mistakes you may have been making or find new options you hadn't noticed before.

Make yourself a cheat sheet (or two!). For your first session, for example, it can be helpful to have the list of skills laid out on the table in front of you so that you can quickly identify what skill tests to call for. Then update your cheat sheet before the next session: There will be some stuff you realise would have been valuable to have at your fingertips. There will be other rules that you memorise so thoroughly that you don't need the quick reference any more.

The 2d20 System at the heart of *Infinity* is designed to be a streamlined and intuitive system, so it's likely that you will quickly master the flexible tools it gives you to work with. Things can get a little more complicated when it comes to gear and adversaries, however, where there are a lot of different options. So, print out copies of the NPCs you are planning to use as part of the next scenario; it's a lot easier to run an encounter if you can just glance at the stats you need instead of needing to flip through a book. Similarly, take a look at the equipment lists for the characters your players are running and make a cheat sheet describing any items you're not familiar with yet. (And when you *are* familiar with them, don't forget to take them off the sheet!) Include page references so that you can look up additional details if you need to.

Finally, do not be afraid to ask for help. Some of your players may know more about the rules of *Infinity* or the setting of the Human Sphere than you do; if you don't know the answer to a question, ask them for their expertise. It may also be prudent to nominate a player to research something in the rulebook while you work on keeping the rest of the scene in motion.

KNOW YOUR SCENARIO
Your scenario is the other half of your toolkit as a GM, because a good RPG scenario – unlike a book or a movie – is not made up of plots, but of tools. Or maybe *toys* are a better way to think of it. Where the rules are your toolkit, your scenario is a toybox. It's filled with a multitude of toys and running the scenario is all about picking up those toys and playing with them in fun and fascinating ways.

Using those toys to best effect is a matter of familiarity. Whether you are running a published scenario or one of your own design, take some time to review it before you run it. Look at the NPCs; figure out how they think and practice the sound of their voice. Look at the adversaries the PCs will be facing; think about the tactics they would use and the unique things they can do in a fight. Look at the locations; picture them in your mind's eye and explore their nooks and crannies.

Consider the premise of your scenario: The subtle shenanigans of the hypercorps. The deadly predations of the Combined Army. The internecine conflicts of the G-5 nations. Understand what the opponents of the PCs are trying to do and how they are planning to do it, so that once the PCs throw a spanner in the works, you will know exactly how those schemes will respond.

LISTEN TO THE PLAYERS

Roleplaying is all about making choices as if you were your character. The cool thing about a roleplaying game is that it allows you — through your character — to play out the impossible upon the fantastical landscape of the imagination.

As a GM, it is your privilege to facilitate these amazing roleplaying experiences for your players. You need to ensure that the choices they are making as their characters are *meaningful*. To do that, you have to remain open to the consequences of those choices: If the PCs decide to unexpectedly join the Atek cult instead of shutting it down, roll with the decision and see where it takes you. These unexpected twists and turns are at the very heart of what makes a roleplaying game special, and it makes things more exciting for you, too, because you will be discovering the adventure right along with your players!

BE PREPARED

In many groups, the GM is the one who is responsible for making the game run smoothly. This may include providing pencils and paper, dice, or other useful gaming aids (such as a dry erase board and glass beads for tracking zones in action scenes) — though, of course, some players may wish to provide their own. Some GMs may prefer to hold onto character sheets between sessions, ensuring that they are all in one place. (Alternatively, you might consider photographing copies of them with your phone just in case a backup is needed.) Keeping track of the little details such as these helps keep the game moving.

RAILROADING

Railroads happen when the GM negates a player's choice in order to enforce a preconceived outcome. Sometimes it can be a little too easy for a GM to want to force the PCs to take some particular action because it fits with their idea of how a scenario is supposed to play out, or to prevent them from "making a mistake". But the most memorable experiences are almost always those which arise organically out of the choices the players make; they are the unique events that nobody could have planned for.

RUNNING THE GAME

Once your preparation is complete, it is time to actually sit down with your players and begin the game. We talk about a GM "running" the game because it is their responsibility to coordinate and manage the session. While being responsive to the actions taken by the players is important, ultimately the GM is the one who controls the flow and pacing of the session.

FRAMING THE SCENE

The first thing you need to do is to describe the environment surrounding the players' characters: The players cannot make choices unless they know where their characters are and what's happening around them.

AGENDA

Start by identifying *why* you are describing this particular moment in the characters' lives instead of another. This is the *agenda* of the scene. Why are we here? Why is this moment important? Not every agenda needs to be portentous, but there should be some *reason* for the scene to exist, and this can often be thought of as a question in search of an answer: Will Rodrigo take the nitrocaine? Can they find the murder weapon? Will the Shasvastii assassin kill them? Will Melissa accept Moto.tronica's offer?

When setting the agenda for a scene, there's a very important maxim to keep in mind:

You may know where the scene begins, but you don't know where it ends.

You are not writing a book or filming a movie. Unlike a traditional author, you may know where you are starting off, but you have no idea where the journey will end.

Your starting point is the *bang*. The bang is the thing that forces the PCs to make one or more meaningful choices (or at least provokes them with the opportunity to do so). It is the explosive force that launches the scene and propels it forward.

Choosing a scene's bang is just as important as setting its agenda. For example, imagine that the PCs are exploring a crashed spaceship. You know that they are going to encounter a hulking Morat that is prowling the ship. Does the scene start when the Morat jumps out and snarls in their faces? Or does it start when they are approaching a compartment and they can hear it smashing apart crates?

Perhaps it starts when they see a corpse of one of the ship's crew strung up and tortured... and then hear the deep thudding of heavy footsteps coming from behind them as the Morat returns?

Each of those is a different bang, and you can see how changing the bang can dramatically shift the nature of the ensuing scene, even if all the other elements remain the same.

FILLING THE FRAME

Now it's time to describe the scene to your players. Here, again, we come back to the idea of *toys*: Take the who, what, where, and when of the scene and fill those elements with all sorts of toys that both you and your players can play with. These toys are the focal points for a liberated imagination, and the more flexible these toys become the more useful they will prove. If you include something with only a single utility, that's pretty good. But if you include something that can be used eight different ways, then you're really cooking with gas.

Location: The "when" and "where" of the scene. It is the immediate environment for the actions of the scene and it can be either claustrophobic ("the back room at the Blockhouse in Franklin County") or absurdly panoramic ("the icy wastes of Huangdi"). You want to try to keep your description of the scene short (minimalising contextualisation makes for a better bang), but you also want to make sure your players can truly see the scene their characters are seeing (and, of course, you want to include lots of toys for them to play with).

Characters: This is the "who" of the scene. You may find it useful to conceptually break these down into three categories: Leads, Features, and Extras.

Leads are the major characters of the scene. They are the characters most affected by the agenda of the scene or who are capable of having the greatest impact on the agenda of the scene.

Features are the supporting cast of the scene. They wield influence over the Leads; or provide crucial information; or are important resources in whatever conflict is being fought.

Extras are scene-dressing. They might find themselves being taken hostage or appealed to for mob justice, but they can usually just be thought of as part of the location instead of as active agents in the scene.

Player characters in a scene are almost always leads. You may find it useful to think of some PCs as being the leads in the scene while other PCs are features (because the agenda of the scene is primarily of interest to the former and of less interest

DESCRIPTION TIPS

Three of Five: Think about your five senses. Try to include three of them in your description. Sight is a gimme and Taste will rarely apply, so that means picking a couple out of Hearing, Smell, and Touch.

Two Cool Details: Try to include two irrelevant-but-cool details that aren't necessary for the scene to work, but are still nifty, interesting, and/or unique. It's the broken AR projector in the corner; the slightly noxious odor with no identifiable source; the Ateks Out! graffiti scrawled on the wall; the bio-luminescent fungal lights of the *avant garde* nightclub, and so forth.

to the latter), but if you have a scene where *none* of the PCs are leads you might want to take a moment and triple-check what you're doing. Unless you have some amazingly good reason for sidelining the PCs, it's probably a good idea to find a way of reframing the agenda of the scene.

Conflict vs. Colour: The "what" of a scene is, essentially, its agenda, but you may find it useful to categorise the scene as being primarily about either *conflict* or *colour*.

Conflict scenes are about two or more characters who want mutually exclusive things. The result might be a firefight, or a formal duel, a boardroom takeover, a political debate, a cyber-assault, or a torrid argument. Whatever form it takes, though, heads are going to butt and dice are probably going to be rolled.

Colour scenes, on the other hand, are about exposition, planning, and/or preparation. They are a time for character development; for showing what the PCs are like (and how they relate to each other) when MULTI rifles are not being shot at their heads. They are the scenes when your crew studies the blueprints and calls in their favours. They also provide a valuable contrast — a negative space to highlight the positive space; a moment of calm to emphasize the frenetic chase.

CUTTING THE SCENE
Not every scene will resolve its agenda. (In fact, it is possible that *most* of them won't.) But however a scene ends — a resolution, a dramatic exit, a victory, a flight — it is important to move the action quickly into the next scene.

To do that, start by asking yourself two questions: What is the current *intention* of the PCs? Does anything interrupt that intention?

If there is, in fact, an *obstacle* that interrupts their intention (an assassin ambushing them, a locked door, an unexpected encounter with an old friend) then the obstacle is your next scene. If there is no obstacle, then the intention is your next scene. (If they say "I want to talk to Yuen again", then the next scene is either about talking to Yuen or about whatever stops them from talking to Yuen.)

In either case, what you are doing is cutting to the next meaningful choice they are making, by either skipping over the "boring bits" inbetween or quickly eliding over them. (If they want to drive across town to Yuen's apartment, you don't need to ask them what route they are taking — unless that choice makes a difference; in which case, it's a *meaningful choice*, right? — you can just say, "Okay, you drive across town and pull up outside his

place." Or even, "Yuen opens the door. He's got a gun pointed at your face," if you want to aim for a stronger bang.

ADJUDICATING ACTION

The fundamental interaction of an RPG can be boiled down to:

> **GM**: What do you want do?
> **Player**: I want to do X.
> **GM**: When you try to do that, this happens. What do you want to do?

Everything else is just a variation of that basic theme. And from this we can see that the GM's core responsibility is *adjudicating action* — taking the player's statement that they want X to happen and determining what the result will be. This creates a cycle:

1. The player states their **intention**.
2. The **method** of achieving that intention is determined.
3. The action being attempted is **resolved**.
4. The **outcome** of the action is narrated.

INTENTION AND METHOD
Intention is the player's statement of what their character wants to accomplish. Method is how the character is accomplishing this. In actual play, intention and method are often conflated together, usually because people jump straight to the method. ("I want to shoot him with my Combi Rifle!" is a commonly stated method which is hiding the generic intention of, "I want to hurt him!")

Understanding the distinction between the two, however, can be valuable when the player declares an action and you do not understand what they are trying to do. If, for example, a player says, "I inspect the carpet," and you do not know *why* they want to do that, you should ask them.

> **Player**: I inspect the carpet.
> **GM**: What are you looking for?
> **Player**: You said it rained last night at 2 AM. If the killer entered through the window after 2 AM, there should be mud on the carpet.
> **GM**: (knowing the murder took place at 4 AM) Yup. It looks like somebody tried to clean it up, but you find some mud scraped onto the moulding near the window.

This is another general principle: *If you don't understand what your players are trying to achieve with a given action, find out before adjudicating the action.*

FORESHADOWING
Colour scenes are also where the facts get established that allow you to minimise contextualisation for later bangs. For example, if you know a character's long-lost brother is going to start randomly ghosting into their AR next week, it's more effective to seed information about the brother into a series of scenes leading up to that bang instead of trying to communicate the full meaning of the bang in the same moment that the brother shows up.

INTENTION, NO METHOD
Sometimes a lack of method can cause confusion. This often happens with social interactions: "I want to seduce the Reverend Moira." or "I convince the Clan Chief to give us the troops we need." These are statements of intention, but they notably lack any method for achieving that intention. Fortunately, the solution to this problem is pretty easy: "How do you do that?"

It should also be noted that intention is not the same thing as outcome. For example, if a player says, "I want to stab him through the chest with my sword!" that is not necessarily what will happen. It is not even necessarily what will happen *with a successful attack test*. (For example, they might make a successful attack test only to discover that the damage is soaked by their would-be victim's armoured clothing.) Determining that outcome is where resolution comes into play, and that requires the GM to make a *ruling* — to determine how the action will be resolved.

SPECTRUM OF GM FIAT
The easiest ruling for a GM to make is, "No."

Player: I want to jump over the chasm.
    GM: No.

Player: I want to convince Yamak Bey, the Silk Tycoon, to help us get hired as guards on the Silk Route.
    GM: He refuses to listen.

Player: I ask around Koryō to see if there are any rumours about Equinox activity in the area.
    GM: You don't find any.

When you use "no" everything is simple: There are no complications. No consequences. It is clean, tidy, and definitive in its finality.

That makes it an incredibly powerful tool. It is also why you should basically never use it. What you want to do is almost the exact opposite: *Default to yes*.

Player: I want to jump over the chasm.
    GM: Okay, you're on the other side.

Player: I want to convince Yamak Bey, the Silk Tycoon, to help us get hired as guards on the Silk Route.
    GM: He listens to your offer and agrees to help you get a position.

Player: I ask around Koryō to see if there are any rumours about Equinox activity in the area.
    GM: A couple of security guards at the Parangsaeui Jib Casino mention a security alert they saw about technical components being stolen from a Kiyometsu subsidiary.

"No" inherently stagnates the action. It leaves the situation unchanged. "Yes", on the other hand, implicitly moves the action forward: It creates a new situation to which both you and the players

will now be forced to respond. Now that they are on the other side of the chasm, what will they do? What dangers will they face on the Silk Route? Will the PCs be able to trace the thefts back to Equinox?

The problem with saying "yes", however, is that it lacks challenge. It is boring and predictable. (It is also not reflective of the way the world works: Failure, or potential failure, is part of life.) This means that we want to add another tool to your repertoire: *Yes, but...*

Player: I want to jump over the chasm.
    GM: Okay, but as you land on the other side you realise it's Paradiso quicksand.

Player: I want to convince Yamak Bey, the Silk Tycoon, to help us get hired as guards on the Silk Route.
    GM: He listens to your offer and seems intrigued, but he wants you to pass him secret information regarding the shipments of his rivals.

Player: I ask around Koryō to see if there are any rumours about Equinox activity in the area.
    GM: A couple of security guards at the Parangsaeui Jib Casino mention a security alert they saw about technical components being stolen from a Kiyometsu subsidiary. But as you're speaking with them, you notice a shadowy figure watching you from nearby...

"Yes, but..." adds to the idea proposed by the player. It enriches the player's contribution by making a contribution of your own. Unlike "no" it doesn't negate. Unlike "yes" it is not predictable.

But what happens if what the players want contradicts the known facts of the Human Sphere? For example, they want rumours of Equinox in the area, but you know there is no local Equinox cell. You may think this brings us back to "no", but we are not quite there yet. Generally speaking, the only time "no" is acceptable is if the intention directly contradicts the reality of the game world. So, before we get back to "no", we are going to make a pit stop at *No, but...*

Player: Can I find an Arachne node?
    GM: Yes.

Player: Can I find an Arachne node?
    GM: Yes, but you'll have to go to Mat'. The Nomads haven't gotten nodes this far out in the Dawn boondocks yet.

THAT WAS EASY
The other reason to default to yes is that, generally speaking, people succeed at most of the things they attempt. You want to drive downtown? Book Circular passage to Neoterra? Find some basic information by looking it up on Maya? Those are all things which are generally going to happen if you decide to do them.

Player: Is there an Arachne node in this town?
  GM: No, but there's one in Mat'.

Player: Is there an Arachne node here?
  GM: On an ALEPH Elysium orbital? No.

As you can see, *No, but...* is in many ways just *Yes, but...* looked at from a slightly different angle. Where a clear distinction does exist is when the method by which the character is attempting to achieve their intention is not viable: "*No*, that will not get you where you want to go. *But* here's an alternate way you could achieve that."

Collectively, this forms the spectrum of GM fiat:
- Yes
- Yes, but...
- No, but...
- No

And the reason we default to yes — i.e., start at the top of this spectrum and work our way down it — is because any requests made by the players generally reflect *things they want to do*. When they say, "I want to do X," what they are saying is, "I would find it fun if I could do X." And unless you have a really, really good reason for prohibiting them from doing those things, it is generally going to result in a better session if you can figure out (and offer them) a path by which they can do the things they want to do.

Sometimes they will reject that path. ("I don't want to go to Mat'. It's too far away.") That's OK. That means they're prioritising something else. But give

them the meaningful choice instead of taking it away. Choice, remember, is what roleplaying is all about.

If you are really struggling to avoid *No*, remember that a close cousin of *Yes, but...* is, "Tell me how you are doing that." It is basically the same thing, except you are prompting the player to think of their own "but".

Player: Can I build a nuclear bomb?
  GM: Okay. Tell me how you're doing that.
Player: Well... I'll need a source of enriched uranium. Can I use human terrain mapping to see if can find a hook-up in the black market?

This last exchange also reminds us that the great thing about a roleplaying game is that you are not limited to the spectrum of GM fiat. The 2d20 System gives you the ability to say, "I'm not sure. Let's find out."

SKILL AND DIFFICULTY

In turning to the game mechanics, you are, at the simplest level, saying that there is a variability in the potential outcome — there is a chance the intention will succeed and a chance the intention will fail.

Before we pick up the dice, however, we should take a moment to consider the potential failure state: Failure should be interesting, meaningful, or both. If it is neither, then you should not be rolling

ILL-SUITED SKILLS
In some cases, although multiple skills could be used, you may feel that one of the skills is less related to the task at hand than the other. In these cases, you might apply a difficulty penalty to the less-appropriate skill.

NOT SO SIMPLE

Severe difficulty factors, or a significant number of such factors, may also raise the difficulty of a Simple (D0) task, forcing a skill test when one would not ordinarily be required.

the dice. The clearest example of this is when the response to failure is to simply try it again:

> **Player**: I try to pick the lock.
> **GM**: You fail. What do you do?
> **Player**: I try to pick the lock again.
> **GM**: You fail. What do you do?
> **Player**: I try to pick the lock again.

This is the gatekeeper of mechanical resolution. If the gate is locked (i.e., failure is neither interesting nor meaningful) then you should go back to the spectrum of GM fiat and remember to *default to yes*.

(It is equally true that *success* should be interesting, meaningful, or both. But this generally takes care of itself because the players are not going to propose actions that they are not interested in achieving.)

USING SKILLS

The most common mechanic you'll use when making rulings as a GM is a skill test. This generally consists of two components: Identifying the skill and setting the difficulty.

Identifying which skill to use is pretty straightforward: The *Skills and Talents* chapter describes each skill and its general parameters. You just need to figure out which skill's parameters the proposed action fits, and this is usually pretty obvious. In some cases, you will find that the proposed action can fall into the purview of multiple skills. Generally speaking, you can just let the character use whichever skill is better for them.

SETTING DIFFICULTY

There are basically two ways of assigning difficulty:

First, you can look at a list of sample difficulties, like those on the *Difficulty Table*, and assign a difficulty by either description or analogy.

Second, you can start with an assumed difficulty of Average (D1) and adjust it by considering the possible difficulty factors that would influence that particular skill test. The *Difficulty Factors Table* provides guidelines for a number of such factors. (For example, trying to patch up a severe wound may be a Challenging (D2) test normally, but attempting

DIFFICULTY TABLE

NAME	SUCCESSES	EXAMPLES
Simple (D0)	0	Opening a slightly stuck door. Researching a widely known subject. Hitting a target at a shooting range with a bullet.
Average (D1)	1	Overcoming a simple lock. Researching a specialised subject. Shooting an enemy at optimal range.
Challenging (D2)	2	Overcoming a complex lock. Researching obscure information. Shooting an enemy at optimal range in poor light.
Daunting (D3)	3	Overcoming a complex lock in a hurry. Researching restricted information. Shooting an enemy at long range in poor light.
Dire (D4)	4	Overcoming a complex lock in a hurry, without the proper tools. Researching classified information. Shooting an enemy at long range, in poor light and heavy rain.
Epic (D5)	5	Overcoming a complex lock in a hurry, without the proper tools, and in the middle of a firefight. Researching a subject where the facts have been thoroughly redacted from official records. Shooting an enemy at extreme range in poor light and heavy rain.

DIFFICULTY FACTORS TABLE

DIFFICULTY FACTOR	EFFECT
Difficult Terrain	Slippery floors, sheer surfaces, deep snow, dense foliage, heaps of refuse, or even dense crowds.
Disruption or Distraction	Something directly interfering with the task or simply distracting from it.
Distance	If a skill is usable at a distance, each range category beyond Close inflicts a cumulative +1 difficulty.
Equipment	Tools that are damaged or of poor quality; or attempting a task with no tools at all.
Encumbrance	Hauling large amounts of material; or while wearing bulky/awkward clothing (like a vac suit).
Environment	Unusual gravity, poor oxygen, caustic atmospheres, or celestial phenomena (radiation, micrometeoroid showers, etc.).
Foreign Language	Social skill tests made in a language the character is not fluent in (assuming comlogs are unavailable for translation).
Lighting	Increasingly dark conditions – ranging from bright moonlight to complete darkness – pose progressively higher difficulty to Observation tests and other tests reliant on sight.
Noise	Loud noises can be detrimental, particularly if the test requires a character to be heard.
Random Motion	Strong winds, crashing waves, or simply the shifting of a moving vehicle.
Social Factors	Interacting with those who don't trust you, are of a rival faction, or otherwise hold an ill opinion of the character (see *Persuasion Factors*, p. 124).
Time	Situations where there is less time than would normally be allotted to the task.
Weather	Severe weather (wind, rain, snow, fog, etc.) can make any physical task difficult.

this in the back of a moving vehicle being driven at full speed might increase the difficulty to Daunting (D3).) Many of these factors can vary in their severity, possibly contributing multiple times to adjusting the difficulty of a test. (For example, spotting something in twilight is harder, but spotting something in the pitch darkness of a moonlit night is even harder yet.)

One feature to note about *Infinity* — particularly if you have experience running other roleplaying games — is that setting a precise difficulty level is not a significant feature of the game. In fact, at least 95% of the time you will basically be deciding whether a task is of Average (D1) difficulty or Challenging (D2) difficulty. (The higher difficulty ratings of Daunting, Dire, and Epic obviously exist, but can be incredibly difficult or even impossible for some characters to achieve under normal circumstances. As such, they should be rare in their application.)

The reason for this is because the *Infinity* system is far less interested in the simple binary of passing or failing the check, and is instead intensely interested in the *quality* of your success, which is measured and leveraged through the use of Momentum.

ENABLING MOMENTUM

Momentum is an incredibly flexible tool for describing the immediate consequences of success and for exploring the lingering or long-term impact of an action on an evolving scene. And the degree to which the relationship between the action that generated the Momentum and the effects created through the use of that Momentum is concrete or abstract is ultimately up to the players. (Although, generally speaking, causal relationships — X happens because of Y — are dramatically more interesting than spontaneous events.)

Regardless of how Momentum is used, the GM's first instinct should be to enable creativity. Here, too, they should *default to yes* — finding ways to make the proposed Momentum spend work.

Of course, that does not mean that they should allow Momentum to be abused. Improvised Momentum spends should generally be proportional to those hard-coded into the rules. In addition, Momentum should never be required to succeed at a test (that is just an increase in difficulty) and it generally should not duplicate a Harm Effect (that is shortcutting the system; if you want to inflict a Harm Effect, inflict a Harm Effect), although there are exceptions.

Momentum as a Moment of Awesome: The most straightforward application of Momentum is

to spike the action of a scene with something amazing, extraordinary, or unusual. These can either be moments of instant gratification (the extra successes from an action are immediately spent to accentuate the action itself) or a delayed reward (paying off later in the scene or even in a different scene).

Momentum as Build: Momentum can also serve as a flexible resource for building towards some ultimate goal over the course of several different actions. (Whether by a single character or the entire group.) The rules for a complex skill test provide a very structured way of doing this, but it can also be improvised through a more freeform accumulation.

Momentum as Preparation: One particular example of this is the explicit preparation for a later action or scene. For example, if a PC wants to get up to a better vantage point for shooting at an enemy, the GM can simply allow them to make an Acrobatics check — any Momentum generated represents the advantage of their newfound position.

Another common example is research, particularly when preparing for a heist or similar scenario. Although it is possible for such research and preparation to reveal specific information, the totality of it can also be represented abstractly through an accumulation of Momentum that can then be spent flexibly throughout the subsequent undertaking. (For example, a PC who has generated Momentum

---

ADVANCED SKILL TESTS

In addition to basic skill tests, *Infinity* includes a number of more advanced options for the GM to use to particular effect.

Complex/Progressive Tests: Use complex skill tests for actions that take longer to resolve compared to other actions being resolved simultaneously. (For example, hacking open a particularly stubborn door while the rest of the group holds off a Druze assault team.) Complex skill tests are statistically favourable to characters who are more skilled, so they can also be appropriate for involved activities where skill can minimise the role of random chance. (Playing a game of Chess, for example.) They can also be useful for abstract, multi-step resolutions when the individual steps are either variable or uncertain, but a single skill test is too simplistic for the situation.

Face-to-Face Tests: Any situation where two characters are competing with each other (either directly or otherwise) should be resolved as a face-to-face test.

Group Tests: Groups tests are, obviously, used to resolve actions where an entire group is acting in concert towards accomplishing a single objective. The GM should make sure that assistants are clearly stating *how* they are assisting; simply being in the vicinity of the character doing the work isn't sufficient.

Complication Tests: Complication tests are a mechanical way of determining if the action will result in a *Yes* or a *Yes, but...* (in the form of a complication). Complication tests can also be a way for PCs to generate Momentum, often making them useful for planning or prep activities.

RESEARCH TESTS

Research tests are used when characters wish to seek out information. They can be performed as general Maya searches or through the use of a specific resource (like the Vatican Archives on Neoterra). Research tests can be resolved with many different skills (depending on the topic being researched or the method of research), but Education, Science, and Tech are the most common skills used.

On a successful Research test, the character will generally receive the basic knowledge they're seeking. In addition, the players can ask the GM one question per Momentum spent. Research tests can also be a good way of using the optional Dedicated Momentum rule (see p. 409).

*O-12 Bureaus and
secondment* – p. 213

studying the blueprints of a black ops research facility might be able to spend that Momentum to duck into a convenient ventilation shaft later on.)

RUNNING ACTION SCENES

Action scenes pose a number of unique challenges for the GM, particularly when it comes to the triple battlefield of Warfare, Infowar, and Psywar.

ENCOUNTER DESIGN
Broadly speaking, an average combat encounter that challenges a group of player characters should consist of a number of Elite adversaries between one-and-a-half to two times the number of PCs.

Troopers count for half an Elite each (whether acting individually or in fireteams). Nemeses, on the other hand, can generally replace two Elites. No more than one Nemesis should be present in most scenes, though an occasional scene with multiple Nemeses can be an exciting change of pace.

Designing an effective encounter, however, still ultimately requires a degree of judgment on the part of the GM. With that in mind, there are a few additional factors to consider.

Number of Actions: If the adversaries have fewer available actions than the PCs, then they are much less likely to present a challenge. Because PCs act before adversaries (in most cases), a degree of redundancy is useful amongst adversaries, so having a few more adversary actions than there are PC actions (at least initially) allows the adversaries to take one or two casualties before they act without severely impacting the difficulty of the encounter.

Environmental Factors: A preponderance of cover or short lines of sight can favour melee and short-ranged shooting over longer-ranged weapons, while large open spaces and difficult terrain favour long-ranged shooting. Terrain can be deliberately set-up to favour one side over another, particularly if one side is defending an objective.

Heat: Spending Heat can amplify the potency of adversaries, or add new adversaries to the fight. By comparison, spending little or no Heat on adversaries during a scene can make them less effective, which can turn a challenging battle into a simple one. This can be used by the GM to scale encounters to the player characters' successes and failures – successful player characters can be met by stronger resistance – and to make later battles in a scenario more difficult.

SCENARIO DESIGN

Infinity is a roleplaying game of infinite possibilities. The Human Sphere – and the strange, alien worlds beyond it – are a limitless playground filled with thrilling adventures, brutal military campaigns, devious corporate machinations, science fiction wonders, top secret direct action missions, transhuman experimentation, Machiavellian political manoeuvres, frontier colonies, strange exoplanets, and deep space orbitals.

BUREAU NOIR CAMPAIGN
The default mode of play, however, is the Bureau Noir Campaign, with the players taking on the role of agents working for O-12's secret service. This agency is the perfect vehicle for exploring the myriad complexities of the Human Sphere because its services can be requested by any of the O-12 Bureaus – whether that's Bureau Aegis' police work; Bureau Gaea's scientific inquiries; Bureau Hermes' hypercorp liaisons; or Bureau Toth's monitoring of artificial intelligence. The process by which Bureau Noir agents can be assigned to these missions is referred to as secondment, and the *O-12* chapter has example mission types listed for every Bureau.

THREE CLUE RULE

The Bureau Noir structure means that most of your scenarios will be based around espionage – intrigue, conspiracy, subterfuge, and, above all, mystery.

When designing a mystery scenario, many GMs make the mistake of thinking of them as "bread crumb trails" – the PCs will find Clue A which tells them where to find Clue B which will tell them where to find Clue C which will tell them where the conclusion of the scenario is. This structure, however, is inherently very fragile and, thus, prone to failure: If the PCs to fail to look for Clue A, or fail to find Clue A, or fail to correctly interpret Clue A, then they will never be able to find Clue B. In order to salvage the scenario at that point, therefore, the GM must try to force one or more of those things to happen, which can be incredibly difficult to do at the best of times, and is frequently impossible to do in a way that is not awkward or unsatisfying.

The way to make a mystery scenario robust – and avoid this problem – is by invariably following the Three Clue Rule:

For any conclusion you want the PCs to make, include at least three clues.

DON'T GO QUIET!
In many RPGs it's not unusual for GMs to quietly resolve the actions of their NPCs during action scenes and then describe the outcome to the players. But you have to remember that, in *Infinity*, the PCs can perform Reactions! That means the players need to know what's happening in order to react to it before you've rolled the dice.

VARYING DIFFICULTY
The difficulty of encounters should be varied. The guidelines presented here offer a baseline designed to challenge the PCs, but they are only a starting point for GMs to create conflicts that are easier or more difficult (by varying the number and type of the opponents being faced).

PLAYTEST TIPS
By the time you've finished running a scenario you'll often have learned a lot about how you could have used it better. Some of these lessons can be applied to future scenarios, but, unfortunately, it's rare for a GM to have an opportunity to run the same scenario a second time. In published *Infinity* scenarios, however, you'll find Playtest Tip sidebars designed to share the insight we've gained during our playtests. They'll include suggestions for how to handle particular encounters, alert you to potential problem areas, and offer other "best practice" recommendations.

This creates redundancy: The players now have three opportunities to find a clue that will point them to Clue B1, B2, and B3. And each additional clue discovered gives them a different perspective (or additional information) that will help them draw the necessary conclusion.

NODE-BASED SCENARIO DESIGN

Let's define each investigatory nexus at which clues can potentially be found as a "node". (These nodes might be locations to physically search, people to be questioned, events to attend, dataspheres to infiltrate, or any number of other possibilities.) The basic implementation of the Three Clue Rule is still a linear structure: The three clues at Node A lead you to Node B; the three clues at Node B lead you to Node C; and so forth.

You can escape the limitations of this linear structure, however, by inverting the Three Clue Rule:

If the PCs have access to ANY three clues, they will reach at least ONE conclusion.

Using this methodology, Node A does not have three clues leading to Node B. Instead it has a clue leading to Node B, another clue leading to Node C, and a third clue leading to Node D. Odds are the PCs will find and figure out at least *one* of those clues and pursue their investigation. Let's say they go to Node C, where they find two clues pointing to Node B and a clue pointing to Node D. At this point they have access to three clues for Node B (including those from Node A) and two clues for Node D. Now they have *lots* of options for pursuing their investigation.

REVELATION LIST

When designing your mystery scenario, make a list of each conclusion you want the PCs to draw.

- Investigate the Jinsuo ammunition factory on Satori.
- Father-Knight Gabrielle de Fersen was there on the night of the murder.
- Journalists Peter Drigenberg and Mark Riley are going to be assassinated.

This is your Revelation List. For each revelation, make a list of three clues and where those clues can be found. (Note that each node is, itself, a revelation: The PCs need to know where to look.)

At its core, the Revelation List *is* your mystery scenario. Everything else is window dressing. During play you will also be able to use the Revelation List as a checklist: What clues have the PCs discovered? What clues have they missed? Is there a crucial revelation that they are in danger of missing?

ADVERSARY ROSTERS

Another common form of scenario structure is the "blueprint": You have a map with different rooms or areas marked with a numbered key and, of course, you have a text which uses the numbered key to describe those keyed areas.

The location described by the blueprint might be just one small part of a larger scenario — a node where clues can be discovered or bad guys can be fought. Or it might be the focal point for an entire scenario. (Like a casino that the PCs need to rob. Or an armed compound of nitrocaine smugglers that they need to root out and destroy. Or a pirate ship that they need to board and commandeer.)

Either way, the advantage of a well-executed blueprint scenario is that each keyed area is effectively "firewalled": As the GM, you generally only need to process and manage a single chunk of material (the current area) until the PCs move on to the next area (at which point you can just look at the next chunk of material). This makes blueprint scenarios very easy to run because everything you need is right there at your fingertips.

The drawback of this approach, however, is that it can result in static scenarios. The firewall, after all, works both ways: It limits the amount of information you need to process at any given time, but it isolates each chunk of content. What would be better is for the security guards in Area 21 to receive the emergency squawk from the remote in Area 20 and come running.

In order to add this dynamic element to location-based scenarios, *Infinity* uses adversary rosters. When using an adversary roster, you separate the occupants of a location from the location key: If the NPCs can move from one area to another, then they do not belong in the key for any specific area; they belong in the adversary roster.

This does increase the complexity of running the scenario, so if you're a first-time GM, you might want to run a few simple blueprint scenarios (with the opponents keyed to specific areas) before tackling the challenge, but you will find it takes surprisingly little practice before you are able to use the adversary roster to play your adversaries' reactions to the PCs in real time, allowing a location to come alive in an organic way which allows for great strategic depth.

ACTION GROUPS

The fundamental building block of the adversary roster is the *action group*. Generally speaking, you don't want to track every single Triad enforcer in a Yu Jing mansion individually, so you group them

PLAYTEST TIP
"OBVIOUS" CLUES
"This clue is really obvious! There is *no way* my players won't figure it out." You're likely wrong about this. For one thing, you're the one designing the scenario. You already know what the solution of the mystery is. *Of course* it's obvious to you. And even if you're right, so what? Having more clues isn't going to cause any problems. Why not be safe rather than sorry?

PLAYTEST TIP
CLUE-GIVING
More clues are always better. There is a natural impulse when designing a mystery to hold back information. After all, a mystery is defined by a lack of information. But the desire to hold back information does more harm than good. So if your players come up with a clever approach to their investigation, err on the side of rewarding that with new information. Don't think of your prepped clues as a straitjacket; think of them as your safety net. And *default to yes*.

OPTIONAL RULE
DEDICATED MOMENTUM
When building Momentum as a form of preparation, the GM may allow players to "bank" Momentum towards a specific purpose. (For example, Momentum gained from researching a Yakuza *oyabun* might be specifically set aside for a psyop targeting the *oyabun* or their associates.) This dedicated Momentum cannot be used for other purposes, but also does not deplete at the end of scenes or during action scenes. (This allows for such Momentum to build up gradually over the course of several scenes.)

together for easy management. For ease of use you can also label and/or number each group. (A label can also be useful for the keywords it provides: If you see a "Death Squad" and a "Perimeter Guard" on your adversary roster, it will be a helpful reminder of how each group will behave when the PCs show up.)

ACTION GROUP TYPES

Generally speaking, you can think of action groups as belonging to one of four different categories, defined by their behaviour.

Patrols make regular circuits through a location. They are indicated by keying their route (Patrol Areas 1, 5, 7, 7, 8, 2, 1).

Mobile is the default action group type. These are keyed to a specific location, but are generally willing and able to respond to the activities of the PCs.

Adversaries – p. 415

Mostly Stationary groups are unlikely to leave the area they are keyed to. This might be a choice on their part (they will not respond when the alarm is raised for whatever reason) or it may not (they are a remote that needs to be turned on). Adversaries waiting in ambush are another common type. But there is the possibility that these action groups might become active (usually because someone fetches them), so they should be included on the adversary roster.

Stationary adversaries will never leave the location they are in. You do not need to include these adversaries on the roster. Instead, they can be placed on the location key. (Since they will only be encountered in that area, there is no reason to clutter up the roster with them.) This might include literally immobile creatures, those simply uninterested in the rest of the complex, or NPCs who are imprisoned or sealed away until the PCs disturb them.

ADVANCED ACTION GROUPS

Variable Areas: Action groups (or individual characters) do not need to be limited to a specific area. This can be indicated on the roster as:

- Area 21 or Area 40: The GM simply decides during play where the NPC begins.
- Area 21 (40%) or Area 40 (60%): The location is randomly determined.
- Area 21 (day) or Area 40 (night): The group's location is dependent on the listed circumstances.

Notes/Footnotes: You can use footnotes to include additional information or cross-referencing. This can include:

- Adversaries carrying a specific item or piece of equipment. (This is useful when you have a bunch of different bad guys all using the same stat block, but only one of them is carrying X, Y, or Z.)
- Brief tactical notes. (Stuff like "monitored by the security geist" or "can see in the infrared spectrum".)
- If they have been classified as mostly stationary, why they have been classified that way (sleeping, in ambush, indifferent, etc.).
- Other notes regarding their activities (disguised as prisoners, playing poker, torturing Sebastian, etc.).

Multiple Rosters: In some cases, you may find it valuable to have multiple rosters of the same location. For example, one roster for Day and another for Night. A Normal and an Alert status are also often useful.

ROSTER UPDATES
Another advantage of using an adversary roster is that you can trivially update a location as adversaries are killed, replaced, or retasked without needing to redo the entire location key. If the PCs attack a Morat advance base on Paradiso and are forced to retreat, for example, they might discover that the Morat position has been reinforced by the time they return. That's easy to do if all you need to do is add additional adversaries to the roster.

FROM THE CIRCULAR FILE
The sample adversary roster on this page is taken from *Circular File*, a scenario which can be found in the *Infinity Quickstart Rules*.

SAMPLE ADVERSARY ROSTER

The Bone Spurs' first priority is notifying Al-Daran of an assault. Al-Daran will dispatch reinforcements to wherever attackers are believed to be. If pressed, the Bone Spurs will fall back to Al-Daran's location. If they feel particularly pressed — and their current location makes it feasible — Al-Daran will attempt to detach the *Sullied Marduk* from the Circular and escape.

BONE SPUR ROSTER–UNAWARE	
Bone Spur Hacker	Area 1
Al-Daran (40%)	Area 3 (40%) or Area 13 (60%)
3 Bone Spurs, 2 Bone Spurs (sleeping)	Area 4
1 Bone Spur	Area 8 or Area 9
1 Bone Spur	Area 11

BONE SPUR ROSTER–PREPARED	
2 Bone Spurs[1]	Area 2
2 Bone Spurs	Area 10
1 Bone Spur[2]	Area 11
2 Bone Spurs, Bone Spur Hacker[3]	Area 12
Al-Daran, 2 Bone Spurs	Area 13

[1] One disguised as a doctor.
[2] Hiding in cargo pod for ambush.
[3] Hiding in cargo pod, opposing quantronic attacks on *Sullied Marduk*.v

ROLEPLAYING TEMPLATES

In published scenarios for the *Infinity* roleplaying game you'll see that we use a roleplaying template to present significant non-player characters. (The featured NPCs in the *Adversaries* chapter also include a roleplaying template.) These templates have been designed to create distinct, easy-to-roleplay characters while also making sure that the essential information they have to present (like clues in a mystery scenario) are easy to find during play. You may find that using the template when designing your own scenarios is useful.

USING THE TEMPLATE

Name: Self-explanatory. (Hopefully.)

Appearance: This brief description is designed to be used when the PCs meet the NPC for the first time. It should be kept pithy. One or two sentences is the sweet spot. Three sentences is pretty much the maximum length you should use unless there is something truly and outrageously unusual about the character. Remember that you don't need to describe every single thing about them: Pick out their most interesting and unique features and let your players' imaginations paint in the rest.

Roleplaying: This is the heart of the template, but it should also be the shortest section. Two or three brief bullet points at most. You are looking to identify the essential elements which will "unlock" the character for you at a glance during play.

There are no firm rules here, but it can be useful to include at least one simple, physical action that you can perform while playing the character at the table. For example, maybe they tap their ear. Or they are constantly wearing a creepy smile. Or they arch their eyebrow. Or they speak with a particular accent or affectation. Or they clap their hands and rub them together. Or snap their fingers and point at the person they are talking to. Or make a point of taking a slow sip from their drink before responding to questions. You do not have to make a big deal of it and it will usually not be something that you do *constantly* (that gets annoying), but this mannerism is your *hook*: You will find that you can quickly get back into the character by simply performing the mannerism. It will make your players remember the NPC as a distinct individual. And it can even make playing scenes with multiple NPCs easier to run (because you can use the mannerisms to clearly distinguish the characters you are swapping between).

You will generally only need one mannerism. Maybe two. More than that and you have lost the simple utility of the mannerism in unnecessary complexity. It is not that the character's entire personality is this one thing; it is that the rest of the character's personality will flow out of you whenever you hit that touchstone.

Round this out with personality traits and general attitude. Are they friendly? Hostile? Greedy? Ruthless? Is there a particular negotiating tactic they like? Will they always offer you a drink? Will they fly into a rage if insulted? Will they always work Dog-Bowl or Aristeia! references into the conversation? But, again, keep it simple and to the point. You want to be able to glance at this section, process the information almost instantaneously, and start playing the character. You don't need a full-blown psychological profile and, in fact, that would be counterproductive.

Background: This section is narrative in nature (although you could certainly use bullet points in your own notes). You can let it breathe a bit more than the other sections if you like, but a little will still go a long way. One way to think of this section is in terms of *essential context* and *interesting anecdotes*. Is it something that will directly influence the decisions they make? Is it information the PCs are likely to discover about them? Is it an interesting story that the NPC might tell about themselves or (better yet) use as context for explaining something? Great. What you generally want to avoid is writing a short story about a random person filled with information that no one will ever see except yourself. Focus your attention on prepping material that is relevant to the players (or making the material you are interested in prepping relevant to them).

Key Info: In bullet point format, lay out the essential interaction or information the PCs are supposed to get from the NPC. The nature of this section will vary depending on the scenario and the NPC's role in it, but the most obvious example is a mystery scenario in which the NPC has a needed clue. Rather than burying that clue in the narrative of the NPC's background, you should yank it out and place it in a list here to make sure you don't lose track of it during play.

You could also use this to lay out the terms of employment being offered by a Warmonger. Or to list the discounts offered by a black market Lhost dealer. It's a flexible tool. In some cases, it might get quite long. But try to keep it well-organised (that's what the bullet points are for).

Stat Block: If you need stats for the NPC, you can drop them in at the bottom of the briefing sheet. (Or include a page reference to the *Adversaries* chapter that you can quickly flip to.)

WILDERNESS OF MIRRORS

Bureau Noir, p. 216: Refer to the *O-12* chapter for details on Bureau Noir commanding officers, black books, mission briefings, and agents.

faction handlers – p. 72

The final element of the Bureau Noir Campaign is the Wilderness of Mirrors. The term "wilderness of mirrors" was originally coined to describe the endless, confusing reflections of espionage, counterintelligence, double crosses, star chambers, and surreptitious secrecy in the intelligence community. It is also how you can reflect the fractious factions of the Human Sphere and vividly bring their conflicts to your gaming table.

Bureau Noir – like O-12 itself – is ostensibly a neutral agency and its agents are impartial and unaligned. But the reality is that the factions of the Human Sphere are pervasive. Every PC belongs to one of them, as determined during character creation. And, in a campaign using the wilderness of mirrors, every PC will have a faction handler who will assign them *covert objectives* in addition to the primary objective of each scenario.

The potential conflict, secrecy, and paranoia spawned by the pursuit of these covert objectives will add an extra layer of compelling complexity, spontaneity, and high-stakes drama to any scenario, creating a dynamic form of game play which is unique to *Infinity*.

SUBTERFUGE INTENSITY

When running an *Infinity* scenario, the GM needs to decide how many covert objectives to include. This is referred to as the *subterfuge intensity* of the scenario.

Using a single covert objective for each mission (while perhaps rotating which team member has a faction goal on subsequent missions) will lightly spice the campaign with complication.

As you raise the subterfuge intensity by adding additional covert objectives to the scenario, the possibility of PCs directly butting their heads as a result of incompatible agendas increases.

At the highest subterfuge intensities – where every PC gets a covert objective – scenarios become laced with paranoia in a complicated loop of espionage and counterintelligence.

Determining the correct subterfuge intensity for a scenario will depend on your group and the situation. Many players will enjoy the layers of nuance and risk which come with covert objectives, partaking with a Machiavellian glee. Others may be unwilling to juggle a covert objective; or become frustrated at the conflicting agendas.

PARANOIA LEVEL

The GM will also want to decide on the *paranoia level* for their campaign.

In a **Deep Cover** campaign, the faction loyalties of the PCs are concealed and their covert objectives for each mission are kept secret. Note-passing and other surreptitious means of communication will form a steady undercurrent in such campaigns as the PCs all invisibly wrangle for advantage and position.

In **Diplomatic Immunity** campaigns, the players, and possibly their PCs, know the faction loyalties of their compatriots, but everybody smiles at the polite fiction that they are all loyal, unbiased O-12 agents. In a campaign like this, it is possible that the covert objectives are openly known at the gaming table, even if the characters are not aware of them. Paranoia is lessened, but with the advantage that the players can all actively spectate on the entertaining machinations of their fellows.

In a **Faction United** campaign, all of the PCs belong to a single faction and they are all working together to pursue both their primary mission objective and their covert objective. In a campaign like this, the PCs could also easily be working for a factional intelligence agency (such as Hexas or the Black Hand) instead of Bureau Noir. (The covert objectives of the Wilderness of Mirrors also allow a GM to easily repurpose published scenarios for *Infinity* for such campaigns: For example, if the PCs are working for Yǎnjīng, the Yu Jing Military Intelligence Service, the GM can often use the Yu Jing factional goal as the scenario hook.)

Finally, in a **Loyal Agents** campaign the PCs have no faction goals and their only objective is the primary mission. As a variant of this paranoia level, it is also possible to have a **Rogue Agent** campaign, in which only one of the PCs is a traitor secretly pursuing faction-based goals.

COVERT OBJECTIVES

Creating effective covert objectives can be a tricky balance.

First, it is strongly recommended that the GM not use covert objectives which contravene the primary objective of the mission. (If the primary objective of the scenario is to save the PanOceanian ambassador, then no faction's covert objective should be to kill the PanOceanian ambassador.) What makes the wilderness of mirrors compelling is the tension between the common goals shared by the group and the conflict which exists between their secret agendas. When the group does not, in fact, share a common agenda (because one or more of them are trying to thwart that agenda), this tension disappears. Such scenarios are also more likely to be frustrating and unsatisfying as they fall apart in internecine conflicts.

The objectives should, obviously, be interesting. They also work best if they tie into the primary content of the scenario: The occasional covert objective which involves "doing this unrelated thing while you happen to be in the area" can be effective, but for the most part it simply distracts from the scenario at hand instead of contributing to it. (On the other hand, a covert objective which initially appears to be unrelated to the investigation only to eventually tie into it can be an effective twist if it is not overused.)

Similarly, it can also be effective for covert objectives to create an independent vector for finding clues in the main scenario. (For example, a PC is asked to tap a diplomatic comlog and the chatter they pick up ends up being related to the group's investigation. How can they explain their newfound lead without compromising their covert objective?) But, at the same time, you should be careful not to use covert objectives that involve one of the PCs already knowing the solution to the central mystery of the primary objective. For example, the group is trying to figure out the mystery of who is doing X, but a covert objective briefing ends up being, "We know that Y is doing X, so we need you to do this, that, or the other thing to X." It is too easy for such objectives to seriously deflate the primary mission.

Keep in mind, however, that covert objectives do not need to be delivered at the beginning of a scenario: A PC's faction handler can choose to contact them at any time (or vice versa). Thus, it is possible to wait until the PCs have figured out some crucial aspect of the case before being asked by the faction handler to pursue it for a covert objective.

It is generally more fun for everyone to have different covert objectives, although if there are multiple members of a single faction on the team they might get used to working together. You can also mix this up by having unexpected faction alliances. This can be particularly effective for non-national factions: For example, the Jingbai Corporation may be interested in getting access to Tohaa weaponry.

O-12 OBJECTIVES

O-12 is, by default, the "neutral faction"—their objective is the mission objective. In practice, however, this means that the covert objective of O-12 characters is often playing spoiler to the covert objectives of the other PCs.

That might result in a covert objective for a PC belonging to the Corporate faction, but, since they are also a Yu Jing-based corporation, it is possible that Yu Jing-allied PCs might get roped into assisting on the same mission.

Finally: Although covert objectives should not directly conflict with the primary mission objective of the scenario, there is absolutely no reason that covert objectives cannot conflict with *each other*. In fact, it is encouraged. It is the surest way to delve deep into the wilderness of mirrors.

THE CAMPAIGN

Most roleplaying games, *Infinity* included, operate on the premise that several sequential scenarios which follow each other will, together, form one whole campaign. An individual scenario may take several sessions of play to complete, whilst a campaign could feasibly run for several months, or even indefinitely.

One of the advantages of the Bureau Noir Campaign is that stringing scenarios together does not require much effort: By default, each scenario is a mission assigned by O-12. When the mission is completed, O-12 can simply assign the PCs another mission and the next scenario can begin.

Even while relying on this simple structure, however, it can be much more rewarding to tie the events of the scenarios together in some way, allowing the campaign to grow and develop as a whole. It can also be more exciting if, rather than having each mission begin as a clean slate, they can instead build upon one another.

FOLLOWING THE CLUES
One simple way to do this is to include clues in one scenario which, when pursued, lead to the next scenario. As you are seeding clues into each scenario, mix it up a bit. Some clues will be the "pay-off" for solving the previous mystery: The PCs clean up the local nitrocaine operation, but in the drug-kingpin's HQ they discover that the money is being used to fund a human-trafficking operation for the Acontecimento Mafia. You can also spread the clues around into earlier parts of the scenario, allowing the clues to slowly accumulate or perhaps even pointing to scenarios which are only tangentially related to the current one.

LAYING GROUNDWORK
A subtler way of giving cohesion to a campaign is to lay the groundwork for a scenario early. These are not direct clues that are designed to be pursued, but rather people, places, or concepts that can be established in the campaign before the scenario begins. For example, you might know that a hypercorp CEO will be playing a major role in an upcoming scenario, so you arrange for him to be at a party the PCs are attending. To prepare for the nitrocaine smuggling operation you might have the PCs begin encountering nitrocaine junkies. If you need a café to blow up on a live Maya broadcast, consider having the PCs coincidentally meet their faction handler there a few sessions earlier.

In published *Infinity* scenarios, you'll find Groundwork sidebars that give examples of how the GM can incorporate elements of the scenario into their campaign prior to running it. (These can make a big difference in helping to make a published scenario an organic part of your home campaign.)

SCENARIO THREADS
Scenario threads are the mirror image of groundwork. Whereas with groundwork you are looking ahead to scenarios you haven't run yet and incorporating their elements into your current scenarios, with scenario threads you are looking at the scenarios you have already run and thinking about how elements from them can be used in future scenarios, weaving them through the tapestry of your campaign.

Pay particular attention to the people or places that particularly resonated with your players: If something interests them or is clicking for them, finding ways to reincorporate it into the campaign is an almost guaranteed success.

As with Groundwork, published *Infinity* scenarios may include Scenario Threads — sidebars that suggest ways in which elements of the scenario could be revisited in later scenarios.

GAMEMASTER ADVERSARIES

The worlds of the Human Sphere are filled with all manner of colourful people, both hostile and personable — and sometimes both, depending on how you interact with them.

FIELDS OF EXPERTISE

The proficiencies and capabilities of characters and creatures are a complex matter. For non-player characters, listing all the same skills a player character is likely to possess provides an unnecessary degree of detail. In their place, non-player characters are listed with six Fields of Expertise, showing their skill in these broad areas as a single number. Whenever an NPC would be required to make a skill test, it uses the relevant Field of Expertise for its Expertise and Focus in the task. For example, a character with an Agility of 9 and Movement +2/1 attempting an Acrobatics test would have a target number of 11 and a Focus of 1 for that test.

The six Fields of Expertise, and the skills they encompass, are as follows:

Combat: This Field of Expertise covers the various tools and techniques for bringing death and destruction. It encompasses the skills Ballistics and Close Combat.

Fortitude: This Field of Expertise covers the means by which a character can survive in a hostile universe. It encompasses the skills Discipline, Extraplanetary, Resistance, and Survival.

Movement: This Field of Expertise covers the ways a character can move around a scene, both personally and using vehicles. It encompasses the skills Acrobatics, Athletics, Pilot, and Stealth.

Senses: This Field of Expertise covers the character's ability to perceive the world's details. It encompasses the skills Analysis and Observation.

Social: This Field of Expertise covers the character's ability to influence other creatures with ways other than force. It encompasses the skills Animal Handling, Command, Lifestyle, Persuade, and Psychology.

Technical: This Field of Expertise covers skills reliant on considerable intellect and knowledge. It encompasses the skills Education, Hacking, Medicine, Science, Tech, and Thievery.

ADVERSARY CATEGORIES

Adversaries in *Infinity* are classified as Troopers, Elites, or Nemeses, with each category representing a certain degree of capability and (in the case of action scenes) danger.

TROOPERS

Troopers are the rank and file. They often form the majority of enemy forces. But while most are talented and capable, against player characters they are only really useful in large numbers.
- Troopers only roll 1d20 on tests (although they can gain bonus dice normally).
- Troopers have Stress equal to one-half the associated attribute (rounding up).
- Troopers can only suffer one Wound or Metanoia before being eliminated, or one Breach before their network is shut down.
- Troopers cannot attempt Reactions.
- Trooper reinforcements cost 1 Heat per Trooper.

ELITES

Elite NPCs are a serious threat. Dangerous individually and more so in numbers, some bring specialist expertise and unusual tactics to bear, while others are simply more skilled and better equipped.
- Elites have Stress equal to the associated attribute.
- Elites can suffer two Wounds or Metanoia before being eliminated, or two Breaches before their network is shut down.
- Elite reinforcements cost 2 Heat per Elite.

NEMESES

A Nemesis is a truly terrifying foe. Possessed of a wide range of skills and abilities, plus the intelligence to wield them with ruthless efficiency, they are often found leading multiple groups of lesser adversaries.

TROOPER OR ELITE?
Some creatures can be used as either Elites or Troopers, representing exceptional individuals within otherwise humble ranks. In addition to being noted as such in the stat block header, these adversaries will include a separate set of Defence stats for their Elite version. Certain gear and special abilities may also be noted as "Elite", meaning that only the Elite version of the adversary possesses them.

BONUS DAMAGE FOR ADVERSARIES
NPCs gain bonus damage to their attacks based on their attributes just like PCs (p. 101). This bonus damage is pre-calculated into the adversary stat blocks found later in this chapter.

NEMESIS STRESS
Firewall: Intelligence + Technical
Resolve: Willpower + Fortitude
Vigour: Brawn + Fortitude

RPG FIRETEAMS

Unlike the miniature wargame, GMs are not limited to a single fireteam in the roleplaying game. They're a convenient tool for breaking up very large groups into discrete chunks that can be easily managed during action scenes.

TOHAA FIRETEAMS

The Tohaa make extensive use of fireteams, often fielding multiple squads in the same engagement, always consisting of exactly three units per fireteam. This has several advantages and drawbacks. First, Tohaa fireteams are always considered to have a leader, even if all the units are Troopers; as such, they always roll 4d20 on tests. On the other hand, they can never have fewer than three members, so if a Tohaa fireteam takes a casualty, it immediately ceases to function as a fireteam.

Called Shot – p. 113

EXAMPLE

FIRETEAM DAMAGE

A fireteam of five KTS mercenaries has ambushed Ken Ryo. Ken dives behind some cover and returns fire with his Vulkan shotgun. His attack is successful, so he rolls the 5+5 🄽 damage for his shotgun and gets a result of 7 damage and one effect. The mercenaries have 6 Vigour, but the first 5 points of damage is enough to inflict a Wound, which eliminates one of them. The mercenaries' Vigour track then resets to 6 and is reduced to 4 by the two remaining points of damage. Ken uses the effect he rolled to trigger the Knockdown quality on the Vulkan shotgun. This would effectively render all of the mercenaries prone (they'll need to wait until their comrade regains his feet), but they choose to instead eliminate one of their members (effectively leaving them behind).

- Nemeses calculate Stress as player characters do, adding the associated attributes and the relevant Field of Expertise together.
- Nemeses suffer damage as player characters do: affected by Harm Effects for the first three Breaches, Metanoia, or Wounds, becoming incapacitated upon the fourth, and being disabled entirely upon the fifth.
- Nemeses can spend 3 Heat to gain 1 Infinity Point.

FIRETEAMS

Many adversaries work effectively in groups, achieving more collectively than they could as individuals. **Fireteams** consist of up to five identical Troopers taking action as a single entity.

Stats: Fireteams have the same stat block as the Troopers which make it up.

Taking Action: When a fireteam takes an action requiring a test, nominate a single character within the group. This character is the one taking the action, for all intents and purposes. The fireteam then rolls a number of d20s equal to the number of characters in the fireteam.

Because the dice granted by a fireteam are a form of assistance (multiple characters contributing towards a single task), they do not count towards the normal limits of three bonus d20s. Consequently, fireteams can still benefit from bonus d20s in the normal ways (spending Heat, using resources, and so forth).

Action Scenes: In an action scene, the following rules apply to fireteams.
- A fireteam gets a single turn each combat round.
- A GM can have a fireteam interrupt the action order normally by spending 1 Heat. (The cost is for a single action, rather than the number of fireteam members.)
- A fireteam is considered a single target for the purposes of making an attack. (If necessary, a single member of the fireteam can be considered the "target" for purposes of calculating range or determining area of effect, although this generally should not be necessary since the fireteam takes action together and should always be in the same zone.)
- Like other Troopers, a fireteam cannot take a Reaction.

Fireteam Damage: If a fireteam takes enough damage to suffer one or more Harms, they suffer a single Harm of the appropriate type and then fully replenish the stress track. Any additional damage is then applied to the next member of the fireteam (i.e., the replenished stress track).

If the Harm was a Wound or Metanoia, instead of suffering the Harm, one member of the fireteam is eliminated.

The personal networks for a fireteam are linked together (to facilitate their cooperation and joint actions). A fireteam's network becomes incapacitated after suffering a number of Breaches equal to the number of members in the fireteam minus one, and their network is eliminated after suffering one additional Breach. All members of the fireteam suffer the effects of any Breach Effect inflicted on their network. If a fireteam member is eliminated, the fireteam also loses one Breach (although they continue suffering from any associated Breach Effect).

If a fireteam suffers a status effect, it can be applied to the entire group equally (a hindrance upon one member will impair all of them), or it can instead be negated by eliminating a single creature in the fireteam (the character is abandoned or voluntarily disengages to keep from slowing down the group).

LEADERS

In some cases, a fireteam will have an Elite or Nemesis NPC as their **leader**. When a fireteam has a leader, the following rules apply:
- The leader is considered a member of the fireteam, and the leader and fireteam act as a single entity, generally with the leader taking action while being assisted by the fireteam.
- When resolving tests, the leader rolls 2d20 plus one additional d20 per fireteam member. (The dice from the fireteam still come from assistance and do not count against the normal maximum of three bonus d20s.)
- When taking damage, the leader is always the last member of a fireteam to take damage, and they use their own Stress values. Attackers can spend 2 Momentum in order perform a Called Shot on the leader.
- Leaders are part of the fireteam's data network and suffer from Breach Effects that have been applied to the fireteam (and vice versa).
- A fireteam whose leader has been eliminated (or which becomes separated from their leader) continues as a normal fireteam.
- Fireteams with leaders are still unable to perform Reactions. (Fireteams normally can't in any case because they're Troopers, and even with a leader they lack the ability to make split-second responses). Leaders can still perform Reactions individually, but they do so without the support of their fireteam.

FIRETEAM HEAT SPENDS

Fireteams have a number of additional ways in which they can spend Heat.

Interpose: If an allied character within Reach is targeted by an attack, the fireteam can spend 1 Heat to have the attack target itself instead.

Special Weaponry: Some fireteams include special weapons or attacks that are employed only by a single character within the group. Using these special weapons or attacks costs 2 Heat; one character makes a separate attack instead of assisting during the rest of the fireteam's attack. This attack can be directed at the same target as the rest of the group or a different one.

CREATING ADVERSARIES

Creating new adversaries for the player characters to confront is as much an art as a science, and there are no hard-and-fast rules. However, GMs may find the following guidelines useful for creating Troopers, Elites, and Nemeses.

Troopers are the weakest category of adversary. Use this category for designing minions, mooks, and cannon fodder.
- Attributes should average 8. (Scores above 10 are rare.)
- Assign 6 ranks of training in Fields of Expertise, with no more than 2 ranks in the Expertise or Focus of any single Field.
- Troopers should have few, if any, special rules.
- Troopers will generally have simple, straightforward gear.

Elites are the default type of NPC. Although not as durable or driven as a player character, they can still provide a decent challenge.
- Attributes should average 9.
- Assign 12 ranks of training in Fields of Expertise, with no more than 3 ranks in the Expertise or Focus of any single Field.
- Some Elites may have one or two special rules and/or unique Heat spends.

Nemeses are unique and potent characters. They're an equal match for a single player character and should be used for significant threats and major rivals.
- Attributes should average 10. (Particularly powerful Nemeses may exceed this limit.)
- Assign 20 ranks of training in Fields of Expertise. One Field of Expertise may have ratings of four or five (equivalent to a player character's signature skills).

- Nemeses should have a number of interesting special rules and/or unique Heat spends, and the GM is encouraged to make them interact in fun and interesting ways.

CONVERTING FROM THE LIFEPATH

For an adversary, it's not necessary to strictly follow the character creation rules. The GM can pick and choose the options that fit the character they're trying to create. Simpler characters can be created by only making a few choices. (For example, Troopers can often be created by simply picking a Faction, Education, and a single Career.)

Once the GM has made the appropriate Lifepath choices, the Expertise and Focus for each skill should be calculated normally. To determine the adversary's Fields of Expertise, gather each skill into the appropriate Field and then pick the second highest Expertise and Focus in each, or the highest in the case of Combat and Senses, which contain only two skills each.

Finally, assign an appropriate category for the adversary using the guidelines above.

Lifepath – p. 38

COMMON SPECIAL ABILITIES

The following are a number of common rules and abilities possessed by creatures in 2d20 System games. These abilities will be referred to by name only in the individual NPC entries, and require you to refer back here for the specifics of each rule.

Fast Recovery (Stress X): Characters with this ability list a type of stress and a number. At the start of each of their turns, the character regains a quantity of stress equal to the number. The character can also expend Momentum to remove Harms associated with that stress. (The cost to remove one Harm is equal to the number of Harms of that type the creature is currently suffering from.)

Fear X: The character's form, nature, or raw presence is deeply unsettling. Whenever the creature attempts a Psywar attack based on fear, it gains bonus Momentum equal to X.

Grasping: On a successful melee attack, the character can grab its target by spending one or more Momentum. A grasped target cannot move or take any action except to attempt an Acrobatics or Athletics test to escape with a difficulty equal

EXAMPLE
FAST RECOVERY

An experimental Charontid with Fast Recovery (Firewall 2) would regain two points of Firewall at the start of each turn. If it had suffered a single Breach, it could also spend 1 Heat to remove it.

to the amount of Momentum spent. While the grasping character has a target grasped, it cannot make attacks against other foes, but it can reduce the difficulty of an Exploit action taken against the grasped target by one step.

Inured to X: The creature is immune to an environment or condition, such as vacuum, extremes of temperature, poison, disease, etc. Common conditions include:

- **Cold**: Provides immunity to the damage and effects of extreme cold.
- **Disease**: Provides immunity to the effects and symptoms of diseases. Immunity does not prevent the creature being a carrier.
- **Heat**: Provides immunity to the damage and effects of extreme heat, including fire.
- **Pain**: Incapable of feeling pain, the creature continues undeterred despite the most horrific agony. It cannot be Dazed or Staggered by physical attacks.
- **Poison**: Provides immunity to all forms of poison, venom, and toxin.
- **Vacuum**: Provides immunity to hard vacuum exposure, extremes of atmospheric pressure, and suffocation.

Keen Senses (sense type): One of the creature's senses — sight, hearing, or smell — is particularly keen. The creature reduces the difficulty of all Observation tests using that sense by two steps.

Unwieldy / Two-Handed weapons – p. 332

Knockdown, p. 337: Target must make Acrobatics/Athletics test with difficulty equal to number of Effects rolled or be knocked prone.

bonus damage, p. 101: Intelligence for Infowar, Personality for Psywar, Brawn for melee, Awareness for ranged.

stress, p. 71: Intelligence for Firewall, Willpower for Resolve, Vigour for Brawn.

NPC ALLIES

The majority of NPCs that interact with the rules are those that the player characters are in conflict with. In some cases, though, NPCs will end up working in direct support of the player characters. These NPC allies have a slightly different way of interacting with the rules. (It's not necessary to use these guidelines for every single friendly NPC. But they should be used for NPCs who are working directly with or under the command of the player characters, particularly if they're participating side-by-side in an action scene.)

Heat: NPC allies cannot use the Heat pool and their complications do not deplete the Heat pool. Instead, they generate and spend Heat and Momentum as if they were player characters. (Adding Heat to take reactions, saving Momentum to assist future actions, and so forth.)

Resources: The expendable resources of NPC allies (Reloads, Serum, Parts, and similar items) can still be handled abstractly, with the NPC ally spending Momentum (instead of the normal Heat) to gain the benefit of a single unit of a resource or to give the resource to a PC. (For particularly significant NPC allies you may wish to track resources explicitly instead of abstractly.)

Fireteams: Trooper NPCs can also form fireteams that support the PCs. In some cases, a PC may even be able to become the leader of an NPC fireteam, following the normal rules for fireteam leaders.

In many cases, it can be useful to let a player take direct control over their NPC allies. Playing multiple characters can be a challenge, but it's an exciting one!

Menacing X: When a Menacing creature enters a scene, the GM immediately adds X points to the Heat pool.

Mindless: The character is an unintelligent being, driven purely by instinct. Mindless creatures cannot attempt Reactions, are immune to any mind-influencing effects, and cannot suffer mental damage.

Monstrous: The considerable bulk and mass of this creature makes it less agile and graceful than smaller creatures and hinders it moving through confined spaces.

- +1 difficulty to tests where great size or weight would be problematic.
- Suffer a Wound following seven or more Vigour damage (instead of five).
- Not required to brace Unwieldy weapons.
- Use 2H weapons in one hand without penalty.
- Spend 1 Momentum before attacking to add Knockdown to its melee attacks for the current turn.

Night Vision: The creature's senses are keen, or use different wavelengths of light, allowing it to pierce the deepest darkness with ease. Tests the creature takes do not increase in difficulty as a result of darkness.

Quantronic Jump: The character has the ability to jump from one quantronic receptacle (such as a Lhost or remote) and into another. If the character is an adversary, the GM can choose to spend Heat to reintroduce them to the scene. Spend 1 Heat to reintroduce them within six rounds, 2 Heat for within four rounds, and 3 Heat for them to reappear at the end of the following round. A maximum of 6 Heat, in any combination, can be spent during each scene on this ability, which represents the total number of proxies hidden nearby.

Superhuman Attribute X: One or more of the character's attributes are beyond human. (Superhuman attributes, in addition to being noted in an adversary's Special Abilities section, will be noted next to the attribute in parentheses.)

- The character adds X automatic successes on tests with the relevant attribute.
- If an attribute normally grants bonus damage to a particular type of attack, the superhuman attribute adds +X damage to those attacks.
- If an attribute is normally used to determine a type of stress, the superhuman attribute adds +X to that damage track.

Threatening X: Powerful, dangerous and possessed of a vitality and drive that allows it to triumph where others might fail, the creature begins each scene with X Heat. Not drawn from the general Heat pool, these may only be used to benefit itself.

DENIZENS OF THE HUMAN SPHERE

TROOPER
112 EMERGENCYSERVICES

The 112 Emergency Service was established in Merovingia when it became clear that they needed a coordinated plan for rescue operations after the First Antipode Offensive. Since many Merovingian villages were often isolated and far apart, the government trained their rescue personnel in a wide array of emergency response methods. The average 112 Emergency Service member is able to provide emergency medical care, assist in putting out dangerous fires, and stand shoulder to shoulder with Ariadnan soldiers in defence of the public. The 112 Emergency Service model was so successful that the Ariadnan government decided to implement it across Dawn, and since its implementation there has been a noticeable decrease in loss of human life to accidents.

A member of the 112 Emergency Service will always put their life on the line to attempt to rescue or administer assistance to those in need, and will only withdraw if they feel the cause is completely lost or their actions would lead to more harm.

ATTRIBUTES

AGI	AWA	BRW	COO	INT	PER	WIL
8	9	9	7	8	7	8

FIELDS OF EXPERTISE

Combat	+1	–	Movement	+1	–	Social	–	–
Fortitude	+1	–	Senses	+1	–	Technical	+1	1

DEFENCES

Firewall	4	Resolve	4	Vigour	5
Security	–	Morale	2	Armour	1

ATTACKS
- **Teseum-Edged Breaching Axe**: Melee, 1+7 🅝 damage, Unbalanced, Anti-Materiel 2, Non-Hackable, Piercing 2, Spread 1, Vicious 2
- **Light Shotgun**: Range C, 1+5 🅝 damage, Burst 1, Unbalanced, Knockdown
- **Pistol**: Range R/C, 1+5 🅝 damage, Vicious 1

GEAR: Armoured Clothing (Firefighter's Uniform), Basic Medical Supplies, Portable Rescue Supply Kit

SPECIAL ABILITIES
- **Courage Under Fire**: Members of the 112 Service rapidly learn to tune out the battle around them. They can reroll one d20 when making a Discipline test, but must accept the new result.
- **Emergency Responder**: 112 Service Members can reroll one d20 when making a Medicine test, but must accept the new result. Additionally, they do not suffer the normal penalty for using a MedIKit to perform a Treat action at range.

TROOPER/ELITE
ACTIVIST

Wherever there is injustice in action, oppressed peoples to defend, or an axe to grind, there are activists. From the repressive regimes of Yu Jing to the anarchistic Nomad ships there are those who fight for an idealised universe. The vast majority of activists are *ad hoc* in their organisation and motivated by personal interest or plight, going to places that symbolise their interpretation of the greatest wrong. These activists include students, disenfranchised youth, family members affected by injustice, or victims of the state. The minority of activists are professional, having found talent and skill in their rabble-rousing efforts and earning a (somewhat) steady pay cheque from the cause *du jour*. Activists tend to be vocal, enthusiastic, and contentious to a fault.

ATTRIBUTES

AGI	AWA	BRW	COO	INT	PER	WIL
7	7	9	7	8	7	11

FIELDS OF EXPERTISE

Combat	+1	1	Movement	+1	1	Social	–	–
Fortitude	+1	1	Senses	–	–	Technical	+1	1

DEFENCES (TROOPER)

Firewall	4	Resolve	6	Vigour	5
Security	–	Morale	–	Armour	1

DEFENCES (ELITE)

Firewall	8	Resolve	11	Vigour	9
Security	2	Morale	1	Armour	2

ATTACKS
- **Improvised Weapon**: Melee, 1+4 🅝 damage, Improvised 2, Stun
- **Improvised Projectile**: Range C, 1+2 🅝 damage, Improvised 2, Thrown
- **Firebomb (Elite)**: Range M, 1+2 🅝 damage, Incendiary 2, Indiscriminate 2, Unsubtle
- **Stun Baton (Elite)**: Melee, 1+5 🅝 damage, Knockdown, Non-Hackable, Stun, Subtle 1

GEAR: Sports Padding

GEAR (ELITE): Anonymising Software (+2 Security), Ballistic Vest, Fake ID 1, MediKit

SPECIAL ABILITIES
- **Hell No! (1–3 Heat)**: Activists can spend 1 Heat to improve their Morale by one, to a maximum of 3 Heat and three bonus Morale.
- **We Won't Go! (2 Heat)**: Attempts to grapple, wrestle, or otherwise force movement on an Activist in a fireteam suffer +2 difficulty.

NEMESIS
ALEPH ASPECT – ASURA

In Vedic mythology, Asuras were the oldest of the gods; terrifying spirits devoted to destruction. In the Human Sphere, the ALEPH Aspects designated as Asura are terrifying operatives devoted to similar pursuits. Working individually or in small units, Asuras assault high-priority objectives, provide armed escort in hostile environments, or any other engagement where ALEPH requires the *crème de la crème* of its armed forces.

Among the finest heavy infantry in the Human Sphere, Asuras combine bleeding-edge Bodhisattva Lhosts with Aspects laser-focused on the art of combat and a disarming comfortability with the brutal calculus of warfare. The living embodiment of heartless arithmetic, they tirelessly carry out their objectives with mathematical precision, killing without hesitation and dying without question.

ATTRIBUTES

AGI	AWA	BRW	COO	INT	PER	WIL
10 (+1)	9 (+1)	11 (+1)	13	10	6	14

FIELDS OF EXPERTISE

Combat	+3	3	Movement	+1	1	Social	–	–
Fortitude	+5	5	Senses	+2	–	Technical	–	–

DEFENCES

Firewall	10	Resolve	19	Vigour	17
Security	–	Morale	6	Armour	4

ATTACKS
- **MULTI Rifle**: Range C/M, 2+6 🅝 damage, Burst 2, 2H, Comms, Expert 1, Medium MULTI, MULTI Light Mod, Vicious 1
  - *DA Mode (Secondary)*: Vicious 2
- **Teseum Chopper**: Melee, 2+7 🅝 damage, Unbalanced, Non-Hackable, Piercing 4, Vicious 2

GEAR: Absorbent Subdermal Armour (Subdermal Plating), Cube 2.0, Multispectral Visor 3

SPECIAL ABILITIES
- **Common Special Abilities**: Inured to Pain, Keen Senses (Hearing, Sight, Smell), Night Vision, Quantronic Jump, Superhuman Agility 1, Superhuman Awareness 1, Superhuman Brawn 1
- **Brutal Calculus**: Mercilessly precise, an Asura can reroll up to 3 🅝 when making a Ballistics or Close Combat attack, but must accept the new results. Additionally, they reduce the penalty for firing at a range other than a weapon's optimal range by one, to a minimum of 0. Finally, each point of Momentum or Heat paid to gain additional dice for a Close Combat test provides two bonus d20s, instead of one.
- **Heartless Arithmetic**: An Asura's calm commitment provides a Morale Soak of 6.
- **Relentless Tenacity**: Asuras are relentless and never weary. When making a Resistance test, they can reroll any dice that did not generate a success on the initial roll, but must accept the new results.

BALA PERDIDA AND ÉIRE

HIGHLANDER MERCENARY & WULVER

BACKER: EDU HERBOSA

Rosita glanced around at her fireteam. Margarida's eyes had the glistening look of having too many MediKit nannies in her blood. The docs would probably be able to save Alex's arm. But that left her and Santos as the only ones operating at full strength.

"We've got a clearing up ahead."

"Okay. Wedge up."

The whole operation had gone pear-shaped. When the Combined drop pods started raining down, Echo Platoon had been sent to form a defensive perimeter along the northern edge of Caracara to protect the villagers. But everything got turned around when the villagers came boiling up from behind them. It had taken them way too long to figure out that the entire settlement had been swarming with Shasvastii. In the chaos, they'd gotten cut off from the rest of their squad and now the comms had been eaten up by the static they called Paradiso pollen (probably from bug-eyed jamming).

"All clear."

The clearing ran parallel to their path. Maybe a hundred feet across, but a long gouge running vertically up to the peak and down towards Caracara. Probably cleared by some flow of lava and already being reclaimed by voracious Paradiso undergrowth. They were about halfway across it when the distinctive sound of a ship's engine caused their heads to turn on a swivel. But it was just a civilian shuttle lifting off from the village. Rosita could see Vulkan Tours—Paradiso emblazoned on its sides. Probably refugees.

But then there was a roaring sound coming from the peak. Turning in the opposite direction, Rosita saw that another round of Morat crash coffins were smashing down. They were being escorted by a uni-ship, but it suddenly turned and began racing down the peak—straight along the clearing; straight towards them; straight towards the shuttle lifting off behind them.

"What the hell is a Highlander doing up here? The AEC isn't part of this op."

Rosita spun back see what Margarida was talking about. Further down the clearing — maybe a half mile or so — there was a figure. Her visor zoomed and enhanced. There was no denying what she was seeing: The distinctive combat kilt was hard to miss.

"Oh my god," Santos muttered. "It's him. El Mercenario Escocés."

Rosita turned to Santos, dizzying herself slightly as the view through her visor snapped back to normal. "What?"

"The Mercenary!"

The distant figure hoisted a missile launcher onto his shoulder. It was as if he was challenging the uni-ship to single combat. There was a plume of smoke, a roar, and then the uni-ship exploded into shrapnel.

* * * * *

The jungle light that filtered through the dense cover barely reached the ground. It helped keep their little camp hidden. As the Highlander came striding up to the tent, Éire dropped out of the trees behind him with a playful little growl.

"It's all right. Your little friend is safe now. And I brought you a souvenir." He dropped a Morat combat medal at her feet. With a cry of glee, she seized it and began gnawing on it enthusiastically.

She really was the cutest little girl.

APPEARANCE

A tousle of brown hair tumbling down around a cheerful face framed by a tidy beard. He wears a tartan kilt and a thick, weatherproof forest green cape. A baby Wulver girl gives a tusky smile from his shoulder.

ROLEPLAYING

- Hides the truth between the endless ironic jokes he tells
- Has a heart for lost causes and large cleavage, will work for almost nothing for these kinds of people
- Never confirms anything about his own past — he hides the truth between his sarcastic jokes

BACKGROUND

Bala Perdida. The Mercenary. That's what the Irmandiños call him, but he's known by other names, too. Sgian dubh. Cat Dubh. One rumour claims he was originally Edward McGrass—corporal in the 45th Highlanders who got caught up in dubious debts and perhaps deeper trouble with off-world corporate fronts like Dia Cash and the *Bakunin Shop*. Joined the Ariadnan Expeditionary Corps to get out from under it. MIA during the Battle of Longxi in the defence of Bái Hai.

That would be where most people's stories end. They walk into war and they don't walk back out. But not Bala Perdida. He walks into legend. Still wearing a Caledonian uniform — although no longer an official one — his kilt and green cape begin cropping up here, there, and everywhere throughout the Human Sphere. And he leaves in his wake a kind of sign: A Jolly Roger of sorts, but with the skull replaced by a black cat and the shinbones by shotguns.

He is said to be unstoppable. He's said to have friends on every world. He works for a bowl of rice, a pretty face, or the promise of a hopeless task. He brings not a flurry of death, but rather the personification of Caledonian stubbornness: Implacable. Ceaseless. Relentless.

He rarely stays long in the same place, or works with the same people. The exception is the wee lass of a Wulver babe he carries on his back. Éire is her name. Bala Perdida and Éire. No one is certain if they share a family tie, but he's known to work with a pair of beautiful Wulver girls from time to time.

STATS (NEMESIS)

ATTRIBUTES

AGI	AWA	BRW	COO	INT	PER	WIL
9	10	11	10	9	9	12

FIELDS OF EXPERTISE

Combat	+3	2	Movement	+2	2	Social	–	–
Fortitude	+2	2	Senses	+2	1	Technical	+2	2

DEFENCES

Firewall	11	Resolve	14	Vigour	13
Security	–	Morale	–	Armour	2

ATTACKS

- **Flash Pulse**: Range M, 1+7 🅝 damage, Burst 1, 2H, Blinding, removes Marked
- **Boarding Shotgun**: Range C, 1+7 🅝 damage, Burst 1, 2H, Knockdown, Medium MULTI
  - *T2 Mode (Primary)*: Anti-Materiel 2, Piercing 2, Vicious 2
  - *DA Mode (Secondary)*: Vicious 2
- **Smoke Grenades**: Disposable, Indiscriminate (Close), Nonlethal, Smoke 2, Speculative Fire, Thrown
- **Claymore**: Melee, 1+8 🅝 damage, 2H, Non-Hackable, Spread 1, Vicious 2
- **Knife**: Melee, 1+5 🅝 damage, 1H, Concealed 1, Non-Hackable, Subtle 2, Thrown, Unforgiving 1

GEAR: Light Combat Armour (with Chameleonwear), Nav Suite, Survival Kit (Jungle) ×2

SPECIAL ABILITIES

- **Behind Enemy Lines**: Bala Perdida has spent an inordinate amount of time plying his trade in the dangerous wilds. He can reroll one d20 when making an Observation test, but must accept the new result.
- **Highlander Trained**: Bala Perdida has further honed his Highlander training over the years. He can reroll up to 3 🅝 when making a Combat test, but must accept the new results.
- **Master and Medic**: Bala Perdida's skills have been shaped by his companionship with different animals, leaving him remarkably self-sufficient. He suffers no penalties for attempting Tech tests without proper tools or facilities.
- **Papa Bear**: Bala Perdida's a jovial sort, quick to see the good in people. Even so, don't poke the bear. If Éire – or anyone else under his care – is placed in immediate danger (whether at the beginning of a scene or during it), immediately add 2 Heat to the GM's pool.

ELITE
ARMS DEALER

"Might makes right" is the motto of the gun traders. When making your point to a group of individuals that do not share your ideas, a loaded gun is a very useful bargaining tool. Arms dealers know this, that's why they offer high-quality merchandise to whoever can afford it. Gangers, paramilitary organisations, crazy cultists, or simple civilians – an arms dealer doesn't care who's buying, as long as the money's right. Loaded with the newest security implants, they are always looking to strike a deal. Make sure that you watch your back, however, or you might end up at the wrong end of the gun you wanted to buy. An arms dealer doesn't deal in loyalty.

ATTRIBUTES

AGI	AWA	BRW	COO	INT	PER	WIL
8	8	7	8	11	10	11

FIELDS OF EXPERTISE

Combat	+1	1	Movement	+1	–	Social	+3	2
Fortitude	–	–	Senses	+2	–	Technical	+1	1

DEFENCES

Firewall	11	Resolve	11	Vigour	7
Security	1	Morale	–	Armour	1

ATTACKS

- **Heavy Pistol**: Range R/C, 2+4 🅝 damage, Burst 1, Unbalanced, Unforgiving 1, Vicious 1

GEAR: AR Eye Implants, Armoured Clothing, Grey Market Firewall (+1 🅝 Security), Negotiator's Kit, Stims (×2)

SPECIAL ABILITIES

- **Common Abilties**: Keen Senses (Sight)
- **Demanding Partner (1–3 Heat)**: Negotiating with the Arms Dealer is mentally draining. At the conclusion of the process, the GM may spend up to 3 Heat to reflect the draining nature of the deal. Anyone that participated in the negotiation must succeed at a Discipline test with a difficulty equal to X or suffer X Resolve damage at the conclusion of the deal, where X is equal to the amount of Heat spent by the GM.

ELITE
ASSAULT PACK LEADER

Given the taks of organising and leading an Antipode pack in the field, the Assault Pack Leader has a job few soldiers envy. They must train for months in gruelling environments among captured or captivity-bred Antipodes (p. 462). Each pack is made up of an Antipodes trinary which has been biochemically altered to be receptive to the Leader's commands and surgically altered to respond to an Antipode Control Device (p. 361). Packs can sniff out enemies or traps with uncanny accuracy, and their speed, stealth, and brutality serve as a disruptive spearhead when thrust directly into enemy lines.

ATTRIBUTES

AGI	AWA	BRW	COO	INT	PER	WIL
10	8	8	10	12	12	10

FIELDS OF EXPERTISE

Combat	+1	1	Movement	+1	1	Social	+2	2
Fortitude	+1	1	Senses	+1	1	Technical	+1	1

DEFENCES

Firewall	12	Resolve	10	Vigour	8
Security	–	Morale	2	Armour	2

ATTACKS

- **Light Grenade Launcher**: Range M, 2+4 🅝 damage, Burst 1, Unbalanced, Munition, Speculative Fire + Grenade qualities
- **Marksman's Rifle**: Range L, 1+5 🅝 damage, Burst 2, 2H, Unforgiving 1
- **Pistol**: Range R/C, 1+4 🅝 damage, Vicious 1
- **Knife**: Melee, 1+3 🅝 damage, 1H, Concealed 1, Non-Hackable, Subtle 2, Thrown, Unforgiving 1

GEAR: Light Combat Armour, Antipode Control Device

SPECIAL ABILITIES

- **Assault Pack**: With their control device, a Pack Leader can coordinate their pack with a single thought. The fireteam formed by their pack can include Elite Antipodes. Unlike other fireteams, the pack can perform Reactions and pays one Heat less than the normal cost for doing so.
- **Pack Leader**: Leaders and pack members draw strength from their packs. They and their pack members benefit from a +2 Morale Soak when leading a pack (included in their profile above).

NOTES

Antipode Warriors fighting under the control of an Assault Pack Leader have a locational beacon implant. If the Pack Leader is no longer capable of controlling them, they will usually retreat.

ELITE
BAKUNIN MODERATOR

Diverse. Colourful. Manic. The corridors of *Bakunin* have been called many things, but conventional is not one of them. In a place with so few rules, who steps in when existing ones are broken? Who maintains a semblance of order in a place that embodies chaos?

Enter *Bakunin*'s tactical police unit, the Moderators, providing unconventional security for an unconventional environment.

As colourful as the communities they serve, and possessed of a disarming friendliness, the Moderators provide rapid crisis response, military security, and counterterrorism actions for the anything-goes playground of *Bakunin*. In this sea of diversity, a Moderator never truly knows what to expect; they have to be ready for anything. One moment, they're removing a Maya star from a vat of candied jelly, the next they're laying down suppressive fire in a counter-terrorism operation, all in the same day. That schedule would drive many insane.

For a Mod, that's Tuesday.

ATTRIBUTES

AGI	AWA	BRW	COO	INT	PER	WIL
10	9	8	9	11	8	8

FIELDS OF EXPERTISE

Combat	+1	1	Movement	+1	–	Social	+2	–
Fortitude	+2	–	Senses	+1	1	Technical	+3	–

DEFENCES

Firewall	11	Resolve	8	Vigour	8
Security	–	Morale	–	Armour	1

ATTACKS
- **Combi Rifle**: Range C/M, 1+6 🅝 damage, Burst 2, 2H, Expert 1, MULTI Light Mod, Vicious 1
- **Modhand**: Melee, 1+4 🅝 damage, 1H, Concealed 2, E/M, Stun, Subtle 1, Vicious 2
- **Modded Hacking Device**: CLAW-1, SWORD-1, SHIELD-1, GADGET-2, IC-2, UPGRADES (pick two), +2 🅝 damage

GEAR: Armoured Clothing, Short ModCoat (with Recorder and Stealth Repeater), SecurCuffs, Spotbot

SPECIAL ABILITIES
- **Paranoid**: This isn't the first time someone's tried to hack the Mods. In fact, it isn't the first time today. As a Reaction, the Moderator can respond to any Infowar attack with an Infowar attack of their own at +2 difficulty. This attack is resolved before the enemy attack, and if it causes a Breach, then the original attack is prevented.
- **Seen It All**: Some of it twice. When making an Observation test, the Moderator can reroll one d20, but must accept the new result.

ELITE
BODYGUARD

Clad in formal clothing and typically the roughest looking person in the room, it's not hard to spot a bodyguard at work. Normally found working for big shot celebrities and important businesspeople, a bodyguard ensures that only the right people can approach their employer and no one else.

Bodyguards routinely find themselves in violent situations that require an immediate resolution. Many bodyguards discretely equip themselves with top of the line personal weaponry and augmentations, to ensure they can eliminate threats and guarantee their charge's safety.

ATTRIBUTES

AGI	AWA	BRW	COO	INT	PER	WIL
9	9	10	9	8	8	10

FIELDS OF EXPERTISE

Combat	+3	1	Movement	+1	–	Social	+1	1
Fortitude	+1	1	Senses	+1	1	Technical	+1	–

DEFENCES

Firewall	8	Resolve	10	Vigour	10
Security	–	Morale	–	Armour	2

ATTACKS
- **Heavy Pistol**: Range R/C, 2+5 🅝 damage, Burst 1, Unbalanced, Unforgiving 1, Vicious 1
- **Collapsible Stun Baton**: Melee, 1+6 🅝 damage, Concealed 1, Knockdown, Stun, Subtle 1

GEAR: AR Eye Implants, Armoured Clothing (Formal), Subdermal Grafts (2 Armour)

SPECIAL ABILITIES
- **Bodyshield**: A Bodyguard can designate an NPC (or player character in some circumstances) to protect. The Bodyguard may take the Guard Reaction without the need to spend 1 Heat, though only in response to their designated charge being declared as the target of an attack.

ELITE
BOUNTY HUNTER

Most bounters are strictly licensed by the Syndicate (p. 208), required to obey the laws of the government whose territory they are operating in, and liable for hefty fines if there are casualties or wanton destruction left in their wake, there is still nothing scarier to someone on the run than the sight of a bounty hunter disembarking at a spaceport and nothing quite as relaxing as seeing one leave. Bounty hunters make a career out of capturing and detaining wanted criminals, becoming tough as the prey that they stalk and ten times meaner. Though they are required to obtain legal authorisation to operate, private and illegal bounty hunters stalk the fringes of society.

ATTRIBUTES

AGI	AWA	BRW	COO	INT	PER	WIL
12	10	9	9	8	7	8

FIELDS OF EXPERTISE

Combat	+3	1	Movement	+1	1	Social	+1	1
Fortitude	+1	–	Senses	+2	1	Technical	–	–

DEFENCES

Firewall	8	Resolve	8	Vigour	9
Security	–	Morale	–	Armour	2

ATTACKS
- **Combi Rifle**: Range C/M, 1+8 🅝 damage, Burst 2, 2H, Expert 1, MULTI Light Mod, Vicious 1
- **Stun Pistol**: Range R/C, 1+7 🅝 damage, Burst 1, 1H, Biotech, Nonlethal, Stun, Vicious 1
- **Breaker Sniper Rifle**: Range L, 1+10 🅝 damage, Burst 2, Unwieldy, Biotech, Breaker, Piercing 1, Unforgiving 2

GEAR: Light Combat Armour, SecurCuffs

SPECIAL ABILITIES
- **Common Special Abilities**: Inured to Pain 1, Menacing 1
- **Prepared**: A bounty hunter always scopes out the lay of land. Unless they are surprised outside of their home base, a bounty hunter has a dedicated pool of 4 Heat which the GM can use to purchase complications representing the booby traps and other preparations they've made (including potential reinforcements).
- **Detailed Anatomical Readouts**: The Bounty Hunter gains +1 🅝 to all damage rolls when making an attack (this is calculated into the attacks listed above).

ELITE
CELESTIAL GUARD

In Yu Jing, there is no greater honour than to serve the Emperor. And among the Imperial Service, there is no higher calling than to serve as part of the renowned Celestial Guard, the Fist of the Dragon.

First and always, the Guard protects the Emperor. But protection can often take a more active form, and the Emperor often deploys these loyal soldiers as military detachments or special police, always reporting directly to the throne; a fact that makes them few friends among their peers in the StateEmpire's army.

Granted functionally limitless authority to carry out arrests, search and seizure, and interrogations, their reputation for expeditious violence is well-earned. Between their robust network of informants, and their tendency to abduct people from their homes in the dead of night — never to be seen again — the average citizen often regards them with a measure of raw terror.

Respectfully.

ATTRIBUTES

AGI	AWA	BRW	COO	INT	PER	WIL
9	10	9	9	10	7	9

FIELDS OF EXPERTISE

Combat	+2	1	Movement	+1	1	Social	+1	1
Fortitude	+1	–	Senses	+2	1	Technical	+1	1

DEFENCES

Firewall	10	Resolve	9	Vigour	9
Security	2	Morale	–	Armour	4

ATTACKS
- **Combi Rifle**: Range C/M, 1+7 🅝 damage, Burst 2, 2H, Expert 1, MULTI Light Mod, Vicious 1
- **Upgraded Hacking Device**: CLAW-1, SWORD-1, SHIELD-1, GADGET-3, IC-3 + 1 🅝 bonus damage

GEAR: Aletheia Kit, Heavy Combat Armour, Recorder

SPECIAL ABILITIES
- **Fearsome Reputation**: It precedes them. The Celestial Guard gains +3 🅝 to Psywar attacks.
- **Tip of the Spear**: When leading a fireteam into action, the Guard can reroll up to 2 🅝 for a ranged attack, but must accept the new results.
- **Voice of the Dragon**: The Celestial Guard speaks with the Emperor's authority, and they're not shy about using it. They generate 1 additional Momentum on Command tests.

TROOPER/ELITE
CHIMERA

Throughout *Bakunin*, the practice of radical body modifications is constantly being pushed in new and different directions. Perhaps no one exemplifies this trend more completely than Chimera; individuals who have so fundamentally altered themselves through biografting and Silk augmentations that they could never be mistaken for "vanilla" humans. From fantastical to nightmarish, the VaudeVille BouBoutiques turn dreams into reality, and anything that clients can dream up is fair game. Provided, of course, they can pay.

Many Chimera consider themselves rising stars, but the reality is that few live to see a happy ending. Prostitution, pornography, and underground combat rings are common "first steps" in a Chimera's career, and most never move on.

A major fad for chimera are animal-like alterations: Cheetah, ram, fox, and wolf traits are common - some selected for fetishists; others for combat prowess.

ATTRIBUTES

AGI	AWA	BRW	COO	INT	PER	WIL
10	8	11	9	7	9	6

FIELDS OF EXPERTISE

Combat	+2	1	Movement	+1	1	Social	+2	1
Fortitude	+1	–	Senses	–	–	Technical	–	–

DEFENCES (TROOPER)

Firewall	4	Resolve	3	Vigour	6
Security	10	Morale	–	Armour	2

DEFENCES (ELITE)

Firewall	7	Resolve	6	Vigour	11
Security	10	Morale	–	Armour	2

ATTACKS
- **Chain-Colt**: Range C, 1+5 🅝 damage, Burst 1, 2H, Concealed 1, Torrent, Vicious 1

GEAR: Armoured Clothing, Cosmetic Augmentation 3, Grey Market Firewall (+1 🅝 to Security), Subdermal Grafts (2 Armour), Surge (×2)

SPECIAL ABILITIES
- **Chimera Ability**: Every chimera is unique. The GM can spend 2 Heat to give a chimera an ability based on their augmentations (+1 zone from movement actions for speed; +4 🅝 to unarmed strike to model claws, +2 Armour Soak to represent a thick hide, etc.). Elite Chimera have one such ability automatically.
- **Savage Charisma**: The Chimera adds +2 🅝 to Psywar attacks.

DANIYAL "WOLF" BAYAR

2ND DRUZE SHOCK TROOP "ALRRAMH"

BACKER: DANIEL MARGOLD

Daniyal schooled his mind to stillness and stopped himself from checking the chrono display of his combat visor again. He knew the waiting was almost over – he could sense it in the almost tangible charging of the air that so often occurred as the moment approached for his team to spring into violent action. The maintenance ducts of the caravanserai lacked heating and seemed to absorb the cold of the asteroid's external ice sheets, but the hours spent lurking within their chilly confines would not hamper him at all thanks to the circuitry of his combat armour.

"Aintalaq." Go. Muttered in Arabic across the team's comm channel, the command finally spurred Daniyal to action. He slipped stealthily from the maintenance duct and dropped into the hangar bay before ghosting between unmarked cargo crates towards the only ship currently docked there: a lightly armed freighter of the Crimson Khan corsair fleet. The soft glow spilling from the yawning ramp of the ship served as the only light source in the darkened interior; maintenance logs would show a critical failure in the hangar's power systems that would eventually lead to the airlock becoming compromised. There would be no calling card left at the end of this mission, it was a simple cleanse and purify. The Druze Elders would let the Crimson Khan know that they were no longer welcome here through more official channels. Checking his visor to confirm the position of his team, he kept his stubby Combi Rifle at the ready in his shoulder and observed over the sights as he hustled towards the waiting ramp.

Daniyal took to one knee beside some heavy crates close to the base of the ramp and kept both his rifle and eyes trained towards the ship's interior as the other three members of his team converged on his position. An innate understanding of their expected roles meant that his comrades rarely spoke unless required, but he wanted to make sure there were no surprises. "How are we looking Zaina?" he whispered as their tech specialist set to work on hacking the freighter's systems.

"Nearly done raqeeb, it shouldn't take longer than a few seconds," but even as she spoke the final few words, the interior lights of the ship flickered and dimmed. Daniyal paused for a moment to let his eyes adjust to his visor's night vision before sweeping his left arm forward in a chopping motion and springing towards the ramp. It was time to teach the Crimson Khan that the Druze were not to be crossed.

APPEARANCE

Tall and imposing, his close-cropped hair and intense grey eyes lend this unquestioning soldier a professional and unflinching aura.

ROLEPLAYING

- Generally appears to be in a grim mood, yet is quite mischievous when off duty
- Highly developed sense of camaraderie and protective of his team
- Extremely focused when on task

BACKGROUND

Daniyal was raised amongst the harsh environments and clandestine practices of the territories on Earth that are firmly under Druze Society "protection". A street urchin of the dusty stone streets, Daniyal brought himself to the attention of a renowned Druze Elder at an early age by sneaking into his high-security compound and stealing food for months before being caught. Rather than waste such talent, the Elder sent Daniyal to join the Druze Shock Troop training grounds located somewhere in the Nur Mountains.

Daniyal mastered every area of his training, but particularly excelled at stealth insertions that would often leave his enemies shocked and disoriented. The harsh training, enforced observances, and mandatory unquestioning loyalty were a small price to pay in Daniyal's eyes for the chance to gain everything that he had dreamed of: respect, the admiration of his peers, and a place in Druze Society.

Daniyal's sponsor, Branimir Yanev, attempted to lure him back into his personal guard once his training was complete, but Daniyal had been given the chance to experience interstellar travel with his new unit and grabbed it with both hands. Now an experienced campaigner, Daniyal has seen action in service to Druze Society across many fronts. His most recent assignment has led him to conduct covert operations from the depths of Druze Society's asteroid caravanserai in the Bourak system.

STATS (ELITE)

ATTRIBUTES

AGI	AWA	BRW	COO	INT	PER	WIL
9	10	10	10	8	8	8

FIELDS OF EXPERTISE

Combat	+3	–	Movement	+1	–	Social	+1	–
Fortitude	+2	2	Senses	+2	1	Technical	–	–

DEFENCES

Firewall	8	Resolve	8	Vigour	10
Security	–	Morale	–	Armour	3

ATTACKS

- **Combi Rifle**: Range C/M, 1+7 🅝 damage, Burst 2, 2H, Expert 1, MULTI Light Mod, Vicious 1
- **Pistol**: Range R/C, 1+6 🅝 damage, Burst 1, 1H, Vicious 1
- **Sword**: Melee, 1+7 🅝 damage, Unbalanced, Non-Hackable, Parry 2

GEAR: Medium Combat Armour, Multispectral Visor 2

SPECIAL ABILITIES

- **Druze Shock Tactics**: Indoctrinated from an early age, Daniyal augmented his natural stealth with deadly commando training. He can reroll one d20 when making a physical Stealth test, but must accept the new results.
- **Clear Shot**: Daniyal reduces the penalty for firing at a range other than the weapon's optimal range by one step (to a minimum of 0).
- **Tough as Nails, Grim as Old Boots**: Daniyal has survived injuries that would end most careers. When making Resistance tests, he can reroll any dice that did not generate a success on the initial roll, but must accept the new result.

NEMESIS

CHIMERA – ÜBERFALLKOMMANDO

Field agents of the Bakunin Moderator Corps, Vice Unit Sport Crimes section, the Überfallkommandos are tasked with breaking up illegal Aristeia! combat rings as well as associated criminals like bookies, loan sharks, and drug dealers. Due to the nature of their skillset, they're also deployed for urban combat and riot control. To accomplish this, they live with one foot in both worlds, as undercover agents.

Which means that every Überfallkommando agent is also a chimera.

With the full backing of the Moderator Corps behind them, they don't have to worry about faulty implants or shortcuts in their modifications, avoiding the patchwork quality that plague other chimera. But no matter how discreet their implants are, all Kommando agents tend to have a swagger in their step – a devil-may-care attitude usually reserved for elite martial artists, or executives with a net worth to rival a minor nation's GDP.

ATTRIBUTES

AGI	AWA	BRW	COO	INT	PER	WIL
11	9	13	8	8	11	10

FIELDS OF EXPERTISE

Combat	+4	4	Movement	+2	1	Social	+3	1
Fortitude	+2	–	Senses	+1	1	Technical	+1	–

DEFENCES

Firewall	9	Resolve	12	Vigour	15
Security	–	Morale	–	Armour	2

ATTACKS

- **Mk12**: Range M, 2+6 🅝 damage, Burst 3, 2H, Salvo (Knockdown)
- **Modhand**: Melee, 1+7 🅝 damage, 1H, Concealed 2, E/M, Stun, Subtle 1, Vicious 2
- **Viral Spiked Chain**: Melee, 1+9 🅝 damage, 1H, Biotech, Concealed 1, Extended Reach, Grievous, Piercing 1
- **Smoke Grenades**: Disposable, Indiscriminate (Close), Nonlethal, Smoke 2, Speculative Fire, Thrown

GEAR: Armoured Clothing (with Thermo-Optical Camouflage), Cosmetic Augmentation 3, Recorder, Subdermal Grafts (2 Armour)

SPECIAL ABILITIES

- **Chimera Abilities**: An Überfallkommando has the same special abilities as a Chimera (p. 423).
- **Natural Born Warrior**: The Überfallkommando's seen every combat style in the Human Sphere, and a few more besides. They do not pay Heat to use the Defence or Guard Reactions, and if successful, they add 1 Heat to the pool.
- **Riot Controller**: The Überfallkommando knows how to manage a crowd, one way or another. They gain an additional 2 Momentum on social skill tests to calm – or incite – a crowd.
- **Undercover Agent**: Years of undercover work have left their mark; the Überfallkommando gains 1 bonus Momentum on face-to-face tests to determine if they are lying.

ELITE

CLUB OWNER

From the trendiest nightclub to the seediest dive bar, there is one universal constant that reliably rears its head, heedless of whatever else is going on: The person in charge.

Club owners come in all shapes and sizes, but whether you're in a Yu Jing *keiretsu's* corporate teahouse, a retired mercenary's dive bar, or a Maya starlet's nightclub *du jour*, the club owners are sharp, savvy, and entirely capable of expressing their displeasure — especially with someone who's disrupted their evening.

Maybe they harbour a mean streak that could turn a Morat green with envy. Maybe they boast a vocabulary to make a Bakunian burlesque dancer blush. Or perhaps they eschew such antics, preferring to make a single politely worded request.

It's the last kind you really need to watch your step around: They tend not to ask twice.

ATTRIBUTES

AGI	AWA	BRW	COO	INT	PER	WIL
7	10	9	7	10	9	11

FIELDS OF EXPERTISE

Combat	+1	–	Movement	–	–	Social	+2	2
Fortitude	+1	–	Senses	+1	1	Technical	+2	2

DEFENCES

Firewall	10	Resolve	11	Vigour	9
Security	–	Morale	–	Armour	2

ATTACKS

- **Stun Baton**: Melee, 1+5 🅝 damage, 1H, Knockdown, Non-Hackable, Stun, Subtle 1
- **Contender**: Range M, 1+6 🅝 damage, Unbalanced, Anti-Materiel 1, Vicious 2

GEAR: Ballistic Vest, SecurCuffs

SPECIAL ABILITIES

- **Intimidator**: When attempting to intimidate an opponent, the Club Owner adds two d20s to their social skills test per Heat paid. The normal limit of three bonus d20s still applies.
- **On My Signal (2 Heat)**: The Club Owner hasn't been watching you since you set foot in the building; they have people for that. In a scene with a Club Owner, the GM reduces the Heat cost to summon reinforcements by 1.
- **Well-Connected**: A Club Owner performs counterintelligence tests at −1 difficulty. When assisting with Human Terrain Mapping, they roll 2d20 (instead of the normal 1d20). For 1 Heat, they can create a dyadic link one step removed from a target.

DANY YEN

ARIADNA SCOUT

BACKER: DENNY YAN

The harsh winds of the Ariadnan winter had been blasting Dany's face for hours with its salty bite. It was different than the wind in Tartary. It had a bitter quality to it. Just like being stuck in USAriadnan territory.

Sighting through his scope, he zoomed in on the figures in the ravine. They had made a tactically sound choice, as the walls shielded them from sight and some sensors. But not from him. He counted at least half a dozen TAGs and around two score infantry, all of them guns for hire. It was definitely Markov's old company. He spat in disgust.

Then his eye caught Markov himself, standing in the vanguard. Which was a problem, because Markov was dead. He'd killed himself. Blood on the winter snow.

Maybe this was some new spacer magic. Shaking his head, he crawled backwards and looked at the sky to appraise the weather. A storm was coming. Trapping the mercenaries here might kill some of them from exposure. If nothing else, it would slow them down. He loosened a charge from his back.

He set to work diligently and placed several charges among the higher parts of the ravine. As he laid in the ninth charge, a quick glance downwards showed him that they were almost past the optimum point of destruction. A shadow in the corner of his eye was the only warning he had. The blast missed him as he rolled aside and the face of a dead man smiled at him as he regained his feet.

"Who are you? Markov is dead." Dany brought up his gun as he circled, though his enemy clearly had the advantage at that close range.

"Ah. You knew him. Too bad. His face is quite useful."

A shiver ran down Dany's spine. Taking a careful step back, he retreated slowly from the edge. The thing followed his every move.

"You even sound like him, damn you," he muttered.

"Time to die," spat the creature.

Dany narrowly avoided a second blast as he triggered the charges. The huge explosion shook the ravine. Caught by surprise, the dead man tried to grasp at anything he could before the rocks started tumbling him down into the ravine. Watching him fall, Dany caught its face as it twitched for a second and something inhuman appeared underneath.

Heaving himself up onto the new edge of the precipice, Dany caught sight of two things before bullets forced him into cover: the dead man crawling out from beneath the rubble and two TAGs buried beneath it.

He rolled away from the edge and opened a channel to the outpost.

"Carson, this is Yen. We've got a problem."

APPEARANCE

Powerfully built and heavily scarred. Dark hair and eyes complement broad cheekbones, but thin lips give him a cold look.

ROLEPLAYING

- A loner, preferring the wilds over company
- Trusts his instincts
- Narrows his eyes in thought

BACKGROUND

Dany's story starts with blood. His mother gave birth to him during a border skirmish between Tartary and USAriadna. She did not survive. His father never recovered from her death and became an alcoholic.

At first, Dany sought company among the deserted streets, then went in search of isolation when he found none. Fortunately, Dawn has a lot of isolation to offer.

Most people he encountered pitied him or ignored him, so he chose to do the latter to most of them as well. His survival skills made him the perfect recruit as a scout for the Minutemen. Staying outside the settlements for weeks or months at a time, he became a ghost amongst legends.

He rarely returns to the settlements and prefers to be alone, pitting himself against the untamed nature of Dawn. A love for his home is the thing that makes him tick and he will defend it against any kind of threat.

STATS (ELITE)

ATTRIBUTES

AGI	AWA	BRW	COO	INT	PER	WIL
9	10	10	9	9	7	9

FIELDS OF EXPERTISE

Combat	+2	1	Movement	+1	1	Social	–	–
Fortitude	+3	1	Senses	+1	1	Technical	+1	–

DEFENCES

Firewall	9	Resolve	9	Vigour	10
Security	–	Morale	–	Armour	2

ATTACKS

- **Sniper Rifle**: Range L, 1+8 🄽 damage, Burst 2, Unwieldy, Unforgiving 2
- **Explosive Mine**: 2+5 🄽 damage, Burst 1, Comms, Disposable, Indiscriminate (Close), Spread 1, Unsubtle, Vicious 2
- **Pistol**: Range R/C, 1+6 🄽 damage, Burst 1, 1H, Vicious 1
- **Knife**: Melee, 1+5 🄽 damage, 1H, Concealed 1, Non-Hackable, Subtle 2, Thrown, Unforgiving 1

GEAR: Light Combat Armour (with Chameleonwear coating), Survival Kit (Arctic) ×2, Nav Suite

SPECIAL ABILITIES

- **Spectre of Dawn**: Dany prefers actions to words, and his actions speak quite clearly to those who threaten his home. He can reduce the penalty for shooting at a range other than weapon's optimal range by one step (to a minimum of 0). Further, taking a Called Shot requires only 1 Momentum (instead of the normal 2 Momentum).
- **Lone Wolf**: Dany has survived longer than most amongst the wilds of Dawn through skill, determination, and a little fortune. He adds 1 bonus Momentum to all Discipline and Resistance tests.
- **Stalking the Horizon**: Dany became a scout to not only fuel his own independence, but to test himself against the unforgiving wilds of his home. He adds one d20 to any Observation, Stealth, or Survival tests related to the Arctic environment.

CORP EXEC

Every corporation has its executives. The people with the power and the money. You can usually tell them from their smiles. It's the kind of smile which is so white you're in danger of being blinded; that's the whole point of course. If you're blind, you won't be able to tell whether it's a handshake or the sharp end of a knife you're being offered. Of course, executives have legions of bodyguards to call upon if things get nasty but that doesn't mean they can't be pretty handy on their own (especially if cornered). Able to afford the best gear, the best augmentations and mods, if you're going after someone who has managed to secure themselves on the executive board you best go heavy or you might not be going home. At least, not in one piece.

ATTRIBUTES

AGI	AWA	BRW	COO	INT	PER	WIL
8	10	7	7	10	10	11

FIELDS OF EXPERTISE

Combat	+1	–	Movement	+1	–	Social	+3	1
Fortitude	+1	–	Senses	+3	1	Technical	+1	–

DEFENCES

Firewall	10	Resolve	11	Vigour	7
Security	3	Morale	–	Armour	1

ATTACKS

- **Defensive Hacking Device**: CLAW-0, SWORD-0, SHIELD-3, GADGET-1, IC-3 +2 🄽 bonus damage
- **Nanopulser Necklace**: Melee, 1+4 🄽 damage, Biotech, Disposable, Subtle 3, Torrent, Vicious 1
- **Swordcane**: Melee, 1+4 🄽 damage, Unbalanced, Concealed 2, Non-Hackable, Parry 1, Vicious 1

GEAR: AR Eye Implants, AutoMediKit, Armoured Clothing (with Locational Beacon), Bespoke Firewall (+1 Security), Inlaid Palm Circuitry, Locational Beacon (implanted), Negotiator's Kit

SPECIAL ABILITIES

- **The Certainty of Wealth**: Any social skills test undertaken by a Corp Exec benefits from 1 bonus Momentum. Additionally, any Momentum or Heat spent to add extra dice to a Social test will add two d20s to the dice pool, instead of one.
- **Get the Big Guy!**: All Corp Execs travel with their bodyguards and keep them close. The GM reduces the Heat cost to summon reinforcements by 1. In addition, the Heat cost for a bodyguard performing a Guard Reaction against an attack targeting the Corp Exec is reduced by 2 (to a minimum of 0).
- **Slippery Bastard**: Corp Execs can regenerate their Firewall by 2, at the cost of 1 Heat.

CORPORATE SECURITY UNIT

Corporate security is an essential part of the Human Sphere. Espionage, hackers, privatised armies; the list of threats against corporations is long and dangerous. It is imperative to protect one's interests on the battlefield of interstellar business, and, where open shows of force fail, Corporate Security Units (CSUs) come into play.

CSU operatives are specially trained mercenaries hired out by SecLock Contingencies (although other outfits also offer comparable services). They offer complete security services to suit every need a client might need: personal protection, home security, corporate security, counter-espionage, counter-insurgency, anti-union actions, surveillance, VIP escorts, and facility security. CSU operatives stand out due to their impeccable training, seamless professionalism, and ultramodern equipment.

ATTRIBUTES

AGI	AWA	BRW	COO	INT	PER	WIL
8	9	9	9	10	10	8

FIELDS OF EXPERTISE

Combat	+1	1	Movement	+2	1	Social	+1	–
Fortitude	+1	–	Senses	+1	–	Technical	+1	–

DEFENCES (TROOPER)

Firewall	5	Resolve	4	Vigour	5
Security	1	Morale	–	Armour	2

DEFENCES (ELITE)

Firewall	10	Resolve	8	Vigour	9
Security	1	Morale	–	Armour	2

ATTACKS

- **CSU Combi Rifle**: Range C/M, 1+6 🄽 damage, Burst 2, 2H, Concealed 2, Expert 1, MULTI Light Mod, Vicious 1
- **Breaker Rifle**: Range M, 1+6 🄽 damage, Burst 2, 2H, MULTI Light Mod, Vicious 1

GEAR: Bespoke Firewall (+1 Security), CSU Armoured Clothing (Hidden Armour 3, Self-Repairing; with Stealth Repeater), Customised Disintegrating Briefcase for CSU Combi Rifle (Concealed 4)

SPECIAL ABILITIES

- **Corporate Infiltration**: CSUs infiltrate and bedevil their targets. They can reroll one d20 when making a Stealth or Thievery test, but must accept the new result. Additionally, they can substitute Stealth for Thievery when attempting to bypass physical security measures.
- **Enhanced Security (Elite)**: Elite CSUs have been physically augmented, possessing one of the following abilities (plus one additional ability for every 2 Heat spent): Fast Recovery (Vigour 1), Inured to X (pick one), Keen Senses (pick type), Night Vision, Superhuman Attribute 1 (pick one), –1 difficulty on Observation tests, +2 Armour Soak (subdermal armour or enhanced skin). The same ability can be selected multiple times; the effects stack where appropriate.

TROOPER/ELITE
CUSTOMS AGENT

Customs agents are empowered officers tasked with intercepting potential threats to their countries and ensuring they are stopped. Utilising lightweight combat gear to allow them to blend into the crowds they police if necessary, they are commonly equipped with ident-scanners or high priority access to the data servers that contain the records of each civilian, criminal, and known foreign agents.

Inquisitive and determined, these agents stand ready at spaceports and docking centres to apprehend those that would threaten their country. They have also been known to be deployed to apprehend illegal immigrants through carefully planned raids in domestic areas.

ATTRIBUTES						
AGI	AWA	BRW	COO	INT	PER	WIL
8	9	8	9	10	8	10

FIELDS OF EXPERTISE						
Combat	+1	1	Movement	+1	–	Social	+1	–
Fortitude	+1	–	Senses	+2	1	Technical	+1	–

DEFENCES (TROOPER)					
Firewall	5	Resolve	5	Vigour	4
Security	1	Morale	–	Armour	2

DEFENCES (ELITE)					
Firewall	10	Resolve	10	Vigour	8
Security	1	Morale	–	Armour	2

ATTACKS
- **Stun Pistol**: Range R/C, 1+5 🄽 damage, Burst 1, 1H, Biotech, Nonlethal, Stun
- **Submachine Gun (Elite)**: Range C, 1+5 🄽 damage, Burst 2, Unbalanced, Spread 1

GEAR: Armoured Clothing (Nondescript), SecurCuffs

SPECIAL ABILITIES
- **Identity Scan (1–2 Heat)**: Customs Agents have access to unique identification databases. The GM can reduce the effective rating of a Fake ID by 1 by spending 1 Heat or by 2 by spending 3 Heat.
- **Keen Eyes (Elite)**: An Elite Customs Agent can reroll one d20 when making an Observation test, but must accept the new result.

ELITE
DETECTIVE

Even detectives who aren't currently on the police force were often officers at some point in the past. But whether working within the police force, as independent contractors, or as hypercorp employees, detectives are skilled in ferreting out concealed truths.

The typical detective is no stranger to fighting. Most are also skilled in both surveillance and counter-surveillance. They're more often than not sharp-minded and charming people.

Of course, some detectives are the last people you expect. (Like the little old lady who leaves a trail of bodies in her wake.)

ATTRIBUTES						
AGI	AWA	BRW	COO	INT	PER	WIL
8	10	8	9	10	9	9

FIELDS OF EXPERTISE						
Combat	+2	–	Movement	+1	–	Social	+2	1
Fortitude	+1	–	Senses	+2	1	Technical	+1	1

DEFENCES					
Firewall	10	Resolve	9	Vigour	8
Security	–	Morale	–	Armour	–

ATTACKS
- **Stun Pistol**: Range R/C, 1+5 🄽 damage, Burst 1, 1H, Biotech, Nonlethal, Stun

GEAR: Analytical Kit, Forensics Kit 1

SPECIAL ABILITIES
- **Case Closed**: Detectives are street savvy and astute. They can reroll one d20 when making an Analysis, Education, or Thievery test, but must accept the new result. Additionally, when making a Persuade or Education test relating to or interacting with the criminal element, they gain 2 bonus Momentum.
- **Undercover Specialist (1–3 Heat)**: The Detective can add the Concealed X property to any item small enough to be held on their body by paying Heat equal to X (to a maximum of 3).

NEMESIS
DETECTIVE, GREAT

The astute mind of a truly great detective is methodical, encyclopaedic, and occasionally labyrinthine in its complexities. Their deep understanding of crime and its perpetrators is an invaluable resource to the circles they operate in, and their help can dramatically speed up an investigation.

Such detectives are skilled in the scientific apparatus of modern criminal investigation, but also capable of astounding intuitive leaps that can seem almost mystical to the layman.

Some of these detectives have earned reputations which have propelled them to minor levels of Maya stardom. Their exploits are recorded by stalkers, companions, and themselves (even, in some cases, through Maya life-casts).

ATTRIBUTES						
AGI	AWA	BRW	COO	INT	PER	WIL
9	11	9	10	11	10	10

FIELDS OF EXPERTISE						
Combat	+1	1	Movement	+1	–	Social	+4	1
Fortitude	+1	1	Senses	+4	4	Technical	+2	1

DEFENCES					
Firewall	12	Resolve	11	Vigour	10
Security	–	Morale	–	Armour	–

ATTACKS
- **Pistol**: Range R/C, 1+6 🄽 damage, Burst 1, 1H, Vicious 1

GEAR: Analytical Kit, AR Eye Implants, Disguise Kit, Forensics Kit 2

SPECIAL ABILITIES
- **Case Closed**: Detectives are street savvy and astute. They can reroll one d20 when making an Analysis, Education, or Thievery test, but must accept the new result. Additionally, when making a Persuade or Education test relating to or interacting with the criminal element, they gain 2 bonus Momentum.
- **Predictive Boxing**: When attacking with an Unarmed Strike, the Great Detective can make their attack using a Senses test (instead of a Combat test). They have the uncanny ability to analyse and predict their opponent's blows and physical movements before they occur.
- **Sleuth's Network (1 Heat)**: By spending 1 Heat, the Great Detective can call in a specialist with a narrow focus in the area of expertise required by the current investigation. This specialist can assist skill tests associated with the investigation by rolling 2d20 (instead of the normal 1d20).

ELITE
DOCTOR

The practice of medicine in the Human Sphere has evolved past the rigid practice of hard science and the pursuit of empirical knowledge. With the advent of geists, Silk tech, genetic applications, and all manner of life-altering implements, a doctor has become more than just a practitioner of the healing arts. Doctors around the Sphere perfect their craft with artistry and precision, marrying technology and aesthetics towards a personal vision of human and posthuman perfection. Most doctors in the Sphere specialise based on technology and intervention, as opposed to specific disease types or parts of the body as was the case in the past. Nanosurgeons, Silkcrafters, graft experts, aesthetic reshapers, genetic composers, and radical traumatists are just a few of these specialties. While they may vary in craft and approach, as a whole they tend to be driven, arrogant, and flirt with amorality when it suits them.

ATTRIBUTES

AGI	AWA	BRW	COO	INT	PER	WIL
7	9	7	11	12	9	8

FIELDS OF EXPERTISE

Combat	–	–	Movement	–	–	Social	+2	1
Fortitude	+1	1	Senses	+1	1	Technical	+3	2

DEFENCES

Firewall	12	Resolve	8	Vigour	7
Security	–	Morale	–	Armour	–

ATTACKS
- **Monomolecular Scalpel**: Melee, 1+3 🟣 damage, Concealed 1, Improvised, Non-Hackable, Subtle 2, Unforgiving 3, loses Unforgiving vs. any armour

GEAR: Basic Medical Supplies, Bioscanner, Medical Clothing (adds +2 BTS), MediKit

SPECIAL ABILITIES
- **Heal Thyself (or Another)**: The Doctor can reroll one d20 when making a Medicine test, but must accept the new result. Additionally, they do not suffer the normal penalty for using a MediKit to perform a Treat action at range. Further, each dose of Serum used by a Doctor adds two bonus d20s to Medicine tests, instead of one. Finally, performing a Treatment test on themselves does not increase the difficulty of the test by two.
- **Spike 'em**: A Doctor can whip up a supplement, stimulant or medical cocktail for any situation to make an ally or adversary more potent. They may spend 2 Heat and attempt a Challenging (D2) treat test on a target. If successful, the target improves one Attribute of the Doctor's choice by two for the remainder of the scene. If unsuccessful, the target must succeed at a Resistance (D2) test or suffer 1+2 🟣 damage with the Stun quality that ignores Soak.
- **Shutdown Protocol(2 Heat)**: Following a successful treat test on a target, a Doctor may spend 2 Heat to shut down any non-vital implant or augmentation. This effect persists until a Hacking (D1) check can be made against the affected implant or augmentation.

ELITE
DIPLOMAT

The Human Sphere is fractured. Nations clash over territory, hypercorps deploy "deniable assets" against their rivals, while PanOceania and Yu Jing seem poised to rip out each other's throats at a moment's notice. If that wasn't enough, here come the Tohaa: pushing an unknown agenda and exacerbating existing tensions. Looking at the situation, it can feel like nothing short of a miracle could prevent a CODE *INFINITY* and stop the Human Sphere from descending into chaos.

Enter the diplomat: miracles are their specialty.

Diplomacy in the Human Sphere can feel like a blindfolded tightrope walk across a volcano, yet somehow these expert negotiators manage the feat with grace and dignity. Skilled at gauging the mood of any room they're in, students of psychology and persuasion, a good diplomat uses every tool at their disposal to benefit those they represent. And sometimes, that takes a miracle.

ATTRIBUTES

AGI	AWA	BRW	COO	INT	PER	WIL
7	9	7	7	9	12	12

FIELDS OF EXPERTISE

Combat	–	–	Movement	–	–	Social	+3	3
Fortitude	–	–	Senses	+3	3	Technical	–	–

DEFENCES

Firewall	9	Resolve	12	Vigour	7
Security	–	Morale	–	Armour	–

ATTACKS
- **Nanopulser Necklace**: Melee, 1+4 🟣 damage, Biotech, Disposable, Subtle 3, Torrent, Vicious 1
- **Banshee Pistol**: Range R/C, 1+5 🟣 damage, Burst 1, 1H, Area (Close), Deafening, Nonlethal, Stun, Terrifying 3, Vicious 1

GEAR: Armoured Clothing, Negotiator's Kit, Strong Painkillers (×2), Stims (×1)

SPECIAL ABILITIES
- **Cooler Heads**: The Diplomat has spent a career talking people off of ledges, not all of them metaphorical. When attempting to inflict a Metanoia Effect to dissuade someone from violent action, the target's Intransigence is lowered by 2 (to a minimum of 1). If their Intransigence was already at 1, the Diplomat generates 2 bonus Momentum on each social skills test.
- **Stubborn**: The Diplomat can reroll one d20 when making a Discipline test, but must accept the new result.

DELPHYNE
SOPHOTECT DINOSAUR

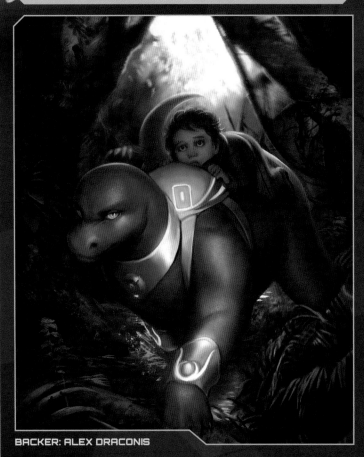

BACKER: ALEX DRACONIS

"Status report on the evac."

"Most children are on board, but I can't see the accompanying Sophotect, sir."

The colourful shuttle emblazoned Vulkan Tours – Paradiso *was ready to go. Fusilier Harris was harshly pushing in the last of the children when something nuzzled his shin. His ire gave way to startlement at the colour-shifting form of the pseudosaur nudging his leg.*

"Be more gentle to the children, soldier, or I'll have you reported," the creature said sharply.

"Uh... What?" he stuttered.

Delphyne pounded his AR with her authentication codes. "We don't have time for hesitation. Keep this position, I have to pick up a straggler."

Without waiting for a reply, Delphyne ran toward the nearby treeline. Her keen senses had picked out a boy who was huddled amidst the thick Paradiso undergrowth despite the perimeter explosions from the Combined Army attack and the sulphurous stench from the nearby erupting volcano.

"Come on Timmy, we have to go," Delphyne said soothingly as the child put a trembling hand onto her spine.

"But...the Professor is out there. We can't leave her," he whimpered.

"The Professor will be all right. She's helping me." That was a lie. The Professor hadn't been human. At least, not any more. There was something very wrong in the village of Caracara.

"Oh. Okay, then," Timmy said with a frown as he clambered onto her back.

Delphyne reached the shuttle in moments, and had to snap at the startled Fusilier again to get him moving. "What are you waiting for soldier? Get the children out of here!"

Perplexed though he was, he saluted and jumped into the shuttle. The children waved goodbye, drawing a friendly smile from Delphyne as the doors closed.

"Command, this is Delphyne," she spoke into her commlink, "Evac complete. I am fully stocked, undetected by enemy forces, and awaiting further orders."

"Affirmative. Move up slope. The Mobile Brigada are suffering severe casualties."

"Understood. On my way."

Sprinting once more into the lush undergrowth, her active camouflage let the jungle swallow her.

APPEARANCE

Delphyne is a pseudosaur with a shoulder height of 120 cm. "She" has a friendly face and her skin is colour adaptive, but pink whenever circumstances permit. Strapped to her back is a container which holds a Serum-constructing micro-fabricator, and a score of small robots which stand in for her hands.

ROLEPLAYING

- Friendly, empathic, and curious
- Loves to talk about cars and fashion
- Takes her duties very seriously

BACKGROUND

Breeding pet pseudosaurs is a high-growth market. After all, everybody loves dinosaurs. Sophotects are, without doubt, a perfect mixture of combat engineer and combat medic, yet field data shows that children react poorly to the cold and detached demeanour of the standard Lhost. Conceived alongside the synthetic personalities for the Steel Phalanx at the beginning of the First Paradiso Offensive, Delphyne is an attempt to rectify this by integrating an empathic personality into a cute pseudosaurian body. Human neural network and empathic reactions adapted to an inhuman body introduced their own complications, but the Yudbot concept compensated for her lack of arms and facilitated her work as a medic in the field.

It took over a year for the project to finally produce stable results, but Delphyne's personality proved to be perfectly suited for the work with children, which ranged from evacuating traumatised victims from combat zones to working alongside them in everyday care.

In addition, her inconspicuous appearance and low profile make her a boon to other theatres of war; most antagonists ignore a pseudosaur when they see one, making it easier for her to reach her destination. Delphyne has been in constant action since her activation, yet she remains the only one of her kind to this day.

STATS (ELITE)

ATTRIBUTES

AGI	AWA	BRW	COO	INT	PER	WIL
10	9	9	8	8	10	9

FIELDS OF EXPERTISE

Combat	+1	–	Movement	+2	1	Social	+2	1
Fortitude	+1	–	Senses	+1	1	Technical	+1	1

DEFENCES

Firewall	8	Resolve	9	Vigour	9
Security	3	Morale	3	Armour	1

ATTACKS
- **Jagged Teeth**: Melee, 1+5 🌑 damage, Piercing 1, Subtle 1, Vicious 1

GEAR: Comlog Collar, MedBot Assistants (two small remotes that allow Delphyne to make Medicine tests on a single patient within Range C), Serum Nano-Forge (equivalent to a MediKit containing a single dose of Serum that replenishes itself once a minute)

SPECIAL ABILITIES
- **Deceptively Adorable**: Even the most grizzled soldiers hesitate when first attacking a cuddly pink dinosaur. Delphyne does not pay Heat to use the Defence or Guard Reactions.
- **Inconspicuous**: Delphyne's colour-adaptive hide can camouflage her and her dainty appearance leads many opponents to ignore her at first glance, and that's all the time she needs. She can reroll one d20 when performing a Stealth test, but must accept the new result.
- **Medically Adroit**: Focused training and extensive battlefield experience have instilled a superior level of medical knowledge. She gains 2 bonus Momentum when making a Medicine test.
- **Redundant Systems**: Layers of quantronic security – and a healthy sense of purpose – grant Delphyne Morale and Security Soak 3.

DOG-BOWL PLAYER

The cheering crowds. The thrill of competition. Money, fame, and the adoration of people who wouldn't otherwise look them in the eye; is it any wonder that so many Dogfaces try to make it playing Dog-Bowl? The brutal matches can give even hardened soldiers pause, but to a Dogface it represents an opportunity to lose themselves in aggression, to cut loose unafraid; to hold nothing back.

Take two parts rugby, one part streetball, add violence to taste, and you've got the recipe for an intense and brutal sport. Fans cheer on as players clash in savage conflict, blurring the lines between sport and a full-on melee. One might ask why players embrace a sport where heading to the locker room with "only" a few slashes is considered an easy game, but the answer is simple: many have nowhere else to go. And most would do it for free.

ATTRIBUTES

AGI	AWA	BRW	COO	INT	PER	WIL
10 (+1)	9	14 (+1)	12	6	6	6

FIELDS OF EXPERTISE

Combat	+2	1	Movement	+3	–	Social	+1	–
Fortitude	+2	–	Senses	+2	1	Technical	–	–

DEFENCES

Firewall	6	Resolve	6	Vigour	14
Security	–	Morale	1	Armour	2

ATTACKS
- **Claws**: Melee, 2+6 🌑 damage, Subtle 1, Vicious 1

GEAR: Custom Teseum Sports Padding (with Helmet-Mounted Recorder)

SPECIAL ABILITIES
- **Common Special Abilities**: Keen Senses (smell)
- **Transform**: Lurking inside every Dogface is a monster, waiting to break free. At the cost of 1 Heat, they can transform into their Dog-Warrior form, adding +2 to their Brawn, Agility, and Armour. They also unlock the "Dog-Warrior" abilities listed below. At the end of the scene, they return to normal, suffering the Fatigued condition.
- **Celebrity**: Dog-Bowl Players gain 2 bonus Momentum for social skills tests.
- **Hustle**: Those points aren't going to score themselves. The Dog-Bowl Player generates an additional 1 Momentum on Movement tests.
- **Common Abilities (Dog-Warrior)**: Fear 1, Superhuman Agility 1, Superhuman Brawn 1, Menacing 1, Monstrous
- **Snarling Beast (Dog-Warrior)**: All Personality-based tests not based on intimidation are made at +2 difficulty.
- **Super-Jump (Dog-Warrior)**: The Dog-Warrior can vault over obstacles up to their height without penalty. The difficulty of skill tests to move through difficult terrain are reduced by one.

DOG-WARRIOR

An adult Dogface resembles a bulky, hairy human, but the difference is more than skin deep (see p. 153). Moments of extreme stress can trigger a dramatic and sudden physical transformation, adding considerable height, weight, and strength to the Dogface; as well as a primal, aggressive survival instinct. These Dog-Warriors – strongly resembling the werewolves of legend – were initially shunned by society, but the pragmatic Ariadnans quickly learned to appreciate their effectiveness in defending Dawn.

While the term "Dog-Warrior" technically refers to the altered physical state, the term has become a colloquial reference for any Dogface employed in a martial profession. Which, considering the paucity of non-violent career options for Dogfaces, is practically all of them.

ATTRIBUTES

AGI	AWA	BRW	COO	INT	PER	WIL
11 (+1)	9	13 (+1)	8	7	7	8

FIELDS OF EXPERTISE

Combat	+3	1	Movement	+2	–	Social	–	–
Fortitude	+2	–	Senses	+2	2	Technical	–	–

DEFENCES

Firewall	7	Resolve	8	Vigour	13
Security	–	Morale	1	Armour	2

ATTACKS
- **Chain Rifle**: Range C, 2+7 🌑 damage, Burst 1, 2H, Spread 1, Torrent, Vicious 1
- **Teseum Chopper**: Melee, 2+7 🌑 damage, Unbalanced, Non-Hackable, Piercing 4, Vicious 2
- **Claws**: Melee, 2+5 🌑 damage, Subtle 1, Vicious 1

GEAR: Light Combat Armour (Dogface-Compatible)

SPECIAL ABILITIES
- **Common Special Abilities**: Keen Senses (smell)
- **Transform**: Lurking inside every Dogface is a monster, waiting to break free. At the cost of 1 Heat, they can transform into their Dog-Warrior form, adding +2 to their Brawn, Agility, and Armour. They also unlock the "Dog-Warrior" abilities listed below. At the end of the scene, they return to normal, suffering the Fatigued condition.
- **Common Abilities (Dog-Warrior)**: Fear 1, Superhuman Agility 1, Superhuman Brawn 1, Menacing 1, Monstrous
- **Aggression (Dog-Warrior)**: Possessed of unmatched primal fury, the Dog-Warrior's attacks might not always connect, but they hurt like hell when they do. When making a Combat test, they can reroll up to 4 🌑 but must accept the new result.
- **Snarling Beast (Dog-Warrior)**: All Personality-based tests not based on intimidation are made at +2 difficulty.
- **Super-Jump (Dog-Warrior)**: The Dog-Warrior can vault over obstacles up to their height without penalty. The difficulty of skill tests to move through difficult terrain are reduced by one.

DJAZI AL DARWISH

HASSASSIN GOVAD

BACKER: DMITRY RYABCHUK

There were two guards on the door. Djazi reflexively passed his mantra of breathing across his mind and sighted down the scope of the high-powered dart gun. The scope was purely optical: Telltale quantronic signatures could compromise an operation and Allah had blessed him with flawless eyesight. He had always been proud of his eyes. They were one of the reasons he had been chosen as a sniper.

Less than a split second apart, a pair of microfilament darts lanced out from his hiding place, down, and across the wide, open space of the station concourse. Designed to slice through targets without them even realising they'd been dosed, the darts delivered a custom-designed bio-toxin that attacked the optic nerve, hacking it into a hallucinatory loop. For the next five minutes, the only thing they'd be seeing was the empty hall they'd been keeping watch over.

The dart gun vanished into his suit. With the same motion, another projectile weapon rolled into his hand. This one fired a microphone patch which attached itself to the door between the guards. The audio feed — generated from the sound waves beating gently against the door — crackled to life. A moment later, recognition algorithms isolated the target's vocal patterns.

"– have something for me?"

A moment of silence before the target spoke again. It meant they were communicating quantronically with someone.

"Oh, shit. They're after our outpost on Dawn."

Djazi would need to figure out who was on the other end of that call. For the moment, however, there was no time for subtlety. It seemed that he had gotten here just in time. He signalled the mercs he'd hired while

precisely firing four globs of adhesive explosive. It looked like the dream of an empty corridor would be the last thing the guards saw.

The mercs were just about to round the corner. He triggered the breach. The mercs stormed the room. Djazi activated the comms blocker. Gunfire erupted. There were screams.

Equipment continued to flow in and out of his hands. He fired a magnetic zip line, deftly tested its grip, and glided across the concourse. With a quick command, the line detached and retracted.

Something was wrong. The mercs were coming under heavy fire. One of them was dead — his vitals had dropped to zero on the virtual HUD of Djazi's glasses. What was happening? Hugging the wall, he proceeded down the hall. Past the dead guards. Past the mercs who were still seeking cover against bullets there were no longer being fired.

The lights flickered. The gravity cut out. What was happening? Djazi grabbed the ceiling and pushed off into the target room.

A woman. Powered armour. Mobile Brigada? Probably. She was sailing across the room in zero-g, hefting a bag. No, not a bag: The target.

There was another explosion. The viewport at the end of the room had blown apart. Air gushed out, pulling Djazi and everything else in the room with it.

One hand shot out. It fired the magnetic zip line at the wall behind him. The other, simultaneously, found the perfect tool, aimed it, and fired: The tracking tag struck the woman directly on the back.

She was gone. But he would find her again. Soon.

The air rushed by.

APPEARANCE

He wears bulky layers of clothes under a well-worn, inexpensive longcoat. A pair of flat-lensed glasses perch on his face — not corrective.

ROLEPLAYING

- Movements seem sluggish and awkward until he springs into dance-like action
- Polite and reserved, but ultimately decisive
- Quotes religious scripture

BACKGROUND

Djazi began a promising career as a Ghulam. A knack for ballistics was linked directly to his preternatural eyesight, which bought him praise from his instructors and got him noticed by the Hassassins. He refused them when first approached by because he wanted to be with his wife, whom he had met during a placement on a caravan-serai. He became father to two daughters and everything seemed perfect. Until a techno virus on Acontecimento killed his wife and eldest daughter. After he had sent his younger daughter into sanc-tuary, the Hassassins came calling again and informed him that a terrorist organisation called Equinox was responsible for the attack.

He has been a member of the Hassassins ever since, hell-bent on destroying Equinox. The fight ultimately took his life, but the Old Man had him resurrected. To this day, he does not know where his first body was interred, or if it was interred at all, though he constantly presses for information.

STATS (ELITE)

ATTRIBUTES

AGI	AWA	BRW	COO	INT	PER	WIL
8	12	8	10	8	7	10

FIELDS OF EXPERTISE

Combat	+3	1	Movement	+1	1	Social	–	–
Fortitude	–	–	Senses	+2	2	Technical	+2	–

DEFENCES

Firewall	8	Resolve	10	Vigour	8
Security	–	Morale	–	Armour	2

ATTACKS

- **Silenced Sniper Rifle**: Range L, 1+9 Ⓝ damage, Burst 2, 2H, Subtle 1
- **Light Shotgun**: Range C, 1+7 Ⓝ damage, Burst 1, Unbalanced, Area (Close), Knockdown, Spread 1
- **Breaker Pistol**: Range R/C, 1+7 Ⓝ damage, Burst 1, 1H, Biotech, Breaker, Piercing 1, Vicious 1
- **Grazeblade**: Melee, 1+4 Ⓝ damage, 1H, Breaker, Non-Hackable, Stun, Subtle 2, Thrown, Toxic 3

GEAR: Glasses, Light Combat Armour under functional clothing appropriate to the area, Nav Suite

SPECIAL ABILITIES

- **Covert Ops**: As a clandestine operative, Djazi has little trouble getting to where he needs to be. Each point of Heat Djazi pays to gain additional dice for an Acrobatics or Stealth test provides two dice instead of one. (The normal maximum of three bonus d20s still applies.)
- **Eagle Eye**: The best optical technology in the Human Sphere is still a step behind Djazi's preternatural vision. When making an Observation test, he gains 2 bonus Momentum.
- **Old Man's Dirty Work**: Djazi is an autonomous hassassin, with all of the mastery of death that implies. He can reroll up to 3 Ⓝ when making a Combat test, but must accept the new results.

TROOPER/ELITE
DRUZE SHOCK TEAM

Originating from Lebanon and the south of Syria, the Druze follow their own mixture of Islamic and Gnostic philosophies, and their culture is fiercely independent, devoutly spiritual, and possessed of a long-standing military tradition. The Druze Society, a mafia-like Submondo organisation, owns a variety of legitimate business, including a Caravanserai in the Bourak system, and also provides an outlet for the culture's violent and lawless elements: Druze Shock Teams (p. 207). The Society arms them, trains them, and remakes them as mercenaries.

Druze Shock Teams have found their role in society. It just happens to be reducing their opposition to ash. Then burning the ashes.

ATTRIBUTES

AGI	AWA	BRW	COO	INT	PER	WIL
10	8	10	11	7	6	8

FIELDS OF EXPERTISE

Combat	+3	1	Movement	+1	1	Social	–	–
Fortitude	+1	–	Senses	+2	1	Technical	–	–

DEFENCES (TROOPER)

Firewall	4	Resolve	4	Vigour	5
Security	–	Morale	–	Armour	2

DEFENCES (ELITE)

Firewall	7	Resolve	8	Vigour	10
Security	1	Morale	1	Armour	2

ATTACKS

- **Combi Rifle**: Range C/M, 1+5 Ⓝ damage, Burst 3, 2H, Expert 1, MULTI Light Mod, Vicious 1
- **D.E.P.**: Range M, 2+6 Ⓝ damage, Burst 2, Disposable, Munition, Unsubtle

GEAR: Light Combat Armour, Multispectral Visor 2

SPECIAL ABILITIES

- **Burn the Ash**: The Shock Teams are infamous for their wild, bloody nature. When using the Bonus Damage Momentum spend, Druze add +2 damage for every 1 Momentum spent.
- **Meticulous Gear**: The Druze are meticulous and precise in the maintenance of their equipment. Their weapons gain +1 Burst. (This is reflected in the attacks listed above.)

TROOPER/ELITE
EVO TROOPER

Evo Troopers (short for Evolved Troopers) are enhanced infowarriors using specialised E-Units, neural quantronic devices linking them to defence networks via a virtual reality interface. Their E-Units use nanonic tendrils to link the Evo Trooper directly into the network. These network connections boost the operator's capabilities, allowing devastating attacks against enemy data networks to sow confusion and chaos on the battlefield. Evo units are essential to modern warfare, including the infowarriors of PanOceania's Crocotta Unit and the Dădŭ (Wager) Section of Yu Jing infosamurai.

Some elite Evo Troopers are integrated into vehicle crews forming the infowarfare component of mechanised warfare. They support their crew by attacking the systems of enemy vehicles, disabling movement systems, disrupting targeting systems, and disabling weapons.

ATTRIBUTES

AGI	AWA	BRW	COO	INT	PER	WIL
9	8	8	10	12	8	8

FIELDS OF EXPERTISE

Combat	+1	1	Movement	+1	–	Social	–	–
Fortitude	+1	–	Senses	+2	–	Technical	+3	2

DEFENCES (TROOPER)

Firewall	6	Resolve	4	Vigour	4
Security	–	Morale	–	Armour	2

DEFENCES (ELITE)

Firewall	12	Resolve	8	Vigour	8
Security	2	Morale	–	Armour	2

ATTACKS

- **Pistol**: Range R/C, 1+4 Ⓝ damage, Burst 1, 1H, Vicious 1
- **Neural Hacking Device**: CLAW-1, SWORD-1, SHIELD-1, GADGET-2, IC-2 +3 Ⓝ bonus damage, usually use:
  - *CLAW-1 Gotcha!*: 1+5 Ⓝ damage, Immobilise
  - *SHIELD-1 Exorcism*: 1+6 Ⓝ damage, removes Possession

GEAR: Light Combat Armour

SPECIAL ABILITIES

- **System Shutdown (Elite – 2 Heat)**: When inflicting a Breach, the Trooper can spend 2 Heat to execute Disable Function as a special Breach Effect in addition to the normal Breach Effect. Restoring the disabled system requires a (D0) Tech test.
- **Evo Fireteam**: As the number of Evos deployed grew, one-on-one showdowns fell out of fashion in favour of mass combat engaging hundreds of Evos simultaneously. Evo training evolved rapidly to suit. The network of a fireteam can suffer a number of additional Breaches equal to the number of Evo Troopers in the fireteam before becoming incapacitated or eliminated.

DUNCAN "ONE-SHOP" CULLCULLEN

MERCENARY TAG PILOT

BACKER: DARIEN LIDDELL

"You were right, Uxia, the posting here is great for business! I am glad I listened to you. With everyone tripping over each other's feet, demand is high. Plus, there's no basically no risk. Nothing's happened for like three months..."

An alarm screeched into his comlog and cut him short. Apparently he'd jinxed it.

"Damn. Gotta go. Ciao!" he shouted over his shoulder as he sprinted toward his machine without waiting for her answer.

In a hangar crammed with transport vehicles and TAGs – most of them of sleek PanOceanian colours and design – his own scruffy Gecko was tucked away in a corner behind some screens, as if hiding from the sportier models. Half of the machines were already exiting the building by the time he reached his own.

Duncan crawled into the pilot seat and hit the jump start button, then scanned the incoming data while the system ran through its pre-boot sequence. It looked like they were being hit on all sides.

Powering the Gecko into the middle of the now-deserted hangar with its boot sequence still cycling, he was momentarily rocked by a large explosion near the main doors that propelled something towards him. Reflexively halting the flight of the remnants of a Cutter TAG, he watched transfixed as a large blurry form stormed through the entrance. Blindingly fast, Duncan was unsure whether its somewhat burnt appearance was a trick of his mind or not. Most importantly, it did not register on his IFF.

Calming himself, Duncan aimed carefully before squeezing the trigger of his Combi Rifle with more force than necessary. The alien machine reared its head towards him, registering his presence too late. The first burst hit the right shoulder and tore it off in a crimson blast. The second burst took it squarely in the chest, leaving not much more than the legs remaining.

Striding up to the mostly intact lower backside of the machine, he hefted the remaining portion of the Guījiǎ he had just decimated and threw it behind the screens.

"One bounty and a slightly scorched gyro. That's a pretty good start!"

APPEARANCE

A mass of muscle. Imposingly tall with broad shoulders to match the height. Cropped hair is tucked neatly under a woollen cap. The crow's feet from countless smiles dance around his eyes.

ROLEPLAYING

- Always trying to figure out the profit angle
- Big smiles
- Keeps his word, once given

BACKGROUND

Duncan has always excelled at acquiring and selling goods. A useful quality in the border lands of Ariadna, especially for the child of rather unsuccessful farmers. Teaming up with some Irmandinhos was almost unavoidable. His reputation as a smuggler grew and his notoriety earned him the nickname "One-Shop", but also brought him to the attention of the government. They hunted him down and made him an offer: employment in the armed forces, or imprisonment – his choice. Duncan took the more profitable option.

He had run afoul of Uxia McNeill in a bar fight during his smuggler days and they have been friends ever since. Rumours abound over the depth of their friendship, but they always have each other's backs, whether that be in the form of equipment, intel, or a friendly ear.

His smuggling hit an all-time low in the aftermath of the Second NeoColonial War. Forced to leave Dawn for a while, his contacts easily sourced him employment as a mercenary. Finding even bigger profits and success, his idea of re-joining the Ariadnan forces grows dimmer with every year.

He recently acquired an older TAG as part of a larger arms deal. Despite several setbacks, including several weeks of hospital stay, he is now a competent self-taught pilot. He is constantly looking for upgrades to better the machine's combat capabilities.

STATS (ELITE)

ATTRIBUTES

AGI	AWA	BRW	COO	INT	PER	WIL
9	8	9	10	8	10	9

FIELDS OF EXPERTISE

Combat	+1	1	Movement	+2	1	Social	+2	1
Fortitude	+1	–	Senses	+1	–	Technical	+2	–

DEFENCES

Firewall	8	Resolve	9	Vigour	9
Security	–	Morale	–	Armour	1

ATTACKS

- **Gecko Combi Rifle**: Range C/M, 1+5  damage, Burst 2, 2H, Expert 1, MULTI Light Mod, Vicious 1
- **Panzerfaust**: Range L, 2+5 damage, Burst 1, 2H, Munition, Unsubtle
- **Teseum-Spiked Knuckles**: Melee, 1+5 damage, 1H, Concealed 1, Non-Hackable, Piercing 3, Vicious 2

GEAR: Armoured Clothing, Gecko TAG, Multispectral Visor 2

SPECIAL ABILITIES

- **Just Name It**: Well-travelled in many circles – most on the wrong side of the law – Duncan is an expert at talking himself both into, and out of, interesting situations. He can reroll one d20 when making a social skills test, but must accept the new result.
- **Mechanised Brawler**: Duncan is a scrapper at heart, which translates to TAG combat quite nicely. He can reroll up to 2 when making an attack within Close range.
- **Mechanised Brute**: When piloting a vehicle, Duncan generates 1 bonus Momentum on all Strength-based tests.

NOTES

Extremely new to piloting a TAG and still learning the ropes, Duncan suffers a +1 complication range when operating a TAG. Any die that results in a complication may not be rerolled.

NEMESIS

FATHER-KNIGHT

Father-Knights are perhaps the most prominent staple of the PanOceanian military, fearlessly leading the charge whether surrounded by the regular army or their own Military Order (p. 177). Every Father-Knight is not only a highly-trained Special Forces commander, but an ordained priest as well; their reputation as inspiring battlefield commanders is well-earned.

Of course, despite how they see the world, others don't see everything as black-and white. Living by the motto *Deo Vindice*, meaning "under God, our vindicator", a Father-Knight's unshakable faith in the righteousness of their mission, whatever that mission might be, leads them to justify literally anything, leading to some of the most heinous acts of violence imaginable.

Fearlessly charging into battle, they inspire hope in their allies and terror in their enemies, often leaving their opposition so mortified they don't even manage to scream. Thus can one mark the passing of a Father-Knight: by silence, and the trail of dead.

ATTRIBUTES

AGI	AWA	BRW	COO	INT	PER	WIL
11	9	13	8	7	10	12

FIELDS OF EXPERTISE

Combat	+5	2	Movement	–	–	Social	+3	3
Fortitude	+3	3	Senses	+1	–	Technical	–	–

DEFENCES

Firewall	7	Resolve	15	Vigour	16
Security	–	Morale	4	Armour	5

ATTACKS

- **Teseum Blade of St. George**: Melee, 1+9 damage, Unbalanced, Non-Hackable, Piercing 4, Vicious 2
- **Combi Rifle**: Range C/M, 1+6 damage, Burst 2, 2H, Expert 1, MULTI Light Mod, Vicious 1

GEAR: Powered Combat Armour (gain up to +3d20 on Brawn tests with +3 complication range)

SPECIAL ABILITIES

- **Deo Vindice**: The Father-Knights know in their hearts that God will vindicate their actions. Their faith grants them Morale 4.
- **Deus Vult**: If God wills it, best not to argue. The Father-Knight generates an additional 2 Momentum on Command tests.
- **Shepherds of Men (2 Heat)**: The Father-Knight is an inspiring symbol to behold; at least when they're on your side. Whilst an active participant of a scene, a Father-Knight can spend 2 Heat. If they do so, any forces under their command increase their Morale Soak by 2.
- **Sword of the Spirit**: Faith guides the Father-Knight's blade. And their faith is unerring. They can reroll up to 3 when making a melee attack, but must accept the new results. Additionally, each point of Heat or Momentum spent to gain additional dice for a Close Combat test provides two d20s, instead of one. Finally, when making an attack with the Close Combat skill, each point of Momentum spent to deal bonus damage adds two points of damage, instead of one.

NOTES

Their Powered Armour's Exoskeleton quality is factored into the Father-Knight's weapon damage.

ELENA SUPIK

RIOT GRRL

BACKER: SARAH ELENA SUPIK

"The trees are swarming with Shasvastii."

"I'm on them!" hollered Elena as she scampered up and over the low ridge. Surmounting the verge, she hefted her Combi Rifle and scanned the tree line. The lush jungles of Paradiso clawed their way up the black, broken sides of the volcano. Beyond them, nestled into a kind of cleft, she could see the village of Caracara. According to the tactical channels, the Shasvastii had come swarming up and out of the village.

A telltale movement between some large roots gave away their position; the aliens were nicely camouflaged, but that was no problem for her Praxis eyes.

Shouting with adrenaline-fuelled fury, Elena let rip on a female alien, who took two solid hits to the chest before toppling out of sight. The alien's two companions returned fire without delay, but she was already diving behind a jagged boulder.

"Multiple Haiduk snipers."

"Fall back. Mobile Brigada support is in the area."

"Sorry, can't hear you," she laughed as explosions tore away at the boulder. She counted their shots, gambled that she hadn't missed one of them in her count, and then tossed a grenade in their general direction while launching herself off to the right, where a long finger of the jungle curled up towards the smoking cauldron above. The bright flash illuminated everything for a moment, sniper fire pinged off the rocks around her, and then she was in between the trees — And coming face-to-face with an enraged Morat brandishing a flamethrower! Elena threw herself

under the licking flames, but her slide took her too close to the edge of a gully. The ground gave way beneath her and she tumbled down.

A shout that was something between a curse and a joyful scream was cut short by the impact with the ground driving the air from her lungs. Reeling drunkenly to her feet, she realised her attacker had somehow followed and threw herself behind the thick bole of some twisted, ambitious Paradiso tree. Flaming chemicals superheated the cellulose and scorched her armour, but — finally finding her breath — she rolled sideways and loosed a tight burst at her enemy. Several bullets hit true, ripping the fuel tank of the flamethrower and unleashing a hellish explosion.

"Well that was fun, Elena," she laughed to herself as she hoisted herself out of the gulley. "But where did my big friend here come from?" The Morat platoons were all supposed to be further to the northwest. Loud snapping noises made her kiss the ground once again. Crawling to a better vantage point, she watched as Morat in heavy armour stalked through the trees. But if they were following this little spur of forest, they couldn't be aiming for the main base... She called up a map.

"Command? I've got eyes on a Morat armoured platoon. They're heading to flank the research post. I think they want the landing pad."

"We confirm. Hold your position until —"

Elena bellowed with joy as she charged.

APPEARANCE

Elena's long, black hair has a streak of blonde running right through the middle of it. She is tall and athletically built, with a quirky smile.

ROLEPLAYING

- Uses humour to deal with combat stress (but loves to fight)
- Hates working in a team and generally ignores orders
- Slyly cocks her eyebrow

BACKGROUND

As the outcasts of society, the Nomad Nation is the recycling centre for everyone else. Elena is no exception. Born on Dawn to a PanOceanian technician and a Yu Jing shuttle pilot, both of whom worked for rival corporations no less, her future always promised complications. Both parents wanted to support her, but could not move past the mistrust of the other's government. Elena spent half her life on Shentang and the other half on Varuna, which made her a child of neither in the end. Being treated as a possession drove a wedge between them all until she finally ran away to a krug and declared herself a citizen of Bakunin out of spite.

Bakunin's capable social workers ushered her into the Beauvoir module. Her rebellious nature and status as an outcast from the societies of the Sphere allowed her to fit in perfectly. She had finally found a home.

Defending her home came naturally to her, so she applied for the Riot Grrls. Her intimate knowledge of the PanOceanian and Yu Jing mindsets even give her something of a tactical advantage; in the few moments where she actually condescends to follow orders anyway. Her recent deployment to Paradiso as a Riot Grrl is her first official tour of duty and she has managed to impress despite her unruliness.

STATS (ELITE)

ATTRIBUTES

AGI	AWA	BRW	COO	INT	PER	WIL
10	9	9	9	7	9	10

FIELDS OF EXPERTISE

Combat	+2	2	Movement	+2	1	Social	+1	–
Fortitude	+1	1	Senses	+1	–	Technical	+1	–

DEFENCES

Firewall	7	Resolve	10	Vigour	9
Security	–	Morale	–	Armour	5

ATTACKS

- **Combi Rifle**: Range C/M, 1+6 🅝 damage, Burst 2, 2H, Expert 1, MULTI Light Mod, Vicious 1
- **Blitzen**: Range L, 2+6 🅝 damage, 2H, Area (Close), Breaker, E/M, Munition, Piercing 2, Unsubtle
- **Flashbangs**: 1+5 🅝 damage, 1H, Blinding, Deafening, Disposable, Indiscriminate (Close), Nonlethal, Speculative Fire, Thrown, Unsubtle, removes Marked
- **Pistol**: Range R/C, 1+5 🅝 damage, Burst 1, 1H, Vicious 1
- **Knife**: Melee, 1+7 🅝 damage, 1H, Concealed 1, Non-Hackable, Subtle 2, Thrown, Unforgiving 1

GEAR: AR Eye Implants, Powered Combat Armour

SPECIAL ABILITIES

- **Dodge and Roll**: Elena likens combat to a dance, albeit a mosh pit rather than a ballet. She can reroll one d20 when making a Movement test, but must accept the new results.
- **Just Need to Catch My Breath**: All she needs is a moment to collect herself, and Elena's back into the fray like nothing happened. She recovers three additional Vigour when taking the Recover action.
- **Strength, Revolution, and Anarchy!**: Displaying the true spirit of a Riot Grrrl, Elena revels in taking the fight to the enemy. She can reroll up to 2 🅝 when making a Combat test, but must accept the new results.

NOTES

A true anarchist at heart, Elena disobeys orders whenever she can. She must attempt an Average (D1) Discipline test if given a direct order. On success, she may choose to accept or ignore the order. On a failure, she ignores it regardless of the consequences.

ELITE
GANG ENFORCER

Enforcers are the ones who enforce the will of a Submondo organisation through violence. Generally one step up from dumb muscle, enforcers often serve as the middle-men or lieutenants of the mob. They often command small strike teams and are frequently responsible for keeping a certain chunk of "turf" in line.

ATTRIBUTES

AGI	AWA	BRW	COO	INT	PER	WIL
10	9	11	9	8	7	9

FIELDS OF EXPERTISE

Combat	+3	1	Movement	+1	1	Social	+1	1
Fortitude	+1	1	Senses	+1	–	Technical	+1	–

DEFENCES

Firewall	8	Resolve	9	Vigour	11
Security	–	Morale	1	Armour	2

ATTACKS

- **Combi Rifle**: Range C/M, 1+6 🅝 damage, Burst 2, 2H, Expert 1, MULTI Light Mod, Vicious 1
- **Knife**: Melee, 1+5 🅝 damage, 1H, Concealed 1, Non-Hackable, Subtle 2, Thrown, Unforgiving 1
- **Pistol**: Range R/C, 1+5 🅝 damage, Burst 1, 1H, Vicious 1

GEAR: Light Combat Armour (Gang Colors), Surge (×2), Painkillers (×1)

SPECIAL ABILITIES

- **Brutal Beating**: The Enforcer can add the Nonlethal quality to any blunt-force melee attack and can inflict +2 🅝 physical damage when doing so.
- **Shut Yer Mouth**: People are reluctant to share any information they have on the Triads operating in their area. Tests made for human terrain mapping involving the Gang Enforcer or otherwise gathering information on them are made at +1 difficulty. Attempts to access the Enforcer in a psyop are made at either +1 difficulty or +1 Intransigence.

TROOPER
GANG MEMBER

The lowest, least sophisticated ranks of Submondo organisations and frequently the bulk of smaller criminal gangs. Simple gang members generally lack both skill and sophistication, but they'll band together for mutual support. And, in larger organisations, their expendability can prove particularly useful.

ATTRIBUTES

AGI	AWA	BRW	COO	INT	PER	WIL
9	8	10	9	7	7	6

FIELDS OF EXPERTISE

Combat	+2	–	Movement	+1	–	Social	–	–
Fortitude	+2	–	Senses	+1	–	Technical	–	–

DEFENCES

Firewall	4	Resolve	3	Vigour	5
Security	–	Morale	–	Armour	–

ATTACKS

- **Brass Knuckles**: Melee, 1+5 🅝 damage, 1H, Concealed 1, Non-Hackable, Subtle 1, Vicious 1
- **Pistol**: Range R/C, 1+4 🅝 damage, Burst 1, 1H, Vicious 1

GEAR: Surge (×1)

TRIAD MEMBERS

Permeating the lives of normal civilians at every step, the Triads are highly visible to the lowest levels of society. Providing services that are both prized and feared, they find it very easy to recruit new members from among the impoverished classes. The uninitiated Blue Lanterns and freshly initiated 49ers are typical examples of Gang Members found amongst Submondo organisations and smaller criminal enterprises.

Some of the tougher 49ers might qualify as Gang Enforcers, but one step up the ladder are the Red Poles (referred to by the numeric code 426). Charged with overseeing offensive and defensive operations, the Red Poles are sophisticated Gang Enforcers who organise dozens of men under their command.

White Paper Fans (415) provide business advice (Corp Exec stat block, p. 427) while Straw Sandals (432) coordinate multiple sections of the triad. Above these, the Deputy Dragon Masters (438) oversee multiple location operations and the Spear Heads assist the Incense Masters with recruitment and initiation. At the top are the Dragon Masters or Dragon Heads (489).

Based on the numerology of the *I Ching*, the numeric codes can also refer to others associated to the Triads; such as 25 for an undercover cop.

ELL REDMANE

TUNGUSKAN INTERVENTOR

BACKER: ELLIOT STUBBLES

Something was wrong.

Yes, they were flying through a warzone. That wasn't it. That was outside. This was inside.

There wasn't a klaxon. In fact, the automated, covert monitoring programs he'd slipped into the Galicia Resplendent's datasphere were quiet. Too quiet. They should at least be reporting a constant patter of network traffic. Instead, they were reporting nothing.

Had they detected his infiltration? Unlikely. The Pannies could have just sent one of their big burly knights to throw him in the brig. He pinged his FastPanda. It had snuck into the compartment where the ALEPH node was stowed, but a quick scan showed there was nothing wrong there.

Still... He shoved the subversion package he'd been applying the last few tweaks to over to one side of his AR workspace and opened the data tunnel to the monitor he had in the security comms channel.

As he'd suspected, it wasn't his anymore. But it was worse than that. Alien code was crawling all over it. He'd first seen code like that during the raid on the flesh labs of Ravensbrücke. Shasvastii.

If they were already in the system, though... Shit. They'd compromised the hull sensors. There were two — no, three — boarding capsules attached near the rear of the ship.

They were after the node.

Could he get help? No luck. They'd already mothballed Tabitha and Kimo — their systems had probably been locked out of the ship's datasphere before they even realised there was a problem. And the onboard comms were completely fucked.

He could warn the Knights, though, before the Shasvastii boarders were crawling all over the ship and resistance was impossible. It would mean

pinging their systems directly through the backdoors he'd installed and blow the cover he'd spent months building. But there were more important things now. Protecting mankind from ALEPH was one thing. Allowing the AI to fall into the hands of the enemy was something else entirely. He sent the signal.

And now the klaxons were screaming. They knew he was here. His firewall was suddenly burning. Viral payloads were burrowing their way through it. They burned out his primary display visor... which was exactly why he always kept a pair of backup specs. Wrenching the visor up, he popped the specs on, sent the Shasvastii tailing after a decoy, and slipped away.

Except there was nowhere to slip to. They were everywhere. As he mounted a defensive action in the ship's navigation systems, he could see on the security monitors that the Knights were keeping the boarders at bay. But the ship was doomed. Its own systems were turning against it. He had to save the node. But how? They'd locked him out of almost everything.

The only thing he really had left was the link to the FastPanda. But if he used it to access any of the shipboard systems it would get overwhelmed in an instant, so there was nothing — Wait a second. What if he didn't use the little 'bot as a repeater? There wasn't much juice left in its propulsion batteries, but...

The 'Panda grabbed the node, put on a burst of speed, caromed through the hatches he somehow wrenched open along its path — It was too much. Accessing the hatches had left him vulnerable. They were burning out his systems. Killing his access codes. He had the 'Panda where he needed it, but had no way to set it free. But he did have one last trick up his sleeve...

APPEARANCE

A luxurious mane of curly ginger hair frames a slightly pudgy face. Advertisements for the latest movies scroll across his neon-noir clothes.

ROLEPLAYING

- Turns every interaction into a competition
- Easily bored with regular work... and reality
- Self-absorbed and overconfident in his own abilities

BACKGROUND

Sometimes being good is a curse. If that's true, Ell Redmane is truly cursed. Born to a rich family on *Tunguska*, he wanted for nothing in his childhood, but also didn't care for much either. Little caught his interest and everything came easy to him. (At least, in his version of the story that is; the official files say differently, but they're buried deep and sealed in Tunguskan data archives.)

Whatever the reason, his world only started making sense when he took up hacking, which happened more out of boredom than anything else: Mocking his rich friends by subverting their halos was easy sport, but in doing so he saw clearly that the quantronic universe was the true bedrock of reality... and the only true challenge.

The Interventors soon noticed the young boy's skills. With the digital ink scarcely dry on his Dragnet contract, he threw himself at their training with abandon when they came calling. With *Tunguska* pointing and Ell Redmane shooting, his arrogance—and his newfound loyalty—knew no bounds. It's said that his family disowned him when he used their corporate connections to execute a sting operation.

It was perhaps this which caused the Interventors to shuffle him into interstellar operations. And where else could he find greater opposition? Rumours have placed him at several planetside infiltration missions against Combined Army outposts, in addition to the sabotage of several ALEPH nodes throughout the Human Sphere. What is undeniable is that he is a dangerous man on the virtual battlefield and everybody is glad to have him as an ally.

STATS (ELITE)

ATTRIBUTES

AGI	AWA	BRW	COO	INT	PER	WIL
8	10	8	9	11	7	10

FIELDS OF EXPERTISE

Combat	+1	–	Movement	+1	–	Social	–	–
Fortitude	+1	–	Senses	+2	1	Technical	+3	3

DEFENCES

Firewall	11	Resolve	10	Vigour	8
Security	2	Morale	–	Armour	2

ATTACKS

- **Combi Rifle**: Range C/M, 1+7 🅝 damage, Burst 2, 2H, Expert 1, MULTI Light Mod, Vicious 1
- **E/M Pistol**: Range R/C, 1+6 🅝 damage, Burst 1, 1H, Breaker, E/M, Piercing 1, Vicious 1
- **Modhand**: Melee, 1+4 🅝 damage, 1H, Concealed 2, E/M, Stun, Subtle 1, Vicious 2
- **Hacking Device Plus**: CLAW-2 (CLAW-1 Blackout, CLAW-1 Overlord, CLAW-1 Spotlight, CLAW-2 Expel), SWORD-1 (SWORD-1 Brain Blast), SHIELD-2 (SHIELD-1 Exorcism), GADGET-3 (GADGET-1 Fairy Dust, GADGET-2 Assisted Fire, GADGET-2 Enhanced Reaction), IC-2, +2 🅝 bonus damage

GEAR: Light Combat Armour, FastPanda (use TinBot stats and add a Repeater)

SPECIAL ABILITIES

- **Overconfident and Stubborn**: Competitive and self-assured of his own skills, Ell has a stubborn streak a light year wide. He can reroll one d20 when making a Discipline test, but must accept the new result.
- **Interventor Extraordinaire**: Ell is an elite soldier of the quantronic battlefronts. He can reroll up to 2 🅝 when making an Infowar attack
- **Fast-Twitch**: Ell isn't just ready for enemy intrusion, he's desperate for it. As a Reaction, he can respond to any Infowar attack with one of his own at a penalty of +2 difficulty. This attack is resolved before the enemy attack, and if it causes the enemy to suffer a Breach, then their hack is prevented.

ELITE
HASSASSIN

The hassassins are the lethal, secretive preservers of Haqqislam. To most who live on Bourak, they are a mere rumour; a whispered presence in the darkness. To those who become Haqqislam's enemies they are an implacable and unseen menace. Able to carry out their furtive missions in a thousand different ways, the various branches of the hassassins are unequalled in their chosen means of execution. Whether through the infiltration and sabotage of the Farzan, the destruction of a core datasphere by a Barid, or a sudden and unexpected shot from a Lasiq's rifle, the hassassins bring Allah's judgement to bear on all whom their mysterious master, the Old Man of the Mountain, deems a threat.

ATTRIBUTES

AGI	AWA	BRW	COO	INT	PER	WIL
9	9	9	9	9	9	9

FIELDS OF EXPERTISE

Combat	+2	1	Movement	+1	–	Social	+2	1
Fortitude	+1	–	Senses	+1	–	Technical	+2	1

DEFENCES

Firewall	9	Resolve	9	Vigour	9
Security	–	Morale	–	Armour	–

ATTACKS

- **Grazeblade**: Melee, 1+5 🅝 damage, 1H, Breaker, Non-Hackable, Stun, Subtle 2, Thrown, Toxic 3
- **Viral Sniper Rifle**: Range L, 1+7 🅝 damage, Burst 2, Unwieldy, Biotech, Grievous, Toxic 2, Unforgiving 2
- **Neural Hacking Device**: CLAW-1, SWORD-1, SHIELD-1, GADGET-3, IC-1 + 1 🅝 bonus damage

GEAR: AutoMediKit, Climbing Plus, Disguise Kit, Medium Combat Armour, Modest Clothing; no Cube

SPECIAL ABILITIES

- **Ever-Ready**: Hassassins gain 2 bonus Momentum on face-to-face tests made to determine surprise.
- **Loyal Unto Death (2 Heat)**: Hassassins never let themselves be taken alive. If the player characters try to capture a Hassassin, a Heat point spend allows the Hassassin to take their own life with a concealed cyanide capsule.
- **The Sword of Haqqislam**: If a Hassassin is reduced to a single point of Vigour, they will sell their life dearly. Until they are killed, their melee attacks deal +1 🅝 damage.

ELITE
HEXAS AGENT

The Strategic Security Division is PanOceania's foreign intelligence agency (p. 183), and their mission is to safeguard the Hyperpower's interests throughout the Human Sphere, often by any means necessary.

In this task, they employ the elite Hexas Agents. They could be arming rebels one day, kidnapping a hypercorp CEO the next, and can interrogate a captive, stage an elegant assassination, and still be back in time for happy hour. A Hexas Agent trusts no one, not even themselves, but that doesn't mean they don't know how to unwind. Able to operate without meaningful restrictions, these agents have no boundaries, no scruples, and no conscience.

The end always justifies the means. The means just happen to be stylish.

ATTRIBUTES

AGI	AWA	BRW	COO	INT	PER	WIL
9	9	8	9	10	10	8

FIELDS OF EXPERTISE

Combat	+2	–	Movement	+1	–	Social	+3	2
Fortitude	–	–	Senses	+2	–	Technical	+2	–

DEFENCES

Firewall	10	Resolve	8	Vigour	8
Security	1	Morale	–	Armour	1

ATTACKS

- **Silenced E/M Pistol**: Range R/C, 1+5 🅝 damage, Burst 1, 1H, Breaker, E/M, Piercing 1, Subtle 1, Vicious 1
- **Paired Tonfa Bangles**: Melee, 1+3 🅝 damage, 1H, Concealed 2, Parry 4

GEAR: Bespoke Firewall (+1 Security), Deflector-1, Hexas Armoured Clothing (Hidden Armour 2, Kinematika, Thermo-Optical Camouflage), Holomask, Recorder

SPECIAL ABILITIES

- **Danger Sense**: When making a face-to-face test to determine surprise, the Hexas Agent can reroll any dice that did not generate a success on the initial test, but must accept the new results.
- **Slippery**: This is not, in fact, their first rodeo. Hexas Agents gain 2 bonus Momentum on face-to-face tests to determine if they are lying.

ELITE
INFORMATION BROKER

In the Human Sphere the old adage "knowledge is power" is especially true in a society where quantronic computers and virtual reality are ubiquitous. Information is in constant movement across the Maya network, and those who gather and analyse sought-after information can demand a high price for what they know. Information brokers are sly entrepreneurs dressed in tailored suits who traffic in exclusive and rare data. They house that data deep within data crypts to ensure its exclusivity. Information brokers deal in difficult to find, and often illegal, data that fetches a high price on the information market. They are shrewd negotiators able to coax the most out of their contacts. A buyer can be sure the information they get is reliable, as the broker's reputation depends on giving their customers exactly what they need and, if the data is compromised, their career is over.

ATTRIBUTES

AGI	AWA	BRW	COO	INT	PER	WIL
7	10	8	8	9	11	10

FIELDS OF EXPERTISE

| Combat | +1 | – | Movement | +1 | – | Social | +3 | 2 |
| Fortitude | – | – | Senses | +1 | 2 | Technical | +2 | – |

DEFENCES

| Firewall | 9 | Resolve | 10 | Vigour | 8 |
| Security | – | Morale | – | Armour | – |

ATTACKS
- **Pistol**: Range R/C, 1+6🅽 damage, Vicious 1

GEAR: Analysis Suite, Negotiator's Kit, Stylish Clothing

SPECIAL ABILITIES
- **Data Hound**: When searching for new information or trying to analyse new data, the Information Broker gains a Technical Focus of 1.
- **Sagacious**: When making an Analysis or Psychology test, the Information Broker can reroll any dice that did not generate a success on the initial roll, but must accept the new results.
- **Key Contacts**: When assisting another character with a research-related task, the Information Broker rolls 2d20 (instead of the normal 1d20).

TROOPER/ELITE
JANISSARY

The Janissary Regiment is formed of the Orphans, the Donated, and the Delivered. The Orphans are those recruited at a very young age from the orphanges of Funduq. The Donated are those given up by poor dhimmi parents (those of non-Islamic faith) in the inhospitable frontiers of Bourak so that they might have a better future in the cities. The Delivered are the children of infidels captured by slave traders; what the traders cannot sell on open market, they sell to Haqqislam. All alike are taken to high performance training centres secreted around Funduq and educated in the Haqqislamite Virtues and the rigours of military life. / When their training is complete, young Janissaries are solid warriors and staunch believers in their (often adopted) faith. The Janissaries are specialised in the use of tactical armoured exoskeletons and dedicated to withstanding the worst of any combat.

ATTRIBUTES

AGI	AWA	BRW	COO	INT	PER	WIL
9	9	10	9	8	8	9

FIELDS OF EXPERTISE

| Combat | +2 | 1 | Movement | – | – | Social | +1 | – |
| Fortitude | +1 | – | Senses | +1 | – | Technical | – | – |

DEFENCES (TROOPER)

| Firewall | 4 | Resolve | 5 | Vigour | 5 |
| Security | – | Morale | 4 | Armour | 2 |

DEFENCES (ELITE)

| Firewall | 8 | Resolve | 9 | Vigour | 10 |
| Security | – | Morale | 4 | Armour | 2 |

ATTACKS
- **AP Rifle**: Range M, 1+6🅽 damage, Burst 2, 2H, MULTI Light Mod, Piercing 2, Vicious 1
- **Light Shotgun**: Range C, 1+5🅽 damage, Burst 1, Unbalanced, Knockdown

GEAR: Powered Combat Armour (gain up to +3d20 on Brawn tests with +3 complication range); no Cube

SPECIAL ABILITIES
- **Religious Troop**: The unshakeable faith and indoctrination of the Janissaries grant them +4 Morale Soak.
- **Tebb al-Nabi (Elite)**: Elite Janissaries are practised in Tebb al-Nabi, the Prophet's Medicine. They gain +3 Expertise and +1 Focus on Medicine tests.
- **Together Since Birth**: Janissary fireteams with three or more members gain 1 bonus Momentum on all skill tests.
- **Warriors of the Faith**: Janissaries have no Cube and have also had their brains altered to make personality recording almost impossible, demonstrating their value as warriors of the faith.

NOTES
Melee bonus damage from Powered Armour's Exoskeleton quality is factored into the Janissary's weapon damage.

NEMESIS
KHAWARIJ

With the red turban for which they are named prominently visible, the Khawarij are immediately distinctive even on the most chaotic of battlefields. Noble, dignified, and deliberate in everything they do, the Khawarij are much more than warriors. Subjected to a rigorous vetting process, only a sel ect few inductees are given the gift of participating in the Runihura (Destructor) super-soldier program.

The primary effect of the Runihura program is massive muscular development and strength. Every Khawarij looks as if they could wrestle a sea serpent into submission with their bare hands. But this physical augmentation is balanced against strenuous and devoted study. Highly honoured by Haqqislamite society, the Khawarij are bound by a strict code of honour as soldiers of Allah. They are, ultimately, sworn defenders of the Word of Allah and the Virtues of Haqqislam.

ATTRIBUTES

AGI	AWA	BRW	COO	INT	PER	WIL
9	10	11 (+2)	10	11	9	10

FIELDS OF EXPERTISE

| Combat | +3 | 2 | Movement | +2 | 1 | Social | +1 | 1 |
| Fortitude | +3 | 1 | Senses | +2 | 1 | Technical | +2 | 1 |

DEFENCES

| Firewall | 13 | Resolve | 13 | Vigour | 14 |
| Security | – | Morale | 5 | Armour | 5 |

ATTACKS
- **Rifle**: Range M, 1+7🅽 damage, Burst 2, 2H, MULTI Light Mod, Vicious 1
- **Light Shotgun**: Range C, 1+6🅽 damage, Burst 1, Unbalanced, Knockdown
- **Grenades**: 1+4🅽 damage, 1H, Indiscriminate (Close), Speculative Fire, Thrown, Unsubtle
- **Teseum-Edged Sword**: Melee, 3+7🅽 damage, 1H, Parry 2, Piercing 3, Vicious 2

GEAR: Khawarij Armour (Light Combat Armour, +3 BTS)

SPECIAL ABILITIES
- **Common Special Abilities**: Inured to Disease, Pain, Poison; Superhuman Brawn 2
- **Indomitable**: The Khawarij benefit from a Morale Soak of 5.
- **Master of Tactics**: The Khawarij are schooled in the arts of warfare and tactics. They may interrupt the player's initiative as a Minor Action without spending Heat.
- **More than Human**: Once per combat, a Khawarij can pass a test automatically, as their genetic enhancements grant them astounding abilities.
- **Super-Jump**: The Kharawij treat any distance fallen as one zone shorter when calculating damage. They may also vault over obstacles up to their own height without penalty and reduce the difficulty of skill tests to move through difficult terrain by one step.
- **Tarik's Legacy (1 Heat)**: Tarik Mansuri is a living legend; one of the first Khawarij to undergo Runihura. For 1 Heat, the Kharawij can become a terrifying dervish and gain the Fear 1 special ability for one round.

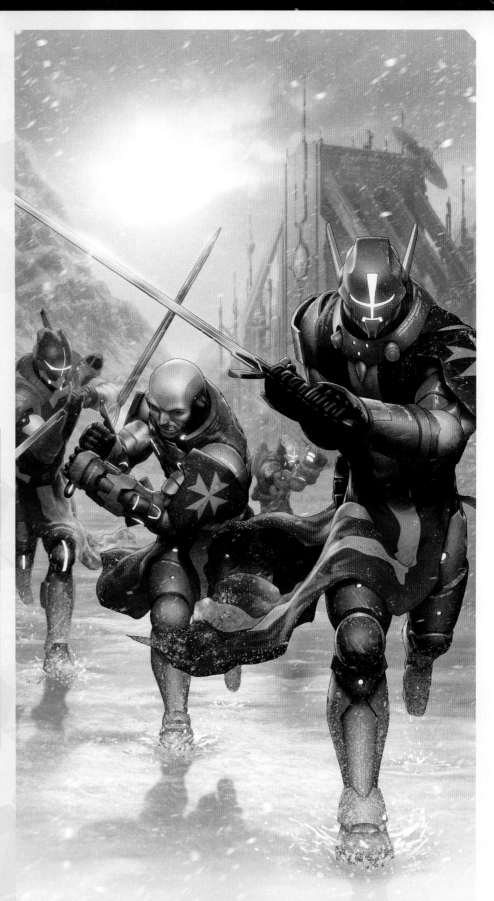

ELITE

KNIGHT

Based on the massive influence of the Catholic Church in PanOceania, the Church's Military Orders (p. 177) enjoy a prominent role in society, both on and off the battlefield. Organisationally, and despite some rivalry existing between them, the Military Orders are highly collaborative. Therefore, it's not unusual to see representatives from multiple orders present in the same combat formations. These *confrère knights* tend to inspire PanOceanian forces to set aside their differences and work towards achieving a common goal.

The orders have a certain degree of autonomy, avoiding much of the military and ecclesiastic red tape that bogs down much of PanOceanian society, in some ways becoming a church inside the Church, and an army inside the Army. A knight is held to a higher standard — not simply by society, but by themselves — and anyone who recklessly opposes them learns just what that entails.

ATTRIBUTES						
AGI	AWA	BRW	COO	INT	PER	WIL
10	8	11	9	7	8	10

FIELDS OF EXPERTISE							
Combat	+3	2	Movement	–	–	Social	+3	2
Fortitude	+2	–	Senses	–	–	Technical	–	–

DEFENCES					
Firewall	7	Resolve	10	Vigour	11
Security	–	Morale	–	Armour	4

ATTACKS
- **Armour-Piercing Sword**: Melee, 1+10 damage, Piercing 2, Parry 2, Vicious 1
- **Combi Rifle**: Range C/M, 1+5 damage, Burst 2, 2H, Expert 1, MULTI Light Mod, Vicious 1

GEAR: AutoMediKit, Heavy Combat Armour (Military Order)

SPECIAL ABILITIES
- **Sword of the Spirit**: Faith guides the Knight's blade, and their faith is unerring. When making a melee attack, they can reroll up to 2 , but must accept the new results.

GRAEME "KOBRA" KORRA

NOMAD TOMCAT ENGINEER

BACKER: GRAHAM KOBZA

"Are you there yet?"

"Ease up, moving in zero-g is not as fast as you might think."

"I read half a dozen intruders, including some remotes judging from their signature. One knight is up to fight them. Hurry!"

Graeme muted the link, instead concentrating on the small, parasitic, alien boarding craft that had come into view as he made his way along the outer hull. Instinct caused him to duck as several rockets passed overhead and struck the parasite. The eerie silence of space made the spectacle even more impressive.

A strange feeling crept over him as he hurried to the gaping hole that the explosion had left behind; probably the thought of defending a PanOceanian ship. Thus is the nature of O-12 operations — *enemies became friends.* Blue lightning flickered across his vision as he reached the breach.

"Someone's firing EMP weapons in there. Don't they know about the cargo?" he bellowed as he reactivated his helmet speakers.

"What? No, they don't!"

"Thus is the nature of secret operations," he muttered under his breath as he once again silenced the link. The Hospitaller was surrounded in there. Time to earn his money.

Crawling carefully against the push of decompression, he edged across the ceiling of the cargo hold. The place was crawling with Shasvastii boarders. The zero-g environment was clearly hindering their movement, but not his own. Graeme was used to it. A carefully aimed

burst from his rifle smashed into the closest intruder and tore it apart, giving the knight it had been engaged with some breathing room. Graeme used the recoil from the shot to launch himself towards the deck and ricocheted off it into a tight, controlled spiral to sight another squid-faced alien. The creature's cover exploded as it spun to face him, throwing it to the deck, before a burst of flame set it alight. The rushing air helped to momentarily convert the scene into a frozen portrait of heroic defence. Graeme smiled.

"Cargo hold secure."

APPEARANCE

Graeme is a broad-shouldered Caucasian in his early thirties. Sporting a ponytail and a full beard of dark brownish hair, his blue eyes are always focused on something, like he does not want any details to elude him.

ROLEPLAYING

- Patient as long as people are patient with him
- Jaded to the dangers and needs of his job
- Angry at those who ignore the dangers of living in space
- Loves art and sees the world with the eyes of a poet

BACKGROUND

Growing up on *Corregidor* is harsh for most people to say the least and Graeme's youth was no different. His father worked in the sanitation services, but hardly earned enough to pay for his own breathing. His mother died on duty when he was four.

A young Graeme loved to daub paint on any wall he could find. His impromptu masterpieces-slash-graffiti saw him frequently swept up by the Alguaciles. He took to sketching portraits of his jail cell guards, however, and the police eventually started fostering him instead of arresting him. In this sort of *ad hoc* squiring, he picked up practical mechanical skills.

When he was just sixteen years old, the fragility of *Corregidor* hit him. A hull breach ripped open the corridor outside Graeme's home. He barely survived. His father didn't.

But he'd witnessed first-hand why the Tomcats are heroes. He saw them rescue many of his friends. He applied to join and they gave him the tag-name of Kobra. It stuck. And so did the job. After a life lacking in discipline — bouncing from one thing to another — he's found his purpose.

STATS (ELITE)

ATTRIBUTES

AGI	AWA	BRW	COO	INT	PER	WIL
9	10	9	10	8	7	10

FIELDS OF EXPERTISE

Combat	+2	–	Movement	+2	1	Social	–	–
Fortitude	+2	2	Senses	+1	1	Technical	+1	–

DEFENCES

Firewall	8	Resolve	10	Vigour	9
Security	–	Morale	–	Armour	3

ATTACKS
- **Combi Rifle**: Range C/M, 1+7🌑 damage, Burst 2, 2H, Expert 1, MULTI Light Mod, Vicious 1
- **Light Flamethrower**: Range C, 1+6🌑 damage, Burst 1, 2H, Incendiary 3, Munition, Terrifying 2, Torrent
- **D-Charge**: 2+6🌑 damage, 1H, Anti-Materiel 2, Comms, Disposable, Piercing 3, Spread 1, Unsubtle, Vicious 2
- **E/M Pistol**: Range R/C, 1+5🌑 damage, Burst 1, 1H, Breaker, E/M, Piercing 1, Vicious 1

GEAR: Medium Combat Armour (with Integrated Vac Suit)

SPECIAL ABILITIES
- **Patchwork Collage**: An artist hides underneath Graeme's gruff exterior, frequently expressed in the repairs that he performs. When making a Tech test to repair an object or construct, (i.e., something with Structure and Faults, as opposed to Vigour and Wounds) he can reroll any dice that did not generate a success, but must accept the new results.
- **Rescue Specialist**: Graeme can assist another character within Reach with movement-based tests even if he is making such checks himself (by rolling 1d20 and using the normal rules for assistance).
- **Zero-G Savant**: Graeme has spent a lifetime thrusting himself along the zero-gravity corridors of *Corregidor's* outer extremities. When making a test in zero-g environments, he generates 2 bonus Momentum.

KUM ENFORCER

HIghwaymen. Asphalt warriors. The Kum are the largest of the motorcycle gangs which roar their way through the Tien Shan mountains on Bourak. Virtually all of their members are of the Kyrgyz people, and they are organised into small, roving fiefdoms each ruled by a Kum Chieftain.

A Kum enforcer has earned their way to a position of respect and honour among their fellow riders. A seasoned veteran who had to prove that they not only possessed the skills to outride opponents, but also to survive the harsh environments of Bourak without support, a Kum enforcer is a deadly adversary on the battlefield. Each is well versed in combat and knows the best way to bring the fight to the enemy. They are not foolhardy, and will not waste their lives or fuel on fool's errands, but will fight for every inch of asphalt if they feel the cause is just and the pay is right.

Some of the best Kum riders were recruited to serve in the Kum Motorized Troops under the Haqqislamite High Command. They served with honour and distinction during the NeoColonial Wars, and continue to harry the Combined Army on Paradiso today.

ATTRIBUTES

AGI	AWA	BRW	COO	INT	PER	WIL
11	11	11	12	12	8	11

FIELDS OF EXPERTISE

Combat	+4	1	Movement	+4	1	Social	+1	1
Fortitude	+1	1	Senses	+3	1	Technical	+1	1

DEFENCES

Firewall	13	Resolve	12	Vigour	12
Security	–	Morale	–	Armour	–

ATTACKS
- **Chain Rifle**: Range C, 1+8🌑 damage, Burst 1, 2H, Spread 1, Torrent, Vicious 1
- **Light Grenade Launcher**: Range M, 2+6🌑 damage, Burst 1, Unbalanced, Area (Close), Munition, Speculative Fire
- **Smoke Grenades**: Disposable, Indiscriminate (Close), Nonlethal, Smoke 2, Speculative Fire, Thrown
- **Light Shotgun**: Range C, 1+6🌑 damage, Burst 1, Unbalanced, Knockdown

GEAR: Motorcycle, War Horn

SPECIAL ABILITIES
- **Common Special Abilities**: Fear 1, Menacing 2
- **Life on the Back of a Bike**: When making a Pilot test while riding a motorcycle, a Kum Enforcer can reroll any dice that did not generate a success, but must accept the new results.
- **Roar of the Bike**: When mounted, a Kum Enforcer has Fear 3 (instead of their normal Fear 1).
- **Take On All Comers (2 Heat)**: For 2 Heat, a Kum Enforcer can ignore any Psywar effect that would cause them to retreat or raise the Intransigence of such a Metanoia Effect by 1.

LAI

Given the near-ubiquitous presence of ALEPH and its Aspects, as well as the existence of the Sole AI Law, some people believe that ALEPH is the only artificial intelligence in the Human Sphere.

But people are wrong about a lot of things.

Ignoring whispers of clandestine AIs crawling through the Arachne shadow web, there are plenty of lesser AIs legally present and active throughout the Human Sphere. Of course, most people have a personal geist that assists them, and have for most of their lives. But that's hardly the only type of LAI in the Human Sphere: security LAIs protect sensitive data, patrol algorithms scour Maya for hackers, and humble helperbots manage sewage treatment facilities and traffic optimization. Lesser Artificial Intelligences are all around us – safe, harmless, and entirely unable to become self-aware.

ATTRIBUTES

AGI	AWA	BRW	COO	INT	PER	WIL
6	10	6	6	12	11	12

FIELDS OF EXPERTISE

Combat	+1	1	Movement	+1	–	Social	+1	–
Fortitude	–	–	Senses	+1	1	Technical	+3	3

DEFENCES

Firewall	12	Resolve	12	Vigour	6
Security	–	Morale	–	Armour	–

ATTACKS
- **Hacking Device**: CLAW-1, SWORD-1, SHIELD-1, GADGET-3, IC-1 +3🌑 bonus damage

SPECIAL ABILITIES
- **Hacker**: When making an Infowar attack, the LAI can reroll up to 5🌑, but must accept the new results.
- **Quantronic Native**: Trying to find a concealed LAI in the datasphere is like searching for a needle in a needle-stack. LAIs benefit from 1 bonus Momentum on face-to-face tests made to detect them.
- **Remote Master**: LAIs gain 1 bonus Momentum on movement-based tests when operating or ghosting a remote.

ELITE

MAYA STAR

Artists, musicians, tastemakers, and commentators; Maya presents more personalities than you could sort through in a lifetime. The datasphere is awash in aspiring hopefuls, but the difference between them and the true stars is simple math: a hobbyist lifecaster may reach hundreds, even thousands of people with their streams. A true star's audience numbers at least a hundred million, maybe more.

Sometimes a lot more.

The very concept of privacy is alien to most Maya personalities; while specific shows and features will always draw the largest crowds, the advent of ever-casting and full-sensorium Maya integration means that every minute detail of their life, everything they see, taste, touch, smell, and feel, is streamed, analysed and discussed in real time by a community the size of a small nation. Some disapprove of their elaborate entourages, but to the Maya Star, it's simple: if you're never alone anyway, why not bring some friends along for the ride?

ATTRIBUTES

AGI	AWA	BRW	COO	INT	PER	WIL
10	8	7	8	9	13	8

FIELDS OF EXPERTISE

Combat	–	–	Movement	+1	–	Social	+3	3
Fortitude	+1	1	Senses	+1	1	Technical	+1	–

DEFENCES

Firewall	9	Resolve	8	Vigour	7
Security	3	Morale	–	Armour	–

ATTACKS

- **Nanopulser Necklace**: Melee, 1+4N damage, Biotech, Disposable, Subtle 3, Torrent, Vicious 1

GEAR: 7 TinBot-Mounted Recorders, Full-Sensorium Maya Integration, Stylish Clothing

SPECIAL ABILITIES

- **Entourage**: When leading a fireteam, the Maya Star can reroll one d20, but must accept the new result.
- **Personal Security Suite**: Maya Stars benefit from increased security versus Infowar attacks and gain a Security Soak of 3.
- **Star Power**: When making social skill tests., the Maya Star gains 2 bonus Momentum.

TROOPER/ELITE

METEOR HEAD

None know the dangers of deep space and the value of a hard day's work better than the meteor heads of *Corregidor*. These men and women are trained to go into zero-g environments in the most dangerous conditions in space to build and repair anything one can imagine. Their skills are so prized that stations and orbitals will delay construction projects until *Corregidor* passes by, knowing they will get the best service if they hire meteor heads. Working with these toughs is a pain in the ass, as they are oftentimes rude, dismissive, and even hostile towards non-Nomads. It is not unheard of for the Nomads to have to intervene with force when native workers clash with meteor heads after a particularly lucrative job has been pulled from the locals and put in more competent hands. Meteor heads are paragons of obstinacy, tough and self-sufficient.

ATTRIBUTES

AGI	AWA	BRW	COO	INT	PER	WIL
10	9	11	8	8	7	10

FIELDS OF EXPERTISE

Combat	+1	–	Movement	+2	1	Social	–	–
Fortitude	+2	–	Senses	–	–	Technical	+1	1

DEFENCES (TROOPER)

Firewall	4	Resolve	5	Vigour	6
Security	–	Morale	–	Armour	3

DEFENCES (ELITE)

Firewall	8	Resolve	10	Vigour	11
Security	–	Morale	–	Armour	3

ATTACKS

- **Heavy Tools**: Melee, 1+6N damage, Improvised 2, Stun

GEAR: Amoured Clothing or XO Suit (when operating in zero-g), Biomonitor, Powered Multitool, Stims in hand-milled autoinjectors (×3), Repair Kit

SPECIAL ABILITIES

- **At Home in the Black**: For each Momentum or Heat spent when making an Interplanetary test, the Meteor Head gains two d20s, instead of one.
- **Groan and Abide (2 Heat)**: Meteor Heads use this phrase in reference to the hardships of their work. By spending 2 Heat, a Meteor Head can eliminate one instance of the Fatigued condition or remove one Metanoia which is impeding a course of action.

NEMESIS

NINJA

This much is certain: ninjas do not exist. At best, they're a common superstition; at worst, an excuse for lazy guards.

So goes the conventional wisdom, and the official line. While they had a place in history, records show that all known ninja clans disappeared in the early 20th century. These ninjas were shadows in human form; experts in stealth, infiltration, disguise, and of course, assassination. Given their diverse array of clandestine skills – to say nothing of their tradition of secretive martial techniques – it's not hard to see how such agents would be useful in modern espionage.

However, their time has clearly long since passed. Any rumours of technologically advanced assassins carrying out the Emperor's will are just that: rumours. Clearly, the Emperor would never permit the politically tumultuous Nipponese to maintain their own caste of mythic assassins.

Unless, of course, they worked for the government (p. 281).

ATTRIBUTES

AGI	AWA	BRW	COO	INT	PER	WIL
14	11	9	8	10	8	10

FIELDS OF EXPERTISE

Combat	+3	2	Movement	+4	4	Social	+2	1
Fortitude	–	–	Senses	+1	–	Technical	+2	1

DEFENCES

Firewall	12	Resolve	10	Vigour	9
Security	–	Morale	–	Armour	2

ATTACKS

- **Ninja Assault Hacking Device**: CLAW-3, SWORD-0, SHIELD-0, GADGET-0, IC-2, UPGRADE White Noise; +2N bonus damage
- **Shock Sword**: Melee, 1+6N damage, Unbalanced, Biotech, Grievous, Non-Hackable, Parry 2, Vicious 1
- **Tactical Bow**: Range C, 1+5N damage, Burst 1, 2H, Non-Hackable, Subtle 2
- **Smoke Grenades**: Disposable, Indiscriminate (Close), Nonlethal, Smoke 2, Speculative Fire, Thrown

GEAR: B&E Kit, Light Combat Armour (with Multispectral Visor 2 and Thermo-Optical Camouflage)

SPECIAL ABILITIES

- **Catlike**: As it so happens, Ninjas leap off of their fair share of buildings. They treat any distance fallen as being three zones shorter when calculating damage.
- **Kenjutsu**: When making a melee attack, the Ninja can reroll up to 3N, but must accept the new results.
- **Living Shadow**: Each point of Momentum or Heat the Ninja spends to gain additional dice for an Acrobatics or Stealth test provides two d20s, instead of one.
- **Quantronic Whisper**: Physical or quantronic, Ninjas don't like to be seen. When attempting to evade detection while hacking, they can reroll one d20, but must accept the new result.

TROOPER/ELITE
NURSE

Nurses are the mainstay of medical practice throughout the Human Sphere, performing many of the functions that have allowed doctors to explore radical specialties. Training for nurses is now more in-depth, allowing them to become more knowledgeable and attend to medical functioning on a more thorough level. While most nurses still function in a support capacity for doctors, they are often the staying force that stabilises and treats the whole patient, where a doctor might treat one specific condition. Nurses are oftentimes responsible for the bulk of communication and interaction with a patient, and when patients become unruly, they are a likely to be involved with intervention. Nurses tend to be dedicated, grounded, and stern figures who wield authority with certainty.

ATTRIBUTES						
AGI	AWA	BRW	COO	INT	PER	WIL
7	7	9	8	10	8	7

FIELDS OF EXPERTISE						
Combat	+1	–	Movement	–	–	Social	+2	1
Fortitude	+1	1	Senses	+2	1	Technical	+2	1

DEFENCES (TROOPER)					
Firewall	5	Resolve	4	Vigour	5
Security	–	Morale	–	Armour	–

DEFENCES (ELITE)					
Firewall	10	Resolve	7	Vigour	9
Security	–	Morale	–	Armour	1

ATTACKS
- **Stun Baton**: Melee, 1+5 🄽 damage, 1H, Knockdown, Non-Hackable, Stun, Subtle 1

GEAR: Clothing (Scrubs), Basic Medical Supplies, MediKit

GEAR (ELITE): Armoured Clothing (Nano-Infused Scrubs, +2 BTS)

SPECIAL ABILITIES
- **Much Needed Assistance (2 Heat)**: A Nurse can act as a synergist for those practising medicine. They can spend 2 Heat to double the Expertise or Focus on the next Medicine test made by a character within Reach. These effects cannot be combined in order to double both Expertise and Focus.
- **Medical Expertise (Elite)**: An Elite Nurse adds +1 Expertise and +1 Focus to their Medicine tests.

NOTES
Psychiatric Nurses specialise in the Psychology skill instead of Medicine. Replace the references to Medicine in the Nurse's special abilities with Psychology for a Psychiatric Nurse.

NEMESIS
ODALISQUE

Trained at the Çember Odalisques Academy in Dar el Funduq on Bourak, Odalisques are celestial houris — deities above mere mortals who have mastered the Arts of Seduction. This is often seen as licentious and wild, but the truth is exactly the opposite: In their training, Odalisques gain complete, precise, and comprehensive understanding and mastery over their bodies and minds... both of which will also be augmented with cutting edge Haqqislamite technology.

The Odalisque's Arts of Seduction also feature multi-faceted combat training, including a wide array of tactics and techniques other warriors would not readily consider, along with intelligence methods that allow them to procure information seemingly at a whim. Upon graduation, Odalisques fulfil numerous military functions, proving their ability to disarm their opponents in either sense with well-practised ease. They are also often employed as bodyguards and VIP escorts by the Haqqislamite elite.

ATTRIBUTES						
AGI	AWA	BRW	COO	INT	PER	WIL
9	8	8	10	12	13	10

FIELDS OF EXPERTISE						
Combat	+3	1	Movement	+3	1	Social	+3	2
Fortitude	+1	–	Senses	+3	2	Technical	+1	–

DEFENCES					
Firewall	13	Resolve	11	Vigour	9
Security	–	Morale	5	Armour	4

ATTACKS
- **Defensive Hacking Device**: CLAW-0, SWORD-0, SHIELD-3, GADGET-1, IC-3; +3 🄽 bonus damage
- **DT Pistol**: Range R/C, 1+4 🄽 damage, Burst 1, 1H, Biotech, Toxic 1, Vicious 1
- **Garrotte**: Melee, 1H, Concealed 2, Non-Hackable, Subtle 2, Unforgiving 1
- **Oneiros Grenade**: Range C, 2+4 🄽 damage, Biotech, Disposable, Immobilising, Indiscriminate (Close), Nonlethal, Speculative Fire, Stun, Thrown

GEAR: AR Eye Implants, Cosmetics Kit, Medium Combat Armour (with Deactivator Kit), Odalisque Subdermal Augmentation (+1 Armour Soak, no complication penalty)

SPECIAL ABILITIES
- **Common Special Abilities**: Keen Senses (Hearing, Sight, Smell)
- **Harem Seduction**: Multiple Odalisques performing a group test to seduce a target roll 2d20 for each assistant, instead of the normal 1d20.
- **Implausible Perfection (2 Heat)**: Beautiful in a way that transcends sexuality and gender, the stare of an Odalisque is a powerful weapon. Odalisque Psywar techniques gain the Grievous quality.
- **Quick Change (1 Heat)**: An Odalisque can spend 1 Heat to perform a quick change, rapidly altering the appearance of their garb and gaining 2 bonus Momentum to a Disguise test.

TROOPER/ELITE
PILOT

As mankind has expanded into the stars, so too has the need for safe and skilled transportation into these new locales. Along the way, the title "pilot" has become somewhat more diffuse as the scope and variety of vehicles in use has grown into a dizzying panoply of disparate options. Some pilots perform aerobatics with single-seaters that can convert from plane to submersible, while others guide craft which are literally kilometres long.

This diversity — in combination with the unimaginably vast vistas across which humans now need to travel — has also, naturally, resulted in pilots being in even higher demand. Thus, even with the ever-encroaching expertise of LAI and pseudo-AI pilots, there are more human pilots in the Human Sphere today than during any other epoch of human history. Oddly, this has not reduced the tendency for pilots to be cocky and confident with a streak of thrillseeking.

ATTRIBUTES						
AGI	AWA	BRW	COO	INT	PER	WIL
9	8	6	10	8	8	7

FIELDS OF EXPERTISE						
Combat	–	–	Movement	+2	1	Social	–	–
Fortitude	+1	–	Senses	+2	1	Technical	+2	–

DEFENCES (TROOPER)					
Firewall	4	Resolve	4	Vigour	3
Security	–	Morale	–	Armour	3*

DEFENCES (ELITE)					
Firewall	8	Resolve	7	Vigour	6
Security	–	Morale	–	Armour	3*

ATTACKS
- **Pistol**: Range R/C, 1+4 🄽 damage, Burst 1, 1H, Vicious 1

GEAR: *Crashsuit (dissolves after a single round of use), Inlaid Palm Circuitry, Parachute Pack, Stim Autoinjectors (×2)

SPECIAL ABILITIES
- **Need for Speed**: Pilots can reroll one d20 when making Pilot tests, but must accept the new result, and additionally gain 1 bonus Momentum on such tests.
- **Slam 'em! (2 Heat)**: A Pilot can ram more effectively, doubling the damage of a ramming attack by spending 2 Heat.

LEPER

POSTHUMAN

BACKER: JOHN SMITH

"What's with the skin? Looks artificial." The Ariadnan guard was peering at him.

"I was caught in a fire when I was young. Needed a full body replacement. Not all of it took." That was a lie. There had been no fire. The glistening burn-scars running from his left hand up to his elbow had been custom-designed.

"Whoa. I'm sorry."

Behind the podunk guard he saw, on the security monitor, his other-self approach the elevators. He leapt away from the bait body – the one which was holding the guard's attention – and stepped through the elevator doors. Jumping between the two bodies took only a fraction of a second, and as he exerted the minimal effort required to keep the conversation alive in the lobby, his main body – the one on the elevator; the one with the trio of ghastly scars running across its left eye and down its cheek – slapped the repeater onto the elevator's security camera, allowing the Wardriver on the orbital caravanserai – the one he'd hired – to hack and loop its feed.

"Who were you here to see?" the guard asked as the elevator camera flickered behind him. Leper set his mouth into motion for the answer and – The third body he had onsite watched the elevator doors open. With a noticeable limp, he hefted the ovoid, gleaming white plastic of the sarcophagus on-board, flitting between steps back to the scarred body which was laying down a circle of breach paste. The doors closed. The elevator went up. He hit the emergency stop button and triggered the paste. A brief flash of light, the smell of melting metal, and a circle dropped out of the floor and plummeted down the shaft. He stepped into the hole (he remained in the elevator) and he fell (he watched) waiting for the laser-calibrated descender to bring him to a gentle halt directly before the door to the sub-basement that wasn't supposed to exist.

Now for the tricky part.

He leapt over the security counter / grabbed the doors / kicked the guard / pushed the sarcophagus towards the hole / took his gun / slammed the separator into / shot / the gap between / shot / the doors / shot the guard three times – Wait. One... two... Alarms. And... Burst the doors / "Phoenix Industries is –" / sight the guards distracted by the alarms / "– a spacer cancer!" / shot / attach the sarcophagus / shot / "This is now –" / the guards drop / "– a hostage situation!"

The third body came sliding down the elevator cable and swung the sarcophagus into the sub-basement.

The hypercorp might guess the real target, but now the Ariadnans would take care of sealing the perimeter for him. He guessed he'd be able to keep the negotiations going with the "terrorist" for at least two hours. He might end up losing the body, but it was just a body, after all.

He shot a wodge of silvery gunk up into the shaft. The aerated steel rapidly expanded, creating a wedge of metal that filled the elevator shaft. That would take care of any additional security personnel trying to breach from above. All he needed to do now was secure the rest of the sub-basement.

"Signal the Professor. We'll be all clear in five minutes."

APPEARANCE

As a Posthuman, Leper has no fixed body and, unlike many Posthumans, no fixed preferences. Except one: he chooses to give each body he inhabits one major disfigurement.

ROLEPLAYING

- Keeps people second guessing him (and themselves)
- Rolls his eyes
- Compulsively checks his six o'clock

BACKGROUND

If anyone knows Leper's true past, it is ALEPH alone. All the official records concerning his history, his qualifications for becoming Posthuman, and his current assignments are either nonexistent or classified. If he's asked about his past, Leper offers a different version every time.

STATS (NEMESIS)

ATTRIBUTES

AGI	AWA	BRW	COO	INT	PER	WIL
12 (+1)	10 (+1)	10 (+1)	10 (+1)	10 (+1)	9	9

FIELDS OF EXPERTISE

Combat	+2	1	Movement	+2	1	Social	+3	2
Fortitude	+2	2	Senses	+1	1	Technical	+2	2

DEFENCES

Firewall	12	Resolve	11	Vigour	12
Security	2	Morale	2	Armour	3

ATTACKS

- **Dual Stun Pistols**: Range R/C, 2+6 🄽 damage, Burst 1, 1H, Biotech, Nonlethal, Stun, Vicious 1
- **Wetspike**: Melee, 2+6 🄽 damage, Biotech, Piercing 1, Subtle 3, Toxic 1

GEAR: Attribute Augmentation (Silk), Bioengineered Physiology, Internal Armour, Light Combat Armour

SPECIAL ABILITIES

- **Common Special Abilities**: Fast Recovery (Firewall 1, Vigour 1), Keen Senses (Hearing, Sight, Smell), Night Vision, Quantronic Jump, Superhuman Agility 1, Superhuman Awareness 1, Superhuman Brawn 1, Superhuman Coordination 1, Superhuman Intelligence 1
- **Connected**: A Posthuman's constant connection to the datasphere illuminates life from a different perspective, and Leper is always working the angles to his benefit. He gains Morale and Security Soak 2.
- **Covertly Deceptive**: Whether deliberate misinformation, inspiring rhetoric, or casual conversation, Leper is incredibly persuasive. When making a social skill test, he can reroll any dice that did not generate a success on the initial roll, but must accept the new result.
- **Proxy Sight**: Leper is constantly cycling between nearby proxies, all while maintaining his link to the datasphere. Needless to say, he's usually quite well-informed. When making an Observation test, he can reroll any dice that did not generate a success on the initial roll, but must accept the new result.

NEMESIS
PIRATE CAPTAIN

A captain of a pirate vessel is a veteran of many sorties, someone who has looked into the eye of fate and lived to tell the tale. These ruthless individuals have long since forgotten about values other than money. They live and die for it. Pirate society is hierarchical, but loyalty is not a virtue shared by many. Some captains try to maintain discipline by the use of intimidation, while others bribe their crews with more generous shares of plunder. In the Human Sphere, captains flying Haqqislamite colours are considered to be the best of the bunch and the most noble, but one should keep in mind that even though a hammerhead is not a great white, it is still a shark.

ATTRIBUTES

AGI	AWA	BRW	COO	INT	PER	WIL
11	9	13	11	7	10	9

FIELDS OF EXPERTISE

Combat	+3	2	Movement	+3	2	Social	+2	1
Fortitude	+2	1	Senses	+1	1	Technical	+2	–

DEFENCES

Firewall	9	Resolve	11	Vigour	15
Security	–	Morale	–	Armour	3

ATTACKS

- **Breaker Pistol**: Range R/C, 1+5 🄽 damage, Burst 1, Biotech, Breaker, Piercing 1, Vicious 1
- **Ceremonial Sabre**: Melee, 1+8 🄽 damage, Unbalanced, Non-Hackable, Parry 2, Vicious 1
- **Nanopulser**: Range C, 1+6 🄽 damage, 1H, Biotech, Subtle 3, Torrent, Vicious 2

GEAR: Medium Combat Armour

SPECIAL ABILITIES

- **All Hands on Deck**: A Pirate Captain's crew is never far from the call of his comlog. When the Pirate Captain is in a scene, the Heat cost of summoning reinforcements is reduced by 2 (to a minimum of 1).
- **Common Special Abilities**: Menacing 1, Threatening 2
- **Promise of Booty**: Pirates are inspired by the presence of their Captain, and fight with increased ferocity, adding +1 🄽 to attacks for the duration of any scene where the Captain is present.
- **Void Vanish**: When piloting a ship, a Pirate Captain gains 2 bonus Momentum on Stealth tests.

TROOPER
PIRATE DECKHAND

The crew of a pirate ship are a nasty lot. The life of a mercenary is not for those faint of heart, as rape, pillage, and plunder are on the daily agenda. This draws a particular type of people into this line of work — hardened people who have decided that they don't fit within the boundaries that the society has set for them. True, some of them are simple free-spirits looking for their place in the world. However, many more are just sociopaths, thieves, and murderers, trying to escape the past that is haunting them. Regardless of the cause of their enlistment with a pirate crew, these ruffians usually find themselves helping with the day-to-day maintenance of the ship and performing menial tasks. They also participate in boarding actions against enemy vessels and, what they lack in training, they more than make up for with numbers.

ATTRIBUTES

AGI	AWA	BRW	COO	INT	PER	WIL
9	7	12	9	6	6	7

FIELDS OF EXPERTISE

Combat	+2	–	Movement	+1	–	Social	–	–
Fortitude	+1	–	Senses	+1	–	Technical	+1	–

DEFENCES

Firewall	3	Resolve	4	Vigour	6
Security	–	Morale	–	Armour	2

ATTACKS

- **Assault Pistol**: Range R/C, 1+4 🄽 damage, Burst 2, Unbalanced, Vicious 1
- **Knife**: Melee, 1+6 🄽 damage, 1H, Concealed 1, Non-Hackable, Subtle 2, Thrown, Unforgiving 1

GEAR: Light Combat Armour

LORNA CLOTILDE

MOBILE BRIGADA

BACKER: NEIL HARVEY

"Are you all right, Mr. Atitarn?" Lorna shouted as she vaulted behind the bar, bullets pinging off her armour. Pausing for a second, she assessed the situation: a breathtaking, floor-to-ceiling, uninterrupted view of Shentang to her left, four angry mercs at the door in front, and a bleeding Phoenix Industries Vice President at her feet who was not responding to her question.

"Obviously not. Time for Plan B." She began firing blindly over the counter towards the door with her right hand — letting the expert systems in the gun handle the aiming — while her left went through the practised motions of opening her MediKit.

"Mr. Atitarn, my name is Lorna Clotilde and I am here to extract you. You're currently going into shock. This is going to hurt."

His scream underlined her statement as she injected him.

"Now, before the sedative kicks in too much, I need you to get into this bag," she ordered, producing something that looked suspiciously like a body bag. "And put this on," she added as she tossed him a flimsy respirator mask. He stared blankly at her. She fired more snap shots over the bar, prompting a satisfying curse from the other side of the room.

"Mr. Atitarn, it is this or a Cube extraction, your choice. You have twenty seconds to decide." As he scrambled for the bag, she popped up and sent a sustained burst towards the end of the room as an advance suppressant.

Turning back, she zipped the bag over the VP as he began adjusting the respirator. Once closed, there was an almost inaudible hiss and the

bag rapidly decompressed. The lights flickered right on cue, a slight shudder raced through the floor, and slowly but surely everything started to float.

Lorna pushed off towards the spectacular view with package in tow, putting the bulk of her armour between Atitarn and the mercs. Half a second before she reached the viewport, it shattered under a barrage of fire from her stealthed remotes outside. In a rush of air, she was pushed out into the silent embrace of nothing.

APPEARANCE

A tall woman in her mid-twenties. She has long blonde hair and brown eyes that generally mimic her often worn smile. A thin, light scar runs up the length of her left bicep.

ROLEPLAYING

- Treats machines like people
- Loves what she is doing and abhors loss of human life
- Very loyal to her comrades

BACKGROUND

Corregidor takes care of its own. When Lorna's parents, both hard-working mine workers, were killed during a revolt on a mining asteroid in the Human Edge, she was taken into the care of an old friend of theirs: a doctor with her own private clinic in the Lazareto slums. With the doctor, Lorna grew up helping to treat the wounded and sick, which became a passion for her.

Paying for medical training is an expensive proposition on *Corregidor* and when her foster mother died in the Second Phantom Conflict, it seemed like her best option was to join the Alguaciles and hope to bootstrap her way into the Daktari medical corps.

Life had other plans for her, however. On her first Alguacil mercenary mission outside *Corregidor*, she came to the rescue of a badly wounded Brigada. Using her rudimentary medical knowledge, she saved his life and, pinned down behind enemy lines, she donned his powered armour and used it to fight their way out.

The grateful soldier told her to keep the Spitfire rifle she'd taken from him. (She still uses it to this day.) And the Mobile Brigada recruited her.

She's continued her medical training and, although she has yet to achieve her doctorate, her comrades are happy to have someone on the squad who knows more about using a MediKit than just jabbing the auto-injectors into their legs. She's also earned a reputation for collecting useful trophies. She acquired a jury-rigged FastPanda during her last tour on Paradiso, for example. Programmed to function as a Tinbot, her squad is grateful for its protection... though some are beginning to question her attachment to it.

STATS (NEMESIS)

ATTRIBUTES

AGI	AWA	BRW	COO	INT	PER	WIL
11	11	9	10	11	9	9

FIELDS OF EXPERTISE

Combat	+2	1	Movement	+2	2	Social	+2	1
Fortitude	+1	1	Senses	+2	1	Technical	+3	2

DEFENCES

Firewall	14	Resolve	10	Vigour	10
Security	–	Morale	–	Armour	5

ATTACKS

- **Spitfire**: Range M, 1+7 🅽 damage, Burst 3, 2H, Spread 2, Unsubtle
- **Pistol**: Range R/C, 1+6 🅽 damage, Burst 1, 1H, Vicious 1
- **Knife**: Melee, 1+7 🅽 damage, 1H, Concealed 1, Non-Hackable, Subtle 2, Thrown, Unforgiving 1

GEAR: BioScanner, Powered Combat Armour (with AutoMediKit and MediKit), Painkillers (×2), Reprogrammed FastPanda (use TinBot stats and add a Repeater), Stims (×2)

SPECIAL ABILITIES

- **Combat Alertness**: Lorna can reroll one d20 when making an Observation test in combat situations, but must accept the new result.
- **Combat Defences**: Lorna is used to high-pressure situations. She never pays more than 1 Heat to use the Defence, Guard, or Return Fire Reactions, and generates 1 Heat if her test is successful.
- **Medicinal Aspirations**: Lorna may not have her MD yet, but all this battlefield experience is starting to add up. When attempting to treat Wounds, any Heat spent to add dice to a Medicine test will add two d20s instead of one (the normal maximum of three bonus d20s still applies).
- **Split Focus (1 Heat)**: By spending 1 Heat, Lorna can make two attacks simultaneously in opposite directions (albeit at +1 difficulty).

TROOPER/ELITE

POLICE

The one commonality shared by almost all human nations is the presence of law enforcement. Varying greatly from Neoterra's specialists to Ariadna's frontiersmen, a significant portion are also contracted to corporations. Whilst the law enforcement of the Human Sphere are as varied as the countries and nations they stand for, all are trained to handle a variety of situations such as combat, negotiation, vehicle operation and technical skills, and other occupational demands.

Most police officers are trained and equipped with weaponry to ensure they will have the advantage over an armed and dangerous civilian, but are rarely issued anything beyond this without special training.

ATTRIBUTES

AGI	AWA	BRW	COO	INT	PER	WIL
8	9	8	9	8	9	9

FIELDS OF EXPERTISE

Combat	+1	1	Movement	+1	–	Social	+2	1
Fortitude	+1	–	Senses	+2	1	Technical	–	–

DEFENCES (TROOPER)

Firewall	4	Resolve	5	Vigour	8
Security	–	Morale	–	Armour	1

DEFENCES (ELITE)

Firewall	8	Resolve	9	Vigour	9
Security	–	Morale	–	Armour	1

ATTACKS

- **Light Shotgun**: Range C, 1+5 🅽 damage, Burst 1, Unbalanced, Knockdown
- **Pistol**: Range R/C, 1+5 🅽 damage, Burst 1, 1H, Vicious 1
- **Stun Baton**: Melee, 1+4 🅽 damage, 1H, Knockdown, Non-Hackable, Stun, Subtle 1

GEAR: Armoured Clothing (Uniform), SecurCuffs, Torch

SPECIAL ABILITIES

- **Blue Line**: A policeman's social zone has Insular 2.
- **Walk the Beat**: When a policeman assists on a skill test for human terrain mapping, they roll 2d20 (instead of the normal 1d20).

NEMESIS

POLICE – SWAT OFFICER

Nothing is more terrifying to a criminal than the sudden, thunderous arrival of SWAT officer. Utilizing close to mid-range weaponry and equipped with heavy armour, SWAT officers breach heavily fortified positions with charges and flashbangs before levelling their weapons and clearing a position without mercy.

Typically withheld until negotiations break down or as a violent preemptive measure against known criminals, SWAT officers are trained to handle close engagements and hostage rescue. Time has done little to change the *modus operandi* of this particular division of law enforcement since the late 19th century. In fact, recent developments in technology have only assisted them, with heat/motion sensors, security worms, and auto-drones allowing the officers to more easily handle situations.

ATTRIBUTES

AGI	AWA	BRW	COO	INT	PER	WIL
9	13	9	12	9	8	10

FIELDS OF EXPERTISE

Combat	+4	2	Movement	+3	1	Social	+1	–
Fortitude	+3	1	Senses	+2	1	Technical	+1	1

DEFENCES

Firewall	10	Resolve	13	Vigour	12
Security	–	Morale	–	Armour	4

ATTACKS

- **Combi Rifle**: Range C/M, 1+8 🅽 damage, Burst 2, 2H, Expert 1, MULTI Light Mod, Vicious 1
- **Boarding Shotgun**: Range C, 1+8 🅽 damage, Burst 1, 2H, Knockdown, Medium MULTI
  - *DA Mode (Secondary)*: Vicious 2

GEAR: Heavy Combat Armour (with Torch)

SPECIAL ABILITIES

- **Blue Line**: A policeman's social zone has Insular 2.
- **Breaching Insertion (1 Heat)**: SWAT Officers are trained in breaching and clearing rooms and facilities. A well-executed breach can leave enemies reeling and easy to pick off. By spending 1 Heat when the SWAT Officer arrives (including from reinforcements) the GM can allow the SWAT to execute a Breaching Insertion. First the GM selects any zone within the current engagement zone for the SWAT Officer to breach. The SWAT Officer can enter that zone through an obstacle and characters within the zone are affected.
- **Tactical Training**: SWAT Officers can reroll up to 2 🅽 when making a ranged attack, but must accept the new results. Additionally, they reduce the penalties for firing at a range other than a weapon's optimal range by one, to a minimum of 0.

MAXIMUS STILTS
INDEPENDENT PATENT ATTORNEY

BACKER: MAXIMILIAN STELZER

Dear Sister,

I hope this message finds you well. I apologise for the lengthy delay between messages, but my work here on Shentang has been both taxing and very rewarding. Preparations for my second office are proceeding apace, and of course the dynamic legacies of so many traditional legal systems – even unified under the purview of the Emperor – continue to provide the most delightful challenges, even when the clients are occasionally delusional.

Actually, I had a consultation yesterday that I think you would have liked. An actual Posthuman – a professor of some sort. Drop dead gorgeous, of course. But even better, she asked for my counsel on the patent implications for the Governance of Exo-Artefacts law under the regulations of the Ariadnan Exclusion Zone Commission. Which is fascinating, because the former is really quite archaic. It actually predates Concilium, and most of it was drafted shortly after the poor Helots were discovered, so it has a bunch of outdated language that sort of implicitly assumes Earth is the centre of the universe. The latter, of course, has sections empowered by authority which didn't even exist until the Accra Truce, and it's all complicated by the fact that the Antipodes' native claims to Dawn have never really been cleared up in the aftermath of the Yu Jing Compromise. Such fun!

You should come and visit! I promise to guide you through the horrific goulash of the local cuisines, because I assure you it's worth the effort. What the Tai Siam and Isan have done with the native Shentang species is a marvel of culinary fusion.

I must stop now. I have another unusual appointment in a few minutes. A private detective named Shoemaker or something like that. If he's half as interesting as the Posthuman, I'll tell you more in my next.

I promise to write again soon.

Love,

Maximus

[Message found on the comlog of patent attorney Maximus Stilts. Current whereabouts unknown. Wanted by Imperial authorities.]

APPEARANCE

A shiny bald pate with surgical implants which can be used to create subtle patterns of multi-coloured light. Attentive, blue-grey eyes are constantly assessing those around him (while seeming somewhat oblivious to his other surroundings). His expensive, fashionable clothing is immaculately tailored.

ROLEPLAYING

- Gregarious and loose in social situations; tightly focused in professional conduct; utterly relaxed in either
- Very competitive and hates losing
- Rubs the top of his head when facing an exciting conundrum

BACKGROUND

As the son of two lawyers, both of whom married other lawyers after they got divorced, it would seem as if Maximus' legal career was almost predetermined. But, in truth, during his youth he wanted nothing to do with "petty legal quarrels". Instead, he first pursued a career in what his parents called the "dirty business of politics" – first in a civil position within the Ministry of Education, and then in the lower echelons of the Zeitgeist Lobby. But there too, as he tells it, he found himself dissatisfied with the "dreary mundanity of the bureaucracy". (The reality is that there was a minor sexual scandal involving members of a Haqqislam diplomatic mission.)

Forced back into a legal education, but still rebelling against his parents, Maximus eschewed the criminal law they prized and instead went into corporate law with a specialisation in intellectual property. Despite his late start, he rose quickly through the ranks, developing a reputation as a shark in the court room, thriving on crushing his opponents and relentlessly pursuing his arguments to the bitter end.

Legal proceedings concerning the reproduction of MULTI weaponry in the Human Edge system brought particular notoriety, and – defying his parents once again – he used it to catapult his legal career out of PanOceania and established a legal office on Shentang.

STATS (ELITE)

ATTRIBUTES

AGI	AWA	BRW	COO	INT	PER	WIL
7	10	8	8	10	10	10

FIELDS OF EXPERTISE

Combat	+1	–	Movement	+1	–	Social	+2	2
Fortitude	+1	–	Senses	+2	1	Technical	+1	1

DEFENCES

Firewall	10	Resolve	10	Vigour	8
Security	–	Morale	–	Armour	1

ATTACKS

- **Briefcase Pistol**: Range R/C, 1+6 🇳 damage, Burst 1, 1H, Concealed 1, Vicious 1

GEAR: AR Eye Implants, Armoured Clothing (Fashionable)

SPECIAL ABILITIES

- **Courtroom Tyrant**: Maximus is a force of nature in the courtroom, harrying both his opponent and their evidence until they crumble. His bonus damage to Psywar attacks is increased by +2 🇳 and an additional +1 🇳 in legal settings.
- **Legal Connections**: Maximus' extensive network of contacts keeps him very well-informed. When spending Heat to call reinforcements in Psywar scenes with Maximus, the GM reduces the total cost by 2 Heat, to a minimum of 1 Heat spent. (If Maximus is incapacitated, the GM can no longer use his Legal Connections ability.)
- **Research Geist Cluster**: Maximus maintains a cluster of multiple geists to assist him with research, making acquiring all types of information much easier.

NEMESIS
POSTHUMAN

Whether they represent the next step in human evolution, a parallel track, or something else entirely, Posthumans are smarter, stronger, and experience life differently than standard humans. Resurrected into Bodhisattva Lhosts by ALEPH itself, these so-called Posthumans are selected from the very best and brightest, which has the side effect of causing a brain drain in humanity proper.

Their constant connection to the Maya datasphere obviates the need for Cubes—their essence is distributed throughout the Datasphere much like ALEPH's—and access to quantronic processing has opened and advanced their minds in ways humanity is still struggling to fully understand. They can fork their personality, merge into and out of a collective with no loss of self, and enjoy all the benefits of a human intellect with the flexibility and power of an AI.

Immortality. Beauty. Powers beyond mortal comprehension. Is it any wonder they're treated like demigods?

ATTRIBUTES

AGI	AWA	BRW	COO	INT	PER	WIL
9 (+1)	10 (+1)	9 (+1)	9	11 (+2)	11	11

FIELDS OF EXPERTISE

Combat	+2	1	Movement	+2	1	Social	+2	2
Fortitude	+2	1	Senses	+2	1	Technical	+2	2

DEFENCES

Firewall	13	Resolve	13	Vigour	11
Security	–	Morale	2	Armour	–

ATTACKS

- **Assault Hacking Device**: CLAW-3, SWORD-0, SHIELD-0, GADGET-0, IC-1; +2 🇳 bonus damage
- **Nanopulser**: Range C, 2+7 🇳 damage, 1H, Biotech, Subtle 3, Torrent, Vicious 2

GEAR: Cube 2.0

SPECIAL ABILITIES

- **Common Special Abilities**: Fast Recovery 1, Keen Senses (Hearing, Sight, Smell), Night Vision, Quantronic Jump, Superhuman Agility 1, Superhuman Awareness 1, Superhuman Brawn 1, Superhuman Intelligence 2
- **Connected**: A Posthuman's constant connection to the datasphere widens their perspective, granting a Morale Soak of 2. If they are unable to connect to the datasphere, they lose these benefits.

TROOPER
PROSPECTOR

Whether it's illegal Teseum mining in the Northern Frontier of Caledonia, an asteroid miner from *Corregidor*, or an off-the-books "asset reclamation team" picking through a battle's aftermath in the jungles of Paradiso, prospectors are a hardy and adventurous lot. They have to be: the life of a prospector is not for the faint of heart, or frankly, anyone with better career options.

Freelance prospectors scour asteroid belts for seams that hypercorp mining companies can exploit, or venture out into dangerous territories, hoping to strike it rich before being struck dead. Radiation burns, collapsing hulks, alien warzones; there's no shortage of occupational hazards. But as anyone who lived through the Helicon Miners' revolt will tell you, if the job doesn't kill you... well, your employers will probably try.

So, while the average prospector doesn't go looking for trouble, they're rarely surprised when it rears its head.

ATTRIBUTES

AGI	AWA	BRW	COO	INT	PER	WIL
9	8	10	8	8	6	7

FIELDS OF EXPERTISE

Combat	+1	–	Movement	+1	–	Social	–	–
Fortitude	+1	–	Senses	+1	–	Technical	+2	–

DEFENCES

Firewall	4	Resolve	4	Vigour	5
Security	–	Morale	–	Armour	3

ATTACKS

- **Boarding Shotgun**: Range C, 1+5 🇳 damage, Burst 1, 2H, Knockdown, Medium MULTI
  - *Normal Shells Mode (Primary)*: Area (Close), Spread 1
  - *AP Slugs Mode (Secondary)*: Piercing 3
- **Explosive Charges**: 2+6 🇳 damage, 1H, Disposable, Indiscriminate, Spread 1, Unsubtle, Vicious 2

GEAR: Powered Multitool, Stims (×1), XO Suit

SPECIAL ABILITIES

- **Explorer**: The Prospector can reroll one d20 when making an Extraplanetary test, but must accept the new result.

TROOPER/ELITE
REPORTER

Technically, reporters are under the protection of the Concilium Convention while working in their protected capacity, and any hostile actions toward them are subject to legal action by interplanetary courts — harming one is a violation of the Concilium Convention.

Of course, so is using a Chain Rifle, and you don't see any shortage of those around.

In reality, reporters often skirt the boundaries of legality while chasing a story, casting their protected status in an ambiguous light, and throwing caution to the wind as a matter of habit. For some, journalism is a calling; a noble pursuit of the truth, even in the face of immediate danger. For others, the lure of bright lights and big paydays clouds their judgement.

Either way, wherever there's trouble, you can bet a reporter is not far behind.

ATTRIBUTES

AGI	AWA	BRW	COO	INT	PER	WIL
9	9	6	8	8	10	10

FIELDS OF EXPERTISE

Combat	–	–	Movement	+1	–	Social	+2	1
Fortitude	+1	–	Senses	+2	1	Technical	+1	–

DEFENCES (TROOPER)

Firewall	4	Resolve	5	Vigour	3
Security	–	Morale	–	Armour	1

DEFENCES (ELITE)

Firewall	8	Resolve	10	Vigour	6
Security	–	Morale	–	Armour	1

ATTACKS
- **Stun Baton**: Melee, 1+4 🅝 damage, 1H, Knockdown, Non-Hackable, Stun, Subtle 1
- **Hacking Device**: CLAW-1, SWORD-1, SHIELD-1, GADGET-3, IC-1

GEAR: Analysis Suite, AR Eye Implants, Nav Suite, Rucksack, TinBot-Mounted Recorder

SPECIAL ABILITIES
- **Danger Sense**: When making a test to determine Surprise, the Reporter can reroll any dice that did not generate a success on the initial roll, but must accept the new results.
- **Sharp Senses**: The Reporter gains again 1 bonus Momentum on Observation tests.

ELITE
RESEARCH SCIENTIST

The relatively recent acceleration into uncharted territory both literally, through the exploration of space, and figuratively, in the expansion of the Human Sphere into new social and technological communities and constructs, has sparked a massive revival of research into a wide array of subjects. Research scientists include the traditional hard sciences such as astrophysics, xenobiology, quantum chemistry, and relativistic mathematics, but also include newer fields including neosociology, alien psychology, and unified linguistics. While many are still affiliated with academic institutions, most research scientists are employed by factions, corporations, and other political entities. Research scientists tend to be introverted, passionate, and blunt when interacting with others.

ATTRIBUTES

AGI	AWA	BRW	COO	INT	PER	WIL
7	8	7	9	13	9	10

FIELDS OF EXPERTISE

Combat	–	–	Movement	–	–	Social	+1	–
Fortitude	–	–	Senses	+3	2	Technical	+3	3

DEFENCES

Firewall	13	Resolve	10	Vigour	7
Security	–	Morale	–	Armour	–

ATTACKS
- **Improvised Weapon**: Melee, 1+2 🅝 damage, Improvised 1, Subtle 1

GEAR: Analytical Kit, Lab Clothing (+1 BTS)

SPECIAL ABILITIES
- **Muddy the Waters (1 Heat)**: A Research Scientist understands how to obscure as well as reveal. They can spend 1 Heat to increase an opponent's Analysis or Science test by +1 difficulty, so long as the Scientist had access to the subject of the check. If this results in a failure, the opponent can attempt a Analysis (D1) test to reveal the interference.
- **Specialisation**: Within the Researcher's field of specialisation, they roll +2d20 on Education tests.

NEMESIS
REVEREND MOIRA

Deep within Praxis is the convent module of the Observance of Mercy, home to the Observants of Saint Mary of the Knife, Our Lady of Mercy. A product of the Great Apostasy when the Catholic Church acknowledged ALEPH, an entity they consider an instrument of the Devil, named after ruthless avengers enforcing fate and punishing gods and men alike, the Reverend Moira enact punishment on those guilty of crimes against the faithful — those who rejected ALEPH and its devilish machinations. Each has proved their devotion through the Seven Rituals and wears blessed nails in their backs.

As some of the best AI experts in Praxis, the Reverend Moira form the backbone of the Bakunin aggression forces and act as the tactical section of the Black Hand, the Nomad Intelligence Agency. Well-equipped and highly trained in multiple combat environments, these infowar experts focus their efforts against ALEPH and other technologically superior enemies of truth.

ATTRIBUTES

AGI	AWA	BRW	COO	INT	PER	WIL
12	10	9	10	10	10	12

FIELDS OF EXPERTISE

Combat	+4	1	Movement	+2	1	Social	+2	2
Fortitude	+2	2	Senses	+1	1	Technical	+2	1

DEFENCES

Firewall	12	Resolve	14	Vigour	11
Security	–	Morale	2	Armour	3

ATTACKS
- **MULTI Rifle**: Range C/M, 1+7 🅝 damage, Burst 2/1, 2H, Expert 1, Medium MULTI, MULTI Light Mod, Vicious 1
  - *DA Mode (Secondary)*: Vicious 3
- **Light Grenade Launcher**: Range M, 2+6 🅝 damage, Burst 1, Unbalanced, Indiscriminate (Close), Munition, Speculative Fire
- **E/M Grenades**: 2+4 🅝 damage, 1H, E/M, Indiscriminate (Close), Piercing 1, Speculative Fire, Thrown, Unsubtle
- **Misericorde**: Melee, 1+4 🅝 damage, Concealed 1, Piercing 2, Subtle 2, Unforgiving 3, Vicious 1
- **Blessed Hacking Device Plus**: CLAW-2, SWORD-1, SHIELD-2, GADGET-2, IC-2, UPGRADE Cybermask, Sucker Punch, White Noise; +2 🅝 bonus damage

GEAR: Medium Combat Armour (with Optical Disruption Device)

SPECIAL ABILITIES
- **Environmental Specialisation (Choose)**: When required to make any form of test as a result of movement within their chosen environment, a Reverend Moira may reroll any dice that did not generate a success on the initial roll, but must accept the new results.
- **Guarded Heart**: A Reverend Moira's faith aids them against mundane setbacks, granting them a Morale Soak of 2. Additionally, when rolling Soak dice for Morale, they instead count each effect rolled as if it were a 2 on those Soak dice.

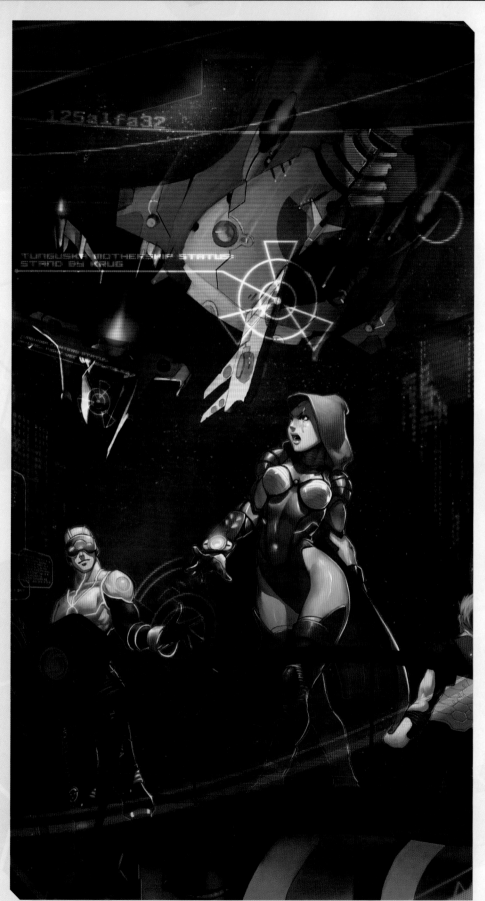

ELITE

RIOT GRRL

Drawn from marginalised neighbourhoods across the Human Sphere, the Riot Grrls are accustomed to street fights and everyday survival. Calling the Beauvoir module of Praxis home, they have coalesced around a radical feminist movement drawing heavily from punk philosophy, aspiring to destroy the dominant Human Sphere society. Though at constant risk of sanction for disrupting Social Energy, the Jurisdictional Command of *Bakunin* saw the advantage of a module driven to create revolution and asked them to unite the "...baddest bitches in the module, the most infamous, tough, and despicable..." to fight for *Bakunin's* interests.

The Beauvoir module became the cradle of a fearsome assault unit which is equipped with the best gear available. The Riot Grrls are true daughters of punk and tactical street combat, anarchist feminists with automatic weapons ready to spit in the face of society and jump into combat for strength, revolution, and anarchy.

ATTRIBUTES						
AGI	AWA	BRW	COO	INT	PER	WIL
11	8	9	10	9	7	9

FIELDS OF EXPERTISE						
Combat	+3	1	Movement	+2	1	Social	–	–
Fortitude	+2	1	Senses	+1	1	Technical	–	–

DEFENCES					
Firewall	9	Resolve	9	Vigour	9
Security	–	Morale	–	Armour	3

ATTACKS

- **Boarding Shotgun**: Range C, 1+5 damage, Burst 1, 2H, Knockdown, Medium MULTI
  - *Normal Shells Mode (Primary)*: Area (Close), Spread 1
  - *AP Slugs Mode (Secondary)*: Piercing 3
- **Flashbangs**: 1+5 damage, 1H, Blinding, Deafening, Disposable, Indiscriminate (Close), Nonlethal, Speculative Fire, Thrown, Unsubtle, removes Marked
- **Knife**: Melee, 1+4 damage, 1H, Concealed 1, Non-Hackable, Subtle 2, Thrown, Unforgiving 1
- **Spitfire**: Range M, 1+5 damage, Burst 3, 2H, Spread 2, Unsubtle

GEAR: Medium Combat Armour

SPECIAL ABILITIES

- **Anarchists Unit!**: When three or more Riot Grrls are in a zone together, they gain +2 Morale Soak.
- **Graceful**: Riot Grrls can reroll one d20 when making an Acrobatics test, but must accept the new result.

ELITE
SCHOLAR

In an age when the collective knowledge of entire planets is accessible at the touch of a comlog, when geists can anticipate your questions, and have an answer ready before you even think to ask — frankly, in a world with ALEPH around — what use is there for scholars?

As it turns out, plenty.

It takes a special sort of person to become an information specialist in the quantronic age. A dedication, bordering on obsession, to delving beyond surface knowledge into the realm of true expertise. Regardless of their field, a scholar asks questions that most never consider, pokes holes in dogma, questions theory, and tackles difficult problems from sophisticated and unorthodox angles.

Demand for scholarly expertise is seeing a resurgence as generals, corporate executives, and lobbyists vie for any possible edge over their competitors. AI strategies are predictable, and safe. Scholarly expertise is anything but.

ATTRIBUTES

AGI	AWA	BRW	COO	INT	PER	WIL
7	10	6	7	13	8	12

FIELDS OF EXPERTISE

| Combat | – | – | Movement | – | – | Social | +1 | 1 |
| Fortitude | – | – | Senses | +3 | 3 | Technical | +2 | 2 |

DEFENCES

| Firewall | 13 | Resolve | 12 | Vigour | 6 |
| Security | – | Morale | – | Armour | – |

ATTACKS

- **Hacking Device Plus**: CLAW-2, SWORD-1, SHIELD-2, GADGET-3, IC-2, UPGRADE White Noise; +3 [N] bonus damage
- **Swordcane**: Melee, 1+4 [N] damage, Unbalanced, Concealed 2, Parry 1, Vicious 1

GEAR: Personal Library Datasphere, Stims (×2)

SPECIAL ABILITIES

- **Disciplined Student**: If the Scholar generates at least one success on an Education test, they can immediately roll one d20 and add the result to the test.
- **Research Specialist**: Across the Human Sphere, people seek Scholars' expertise, and with good reason. When making a skill test to research a topic, the Scholar gains 3 bonus Momentum.

NEMESIS
SILK LORD

Silk is the most precious and valuable substance in the Human Sphere. That makes the people who control its distribution the most powerful individuals. The Silk Lords are those people; a small coterie of men and women who, between them, control the ability to cheat death, sharing it amongst those who can afford to pay to have it. Silk Lords are secretive, constantly on guard against attempts to kidnap or kill them. Master manipulators, their will is carried out by thousands of agents, many of whom have no conception of who it is they work for. A Silk Lord is the deadliest of foes; implacable, brilliant and able to call upon resources beyond imagining.

ATTRIBUTES

AGI	AWA	BRW	COO	INT	PER	WIL
8	12	8	9	12	11	10

FIELDS OF EXPERTISE

| Combat | +2 | 1 | Movement | +2 | | Social | +3 | 1 |
| Fortitude | +2 | 1 | Senses | +3 | 1 | Technical | +3 | 1 |

DEFENCES

| Firewall | 15 | Resolve | 12 | Vigour | 10 |
| Security | – | Morale | 4 | Armour | 1 |

ATTACKS

- **Defensive Hacking Device**: CLAW-0, SWORD-0, SHIELD-3, GADGET-1, IC-3; +3 [N] bonus damage
- **Grazeblade**: Melee, 1+4 [N] damage, 1H, Breaker, Non-Hackable, Stun, Subtle 2, Thrown, Toxic 3

GEAR: Armoured Clothing, AutoMediKit

SPECIAL ABILITIES

- **With Great Power**: Silk Lords are used to issuing orders and being immediately obeyed. They benefit from an increased Morale Soak (already included in the profile). Additionally, all Psywar attacks made by a Silk Lord cause +2 [N] extra damage.
- **Falsafa**: Silk Lords can reroll one d20 when making an Education or Discipline test, but must accept the new result, and generate one additional Momentum on such tests.
- **Never Alone**: A Silk Lord is never left unguarded. The GM can summon twice the normal number of reinforcements through Heat expenditure.
- **Plentiful Silk**: The Silk Lord gets two doses of Silk for each Heat spent by the GM.

ELITE
SOPHOTECT

Expert technicians, fast-response medics, and all-purpose engineers, the Sophotects are first on the scene when ALEPH needs something fixed. Originally designated Rbhu — minor Vedic gods, and unparalleled artisans — ALEPH field teams nicknamed them "the Sophotects", a Classical Greek word meaning "wisdom creators". Given their reputation for pulling solutions literally out of thin air, the designation stuck.

Whether it's wounded soldiers of the Special Situations Section, misbehaving quantronic infrastructure, or when ALEPH decides that humanity really needs a bridge on Paradiso, the Sophotects are equipped for the job. To that end, Sophotects carry a piece of equipment known as a Mother-Forge, a sophisticated personal-scale fabricator and nanomachine reprogrammer.

ATTRIBUTES

AGI	AWA	BRW	COO	INT	PER	WIL
9	8	7	9	12	6	12

FIELDS OF EXPERTISE

| Combat | +1 | – | Movement | +3 | – | Social | – | – |
| Fortitude | – | – | Senses | +2 | – | Technical | +3 | 3 |

DEFENCES

| Firewall | 12 | Resolve | 12 | Vigour | 7 |
| Security | 3 | Morale | – | Armour | 2 |

ATTACKS

- **Combi Rifle**: Range C/M, 1+5 [N] damage, Burst 2, 2H, Expert 1, MULTI Light Mod, Vicious 1
- **D-Charges**: 2+6 [N] damage, 1H, Anti-Materiel 2, Comms, Disposable, Piercing 3, Spread 1, Unsubtle, Vicious 2

GEAR: Deflector-2, ECM, Mother-Forge, Reinforced Shell (2 Amour)

SPECIAL ABILITIES

- **Battle-Forged**: Due to their specialised nanofactories, Sophotects gain 2 bonus Momentum for Medicine and Tech tests.
- **Redundant Systems**: Additional layers of quantronic security grant the Sophotect Security 3.
- **Sophotect Lhost**: Sophotects have the Inured to Pain, Keen Senses (Sight), Quantronic Jump, Superhuman Intelligence 1, and Superhuman Willpower 1 common abilities. Their Lhosts are also extremely fast, allowing them to move one additional zone when taking any movement action.

NOTES

Mother-Forges are among the most coveted pieces of technology in the Human Sphere, and are closely guarded. Unless properly removed with a Tech (D4) test, automatic protocols quickly disable the device, rendering it a very distinctive paperweight.

TROOPER/ELITE
SPEC OPS

Warfare has changed in the Human Sphere. Full-scale wars are few and far between, but limited-window conflict zones? Nearly ubiquitous. This new battlefield requires an agile, flexible soldier, able to adapt to any number of disparate challenges anywhere in the Human Sphere.

In this constantly shifting landscape, the traditional role of Special Operations forces has drastically expanded, leading to widespread adaptation of the Spec Ops trooper. No longer the exclusive domain of national militaries, the modern operative could be a corporate security high-threat responder, a PanOceanian lobbyist's counterintelligence team, or simply an asset hidden up the proverbial sleeve of a Submondo crime boss.

Regardless of how they pay the rent, operatives are experts in reconnaissance, surveillance, and hit-and-run guerrilla tactics, as well as focused combat actions.

ATTRIBUTES

AGI	AWA	BRW	COO	INT	PER	WIL
9	9	8	9	7	7	8

FIELDS OF EXPERTISE

Combat	+2	1	Movement	+1	–	Social	–	–
Fortitude	–	–	Senses	+2	1	Technical	+1	–

DEFENCES (TROOPER)

Firewall	4	Resolve	4	Vigour	4
Security	–	Morale	–	Armour	2

DEFENCES (ELITE)

Firewall	7	Resolve	8	Vigour	8
Security	–	Morale	–	Armour	2

ATTACKS
- **Stun Baton**: Melee, 1+4 🅝 damage, 1H, Knockdown, Non-Hackable, Stun, Subtle 1
- **Submachine Gun**: Range C, 1+5 🅝 damage, Burst 2, 1H, Unbalanced, Piercing 2, Spread 1

GEAR: Light Combat Armour (with Climbing Kit), Multispectral Visor 1

SPECIAL ABILITIES
- **Bulletstorm**: The Operative can reroll up to 2 🅝 when making a ranged attack, but must accept the new results.

ELITE
SPEC OPS, HEAVY

Sometimes, a conventional response just isn't enough. Sometimes, even highly trained, well-equipped special forces are neither special nor forceful enough to address the threat at hand. In these situations, elite units in powered armour are deployed to the scene. One part soldier, two parts cowboy, sporting bleeding-edge powered armour, and packing heavy ordinance, these units are effective, if unsubtle; once they hit the ground, the local architecture is never quite the same.

For the discerning commander willing to accept a little property damage, these dynamos are like a TAG's little sibling; durable, intimidating, and able to neutralise multiple hostiles in short order.

ATTRIBUTES

AGI	AWA	BRW	COO	INT	PER	WIL
9	8	10	11	9	7	9

FIELDS OF EXPERTISE

Combat	+3	3	Movement	+1	–	Social	–	–
Fortitude	+1	1	Senses	+1	–	Technical	+2	–

DEFENCES

Firewall	9	Resolve	9	Vigour	10
Security	–	Morale	–	Armour	5

ATTACKS
- **Heavy Machine Gun**: Range L, 2+6 🅝 damage, Burst 3, Unwieldy, Spread 1, Unsubtle
- **Spiked Knuckles**: Melee, 1+9 🅝 damage, 1H, Concealed 1, Non-Hackable, Piercing, Vicious 1

GEAR: Drop Bears (×2), Powered Combat Armour (gain up to +3d20 on Brawn tests with +3 complication range)

SPECIAL ABILITIES
- **Bullethell**: The Operative unleashes a torrent of ammunition, rendering a small area decidedly inhospitable. As a Free Action, they can grant their HMG the Indiscriminate quality, but this reduces the weapon's damage by 2 🅝.
- **Bulletstorm**: The Operative can reroll up to 2 🅝 when making a ranged attack, but must accept the new results.

MIKE "VANDAL" OMDAHL

MOBILE BRIGADA

BACKER: MICHAEL VENDERDAHL

Bullets were flying overhead as he reached the defensive wall and hunkered down beside his sergeant. The reinforced concrete did little to stop the projectiles that tore through it and took down half a dozen of the lightly armoured Alguaciles. One of the Morat Raicho up there had something like a chain rifle firing *malditos K1* rounds as if he was pissing *skënder*.

"Get rid of that damn gunner, Vandal."

"Aye, sergeant."

A quick glance at his tactical screens revealed the enemy positions. The Riot Grrls had warned them that the Morat were heading towards this landing pad, but by the time they'd been able to mobilise, the alien *puto* had already seized it. And now they knew why: HQ needed to get *Zúyǒng* reinforcements here pronto, and this landing pad was the only way to do it.

Mike rose, aimed, and let loose. The missile's fiery trail entranced him as it sped towards the enemy gunner. He caught the explosion just before a ricocheting bullet reminded him that they were still well and truly in the mix.

"Good shot, Vandal."

"Thanks. Looks bad out there."

"They're giving us a lot of heat. Their high ground support was taken out, but the TAG on eleven will beat us down before reinforcements arrive."

"Copy That." He tabbed over to the Alguacil comms chanel. "Cover me and I'll take that thing down."

The Alguaciles gave curt nods. Mike waited until they opened up in the enemy's direction, then jumped from cover and ran for the nearby wreck of a drop carrier that was blocking half of the landing field. The tactical data did not look good. Life monitors were going black all across their line. The Alguaciles weren't going to last long unless he could take that rampaging firebird down.

The thing popped into view as if summoned by his thoughts, towering over everything around it and swinging its ape-like head back and forth. He only had a clear shot for three seconds, but Michael shot on instinct. The missile struck true and caused the beast to stumble back with the explosion. Not lingering to observe his handiwork, Michael sprinted up the slope and ducked in behind one of the support pillars.

True to Morat form, the beast annihilated his previous cover. Worse yet, it had barely been scratched by the direct hit. He could wear it down with surgical strikes, but that was going to take time the Alguaciles didn't have. The beast was roaring now, bellowing its rage out over the valley and turning its guns back towards the retaining wall.

Then Vandal saw his shot. Taking aim at the support pillar directly below the blustering Morat, he opened a commline and pre-empted his shot with a brief message: "Landing pad is clear."

He fired.

APPEARANCE

Short but powerfully built, his movements have a threatening quality to them. He has a tattooed head and clear blue eyes.

ROLEPLAYING

- Very literal minded
- Has a knack for finding weak spots, in plans as well as people
- Likes destruction

BACKGROUND

Vandal grew up among the *vatos* gangs of *Corregidor*. His nickname, taken from the barbaric tribe of Earth that revelled in destruction, comes from that time. He still takes after his namesake, more a force of nature than a soldier.

When the corridor boys ask him why he joined the Mobile Brigada, he tells them the obvious truth: They won't throw him in jail for doing what he does best. The pay is more reliable. And they gave him a missile launcher.

The real truth is that he found love. Not with Miranda. She's a pain in the ass. But with the little girl that Miranda gave him. When he saw her for the first time he knew two things: First, he wanted to live long enough to see her grow up. Second, he wanted to give her everything he had never had.

Unfortunately, there's only one thing Mike Omdahl is really good at. Ironically, though, he's statistically more likely to see his thirty-fifth birthday on the battlefields of the Human Sphere than running the corridors. And if he doesn't... well, the resurrection package isn't half bad.

STATS (ELITE)

ATTRIBUTES

AGI	AWA	BRW	COO	INT	PER	WIL
10	10	9	9	8	7	10

FIELDS OF EXPERTISE

Combat	+2	2	Movement	+1	–	Social	–	–
Fortitude	+1	1	Senses	+1	–	Technical	+2	2

DEFENCES

Firewall	8	Resolve	10	Vigour	9
Security	–	Morale	2	Armour	5

ATTACKS

- **Missile Launcher**: Range L, 2+9 (N) damage, Burst 1, Unwieldy, Munition
  - *EXP Mode:* Area (Close), Spread 1, Unsubtle, Vicious 2
  - *Needle Mode:* Piercing 2, Spread 1, Vicious 2
- **Pistol**: Range R/C, 1+6 (N) damage, Burst 1, 1H, Vicious 1
- **Knife**: Melee, 1+4 (N) damage, 1H, Concealed 1, Non-Hackable, Subtle 2, Thrown, Unforgiving 1

GEAR: Powered Combat Armour (gain up to +3d20 on Brawn tests with +3 complication range)

SPECIAL ABILITIES

- **Menacing 2**: When Vandal shows up for work, the local geography is never quite the same. When he enters a scene, the GM immediately adds 2 Heat to the pool.
- **Fatal Flaw**: Plans, structures, people; they all have weak points; and that tells Vandal where to apply pressure. When he takes an Exploit action, he also adds the Grievous and Knockdown weapon qualities to his subsequent attack.
- **Stoic and Stubborn**: The Brigada are renowned for their bravery and honour. Vandal possesses neither of these; he just never relents. He can reroll one d20 when making a Fortitude test, but must accept the new results.
- **Unrelenting**: Arguing with Vandal is like shouting at a brick wall with a turret on top. He has an innate Morale Soak of 2.

TAG PILOT

The life of a TAG pilot is a dangerous one, fraught with perils both from the environments that they work or fight in as well as the fighting itself. As a result, there is a strong sense of unity within those who share the common bond of piloting a massive death-dealing machine. TAG Pilots have a great deal of specialised knowledge to go with their honed combat skills, with many pilots assisting with or performing maintenance, upgrades of their units and having capacious technical knowledge of virtually all TAGs. While TAGs have become a mainstay of many of the armed services within the various factions, they have also had expanded roles in construction, demolition, mining, and other less glorious aspects of day-to-day function. TAG Pilots tend to be aggressive, reactive, and loyal to those that they consider a part of their breed.

ATTRIBUTES

AGI	AWA	BRW	COO	INT	PER	WIL
8	10	8	11	8	7	8

FIELDS OF EXPERTISE

Combat	+2	1	Movement	+1	1	Social	–	–
Fortitude	+1	–	Senses	+1	–	Technical	+1	–

DEFENCES (TROOPER)

Firewall	4	Resolve	4	Vigour	4
Security	–	Morale	–	Armour	2

DEFENCES (ELITE)

Firewall	8	Resolve	8	Vigour	8
Security	–	Morale	–	Armour	3*

ATTACKS

- **Heavy Pistol**: Range R/C, 2+6 (N) damage, Burst 1, Unbalanced, Unforgiving 1, Vicious 1

GEAR: *Crashsuit (dissolves after a single round of use), Stims (×1), Surge (×1)

SPECIAL ABILITIES

- **Natural Equilibrium**: A TAG Pilot can reroll any number of dice when using the Pilot skill to make a terrain test, but must accept the new result.
- **Rock 'Em, Sock 'Em (Elite)**: When piloting a vehicle, a TAG Pilot can spend 2 Heat to ignore the effect of the first Fault suffered by the vehicle.

TECH SUPPORT

When a soldier's rig goes down mid-fire fight, Nomad intrusion counter-measures wreak havoc on a secure network, or a possessed TAG is on a rampage, it's time to call in Tech Support. These support specialists provide network security for facilities and their personnel countering enemy hackers and operatives.

Fighting enemy hackers from the safety of a bunker demands detached calm while working, making "Tech Support" a derisive phrase used by field operatives. While it's true they rarely see combat, the security centre of any facility is a prime target for any enemy operatives, and Tech Support personnel have basic security and combat training. Most carry a sidearm in case the security room is breached and the fight has to go offline.

ATTRIBUTES

AGI	AWA	BRW	COO	INT	PER	WIL
7	9	7	8	10	7	8

FIELDS OF EXPERTISE

Combat	+1	–	Movement	–	–	Social	–	–
Fortitude	–	–	Senses	+1	–	Technical	+2	2

DEFENCES

Firewall	5	Resolve	4	Vigour	4
Security	2	Morale	–	Armour	–

ATTACKS

- **Defensive Hacking Device**: CLAW-0, SWORD-0, SHIELD-3, GADGET-1, IC-3; +2 (N) bonus damage
- **Pistol**: Range R/C, 1+5 (N) damage, Burst 1, 1H, Vicious 1

GEAR: Powered Multitool, Repair Kit

SPECIAL ABILITIES

- **Remote Reboot (2 Heat)**: For 2 Heat, Tech Support takes an action and performs the Reset action, applying the effects to a friendly target. The target does not suffer the normal penalties for using the Reset action.
- **Fast Repair**: When repairing objects, Tech Support can perform a Recover or Treat action as a Minor Action (instead of the normal Standard Action).

MIN-KI MOK, BIRD OF PREY

IMPERIAL AGENT, CRANE RANK

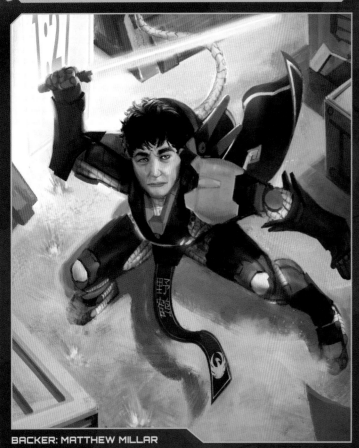

BACKER: MATTHEW MILLAR

"I am taking charge of this operation. Step down."

The plain statement sent ripples through the assembled policemen facing the unhappy crowd of mixed perpetrators filling the street. It had started as a peaceful protest for better housing in the Korean quarter of Shaoshang, but was now a full-blown riot waiting to happen.

The former commanding officer on the scene stammered. "What do you want my men to do?"

"Nothing," the Xiān Hè (Crane Rank) Imperial Agent said. "I dislike distractions."

The policeman did nothing to stop him as he shouldered his way to the front. At the sight of his crisp, distinct uniform the crowd quieted somewhat. He activated a subdermal voice amplifier in his throat. "Subjects of the Dragon. Your concerns have been noted and will be transmitted to the proper ears. There is no need for this demeaning behaviour. This crowd will disperse. Anyone still here in two minutes will be taken into custody with full force."

A flick of his wrist projected a large timer into the air. Panic gripped the crowd as everyone tried to be the first to get away. The agent watched impassively.

The distinctive glint of a sniper's scope caused his autonomic expert systems to kick in, jerking his body out of the way moments before the shot struck. Tucking into a roll, he came to his feet several metres away. More bullets strafed his former position.

"Shooter on the roof. One o'clock!" he bellowed. As the policemen began a clumsy barrage of return fire, he flowed into and through the crowd of protesters, gliding to a nearby ladder and hustling up to the roof above.

The sniper heard him coming and spun around. At this range he could hardly miss, but it didn't matter: Mok's sidearm was already snapping up and a bullet smashed through the sniper's forehead, sending him tumbling back over the edge of the roof.

A few moments later, the agent returned to the street by a gentler way. He tore open the sniper's mask. He knew the face.

With a definitive tick, the countdown expired. The crowd was gone. The agent's comlog flicked out a confirmation code. He was done here. And now he had an appointment with Phoenix Industries.

APPEARANCE

Broad-shouldered and muscular, his movements are that of a hunter on the prowl. His black curls are generally cut short and Korean ancestry is clearly visible in his features.

ROLEPLAYING

- No-nonsense approach to problems, either you are a problem or an asset
- Rarely smiles, speaks with a clipped, precise tone
- Prefers bullying to persuasion

BACKGROUND

Maeng-geum. Bird of Prey. It began as an insult during his rise to the rank of the Crane. Few believed a word about the famous exploits that had garnered him an invite into their illustrious ranks. A Korean with a Dragon license? It had to be a political move. Calling him Bird of Prey indicated that someone had let him loose. He took to wearing the name as a badge of honour.

Contrary to popular belief, however, he became an Imperial Agent of his own accord and on his own merits. A child of the Seoul slums in old Korea, he knew the disdain Imperial Agents held for his kind. His parents had been killed in a shooting when he was twelve, his sisters two years later through food poisoning. Those responsible were barely investigated. Justice became a mantra and so he did everything necessary to enter the ranks of those who adjudicated it. Hardship and prejudice hindered his way at first, but he endured and finally prevailed after saving the life of one of the Emperor's daughters.

Those who do not know him struggle to believe he is a legitimate agent at first, but this only raises his ire. Imperial Agents are not known for their leniency, but he is a terror. He shows no mercy to perpetrators and hounds a trail with dogged determination. His standing with the Imperial family makes him a very useful political tool; a tool to intimidate. When the *Maeng-geum* arrives, it is a guarantee that the Emperor is taking the matter seriously. This gives him serious political clout, a fact he enjoys almost as much as capturing criminals.

STATS (NEMESIS)

ATTRIBUTES

AGI	AWA	BRW	COO	INT	PER	WIL
10	10	11	10	10	9	10

FIELDS OF EXPERTISE

Combat	+4	2	Movement	+2	2	Social	+2	2
Fortitude	+1	—	Senses	+2	1	Technical	+1	1

DEFENCES

Firewall	11	Resolve	11	Vigour	12
Security	—	Morale	3	Armour	5

ATTACKS

- **MULTI Rifle**: Range C/M, 1+7 🅝 damage, Burst 2/1, 2H, Comms, Expert 1, Medium MULTI, MULTI Light Mod, Vicious 1
  - *DA Mode (Secondary):* Vicious 2
- **Heavy Pistol**: Range R/C, 2+6 🅝 damage, Burst 1, Unbalanced, Unforgiving 1, Vicious 1
- **Monofilament Sword**: Melee, 1+5 🅝 damage, Unbalanced, Monofilament, Parry 2, Vicious 1

GEAR: Dragon Class License, Powered Combat Armour (gain up to +3d20 on Brawn tests with +3 complication range)

SPECIAL ABILITIES

- **Dragon-Class Operative**: Bird of Prey is a senior Imperial Agent of the Crane rank; one of the best the StateEmpire can offer. He can reroll up to 3 🅝 when making a Combat test, but must accept the new results.
- **Decisive Action**: Bird of Prey is many things, but indecisive is not one of them — when he commits to an attack, he rarely holds back. Each point of Heat spent to deal bonus damage will ignore an equal amount of Soak.
- **Grim Determination**: Bird of Prey found success through bitter determination and vengeance-fuelled obstinacy. This stubbornness grants him Morale Soak 3.
- **Preceded by Reputation**: Bird of Prey's reputation and training ensure that every command is obeyed without hesitancy. He can reroll one d20 when making a social skills test, but must accept the new result.
- **The Emperor's Will**: A direct link to the emperor is no small matter; a detail that Bird of Prey is keenly aware of. He possesses a Psywar attack form called Air of Authority that has a range of Close and inflicts 1+6 🅝 damage with the Area (Close) and Stun qualities, although he must be recognised as an Imperial Agent in order to use the attack.

ELITE
TERRORIST

Although the phenomenon of terrorism is as old as humanity itself, it would be blind to ignore that terrorists have adapted to the modern times. Masters of stealth and subterfuge, they strike from the shadows and withdraw quickly to avoid retribution. Although idealistic terrorism is still popular in some parts of the Human Sphere, more often than not the terrorists of today are industrial mercenaries, eager to take the coin from whoever wants to hire them. Corporations looking to crash the stock market, warlords looking for a way to dislodge their competition, or black ops operators requiring a distraction — no one is below hiring a professional to do their dirty work.

ATTRIBUTES

AGI	AWA	BRW	COO	INT	PER	WIL
10	9	11	9	8	7	9

FIELDS OF EXPERTISE

Combat	+3	2	Movement	+1	1	Social	—	—
Fortitude	+1	1	Senses	+1	—	Technical	+2	—

DEFENCES

Firewall	8	Resolve	9	Vigour	11
Security	—	Morale	—	Armour	—

ATTACKS

- **Assault Pistol**: Range R/C, 1+5 🅝 damage, Burst 2, Unbalanced, Vicious 1
- **Combi Rifle**: Range C/M, 1+6 🅝 damage, Burst 2, 2H, Expert 1, MULTI Light Mod, Vicious 1
- **DT Grenades**: 2+4 🅝 damage, Biotech, Comms, Indiscriminate (Close), Speculative Fire, Thrown, Toxic 2, Unsubtle, Vicious 1
- **Haunt Charges**: Poison damage, Comms, Indiscriminate (Close), Nonlethal, Subtle 2

GEAR: Chameleonwear

SPECIAL ABILITIES

- **Another's Freedom Fighter**: Terrorists have long learned how to blend in and operate from the shadows. They only need to spend 1 Momentum (instead of two) in order to reduce a noisy action to sneaky or a sneaky action to silent.
- **I Came With Bombs**: When a Terrorist is part of a scene, the GM can spend Heat to trigger prepared bombs and similar booby traps. These function as hazards (p. 34), but include the Indiscriminate (Close) quality at no cost.

TROOPER
THUG A

Every society has its dregs. Motivated by addiction, greed, or even desperation, they gravitate towards violence to achieve their goals and take what they want by force. Some join gangs of like-minded individuals, others rob stores or civilians. The unchanging fact is that they are armed and willing to hurt others to achieve their goals.

Thugs are usually armed with simple weapons — knives, blunt objects, and basic firearms — which they use to intimidate potential targets. Only a rare few are adept with these weapons, but in numbers they can pose a formidable threat.

ATTRIBUTES

AGI	AWA	BRW	COO	INT	PER	WIL
9	7	9	8	7	8	8

FIELDS OF EXPERTISE

Combat	+1	1	Movement	+1	—	Social	+1	—
Fortitude	+1	1	Senses	—	—	Technical	—	—

DEFENCES

Firewall	4	Resolve	4	Vigour	5
Security	—	Morale	—	Armour	—

ATTACKS

- **Knife**: Melee, 1+4 🅝 damage, 1H, Concealed 1, Non-Hackable, Subtle 2, Thrown, Unforgiving 1
- **Pistol**: Range R/C, 1+4 🅝 damage, Burst 1, 1H, Vicious 1

TROOPER
THUG B

Mob heavies. Maras enforcers. The bottom rung of *Corregidor's* infamous muscle-for-hire. Whatever form they take, there seems to be an increasing demand for individuals with more brawn than conscience, especially if they work cheap. In other words, it's a comparatively good time to be a common thug.

Straightforward to a fault, your average street tough bears little resemblance to a trained soldier, and usually isn't involved in anything more sophisticated than intimidation or muggings. Drunk on power — and sometimes just plain drunk — violence is a first, second, and third option when they get their way.

Undisciplined, and quick to falter when faced with a genuine threat, they can nevertheless be dangerous in groups, or under a charismatic leader's command; one should never underestimate the power of narrow-minded, violent people in large groups.

ATTRIBUTES						
AGI	AWA	BRW	COO	INT	PER	WIL
10	7	10	10	6	7	6

FIELDS OF EXPERTISE						
Combat	+2	1	Movement	+1	–	Social	+1	1
Fortitude	–	–	Senses	–	–	Technical	–	–

DEFENCES						
Firewall	3	Resolve	3	Vigour	5
Security	–	Morale	–	Armour	1

ATTACKS
- **Brass Knuckles**: Melee, 1+5 Ⓝ damage, 1H, Concealed 1, Subtle 1, Vicious 1
- **Chain Rifle**: Range C, 1+5 Ⓝ damage, Burst 1, 2H, Spread 1, Torrent, Vicious 1

GEAR: Hard Hat, Surge (×1)

ELITE
TRADER

At every spaceport, outpost, or market you'll find traders haggling for the best price on goods and services. They ply the Circulars, journey between caravanserai, or serve Nomad Commercial Missions. They come from all backgrounds and cultures, but their nomadic life brings them to the far reaches of the Human Sphere where danger lurks in the shadow of every asteroid. The ever-present threat of pirates and raiders means that most traders know how to handle themselves, and many of them also know how to make a tidy profit from a time of troubles.

ATTRIBUTES						
AGI	AWA	BRW	COO	INT	PER	WIL
8	10	8	9	10	10	8

FIELDS OF EXPERTISE						
Combat	+1	–	Movement	–	–	Social	+3	2
Fortitude	–	–	Senses	+3	1	Technical	+1	1

DEFENCES						
Firewall	10	Resolve	8	Vigour	8
Security	–	Morale	–	Armour	1

ATTACKS
- **Light Shotgun**: Range C, 1+6 Ⓝ damage, Burst 1, Unbalanced, Knockdown

GEAR: Cargo Shuttle, Freighter, or Ground Transport

SPECIAL ABILITIES
- **Haggler**: When negotiating the price of goods or services, a Trader can reroll any dice that did not score a success, but must accept the new results.
- **Lie Detector**: The Trader gains 1 bonus Momentum when making a test to determine if someone is lying.

NOTES
Elite Traders may own a spaceship or a small fleet of cargo vessels.

NEMESIS
TRIAD BOSS

Called the "Dragon Head" in Triad jargon, the Triad Boss is the man pulling all the strings. He is the grey eminence behind the local politician, the mysterious benefactor of the local charity, the true mastermind behind the Triad's operations. Usually one of the oldest and most experienced members in the organisation, the Dragon Head is responsible for long-term policy planning and for oversight of all the individual Red Poles (p. 437). He offers advice and is a voice of reason, as well as acts as an intermediary in case of any internal conflicts. Usually hiding his real identity behind many layers of masking technology, the Triad Boss is a figure of mystery, a true ghost.

ATTRIBUTES						
AGI	AWA	BRW	COO	INT	PER	WIL
7	12	6	8	13	13	12

FIELDS OF EXPERTISE						
Combat	+1	1	Movement	+1	–	Social	+4	3
Fortitude	+2	1	Senses	+3	1	Technical	+2	1

DEFENCES						
Firewall	15	Resolve	14	Vigour	8
Security	–	Morale	–	Armour	2

ATTACKS
- **Silenced Assault Pistol**: Range R/C, 1+7 Ⓝ damage, Burst 2, Unbalanced, Subtle 1, Vicious 1

GEAR: Aletheia Kit, Ballistic Vest, Holomask

SPECIAL ABILITIES
- **Grey Eminence**: The Triad Boss can influence conflict via meticulous planning before first shots are fired. When his underlings are working according to the plan he laid out, all their tests are made at −1 difficulty.
- **Dominating Presence**: The Triad Boss gains 2 bonus Momentum when using Psywar techniques.
- **Shield of the Secret Society**: When targeting the Triad Boss with human terrain mapping, add +2 zones to the contact distance of the contact point.

ELITE
WARCOR

A portmanteau for war correspondents, warcors might be the single largest contributing factor to the Human Sphere's military news addiction. Bravely embedding themselves among active troops, a warcor's presence means that any soldier is just one heroic moment away from Maya stardom, and one act of cowardice from eternal shame.

Most warcors are civilians — professional journalists, videographers, and the occasional actor — usually assigned to specific units or operations. Sometimes the public relations division of the armed forces sends one of their own, like ALEPH's Aoidoi, whose tales of the heroic Myrmidons dominate popular media.

In combat situations, freedom of the press is often a distant memory; every last word has been scrutinised, critiqued, and approved by military officials before it sees daylight. But for their part, warcors see themselves like the bards of old; theirs is the task of exalting heroes, to create and magnify their legend.

ATTRIBUTES						
AGI	AWA	BRW	COO	INT	PER	WIL
8	10	7	8	8	11	11

FIELDS OF EXPERTISE						
Combat	+1	–	Movement	+1	–	Social	+2	1
Fortitude	–	–	Senses	+3	1	Technical	+3	–

DEFENCES					
Firewall	8	Resolve	11	Vigour	7
Security	–	Morale	–	Armour	2

ATTACKS
- **Flash Pulse**: Range M, 1+7 🅝 damage, Burst 1, 2H, Blinding, removes Marked
- **Stun Pistol**: Range R/C, 1+6 🅝 damage, Burst 1, 1H, Biotech, Nonlethal, Stun, Vicious 1

GEAR: AR Eye Implants, Ballistic Vest, Painkillers (×2), Survival Kit, TinBot-Mounted Recorder ×2

SPECIAL ABILITIES
- **Everything for the Audience**: A Warcor can reroll one d20 when making a Persuade test, but must accept the new result.
- **Embedded Correspondent**: The Warcor's presence lifts the spirits of nearby allies. Any time forces allied with them are subject to a Psywar attack, those forces increase their Morale Soak by 2.

ELITE
WARDRIVER

The term "wardriving" dates from the 21st century when hackers searched for vulnerable wireless networks from moving vehicles. In the modern world of the Human Sphere, mercenary hackers offering their services for hire as cybercombat operatives have repurposed the term. Wardrivers hail from all walks of life. Some are street hackers running stock programs, while others are decorated combat veterans who've left the military for more freedom and better pay. Their community demands anyone wearing a wardriver patch meet certain qualifications. In their secretive Maya enclaves, they trade tips on combat programming, information on clients, and the latest tactical training programs. To the wardrivers, reputation and prestige is everything and more valuable than any amount of money. In turn, they'll aggressively protect said reputation.

ATTRIBUTES						
AGI	AWA	BRW	COO	INT	PER	WIL
9	10	8	9	11	8	8

FIELDS OF EXPERTISE						
Combat	+1	1	Movement	+1	–	Social	+1	–
Fortitude	+1	–	Senses	+2	–	Technical	+3	2

DEFENCES					
Firewall	11	Resolve	8	Vigour	8
Security	1	Morale	–	Armour	2

ATTACKS
- **Boarding Shotgun**: Range C, 1+7 🅝 damage, Burst 1, 2H, Knockdown, Medium MULTI
  - *Normal Shells Mode (Primary)*: Area (Close), Spread 1
  - *AP Slugs Mode (Secondary)*: Piercing 3
- **Assault Hacking Device**: CLAW-3, SWORD-0, SHIELD-0, GADGET-0, IC-1; +2 🅝 bonus damage

GEAR: Light Combat Armour, Grey Market Firewall (+1 🅝 Security)

SPECIAL ABILITIES
- **Sharp Senses**: The Wardriver can reroll one d20 when making an Observation test, but must accept the new result.

TROOPER
WULVER

Wulvers are the children of human and Dogface parents (p. 153). Sterile and distrusted because of their notorious tempers, Wulvers are few in number and have struggled to find a place in Ariadnan society, with many ending up as muscle for local gangs and other disreputable organisations. Unlike Dogfaces, Wulvers cannot transform. However their natural form is much larger than an average human to begin with and covered with long, thick fur, lending themselves readily to nicknames like "wolf-man" and slurs like "lycan". Although statistically more intelligent than Dogfaces, their reputation is muddied because they cannot avoid being carried away by the blood fever inherited from their Antipodean forebears. The wild look, the furious cries, and the instinctive movement towards danger are the warning signs of a Wulver charge.

ATTRIBUTES						
AGI	AWA	BRW	COO	INT	PER	WIL
8	8	14 (+1)	7	7	5	7

FIELDS OF EXPERTISE						
Combat	+1	1	Movement	+1	–	Social	–	–
Fortitude	+1	1	Senses	+1	–	Technical	–	–

DEFENCES					
Firewall	4	Resolve	4	Vigour	8
Security	–	Morale	–	Armour	2

ATTACKS
- **AP Rifle**: Range M, 1+5 🅝 damage, Burst 2, 2H, Piercing 2, Vicious 1
- **Claws**: Melee, 2+6 🅝 damage, Subtle 1, Vicious 1

GEAR: Ballistic Vest; no Cube

SPECIAL ABILITIES
- **Common Special Abilities**: Fast Recovery (Vigour 1), Fear 1, Keen Senses (Smell), Menacing 1, Monstrous, Superhuman Brawn 1
- **Blood Fever**: After suffering any Wound in combat, a Wulver must make a successful Discipline test with a difficulty equal to the number of Wounds they have suffered or succumb to the blood fever — an overwhelming bloodlust that urges them to destroy the source of thier pain and frustration even if it's to their own detriment. (This effect can also be triggered as a Metanoia Effect.) In this state they receive +4 Morale and +2 🅝 to the damage of melee attacks, but suffer a +2 difficulty to all Discipline tests and other tests requiring mental concentration. Exiting the Berserk mode requires a Standard Action and a successful discipline test with a difficulty equal to the number of Wounds they have suffered (minimum 1).
- **Wulver Charge**: When suffering from the Blood Fever, Wulvers can move up to two combat zones and make a melee attack as a Standard Action.

ALIENS

ELITE
ANTIPODE WARRIOR

The original inhabitants of Dawn, the Antipodes are a fierce race of pack hunting predators who would have come to dominate their planet if not for the unexpected arrival, or invasion as they see it, of mankind. Their warriors are led by war chiefs (p. 152), although some are enslaved and controlled by human Assault Pack Leaders (p. 421).

ATTRIBUTES

AGI	AWA	BRW	COO	INT	PER	WIL
11 (+1)	7	10 (+1)	9	6	5	8

FIELDS OF EXPERTISE

Combat	+2	1	Movement	+1	1	Social	–	–
Fortitude	+1	1	Senses	+1	1	Technical	–	–

DEFENCES

Firewall	6	Resolve	8	Vigour	11
Security	-	Morale	–	Armour	–

ATTACKS
- **Antipode War Bow**: Range C/M, 1+5 🅝 damage, Burst 1, 2H, Biotech, Subtle 2, Toxic 2, Vicious 3
- **Poison-Coated Knife**: Melee, 1+5 🅝 damage, Biotech, 1H, Concealed 1, Non-Hackable, Subtle 2, Thrown, Toxic 2, Unforgiving 1, Vicious 1

SPECIAL ABILITIES
- **Common Special Abilities**: Fear 1, Keen Senses (Smell)
- **Clever Hunters**: When in tall grass or forested terrain the Antipode can spend 1 Heat for +2 difficulty to tests to detect them.
- **Feral Roar (2 Heat)**: As a Minor Action, an Antipode Warrior's Feral Roar is a mental attack that targets all enemies within Close range and inflicts 1+2 🅝 (Stun, Unsubtle) mental damage.
- **Super-Jump**: Antipode Warriors treat any distance fallen as one zone shorter when calculating damage. Additionally, they can also vault over obstacles up to their own height without penalty and reduce the difficulty of skill tests to move through difficult terrain by one step.
- **Trinary**: The three Antipodes forming a trinary individual can each roll 2d20 when assisting each other (instead of the normal 1d20). Antipodes who are not members of a trinary, however, suffer a +1 difficulty to all tests. If a member of a trinary is killed or removed from their trinary, the remaining members enter mind-shock, suffering an additional +1 difficulty to all tests until they can succeed on a Discipline (D4) test. The difficulty of this test is reduced by one step per minute to a minimum of D1.

TROOPER
CHAKSA

A young pupil race of the Tohaa, the Chaksa are hardy, clever, and utterly dedicated to their mentors (p. 323). Broad and muscular, with yellowish skin, vestigial bobtails, and three-toed digitigrade legs, Chaksa exhibit a mixture of reptilian, mammalian, and cephalopod traits unlike anything found in the Human Sphere. But despite their imposing appearance, peering into the red eyes of a Chaksa reveals a gentle soul as often as not.

The Chaksa government is wholly subsumed by the Trinomial, and Chaksa military enrolment is widespread. Sceptics whisper that Exaltation involves a significant indoctrination component, engineering the Chaksa to be loyal to their Tohaa superiors, be they Trihedron or Trinomial, as little more than slaves.

The Chaksa themselves regard this attitude with confusion; why wouldn't they be grateful for the gift of Exaltation? To them, it's a debt they may never be able to repay, but the only honourable thing to do is try.

ATTRIBUTES

AGI	AWA	BRW	COO	INT	PER	WIL
10	7	10	8	7	6	8

FIELDS OF EXPERTISE

Combat	+1	1	Movement	+1	–	Social	–	–
Fortitude	+2	–	Senses	+1	–	Technical	–	–

DEFENCES

Firewall	4	Resolve	4	Vigour	5
Security	–	Morale	–	Armour	–

ATTACKS
- **HMG**: Range L, 2+6 🅝 damage, Burst 3, Unwieldly, Spread 1, Unsubtle
- **Hedgehog**: Melee, 1+6 🅝 damage, Aug (Implant), Subtle 1, Toxic 4, Vicious 2

GEAR: Sensor Suite (pick two)

SPECIAL ABILITIES
- **Hyper-Dynamics**: Chaksa are extremely fast, allowing them to move one additional zone when taking any movement action. They also gain 1 bonus Momentum on Defence actions in Warfare scenes due to their ultra-fast reflexes.
- **Sly Servants**: Chaksa gain 1 bonus Momentum on Stealth tests.

NEMESIS
EI–AVATAR

The Ur Rationalists' ultimate war machine, Avatars are roving battle platforms designed to carry an aspect of the Evolved Intelligence onto the battlefield. This gives the EI a first-hand perspective, as well as the opportunity to directly impact its surroundings. These hulking masses of biosynthetics employ optical disruptor technology – a bewildering array of photon-bending gravitic fields, twisting and churning local space around the armoured colossi – which cause them to appear as massive blurry outlines. On top of that, their weapon platforms, heavy armour plating, and advanced targeting solutions rival even the most powerful TAGS.

The Combined Army posits that opposing the EI is an expression of suicidal futility. Where the Avatar is concerned, they're not entirely wrong.

ATTRIBUTES

AGI	AWA	BRW	COO	INT	PER	WIL
9	9	14	12	11	6	11

FIELDS OF EXPERTISE

Combat	+5	3	Movement	+3	–	Social	–	–
Fortitude	+3	2	Senses	+3	1	Technical	–	–

DEFENCES

Firewall	11	Resolve	14	Vigour	17
Security	–	Morale	–	Armour	9

ATTACKS
- **Claws**: Melee, 2+8 🅝 damage, Piercing 1, Spread 1, Vicious 1
- **MULTI HMG**: Range L, 2+6 🅝 damage, Burst 3, Unwieldy, Medium MULTI, MULTI Heavy Mod, Spread 1, Unsubtle
  - *DA Mode (Default Secondary)*: Vicious 2
- **Sepsitor Plus**: Range C, 1+5 🅝 mental damage, Burst 1, Mounted, Terrifying 4, Torrent, Toxic 3

GEAR: ECM, Optical Disruption Device, Sensor Suite (Motion, Heat)

SPECIAL ABILITIES
- **Common Special Abilities**: Inured to Pain, Poison, and Vacuum; Menacing 4, Monstrous, Quantronic Jump
- **Assurance of Victory**: When an Avatar takes the field, the possibility of defeat does not occur to its troops. While an Avatar is an active participant in a conflict, allied forces gain +6 🅝 Morale Soak.
- **Death Incarnate**: The EI hasn't come this far by holding back. When making a Combat test, an Avatar can reroll up to 6 🅝, but must accept the new result.
- **Semi-Autonomous Weapon Platform**: As a Reaction, the Avatar can make a single attack with its MULTI HMG. The extra attack is made at +2 difficulty.

EI–CHARONTID

An upgrade to the outdated Skiávoros model, the Charontid is an EI heavy tactical unit capable of operating in the harshest of environments.

These creatures are the perfect soldiers. They can march for a week without sleep. They can withstand any level of solar radiation and any gravity. They can breathe any atmosphere, untroubled by the stench of an alien planet. They can slumber anywhere, and regain full awareness in an instant. They can feed off any organic matter. They are equipped with the best in Voodoo Technology. Their helmets are fitted with a next-generation wide-angle image intensifier, a multi-directional microphone, a wide-spectrum telemeter and a set of active and passive infrared sensors. Sensory hypersensitivity and radar/sonar systems are spread over a number of armour plates for full awareness of its surroundings. In the field, these operatives receive a constant information feed from the satellite network and geosynchronous EI command centres. All transmissions are redundant, with different sources and encryption methods, to guarantee the integrity of the information and avoid enemy tampering.

ATTRIBUTES

AGI	AWA	BRW	COO	INT	PER	WIL
11	10	12	12	11	6	12

FIELDS OF EXPERTISE

Combat	+5	3	Movement	+2	1	Social	–	–
Fortitude	+2	2	Senses	+3	2	Technical	–	–

DEFENCES

Firewall	11	Resolve	14	Vigour	14
Security	–	Morale	–	Armour	4

ATTACKS

- **Hacking Device Plus**: CLAW-2, SWORD-1, SHIELD-2, GADGET-3, IC-2, UPGRADE Cybermask, Sucker Punch, White Noise; +2 🅽 bonus damage
- **Styx Knife**: Melee, 1+6 🅽 damage, 1H, Concealed 1, Non-Hackable, Subtle 2, Thrown, Unforgiving 3
- **Plasma Rifle**: Range R/C, 1+8 🅽 damage, Burst 3, Unbalanced, Area (Close), Knockdown, Unforgiving 3, Unsubtle, Vicious 1
- **Sepsitor**: Range C, 1+6 🅽 mental damage, Burst 1, 1H, Terrifying 3, Torrent, Toxic 3

GEAR: Multispectral Visor 3, Sensor Suit (Motion, Heat)

SPECIAL ABILITIES

- **Common Special Abilities**: Inured to Cold, Disease, Heat, Pain, and Poison, Menacing 2, Night Vision, Quantronic Jump
- **Integrated Armour**: A Charontid has 4 Armour Soak from its integrated armour plating.
- **Omni-Awareness**: The synergy of their advanced technology allows Charontids to see everything and process every detail of the battlefield. They gain +2d20 on Observation tests.

EI–SKIÁVOROS

The template race from which the EI built the insectoid Skiávoros ("Shadow Devourers") was originally known merely as the Colonizers. Created millennia ago as eternal bodies that could carry copies of their creators to distant star systems via slower-than-light travel, the Colonizers were physically resistant and adaptable to almost any environment. Their Makers, however, feared their possible return, and so their point of origin was deleted from the navigation systems of their Ark-Ships: the Colonizers could explore the galaxy, but could never return home.

The EI intercepted an Ark-Ship that had been damaged and become lost. The Colonizers had placed their bodies in stasis, but aeons of drifting through the void degraded their memory storage. The EI took the empty, soulless bodies, loaded them with weapons, and turned them to its own purposes as hosts for its aspects.

ATTRIBUTES

AGI	AWA	BRW	COO	INT	PER	WIL
9	9	10	10	9	6	10

FIELDS OF EXPERTISE

Combat	+3	3	Movement	–	–	Social	–	–
Fortitude	+2	2	Senses	+1	1	Technical	–	–

DEFENCES

Firewall	9	Resolve	10	Vigour	10
Security	–	Morale	–	Armour	–

ATTACKS

- **Nanopulser**: Range C, 1+6 🅽 damage, 1H, Biotech, Subtle 3, Torrent, Vicious 2
- **Plasma Rifle**: Range R/C, 1+7 🅽 damage, Burst 3, Unbalanced, Area (Close), Knockdown, Unforgiving 3, Unsubtle, Vicious 1
- **Sepsitor**: Range C, 1+5 🅽 mental damage, Burst 1, 1H, Terrifying 3, Torrent, Toxic 3

SPECIAL ABILITIES

- **Common Special Abilities**: Inured to Cold, Heat, and Pain; Quantronic Jump
- **Mimetism**: Skiávoros benefit from 2 bonus Momentum when making face-to-face tests to remain in the detected stealth state.
- **Strategos**: A Skiávoros is in constant communication with Combined Army forces. As long as they are present in a scene, the GM reduces the Heat cost to summon reinforcements by 6 (to a minimum of 1).

MIURA KAYON

MERCENARY, EX-HARAMAKI

BACKER: JEFF HOFER

Blood spattered across his helmet, and he felt the old urge rise fresh in his breast.

He fought it down and knelt beside the poor bastard. The body twitched, and he wanted to ram his blade into it again. To make it stop. To feel metal penetrating flesh. To own the finality of it. The purging of it.

Beneath the ashy grime which coated the body, his former regiment's insignia was visible. He swallowed his resentment of the turncoat. Instead, he reached out and closed the treacherous, accusing eyes which were staring into his. Then he stood and bowed from the waist as a sign of his sorrow and respect.

He detested traitors, but here on alien-infested Paradiso not all of the traitors had a choice. The Shasvastii were on the move.

He stepped back and looked back up the long slope.

He had no love for the base. Beautifully crafted and lodged into the side of Mount Cristol, it deserved a poem, but he lacked the education to do it justice. He hated it for that.

He turned back to the jungle. Listening again for the sound he had heard. The Shasvastii were clever to send their puppet out, but it was no puppet that he had heard. The distinct, slowly encroaching sounds of the battle were making it indistinct and hard to pinpoint, but it was still there.

He disabled the tactical map in his HUD. He didn't need it to tell him that they were encircled by aliens, and he didn't need the distraction.

He envisioned himself springing into action as something broke the treeline, sweeping out his blade and striking down the assailant with a fast slash to the right before landing in a crouch, side-stepping to the left, and bringing his blade into both hands ready to face more foes.

The call to action surged within him with each deep breath. His muscles tensed. The urge to kill pulsed stronger and stronger. Still he calmed himself to patience.

Finally, an inhuman form entered his field of vision. He leapt like a coiled spring. Unleashed his fury through a flashing blade.

The move was perfect.

APPEARANCE

Chiselled features, clear blue eyes, and a military haircut.

ROLEPLAYING

- Tries to hide his humble origins
- Takes deep breaths to calm his boiling emotions
- Craves perfection

BACKGROUND

Miura's life could easily be the blueprint for a Maya commercial on the advancement possibilities of the armed services. Born to the lower echelons of Nipponese society, he entered training as a soldier at an early age by enlisting with the Gekken Kogyo – the "sword show" combat-sport spectacles fought among the ranks of the Nipponese Army – when he felt ready. His success there brought him rapidly to the attention of the recruiters for the Haramaki Zensenbutai (腹巻前線部隊), a samurai regiment created expressly to mitigate the otherwise extreme class-segregation of the Nipponese Army.

His astronomic career, however, was waylaid when he was killed on the battlefield during the First Paradiso Offensive and resurrected in a European-styled Lhost, much to his shame. His new body caused no end of grief as others in the Nipponese Army constantly challenged his honour. This led to him cutting down two officers in anger in an act that led to a court martial and dishonourable discharge. He has since become a mercenary, drifting from one war to another as he seeks to hone his skill.

STATS (ELITE)

ATTRIBUTES

AGI	AWA	BRW	COO	INT	PER	WIL
9	9	10	10	8	7	10

FIELDS OF EXPERTISE

Combat	+2	2	Movement	+1	1	Social	+1	–
Fortitude	+1	–	Senses	+2	1	Technical	+1	–

DEFENCES

Firewall	8	Resolve	10	Vigour	10
Security	–	Morale	–	Armour	5

ATTACKS
- **Combi Rifle**: Range C/M, 1+6  damage, Burst 2, 2H, Expert 1, MULTI Light Mod, Vicious 1
- **DT-Coated Sword**: Melee, 1+7 damage, Unbalanced, Biotech, Non-Hackable, Parry 2, Toxic 1, Vicious 2
- **Knife**: Melee, 1+5 damage, 1H, Concealed 1, Non-Hackable, Subtle 2, Thrown, Unforgiving 1

GEAR: Powered Combat Armour (with AutoMediKit and Surge AutoInjector; gain up to +3d20 on Brawn tests with +3 complication range), Surge ×3

SPECIAL ABILITIES
- **Aspirations Above His Station**: Even though his formal military career has been buried alongside two corpses, Miura still labours to shed his low birth status. He compensates with perfect social graces. He can reroll one d20 when making a Lifestyle test, but must accept the new result.
- **Hew and Cleave**: Miura prefers to let his blade do the talking. He can reroll up to 4 when making a melee attack, but must accept the new results.
- **Living Weapon**: Miura's blade is an extension of his body, though it's far from the only one. He can draw a melee weapon as a Free Action (instead of a Minor Action), and is always considered armed for the purposes of the Defence Reaction.
- **Perfect Strike**: Obsessed with perfecting his technique, Miura can strike at a moment's notice, and does so with alarming ferocity. When spending Heat to interrupt turn order, he also gains the benefits of an Exploit action.

NOTES
Ashamed of his birth status and possessed of a hair-trigger temper, Miura suffers a +1 complication range when making tests based on Willpower.

MORAT

A quintessentially militaristic race, the Morat pursue excellence in warfare above all things. To an outsider, their gregarious collectivism might be surprising, but there's no contradiction to a Morat. To take down dangerous prey, you hunt in groups. A strong group beats a strong individual every time. Simple.

As such, Morats think of themselves as soldiers first and foremost; personal notions of honour are superseded by loyalty to the Morat Supremacy, and their comrades-in-arms. To fight for the Supremacy is to embrace destiny, to kill its enemies is to know satisfaction, and to die in its service worthy. As one Morat saying goes, "it is a great tragedy to watch the hour of death pass you by."

Needless to say, the Morat aren't fond of being taken prisoner, as this means they've failed their duty twice – both to kill their opponent, and to die in battle.

ATTRIBUTES

AGI	AWA	BRW	COO	INT	PER	WIL
10	8	12	10	8	7	8

FIELDS OF EXPERTISE

Combat	+2	2	Movement	+1	1	Social	–	–
Fortitude	+2	2	Senses	+1	1	Technical	–	–

DEFENCES

Firewall	8	Resolve	8	Vigour	12
Security	–	Morale	2	Armour	2

ATTACKS
- **Combi Rifle**: Range C/M, 1+5 damage, Burst 2, 2H, Expert 1, MULTI Light Mod, Vicious 1
- **Knife**: Melee, 1+6 damage, 1H, Concealed 1, Non-Hackable, Subtle 2, Thrown, Unforgiving 1

GEAR: Light Combat Armour

SPECIAL ABILITIES
- **Morat Aggression**: The Morat's brutal outlook grants them a Morale Soak of 2.

MR. PATCH

NOMAD CYBER-ASSAULT OPERATOR

SYSTEM BREACHED --
SHUTTING DOWN WEAPONS

BACKER: RAUL PACHECO

"Repeater deployed. Have fun!"

As the system came up, in the video feed he could see the Riot Grrl skipping down the side of the volcano. It was a weird gig. Zhiyong must really be behind the eight ball if he was calling him in. And far be it from him to turn down an offer of access to the Dărăo network.

He started by deploying an automatic scanning program. Then his system was screaming at him. A Nomad emergency beacon. His eyes darted to the mercs he'd sent to infiltrate the Navaria Nightmares club here on Neoterra, but everything there was fine. The signal had pinged the repeater on Paradiso from a couple clicks away. And then it had been cut off.

He cracked the package it had left behind: Access codes to some sort of quantronic backdoor. And a single word: OPEN. What the hell – ?

His scanners nabbed a different quantronic signature. Closer this time: A TAG in full combat mode. Its firewall reared its head as he probed its code, so he retreated and looked for another door. The code, however, had allowed him to tag the machine as a Morat Raicho. Nasty bit of business that. Trust his dumb luck.

It took about two seconds to backdoor the code and slip in, suppressing the intruder systems as he went. Heading straight for the ejection system, he was not disappointed to find it less defended than the TAG's other controls. Sending one final message to the pilot's HUD–With Regards from Mr. Patch ☺–he enacted the ejection protocols.

He set some CLAW programs running, hoping to crack the Morat combat datasphere through the compromised Raicho. Curiosity beckoned, however. Using a quantronic repeater to isolate himself from any possible viral payload, he activated the access point encoded in the emergency beacon.

He found himself logged into a FastPanda, its propulsion batteries completely drained, in what appeared to be an airlock. This was totally bizarre, what was he – a red flag alerted him to a faulty weapon among the Riot Grrls; an HMG with a malfunctioning ammo count. He gave it a quick reboot – supposed to do with this? Wait. Open? This guy was crazier than he was!

He sent the command. The airlock door cycled. The FastPanda – and something else? – was sucked out in a sudden blast of air. He applied some visual stabilisation routines to the rapidly rotating footage streaming from the 'Panda and could see the smoking plume of Mount Cristol. This thing was almost directly above his repeater!

And falling fast.

He rerouted and reached for the satellite network. He found one that hadn't patched the zero day exploit he'd lifted off an AccessTel mainframe nearly a year go. Amateurs. He pulled down its orbital imagery, tracked the path of the errant FastPanda, and shot the whole thing over to Zhiyong in a memetic bundle. Maybe the mastermind could figure out what this had all been about.

Just before severing his connection, he couldn't resist leaving a message: Fixed your access files, Regards from Mr. Patch ☺. A fresh ping found no immediate threats near the repeater and the team on Neoterra were still right on schedule. So he pulled up a suite of news channels from Shentang and then popped over to place a quick bet on a catamaran race on Varuna.

APPEARANCE

His eyes are glistening black with snake-like irises glowing faintly blue. Full, thick black curls top a tall, gaunt frame.

ROLEPLAYING

- Attention deficit disorder, but dead serious beneath his façade
- Always leaves a quantronic calling card
- Enraged by anyone trying to find out his true identity

BACKGROUND

The Echo of Arachne, as he is also called, is a mystery. He's believed to be Bakunian, but any documentation of his true identity appears to have been wiped before "Mr. Patch" made his first appearance in the Arachne hacker clusters, offering his services as a mercenary hacker. Some theories hold that he's a PanOceanian ex-pat; or an Hassassin infiltrator; or a clone created *tabula rasa* by the Black Hand. Whatever the case may be, he has demonstrated a fierce loyalty to the Nomad Nation.

STATS (ELITE)

ATTRIBUTES

AGI	AWA	BRW	COO	INT	PER	WIL
8	10	7	8	12	9	9

FIELDS OF EXPERTISE

Combat	+1	–	Movement	–	–	Social	+1	–
Fortitude	–	–	Senses	+2	2	Technical	+3	3

DEFENCES

Firewall	12	Resolve	9	Vigour	7
Security	4	Morale	–	Armour	1

ATTACKS

- **E/M Pistol**: Range R/C, 1+6 🄽 damage, Burst 1, 1H, Breaker, E/M, Piercing 1, Vicious 1
- **Modhand**: Melee, 1+4 🄽 damage, 1H, Concealed 2, E/M, Stun, Subtle 1, Vicious 2
- **Neural Hacking Device Plus**: CLAW-2 (CLAW-1 Blackout, CLAW-1 Overlord, CLAW-1 Spotlight, CLAW-2 Expel), SWORD-1 (SWORD-1 Brain Blast, SWORD-1 Slasher), SHIELD-2 (SHIELD-1 Exorcism, SHIELD-2 Breakwater), GADGET-2 (GADGET-1 Fairy Dust, GADGET-2 Assisted Fire, GADGET-2 Enhanced Reaction), IC-2, UPGRADE Cybermask, Sucker Punch, White Noise; +3 🄽 bonus damage

GEAR: Armoured Clothing (with Backup Hacking Device Plus), Short ModCoat (with Stealth Repeater)

SPECIAL ABILITIES

- **Finger on the Pulse**: Mr. Patch has a highly analytical mind that rapidly assimilates all of the data at his fingertips. He can reroll one d20 when making an Analysis test, but must accept the new result.
- **Patch is the Name, Hacking the Game (1 Heat)**: Mr. Patch slices through quantronic networks with distressing ease. He can reroll up to 6 🄽 when making an Infowar attack.
- **Closer Than You Think**: Mr. Patch's techniques are so far ahead of the curve that they'll be cutting-edge five years from now. Of course, that's left little time for testing. He can extend his usual hacking range from Close to Medium by spending 1 Heat, or from Close to Long by spending 3 Heat. This effect lasts until the end of the round.

MORAT – DĀTURAZI WITCH-SOLDIER

First appearing as part of the Knife Renaissance that followed the coming of the EI, the Dāturazi are simultaneously a pillar of Morat philosophy, and a bizarre outlier. Followers of Cotoya, the Morat god of war, the Dāturazi employ meditation techniques in harmony with the analytic prowess of the EI comlog to deadly effect.

Morats generally take a detached outlook toward religion, and the concept of meditation had traditionally been met with scorn; but no one could deny the brutal efficiency of these warrior-monks and their innovative combat techniques. The Dāturazi see virtue in personal combat, in tearing the life out of an enemy with their own hands, and their signature martial art, "Dirty War", reflects this.

Many young Morats look to advance their careers by joining the Witch-Soldiers, even though the ceremony that new initiates undergo is so brutal that even most Morats prefer to skip the details.

ATTRIBUTES

AGI	AWA	BRW	COO	INT	PER	WIL
13	11	12	7	9	7	11

FIELDS OF EXPERTISE

Combat	+4	4	Movement	+2	–	Social	–	–
Fortitude	+3	1	Senses	+3	1	Technical	+2	–

DEFENCES

Firewall	11	Resolve	14	Vigour	15
Security	–	Morale	2	Armour	2

ATTACKS

- **AP Axe**: Melee, 1+8 🄽, Unbalanced, Non-Hackable, Piercing 2, Spread 1, Vicious 2
- **Vulkan Shotgun**: Range C, 1+7 🄽 damage, Burst 1, 2H, Knockdown, Medium MULTI
  - *Normal Shells Mode (Primary)*: Area (Close), Spread 1
  - *Fire Shells Mode (Secondary)*: Area (Close), Incendiary 3, Terrifying 1
- **Smoke Grenades**: Disposable, Indiscriminate (Close), Nonlethal, Smoke 2, Speculative Fire, Thrown

GEAR: Light Combat Armour (Kinematika)

SPECIAL ABILITIES

- **Baptised in Fire**: They'd rather not talk about it. The Dāturazi can reroll one d20 when making a Discipline test, but must accept the new result.
- **Dirty War**: As a Minor Action, the Dāturazi can make a Senses (D1) test against an opponent; if successful, their next attack against that target gains the benefits of an Exploit.
- **Morat Aggression**: The Morat's brutal outlook grants them a Morale Soak of 2.
- **Scout**: The Dāturazi can reroll one d20 when making a Stealth test, but must accept the new result.

MORAT – RAICHO PILOT

Understanding how *raichō* — meaning "thunderbird" in Japanese — became the unofficial designation for the Morat Armoured Brigade's Raizot pilots goes a long way toward understanding these firebrands. The term was coined by Yu Jing's Nipponese troops, who first encountered the Raicho piloting TAGs decorated in Demarok pelts — trophies from a mighty predator on Ugarat — and unleashing cacophonous torrents of ammunition upon the battlefield. The mottled white pelt reminded them of the *raichō* bird from Toyama Prefecture, and "Thunderbird" certainly described these alien terrors.

The Raicho, for their part, neither knew nor cared. But they weren't about to turn down a sobriquet their enemies shrieked before dying, so they adopted the term themselves, and have used it ever since.

Daredevils with a particularly nasty sense of humour, Raicho are bullish, unsubtle, and hard to divert once they've built up a head of steam; traits they share with their signature TAG.

ATTRIBUTES

AGI	AWA	BRW	COO	INT	PER	WIL
12	10	10	12	9	8	9

FIELDS OF EXPERTISE

Combat	+3	3	Movement	+4	–	Social	+2	1
Fortitude	+2	1	Senses	+1	1	Technical	+2	–

DEFENCES

Firewall	11	Resolve	11	Vigour	12
Security	–	Morale	2	Armour	1

ATTACKS

- **Assault Pistol**: Range R/C, 1+6 🄽 damage, Burst 2, Unbalanced, Vicious 1

GEAR: Armoured Clothing

SPECIAL ABILITIES

- **Berserker Rage**: Sometimes, Raicho just get mad. As a Minor Action, they can enter a Berserker Rage, adding +4 🄽 to all attacks. While in this state, they may not make Defence Reactions, and gain no benefit from cover. They can spend a Minor Action and attempt a Discipline (D1) test to calm themselves down, exiting the state and removing all of its effects if they succeed.
- **Thundering Fire**: Raicho aren't the most accurate gunners in the Combined Army, a fact they remedy with sheer volume. When piloting a vehicle and spending Heat to gain the effects of a Reload, they gain the benefit of two Reloads per Heat spent. They also increase the effective Burst of any vehicle-based weapons by +1.
- **Expert Maneuverers**: Raicho like to be in the middle of the action; they waste little effort in getting there. They can reroll one d20 when making a Movement test, but must accept the new result.
- **Morat Aggression**: The Morat's brutal outlook grants them +2 Morale Soak.

OLEN "GRAVEL" EMMER

HELLCAT/COMM SUPPORT

BACKER: OLEN GRAVEL

The ratcheting clank vanquished the darkness as the shady light of dawn spilled into the workshop. Gravel ducked beneath the partly open shutter and made his way towards the three repeaters and two helmets that were scattered across the central workbench, wrinkling his nose at the unseemly state of the workshop and the stench of cheap vodka. Putting his rifle carefully on the workbench as he sat, he took out his personal toolkit and set to work disassembling one of the repeaters.

His motions were precise, delicate, and executed with neither haste nor sloth. Like a mantra, he repeated the procedure three times. Then he turned his attention to the first helmet.

"Knock, knock." The flirtatious voice drew his attention to the slender silhouette that had appeared at the shutter. He squinted his eyes against the glare. Sasha.

"Is your comlog broken now, too?" asked Olen, his voice a rocky rumble.

"Maybe just hearing that gravelly voice of yours isn't enough for me," Sasha grinned, throwing a leg over the bench next to him. "And maybe letting you feast your eyes on me is just my way of saying thank you. Is that mine?"

"Da, I fixed the transmission errors in your receiver."

"Gracias, I knew you were good for something."

"You really should take better care of your equipment. Înțelegi?" Sasha put on a sarcastic pout. "That sounds boring."

A klaxon sounded. Their comlogs squawked. "Hostiles inbound at Foxtrot. All Hellcats, depart in five. Repeat. All Hellcats, report to drop shuttles in five minutes."

Sasha's grin broadened with a cat-like gleam. "I guess the comlog is good for something." She grabbed her helmet, bounced off the bench, and giddily pranced through the door.

With a sigh, Gravel turned back to one of the offending helmets and ran through one final check before putting it on, slinging his rifle around his shoulder, and hefting the repeaters. He slapped them onto their holding magnets as he strode towards the waiting shuttles. A glance at his HUD told him they were still two minutes from departure and displayed the deployment intel across his vision. Dangerous, rear-line disruption of the encroaching Morat forces. Gravel strapped himself into a seat and leaned back.

"Wake me when we get there."

APPEARANCE

Olen is a man in his forties, of slender build, and clearly of Romanian descent. His black hair is always short and somewhat deranged. The rest of his appearance is otherwise flawless.

ROLEPLAYING

- Uncannily cool, with perfectly placid features
- Sighs often when someone does something reckless
- Grinds his teeth
- Always has a contingency plan

BACKGROUND

Olen took his nickname from the grinding sound he makes with his teeth when angry at someone. Born and raised on *Corregidor*, he is a perfect representation of this heritage. He is very pragmatic, professional, and free-spirited. He rarely talks about life before joining the Hellcats, and no one asks. His service record places him amidst all major engagements of the past twenty years: the Commercial Conflicts. Second Phantom Conflict. The Outer Mercantile Crisis and the Union Revolts of the Jupiter-Pluto Circuit. Even the Fourth Antipode Offensive on Ariadna for some godforsaken reason.

He ended up on Paradiso during the First Offensive. (The way the story goes is that he was visiting friends on the ground when the invasion started.) Then he got off-planet for awhile with a mercenary contract in the Human Edge, only to be rotated back to Paradiso just in time for the Second Offensive to kick off.

If it was someone else, people might start thinking of him as bad luck. But Olen approaches everything with such suave professionalism that his litany of experience mostly seems to just fill those around him with confidence. Sometimes, despite his best efforts, too much confidence.

STATS (ELITE)

ATTRIBUTES

AGI	AWA	BRW	COO	INT	PER	WIL
8	9	10	9	10	7	10

FIELDS OF EXPERTISE

Combat	+2	1	Movement	+1	–	Social	–	–
Fortitude	+1	1	Senses	+1	1	Technical	+2	2

DEFENCES

Firewall	10	Resolve	10	Vigour	10
Security	–	Morale	1	Armour	4

ATTACKS

- **Combi Rifle**: Range C/M, 1+6  damage, Burst 2, 2H, Expert 1, MULTI Light Mod, Vicious 1
  - *Light Shotgun:* Range C, 1+5 damage, Burst 1, Unbalanced, Knockdown
- **Hacking Device**: CLAW-1, SWORD-1, SHIELD-1, GADGET-3, IC-1; +2 bonus damage

GEAR: Heavy Combat Armour (with Combat Jump Pack and Deployable Repeater ×3)

SPECIAL ABILITIES

- **Battlefield Survivor**: A survivor of numerous campaigns across countless battlefields, some consider him to be a lucky talisman, others just a tough old boot. As long as he is not incapacitated, he generates +1 Morale Soak to his allies, including himself. (This is already included in his stats.)
- **Custom Repeaters**: Olen takes care of his gear, and it returns the favour. He can reroll up to 4 when making Infowar attacks using his repeaters, but must accept the new result.
- **Hellcat Jump Pack**: Olen's old pack has seen him through a lot, and he knows it inside and out. In addition to the gear's normal benefits, he generates 1 additional Momentum on Movement tests when wearing his jump pack.

MORAT—RASYAT

Joining the EI's Combined Civilisation was a difficult time for the Morat Supremacy. For the first time in their history, they were required to have a diplomatic service; a problematic concept for the Morat, who'd traditionally derided diplomacy as a tool of the weak. However, the Supremacy found an elegant solution to this conundrum: train up the toughest, most vicious, and xenophobic Surats for an elite combat force, then task them with making incursions into enemy territory to learn their weaknesses in anticipation of future strikes.

Thus was the Rasyat Diplomatic Division born.

The Rasyatnat is a distillation of Morat negotiation principles; specifically, the biggest gun makes the best argument, and persuasion is best delivered in high-impact bursts. Through this philosophy, the Rasyat have refined coercion and bullying to unprecedented degrees.

If they'd only known that diplomacy meant scaring the hell out of people, they'd have done this ages ago.

ATTRIBUTES

AGI	AWA	BRW	COO	INT	PER	WIL
11	9	12	8	9	11	10

FIELDS OF EXPERTISE

Combat	+3	1	Movement	+1	1	Social	+4	4
Fortitude	+3	1	Senses	+1	–	Technical	+1	–

DEFENCES

Firewall	10	Resolve	13	Vigour	15
Security	–	Morale	2	Armour	3

ATTACKS

- **D-Charges**: 2+6 damage, 1H, Anti-Materiel 2, Comms, Disposable, Piercing 3, Spread 1, Unsubtle, Vicious 2
- **Haunt Charges**: Poison damage, Comms, Indiscriminate (Close), Nonlethal, Subtle 2
- **E/M Combi Rifle**: Range C/M, 1+5 damage, Burst 2, 2H, Breaker, E/M, Expert 1, Piercing 2, Vicious 1
- **Eclipse Grenades**: Disposable, Indiscriminate (Close), Reflective 2, Speculative Fire, Thrown, Unsubtle

GEAR: Medium Combat Armour (with Combat Jump Pack)

SPECIAL ABILITIES

- **Heated Negotiation**: The Rasyat are trained instigators; as such, they're rarely surprised. When making a face-to-face test to determine Surprise, they can reroll any dice that did not generate a success on the initial test, but must accept the new results.
- **Interpersonal Communication**: The Rasyat like to get up close and personal. When making social skill tests. to intimidate, they gain 2 bonus Momentum if the target is within Close range.
- **Morat Aggression**: The Morat's brutal outlook grants them +2 Morale Soak.
- **Traditional Diplomacy**: The Rasyat adds +4 to Psywar attacks.

PROFESSOR VITRIARIUS

POSTHUMAN ARCHAEOLOGIST

BACKER: THOMAS SMITH

"Thank you, counsellor, for your help."

"My pleasure!" The lawyer rubbed his bald head. "You've given me quite the puzzle to unravel, but I think I should have some answers for you by the end of the week."

Professor Vitriarius nodded and turned away. As the door slid shut behind him, he hopped out of the shell on Shentang. The body's programming would ensure that it found its way to the hotel on its own. He was glad to be out of it, at least for the moment. It had just been a communal carrier—shared by any Posthuman in need—and he wasn't new-fangled enough to really be comfortable in a female body.

In the next moment, he opened his eyes on the Black Elysium station in the Paradiso system. Checking his internal chronometer, however, he could see that several hours had elapsed—the time necessary for his conscious-ness-diff to transmit at light speed through the wormhole network.

He hoisted himself out of the cradle that held his body here and went out into the laboratory.

"Ah! Professor Vitriarius! Your morning meeting went well?"

"Very well, Betty. Thank you." He nodded and smiled at her. "Have you man-aged to equalise the neuroplasticity on the zeta set of psychogenetic templates?"

"We're running the random samples through a battery of tests, but it's looking good." Betty double-checked something on her private AR displays. "The compatibility ratings are very high."

"That's great work. Look, I need to meet with Dr. Sharrakin, but I should be free in about an hour—" A high-priority alert blazed across his consciousness. "Excuse me, Dr. Straub."

They were ready for him. That was quicker than he'd expected. But it meant he didn't have any time to spare. He left a copy of his geist in

charge of handling the meeting with Dr. Sharrakin and triggered another transfer, this time queuing it through the Metatron network. It was expen-sive—and a mild security risk if the Dărăo satellites were monitoring the right channels—but necessary. There was the strange-yet-familiar sen-sation of being squeezed, which was something he had never overcome, and twenty seconds later he opened his eyes on Dawn.

He levered himself out of the sarcophagus. He was in a cavern. Large and mostly being used as a storeroom, although he had to step over the uncon-scious bodies of several guards in order to reach the door. He could feel his pulse beating a little faster—knowing it to be a psychosomatic vestige of his humanity, but nonetheless thrilled at the thought of what Phoenix Industries had discovered here three hundred feet below the city of Skara Brae.

As the door opened, his advance agent turned and looked at him twice. "Welcome to Project Blacklight, Professor."

APPEARANCE

As a Posthuman, Vitriarius is able to assume many forms. But he often resembles his old body at age twenty-seven—long black hair, a beard, and the perfect physique of a Boddhisatva Lhost. (He is also known to occasionally use digging machines and laser scanners as hosts.)

ROLEPLAYING

- Scrupulously polite, always practicing the perfect etiquette
- Tends to expostulate lengthily on any given topic
- Values curiosity more than personal safety

BACKGROUND

Older than ALEPH itself and hailing from a wealthy PanOceanian family which had made its fortune during the colonisation of Neoterra, Vitriarius was a young university student when the AI was activated. Fascinated by the dream of mankind's birthplace, he emigrated back to Earth and putt-ered about in the moribund field of archaeology for a number of decades.

He was killed in a traffic accident in 6 NC, but was lucky enough to have lived long enough (and be wealthy enough) to be resurrected. He was killed again in 14 NC, and this time it took half a decade before he was resurrected (narrowly skirting under the Resurrection Pacts). In the wake of his second death, he found himself weary of the dead end he had trapped himself in. Leaving Earth, he journeyed to Varuna and became a premiere exo-archaeologist and one of the leading authorities on Helot culture.

In 47 NC, with this third body once gain turning venerable, he was on Paradiso when the first alien artefacts were discovered at ZuluPoint. Initially it was a case of having the perfect skills in the perfect place at the perfect time, and Vitriarius became fascinated by the discoveries being made. But then, when the project became heavily classified, he was abruptly shut out. Unwilling to accept the mysteries he had been unravelling, the professor spearheaded several expeditions into the NiemandsZone, gathering an enormous amount of data that couldn't be shared without fear of being persecuted for his crimes.

Through contacts he had cultivated, he became aware of the mission to the Last Cosmolite in the Sisargas Islands. At great personal expense, he attempted to infiltrate the islands himself. His flight was instead mistaken for a Combined Army attack and shot down. Members of the S.S.S. were the first to reach his crash site and, strangely, ALEPH chose to reach out to the fatally injured professor, who could hardly refuse the AI's enigmatic offer to become Posthuman. After all, he still had so much work to complete.

It took some time to adapt to his limitless existence, but with a countless number of years ahead of him, Vitriarius is more commit-ted than ever to bridging the gap between the mind of man and the riddling conundrums of alien existence.

STATS (NEMESIS)

ATTRIBUTES

AGI	AWA	BRW	COO	INT	PER	WIL
10 (+1)	11 (+1)	9 (+1)	8	12 (+2)	10	10

FIELDS OF EXPERTISE

Combat	+1	1	Movement	+1	1	Social	+1	1
Fortitude	+1	–	Senses	+2	2	Technical	+4	4

DEFENCES

Firewall	16	Resolve	12	Vigour	2
Security	2	Morale	2	Armour	2

ATTACKS

- **Nanopulser**: Range C, 1+7 🅝 damage, 1H, Biotech, Subtle 3, Torrent, Vicious 2
- **Pistol**: Range R/C, 2+6 🅝 damage, Burst 1, 1H, Vicious 1
- **Knife**: Melee, 2+4 🅝 damage, 1H, Concealed 1, Non-Hackable, Subtle 2, Thrown, Unforgiving 1

GEAR: Armoured Clothing (with Chameleonwear), Bioengineered Physiology, Cube 2.0, Silk Attribute Augmentation 2 (Intelligence)

SPECIAL ABILITIES

- **Common Special Abilities**: Fast Recovery (Firewall 1, Vigour 1), Keen Senses (Hearing, Sight, Smell), Night Vision, Quantronic Jump, Superhuman Agility 1, Superhuman Awareness 1, Superhuman Brawn 1, Superhuman Intelligence 2
- **Connected**: A Posthuman's constant connection to the datasphere widens their perspective and Vitriariaus has been connected for a long time. He gains Morale and Security Soak 2. If he is unable to connect to the datasphere, he loses these benefits.
- **Enlightened Scholar**: Vitriarius was an expert in his field before becoming Posthuman; now he is an expert in any field he sets his mind to. When making a Technical test, he can reroll any dice that did not generate a success on the initial roll, but must accept the new result.

SHASVASTII

Any Shasvastii (p. 313) operating within the Human Sphere are likely part of the Pioneer or Deep Incursion Corps. Operatives from both are masters of deception, camouflage, guerrilla warfare, and sabotage. Most often, the greatest challenge in overcoming a Shasvastii foe is finding them. Their bio-quantronic clothing and stealth gear allow them to deceive even the most advanced sensor systems, and they lay plans within plans to ensure their own survival and that of their race. The combination of technology and patient planning gives them the means to access corporate, military, and criminal organisations across the Sphere. Wherever they're found, Shasvastii work tirelessly and invisibly to sow confusion and discord, weakening Sphere institutions by turning them against one another.

ATTRIBUTES

AGI	AWA	BRW	COO	INT	PER	WIL
10	9	9	9	9	6	8

FIELDS OF EXPERTISE

Combat	+2	1	Movement	+2	1	Social	–	–
Fortitude	+1	–	Senses	+1	1	Technical	+1	1

DEFENCES (TROOPER)

Firewall	5	Resolve	4	Vigour	5
Security	–	Morale	–	Armour	–

DEFENCES (ELITE)

Firewall	9	Resolve	8	Vigour	9
Security	–	Morale	–	Armour	–

ATTACKS

- **D-Charges**: 2+6 🅝 damage, 1H, Anti-Materiel 2, Comms, Disposable, Piercing 3, Spread 1, Unsubtle, Vicious 2
- **Needle Mines**: 2+5 🅝 damage, 1H, Comms, Disposable, Indiscriminate (Close), Piercing 2, Spread 1, Unsubtle, Vicious 2
- **Assault Pistol**: Range R/C, 1+5 🅝 damage, Burst 2, Unbalanced, Vicious 1
- **Combi Rifle**: Range C/M, 1+6 🅝 damage, Burst 2, 2H, Expert 1, MULTI Light Mod, Vicious 1
- **Knife**: Melee, 1+4 🅝 damage, 1H, Concealed 1, Non-Hackable, Subtle 2, Thrown, Unforgiving 1

GEAR: Aletheia Kit, AutoMediKit

SPECIAL ABILITIES

- **Covert by Nature (Elite)**: When attempting to remain unseen or unnoticed, any Momentum or Heat spent to add dice to their Stealth pool adds two d20s, instead of one.
- **Pioneer**: The Shasvastii can reroll one d20 when making a Stealth test, but must accept the new result.

SHASVASTII –SEED SOLDIER

Heavily cloaked, nearly undetectable deployment ships bury Shasvastii Seed capsules in remote, hidden locations where soldiers or operatives will be needed. Each Seed contains a Shasvastii who remains hidden inside while receiving a continuous intelligence and information stream from the EI network. The Shasvastii inside deploys from the Seed capsule either on command or time trigger. While the operative moves away from the deployment site, the opened Seed emits electronic interference and false data signals affecting any nearby detection or sensor arrays, effectively covering initial deployment. Seed Soldiers can then wreak havoc in areas previously considered secure.

The need for an insertion vessel means that most Seed Soldiers deploy into combat zones, but stealth dropships can place intelligence and insurgent operatives deep behind friendly lines on planets with a Shasvastii presence. The Seed also provides a standard equipment loadout, giving them the means to accomplish their mission.

ATTRIBUTES

AGI	AWA	BRW	COO	INT	PER	WIL
11	11	8	9	8	7	9

FIELDS OF EXPERTISE

Combat	+2	2	Movement	+1	1	Social	–	–
Fortitude	+1	1	Senses	+1	1	Technical	+1	1

DEFENCES

Firewall	8	Resolve	9	Vigour	8
Security	–	Morale	–	Armour	–

ATTACKS

- **Assault Pistol**: Range R/C, 1+6 🅝 damage, Burst 2, Unbalanced, Vicious 1
- **Knife**: Melee, 1+3 🅝 damage, 1H, Concealed 1, Non-Hackable, Subtle 2, Thrown, Unforgiving 1
- **Combi Rifle**: Range C/M, 1+7 🅝 damage, Burst 2, 2H, Expert 1, MULTI Light Mod, Vicious 1
  - *Light Shotgun*: Range C, 1+6 🅝 damage, Burst 1, Unbalanced, Knockdown

GEAR: AutoMediKit, Survival Kit

SPECIAL ABILITIES

- **Pioneer**: The Seed Soldier can reroll one d20 when making a Stealth test, but must accept the new result.
- **Military Training**: Seed Soldiers can reroll up to 2 🅝 on ranged attacks, but must accept the new results.

REVIC "ICARUS"

DACTYL ENGINEER

BACKER: MICHAEL WILSON

"Package has landed. Hostiles inbound. Ekdromoi in pursuit."

But they would be too late. That's what his calculations showed. It was pure dumb luck that he was up this high. Looking up from the edge of the smoking caldera, Revic watched the fiery trail of more Combined Army crash coffins blazing across the sky.

"I am en route to secure the LZ," he reported as he sprinted precariously along the precipice. Thankfully, the two suns stayed visible in the darkening sky long enough to illuminate his path as he ran to the dropsite. The smothering heat and ash-choked air would make it a difficult task for most, but posed little challenge for his inhuman lungs.

He ground to a halt and unleashed a bolt of glue at a large Morat that sprang up in front of him. Apparently not expecting him to react so quickly, the alien was taken by surprise and rooted to the spot within seconds as the substance hardened. If he had been a scout, then the terrain suggested that his squad would be using a Morat rek wedge... Revic primed an explosive, placed it in the Morat's hand, and push him over the ridge. 5... 4... 3... 2... He triggered the explosive.

That had bought him about thirty seconds. The Ekdromoi were five minutes out.

Rounding a jagged outcropping of rock, he spotted the escape pod. It had lodged itself into a thick sweep of ash only a couple of yards from the edge of the caldera. Just more dumb luck that it hadn't plunged straight into the volcano. He skidded to a halt in front of it and had half a second to analyse the situation before an incoming volley forced him to whip behind the pod and use it for cover. Eight... No, nine of them. Not enough goo and his pistol wasn't going to be worth much against their powered armour.

If he could get the pod open, then he could grab the cargo and try to make a run with it. But he couldn't. The pod had impacted hard – he fired a burst of shots around the edge of the pod, his fingers playing the tarantella on the trigger; might as well try to keep them honest – and the framing had collapsed in, jamming the door shut.

Ekdromoi still four minutes out.

If he couldn't save the cargo, then he needed to destroy it.

A trio of the most daring Morat were charging towards him now. Two birds with one stone? Tapping into the pod's system, Revic accessed the cooling mechanisms, overrode the safety protocols, and vented the coolant hard. It blasted out, sending the Morat fireteam (the joints of their armour frozen up) tumbling down the rocky slope while also carrying the pod up and – if his calculations were right – to its fiery doom.

Unfortunately, it also carried away his cover. He bolted down the slope – skidding and sliding through the ash and rock into a narrow cleft that provided a minimal cover profile from the bullets flying past him... and also through him. He'd been hit in the left arm. He shut off the pain receptors and glanced back up.

The pod hadn't gone over. The uncontrolled venting had twisted its trajectory instead of giving it a straight shot. It was poised on the very cusp of the caldera.

Revic jolted back to his feet and started running towards it. If he could overload the propellant on his adhesive launcher, then – There was a sharp jolt and his legs stopped working. Looking down he saw that something had punched through his chest. Something large. He looked back up at the escape pod. It was so close and yet so impossibly far. Maybe he could... Or...

"I've got this!"

From off to his right a purple pseudosaur rushed out from between the rocks and rammed her head into the escape pod. It tottered... tipped... fell... Far below it cracked through the lava crust and a plume of molten rock lit the scene with a sepulchral red light.

Revic blinked. His final thought, as he felt his consciousness uploading into the Maya datasphere, echoed with the heart of ALEPH: "I never cease to amaze myself."

APPEARANCE

Short, ashy blonde hair with a beard to match and slate grey eyes. His movements are short, quick, and precise.

ROLEPLAYING

- He's irritated when others don't share his conclusions
- Assesses situations quickly and acts impulsively on the analysis
- Peppers his conversation with weird trivia from 20th century video games

BACKGROUND

Revic's personality is based on an obscure Silicon Valley engineer who worked at a company called Atari in the 1970s and somehow got stuck in the craw of the psychogenesis matrix. His eccentricities didn't make him any less effective as a Dactyl, however, and with the frontlines on Paradiso stretched to the breaking point an imperfect engineer was better than none. Revic was deployed and left his mark by boarding an alien troop transport and crash-landing it on an enemy position. A warcor caught footage of him emerging from the burning wreck and he became a viral sensation, with Maya collectively dubbing him "Icarus" for the deed.

STATS (ELITE)

ATTRIBUTES

AGI	AWA	BRW	COO	INT	PER	WIL
10	10	8	9	10	8	8

FIELDS OF EXPERTISE

Combat	+1	1	Movement	+2	1	Social	–	–
Fortitude	+1	–	Senses	+1	–	Technical	+3	2

DEFENCES

Firewall	10	Resolve	8	Vigour	8
Security	–	Morale	–	Armour	2

ATTACKS

- **Adhesive Launcher**: Range M, 1+8  damage, Burst 1, Unwieldy, Area (Close), Immobilising, Knockdown, Munition, Nonlethal
- **D-Charge**: 2+6 damage, 1H, Anti-Materiel 2, Comms, Disposable, Piercing 3, Spread 1, Unsubtle, Vicious 2
- **Pistol**: Range R/C, 1+6 damage, Burst 1, 1H, Vicious 1
- **Knife**: Melee, 1+3 damage, 1H, Concealed 1, Non-Hackable, Subtle 2, Thrown, Unforgiving 1

GEAR: Bioengineered Physiology, Light Combat Armour (with Repair Kit)

SPECIAL ABILITIES

- **Deft Destruction**: Dactyls are renowned for their finesse and adroitness with explosives; Revic exemplifies these attributes. He can reroll one d20 when making a Technical test related to explosives or demolitions, but must accept the new result.
- **Decisive Destruction**: Applied demolitions is no place for indecision. Luckily, Revic doesn't have that problem. He gains 2 bonus Momentum when setting an explosive charge.
- **Overlaid Characteristics**: An Ekdromoi trapped inside a Dactyl's body, Revic displays characteristics of both. He can reroll one d20 when making a Movement test, but must accept the new result.

NEMESIS

SHASVASTII–SPECULO KILLER

The ultimate mimics and sleeper agents, Speculo Killers eliminate their targets and use sampled DNA to transform themselves into a perfect replica. They often live the role for years with amazing subtlety, spreading lies, deception, and often extreme violence, infiltrating or eliminating targets thought to be unassailable. Their biosynthetic bodies transform at a genetic level, producing near perfect physical replication. After only a few hours, even advanced genetic verification cannot distinguish them from their target. In addition to physical replication, they can download and overlay a target's Cube data over their own, creating a flawless personality match as well. Combine this with the most advanced shape- and holo-morphing clothing in the EI's arsenal, and you have an undetectable doppelgänger, waiting for the perfect time to strike.

O-12 actively works to silence any rumours of Speculo Killers — only allowing select hunters to know about the foe — to prevent the spread of distrust and paranoia amongst a populace who can no longer be sure if their best friends might be alien agents. Speculo Killers share the same paranoid, long-term survival traits as the rest of the Shasvastii race, and are never far from a cache of weapons and equipment geared to aid both in their escape and the elimination of any that get in their way.

ATTRIBUTES

AGI	AWA	BRW	COO	INT	PER	WIL
16	11	10	11	9	6	9

FIELDS OF EXPERTISE

Combat	+3	2	Movement	+2	1	Social	+1	1
Fortitude	+2	1	Senses	+3	1	Technical	+2	1

DEFENCES

Firewall	11	Resolve	11	Vigour	12
Security	–	Morale	–	Armour	–

ATTACKS

- **Assault Pistol**: Range R/C, 1+6 damage, Burst 2, Unbalanced, Vicious 1
- **Combi Rifle**: Range C/M, 1+7 damage, Burst 2, 2H, Expert 1, MULTI Light Mod, Vicious 1
- **Monofilament Garrotte**: Range C, 1+4 damage, 2H, Concealed 2, Monofilament, Subtle 2, Unforgiving 2
- **Smoke Grenades**: Disposable, Indiscriminate (Close), Nonlethal, Smoke 2, Speculative Fire, Thrown

GEAR: AutoMediKit, Holomask, Thermo-Optical Camouflage

SPECIAL ABILITIES

- **Common Special Abilities**: Fear 1, Threatening 2
- **Hard to Hit**: When taking a Defence Reaction against ranged attacks, a Speculo Killer increases their Movement Focus by 2.
- **Many Unseen Faces**: A Speculo Killer gains 2 bonus Momentum when attempting a Stealth test to make or use a disguise. When attempting to remain unseen or unnoticed, each point of Momentum or Heat spent to add dice to the Stealth pool adds two d20s, instead of one.
- **Morpho-Scan (2 Heat)**: By spending 2 Heat, a Speculo Killer can take the genetic sample of a character within Reach with a melee attack test (D0). This sample will allow them to assume their form (a process which generally cannot be undertaken in the midst combat). If the target is incapacitated, the Speculo Killer does not need to spend Heat and can also make a Hacking (D2) test to duplicate their Cube.

SHANE SCHOON
NOMAD DETECTIVE

BACKER: SEAN SCHOONMAKER

He checked the squalid corridor in both directions. The communal AR channel had been programmed to scroll the news, and video headlines were crawling past about a security lockdown here in Paekche. This was why he hated working in the Jade Empire. He took out his electric pick and bypassed the door's security.

Blue and red neon streetlights lent the bedsit apartment a surreal quality. Rotting food hit his nostrils and drew his attention to two empty cartons, each containing a pair of chopsticks, that had been left on the narrow counter that ran long one side of the room. Judging from the remains, they were no more than a week old. A glance through the window revealed a market street packed with vendors a couple stories below.

There was a lot of garbage strewn around. Miscellaneous papers scrawled in a combination of Korean and Chinese were mixed in with it – enticing at first glance, but clearly junk. Deliberate junk, actually, put on hardcopy to obfuscate how fake it was and waste his time. But his custom OCR eye scanner had already pulled it and his geist was running analysis on it.

It was a professional cleaning... despite the place looking like a dump.

There was one trick he could pull. Using a hacked omni-directional microphone, he sent a small burst of broadcast power through the room – basically just a little frizzle of static electricity. If it worked, then it would jump-start any dormant QIDs in the room and – jackpot. A dead tag sputtered back to life and sent a burst of shipping data:

someone named Naaman Aram had received a package here. And not too long ago

He tossed the name and shipping details to Thema with an urgent flag. Can you track this down for me ASAP? A second later the ghostly words You'll owe me lunch at Victor's floated across his field of view.

Next was the toilet, which was as grubby as everything else. But he got a little lucky: an empty vial wedged behind the toilet bowl. Fingerprints went nowhere according to Shaeng, his contact in the local police, but passing it through his portable chemistry kit revealed it to be even more interesting than he'd hoped. Not street drugs. Vaccines. And the mix meant off-world travel. They were hitting the Circulars.

Thema pinged him. He tuned her in. "What have you got for me?"

She flickered into his AR, as if she was standing in the room next to him. "Well, whoever he is, Naaman Aram isn't his real name. Limited financial track, but he did rent a data storage platform. I checked it out, but it's been thoroughly wiped." Schoon groaned, but Thema grinned. "You owe me a lot more than lunch."

"What did you find?"

"The server was wiped, but not the access logs. So I tracked those and one of the users was sloppy. I was only able to pull the list of files he accessed. I'm checking those out now, but I've got several hits on something called 'Project Blacklight.'"

"Thanks, Thema. Let me know if you find anything else." She nodded and winked out in a flurry of illuminated motes. He tabbed open a new communications channel. "Mr. Atitarn?"

"Yes, Mr. Schoon? You have something for me?"

"Not a lot. Just a name: Project Blacklight."

There was a beat of silence from the other end of the line. Then: "Oh, shit. They're after our outpost on Dawn."

"Is there anything you can tell me about –"

There was an explosion on the other end of the line and, with a crackle of static, the connection went dead.

"Shit," Schoon said to the empty room. "I hope I still get paid."

APPEARANCE

Two metres of lean muscle topped with greying blonde hair, a grizzled goatee, and haunted, soul-searching eyes.

ROLEPLAYING

- Moans about circumstances and incompetence of others
- Reserved, hardly talks, but extremely attentive to detail
- Never lets on what he knows

BACKGROUND

After his father was killed by Submondo moneylenders, Shane's mother took her son and fled to *Corregidor*. He hated life on the mothership, and took every odd job and opportunity to head planet-side or station-side in whatever system the ship was passing through at the time. Schoon proved adept at striking up friendships wherever he went (and ended up with a reputation for having a lady in every port). He eventually bounced off the mothership entirely, landing almost by accident into the role of a private detective.

STATS (ELITE)

ATTRIBUTES

AGI	AWA	BRW	COO	INT	PER	WIL
8	10	10	8	9	8	10

FIELDS OF EXPERTISE

Combat	+1	1	Movement	+1	1	Social	+1	–
Fortitude	+1	–	Senses	+2	2	Technical	+1	1

DEFENCES

Firewall	9	Resolve	10	Vigour	10
Security	–	Morale	–	Armour	2

ATTACKS

- **Stun Pistol**: Range R/C, 1+6 🅝 damage, Burst 1, 1H, Biotech, Nonlethal, Stun, Vicious 1
- **Collapsible Baton**: Melee, 1+6 🅝 damage, Concealed 1, Stun, Subtle 1

GEAR: B&E Kit, Forensics Kit 2, Light Combat Armour, Micro-Torch, SecurCuffs

SPECIAL ABILITIES

- **In Another Life**: Shane grew up bucking the system, right up until the system caught up with him. He can reroll one d20 when making social skill tests related to interacting with the criminal element.
- **Eye for Detail**: Shane has an eye for minutia, and a razor-sharp mind. He can reroll one d20 when making a an Analysis or Observation test, but must accept the new result.
- **Eidetic Memory**: Better than a recording, Shane can recall events with crystal precision. By spending 2 Heat, he can perfectly recall prior events, essentially succeeding on a retroactive Observation test.

SHASVASTII–SPHINX (SPECIAL ARMOURED CORPS)

The Sphinx is a TAG fitted with every stealth technology available to a race renowned for covert operations. Forensic analysis from rare, destroyed units have revealed an array of both active and passive systems that make this TAG effectively invisible. Non-magnetic and non-conductive composite polymers wrap its armoured shell. This surface can also emit directional polarised holograms and thermal patterns under the direction of a specialised semi-intelligent computer, more effective than any Thermo-Optical Camouflage available in the Human Sphere. Offensively, the Sphinx excels at ambush tactics, its loadout filled with devastating melee and close range weaponry.

Sphinx units are – thankfully – a rarity for the Shasvastii. They are utilized either for reconnaissance of highly contested environments or in support of Deep Incursion Corps operations requiring the impressive firepower and ambush capabilities it brings to the table. The presence of a Sphinx means that the area is, or very soon will be, the focus of intense Shasvastii attention.

ATTRIBUTES

AGI	AWA	BRW	COO	INT	PER	WIL
12	9	10	9	9	6	8

FIELDS OF EXPERTISE

Combat	+3	2	Movement	+1	1	Social	–	–
Fortitude	+2	1	Senses	+1	1	Technical	–	–

DEFENCES

Firewall	9	Resolve	8	Vigour	10
Security	2	Morale	1	Armour	5

ATTACKS

- **Integrated Close Combat Weaponry**: Range C, 1+6 🅝 damage, Area (Close), Spread 1, Vicious 2
- **Heavy Flamethrowers**: Range C, 2+6 🅝 damage, Burst 1, Incendiary 3, Munition, Terrifying 2, Torrent
- **Spitfire**: Range M, 1+6 🅝 damage, Burst 3, 2H, Spread 2, Unsubtle

GEAR: ECM, Climbing Plus, Thermo-Optical Camouflage

SPECIAL ABILITIES

- **Common Special Abilities**: Menacing 2, Monstrous
- **Advanced Thermal Optics**: When active, the stealth suite of this TAG adds two d20s per Momentum or Heat spent to add dice to Stealth tests, instead of one.
- **Devastating Up Close**: Sphinx are trained to be devastating in combat. Each point of Momentum or Heat spent to gain additional dice for a Close Combat test provides two d20s, instead of one. Additionally, each point of Momentum spent to deal bonus damage adds two points of damage, instead of one.
- **TAG Augmentation**: Whilst active and powered, a Sphinx's TAG provides it with additional Momentum for all Strength-based tests and increases their melee damage bonus by +1 🅝. Additionally, they can ignore the first Fault suffered during a scene.

TOHAA

Possessed of a gregarious nature, striking features, and a primal grace, the Tohaa make a strong impression, though no one would ever mistake them for human. Humanity's new allies have provided much-needed support in an hour of need, but their actions remain enigmatic at best. In the short time since first contact, they've proven to be ruthless, cagey, and entirely capable of cold-blooded pragmatism.

The average Tohaa is tall and slender, and while they can look almost delicate to the human eye, their lithe frames possess a deceptive strength. Most Tohaa will avoid conflict if they can help it, but that in no way makes them passive. Indeed, their ability to communicate discreetly means that Tohaa often conduct operations right under the noses of nearby humans; even the most insignificant-seeming functionary could be a Trihedron – or Trinomial – operative, and seemingly ornamental pets and plants often contain biotechnological assets.

ATTRIBUTES

AGI	AWA	BRW	COO	INT	PER	WIL
9	9	7	9	8	9	8

FIELDS OF EXPERTISE

Combat	+1	1	Movement	+1	1	Social	+2	1
Fortitude	–	–	Senses	+1	–	Technical	+1	–

DEFENCES (TROOPER)

Firewall	4	Resolve	4	Vigour	4
Security	–	Morale	–	Armour	1

DEFENCES (ELITE)

Firewall	8	Resolve	8	Vigour	7
Security	–	Morale	–	Armour	1

ATTACKS

- **DT Pistol**: Range R/C, 1+5 🅝 damage, Burst 1, 1H, Biotech, Toxic 2, Vicious 2
- **Wetspike**: Melee, 1+4 🅝 damage, Biotech, Piercing 1, Subtle 3, Toxic 1

GEAR: Armoured Clothing

SPECIAL ABILITIES

- **Corahtaa**: The Tohaa can speak the Tohaa pheromonal language; communicating silently and securely with other speakers within Close range. They cannot use Psywar actions or techniques which require deception when using Corahtaa.
- **Custom Biotech (Elite – 1 Heat)**: Tohaa biotechnology is incredibly subtle and difficult to detect. For 1 Heat, the GM can reveal that an Elite Tohaa has a previously unnoticed augmentation.

SITHI MASTERS
MINUTEMEN

BACKER: JEFFREY SITHI-AMNUAI

"Will you stop complaining, Sithi?" Beth shoved a stack of poker chips into the pot.

"C'mon guys. I'm just asking why we're way outside the Wall in the middle of Antipode hunting season."

"I'm guessing it's got something to do with the O-12 guy hanging out in the lieutenant's tent. What's his name? Carson?"

"That just makes it worse. O-12 agents. Space freaks." Sithi called the bet.

"You got to admit that there are perks, though," Yanni said, grabbing a cold beer out of the automated fridge which had trundled its way up to the campsite with them.

"The beer is great," Sithi conceded. "But don't you find that thing a little creepy?"

As if in protest, the fridge gave an irate beep. Yanni swung the door shut.

"Read 'em and weep," Beth grinned, spreading three kings on the table.

"Ladies first, I guess," Sithi said. "By which I mean my ladies." He dropped three queens. "Assisted by a pair of handsome jacks." Beth cursed as he dropped his full house and scooped up the chips.

The tent flap swung aside and a small man – the guy out from Bureau Noir – stepped in. Sithi was tempted to ignore him, but he was followed by Lieutenant Timmons, and that brought everyone to their feet.

The space freak crossed his hands behind his back and swept them with a cold gaze. "All right. You might all be wondering why we've brought you out here. We suspect – "

The radio crackled. "This is Yen. We're hauling ass with hostiles on our tail. Inbound on three."

"Ready in a minute!"

"I don't think we've got it!" The burst of gunfire ripped static across the radio.

Commotion. Sithi grabbed his rifle and sprinted out of the tent. By the time the others came rumbling out in his wake, he was already half way up the tree he had scoped out earlier. He scanned the eastern horizon: there they were. Yen and the other two scouts, hustling over the top of the hill. And behind them a half dozen howling Antipodes.

"Permission to fire, Lieutenant?"

"Granted."

One of the Antipodes was leaping now – heading straight at Yen's back. Sithi squeezed the trigger and the beast's body jerked back. Its two trinary mates stumbled in mind-shock.

"Dany! Down!" Sithi barked into the commlink. The scout did as he was told, allowing Sithi to put three bullets into another Antipodes' chest and one into the head of its pack mate. "Up. Run!"

The Antipodes had lost a step on the scout group. They should be able to make it back to the defensive line the rest of the squad was forming below. Sithi started lining up his next shot – There were more howls coming from the south. A lot of them.

APPEARANCE

Somewhere in his mid-thirties, Sithi has honey-brown skin, black hair, and mischievous eyes.

ROLEPLAYING

- Pessimistic, always painting pictures of the worst that could happen
- But optimistic, gregarious, and cracking jokes about the inevitable doom he foresees
- Obeys orders without question

BACKGROUND

Sithi grew up in the southern reaches of USAriadna. His family was fiercely patriotic, with most of them hardcases in the Irregular Frontiersmen battalions. His father and grandmother were actually both killed on the same patrol during the first raids of the Third Antipode Offensive. His mother mourned, but never regretted the man she had married nor the mother she had lost. As he grew up, she played the dozens of recordings his father had made, proudly recounting family stories of Antipodean war stretching back for generations.

When he became of age, Sithi joined the Irregulars himself. He complained all the time, but somehow he was always the first into any fray. His talents came to the attention of the USAriadna Rangers, who scooped him up and placed him with the 5th Minutemen. Now the Ariadnan Expeditionary Corps has been knocking at his door. Sithi honestly sees nothing but bad things if he heads for Paradiso, but he is, after all, a patriot.

STATS (ELITE)

ATTRIBUTES

AGI	AWA	BRW	COO	INT	PER	WIL
8	9	10	9	9	8	10

FIELDS OF EXPERTISE

Combat	+1	1	Movement	+1	1	Social	+1	–
Fortitude	+1	–	Senses	+2	2	Technical	+1	1

DEFENCES

Firewall	9	Resolve	10	Vigour	10
Security	–	Morale	–	Armour	4

ATTACKS

- **AP Rifle**: Range M, 1+6 N damage, Burst 2, 2H, Non-Hackable, Piercing 2, Vicious 1
- **Light Flamethrower**: Range C, 1+5 N damage, Burst 1, 2H, Incendiary 3, Munition, Non-Hackable, Terrifying 2, Torrent
- **Breaker Pistol**: Range R/C, 1+5 N damage, Burst 1, 1H, Biotech, Breaker, Non-Hackable, Piercing 1, Vicious 1
- **Teseum-Edged Knife**: Melee, 1+5 N damage, 1H, Concealed 1, Non-Hackable, Piercing 2, Subtle 2, Thrown, Unforgiving 1

GEAR: Heavy Combat Armour

SPECIAL ABILITIES

- **Crack Shot**: Sithi consistently outscores his platoon on the targeting range. He can reroll up to 4 N when making a ranged attack, but must accept the new results.
- **Reckless Bravery**: Being quick to action has its risks, but puts Sithi in position to save lives. For him, the answer is simple: keep moving. When spending Heat to interrupt turn order, he also gains the benefits of Light Cover until the end of the turn.
- **Smooth Operator**: Despite his pessimistic outlook, Sithi rarely sleeps alone. He gains one bonus d20 when using affection, physical attraction, or the promise of sexual favours as part of a social interaction.

NOTES

Off the grid, and happy that way, Sithi distrusts any equipment that can be hacked. Given a choice, he never uses equipment with a datasphere or network connection, and cannot perform, nor be targeted by, Infowar attacks.

TOHAA – DIPLOMAT

A civilisation of explorers, the Tohaa frequently make first contact with other species. These meetings are important and dangerous in equal measure, to successfully navigate them requires operatives with exceptional diplomatic skills as well as ice in their veins.

Enter the diplomatic delegates. Social elites outranking most politicians, Tohaa diplomats are renowned for their flexibility in approach, methodology, and ethics. Rumour has it that these elite negotiators are even capable of lying through the Corahtaa pheromone language, causing other Tohaa to regard them with a mixture of fear and awe. Tohaa pop culture has embraced diplomatic delegates as the perfect ideal of elegant, glamourous, and deadly operatives, as skilled in espionage as in negotiation.

Their actual intelligence work tends to be of a subtler nature; intrigue and conspiracy rather than high-stakes action. Still, they are neither incapable nor unwilling to use direct methods when the need arises.

ATTRIBUTES

AGI	AWA	BRW	COO	INT	PER	WIL
9	9	7	8	8	12	10

FIELDS OF EXPERTISE

Combat	+1	–	Movement	+1	–	Social	+3	3
Fortitude	–	–	Senses	+2	1	Technical	+1	–

DEFENCES

Firewall	8	Resolve	10	Vigour	7
Security	–	Morale	–	Armour	1

ATTACKS

- **Tohaa Nanopulser**: Range C, 1+6 N damage, Biotech, Subtle 3, Torrent, Vicious 2, evidence dissolves after 1d20 minutes
- **Wetspike Augmentation**: Melee, 1+4 N damage, Biotech, Piercing 1, Subtle 3, Toxic 3
- **Pheroware Tactics**: See Diplomatic Corahtaa below

GEAR: Symbiont graft, Unique & Bespoke Clothing + Tohaa Nanopulser

SPECIAL ABILITIES

- **Diplomatic Corahtaa**: The Diplomat can speak the Tohaa pheromonal language; communicating silently and securely with other speakers within Close range, and controlling SymbioMates and SymbioBombs. Unlike most Tohaa, Diplomats can use Psywar actions and techniques featuring deception when using Corahtaa, and generate and use one Pheroware tactic per round without assistance.
- **Veteran Negotiator**: Tohaa Diplomats generate 2 bonus Momentum on social skill tests.
- **VIP Symbiont**: The Diplomat's symbiont graft grants them the Fast Healing 1 ability.

TOHAA – FRAACTA DROP UNIT

Perhaps no sane person would cackle with unrestrained joy while hurtled at ballistic speeds into a war zone. Perhaps no sane person could giggle with simple pleasure while evading anti-aircraft guns. Then again, anyone who's seen these all-female Drop Units at work would be hard-pressed to describe them as sane. Behind that thrillseeking antics and gravity-defying movements and thirst for danger, however, the Fraacta are brutally efficient purveyors of violence.

The Fraacta have manoeuvring thrusters that jut out like angelic wings from their distinctive red combat armour. They're the most technologically sophisticated airborne brigade operating on Paradiso.

ATTRIBUTES

AGI	AWA	BRW	COO	INT	PER	WIL
13	10	10	12	8	7	10

FIELDS OF EXPERTISE

Combat	+3	3	Movement	+5	3	Social	+1	–
Fortitude	+2	–	Senses	+1	1	Technical	+1	–

DEFENCES

Firewall	9	Resolve	12	Vigour	12
Security	–	Morale	2	Armour	2

ATTACKS

- **Spitfire**: Range M, 1+7 N damage, Burst 3, 2H, Spread 2, Unsubtle
- **Tohaa Nanopulser**: Range C, 1+7 N damage, Biotech, Subtle 3, Torrent, Vicious 2, evidence dissolves after 1d20 minutes

GEAR: Fraacta Combat Jump Suit (2 Armour)

SPECIAL ABILITIES

- **Corahtaa**: The Fraacta can speak the Tohaa pheromonal language; communicating silently and securely with other speakers within Close range. They cannot use Psywar actions or techniques which require deception when using Corahtaa.
- **Courageous**: The Fraacta benefits from a Morale Soak of 2.
- **Drop Unit**: When called in as a reinforcement, the Fraacta begin play in a zone of their choosing, provided it's accessible from above.
- **Hypermobile**: The Fraacta can move one additional zone when performing a movement action.
- **Survival Mode**: A Fraacta can retract its wings in a defensive posture, forfeiting the benefits of Hypermobile, but increasing its Armour and Security Soak by 2.

ELITE

TOHAA—KUMOTAIL BIOENGINEER

Dedicated mecha-geneticists, the Kumotail Bioengineers are the intellectual aristocracy of the Tohaa Trident. Tohaa technology inexorably combines mechanics and biomedicine, and the Kumotail are the undisputed masters of this synthesised discipline, able to repair anything, or for that matter, anyone.

A deeply spiritual corps of military scientists, they consider the pursuit of bioengineering as the only true path to enlightenment, that to create — and improve upon — nature is a fundamentally virtuous endeavour. Their obsessive sense of purpose drives the Kumotail on; life is a series of challenges to be met. Nothing is trivial, anything is possible.

The Kumotail believe that adversity breeds excellence, so their ranks are forged in the crucible of crisis. Whether on the battlefields of Paradiso, supporting clandestine actions in the Human Sphere, or pursuing their own agendas regardless of where they might lead, Kumotail spend significantly more time in the field than the lab.

ATTRIBUTES

AGI	AWA	BRW	COO	INT	PER	WIL
9	9	9	9	14	8	12

FIELDS OF EXPERTISE

| Combat | +2 | 2 | Movement | +1 | – | Social | +2 | – |
| Fortitude | +2 | – | Senses | +2 | 1 | Technical | +4 | 4 |

DEFENCES

| Firewall | 14 | Resolve | 12 | Vigour | 9 |
| Security | 2 | Morale | – | Armour | 2 |

ATTACKS
- **Combi Rifle**: Range C/M, 1+6 🅝 damage, Burst 2, 2H, Expert 1, MULTI Light Mod, Vicious 1
- **D-Charges**: 2+6 🅝 damage, 1H, Anti-Materiel 2, Comms, Disposable, Piercing 3, Spread 1, Unsubtle, Vicious 2
- **Tohaa White Hacking Device**: CLAW-0, SWORD-0, SHIELD-3, GADGET-1, IC-3, UPGRADE Cyberalert Systems; +4 🅝 bonus damage

GEAR: MediKit, Nu-El Armour, Powered Multitool

SPECIAL ABILITIES
- **Battle-Hardened**: Kumotail Bioengineers are used to suboptimal conditions; they suffer no penalties for Technical tests attempted without proper tools or facilities.
- **Corahtaa**: The Bioengineer can speak the Tohaa pheromonal language; communicating silently and securely with other speakers within Close range. They cannot use Psywar actions or techniques which require deception when using Corahtaa.
- **Mecha-Geneticist**: The Bioengineer can reroll one d20 when making a Medicine or Tech test, but must accept the new result.

NEMESIS

TOHAA—MAAKREP TRACKER

Maakrep Trackers are the secret police of the Sygmaa Trihedron. Ruthless, driven, and entirely cold-blooded, in their home systems they are primarily charged with hunting down Trigon cells and other revolutionary groups and empowered to use any means necessary, including summary executions. On Paradiso their ruthless skills are used primarily for infiltration missions, often operating as undercover agents within Tohaa Trinomial facilities.

When they find their target, they put it down without hesitation or remorse. If that's in a quiet alleyway, fine; in a crowded marketplace, so much the better. They want their work to be seen, to send a message to the EI's enemies: if the Maakrep Trackers are hunting you, nowhere is safe. And nothing can save you

ATTRIBUTES

AGI	AWA	BRW	COO	INT	PER	WIL
9	12	9	10	10	11	9

FIELDS OF EXPERTISE

| Combat | +2 | 2 | Movement | +1 | – | Social | +2 | 1 |
| Fortitude | +1 | – | Senses | +4 | 4 | Technical | +2 | 1 |

DEFENCES

| Firewall | 12 | Resolve | 10 | Vigour | 10 |
| Security | – | Morale | – | Armour | 2 |

ATTACKS
- **Boarding Shotgun**: Range C, 1+8 🅝 damage, Burst 1, 2H, Knockdown, Medium MULTI
  - *Normal Shells Mode (Primary)*: Area (Close), Spread 1
  - *AP Mode (Secondary)*: Piercing 2
- **EI Hacking Device**: CLAW-2, SWORD-2, SHIELD-2, GADGET-3, IC-3, UPGRADE [Sucker Punch] +2 🅝 bonus damage

GEAR: Multispectral Visor 2, Nu-El Armour (with AutoMediKit)

SPECIAL ABILITIES
- **Corahtaa**: The Tracker can speak the Tohaa pheromonal language; communicating silently and securely with other speakers within Close range. They cannot use Psywar actions or techniques which require deception when using Corahtaa.
- **Data Tracker**: When making an Infowar attack, the Tracker can reroll up to 3 🅝.
- **I Am the Law**: When gathering information on their quarry, the Tracker can reroll one d20 on research tests, but must accept the new result. Further, they benefit from one bonus Momentum for any social skill tests taken during their information gathering.
- **Nowhere to Hide**: The Tracker can reroll one d20 on Observation tests, but must accept the new result.

TROOPER/ELITE
TOHAA —MAKAUL TROOPER

Makaul Troopers are consistently among the most decorated — and delinquent — soldiers in the Tohaa Trident. A holdover from the old Colonial Force, their unit designation — Makaul, the 10100, a number symbolic of mythic strength, courage, and salvation from physical danger — retains its significance in modern times. Troopers train for high-risk deployments across the galaxy, and are frequently dispatched to frontier outposts, facing numerically superior foes with little to no backup. Their continued success in the face of overwhelming odds has made them the stuff of legend; Tohaa fiction often features heroic Makaul protagonists rushing boldly into danger, heedless of their personal safety.

ATTRIBUTES

AGI	AWA	BRW	COO	INT	PER	WIL
9	8	8	10	8	6	8

FIELDS OF EXPERTISE

Combat	+3	2	Movement	+1	1	Social	–	–
Fortitude	+2	1	Senses	+1	–	Technical	–	–

DEFENCES (TROOPER)

Firewall	4	Resolve	4	Vigour	4
Security	–	Morale	–	Armour	3

DEFENCES (ELITE)

Firewall	8	Resolve	8	Vigour	8
Security	–	Morale	2	Armour	3

ATTACKS
- **Combi Rifle**: Range C/M, 1+5 🌑 damage, Burst 2, 2H, Expert 1, MULTI Light Mod, Vicious 1
  - *Light Flamethrower*: Range C, 1+4 🌑 damage, Burst 1, 2H, Incendiary 3, Munition, Terrifying 2, Torrent)

GEAR: Sakiel Armour

SPECIAL ABILITIES
- **Corahtaa**: The Makaul can speak the Tohaa pheromonal language; communicating silently and securely with other speakers within Close range. They cannot use Psywar actions or techniques which require deception when using Corahtaa.
- **Thrillseeker**: To a Makaul, getting hit in the face is preferable to sitting around. When making an attack at Close range, each point of Heat paid to gain additional d20s provides two dice instead of one.
- **Martial Master (Elite)**: An Elite Makaul Trooper gains +2 🌑 physical damage on all melee and ranged attacks.

NEMESIS
UMBRA LEGATE

The Umbra Legates serve as heralds, enforcers, mediators, lieutenants, judges, executioners, and right-hand attendants for the EI. They are powerful and deadly, cruel and violently efficient, tall and graceful, strong and swift, and exude an aura of fear and frightening competence. Supremely aware of their surroundings, their every movement a sculpted and deliberate act, poised and balanced.

Legates have thickly corded, crimson skin, a colour which is also commonly echoed by their clothing and armour. To human eyes, their faces bear a disturbing resemblance to an anatomical diagram in which all the skin has been peeled back from raw muscle. Their eyes are blue, burning coals that relentlessly track their foes.

ATTRIBUTES

AGI	AWA	BRW	COO	INT	PER	WIL
13 (+1)	9	10	9	10	10 (+1)	12

FIELDS OF EXPERTISE

Combat	+4	2	Movement	+2	2	Social	+2	–
Fortitude	+3	3	Senses	+2	–	Technical	–	–

DEFENCES

Firewall	10	Resolve	15	Vigour	13
Security	–	Morale	–	Armour	2

ATTACKS
- **Combi Rifle**: Range C/M, 1+6 🌑 damage, Burst 3, 2H, Expert 1, Vicious 1
- **EI Hacking Device**: CLAW-2, SWORD-2, SHIELD-2, GADGET-3, IC-3, UPGRADE Sucker Punch; +2 🌑 bonus damage
- **Nano-Coated Shock Sword**: Melee, 1+7 🌑 damage, Unbalanced, Parry 2, Stun, Vicious 4

GEAR: Umbra Thrust Armour (Light Combat Armour with Kinematika, Umbra Thrust Pack), Satellite Uplink

SPECIAL ABILITIES
- **Common Special Abilities**: Fear 2, Inured to Pain, Menacing 1, Superhuman Agility 1, Superhuman Personality 1, Threatening 2
- **EI Enforcers**: The Umbra Legates are an unsubtle blade that enforce the will of the EI wherever directed. They can reroll up to 2 🌑 when making ranged or melee attacks, but must accept the new results. Additionally, they reduce the penalty for firing at a range other than the weapon's optimal range by one, to a minimum of 0. Further, they can draw a weapon as a Free Action and do not need to have a weapon in their hand in order to respond to attacks — any weapon within Reach may be used to respond to attacks. Finally, they may make a special Psywar attack that has a range of Close and inflicts 1+3 🌑 damage with the Area and Stun qualities.
- **Red Shadow**: Umbra Legates benefit from 2 bonus Momentum when making face-to-face tests to remain in the detected stealth state.
- **Umbra Thrust Pack**: Special thrusters built into the back of a Legate's armour allow them to move one additional zone when taking a movement action.
- **Weapon Specialist**: Umbra Legates add +1 Burst to all of their weapons. (This is reflected in the attacks listed above.)

TROOPER
UNIDRON BATROIDS

When the EI requires soldiers, it does not always bother to recruit them. It can also harvest them.

Tall and frightening, Unidron Batroids are a mix of biological and robotic components. The body is a mixture of armoured plating with patches of visible musculature and sinews, the movements sharp and deliberate, in some regards animal-like, but wholly controlled, deadly and deliberate. These silicon-based/carbon-based hybrids are cultivated in rapid-growth plantations hidden throughout the EI's territories using a monitored pseudo-intelligent substrate.

The bulk of the Ur armed forces that the EI used to jumpstart its campaign of conquest was comprised of Batroids, techno-organic units designed for action in hostile environments. In the Ur culture, the use of Batroids as operatives predates even the creation of the Evolved Intelligence, but the EI continues to utilize them and maintains a Batroid contingent of varying size as an element against insurrectionist tendencies.

ATTRIBUTES

AGI	AWA	BRW	COO	INT	PER	WIL
6	10	9	6	7	5	9

FIELDS OF EXPERTISE

Combat	+2	–	Movement	+1	–	Social	–	–
Fortitude	+1	–	Senses	+1	–	Technical	–	–

DEFENCES (TROOPER)

Firewall	4	Resolve	5	Vigour	5
Security	–	Morale	–	Armour	–

ATTACKS
- **K1 Combi Rifle**: Range C/M, 1+7 🌑 damage, Burst 2, 2H, Anti-Materiel 1, Expert 1, Monofilament, Vicious 1

SPECIAL ABILITIES
- **Common Special Abilities**: Keen Senses (Hearing), Quantronic Jump
- **Autotool Remote**: Unidron Batroids are usually controlled by a limited AI system developed during the heyday of the Ur Civilization and modeled after Ruaria behavioural patterns. They can also be operated as remotes.

CREATURES AND ANIMALS

ELITE

ARIADNAN BROWN BEAR

Given some of the strange, alien creatures discovered on the planet Dawn, settlers could be forgiven for seeking some normality. So when *Ursus Ariadna* was first encountered, the Rodinan explorers who found it experienced a complex mix of emotions. The thrill of discovery. Relief at something normal-seeming. And raw terror, because, as it turns out, bears are still terrifying.

Colloquially known as the Ariadnan Brown Bear, despite being more of a dull, grayish green colour, the first settlers viewed the creature as something of a calming, normalising presence in the wilds of Ariadna. Even light years from Earth, a "bear is still just a bear" (as the popular saying goes on Dawn)... even if it really looks more like a bipedal buffalo when you get right down to it.

And when you understand how that could be comforting, you're on your way to understanding Ariadna.

ATTRIBUTES

AGI	AWA	BRW	COO	INT	PER	WIL
9	11	15	5	5	10	8

FIELDS OF EXPERTISE

Combat	+1	1	Movement	+1	1	Social	+1	1
Fortitude	+1	1	Senses	+2	2	Technical	–	–

DEFENCES

Firewall	N/A	Resolve	8	Vigour	15
Security	N/A	Morale	–	Armour	2

ATTACKS
- **Claws:** Melee, 2+7 🔘 damage, Piercing 1, Vicious 1

SPECIAL ABILITIES
- **Common Special Abilities:** Grasping, Keen Senses (Smell)
- **Force of Nature:** Don't poke the bear. Each point of Momentum or Heat spent to gain additional dice for close combat attacks or Resistance tests provides two dice instead of one. (The normal maximum of three bonus d20s still applies.)
- **Natural Armour:** The Bear's thick hide provides an Armour Soak of 2.
- **Sometimes the Bear Eats You:** When the Bear makes a melee attack on a grabbed target, it can reroll up to 7 🔘

TROOPER/ELITE

ARIADNAN RAPTOR

The Ariadnan Raptor combines avian and reptilian traits. It can glide for long distances before swooping down on its prey, the Ariadnan Raptor is an incredibly graceful predator, right up to the moment where it becomes mercilessly savage.

Unlike many predatory venoms which cause paralysis, an Ariadnan Raptor's sting seems primarily designed to cause anaphylactic shock. Lashing with its tail-like stinger when its talons dig into a target, the Raptor proceeds to begin its meal while its victim is still alive, often tearing chunks out of much larger creatures.

ATTRIBUTES

AGI	AWA	BRW	COO	INT	PER	WIL
12	10	8	11	7	4	8

FIELDS OF EXPERTISE

Combat	+2	2	Movement	+1	1	Social	+3	–
Fortitude	+1	–	Senses	–	–	Technical	–	–

DEFENCES (TROOPER)

Firewall	N/A	Resolve	4	Vigour	4
Security	N/A	Morale	–	Armour	–

DEFENCES (ELITE)

Firewall	N/A	Resolve	8	Vigour	8
Security	N/A	Morale	–	Armour	–

ATTACKS
- **Claws:** Melee, 1+5 🔘 damage, Biotech, Toxic 2, Vicious 2

SPECIAL ABILITIES
- **Common Special Abilities:** Grasping, Keen Senses (Smell)
- **Swoop (Elite - 2 Heat):** After diving from the air and successfully performing a melee attack, an Elite Ariadnan Raptor can spend 2 Heat to immediately perform a second Minor movement action in the same turn (allowing them to swoop back up into the air).

NEMESIS

BOURAKIAN SEA SERPENT

Leviathans. Jörmungandr. The Loch Ness Monster. Human history is riddled with tales of legendary sea serpents; massive creatures capable of cracking a ship in half, mythical behemoths capable of legendary feats. We now know that these were just stories, as there's nothing remotely like that in Earth's oceans.

Turns out they were all on Bourak.

The planet's oceans are dominated by sea serpents of all shapes and sizes, but for sheer scope, nothing compares to *Hydrophis praegandis*, more commonly stylised as the Bourakian Sea Serpent. They commonly surface during particularly violent storms, or when ships disturb the water. They have been observed eating clusters of ophidian minnows, other serpentine gargantua... and snacking on sailors after cracking open ships.

ATTRIBUTES

AGI	AWA	BRW	COO	INT	PER	WIL
13	10	16 (+1)	9	8	6	8

FIELDS OF EXPERTISE

Combat	+3	3	Movement	+4	4	Social	+1	–
Fortitude	+3	1	Senses	+1	–	Technical	–	–

DEFENCES

Firewall	N/A	Resolve	11	Vigour	19
Security	N/A	Morale	–	Armour	1

ATTACKS
- **Bash:** Melee, 4+8 🔘 damage, Indiscriminate (Close), Unforgiving 4
- **Constriction:** Melee (only against a grabbed target), 4+9 🔘 damage, Piercing 5, Stun, Vicious 4

SPECIAL ABILITIES
- **Common Special Abilities:** Fear 3, Grasping, Inured to Aquatic Pressure and Cold, Menacing 3, Monstrous, Night Vision, Superhuman Brawn 3
- **Natural Armour:** The Sea Serpent's dense scales provide 1 Armour.
- **Terror of the Seas:** The Sea Serpent's massive size allows it to use its Grasping ability on vehicles at no penalty.

TROOPER
FUNDUQ VIPER

In all of Bourak, no creature is as recognisable, nor seemingly omnipresent as the Funduq Viper. A fixture in urban environments, the snakes have found a comfortable coexistence alongside their human neighbours. While not strictly domesticated, many industrious Haqqislamites have found that by creating a pleasant and welcoming habitat — and maintaining a respectful distance — the Vipers are only too happy to provide a vermin-free environment in exchange.

This arrangement has led some to refer to the Funduq Viper as the "Haqqislam Housecat", but locals are quick to point out the differences: while many citizens do take advantage of the viper's services, the Funduq Viper is neither tame, nor a social animal; it attacks when approached, and its bite carries a distinctly unpleasant venom. Most Haqqislamites consider them touchy, easily agitated neighbours, who can nevertheless provide a useful service if kept at arm's length and appropriately flattered; not unlike PanOceania or Yu Jing.

ATTRIBUTES

AGI	AWA	BRW	COO	INT	PER	WIL
10	9	6	5	6	11	9

FIELDS OF EXPERTISE

| Combat | +1 | – | Movement | +3 | – | Social | +1 | – |
| Fortitude | – | – | Senses | +1 | – | Technical | – | – |

DEFENCES

| Firewall | N/A | Resolve | 5 | Vigour | 3 |
| Security | N/A | Morale | – | Armour | – |

ATTACKS
- **Venomous Bite**: Melee, 1+3 🅝 damage, Biotech, Toxic 2, Vicious 2

ELITE
GĀYATRĪ MOEHAU

Thylarctos melodious is a nocturnal arboreal predator native to Paradiso, and the inheritor of several different cultural legacies. Weighing in around 100 kilograms, and measuring roughly 1.3 metres, the Gāyatrī Moehau owes its name to two of its most distinct features. Firstly, it has a distinct mating call comprised of long, shrill notes with eight distinct rhythmic disruptions, repeated three times. Scientists were reminded of *gāyatrī*, a twenty-four-syllable Vedic poetic metre, and the name stuck.

The other distinction calls to a different manner of heritage. PanOceanian soldiers carried the New Zealand myth of the Moehau — a cryptid the size of a normal man, with an ape-like face, shaggy hair, and extremely long fingers ending in sharp claws that was said to drop on its prey from above. Legend has it that while patrolling the jungle, a PanOceanian soldier was suddenly ambushed by a furry predator from above, much to their company's shock, horror, and indeed, amusement.

True or not, the story has endured. Thus was the Gāyatrī Moehau born.

ATTRIBUTES

AGI	AWA	BRW	COO	INT	PER	WIL
13	12	11	7	5	8	7

FIELDS OF EXPERTISE

| Combat | +3 | 3 | Movement | +2 | 2 | Social | +1 | – |
| Fortitude | – | – | Senses | +1 | – | Technical | – | – |

DEFENCES

| Firewall | N/A | Resolve | 7 | Vigour | 11 |
| Security | N/A | Morale | – | Armour | – |

ATTACKS
- **Claws**: Melee, 2+5 🅝 damage, Piercing 1, Vicious 1

SPECIAL ABILITIES
- **Death from Above**: When attacking from an elevated position, the Gāyatrī Moehau gains 2 bonus Momentum on melee attacks.
- **Lurker**: The Gāyatrī Moehau is always waiting. They benefit from one bonus Momentum on Stealth tests to remain hidden.

TROOPER
GUARD DOG

Known as "man's best friend", dogs of all kinds accompanied humanity as they departed Earth. Larger, more aggressive breeds are employed by the corporations as trackers and sentries, their keen noses helping humans hunt as they have for tens of thousands of years.

The following profile represents a keen and aggressive breed of dog, of a kind popular amongst the frontier settlers. The same profile can be easily used for other search and retrieval or guard and attack working animals with little or no modification.

ATTRIBUTES

AGI	AWA	BRW	COO	INT	PER	WIL
10	12	9	5	5	8	7

FIELDS OF EXPERTISE

| Combat | +1 | – | Movement | +1 | – | Social | – | – |
| Fortitude | +1 | – | Senses | +2 | 1 | Technical | – | – |

DEFENCES

| Firewall | N/A | Resolve | 3 | Vigour | 5 |
| Security | N/A | Morale | – | Armour | – |

ATTACKS
- **Bite**: Melee, 1+4 🅝 damage, Vicious 1
- **Growl and Bark**: Range C, 1+3 🅝 mental damage, Stun

SPECIAL ABILITIES
- **Common Special Abilities**: Grasping, Keen Senses (Smell)
- **Companion Animal**: A companion animal is considered to be part of a fireteam led by its owner. However, due to the animal's limited capabilities, it can only assist on Awareness tests made by the owner, or when the owner makes a melee or mental attack. The owner can attack using the animal's melee attacks in place of their own by ordering the animal to attack.

STEPHEN "VOLKBANE" MILLER

FATHER-KNIGHT

BACKER: STEPHEN MILLER

A piercing alarm was ordering everyone to abandon the vicinity of the large gate. Stephen found himself marvelling at the beauty of the volcano's eruption – its pillars of lava coursing up into the air. A shout broke his reverie.

"Father Miller, Father Miller!" The voice belonged to Sergeant Cross, the young man whose field promotion had placed him in command of a company of Fusiliers. He looked very worried.

"Yes, Sergeant Cross."

"The enemy is at the gates! The base has fallen!"

"Calm yourself, my son. Are we not still here?"

"Yes, but there are Raicho swarming at the perimeter! When those TAGs break through we're done for!"

"Look around you."

With a frown, Cross did as he was asked.

"Do you see the men taking position at the barricades behind the gates? Do you see the messengers of ALEPH on the walls above us? And do you see yourself?"

"Myself?"

"Yes, yourself. Are you not a defender of all that is true and good? Are you not here to stand against the alien darkness?"

"I... guess so."

"Then soothe your worry. We are not forgotten, neither by our allies, nor by the Lord. They are on the way to aid us right now. All we need is some time and faith."

Stephen plucked a flower from the ground with his left hand.

"See, beauty has already set in, even here on these molten stone grounds. Should we yet fall so far from home, beauty and life will sprout from our sacrifice. Do not despair. The Lord walks with us, and those who walk with the Lord will not falter."

Confusion and fear still lurked behind the boy's eyes, but the panic had passed from them.

"Come pray with me."

The boy knelt beside him. His eyes shut, sealing the fear behind them. Some minutes later the gates blew open.

They rose as one.

APPEARANCE

Clear blue eyes and short blonde hair frame a placid face. Short in stature, his shoulders are broad. A simple, wooden crucifix hangs around his neck.

ROLEPLAYING

- Often holds his crucifix in a calm grip when speaking
- Impossible to anger
- Never talks about himself

BACKGROUND

Silence is the hallmark of the Father-Knights, and that is exactly what one gets when enquiring after Father Miller's past. Nothing is known about his history before joining the Military Orders. His only answer is: God knows. Whatever came before, he is a terrific soldier and leader who is always where the fighting is thickest. His combat skills are the equal of his teaching and men rally around him naturally; though his speeches can whip them into a frenzy, he always remains calm and exterminates God's enemies with precision.

STATS (ELITE)

ATTRIBUTES

AGI	AWA	BRW	COO	INT	PER	WIL
10	8	9	9	8	10	9

FIELDS OF EXPERTISE

Combat	+2	2	Movement	–	–	Social	+2	1
Fortitude	+1	1	Senses	+1	1	Technical	+1	–

DEFENCES

Firewall	8	Resolve	9	Vigour	9
Security	–	Morale	–	Armour	5

ATTACKS

- **Combi Rifle**: Range C/M, 1+5  damage, Burst 2, 2H, Expert 1, Light Mod, Vicious 1
- **DA-Coated Sword**: Melee, 1+9 damage, Unbalanced, Non-Hackable, Parry 2, Vicious 3
- **Breaker Pistol**: Range R/C, 1+4 damage, Burst 1, 1H, Biotech, Breaker, Piercing 1, Vicious 1

GEAR: Powered Combat Armour (Vestments; gain up to +3d20 on Brawn tests with +3 complication range)

SPECIAL ABILITIES

- **Incarnate Vengeance of God**: A soldier of faith, Stephen is an accomplished warrior. He can reroll up to 2 when making a Combat test, but must accept the new results.
- **Inspire by Faith**: Stephen's steadfast belief is like a beacon to those around him. Any time forces under his command within line of sight are subjected to a Psywar attack, those forces gain +2 Morale Soak.
- **Lead by Example**: Stephen is a natural leader who easily gains the respect of those he commands. When dealing with allied forces, spending 1 Heat to add dice to a Command test will add three d20s instead of one (the normal maximum of three bonus d20s still applies).

JORŌGUMO

A type of *yōkai*, or "bewitching spectre", from Japanese mythology, Jorōgumo were shape-shifting spider demons that would take the form of an attractive maiden to trick unsuspecting prey. Yu Jing's Nipponese soldiers carried their homeland's tales with them in their travels, providing them with a fitting classification for the arthropods of Paradiso collectively known as Jorōgumo.

Referring to a variety of species, Jorōgumo resemble tall, stick-like spiders, standing about five metres tall. This plays into a favoured hunting strategy, where the creatures stand upright and fold in their limbs; swaying gently in the wind, their upright posture combined with their wispy antennae camouflages them as trees. If one catches the light just so, they can also vaguely resemble a human woman, at least in silhouette.

A hunting Jorōgumo endeavours to quickly kill its prey, often depositing clusters of eggs within still-warm corpses, to the horror of any unfortunate witnesses.

ATTRIBUTES

AGI	AWA	BRW	COO	INT	PER	WIL
12	14	10	9	7	4	7

FIELDS OF EXPERTISE

Combat	+2	2	Movement	+2	2	Social	–	–
Fortitude	–	–	Senses	+2	2	Technical	–	–

DEFENCES

Firewall	N/A	Resolve	7	Vigour	10
Security	N/A	Morale	–	Armour	–

ATTACKS

- **Venomous Bite**: Melee, 1+5 damage, Biotech, Toxic 2, Vicious 2
- **Corrosive Saliva**: Range C, 1+6 damage, Immobilising, Terrifying 1, Torrent, Vicious 1

SPECIAL ABILITIES

- **Common Special Abilities**: Grasping, Inured to Pain
- **Patient Predation**: The Jorōgumo's uncanny ability to blend into its environment makes it difficult to spot, even if you know what to look for. They benefit from 2 bonus Momentum on Stealth tests to remain hidden.

STEVEN PARK

USARIADNA COMMTECH/HACKER

BACKER: RICHARD CHOI

"Hurry, Steven, hurry."

He was alone, talking to himself, and frantically plucking cables from a transmitter. A glance at the display of his hacking device told him that his comrades were about to double their trouble; the police were drawing closer.

With one final yank, he popped open a protective cover and smirked at the Chinese script labelling the inner circuitry beyond. "Thank you for teaching me, Mother," he sighed thankfully, before gently removing the rerouting chip and sliding in his own replacement.

"With compliments from USAriadna, you suckers!" he chortled as he began hastily replacing the cover and reconnecting the cables. A short key sequence on his computer rebooted the line and allowed him to notify his comrades via the new link, just as he picked up approaching footsteps.

"Hurry, Steven," prompted him to jump to his feet; a tricky prospect inside the cramped interior of the comms server room.

A shout in Chinese instantly drew his attention to the police officer taking aim from further along the corridor. With barely a pause, the officer let rip, causing shots to ricochet off the walls and sparks to erupt from his computer thanks to a stray bullet.

Backpedalling, Steven threw a grenade to the ground then sprinted for the closest exit as the dense smoke began to fill the corridor. Tearing the door open, he tackled the second, startled police officer standing in front of it, causing them both to tumble down the flight of steps leading up to it.

Steven came out on top and slammed his broken computer on the officer's head, causing her to go limp. Several people had stopped to stare at the scene, before choosing to swiftly move on as his cool eyes swept across them. Exhaling sharply, he strode into the throng of people and was swallowed by the crowd just as two more members of the Judicial Police emerged from the smoking door.

APPEARANCE

In his late twenties, standing 1.6 metres tall, Steven has a more lean than muscular body. His black hair curls naturally and he sports just enough length for that to be seen.

ROLEPLAYING

- Dry and black sense of humour
- Talks to himself to ease his mind
- Open to new ideas

BACKGROUND

Steven is a man haunted by his ancestry. He grew up in the Hifz Commune, a community founded by soldiers of Chinese and Korean descent who had come to Dawn as part of the U.S. Rangers and, when it became clear that Earth was lost to them, sought to preserve Asian cultures on their new homeworld. Like many of the Hifz, he felt isolated from the rest of Ariadnan culture. But unlike previous generations, which had increasingly withdrawn from mainstream life on Dawn, in the wake of the Commercial Conflicts, Steven's curious nature led him to spend as much time as he could amongst the off-worlders swarming into Merovingia and Tartary.

This made him a double outcast of sorts, but Steven isn't bothered by this any more. He chooses to follow his own path, wherever it may take him. He developed a black sense of humour and a certain indifference to other peoples´ opinions, which also induced a sense of disdain for small mindedness.

Fascinated by modern computing and with a knack for all things technical, he was the perfect candidate for the Dozer corps, where he served throughout the Fourth Antipode Offensive. When the Antipodean threat was finally put down, he found himself recruited by the Stavka Intelligence Department, who wanted to train him for Yu Jing infiltration missions "because he could easily blend into the Jade Empire". It sounded like a bad joke. But for once he had been *chosen* for being different — for being an outsider — and that felt pretty good.

He has since enjoyed several tours on Paradiso, Shentang, and Yutang, and made himself a valuable asset for the Ariadnan people; an asset they rarely share with others. Steven enjoys the work. He gets to visit new places and meet plenty of people, although he remains adamant he would never trade his home for any of these alien vistas.

STATS (NEMESIS)

ATTRIBUTES

AGI	AWA	BRW	COO	INT	PER	WIL
10	10	9	9	11	10	11

FIELDS OF EXPERTISE

Combat	+2	1	Movement	+1	1	Social	+2	2
Fortitude	+1	1	Senses	+2	1	Technical	+4	2

DEFENCES

Firewall	15	Resolve	12	Vigour	10
Security	4	Morale	–	Armour	2

ATTACKS

- **Submachine Gun**: Range C, 1+6 🅝 damage, Burst 2, Unbalanced, Spread 1
- **Knife**: Melee, 1+4 🅝 damage, 1H, Concealed 1, Non-Hackable, Subtle 2, Thrown, Unforgiving 1
- **Smoke Grenades**: Disposable, Indiscriminate (Close), Nonlethal, Smoke 2, Speculative Fire, Thrown
- **Hacking Device Plus**: CLAW-2 (CLAW-1 Overlord, CLAW-2 Oblivion), SWORD-1 (SWORD-1 Brain Blast, SWORD-1 Slasher), SHIELD-2 (SHIELD-1 Exorcism, SHIELD-2 Breakwater), GADGET-3 (GADGET-1 Fairy Dust), IC-2, UPGRADE Cybermask, Sucker Punch, White Noise; +2 🅝 bonus damage

GEAR: Light Combat Armour (with Repair Kit)

SPECIAL ABILITIES

- **Double Outcast**: Steven's wide-ranging careers have not only taught him a diverse skillset, but granted familiarity with a variety of cultures. He can reroll one d20 when making a social skill test, but must accept the new result.
- **Swift**: Whether it's parkour, infiltration, or hacking, Steven moves with speed and discretion. Any Heat spent to add dice to an Acrobatics test or Hacking-based movement test will add two d20s instead of one (the normal maximum of three bonus d20s still applies).
- **Technological Adept**: Steven has plied his skills across many combat zones, and adapted various systems to overcome virtually insurmountable difficulties. When making a Tech test, he can reroll any dice that did not generate a success on the initial roll, but must accept the new result.

TROOPER

KARAVA VINETRAP

A "catapult flytrap", the Karava Vinetrap (named after the Punjabi word for "curve" due to the shape of its vines) is an invasive species that covers wide areas of the Paradiso jungle, and flowers into a beautiful array of iridescent sundew blossoms, which produce a succulent fruit with a flavour reminiscent of peaches and strawberries.

This is, of course, a trap.

Once a potential meal is within its grasp, the Karava's snap tentacles contract, delivering a potent mix of neurotoxins not unlike a scorpion's sting, and pulling its prey toward the centre of the blossom. Once ensnared, the plant secretes an acidic substance that breaks down organic matter into a digestible slurry.

Removing its prey is an incredibly unpleasant process, as hundreds of toxic nettles hook their way under the skin during the ensnarement process. More than one incautious soldier has observed that the process of being freed from the plant is often more painful than becoming ensnared in the first place.

ATTRIBUTES

AGI	AWA	BRW	COO	INT	PER	WIL
13	13	15	15	–	–	–

FIELDS OF EXPERTISE

Combat	+1	1	Movement	–	–	Social	–	–
Fortitude	–	–	Senses	+2	2	Technical	–	–

DEFENCES

Firewall	N/A	Resolve	N/A	Vigour	8
Security	N/A	Morale	N/A	Armour	–

ATTACKS

- **Snap Tentacles**: Melee, 1+7 🅝 damage, Concealed 2, Toxic 1, Vicious 1
- **Digestion**: Melee (only against a grasped target) Damage 1+3 🅝, Biotech, Toxic 3, Vicious 2

SPECIAL ABILITIES

- **Common Special Abilities**: Grasping, Mindless, Threatening 2
- **Traps All the Way Down**: When a grasped character escapes, the Karava Vinetrap can spend 1 Heat to immediately attack with Snap Tentacles.

NOTES

While the Karava Vinetrap has some degree of mobility, it is still a plant, and cannot take movement actions.

ELITE

KI-RIN

Auspicious. There's really no other way to describe laying eyes on one of these gregarious creatures; meeting a Ki-Rin – even as new domestication programs make such encounters increasingly common – is nothing short of auspicious.

Named for the beatific creatures from China's mythic history, images don't do these equine quadrupeds justice. Cameras can capture their jewel-toned, iridescent fur, but misses how it refracts the light like a prism, how the wispy tufts of hair dance as they move, or the impossible grace with which such a large, fast creature moves; seeming almost to glide across the ground. Little wonder that they seemed a myth sprung to life.

Ki-Rin are as easily identified by their horn or antler-like keratin deposits – naturally filed to a sharp edge – as by their languid, ambling gait. A Ki-Rin always keeps one hoof on the ground; only making exceptions for their annual migration, or in times of great danger. "The Ki-Rin are flying" is a common Yu Jing euphemism for a bad situation, likely to get worse.

ATTRIBUTES

AGI	AWA	BRW	COO	INT	PER	WIL
14	12	12	4	5	8	8

FIELDS OF EXPERTISE

Combat	+1	1	Movement	+3	3	Social	–	–
Fortitude	–	–	Senses	+2	2	Technical	–	–

DEFENCES

Firewall	N/A	Resolve	8	Vigour	12
Security	N/A	Morale	1	Armour	–

ATTACKS

- **Kick**: Melee, 1+6 🅝 damage, Knockdown, Stun
- **Gore**: Melee, 2+7 🅝 damage, Piercing 1, Vicious 1

SPECIAL ABILITIES

- **Ambling Gait**: A Ki-Rin dances across the landscape with effortless grace. It can move an additional zone when performing a movement action.
- **Charging Gore (Elite)**: If an elite Ki-Rin moves at least two zones on the same turn as performing a Gore attack, they add +2 🅝 to the damage of the attack.

TEÓFILO HURTADO NAVARRO

KNIGHT OF SANTIAGO

BACKER: TEÓFILO HURTADO NAVARRO

An explosion rocks the compartment. His prayers murmur on, uninterrupted. The klaxon of a hull breach echoes through the corridors. Teófilo rises without hurry. He crosses himself. He turns and leaves the chapel.

A quick look at his comlog. Intruders in the aft cargo bay. The chapel isn't far from there.

He signals his location and intention to his Captain-Brother as he breaks into a run. The halls around him are desolate – the secret cargo run of the Galicia Resplendent bringing with it no passengers and few crew. No harm shall come to any of them as long as a son of Santiago can still take breath to protect them.

The cargo bay doors come into sight. His geist collects surveillance footage and superimposes disparate angles onto his field of view. Six intruders. He preps a grenade, overrides the airlock, and enters on a surge of decompressing air.

His Spitfire roars to life. He doesn't need to look because he's already seen – expert systems extrapolating the surveillance cameras into a 3D overlay which let him peer behind crates and through walls. Bullets rip through aluminium sheeting and tear into the purplish-grey flesh of a slender alien.

The HE rounds rupture its meat. But it doesn't fall. A technological carapace keeps it up. He slides to a halt next to a magnetised crate, hurls a grenade – one of the icons vanishes from his tac-display.

But then his cover is exploding in fiery plasma. He's running sideways. Dodging another fusillade. They're well positioned around him. There's

no cover in the centre of the room. Another grenade provides it, and he moves at blinding speed amidst the blue lightning sizzling through the room. Straight at one of them. He slams into shelving, powered armour ripping bolts from the floor and sending it toppling down on top of the alien.

Then he's up and over and behind the shelf. Outside of their circle. Behind cover again.

But the fight is far from over.

APPEARANCE

A body steeled though years of constant training, dark eyes, and of Spanish descent. Not particularly tall, but with an impressive physical presence. A miniature crucifix is tattooed just inside the suprasternal notch at the bottom of his neck.

ROLEPLAYING

- Calm and serene outside of battle
- Tends to display foolish bravery in a fight
- Loves to discuss stock markets and theology

BACKGROUND

Born to a working-class family on Acontecimento, Hurtado enjoyed a comfortable childhood. He respected his parent's hard work, but dreamed of bigger things. From an early age, he saved and invested as much as he could, always seeking the best returns. He had an aptitude for these things and had begun to make serious money while he was still a teenager. By the time he was twenty-one, however, he realised that he had a different calling to pursue.

A career at an avionics company that produced ships for the Knights of Santiago led him to the decision that a stint in the Order would be beneficial to the political career he was beginning to map out for himself. After all, buying oneself into the ranks is a perfectly normal occurrence these days.

His first day aboard a pilgrim ship almost broke him. Manual labour was a shock to the system and he almost quit immediately.

On the second day, he found some time to talk to one of the pilgrims. Hurtado had no interest in what he had to say, but there was no one else to talk to. The honest faith of the man impressed him deeply, however, and over the course of the next week he found the same conviction in several other pilgrims. Not every pilgrim was an honest believer, but the faith of those who were struck him to the core.

His application to the Order took on a seriousness that it had lacked before. Four years of intense training finally saw him join the ranks. That was two decades ago. So long as there remains even one faithful pilgrim, Teófilo will never look back.

STATS (ELITE)

ATTRIBUTES

AGI	AWA	BRW	COO	INT	PER	WIL
10	9	9	8	9	8	10

FIELDS OF EXPERTISE

Combat	+2	2	Movement	+1	–	Social	+1	–
Fortitude	+2	–	Senses	+1	1	Technical	+2	–

DEFENCES

Firewall	9	Resolve	10	Vigour	9
Security	–	Morale	–	Armour	5

ATTACKS

- **Spitfire**: Range M, 1+6 🌑 damage, Burst 3, 2H, Spread 2, Unsubtle
- **DA Pistol**: Range R/C, 1+5 🌑 damage, Burst 1, 1H, Vicious 3
- **AP Axe**: Melee, 1+6 🌑 damage, Unbalanced, Non-Hackable, Piercing 2, Thrown, Vicious 1
- **EXP Grenades**: 2+4 🌑 damage, Comms, Disposable, Indiscriminate (Close), Speculative Fire, Spread 1, Thrown, Unsubtle, Vicious 2

GEAR: Powered Combat Armour (gain up to +3d20 on Brawn tests with +3 complication range)

SPECIAL ABILITIES

- **Knight Among the Stars**: Hurtado is a tireless member of the Order of Santiago. He can reroll up to 2 🌑 when making a Combat test, but must accept the new results.
- **Seasoned Investor**: A lifetime of dabbling in stock speculation has left Hurtado both wealthy and worldly. He can reroll one d20 when making a social skills test, but must accept the new results.
- **Stalwart Protector**: Hurtado takes his role as a guardian incredibly seriously, fighting tirelessly to defend his charges. He reduces the Heat cost of all Defence or Guard Reactions by one.

ELITE

KING TIGER SEAL

Upon learning of the King Tiger Seal, many remark that Paradiso seems rife with wildlife that strongly resembles creatures back on Earth, only bigger. Certainly, weighing in at 600 kilograms and measuring four metres long, the King Tiger Seal is an intimidating specimen. However, they're still dwarfed by Earth's southern elephant seal, weighing as much as 4,000 kilograms, and nearly six metres long. No, the thing that sets Paradiso's King Tiger Seal apart from their Earthly counterparts is their potent combination of size, strength, and acclimation to a tropical climate.

And their temper. Their horrible, horrible temper.

The King Tiger Seal — *Hydrurga rex* to be exact — is a belligerent predator, using its bulk and strength to take down its prey, defend its territory, and drive off rivals. It is worth noting that explorers, Kragodons, and tanks have all been deemed worthy of its attention at one point or another.

ATTRIBUTES

AGI	AWA	BRW	COO	INT	PER	WIL
9	14	15	3	3	9	10

FIELDS OF EXPERTISE

Combat	+3	3	Movement	+1	–	Social	+1	–
Fortitude	+3	–	Senses	+1	–	Technical	–	–

DEFENCES

Firewall	N/A	Resolve	10	Vigour	15
Security	N/A	Morale	–	Armour	–

ATTACKS

- **Slam**: Melee, 1+8 🌑 damage, Anti-Materiel 1, Knockdown, Vicious 1

SPECIAL ABILITIES

- **Common Special Abilities**: Monstrous
- **Alpha Predator**: When making a melee attack, the King Tiger Seal can reroll up to 4 🌑.
- **King's Court**: The King Tiger Seal would like you to leave. Now. When making a Psywar attack, they can reroll one d20, but must accept the new result.

ELITE

KRAGODON

A massive predatory lizard, the Kragodon seems to have historically dominated every ecosystem it inhabited. Commonly growing as long as three metres, they use their massive size and strength to hunt and feed at their leisure, spending most of their waking hours sunning themselves on Molokai's beaches, and occasionally defending their territory from King Tiger Seals. However, the recent warfare on Paradiso has caused a migration of said Tiger Seals, causing an intense battle for hunting grounds in game-rich Molokai.

As a result, Kragodons are increasingly likely to view anything sufficiently loud and large as a potential rival, causing them to act with uncharacteristic aggression. And of course, they've never been shy about considering humans an appropriate food source.

ATTRIBUTES

AGI	AWA	BRW	COO	INT	PER	WIL
13	12	14	3	3	7	11

FIELDS OF EXPERTISE

Combat	+3	1	Movement	+1	1	Social	+3	–
Fortitude	+1	–	Senses	+1	1	Technical	–	–

DEFENCES

Firewall	N/A	Resolve	11	Vigour	14
Security	N/A	Morale	–	Armour	1

ATTACKS

- **Claws**: Melee, 2+7 🌑 damage, Concealed 1, Piercing 1, Vicious 1

SPECIAL ABILITIES

- **Common Special Abilities**: Grasping, Night Vision
- **Alpha Predator**: When making a melee attack, the Kragodon can reroll up to 4 🌑.
- **Natural Armour**: The Kragodon's scaly hide provides an Armour Soak of 1.

WILLEM HERON
ARIADNA SPY/TAG PILOT

BACKER: BILL HERON

He looked out over the sprawling, crowded hills of Paekche from his perch on the third floor balcony of the Kang Imperial Hotel. The encrypted commbud in his ear chirruped.

"The meeting with the Bourakian was fruitful. We should meet up and then get the hell —" The voice cut off. The hiss of severed comms line set Willem instantly on edge.

The door behind him burst open. "Lìding!"

He didn't speak Chinese, but the tone gave him all the command he needed. He raised his arms. Slow. Count to three and...

Willem stepped forward, off the edge of the balcony, and dropped to the street below. Specialised gel in the soles of his boots absorbed some of the impact, but his calves still ached.

Fifteen steps. And then down the stairs to the subway station. Shift into crowd. Forty steps to the platform below. The jammed comms were preventing him from contacting his team. Assume drastic measures are needed. Shed the coat. As it falls to the ground, let it cover the hands that yank the hidden drive free from the fake notebook in your pocket. Let the crowd move you. Dump the notebook into the trash can. Follow the crowd onto the subway car.

Count to thirty. Pull the emergency brake. Let the crowd's panic take hold. Count to ten. Slip out the door and onto the tracks.

Twenty-two steps. Up the exit ladder. Back onto the streets, where everything is quiet. Everything including the commbud.

No. Not the commbud. It crackled back to life. The jammers they were using must have had a limited range. "Bill. I'm getting your ping now. What the hell happened?"

"A close call, but I think I've gotten outside the immediate cordon."

"But not the larger one. They're blasting all the major Maya channels and issuing a security lockdown. Some story about an Imperial Agent getting attacked."

That meant his path to the extraction point would be blocked. That was all right. He still had an ace up his sleeve.

APPEARANCE

Dark curls and a long face are perfectly complimented by the warm and sincere smile offered to most people he meets. British ancestry shines through clearly in his voice and manners.

ROLEPLAYING

- Easily discerns what others want and has no scruples to exploit it
- Likes the thrill of a close call and works best under pressure
- Cocks an eyebrow while dealing with a problem

BACKGROUND

Willem got around a lot during his childhood; at least, as much as you can on somewhere like Dawn. Born the son of a diplomatic envoy of USAriadna and a Merovingian merchant, the road became his cradle. He had extensively travelled Dawn by the age of thirteen and showed a certain aptitude for machines, which was showcased by his short-circuiting of a heavy cargo lifter exoskeleton that he then used to pin an enraged Dogface until the Loup-Garou arrived.

He was approached by the Stavka shortly before his term in the armed forces of Dawn was due to begin and offered a position with off-world duties. As much as he loved Ariadna, Willem jumped at the chance to see other planets and cultures. He undertook extensive training before being given his first off-world assignments, which taught him to use his likable manner as a means to gain exploitable data on acquaintances.

He gained first-hand experience in TAG combat during a posting in the Human Edge — and he was in love. He harvests every bit of information that he can about these machines, which better equips him for stealing them when on assignment; something he finds an excuse to partake in with increasing regularity. There is hardly a TAG that he could not pilot or hotwire for that matter, which is a very handy skill that sees him assigned to any mission that might require his expertise; his stationing with a unit of Geckos from *Corregidor* during his last tour on Paradiso was not a coincidence.

STATS (NEMESIS)

ATTRIBUTES

AGI	AWA	BRW	COO	INT	PER	WIL
10	10	10	9	11	11	9

FIELDS OF EXPERTISE

Combat	+2	1	Movement	+1	1	Social	+2	2
Fortitude	+1	–	Senses	+2	1	Technical	+4	3

DEFENCES

Firewall	15	Resolve	10	Vigour	11
Security	–	Morale	–	Armour	1

ATTACKS

- **Assault Pistol**: Range R/C, 1+6 (N) damage, Burst 2, Unbalanced, Vicious 1
- **Knife**: Melee, 1+5 (N) damage, 1H, Concealed 1, Non-Hackable, Subtle 2, Thrown, Unforgiving 1
- **Hacking Device Plus**: CLAW-2 (CLAW-1 Gotcha!, CLAW-1 Overlord), SWORD-1, SHIELD-2, GADGET-3 (GADGET-1 Lockpicker), IC-2, UPGRADE Cybermask, Sucker Punch, White Noise; +2 (N) bonus damage

GEAR: Armoured Clothing, B&E Kit, Fake ID 3, Powered Multitool, Short ModCoat (with Hacking Device Plus and Recorder)

SPECIAL ABILITIES

- **Contingency Plan**: Willem spends a great deal of time preparing for things to go wrong; that way, he's rarely surprised when they do. As a Reaction, he can spend 1 Heat to grant himself Light Cover or Minor Interference, regardless of circumstance.
- **Efficiency of Motion**: Whether on foot, or piloting his beloved TAGs, Willem possesses a determined sort of grace. He can reroll one d20 when making an Acrobatics or movement-related Pilot test, but must accept the new result.
- **Multifarious Mirror Agent**: Willem's cocky nature and ability to exploit others has seen him excel as an undercover agent. He can reroll one d20 when making a social skills test undercover or in disguise, but must accept the new result.
- **TAG-Induced Kleptomania**: Willem's technical prowess is near legendary amongst his Stavka peers, as is his ability to requisition massive armoured platforms. He reduces the difficulty of all Technical tests involving TAGs by one step, to a minimum of Simple (D0).

NEOTERRAN EMERALD DRAGON

A living window into history, the Neoterran Emerald Dragon (*Draconis Magnavenator*) would have fit in perfectly alongside the dinosaurs of Earth's Mesozoic Era. Measuring thirty metres from tail to snout with twenty-five-centimetre-long talons, a scaly hide and iridescent viridian feathers, the Dragon was unquestionably the apex predator of Neoterra before humanity's arrival. Possessed of semi-vestigial wings, the Emerald Dragon prefers to swoop down from an elevated position, gliding its way to the ground and diving into unsuspecting prey. It has a caustic venom, used primarily as a deterrent to other predators, or in fights to establish dominance with other Dragons.

First encountered by the explorer Georgia Kawhau-Stanley — affectionately referred to as the "Neoterran Stanley" — this extremely dangerous creature has become a PanOceanian treasure, an avatar that embodies traits the Hyperpower sees in itself. But despite the mascots, toys, and pageantry, underestimating these fearsome creatures can be a fatal mistake.

ATTRIBUTES

AGI	AWA	BRW	COO	INT	PER	WIL
9	10	16 (+3)	7	5	11 (+1)	10

FIELDS OF EXPERTISE

Combat	+3	3	Movement	+3	3	Social	+1	1
Fortitude	+4	–	Senses	+1	1	Technical	–	–

DEFENCES

Firewall	N/A	Resolve	14	Vigour	23
Security	N/A	Morale	–	Armour	–

ATTACKS

- **Toxic Spit**: Range C, 1+6 (N) damage, Area (Close), Biotech, Toxic 2, Vicious 2
- **Claws**: Melee, 4+8 (N) damage, Piercing 1, Vicious 1

SPECIAL ABILITIES

- **Common Special Abilities**: Grasping, Menacing, Superhuman Brawn 3, Superhuman Personality 1, Threatening 3
- **Apex Predator**: When making a melee attack, the Dragon can reroll up to 6 (N).
- **Colossal Creature**: A Dragon is an immense creature, many metres long. A Dragon can treat any creature within Close range as being within Reach. Close combat attacks against a Dragon are at +1 difficulty, but ranged attacks are at −1 difficulty. The Dragon inflicts an automatic 1+3 (N) damage with the Knockdown quality on any creature that attempts to make a close combat attack against it and fails.
- **Cumbersome**: A Dragon is a slow and awkward creature, unable to move quickly due to its sheer size and bulk. It cannot take the Sprint Standard Action or any Response Action.
- **Death from Above**: When attacking from an elevated position, the Dragon gains 2 bonus Momentum on melee attacks.
- **Rule the Roost**: When making a Psywar attack, the Dragon can reroll one d20, but it must accept the new result.

RIDING HORSE

Though horses are amongst the oldest and most widespread riding animals, they are far from the only kind. The following profile represents a swift and sturdy breed of horse, of a kind popular amongst the frontier settlers. The same profile can be easily used for other riding or harness working animals with little or no modification.

ATTRIBUTES

AGI	AWA	BRW	COO	INT	PER	WIL
10	10	14	4	5	6	7

FIELDS OF EXPERTISE

Combat	+1	–	Movement	+2	1	Social	–	–
Fortitude	+1	–	Senses	+1	–	Technical	–	–

DEFENCES

Firewall	N/A	Resolve	4	Vigour	7
Security	N/A	Morale	–	Armour	–

ATTACKS

- **Kick**: Melee, 1+7 (N) damage, Knockdown, Stun

SPECIAL ABILITIES

- **Gallop**: A horse is quick over short distances. A horse can Run as a Minor Action.
- **Mount**: A ridden animal is considered to be part of a fireteam led by its rider. However, due to the animal's limited capabilities, it can only assist on melee attack tests, movement-based tests, or Awareness tests. The rider can attack using the mount's melee attacks instead of their own.

WOO BONG-GYUN

EX-FUSILIER WARCOR

BACKER: WOO BONG-GYUN

<The explosion's concussive blast sends a shudder through the CamBot. Flames glisten on the hard, blue armours of the Fusiliers.>

"*The Morat forces remain pinned down in the ruins of the main gate. Led by Volkbane, the Father-Knight whose exploits during the Evacuation of Silvania were immortalised by Melissa Oso* – (Puff, patch in the archive footage from *Deeds of the New Crusaders and link it) – has rallied a platoon of fusiliers to keep them bottled up while the Ekdromoi on the walls above pour Teseum death down upon the Yaogat.*"

<The camera pans up and across the wall. Plumes of smoke billow across the sky behind the porcelain perfection of the Ekdromoi, streamers of tracer fire lancing down from their HMGs.>

"*The scene could not be more different than just a few hours ago –* (give me the queued footage now, Puff) *–*"

<A sharp cut. Looking down from the wall to the green sward in the centre of the fort where twenty or so soldiers are seen kneeling.>

"*– when the Father-Knight led two squads of Fusiliers in prayer. Many of those who then knelt to ask for strength and courage and hope now lie dead in the defence of the innocent.*"

<The camera begins to pan to the right, following the curve of the fort's wall.>

"*But if those brave Fusiliers should fail or if Volkbane should fall, then the last desperate hope of that defence will be lost. Worse yet, the plan only works for as long as the wall holds –*"

<The image pans cross a section of wall that looks like swiss cheese. Huge, gaping holes are torn into it.>

"*Ten minutes ago, the Ekdromoi guarding the east wall abandoned it – cutting a swath out of that weakly defended side of the base and*

disappearing up the side of the volcano, leading many to believe that ALEPH may have written this facility off as a – Whoa! – (Puff, cut that last.)"

<An abrupt tilt skywards. A flaming ship sears its way across the sky towards Valkenswijk in the west. It's a stunning sight. Something explodes out the side of the ship, plunging towards the volcano's peak. A much nearer explosion rocks the footage. The CamBot's lens is wrenched back down to the wall.>

"*The Morat have breached the wall! There are – There are TAGS – I'm seeing a half dozen Raicho. They've brought the –*"

<The wall collapses into slag, drowning out his words. The CamBot zooms back, bringing the reporter back into frame as he dives for cover.>

"*This is Woo Bong-Gyun, signing off from the final stand of Mount Cristol. Do not fear the Death! PUFF! SEND IT! GET IT OUT NOW BEFORE IT'S TOO LATE!*"

* * * * *

Bong-Gyun kept his cameras running. The Fusiliers rallied. Held for a long moment, and then another. But then one of the Raicho charged forward, heedless of its own safety, and released a nanopulser. The Fusiliers were broken, falling back. The first ranks of the Raicho stepped through their breach.

And then there was an explosion from behind the Raicho. Confusion was sown in their ranks. The Zúyǒng – the Invincibles – had arrived.

The day was won.

APPEARANCE

The huge grin plastered across Woo's face is infectious enough to almost make you forget the cam-glasses he's wearing. A press pass is clipped to his shirt with QID credentials dripping off it, his pants are covered with a multitude of pockets, and a small green fairy dragon flits around his halo.

ROLEPLAYING

- Fearless, jaded, nosy, and curious
- Uses the flask he always keeps in his hip pocket to break the ice. (And to take a swig when the situation gets tense.)
- His sign-off and catchphrase is, "Do not fear the Death"

BACKGROUND

Hailing from a family of freighter captains – Korean ex-pats who had fled to the welcoming embrace of PanOceania when the Yu Jing hammer fell on their homeland – Bong-Gyun wanted to get his feet on the ground from an early age and the army seemed the best idea.

He enlisted as a Fusilier, as they *are* the army – so the advertisements say at least. He learned the truth of that statement when he witnessed the death of his entire platoon during an expedition to Dawn. Neither their deaths, nor the atrocities of their mercenary support, received any publicity. Bong-Gyun, however, wanted answers.

A transfer to Paradiso was intended to shut him up, but he bore witness to similar atrocities that were once again buried. Intent on getting answers, he requested a discharge and became a reporter, which made him a lot of friends in the ranks, but alienated him further from the brass.

His two constant companions are Puff (his geist, which manifests as a small dragon) and the flask of liquor he keeps in his hip pocket.

STATS (ELITE)

ATTRIBUTES

AGI	AWA	BRW	COO	INT	PER	WIL
8	10	8	9	9	10	9

FIELDS OF EXPERTISE

| Combat | +1 | – | Movement | +1 | – | Social | +2 | 2 |
| Fortitude | +1 | – | Senses | +2 | 1 | Technical | +1 | 1 |

DEFENCES

| Firewall | 9 | Resolve | 9 | Vigour | 8 |
| Security | – | Morale | – | Armour | 2 |

ATTACKS

- **Flash Pulse**: Range M, 1+7 damage, Burst 1, 2H, Blinding, removes Marked
- **Stun Pistol**: Range R/C, 1+6 damage, Burst 1, 1H, Biotech, Nonlethal, Stun, Vicious 1
- **Knife**: Melee, 1+3 damage, 1H, Concealed 1, Non-Hackable, Subtle 2, Thrown, Unforgiving 1

GEAR: AR Eye Implants, Armoured Clothing, Ballistic Vest, Flask of "The Good Stuff", CamBot (TinBot + Recorder)

SPECIAL ABILITIES

- **Bad Things Happen**: An ex-Fusilier with experience on the front lines of both Dawn and Paradiso, Bong-Gyun has witnessed some of the worst that war has to offer. He can take a Defence Reaction against any attacks, including those that he may not have any apparent reason to know about, although he must still pay the normal Heat cost for taking a Reaction.
- **Feet on the Ground**: Bong-Gyun's reporting has made him a lot of friends amongst the ordinary ranks, and they're quick to lend a hand if he's in trouble. When spending Heat to call Reinforcements, the GM may call three Troopers per 2 Heat spent. (If Bong-Gyun is incapacitated, the GM can continue using his Feet on the Ground Ability until the end of the scene.)
- **Slug of The Good Stuff**: Bong-Gyun is able to summon a significant amount of courage from the depths of his hip flask. When exposed to a traumatic event, he may spend 1–2 Heat in order to gain twice the amount of Heat spent as Morale Soak. This effect lasts until the end of the current scene and stacks with all other sources of Morale Soak.

ELITE
SHRIKE TARDIGRADE

Space is cold and uncaring. The thought that anything could survive in that harsh vacuum was always improbable; outside of the tardigrade – a micro-animal found on Earth – humanity was unaware of anything that could survive such a hostile environment. So when explorers discovered a dog-sized, six-legged, mole-like creature hibernating on an asteroid in the Varuna system, scientists were understandably elated by the discovery.

This enthusiasm would be somewhat dampened as the creatures' nature revealed itself, and humanity encountered its first interstellar invasive species.

Capable of surviving just about anything by entering a sort of hibernation, the Shrike Tardigrade awakens from this state by absorbing ambient moisture and heat; they rehydrate, and wake up extremely hungry. Omnivores in the truest sense, they indiscriminately devour organic material of all types, and their claws have been known to crack open the hulls of small ships in hopes of finding sustenance inside.

The creature's odd properties – and the seeming lack of any supporting lineage or ecosystem – has lead some scientists to theorise that the Shrike Tardigrade may have been conceived as some kind of bioweapon, like a space mine left behind in a scorched earth manoeuvre.

ATTRIBUTES

AGI	AWA	BRW	COO	INT	PER	WIL
12	9	14	5	4	4	15

FIELDS OF EXPERTISE

| Combat | +1 | 1 | Movement | +1 | 1 | Social | – | – |
| Fortitude | +3 | 3 | Senses | +1 | 1 | Technical | – | – |

DEFENCES

| Firewall | N/A | Resolve | 15 | Vigour | 14 |
| Security | N/A | Morale | – | Armour | 2 |

ATTACKS

- **Claws**: Melee, 2+7 damage, Piercing 3, Vicious 1

SPECIAL ABILITIES

- **Common Special Abilities**: Grasping, Inured to Cold, Disease, Heat, Poison, Radiation, and Vacuum
- **Impaler**: Like its namesake bird, the Shrike Tardigrade prefers to impale its meals on something sharp. When it successfully causes a Wound with a Melee attack, it can reduce the Heat cost for its Grasping ability by 2, to a minimum of 0.

YASHA THENOR

NOMAD HELLCAT

BACKER: GEORGES THENOR-LOUIS

The countdown was the only thing visible in the darkness of the passenger hold. Each second that ticked away seemed to stretch out longer and longer for Yasha. "Wake up, jump ahead," he said as he tapped his neighbour on the shoulder at the thirty count. Not waiting for a reply, he took up position near the jump door and scanned the latest frontline intel.

"Hey, hot zone. Almost makes up for the low jump," he said mirthlessly to himself. Which was apparently the code phrase to open the jump door. A smile crept onto his lips as the wind struck him.

Yasha leapt without delay on his turn, letting the soaring wind embrace him as he dove head first. The ground was a greyish-white blur, but details were becoming clearer very fast even with his comlog placing a tactical grid in front of his vision. He chose a landing spot and angled his body towards it, picking out the different elevations in the rocks as he flew and watching the small specks resolve into buildings and trees. A final veer to the right brought him into position and angled his feet toward the ground. He waited for a count of two before firing the jets when the altimeter warning sounded and laughed hard as the deceleration hit him like a brick wall. A huge fountain of snow and slush exploded around his impact.

Not wasting any time, he rolled sideways, brought his weapons up, and checked his position before running towards a small wood that was under assault. Two Geckos were using the cover of a rock formation to hide from an outpost's intense bursts. Yasha carefully took aim at the

furthest before squeezing the trigger. The projectile struck true, causing green gel to spread rapidly around the TAG's torso and freeze it in place, despite a last frantic movement to dislodge the chemical. Yasha ran for cover as return fire from the Gecko's companion lanced out towards him.

APPEARANCE

Yasha is tall, muscular, and somewhat slim. His movements always have a sense of readiness to them. Short-cropped black hair crowns his Haitian features and broad, infectious smile.

ROLEPLAYING

- Hardly ever at rest, his body is in constant motion
- Lopsided grin
- Often mutters happily to himself

BACKGROUND

They say everybody has a vice. If Yasha has one, it is a longing for air. Born and raised in the modules of *Corregidor* he — as with so many others — had never once tasted fresh air. When he was young, however, his mother gave him a holo-recording of a green hill under blue skies with a fierce wind whipping the trees. Family heirloom she said. It was the only thing she ever gave him.

His days began in the same gang that had been the lifelong home of his parents. He was a regular guest in the cells of the Alguaciles. A daredevil and thrillseeker at heart, the opportunity to join the armed forces seemed a natural way to escape from the corridor-crawlers. His first two missions were disasters that he only managed to survive due to cunning and sheer stubbornness. Then the Hellcats came calling.

A lot of Corregidorans are hesitant when making the leap (literally) to planet-side missions. But not Yasha. He still meditated to the sight of those wind-whipped trees and he wanted to feel that wind for himself.

And it turned out that high-speed insertions and high-risk threshold operations were just the thing to get him smiling… and never stop.

He has seen fighting on Paradiso, Svalarheima, and Dawn during the last ten years. When command needs a last resort, he's the man they send.

STATS (ELITE)

ATTRIBUTES

AGI	AWA	BRW	COO	INT	PER	WIL
10	9	10	9	8	9	8

FIELDS OF EXPERTISE

Combat	+2	2	Movement	+2	1	Social	+1	–
Fortitude	+1	1	Senses	+1	–	Technical	+1	–

DEFENCES

Firewall	8	Resolve	8	Vigour	10
Security	–	Morale	2	Armour	4

ATTACKS

- **Combi Rifle**: Range C/M, 1+6 🔘 damage, Burst 2, 2H, Expert 1, MULTI Light Mod, Vicious 1
- **Adhesive Launcher**: Range M, 1+7 🔘 damage, Burst 1, Unwieldy, Area (Close), Immobilising, Nonlethal, Munition, Knockdown
- **Pistol**: Range R/C, 1+5 🔘 damage, Burst 1, 1H, Vicious 1
- **Knife**: Melee, 1+5 🔘 damage, 1H, Concealed 1, Non-Hackable, Subtle 2, Thrown, Unforgiving 1

GEAR: Heavy Combat Armour (with Hellcat Combat Jump Pack)

SPECIAL ABILITIES

- **Fighting for Air**: Yasha fights not only for the fresh air he relishes, but because he seeks to provide the same to his people. He can reroll up to 3 🔘 when making a Combat test, but must accept the new results.
- **Hellcat Jump Pack**: A daredevil's best friend, Yasha's pack is never far from hand. In addition to the gear's normal benefits, he can reroll one d20 on Movement tests when wearing his Jump Pack, but he must accept the new result.
- **Life on the Edge**: An effervescent thrillseeker, Yasha is well-liked by his comrades, despite the fact that they find themselves shaking their heads at his antics. He can reroll one d20 when making a Social test, but must accept the new result.
- **Daredevil**: There is precious little in this world – or any other – that gives Yasha pause. He has an innate Morale Soak of 2.

SCORPIONETTE

Measuring roughly thirty centimetres from pincer to stinger, the double-tailed *Heterometrus terribilis* has caused more casualties than any forces on Paradiso care to admit. A solitary hunter, the Scorpionette lies in wait beneath the layers of vegetation that blanket Paradiso, its dorsal stinger poised and ready to strike.

Other than a high concentration of carrion-eaters, there are few signs of its presence.

It preys primarily on large mammals who fail to notice its presence, treading directly on its exposed dorsal stinger; which delivers a potent paralytic venom that can kill an adult human in less than twenty-four hours. If that doesn't suffice, its tail stinger packs a vicious neurotoxin it uses to hunt larger mammals. One sting can stop a human heart in less than twenty minutes.

So naturally, there's a robust community of Scorpionette breeders in the Paradiso animal trade, and an illegal underground Scorpionette fighting ring.

ATTRIBUTES

AGI	AWA	BRW	COO	INT	PER	WIL
12	11	6	5	8	7	10

FIELDS OF EXPERTISE

Combat	+2	2	Movement	+1	1	Social	–	–
Fortitude	–	–	Senses	+2	1	Technical	–	–

DEFENCES (TROOPER)

Firewall	N/A	Resolve	5	Vigour	3
Security	N/A	Morale	–	Armour	–

ATTACKS

- **Dorsal Stinger**: Melee, 1+2 🔘 damage, Biotech, Immobilising
- **Tail Stinger**: Melee, 1+3 🔘 damage, Biotech, Toxic 3, Vicious 3

SPECIAL ABILITIES

- **Entrapment**: In tall grass, jungle floors, or other suitably concealing terrain, Scorpionettes benefit from 1 bonus Momentum on Stealth tests to remain hidden.
- **Paralytic Poison**: The Scorpionette's dorsal stinger can deliver a dose of paralytic poison equivalent to tetrodotoxin (p. 383).

TITAN JELLYFISH

The Titan Jellyfish (*Cyanea titania*) – twenty metres in diameter with six clusters of seventy or more sticky tentacles that can trail up to forty-five metres – live in the abyssal depths of the Svalarheiman oceans. Their coloration is dictated by size, with larger specimens a dark purple and smaller specimens grading down to a light blue. Though they normally feed on smaller fishes and other jellyfish, they can pose a serious danger to the sailors and divers that hunt them for their valuable and complex toxins, precious to PanOceanian, Yu Jingese, and especially Haqqislamite pharmaceutical researchers and bio-prospectors.

Titans dive deep in summertime, requiring specialised bathyscaphes to reach their abyssal habitats – while unmanned drones can help, Titans' cunning, deft tentacles, and deadly neurotoxins demand onsite manned vehicles to direct the hunt. In winter, strong storms drive the Titans to the surface, requiring whale hunt-like techniques to pursue them across Svalarheima's vicious storm-wracked seas. Whatever the season, many hunters never make it back to harbour.

ATTRIBUTES

AGI	AWA	BRW	COO	INT	PER	WIL
17	16	18	5	7	2	5

FIELDS OF EXPERTISE

Combat	+3	3	Movement	+3	3	Social	–	–
Fortitude	+2	2	Senses	+2	2	Technical	–	–

DEFENCES

Firewall	N/A	Resolve	7	Vigour	20
Security	N/A	Morale	–	Armour	–

ATTACKS

- **Billions of Nematocysts**: Melee (only against a grabbed target), 1+8 🔘 damage, Stun, Toxic 3, Vicious 3
- **Grasping Tentacles**: Melee, 1+9 🔘 damage, Area (Close), Immobilising, Nonlethal
- **Lashing Tentacles**: Melee, 2+9 🔘 damage, Indiscriminate (Close), Spread 1

SPECIAL ABILITIES

- **Common Special Abilities**: Grasping, Inured to Aquatic Pressure, Cold, Pain, and Poison; Menacing 4, Monstrous, Night Vision
- **Aquatic Rush (1 Heat)**: Once per round for 1 Heat, a Titan Jellyfish can make a Run Action (through water) as a Free Action, in addition to any Run Action made as a Standard Action.

ZHIYONG LOH

YU JING MILITARY STRATEGIST

BACKER: LOH CHI YONG

He strode with haste and purpose into the centre of the holographic sphere and perched himself on a barren stool, without once taking his gaze from the projection. The colour-coded map laid bare the entirety of the Paradiso system, displaying blue for allies, red for enemies. There was a lot of red today.

A new wave of attackers had broken through the Acheron Blockade, with most of them now attempting planetfall. Zhiyong had been tasked to coordinate a tandem defence and several allied battalions were already on the move, although he was not so fast to judge; the projections were still inconclusive.

A cursory check of incoming reports from the Intermediate Blockade revealed that several ships were missing, prompting him to request an updated status list and warn all approaching vessels that hostiles were in the vicinity.

Zhiyong countermanded an order that would have automatically deployed a platoon of Zúyŏng Invincibles to the drop point of a ship tagged with EI aspects. Two platoons of light troops and supporting Hac Tao would have the honour of figuring out how to deal with them. The Zúyŏng were needed to protect a rear echelon water purification plant that was simultaneously put on high alert.

The list of incoming ships twisted again in the right-hand display of his glasses. Updated projections burst into existence, but not enough of them. Where were the rest? One vessel in blue – an Order of Santiago vessel named the Galicia Resplendent – caught his eye. Not part of the combat contingent, but its readout was flickering... why? Ah! The eruption of Mount Cristol!

Sending an attack warning to the Santiago, he opened a channel to his PanOceanian counterpart. "They're using the volcanic ash to disrupt our sensors. Diverting forces."

The Zúyŏng – their work already done at the water purification plant – were redeployed again, this time to the volcano. He'd have to trust that the Zhànshì mop-up squads could finish the job.

APPEARANCE

Zhiyong is a man in his early forties, though his youthful features make this hard to judge. His black hair is kept short, whilst his eyes are often ff behind glasses that serve a dual purpose as comlog displays.

ROLEPLAYING

- Cheery and talkative, but only shares vital information if necessary
- Continually formulating plans and projections
- Habitually adjusts his glasses while speaking

BACKGROUND

Tradition is a powerful force in Yu Jing society. As the son of two middle ranking party members, Zhiyong's career appeared set in stone from the day of his conception. His future lay clearly mapped out before him, and he hated what he saw. As an honourable son, however, he learned to accept what was to come, and perfected the proper reactions to any situation. No one ever took him by surprise. Not even his wife or his children.

He found escape in games of planning and strategy, from ancient classics to modern incarnations. During the NeoColonial Wars he participated in the Sakuramachi Go Tournament, and found himself – by at least seeming chance – seated opposite Sun Tze himself during an early round. He lost decisively, despite drawing black, and was disappointed in his rapid elimination. The next day, however, a high-ranking official requested his application for the strategic division of the StateArmy.

Training was intense, but his highly developed ability for prediction and an amiable nature ingratiated him with his military colleagues. Zhiyong has served his people in this function ever since, throughout most theatres of war. He openly admits that he finds pleasure in predicting difficult strategic matters, even though he is aware that many lives depend on these decisions.

He has made both good and bad calls, though luckily the former have outweighed the latter. Statistically speaking, his assignment to a theatre of operations improves the survival rate of troops by approximately ten percent, so there is no shortage of requests for his expertise.

STATS (ELITE)

ATTRIBUTES

AGI	AWA	BRW	COO	INT	PER	WIL
8	9	8	8	11	9	10

FIELDS OF EXPERTISE

Combat	+1	–	Movement	–	–	Social	+1	1
Fortitude	+1	–	Senses	+2	2	Technical	+2	2

DEFENCES

Firewall	11	Resolve	10	Vigour	8
Security	–	Morale	–	Armour	1

ATTACKS

- **Pistol**: Range R/C, 1+5 Ⓝ damage, Burst 1, 1H, Vicious 1

GEAR: Analysis Suite, AR Glasses, Armoured Clothing

SPECIAL ABILITIES

- **Deft Analyst**: Zhiyong sees the world through a strategist's eyes. He can reroll one d20 when making an Analysis test, but must accept the new result.
- **Diverting Forces**: Renowned for his ability to rapidly process information, Zhiyong is never without a backup plan. When spending Heat to call reinforcements, the GM reduces the total cost by two, to a minimum of 1 Heat spent. (If Zhiyong is incapacitated, the Gamemaster can no longer use his Diverting Forces ability.)
- **Urbane Chatter**: Zhiyong is comfortable amongst peers and strangers alike. He can reroll one d20 when making a social skills test, but must accept the new result.

TROLLHÄTTAN TROLL

The Human Sphere is fond of mythological trappings; Svalarheima more so than most. Discovered by the vessel *Midgard*, home to Fimbul Storms and Mjolnir's Handle, when massive lumbering simians were discovered in Trollhättan, there was really only one thing to call them.

But perhaps they should have chosen a different name.

A nightmare on two legs, these lumbering monstrosities have evolved to become the apex predator in the blasted wastelands of Trollhättan. Like giant, icy vultures, Trolls will also engage in pursuit predation - relentlessly dogging their prey's trail and waiting until they are too weak to fight back. Wasting no time in hunting, they secrete a digestive enzyme when attacking their prey; not only do Trolls not bother waiting for their victims to die before eating them, they don't even have the decency to chew.

ATTRIBUTES

AGI	AWA	BRW	COO	INT	PER	WIL
8	11	15	5	5	14	12

FIELDS OF EXPERTISE

Combat	+3	3	Movement	+1	1	Social	+1	1
Fortitude	+4	4	Senses	+1	1	Technical	–	–

DEFENCES

Firewall	N/A	Resolve	16	Vigour	19
Security	N/A	Morale	–	Armour	–

ATTACKS

- **Bludgeon**: Melee, 1+7 Ⓝ damage, Knockdown, Vicious 2
- **Digestion**: Melee (only against a grabbed target), 1+6 Ⓝ damage, Biotech, Toxic 2, Vicious 2

SPECIAL ABILITIES

- **Common Special Abilities**: Grasping, Fear 3, Inured to Cold, Monstrous
- **Alpha Predator**: When making a melee attack, the Trollhättan Troll can reroll up to 5 Ⓝ.

VARUNAN WATER-SNAKE

The *Laticauda musculus*, better known as the Varunan Water-Snake, is a venomous elapid serpent native to the shoals of Varuna, measuring between five and seven metres from fanged mouth to paddle-shaped tail, and roughly as wide around as the average human. While on the surface, these semi-aquatic serpents resemble Earth's anacondas — primarily in their size, diet, and use of constriction to hunt, they share many more traits with sea kraits, notably their impressive underwater mobility, and their deceptive speed when scaling rock faces.

Though venomous, their bite is used primarily when threatened; they prefer to subdue their prey by lying in wait near the coast, and suddenly pouncing. Able to coil and constrict their quarry with alarming speed, they often drag their victims back underwater, making short work of them. Their diet has long included Helots, and has expanded to include humans since their arrival on Varuna.

ATTRIBUTES

AGI	AWA	BRW	COO	INT	PER	WIL
12	14	13	5	5	5	9

FIELDS OF EXPERTISE

Combat	+2	2	Movement	+2	2	Social	–	–
Fortitude	–	–	Senses	+2	2	Technical	–	–

DEFENCES

Firewall	N/A	Resolve	9	Vigour	14
Security	N/A	Morale	–	Armour	–

ATTACKS

- **Pounce**: Melee, 1+5 Ⓝ damage, Unforgiving 4, Subtle 2
- **Constriction**: Melee (only against a grabbed target), 2+6 Ⓝ damage, Stun, Vicious 3
- **Venomous Bite**: Melee, 1+6 Ⓝ damage, Biotech, Toxic 2, Vicious 2

SPECIAL ABILITIES

- **Common Special Abilities**: Grasping, Night Vision
- **Ambush Predator**: When attacking from the Hidden State, the Water-Snake adds 2d20 to melee attacks.
- **Ensnaring Coils**: Attempts to escape a Water-Snake's grasp are at +1 difficulty.

PROGRAM TEMPLATES

Hackers have a great deal of flexibility in the programming load outs they choose for their hacking devices. Adversaries are no exception to this. Throughout the *Adversaries* chapter, therefore, stat blocks will only list the specific hacking device typically used by a particular type of adversary. These hacking devices can then be combined with one of the program templates listed below. This will allow the GM to rapidly customize their hacker NPCs, and get maximum utility out of Infowar-focused adversaries like Evo Troopers (p. 433), Reverend Moiras (p. 452), and Wardrivers (p. 461), along with any other NPCs who might want to employ a hacking device.

ASSAULT HACKING DEVICE

- *Black Hat*: IC-1 Black ICE, CLAW-1 Blackout, CLAW-3 Total Control

- *TAG-Killer*: IC 1 Countermeasures, CLAW-2 Expel, CLAW-2 Oblivion, CLAW-3 Basilisk

- *Wight*: IC-1 Hivemines, CLAW 2 Oblivion, CLAW-3 Carbonite

DEFENSIVE / WHITE HACKING DEVICE

- *Meticulous Admin*: IC-3 Crybaby, IC-3 Redtape, SHIELD-3 Counterstrike

- *Rook*: IC-3 Countermeasures, SHIELD-1 Exorcism, SHIELD-1 U-Turn, SHIELD-3 Counterstrike

- *White Hat*: IC-3 Countermeasures, SHIELD-1 Exorcism, SHIELD-2 Breakwater, SHIELD-3 Zero Pain

EI HACKING DEVICE

- *Halo Hunter*: CLAW 2 Oblivion, SWORD-1 Slasher, SWORD-2 Redrum, SHIELD-2 Breakwater

- *Mindworm*: CLAW-2 Oblivion, IC-3 Mirrormaze, SWORD-2 Trinity

- *Pax*: CLAW 2 Expel, SHIELD-1 Exorcism, SHIELD-1 U-Turn, SWORD-2 Redrum

HACKING DEVICE

- *Combat Support*: CLAW-1 Spotlight, GADGET-1 Controlled Jump, GADGET-1 Fairy Dust, SHIELD-1 U-Turn

- *Infiltrator*: CLAW-1 Blackout, CLAW-1 Overlord, GADGET-1 Lockpicker, SWORD-1 Slasher

- *Lurking Admin*: CLAW-1 Brain Blast, IC-1 Deadfall, IC-1 Redtape, SWORD-1 Slasher

- *Remote Jockey*: GADGET-2 Assisted Fire, GADGET-2 Enhanced Reaction, SHIELD-1 Exorcism

HACKING DEVICE PLUS

- *D.F.A*: IC-2 Black ICE, CLAW-2 Expel, GADGET-1 Controlled Jump, SHIELD-2 Breakwater

- *Grey Hat*: CLAW-2 Oblivion, IC-2 Gaslight, SHIELD-2 Breakwater, SWORD-1 Brain Blast

- *Infiltrator Plus*: CLAW-2 Oblivion, GADGET-1 Lockpicker, SHIELD-2 Breakwater, SWORD-2 Trinity

KILLER HACKING DEVICE

- *MIRV*: IC-1 Hivemines, IC-1 Deadfall, SWORD-2 Skullbuster

- *Redcap*: IC-1 Red Tape, SWORD-1 Slasher, SWORD-2 Redrum

- *Czar*: IC-1 Black ICE, SWORD-2 Trinity

infinity
THE ROLEPLAYING GAME

NAME

PLAYER

FACTION

HOMEWORLD

HERITAGE

SOCIAL STATUS

INFINITY POINTS

REFRESH

REACTION TRACKER

DAMAGE BONUS

	MELEE	RANGED
PSYWAR		
INFOWAR		

XP

TOTAL	SPENT

DEFENCES

SECURITY	MORALE	BTS

FIREWALL

HEAD 1-2

RIGHT ARM 3-5

LEFT ARM 6-8

TORSO 9-14

RIGHT LEG 15-17

LEFT LEG 18-20

DAMAGE

BREACHES

RESOLVE

METANOIA

VIGOUR

WOUNDS

ARMOUR EQUIPPED

QUALITIES

HARM EFFECTS

ATTRIBUTES & SKILLS

AGILITY

SKILL	SIGNATURE	EXP	FOC	TN
ACROBATICS				
CLOSE COMBAT				
STEALTH				

AWARENESS

SKILL	SIGNATURE	EXP	FOC	TN
ANALYSIS				
EXTRAPLANETARY				
OBSERVATION				
SURVIVAL				
THIEVERY				

BRAWN

SKILL	SIGNATURE	EXP	FOC	TN
ATHLETICS				
RESISTANCE				

COORDINATION

SKILL	SIGNATURE	EXP	FOC	TN
BALLISTICS				
PILOT				
SPACECRAFT				

INTELLIGENCE

SKILL	SIGNATURE	EXP	FOC	TN
EDUCATION				
HACKING				
MEDICINE				
PSYCHOLOGY				
SCIENCE				
TECH				

PERSONALITY

SKILL	SIGNATURE	EXP	FOC	TN
ANIMAL HANDLING				
COMMAND				
LIFESTYLE				
PERSUADE				

WILLPOWER

SKILL	SIGNATURE	EXP	FOC	TN
DISCIPLINE				

GEIST

GEIST NAME

	AGI	AWA	BRW	COO	INT	PER	WIL

DEFENCES

FIREWALL		RESOLVE		STRUCTURE
SECURITY		MORALE		ARMOUR

HARMS

BREACHES		METANOIA		FAULTS

SKILL	EXP	FOC	TN

SKILL	EXP	FOC	TN

TRAITS

1	4
2	5
3	6

FACTION HANDLER

IDENTITY

FACTION

CONTACT PROTOCOL

COVERT OBJECTIVE

WEAPONS

WEAPON NAME

RANGE	DAMAGE	BURST	SIZE	AMMO

QUALITIES

WEAPON NAME

RANGE	DAMAGE	BURST	SIZE	AMMO

QUALITIES

TALENTS

NAME	SKILL	RANKS
EFFECT		

NAME	SKILL	RANKS
EFFECT		

NAME	SKILL	RANKS
EFFECT		

NAME	SKILL	RANKS
EFFECT		

NAME	SKILL	RANKS
EFFECT		

NAME	SKILL	RANKS
EFFECT		

NAME	SKILL	RANKS
EFFECT		

NAME	SKILL	RANKS
EFFECT		

NAME	SKILL	RANKS
EFFECT		

NAME	SKILL	RANKS
EFFECT		

NAME	SKILL	RANKS
EFFECT		

NAME	SKILL	RANKS
EFFECT		

NAME	SKILL	RANKS
EFFECT		

HOST

TYPE	AGI	AWA	BRW	COO	INT	PER	WIL

AUGMENTATIONS

NAME	TYPE	LOCATION

HOST ATTRIBUTES

CHARACTER DESCRIPTION

HEIGHT	WEIGHT	HAIR	EYES

GEAR

NAME	ASSETS	EARNINGS	CASHFLOW	SHORTFALLS
		QUANTITY	MAINT	

AMMUNITION

AMMO	CATEGORY	RELOADS
QUALITIES		

AMMO	CATEGORY	RELOADS
QUALITIES		

AMMO	CATEGORY	RELOADS
QUALITIES		

AMMO	CATEGORY	RELOADS
QUALITIES		

RESOURCES

NAME	QUANTITY

iNFiNiTY
THE ROLEPLAYING GAME

CHARACTER ADDENDUM

BACKGROUND

AGE		LANGUAGES

LIFEPATH CHARACTERISTICS

FAMILY SOCIAL STATUS	
HOME ENVIRONMENT	
YOUTH EVENT	
EDUCATION	
ADOLESCENT EVENT	
FIRST CAREER	
SECOND CAREER	
THIRD CAREER	
FOURTH CAREER	

PREVIOUS FACTIONS	

ADDITIONAL LIFEPATH NOTES / EVENTS

ADDITIONAL INFORMATION

PORTRAIT

LIFESTYLES

NAME	RATING	MAINT

FAMILY

PARENTS	
SPOUSE	
SIBLINGS	
CHILDREN	
EXTENDED FAMILY	

FAKE IDs

NAME	RATING

PERSONALITY

LIKES	
DISLIKES	
QUIRKS	
PHOBIAS	
CATCHPHRASES & BATTLE CRIES	

CONTACTS

NAME	NOTES

ADDITIONAL TALENTS

NAME	SKILL	RANKS
EFFECT		

NAME	SKILL	RANKS
EFFECT		

NAME	SKILL	RANKS
EFFECT		

NAME	SKILL	RANKS
EFFECT		

NAME	SKILL	RANKS
EFFECT		

NAME	SKILL	RANKS
EFFECT		

NAME	SKILL	RANKS
EFFECT		

NAME	SKILL	RANKS
EFFECT		

NAME	SKILL	RANKS
EFFECT		

NAME	SKILL	RANKS
EFFECT		

NAME	SKILL	RANKS
EFFECT		

HACKING DEVICE

	CLAW	SWORD	SHIELD	GADGET	IC

DEVICE PROGRAMS

NAME	DAMAGE	QUALITIES / SPECIAL EFFECTS

ADDITIONAL WEAPONS

WEAPON NAME

RANGE	DAMAGE	BURST	SIZE	AMMO
QUALITIES				

WEAPON NAME

RANGE	DAMAGE	BURST	SIZE	AMMO
QUALITIES				

WEAPON NAME

RANGE	DAMAGE	BURST	SIZE	AMMO
QUALITIES				

WEAPON NAME

RANGE	DAMAGE	BURST	SIZE	AMMO
QUALITIES				

ADDITIONAL GEAR

NAME	QUANTITY	MAINT

NOTES

ADVERSARY

DESCRIPTION

NOTES

ADVERSARY NAME

AGI	AWA	BRW	COO	INT	PER	WIL

FIELDS OF EXPERTISE

COMBAT		MOVEMENT		SOCIAL	
FORTITUDE		SENSES		TECHNICAL	

DEFENCES

FIREWALL		RESOLVE		VIGOUR	
SECURITY		MORALE		ARMOUR	

HARMS

BREACHES		METANOIA		WOUNDS	

ATTACK NAME

RANGE	DAMAGE	BURST	SIZE	AMMO

QUALITIES

ATTACK NAME

RANGE	DAMAGE	BURST	SIZE	AMMO

QUALITIES

ATTACK NAME

RANGE	DAMAGE	BURST	SIZE	AMMO

QUALITIES

GEAR

SPECIAL ABILITIES

REMOTE

REMOTE NAME

AGI	AWA	BRW	COO	INT	PER	WIL

FIELDS OF EXPERTISE

COMBAT	MOVEMENT	SENSES	SOCIAL
FORTITUDE			TECHNICAL

DEFENCES

FIREWALL	RESOLVE	STRUCTURE
SECURITY	MORALE	ARMOUR

HARMS

BREACHES	METANOIA	FAULTS

ATTACK NAME

RANGE	DAMAGE	BURST	SIZE	AMMO
QUALITIES				

ATTACK NAME

RANGE	DAMAGE	BURST	SIZE	AMMO
QUALITIES				

ATTACK NAME

RANGE	DAMAGE	BURST	SIZE	AMMO
QUALITIES				

GEAR

SPECIAL ABILITIES

DESCRIPTION

NOTES

GEIST

GEIST NAME

AGI	AWA	BRW	COO	INT	PER	WIL

DEFENCES

FIREWALL	RESOLVE	STRUCTURE
SECURITY	MORALE	ARMOUR

HARMS

BREACHES

METANOIA	FAULTS

SKILL	EXP	FOC	TN		SKILL	EXP	FOC	TN

TRAITS

1	
2	
3	
4	
5	
6	

TALENTS

NAME		SKILL	RANKS
EFFECT			
NAME		SKILL	RANKS
EFFECT			
NAME		SKILL	RANKS
EFFECT			
NAME		SKILL	RANKS
EFFECT			
NAME		SKILL	RANKS
EFFECT			
NAME		SKILL	RANKS
EFFECT			
NAME		SKILL	RANKS
EFFECT			

AR AVATAR

ROLEPLAYING

BACKGROUND

OTHER NOTES

INFINITY
BACKERS

A Curtis, A Thomson, A.T., Aaron, Aaron A Gonzales, Aaron England, Aaron Fortner, Aaron J. Schrader, Aaron J. Wong, Aaron Mitton, Aaron Pothecary, Aaron 'Random' Brown, Aaron Reimer, Aaron Smithies, Aaron Weinz, Aaron Woodside, Abba Elfman, Abel "SrProu" Vázquez Bayón, Abhishek Ray, Abraham Garcia, Abstract Turtle, Abydog, ace, Adam "Ace" Krump, Adam "Yuusha" Peters, Adam (Minmax) Abramson, Adam Ackerman, Adam Atencio, Adam Benedict Canning, Adam Bienvenu, Adam Bysko, Adam Cortes, Adam Crumpton, Adam Ezra, Adam Hyz, Adam I. Shagan, Adam Kibbler, Adam Masishin, Adam Neisius, Adam Paciorek, Adam R Johnson, Adam R. Stein, Adam Reynolds, Adam Richardson, Adam 'Rolo' Rolan, Adam Skelton, Adam Swift, Adam Walck, Adam Waller, Adam Whitworth, Adam, Peter & Emma Spence, Admael Stark, Admiral JCJ Farley, Adnan Ali Khan Choudhury, Adrià Antón Peidró, Adrián Muñoz Antón, Adrian Praetorius, adumbratus, Adventurer's Quarter, Aeious, Aeyran, AikasMX, AikiGhost, Aiwe & Indael, AixAthanatos, Aj Comfort, AJ Whitfield, Åke Argéus, Akesh, Akrabat The Goblin, Al Shirey, Alain Sarti, Alain Y. Poli, Alan Borthwick, Alan Jaeger, Alan Klaebel Weisdorf, Alan Mort, Alan Washburn, AlaNegra, Alasdair MacIver, Alastair "dulydude" Duly, Albek, Alberto Elortegui, Alberto Maran, Alberto Mosquera Villarino, Alcethenecromancer, Alec MacKinnon, Alejandro, Alejandro Dell'Olio, Alejandro J. Sánchez Sotano, Alejandro Luna Martínez, Alejandro Villagrana, Alesander Robleño, Alessandro Arduino, Alessandro Bertuccelli, Alessandro Guardigli, Alessandro Pantani, Alex, Alex "Nailbomb" Donald, Alex Bast Jensen, Alex Born, Alex Char, Alex Cropp, Alex Erhardt, Alex Fashandi, Alex Geiger-Wagner, Alex Hagerman, Alex Kartzoff, Alex Koza, Alex Lexxman Fueller, Alex Manduley, Alex Osborne, Alex R, Alex Redshaw, Alex Sawinski, Alex Sinkowski, Alex Torres, Alex Tynan, Alex Withycombe, Alexander, Alexander "F9SSS" Loginov, Alexander Allan, Alexander Ballis, Alexander Brethouwer, Alexander Chan, Alexander Chang, Alexander Eriksson, Alexander Gage, Alexander Gray, Alexander Herbert, Alexander Howell, Alexander K. Haynes, Alexander Kunze, Alexander Landmann, Alexander Lang, Alexander Mole, Alexander Sawyer, Alexander Shvarts, Alexandre "Magnamagister" Joly, Alexandre Bouchard, Alexandre Dupuis, Alexandre Larivee, Alexandre SAUTER, Alexandrite Draconis, Alexey "Ariwch" Ksenzov, Alexis [Khalaiiss] Stacke, Alfonso Botas, Alin, Alistair Cleave, Alistair Gillies, Alistair Higgins, Allan Wilson, Allen "Wildchevy" Emlet, Allen Cantrell, Allen Guise, Alninio, Alosia Sellers, Aloysius Ewing, Alphaspel, Alphatier, Altorinne, Álvaro Canda Tovar, Álvaro López Aránguez, Álvaro Marfil, Álvaro Sánchez Gómez, Alwin Penterman, Amber Ryan, Amertes, Amie kievit, Amonchakai, Anarkhan, Anastasia Patterson & Garrett O'brien, Anders Björnberg, Anders Vestermark, Anderson Saw, André "Hoargald" Kleilein, André Buchheim, Andre Feliz, Andre Harmon, Andre Herpertz, Andre J, André Kießelbach, André Norell, Andre/Ryan, Andrea Carbone, Andrea Dalle Vedove, Andrea Filisetti, Andrea Gualano, Andrea Pedrani, Andrea Peruggini, Andrea Sasso, Andreas, Andreas "Dante" Timel, Andreas ESSO Jensen, Andreas Felde, Andreas Gruber, Andreas Hötzel, Andreas K., Andreas Lundmark, AndreRow87, Andres Villaseca, Andreu Albert Correa, Andrew "Ikomajedi" Howell, Andrew Bailey, Andrew Bowles, Andrew Brandt, Andrew Broxham, Andrew C., Andrew Campbell, Andrew Comery, Andrew Craghead, Andrew Cumming, Andrew Deignan, Andrew Don, Andrew Doucet, Andrew Dynon, Andrew Gorman, Andrew Gould, Andrew Green, Andrew Guentert, Andrew J Garbade, Andrew J. Hayford, Andrew Jankovic, Andrew 'JoeKano' Godde, Andrew Johnson, Andrew Knipfer, Andrew Laliberte, Andrew Lewis, Andrew Lloyd, Andrew Lubich, Andrew MacD, Andrew Markell, Andrew Marshall, Andrew McKinney, Andrew Moreton, Andrew Newton, Andrew Ng Yun Ru, Andrew Niekamp, Andrew P. Moore, Andrew Parent, Andrew Pearson, Andrew Puchnin, Andrew R Bussey, Andrew Rout, Andrew Sinclair, Andrew Travers, Andrew Urbanski, Andrew viking Gill, Andrew Wells, Andrew 'whitenoise' Rogers, Andrew Zucker, Andrey 'asm0dai' Lazarev, Andy Akins, Andy Bethell, Andy Dorman, Andy el Sabio, Andy G, Andy Nicholson, Andy Rennard, Andy Slack, Andy Walmsley, AndyE, Anestis Kozakis, Aneurin ap John Williams-Harrow, Angel "Badgerfish" Llera, Ángel L. Jarillo (ALJO), Ángel Osuna (Conanelectronico), Angela Nichols, Angelic Despot, Angelo Pileggi, Angry norwegians, Annette, Anson LeBrid Bird, Antero, Anthony "Fixer" Hansen, Anthony "Infornographie" Avila, Anthony 'Anfernee' Mason, Anthony Careatti, Anthony Contoleon, Anthony Craig Senatore, Anthony Funaro, Anthony Howell, Anthony Marks, Anthony Pavone, Anthony Trainer, Anthony Wilson (Ouchies), ANTi-GRAV, antoine (eorl) BISCH, Antoni Diaz, Antonin Dussaix, Antonio Ignacio Gutiérrez Caride, Antonio Martín Yuste, Antonio Perez Sanchez, Antonio Rodriguez Lopez, Antonio Sánchez Sánchez (Jehuty), Antonio Santos, Antti Ilmavirta, Antti Kautiainen, Antwan R, Aoren, apHywel, Apocryphal Lore, Arakas, Arckane, Ardegrath, Aric Wieder, Arjan de Koning, Arkhosh, Armihaul, Arnau "Duncan" Pérez-Torné, Arno.Nico.Steph, Aron Britchford, Aron Bud Burton, Aron Hoskins, Arron Hooks, Arthur "SebsokK" Duthoo, Arthur Chang, Arthur Gibbs, ArthurDent, ArTrodes, Artur Jeziorski, Arvin "KAZEfirst" Kayz, Ash Brown, Ashley "Warpstone" Barrot, Asier Serras Gorostizagoiza, Asociación 6D6, Associazione Cavalieri Dell'Esagono - Trieste, atarola, Atlictoatl, Attila 'Atis' Bodrogi, Aubrey Knight, Aurioch, Austin Enriquez, Australoup, Avelino J. Avelenda, Aven Lee, Avery Lee, Aviad Madar, AVS, Axelle Vidal, Aymeric DORIDOU, Ayron Atkinson, Azhacael, B. Griffiths, BA Sparks, Bad Syntax, Badula, Baiyuan, Bajorque aka Anne-Sylvie, Baradaelin, Barney Hanlon (shrikeh), Barrie Voice, Barry Gingell, Barry Watson, Bart Kersteter, Bartosz "Asar" Skorupa, Bartosz "Stoperssonn" Stopczyk, Basil Lisk, Bastian Dornauf, Batronoban, Bawon Samdi, BD Davis, BeardedBrigand, Beerbarian, Belakar, Ben Bogaerts, Ben Corcoran, Ben Cunningham, Ben Drake, Ben Franzen, Ben Frost, Ben Hayes, Ben Jones, Ben Lambert, Ben 'Red Rook' Nettleship, Ben Rogers, Ben Rowe, Ben Seager, ben shultz, Ben Sorrie, Ben Stones, Ben Warner, Ben Wood, Benj 'kerberos' Hanson, Benjamin Kenner, Benjamin Koch, Benjamin W Royal, Benn Graybeaton, Benoît "Aybarra" Pisani, Benoit Heslouin, Bentley, Bernardo Tacchini, Bernd Sommeregger, Bernd W.E. Petermann, Bernie, Bertrand Dehouck, Beto Serna, Bibi, Bill Heron, Billy Clabough, Billy 'wildbill' Young, BionicRope, Björn Berg, Björn Löb, Björn Söderström, black2k, BlackTalon 588, Blair MacDougall, Blake Graumann, Blake Jolly, Blake McCormack, Blangis, blix, BlkBunny, bluesickboy (N8), Bo Fahlberg Madsen, Bob Fletcher, Theo McGuckin and Noah Ingram, Bob Huss, Bob Lewis, Bob McConnell, Bob Munsil, Bob Thomas, Bobby Erlichman, Boman Hwang, Bomster, Bonsai, Boon Hwee "Bonkers" Yeo, Börds, Borednlost, Boring Sid, Boris Rothmund, Boris Volk, boxer6, Brad Bell, Brad Clark, Brad D. Kane, Brad Evans, Brad Hickman, Brad Kim, Brad Madden, Brad Petrie, Bradley Bennett, Bradley Dunn, Bradley Ingram, Bradley Lyons, Brady Cox, Brady Webb, Bram Dyckmans, Brandon "Xar" McKee, Brandon Boulter, Brandon Busby, Brandon Hodgins, Brandon K. Fero, Brandon Kreager, Brandon Morgan, Brandon Robinson, Brandon Tneh, Brant & Calhon Waterson, Brax, Braz, brazil808, Bremy, Brendan Hutchison, Brendan Murphy, Brendan O'Connor, Brendan Toliver, Brennan Dawson, Brennan See, Brent "Quorum Of 4" Ahern, Brent Evans, Brent Shadwell, Brepost, Brett Adams, Brett Easterbrook, Brett Tennant and Ryan Hart, Brian "Lexington" Solomon, Brian "Snugs" Stout, Brian "The Gnome" D., Brian A. Nichols, Brian Boese, Brian Browne, Brian Collins, Brian 'Doc Bacon' Smith, Brian Fowler, Brian Freund, Brian Hart, Brian Kirchhoff, Brian L Smith, Brian Orban, Brian Pugh, Brian Ross Edwards, Brian Skov-Nielsen, Brian Stelter, Brian Woods, Brittle, Brody "Madzerker" States, Brother Domitian, Brother Faust, Brother Knight Manuel A. Moya of the Holy Sepulcher Military order, Bruce Turner, Bryan D., Bryan Harclerode, Bryan Launier, Bryan Patraw, Bryan Zancanella, Bryce Bonzo, Bryce Deakin, Bryce Undy, Bryton Tateishi, BuckDharma, Bucky0, Buddajaxx Brothwood, Bulleye, Burke Snow, burningcrow, Burny, Buscador95, Byron Bornhorst, Byron D. Molix, C Scarr, "Casata Lannister" Infinity Combat Group - Alessandria, C. B. Ash, C. MacLean, C. Preston Richards, C.J. Hill, C.Whelan, Caleb Gordon, Caleb Twitchell, Calibur_ex, Calindor, Callum Smith, Cam G, Cameron "Khalus" Haggett, Cameron A McGinley, Cameron Wassom, Caoimhe Brennan, Captain Agrippa, Captain Pipebeard, Captain Protagon,

Captian Ahab, Cargo Manshark, Carl Beard, Carl Grant Lehmann, Carl Powell, Carl Tees, Carlo Desiderio Zanella, Carlo Krebs, Carlos "Eddorre" Rodriguez, Carlos "Pyttman" Mangas, Carlos Calabuig, Carlos Manuel Luna Cuenca, Carlos Mimoso, Carlos Restrepo, Carlos the Dwarf, Carsten "semiomant" Husek, Carsten Bärmann, Carter Brent AKA Wrathmaur, Casey Gilliland, Casey Goss (Deltabeoulve), Casey Roberts, Casper Fertier, Casper Raundorf, Cassiar Beaver, Caz and Del, CBudworth, CE Chua, Cedric "Cedwfox" FERRUT, Cedric "Le Dindon" Gillmann, Cédric "Lilan" LIGEONNET, Cedric dubbiosi, CelestialDoggie, Celoy, Cesare Verzini, Chad Bartlett, Chad Booth, Chad Verrall, Chance Medlin, Chaoran Cheng, Chaosmeister, Chaosnight, Chaostroll, Charles "Dreamstreamer" Alston, Charles Coleman, Charles Kinter, Charles Shepherd, Charles Sousa, Charles St-Laurent, Charles Tibbals, Charles Wilkinson, Charlie Heckman, Charlie St Clair, Charno, Chase Murphy, Chase Smith, Che "UbiquitousRat" Webster, Cheston P. Keck, Chip Dickerson, Choucas, Chrarm, Chris "Durty B" Broeska, Chris "Grimtooth" Colborn, Chris "Jimmy2Shot" Grinstead, Chris "The Tilean" Mumford, Chris A Challacombe, Chris A. Johnson, Chris Adams, Chris Avery, Chris Ball, Chris Barney, Chris Buck, Chris Carpenter, Chris Chambers, Chris Charlton II, Chris Collins, Chris Corvus, Chris D, Chris Dorfschmidt, Chris Dunn, Chris Edwards, Chris Halverson, Chris Hartford, Chris Hodge, Chris Jackson, Chris Jarratt, Chris Johnson, Chris Kenna, Chris Kornfeld, Chris Laude, Chris Law, Chris Maggard, Chris Matthews, Chris May, Chris Menking, Chris Michael Jahn, Chris Milne (aka Milney), Chris Mitchell, Chris Moak, Chris Naj, Chris Newman, Chris Otton, Chris Parson, Chris piatt, Chris Poon, Chris Rouse, Chris Snyder, Chris Sousa, Chris Thomas, Chris V., Chris Visser, Chris Walker, Chris Welsh, Chris Young, Chris 'Yvraith' Barton, Christer, Christer Malmberg, Christian "Cohinor" Krieger, Christian & Hendrik Klee, Christian "Corvus" Häusler, Christian A. Nord, Christian Curado, Christian Douven, Christian Klinkewitz, Christian Lacerte, Christian Mejstrik, Christian Ø.Jensen, Christian Probst, Christian Svalander, Christian Taylor, Christian van den Boom, Christian Weinert, Christoph B., Christoph 'Keladryel' Schrage, Christoph Sueka, christophe ECKENFELS, Christopher Avery, Christopher Barney, Christopher Barrett, Christopher Bohdaniuk, Christopher Cecil, Christopher Corayer, Christopher Curtis de Diego, Christopher D. Garland, Christopher Evans, Christopher Feola, Christopher Fodge, Christopher Gebhart, Christopher Goundry, Christopher Gunning, Christopher Harris, Christopher J. Lees, Christopher L Jones, Christopher L. Moore, Christopher Malone, Christopher Niziol, Christopher Reid, Christopher Sanders, Christopher Segerson, Christopher Weuve, Christopher Willett, Christopher Wordekemper, Chrystian Silva, Chuck Cordivano, Chuck Rodgers, CJ Brenner, Claude Westmoreland, Claudius Sol, Claus Bo Christensen, Clayton Schmitt, Clifford Cordingley, Clinton Williams, Clio51, Clive Parkin, Clunker, Clyde Lee Graham, Cobra Burbuja, Cody A. Hobbs, Cody Black, Cofradía del Dragón, Cole "Martok" Olson, Cole Webber, Colen McAlister, Coleslaw, Colgrevance, Colin Brook, Colin Chapman, Colin Lloyd, Colin M Morrison, Colin Miller, Colin Padgett Arnold, Colin Pyle, Colin Thomas, Coman "Niraco" Razvan, Companero, Confanity, Connor Butler, Connor Holden, Connor Kelly, Conor degroot, Conor Warde, Constantí Montsó i Cadena, Constantin Patrascu, Constanze Schmidt-Sinn, Corey Gajajiva, Corey Spillis, Cornelius Milertens, Corvo Lee, Cory "Korva" Cass, Cory Cook, Cottar "Nnay" Yann, Count Thalim, crabmancer, Craig "Stevo" Stephenson, Craig Gaddis, Craig Irvine, Craig J. Morgan, Craig Namvar, Craig Richards, Craig Wright, CraigS, Crazy French guy, Crazy Paul, CrazyBaldHead, Crazypaul, Create And Play - Gregor Lengsfeld, Creative play and podcast Network, Cristiano Tomba, Cristobal Mera, Crossbones, Crunkbeard, Cryoban, CS20Gaming, Cullen Knappen, Curt Loudon, Czech Drop Team, D. Böhmer, D. Hargart, D. Heckman, D. McElroy, D. S. Kelly, d.factorial, DJ. Safady, D.M. Whitten, Da_Baron, DaBoss, Daenauriel Fakespike, Dagda, Daixomaku, Daje,né Club!, Dale C. Blessing, Dalmat Red, Dalton weir, Damian Fitzpatrick, Damian Leszek Jaśkiewicz, Damiel, Damien Gour, Damien Porter, Dan, Dan "Sandwich" Adams, Dan Aguirre-Zeder, Dan Bennett, Dan Friis-Christensen, Dan Gimmelli, Dan Grothe, Dan Hope, Dan Jones, Dan Kotlewski, Dan Massey, Dan Molzan, Dan Rees, Dan Reilly, Dan Sprietzer, Dangerousllama, Dani Havn, Daniel "Bane of Humanity" Blais, Daniel B. Nissman, Daniel Bauer, Daniel Belfrage-Young, Daniel Bell, Daniel Berglund, Daniel 'Berli' Brown, Daniel Brewer, Daniel Brian England, Daniel Casey O'Donovan, Daniel Coto Rodríguez (TirMcdhol), Daniel Crisp, Daniel Díaz Capó, Daniel Domke, Daniel Dönigus, Daniel Fruchterman, Daniel Gaghan, Daniel Gardiner, Daniel Granstrand, Daniel Gregory, Daniel Grigg, Daniel H., Daniel Herink, Daniel Hermle, Daniel HUERTOS, Daniel Ing, Daniel Joelsson, Daniel John Richardson, Daniel jun, Daniel L Thompson, Daniel Leggett, Daniel Martindale, Daniel Melchin, Daniel Mortensen, Daniel Mosley, Daniel O, Daniel Plastic Caton, Daniel Ridley, Daniel Scheuss, Daniel Scholefield, Daniel Shaw, Daniel Sturgiss, Daniel T. Kulhanek, Daniel Thornton and Matthew Young, Daniel Whitmee, Daniel Wilkinson, Daniel Willuweit, Daniel Wixson, Daniel Yauger, Daniele "I'Biondo" Ermini, Danny Babin, Danny Seedhouse, Danny Tan, dansterd, Dante Sanders, Darien "SabotSsnake" Liddell, Darin Belcher, Dario Vojnic, Dariusz Wesołowski, Darkside, Darnok, Darren, Darren "littlebear" Pearce, Darren Buckley, Darryl Roberds, das_ninja, Dasha Melnikova & Egor Zajcev, DaSilva, Dave, Dave "Felix" Pike, Dave "KingDaveTheBest" Hood, Dave "Mefisto" Laithwaite, Dave "Obscuro" Ward, Dave "Wintergreen" Harrison, Dave Duerschlag, Dave Edwards, Dave Godwin, Dave Holliday, Dave Kelly, Dave Keyser, Dave Muench, Dave Pinches, Dave Satterthwaite, Dave Schatz, Dave Seitz, Dave Stolarski, Dave Tiberius Curran, Davezilla Chris Sprules, David "Cervantes3773" Seley, David "Claidhmor" Garbowski, David "Kodo" Codosero, David "MarcoSkoll" Fincher, David "Overkill" Peers, David "Zleapy" Rindbäck, David A. Baird, David Abad Vich, David Andrews, David Bayless, David Berry, David Blount, David Briski, David Bruce, David 'Bunniegodd' Webster, David Chervanik, David Clarke, David Cousins, David Dalton, David Dauterive, David E Durrett Jr, David Ellery, David Fernàndez López, David Flores Pires, David Fry II, David Gibbings, David Gröbner, David Haidon, David Harrison, David Hibbs, David J. Clark, David Johnston, David Khoo, David Kirlin, David Lamarre, David Lavictoire, David Leong, Adi Farhan Jumali, Joshua Tan and Timothy Leong, David Lyons, David Marc Gardiner, David McGuire, David Morgans, David Morris, David N Stevens, David Nadj, David O., David Ogea, David P. Karcher III, David Paul Guzmán, David R Cunningham, David R. Graham, David Rache, David Rhode, David Rolton, David Schweighofer, David Snart, David 'Spin' Springbett, David Stewart, David Stillberg, David Trew, David Un, David W Smith, David W. Kaufman II, David Waldron, David Whitworth, David Wilcox, David Wolf, Davide, Dawfydd Kelly, Dawid Kępa, Dean Brown, Dean Burling,Dean Harvey, Dean Kirkpatrick, Declan Ellery, Dee Ramsey, Deep_Winter, delirium, Demarcosg, Demihuman, Denis Darwish, Denis Frédéric-Martin, Denis Großmann, Dennis D. Carter, Dennis K. Cross, Dennis Kieper, Dennis Kripzak, Dennis McCollum, Dennis Ovens, Dennis Rx, Dennis Seeliger, Dennis Walter, Denny "the_eldar" Buhle, Denny Yan, Derek Briscoe, Derek Carnell, Derek D Young (Winnipeg, Canada), Derek Fleetwood, Derek Hand, Derek Martin, Derek Mayne, Derek Schmidt, Derek Stiles, Derrick Cochran, Derrick Schwartz, Deshkorgos, Despoulain F-Xavier, Dess, Deven Selikha Tooze, Devon "Popinfrsh" Golub, Dewar Gray Peterkin, Dhed Jr, Dice Saloon, Diego (Oda) Tomé, Diego Morales Quintana, Diego Moura, Dietmar Böhmer, Dillon Burke, Dimitri Achminov, Diodoro Alegre Ontavilla, Dirk Keienburg, Dirk Koch, Dirk Lancer, Dirk Lange, Dirk Vanleeuw, Dittrich Christoph, Dizzy, DJ & Leigh Rost, Dj Ludowici, Dmitrij "DTR" Semionov, Dmitry Bogdanov, Dmitry Ryabchuk, Dom "by the tentacles" Toghill, Domenico Radogna Ermes Cellot, Dominic "Domo" Woods, Dominic A. Nursey, Dominic Rawle, Dominic wai, Dominik "Frischi" Frischknecht, Dominique 'Dee' Hendrikx, Domus, Don, Don Penney, Donald Gardner, Donald Johnson, Donald Lang, Donald Trump, Donavon Boyd, Dongkyu Uh, DonGlo, Donnie Rose, Dorian Knight, Dorian Zaharia, Dorothy Sich, Doug Hooker, Doug McKerracher, Douglas "Dahigi" Grimes, Douglas Gardiner, Douglas Hamilton, Douglas Jessup, Douglas Laedtke, Douglas M. Akin, Douglas Triggs, Dr JW, Dr. Arnd Felten, Dr. Christian Brandt, Dr. David Rodríguez Sanfiorenzo, Dr. Edward Guernica, Dr. Seth A Jones, Dragon's Lair Comics & Fantasy, Dragon's Lair Comics & Fantasy®, Dragonstriker, Dreamseed, Drew Hallenbeck, Drew M., Drew Pearson, Drew Pessarchick, Dropzone Games, Dru Pifel, Drungdrakki, Duatha, Dujek Onearm, DukeFluffy, DumbparameciuM, Duncan "Dude" Wright, Duncan K Wong, Duncan Parton, Duncan Stewart, Duncan Watson, Duncan Webster, Dunni, Dustin Rector, Dwayne Hauser, Dylan "Varis" Svedvik, Dylan Chesworth, Dylan Friesen, Dylan Gould, Dylan Rogers, Dylan Stowell, E Bateman, E Whitten, e. carletti, eadbasher, Eammon Grosek, Eamon Duffy, Eamon Sheehy, Ed Kowalczewski, Ed Lykos, Ed andomOne, Ed Ross, Ed Vetter, Eddie Ho, Eden Janissen, Edgar G Flores, Edouard Foraz (Jean-edou Artwork), Eduardo Lasso Lajarin, Edward "MilesAnP" Miles, Edward Deguzman, Edward E Cook, Edward Gray, Edward Saxton, Edward Sykes, Edwin Wessels, Eero Bodien, Eganra, Eika Forge, Einheijar, Éire y Edu Herbosa, Elizabeth Robson, Elldaryck,

Elliot Stubbles, Elsydeon, Embers Design Studios, Emil Scott, Emil Wulff Nelander, Emily kindleysides, Emma (Peg) Howe, Emmanuel MORSEAU, Emmanuel Papst, Endeus, Eneko Hernanz, Enff, Engin Cekic, Enkufka, Enoch Wan, Eoin Burke, Eorahil, epeeguy, Erahard, Eran Aviram, Eric "Gonzo" Gunsolus, Eric Benaresh, Eric Bonnet, Eric Bos, Eric Brousseau, Eric Chou, Eric D. Bassett, Eric DeSnyder, Eric Edwards, Eric Falsken, Eric Freedlund, Eric Freeland - ski2060, Eric Harris, Eric Haste, Eric L Wong, Eric L. Anderson, Eric Larrivee, Eric Leach, Eric M Jackson, Eric M. Rupert, Eric Massicotte, Eric McDowell, Eric McIntosh - Lord Shiv, Eric Meske, Eric Oestrich, Eric Pasche, Eric V Walker, Erich Brackmann, Erik Jacobson, Erik Jung, Erik Olsen, Erik Parasiuk, Erik Raab, Erik Reiersen, Eriol, Erland Hakon, Ernest Fessenden, Ernesto Lorini Martell, Erwin Loubet, Erwin Sablon, Esteban Jauregui, Ethan "Snowball" Pearson, Ethan C, Ethan Eberle, Ev0k, Eva Johanna Hartel, Evan "Blooterman" Borgman, Evan Brownfield, Evan Jones, Evan Miller, Evan Scholl, Evert Koopman, Evil Stu, EvilMegan, Excelsior! Comics, Excubitor, Fabian Hochreuther, Fabian Nürnberger, FabianS, Fabien "bjorn29" NOURRISSON, Fabien FARENQ, Fabri Pérez Fernandez, Fabrice (Cabfire) Depierre, Fabrice Breau, Fabrizio Borgo, Fabrizio Merengo, Faisho, Faiz Sheikh, Falamore, FallenLeaf, "Fanatix of Enterprise", Farid Kutyev, Farstrider, Farun, FatherKnight, Fatsquirrel, Faultie, Fed Kassatkin, Federico "1MINUTEWAR" Pinci, Federico "Flamberga" Cortonesi, Federico Franceschi, Fedric Avian, Feliciano Bethencourt Herrera (Pipoboy), Felix Shafir, Felix-Maximilian Harre, Fenge Jørgensen, Fenswick, Ferben "Yaz" Yazicioglu, Ferji, Fernando Autran, Fernando Souto Redondo, Fernando Tucci and Fallon Baxter, Findreans (Eduardo Henrique Castelhano Dias), Finin Chisholm, Finlas, Finlay Hunter, Fireside, Flaktower, F'lar Burrill, Flecha, Flip PS, FloKo, Florentine Hlawatsch, Florian Hanke, Florian Hollauer, Florian Huggenberger, Florian Nimtsch, Florian Samsony, Florian Stitz, Floyd Daye, Flums, FNS187, Fran, Fran Miller "Solo", Francesco "ElvenKnight" Zotti, Francis Budden-Hinds, Francis 'Eon' Stabile, Francis Garot, Francis Li, Francisco de Borja Masip Torre, Francisco Javier García Sanchéz, François 'Doogy' THOMAS, Francois HIlton Jones, François M., Frank a Roberts III, Frank Benke, Frank Blau, Frank Falkenberg, Frank Guti Isco, Frank Moran, Frank Schulze, Frank Wenzel, Frankie Mundens, Franklin Crosby, Franz Georg Rösel, Frazer Slack, Fred CHO Seongjoon, Fred Schwe, Frédéri "Volk Kommissar Friedrich" POCHARD, Frederic Granet, Frederic Methot, Frédéric UTZI, Frederik Theill Jørgensen, FredRaider, Fredrik Lyngfalk, friareriner, Frikitorium Valladolid, Frits Kuijlman, Friz86, Frost Holliman, Frozenpyro, Fulgrim, Fulman, G Rowland, G. Bryan Miller, Gabe Laserhead Waluconis, Gábor Felméry, Gabor Kovacs, Gabriele Marino, Gabrielle Lopez, Gaëtan Boscher, Gaizka 'eXar-khun' Isusquiza, Galen Teschendorf, Gallant Lee, Gallowglass, Game Knight (Australia), Game Wizard Hobbies, gamers haven, Gamers Pair a Dice Toledo, OH, Gamerz Nexus, Gaming with The Cooler, Gangrol, Gareth Davies, Gareth Edwards, Gareth Jones, Gareth Lawrence, Gareth Mackay, Gareth Mekwinski, Gareth Wilson, Garion Hamilton, Garrett Book, Garrett Bruce, Garrett Copeland, Garry JW Jones, Garry Shortland, Gary Barrett, Gary de Vink, Gary Lee, Gaspard Levavasseur, Gasser Alain, Gavin "Carbide" Sullivan, Gavin Bateman, Gavin Mutter, Gavin O'Reilly, Gavin Peace, Gavin Willins, Geckilian, Geijhan, Genester, Genndy Sobolev, Geoff "Ontos" Strain, Geoff Core, Geoffrey Dibb, Geoffrey Nicholls, Georges Yasha Thenor-Louis, Geraint Osborn, Gerald A Burns, Gerald Rose Jr, gerard stephan, Gerd Davids, Gerhardus Klopper, Gero Burgard, gfjghj, ghalgor, Ghentec, Ghislain Lerda, -Ghost Wolves-, ghostinthemachine, Giacomo Fontana, Gian Holland, Giantcavecrab, Gideon "gernesto" Ernst, Gideon Lim, Giga-Bites Tabletop Cafe, Gilbert Bolof, Giles H Towers, Gilles Cherrier, Gino Sciarra, Giuliano "gr1mR36p3r" Liguori, Giulio "ingcaz" Cazzoli, Giuseppe "Bishop" Zeuli, Gkarilas Petros, GLEis, Glen Stones, Glenn Brunmar, Glenn Matthews, Glenn Mochon, Glenn Murphy, Gonzalo 'Gozillah' de Balanzó Lajusticia, Goonius Maximus, Goran Narančić, Gordon Glock, Gordy Dupuis, Gothmog, Grady S Harris, Graeme J. Inglis, Graham Bennett, Graham Cleary, Graham Cooke, Graham Goodwin, Graham Kobza, Graham Spearing, Graham T. Owens, Grant Frydenlund, Grant Huddleston, Grant Scullard, Grant Sims, Grantt Josh paul, Great Canadian Games & Hobbies, Greg "chroniclés" Cueto, Greg Brandell, Greg Chapman, Greg Childress, Greg Daniel, Greg Fawcett, Greg H., Greg M Lee, Greg Maroda, Greg Millsopp, Greg Morris, Greg Patterson, Greg Romano, Greg Walters, Greg Wilson, Gregdorf, Grégoire Veauléger, Gregor Mascher, Gregory Cox Jr., Gregory D. Ford, Gregory M. Terrell, Gregory Marlin, Gregory S. Small, Gregory Toews, Gregory Zuniga,

Greig Burges, Grenadier Games crew, Greysturm, Grigorakakis Panagiotis, Gritche, Grogian, Grzegorz Bagiński, Guido Guenther, Guillaume "Graider" Girard, Guillaume Bernard, Guillaume C, Guillaume GALDEANO, Guillaume Robert, Guillernaut, Gurkham, Gurlick, Gustaf Lundegren, Gustave E. Leibbrandt, Gustavo Barona, Guy, Guy Licata, H, H Dalton, H Thomas, H. Grillenberger, H. Joe Muffly, H. M. 'Dain' Lybarger, Hagen von Oelsen, Haiwire01, Håkan Jansson, Hal "Venjack" Neat, Hamish Gordon, hamsterhill, Hank Bao, Hans Fellhauer, Harju Pasi, Harley Gardias, harlokin, Harold Reavley, Haroon Alsaif, Harpyja, Harry Dunn, HarryG702, Harti, Harvey and Jennifer Collins, HD-Logan, Heath Borton, HeavyBana (a.k.a. 너불레기), Heinrich Wallesh, Heitter Ákos, Hellraiser, Henning "Auglim" Elfwering, Henning Harrer, Henrik Collin, Herb seifert, HH3818919, Hillfood, Hinterlight,His Eminence and Benevolent Grace Lord Ivan Rajic, hitmahip, Hobbes,Hoffen,Hooch, Hosea Lueke, HubbaBubba, Hugh "Fenton" Ashman, Hugh Badham, Hugh Montgomerie, Hugosemievil, Hugues Pauget, Hunni Bear, Hunter Domingue, Hydraxus, i0003, Iago Torres Piñeiro (Hombrequerie), Iain, Iain McGregor, Iain Milligan, Ian A. McCreery, Ian Clark, Ian Date, Ian Fielder, Ian Harris, Ian 'IJW Wartrader' Wood, Ian J. Throckmorton, Ian Kimmell, Ian Lathem, Ian M Kirby, Ian Magee, Ian Porter, Ian R. Magill, Ian Simpson, Ian Stewart, Ian Stewart-Shelafo, ian 'van' miller, Ian Woodley, Ian Zaglen, Iban Ruiz, Icemeld, IdMode, Ierim de Lis, Iker, illenvillen, Illya "Hunter"Kondratov, Illyan, Iluminus, Imperial Outpost Games, Infinite Monkey, Infinityharbour.com, Ingo | obskures.de, Innis & Avelynn P., inRemote, iolaran, Isaac Lee, Israel Salcedo Jiménez, Istrian, Itthi Mongkolwat, Ivan Caprioli, Ivan Daskalov, Ivan Finch, Iván Gimeno, Ivan Solla, Ivan Tam, Ivan_M, Ivar Ofärd, Ix Adams, J Wood, J. Luebben, J. Stephen Strain, J.B. Smith, J.c., JJ, JJ. & Lana Mason, JJ.B., J.K. Meisen, Jaakko Saari, Jace Boatrite, Jack "Shinlocke" Sweek, Jack Crease, Jack Gulick, Jack Marroquin, Jack Mills, Jack Mooney Jr., Jack Mottershead, Jack Newton, Jack Norris, Jack of Arc, Jack Ramstad, Jack Skratch, Jack Thomas, Jackson Brantley, Jacob Boersma, Jacob Connor, Jacob 'Crimson' Dawson, Jacob E Bliss, Jacob Evans, Jacob Gilbar, Jacob Kemp, Jacob Pacholski, Jacob Preisig, Jacob Sorensen, Jacob Torgerson, Jacob Wisner, Jacobo Morère, Jaime and Moira, Jaime Herazo B., Jaime T. Matthew, Jaime Tiampo, Jak Van Der Graaf, Jake B, Jake Baker, Jake Shepherd, Jake the Junkman, Jakub Palm, Jakub Vosahlo, James Dezomits, James & Jean Meisenburg, James & Silvia Soares Reid, James Allen, James Anh Dung Ho, James Carpendale, James Carus, James Casey, James Clarke, Jon Clemens, Jay-daniel Clemens and Jamie Thomas, James Conason, James Cruise, James Cunningham, James Dugdale, James F Tillman, James Faltum, James 'Flashman' Harper, James Funnell, James Goddard, James Gorman, James Griswold, James Hartwell, James Henderson, James Keast, James Keatley, James N Baldwin, James Payne, James Phelan, James Pittman, James Powell, James R. Chance, James R. Lynch, James Reason, James Roberts, James S. King, James Sadkovich, James Sanderson, James Sheahan, James Sherlock, James Studer, James Talbot, James Taylor, James 'The Great Old One' Burke, Jamie Heidenreich, Jamie Sanchez, Jamie Shirlaw, Jamie Wheeler, Jamie Wright, Jan, Jan "0rph3u5" Dombert, Jan Eriksson, Jan Mäkinen, Jan Malte Riedel, Jan Senten, Jan Thiele, Jan-Hendric Besching, Jani Waara, Janne Jaakola, Jared Cook, Jared Staub, Jared Thibault, Jarek J. Jarzębiak, Jaret Brzezniak, Jase Duncum, Jason "Data" Dawson, Jason "Joker" Henwood, Jason "SKEE" Nechanicky, Jason A Longden, Jason A. Childs, Jason Ball, Jason Bell, Jason Cabral, Jason Cook, Jason Craig Spencer, Jason DeForest, Jason Dickerson, Jason Dosier, Jason Ellsworth-Aults, Jason G. Rak, Jason H, Jason H Gauthier, Jason Hawkes, Jason Holt, Jason Italiano, Jason Johnsto, Jason Jordan Brasie, Jason LeBeau, Jason Lescalleet, Jason Lindsey, Jason Luff, Jason M Martin, Jason MacDougall, Jason March, Jason McKenzie, Jason McQuain, Jason meeker, Jason Ong, Jason Pasch, Jason Pocino, Jason R Weimer, Jason Sharp, Jason T Roe, Jason Thompson, "Jason Thompson ", Jason Whittle, Jason Williams, javel, Javier Díaz Suso, Jay, Jay "Doughnut" Richards, Jay A. Hix, Jay Baxter, Jay Draper, Jay Guo, Jay Watson, Jaysom, Jazzman Lewis, JDSeibert, Jean-baptise Avanzini, Jean-Baptiste "Alphast" Perrin, Jean-Enric Courvoisier, Jean-Romain Barrau, Jeb Boyt, Jebilo, Jeff "Shriggs" Longa, Jeff Bidstrup, Jeff Briggs, Jeff Burton, Jeff Carter, Jeff Clark, Jeff Craft, Jeff 'Erion' Hoffman, Jeff Hofer, Jeff Ivey, Jeff Knobloch, Jeff McDowall, Jeff Robinson, Jeff Rossiter, Jeffrey "König-Wolf" James, Jeffrey Andres Williams, Jeffrey Chow, Jeffrey Palmer, Jeffrey Sithi-Amnuai, Jen Parr, Jenny and Andre Fleitmann, Jens Arnold, Jens Henrik Skuldbøl, Jens Hoelderle, Jens Ploug, Jere Manninen, Jeremiah Conley, Jeremiah Halstead, Jeremy "Knil" Andre, Jeremy "Raz" Asbury, Jeremy Bailey,

Jeremy Baker, Jeremy Brown, Jeremy Busse-Jones, Jeremy Cox, Jeremy Geib, Jeremy Goens, Jeremy Griffin, Jeremy Hendrix, Jeremy Kear, Jeremy Kinser, Jeremy kofoot, Jeremy R. Smith, Jeremy S. Hicks, Jeremy Scranton, Jeremy Seeley, Jeremy Wininger, Jerome Devie, Jérôme Draussin, Jerumiah, the Damned Prophet, Jerzy Bogusławski, Jesper Fogelholm, Jesper Fonvig, Jesper T. Hansen "Pyromadness", Jess Stanley, Jesse Busch, Jesse C., Jesse Clark, Jesse Escobedo, Jesse Goble, Jesse Stern, JesterEves, Jestertales, Jez Fairclough, JG Cully, Jico, Jim D. McGovern, Jim Dice, Jim Graham,Jim Kitchen, Jim Sharples, Jimmie Rush jr, Jimmy Czodli, Jimmy Edwards, Jimmy Karlsson, Jimmy Law, Jimmy Lindqvist, Jimmy Pigott, JKW, JM Owen, JMH621Nova aka Jonathan Harris, Joachim Schenkel, Jody Gorton, Joe "joerocks1981" Martin, Joe Banner, Joe Burnham, Joe Cirillo, Joe Dogonniuck, Joe Leggatt, Joe 'Union Jackal' Hill, Joe Wojtas, Joel "Pikutiku" Sanchez, Joel Craig, Joel Müller, Joel Purton, Joel Simpson, Joel Smythe, Joel Swankhuizen, Joel Vaughan, Joerg Gering, Joerg Herz, Johan Grønstad, Johannes Forster, Johannes M., John "All Voices Anonymous " Kraemer, John "BLOODGOD" Junghans, John "evernevermore" Scheib, John "Leper" Smith, John "Prezius" angelosi, John "Smiley" Adams, John "Sniper X" Aridi, john "Xaoseac" Marshall, John A W Phillips, John Bates, John Bishop, John Casey, John Corley, John D Prins, John 'Diesel Fox' Lilley, John Dobbins, John Doyle, John F. Zmrotchek, John Flitcroft, John G. Colon, John Gustafson, John Hardey, John Hay, John Hildebrand, John Hobbs, John Horton, John W.T. Kirkpatrick, John Lambert, John Law, John Lorinskas, John Lowney, John MacKenzie, John McGill, John McLeish, John McShane, John Murdoch, John Myers, John Nellis, John Oram, John Philip Corpuz, John Polack, John Pope, John Ralston, John Roberts, John Robertson, John Rogers - KFM, John Sheffield, John Simutis, ויטש ותנוהי, John Stiles, john taylor, John Trace, John W. Hess II, John Watson, John Wilkinson, John Wille, Johnathon Pittman, Johnnie Chau, Johnny Killstring, Johnny Peralta, Johnson Thurston, "JOjo the barb", Jon "Saberzero" Chin, Jon Ander "Headok" Maiz, Jon Dennis, Jon Geraghty, Jon Jones, Jon Kjellberg, Jon McDermott, Jon Morrison, Jon Smejkal, Jonah Benterbusch, Jonas Beardsley, Jonas Gabel, Jonas Hansson, Jonas Skadberg, Jonathan, Jonathan "Calamar" Marqués Mansilla, Jonathan Aylmer, Jonathan Beer, Jonathan Breese, Jonathan Chew, Jonathan Crane, Jonathan Crow, Jonathan Dominguez, Jonathan Fenwick, Jonathan Fish, Jonathan Gerber, Jonathan Greeley, Jonathan Haskins, Jonathan Johnson, Jonathan Konig, Jonathan Lloyd, Jonathan Lucas, Jonathan Morris, Jonathan R. Nicol, Jonathan Smith, Jonathan Souza, Jonathan Stromberg, Johnathan "Jt" Turner, Jonjo, Joobi, Joonas Selin, Joost Hendriks, Jopy Kaibel Val, Jordan "Chikki" Ciccarelli, Jordan Brezer, Jordan Carasa, Jordan Kaase, Jordan Lennard, Jordan Sanderson, Jordan Smock, Jordan 'Sylvar' Dixon, Jordan Tytler, Jordi "Dimuscul" Franch, Jordi José Bazán, Jordi Mundet Mas, Jordi Rabionet, Jordi Salvador, Jörg Bours, Jorge Idarraga, Jorge Worlders, Joris Van der Vorst, Jose M.A. Blanco, Jose I Cavero, José Ignacio Macaya Sanz, Jose Luis "devBadger" Castro, Jose M. Nieto, Jose Palma Gil, Jose Pedro Fernández Pascual, Josep Maria Serres, Joseph "mayday" Miles, Joseph (Joe) Edge, Joseph A. Zdanavage, Joseph 'BEAR' Thompson, Joseph Cortese, Joseph Evenson, Joseph G, Joseph J Batz, Joseph Kerstetter, Joseph Mazurek, Joseph Noll, Joseph Perez, Joseph Phillip Robles Figueroa, Joseph Scanlon, Josh "Maverick" Helton, Josh Affrime, Josh Allen, Josh Hatch, Josh Levan, Josh Nuttall, Josh Olivieri, Josh Rasey, Josh Riggins, Josh Schonaerts, Josh Wolski, Joshua Allen, Joshua Belcher, Joshua C. Varrone, Joshua Freitas, Joshua Gordon, Joshua Himebaugh, Joshua Nanke-Mannell, Joshua Nassir Hernandez, Joshua Nuttall, Joshua O'Connor, Joshua Patenaude, Joshua Ray, Joshua Van Zaane, JoskCB, Josu Garhex Castro, JPtheBrit, JR Gonzalez, JSE, JT Wanner, Juan A. Valdez, Juan Carlos Ruiz Maroto, Juan Francisco Gutiérrez Gutiérrez, Juan Jacobo Yarce Velez, Juan José Gracia Roche, Juan Malvido Gonzalez, Judson Brislin, Judy Johnson, Juhana "Wouho" Oukka, Juice Pan, Julian C, Julien Bortoli Chapalay, Julien Graf, Julio C. Saiz, Julius Wu, Jun Yong Kim, Jürgen Pünter, Jussi Myllyluoma, Justin "Vandraven" Ragan, Justin Allred, Justin Cranford, Justin D, Justin Enders, Justin Hayes, Justin Inman, Justin Lance, Justin M. Flint, Justin Orion Everman, Justin Richt, Justin Williamson, K,K Reavy, K. Pickett, K. Shirk, K. Watt, k.wilson, Kaleb Reisner, Kaleb Shissler, Kalu Ekeh, Kamil Pawlowski, Kapton Morgunz, Karen J. Grant, KarethRahl, Karim Zendougui, Karl A. Rodriguez, Karl Ancell, Karl Kreutzer, Karl Moy, Kashch3i, Kason Cheng, Kasper Luiten, Kavnorak, KazakMatt, Kaze, Kazgarom, KDLynch, Kean P Stuart, Keasar, Keegan "Tinkergoth" Bateman, Keith "Big K" Hoffman, Keith gray, Keith Higdon, Keith O'Sullivan, Keith Romero, Keith "Kurrelgyre" Shutler, Keith St Peter,

Keith Trost, keith wilson, Keith Woodsum, Kel, Keld Hjortskov, Kele' Mendell, Kelreth, Kelvin 'mewmew' Porter, Ken Foster, Ken Perry, Ken Robinson, Ken Sieffert, Kenneth Djuwidja, Kenneth Fornal, Kenneth Johnson, Kennie Poulsen, Kenny Hall, Kenomi, Kent B. Shuford, Kergonan, Kevbo, Kevin "MightyBroden" Oden, Kevin Allen, Kevin B Madison, Kevin C., Kevin Comer, Kevin Cook, Kevin Dickens, Kevin Doherty, Kevin Duncan, Kevin Flynn, Kevin Foxall, Kevin Heath, Kevin Henley, Kevin Rau, Kevin Ray, Kevin Rougas, Kevin Satra Schwarz, Kevin Wine, Kevin Zhang, Kevyn K Dietz, Khatre, Khayloth - Javier Arteagoitia, Kheev, Khi-Jon, Chua, Kieran Wallace, Killerbienchen0684, Killian "Deep-Green-X" Mc Keever, Kim Brown, Kim Hocking, Kim Starkey, KinetikSky, Kiri RR, Kirk Penner, Kirk Severson, Kiruna Gaming Club SODA, Kirzai, Kiwihiker, KJ Miller, Kjedoran, Kjell Kenneth Moens, Klaus Kristensen, Klaus Ostrom, Klendathu, Knight's Blade Gaming & Hobby, Koen de Rooster, Koen Theys, Koloman Varady, Konstantin Kirilin, Konstantinos "Psychotic Storm" karayiannis, Konstantinos Lamprou, Korlie, Kosta Kostulas, Kosuno, Kota Simonson, Krasnov, Kristof "Yindaka" Vandewynckel, Kristofer Barr (Mama Luigi), Krofinn, Krzysztof Leszczyński, Krzysztof Zajac, Kurenai Sasori, Kurt McMahon, Kustross, Kwondae, Kyle Addy, Kyle Bonderud, Kyle Burckh, Kyle Collins, Kyle Kolbe, Kyle Kroening, Kyle Radtke, Kyle Raen, Kyle Randolph "Pride of Rodina", Kyle Rimmer, Kyle Thompson, Kyone Akashi, Kyorou, Lachlan "Raith" Conley, Lachlan Carter, Lael B., Lakshman Godbole, Lalo Halcon, Lance Becker, Lance Wente, Lane Shutt, Larry Correia, Lars Emil "TheHolyMage" Nielsen, Lars Holgaard, Lars Molls, Lasse Rasmussen, Laszlo Scholz, Lathuran, Laurence Bates, Laurent BABAULT, Laurent Dumas, Lauri Hirvonen, Lauri Marx, Lawrence "Saker" Collins, Lawson Tong, Lazar Stojkovic, Lazytanker, Lee Long, Lee Pickett, Lee Rossi, Lee T Wendel, Leithius, lemiss, Len852, Leni, Lennart Schmidt, Leo Lingas, Leo Paixao, Leonard Kelly, Leonardo Chavez Weyand, Leonardo Darkvortex87 Ciferri, Leonardo Lee, LeRag, Leszek Zieliński 'XLS', Levi, Levi Geiger, LeWhite, Lewis Allen, Lewis Bracey-Forde, Lewis Frasch, Liam Elliott, Liam Eyers, Limsk, Lin Wyeth, Lindel Kinchen, Lindhrive, Lindon Paxton, Linuo, Lionel Dou, Liryel, Living Worlds Games, LLC., Llalowar, Lluis Pons (Muerde), Lobo, Locksmith, Locustron, Loddfafnir, Logan Hudson, Logan Laren Liuzzo, Logan RR Batty, Loh "Elldane" Chi Yong, Loke Wallmo, Lonni Swanson, Lord Nocturin Lacey-Clarke III, Lordfient, Lordtehuti, Loris Lentini, Lsathranil, Lt. Robert Dolan Logan, Luc Charbonneau, Luc Phaneuf, Luc Teunen, Luca Beltrami, Luca Ceriola, Lucas Joyce, Lucas Lachaux, Luciano Marchetti (El_Mariacheat), Luciano Vieira Velho, Lucky Eddy, Ludo, Ludus In Fabula, luferox, Luide, Luis Carretero, Luis Chavez, Luis La Luz Montañez, Luis Manuel Galiano Baragaño, Luis Miguel Aguirre Sánchez-Bermejo (Azakel), Lukas Zarychta, Łukasz "zulus" Mazur, Łukasz 'cielaq' Cieluba, Luke Busler, JM DeFoggi, Chris Pileggi, Luke Day, Luke Liu, Luke 'Mecha' Giesemann, Luke Miller, Luke Moran, Luke Morton, Luke Stundon, Luke Taylor, Luke Tickle, Luke Trist, Luke Turner, Luther Chip Harris IV, Lutwolf, M Kevin Chau, M Vamp, M Wright, M. Fang, M. Gatzke, M. Rauscher, M. Schoenstein & the Pack, M.Bariat, M.Tyson, M3rauer, MacD, Maciej Kotowicz, Maciej Rakowski, Mack Nolte, Mad Gav, Mad Ivan, Madahades, Mads F. Johansen, Maerlyn the Solitaire, Magno, Maguila, Mahmoud A. Al Mahmoud, Maj, Major_Gilbear, Maki Games, MakorDal, Malcolm Pritchard, Malibu Road Pictures LLC, Malone Screen, Malte & Thore Schmidt, Malte Hansson, Manu Forget, Manuel Ángel Fidalgo Vega, Manuel Lorenz, Manuel Putz, "Manuel Rodrigo Calvo Iglesias(Bogatyr), "ManuSan, Maqywhaq, Marc "Marx" Quaglia, Marc "Wraithinshadow" Pearce, Marc Bevan, Marc Callaghan, Marc Espresate "Burning Tear", Marc Langworthy, Marc Marti, Marc Moragrega, Marc Taylor, Marc Tetlow, Marc-André Boyer, Marc-Antoine Rondeau, Marcel Basmer, Marcel Schlicher (Gorim), Marcel Zons, Marcin, Meeks" Kosiedowski, Marcin Tysler, Marco Ambrosini, Marco DivaZ, Marco Mazza, Marco Ponso, Marco Zimmermann, Marcos Martin Davila aka Linksamaru, Marc-Philip Hoffmann, Marcus "Lasse" Folz, Marcus "Naknut" Isaksson, Marcus A, Marcus Archer, Marcus Mitzel, Marcus Rendell, Marcus Rounds, Mario Croner, Mario Fahlandt, Mario Iglesias, Mario Morales, Mario N. Bonassin, Marius E., Marius Laub, Mark "Feric" N., Mark "Hatchetboy" Alexander, Mark "WarHound" Stumpf, Mark Aksel, Mark Balakrishnan, Mark Bishop, Mark Bjorkman, Mark C. Ratter, Mark Cunningham, Mark D. Taylor, Mark E. O'Mealey, Mark Galvez, Mark Geller, Mark Green, Mark Hanna, Mark Horne, Mark Kehl, Mark Lesny, Mark Lorriman, Mark Pattison, Mark Peyton, Mark Quartermain, Mark Renshaw, Mark Richardson, Mark Roberts, Mark Rosete, Mark Roy, Mark Ruffles, Mark S, Mark Saniter, Mark Spaeth, Mark

Stone, Mark Sykes, Mark T. Jefferies, Mark Thompson, Mark Threlfall, Mark Wilson, Markus "Malagrim" Steiner, Markus Boehner, Markus Gawenda, Markus Grapendal, Markus 'Harlekin' Goettfert, Markus Kemper, Markus Raab, Marley Griffin, Martin, Martin "Duster" Cloutier, Martin Kreuter, Martin "Mautzy" Mautz, Martin "Picken" P., Martin An Nguyen, Martin Bailey, Martin Carlsson, Martin Crane, Martin Eckert, Martin Ellermeier, Martin Greening, Martin Hammerich Lund, Martin Lundegren, Martin Kanshige, Martin Krebs, Martin Kühne, Martin Kvolbæk, Martin Legg, Martin Mckeown - ShRiLLeR, Martin Monrad, Martin Munke, martin neal, Martin Noras, Martin Ritter, Martin Takaichi, Martin Thompson, Martin Whitworth, Martin Winter, Martin Woels, Martyn Findley, Martyn R, Massimo Malpezzi, Mat Masding-Grouse, Mateo "Gattou" Cano, Mathias "TheQuest" Tolksdorf, Mathias Gehl, Mathieu "orion" durand, Mathieu Thérézien, Matias "m0ca" Grönqvist, Matija Prekslavec, Mats "Deadit" Peltola, Matt, Matt Parker, Matt Barker, Matt Beech, Matt Blackwell, Matt Carey, Matt Doidge, Matt G, Matt Gregory, Matt Jameson, Matt Leitzen, Matt MacGregor, Matt MacMurray, Matt "TheWildFerret" Mayer, Matt Mollison, Matt N., Matt Parks, Matt Rowan, Matt Scott, Matt Screng Paluch, Matt Shinners, Matt Valgardson, USAriadna Community Radio, Matteo "Nthpower" Sebastiani, Matteo Signorini, Matthew "Scar137" Hamilton, Matthew & Nigel Morocco, Matthew Banning, Matthew Bates, Matthew Blair, Matthew Brooks, Matthew Brooksby, Matthew Broome, Matthew Cataldo, Matthew Dickey, Matthew Dive, Matthew Eastwood, Matthew Edgeworth, Matthew Fundaun, Matthew Garmon, Matthew Green, Matthew Harrell, Matthew Haupt, Matthew Hayward, Matthew Hoeveler, Matthew Howlett, Matthew Jorgenson, Matthew Lane, Matthew Lea, Matthew Madden, "Matthew McCann, Adam Watkins, Matthew McCoulough-Fry, Matthew Millar, Matthew Percival, Matthew Plank, Matthew Prather, Matthew Pryor, Matthew Rhodes, Matthew Ruane, Matthew S. Robertson, Matthew Sullivan, Matthew Taylor, Matthew Underwood, Matthew Wasiak, Matthew Yeomans, Matthias "Logan McCormack" Platzer, Matthias Grzib, Matthias Hochmuth, Matthias Niel, Matthieu Renoult, Matthieu T., Mattias "Ingenting" Elblaus, MattSJ, Matty Maple, Matze, Mauro 'Kilroy' Giordano, Maurycy Stefański, Max, Max Glasner, Max Grüntgens, Max Hardenbrook, Max L Chapman, Max Stelzer, Max Thell, Maxence Delsaut, Maxime Mackie, Maximilian Müller, MaxMahem, MaxOrion, Meeple Madness, Meldinov, Melinda R. Nelson, Mergar, Meribast, Merioch, Merlin Stein, Mgchu, Micha Granit, Michael "BigButaiBoss" Ordidge, Michael "Burge" Burgess, Michael "Dameon Black" Dunsch, Michael "KingNova3000" Hurrell, Michael "Laserburn" Smith, Michael "TaShadan" Leppert, Michael "winter" Watson, Michael A Guerra, Michael A Miller AKA: Gideon Wolf, Michael Baker, Michael Bauer, Michael Beck, Michael Boone, Michael Browne "Mal", Michael C. Leonard, Michael Cefaratti, Michael Christensen, Michael Cortez, Michael De Rosa, Michael Eder, Mike 'Lightbulb' Evans, Michael F. Foran Jr., Michael Feldhusen, Michael Filatov, Michael G. Palmer, Michael Gallagher, Michael Gellar, Michael Herz, Michael Hixenbaugh, Michael Hocutt, Daniel Taylor, Kenneth Hackinson, Alex Brotherton, Michael Inose, Michael J McLaughlin, Michael J. Wypyszinski, Michael Jaszmann, Michael Jay Ford, Michael Kaplan, Michael Klein, Michael oraszewski, Michael Koutsoukos, Michael Krzak, Michael Kullmann, Michael Layton, Michael Lessau, Michael Lovell, Michael Ma, Michael Maraszkiewicz, Michael Marquez, Michael Mattner, Michael McKenzie, Michael Meyer, Michael Mooney The Tyranny of Books, Michael Moran, Michael Naber, Michael Perry, Michael Ratzka, Michael Readhead, Michael Riber, Michael Rivero, Michael Roberts, Michael Roebling, Michael Ryan, Michael S., Michael Say, Michael Scott, Michael Sim CH, Michael Soar, Michael Southern, Michael Spinks, Michael T McDonnell, Michael Ulanski, Michael Venderdahl, Michael Wood, Michael Wright, Michal "costi" Koscielak, Michal 'Xaos' Lewandowski, Michał Jaroszuk, Michał Szczepaniak, Micheal J Wright, Michele, Michele "Cugino" Poggi, Michiel Koning, Mickey O'Hagan, Micro Art Studio Infinity players, Midnightcrash, Miguel A. Joga, Miguel Ángel Guerrero Pozo (Shirloth), Miguel Angel Riera, Miguel Angel Rodriguez, III, Miguel Luis "Dindo" N. Moreno, Miha Mužič, Mihai Bolda, Mik Neville, Mikael Suominen, Mikarl Carl Fredrik Karlsson, Mike "Laz" MacMartin, Mike "TheFailBus" Williams, Mike Beanland, Mike Bowie, Mike Burt, Mike Buse, Mike Clancy aka Mohgreen, Mike Coleman, Mike Follis, Mike Haire, Mike Harper, MD, Mike Johnson, Mike Krog, Mike McArthur, Mike Ortiz, Mike Rogers, Mike Rossmassler, Mike Schmitz, Mike Spector, "Mike Stevens Sisco Martinez, "Mike Strefford, Mike Thomas, Mike

Williams of I Talk to Planets, Mike Wilson, Mike Zocchi, Mikfard, Mikhail Gordin, Mikko Iivonen, Mikko Julen, Miles Pattingale, MindlessCalm, Miniature Tim, Miquel Galiana, Mirko Mazzi, Misiolak, Miska Fredman, Mistlynx, Mitch Johnston, Mitch Nelson, Mitch W., Mitchell "Haematite" Christov, Mitchell German, Mitchell McBroom, MitchTT, MJ Newcomb, MJ12, "MKL", Mohammed Forsad, Moisés Reina Perez, Monica Lopez Laujac, Moraxus (Anthony Williams), Morgan J Boyd, Morgan Llewellyn, Morgan Weeks, Morten Birch, Morten Grubbe, Morticutor, Mostafa Ali, Mostroneddo, Mothman, Moto, moxou, Mr Andy, Mr C Moses!, Mr Clarke, Mr. Nickel, mreule, mrhuettel, MSB, Mus Marzuki, Myaori, Mycheal Kelly, Myrmir, N. E. Regnat, N.Danielsson, N.W., n0Face, N21LV, NA, Nachtpfiffel, Nakodo, Namal Dayarathna, Nasca, Nat Lanza, Nate Feyma, Nate Moore, Nate Owen, Nathan "Prost" Williams, Nathan A. R. McGee, Nathan Carraway, Nathan Falconer, Nathan Jones, Nathan Little, Nathan Sharp, Nathan Westcott, Nathan Wise, Nathaniel Baker, Nathaniel Beers, Nathaniel Heironimus, Nathaniel Lindén, Nathaniel McMerdie Smith, Nathaniel Mericle, Nathaniel Slivka, Nathaniel Southworth-Barlow, Nauzet "Valdrak", Nawaf Mesad, nechaka, Neil Bennett, Neil Bevan, Neil Cruickshank, Neil Hamilton, Neil 'Jag' Jagger, Neil James Harvey, Neil Mahoney, Neil Shields, Neil Thompson, Neill Ramsey, Nelson P Hernandez, Nemesis, Nephusis, Nesox Kalim, Nespar, Nestor A. Medina Jr, Netpak, Newton Grant, Nic Ellis, Nicholas "Tubmaster General" Carreau, Nicholas Aldrich, Nicholas Barabach, Nicholas Brawn, Nicholas G. Rais, Nicholas Koutsouliotas, Nicholas Vessey, Nicholas Whittington, Nicholas Wright, Nick "Ambisinister" Vale, Nick "Dysartes" Johnson, Nick "Gertje" Rebergen, Nick "W1tcher", Nick Bate, Nick Chew, Nick Fallon, Nick H., Nick Hansen, Nick Hart, Nick Hintz, Nick Irish, Nick Keyuravong, Nick Macdonald, Nick Neill, Nick pater, Nick Rasch, Nick Riggs, Nick Rowe, Nick Scherdnik, Nick Shoemaker, Nick Simpson, Nick Thomas, Nick wingedferret Brown, Nickolas Perez, Nico "Mirà" Fichino, Nicolas D'Aversa, Nicolas Hamilton, Nicolas Middendorff, Nicolas Vandemaele-Couchy, nicolas vialettes, Nicolo' Sfriso, Nie Wieder Bakunin, Niels Hamersma, Niels Quaade Jensen, Niels Sørensen, Nigel Cobb, Nigel Hyde, Nigel Robinson, Nigel V Wright, Niguel Vega, Niki Strøh, Nikica Puksic, Niklas Benzein, Niko Nevala, Nikolai Tsekov, Nikolaus Poenisch, Nils Hanke, NinjaCyborg, Ninkasi, Nino Bagus, Noah Heck, Noah Yablong, Noctum, Noel Black, NomadSoul, Norillo, Norrie Thompson, Noursetdou, Novafan, Nul'taar Shalrac, Nurkolai, Odalma, Odium, Oisin O'Higgins Benton, Oleg Gorelkin, Olen "Dozer" Gravel, Oli Barker, Oliver "Malnox" Vogt, Oliver Haywood, Oliver 'Noly' Neary, Oliver Schneider, Olivier Cauchois, Olivier Gribaudo, Omadon, Omer Ahmed, Omikoron, Onehly49, Onlyonepinman, Orfeas Iatrou, Dimitrios Karametos, Fotis Liakeas, Orlando Soage Sánchez, Orlean, Ö-viksgänget, Owain Cooke, Owen Camber, Owen Glover, OwenOS, P. "Kobold" Klemm, Pablo Gil Fuentes, Pablo Palacios, Pablo Quintana, Padde and Ilka for infinity!, Pádraig Donnelly, Padre Santiago, PaganDude, Paladin von Korff, Pandabear, Panzerbaer Walbauch, Paolo Biggio, Paris (Pure Mongrel) Conte, Parker, Patrice Mermoud, Patrick, Patrick Adams, Patrick Alexander, Patrick Chambers, Patrick Crisostomo, Patrick de la Vega Justice, Patrick Dwyer, Patrick Farrell, Patrick Forbeck, Patrick Fowler, Patrick Healey, Patrick Hickey, Patrick 'JiaoshouX' Taylor, Patrick Knight, Patrick Mastrobuono, Patrick Noble Brewington, Patrick Phillips, Patrick Seyfarth, Patrick Stalter, Patrick St-Amand, Patrick Wallen, Patrick Wenzlaff, Patrik Hallberg, Patrik Lejon, Patriot Games, Patrycjusz "Alkasyn" Piechowski, Pau Martín Bosch, Paul, Paul "Firellon" Tightbow, Paul "Stormwatcher" Beck, Paul "XpresoAdct" Haban, Paul Atreides, Paul Barton, Paul Carolan, Paul Dawson, Paul Dempsey, Paul Edwards, Paul Eyles, Paul G. Harris, Paul Gibson, Paul Hayes, Paul Hurd, Paul Kolo, Paul Kutscha, Paul Lell, Paul Lu, Paul May, Paul Moore III, Paul Ryan Kuykendall, Paul Simms, Paul Smith, Paul Steffens, Paul Thomas, Paul Thompson, Paul Woodward, Pavel Ilin, Pavel Sedov, Pawel Daruk, Pax Aeterna Nerdclub, payday4ray, Peacock, Pedion Modular Battlefields, Pedro Cortez Pinto, Pedro Gonzalez, Pedro J. Deyo, Pedrom Adeli, Per Hyyrynen, Pere Capellades i Rais, Per-Olov Gothe, Pete and Jenni Harper, Pete Mason, Pete Middaugh, Pete Miller, Pete Wylie, Peter "Lenin" Edlin, Peter "Lilith" Balogh, Peter "Pskion" Rivera, Peter (CrispyPete) Green, Peter Boze, Peter Dean, Peter Egeriis, Peter Engebos, Peter F., Peter Gates, Peter Hemken, Peter Holland, Peter Ian Hughes, Peter K.W. Wong, Peter Loeb Caldenhof, Peter Marič, Peter Newson, Peter Orrmalm, peter peretti, Peter 'Phlyk' Acs, Peter Risby, Peter Sinkis, Peter Smyk, Peter Sykora, Petey R, Petter Wäss, Phil Abramowitz, Phil Brown, Phil Harvey, Phil Ingham, Phil Manwaring, Phil Vint, Phil

Wilson, Phil Wong, Philip Gray, Philip Hippeau, Philip Malone, Philip Williams, Philipp Gaidar, Philippe De Braekeleer, Philippe Devillé, Philippe Hermiz, Phillip Bailey, Phillip Dishon, Phillip Dunn, Phillip Gates-Shannon, Phillip McGregor, Phillip Wolf, Philo Sluijsmans, Philou, Phubar, Pierre "lyzech" Allegraud, Pierre Chaloux, Pierre G, Pierre Waldfried, Pierre-Andre Lepine, Pinky, Pinsel, PJ Frack, PJ Holmes, Placator, plastictrees, PlatypusPal320, POGMONSTA, Pointman, Poulpiche, powerful hallucinogens, Praetorian, Preston Thomas, Primož P, PrometheusUB, Prototheca, Pustik, Qali Va'Shen, Queen Ardana, Quickit, Quinton Sung, R Coit, R Silvers, R. Hillmann, R. Sean Callahan, R. W. Carlson, Rachael G Wright, Radoslaw Bozek, Rafaël, Rafael " The Goochman" Gu, Rafael "Primo", Rafael Cerrato, Rafael Klosowski, Rafael Moreno, Rafael Sabino, Rafal "mirai" Zygadlo, Rafał 'Artein' Lehnert, Rafał Oprych, Rain & Aidenn, Raj Kapila, rambol, RAM-Kay, Ramon Bernardo Masalias Lascosqui, Ramunas 'Animus' Kulvelis, Rand Eaton, Randall Burt, Randolph "A Mão Esquerda" Johnson, Randy Eckenrode, Randy Mora, Randy Mosiondz, Rasmus Petersen, RattlerNxt, Ratty, Raul Pacheco Santander, Ravele, Raxs, Raymon Rodenburg, Raymond Bennett, Raymond Nagle, RC_Sparrow, Redfuji6, Redmaw69 aka. Gib-San (Andrew Gibson), Reece Gordon, Rekeiji, Remi Letourneau, Renaat, Renzo Crispieri, Reto M. Kiefer, Reuben Rees, Reuben Timineri, Rev. Adrian Milik, Reverance Pavane, RG Bilton, Rhelyk, Rhys Steele, Ricardo Bibiloni, Ricardo García Plaza., Ricardo Nacarini, Riccardo Ciliberti (Cilibeo), Ricey, Rich Jeffords, Rich Riddle, Richard "Ironburn" Hickman, Richard A M Green, Richard Anstey, Richard Coates, Richard Convery, Richard Fancher, Richard G.W. Cook, Richard Heales, Richard Hohne, Richard Howe, Richard Latwaitis, Richard Moonil Choi, Richard p Creighton, Richard Poffley, Richard Rush, Richard Scorpius Zhang, Richard Thrower, Richard Tighe, Richard 'Vidiian' Greene, Richard Wagener/Darkeldar, Rick Hewitt, Rick Marston, Rick Smith, Ricky A Perez, Ricky Morales, Rik Geuze, Riley Esmond, Rob "BlueDagger" Brock, Rob "The MoonDoggy' Bent, Rob Barley, Rob Griffiths, Rob Huckabay, Rob Hynes, Rob Lawrence, Rob Randolph, Rob Schubert, Rob Silvester, Rob Thomas, Rob Waller, Robby Beatty, Robby Dunn, Robby Payne, Robert "Lobster" Long, Robert "Neoscream" Angliss, Robert Allen, Robert Biddle,Robert C. Kim, Robert Calpo, Robert Christiansen, Robert De Luna, Robert Duffy, Robert G. Male, Robert H. Mitchell Jr., Robert Havoc, Robert J Bennett, Robert Jacques, Robert Lowndes, Robert Mahoney, Robert McNeal, Robert O. Hoffman, Robert Phanelson, Robert Small, Robert Spaulding, Roberto Padron, Robey Jenkins, Robin Finney, Robin Paterson, Rocky Randalls, Rocky Viet Tran, Rodgher De Steele, Rodney Brice, Rodrigo, Rodrigo Olalla (Rod), Rodrigo Vergueiro, Rodrigo Vilanova, Rodrigo y Xabi Barcia, Roger 4bit, Roland Everaert, Rolf Kunisch, Romain Darmon, Roman "Do Fel" Nechiporenco, Roman "Romiras" Zorin, Roman G Basurto, Roman Kuzyk, ron beck, Ron Fuentes, Ron James, Ron Niabati, Ron Reamey, Ron Tracey, Ronald Martin, Ronald Scheuermann, Ronan"Sixpiedsousterre"Helies, Roofpig, Rory Warman MacLeod, Ross H. Bluth, Ross Holt, Ross Salerno, Ross Webb-Wagg, Roy, Roy Davis, Roy Oliver, Royden Clark, RSRD, RT, Ruben 'D1' de Jong, Ruben 'Uezguersmaster' Jochheim, Ruben Vargas, Rudolf Spennemann, RumDrum37, Ruslan Khamdulaev, Russell Higgins, Russell Housby, Russell Litzkow, Russell Staughton, Russell Warfield, Ryan "stormbringrr" Duncan, Ryan bowles, Ryan Chamberlain, Ryan Clarke, Ryan Crowell, Ryan Kent, Ryan Lambert, Ryan M. Ford, Ryan Olds, Ryan Percival, Ryan Powell, Ryan Robinson, Ryan Upjohn, Ryan Waite, Ryu Li, (Solav) James lofshult, S. Lacy, S. Finke, S. Godkin, S. Smigielski, S.Emery, Sam, Sam Billings, Sam Cooper, Sam Feipel, Sam G May, Sam Gulliver-Goodall, Sam Metcalfe, Sam Olley, Sam S, Sam Slocum, Sam Wong, Sam Wright, Sampo Lappalainen, Samuel, Samuel Mah, Samuel Ridge-Ward, Samuel Vera, Samuel Ward, Samuele Rossi, Sander van Zuidam, Sandro "Yoritomo" Cipiccia, Sandy Fesq, Santiago Checa, Santiago J. "El enemigo" Lupiañez Lopez, Sarah A Thompson, Sarah Antonelli, Sarry, Sarwat Chadda, Saskia Wyville, Satoshi Nakamoto, Satsu Kuong, SaturnAttack, Saul Wright, Scelus Sceleris, Scorch_13, Scot MacNaughton, Scott, Scott B. Peiterson, Scott Butcher, Scott Butler, Scott 'Captain Sparks' Parkin, Scott Carmody, Scott Charnick, Scott E. Bowen, Scott J. Brandt, Scott Kunian, Scott McNair, Scott Miller, Scott MoonHunter Fitzpatrick, Scott Neal, Scott Raby, Scott Spicer, Scott Synowiez, Scott Tipsword, Scott Yanos, Scott Zaloudek, Seamas, Sean "Garg" McAlister, Sean "GreenLupin" Mooney, Sean "Grimace" Houston, Sean "Regnirok" Poeschl, Sean Chavira, Sean Connolly, Sean Edward R Mercado, Sean H., Sean Jamison, Sean Kuhl, Sean M Smith, Sean O'Connor, Sean Poindexter, Sean

Ryan Frank, Ryan Stewart, Sean Schoonmaker, Sean Silva-Miramon, Sean Stevens, Sean Stockton, Sean Tracy, Sean W. Cravens, Sebastiaan Vandekerkhove, Sebastian Garcia, Sebastian Lange, Sebastian Mathias, Sebastian Muhs, Sebastian Schmidt, Sebastian Schommer, Sebastian Schwott, Sebastian Zankl, Sebastian"Enache"este, Sebastien "Kayn" Corne, Seiji Kato, Selwyn Percival, Seneca, Sentaph, Seon Arikale, Seraphmoon, Sergeant Michele Giammarroni, Corregidor, Sergio van Pul, Seth Gupton, Seth Hartley, Seth Keeler, Seth Stephens, Seth Tupper, Seukjin Choi (Nosferatu), sev, Sgt. Frazer Barnard "6th Scots Guards of Ariadna", Shadow-pm, Shan Lewis, Shane Coates, Shane Everly, Shane Mclean, Shane Peabody, Shane T. Bennett, Shaun Khiu, Shaun Lane, Shaun O'Hara, Shawn & Jessica Lavoie, Shawn Hagen, Shawn Lamb, Shawn P, Shawn P Ausherman, Shawn R. Maxwell, Shawn Zumwalt, Shay Wallace, Shea Shortridge, Shelton, Shen Hung-Yang, Sherlock Holmes, Shi Won On, Shin Jin Woo, Shiny Games, Shivan Rage, Shogran, Shunkaha, 'Sifu' Steve Martin, Signal and Noise, Sigurd Rubech Hartmeyer-Dinesen, Silas Marr, Silvio Herrera Gea, Simon "imonsei" Kristensen, Simon "Rizzy" Voelker, Simon "Sihook" Hooker, Simon Barlow, Simon Booth, Simon Brunning, Simon Cotterill, Simon Crowe, Simon D. McAleney, Simon Earl, Simon Elliott, Simon Hutchinson, Simon Inglis, Simon Landmine, Simon Laurenz Rauschmayer, Simon Layton, Simon M, Simon Stroud, Simon Vernon French, Simon Wellsted, Simon York, Simon 'Zed' Roe, Simone Giuliani, Sir William de le weir, Sirez, Siriux, SirPadras, Sjoerd de Zwart, skelley, skibble, Skoll Rodriguez, Skyler Slafsky, Skyler Taylor, Slaz, Smiler, SNAFU, Snaïl Belkhala, Snowflake337, Sobakaa, Socky D & Bitterness, SombreroDeLaNuit, Soren A, Hjorth, Soulsorcerer, Southern Oregon Infinity, SpaceThor, SpadesCT, Sparco (Bakunin Shop), Spectre Studios.us, Spellscape /Svyatoslav Karyagin, Spencer "IridiumFire" Moulds, Spencer JK Murray, Spenser Clark, Sphärenmeisters Spiele, Spinach Chin, Spkt0r, SquidGoggles, Sr_Garcia, SrBarrod, Stahlzombie, Starkmad, Stavros "Stav" Makris, SteelSpyder, steelwraith, Stefan Lammer, Stefan "ToastyJustice" M., Stefan Bogen, Stefan Brammer, Stefan Faber, Stefan Heuer, Stefan Kahler, Stefan Kozemchak, Stefan Locklair, Stefan Lovingood, Stefan Nilsson, Stefan Posselt, Stefan shecke, Stefan Sova (Theradrussian), Stefan Wertheimer, Stefano Padelli, Steffen Gauss, Steffen Rasmussen, Stephan Szabo, Stephan Waider, Stephane Henry, Stephane Pouderoux, Stephen A Turner, Stephen A. Reeves, Stephen Cox, Stephen Davies, Stephen Esdale, Stephen Fletcher, Stephen G. Rider, Stephen Justice, Stephen Lopaz, Stephen McCool, Stephen McGee, Stephen Micheal James Mckay, Stephen Miller, Stephen Mortimer, Stephen peacock, Stephen Peterka, Stephen Peters, Stephen Rubin, Stephen Thomas, Stephen Wilcoxon, stephen wilkinson, Sterling Rutherford, Steve "Hollowpoint" Leach, Steve Bladen, Steve Chan, Steve Elkington, Steve Fase, Steve Gardner, Steve Harbron, Steve Jasper, Steve Jones, Steve Moos, Steve Noia, Steve Piper, Steve Rubino, Steve Wagner, Steve Yates (Zero), Steven "The Farnablaster" Farnaby, Steven & Charmaine Thornton-Cook, Steven Baker, Steven Barrett, Steven Bledsoe, Steven Goddard, Steven Hinson, Steven Humphries, Steven K Cheng, Steven Kerampran, Steven Law, Steven Moy, Steven Siddall, Steven Thesken, Steven Weidner, Stimpson Clan, Stolby, Storm Luna, Stormbrook Thunderbringer (Davy), Stormquiss, Stosh W, Strahan Groves, strelKa, Stu Liming, Stuart Christie, Stuart Climpson, Stuart Coutts, Stuart Fores, Stuart Park, Stuart Watkins, StuG, Sullivan Thompson, Supasan Joonkiat, Superfritz, Suzushiro Aoi, Sven "Gorasa" Braun, Sven Ecke, Sven Heitbrink, Sven Holz, Svend Andersen, Swen Barth, Swindleous, Swole Mole, Sydney A Marsden, Sydney Bridges, Sylpherion, Sylvannas, Syph, Szymon Marcjanek, T. Osborne, Tad Duncan, Tad Kelson, Tad Rudnicki, Tad Simmons, Tako, Taliesin Morgan, Tamachan, TanKoL, Tarek Alatrach, Tartufu, Tauréolé, Taylor Henrickson, Taylor Holloway, Taylor Ogg, Taylor Wilson, Tazzz, Tchazzar, Team Total Reaction, Ted Soper, Teddy Lindsey, Telliez Jean-Christophe, Temoore Baber, Tempedius, Templar Denis, Tenabrae, Teófilo Hurtado Navarro, Terrance Mobley, Terrence Rideau, Tezeech, That Game Place, The Arbitor, The brothers Toivonen, The Dark Canuck, The Gamers' Emporium - Swansea, The Iron Mandarin, The Phalanx Consortium, The Startled Mole, The Tekwych, The Wrecking Crew, TheArnold, TheBaron Keskel, TheBearIsDriving, The-Flip, Theharper, Theo, Theodor Gehrer, TheWildFerret, Thierry DELPIERRE, Thilo Goerke, Thingus, Thom Shartle, Thomas "Jumbo" Lerch, Thomas "Tnibs" Niblock, Thomas "Vondi" Vonderbank, Thomas 'advi' Brandt, Thomas Alexander Chudo, Thomas DENIS, Thomas East, Thomas Foo, Thomas Fucke, Thomas George, Thomas Harbert, Thomas Jason, Thomas Joseph

Henderson, Thomas Kay, Thomas Kühn, Thomas Kurilla, Thomas Laguillon, Thomas M. Forsko, Thomas Pizon, Thomas Scarlett, Thomas Shook, Thomas Tramantano, Thomas Vierling, Thomas Walmsley, Thomas Young, Thor-Bear the Heinous, Thorbjørn Steen, Thorg, Thorsten Fischer, Thorsten Holler, Thorsten Kühn, Thorsten Schreck, Thorsten Senger, Thunder Gundersen, Ti Dinzeo, TiberiousFox, Till "Zephro" Schlusen, Tim Aubel, Tim C., Tim Coates, Tim Edwards, Tim Franklin and David Miles, Tim Goodlett, Tim Peasgood, Tim Pskowski, Tim Rasely, Tim van Leeuwen, Tim W White, Timo Mattes, Timo Scala, Timo W., Timothy Carroll, Timothy Cummings, Timothy E. Adams, Timothy G. Williamson (Zinistar), Timothy Inglefinger, Timothy Jackson, Timothy Leonard, Timothy Link, Timothy Martin, Timothy Morton, Timothy Ryan, Timothy S Schmidt, Timothy Steed, Tino"TJE"Elsner, Tirlista, TJ Weller, TJames, tleilax, To my wife Denise Drzewiecki, I love you (Scott Drzewiecki), toadchild & inkybrushes, Tobias, Tobias Blüm, Tobias Dworschak, Tobias 'eLi' Breuer, Tobias G., Tobias Schulte-Krumpen, Tobias Tröger, Toby Datson, Toby Hall, Toby Leigh, Toby O'Hara, Toby Williamson, Tod Allen Smith, Todd Peters, Todd V. Ehrenfels, Todd Walker, Todd Young, Toffi, Tom, Tom "CmdrKiley" Kiley, Tom "The Monster" Hoefle, Tom Baxendale, Tom Blake, Tom Breeze (0-0-17), Tom Eddy, Tom Granados, Tom Jensen, Tom Killingbeck, Tom Ladegard, Tom 'Lord Farfhocel' Kapel, Tom M., Tom Norris, Tom Olivieri, Tom Richards, Tom Saddler, Tom Schadle, MayaCast, Tom Smith, Tomas Enrique Diaz, Tomáš Gregovský, Tomas Lennvall, Tomasz Stanisławski, Tomato Jam, Tomaz Susic, TomBullet, Tomislav Rac, Tommaso Gollini, Tommi Malkki, Tommy Beaudry, Tommy Moore, Tommy Svensson, Töni, Tony E. Calidonna, Tony Rushowrth (Battleship Bismarck), Tony Strongman, Tony Wallace, Top Deck Games, Torsten Pluschke, TotallyMunted, Totus Gnarus, Tracy and Masako Castile, Tracy and Nicole Vierra, Tracy S. Landrum, Trageser, Travis "T3" Keating, Travis Bryant, Travis Teitsch, TreasureX, Trevor Seeton, Trevor Younghusband, Trey Mercer, Triof, Trip Space-Parasite, Tripleyew, Trismoonfarmer, Tristan, Tristan Danner, Trojan Points, Trolkor, Troy C. Yarbrough, Troy Cota, Troy Ellis, Troy Stuart, Tshonka, TTS TableTopShop, Tusochiso, twentysix, Twisted Cauldron, Tye Rougas, Tyler Berard, Tyler Doyon, Tyler G Brodell, Tyler Norman, Tyler Ricotta, Tyler Svancara, Tyson Villeneuve, U Majuran, Uiliam O' Regan, Ujka Kevin, Ulf Hillebrecht, Ulrich Drees, Umbarthio Daniaux, Unai Mujika, Unai Usin Bengoa, Uraziel Nomolos, Uriah J. Mach,

Ursula Searle, Ursun, Uwe Bachmann, Valentin Pacquet, Valerio Cossari, Vanve, Vaughan Cockell, vCJD, Verkath, VerrDon Mason, Versino of Malfeas, Vicente Sampedro, Victor (Wonkateuton) Febres, Victor "Freaktor" Pérez, Victor Alfonso Perez Sanchez, Victor Fajardo Lopez, Víctor Guerrero Vilches, Victor Lopes, Victor Manuel Sanchez Esparza, Victor Sanchez Pintado, Victor St-Cyr Robitaille, Viet Tran, Viktor "Sikil" Carlson, Ville Ojanperä, Vincent "Bwarevince" Henrotte, Vincent Arebalo, Vincent Bordes, Vincent Brousse, Vincent David "El Jeffe", Vincent Douchamps, Vincent FURSTENBERGER, Vincent GOUDE, Vincent Hatakeyama, Vinsc, Visarion, Vise, Vitali, Vitaly Chernishov, Vito Alonso, Vivier de la Vialle - Fièvre de la Bulle, Vladimir Rebchenko, VoidWolf, Volker Jacobsen, Volker Marx, VonScamp, Vortex, Vorzakk, Vyse, W H, "Witch Hunter" Joe Lawrence, Wabi Sabi Will, Wacey "Drunder" Stavinoha, Wade Geer, Wade Jones, Wajanai Snudvongs, Walker FitzRoy, Walo von Greyerz, Walt J Rickells, Walter B. Schirmacher, Walter Simpson, Wargamers Consortium, Warheit, Warren P Nelson, Warren Walker, Warrick Voyzey, Wasim R. Fernandez, Wax, Waylon Wyatt, Wayne Rankin, Jr., wefra, Weltenschatz, Weltenwolf, Wenqing Du, Werner Ceelen, Wes, Wes "Pimiento" Smith, Wesley Keen, Weyenbergh Kevin, White Kitsune, Wilbert & Meow Galapon, Wild Boyz, Will Cassey, Will Hochella, Will Lennon, Will McKeever, Will Pitts, Will Urban, Willem van der Horst, William (Hoppy) Davisson, William Byrne, William Håkansson, William Holmes, William Rullenraad, William T. Burch, William Victor Janak the Fourth, William Witchalls, Willow Sheard, Willy "Raven" Mangin, Wilson Badillo, Wojciech Słowacki, Wolfen Loki, Wolfengil, Wolfgang_ TrueCorrupt, WookieeGunner, World's Best Comics and Games, Wouter, Wulpertinger, WWS Louie, www.thewarstore.com, Wyatt Douglas McRae, x4RsOL, Xaierrre Hernandez, Xale'Endar, Xones, Yan Duranceau, Yan Shen, Yann Laot, Yashia, Yehuda Halfon, Yeon Chang, Choi, Yong Jun Park, YouriJ, Yu-Cheng Hsu, Yumpus Chen, Yuri Surovtsev, Yuri Tigelaar, Yves Dubois, Yves Fréchette, Z Gomez, Zach, Zach Churcher, Zach Ross, Zachary Devokai, Zadakiel, Zah, Zak Anderson, Zak Kellaway, Zalabar, Zane Gunton, Zanntos, Zarpas, Zendoku, Zengo, Zenon Berg, Zergash, Zewrath, Zhaoqi Peng, Zhaxtbrecht, Zhexiao Huang, Zoddl, Zöldi-Kovács Róbert, Zreef, 우 봉균(Woo Bong-Gyun), 盧德揚

INFINITY

INDEX

EXPLORE NEW WORLDS

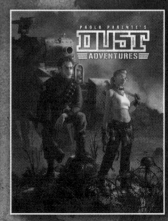

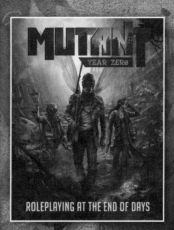

MŌDIPHIÜS™ ENTERTAINMENT

modiphius.com
facebook.com/modiphius

Sol

Dawn

Yu Jing

Bourak

Acontecimento